WILEY PLUS for **Management**, Canadian Edition

Check with your instructor to find out if you have access to *WileyPLUS!*

Study More Effectively with a Multimedia Text

WileyPLUS: Home | Help | Contact us | Logout

Schermerhorn, Wright, Management, Canadian Edition

Schermerhorn, Wright, Management, Canadian Edition

WILEY PLUS

Chapter 8. Planning and Controlling ▸ GO

Standard View | Printer View | < Back | Next >

Reading content
Chapter Opener
Chapter 8 Learning Preview
How and Why Managers Plan
Types of Plans Used by Manage
Planning Tools and Techniques
The Control Process
Organizational Control
Chapter 8 Study Guide
Chapter 8 Integrated Learning
Self-test 8
References
Key Terms Review

Visualization Resources
Chapter 8 PowerPoint Presenta
Manager's Notepad Chapter 8 !

Study Resources
Chapter 8 Personal Managemei
Chapter 8 Flash Cards
Chapter 8 Puzzle Part 1
Chapter 8 Puzzle Part 2

Planning Improves Action Orientation

Planning is a way for people and organizations to stay ahead of the competition and always become better at what they are doing. It helps avoid the complacency trap of simply being carried along by the flow of events or of being distracted by successes or failures of the moment. It keeps the future visible as a performance target and reminds us that the best decisions are often made before events force them upon us. Management consultant Stephen R. Covey talks about the importance of priorities. He points out that the most successful executives "zero in on what they do that 'adds value' to an organization." Instead of working on too many things, they work on the things that really count. Covey says that good planning makes us more (1) results oriented—creating a performance-oriented sense of direction; (2) priority oriented—making sure the most important things get first attention; (3) advantage oriented—ensuring that all resources are used to best advantage; and (4) change oriented—anticipating problems and opportunities so they can be best dealt with.8

Planning Improves Coordination

Planning improves coordination. The many different individuals, groups, and subsystems in organizations are each doing many different things at the same time. But even as they pursue their specific tasks and objectives, their accomplishments must add up to meaningful contributions to the needs of the organization as a whole. Good planning throughout an organization creates a means–ends chain o~~f~~ ~~~~ ~~~~ objectives lead to the accomplishment of higher-level ones. Higher-level objectives as ends are directly tied to lower-level objectives as the means for their accomplishment. Figure 8-2 uses the example of quality management to show how a means–ends chain helps guide and integrate quality efforts within a large manufacturing firm.

References

In a **means–ends chain**, lower-level objectives help accomplish higher-level ones.

Corporate quality objectives	Manufacturing division quality objectives	Plant quality objectives	Shift supervisor quality objectives
Deliver error-free products that meet customer requirements 100% of the time.	Become a preferred supplier by achieving 100% on-time delivery of all products.	Increase customer delivery acceptance rate by 5%.	Assess capabilities of machine operators and provide/arrange appropriate training.

This multimedia version of your text brings your readings to life by integrating self-assessment quizzes, student polls, and hyperlinks throughout. *WileyPLUS* gives you control over how you learn.

Click on an e-book hyperlink to instantly access extra resources.

WileyPLUS: Home | Help | Contact us | Logout

Schermerhorn, Wright, Management, Canadian Edition

Schermerhorn, Wright, Management, Canadian Edition

WILEY PLUS

Chapter 10. Organizing ▸ GO

Standard View | Printer View | < Back | Next >

Reading content
Chapter Opener
Chapter 10 Learning Preview
Organizing as a Management F
Traditional Organization Structi
Directions in Organization Stru
Organizing Trends and Practice
Chapter 10 Study Guide
Chapter 10 Integrated Learning
Self-test 10
References
Key Terms Review

Visualization Resources
Chapter 10 PowerPoint Present
Manager's Notepad Chapter 10

Study Resources
Chapter 10 Personal Managem
Chapter 10 Flash Cards
Chapter 10 Puzzle Part 1
Chapter 10 Puzzle Part 2

Case 10: Nike

take it to the case!

Nike

Spreading Out to Stay Together

The next time you are looking for a company that uses outsourcing to capitalize on their core competencies, look no further than your feet. With one of the world's most recognized brands, their trademark "swoosh", Nike is among the most successful companies in North America. But how can a company that outsources most of their production remain connected to their products and their customers' needs? By focusing on what they do best! Nike adopted a decentralized structure in order to focus resources directly on their core competencies: comprehensive market research, advertising, and innovative research and design. As a result, Nike continues to dominate the highly competitive athletic market.

References

Case 10

Nike: Spreading Out to Stay Together

Nike is, indisputably, a giant in the athletics industry. Yet the Portland, Oregon, company has grown so large precisely because it knows how to stay small. By focusing on its core competencies, and outsourcing the rest, Nike has managed to become a sharply focused industry leader. But can it keep the lead?

What do You call A Company of Thinkers?

It's not a joke or a riddle. Rather, it's a conundrum that applies to one of the most successful companies in the United States. Nike is known worldwide for its products, none of which it actually makes. This begs two questions: if you don't make anything, what do you actually do, and if you outsource everything, what's left?

Grasp key concepts by exploring the various interactive tools in Read, Study & Practice.

Preparing for a test has never been easier! *WileyPLUS* brings all of your course materials together and takes the stress out of organizing your study aids. A streamlined study routine saves you time and lets you focus on learning.

John Wiley & Sons Canada, Ltd.

WILEY PLUS *for Management*, Canadian Edition

Complete and Submit Assignments On-line Efficiently

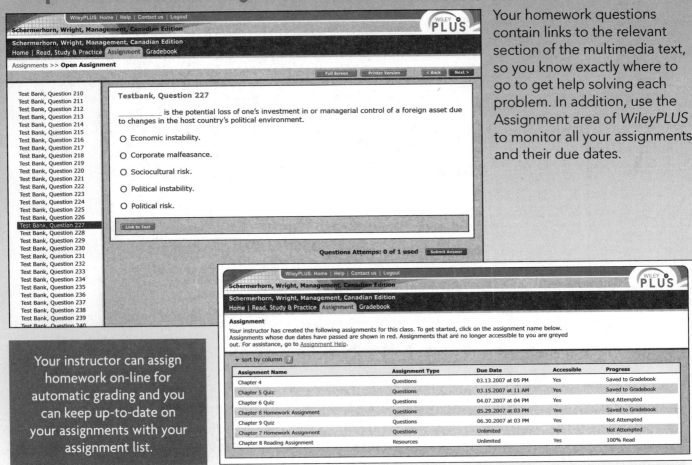

Your homework questions contain links to the relevant section of the multimedia text, so you know exactly where to go to get help solving each problem. In addition, use the Assignment area of *WileyPLUS* to monitor all your assignments and their due dates.

Your instructor can assign homework on-line for automatic grading and you can keep up-to-date on your assignments with your assignment list.

Keep Track of Your Progress

Your personal Gradebook lets you review your answers and results from past assignments as well as any feedback your instructor may have for you.

Keep track of your progress and review your completed questions at any time.

Technical Support: http://hesupport.wiley.com/wileyplus
Student Resource Centre: http://www.wileyplus.com

For further information regarding *WileyPLUS* and other Wiley products, please visit www.wiley.ca.

MANAGEMENT

CANADIAN EDITION

John R. Schermerhorn, Jr.

Barry Wright

John Wiley & Sons Canada, Ltd.

Library and Archives Canada Cataloguing in Publication

Schermerhorn, John R.
    Management / John R. Schermerhorn. -- Canadian ed. / Barry Wright

ISBN 978-0-470-15457-1

    1. Management.   I. Wright, Barry, 1954- II. Title.
HD31.S34 2007a   658   C2007-904542-1

Production Credits

Acquisitions Editor: Darren Lalonde
Editorial Manager: Karen Staudinger
Publishing Services Director: Karen Bryan
Developmental Editor: Daleara Hirjikaka
Editorial Co-ordinator: Tamara Capar
Design: Interrobang Graphic Design Inc.
Cover Photo: Digital Vision, Getty Images
Printing & Binding: Quebecor World—Dubuque

Printed and bound in the United States of America
1 2 3 4 5 QW 11 10 09 08 07

John Wiley and Sons Canada Ltd.
6045 Freemont Blvd.
Mississauga, Ontario L5R 4J3
Visit our website at www.wiley.ca

About the Authors

Barry Wright is an Associate Professor in the Faculty of Business at Brock University in St. Catharines, Ontario. Dr. Wright has over 20 years of experience in the classroom. Prior to joining the faculty at Brock he worked as a professor at St. Francis Xavier University, and taught at the International Study Centre in Herstmonceux, UK and at Queen's University in Kingston, Ontario. He has also worked as an administrator with the City of Red Deer. During his career as an educator, Barry has been nominated several times for teaching awards and was the recipient of the "PHESA Award" for excellence in academic teaching given by Queen's University.

At home in the classroom, Barry is also comfortable in the boardroom. He has provided a variety of training and research consultations to a number of Canadian private and public organizations. These services have included the development and implementation of programs in leadership, employee motivation, strategic planning, diversity management, stress management, and managing organizational change. Barry also provides one-on-one "coaching" sessions for senior executives who have expressed a desire for outside counsel.

He received his MA (Sport Psychology) and Ph.D. (Management) degrees from Queen's University. His academic research focuses on understanding and solving leadership challenges, change and its influence on organizational members, and creating effective work environments.

Barry enjoys being married and being a father, coaching sports, a trip to the art gallery, travelling, and a good laugh.

John R. Schermerhorn, Jr. is the Charles G. O'Bleness Professor of Management in the College of Business at Ohio University, where he teaches graduate and undergraduate courses in management. Dr. Schermerhorn earned a Ph.D. in Organizational Behaviour from Northwestern University, an MBA (with distinction) in Management and International Business from New York University, and a BS in Business Administration from the State University of New York at Buffalo. He has taught at Tulane University, the University of Vermont, and Southern Illinois University at Carbondale, where he also served as Head of the Department of Management and Associate Dean of the College of Business Administration.

At Ohio University Dr. Schermerhorn has been named a University Professor, the university's highest campus-wide honour for excellence in undergraduate teaching. He is committed to instructional excellence and curriculum innovation, and is working extensively with technology utilization in the classroom. He serves as a guest speaker at colleges and universities, lecturing on developments in higher education for business and management, as well as on instructional approaches and innovations. He is co-author of *Organizational Behaviour* (Wiley, 2005).

Preface

Welcome to *Management*, Canadian Edition, and its theme—"personal management." As the cover image suggests, a major goal of this text is to help set your students apart positively from the competition—others, who like them, want satisfying careers in today's challenging business environment. To do this, the text emphasizes personal management—the ability to understand yourself individually and in the social context, to access personal strengths and weaknesses, to exercise initiative, to accept responsibility for accomplishments, to work well with others, and to adapt, by continually learning from experience in the quest for self improvement.

MANAGEMENT PHILOSOPHY

Today's students are tomorrow's leaders and managers. Just as the workplace in this new century will be vastly different from today's, so too must our teaching and learning environments be different from days gone by. New values and management approaches are appearing; the nature of work and organizations is changing; the age of information is not only with us, it is transforming our lives.

Management is part of the same transformation. It is based on four constructive balances that we believe remain essential to the agenda of higher education for business and management.

- *The balance of research insights with formative education.* As educators we must be willing to make choices when bringing the theories and concepts of our discipline to the attention of the introductory student. We cannot do everything in one course. The goal should be to make good content choices and to set the best possible foundations for lifelong learning.

- *The balance of management theory with management practice.* As educators we must understand the compelling needs of students to understand and appreciate the applications of the material they are reading and thinking about. We must continually bring to their attention good, interesting, and recognizable examples.

- *The balance of present understandings with future possibilities.* As educators we must continually search for the directions in which the real world of management is heading. We must select and present materials that can both point students in the right directions and help them develop the confidence and self-respect needed to best deal with them.

- *The balance of what "can" be done with what is, purely and simply, the "right" thing to do.* As educators we are role models; we set the examples. We must be willing to take stands on issues like managerial ethics and corporate social responsibility. We must be careful not to let the concept of "contingency" betray the need for positive "action" and "accountability" in managerial practice.

Today, more than ever before, our students have pressing needs for direction as well as suggestion. They have needs for application as well as information. They have needs for integration as well as presentation. Our instructional approaches and materials must deliver on all of these dimensions and more. Our goal is to put into your hands and into those of your students a learning resource that can help meet these needs. *Management* and its website are our contributions to the future careers of your students and ours.

MANAGEMENT HIGHLIGHTS

Management introduces the essentials of management as they apply within the contemporary work environment. The subject matter is carefully chosen to meet AACSB accreditation guidelines while allowing extensive flexibility to fit various course designs and class sizes.

Organization

- The book is organized into five parts with themes relevant to today's organizations: (1) Introducing Management, (2) Context, (3) Mission, (4) Organization, (5) Leadership.

- *Part 1: Management Today*—focuses on understanding managers, what they do, the exciting new workplace, lessons of the past and present, and ethics and social responsibility.

- *Part 2: Context*—explores the contemporary environment in terms of competition, diversity, organization cultures, globalization, crosscultural management, entrepreneurship, and small business.

- *Part 3: Mission*—addresses how managers use information, information technology, and decision making for planning and controlling, and in the process of strategic management.

- *Part 4: Organization*—reviews traditional and new developments in organization structures, organizational design contingencies and alternatives, as well as systems and work processes.

- *Part 5: Leadership*—presents the major models and current perspectives on leadership, individual behaviour and performance, teams and teamwork, communication and interpersonal skills, and change leadership.

Content

In addition to core themes of ethics, diversity, competitive advantage, quality, globalization, and empowerment, *Management* also covers the following topics:

- intellectual capital • multicultural organizations • ethnocentrism • cultural relativism • strategic leadership • competitive advantage • self-management • crisis management • change leadership • customer relationship management • e-business • entrepreneurship • organizational learning • emotional intelligence • horizontal organizations • cross-functional teams • virtual teams • career readiness • virtual organizations • reengineering • work–life balance • strategic human resource planning • boundaryless organizations • performance-based rewards • personality • job stress • alternative work arrangements • crosscultural communication • conflict management • negotiation • teamwork • innovation processes

Chapter Features

A most important feature of *Management* is the use of an integrated learning model to help guide students as they read and study for exams. Look for the following features in each chapter:

Planning Ahead—

- Key learning objectives and study questions
- Opening vignette
- In the Workplace—a scenario that provides students with a realistic opportunity to apply the material covered in each chapter

In Text—

- Learning Preview linking opening vignette to a visual chapter guide
- Learning Checks for each major section and learning objective
- Personal Management feature with recommended self-assessments
- Thematic boxes with current examples on timely themes
- Manager's Notepads with practical guidelines and suggestions
- Take it to the case! feature introducing chapter case
- Margin running glossary with definitions of key terms

End-of-Chapter Study Guide—

- Where We've Been linking back to opening vignette
- The Next Step guide to cases, projects, exercises, and assessments
- Chapter Summary in bullet-list format
- Key Terms Review for major terms and concepts
- Chapter Self-Test with multiple-choice, short-answer, and essay questions

Management Learning Workbook

The *Management Learning Workbook* provides students and instructors with a rich variety of suggested learning activities.

- Chapter Cases—18 timely cases on well-recognized organizations
- Integrated Case—a multi-faceted cross-functional case that allow students to apply an extensive amount of course material

- Active Learning Projects—10 suggestions for student projects (individual or group), including management in popular culture and service learning

- Exercises in Teamwork—30 exercises for in-class and out-of-class use

- Self-Assessments—30 personality and self-reflection instruments

- Student Portfolio Builder—a special guide to building a student portfolio complete with professional resumé and competency documentations

Student Website: wiley.com/canada/management

A robust Student Website supports *Management* for classroom application. This site includes the following special student learning resources:

- PowerPoint downloads for text and supplementary figures

- Student Polls introduce a key fact or survey result for every chapter

- Interactive online versions of self-assessments

- An online study guide for students, including PowerPoint chapter reviews and chapter self-tests

Instructor's Support

Management comes with a comprehensive resource package that assists the instructor in creating a motivating and enthusiastic learning environment.

- *Complete Instructor's Resource Guide* offers helpful teaching ideas, advice on course development, sample assignments, and chapter-by-chapter text highlights, learning objectives, lecture outlines, class exercises, lecture notes, answers to end-of-chapter material, and tips on using cases.

- *The Authors' Classroom*—a unique Web resource offering the authors' personal classroom materials from special PowerPoint slides to quick-hitting learning activities.

- *Comprehensive Test Bank*—completely updated and linked to the chapter "Learning Checks," questions are categorized by pedagogical element, margin terms, or general text knowledge, page number, and type of questions. The entire test bank is available in a computerized version, MICROSOFT Diploma for windows, created by Brownstone Research Group.

- *Video Package*—offering video selections from business news clips.

- *MP3 Chapter Reviews*—MP3 files that provide a review of the chapter are available for students to download and play back at their convenience using MP3 players, computer multimedia players, and other devices.

- *Wiley PLUS*—an integrated suite of resources including the full online version of the textbook, plus easy-to-use homework management tools, interactive presentation resources, and a range of practice and study activities-—with instant feedback—for your students.

Acknowledgements

Writing a book is always a big task and there are many people who have contributed greatly to this project. Special thanks go to Darren Lalonde, Acquisitions Editor, for his support and vision for the project, and to Daleara Hirjikaka, Developmental Editor, for her strong, steady, and unwearied guidance on the day-to-day aspects of the project. I would also like to thank Alison Arnot for her work on the feature boxes that are an integral part of each chapter and Laurel Hyatt for her editorial contributions. I would like to offer my particular thanks to my team of exceptional researchers who individually and collectively did an outstanding job—Wendy Dueck, Jessica Srivastava, and Michelle Leece.

I am grateful to the following colleagues who offered their insightful and very useful comments for the initial proposal for the text and those who reviewed drafts of the chapters.

Colin Boyd	University of Saskatchewan
Lewie Callahan	University of Lethbridge
Tyler Chamberlin	University of Ottawa
Choon Hian Chan	Kwantlen University College
Kay Devine	Athabasca University
Victoria Digby	Fanshawe College
Richard Field	University of Alberta
Douglas Fletcher	Kwantlen University College
Paul Gallina	Bishop's University
Jane Haddad	Seneca College
Don Haidey	Mount Royal College
Don Hill	Kwantlen University College
Cyndi Hornby	Fanshawe College
Barbara Lipton	Seneca College
Brad Long	St. Francis Xavier University
Sean MacDonald	University of Manitoba
Bonnie Milne	British Columbia Institute of Technology
Kerry Rempel	Okanagan College
Ron Shay	Kwantlen University College
Patricia Stoll	Seneca College
Susan Thompson	Trent University
Joe Trubic	Ryerson University
Debra Warren	Centennial College
Bruce Weir	Kwantlen University College
Wallace John Whistance-Smith	Ryerson University
Don Valeri	Douglas College
Heather White	Georgian College
David Wright	Kwantlen University College

I would especially like to thank my family—my lovely wife Mary, darling daughters Monica and Kit, and happy son John Emmett, who graciously allowed me the time to take on this project. It is to my family that I dedicate this book.

Barry Wright
St. Catharines, Ontario
November 12, 2007

How to Use This Book

1. What is ethical behaviour?

2. How do ethical dilemmas complicate the workplace?

3. How can high ethical standards be maintained?

4. What is corporate social responsibility?

5. How do organizations and governments work together in society?

Each chapter opens with **Planning Ahead**—a set of study questions that provides learning objectives for the chapter and a framework for the end-of-chapter review.

The **Opening Vignette** is a timely, real-world example that highlights chapter themes. The example is visited again in the end-of chapter **Where We've Been**.

The **In The Workplace** feature provides hypothetical scenarios that offer students a realistic opportunity to apply the material covered in each chapter.

Aldo Shoes

Creating a better world

Creating a better world is important to Aldo Bensadoun, owner of the Montreal-based company, ALDO shoes. Perhaps his own multi-cultural background has provided him with this global view. Born in Morocco, he grew up in France, and fell in love with Montreal during a weekend trip while at university.

Flash back to 1972; ALDO is founded, continuing a family tradition of working within the shoe industry. Starting with concessions in Le Château stores in Montreal, Ottawa, Quebec City, and Winnipeg,

In addition to being a successful company, ALDO has valued the role of being a good corporate citizen. It sees itself as a "brand with a conscience, a brand that cares." While supporting local communi-

countries, featuring many celebrities and media outlets. ALDO has also developed a limited edition "empowerment tag necklace," which is being sold worldwide and through the internet, with 100 per

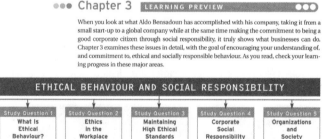

IN THE WORKPLACE

You ponder the confidential report that you have just received. Drawn up by a team of outside consultants, the report suggests that your company close one of its manufacturing plants in a small town in rural Canada and, instead, sign a long-term contract with a plant in Asia to produce its new product line. The report suggests that while there will be high initial costs to the plant closure, such as paying severance fees to the approximately 250 workers, in the medium to long term, the company should realize a greater profit due to the Asian plant's lower operating costs.

Your supervisor has asked you to highlight considerations other than just economic issues that senior management should also consider before deciding to go "off-shore." What is your response?

PERSONAL MANAGEMENT

PERSONAL CHARACTER is a foundation for all that we do. It establishes our integrity and provides an ethical anchor for our behaviour in the workplace and in life overall. Persons of high integrity can always be confident in the self-respect it provides, even in the most difficult of situations. Those who lack it are destined to perpetual insecurity, acting inconsistently, and suffering not only in self-esteem but also in the opinion of others. How strong is your personal character? How well prepared are you to deal with the inevitable ethical dilemmas and challenges in work and in life? Can you give specific examples showing how your behaviour lives up to these Six Pillars of Character identified by the Josephson Institute of Ethics?[34]

- Trustworthiness—honesty, integrity, reliability in keeping promises, loyalty
- Respect—civility, courtesy and decency, dignity, tolerance, and acceptance
- Responsibility—sense of accountability, pursuit of excellence, self-restraint
- Fairness—commitment to process, impartiality, equity
- Caring—concern for others, benevolence, altruism
- Citizenship—knowing the law, being informed, volunteering

Get to know yourself better

Complete Self-Assessments #5—**Terminal Values Survey**, and #6—**Instrumental Values Survey**; and Exercises #6—**Confronting Ethical Dilemmas** from the Workbook and Personal Management Activity #1 on the companion website.

Chapter 3   LEARNING PREVIEW

When you look at what Aldo Bensadoun has accomplished with his company, taking it from a small start-up to a global company while at the same time making the commitment to being a good corporate citizen through social responsibility, it truly shows what businesses can do. Chapter 3 examines these issues in detail, with the goal of encouraging your understanding of, and commitment to, ethical and socially responsible behaviour. As you read, check your learning progress in these major areas.

ETHICAL BEHAVIOUR AND SOCIAL RESPONSIBILITY

Study Question 1 What Is Ethical Behaviour?	Study Question 2 Ethics in the Workplace	Study Question 3 Maintaining High Ethical Standards	Study Question 4 Corporate Social Responsibility	Study Question 5 Organizations and Society
• Laws, values, and ethical behaviour • Alternative views of ethics • Cultural issues in ethical behaviour	• Ethical dilemmas at work • Rationalizations for unethical behaviour • Factors influencing ethical behaviour	• Ethics training • Whistle-blower protection • Ethical role models • Codes of ethical conduct	• Stakeholder issues and analysis • Perspectives on corporate social responsibility • Evaluating corporate social performance • Social entrepreneurship	• How governments influence organizations • How organizations influence governments • Role of corporate governance
Learning check ❶	Learning check ❷	Learning check ❸	Learning check ❹	Learning check ❺

The **Learning Preview** links the Opening Vignette with the major topics of the chapter and includes a graphic outline of major topics.

The **Personal Management** feature integrates each chapter with personal development issues, including how to "get to know yourself better" by using key learning resources in the end-of-chapter **Management Learning Workbook**.

CANADIAN COMPANY
IN THE NEWS   Mountain Equipment Co-op

CANADIAN STORE IS NUMBER ONE AT DOING GOOD

Vancouver-based Mountain Equipment Co-op (MEC) ranks at the top of big retail chains when it comes to corporate social responsibility (CSR), according to *Report on Business* magazine. ROB ranked companies that operate in Canada on the basis of their CSR performance, focusing on five specific industries, rather than on a broad range of sectors. MEC scored well above its peer group in the big retail category. The main reasons for this are the co-operative membership structure, which encourages employee and customer involvement, and the fact that it's the only Canadian retailer participating in the Fair Labour Association, a non-profit coalition working to improve labour standards and working conditions worldwide. Also, MEC is committed to generating zero waste in its operations. In 2004, it diverted about 76 percent of waste from its stores that would otherwise have gone to landfill.

Source: "Corporate Social Responsibility Ranking," *Report on Business*, February 23, 2006.

Canadian Managers
Volunteer Now!

Marc Kielburger is a Canadian social entrepreneur. He started Volunteer Now! in order to make social advocacy "cool" in Toronto high schools. His organization was founded on the principle that young people have within them the power to change the world. Volunteer Now! seeks to motivate young people to become active in both their local and global communities. It is primarily a student-run program that serves to educate teachers about how to introduce the concept into classrooms, organizes student leadership programs, and educates student "volunteer ambassadors" who go out to inspire fellow students to work with their communities as agents of positive change.

Source: Information taken from <www.volunteernow.ca> (January 2007).

The **Canadian Company in the News** and the **Canadian Managers** features bring real-life examples of management skills and innovation into the classroom.

AROUND THE WORLD

The enormous success of the Real Madrid soccer team on the field is rivalled only by its success off the field. The Spanish club is not only the winningest team in European soccer history, but it's the richest soccer team in the world, pulling in 292 million Euros in 2005-06. The 100-year-old club has developed into one of the world's most recognizable brands in any type of business, spawning a video game, TV channel, and even a movie. Real Madrid players, employees, shareholders (who are members of the public), advertisers, and its loyal fans stick to traditional values of honesty, discipline, fighting spirit, leadership, camaraderie, chivalry, nobility, fair play, continual self-improvement, and respect for adversaries. The century-old team spirit inspires Real Madrid's backroom employees. In fact, it's said that if a management directive is ever unclear, employees instinctively know what to do because the values are so enshrined.

Teaming up for worldwide soccer success

Source: "Real Madrid stays at the top," Deloitte and Touche press release, Feb. 8, 2007; Kimio Kase, Ignacio Urrutia de Hoyos, Carlos Martí Sanchis, and Magdalena Opazo Bretón, "The proto-image of Real Madrid: Implications for marketing and management," International *Journal of Sports Marketing and Sponsorship*, April 2007, pp. 212 -233; corporate website: <www.realmadrid.com>.

The **Around the World** feature introduces students to global management trends and practices.

A Critical Thinking Case for each chapter is introduced with **Take it to the case!**, which applies the case to the material being discussed.

take it to the case!

Barenaked Ladies
Changing the world one song at a time

Is it possible for a rock band to be popular, profitable, and not pollute? The Barenaked Ladies, five Canadians who are self-effacing celebrities and nice lads, certainly hope so. From their basement beginnings in the late 1980s, their focus has grown from being a successful band to being a successful band that makes a difference. BNL has matured from merely singing about things to taking action as engaged activists on issues important to band members. Actions include voicing their opinion on issues by wearing "Vote Solar" T-shirts onstage to actually walking the talk by using greener fuels like biodiesel in their tour vehicles, composting material backstage, and setting up eco-villages at their concerts. Learn more about their approach to corporate social responsibility by reading the case in the *Management Learning Workbook*.

Source: With information from the corporate website: <www.bnlmusic.com>.

■ **Procedural justice** is concerned that policies and rules are fairly applied.

■ **Distributive justice** is concerned that people are treated the same regardless of personal characteristics.

■ **Interactional justice** is the degree to which others are treated with dignity and respect.

Key terms are called out and defined in the margins, forming a **Margin Running Glossary**.

Manager's Notepads in each chapter offer lists of helpful "do's" and "don'ts" of managerial behaviour.

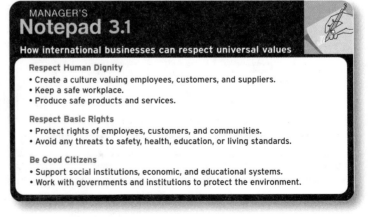

MANAGER'S
Notepad 3.1

How international businesses can respect universal values

Respect Human Dignity
• Create a culture valuing employees, customers, and suppliers.
• Keep a safe workplace.
• Produce safe products and services.

Respect Basic Rights
• Protect rights of employees, customers, and communities.
• Avoid any threats to safety, health, education, or living standards.

Be Good Citizens
• Support social institutions, economic, and educational systems.
• Work with governments and institutions to protect the environment.

BE SURE YOU CAN

✓ Learning check ❶ • define ethics • list and explain four views of ethical behaviour • discuss the types of ethical problems faced by people at work • differentiate the implications of cultural relativism and universalism in international business ethics

At the end of each section, **Learning Checks** prompt you to stop and review the key points you have just studied. If you cannot answer these questions, you should go back and read the section again.

●●● Chapter 3 STUDY GUIDE

WHERE WE'VE BEEN

Back to Aldo Shoes

The opening example of Aldo Shoes provided a clear benchmark for how business performance, ethical behaviour, and social responsibility can go hand in hand. Aldo Shoes, along with other positive examples in the chapter, helps offset the bad side of business and managerial behaviour sensationalized in the cases of Bre-X, Enron, Andersen, WorldCom, and others. In Chapter 3 you learned more about the issues and complexities of personal ethics and corporate social responsibility. As you read further in *Management*, always keep these themes in mind as a learning context. Never forget that there is no substitute for ethical and socially responsible behaviour.

Each chapter ends with **Where We've Been**, which looks back at the chapter opening vignette as a helpful reminder for summary and review purposes.

THE NEXT STEP
INTEGRATED LEARNING ACTIVITIES

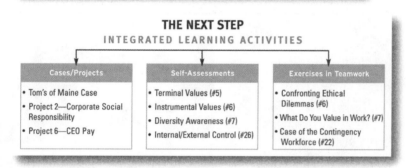

Cases/Projects	Self-Assessments	Exercises in Teamwork
• Tom's of Maine Case • Project 2—Corporate Social Responsibility • Project 6—CEO Pay	• Terminal Values (#5) • Instrumental Values (#6) • Diversity Awareness (#7) • Internal/External Control (#26)	• Confronting Ethical Dilemmas (#6) • What Do You Value in Work? (#7) • Case of the Contingency Workforce (#22)

The Next Step directs you to cases, projects, self-assessments, and experiential exercises included in the **Management Learning Workbook** at the back of the text.

STUDY QUESTION SUMMARY

1. What is ethical behaviour?

• Ethical behaviour is that which is accepted as "good" or "right" as opposed to "bad" or "wrong."

• Simply because an action is not illegal does not necessarily make it ethical in a given situation.

• Because values vary, the question of "What is ethical behaviour?" may be answered differently by different people.

• Four ways of thinking about ethical behaviour are the utilitarian, individualism, moral-rights, and justice views.

• Cultural relativism argues that no culture is ethically superior to any other.

2. How do ethical dilemmas complicate the workplace?

• When managers act ethically they have a positive impact on other people in the workplace and on

others in organizations, even while facing career risks for doing so.

• Top management sets an ethical tone for the organization as a whole, and all managers are responsible for acting as positive models of appropriate ethical behaviour.

• Written codes of ethical conduct formally state what an organization expects of its employees regarding ethical conduct at work.

4. What is corporate social responsibility?

• Corporate social responsibility is an obligation of the organization to act in ways that serve both its own interests and the interests of its many external publics, often called stakeholders.

• Criteria for evaluating corporate social performance include economic, legal, ethical, and discretionary responsibilities.

The **Summary** is a bullet list summary of key points for each chapter opening Study Question.

An end-of-chapter **Self-Test** helps assess your understanding of key chapter topics, including multiple-choice, short response, and essay questions.

SELF-TEST 3

MULTIPLE-CHOICE QUESTIONS:

1. Values are personal beliefs that help determine whether a behaviour will be considered eth
   example of a terminal value is _____ .
   (a) ambition (b) self-respect (c) courage (d) imagination

2. Under the _____ view of ethical behaviour, a business owner would be considered eth
   plant's workforce by 10 percent in order to cut costs and be able to save jobs for the other 9(
   (a) utilitarian (b) individualism (c) justice (d) moral-rights

KEY TERMS REVIEW

Accommodative strategy (p. 72)	Defensive strategy (p. 72)	Ethics training (p. 65)
Code of ethics (p. 67)	Distributive justice (p. 59)	Individualism view (p. 58)
Corporate governance (p. 76)	Ethical behaviour (p. 57)	Instrumental values (p. 58)
Corporate social responsibility (p. 68)	Ethical dilemma (p. 61)	Interactional justice (p. 59)
	Ethical imperialism (p. 60)	Justice view (p. 59)
Cultural relativism (p. 59)	Ethics (p. 57)	Lobbying (p. 76)

The **Key Terms List** is a reminder about key concepts, along with page references where they are defined.

The *Management Learning Workbook* is an end-of-text learning resource complete with a wide variety of cases, active learning projects, experiential exercises, self-assessments, and student portfolio builder to enrich and extend student learning.

The Integrated Case is a multi-faceted cross-functional case that allows students to apply an extensive amount of course material.

The Cases for Critical Thinking section in the *Management Learning Workbook* contains 18 cases, based on actual organizations and specifically developed for a text chapter.

Ten Active Learning Projects in the *Management Learning Workbook* engage students in research and presentation projects on timely management topics, as well as in an exploration of management themes in popular culture.

A portfolio of 30 Exercises in Teamwork in the *Management Learning Workbook* help students experience through teamwork various issues and practical aspects of each chapter.

A set of 30 Self-Assessment inventories in the *Management Learning Workbook* involves students in exploring their personal managerial tendencies and perspectives.

The Student Portfolio section of the *Management Learning Workbook* provides students with a template for building a student portfolio to summarize academic outcomes and display career credentials to potential employers.

How Do You Learn Best?

This questionnaire aims to find out something about your preferences for the way you work with information. You will have a preferred learning style. One part of that learning style is your preference for the intake and the output of ideas and information. Circle the letter of the answer that best explains your preference. Circle more than one if a single answer does not match your perception. Leave blank any question that does not apply.

1. You are helping someone who wants to go to your airport, town centre, or railway station. You would:
   V) draw, or give her a map.
   A) tell her the directions.
   R) write down the directions (without a map).
   K) go with her.
2. You are not sure whether a word should be spelled "dependent" or "dependant." You would:
   V) see the words in your mind and choose by the way they look.
   A) think about how each word sounds and choose one.
   R) find it in a dictionary.
   K) write both words on paper and choose one.
3. You are planning a holiday for a group. You want some feedback from them about the plan. You would:
   V) use a map or website to show them the places.
   A) phone, text, or e-mail them.
   R) give them a copy of the printed itinerary.
   K) describe some of the highlights.
4. You are going to cook something as a special treat for your family. You would:
   V) look through the cookbook for ideas from the pictures.
   A) ask friends for suggestions.
   R) use a cookbook where you know there is a good recipe.
   K) cook something you know without the need for instructions.
5. A group of tourists wants to learn about the parks and wildlife reserves in your area. You would:
   V) show them Internet pictures, photographs, or picture books.
   A) talk about, or arrange a talk for them to learn about parks or wildlife reserves.
   R) give them a book or pamphlets about the parks or wildlife reserves.
   K) take them to a park or wildlife reserve and walk with them.
6. You are about to purchase a digital camera or mobile phone. Other than price, what would most influence your decision?
   V) It is a modern design and looks good.
   A) The salesperson telling me about its features.
   R) Reading the details about its features.
   K) Trying or testing it.
7. Remember a time when you learned how to do something new. Try to avoid choosing a physical skill, e.g., riding a bike. You learned best by:
   V) diagrams and charts—visual clues.
   A) listening to somebody explaining it and asking questions.

R) written instructions—e.g., a manual or textbook.
   K) watching a demonstration.
8. You have a problem with your knee. You would prefer that the doctor:
   V) showed you a diagram of what was wrong.
   A) described what was wrong.
   R) gave you a web address or something to read about it.
   K) used a plastic model of a knee to show what was wrong.
9. You want to learn a new program, skill, or game on a computer.
   You would:
   V) follow the diagrams in the book that came with it.
   A) talk with people who know about the program.
   R) read the written instructions that came with the program.
   K) use the controls or keyboard.
10. I like websites that have:
    V) interesting design and visual features.
    A) audio channels where I can hear music, radio programs, or interviews.
    R) interesting written descriptions, lists, and explanations.
    K) things I can click on, shift, or try.
11. Other than price, what would most influence your decision to buy a new, non-fiction book?
    V) The way it looks is appealing.
    A) A friend talks about it and recommends it.
    R) Quickly reading parts of it.
    K) It has real-life stories, experiences, and examples.
12. You are using a book, CD, or website to learn how to take photos with your new digital camera. You would like to have:
    V) diagrams showing the camera and what each part does.
    A) a chance to ask questions and talk about the camera and its features.
    R) clear written instructions with lists and bullet points about what to do.
    K) many examples of good and poor photos and how to improve them.
13. Do you prefer an instructor who likes to use
    V) diagrams, charts, or graphs?
    A) question and answer, talk, group discussions, or guest speakers?
    R) handouts, books, or readings?
    K) demonstrations, models, or practical sessions?
14. You have finished a competition or test and would like some feedback. You would like to have feedback:
    V) using graphs showing you what you had achieved.

A) from somebody who talks it through with you.

R) using a written description of your results.

K) using examples from what you have done.

15. You are going to choose food at a restaurant or café. You would:

V) look at what others are eating or look at pictures of each dish.

A) listen to the waiter or ask friends to recommend choices.

R) choose from descriptions on the menu.

K) choose something that you have had there before.

16. You have to make an important speech at a conference or special occasion. You would:

V) make diagrams or get graphs to help explain things.

A) write a few key words and practise saying your speech over and over.

R) write your speech and learn from reading it over several times.

K) gather many examples and stories to make the talk real and practical.

Count your choices: ☐   ☐   ☐   ☐
                     V   A   R   K

Determine whether your learning style is primarily visual (V), aural (A), reading/writing (R), or kinesthetic (K). You may have more than one learning style preference—many people do. This is known as a multimodal (MM) style. Look at the learning styles chart on the next page to determine what will help you learn the best.

© Copyright for this version of VARK is held by Neil D. Fleming, Christchurch, New Zealand and Charles C. Bonwell, Green Mountain, Colorado, USA.

LEARNING STYLES CHART

Visual

WHAT TO DO IN CLASS	WHAT TO DO WHEN STUDYING	TEXT FEATURES THAT MAY HELP YOU	WHAT TO DO PRIOR TO EXAMS
• Pay close attention to charts, drawings, and handouts your instructor uses. • Underline and highlight. • Use different colours. • Use symbols, flow charts, graphs, different arrangements on the page, white space.	Convert your lecture notes into "page pictures." To do this: • Reconstruct images in different ways. • Redraw pages from memory. • Replace words with symbols and initials. • Look at your pages.	• Chapter opener vignettes • Chapter learning preview chart • Photos • Illustrations • Key Terms in orange • Words in italics • Learning Checks • Self-Tests • Video news clips (available in your instructor's Video Package)	• Recall your "page pictures." • Draw diagrams where appropriate. • Practise turning your visuals back into words

Aural

WHAT TO DO IN CLASS	WHAT TO DO WHEN STUDYING	TEXT FEATURES THAT MAY HELP YOU	WHAT TO DO PRIOR TO EXAMS
• Attend lectures and tutorials. • Discuss topics with students and instructors. • Explain new ideas to other people. • Use a tape recorder. • Leave spaces in your lecture notes for later recall. • Describe overheads, pictures, and visuals to somebody who was not in class.	You may take poor notes because you prefer to listen. Therefore: • Expand your notes by talking with others and with information from your textbook. • Listen to the pre-recorded chapter summaries (available on the companion website). • Read summarized notes out loud. • Explain your notes to another "aural" person.	• Chapter study questions • Chapter learning preview chart • Photos/Illustrations • Study Question Summary • Self-Tests • Cases for Critical Thinking • Active Learning Projects • Exercises in Teamwork • Self-Assessments • Glossary	• Talk with the instructor. • Spend time in quiet places recalling the ideas. • Practise writing answers to old exam questions. • Say your answers out loud.

Reading/Writing

WHAT TO DO IN CLASS	WHAT TO DO WHEN STUDYING	TEXT FEATURES THAT MAY HELP YOU	WHAT TO DO PRIOR TO EXAMS
• Use lists and headings. • Use dictionaries, glossaries, and definitions. • Read handouts, textbooks, and supplemental library readings. • Use lecture notes.	• Write out words again and again. • Reread notes silently. • Rewrite ideas and principles into other words. • Turn charts, diagrams, and other illustrations into statements.	• Chapter opener vignettes • Chapter study questions • Chapter learning preview chart • Manager's Notepad • Learning Checks • Key term definitions in margins • Study Question Summary • Self-Tests, especially the Short Response Questions and the Application Questions • Cases for Critical Thinking • Glossary	• Write exam answers. • Practise with multiple choice questions. • Write paragraphs, beginnings and endings. • Write your lists in outline form. • Arrange your words into hierarchies and points.

Kinesthetic

WHAT TO DO IN CLASS	WHAT TO DO WHEN STUDYING	TEXT FEATURES THAT MAY HELP YOU	WHAT TO DO PRIOR TO EXAMS
• Use all your senses. • Go to labs, take field trips. • Listen to real-life examples. • Pay attention to applications. • Use hands-on approaches. • Use trial-and-error methods.	You may take poor notes because topics do not seem concrete or relevant. Therefore: • Put examples in your summaries. • Use case studies and applications to help with principles and abstract concepts. • Talk about your notes with another "kinesthetic" person. • Use pictures and photographs that illustrate an idea.	• Chapter opener vignettes • Chapter learning preview chart • Canadian Company in the News boxes • Canadian Managers boxes • Take it to the case! boxes • Around the World boxes • Personal Management boxes • Study Question Summary • Self-Tests • Integrated Case • Cases for Critical Thinking, especially the questions on You Do the Research • Active Learning Projects • Exercises in Teamwork • Self-Assessments	• Write practice answers. • Role-play the exam situation.

For all learning styles: Be sure to use the learning aids on the companion website to enhance your understanding of the concepts and procedures of the text. In particular, use the animated tutorials, study aids (including the searchable glossary, PowerPoint presentations, and problem-solving techniques), and practice tools (including additional demonstration problems, key term matching activities, self-assessment quizzes, and working with annual reports).

Brief Contents

PART ONE ■ MANAGEMENT TODAY

CHAPTER 1   The Dynamic New Workplace   2
CHAPTER 2   Management—Past to Present 30
CHAPTER 3   Ethical Behaviour and Social Responsibility 54

PART TWO ■ CONTEXT

CHAPTER 4   Environment, Organizational Culture, and Diversity 82
CHAPTER 5   Global Dimensions of Management 106
CHAPTER 6   Entrepreneurship and Small Business 134

PART THREE ■ MISSION

CHAPTER 7   Information and Decision Making 156
CHAPTER 8   Planning and Controlling 180
CHAPTER 9   Strategic Management 210

PART FOUR ■ ORGANIZATION

CHAPTER 10   Organizing 236
CHAPTER 11   Organizational Design and Work Processes 260
CHAPTER 12   Human Resource Management 282

PART FIVE ■ LEADERSHIP

CHAPTER 13   Leading 308
CHAPTER 14   Motivation—Theory and Practice 334
CHAPTER 15   Individual Behaviour and Performance 358
CHAPTER 16   Teams and Teamwork 382
CHAPTER 17   Communication and Interpersonal Skills 412
CHAPTER 18   Change Leadership 440

MANAGEMENT LEARNING WORKBOOK ■

Integrated Case W-4
Cases for Critical Thinking W-13
Active Learning Projects W-62
Exercises in Teamwork W-68
Self-Assessments W-88
Student Portfolio Builder W-124

Contents

PART ONE ■ MANAGEMENT TODAY

C H A P T E R   1

THE DYNAMIC NEW WORKPLACE 2

Planning Ahead 2
Study Questions 2
Workopolis.com—*Putting technology–and people–to work* 3
Learning Preview 4

WORKING IN THE NEW ECONOMY 5

Intellectual Capital 6
Globalization 7
Technology 7
Diversity 8
Ethics 8
Careers 9

ORGANIZATIONS IN THE NEW WORKPLACE 10

What Is an Organization? 11
Organizations as Systems 11
Organizational Performance 12
Changing Nature of Organizations 13

MANAGERS IN THE NEW WORKPLACE 14

What Is a Manager? 14
Levels and Types of Managers 15
Managerial Performance 16
Changing Nature of Managerial Work 17

THE MANAGEMENT PROCESS 18

Functions of Management 18
Managerial Activities and Roles 20
Managerial Agendas and Networking 21

LEARNING HOW TO MANAGE 22

Essential Managerial Skills 22
Skill and Outcome Assessment 23
Management Learning Framework 24
Chapter 1 Study Guide 25
Where We've Been: Back to Workopolis.com 25
The Next Step: Apple Computer Case, Projects, Exercises, Assessments 25
Study Question Summary 26
Key Terms Review 27
Self-Test 1 27

C H A P T E R   2

MANAGEMENT–PAST TO PRESENT 30

Planning Ahead 30
Study Questions 30
Google, Inc—*Web-crawler extraordinaire!* 31
Learning Preview 32

CLASSICAL MANAGEMENT APPROACHES 33

Scientific Management 33
Administrative Principles 35
Bureaucratic Organization 37

BEHAVIOURAL MANAGEMENT APPROACHES 38

The Hawthorne Studies and Human Relations 39
Maslow's Theory of Human Needs 40
McGregor's Theory X and Theory Y 41
Argyris's Theory of Adult Personality 42

QUANTITATIVE MANAGEMENT APPROACHES 43

Management Science 43
Applied Quantitative Analysis Today 44

MODERN MANAGEMENT APPROACHES 44

Organizations as Systems 44
Contingency Thinking 45

CONTINUING MANAGEMENT THEMES 46

Quality and Performance Excellence 46
Global Awareness 48
Learning Organizations 48
21st-Century Leadership 49
Chapter 2 Study Guide 50
Where We've Been: Back to Google, Inc. 50
The Next Step: Coca-Cola Case, Projects, Exercises, Assessments 51
Study Question Summary 51
Key Terms Review 52
Self-Test 2 52

C H A P T E R   3

ETHICAL BEHAVIOUR AND SOCIAL RESPONSIBILITY 54

Planning Ahead 54
Study Questions 54

ALDO Shoes—*Creating a better world* 55
Learning Preview 56

WHAT IS ETHICAL BEHAVIOUR? 57
  Laws, Values, and Ethical Behaviour 57
  Alternative Views of Ethics 58
  Cultural Issues in Ethical Behaviour 59

ETHICS IN THE WORKPLACE 61
  Ethical Dilemmas at Work 61
  Rationalizations for Unethical Behaviour 61
  Factors Influencing Ethical Behaviour 62

MAINTAINING HIGH ETHICAL STANDARDS 65
  Ethics Training 65
  Whistle-blower Protection 66
  Ethical Role Models 66
  Codes of Ethical Conduct 67

CORPORATE SOCIAL RESPONSIBILITY 67
  Stakeholder Issues and Analysis 68
  Perspectives on Corporate Social
    Responsibility 69
  Evaluating Corporate Social Performance 71
  Social Entrepreneurship 72

ORGANIZATIONS AND SOCIETY 74
  How Governments Influence Organizations 75
  How Organizations Influence Governments 76
  Role of Corporate Governance 76
Chapter 3 Study Guide 77
  Where We've Been: Back to ALDO Shoes 77
  The Next Step: Barenaked Ladies Case,
    Projects, Exercises, Assessments 77
  Study Question Summary 78
  Key Terms Review 78
  Self-Test 3 79

PART TWO ■ CONTEXT

CHAPTER 4

**ENVIRONMENT, ORGANIZATIONAL CULTURE,
  AND DIVERSITY 82**
Planning Ahead 82
Study Questions 82
BMO Financial Group—*An employer of choice* 83
Learning Preview 84

**ENVIRONMENT AND COMPETITIVE
  ADVANTAGE 84**
  What Is Competitive Advantage? 85
  The General Environment 85
  Stakeholders and the Specific

  Environment 86
  Environmental Uncertainty 88

CUSTOMER-DRIVEN ORGANIZATIONS 88
  Who Are the Customers? 89
  What Customers Want 89
  Customer Relationship Management 90

QUALITY-DRIVEN ORGANIZATIONS 90
  Total Quality Management 91
  Quality and Continuous Improvement 91
  Quality, Technology, and Design 92

ORGANIZATIONAL CULTURE 93
  What Strong Cultures Do 93
  Levels of Organizational Culture 94
  Value-Based Management 95
  Symbolic Leadership 95

**MULTICULTURAL ORGANIZATIONS AND
  DIVERSITY 96**
  What Is a Multicultural Organization? 97
  Organizational Subcultures 97
  Challenges Faced by Minorities and Women
    98
  Managing Diversity 100
Chapter 4 Study Guide 102
  Where We've Been: Back to BMO Financial
    Group 102
  The Next Step: UPS Case, Projects,
    Exercises, Assessments 102
  Study Question Summary 102
  Key Terms Review 103
  Self-Test 4 104

CHAPTER 5

GLOBAL DIMENSIONS OF MANAGEMENT 106
Planning Ahead 106
Study Questions 106
Gildan—*Taking on the giants* 107
Learning Preview 108

**INTERNATIONAL MANAGEMENT AND
  GLOBALIZATION 109**
  Europe 110
  The Americas 110
  Asia and the Pacific Rim 111
  Africa 112

INTERNATIONAL BUSINESS CHALLENGES 113
  Why Companies Go International 113
  Forms of International Business 114
  Complications in the Global Business

Environment 116

MULTINATIONAL CORPORATIONS 117
Types of Multinational Corporations 117
Pros and Cons of Multinational Corporations 118
Ethical issues for Multinational Corporations 119

CULTURE AND GLOBAL DIVERSITY 120
Popular Dimensions of Culture 120
Values and National Cultures 122
Understanding Cultural Diversity 124

MANAGEMENT ACROSS CULTURES 125
Planning and Controlling 126
Organizing and Leading 126
Are Management Theories Universal? 127
Global Organizational Learning 128
Chapter 5 Study Guide 129
Where We've Been: Back to Gildan Activewear Inc. 129
The Next Step: Bata Case, Projects, Exercises, Assessments 129
Study Question Summary 130
Key Terms Review 131
Self-Test 5 131

C H A P T E R   6

ENTREPRENEURSHIP AND SMALL BUSINESS   134
Planning Ahead 134
Study Questions 134
ACE—*Support for the budding student entrepreneur* 135
Learning Preview 136

THE NATURE OF ENTREPRENEURSHIP 136
Who Are the Entrepreneurs? 137
Characteristics of Entrepreneurs 139
Diversity and Entrepreneurship 140

ENTREPRENEURSHIP AND SMALL BUSINESS 142
Entrepreneurship and the Internet 142
International Business Entrepreneurship 143
Family Businesses 143
Why Many Small Businesses Fail 145

NEW VENTURE CREATION 146
Life Cycles of Entrepreneurial Firms 146
Writing the Business Plan 147
Choosing the Form of Ownership 148
Financing the New Venture 148

ENTREPRENEURSHIP AND BUSINESS DEVELOPMENT 150
Entrepreneurship in Large Enterprises 150
Business Incubation 151
Small Business Development Centres 151
Chapter 6 Study Guide 152
Where We've Been: Back to ACE 152
The Next Step: Hannah's Ice Cream Case, Exercises, Assessments 152
Study Question Summary 152
Key Terms Review 153
Self-Test 6 154

PART THREE ■ MISSION

C H A P T E R   7

INFORMATION AND DECISION MAKING 156
Planning Ahead 156
Study Questions 156
Chapters-Indigo—*A passion for books leads to success* 157
Learning Preview 158

INFORMATION TECHNOLOGY AND THE CHANGING WORKPLACE 159
How IT Is Changing Business 159
How IT Is Changing Organizations 159
How IT Is Changing the Office 161

INFORMATION AND THE MANAGEMENT PROCESS 161
What Is Useful Information? 161
Information Needs in Organizations 162
Information Systems 163
Managers as Information Processors 164

INFORMATION AND MANAGERIAL DECISIONS 165
Types of Managerial Decisions 165
Decision Environments 167
Problem-Solving Styles 168

THE DECISION-MAKING PROCESS 169
Identify and Define the Problem 169
Generate and Evaluate Alternative Courses of Action 170
Decide on a Preferred Course of Action 171
Implement the Decision 172
Evaluate Results 172

ISSUES IN MANAGERIAL DECISION MAKING 173
Decision-Making Errors and Traps 173
Individual vs. Group Decision Making 174

Ethical Decision Making 175
Knowledge Management and Organizational
Learning 175
Chapter 7 Study Guide 176
Where We've Been: Back to Chapters-Indigo
176
The Next Step: Spin Master Case, Projects,
Exercises, Assessments 176
Study Question Summary 177
Key Terms Review 177
Self-Test 7 178

C H A P T E R   8

PLANNING AND CONTROLLING   180
Planning Ahead 180
Study Questions 180
Cognos Inc.—*Crunching the numbers to succeed*
181
Learning Preview 182

HOW AND WHY MANAGERS PLAN 183
Importance of Planning 183
The Planning Process 183
Benefits of Planning 184
Planning Theories 186

TYPES OF PLANS USED BY MANAGERS 187
Short-Range and Long-Range Plans 187
Strategic and Operational Plans 188
Policies and Procedures 189
Budgets and Projects 189

PLANNING TOOLS AND TECHNIQUES 190
Forecasting 190
Contingency Planning 191
Scenario Planning 191
Benchmarking 191
Use of Staff Planners 191
Participation and Involvement 192

THE CONTROL PROCESS 193
Importance of Controlling 193
Steps in the Control Process 193
Types of Controls 195
Internal and External Control 197

ORGANIZATIONAL CONTROL 197
MBO: Integrated Planning and Controlling 197
Employee Discipline Systems 199
Information and Financial Controls 199
Break-Even Analysis 200
Operations Management and Control 201

Controlling the Unexpected 203
Chapter 8 Study Guide 205
Where We've Been: Back to Cognos Inc. 205
The Next Step: Wal-Mart Case, Projects,
Exercises, Assessments 205
Study Question Summary 205
Key Terms Review 206
Self-Test 8 207

C H A P T E R   9

STRATEGIC MANAGEMENT   210
Planning Ahead 210
Study Questions 210
Taxi invites you to be part of the future 211
Learning Preview 212

STRATEGIC COMPETITIVENESS 213
What Is Strategy? 213
Strategic Management 213
Strategic Management Goals 214

THE STRATEGIC MANAGEMENT PROCESS 215
Analysis of Mission, Values, and Objectives 216
Analysis of Organizational Resources and
Capabilities 218
Analysis of Industry and Environment 219

STRATEGIES USED BY ORGANIZATIONS 220
Levels of Strategy 221
Growth and Diversification Strategies 222
Restructuring and Divestiture Strategies 222
Global Strategies 223
Co-operative Strategies 224
E-Business Strategies 224

STRATEGY FORMULATION 225
Porter's Generic Strategies 226
Portfolio Planning 227
Adaptive Strategies 229
Incrementalism and Emergent Strategy 229

STRATEGY IMPLEMENTATION 230
Management Practices and Systems 230
Corporate Governance 231
Strategic Leadership 231
Chapter 9 Study Guide 233
Where We've Been: Back to Taxi 233
The Next Step: Toyota Canada Case, Projects,
Exercises, Assessments 233
Study Question Summary 233
Key Terms Review 234
Self-Test 9 234

PART FOUR ■ ORGANIZATION

CHAPTER 10

ORGANIZING 236
Planning Ahead 236
Study Questions 236
Edward Jones—*Structures supporting strategies* 237
Learning Preview 238

ORGANIZING AS A MANAGEMENT FUNCTION 239
What Is Organization Structure? 239
Formal Structures 240
Informal Structures 240

TRADITIONAL ORGANIZATION STRUCTURES 241
Functional Structures 241
Divisional Structures 242
Matrix Structures 244

DIRECTIONS IN ORGANIZATION STRUCTURES 246
Team Structures 247
Network Structures 248
Boundaryless Organizations 250

ORGANIZING TRENDS AND PRACTICES 252
Shorter Chains of Command 252
Less Unity of Command 253
Wider Spans of Control 253
More Delegation and Empowerment 254
Decentralization with Centralization 255
Reduced Use of Staff 256
Chapter 10 Study Guide 257
Where We've Been: Back to Edward Jones 257
The Next Step: Nike Case, Projects, Exercises, Assessments 257
Study Question Summary 257
Key Terms Review 258
Self-Test 10 258

CHAPTER 11

ORGANIZATIONAL DESIGN AND WORK PROCESSES 260
Planning Ahead 260
Study Questions 260
KPMG International—*Design for integration, empowerment, and flexibility* 261
Learning Preview 262

ORGANIZATIONAL DESIGN ESSENTIALS 263
What Is Organizational Design? 263
Organizational Effectiveness 263

Organizational Design Choices 264

CONTINGENCIES IN ORGANIZATIONAL DESIGN 268
Environment 268
Strategy 269
Technology 270
Size and Life Cycle 270
Human Resources 272

SUBSYSTEM DESIGN AND INTEGRATION 273
Subsystem Differentiation 274
Subsystem Integration 275

WORK PROCESS DESIGN 276
What Is a Work Process? 276
How to Re-engineer Core Processes 276
Process-Driven Organizations 277
Chapter 11 Study Guide 278
Where We've Been: Back to KPMG International 278
The Next Step: BET Case, Projects, Exercises, Assessments 278
Study Question Summary 279
Key Terms Review 279
Self-Test 11 280

CHAPTER 12

HUMAN RESOURCE MANAGEMENT 282
Planning Ahead 282
Study Questions 282
DOFASCO—*"Take care of people; they'll take care of business"* 283
Learning Preview 284

WHY PEOPLE MAKE THE DIFFERENCE 285
Valuing Human Capital 285
The Diversity Advantage 285

HUMAN RESOURCE MANAGEMENT 287
Human Resource Management Process 287
Strategic Human Resource Management 287
Laws Against Employment Discrimination 288
Current Legal Issues in Human Resource Management 289

ATTRACTING A QUALITY WORKFORCE 291
Human Resource Planning 291
The Recruiting Process 292
How to Make Selection Decisions 293

DEVELOPING A QUALITY WORKFORCE 296
Employee Orientation 296
Training and Development 296
Performance Management Systems 298

MAINTAINING A QUALITY WORKFORCE 300
  Career Development 300
  Work-Life Balance 301
  Compensation and Benefits 301
  Retention and Turnover 302
  Labour-Management Relations 303
Chapter 12 Study Guide 304
  Where We've Been: Back to Dofasco 304
  The Next Step: Royal Bank Case, Projects,
    Exercises, Assessments 304
  Study Question Summary 305
  Key Terms Review 305
  Self-Test 12 306

PART FIVE ■ LEADERSHIP

CHAPTER 13

LEADING 308
Planning Ahead 308
Study Questions 308
J.-Robert Ouimet—*Leading with vision, cordon
bleu and spirituality* 309
Learning Preview 310

THE NATURE OF LEADERSHIP 310
  Leadership and Vision 311
  Power and Influence 312
  Ethics and the Limits to Power 314
  Leadership and Empowerment 314

LEADERSHIP TRAITS AND BEHAVIOURS 316
  Search for Leadership Traits 316
  Focus on Leadership Behaviours 317
  Classic Leadership Styles 318

CONTINGENCY APPROACHES TO LEADERSHIP 318
  Fiedler's Contingency Model 318
  Hersey-Blanchard Situational Leadership
    Model 320
  House's Path-Goal Leadership Theory 321
  Vroom-Jago Leader-Participation Model 322

TRANSFORMATIONAL LEADERSHIP 323
  Transformational and Transactional
    Leadership 324
  Qualities of a Transformational Leader 325

**CURRENT ISSUES IN LEADERSHIP DEVELOPMENT
325**
  Emotional Intelligence 325
  Gender and Leadership 326
  Drucker's "Old-Fashioned" Leadership 327

  Moral Leadership 327
Chapter 13 Study Guide 329
  Where We've Been: Back to J.-Robert
    Ouimet 329
  The Next Step: Lakeport Brewing Case,
    Projects, Exercises, Assessments 329
  Study Question Summary 330
  Key Terms Review 330
  Self-Test 13 331

CHAPTER 14

MOTIVATION—THEORY AND PRACTICE 334
Planning Ahead 334
Study Questions 334
Genentech—*Passion for science and people* 335
Learning Preview 336

WHAT IS MOTIVATION? 337
  Motivation and Rewards 337
  Rewards and Performance 338

CONTENT THEORIES OF MOTIVATION 339
  Hierarchy of Needs Theory 339
  ERG Theory 340
  Two-Factor Theory 340
  Acquired Needs Theory 341
  Questions and Answers on Content Theories
    342

PROCESS THEORIES OF MOTIVATION 343
  Equity Theory 343
  Expectancy Theory 345
  Goal-Setting Theory 346

REINFORCEMENT THEORY OF MOTIVATION 347
  Reinforcement Strategies 348
  Positive Reinforcement 348
  Punishment 349
  Ethical Issues in Reinforcement 350

MOTIVATION IN THE NEW WORKFORCE 350
  Integrated Model of Motivation 351
  Pay for Performance 351
  Incentive Compensation Systems 352
Chapter 14 Study Guide 355
  Where We've Been: Back to Genentech 355
  The Next Step: SC Johnson Canada Case,
    Projects, Exercises, Assessments 355
  Study Question Summary 355
  Key Terms Review 356
  Self-Test 14 356

CHAPTER 15

INDIVIDUAL BEHAVIOUR AND PERFORMANCE 358

Planning Ahead 358

Study Questions 358

Monitor Company—*Unlocking everyone's performance potential* 359

Learning Preview 360

UNDERSTANDING PEOPLE AT WORK 361

Organizational Behaviour 361

Psychological Contracts 362

Work and the Quality of Life 362

Personality Traits 363

WORK ATTITUDES AND BEHAVIOUR 365

What Is an Attitude? 365

Job Satisfaction 366

Individual Performance 367

JOB DESIGN ALTERNATIVES 369

Scientific Management 369

Job Rotation and Job Enlargement 370

Job Enrichment 370

DIRECTIONS IN JOB ENRICHMENT 371

Core Characteristics Model 371

Technology and Job Enrichment 373

Questions and Answers on Job Enrichment 373

ALTERNATIVE WORK ARRANGEMENTS 374

The Compressed Workweek 374

Flexible Working Hours 375

Job Sharing 375

Telecommuting 376

Part-Time Work 377

Chapter 15 Study Guide 378

Where We've Been: Back to Monitor Company 378

The Next Step: Steinway Piano Case, Projects, Exercises, Assessments 378

Study Question Summary 378

Key Terms Review 379

Self-Test 15 380

CHAPTER 16

TEAMS AND TEAMWORK 382

Planning Ahead 382

Study Questions 382

C.O.R.E Digital Pictures—*Teamwork in a pod* 383

Learning Preview 384

TEAMS IN ORGANIZATIONS 385

Teamwork Pros and Cons 385

Why Meetings Fail 386

Synergy and the Usefulness of Teams 387

Formal and Informal Groups 388

TRENDS IN THE USE OF TEAMS 388

Committees, Project Teams, and Task Forces 388

Cross-Functional Teams 389

Employee Involvement Teams 389

Virtual Teams 390

Self-Managing Work Teams 390

HOW TEAMS WORK 392

What Is an Effective Team? 392

Stages of Team Development 394

Norms and Cohesiveness 396

Task and Maintenance Needs 398

Communication Networks 399

DECISION MAKING IN TEAMS 400

How Teams Make Decisions 400

Assets and Liabilities of Group Decisions 401

Groupthink 402

Creativity in Team Decision Making 403

LEADING HIGH-PERFORMANCE TEAMS 404

The Team-Building Process 404

Success Factors in Teams 406

Team Leadership Challenges 407

Chapter 16 Study Guide 408

Where We've Been: Back to C.O.R.E. 408

The Next Step: Callaway Golf Case, Projects, Exercises, Assessments 408

Study Question Summary 408

Key Terms Review 409

Self-Test 16 410

CHAPTER 17

COMMUNICATION AND INTERPERSONAL SKILLS 412

Planning Ahead 412

Study Questions 412

Center for Creative Leadership—*Lead the way with communication* 413

Learning Preview 414

THE COMMUNICATION PROCESS 415

What Is Effective Communication? 415

Persuasion and Credibility in Communication 416

Communication Barriers 417

IMPROVING COMMUNICATION 420
Active Listening 420
Constructive Feedback 421
Use of Communication Channels 422
Interactive Management 422
Proxemics and Space Design 423
Technology Utilization 424
Valuing Culture and Diversity 425

THE PERCEPTION PROCESS 425
Perception and Attribution 426
Perceptual Tendencies and Distortions 426

CONFLICT 428
Functional and Dysfunctional Conflict 428
Causes of Conflict 429
How to Deal with Conflict 430
Conflict Management Styles 430

NEGOTIATION 432
Negotiation Goals and Approaches 432
Gaining Integrative Agreements 433
Avoiding Negotiation Pitfalls 434
Dispute Resolution 434
Ethical Issues in Negotiation 435
Chapter 17 Study Guide 436
Where We've Been: Back to Center for
   Creative Leadership 436
The Next Step: United Nations Case,
   Projects, Exercises, Assessments 436
Study Question Summary 436
Key Terms Review 437
Self-Test 17 438

CHAPTER 18

CHANGE LEADERSHIP 440
Planning Ahead 440
Study Questions 440
Meridian Credit Union—*The call that changed the
   face of the neighbourhood credit union* 441
Learning Preview 442

STRATEGIC LEADERSHIP AND INNOVATION 443
What Is Strategic Leadership? 443
Creativity and Innovation 444
Characteristics of Innovative Organizations 446

ORGANIZATIONAL CHANGE 448
Change Leaders 448
Models of Change Leadership 448

Transformational and Incremental Change 450
Forces and Targets for Change 451

LEADING PLANNED CHANGE 452
Phases of Planned Change 452
Change Strategies 454
Resistance to Change 456
Challenges of Technological Change 457

ORGANIZATION DEVELOPMENT 458
Organization Development Goals 458
How Organization Development Works 459
Organization Development Interventions 460

STRESS AND STRESS MANAGEMENT 461
Sources of Stress 462
Consequences of Stress 463
Stress Management Strategies 464
Chapter 18 Study Guide 465
Where We've Been: Back to Meridian Credit
   Union 465
The Next Step: BC Ferries Case, Projects,
   Exercises, Assessments 465
Study Question Summary 466
Key Terms Review 467
Self-Test 18 467

**MANAGEMENT LEARNING
WORKBOOK** ■

Integrated Case W-4

Cases for Critical Thinking W-13

Active Learning Projects W-62

Exercises in Teamwork W-68

Self-Assessments W-88

Student Portfolio Builder W-124

Notes EN-1

Name Index NI-1

Subject Index SI-1

The Dynamic New Workplace

Planning Ahead

After reading Chapter 1, you should be able to answer these questions in your own words.

1. What are the challenges of working in the new economy?

2. What are organizations like in the new workplace?

3. Who are managers and what do they do?

4. What is the management process?

5. How do you learn the essential managerial skills and competencies?

workopolis.com

Putting technology— and people—to work!

True to many great business deals, the concept for Workopolis was sketched out on a napkin over lunch. In 1999, two competitors, the head of *The Toronto Star's* electronic division and the head of the electronic division of *The Globe and Mail,* looked at the evolving online job market in the US and determined that if newspapers were to survive in the employment category they needed to embrace new technologies. Workopolis was launched in 2000 with 15,000 job listings and was a phenomenal success. The company is now Canada's leading provider of Internet recruitment and job search solutions, currently offering more than 40,000 jobs daily.

The company's initial success didn't lead to complacency. The founders continued to seek opportunities to provide greater services for their clients. Forming a partnership with Quebec-based Gesca Ltd led to the launch of a French edition of workopolis.com. With the Canadian National Institute for the Blind (CNIB) as its exclusive recruiting partner, Workopolis helped to launch the careers of blind, visually impaired, and deaf-blind Canadians. To counter threats from competitors in the United States such as monster.com, the company also teamed up with Chicago-based CareerBuilder.com to provide a one-stop North American online job-search destination. Also, Workopolis TV was launched—the first nationally broadcast, interactive TV match-making service for employers and employees, focusing on the latest employment trends, career planning, placement opportunities, and advice such as how to get and prepare for a job interview.

The company has now evolved into three distinct business lines: workopolis.com, Canada's biggest job site; workopolisCampus.com, Canada's biggest student job site; and CorporateWorks, an applicant tracking system installed by 85 of Canada's largest employers, including Bell, Dofasco, Petro-Canada, and the Bank of Canada.

The management team believes that the key to their success lies with the talent and passion of an incredibly dedicated team of employees. Workopolis president, Patrick Sullivan states, "There is a strong business model and an excellent team in place at Workopolis." The Workopolis model for online recruitment aims to bring together people and technology to provide an integrated "high tech" and "high touch" service for employers and job seekers. "I'm looking forward to taking the business forward to achieve even greater growth and success." [1]

IN THE WORKPLACE

On the first day at your new job, you are excited but nervous. Your supervisor, Darren Smith, has outlined what is expected of you in the next few months, set up a meeting with the human resources department to do your paperwork, and invited you to the company's Learning Day. He gives you a registration form that needs to be sent back in the next 15 minutes. Darren says you could go to one seminar or could use that time to get settled in to your office.

Several activities interest you, including a workshop on an unfamiliar but potentially useful software program, a "new hires" networking session, and a seminar on excelling as a team leader. Do you decide to sign up for a session (and if so, which one) or organize your workspace?

●●● Chapter 1

The purpose of Chapter 1 is to introduce you to the many dynamics of the workplace and to demonstrate the importance of management in creating high-performance organizations. As you read, keep this purpose in mind while checking your learning progress step-by-step in these major areas.

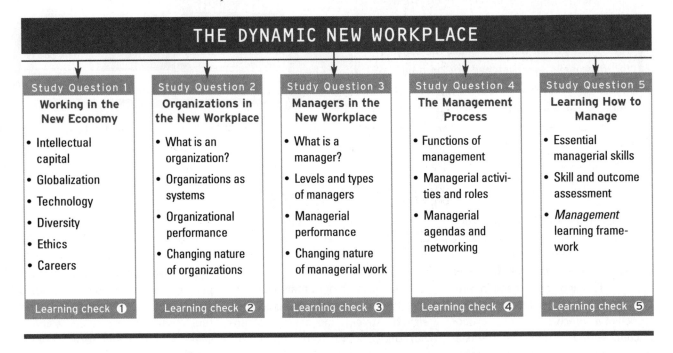

THE DYNAMIC NEW WORKPLACE				
Study Question 1 **Working in the New Economy**	**Study Question 2** **Organizations in the New Workplace**	**Study Question 3** **Managers in the New Workplace**	**Study Question 4** **The Management Process**	**Study Question 5** **Learning How to Manage**
• Intellectual capital • Globalization • Technology • Diversity • Ethics • Careers	• What is an organization? • Organizations as systems • Organizational performance • Changing nature of organizations	• What is a manager? • Levels and types of managers • Managerial performance • Changing nature of managerial work	• Functions of management • Managerial activities and roles • Managerial agendas and networking	• Essential managerial skills • Skill and outcome assessment • *Management* learning framework
Learning check ①	Learning check ②	Learning check ③	Learning check ④	Learning check ⑤

The 21st century has brought with it a new workplace, one in which everyone must adapt to a rapidly changing society with constantly shifting demands and opportunities. As workopolis.com has taught us, learning and speed are in; habit and complacency are out. Organizations are fast changing, as is the nature of work itself. The economy is global, driven by innovation and technology. Even the concept of success, personal and organizational, is evolving as careers take new forms and organizations transform to serve new customer expectations. These developments, say the editors of *Fast Company* magazine, affect us all, offering both "unparalleled opportunity and unprecedented uncertainty." In this age of continuous challenge, a compelling message must be heard by all of us—smart people and smart organizations create their own futures.[2]

In the quest to create this future, the best employers share an important commitment—they value people! They offer supportive work environments that allow people's talents to be fully utilized while providing them with both valued rewards and respect for work-life balance. In progressive organizations, employees benefit from flexible work schedules, on-site child care, health and fitness centres, domestic partner benefits, as well as opportunities for profit sharing, cash bonuses, and competitive salaries. In short, the best employers are not just extremely good at attracting and retaining talented employees, they also excel at creating a high-performance context in which everyone's abilities are highly valued.

After studying high-performing companies, management scholars Charles O'Reilly and Jeffrey Pfeffer conclude that success is achieved because they are better than their competitors at getting extraordinary results from the people working for them. "These companies have won the war for talent," they say, "not just by being great places to work—although they are that—but by figuring out how to get the best out of all of their people, every day."[3] This, in large part, is what *Management* and your management course are all about. Both are designed to introduce you to the concepts, themes, and directions that are consistent with career success and organizational leadership in today's high-performance work settings. As you begin, let your study of management be devoted to learning as much as you can in order to prepare for a career-long commitment to getting great things accomplished through working with, and valuing, people.

WORKING IN THE NEW ECONOMY

Yes, we now live and work in a new economy ripe with challenging opportunities and dramatic uncertainty.[4] It is a networked economy in which people, institutions, and nations are increasingly influenced by the Internet and continuing developments in information technology.[5] The chapter opener on workopolis.com is but one example of how the Web and its vast networking capabilities are changing our lives. The new economy is global, and the nations of the world are increasingly interdependent. The new economy is also knowledge based, and success is forged in workplaces that are continually being reinvented to unlock the great potential of human intelligence. The themes of the day are "respect," "participation," "empowerment," "involvement," "teamwork," "self-management," and more.

Undoubtedly, too, the new economy is performance driven. Expectations for organizations and their members are very high. Success must be earned in a society that demands nothing less than the best from all its institutions. Organizations are expected to continuously excel on performance criteria that include concerns for ethics and social responsibilities, innovativeness, and employee development, as well as more traditional measures of profitability and investment value. When they fail, customers, investors, and employees are quick to let them know. For individuals, there are no guarantees of long-term employment. Jobs are increasingly earned and re-earned every day through one's performance accomplishments. Careers are being redefined in terms of "flexibility," "free

---

CANADIAN COMPANY IN THE NEWS   Research in Motion

RIM ALLOWS THE WORKPLACE TO GO WITH YOU

Waterloo, Ontario-based Research in Motion (RIM) has carved a firm place in today's workplace. RIM has been successful in the new economy because it recognized consumer desires to keep connected. With its handheld BlackBerry pager and the technology that goes with it, RIM has cornered the market on the way many communicate in the new economy. The corporate world is so dependent on its technology that the prospect of it being shut down while a patent battle raged in courts sent panic waves across the business world. Despite losing US $612.5 million in settling the patent infringement suit, RIM continues to grow. "We recently passed the $2 billion annual revenue and five million subscribers milestones, and we have begun the new fiscal year with over 150 carrier partners around the world," said Chairman and CEO Jim Balsillie in April 2006.

Source: RIM news release, "Fourth Quarter and Year-End Results for Fiscal 2006," April 6, 2006.

agency," "skill portfolios," and "entrepreneurship." Today, it takes initiative, discipline, and continuous learning to stay in charge of your own career destiny. Tomorrow's challenges are likely to be even greater.

Just what are the challenges ahead?

●●●● INTELLECTUAL CAPITAL

The dynamic pathways into the future are evident among new benchmarks being set by progressive organizations everywhere. At Herman Miller, the innovative manufacturer of designer furniture, respect for employees is central to organizational success. The firm's core values include the statement: "Our greatest assets as a corporation are the gifts, talents, and abilities of our employee-owners....When we as a corporation invest in developing people, we are investing in our future." Former CEO Max DePree says, "At Herman Miller, we talk about the difference between being successful and being exceptional. Being successful is meeting goals in a good way—being exceptional is reaching your potential."[6]

Canadian Managers
Leadership in Team Building

Kerri Molinaro's employer, IKEA, values her ability to bring employees together to work as a team, so much so that in 2005, Molinaro became the first Canadian and the first woman to run IKEA's Canadian operations, which include 11 stores across the country. Molinaro returned to Canada after five years in Helsingborg, Sweden, where she was the first woman and foreigner to run IKEA's 14 superstores. The Swedish retailer encourages management mobility, which Molinaro has experienced in her years with the company. She joined IKEA in 1992 as manager of its North York store. After overseeing the Toronto store's expansion, she moved to Chicago to open the first IKEA in the U.S. Midwest. She hired 500 employees, brought in four Canadian managers, and watched sales grow for three years. From there, she was promoted and sent to Sweden in 2000.

Source: Marina Strauss, "Fortysomething Canadian: Swedish for common sense," *The Globe and Mail*, April 13, 2005.

■ **Intellectual capital** is the collective brainpower or shared knowledge of a workforce.

■ **A knowledge worker** is someone whose mind is a critical asset to employers.

The point of these examples is clear. People—what they know, what they learn, and what they do with it—are the ultimate foundations of organizational performance. They represent an **intellectual capital**, defined as the collective brainpower or shared knowledge of a workforce that can be used to create value.[7] Indeed, the ultimate elegance of the new workplace may well be its ability to combine the talents of many people, sometimes thousands of them, to achieve unique and significant results.

This is the new age of the **knowledge worker**—someone whose mind is a critical asset to employers and who adds to the intellectual capital of the organization.[8] If you want a successful career in the new economy, you must be willing to reach for the heights of personal competency and accomplishment. You must be a self-starter and willing to continuously learn from experience even in an environment that increasingly grows more complex and challenging.

●●● GLOBALIZATION

Japanese management consultant Kenichi Ohmae suggests that the national boundaries of world business have largely disappeared.[9] Who can state with confidence where their favourite athletic shoes or the parts for their personal computer were manufactured? More and more products are designed in one country, while their component parts are made in others, and the assembly of the final product takes place in still another. Top managers at Ford, IBM, Sony, and other global corporations have no real need for the word "overseas" in everyday business vocabulary. They operate as global businesses that view themselves as equidistant from customers and suppliers, wherever in the world they may be located.

Ballard Power Systems, based in Burnaby, B.C., is a good example of a Canadian company going global. Ballard is recognized as a world leader in the design, development, and manufacturing of automotive fuel cells. Their automotive fuel cells use hydrogen and oxygen to generate electrical energy to power a car and, unlike gasoline engines, produce zero emissions or pollutants. With research and production centres in three countries, suppliers located around the world, and production partners in China, Ballard is indeed a global company.[10]

This is part of the force of **globalization**, the worldwide interdependence of resource flows, product markets, and business competition that characterizes our new economy.[11] This process is described as one in which "improvements in technology (especially in communications and transportation) combine with the deregulation of markets and open borders to bring about vastly expanded flows of people, money, goods, services, and information."[12] In a globalized world, countries and people are increasingly interconnected through the news, in travel and lifestyles, in labour markets and employment patterns, and in business dealings. Government leaders now worry about the competitiveness of nations, just as corporate leaders worry about business competitiveness.[13] The world is increasingly arranged in regional economic blocs, with Asia, North and Latin America, and Europe as key anchors, and with Africa fast emerging to claim its economic potential. Like any informed citizen, you too must understand the forces of globalization.

■ **Globalization** is the worldwide interdependence of resource flows, product markets, and business competition.

●●● TECHNOLOGY

The global economy isn't the only beneficiary of developments with new technology. Who hasn't been affected by the Internet and the World Wide Web? For better or worse, we now live in a technology-driven world increasingly dominated by bar codes, automatic tellers, computerized telemarketing campaigns, electronic mail, Internet resources, electronic commerce, and more.

From the small retail store to the large multinational firm, technology is an indispensable part of everyday operations—whether one is checking inventory, making a sales transaction, ordering supplies, or analyzing customer preferences.[14] And when it comes to communication in organizations, geographical distances hardly matter anymore. Computer networking can bring together almost anyone from anywhere in the world at the mere touch of a keyboard. In "virtual space" people hold meetings, access common databases, share information and files, make plans, and solve problems together—all without ever meeting face-to-face. As the pace and complexities of technological change accelerate, the demand for knowledge workers with the skills to best utilize technology is increasing. Computer literacy must be mastered and continuously updated as a foundation for career success.

●●● DIVERSITY

When published by the Hudson Institute, the report *Workforce 2000: Work and Workers for the 21st Century* created an immediate stir in business circles, among government policymakers, and in the public eye.[15] It called attention to the slow growth of the North American workforce, fewer younger workers entering the labour pool, the higher average age of the workforce, more women entering the workforce, and the increased proportions of minorities and immigrants in the workforce. A follow-up report, *Workforce 2020*, focusing on diversity themes and trends, was referred to as "a wake-up call for…workers, corporations, educators, parents and government offcials."[16]

> ■ **Workforce diversity** describes differences in gender, race, age, ethnicity, able-bodiness, religious affiliation, and sexual orientation among workers.

The term **workforce diversity** describes the composition of a workforce in terms of differences among the members.[17] These differences include gender, age, race, ethnicity, religion, sexual orientation, and able-bodiness. The *Canadian Human Rights Act* is very strict in prohibiting the use of demographic characteristics in human resource management decisions.[18] And indeed, today's increasingly diverse and multicultural workforce is increasingly viewed as an asset offering great opportunities for performance gains.[19] By "valuing diversity," organizations can tap a rich talent pool and help everyone work to their full potential. But what does this really mean? According to one consultant, it should mean "enabling every member of your workforce to perform to his or her potential." A female vice-president at Avon once posed the challenge of managing diversity this way: "consciously creating an environment where everyone has an equal shot at contributing, participating, and most of all advancing."[20]

Even though progress in valuing diversity continues to be made, lingering inequalities remain in the workplace. A study by Catalyst, a non-profit research group focusing on corporate women, reports that among Fortune 500 companies women held 15.7 percent of top jobs in 2002, up from 8.7 percent in 1995. There were six woman CEOs, up from one in 1995.[21] That's quite an increase; however, the figures still leave a lot of room for future progress. In terms of wage comparisons, Catalyst found that for each $1 earned by men, women earn 86 cents. Catalyst also found that 66 percent of minority women in management are dissatisfied with their career advancement opportunities.[22]

> ■ **Prejudice** is the display of negative, irrational attitudes toward women or minorities.

> ■ **Discrimination** actively denies women and minorities the full benefits of organizational membership.

In respect to racial diversity in the workplace, a *Fortune* magazine article once concluded: "The good news is, there's plenty of progress for companies and employees to talk about… But what often doesn't get said, especially in mixed-race settings, is how much remains to get done."[23] A recent study revealed, for example, that when resumés are sent to potential employers, those with white-sounding first names, like Brett, received 50 percent more responses than those with black-sounding first names, such as Kareem.[24] The fact that these resumés were created with equal credentials reveals once again that diversity bias can still be a limiting factor in too many work settings.[25] **Prejudice**, or the holding of negative, irrational opinions and attitudes regarding members of diverse populations, sets the stage for bias. It becomes active **discrimination** when minority members are unfairly treated and denied the full benefits of organizational membership. A subtle form of discrimination is called the **glass ceiling effect**, an invisible barrier or "ceiling" that prevents women and minorities from rising above a certain level of organizational responsibility.[26] Scholar Judith Rosener suggests that the organization's loss for any discriminatory practices is "undervalued and underutilized human capital."[27]

> ■ The **glass ceiling effect** is an invisible barrier limiting career advancement of women and minorities.

●●● ETHICS

> ■ **Ethics** set moral standards of what is "good" and "right" in one's behaviour.

Surely you remember the recent sensational cases of ethical failures in business—WorldCom, Bre-X, Enron, and Arthur Andersen, among others.[28] In Chapter 3, **ethics** is defined as a code of moral principles that sets standards of what is "good" and "right" as opposed to "bad" or "wrong" in the conduct of a person or group. There is a lot to be concerned about in the behaviour of the corporations and people behind the scandals. Senior executives acted unethically, and organizational systems tolerated actions that enriched the few while damaging many—from company employees losing retirement savings, to stock-holders whose investments lost value, to customers and society who paid the price as business performance deteriorated.

Even though ethical failures are well publicized, there is a plethora of positive cases and ethical role models to be studied as well. You will find in this book many examples of people and organizations that are exemplars of ethical leadership and whose integrity is unquestioned. They meet the standards of an ethical reawakening that places high value on social responsibility in business and organizational practices. The expectations include integrity and ethical leadership at all levels in an organization, sustainable development and protection of the natural environment, protection of consumers through product safety and fair practices, and protection of human rights in all aspects of society, including employment.[29]

Society is becoming strict in requiring businesses and other social institutions to operate according to high moral standards. Businesses, by law, must have boards of directors that are elected by stockholders to represent their interests. One of the issues raised by the rash of business ethics failures is the role of corporate governance, the active oversight of management decisions and company actions by boards of directors. Many argue that **corporate governance** failed in cases like Enron, Hollinger Inc., and Andersen. The result is more emphasis today on restoring the strength of corporate governance. The expectation is that boards will hold management accountable for ethical and socially responsible behaviour by the businesses they are hired to lead. Consider, for example, the ethical framework set by this statement from the credo of Johnson & Johnson:[30]

◾ **Corporate governance** is oversight of a company's management by a board of directors.

We are responsible to the communities in which we live and work, and to the world community as well. We must be good citizens—support good works and charities and bear our fair share of taxes. We must encourage civic improvements and better health and education. We must maintain in good order the property we are privileged to use, protecting the environment and natural resources.

●●● CAREERS

The career implications of the new economy and the challenges of change make personal initiative and self-renewal hallmarks of the day. British scholar Charles Handy suggests the analogy of the Irish shamrock to describe and understand the new employment patterns characteristic of this dynamic environment.[31] Each of a shamrock's three leaves has a different career implication. In one leaf are the core workers. These full-time employees pursue traditional career paths. With success and the maintenance of critical skills, they can advance within the organization and may remain employed for a long time. In the second leaf are contract workers. They perform specific tasks as needed by the organization and are compensated on a fee-for-services basis rather than by a continuing wage or salary. They sell a skill or service and contract with many different employers over time. In the third leaf are part-time workers hired only as needed and for only the number of hours needed. Employers expand and reduce their part-time staffs as business needs rise and fall. Part-time work can be a training ground or point of entry to the core when openings are available.

The Bank of Nova Scotia is an example of a "shamrock" organization. Core workers include branch managers, full-time tellers, HRM (human resource management) professionals, financial traders, and senior managers. Contract workers might include information technology specialists, project leaders, or managerial consultants; part-time employees would include customer service representatives and co-op students who are brought in during key times.

You must be prepared to prosper in any of the shamrock's three leaves. The typical career of the 21st century won't be uniformly full-time and limited to a single large employer. It is more likely to unfold opportunistically and involve several employment options over time. Not only must you be prepared to change jobs and employers over time, but your skills must be portable and always of current value in the employment markets. Skills are not gained once and then forgotten; they must be carefully maintained and upgraded all the time. One career consultant describes this career scenario with the analogy of a surfer: "You're always moving. You can expect to fall into the water any number of times, and you have to get back up to catch the next wave."[32] Handy's advice is that you maintain a "portfolio of skills" that is always up-to-date and valuable to potential employers.

✓ Learning check ①

BE SURE YOU CAN
• describe how intellectual capital, ethics, diversity, globalization, technology, and the changing nature of careers influence working in the new economy • define the terms intellectual capital, workforce diversity, and globalization • explain how prejudice, discrimination, and the glass ceiling effect can hurt people at work

ORGANIZATIONS IN THE NEW WORKPLACE

The new world of work is closely tied to the connectivity made possible by information technology. Management consultant Tom Peters describes it this way:[33]

> *In the next few years, whether at a tiny company or behemoth, we will be working with an eclectic mix of contract teammates from around the globe, many of whom we'll never meet face-to-face. Every project will call for a new team, composed of specially tailored skills....Every player on this team will be evaluated—pass-by-pass, at-bat by at-bat—for the quality and uniqueness and timeliness and passion of her or his contribution.*

MANAGER'S
Notepad 1.1

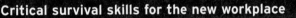

Critical survival skills for the new workplace

Mastery: You need to be good at something; you need to be able to contribute something of value to your employer.

Network: You need to know people; links with peers and others within and outside the organization are essential to get things done.

Entrepreneurship: You must act as if you are running your own business: spotting ideas and opportunities, and stepping out to embrace them.

Embrace technology: You have to understand and utilize technology effectively; you don't have to be a technician, but you must be willing and able to fully utilize IT.

Marketing: You need to be able to communicate your successes and progress: both yours personally and those of your work group.

Passion for renewal: You need to be continuously learning and changing, always updating yourself to best meet future demands.

Organizations in the new workplace are challenging settings, but exciting for their great opportunities and possibilities. Whether large or small, business or non-profit, each should make real and positive contributions to society. Everyone has a stake in making sure that they perform to expectations, including how well they serve as a principal source of careers and economic livelihood. In his article "The Company of the Future," Robert Reich says: "Everybody works for somebody or something—be it a board of directors, a pension fund, a venture capitalist, or a traditional boss. Sooner or later you're going to have to decide who you want to work for."[34] In order to make good employment choices and perform well in a career, you must have a fundamental understanding of the nature of organizations in the new workplace. *Manager's Notepad 1.1* provides a first look at some of the critical survival skills that you should acquire in order to work well in the organizations of today…and tomorrow.[35]

●●● WHAT IS AN ORGANIZATION?

An **organization** is a collection of people working together to achieve a common purpose.[36] It is a unique social phenomenon that enables its members to perform tasks far beyond the reach of individual accomplishment. This description applies to organizations of all sizes and types, from large corporations, to the small businesses that make up the life of any community, to non-profit organizations such as schools, government agencies, and community hospitals.

All organizations share a broad purpose—providing useful goods or services. Each one should return value to society and satisfy customers' needs in order to justify its continued existence. A clear sense of purpose that is tied to "quality products" and "customer satisfaction" is an important source of organizational strength and performance advantage. At Medtronic, a large Minnesota-based medical products company, for example, employees are noted for innovation and their commitment to a clear and singular corporate mission—helping sick people get well. The sense of common purpose centres attention and focuses their collective talents on accomplishing a compelling goal: improving the health and well-being of those who use Medtronic products.[37]

■ An **organization** is a collection of people working together in a division of labour to achieve a common purpose.

●●● ORGANIZATIONS AS SYSTEMS

Organizations are systems composed of interrelated parts that function together to achieve a common purpose.[38] They are **open systems** that interact with their environments in the continual process of transforming resource inputs into product outputs in the form of finished goods and/or services. As shown in *Figure 1.1*, the external environment is a critical element in the open-systems view of organizations. It is both a supplier of resources and the source of customers. Feedback from the environment tells an organization how well it is doing. Without customer willingness to use the organization's products, it is difficult to operate or stay in business over the long run. The recent bankruptcies of Canada 3000, The Bombay Company, and Planet Hollywood give stark testimony to this fact of the marketplace: without customers, a business can't survive.

■ In an **open system**, organizations interact with their environment to transform resources into product outputs.

The environment supplies

Resource inputs
People
Money
Materials
Technology
Information

The organization creates

Work activities turn resources into outputs
Transformation process

The environment consumes

Product outputs
Finished goods and/or services

Customer and client feedback

Figure 1.1 Organizations as open systems.

●●● ORGANIZATIONAL PERFORMANCE

For an organization to perform well, resources must be well utilized and customers well served. The notion of *value creation* is very important in this context. If operations add value to the original cost of resource inputs, then (1) a business organization can earn a profit—that is, sell a product for more than the cost of making it (e.g., fast-food restaurant meals), or (2) a non-profit organization can add wealth to society—that is, provide a public service that is worth more than its cost (e.g., fire protection in a community). Value is created when an organization's resources are utilized in the right way, at the right time, and at minimum cost to create high-quality goods and services for customers.

The best organizations utilize a variety of performance measures. On the customer side, high-performing firms measure customer satisfaction and loyalty, as well as market share. On the employee side, they measure retention, career development, job satisfaction, and task performance. A common measure of overall performance is **productivity**, the quantity and quality of work performance, relative to resources used. Productivity can be measured at the individual, group, as well as organizational levels.

Figure 1.2 links productivity with two terms commonly used in management: effectiveness and efficiency. **Performance effectiveness** is an output measure of task or goal accomplishment. If you are working in the manufacturing area of a computer firm, for example, performance effectiveness may mean that you meet a daily production target in terms of the quantity and quality of keyboards assembled. By so doing, you help the company as a whole to maintain its production schedule and meet customer demands for timely delivery and high-quality products.

■ **Productivity** is the quantity and quality of work performance, with resource utilization considered.

■ **Performance effectiveness** is an output measure of task or goal accomplishment.

Figure 1.2 Productivity and the dimensions of organizational performance.

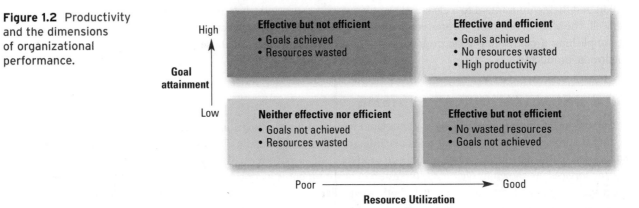

■ **Performance efficiency** is an input measure of resource costs associated with goal accomplishment.

Performance efficiency is a measure of the resource costs associated with goal accomplishment. Cost of labour is a common efficiency measure. Others include equipment utilization, facilities maintenance, and supplies or materials expenses. Returning to the example of computer assembly, the most efficient production is accomplished at a minimum cost in materials and labour. If you were producing fewer computer keyboards in a day than you were capable of, this amounts to inefficiency. Likewise, if you made a lot of mistakes or wasted materials in the assembly process, this is also inefficient work. In summary, efficiency means doing things right while effectiveness means doing the right things. To achieve high productivity, a company must be both efficient and effective.

●●● CHANGING NATURE OF ORGANIZATIONS

Change is a continuing theme of this book, and organizations are certainly undergoing dramatic changes today. Among the many trends in the new workplace, the following organizational transitions are important to your study of management:[39]

- *Belief in human capital:* Demands of the new economy place premiums on high involvement and participatory work settings that rally the knowledge, experience, and commitment of all members.

- *Demise of "command-and-control":* Traditional hierarchical structures with "do as I say" bosses are proving to be too slow, conservative, and costly for today's competitive environments.

- *Emphasis on teamwork:* Today's organizations are less vertical and more horizontal in focus; they are increasingly driven by teamwork that pools talents for creative problem solving.

- *Pre-eminence of technology:* New opportunities appear with each new development in computer and information technology; they continually change the way organizations operate and how people work.

- *Embrace of networking:* Organizations are networked for real-time communication and coordination, both internally and externally with partners, contractors, suppliers, and customers.

- *New workforce expectations:* A new generation of workers brings to the workplace less tolerance for hierarchy, more informality, and more attention to performance merit than to status and seniority.

- *Concern for work-life balance:* Today, workers are forcing organizations to pay more attention to balance in the often conflicting demands of work and personal affairs.

take it to the case!

Apple Computer Inc.
Where people and design create the future

Innovative design is a mainstay of Apple's business model. But there's more to the company than that. Under the leadership of co-founder Steven Jobs, Apple Computer is a model of operating efficiency and marketing savvy. Jobs claims we are entering the third and "golden age" of personal computing. With this vision, there is no doubt that Jobs brings passion, inventiveness, and a great eye for customer markets to the company. But the execution comes from people and the team driven, technology rich, and talent based high-performance environment that represents life within Apple. If you want to study a company that operates with a keen eye for new technology and market adaptability in the fast-paced world of the new economy, take a look at Apple. Even in the intensely competitive computer industries, the wizardry of Apple sets a benchmark for the rest of the pack. Recently, Apple topped the *Business Week*/Boston Consulting Group's list as "The Worlds's Most Innovative Company"—check out the case to learn more about how they did it!

Sources: "Apple," *Business Week* (July 31, 2000), pp. 102–13, "Apple Wins with Design," *Business Week* (July 31, 2000), pp. 144, and "Apple Putting Hopes on New Macintosh Line," *New York Times* (January 10, 2001), p. C7. "The Worlds's Most Innovative Companies," *Business Week* (May 4, 2007)

- *Focus on speed:* In business those who get products to market first have an advantage, and in any organization work is expected to be both well done and timely.

There are many forces driving these changes in organizations. Key among them is unrelenting demand for quality products and services. Organizations that fail to listen to their customers and fail to deliver quality goods and services at reasonable prices will be left struggling in a highly competitive environment. References will be made throughout this book to the concept of **total quality management (TQM)**—managing with an organization-wide commitment to continuous improvement and meeting customer needs completely.[40] For the moment, the quality commitment can be recognized as a hallmark of enlightened productivity management in any organization.

■ **Total quality management (TQM)** is managing with commitment to continuous improvement, product quality, and customer satisfaction.

✔ Learning check ❷

BE SURE YOU CAN

- describe how organizations operate as open systems • explain productivity as a measure of organizational performance • list several ways in which organizations are changing today • distinguish between performance effectiveness and performance efficiency • explain the concept of TQM

MANAGERS IN THE NEW WORKPLACE

In an article entitled "Putting People First for Organizational Success," Jeffrey Pfeffer and John F. Veiga argue forcefully that organizations perform better when they treat their members better. They also point out that too many organizations fail to operate in this manner and, as a consequence, suffer performance failures. Pfeffer uses the term "toxic workplaces" to describe organizations that treat their employees mainly as costs to be reduced. True high-performing organizations are very different. They treat people as valuable strategic assets that should be carefully nurtured.[41]

The themes and concepts of *Management* support this view that organizations should operate with a commitment to people as their most important assets. In the day-to-day flow of events in any workplace, those who serve in managerial roles have a special responsibility for ensuring that this commitment is fulfilled.

●●● WHAT IS A MANAGER?

You find them in all organizations. They work with a wide variety of job titles—supervisor, team leader, department head, project manager, dean, president, administrator, and more. They always work directly with other persons who rely on them for critical support and assistance in their own jobs. We call them **managers**, people in organizations who directly support and help activate the work efforts and performance accomplishments of others.

For those serving as managers, the job is challenging and substantial. Any manager is responsible not just for his or her own work but for the overall performance and accomplishments of a team, work group, department, or even organization as a whole. Research conducted by the Saratoga Institute reports that the average manager oversees the work of 10.75 other people.[42] Whether they are called direct reports, team members, work associates, or subordinates, these "other people" are the essential human resources whose contributions represent the real work of the organization.

Every manager's job thus entails a key responsibility—to help other people achieve high performance. Those persons working with and reporting to managers are the critical human capital upon whose intellects and efforts the performance of any organization is ultimately

■ A **manager** is a person who supports and is responsible for the work of others.

built. As pointed out by McGill University management theorist Henry Mintzberg, being a manager in this sense is a most important and socially responsible job:[43]

> *No job is more vital to our society than that of the manager. It is the manager who determines whether our social institutions serve us well or whether they squander our talents and resources. It is time to strip away the folklore about managerial work, and time to study it realistically so that we can begin the difficult task of making significant improvement in its performance.*

●●● LEVELS AND TYPES OF MANAGERS

The nature of managerial work is evolving as organizations change and develop with time. In addition to being responsible for the people who report directly to them, managers must influence others as well. A *Wall Street Journal* report described the transition of managers as follows: "Not so long ago they may have supervised 10 people sitting outside their offices. Today they must win the support of scores more—employees of different backgrounds, job titles, and even cultures. These new managers are expected to be skilled at organizing complex subjects, solving problems, communicating ideas, and making swift decisions."[44]

Levels of Managers

At the highest levels of organizations, common job titles are chief executive officer (CEO), president, and vice president. These **top managers** are responsible for the performance of an organization as a whole, or for one of its larger parts. They pay special attention to the external environment, are alert to potential long-run problems and opportunities, and develop appropriate ways of dealing with them. The best top managers are future-oriented strategic thinkers who make many decisions under highly competitive and uncertain conditions. They scan the environment, create and communicate long-term vision, and ensure that strategies and objectives are consistent with the organization's purpose and mission. Before retiring as Medtronic's CEO, Bill George crafted "Vision 2010" to position the firm as a client-centred deliverer of medical services. The hours were long and the work demanding, but George also loved his job, saying: "I always dreamed…of being head of a major corporation where the values of the company and my own values were congruent, where a company could become kind of a symbol for others, where the product that you represent is doing good for people."[45]

■ **Top managers** guide the performance of the organization as a whole or of one of its major parts.

Middle managers are in charge of relatively large departments or divisions consisting of several smaller work units. Examples are clinic directors in hospitals; deans in universities; and division managers, plant managers, and branch sales managers in businesses. Middle managers work with top managers and coordinate with peers to develop and implement action plans to accomplish organizational objectives. They must be team oriented and able to work well with people from all parts of an organization. An important example is the job of **project manager**, someone who coordinates complex projects with task deadlines while working with many persons within and outside the organization. At General Electric, for example, corporate troubleshooting groups solve problems and create change across divisions and geographic boundaries within the company. One cross-functional team brought together managers from marketing, human resources, and field operations to design a new compensation system.[46]

■ **Middle managers** oversee the work of large departments or divisions.

■ **Project managers** coordinate complex projects with task deadlines.

Even though most people enter the workforce as technical specialists, sooner or later they advance to positions of initial managerial responsibility. A first job in management typically involves serving as a **team leader** or **supervisor**—someone in charge of a small work group composed of nonmanagerial workers. Job titles for these *first-line managers* vary greatly but

■ **Team leaders** or **supervisors** report to middle managers and directly supervise nonmanagerial workers.

include such designations as department head, group leader, and unit manager. For example, the leader of an auditing team is considered a first-line manager, as is the head of an academic department in a university. *Manager's Notepad 1.2* offers advice on the performance responsibilities of team leaders and supervisors.[47] Such managers ensure that their work teams or units meet performance objectives that are consistent with higher-level organizational goals. Justine Fritz led a 12-member Medtronic team to launch a new product. "I've just never worked on anything that so visibly, so dramatically changes the quality of someone's life," she says, while noting that the demands are also great. "Some days you wake up, and if you think about all the work you have to do it's so overwhelming, you could be paralyzed." That's the challenge of managerial work at any level. Fritz says: "You just have to get it done."[48]

MANAGER'S
Notepad 1.2
Nine responsibilities of team leaders

1. Plan meetings and work schedules.
2. Clarify goals and tasks, and gather ideas for improvement.
3. Appraise performance and counsel team members.
4. Recommend pay increases and new assignments.
5. Recruit, train, and develop teams to meet performance goals.
6. Encourage high performance and teamwork.
7. Inform team members about organizational goals and expectations.
8. Inform higher levels of team needs and accomplishments.
9. Coordinate with other teams and support the rest of the organization.

Types of Managers

In addition to serving at different levels of authority, managers work in different capacities within organizations. **Line managers** are responsible for work activities that make a direct contribution to the organization's outputs. For example, the president, retail manager, and department supervisors of a local department store all have line responsibilities. Their jobs in one way or another are directly related to the sales operations of the store. **Staff managers**, by contrast, use special technical expertise to advise and support the efforts of line workers. In a department store, the director of human resources and chief financial offcer would have staff responsibilities.

In business, **functional managers** have responsibility for a single area of activity, such as finance, marketing, production, personnel, accounting, or sales. **General managers** are responsible for more complex units that include many functional areas. An example is a plant manager who oversees many separate functions, including purchasing, manufacturing, warehousing, sales, personnel, and accounting. It is common for managers working in public or non-profit organizations to be called **administrators**. Examples include hospital administrator, public administrator, city administrator, and human-service administrator.

●●● MANAGERIAL PERFORMANCE

All managers help people, working individually and in groups, to achieve productivity while using their talents to accomplish organizational goals. Importantly, managers do this while being held personally "accountable" for results achieved. **Accountability** is the requirement

---

■ **Line managers** directly contribute to the production of the organization's basic goods or services.

■ **Staff managers** use special technical expertise to advise and support line workers.

■ **Functional managers** are responsible for one area of activity, such as finance, marketing, production, personnel, accounting, or sales.

■ **General managers** are responsible for complex multi-functional units.

■ An **administrator** is a manager in a public or non-profit organization.

■ **Accountability** is the requirement to show performance results to one's immediate supervisor.

of one person to answer to a higher authority for performance results achieved in his or her area of work responsibility. The team leader is accountable to a middle manager, the middle manager is accountable to a top manager, and even the top manager is accountable to a board of directors.

But the concept of managerial performance is multi-dimensional. Superior managers help others to both achieve high performance by working effectively and efficiently, and experience satisfaction in their work. This dual concern for performance and satisfaction is a central theme in the new workplace, and it runs throughout *Management*. It is represented in the concept of **quality of work life,** an indicator of the overall quality of human experiences in the workplace. A "high-QWL" workplace expresses a true respect for people at work by offering such things as fair pay, safe working conditions, opportunities to learn and use new skills, room to grow and progress in a career, protection of individual rights, and pride in the work itself and in the organization. Part of any manager's accountability is to achieve high-performance outcomes while maintaining a high-quality work life environment.[49] Simply put, in the new workplace, performance, satisfaction, and a high-quality work life can, and should, go hand in hand.

■ **Quality of work life** is the overall quality of human experiences in the workplace.

●●● CHANGING NATURE OF MANAGERIAL WORK

In today's organizations the words "coordinator," "coach," and "team leader" are heard as often as "supervisor" or "manager." The work managers perform is less directive and more supportive than in the past. There is little tolerance or need in today's organizations for those who simply sit back and tell others what to do. The best managers are well informed regarding the needs of those reporting to or dependent on them. They can often be found working alongside those they supervise. They will always be found providing advice and developing the support needed for others to perform to the best of their abilities. High-performing managers are good at building working relationships with others, helping others develop their skills and performance competencies, fostering teamwork, and otherwise creating a work environment that is both performance driven and satisfying to those who do the required work.

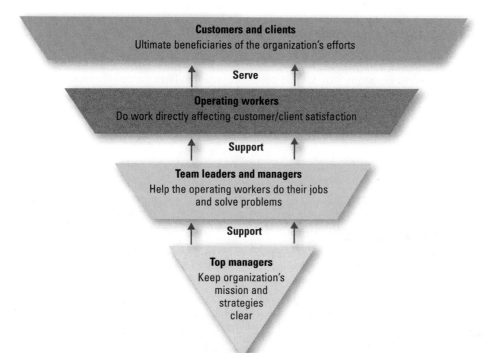

Customers and clients
Ultimate beneficiaries of the organization's efforts

Serve

Operating workers
Do work directly affecting customer/client satisfaction

Support

Team leaders and managers
Help the operating workers do their jobs and solve problems

Support

Top managers
Keep organization's mission and strategies clear

Figure 1.3 The organization viewed as an upside-down pyramid.

Among the many changes taking place in managerial work, the concept of the "upside-down pyramid" is insightful. Shown in *Figure 1.3*, it offers an alternative way of viewing organizations and the role played by managers within them. The operating workers are at the top of the upside-down pyramid, just below the customers and clients that they serve. They are supported in their work efforts by managers located at the bottom. These managers aren't just order givers; they are there to mobilize and deliver the support others require to best serve customer needs. Each member of the upside-down pyramid is a value-added worker—someone who creates eventual value for the organization's customers or clients. The whole organization is devoted to serving the customer, and this is made possible with the support of managers. As noted earlier, we are in a time when the best managers are known more for "helping" and "supporting" than for "directing" and "order giving." Even in an age of high technology and "smart" machines, the human resource is indispensable. Worker involvement and empowerment are critical building blocks of organizational success. Full human resource utilization increasingly means changing the way work gets done by pushing decision-making authority to the point where the best information and expertise exist—with the operating workers.

✓ Learning check ❸

BE SURE YOU CAN

• describe the various types and levels of managers • define the terms accountability and quality of work life and explain their importance to managerial performance • explain the role of managers in the upside-down pyramid view of organizations • list the several ways in which managerial work is changing

THE MANAGEMENT PROCESS

The ultimate "bottom line" in every manager's job is to succeed in helping an organization achieve high performance by best utilizing its human and material resources. If productivity in the form of high levels of performance effectiveness and efficiency is a measure of organizational success, managers are largely responsible for its achievement. It is their job to mobilize technology and talent by creating environments within which people work hard and perform to the best of their abilities.

●●● FUNCTIONS OF MANAGEMENT

Managers must have the capabilities to recognize performance problems and opportunities, make good decisions, and take appropriate actions. They do this through the process

Figure 1.4 Four functions of management.

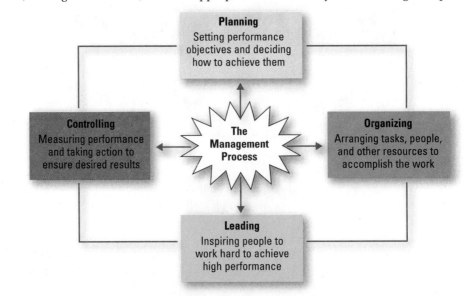

Planning
Setting performance objectives and deciding how to achieve them

Organizing
Arranging tasks, people, and other resources to accomplish the work

The Management Process

Controlling
Measuring performance and taking action to ensure desired results

Leading
Inspiring people to work hard to achieve high performance

AROUND THE WORLD

Ernst & Young is one of the world's top professional services firms. With operations in 130 countries, it serves the needs of business customers in all areas of public accounting as well as online security, enterprise risk management, and other business areas. Wherever in the world Ernst & Young operates, its performance commitment is expressed in the slogan "Quality in Everything We Do." Recently, Ernst & Young Poland was named by the local edition of *Newsweek* as the country's most desired employer. The firm's goal of valuing people is expressed in its emphasis on teamwork, continuous learning, work-life balance, and leadership for all employees.

Source: information from the corporate website: <www.ey.com>

Professionalism travels the world

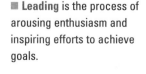

of **management**—planning, organizing, leading, and controlling the use of resources to accomplish performance goals. These four management functions and their interrelationships are shown in *Figure 1.4*. All managers, regardless of title, level, type, and organizational setting, are responsible for the four functions.[50] However, they are not accomplished in linear step-by-step fashion. The reality is that all functions are continually engaged as a manager moves from task to task and opportunity to opportunity in his or her work.

■ **Management** is the process of planning, organizing, leading, and controlling the use of resources to accomplish performance goals.

Planning

In management, **planning** is the process of setting performance objectives and determining what actions should be taken to accomplish them. Through planning, a manager identifies desired results and ways to achieve them. Take, for example, an Ernst & Young initiative that was developed to better meet the needs of the firm's female professionals.[51] Top management grew concerned about the firm's retention rates for women and by a critical report from the research group Catalyst. Chairman Philip A. Laskawy, who personally headed Ernst & Young's Diversity Task Force, responded by setting a planning objective to reduce turnover rates for women. Rates at the time were running some 22 percent per year and costing the firm about 150 percent of each person's annual salary to hire and train new staff.

■ **Planning** is the process of setting objectives and determining what should be done to accomplish them.

Organizing

Even the best plans will fail without strong implementation. Success begins with **organizing**, the process of assigning tasks, allocating resources, and coordinating the activities of individuals and groups to implement plans. Through organizing, managers turn plans into actions by defining jobs, assigning personnel, and supporting them with technology and other resources. At Ernst & Young, Laskawy organized to meet his planning objective by first creating a new Office of Retention and then hiring Deborah K. Holmes to head it. As retention problems were identified in various parts of the firm, Holmes convened special task forces to tackle them and recommend location-specific solutions. A Woman's Access Program was started to give women access to senior executives for mentoring and career development.

■ **Organizing** is the process of assigning tasks, allocating resources, and coordinating work activities.

Leading

In management, **leading** is the process of arousing people's enthusiasm to work hard and inspiring their efforts to fulfill plans and accomplish objectives. Through leading, managers

■ **Leading** is the process of arousing enthusiasm and inspiring efforts to achieve goals.

build commitments to a common vision, encourage activities that support goals, and influence others to do their best work on the organization's behalf. At Ernst & Young, Deborah Holmes identified a core problem—work at the firm was extremely intense and women were often stressed because their spouses also worked. She became a champion for improved work-life balance and pursued it relentlessly. Although admitting that "there's no silver bullet" in the form of a universal solution, new initiatives from her office supported and encouraged better balance. She started "call-free holidays" where professionals did not check voice mail or e-mail on weekends and holidays. She also started a "travel sanity" program that limited staffers' travel to four days a week so that they could get home for weekends.

Controlling

> ■ **Controlling** is the process of measuring performance and taking action to ensure desired results.

The management function of **controlling** is the process of measuring work performance, comparing results to objectives, and taking corrective action as needed. Through controlling, managers maintain active contact with people in the course of their work, gather and interpret reports on performance, and use this information to plan constructive action and change. At Ernst & Young, Laskawy and Holmes both knew what the retention rates were when they started the new program, and they were subsequently able to track improvements. Through measurement they were able to compare results with objectives, and track changes in work-life balance and retention rates. They continually adjusted the program to improve it. In today's dynamic times, such control and adjustment are indispensable. Things don't always go as anticipated, and plans must be modified and redefined for future success.

●●● MANAGERIAL ACTIVITIES AND ROLES

Although the management process may seem straightforward, things are more complicated than they appear at first glance. In his classic book *The Nature of Managerial Work*, Henry Mintzberg describes the daily work of corporate chief executives as: "There was no break in the pace of activity during office hours. The mail…telephone calls…and meetings…accounted for almost every minute from the moment these executives entered their offices in the morning until they departed in the evenings."[52] Today, we would have to add ever-present e-mail to Mintzberg's list of executive preoccupations.[53]

In trying to systematically describe the nature of managerial work and the demands placed on those who do it, Mintzberg identified the set of 10 roles depicted in *Figure 1.5*. The roles involve managing information, people, and action. The roles are interconnected, and all managers must be prepared to perform all of them.[54] In Mintzberg's framework, a manager's *informational roles* involve the giving, receiving, and analyzing of information. The *interpersonal roles* involve interactions with people inside and outside the work unit. The *decisional roles* involve using information to make decisions to solve problems or address opportunities.

Mintzberg is careful to note that the manager's day is unforgiving in the intensity and pace of these role requirements. The managers he observed had little free time because unexpected problems and continuing requests for meetings consumed almost all the time that became available. Their workdays were hectic, and the pressure for continuously improving performance was all-encompassing. Says Mintzberg: "The manager can never be free to forget the job, and never has the pleasure of knowing, even temporarily, that there is nothing else to do.… Managers always carry the nagging suspicion that they might be able to contribute just a little bit more. Hence they assume an unrelenting pace in their work."[55]

Managerial work is busy, demanding, and stressful not just for chief executives but for managers at all levels of responsibility in any work setting. A summary of research on the nature of managerial work offers this important reminder.[56]

Interpersonal roles	Informational roles	Decisional roles
How a manager interacts with other people • Figurehead • Leader • Liaison	How a manager exchanges and processes information • Monitor • Disseminator • Spokesperson	How a manager uses information in decision making • Entrepreneur • Disturbance handler • Resource allocator • Negotiator

Figure 1.5 Mintzberg's 10 managerial roles.

- Managers work long hours.

- Managers work at an intense pace.

- Managers work at fragmented and varied tasks.

- Managers work with many communication media.

- Managers accomplish their work largely through interpersonal relationships.

●●● MANAGERIAL AGENDAS AND NETWORKING

On her way to a meeting, a general manager (GM) bumped into a staff member who did not report to her. Using this opportunity, in a two-minute conversation she (a) asked two questions and received the information she needed; (b) reinforced their good relationship by sincerely complimenting the staff member on something he had recently done; and (c) got the staff member to agree to do something that the GM needed done.

This description of a brief incident provides a glimpse of an effective general manager in action.[57] It portrays two activities that management consultant and scholar John Kotter considers critical to a general manager's success—agenda setting and networking. Through agenda setting, good managers develop action priorities that include goals and plans spanning long and short time frames. These agendas are usually incomplete and loosely connected in the beginning, but become more specific as the manager utilizes information continually gleaned from many different sources. The agendas are always kept in mind and are "played out" whenever an opportunity arises, as in the preceding quotation. Good managers implement their agendas by working with a variety of people inside and outside the organization. In Kotter's example, the GM was getting things done through a staff member who did not report directly to her. This is made possible by networking, the process of building and maintaining positive relationships with people whose help may be needed to implement one's work agendas. In this example, the GM's networks would include relationships with peers, a boss, and higher-level executives, subordinates, and members of their work teams, as well

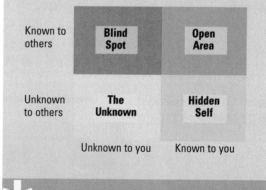

as with external customers, suppliers, and community representatives. Such networks are indispensable to managerial success in today's complex work environments, and excellent managers devote much time and effort to their development.

✓ Learning check ❹

BE SURE YOU CAN

• define and give examples of each of the four major functions in the management process—planning, organizing, leading, and controlling • explain Mintzberg's view of what managers do, including the key managerial roles • explain how managers use agendas and networks to fulfill their work responsibilities

LEARNING HOW TO MANAGE

Today's turbulent times present an ever-shifting array of problems, opportunities, and performance expectations to organizations and their members. Change is a way of life, and it demands new organizational and individual responses. The quest for high performance is relentless, with workers everywhere expected to find ways to achieve high productivity under new and dynamic conditions. They are expected to become involved, participate fully, demonstrate creativity, and find self-fulfillment in their work. They are expected to be team players who understand the needs and goals of the total organization, and who use new technologies to their full advantage.

■ **Lifelong learning is continuous learning from daily experiences.**

All of this, of course, means that your career success depends on a real commitment to learning—not just formal learning in the classroom, but also **lifelong learning**. This is the process of continuously learning from our daily experiences and opportunities. Especially in a dynamic and ever-changing environment, a commitment to lifelong learning helps us build portfolios of skills that are always up to date, job relevant, and valuable in the emerging economy.

●●● ESSENTIAL MANAGERIAL SKILLS

■ **A skill is the ability to translate knowledge into action that results in desired performance.**

A **skill** is the ability to translate knowledge into action that results in desired performance. Obviously, many skills are required to master the challenging nature of managerial work. The most important ones are those that allow managers to help others become more productive in their work. Harvard scholar Robert L. Katz has classified the essential skills of managers into three categories: technical, human, and conceptual.[59] Although all three skills are necessary for managers, he suggests that their relative importance tends to vary by level of managerial responsibility, as shown in *Figure 1.6*.

Figure 1.6 Katz's essential managerial skills.

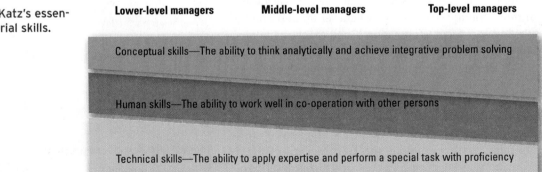

| Lower-level managers | Middle-level managers | Top-level managers |

Conceptual skills—The ability to think analytically and achieve integrative problem solving

Human skills—The ability to work well in co-operation with other persons

Technical skills—The ability to apply expertise and perform a special task with proficiency

A **technical skill** is the ability to use a special proficiency or expertise to perform particular tasks. Accountants, engineers, market researchers, financial planners, and systems analysts, for example, possess technical skills. These skills are initially acquired through formal education and are further developed by training and job experience. Technical skill in the new economy is also increasingly tied to computer literacy and utilization of the latest information technology. *Figure 1.6* shows that technical skills are very important at career entry levels. The critical question to be asked and positively answered by you in this respect and in preparation for any job interview comes down to this simple test: "What can you really do for an employer?"

The ability to work well in co-operation with other persons is a **human skill**. It emerges in the workplace as a spirit of trust, enthusiasm, and genuine involvement in interpersonal relationships. A manager with good human skills will have a high degree of self-awareness and a capacity to understand or empathize with the feelings of others. An important component of the essential human skills is **emotional intelligence**.[60] Discussed in Chapter 13 for its leadership implications, "EI" is defined by scholar and consultant Daniel Goleman as the "ability to manage ourselves and our relationships effectively."[61] Given the highly interpersonal nature of managerial work, human skills and emotional intelligence are critical for all managers. *Figure 1.6* shows that they are consistently important across all the managerial levels. Again, a straightforward question puts your interpersonal skills and emotional intelligence to the test: "How well do you work with others?"

All good managers ultimately have the ability to view situations broadly and to solve problems to the benefit of everyone concerned. This ability to think critically and analytically is a **conceptual skill**. It involves the capacity to break problems into smaller parts, to see the relations between the parts, and to recognize the implications of any one problem for others. As we assume ever-higher responsibilities in organizations, we are called upon to deal with more ambiguous problems that have many complications and longer-term consequences. *Figure 1.6* shows that conceptual skills gain in relative importance for top managers. At this point, you should ask: "Am I developing critical thinking and problem-solving capabilities for long-term career success?"

●●● SKILL AND OUTCOME ASSESSMENT

Business and management educators are increasingly interested in helping people acquire the essential skills and develop specific competencies that can help them achieve managerial success. A **managerial competency** is a skill-based capability that contributes to high performance in a management job.[62] A number of these competencies have been implied in the previous discussion of the management process, including those related to planning, organizing, leading, and controlling. Competencies are also implicit in the information, interpersonal, and decision-making demands of managerial roles, as well as in agenda setting and networking as managerial activities.

Listed here are some of the skills and personal characteristics business schools emphasize as foundations for continued professional development and career success. You can use this as a preliminary checklist for assessing your career readiness.

- *Communication*—ability to share ideas and findings clearly in written and oral expression—includes writing, oral presentation, giving/receiving feedback, technology utilization

- *Teamwork*—ability to work effectively as a team member and team leader—includes team contribution, team leadership, conflict management, negotiation, consensus building

■ **Technical skill** is the ability to use expertise to perform a task with proficiency.

■ A **human skill** is the ability to work well in co-operation with other people.

■ **Emotional intelligence** is the ability to manage ourselves and our relationships effectively.

■ **Conceptual skill** is the ability to think analytically and solve complex problems.

■ **Managerial competency** is a skill-based capability for high performance in a management job.

- *Self-management*—ability to evaluate oneself, modify behaviour, and meet performance obligations—includes ethical reasoning and behaviour, personal flexibility, tolerance for ambiguity, performance responsibility

- *Leadership*—ability to influence and support others to perform complex and ambiguous tasks—includes diversity awareness, global understanding, project management, strategic action

- *Critical thinking*—ability to gather and analyze information for creative problem solving—includes problem solving, judgement and decision making, information gathering and interpretation, creativity/innovation

- *Professionalism*—ability to sustain a positive impression, instill confidence, and maintain career advancement—includes personal presence, personal initiative, and career management

●●● *MANAGEMENT* LEARNING FRAMEWORK

Management introduces management as an academic discipline whose understanding is important for anyone seeking career success in the new workplace. The focus is on helping you to become familiar with key concepts, theories, and terms, and to understand their practical implications. The five major parts of the book are presented in a systematic building-block fashion: (1) Introducing Management, (2) Context, (3) Mission, (4) Organization, (5) Leading. The subject matter in each has been carefully chosen, described, and illustrated in ways that encourage you to actively think about your developing managerial skills and competencies. As you read *Management* remember to take full advantage of the built-in learning framework. The chapters are written with an integrated pedagogy that makes it easier for you to do well on assignments and examinations. From the chapter-opening study questions, to the learning preview, to the embedded learning checks, through the many examples, to the end-of-chapter study guide with its summary, key terms review, and self-test, you have the opportunity to learn as you read. If you allow the book's pedagogy to work for you, the learning opportunities summarized in *Figure 1.7* should pay off in solid understanding and enhanced course performance.

Figure 1.7 *Management–* Understanding Management from Theory to Practice.

Part 1 Management Today
- The Dynamic New Workplace
- Management—Past to Present
- Ethical Behaviour and Social Responsibility

Managerial Skills and Competencies
Management Learning Workbook

Part 2 Context
- Environment and Diversity
- Global Dimensions
- Entrepreneurship and Small Business

Part 3 Mission
- Information and Decision Making
- Planning and Controlling
- Strategic Management

Part 4 Organization
- Organizing
- Organizational Design and Processes
- Human Resource Management

Part 5 Leadership
- Leading
- Motivation–Theory and Practice
- Individual, Behaviour and Performance
- Teams and Teamwork
- Communication and Interpersonal Skills
- Change Leadership

A special and unique learning resource is found in the end-of-text *Management Learning Workbook*. This feature offers the critical "next step" in learning, providing you with a rich variety of resources and activities. Explore the cases, pursue the active-learning projects, engage in the experiential exercises, take the self-assessments, and build a student portfolio. Many opportunities for learning are present in the workbook, but only you can take advantage of them. Only you can step forward and take personal responsibility for advancing your managerial skills and career readiness in today's challenging world. *Management*, from cover to cover, is a great learning resource. Now is the time to read, study, and benefit from it. Get connected with your future!

BE SURE YOU CAN

• define three essential managerial skills—technical, human, and conceptual skills • explain Katz's view of how these skills vary in importance across management levels • define emotional intelligence as an important human skill • list and give examples of several personal characteristics important for managerial success

✓ Learning check ⑤

●●● Chapter 1   STUDY GUIDE

WHERE WE'VE BEEN

Back to workopolis.com

The opening example of workopolis.com focused on you, your career, and the great opportunities for career success that exist in today's dynamic environment. You don't need to create your own company to achieve career success, although you could. What you must do is discover the willingness to learn within yourself, and commit it to academic success and career development. In Chapter 1 you learned about the new work environment—from the challenges of technology utilization, to the forces of globalization, to diversity and ethical behaviour, and more. You also gained insight into the nature of organizations, the managerial roles, and the critical importance of developing essential managerial and leadership skills.

THE NEXT STEP
INTEGRATED LEARNING ACTIVITIES

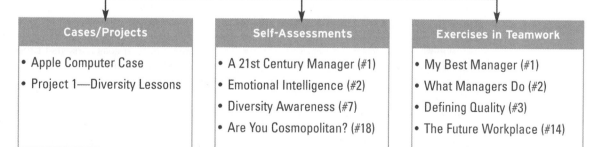

Cases/Projects	Self-Assessments	Exercises in Teamwork
• Apple Computer Case	• A 21st Century Manager (#1)	• My Best Manager (#1)
• Project 1—Diversity Lessons	• Emotional Intelligence (#2)	• What Managers Do (#2)
	• Diversity Awareness (#7)	• Defining Quality (#3)
	• Are You Cosmopolitan? (#18)	• The Future Workplace (#14)

STUDY QUESTION SUMMARY

1. What are the challenges of working in the new economy?

- Today's turbulent environment challenges everyone to understand and embrace continuous change and developments in a new information-driven and global economy.

- Work in the new economy is increasingly knowledge based, and people, with their capacity to bring valuable intellectual capital to the workplace, are the ultimate foundation of organizational performance.

- The forces of globalization are bringing increased interdependencies among nations and economies, as customer markets and resource flows create intense business competition.

- Ever-present developments in information technology and the continued expansion of the Internet are reshaping organizations, changing the nature of work, and increasing the value of knowledge workers.

- Organizations must value the talents and capabilities of a workforce whose members are increasingly diverse with respect to gender, age, race and ethnicity, able-bodiedness, and lifestyles.

- Society has high expectations for organizations and their members to perform with commitment to high ethical standards and in socially responsible ways, including protection of the natural environment and human rights.

- Careers in the new economy require great personal initiative to build and maintain skill "portfolios" that are always up to date and valuable to employers challenged by the intense competition and the information age.

2. What are organizations like in the new workplace?

- Organizations are collections of people working together to achieve a common purpose.

- As open systems, organizations interact with their environments in the process of transforming resource inputs into product outputs.

- Productivity is a measure of the quantity and quality of work performance, with resource costs taken into account.

- High-performing organizations are both effective, in terms of goal accomplishment, and efficient, in terms of resource utilization.

- Organizations today emphasize total quality management in a context of technology utilization, empowerment and teamwork, and concern for work-life balance, among other trends.

3. Who are managers and what do they do?

- Managers directly support and facilitate the work efforts of other people in organizations.

- Top managers scan the environment, create vision, and emphasize long-term performance goals; middle managers coordinate activities in large departments or divisions; team leaders and supervisors support performance at the team or work-unit level.

- Functional managers work in specific areas such as finance or marketing; general managers are responsible for larger multifunctional units; administrators are managers in public or non-profit organizations.

- Managers are held accountable for performance results that the manager depends on other persons to accomplish.

- The upside-down pyramid view of organizations shows operating workers at the top serving customer needs while being supported from below by various levels of management.

- The changing nature of managerial work emphasizes being good at "coaching" and "supporting" others, rather than simply "directing" and "order-giving."

4. What is the management process?

- The management process consists of the four functions of planning, organizing, leading, and controlling.

- Planning sets the direction; organizing assembles the human and material resources; leading provides the enthusiasm and direction; controlling ensures results.

- Managers implement the four functions in daily work that is intense and stressful, involving long hours and continuous performance pressures.

- Managerial success in this demanding context requires the ability to perform well in interpersonal, informational, and decision-making roles.

- Managerial success also requires the ability to utilize interpersonal networks to accomplish well-selected task agendas.

5. How do you learn the essential managerial skills and competencies?

- Careers in the new economy demand continual attention to lifelong learning from all aspects of daily experience and job opportunities.

- Skills considered essential for managers are broadly described as technical—ability to use expertise; human—ability to work well with other people; and conceptual—ability to analyze and solve complex problems.

- Skills and outcomes considered as foundations for managerial success include communication, teamwork, self-management, leadership, critical thinking, and professionalism.

- *Management* focuses attention on building your career potential through understanding the practical implications of important concepts and theories.

KEY TERMS REVIEW

Accountability (p. 16)

Administrator (p. 16)

Conceptual skill (p. 23)

Controlling (p. 20)

Corporate governance (p. 9)

Discrimination (p. 8)

Emotional intelligence (p. 23)

Ethics (p. 8)

Functional managers (p. 16)

General managers (p. 16)

Glass ceiling effect (p. 8)

Globalization (p. 7)

Human skill (p. 23)

Intellectual capital (p. 6)

Knowledge worker (p. 6)

Leading (p. 19)

Lifelong learning (p. 22)

Line managers (p. 16)

Management (p. 19)

Manager (p. 14)

Managerial competency (p. 23)

Middle managers (p. 15)

Open system (p. 11)

Organization (p. 11)

Organizing (p. 19)

Performance effectiveness (p. 12)

Performance efficiency (p. 12)

Planning (p. 19)

Prejudice (p. 8)

Productivity (p. 12)

Project managers (p. 15)

Quality of work life (p. 17)

Skill (p. 22)

Staff managers (p. 16)

Supervisors (p. 15)

Team leaders (p. 15)

Technical skill (p. 23)

Top managers (p. 15)

Total quality management (TQM) (p. 14)

Workforce diversity (p. 8)

SELF-TEST 1

MULTIPLE-CHOICE QUESTIONS:

1. The process of management involves the functions of planning, _____, leading, and controlling.
   (a) accounting (b) creating (c) innovating (d) organizing

2. An effective manager achieves both high-performance results and high levels of _____ among people doing the required work. (a) turnover (b) effectiveness (c) satisfaction (d) stress

3. Performance efficiency is a measure of the _____ associated with task accomplishment.
   (a) resource costs (b) goal specificity (c) product quality (d) product quantity

4. The requirement that a manager answer to a higher-level boss for results achieved by a work team is called
_____.

    (a) dependency (b) accountability (c) authority (d) empowerment

5. Productivity is a measure of the quantity and _____ of work produced, with resource utilization taken into account. (a) quality (b) cost (c) timeliness (d) value

6. _____ managers pay special attention to the external environment, looking for problems and opportunities and finding ways to deal with them.
    (a) Top (b) Middle (c) Lower (d) First-line

7. The accounting manager for a local newspaper would be considered a _____ manager, whereas the editorial manager would be considered a _____ manager.
    (a) general, functional (b) middle, top (c) staff, line (d) senior, junior

8. When a team leader clarifies desired work targets and deadlines for a work team, he or she is fulfilling the management function of _____.
    (a) planning (b) delegating (c) controlling (d) supervising

9. The process of building and maintaining good working relationships with others who may help implement a manager's work agendas is called _____.
    (a) governance (b) networking (c) authority (d) entrepreneurship

10. In Katz's framework, top managers tend to rely more on their _____ skills than do first-line managers.
    (a) human (b) conceptual (c) decision-making (d) technical

11. The research of Mintzberg and others concludes that managers _____.
    (a) work at a leisurely pace (b) have blocks of private time for planning (c) always live with the pressures of performance responsibility (d) have the advantages of short work weeks

12. When someone with a negative attitude toward minorities makes a decision to deny advancement opportunities to an Indo-Canadian worker, this is an example of _____. (a) discrimination (b) emotional intelligence (c) control (d) prejudice

13. Among the trends in the new workplace, one can expect to find _____.
    (a) more order giving (b) more valuing people as human assets (c) less teamwork (d) reduced concern for work-life balance

14. The manager's role in the "upside-down pyramid" view of organizations is best described as providing _____ so that operating workers can directly serve _____.
    (a) direction, top management (b) leadership, organizational goals (c) support, customers (d) agendas, networking

15. The management function of _____ is being perfomed when a retail manager measures daily sales in the dress department and compares them with daily sales targets.
    (a) planning (b) agenda setting (c) controlling (d) delegating

SHORT-RESPONSE QUESTIONS:

16. List and explain the importance of three pressures of ethics and social responsibility that managers must be prepared to face.

17. Explain how "accountability" operates in the relationship between (a) a manager and her subordinates, and (b) the same manager and her boss.

18. Explain how the "glass ceiling effect" may disadvantage newly hired female university graduates in a large corporation.

19. What is "globalization" and what are its implications for working in the new economy?

APPLICATION QUESTION:

20. You have just been hired as the new supervisor of an audit team for a national accounting firm. With four years of experience, you feel technically well prepared for the assignment. However, this is your first formal appointment as a "manager." Things are complicated at the moment. The team has 12 members of diverse demographic and cultural backgrounds, as well as work experience. There is an intense workload and a lot of performance pressure. How will this situation challenge you to develop and use essential managerial skills and related competencies to successfully manage the team to high levels of auditing performance?

Management—
Past to Present

●●● CHAPTER 2 STUDY QUESTIONS

Planning Ahead

After reading Chapter 2, you should be able to answer these questions in your own words.

1. What can be learned from classical management thinking?

2. What ideas were introduced by the human resource approaches?

3. What is the role of quantitative analysis in management?

4. What is unique about the systems view and contingency thinking?

5. What are continuing management themes of the 21st century?

Google, Inc.

Web-crawler extraordinaire!

Since its origins in a Stanford University dorm room in 1998, Google has built a reputation that usually takes most companies decades to achieve. The company recently placed third among 60 of the most prominent companies in the world, ranking behind No. 1 Johnson & Johnson and No. 2 Coca-Cola Co., business icons that are both more than a century old. Started by two young university students, Larry Page and Sergey Brin, the company has grown to 4,138 employees. In August 2004, Google became a publicly traded company; one year later its share prices had tripled and it had a market capitalization of US $125 billion.

Today, Google is the world's largest search engine with 40 percent of the search market, offering its service in over 100 languages; 400 million people use Google for online searches each month. Survey respondents have called Google "indispensable" and "priceless." It's also the engine that drives both AOL and Yahoo searches. How did the company attain such success? What is the Google difference? The answer is performance excellence based on speed, accuracy, and ease of use. These have been the guiding performance criteria from the beginning, the basis for generating user appeal and competitive advantage in the marketplace. Page and Brin wanted to create the "perfect search engine" that "understands exactly what you mean and gives you back exactly what you want," says Page. With such goals, talent and motivation drive the system. The company uses unique strategies to recruit the best and the brightest, once posting a billboard on a stretch of highway running through Silicon Valley that read: "Solve the complex math problem on the ad, plug the correct answer into an Internet site and you could wind up working for the world's most popular search engine." The company website describes its approach to talent this way: "Google's hiring policy is aggressively non-discriminatory, and favors ability over experience." The result is a staff that reflects the global audience the search engine serves.

In all, 34 languages are spoken by Google staffers—from Turkish to Telugu. In the continuing search for motivation, the firm sticks to its historical roots—an informal culture with a small company feel. At Google, bright, creative people with diverse backgrounds and skills come together to build an ever-better search engine. [1]

IN THE WORKPLACE

You have just met with Edgar Old, a manager from another division at your company. Edgar told you that most of the new hires are weak, lack ambition, and need a "boot" to keep them going. He hoped that you were not "one of them."

Your next assignment involves working closely with Edgar. He has drawn a list of tasks to complete. You think several will be easy to do, some a little more challenging, and others will be very difficult. You also think that many are simply to keep you busy and that there are several important tasks missing. What would be your best strategy: keep quiet and work through the list, keep quiet until you have completed a number of tasks, or express your concerns right now? Or is there another strategy?

●●● **Chapter 2**   LEARNING PREVIEW   ●●●

Just as a Google search churns through billions of websites, Google's founders and staffers continuously strive to learn from past experience and apply their expertise to continuously improving the company. The same holds as scholars work within the field of management itself. In Chapter 2 you will become acquainted with the historical roots of management and learn how they created the knowledge base that today helps you and others become better managers.

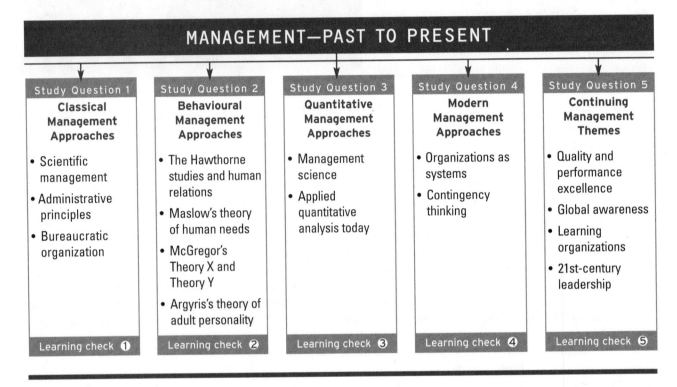

MANAGEMENT—PAST TO PRESENT

Study Question 1	Study Question 2	Study Question 3	Study Question 4	Study Question 5
Classical Management Approaches	**Behavioural Management Approaches**	**Quantitative Management Approaches**	**Modern Management Approaches**	**Continuing Management Themes**
• Scientific management • Administrative principles • Bureaucratic organization	• The Hawthorne studies and human relations • Maslow's theory of human needs • McGregor's Theory X and Theory Y • Argyris's theory of adult personality	• Management science • Applied quantitative analysis today	• Organizations as systems • Contingency thinking	• Quality and performance excellence • Global awareness • Learning organizations • 21st-century leadership
Learning check ❶	Learning check ❷	Learning check ❸	Learning check ❹	Learning check ❺

The problems and opportunities facing organizations today are complex, ever-present, and always changing. From the anxieties of terrorism to the uncertainties of international politics to the challenges of globalization, all of society's institutions feel the pressures of a new and very challenging environment. The world of work and business as we have known it is being transformed as traditional ways of doing things are replaced by new practices and viewpoints. But even in the rush toward an exciting future, one shouldn't sell history short. Knowledge gained through past experience can and should be used as a foundation for future success.

When Harvard University Press released *Mary Parker Follett—Prophet of Management: A Celebration of Writings from the 1920s*, it clearly reminded us of the wisdom of history.[2] Although Follett wrote in a different day and age, her ideas are rich with foresight. She advocated co-operation and better horizontal relationships in organizations, taught respect for the experience and knowledge of workers, warned against the dangers of too much hierarchy, and called for visionary leadership. Today we pursue similar themes while using terms like "empowerment," "involvement," "flexibility," and "self-management." Rather than naively believe that we are reinventing management practice, it is better to recognize the historical roots of many modern ideas and admit that we are still trying to perfect them.[3]

In *The Evolution of Management Thought*, Daniel Wren traces management as far back as 5000 BC, when ancient Sumerians used written records to assist in governmental and commercial activities.[4] Management was important to the construction of the Egyptian pyramids, the rise of the Roman Empire, and the commercial success of 14th-century Venice. By the time of the Industrial Revolution in the 1700s, great social changes helped prompt a great leap forward in the manufacture of basic staples and consumer goods. Industrial development was accelerated by Adam Smith's ideas of efficient production through specialized tasks and the division of labour. By the turn of the 20th century, Henry Ford and others were making mass production a mainstay of the emerging economy. Since then, the science and practices of management have been on a rapid and continuing path of development.

To frame our "Past to Present" discussion, the history of management theory has been grouped into five eras or phases of development. The first era, the classical management approaches, begins with the work of Frederick W. Taylor and examines developments in management thinking at the beginning of the 20th century. In a search for efficiency, the classical approaches move through a number of management models, all of them based on the rationale that people will work in a manner most economically beneficial to themselves. In the 1930s the focus shifts to theories of behavioural management, which look for a more progressive workplace where employee morale and relationships are found to be important. It is in this era that the dominant thinking of "man as machine" is challenged and the human side of business examined. As a result of the demands of the Second World War, the 1940s bring in a quantitative approach to management that focuses on producing goods quickly and achieving the greatest output possible. Beginning with the 1960s, the modern era of management theory concerns itself with an examination of organizations within their environment and the things that could be learned from the interactions between the two. Strategy and structure discussions are in vogue as management fully explores contingency theories. In the 1980s, up until the present, management theory focuses on the issues of quality, excellence, globalization, learning, technology, and cross-cultural aspects of management. You will discover that much of current management thought is built on the theories and lessons of the past.

CLASSICAL MANAGEMENT APPROACHES

Our study of management begins with the classical approaches: (1) scientific management, (2) administrative principles, and (3) bureaucratic organization.[5] *Figure 2.1* associates each with a prominent person or people in the history of management thought. These names are important to know since they are still widely used in management conversations today. Also, the figure shows that the classical approaches share a common assumption: people at work act in a rational manner that is primarily driven by economic concerns. Workers are expected to rationally consider opportunities made available to them and do whatever is necessary to achieve the greatest personal and monetary gain.[6]

●●● SCIENTIFIC MANAGEMENT

In 1911 Frederick W. Taylor published *The Principles of Scientific Management*, in which he makes the following statement: "The principal object of management should be to secure maximum prosperity for the employer, coupled with the maximum prosperity for the employee."[7] Taylor, often called the "father of scientific management," noticed that many workers did their jobs their own way and without clear and uniform specifications. He believed that this caused them to lose efficiency and perform below their true capacities. He also believed that this problem could be corrected if workers were taught and then helped by supervisors to always perform their jobs in the right way.

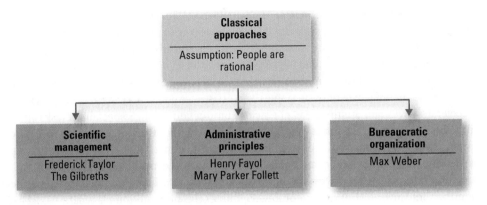

Figure 2.1 Major branches in the classical approach to management.

Taylor's goal was to improve the productivity of people at work. He used the concept of "time study" to analyze the motions and tasks required in any job and to develop the most efficient ways to perform them.[8] He then linked these job requirements with both training for the worker and support from supervisors in the form of proper direction, work assistance, and monetary incentives. The implications of his efforts are found in many management settings today, as summarized in *Manager's Notepad 2.1*. Taylor's approach is known as **scientific management** and includes these four guiding action principles.

■ **Scientific management** emphasizes careful selection and training of workers and supervisory support with an emphasis on improving efficiency.

1. Develop for every job a "science" that includes rules of motion, standardized work implements, and proper working conditions.

2. Carefully select workers with the right abilities for the job.

3. Carefully train workers to do the job and give them the proper incentives to cooperate with the job "science."

4. Support workers by carefully planning their work and by smoothing the way as they go about their jobs.

Expanding on his first guiding principle, Taylor highlighted the importance of studying the motions involved in a task in order to understand the most efficient way of working. This approach, called **motion study**, is the science of reducing a job or task to its basic physical motions. Two contemporaries of Taylor, Frank and Lillian Gilbreth, pioneered motion studies

■ **Motion study** is the science of reducing a task to its basic physical motions.

MANAGER'S
Notepad 2.1

Practical lessons from scientific management

- Produce safe products and services.
- Make results-based compensation a performance incentive.
- Carefully design jobs with efficient work methods.
- Carefully select workers with the abilities to do these jobs.
- Train workers to perform jobs to the best of their abilities.
- Train supervisors to support workers so that they can perform jobs to the best of their abilities.

as a management tool. In one famous study, they reduced the number of motions used by bricklayers and tripled their productivity.[9] The Gilbreths' work established the foundation for later advances in the areas of job simplification, work standards, and incentive wage plans—all techniques still used in the modern workplace.

An example of the continuing influence of Taylor and the Gilbreths can be seen at United Parcel Service (UPS), where workers are guided by carefully calibrated productivity standards. At regional centres, sorters are timed according to strict task requirements and are expected to load vans at a set number of packages per hour. Delivery stops on regular van routes are studied and carefully timed, and supervisors generally know, within a few minutes, how long a driver's pickups and deliveries will take. Industrial engineers devise precise routines for drivers, who are trained to knock on customers' doors rather than spend even a few seconds looking for the doorbell. Handheld computers further enhance delivery efficiencies. At UPS, savings of seconds on individual stops add up to significant increases in productivity.

●●● ADMINISTRATIVE PRINCIPLES

A second branch in the classical approaches to management includes attempts to document and understand the experiences of successful managers. Two prominent writers in this school of thought are Henri Fayol and Mary Parker Follett.

Henri Fayol

In 1916, after a career in French industry, Henri Fayol published *Administration Industrielle et Générale*.[10] The book outlines his views on the proper management of organizations and the people within them. Henri Fayol identified 14 principles of management that he felt should be taught to all aspiring managers like yourselves. Fayol derived these principles from his own experiences as an engineer leading large-scale enterprises of thousands of employees. His 14 principles are as follows:

1. *Division of Labour*—Specialization of work will result in continuous improvements in skills and methods.

2. *Authority*—Managers and workers need to understand that managers have the right to give orders.

3. *Discipline*—Behaviour needs to be grounded in obedience and derived from respect. There will be no slacking or bending of rules.

4. *Unity of Command*—Each employee should have one, and only one, manager.

5. *Unity of Direction*—The leader generates a single plan, and all play their part in executing that plan.

6. *Subordination of Individual Interests*—While at work, only work issues should be undertaken or considered.

7. *Remuneration*—All should receive fair payment for their work; employees are valuable and not simply an expense.

8. *Centralization*—While recognizing the difficulties in large organizations, decisions are primarily made from the top.

9. *Scalar Chain* (line of authority)—Organizations must have clear, formal chains of command running from the top to the bottom of the organization.

10. *Order*—There is a place for everything, and all things should be in their place.

11. *Equity*—Managers should be kind and fair.

12. *Personnel Tenure*—Unnecessary turnover is to be avoided, and there should be lifetime employment for good workers.

13. *Initiative*—Undertake work with zeal and energy.

14. *Esprit de corps*—Work to build harmony and cohesion among personnel.

The following five "rules" or "duties" of management identified by Fayol in his book closely resemble the four functions of management—planning, organizing, leading, and controlling—that we talk about today:

1. *Foresight*—to complete a plan of action for the future.

2. *Organization*—to provide and mobilize resources to implement the plan.

3. *Command*—to lead, select, and evaluate workers to get the best work toward the plan.

4. *Coordination*—to fit diverse efforts together, and ensure information is shared and problems solved.

5. *Control*—to make sure things happen according to plan, and to take necessary corrective action.

What lessons can we derive from Fayol today? Most importantly, Fayol believed that management could be taught. He was very concerned about improving the quality of management and set forth a number of "principles" to guide managerial action. Fayol showed us that management can be seen as a variety of activities or actions that can be worked on in order to improve one's managerial skill set. A number of them are still part of the management vocabulary. They include Fayol's *scalar chain principle*—there should be a clear and unbroken line of communication from the top to the bottom in the organization; the *unity of command principle*—each person should receive orders from only one boss; and the *unity of direction principle*—one person should be in charge of all activities that have the same performance objective.

AROUND THE WORLD

When Mercedes Benz started manufacturing in North America, the best of its German management practices came, too. The German automaker expects and teaches its American workers to follow precise standard methods and procedures (SMPs), which specify everything right down to the way a lug nut should be tightened. Mercedes believes this is the key to maintaining high-quality and high-performance standards, no matter where in the world its automobiles are manufactured. In 2007, Mercedes-Benz received three awards for the highest ranked vehicle quality in its respective market segments by J.D. Power and Associates. Collectively, Mercedes-Benz ranked fifth overall. It looks like Mercedes-Benz follows a "one-best way approach."

Sources: Information from Justin Martin, "Mercedes: Made in Alabama," *Fortune* (July 7, 1997), pp. 150-158; and "A Plant Grows in Alabama," *Mercedes Momentum* (Spring 1998), pp. 56-61. With information from the J.D. Power and Associates report on 2007 initial quality study (IQS) rankings (June 6, 2007) : <www.jdpower.com/press-releases>

Mary Parker Follett

Another contributor to the administrative principles school was Mary Parker Follett, who was eulogized at her death in 1933 as "one of the most important women America has yet produced in the fields of civics and sociology."[11] In her writings about businesses and other organizations, Follett displayed an understanding of groups and a deep commitment to human co-operation—ideas that are highly relevant today. For her, groups were mechanisms through which diverse individuals could combine their talents for a greater good. She viewed organizations as "communities" in which managers and workers should labour in harmony, without one party dominating the other and with the freedom to talk over and truly reconcile conflicts and differences. She believed it was the manager's job to help people in organizations co-operate with one another and achieve an integration of interests.

A review of *Dynamic Administration: The Collected Papers of Mary Parker Follett* helps to illustrate the modern applications of her management insights.[12] Follett believed that making every employee an owner in the business would create feelings of collective responsibility. Today, we address the same issues under such labels as "employee ownership," "profit sharing," and "gain-sharing plans." Follet believed that business problems involve a wide variety of factors that must be considered in relationship to one another. Today, we talk about "systems" when describing the same phenomenon. Follett believed that businesses were services and that private profits should always be considered vis-à-vis the public good. Today, we pursue the same issues under the labels of "managerial ethics" and "corporate social responsibility."

●●●● BUREAUCRATIC ORGANIZATION

Max Weber was a late-19th-century German intellectual whose insights have had a major impact on the field of management and the sociology of organizations. His ideas developed somewhat in reaction to what he considered to be performance deficiencies in the organizations of his day. Among other things, Weber was concerned that people were in positions of authority not because of their job-related capabilities, but because of their social standing or "privileged" status in German society. For this and other reasons, he believed that organizations largely failed to reach their performance potential.

At the heart of Weber's thinking was a specific form of organization he believed could correct the problems just described—a **bureaucracy**.[13] This is an ideal, intentionally rational, and very efficient form of organization founded on principles of logic, order, and legitimate authority. The defining characteristics of Weber's bureaucratic organization are as follows:

■ A **bureaucracy** is a rational and efficient form of organization founded on logic, order, and legitimate authority.

- *Clear division of labour:* Jobs are well defined, and workers become highly skilled at performing them.

- *Clear hierarchy of authority:* Authority and responsibility are well defined for each position, and each position reports to a higher-level one.

- *Formal rules and procedures:* Written guidelines direct behaviour and decisions in jobs, and written files are kept for historical record.

- *Impersonality:* Rules and procedures are impartially and uniformly applied with no one receiving preferential treatment.

- *Careers based on merit:* Workers are selected and promoted on ability and performance, and managers are career employees of the organization.

Weber believed that organizations would perform well as bureaucracies. They would have the advantages of efficiency in utilizing resources and of fairness or equity in the treatment of employees and clients. In his words:

> *The purely bureaucratic type of administrative organization…is, from a purely technical point of view, capable of attaining the highest degree of efficiency. …It is superior to any other form in precision, in stability, in the stringency of its discipline, and in its reliability. It thus makes possible a particularly high degree of calculability of results for the heads of the organization and for those acting in relation to it. It is finally superior both in intensive efficiency and in the scope of its operations and is formally capable of application to all kinds of administrative tasks.*[14]

This is the ideal side of bureaucracy. However, the terms "bureaucracy" and "bureaucrat" are now often used with negative connotations. The possible disadvantages of bureaucracy include excessive paperwork or "red tape," slowness in handling problems, rigidity in the face of shifting customer or client needs, resistance to change, and employee apathy. These disadvantages are most likely to cause problems for organizations that must be flexible and quick in adapting to changing circumstances—a common situation today. Thus researchers now try to determine when and under what conditions bureaucratic features work best. They also want to identify alternatives to the bureaucratic form. Current trends in management include many innovations that seek the same goals as Weber but with different approaches to how organizations can be structured.

Learning check ❶

BE SURE YOU CAN
• list the principles of Taylor's scientific management • list key points raised by Fayol such as "unity of command" • understand Follett's view of an "integration of interests" • list the key characteristics of bureaucracy and explain why Weber considered it an ideal form of organization • identify possible disadvantages of bureaucracy in today's environment

BEHAVIOURAL MANAGEMENT APPROACHES

During the 1920s, an emphasis on the human side of the workplace began to influence management thinking. Major branches in the behavioural, or human resource, approaches to management are shown in *Figure 2.2*. They include the famous Hawthorne studies and Maslow's theory of human needs, as well as theories generated from these foundations by Douglas McGregor, Chris Argyris, and others. The behavioural approaches maintain that people are social and self-actualizing. People at work are assumed to seek satisfying social relationships, respond to group pressures, and search for personal fulfillment.

Figure 2.2 Foundations in the behavioural or human resource approaches to management.

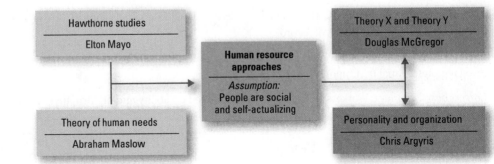

●●● THE HAWTHORNE STUDIES AND HUMAN RELATIONS

In 1924, the Western Electric Company (predecessor to today's Lucent Technologies) commissioned a research program to study individual productivity at the Hawthorne Works of the firm's Chicago plant.[15] The initial "Hawthorne studies" had a scientific management perspective and sought to determine how economic incentives and the physical conditions of the workplace affected the output of workers. An initial focus was on the level of illumination in the manufacturing facilities; it seemed reasonable to expect that better lighting would improve performance. After failing to find this relationship, however, the researchers concluded that unforeseen "psychological factors" somehow interfered with their illumination experiments. This finding and later Hawthorne studies directed attention toward human interactions in the workplace and ultimately had a major influence on the field of management.

Relay Assembly Test-Room Studies

In 1927, a team led by Harvard's Elton Mayo began more research to examine the effect of worker fatigue on output. Care was taken to design a scientific test that would be free of the psychological effects thought to have confounded the earlier illumination studies. Six workers who assembled relays were isolated for intensive study in a special test room. They were given various rest pauses and workdays and workweeks of various lengths, and production was regularly measured. Once again, researchers failed to find any direct relationship between changes in physical working conditions and output. Productivity increased regardless of the changes made.

Mayo and his colleagues concluded that the new "social setting" created for workers in the test room accounted for the increased productivity. Two factors were singled out as having special importance. One was the group atmosphere; the workers shared pleasant social relations with one another and wanted to do a good job. The other was more participative supervision. Test-room workers were made to feel important, were given a lot of information, and were frequently asked for their opinions. This was not the case in their regular jobs elsewhere in the plant.

CANADIAN COMPANY
IN THE NEWS   **Four Seasons Hotels and Resorts**

PEOPLE HOLD THE KEYS TO LONG-TERM PERFORMANCE SUCCESS

Toronto-based Four Seasons Hotels and Resorts seeks employees who are friendly, committed to teamwork, and, of course, highly talented. The firm declares that quality of service is "so critically important to our guests, and the degree to which we can provide and evolve it, worldwide, is also the degree to which we can differentiate ourselves and stay ahead of the rest." Four Seasons is a leader in the luxury segment of the hospitality industry. Its strengths and reputation are cultivated with leadership commitment to a fundamental principle: The key to sustained performance success is people. Among the guiding values of the firm is: "we believe that each of us needs a sense of dignity, pride, and satisfaction in what we do."

Source: Information from corporate website: <www.fourseasons.com>

Employee Attitudes, Interpersonal Relations, and Group Processes

Mayo's research continued until the worsening economic conditions of the Depression forced its termination in 1932. By then, interest in the human factor had broadened to include employee attitudes, interpersonal relations, and group relations. In one study, over 21,000 employees were interviewed to learn what they liked and disliked about their work environment. "Complex" and "baffling" results led the researchers to conclude that the same things (e.g., work conditions or wages) could be sources of satisfaction for some workers and of dissatisfaction for others. The final Hawthorne study was conducted in a bank wiring room and centred on the role of the work group. A surprise finding here was that people would restrict their output in order to avoid the displeasure of the group, even if it meant sacrificing pay that could otherwise be earned by increasing output. Thus, it was recognized that groups can have strong negative, as well as positive, influences on individual productivity.

Lessons of the Hawthorne Studies

As scholars now look back, the Hawthorne studies are criticized for poor research design, weak empirical support for the conclusions drawn, and the tendency of researchers to over-generalize their findings.[16] Yet their significance as turning points in the evolution of management thought remains intact. The Hawthorne studies helped shift the attention of managers and management researchers away from the technical and structural concerns of the classical approach and toward social and human concerns as keys to productivity. They showed that people's feelings, attitudes, and relationships with co-workers affected their work. They recognized the importance of group influences on individuals. They also identified the **Hawthorne effect**—the tendency of people who are singled out for special attention to perform as anticipated merely because of expectations created by the situation.

The Hawthorne studies contributed to the emergence of the **human relations movement**, which influenced management thinking during the 1950s and 1960s. This movement was largely based on the viewpoint that managers who used good human relations in the workplace would achieve productivity. Importantly, this movement combined with related developments in the social sciences to set the stage for what has now evolved as the field of **organizational behaviour**, the study of individuals and groups in organizations.

●●● MASLOW'S THEORY OF HUMAN NEEDS

Among the insights of the human relations movement, the work of psychologist Abraham Maslow in the area of human "needs" is a key foundation.[17] A **need** is a physiological or psychological deficiency a person feels the compulsion to satisfy. This is a significant concept for managers because needs create tensions that can influence a person's work attitudes and behaviours.

Maslow identified the five levels of human needs, shown in *Figure 2.3*. From lowest to highest in order, they are physiological, safety, social, esteem, and self-actualization needs. Maslow's theory is based on two underlying principles. The first is the *deficit principle*—a satisfied need is not a motivator of behaviour. People act to satisfy "deprived" needs, those for which a satisfaction "deficit" exists. The second is the *progression principle*—the five needs exist in a hierarchy of "prepotency." A need at any level is only activated when the next-lower-level need is satisfied.

According to Maslow, people try to satisfy the five needs in sequence. They progress step by step from the lowest level in the hierarchy up to the highest. Along the way, a deprived need

■ The **Hawthorne effect** is the tendency of persons singled out for special attention to perform as expected.

■ The **human relations movement** suggests that managers using good human relations will achieve productivity.

■ **Organizational behaviour** is the study of individuals and groups in organizations.

■ A **need** is a physiological or psychological deficiency that a person wants to satisfy.

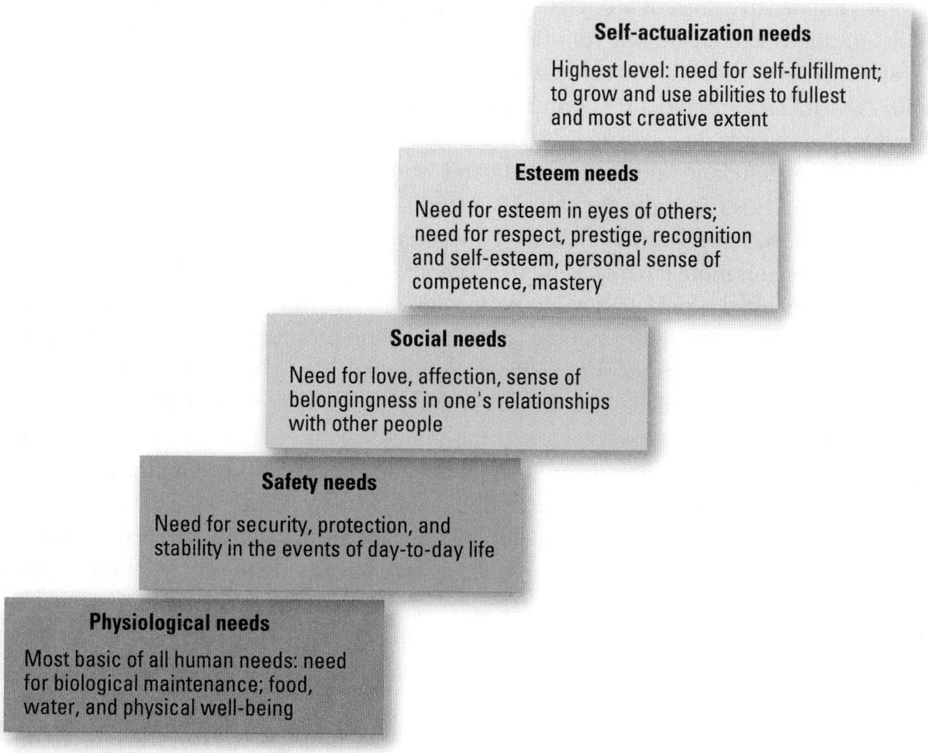

Figure 2.3 Maslow's hierarchy of human needs.

Self-actualization needs

Highest level: need for self-fulfillment; to grow and use abilities to fullest and most creative extent

Esteem needs

Need for esteem in eyes of others; need for respect, prestige, recognition and self-esteem, personal sense of competence, mastery

Social needs

Need for love, affection, sense of belongingness in one's relationships with other people

Safety needs

Need for security, protection, and stability in the events of day-to-day life

Physiological needs

Most basic of all human needs: need for biological maintenance; food, water, and physical well-being

dominates individual attention and determines behaviour until it is satisfied. Then, the next-higher-level need is activated. At the level of self-actualization, the deficit and progression principles cease to operate. The more this need is satisfied, the stronger it grows.

Consistent with human relations thinking, Maslow's theory implies that managers who help people satisfy their important needs at work will achieve productivity. Although scholars now recognize that things are more complicated than this, as discussed in Chapter 14 on motivation, Maslow's ideas are still relevant. Consider, for example, the case of volunteer workers who do not receive any monetary compensation. Managers in non-profit organizations have to create jobs and work environments that satisfy the many different needs of volunteers. If their work isn't fulfilling, the volunteers will lose interest and probably redirect their efforts elsewhere.

●●● McGREGOR'S THEORY X AND THEORY Y

Douglas McGregor was heavily influenced by both the Hawthorne studies and Maslow. His classic book *The Human Side of Enterprise* advances the thesis that managers should give more attention to the social and self-actualizing needs of people at work.[18] McGregor called upon managers to shift their view of human nature away from a set of assumptions he called "Theory X" and toward ones he called "Theory Y."

According to McGregor, managers holding **Theory X** assumptions approach their jobs believing that those who work for them generally dislike work, lack ambition, are irresponsible, are resistant to change, and prefer to be led rather than to lead. McGregor considers such thinking inappropriate. He argues instead for the value of **Theory Y** assumptions in which the manager believes people are willing to work, are capable of self-control, are willing to accept responsibility, are imaginative and creative, and are capable of self-direction.

■ **Theory X** assumes people dislike work, lack ambition, are irresponsible, and prefer to be led.

■ **Theory Y** assumes people are willing to work, accept responsibility, are self-directed and creative.

■ A **self-fulfilling prophecy** occurs when a person acts in ways that confirm another's expectations.

An important aspect of McGregor's ideas is his belief that managers who hold either set of assumptions can create **self-fulfilling prophecies**: that is, through their behaviour they create situations where others act in ways that confirm the original expectations. *Managers with Theory X assumptions*, for example, act in a very directive "command-and-control" fashion that gives people little personal say over their work. These supervisory behaviours create passive, dependent, and reluctant subordinates who tend to do only what they are told to or required to do. This reinforces the original Theory X viewpoint.

In contrast, *managers with Theory Y perspectives* behave in "participative" ways that allow subordinates more job involvement, freedom, and responsibility. This creates opportunities to satisfy esteem and self-actualization needs, and workers tend to perform as expected with initiative and high performance. The self-fulfilling prophecy thus becomes a positive one. Theory Y thinking is consistent with developments in the new workplace and its emphasis on valuing workforce diversity. It is also central to the popular notions of employee participation, involvement, empowerment, and self-management.[19] In summary, Theory X and Y are assumptions about human nature that guide our thoughts, but this approach to managing people has its limitations. Rather than thinking that all workers belong to either the X or Y camp, managers need to understand that both approaches to dealing with people work (and do not work) under certain conditions. We will discuss this later in the chapter under the topic "contingency thinking."

●●● ARGYRIS'S THEORY OF ADULT PERSONALITY

Ideas set forth by the well-regarded scholar and consultant, Chris Argyris, also reflect the belief in human nature advanced by Maslow and McGregor. In his book *Personality and Organization*, Argyris contrasts the management practices found in traditional and hierarchical organizations with the needs and capabilities of mature adults.[20] He concludes that some practices, especially those influenced by the classical management approaches, are inconsistent with the mature adult personality.

Canadian Managers
Measuring Innovation

Zenon Environmental, known for its innovative membrane for water filtration, has thrived largely due to the quantitative management approach of former COO Rafael Simon. While at Zenon, Simon created a single metric to measure all costs at Zenon: the cost per gallon of water treated. This encompasses everything that goes into the final product, and links the company's efforts with customers' interests. In the three years after Simon introduced the metric in 2001, the cost per gallon of water treated fell more than 25 percent. Simon's approach has become part of the corporate culture. It has changed the way the company works—how it bids on contracts and how departments collaborate. Still, simple cost-cutting isn't enough. In an interview Simon once said that as COO he faced the challenge "to make sure that, as we improve our profitability, as we tighten up our operations, and as we install the necessary policies and procedures, we never lose that entrepreneurial spark."

Source: Andrew Wahl, "The Best Managers in Canada: Top in Operations," *Canadian Business*, April 26–May 9, 2004, Vol. 77, Iss. 9.

Consider these examples. In scientific management, the principle of specialization assumes that people will work more efficiently as tasks become better defined. Argyris believes that this may inhibit self-actualization in the workplace. In Weber's bureaucracy, people work in a clear hierarchy of authority, with higher levels directing and controlling lower levels. Argyris worries that this creates dependent, passive workers who feel they have little control over their work environments. In Fayol's administrative principles, the concept of unity of direction assumes that efficiency will increase when a person's work is planned and directed by a supervisor. Argyris suggests that this may create conditions for psychological failure; psychological success occurs when people define their own goals.

Like McGregor, Argyris believes that managers who treat people positively, and as responsible adults, will achieve the highest productivity. His advice is to expand job responsibilities, allow more task variety, and adjust supervisory styles to allow more participation and promote better human relations. He believes that the common problems of employee absenteeism, turnover, apathy, alienation, and low morale may be signs of a mismatch between management practices and mature adult personalities.

BE SURE YOU CAN
• define the term Hawthorne effect • explain how the Hawthorne findings influenced the development of management thought • explain how Maslow's hierarchy of needs operates in the workplace • distinguish between Theory X and Theory Y assumptions, and explain why McGregor favoured Theory Y • explain Argyris's criticism that traditional organizational practices are inconsistent with mature adult personalities

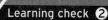 ✓ Learning check ❷

QUANTITATIVE MANAGEMENT APPROACHES

About the same time that some scholars were developing human resource approaches to management, others were investigating how quantitative techniques could improve managerial decision making. The foundation of the quantitative approaches is the assumption that mathematical techniques can be used for better problem solving. Today these applications are increasingly supported and driven by computer technology and software programs.

●●● MANAGEMENT SCIENCE

The terms **management science** and *operations research* are often used interchangeably to describe the scientific applications of mathematical techniques to management problems. A typical approach proceeds as follows. A problem is encountered, it is systematically analyzed, appropriate mathematical models and computations are applied, and an optimum solution is identified. There are a variety of management science applications that can be used in this way. *Mathematical forecasting* helps make future projections that are useful in the planning process. Inventory modelling helps control inventories by mathematically establishing how much to order and when. *Linear programming* is used to calculate how best to allocate scarce resources among competing uses. *Queuing theory* helps allocate service personnel or workstations to minimize customer waiting time and service cost. *Network models* break large tasks into smaller components to allow for better analysis, planning, and control of complex projects. *Simulations* create models of problems so different solutions under various assumptions can be tested.

Regardless of the specific technique used, the essence of quantitative management approaches includes these characteristics. There is a focus on rational decision making that has clear action implications. The techniques use "economic" decision criteria, such as costs,

■ **Management science** uses mathematical techniques to analyze and solve management problems.

revenues, and return on investment. They also involve mathematical models that follow sophisticated rules and formulas.

●●● APPLIED QUANTITATIVE ANALYSIS TODAY

University courses in management science, operations research, and quantitative business analysis provide a good introduction to these quantitative management foundations. Courses in operations management apply them to the physical production of goods and services. Since many of the techniques are highly sophisticated, organizations often employ staff specialists to help managers take advantage of them effectively. Software developments are now making these techniques more readily available through easy-to-use applications for desktop and even handheld personal computers. This greatly expands their use throughout the workplace and makes it even more important for managers to understand the value of each technique. Always, of course, mathematical solutions to problems must be supported by good managerial judgement and an appreciation of the human factor.

✓ **Learning check ❸**

BE SURE YOU CAN

• define the term management science • list three quantitative techniques that are used in management today • explain how these techniques help managers solve problems

MODERN MANAGEMENT APPROACHES

The modern approaches to management grew from the rich foundations established by the classical, human resource, and quantitative schools of thought. According to the modern management approaches, people are complex and variable. They have many varied needs that can change over time. They possess a range of talents and capabilities that can be continually developed. Organizations and managers, therefore, should respond to individual differences with a wide variety of managerial strategies and job opportunities. Key foundations of the modern management approaches include the systems view of organizations and contingency thinking. Importantly, they recognize that no one model or theory applies universally in all situations or to the exclusion of the others.

●●● ORGANIZATIONS AS SYSTEMS

▥ A **system** is a collection of interrelated parts working together for a purpose.

▥ A **subsystem** is a smaller component of a larger system.

Formally defined, a **system** is a collection of interrelated parts that function together to achieve a common purpose. A **subsystem** is a smaller component of a larger system.[21] One of the earliest management writers to adopt a systems perspective was Chester Barnard. His 1938 groundbreaking book *Functions of the Executive* was based on years of experience as a telephone company executive.[22] Barnard described organizations as co-operative systems that achieve great things by integrating the contributions of many individuals to achieve a common purpose. Importantly, Barnard considered co-operation a "conscious, deliberate, and purposeful" feature of organizations. In other words, it had to be created. For him, using communication to make this co-operation happen was the principal executive responsibility. Management theory and practice today are influenced by the complexity of organizational systems and subsystems.[23] One application is described in *Figure 2.4,* which is an extension of the systems view of organizations described in Chapter 1. This figure first depicts the larger organization as an **open system** that interacts with its environment in the continual process of transforming inputs from suppliers into outputs for customers. Within the organization, any number of critical subsystems can be described as part of the transformation process. In the figure, the operations and service management systems are a central point. They provide the integration among other subsystems, such as purchasing, accounting, sales, and information, that are essential to the work of the organization. Importantly, and as suggested by Barnard, high performance by the organization as a whole occurs only when each subsystem both performs its tasks well and works well in co-operation with others. It is the job of managers throughout the organization to make this coordinated action possible.

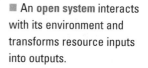

■ An **open system** interacts with its environment and transforms resource inputs into outputs.

●●● CONTINGENCY THINKING

Modern management is situational in orientation; that is, it attempts to identify practices that are the best fit with the unique demands of a situation. It utilizes **contingency thinking** that tries to match managerial responses with the problems and opportunities specific to different settings, particularly those posed by individual and environmental differences. In the modern management approach, there is no expectation that one can, or should, find the "one best way" to manage in all circumstances. Rather, the contingency perspective tries to help managers understand situational differences and respond to them in ways appropriate to their unique characteristics.[24]

■ **Contingency thinking** tries to match management practices with situational demands.

Contingency thinking is an important theme in this book, and its implications extend to all of the management functions—from planning and controlling for diverse environmental conditions, to organizing for different environments and strategies, to leading in different performance situations. For example, consider again the concept of bureaucracy. Weber offered it as an ideal form of organization. But from a contingency perspective, the strict bureaucratic form is only one possible way of organizing things. What turns out to be the "best" structure in any given situation will depend on many factors, including environmental uncertainty, an organization's primary technology, and the strategy being pursued. The strict bureaucracy works best only when the environment is relatively stable and operations are predictable. In other situations, alternative and more flexible structures are needed. Contingency thinking

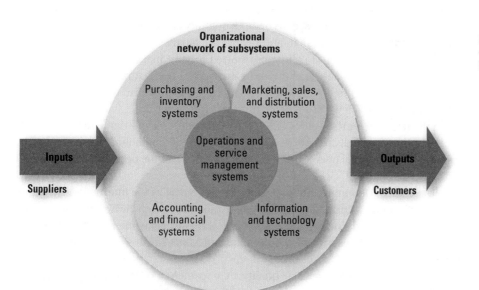

Figure 2.4 Organizations as complex networks of interacting subsystems.

recognizes that what is a good structure for one organization may not work well for another, and what works well at one time may not work as well in the future as circumstances change.[25] This contingency approach to organization structure and design will be examined further in Chapters 10 and 11.

✓ Learning check ④

BE SURE YOU CAN

• define the terms system, subsystem, and open system • apply these concepts to describe the operations of an organization in your community • define the term contingency thinking • explain how contingency thinking might influence a manager's decision to use or not use a bureaucratic approach to organization structure

---

CONTINUING MANAGEMENT THEMES

The many accumulating insights discussed so far helped set the foundation for important trends and directions in management thought that are evident as we begin the 21st century. Among the most important is the recognition that we live and work in a dynamic and ever-changing environment that puts unique and never-ending pressures on organizations. In this context, the themes reflected throughout *Management* include quality and performance excellence, ethics and social responsibility, global awareness, and the importance of new leadership in an age of information, knowledge workers, and highly competitive business environments.

●●● QUALITY AND PERFORMANCE EXCELLENCE

The theme of quality first introduced in Chapter 1 remains a very important direction in management today.[26] Managers and workers in truly progressive organizations are quality conscious. They understand the basic link between competitive advantage and the ability to always deliver quality goods and services to their customers. The best organizational cultures include quality as a core value and reinforce the quality commitment in all aspects of the work environment.

Perhaps the best known proponent of quality management for business was Edward Demming. A statistical expert, Demming first applied his expertise to the Second World War effort. He helped manufacturers focus on both quantity and quality. After the war, he lectured and consulted extensively in Japan and helped the Japanese develop a quality approach to management. When Japanese companies started to gain market share, particularly in the automobile sector, his quality focus made its way back to North American managers. Another key and expert quality proponent was Joseph Juran. His approach to solving quality issues was to begin with the "vital few" issues before moving on to tackle the "trivial many" problems. He coined the term the "Pareto Principle," or the 80/20 rule, to give a name to his theory that 80 percent of the problems are caused by 20 percent of the operations. Juran showed that by focusing on the few vital operations first, a large number of the operational problems would be resolved.

As a result of Demming and Juran's efforts, programs like the International Organization for Standardization (ISO), the Balderidge Awards, and the Canada Awards for Excellence (CAE) have become standards for businesses to strive toward. Recent winners of the CAE include 3M Canada of Ontario, Telus in British Columbia, and Xerox North American TeleWeb in Nova Scotia.[27]

Every effort is made in total quality management (TQM) to build quality into all aspects of operations from initial acquisition of resources, through the transformation processes and work systems, all the way to ultimate product delivery to customers or clients. *Figure 2.5* describes the systems context for TQM with respect to the **value chain**— a specific sequence of activities that transforms raw materials into a finished good or service.[28] Quality must be maintained at each point in the value chain, whether it is performed directly by the organization or is part of its network of relationships with suppliers and contractors. Closely aligned with the pursuit of quality is management commitment to performance excellence, a theme that rose to special prominence over 20 years ago when *In Search of Excellence: Lessons from America's Best-Run Companies* was published by Thomas Peters and Robert Waterman.[29] Based on case investigations of successful companies, they identified the eight attributes of performance excellence shown in *Manager's Notepad 2.2*. Although we now recognize that these attributes are but modest insights into a far more complex performance picture, they are useful starting points. In them you will find many themes and directions that are now common practice in organizations today.

■ A **value chain** is the sequence of activities that transforms raw materials into finished goods or services.

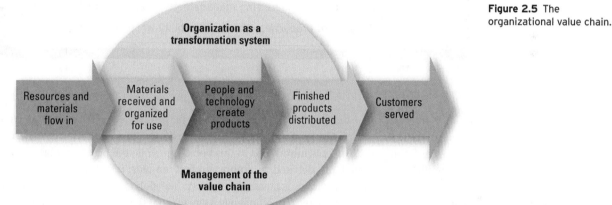

Figure 2.5 The organizational value chain.

---

take it to the case!

The Coca-Cola Company
Coke gets back to business

Talk about history! Coca-Cola for decades has been one of the world's best-known brands. Where in the world can you go and not be able to get a Coke? But the firm's glorious past can't guarantee the same future. Coke must prosper in a highly competitive soft drink industry, and successfully counter all attacks by arch rival Pepsi as well as those of discount beverage sellers and new entrants like Virgin Cola. Past achievements (Diet Coke) and failures ("New Coke") provide a learning base from which to craft future strategy and plans. In 2007, the beverage giant claimed the top spot for the seventh year in a row as the Best Global Brand mostly because it is big and everywhere; however, its move into healthier drinks and snacks has yet to add value. Like all growth companies, Coke has to deal with the inevitable problems brought on by increasing size such as organizational structural issues, changing consumer demands, challenges from competitors, and the management of people.

Source: Information from Ann Harrington, "Coke Denied: Prevention Is the Best Defense," *Fortune* (July 10, 2000), p. 188. "Best Global Brands," *Business Week* (Aug. 6, 2007).

MANAGER'S
Notepad 2.2

Eight attributes of performance excellence

- *Bias toward action*—making decisions and making sure things get done.
- *Closeness to the customers*—knowing their needs and valuing customer satisfaction.
- *Autonomy and entrepreneurship*—supporting innovation, change, and risk taking.
- *Productivity through people*—valuing people as keys to quality and performance.
- *Hands-on and value-driven*—having a clear sense of organizational purpose.
- *Sticking to the knitting*—focusing resources and attention on what the organization does best.
- *Simple form and lean staff*—minimizing management levels and staff personnel.
- *Simultaneous loose-tight properties*—allowing flexibility while staying in control.

●●● GLOBAL AWARENESS

We have emerged from a decade in which the quality and performance excellence themes were reflected in the rise of "process re-engineering," "virtual organizations," "agile factories," "network firms," and other concepts introduced in this book. But while the best formulas for success continue to be tested and debated, an important fact remains: much of the pressure for quality and performance excellence is created by the forces of globalization and a highly competitive global economy. Nowhere is this challenge more evident than in the continuing efforts of businesses around the globe to transform themselves into truly world-class operations.

Like the lessons of performance excellence, current trends and directions in global awareness have ties back to the 1980s. That was a time when the success of Japanese industry caught worldwide attention, and both scholars and consultants rushed to identify what could be learned from Japanese management practices. The books *Theory Z*, by William Ouchi, and *The Art of Japanese Management*, by Richard Tanner Pascale and Anthony G. Athos, were among the first that called attention to the possible link between unique Japanese practices and business success.[30] Ouchi used the term "Theory Z" to describe a management framework that uses insights found in the Japanese models.[31] Prominent in the **Theory Z** management approach are such things as long-term employment, slower promotions and more lateral job movements, greater attention to career planning and development, more use of consensus decision making, and high emphasis on use of teamwork and employee involvement. And even though the Japanese economy and management systems face pressures of their own today, these early insights into the Japanese business experience helped to establish a global awareness that continues to enrich management thinking today. This international dimension will be emphasized throughout *Management*. Chapter 5 gives special attention to understanding cultural influences on management practices.

■ **Theory Z** describes management emphasizing long-term employment, consensus, and teamwork.

●●● LEARNING ORGANIZATIONS

■ A **learning organization** continuously changes and improves, using the lessons of experience.

The change and uncertainty in today's environment have given rise to an emphasis on creating **learning organizations**, ones that are able to continually learn and adapt themselves to new circumstances. Such organizations are successful because they are uniquely capable of improving themselves by learning from experience. Consultant Peter Senge popularized the concept of the learning organization in his book *The Fifth Discipline*, and he identifies the following as its core ingredients:[32]

1. Mental models—everyone sets aside old ways of thinking.

2. Personal mastery—everyone becomes self-aware and open to others.

3. Systems thinking—everyone learns how the whole organization works.

4. Shared vision—everyone understands and agrees to a plan of action.

5. Team learning—everyone works together to accomplish the plan.

Organizations that meet Senge's criteria for learning organizations offer work settings in which members develop their abilities to learn and are encouraged and helped to make that learning continuously available to everyone else. They have value-driven organizational cultures that emphasize information sharing, teamwork, empowerment, participation, and learning. Importantly, the leaders of learning organizations set an example for others by embracing change and communicating enthusiasm for solving problems and growing with new opportunities.

●●● 21ST-CENTURY LEADERSHIP

There is no doubt that today's social, political, and economic forces make it necessary for people and organizations to continually adapt to new situations if they are to survive and prosper over the long run. Learning, learning, and more learning is the new reality of work in the 21st century. This fact carries with it distinctive personal development and leadership challenges. And when it comes to leadership, history once again sets the stage for the future. In his book *No Easy Victories*, John Gardner speaks of leadership as a special responsibility, and his words are well worth considering today:

> *Leaders have a significant role in creating the state of mind that is the society. They can serve as symbols of the moral unity of the society. They can express the values that hold the society together. Most important, they can conceive and articulate goals that lift people out of their petty preoccupations, carry them above the conflicts that tear a society apart, and unite them in the pursuit of objectives worthy of their best efforts.[33]*

Leadership and the new directions of learning organizations are singled out again and again in *Management* as important keys to personal and organizational performance.

Managers of the 21st century will have to excel as never before to meet the expectations held of them and of the organizations they lead. Importantly, we must all recognize that new managerial outlooks and new managerial competencies

PERSONAL MANAGEMENT

NOW IS A very good time for you to examine your learning style. Every person a manager deals with is unique, most problem situations are complex, and things are always changing. Success in management only comes to those who thrive on learning. Some people learn by watching; they observe others and model what they see. Others learn by doing; they act and experiment, learning as they go. There is no one best way to learn about managing—there is only the need to learn…all the time, from others, from formal training, and from real experiences. An organization development manager at PepsiCo once said: "I believe strongly in the notion that enhancing managers' knowledge of their strengths and particularly their weaknesses is integral to ensuring long-term, sustainable performance improvement and executive success."[34] The problem is that many of us never dig deep enough to both get this depth of personal understanding and use it to set learning goals. You can start here by keeping a personal strengths and weaknesses scorecard.

Strengths

Where I am now	*Learning goals*

Weaknesses

Where I am now	*Learning goals*

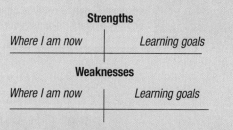

Get to know yourself better

Complete Self-Assessments #3—**Learning Tendencies**, and #4—**What Are Your Managerial Assumptions?**, from the Workbook and Personal Management Activity #2 on the companion website.

appropriate to the new times are requirements for future leadership success. At the very least, the 21st-century manager must display these attributes:

- *Global strategist*—understanding the interconnections among nations, cultures, and economies; planning and acting with due consideration of these interconnections.

- *Master of technology*—comfortable with information technology, understanding technological trends and their implications, able to use technology to best advantage.

- *Inspiring leader*—attracting highly motivated workers and inspiring them with a high-performance culture where individuals and teams can do their best work.

- *Model of ethical behaviour*—acting ethically in all ways, setting high ethical standards for others to follow, building a work culture that values ethics and social responsibility.

Management scholar and consultant Peter Drucker called this the age of information and considered knowledge the principal resource of a competitive society. Drucker also cautioned that knowledge constantly makes itself obsolete.[35] In a society where knowledge workers are increasingly important, this means that new managers must be well educated...and they must continue that education throughout their careers. Success in turbulent times comes only through learning and continuous improvement.

The new economy requires everyone—you included—to be unrelenting in efforts to develop, refine, and maintain job-relevant skills and competencies. It requires leaders with strong people skills, ones attuned to the nature of an information/service society, ones who understand the international dimensions, and ones who establish commitments to work-life balance. And the new economy places a premium on high-performance leadership. Consider, for example, this comment by former corporate CEO and college president Ralph Sorenson: "It is the ability to make things happen that most distinguishes the successful manager from the mediocre or unsuccessful one....The most cherished manager is the one who says 'I can do it,' and then does."[36]

"Do it," advises Sorenson. "Of course," you may quickly answer. But don't forget that the 21st-century manager must also do the "right" things—the things that really count, the things that add value to the organization's goods and/or services, the things that make a real difference in performance results and competitive advantage, and the ethical things. Those are challenging directions for leadership and career success in the new economy.

✓ Learning check ⑤

BE SURE YOU CAN
• define the term value chain • illustrate how the value chain operates in an organization that you know • explain Theory Z • list the characteristics of a learning organization • discuss special characteristics of 21st-century leaders • discuss your personal responsibilities for learning and performance

●●● Chapter 2   STUDY GUIDE

WHERE WE'VE BEEN

Back to Google, Inc.

The opening example of Google, Inc. introduced you to the world of high technology and the opportunities of getting connected in our digital world. But it is important to remember that Google couldn't have been created without the knowledge made available by the full history of research and development in computer science. Now it is an organization that is turning its founders' commitments to learning into the pathway toward the future. At the beginning of the chapter we posed a question about which management practices from the past helped guide Google's development; what did you find? Do you think that quantitative analysis, a focus on quality, or the creation of a learning organization were important? In Chapter 2 you learned the major historical roots that influence the study of management. As you read further in *Management*, keep the lessons of history in mind. The management theories and concepts we value today have strong links to the past.

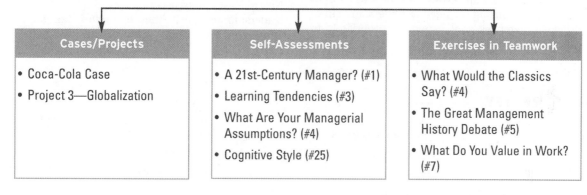

STUDY QUESTION SUMMARY

1. What can be learned from classical management thinking?

- Frederick Taylor's four principles of scientific management focused on the need to carefully select, train, and support workers for individual task performance.

- Henri Fayol suggested that managers should learn what are now known as the management functions of planning, organizing, leading, and controlling.

- Max Weber described bureaucracy with its clear hierarchy, formal rules, and well-defined jobs as an ideal form of organization.

2. What ideas were introduced by the human resource approaches?

- The human resource or behavioural approaches shifted attention toward the human factor as a key element in organizational performance.

- The historic Hawthorne studies suggested that work behaviour is influenced by social and psychological forces and that work performance may be improved by better "human relations."

- Abraham Maslow's hierarchy of human needs introduced the concept of self-actualization and

the potential for people to experience self-fulfillment in their work.

- Douglas McGregor urged managers to shift away from Theory X and toward Theory Y thinking, which views people as independent, responsible, and capable of self-direction in their work.

- Chris Argyris pointed out that people in the workplace are adults and may react negatively when constrained by strict management practices and rigid organizational structures.

3. What is the role of quantitative analysis in management?

- The availability of high-power desktop computing provides new opportunities for mathematical methods to be used for managerial problem solving.

- Many organizations employ staff specialists who are experts in quantitative management science and operations research.

- Quantitative techniques used by managers include forecasting, linear programming, and simulation, among others.

4. What is unique about the systems view and contingency thinking?

- Organizations are complex open systems that interact with their external environments to transform resource inputs into product outputs.

- Resource acquisition and customer satisfaction are important requirements in the organization–environment relationship.

- Organizations are composed of many internal subsystems that must work together in a coordinated way to support the organization's overall success.

- Contingency thinking avoids "one best way" arguments, recognizing the need to understand situational differences and respond appropriately to them.

5. What are continuing management themes of the 21st century?

- The commitment to meet customer needs guides organizations toward total quality management and continuous improvement of operations.

- Interest in Japanese management practices illustrates the opportunities to learn new ways of managing from practices in other countries.

- Changing times place great value on learning organizations, ones that are able to continually learn and adapt themselves to changing circumstances.

- New managers must accept and excel at 21st-century leadership responsibilities to perform as global strategists, technology masters, sensitive politicians, leader/motivators, and ethical role models.

KEY TERMS REVIEW

Bureaucracy (p. 37)	Motion study (p. 34)	Subsystem (p. 44)
Contingency thinking (p. 45)	Need (p. 40)	System (p. 44)
Hawthorne effect (p. 40)	Open system (p. 45)	Theory X (p. 41)
Human relations movement (p. 40)	Organizational behaviour (p. 40)	Theory Y (p. 41)
Learning organization (p. 48)	Scientific management (p. 34)	Theory Z (p. 48)
Management science (p. 43)	Self-fulfilling prophecies (p. 42)	Value chain (p. 47)

SELF-TEST 2

MULTIPLE-CHOICE QUESTIONS:

1. The assumption that people are complex with widely varying needs is most associated with the _____ management approaches.
   (a) classical (b) neoclassical (c) behavioural (d) modern

2. The father of scientific management is _____.
   (a) Weber (b) Taylor (c) Maslow (d) Hawthorne

3. The Hawthorne studies are important because they raised awareness of the important influences of _____ on productivity.
   (a) structures (b) human factors (c) physical work conditions (d) pay and rewards

4. Advice to study a job and carefully train workers to do that job with financial incentives tied to job performance would most likely come from _____.
   (a) scientific management (b) contingency management (c) Henri Fayol (d) Abraham Maslow

5. The highest level in Maslow's hierarchy is the level of _____ needs.
   (a) safety (b) esteem (c) self-actualization (d) physiological

6. Conflict between the mature adult personality and a rigid organization was a major concern of _____.
   (a) Argyris (b) Follett (c) McGregor (d) Fayol

7. When people perform in a situation as they are expected to, this is sometimes called the _____ effect.
   (a) Hawthorne (b) bureaucratic (c) contingency (d) open-systems

8. Linear programming and queuing theory are examples of techniques found in the _____ approach to management.
   (a) classical (b) quantitative (c) bureaucratic organization (d) modern

9. Resource acquisition and customer satisfaction are important when an organization is viewed as a(n) _____.
   (a) bureaucracy (b) closed system (c) open system (d) pyramid

10. Long-term employment and consensus decision making are characteristic of the _____ management framework.
    (a) Theory X (b) Theory Y (c) Theory Z (d) contingency

11. When your local bank or credit union is viewed as an open system, the loan-processing department would be considered a _____.
    (a) subsystem (b) closed system (c) resource input (d) value centre

12. When a manager notices that Sheryl has strong social needs and puts her in a job that involves customer relations, while also being sure to give Kwabena lots of praise because of his strong ego needs, the manager is displaying _____.
    (a) systems thinking (b) Theory X (c) motion study (d) contingency thinking

13. If you conducted a value chain analysis of a business, you would study _____.
    (a) customer satisfaction with products (b) how much TQM affects profits (c) the flow of activities that transform resources into goods and services (d) the links between performance and rewards

14. In a learning organization, as described by Peter Senge, one would expect to find _____.
    (a) priority placed on following rules and procedures (b) promotions based on seniority (c) employees who are willing to set aside old thinking and embrace new ways (d) a strict hierarchy of authority

15. 21st-century leaders must, according to Ralph Sorenson, be able to add value to organizations by _____.
    (a) taking action to make things happen (b) building efficient structures (c) keeping customers happy (d) using mathematics for decision making

SHORT-RESPONSE QUESTIONS:

16. Explain how McGregor's Theory Y assumptions can create self-fulfilling prophecies consistent with the current emphasis on participation and involvement in the workplace.

17. How do the deficit and progression principles operate in Maslow's hierarchy-of-needs theory?

18. Define "contingency thinking" and give an example of how it might apply to management.

19. Explain why the external environment is so important in the open-systems view of organizations.

APPLICATION QUESTION:

20. Enrique Temoltzin has just been appointed the new manager of your local bookstore. Enrique would like to make sure the store operates according to Weber's bureaucracy. Describe the characteristics of bureaucracy and answer this question: Is the bureaucracy a good management approach for Enrique to follow? Discuss the possible limitations of bureaucracy and the implications for managing people as key assets of the store.

Ethical Behaviour and Social Responsibility

Planning Ahead

After reading Chapter 3, you should be able to answer these questions in your own words.

1. What is ethical behaviour?

2. How do ethical dilemmas complicate the workplace?

3. How can high ethical standards be maintained?

4. What is corporate social responsibility?

5. How do organizations and governments work together in society?

Aldo Shoes

Creating a better world

Creating a better world is important to Aldo Bensadoun, owner of the Montreal-based company, ALDO shoes. Perhaps his own multicultural background has provided him with this global view. Born in Morocco, he grew up in France, and fell in love with Montreal during a weekend trip while at university.

Flash back to 1972; ALDO is founded, continuing a family tradition of working within the shoe industry. Starting with concessions in Le Château stores in Montreal, Ottawa, Quebec City, and Winnipeg, the company expands to include 95 free-standing stores across Canada by 1993. With the vision "to make people feel good through the products and the service we provide everyday," ALDO moves into the American market, opening its first store in Boston, Massachusetts.

According to Bensadoun, "being a Montreal-based company has been instrumental in ALDO's ability to become a global player." At a time when Canadian companies are criticized for being unable to expand successfully into the American market, the ALDO group continues to grow and operate 300 stores, with Bensadoun saying, "Honestly, I think Canada is a fantastic place from which to become a global player."

Fast forward to today, and you see a company that has expanded globally, now including stores in the United Kingdom, Australia, Poland, Switzerland, and Denmark.

In addition to being a successful company, ALDO has valued the role of being a good corporate citizen. It sees itself as a "brand with a conscience, a brand that cares." While supporting local communities, ALDO has aligned itself with the fight against AIDS since 1985. It recently launched the "ALDO FIGHTS AIDS" campaign in 20 countries, featuring many celebrities and media outlets. ALDO has also developed a limited edition "empowerment tag necklace," which is being sold worldwide and through the Internet, with 100 percent of the proceeds going to YouthAIDS. As their website notes, "Together with you our customer, ALDO is making a difference."[1]

IN THE WORKPLACE

You ponder the confidential report that you have just received. Drawn up by a team of outside consultants, the report suggests that your company close one of its manufacturing plants in a small town in rural Canada and, instead, sign a long-term contract with a plant in Asia to produce its new product line. The report suggests that while there will be high initial costs to the plant closure, such as paying severance fees to the approximately 250 workers, in the medium to long term, the company should realize a greater profit due to the Asian plant's lower operating costs.

Your supervisor has asked you to highlight considerations other than just economic issues that senior management should also consider before deciding to go "offshore." What is your response?

●●● **Chapter 3**   LEARNING PREVIEW   ●●●

When you look at what Aldo Bensadoun has accomplished with his company, taking it from a small start-up to a global company while at the same time making the commitment to being a good corporate citizen through social responsibility, it truly shows what businesses can do. Chapter 3 examines these issues in detail, with the goal of encouraging your understanding of, and commitment to, ethical and socially responsible behaviour. As you read, check your learning progress in these major areas.

ETHICAL BEHAVIOUR AND SOCIAL RESPONSIBILITY

Study Question 1	Study Question 2	Study Question 3	Study Question 4	Study Question 5
What Is Ethical Behaviour?	**Ethics in the Workplace**	**Maintaining High Ethical Standards**	**Corporate Social Responsibility**	**Organizations and Society**
• Laws, values, and ethical behaviour • Alternative views of ethics • Cultural issues in ethical behaviour	• Ethical dilemmas at work • Rationalizations for unethical behaviour • Factors influencing ethical behaviour	• Ethics training • Whistle-blower protection • Ethical role models • Codes of ethical conduct	• Stakeholder issues and analysis • Perspectives on corporate social responsibility • Evaluating corporate social performance • Social entrepreneurship	• How governments influence organizations • How organizations influence governments • Role of corporate governance
Learning check ❶	Learning check ❷	Learning check ❸	Learning check ❹	Learning check ❺

It wasn't very long ago that we were shocked and dismayed when a rash of sensational news reports communicated the worst of business behaviour, among them WORLDCOM FACING CHARGES OF FRAUD—HOW ENRON BOSSES CREATED A CULTURE OF PUSHING LIMITS—ANDERSEN'S WRONG TURNS GREW OBVIOUS—A "STELLAR REPUTATION" SHATTERED.[2] The stories behind the headlines revealed ethical failures by prominent businesses and their leaders. They were hard facts of the new century, not just textbook possibilities. In December 2001, three months after the attack on the World Trade Center, Enron declared bankruptcy, the largest in US history. In July 2002, the WorldCom bankruptcy bettered Enron by 60 percent, coming in at US $104 billion. Caught in Enron's web of ethical catastrophe, Arthur Andersen, LLP, fell from being one of the largest certified public accounting firms in the world to being out of business.[3]

In Canada we must also recognize ethical failures that are homegrown—from Bre-X's "unusual rock sampling methods" that were kept quiet by the company as their stock rose dramatically in value to the sponsorship scandal where federal government sponsorship money was funnelled to government-friendly advertising agencies.[4] Ethical challenges occur everywhere.

The root causes of these and many other bankruptcies were not poor business models or bad market calculations. They were failures of ethics. Employees and officers lied and cheated about important financial information. They cajoled and threatened others to do the same. They modelled unethical conduct to the point that such behaviour became accepted practice within the firms.[5] Such cases can easily leave us feeling cynical, pessimistic, and even helpless regarding the state of ethical leadership in our society. But even in the face of so much bad news, a more positive and promising perspective can be taken. Jana Matthews, founder and CEO of Boulder Quantum Ventures, a consulting firm that helps businesses grow, says:

> After watching WorldCom, Enron, Arthur Andersen and other companies "cook the books" and artificially inflate profits, I understand the public skepticism about business. But I maintain that there are thousands and thousands of companies employing millions and millions of people who operate honestly, with the right values.[6]

It is time to get serious about the moral aspects and social implications of decision making in organizations. In your career and in the work of any manager, performance goals must always be achieved through ethically and socially responsible action. The following reminder from Desmond Tutu, archbishop of Capetown, South Africa, and winner of the Nobel Peace Prize, is applicable to managers everywhere:[7]

> You are powerful people. You can make this world a better place where business decisions and methods take account of right and wrong as well as profitability. . . . You must take a stand on important issues: the environment and ecology, affirmative action, sexual harassment, racism and sexism, the arms race, poverty, the obligations of the affluent West to its less-well-off sisters and brothers elsewhere.

WHAT IS ETHICAL BEHAVIOUR?

For our purposes, **ethics** can be defined as the code of moral principles that sets standards of good or bad, or right or wrong, in one's conduct.[8] Ethics provides principles to guide behaviour and help people make moral choices among alternative courses of action. In practice, **ethical behaviour** is that which is accepted to be "good" and "right" as opposed to "bad" or "wrong" in the context of the governing moral code.

■ **Ethics** sets standards of good or bad, or right or wrong, in one's conduct.

■ **Ethical behaviour** is "right" or "good" in the context of a governing moral code.

●●●● LAWS, VALUES, AND ETHICAL BEHAVIOUR

It makes sense that anything that is legal should be considered ethical. Yet slavery was once legal in the United States and laws once permitted only men to vote. That doesn't mean that these practices were ethical; rather, we consider these laws unethical today. Furthermore, just because an action is not strictly illegal doesn't make it ethical. Living up to the "letter of the law" is not sufficient to guarantee that one's actions will or should be considered ethical.[9] Is it truly ethical, for example, for an employee to take longer than necessary to do a job? To make personal telephone calls on company time? To call in sick to take a day off for leisure? To fail to report rule violations by a co-worker? None of these acts are strictly illegal, but many people would consider any one or more of them to be unethical.

Most ethical problems in the workplace arise when people are asked to do, or find themselves about to do, something that violates their personal beliefs. For some, if the act is legal they proceed with confidence. For others, the ethical test goes beyond the legality of the act alone. The ethical question extends to personal **values**—the underlying beliefs and attitudes

■ **Values** are broad beliefs about what is appropriate behaviour.

take it to the case!

Barenaked Ladies
Changing the world one song at a time

Is it possible for a rock band to be popular, profitable, and not pollute? The Barenaked Ladies, five Canadians who are self-effacing celebrities and nice lads, certainly hope so. From their basement beginnings in the late 1980s, their focus has grown from being a successful band to being a successful band that makes a difference. BNL has matured from merely singing about things to taking action as engaged activists on issues important to band members. Actions include voicing their opinion on issues by wearing "Vote Solar" T-shirts onstage to actually walking the talk by using greener fuels like biodiesel in their tour vehicles, composting material backstage, and setting up eco-villages at their concerts. Learn more about their approach to corporate social responsibility by reading the case in the *Management Learning Workbook.*

Source: With information from the corporate website: <www.bnlmusic.com>.

that help determine individual behaviour. To the extent that values vary among people, we can expect different interpretations of what behaviour is ethical or unethical in a given situation.

The psychologist Milton Rokeach makes a popular distinction between "terminal" and "instrumental" values.[10] **Terminal values** are preferences about desired ends, such as the goals one strives to achieve in life. Examples of terminal values considered important by managers include self-respect, family security, freedom, inner harmony, and happiness. **Instrumental values** are preferences regarding the means for accomplishing these ends. Among the instrumental values held important by managers are honesty, ambition, courage, imagination, and self-discipline. Both terminal and instrumental values vary from one person to the next, but the value pattern for any one person is very enduring. This variation among value profiles is a reason why different people respond quite differently to a situation with ethical challenges.

> ■ **Terminal values** are preferences about desired end states.
>
> ■ **Instrumental values** are preferences regarding the means to desired ends.

●●● ALTERNATIVE VIEWS OF ETHICS

Figure 3.1 shows four views of ethical behaviour that philosophers have discussed over the years.[11] Behaviour that would be considered ethical from the **utilitarian view** delivers the greatest good to the greatest number of people. Founded in the work of 19th-century philosopher John Stuart Mill, this results-oriented point of view tries to assess the moral implications of decisions in terms of their consequences. Business decision makers, for example, are inclined to use profits, efficiency, and other performance criteria to judge what is best for the majority. A manager may make a utilitarian decision to cut 30 percent of a plant's workforce in order to keep the plant profitable and save the remaining jobs.

> ■ In the **utilitarian view** ethical behaviour delivers the greatest good to the majority.

The **individualism view** of ethical behaviour is based on the belief that one's primary commitment is long-term advancement of self-interests. People supposedly become self-regulating as they pursue long-term individual advantage. For example, lying and cheating for short-term gain should not be tolerated. If one person does it, and profits from it, everyone will do it, and no one's long-term interests will be served. Thus, the individualism view is supposed to promote honesty and integrity. But in business practice it may result in a *pecuniary ethic*, described by one executive as the tendency to "push the law to its outer limits" and "run roughshod over other individuals to achieve one's objectives."[12]

> ■ In the **individualism view** ethical behaviour advances long-term self-interests.

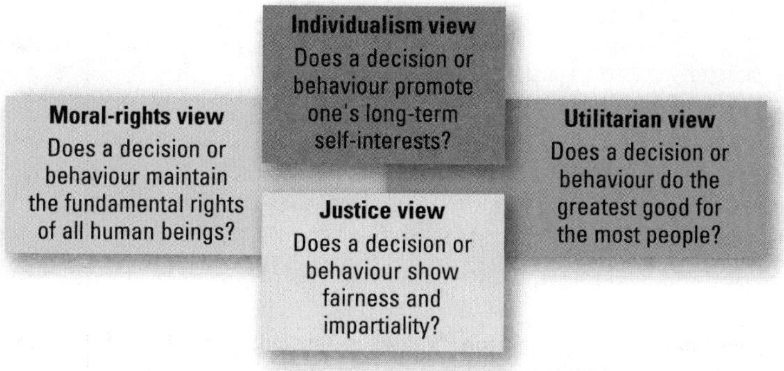

Figure 3.1 Four views of ethical behaviour.

Ethical behaviour under a **moral-rights view** is that which respects and protects the fundamental rights of people. From the teachings of John Locke, for example, the rights of all people to life, liberty, and fair treatment under the law are considered inviolate. In organizations, this concept extends to ensuring that employees are always protected in terms of rights to privacy, due process, free speech, free consent, health and safety, and freedom of conscience. The issue of human rights, a major ethical concern in the international business environment, is central to this perspective. The United Nations stands by the Universal Declaration of Human Rights passed by the General Assembly in 1948.

Finally, the **justice view** of moral behaviour is based on the belief that ethical decisions treat people impartially and fairly, according to legal rules and standards. This approach evaluates the ethical aspects of any decision on the basis of whether it is "equitable" for everyone affected.[13] The justice view encompasses three different but complementary perspectives—procedural, distributive, and interactional.

Procedural justice involves the degree to which policies and rules are fairly administered. For example, does a sexual harassment charge levied against a senior executive receive the same full hearing as one made against a first-level supervisor? To be seen as being procedurally just, due process must be followed in both cases.

Distributive justice involves the degree to which outcomes are allocated without respect to individual characteristics based on ethnicity, race, gender, age, or other particular criteria. For example, does a woman with the same qualifications and experience as a man receive the same wage? If not, there is a problem.

Interactional justice involves the degree to which others are treated with dignity and respect. For example, does a bank loan officer take the time to fully explain to an applicant why he or she was turned down for a loan?[14]

●●● CULTURAL ISSUES IN ETHICAL BEHAVIOUR

The influence of culture on ethical behaviour is increasingly at issue in this time of globalization. Corporate leaders must master difficult challenges when operating across borders that are cultural as well as national. Former Levi Strauss CEO Robert Haas once said that an ethical dilemma "becomes even more difficult when you overlay the complexities of different cultures and values systems that exist throughout the world."[15]

Those who believe that behaviour in foreign settings should be guided by the classic rule of "When in Rome, do as the Romans do" reflect an ethical position of **cultural relativism**.[16] This is the belief that there is no one right way to behave and that ethical behaviour is always determined by its cultural context. A Canadian international business executive guided by rules of cultural relativism, for example, would argue that the use of child labour is okay in another country if it is consistent with local laws and customs.

Figure 3.2 contrasts cultural relativism with the alternative of **universalism**. This ethical position suggests that if a behaviour or practice is not okay in one's home environment, it is

■ In the **moral-rights view** ethical behaviour respects and protects fundamental rights.

■ In the **justice view** ethical behaviour treats people impartially and fairly.

■ **Procedural justice** is concerned that policies and rules are fairly applied.

■ **Distributive justice** is concerned that people are treated the same regardless of personal characteristics.

■ **Interactional justice** is the degree to which others are treated with dignity and respect.

■ **Cultural relativism** suggests there is no one right way to behave; ethical behaviour is determined by its cultural context.

■ **Universalism** suggests ethical standards apply absolutely across all cultures.

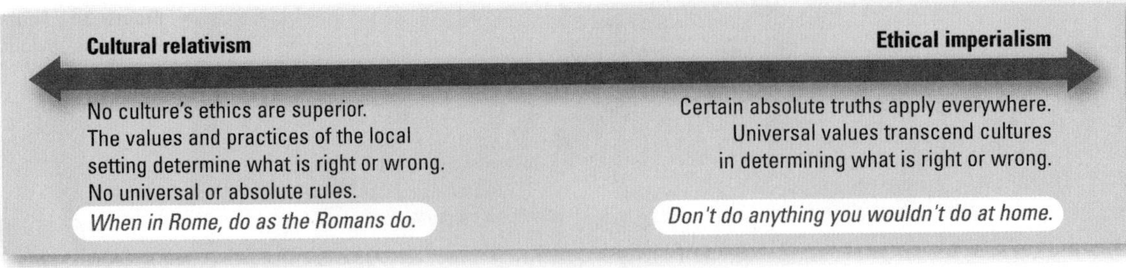

Cultural relativism	Ethical imperialism
No culture's ethics are superior. The values and practices of the local setting determine what is right or wrong. No universal or absolute rules.	Certain absolute truths apply everywhere. Universal values transcend cultures in determining what is right or wrong.
When in Rome, do as the Romans do.	*Don't do anything you wouldn't do at home.*

Figure 3.2 The extremes of cultural relativism and ethical imperialism in international business ethics.

Source: Developed from Thomas Donaldson, "Values in Tension: Ethics Away from Home," *Harvard Business Review*, vol. 74 (September–October 1996), pp. 48–62.

not acceptable practice anywhere else. In other words, ethical standards are universal and should apply absolutely across cultures and national boundaries. In this example, the Canadian executive would not do business in a setting where child labour was used, since it is unacceptable at home. Critics of such a universal approach claim that it is a form of **ethical imperialism**, or the attempt to externally impose one's ethical standards on others.

■ **Ethical imperialism** is an attempt to impose one's ethical standards on other cultures.

Business ethicist Thomas Donaldson discusses the debate between cultural relativism and ethical imperialism. Although there is no simple answer, he finds fault with both extremes. He argues instead that certain fundamental rights and ethical standards can be preserved while values and traditions of a given culture are respected.[17] The core values or "hyper-norms" that should transcend cultural boundaries focus on human dignity, basic rights, and good citizenship. With a commitment to core values creating a transcultural ethical umbrella, Donaldson believes international business behaviours can be tailored to local and regional cultural contexts. In the case of child labour, again, the Canadian executive might ensure that any children working in a factory under contract to his or her business would be provided schooling as well as employment. *Manager's Notepad 3.1* summarizes Donaldson's suggestions on how corporations can respect the core or universal values.[18]

✓ **Learning check ❶**

BE SURE YOU CAN

• define ethics • list and explain four views of ethical behaviour • discuss the types of ethical problems faced by people at work • differentiate the implications of cultural relativism and universalism in international business ethics

MANAGER'S
Notepad 3.1

How international businesses can respect universal values

Respect Human Dignity
• Create a culture valuing employees, customers, and suppliers.
• Keep a safe workplace.
• Produce safe products and services.

Respect Basic Rights
• Protect rights of employees, customers, and communities.
• Avoid any threats to safety, health, education, or living standards.

Be Good Citizens
• Support social institutions, economic, and educational systems.
• Work with governments and institutions to protect the environment.

ETHICS IN THE WORKPLACE

A classic quotation states, "Ethical business is good business." The same can be said for all persons and institutions throughout society. But the real test is when a manager or worker encounters a situation that challenges his or her ethical beliefs and standards. Often ambiguous and unexpected, these ethical challenges are inevitable and everyone has to be prepared to deal with them, even students. A college student may get a job offer and accept it, only to get a better offer two weeks later. Is it right for her to renege on the first job to accept the second? A student knows that in a certain course his roommate submitted a term paper purchased on the Internet. Is it right for him not to tell the instructor? One student tells another that a faculty member promised her a high final grade in return for sexual favours. Is it right for him not to vigorously encourage her to inform the instructor's department head?

●●● ETHICAL DILEMMAS AT WORK

An **ethical dilemma** is a situation that requires a choice regarding a possible course of action that, although offering the potential for personal or organizational benefit or both, may be considered unethical. It is often a situation in which action must be taken but for which there is no clear consensus on what is "right" and "wrong." The burden is on the individual to make good choices. An engineering manager speaking from experience sums it up this way: "I define an unethical situation as one in which I have to do something I don't feel good about."[19] Examples of some problem areas where managers make unethical decisions include:[20]

■ An **ethical dilemma** is a situation that, although offering potential benefit or gain, may be considered as unethical.

- *Discrimination*—denying promotion or appointment to a job candidate because of the candidate's race, religion, gender, age, or other non-job-relevant criterion.

- *Sexual harassment*—making a co-worker feel uncomfortable through inappropriate comments or actions regarding sexuality; or a manager requesting sexual favours in return for favourable job treatment.

- *Conflicts of interest*—taking a bribe or kickback or extraordinary gift in return for making a decision favourable to the gift giver.

- *Customer confidence*—giving another party privileged information regarding the activities of a customer.

- *Organizational resources*—using official stationery or a company e-mail account to communicate personal opinions or make requests from community organizations.

In a survey of *Harvard Business Review* subscribers, many of the ethical dilemmas reported by managers involved conflicts with superiors, customers, and subordinates.[21] The most frequent issues involved dishonesty in advertising and communications with top management, clients, and government agencies. Problems in dealing with special gifts, entertainment, and kickbacks were also reported. Significantly, the managers' bosses sometimes pressured them to engage in such unethical activities as supporting incorrect viewpoints, signing false documents, overlooking the boss's wrongdoings, and doing business with the boss's friends.

●●● RATIONALIZATIONS FOR UNETHICAL BEHAVIOUR

Why do otherwise reasonable people justify unethical acts? Think back to the earlier examples and to those from your experiences. Consider the possibility of being asked to place a bid for a business contract using insider information, paying bribes to obtain foreign business, falsifying expense account bills, and so on. "How," you should be asking, "do people explain doing things like this?" There are at least four common rationalizations that may be used to justify misconduct in these and other ethical dilemmas.[22]

- Convincing yourself that the behaviour is not really illegal.

- Convincing yourself that the behaviour is in everyone's best interests.

- Convincing yourself that nobody will ever find out what you've done.

- Convincing yourself that the organization will "protect" you.

After doing something that might be considered unethical, a rationalizer says, "*It's not really illegal.*" This expresses a mistaken belief that one's behaviour is acceptable, especially in ambiguous situations. When dealing with shady or borderline situations in which you are having a hard time precisely determining right from wrong, the advice is quite simple: when in doubt about a decision to be made or an action to be taken, ask yourself a few questions:

- Does this action make sense?

- Is this action or decision compatible with my concept of myself at my best?

- Do I think this action is right primarily because someone with appropriate authority says it is right?

Answering "No" to the first two questions and "Yes" to the last would indicate that you should not do it. Another strong sign that you are going too far is if you "gag" at the thought of carrying it out. An additional approach is to share your plan with others and get their thoughts on it before you proceed.

Another common statement by a rationalizer is, "*It's in everyone's best interests.*" This response involves the mistaken belief that because someone can be found to benefit from the behaviour, the behaviour is also in the individual's or the organization's best interests. Overcoming this rationalization depends in part on the ability to look beyond short-run results to address longer-term implications, and to look beyond results in general to the ways in which they are obtained. For example, in response to the question "How far can I push matters to obtain this performance goal?," the best answer may be, "Don't try to find out."

Sometimes rationalizers tell themselves, "*No one will ever know about it.*" They mistakenly believe that a questionable behaviour is really "safe" and will never be found out or made public. Unless it is discovered, the argument implies, no crime was really committed. Lack of accountability, unrealistic pressures to perform, and a boss who prefers "not to know" can all reinforce such thinking. In this case, the best deterrent is to make sure that everyone knows that wrongdoing will be punished whenever it is discovered.

A good way to question one's ethical conduct around "no one will ever know about it" is to take the "Front Page Challenge." If your actions were reported on the front page of your local paper, would you still undertake the same action? If your answer is no, then likely you should reconsider your course of action.

Finally, rationalizers may proceed with a questionable action because of a mistaken belief that "*the organization will stand behind me.*" This is misperceived loyalty. The individual believes that the organization's best interests stand above all others. In return, the individual believes that top managers will condone the behaviour and protect the individual from harm. But loyalty to the organization is not an acceptable excuse for misconduct; it should not stand above the law and social morality.

●●●● FACTORS INFLUENCING ETHICAL BEHAVIOUR

It is almost too easy to confront ethical dilemmas from the safety of a textbook or a classroom. In practice, people are often challenged to choose ethical courses of action in situations where

Figure 3.3 Factors influencing ethical managerial behaviour— the person, organization, and environment.

the pressures may be contradictory and great. Increased awareness of the factors influencing ethical behaviour can help you better deal with them in the future. *Figure 3.3* shows these influences emanating from the person, the organization, and the environment.

The Person

Family influences, religious values, personal standards, and personal needs, financial and otherwise, will help determine a person's ethical conduct in any given circumstance. Managers who lack a strong and clear set of personal ethics will find that their decisions vary from situation to situation as they strive to maximize self-interests. Those with solid ethical frameworks, personal rules, or strategies for ethical decision making will be more consistent and confident. Their choices are always guided by a stable set of ethical standards. Personal values that give priority to such virtues as honesty, fairness, integrity, and self-respect provide *ethical anchors* that help people make correct decisions even when circumstances are ambiguous and situational pressures are difficult.

It isn't easy to stand up for what you believe in as a person, especially in a social context full of contradictory or just plain bad advice. Consider these words from a commencement address delivered a few years ago at a well-known school of business administration. "Greed is all right," the speaker said. "Greed is healthy. You can be greedy and still feel good about yourself." The students, it is reported, greeted these remarks with laughter and applause. The speaker was Ivan Boesky, once considered the "king of the arbitrageurs."[23] It wasn't long after his commencement speech that Boesky was arrested, tried, convicted, and sentenced to prison for trading on inside information.

The Organization

The organization is another important influence on ethics in the workplace. We noted earlier that bosses can have a major impact on their subordinates' behaviours. Just exactly what a supervisor requests, and which actions are rewarded or punished, can certainly affect an individual's decisions and actions. The expectations and reinforcement provided by peers and group norms are likely to have a similar impact. Formal policy statements and written rules are also helpful. They support and reinforce the ethical climate for the organization as a whole.

At The Body Shop, founder Anita Roddick created an 11-point charter to guide the company's employees: "Honesty, integrity and caring form the foundations of the company and should flow through everything we do—we will demonstrate our care for the world in which we live by respecting fellow human beings, by not harming animals, by preserving our forests." The fact that The Body Shop still gets occasional ethical criticisms demonstrates the inadequacy of formal policies alone to guarantee consistent ethical behaviour. A visit to The Body Shop website, however, shows the firm's ongoing ethical commitments and provides answers to frequently asked questions regarding such controversial issues as animal testing in the cosmetics industry.[24]

Further evidence also suggests that having a charter is not enough to ensure an ethical environment. In 1994, Nortel Networks hired a senior ethical advisor, Megan Barry, to write a code of conduct entitled "Acting with Integrity," establish an internal hotline for ethical guidance and to report wrongdoing, and to share ethical principles with employees. At the time, Nortel was seen as a trailblazer in corporate ethics. However, with a change of top leadership, the ethics department increasingly became less visible and Barry left the company in 1999. Although the code of conduct was still on the books, there was little to suggest that it was being read anymore and lots to suggest that it was being ignored. Recent investigations have signalled accounting abuses by former executives that resulted in millions of dollars of bonuses being misappropriated. It has been suggested that Nortel's ethics were not destroyed by a few executives but by years of serious neglect. In 2005, Nortel Networks hired a new ethical guru, Susan Sheppard, to reaffirm the company's standards of ethics and integrity.[25]

The Environment

Organizations operate in competitive environments influenced by government laws and regulations and social norms and values. Laws interpret social values to define appropriate behaviours for organizations and their members; regulations help governments monitor these behaviours and keep them within acceptable standards. For example, the recent Enron and Arthur Andersen scandals led to new legislation that attempts to substitute for any lack of ethical leadership at the firm and industry levels in business. In the United States, the *Sarbanes-Oxley Act* of 2002 now makes it easier for corporate executives to be tried and sentenced to jail for financial misconduct. In Canada, the Canadian Securities Administrators (CSA) proposed new legislation. The CSA is a council of 13 provincial and territorial regulatory agencies that protects Canadian investors from unfair or fraudulent practices in order to ensure fair and efficient capital markets.

The climate of competition in an industry also sets a standard of behaviour for those who hope to prosper within it. Sometimes the pressures of competition contribute further to the ethical dilemmas of managers. Former American Airlines president Robert Crandall once telephoned Howard Putnam, then president of now-defunct Braniff Airlines. Both companies were suffering from money-losing competition on routes from their home base of Dallas. A portion of their conversation follows:[26]

Putnam: Do you have a suggestion for me?

Crandall: Yes. . . . Raise your fares 20 percent. I'll raise mine the next morning.

Putnam: Robert, we—

Crandall: You'll make more money and I will, too.

Putnam: We can't talk about pricing.

Crandall: Oh, Howard. We can talk about anything we want to talk about.

The U.S. Justice Department disagreed. It alleged that Crandall's suggestion of a 20 percent fare increase amounted to an illegal attempt to monopolize airline routes. The suit was later settled when Crandall agreed to curtail future discussions with competitors about fares.

✔ Learning check ❷

BE SURE YOU CAN

• define an ethical dilemma • list at least three ethical problem areas common in the workplace • list four common rationalizations for unethical behaviour • explain how ethics are influenced by the person, the organization, and the environment

MAINTAINING HIGH ETHICAL STANDARDS

The bad news is, as we well know, that news from the corporate world is not always positive. Consider these actual reports from past news stories. Item: Firm admits lowering phone contract bid after receiving confidential information from an insider that an initial bid "was not good enough to win." Item: Company admits overcharging consumers and insurers more than $13 million for repairs to damaged rental cars. Item: Executives get prison terms for selling adulterated apple juice; the juice, labelled "100% fruit juice," was actually a blend of synthetic ingredients.

The good news is that progressive organizations support a variety of methods for maintaining high ethical standards in workplace affairs. Some of the most important efforts in this area involve ethics training, whistle-blower protection, top management support, formal codes of ethics, and strong ethical cultures.

MANAGER'S
Notepad 3.2

Checklist for dealing with ethical dilemmas

Step 1. Recognize the ethical dilemma.

Step 2. Get the facts.

Step 3. Identify your options.

Step 4. Test each option: Is it legal? Is it right? Is it beneficial?

Step 5. Decide which option to follow.

Step 6. Double-check decision by asking the "spotlight" questions:

"How would I feel if my family found out about my decision?"

"How would I feel about this if my decision were printed in the local newspaper?"

Step 7. Take action.

●●● ETHICS TRAINING

Ethics training takes the form of structured programs to help participants understand the ethical aspects of decision making. It is designed to help people incorporate high ethical standards into their daily behaviours. An increasing number of university and college curricula now include required courses on ethics, and seminars on this topic are popular in the corporate world. But it is important to keep ethics training in perspective. An executive at Chemical Bank once put it this way: "We aren't teaching people right from wrong—we assume they know that. We aren't giving people moral courage to do what is right—they should be able to do that anyhow. We focus on dilemmas."[27]

Many ethical dilemmas arise as a result of the time pressures often associated with decision making. Ethics training can help people learn how to deal with ethical issues while under pressure. *Manager's Notepad 3.2* presents a seven-step checklist for dealing with an ethical dilemma. It offers an important reminder to double-check decisions before taking action. The key issue in the checklist may well be Step 6—the risk of public disclosure. Asking and answering the "spotlight" questions is a powerful way to test whether a decision is consistent with your personal ethical standards.

> **■ Ethics training** seeks to help people understand the ethical aspects of decision making and to incorporate high ethical standards into their daily behaviour.

●●● WHISTLE-BLOWER PROTECTION

Agnes Connolly pressed her employer to report two toxic chemical accidents; Dave Jones reported that his company was using unqualified suppliers in the construction of a nuclear power plant; Margaret Newsham revealed that her firm was allowing workers to do personal business while on government contracts; Herman Cohen charged that the ASPCA in New York was mistreating animals; Barry Adams complained that his hospital followed unsafe practices.[28] In Canada, more than 10 years ago, government accountant Allan Cutler began complaining about all kinds of problems in the awarding of federal advertising contracts. If his warnings had been heeded, the sponsorship scandal may never have happened.[29] They were whistle-blowers, persons who expose the misdeeds of others in organizations in order to preserve ethical standards and protect against wasteful, harmful, or illegal acts.[30] All were fired from their jobs. Indeed, whistle-blowers face the risks of impaired career progress and other forms of organizational retaliation, up to and including termination.

■ A whistle-blower exposes the misdeeds of others in organizations.

Today, federal and provincial laws increasingly offer whistle-blowers some defence against "retaliatory discharge." While signs indicate that the courts are growing more supportive of whistle-blowers, legal protection can still be inadequate. Furthermore, even with legal protection, potential whistle-blowers may find it hard to expose unethical behaviour in the workplace.

Some organizational barriers to whistle-blowing include a *strict chain of command* that makes it hard to bypass the boss; *strong work group identities* that encourage loyalty and self-censorship; and *ambiguous priorities* that make it hard to distinguish right from wrong.[31] A survey by the Ethics Resource Center reports that some 44 percent of workers still fail to report the wrongdoings they observe at work. The top reasons for not reporting are (1) the belief that no corrective action would be taken and (2) the fear that reports would not be kept confidential.[32]

In the attempt to remove these and other blocks to the exposure of unethical behaviours, some organizations have formally appointed staff members to serve as *ethics advocates*. One novel proposal suggests the use of *moral quality circles* to help create shared commitments for everyone to work at their moral best.[33]

PERSONAL MANAGEMENT

PERSONAL CHARACTER is a foundation for all that we do. It establishes our integrity and provides an ethical anchor for our behaviour in the workplace and in life overall. Persons of high integrity can always be confident in the self-respect it provides, even in the most difficult of situations. Those who lack it are destined to perpetual insecurity, acting inconsistently, and suffering not only in self-esteem but also in the opinion of others. How strong is your personal character? How well prepared are you to deal with the inevitable ethical dilemmas and challenges in work and in life? Can you give specific examples showing how your behaviour lives up to these Six Pillars of Character identified by the Josephson Institute of Ethics?[34]

- Trustworthiness—honesty, integrity, reliability in keeping promises, loyalty
- Respect—civility, courtesy and decency, dignity, tolerance, and acceptance
- Responsibility—sense of accountability, pursuit of excellence, self-restraint
- Fairness—commitment to process, impartiality, equity
- Caring—concern for others, benevolence, altruism
- Citizenship—knowing the law, being informed, volunteering

Get to know yourself better

Complete Self-Assessments #5—**Terminal Values Survey**, and #6—**Instrumental Values Survey**; and Exercises #6—**Confronting Ethical Dilemmas** from the Workbook and Personal Management Activity #1 on the companion website.

●●● ETHICAL ROLE MODELS

Top managers, in both large and small enterprises, have the power to shape an organization's policies and set its moral tone. They also have a major responsibility to use this power well by serving as ethical role models. Not only must their day-to-day behaviour be the epitome of high ethical conduct, they must also create ethical cultures and communicate similar expectations throughout the organization.

Even though top managers bear a special responsibility for setting the ethical tone of an organization, all managers are in a position to influence the ethical behaviour of the people who work for and with them. All managers must act as ethical role models, and both expect and support ethical behaviour by others. The important supervisory act of setting goals and communicating performance expectations is a good case in point. A surprising 64 percent of 238 executives in one study, for example, reported feeling pressure to compromise personal standards to achieve company goals. A *Fortune* survey also reported that 34 percent of its respondents felt a company president can create an ethical climate by setting reasonable goals "so that subordinates are not pressured into unethical actions."[35] Any manager may unknowingly encourage unethical practices by exerting too much pressure on others to accomplish goals that are too difficult. Part of the manager's ethical responsibility is to be realistic about performance goals.

●●● CODES OF ETHICAL CONDUCT

A **code of ethics** is a formal statement of an organization's values and beliefs. It offers guidelines on how to behave in situations susceptible to ethical dilemmas. Such codes are important anchor points in professions such as engineering, medicine, law, and public accounting. In organizations they identify expected behaviours in such areas as general citizenship, the avoidance of illegal or improper acts in one's work, and good relationships with customers. Specific guidelines are often set for bribes and kickbacks, political contributions, honesty of books or records, customer–supplier relationships, and confidentiality of corporate information.

■ A **code of ethics** is a formal statement of an organization's values and beliefs.

At Bell Canada Enterprises (BCE) their code of ethical conduct offers that "what we do is who we are." As President and CEO, Michael Sabia, states, "To maintain these high standards and our reputation, we cannot just read the code and sign compliance forms. We must live it and apply the code to every action and decision we take."[36]

In the increasingly complex world of international business, codes of conduct for manufacturers and contractors are becoming more prevalent. At Gap Inc., global manufacturing is governed by a formal Code of Vendor Conduct.[37] The document specifically deals with *discrimination*—"Factories shall employ workers on the basis of their ability to do the job, not on the basis of their personal characteristics or beliefs"; *forced labour*—"Factories shall not use any prison, indentured or forced labour"; *working conditions*—"Factories must treat all workers with respect and dignity and provide them with a safe and healthy environment"; and *freedom of association*—"Factories must not interfere with workers who wish to lawfully and peacefully associate, organize, or bargain collectively."

Although codes of ethical conduct are now common, it must be remembered that they have limits. While helpful, codes alone cannot guarantee ethical conduct. Ultimately, the value of any ethics code still rests on the human resource foundations of the organization. There is no replacement for effective hiring practices that staff organizations with honest and moral people. And there is no replacement for leadership by committed managers who set positive examples and always act as ethical role models.

> **BE SURE YOU CAN**
> • define the term whistle-blower • list three organizational barriers to whistle-blowing • compare and contrast ethics training, codes of ethical conduct, and ethical role models as methods for encouraging ethical behaviour in organizations

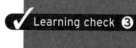 **✔ Learning check ❸**

CORPORATE SOCIAL RESPONSIBILITY

It is now time to shift our interest in ethical behaviour from the level of the individual to that of the organization. To begin, it is important to remember that all organizations exist in an "open system" or in a complex relationship with elements in their external environment. In

■ **Corporate social responsibility** is the obligation of an organization to serve its own interests and those of society.

this context, **corporate social responsibility** is defined as an obligation of the organization to act in ways that serve both its own interests and the interests of society at large.[38]

●●● STAKEHOLDER ISSUES AND ANALYSIS

A popular and useful way to examine the concept of corporate social responsibility is through a stakeholder analysis. *Figure 3.4* describes the environment of a typical business as a network of **organizational stakeholders**—those persons, groups, and other organizations directly affected by the behaviour of the organization and holding a stake in its performance.[39] In this perspective, the organization has a social responsibility to serve the interests of its many stakeholders, including:

■ **Organizational stakeholders** are directly affected by the behaviour of the organization and hold a stake in its performance.

- *Employees*—employees and contractors who work for the organization.

- *Customers*—consumers and clients who purchase the organization's goods and/or use its services.

- *Suppliers*—providers of the organization's human, information, material, and financial resources.

- *Owners*—stockholders, investors, and creditors with claims on assets and profits of the organization.

- *Competitors*—other organizations producing the same or similar goods and services.

- *Regulators*—the local, provincial, and federal government agencies that enforce laws and regulations.

- *Interest groups*—community groups, activists, and others representing interests of citizens and society.

Figure 3.4 Multiple stakeholders in the environment of organization.

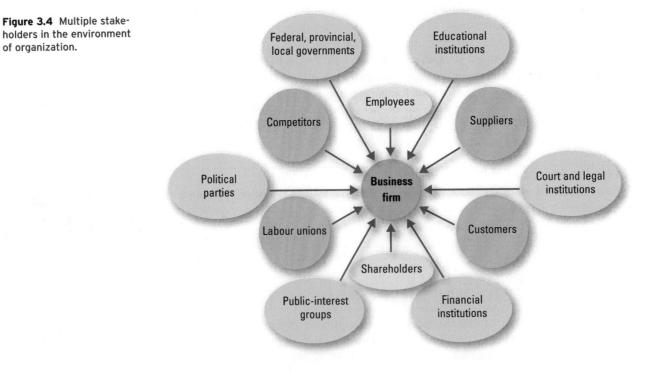

The unethical practices at Bre-X, WorldCom, Enron, and Andersen, as discussed previously, had an adverse impact on these firms' stakeholders. Everyone from investors to employees to customers suffered, with even competitors feeling the spillover effects as new government regulations were put into place. But even when it seems that "bad" things dominate the news, remember that there are also a lot of good things happening in organization–stakeholder relationships.

Several Canadian organizations have worked extensively with stakeholders to achieve positive results within their communities. Dupont Canada initiated a multi-stakeholder round table entitled the Social Innovation Enterprise Program in order to ensure that the company is contributing to the communities in which it operates. Home Depot encourages a culture of volunteerism among their employees. The company's community investments target four priority areas: environment, affordable housing, at-risk youth, and emergency preparedness. The Moose Deer Point First Nations Sustainable Community Project, initiated by Husky Injection Molding, has proven to be a truly innovative partnership successfully linking private industry, the government, and First Nations communities.[40]

Consumers, activist groups, non-profit organizations, and governments are increasingly vocal and influential in directing organizations toward socially responsible practices. In today's information age, business activities are increasingly transparent. Irresponsible practices are difficult to hide for long, wherever in the world they take place. Not only do news organizations find and disseminate the information, activist organizations also lobby, campaign, and actively pressure organizations to respect and protect everything from human rights to the natural environment. Increasingly important too are investor groups such as the Ethical Funds Company.

Ultimately, leaders exert a critical influence on the behaviour of organizations and their members. The leadership beliefs that guide socially responsible practices have been described as:[41]

- *People*—people do their best in healthy work environments with a balance of work and family life.

- *Communities*—organizations perform best when located in healthy communities.

- *Natural environment*—organizations gain by treating the natural environment with respect.

- *Term*—organizations must be managed and led for long-term success.

- *Reputation*—one's reputation must be protected to ensure customer and stakeholder support.

●●● PERSPECTIVES ON CORPORATE SOCIAL RESPONSIBILITY

Two contrasting views of corporate social responsibility have stimulated debate in academic and public-policy circles.[42] The *classical view* holds that management's only responsibility in running a business is to maximize profits. In other words, "the business of business is business," and the principal concern of management should always be to maximize shareholder value. This view is supported by Milton Friedman, a respected economist and Nobel Laureate. He says, "Few trends could so thoroughly undermine the very foundations of our free society as the acceptance by corporate officials of social responsibility other than to make as much money for their stockholders as possible."[43] The *arguments against corporate social responsibility* include fears that its pursuit will reduce business profits, raise business costs, dilute business purpose, give business too much social power, and do so without business accountability to the public.

By contrast, the *socio-economic view* holds that management of any organization must be concerned with broader social welfare and not just with corporate profits. This broad-based stakeholder perspective is supported by Paul Samuelson, another distinguished economist and Nobel Laureate. He states, "A large corporation these days not only may engage in social responsibility, it had damn well better try to do so."[44] Among the *arguments in favour of corporate social responsibility* are that it will add long-run profits for businesses, improve the public image of businesses, and help them avoid government regulation. Furthermore, businesses have the resources and ethical obligation to act responsibly.

Today, there is little doubt that the public at large wants businesses and other organizations to act with genuine social responsibility. Stakeholder expectations are increasingly well voiced and include demands that organizations integrate social responsibility into their core values and daily activities. And research indicates that social responsibility can be associated with strong financial performance and, at worst, has no adverse financial impact.[45] The argument that acting with a commitment to social responsibility will negatively affect the "bottom line" is hard to defend. Indeed, evidence points toward a *virtuous circle* in which corporate social responsibility leads to improved financial performance for the firm and this in turn leads to more socially responsible actions in the future.[46]

There seems little reason to believe that businesses cannot serve the public good while advancing the financial interests of their shareholders. Even as the research continues on this important concept, these historical comments by management theorist Keith Davis still confirm the importance of corporate social responsibility.[47]

> *Society wants business as well as all other major institutions to assume significant social responsibility. Social responsibility has become the hallmark of a mature, global organization. . . . The business which vacillates or chooses not to enter the arena of social responsibility may find that it gradually will sink into customer and public disfavour.*

CANADIAN COMPANY
IN THE NEWS   **Mountain Equipment Co-op**

CANADIAN STORE IS NUMBER ONE AT DOING GOOD

Vancouver-based Mountain Equipment Co-op (MEC) ranks at the top of big retail chains when it comes to corporate social responsibility (CSR), according to *Report on Business* magazine. ROB ranked companies that operate in Canada on the basis of their CSR performance, focusing on five specific industries, rather than on a broad range of sectors. MEC scored well above its peer group in the big retail category. The main reasons for this are the co-operative membership structure, which encourages employee and customer involvement, and the fact that it's the only Canadian retailer participating in the Fair Labour Association, a non-profit coalition working to improve labour standards and working conditions worldwide. Also, MEC is committed to generating zero waste in its operations. In 2004, it diverted about 76 percent of waste from its stores that would otherwise have gone to landfill.

Source: "Corporate Social Responsibility Ranking," *Report on Business*, February 23, 2006.

⬤⬤⬤ EVALUATING CORPORATE SOCIAL PERFORMANCE

A **social responsibility audit** can be used at regular intervals to report on, and systematically assess, an organization's accomplishments in various areas of corporate social responsibility. You might think of social responsibility audits as attempts to assess the social performance of organizations, much as accounting audits assess their financial performance. Typical audit areas include concerns for ecology and environmental quality, truth in lending, product safety, consumer protection, and aid to education. They also include service to communities, employment practices, diversity practices, progressive labour relations and employee assistance, and general corporate philanthropy, among other possibilities.

▦ **A social responsibility audit** assesses an organization's accomplishments in areas of social responsibility.

Criteria for Evaluating Social Performance

The social performance of business firms and other organizations can be described as driven by *compliance*—acting to avoid adverse consequences, or by *conviction*—acting to create positive impact.[48] Obviously, those of us who highly value corporate social responsibility believe that organizations should act with both. *Figure 3.5* links compliance and conviction with four criteria of social responsibility identified by management scholar Archie Carroll—economic, legal, ethical, and discretionary.[49] An audit of corporate social performance might include questions posed for each criterion: (1) Is the organization's *economic responsibility* met—is it profitable? (2) Is the organization's *legal responsibility* met—does it obey the law? (3) Is the organization's *ethical responsibility* met—is it doing the "right" things? (4) Is the organization's *discretionary responsibility* met—does it contribute to the broader community?

As the audit moves step by step through these criteria, the assessment inquires into ever-greater demonstrations of social performance. An organization is meeting its economic responsibility when it earns a profit through the provision of goods and services desired by customers. Legal responsibility is fulfilled when an organization operates within the law and according to the requirements of various external regulations. An organization meets its ethical responsibility when its actions voluntarily conform not only to legal expectations but also to the broader values and moral expectations of society. The highest level of social performance comes through the satisfaction of an organization's discretionary responsibility. Here, the organization voluntarily moves beyond basic economic, legal, and ethical expectations to provide leadership in advancing the well-being of individuals, communities, and society as a whole.

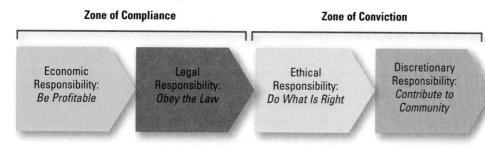

Figure 3.5 Criteria for evaluating corporate social performance.

Social Responsibility Strategies

The social performance of organizations can also be analyzed in respect to the apparent "strategy" being followed. *Figure 3.6* describes a continuum of four corporate social responsibility strategies, with the commitment increasing as the strategy shifts from "obstructionist" at the lowest end to "proactive" at the highest.[50]

■ An **obstructionist strategy** avoids social responsibility and reflects mainly economic priorities.

An **obstructionist strategy** ("Fight the social demands") reflects mainly economic priorities; social demands lying outside the organization's perceived self-interests are resisted. If the organization is criticized for wrongdoing, it can be expected to deny the claims. A **defensive strategy** ("Do the minimum legally required") seeks to protect the organization by doing the minimum legally necessary to satisfy expectations. Corporate behaviour at this level conforms only to legal requirements, competitive market pressure, and perhaps activist voices. If criticized, intentional wrongdoing is likely to be denied.

■ A **defensive strategy** seeks protection by doing the minimum legally required.

■ An **accommodative strategy** accepts social responsibility and tries to satisfy economic, legal, and ethical critera.

Organizations pursuing an **accommodative strategy** ("Do the minimum ethically required") accept their social responsibilities. They try to satisfy economic, legal, and ethical criteria. Corporate behaviour at this level is congruent with society's prevailing norms, values, and expectations. But, it may be so only because of outside pressures. An oil firm, for example, may be willing to "accommodate" with cleanup activities when spills occur but remain quite slow in taking actions to prevent them in the first place. The **proactive strategy** ("Take leadership in social initiatives") is designed to meet all the criteria of social performance, including discretionary performance. Corporate behaviour at this level takes preventive action to avoid adverse social impacts from company activities, and it takes the lead in identifying and responding to emerging social issues.

■ A **proactive strategy** meets all the criteria of social responsibility, including discretionary performance.

Figure 3.6 Four strategies of corporate social responsibility—from obstructionist to proactive behaviour.

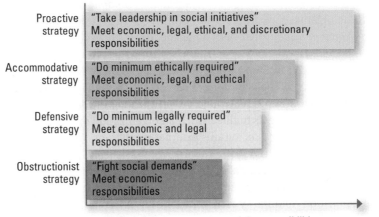

Commitment to corporate social responsibilities

●●● SOCIAL ENTREPRENEURSHIP

Social entrepreneurs recognize that certain groups in their communities are experiencing difficulties and they seek new ways to solve the problems. Loosely defined, social entrepreneurial behaviour involves undertaking tasks for the benefit of society rather than for personal profit. For example, as a nurse, Veronica Khosa was frustrated with the health care system in her native country of South Africa. She saw sick people not being helped and thus becoming sicker, aged people physically unable to make the trip to a doctor, and hospitals with empty beds but apparently with no room for people with HIV-related illnesses. In response to these things, Khosa began a "home care" program in her country, calling it Tateni Home Care Nursing Services.[51] Her not-for-profit team took to the streets to provide care to the sick in the comfort and security of their own homes. Years later, the South African government recognized the wisdom of this plan and adopted her model of health care. Social entrepreneurs like Veronica Khosa redefine their field and go on to solve systemic social problems on a larger scale.

Social entrepreneurs search out things that are not working for those who need them. They seek to solve the problem first by changing the system, then by spreading the solution, and lastly by working to persuade entire societies to take up the challenge to change. For example, Ashoka, which serves to develop the concept of social entrepreneurship and support these individuals, sees social entrepreneurs as people who "are not content just to give a fish to a starving person nor are they satisfied with teaching them how to fish. Social entrepreneurs will not rest until they have revolutionized the fishing industry."[52]

Social Entrepreneurship and Business

Central to any discussion of social entrepreneurship is the question of who should take responsibility for the needs of our collective society. As such, you might ask how social entrepreneurship fits within the business world. Traditionally, governments have been regarded as having responsibility for social initiatives. As discussed earlier in the chapter, modern perspectives now recognize that our communities are everyone's responsibility. The growing number of businesses helping out in communities indicates that many social entrepreneurs are experienced and successful business executives who clearly wish to "give something back" to the communities in which their businesses operate.

For example, business social entrepreneurs ensure that profits generated from a specific project are used for the benefit of a specific group. An example of this is the CIBC's partnership with the Canadian Breast Cancer Foundation in order to organize and promote the "Run for the Cure" event. Overall, there is a movement to formalize the links between corporate donations and social causes. A key focus of Imagine Canada, a non-profit organization, is to champion corporate citizenship and help businesses partner in the community. The Imagine challenge asks Canadian companies to donate a minimum of 1 percent of their domestic, pre-tax profits to a Canadian charitable or non-profit organization.

Taking the social entrepreneurship idea a step further, others have argued that a realistic and desirable way for businesses to be socially responsible is through "strategic philanthropy," whereby a business makes donations in areas that support the company's interests and to organizations that they might have a connection with. For example, a construction company might be active in social initiatives that promote the building of low-cost housing in a community. This is the case with Home Depot. Through employee engagement programs, Home Depot has given paid time off to employees to allow them to help build affordable housing in their communities.

Many Canadian organizations, both for profit and not-for-profit, encourage employees to take up the change the community for the better challenge. Microsoft donates $17 per hour to a registered charity for each hour their employee volunteers there, and also loans out their executives to volunteer for the United Way. PricewaterhouseCoopers Canada also provides funding to organizations where their employees volunteer; recently, over 1,000 employees were active in making a difference in their communities. The term "caring capitalism" has been coined to describe this type of activity in which the achievement of relevant social goals relies on competitiveness in the marketplace.

On Becoming a Social Entrepreneur

In one of the first studies aimed at understanding social entrepreneurs, Charles Leadbeater, a visiting fellow at Oxford University, identified several social entrepreneurs and looked for common traits among them. These individuals endeavoured to address local issues, some of which, over time, spread from their neighborhood beginnings to have a national or even international focus. Leadbeater established that while social entrepreneurs possessed many of the

Canadian Managers

Volunteer Now!

Marc Kielburger is a Canadian social entrepreneur. He started Volunteer Now! in order to make social advocacy "cool" in Toronto high schools. His organization was founded on the principle that young people have within them the power to change the world. Volunteer Now! seeks to motivate young people to become active in both their local and global communities. It is primarily a student-run program that serves to educate teachers about how to introduce the concept into classrooms, organizes student leadership programs, and educates student "volunteer ambassadors" who go out to inspire fellow students to work with their communities as agents of positive change.

Source: Information taken from <www.volunteernow.ca> (January 2007).

qualities of successful business entrepreneurs, they also had a strong commitment to help others.[53] These attributes and abilities allowed a social entrepreneur to follow a distinctive course of action, which was often characterized by the following steps:

1. identify a "needs gap" and fully understand the related opportunity,

2. inject imagination and vision into their approach,

3. recruit and motivate others to the cause and build essential networks,

4. secure the needed resources,

5. overcome obstacles and challenges and handle the associated risks, and

6. introduce proper control systems for the venture.

Social entrepreneurship is a growing opportunity. How might you make a difference in your community?

Learning check ❹

BE SURE YOU CAN
• define the term corporate social responsibility • summarize the arguments for and against social responsibility by businesses • defend a personal preference between these arguments • identify four criteria for measuring corporate social performance • identify these criteria with four possible social responsibility strategies • understand the goals of social entrepreneurs

ORGANIZATIONS AND SOCIETY

The fact remains that not all managers and not all organizations accept the challenge of acting with conviction and proactive commitment to social responsibility. Government, as the voice and instrument of the people, is often called upon to step in and act on the public's behalf.

●●● HOW GOVERNMENTS INFLUENCE ORGANIZATIONS

Governments influence organizations by passing laws and establishing regulating agencies to control and direct their behaviour. It may not be too far-fetched to say that behind every piece of legislation—federal, provincial, or municipal—is a government agency charged with the responsibility of monitoring and ensuring compliance with its mandates. These include groups like the Transportation Safety Board of Canada, provincial ministries of the environment and of health, and the Canadian Food Inspection Agency.

Business executives often complain that many laws and regulations are overly burdensome. Public outcries to "dismantle the bureaucracy" and/or "deregulate business" express concerns that some agencies and legislation are not functional. But the reality is that the legal environment is both complex and constantly changing. Managers must stay informed about new and pending laws as well as existing ones. As a reminder, consider four areas in which the Canadian government takes an active role in regulating business affairs.

The first area is *occupational health and safety*. The *Occupational Health and Safety Act* of 1973 firmly established that the federal government is concerned about worker health and safety on the job. Even though some complain that the regulations are still not strong enough, the act continues to influence the concerns of employers and government policy-makers for worker safety. Second is the area of *fair labour* practices. Legislation and regulations that prohibit discrimination in labour practices are discussed in Chapter 12, which deals with human resource management. For example, in Canada, the *Employment Equity Act*, originally passed in 1985 and adapted in 1995, is designed to reduce employment barriers for visible minorities, women, Aboriginals, and persons with disabilities. Unfortunately, the act applies only to federal government employees or employees of companies that have contracts with the federal government or are federally regulated. Third is *consumer protection*. The *Hazardous Products Act* gives government the authority to examine and force a business to withdraw from sale any product that it feels is hazardous to the consumer. Children's toys and flammable fabrics are within the great range of products affected by such regulation. The fourth area concerns *environmental protection*. Several anti-pollution acts, including the Canadian *Environmental Protection Act* of 1999, are designed to eliminate careless pollution of the air, water, and land.

AROUND THE WORLD

Among the important social contributions of non-profit organizations, Social Accountability International stands tall for its dedication to workers and their communities around the world. Its mission is described as, "Setting standards for a just world." In practice, this involves the organization's commitment to improving workplaces and combatting sweatshops through the expansion and further development of the international workplace standards known as SA8000 and S8000. The nine dimensions of accountability it measures are child labour, forced labour, health and safety, freedom of association and the right to collective bargaining, discrimination, discipline, working hours, remuneration, and management systems. Certification is voluntary but is highly regarded by unions and non-governmental organizations (NGOs). At present there are certified firms in more than 30 countries and industries.

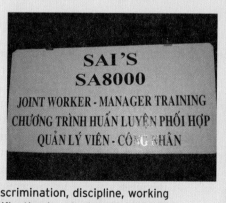

Non-profit supports social accountability worldwide

Source: Information from <www.cepaa.org/AboutSAI/>.

●●● HOW ORGANIZATIONS INFLUENCE GOVERNMENTS

Just as governments influence organizations, the leaders of organizations may take action to influence governments. There are a number of ways in which businesses in particular attempt to influence government to adopt and pursue policies favourable to them.

■ **Lobbying** expresses opinions and preferences to government officials.

■ **Political action committees** collect money for donation to political campaigns.

Through *personal contacts and networks*, executives get to know important people in government and try to gain their support for special interests. Through *public relations campaigns*, executives try to communicate positive images of their organizations to the public at large. Through **lobbying**, often with the assistance of professional lobbyists, executives can have their desires communicated directly to government officials. Executives also seek influence through financial contributions to **political action committees** (PACs) that collect money and donate it to support favoured political candidates. Unfortunately, illegal acts also occur. Executives sometimes resort to bribes or illegal financial campaign contributions in the attempt to gain influence over public officials.

Figure 3.7 Centrality of ethics and social responsibility in leadership and the managerial role.

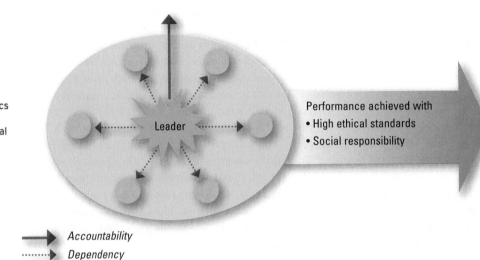

Leader

Performance achieved with
• High ethical standards
• Social responsibility

→ *Accountability*
⋯▸ *Dependency*

●●● ROLE OF CORPORATE GOVERNANCE

■ **Corporate governance** is the oversight of top management by a board of directors.

In Chapter 1, **corporate governance** was defined as oversight of the top management of an organization by a board of directors. Governance most typically involves hiring, firing, and compensating the CEO, assessing strategy, and verifying financial records. One board member describes the responsibilities of corporate governance as, "It's really about setting and maintaining high standards."[54] But even though the purpose is clear, there is a lot of concern that corporate governance can be inadequate and in some cases ineffectual. For example, the news contains critical reports that CEO pay is too high; we also read about continuing accounting scandals that reveal misuse of corporate assets and wrongful financial reporting.[55] All this raises stakeholder concerns to ensure high standards of ethical conduct by executives and socially responsible behaviour by organizations.

There is no doubt that the pressure is on to restore corporate governance to its rightful place as a key guarantor that businesses and other organizations are run properly. And importantly, the responsibilities of "governance" in respect to day-to-day managerial control are being well communicated throughout organizations. Trends in social values are reflected in ever-increasing demands, from governments and other stakeholders, that managerial decisions reflect ethical as well as high-performance standards. All managers must accept personal responsibility for doing the "right" things. Decisions must be made and problems solved with ethical considerations standing side by side with performance objectives.

Management focuses your attention throughout on the responsibilities depicted in *Figure 3.7.* It presents the manager's or team leader's challenge this way: to fulfill an accountability for achieving performance objectives, while always doing so in an ethical and socially responsible manner. The full weight of this responsibility applies to every organizational setting from small to large and from private to non-profit. It applies also at every managerial level, from bottom to top. There is no escaping the ultimate reality—being a manager is a very socially responsible job!

BE SURE YOU CAN   ✓ Learning check ❺

• explain and give examples of how governments use legislation to influence business behaviour • identify methods used by businesses to influence governments to adopt favourable policies toward them • define corporate governance and discuss its importance in organization–society relationships

---

●●● Chapter 3 STUDY GUIDE

WHERE WE'VE BEEN

Back to Aldo Shoes

The opening example of Aldo Shoes provided a clear benchmark for how business performance, ethical behaviour, and social responsibility can go hand in hand. Aldo Shoes, along with other positive examples in the chapter, helps offset the bad side of business and managerial behaviour sensationalized in the cases of Bre-X, Enron, Andersen, WorldCom, and others. In Chapter 3 you learned more about the issues and complexities of personal ethics and corporate social responsibility. As you read further in *Management,* always keep these themes in mind as a learning context. Never forget that there is no substitute for ethical and socially responsible behaviour.

THE NEXT STEP
INTEGRATED LEARNING ACTIVITIES

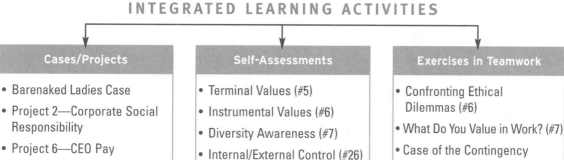

Cases/Projects	Self-Assessments	Exercises in Teamwork
• Barenaked Ladies Case	• Terminal Values (#5)	• Confronting Ethical Dilemmas (#6)
• Project 2—Corporate Social Responsibility	• Instrumental Values (#6)	• What Do You Value in Work? (#7)
• Project 6—CEO Pay	• Diversity Awareness (#7)	• Case of the Contingency Workforce (#22)
	• Internal/External Control (#26)	

STUDY QUESTION SUMMARY

1. What is ethical behaviour?

- Ethical behaviour is that which is accepted as "good" or "right" as opposed to "bad" or "wrong."

- Simply because an action is not illegal does not necessarily make it ethical in a given situation.

- Because values vary, the question of "What is ethical behaviour?" may be answered differently by different people.

- Four ways of thinking about ethical behaviour are the utilitarian, individualism, moral-rights, and justice views.

- Cultural relativism argues that no culture is ethically superior to any other.

2. How do ethical dilemmas complicate the workplace?

- When managers act ethically they have a positive impact on other people in the workplace and on the social good performed by organizations.

- An ethical dilemma occurs when someone must decide whether to pursue a course of action that, although offering the potential for personal or organizational benefit or both, may be considered potentially unethical.

- Managers report that their ethical dilemmas often involve conflicts with superiors, customers, and subordinates over such matters as dishonesty in advertising and communications as well as pressure from their bosses to do unethical things.

- Common rationalizations for unethical behaviour include believing the behaviour is not illegal, is in everyone's best interests, will never be noticed, or will be supported by the organization.

3. How can high ethical standards be maintained?

- Ethics training in the form of courses and training programs helps people better deal with ethical dilemmas in the workplace.

- Whistle-blowers expose the unethical acts of others in organizations, even while facing career risks for doing so.

- Top management sets an ethical tone for the organization as a whole, and all managers are responsible for acting as positive models of appropriate ethical behaviour.

- Written codes of ethical conduct formally state what an organization expects of its employees regarding ethical conduct at work.

4. What is corporate social responsibility?

- Corporate social responsibility is an obligation of the organization to act in ways that serve both its own interests and the interests of its many external publics, often called stakeholders.

- Criteria for evaluating corporate social performance include economic, legal, ethical, and discretionary responsibilities.

- Corporate strategies in response to social demands include obstruction, defence, accommodation, and proaction, with more progressive organizations taking proactive stances.

5. How do organizations and governments work together in society?

- Government agencies are charged with monitoring and ensuring compliance with the mandates of law.

- Managers must be well informed about existing and pending legislation in a variety of social responsibility areas, including environmental protection and other quality-of-life concerns.

- Organizations exert their influence on government in many ways, including interpersonal contacts of executives, use of lobbyists, and financial contributions to PACs.

- All managerial decisions and actions in every workplace should fulfill performance accountability with commitments to high ethical standards and socially responsible means.

KEY TERMS REVIEW

Accommodative strategy (p. 72)

Code of ethics (p. 67)

Corporate governance (p. 76)

Corporate social responsibility (p. 68)

Cultural relativism (p. 59)

Defensive strategy (p. 72)

Distributive justice (p. 59)

Ethical behaviour (p. 57)

Ethical dilemma (p. 61)

Ethical imperialism (p. 60)

Ethics (p. 57)

Ethics training (p. 65)

Individualism view (p. 58)

Instrumental values (p. 58)

Interactional justice (p. 59)

Justice view (p. 59)

Lobbying (p. 76)

Moral-rights view (p. 59)

Obstructionist strategy (p. 72)

Organizational stakeholders (p. 68)

Political action committees (p. 76)

Proactive strategy (p. 72)

Procedural justice (p. 59)

Social responsibility audit (p. 71)

Terminal values (p. 58)

Universalism (p. 59)

Utilitarian view (p. 58)

Values (p. 57)

Whistle-blowers (p. 66)

SELF-TEST 3

MULTIPLE-CHOICE QUESTIONS:

1. Values are personal beliefs that help determine whether a behaviour will be considered ethical or unethical. An example of a terminal value is _____ .
   (a) ambition (b) self-respect (c) courage (d) imagination

2. Under the _____ view of ethical behaviour, a business owner would be considered ethical if she reduced a plant's workforce by 10 percent in order to cut costs and be able to save jobs for the other 90 percent.
   (a) utilitarian (b) individualism (c) justice (d) moral-rights

3. A manager's failure to enforce a late-to-work policy the same way for all employees is an ethical violation of _____ justice.
   (a) ethical (b) moral (c) distributive (d) procedural

4. The *Sarbanes-Oxley Act* of 2002 makes it easier for corporate executives to _____.
   (a) protect themselves from shareholder lawsuits (b) sue employees who commit illegal acts (c) be tried and sentenced to jail for financial misconduct (d) shift blame for wrongdoing to boards of directors

5. Two "spotlight" questions for conducting the ethics double-check of a decision are: (a) "How would I feel if my family found out about this?" and (b) "How would I feel if _____?"
   (a) my boss found out about this (b) my subordinates found out about this (c) this was printed in the local newspaper (d) this went into my personnel file

6. Research on ethical dilemmas indicates that _____ is/are often the cause of unethical behaviour by people at work.
   (a) declining morals in society (b) lack of religious beliefs (c) the absence of whistle-blowers (d) pressures from bosses and superiors

7. Customers, investors, employees, and regulators are examples of _____ that are important in the analysis of corporate social responsibility.
   (a) special-interest groups (b) stakeholders (c) ethics advocates (d) whistle-blowers

8. A(n) _____ is someone who exposes the ethical misdeeds of others.
   (a) whistle-blower (b) ethics advocate (c) ombudsman (d) stakeholder

9. Two employees are talking about their employers. Sean says that ethics training and codes of ethical conduct are worthless; Maura says these are the best ways to ensure ethical behaviour in the organization. Who is right and why?
   (a) Sean—no one cares. (b) Maura—only the organization can influence ethical behaviour. (c) Neither Sean nor Maura—training and codes can aid but never guarantee ethical behaviour. (d) Neither Sean nor Maura—only the threat of legal punishment will make people act ethically.

10. A proponent of the classical view of corporate social responsibility would most likely agree with which of these statements?
   (a) Social responsibility improves the public image of business. (b) The primary responsibility of business is to maximize business profits. (c) By acting responsibly, businesses avoid government regulation. (d) Businesses can and should do "good" while doing business.

11. Which criterion for evaluating corporate social performance ranks highest in terms of conviction to operate in a responsible manner?
    (a) economic (b) legal (c) ethical (d) discretionary

12. An organization that takes the lead in addressing emerging social issues is being _____, showing the most progressive corporate social responsibility strategy.

    (a) accommodative (b) defensive (c) proactive (d) obstructionist

13. _____ seek to influence governments to adopt favourable policies toward business by raising money and donating it to support political candidates.
    (a) Stakeholders (b) Lobbyists (c) PACs (d) Auditors

14. In the final analysis, managers must make sure that high-performance goals in and by organizations are achieved by _____ means.
    (a) any possible (b) cultural relativism (c) ethical imperialism (d) ethical and socially responsible

15. A social entrepreneur _____ . (a) looks for opportunities to make money (b) seeks out social problems and works to find solutions (c) adheres to the status quo (d) is a small business owner

SHORT-RESPONSE QUESTIONS:

16. Explain the difference between the individualism and justice views of ethical behaviour.

17. List four common rationalizations for unethical managerial behaviour.

18. What are the major elements in the socio-economic view of corporate social responsibility?

19. What role do government agencies play in regulating the socially responsible behaviour of businesses?

APPLICATION QUESTION:

20. A small outdoor clothing company has just received an attractive offer from a business in Bangladesh to manufacture its work gloves. The offer would allow for substantial cost savings over the current supplier. The company manager, however, has read reports that some Bangladeshi businesses break their own laws and operate with child labour. How would differences in the following corporate responsibility strategies affect the manager's decision regarding whether to accept the offer: obstruction, defence, accommodation, and proaction?

Environment, Organizational Culture, and Diversity

●●● CHAPTER 4 STUDY QUESTIONS

Planning Ahead

After reading Chapter 4, you should be able to answer these questions in your own words.

1. What is the external environment of organizations?

2. What is a customer-driven organization?

3. What is a quality-driven organization?

4. What is organizational culture?

5. How is diversity managed in a multicultural organization?

of direct consequence to the organization as it operates
environment is often described in terms of **stakeholder**
sons, groups, and institutions who are affected in one w
performance. They are key constituencies that have a s
ance, are influenced by how it operates, and can influen

Sometimes called the *task environment*, the specific
are distinct for each organization. They can also change o
unique customer base, operating needs, and circumstance
to the specific environment of most organizations include
regulators, and investors/owners from the external enviror
internal environment.

Figure 4.1 shows the typical business firm as an ope
eral stakeholder groups linked by stages in the input-tr
type of stakeholder analysis can be used to both assess
zations vis-à-vis *strategic constituencies* and to develop
in the future. The analysis helps focus management atte
to which the organization is creating value for, and s
constituencies.

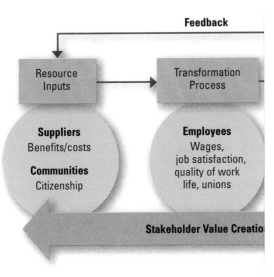

Feedback

Resource Inputs → Transformation Process

Suppliers
Benefits/costs

Communities
Citizenship

Employees
Wages,
job satisfaction,
quality of work
life, unions

Stakeholder Value Creatio

As suggested in *Figure 4.1*, value creation is impor
specific environment, reflected in the input and output
an open system, and from the internal environmen
process itself. In respect to product outputs, for examp
tomers through product price and quality, and for owne
respect to inputs, businesses create value for suppliers
business relationships, and for communities in such a
in using and contributing to public services. And in resp
ate value for employees through the wages and satisfa
transforming resource inputs into product outputs. Wa
zation that manages the value creation chain quite w
input and throughput stages, they are able to offer pi
appeal to customers.

BMO Financial Group

An employer of choice

Would you like to work for a company that is "committed to ensuring a workplace where the voice of every colleague is listened to and encouraged"? That's what BMO Financial Group prides itself in providing. Established in 1817 as Bank of Montreal, BMO Financial Group's core values have been fundamental in the development of many diverse and innovative programs. These have helped drive the institution's stated vision to be the top performing financial services company in North America. The bank's core values create an inclusive organizational culture:

- We care about our customers, shareholders, communities, and each other.
- We draw our strength from the diversity of our people and our businesses.
- We insist upon respect for everyone and encourage all to have a voice.
- We keep our promises and stand accountable for our every action.
- We share information, learn, and innovate to create consistently superior customer service.

Since 1990, there have been several groundbreaking task forces within the company to ensure a diverse and equitable working population. This, coupled with the flexible working hours and generous allowances for employee education, have resulted in continuing high job satisfaction rates reported by employees. The bank believes that "its revenue growth and the advancement of workplace equality are inextricably linked."

It's not surprising then that the institution was recently awarded the 2005 Canada's Best Corporate Citizen of the Year award by the magazine *Corporate Knights*, that it is consistently ranked as one of the best places to work in Canada and, according to *Canadian Business* magazine's annual corporate governance survey, ranked among the top 25 boards in Canada. BMO Financial Group is an "employer of choice."[1]

IN THE WORKPLACE

Over coffee, you talk with some colleagues about how to improve customer service at your company.

You suggest considering the customer service approach of the successful US department store Nordstrom. You show them its one-page employee handbook:

WELCOME TO NORDSTROM
We're glad to have you with our Company. Our number one goal is to provide outstanding customer service. Set both your personal and professional goals high. We have great confidence in your ability to achieve them.

Nordstrom Rules: Rule #1:
Use your good judgment in all situations. There will be no additional rules.
Please feel free to ask your department manager, store manager, or division general manager any question at any time.

A skeptical colleague wonders how the employee handbook can develop Nordstrom's core value of superior customer service. How do you respond?

- *Legal-political conditions*—prevail
  ties running the government, as w

- *Technological conditions*—develor
  advancements.

- *Natural environment conditions*
  including levels of public concern

If we take the natural environ
Toyota seem to be finding the poter
leading edge of new markets for hyb
America's automakers were betting
often gas-hungry vehicles, their Ja
advantage. Now they have experienc
the more environmentally friendly

In respect to the socio-cultural
Managers who understand demogra
tomer base and labour markets t
Notepad 4.1 highlights important
Canadian society.[8] These and other
noticeable internationally. External
ture to the next, and managers mus
pharmaceutical giant Merck derive:
ations. Its executives recognize the
ing local conditions. In Europe, for
with local companies, conducted re
ments on legal matters.

MANAGER'S
Notepad 4.1

Diversity trends in the so

- Visible minority groups and
  ethnic populations are an ir

- More women are working.

- People with disabilities are

- More workers come from n
  wage earners).

- The average age of workers

- The number of different fai

■ The **specific environment**
includes the people and
groups with whom an
organization interacts.

●●● STAKEHOLDERS A

The **specific environment** consis
whom an organization interacts a

Japanese were straightforward . . . and they worked: tally defects, analyze and trace them to the source, make corrections, and keep a record of what happens afterward.[18] Deming's "14 points of quality" emphasize constant innovation, use of statistical methods, and commitment to training in the fundamentals of quality assurance.

■ **Continuous improvement**
involves always searching for
new ways to improve work
quality and performance.

The search for quality is closely tied to the emphasis on **continuous improvement**—always looking for new ways to improve on current performance.[19] The notion is that one can never be satisfied; something always can and should be improved on. Continuous improvement must be a way of life. Another important aspect of total quality operations is cycle time—the elapsed time between receipt of an order and delivery of the finished product. The quality objective here is to reduce cycle time by finding ways to serve customer needs more quickly.

■ Members of a **quality
circle** meet periodically to
discuss ways of improving
the quality of products or
services.

One way to combine employee involvement and continuous improvement is through the popular **quality circle** concept.[20] This is a small group of workers that meets regularly to discuss ways of improving the quality of their products or services. Their objective is to assume responsibility for quality and apply every member's full creative potential to ensure that it is achieved. Such worker empowerment can result in cost savings from improved quality and greater customer satisfaction. It can also improve morale and commitment, as the following remarks from quality circle members indicate: "This is the best thing the company has done in 15 years." . . . "The program proves that supervisors have no monopoly on brains." . . . "It gives me more pride in my work."[21]

●●● QUALITY, TECHNOLOGY, AND DESIGN

Technology utilization is improving the quality of manufacturing today by helping firms better integrate their operations with customer preferences, and by allowing production changes to be made quickly and at low cost. For example, *lean production* uses technologies to streamline systems and allow work to be performed with fewer workers and smaller inventories. *Flexible manufacturing* allows processes to be changed quickly and efficiently to produce different products or modifications to existing ones. Through such techniques as *agile manufacturing* and *mass customization*, organizations are able to make individualized products quickly and with production efficiencies once only associated with the mass production of uniform products.[22]

Another timely and important contribution to quality management is found in *product design*. We are all aware of design differences among products, be they cars, computers, cell phones, stereos, watches, clothes, or whatever. But what may not be recognized is that design makes a difference in how things are produced and at what level of cost and quality. In today's competitive global economy, product designs are strategic weapons. A "good" design has both eye appeal to the customer and is easy to manufacture with regards to productivity. *Design for manufacturing* means that products are styled to lower production costs and smooth the way toward high-quality results in all aspects of the manufacturing processes. A manufacturing approach that shows respect for the natural environment is *design for disassembly*. The goal is to design products while taking into account how their component parts will be recycled at the end of their lives.

✓ **Learning check ❸**

BE SURE YOU CAN

- define the term **ISO certification** • explain the role of continuous improvement in TQM • describe what a quality circle is and how its use can increase performance quality • discuss how good use of technology and product design can improve quality

BMO Financial Group

An employer of choice

Would you like to work for a company that is "committed to ensuring a workplace where the voice of every colleague is listened to and encouraged"? That's what BMO Financial Group prides itself in providing. Established in 1817 as Bank of Montreal, BMO Financial Group's core values have been fundamental in the development of many diverse and innovative programs. These have helped drive the institution's stated vision to be the top performing financial services company in North America. The bank's core values create an inclusive organizational culture:

- We care about our customers, shareholders, communities, and each other.

- We draw our strength from the diversity of our people and our businesses.

- We insist upon respect for everyone and encourage all to have a voice.

- We keep our promises and stand accountable for our every action.

- We share information, learn, and innovate to create consistently superior customer service.

Since 1990, there have been several groundbreaking task forces within the company to ensure a diverse and equitable working population. This, coupled with the flexible working hours and generous allowances for employee education, have resulted in continuing high job satisfaction rates reported by employees. The bank believes that "its revenue growth and the advancement of workplace equality are inextricably linked."

It's not surprising then that the institution was recently awarded the 2005 Canada's Best Corporate Citizen of the Year award by the magazine *Corporate Knights*, that it is consistently ranked as one of the best places to work in Canada and, according to *Canadian Business* magazine's annual corporate governance survey, ranked among the top 25 boards in Canada. BMO Financial Group is an "employer of choice."[1]

IN THE WORKPLACE

Over coffee, you talk with some colleagues about how to improve customer service at your company.

You suggest considering the customer service approach of the successful US department store Nordstrom. You show them its one-page employee handbook:

WELCOME TO NORDSTROM

We're glad to have you with our Company. Our number one goal is to provide outstanding customer service. Set both your personal and professional goals high. We have great confidence in your ability to achieve them.

Nordstrom Rules: Rule #1: Use your good judgment in all situations. There will be no additional rules.

Please feel free to ask your department manager, store manager, or division general manager any question at any time.

A skeptical colleague wonders how the employee handbook can develop Nordstrom's core value of superior customer service. How do you respond?

●●● Chapter 4 **LEARNING PREVIEW** ●●●

The BMO Financial Group keeps its high-performance edge with a unique commitment to environment and diversity. Externally, the firm values all stakeholders, including its communities. Internally, it values people, respects diversity, and engages employees through participation in the affairs of the enterprise. The purpose of Chapter 4 is to introduce you to the external and internal environments of organizations. As you read, check your learning progress in these major areas.

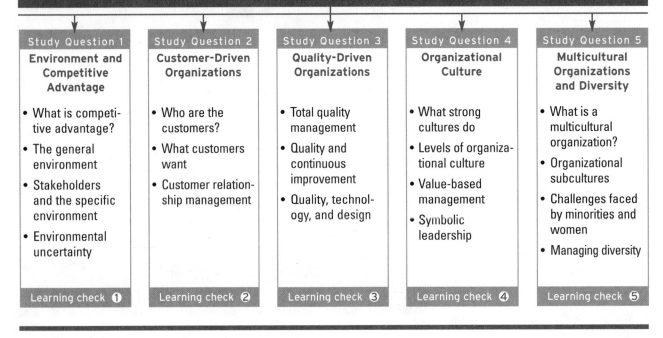

ENVIRONMENT, ORGANIZATIONAL CULTURE, AND DIVERSITY

Study Question 1	Study Question 2	Study Question 3	Study Question 4	Study Question 5
Environment and Competitive Advantage	**Customer-Driven Organizations**	**Quality-Driven Organizations**	**Organizational Culture**	**Multicultural Organizations and Diversity**
• What is competitive advantage? • The general environment • Stakeholders and the specific environment • Environmental uncertainty	• Who are the customers? • What customers want • Customer relationship management	• Total quality management • Quality and continuous improvement • Quality, technology, and design	• What strong cultures do • Levels of organizational culture • Value-based management • Symbolic leadership	• What is a multicultural organization? • Organizational subcultures • Challenges faced by minorities and women • Managing diversity
Learning check ❶	Learning check ❷	Learning check ❸	Learning check ❹	Learning check ❺

Once a benchmark for science fiction writers, the dawning of the 21st century is now placing unrelenting new demands on organizations and their members. Managers today are learning to operate in a world that places a premium on information, technology utilization, quality, customer service, and speed. They are learning how to succeed in a world of intense competition, continued globalization of markets and business activities, and rapid technological change. And they are facing renewed demands for ethical behaviour and social responsibility.

This chapter introduces the external and internal environments of organizations, along with their performance implications. The chapter opening example, the BMO Financial Group, sets the stage. It introduces the importance of core values and it raises the following question: What must organizations do to remain successful in our dynamic, complex, and ever-changing environment?

ENVIRONMENT AND COMPETITIVE ADVANTAGE

In his book *The Future of Success*, Robert Reich writes: "The emerging economy is offering unprecedented opportunities, an ever-expanding choice of terrific deals, fabulous products, good investments, and great jobs for people with the right talents and skills. Never before in human history have so many had access to so much so easily."[2] In these terms, things couldn't be better for organizations and career seekers. But there are also major challenges to be faced. When looking at things from a business vantage point, IBM's former CEO Louis V. Gerstner, Jr., described the challenge this way: "We believe very strongly that the age-old levers of competition—labour, capital, and land—are being supplemented by knowledge, and that most successful companies in the future will be those that learn how to exploit knowledge—knowledge about customer behaviour, markets, economies, technology—faster than their competitors."[3]

Knowledge and speed are indispensable to success in this new economy. Even as managers strive to lead their organizations toward a high-performance edge, they cannot afford for a minute to rest on past laurels. The world is too uncertain and the competition too intense for that. "In order to survive," Reich points out, "all organizations must dramatically and continuously improve—cutting costs, adding value, creating new products."[4]

●●● WHAT IS COMPETITIVE ADVANTAGE?

Astute executives understand the management implications in the prior observations. They are ever alert to environmental trends that require adjustments in the ways their organizations operate and that offer opportunities to gain **competitive advantage**.[5] This term refers to a core competency that clearly sets an organization apart from its competitors and gives it an advantage over them in the marketplace. Simply put, it comes from an ability to do things better than one's competitors. An organization may achieve competitive advantage in many ways, including through its products, pricing, customer service, cost efficiency, and quality, among other aspects of operating excellence. But regardless of how competitive advantage is achieved, the key result is the same—an ability to consistently do something of high value that one's competitors cannot replicate quickly or do as well.

■ **A competitive advantage** allows an organization to deal with market and environmental forces better than its competitors.

Some years ago, at a time when the North American industry was first coming to grips with fierce competition from Japanese products, quality pioneer J. M. Juran challenged an audience of Japanese executives with a prediction. He warned them against complacency, suggesting that North America would bounce back in business competitiveness.[6] There seems little doubt today that Juran's prediction was accurate.

There was a resurgence of business excellence in North America partly because business leaders could better understand the interdependencies of their organizations with the external environment. Competitive advantage in the demanding global economy can be achieved only by continuously scanning the environment for opportunities and taking effective action based on what is learned.[7] The ability to do this begins with the answer to a basic question: What is present in the external environment of organizations?

●●● THE GENERAL ENVIRONMENT

The **general environment** consists of all conditions in the external environment that form a background context for managerial decision making. The following are typical external environmental issues:

■ The **general environment** is composed of cultural, economic, legal-political, and educational conditions.

- *Economic conditions*—health of the economy in terms of inflation, income levels, gross domestic product, unemployment, and job outlook.

- *Social-cultural conditions*—norms, customs, and social values on such matters as human rights, trends in education and related social institutions, as well as demographic patterns in society.

- *Legal-political conditions*—prevailing philosophy and objectives of the political party or parties running the government, as well as laws and government regulations.

- *Technological conditions*—development and availability of technology, including scientific advancements.

- *Natural environment conditions*—nature and conditions of the natural environment, including levels of public concern expressed through environmentalism.

If we take the natural environment as an example, Japanese automakers Honda and Toyota seem to be finding the potential for competitive advantage. The two firms are on the leading edge of new markets for hybrid cars that combine gas and electric power. While North America's automakers were betting that customers would stay loyal to large gas-fuelled and often gas-hungry vehicles, their Japanese competitors saw the potential for competitive advantage. Now they have experience and a reputation gained from being first to market with the more environmentally friendly vehicles.

In respect to the socio-cultural environment, population demographics are a key feature. Managers who understand demographic profiles and trends can anticipate shifts in the customer base and labour markets that affect their organizations. For example, *Manager's Notepad 4.1* highlights important diversity trends in the demographic characteristics of Canadian society.[8] These and other differences in general environment factors are especially noticeable internationally. External conditions vary significantly from one country and culture to the next, and managers must understand these differences. Like many large firms, the pharmaceutical giant Merck derives a substantial portion of its business from overseas operations. Its executives recognize the need to be well informed about, and responsive to, differing local conditions. In Europe, for example, they have entered into co-operative agreements with local companies, conducted research with local partners, and worked with local governments on legal matters.

MANAGER'S
Notepad 4.1

Diversity trends in the socio-cultural environment

- Visible minority groups and new Canadians from a variety of ethnic populations are an increasing percentage of the workforce.

- More women are working.

- People with disabilities are gaining more access to the workplace.

- More workers come from non-traditional families (e.g., single parents, dual wage earners).

- The average age of workers is increasing.

- The number of different faith backgrounds is increasing.

■ The specific environment includes the people and groups with whom an organization interacts.

●●● STAKEHOLDERS AND THE SPECIFIC ENVIRONMENT

The **specific environment** consists of the actual organizations, groups, and persons with whom an organization interacts and conducts business. These are environmental elements of direct consequence to the organization as it operates on a day-to-day basis. The specific environment is often described in terms of **stakeholders**, defined in Chapter 3 as the persons, groups, and institutions who are affected in one way or another by the organization's performance. They are key constituencies that have a stake in the organization's performance, are influenced by how it operates, and can influence it in return.

> ■ **Stakeholders** are the persons, groups, and institutions directly affected by an organization.

Sometimes called the *task environment*, the specific environment and the stakeholders are distinct for each organization. They can also change over time according to the company's unique customer base, operating needs, and circumstances. Important stakeholders common to the specific environment of most organizations include customers, suppliers, competitors, regulators, and investors/owners from the external environment, as well as employees from the internal environment.

Figure 4.1 shows the typical business firm as an open system, with the interests of several stakeholder groups linked by stages in the input-transformation-output process. This type of stakeholder analysis can be used to both assess the current performance of organizations vis-à-vis *strategic constituencies* and to develop ideas for improving performance in the future. The analysis helps focus management attention on **value creation**, the extent to which the organization is creating value for, and satisfying the needs of, important constituencies.

> ■ **Value creation** is creating value for, and satisfying needs of, constituencies.

> **Figure 4.1** Stakeholder analysis of value creation for key constituencies of a business firm: an open-systems approach.

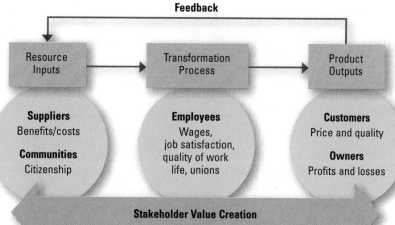

As suggested in *Figure 4.1*, value creation is important to stakeholders from both the specific environment, reflected in the input and output boundaries of the business firm as an open system, and from the internal environment, reflected in the transformation process itself. In respect to product outputs, for example, businesses create value for customers through product price and quality, and for owners by realized profits and losses. In respect to inputs, businesses create value for suppliers through the benefits of long-term business relationships, and for communities in such areas as the citizenship they display in using and contributing to public services. And in respect to throughputs, businesses create value for employees through the wages and satisfaction gained through their work of transforming resource inputs into product outputs. Wal-Mart is an example of an organization that manages the value creation chain quite well. By managing costs at both the input and throughput stages, they are able to offer products at a price and quality that appeal to customers.

●●● ENVIRONMENTAL UNCERTAINTY

■ **Environmental uncertainty** is a lack of complete information about the environment.

There is a lot of uncertainty in the external environments of many organizations. **Environmental uncertainty** means that there is a lack of complete information regarding what exists and what developments may occur. This makes it difficult to analyze constituencies and their needs, predict future states of affairs, and understand their potential implications for the organization. *Figure 4.2* describes two dimensions of environmental uncertainty: (1) complexity, or the number of different factors in the environment, and (2) the rate of change in these factors.[9]

Environmental uncertainty presents a host of management challenges. Greater uncertainty requires more concentrated attention. An uncertain environment has to be continually studied and monitored to spot emerging trends. Also, the greater the environmental uncertainty, the greater the need for flexibility and adaptability in organizational designs and work practices. Because of uncertainty, organizations must be able to respond quickly as new circumstances arise and information becomes available. The airline industry is an example of an uncertain environment arising from a number of factors: threats of terrorism, fuel costs, deregulation, and currency fluctuations. One need only look at the management challenges faced by companies such as the now-defunct Jetsgo to appreciate this fact. Throughout this book you will find many examples of how organizations try to stay adaptable in order to best deal with the high uncertainty that so often prevails in their environments.

Figure 4.2 Dimensions of uncertainty in organizational environments.

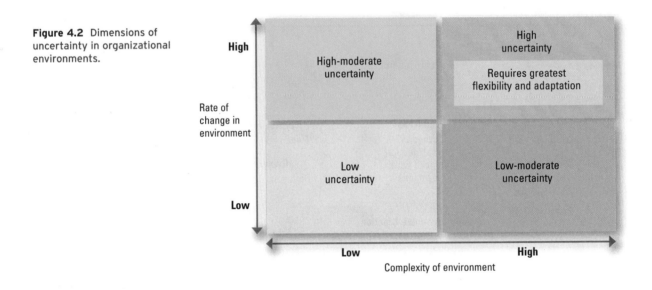

Learning check ❶

BE SURE YOU CAN

• list key elements in the general and specific environments of organizations • define the terms competitive advantage, stakeholders, and environmental uncertainty • describe the stakeholders for a business in your local community

CUSTOMER-DRIVEN ORGANIZATIONS

Question: What's your job?

Answer: I run the cash register and sack groceries.

Question: But isn't it your job to serve the customer?

Answer: I guess, but it's not in my job description.

This conversation illustrates what often becomes the missing link in the quest for competitive advantage: customer service. Contrast this conversation with the example of a customer who called the Vermont Teddy Bear Company to complain that her new mail-order teddy bear had a problem. The company responded promptly, she said, and arranged to have the bear picked up and replaced. She wrote the firm to say "thank you for the great service and courtesy you gave me."[10] As demonstrated, responding quickly to customer requests can turn a potentially negative situation into a very positive one.

●●● WHO ARE THE CUSTOMERS?

Figure 4.3 expands the open-systems view of organizations to now depict the complex internal operations of the organization as well as its interdependence with the external environment. In this figure the organization's *external customers* purchase the goods produced or utilize the services provided. They may be industrial customers, that is, other firms that buy a company's products for use in their own operations; or they may be retail customers or clients who purchase or use the goods and services directly. *Internal customers*, by contrast, are found within the organization. They are the individuals and groups who use or otherwise depend on one another's work in order to do their own jobs well. The notion of customer service applies equally well to external and internal customers. For example, the customer is "captain" of the supply chain for Dell Computer. Founder and chairman Michael Dell firmly believes that customers drive competitive advantage. The firm is a leader in using information technology to efficiently deliver products meeting customer preferences.

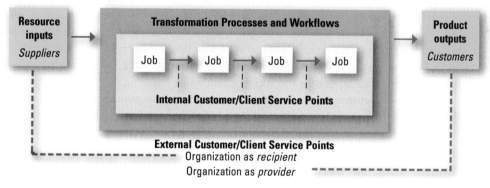

Figure 4.3 The importance of external and internal customers.

●●● WHAT CUSTOMERS WANT

Customers are always key stakeholders; they sit at the top when organizations are viewed as the upside-down pyramids described in Chapter 1. And without any doubt, customers put today's organizations to a very stiff test. They primarily want at least one of four things in the goods and services they buy: (1) high quality, (2) reasonable price, (3) on-time delivery, and (4) excellent service.

Organizations that can't meet customer expectations suffer the market consequences; they lose competitive advantage. Some time ago, for example, Intel Corporation faced a crisis in customer confidence when a defect was found in one of its computer chips. At first, top management of this highly regarded company balked at replacing the chips, suggesting that the defect wasn't really important. But customers were angry and unrelenting in their complaints. Eventually the customers won, as they should. Intel agreed to replace the chips without any questions asked. Company executives also learned two important lessons of successful business practices: (1) always protect your reputation for quality products—it is hard to get and easy to lose, and (2) always treat your customers well—they, too, are hard to get and easy to lose.

●●● CUSTOMER RELATIONSHIP MANAGEMENT

A *Harvard Business Review* survey reports that North American business leaders rank customer service and product quality as the first and second most important goals in the success of their organizations.[11] In a survey by the market research firm Michelson & Associates, poor service and product dissatisfaction were the first and second reasons respectively for customers abandoning a retail store.[12] Reaching the goals of providing great service and quality products isn't always easy. But when pursued relentlessly they can be important sources of competitive advantage. Just imagine the ramifications if every customer or client contact for an organization were positive. Not only would these customers return again and again, they would also tell others and expand the customer base.

■ **Customer relationship management** strategically tries to build lasting relationships with, and add value for, customers.

Progressive managers use the principles of **customer relationship management** to establish and maintain high standards of customer service. Known as "CRM," this approach uses the latest information technologies to maintain intense communication with customers as well as to gather and utilize data regarding their needs and desires. At Marriott International, for example, CRM is supported by special customer management software that tracks information on customer preferences. When you check in, the likelihood is that your past requests for things like a king-size bed, no-smoking room, and Internet access are already in your record. Says Marriott's chairman: "It's a big competitive advantage."[13]

■ **Supply chain management** strategically links all operations dealing with resource supplies.

Just as organizations need to manage their customers on the output side, supplier relationships on the input side must be well managed, too. The concept of **supply chain management** (SCM) involves strategic management of all operations involving an organization's suppliers. This includes the use of information technology to improve purchasing, manufacturing, transportation, and distribution.[14] The goals of SCM are straightforward: achieve efficiency in all aspects of the supply chain while ensuring on-time availability of quality resources for customer-driven operations. As retail sales are made at Wal-Mart, for example, an information system updates inventory records and sales forecasts. Suppliers access this information electronically, allowing them to adjust their operations and rapidly ship replacement products to meet the retailer's needs.

✓ Learning check ❷

BE SURE YOU CAN

• explain the difference between internal and external customers of a firm • list the four primary things customers want in what they buy • discuss the importance of customer relationship management in a competitive business environment

QUALITY-DRIVEN ORGANIZATIONS

If managing for high performance and competitive advantage is the theme of the day, "quality" is one of its most important watchwords. Customers want quality whether they are buying a consumer product or receiving a service. The achievement of quality objectives in all aspects of operations is a global criterion of organizational performance in manufacturing and service industries alike. **ISO certification** by the International Organization for Standardization in Geneva, Switzerland has been adopted by many countries of the world as a quality benchmark. Businesses that want to compete as "world-class companies" are increasingly expected

■ **ISO certification** indicates conformance with a rigorous set of international quality standards.

to have ISO certification at various levels. To do so, they must refine and upgrade quality in all operations and then undergo a rigorous assessment by outside auditors to determine whether they meet ISO requirements.

●●● TOTAL QUALITY MANAGEMENT

The term **total quality management** (TQM) was introduced in Chapter 1. It describes the process of making quality principles part of the organization's strategic objectives, applying them to all aspects of operations, committing to continuous improvement, and striving to meet customers' needs by doing things right the first time.[15]

Most TQM approaches begin with an insistence that the total quality commitment apply to everyone in an organization and to all aspects of operations, right from resource acquisition through to the production and distribution of finished goods and services.[16] Philip Crosby, a consultant, became quite famous for offering these "four absolutes" of management for total quality control: (1) *quality means conformance to standards*—workers must know exactly what performance standards they are expected to meet; (2) *quality comes from defect prevention, not defect correction*—leadership, training, and discipline must prevent defects in the first place; (3) *quality as a performance standard must mean defect-free work*—the only acceptable quality standard is perfect work; and (4) *quality saves money*—doing things right the first time saves the cost of correcting poor work.[17]

■ **Total quality management** is managing with an organization-wide commitment to continuous improvement, product quality, and customer needs.

---

take it to the case!

United Parcel Service
Where technology rules a total quality road

Once named company of the year by *Forbes* magazine, UPS is the world's largest package delivery company. It's also a leader in technology utilization for competitive advantage. Log on to the UPS website and the company literally takes you around the world of package delivery. Operating efficiency and customer service are rules of the day every day at UPS. The company claims "a technology infrastructure second to none, enabling customers to link product shipments, services and information throughout the transaction value chain." Customers find IT working for them through an efficient online package tracking system and transit and delivery times. Operations are streamlined through the firm's seamless supply chain.

Source: With information from the corporate websites: <www.ups.com> and <www.ups-scs.ca>.

●●● QUALITY AND CONTINUOUS IMPROVEMENT

The work of W. Edwards Deming is a cornerstone of the total quality movement. The story begins in 1951 when he was invited to Japan to explain quality control techniques that had been developed in the United States. The result was a lifelong relationship epitomized in the Deming Prize, which is still annually awarded in Japan for excellence in quality. "When Deming spoke," we might say, "the Japanese listened." The principles he taught the

Japanese were straightforward . . . and they worked: tally defects, analyze and trace them to the source, make corrections, and keep a record of what happens afterward.[18] Deming's "14 points of quality" emphasize constant innovation, use of statistical methods, and commitment to training in the fundamentals of quality assurance.

■ **Continuous improvement** involves always searching for new ways to improve work quality and performance.

The search for quality is closely tied to the emphasis on **continuous improvement**— always looking for new ways to improve on current performance.[19] The notion is that one can never be satisfied; something always can and should be improved on. Continuous improvement must be a way of life. Another important aspect of total quality operations is cycle time—the elapsed time between receipt of an order and delivery of the finished product. The quality objective here is to reduce cycle time by finding ways to serve customer needs more quickly.

■ Members of a **quality circle** meet periodically to discuss ways of improving the quality of products or services.

One way to combine employee involvement and continuous improvement is through the popular **quality circle** concept.[20] This is a small group of workers that meets regularly to discuss ways of improving the quality of their products or services. Their objective is to assume responsibility for quality and apply every member's full creative potential to ensure that it is achieved. Such worker empowerment can result in cost savings from improved quality and greater customer satisfaction. It can also improve morale and commitment, as the following remarks from quality circle members indicate: "This is the best thing the company has done in 15 years." . . . "The program proves that supervisors have no monopoly on brains." . . . "It gives me more pride in my work."[21]

●●● QUALITY, TECHNOLOGY, AND DESIGN

Technology utilization is improving the quality of manufacturing today by helping firms better integrate their operations with customer preferences, and by allowing production changes to be made quickly and at low cost. For example, *lean production* uses technologies to streamline systems and allow work to be performed with fewer workers and smaller inventories. *Flexible manufacturing* allows processes to be changed quickly and efficiently to produce different products or modifications to existing ones. Through such techniques as *agile manufacturing* and *mass customization*, organizations are able to make individualized products quickly and with production efficiencies once only associated with the mass production of uniform products.[22]

Another timely and important contribution to quality management is found in *product design*. We are all aware of design differences among products, be they cars, computers, cell phones, stereos, watches, clothes, or whatever. But what may not be recognized is that design makes a difference in how things are produced and at what level of cost and quality. In today's competitive global economy, product designs are strategic weapons. A "good" design has both eye appeal to the customer and is easy to manufacture with regards to productivity. *Design for manufacturing* means that products are styled to lower production costs and smooth the way toward high-quality results in all aspects of the manufacturing processes. A manufacturing approach that shows respect for the natural environment is *design for disassembly*. The goal is to design products while taking into account how their component parts will be recycled at the end of their lives.

✓ **Learning check ❸**

BE SURE YOU CAN

• define the term ISO certification • explain the role of continuous improvement in TQM • describe what a quality circle is and how its use can increase performance quality • discuss how good use of technology and product design can improve quality

ORGANIZATIONAL CULTURE

"Culture" is a popular word in management these days. Important differences in national cultures will be discussed in Chapter 5 on the global dimensions of management. Here, it is time to talk about cultural differences in the internal environments of organizations. **Organizational culture** is defined by noted scholar and consultant Edgar Schein as the system of shared beliefs and values that develops within an organization and guides the behaviour of its members.[23] Sometimes called the *corporate culture*, it is a key aspect of any organization and work setting. Whenever someone, for example, speaks of "the way we do things here," they are talking about the culture.

■ **Organizational culture** is the system of shared beliefs and values that guides behaviour in organizations.

MANAGER'S
Notepad 4.2
S C O R E S—How to read an organization's culture

S-How tight or loose is the *structure?*

C-Are decisions *change* oriented or driven by the status quo?

O-What *outcomes* or results are most highly valued?

R-What is the climate for *risk taking*, innovation?

E-How widespread is *empowerment*, worker involvement?

S-What is the competitive *style*, internal and external?

●●● WHAT STRONG CULTURES DO

Although it is clear that culture is not the sole determinant of what happens in organizations, it is an important influence on what they accomplish . . . and how. The internal culture has the potential to shape attitudes, reinforce beliefs, direct behaviour, and establish performance expectations and the motivation to fulfill them. A widely discussed study of successful businesses concluded that organizational culture made a major contribution to their long-term performance records.[24] Importantly, the cultures in these organizations provided for a clear vision of what the organization was attempting to accomplish, allowing individuals to rally around the vision and work hard to support and accomplish it.[25] *Manager's Notepad 4.2* offers ideas for reading differences among organizational cultures.

Strong cultures, ones that are clear and well defined and widely shared among members, discourage dysfunctional work behaviours and encourage positive ones. They commit members to doing things for and with one another that are in the best interests of the organization. The best organizations are likely to have cultures that are performance oriented, emphasize teamwork, allow for risk taking, encourage innovation, and make the well-being of people a top management priority.[26] Only 36 percent of Canadian executives surveyed by Waterstone Human Capital Ltd., a Toronto-based executive search firm, felt that their companies could be classified as having strong, adaptive cultures, while a large portion (55 percent) felt that their organizations were weak and plagued by problems such as top-down managerial haughtiness, a fear of risk taking, too much of an inward focus, and too much bureaucracy.[27] In the recent study by Waterstone, WestJet stood out as having the most admired Canadian corporate culture. WestJet, based in Calgary, Alberta, is noted for its "entrepreneurial spirit," "delivering what they promise," and its "winning attitude."[28] Honda is another good example. The firm's culture is tightly focused around what is known as "The Honda Way"—a set of principles emphasizing ambition, respect for ideas, open communication, work enjoyment, harmony, and hard work.

●●● LEVELS OF ORGANIZATIONAL CULTURE

Organizational culture is usually described from the perspective of the two levels shown in *Figure 4.4*—the "observable" culture and the "core" culture.[29] The *observable culture* is visible; it is what one sees and hears when walking around an organization as a visitor, a customer, or an employee. The observable culture is apparent in the way people dress at work, how they arrange their offices, how they speak to and behave toward one another, the nature of their conversations, and how they talk about and treat their customers. It is also found in the following elements of daily organizational life—through them, new members learn the organization's culture and all members share and reinforce its special aspects over time:

- *Stories*—oral histories and tales, told and retold among members, about dramatic sagas and incidents in the life of the organization.

- *Heroes*—the people singled out for special attention and whose accomplishments are recognized with praise and admiration among members; they include founders and role models.

- *Rites and rituals*—the ceremonies and meetings, planned and spontaneous, that celebrate important occasions and performance accomplishments.

- *Symbols*—the special use of language and other non-verbal expressions to communicate important themes of organizational life.

For example, at the eBay Canada office in Toronto, an organizational ritual has all 30 employees voting on the "Hat Trick Award." The award is given quarterly to a person who has achieved "great performance." As Jordon Banks, eBay Canada's managing director, states, the award is given for "not only what is done, but more importantly, how it is done."[30]

Figure 4.4 Levels of organizational culture—observable culture and core culture.

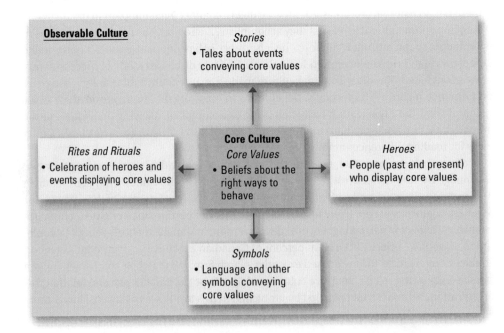

The second and deeper level of organizational culture is the *core culture*. It consists of the **core values** or underlying assumptions and beliefs that shape and guide people's behaviours, and actually contribute to the aspects of observable culture just described. Strong-culture organizations operate with a small but enduring set of core values. Researchers point out that commitment to core values is a major contributor to long-term success.[31] Highly successful companies typically emphasize the values of performance excellence, innovation, social responsibility, integrity, worker involvement, customer service, and teamwork. Examples of core values that drive the best firms include "service above all else" at Nordstrom; "science-based innovation" at Merck; "encouraging individual initiative and creativity" at Sony; and "fanatical attention to consistency and detail" at Disney.

■ **Core values** are beliefs and values shared by organization members.

●●● VALUE-BASED MANAGEMENT

The core values espoused by organizations are widely publicized in corporate mission statements and on their official websites. But mere testimonies to values are not enough to create a strong core culture and derive its benefits. The values must be practised. They must be real, they must be shared, and they must be modelled and reinforced by managers from top to bottom. The term value-based management describes managers who actively help develop, communicate, and enact shared values within an organization. Importantly, one area where **value-based management** has a major impact is with respect to ethics and social responsibility. As discussed in the last chapter, core values are powerful influences on the ethical behaviour of organization members.

■ **Value-based management** actively develops, communicates, and enacts shared values.

The responsibility for value-based management extends to all managers and team leaders working at all levels. Like the organization, any work team or group will have a culture. How well this culture operates to support the group and its performance objectives will depend in part on the strength of the core values and the manager's role as a values champion. Just as with the organization as a whole, the value-based management of any work unit or team should meet the test of these criteria.[32]

- *Relevance*—Core values should support key performance objectives.

- *Integrity*—Core values should provide clear, consistent ethical anchors.

- *Pervasiveness*—Core values should be understood by all members.

- *Strength*—Core values should be accepted by everyone involved.

●●● SYMBOLIC LEADERSHIP

A **symbolic leader** is someone who uses symbols to establish and maintain a desired organizational culture. Symbolic managers and leaders both act and talk the "language" of the organization. They are always careful to behave in ways that live up to the espoused core values; they are ever-present role models for others to emulate and follow. Symbolic leaders also communicate values in their spoken and written words, taking advantage of every opportunity to do so. They use language very well to describe people, events, and even the competition in ways that reinforce and communicate core values. *Language metaphors*—the use of positive examples from another context—are very powerful in this regard. For example, newly hired workers at Disney World and Disneyland are counselled to always think of themselves as more than employees; they are key "members of the cast," and they work "on stage." After all, they are told, Disney isn't just any business, it is an "entertainment" business.

■ A **symbolic leader** uses symbols to establish and maintain a desired organizational culture.

Good symbolic leaders highlight and even dramatize core values and the observable culture. They tell key stories over and over again, and they encourage others to tell them.

AROUND THE WORLD

Value-based initiative encourages Latin American entrepreneurs

Entrepreneurship accounts for most new job creation, business innovation, and inventions around the world. With the vision of helping Latin America's sagging economies, Linda Rottenberg and Peter Kellner formed the non-profit organization Endeavor Global to help owners of small and medium-sized businesses in Latin America to become entrepreneurs. In six years their approach has created over 6,000 new jobs and generated more than $400 million in local entrepreneurial revenues. Former World Bank president, James D. Wolfensohn, calls the firm "a model that should be replicated around the world." After examining its successes in Latin America, he wants to support its expansion to Africa. Endeavor's founders Rottenberg and Kellner are committed to the belief that "new ventures create jobs, spread wealth, expand opportunity and increase social mobility."

Source: Information from Michael Allen, "Endeavor Bets on Latin American entrepreneurs," *Wall Street Journal* (April 15, 2002), p. B4.

They often refer to the "founding story" about the entrepreneur whose personal values set a key tone for the enterprise. They remind everyone about organizational heroes, past and present, whose performances exemplify core values. They often use rites and rituals to glorify the performance of the organization and its members. At Mary Kay Cosmetics, gala events at which top sales performers share their tales of success are legendary. So, too, are the lavish incentive awards presented at these ceremonies, especially the pink luxury cars given to the most successful salespeople.[33]

Learning check 4

BE SURE YOU CAN

- define the term organizational culture and explain the importance of strong cultures to organizations
- distinguish between the observable and core cultures • explain the concept of value-added management
- discuss how symbolic leaders build high-performance organizational cultures

MULTICULTURAL ORGANIZATIONS AND DIVERSITY

At the very time that we talk about the culture of an organization as a whole, we must also recognize diversity in its membership. Organizations are made up of many individuals, each of them unique. An important key to competitive advantage is respecting this diversity and allowing everyone's talents to be fully utilized.

■ The term **diversity** describes race, gender, age, and other individual differences.

As first introduced in Chapter 1, **diversity** is a term used to describe differences among people at work. Primary dimensions of diversity include age, race, ethnicity, gender, physical ability, and sexual orientation. But workplace diversity also includes differences in religious beliefs, education, experience, and family status, among others.[34] In his book *Beyond Race and Gender*, consultant R. Roosevelt Thomas, Jr., makes the point that "diversity includes everyone." He says, "In this expanded context, white males are as diverse as their colleagues."[35] Thomas also links diversity with organizational culture, believing that the way people are treated at work—with respect and inclusion, or with disrespect and exclusion—is a direct reflection of the organization's culture.

Thomas's diversity message to those who lead and manage organizations is pointed. Diversity is a potential source of competitive advantage, offering organizations a mixture of talents and perspectives that is ready and able to deal with complexities and uncertainty in the ever-changing 21st-century environment. If you do the right things in organizational leadership, in other words, you'll gain competitive advantage through diversity. If you don't, you'll lose it. This message is backed by recent research on the relationship of diversity and performance. In a study of the business case for diversity, Thomas Kochan found that the presence of diversity alone does not guarantee a positive performance impact.[36] Only when diversity is leveraged through training and supportive human resource practices are the advantages gained. The study offers this guidance:

To be successful in working with and gaining value from diversity requires a sustained, systemic approach and long-term commitment. Success is facilitated by a perspective that considers diversity to be an opportunity for everyone in an organization to learn from each other how better to accomplish their work and an occasion that requires a supportive and cooperative organizational culture as well as group leadership and process skills that can facilitate effective group functioning.

●●● WHAT IS A MULTICULTURAL ORGANIZATION?

A key issue in the culture of any organization is *inclusivity*—the degree to which the organization is open to anyone who can perform a job, regardless of their race, sexual preference, gender, or other diversity attribute.[37] The term **multiculturalism** refers to inclusivity, pluralism, and respect for diversity in the workplace. There is no reason why organizational cultures cannot communicate core values that respect and empower the full demographic and cultural diversity that is now characteristic of our workforces. The "best" organizational cultures in this sense are inclusive. They value the talents, ideas, and creative potential of all members. The model in this regard is the truly **multicultural organization** with these characteristics:[38]

- *Pluralism*—Members of both minority cultures and majority cultures are influential in setting key values and policies.

- *Structural integration*—Minority-culture members are well represented in jobs at all levels and in all functional responsibilities.

- *Informal network integration*—Various forms of mentoring and support groups assist in the career development of minority-culture members.

- *Absence of prejudice and discrimination*—A variety of training and task force activities address the need to eliminate culture-group biases.

- *Minimum inter-group conflict*—Diversity does not lead to destructive conflicts between members of majority and minority cultures.

●●● ORGANIZATIONAL SUBCULTURES

Like society as a whole, organizations contain a mixture of **subcultures**; that is, cultures common to groups of people with similar values and beliefs based on shared work responsibilities and personal characteristics. Whereas the pluralism that characterizes multicultural organizations conveys respect for different subcultures, working relations in organizations are too

■ **Multiculturalism** involves pluralism and respect for diversity.

■ A **multicultural organization** is based on pluralism and operates with inclusivity and respect for diversity.

■ Organizational **subcultures** exist among people with similar values and beliefs based on shared work responsibilities and personal characteristics.

■ Ethnocentrism is the belief that one's membership group or subculture is superior to all others.

often hurt by the opposite tendency. Just as with life in general, **ethnocentrism**—the belief that one's membership group or subculture is superior to all others—can creep into the workplace and adversely affect the way people relate to one another.

The many possible subcultures in organizations include *occupational subcultures*.[39] Salaried professionals such as lawyers, scientists, engineers, and accountants have been described as having special needs for work autonomy and empowerment that may conflict with traditional management methods of top-down direction and control. Unless these needs are recognized and properly dealt with, salaried professionals may prove difficult to integrate into the culture of the larger organization.

There are also *functional subcultures* in organizations, and people from different functions often have difficulty understanding and working well with one another. For example, employees of a business may consider themselves "systems people" or "marketing people" or "manufacturing people" or "finance people." When such identities are overemphasized, members of the functional groups may spend most of their time with each other, develop a "jargon" or technical language that is shared among themselves, and view their role in the organization as more important than the contributions of the other functions.

Differences in *ethnic or national cultures* will be discussed in Chapter 5 on the global dimensions of management.[40] Although it is relatively easy to recognize that people from various countries and regions of the world have different cultures, it is far harder to turn this awareness into the ability to work well with persons whose backgrounds differ from our own. The best understanding is most likely gained through direct contact and being open-minded. The same advice holds in respect to *racial subcultures*. Although one may speak in everyday conversations about "African-American" or "Aboriginal" or "Asian" cultures, one has to wonder what we really know about them.[41] Importantly, a key question remains largely unanswered: Where can we find frameworks for understanding them? If improved cross-cultural understandings can help people work better across national boundaries, how can we create the same to help people from different racial subcultures work together better?

We live at a time when the influence of *generational subcultures* at work is of growing importance. But the issues are more subtle than young–old issues alone. It is possible to identify "generational gaps" among "baby boomers" now in their 50s, "Generation Xers" now in their 30s and early 40s, "Nexters" now in their 20s, and the "Millennial Generation" in high school at the turn of the century. Members of these generations grew up in quite different worlds and were influenced by different values and opportunities. Their work preferences and attitudes tend to reflect these differences. Someone who is 60 years old today, a common age for senior managers, was a teenager in the 1960s. Such a person may have difficulty understanding, supervising, and working with younger managers who were teens during the 1970s, 1980s, and even the 1990s.[42]

Issues of relationships and discrimination based on *gender subcultures* also continue to complicate the workplace. Some research shows that when men work together, a group culture forms around a competitive atmosphere. Sports metaphors are common, and games and stories often deal with winning and losing.[43] When women work together, a rather different culture may form, with more emphasis on personal relationships and collaboration.[44]

●●● CHALLENGES FACED BY MINORITIES AND WOMEN

The very term "diversity" basically means the presence of differences. But what does it mean when those differences are distributed unequally in the organizational power structure? What difference does it make when one subculture is in "majority" status while others become "minorities" in respect to representation within the organization? Even though organizations are changing today, most senior executives in large organizations are older, white, and male.

There is still likely to be more workforce diversity at lower and middle levels of most organizations than at the top.

Take a look at the situation shown by *Figure 4.5*. It depicts the operation of the **glass ceiling**, defined in Chapter 1 as an invisible barrier that limits the advancement of women and minorities in some organizations. What are the implications for visible minorities and women, seeking to advance and prosper in organizations traditionally dominated by a majority culture, such as white males?

The daily work challenges faced by minorities and women can range from misunderstandings and lack of sensitivity on the one hand, to glass ceiling limitations, to even outright harassment and discrimination. *Sexual harassment* in the form of unwanted sexual advances, requests for sexual favours, and sexually laced communications is a problem female employees in particular may face. Minority workers can also be targets of cultural jokes; one survey reports some 45 percent of respondents had been the targets of such abuse. *Pay discrimination*

■ The **glass ceiling** is a hidden barrier to the advancement of women and minorities.

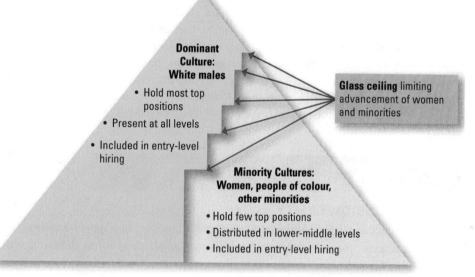

Figure 4.5 Glass ceilings as barriers to women and minority cultures in traditional organizations.

Canadian Managers
Balanced Leadership

Annette Verschuren is a leader in the traditionally male-dominated world of home renovation. As head of Home Depot Canada, Verschuren is responsible for the retailer's operations in all 10 provinces. Verschuren ventured into big-box retailing by bringing the arts and crafts store Michaels to Canada. She left Michaels in 1996, taking over Home Depot's Canadian operations when it had 19 stores with 4,500 associates. A decade later, it has approximately 151 stores and 23,000 associates. How does she manage such a large company? "I delegate and juggle well," Verschuren says. "I think a lot of my success comes from putting a team together... I believe better teams usually have a more diverse group of people... I like to be among balanced groups."

Source: "Flexibility is key, says Home Depot chief," *Business Edge*, May 12, 2005; Sarah Thomson, "Annette Verschuren: president of Home Depot," *Women's Post*, November 2005.

is also an issue. A senior executive in the computer industry reported her surprise at finding out that the top performer in her work group, an African-American male, was paid 25 percent less than anyone else. This wasn't because his pay had been cut to that level, she said, but because his pay increases over time had always trailed those given to his white co-workers. The differences added up significantly over time, but no one noticed or stepped forward to make the appropriate adjustment.[45] Minority members may also face *job discrimination*. Microsoft, for example, has been criticized for treating the firm's 5,000 or more temporary workers unfairly in terms of access to benefits and work assignments. Some temporary employees (who wore orange identification badges at work) claimed that they were treated as second-class citizens by the permanent employees (who wore blue badges).[46]

■ **Biculturalism** is when minority members adopt characteristics of majority cultures in order to succeed.

Sometimes the adaptation of minorities to organizations dominated by a majority culture takes the form of tendencies toward **biculturalism**. This is the display, by members of minority cultures, of majority-culture characteristics that seem necessary to succeed in the work environment. For example, one might find gays and lesbians hiding their sexual orientation from co-workers out of fear of prejudice or discrimination. Similarly, one might find an employee of colour carefully training herself to not use, at work, certain words or phrases that might be considered by white co-workers as subculture slang.

The special economic and work challenges faced by minorities are not always highly visible. Over a recent period of economic expansion, most Canadians and Americans benefitted from a growth in jobs and employment opportunities. But how many of us know that disabled workers largely failed to share in the gains? At the same time that demand for workers in general rose, the employment rate of the disabled fell over 10 percent for men and 5 percent for women.[47]

CANADIAN COMPANY IN THE NEWS   Xerox Canada

RECOGNIZING DIVERSITY

The Canadian Council for Aboriginal Business's Progressive Aboriginal Relations (PAR) program assesses the performance of corporations and their relations and involvement with Native Canadian communities. PAR provides a framework for setting organizational objectives, developing action plans, measuring performance, and achieving results. PAR participants measure their performance through a self-assessment and external verification process, and use the results to determine the success of their efforts.

Toronto-based Xerox Canada achieved gold-level recognition in 2006, after receiving silver-level recognition in 2003. In addition to financial and in-kind donations, employee recruitment, and cultural awareness training, Xerox Canada's support includes an annual Aboriginal Scholarship Program, a "CEO for a Day" program, and the creation of the Aboriginal Community Records Information Management program at the Southern Alberta Institute of Technology.

Sources: "Xerox recognized for work with Native community," *The Globe and Mail*, February 21, 2006. CCAB web site: <http://www.ccab.com/par.htm>

■ **Managing diversity** is building an inclusive work environment that allows everyone to reach their full potential.

●●● MANAGING DIVERSITY

There's no doubt today what minority workers want.[48] They want the same thing everyone wants. They want respect for their talents and a work setting that allows them to achieve their full potential. It takes the best in diversity leadership at all levels of organizational management to meet these expectations. R. Roosevelt Thomas defines **managing diversity**

Figure 4.6 Leadership approaches to diversity—from advancing action to managing diversity.

Source: Adapted by permission of the publisher, from *Beyond Race and Gender* by R. Roosevelt Thomas © 1991 R. Roosevelt Thomas Jr., AMACOM books, division of American Management Association, New York, NY. All rights reserved. www.amacombooks.org

as building an organizational culture that allows all members, minorities and women included, to reach their full potential.

Figure 4.6 describes a continuum of leadership approaches to diversity. The first is *advancing action*, in which leadership commits the organization to hiring and advancing minorities and women. The second is *valuing diversity*, in which leadership commits the organization to education and training programs designed to help people better understand and respect individual differences. The third, and most comprehensive, is *managing diversity*, in which leadership commits to changing the organizational culture to empower and include all people.

Thomas believes that managing diversity holds the most value in respect to competitive advantage.[49] A diverse workforce offers a rich pool of talents, ideas, and viewpoints for solving the complex problems of often-uncertain environments. And a diverse workforce is best aligned with the needs and expectations of a diverse customer and stakeholder base. Organizations that Thomas calls "diversity mature" are well positioned to derive these and other sources of competitive advantage. In these organizations there is a diversity mission as well as an organizational mission; diversity is viewed as a strategic imperative, and the members understand diversity concepts.[50] Ultimately, however, he considers the basic building block of a diversity-mature organization to be the *diversity-mature individual*.[51]

Perhaps the most important word in human resource management today is "inclusiveness." By valuing diversity and building multicultural organizations that include everyone, organizations of all types can be strengthened and brought into better alignment with the challenges and opportunities of today's environment. Research reported in the *Gallup Management Journal*, for example, shows that establishing a racially and ethnically inclusive workplace is good for morale.[52] In a study of 2,014 workers, those who felt included were more likely to stay with their employers and recommend them to others. Survey questions asked such things as: "Do you always trust your company to be fair to all employees?" "At work, are all employees always treated with respect?" "Does your supervisor always make the best use of employees' skills?" Clearly, inclusivity counts; it counts in terms of respect for people, and it counts in building organizational capacities for high performance and sustainable competitive advantage. As Michael R. Losey, president of the Society for Human Resource

PERSONAL MANAGEMENT

DIVERSITY MATURITY is essential if you are to work well in today's organizations. It is a cornerstone for personal inclusivity. Consultant Roosevelt Thomas uses the following questions when testing diversity maturity among people in the workplace. Answer the questions. Be honest; admit where you still have work left to do. Use your answers to help set future goals to ensure that your actions, not just your words, consistently display positive diversity values.

- Do you accept responsibility for improving your performance?
- Do you understand diversity concepts?
- Do you make decisions about others based on their abilities?
- Do you understand that diversity issues are complex?
- Are you able to cope with tensions in addressing diversity?
- Are you willing to challenge the way things are?
- Are you willing to learn continuously?

Get to know yourself better

Complete Self-Assessments #7—**Diversity Awareness**, and Exercise #7—**What Do You Value in Work?**, from the Workbook and Personal Management Activity #4 on the companion website.

Management (SHRM), says: "Companies must realize that the talent pool includes people of all types, including older workers; persons with disabilities; persons of various religious, cultural, and national backgrounds; persons who are not heterosexual; minorities; and women."[53]

✓ Learning check ❺

BE SURE YOU CAN

• explain multiculturalism and list key characteristics of multicultural organizations • identify typical organizational subcultures • discuss the common employment problems faced by minorities and women • explain Thomas's concept of managing diversity • realistically assess your diversity maturity

●●● Chapter 4 STUDY GUIDE

WHERE WE'VE BEEN

Back to BMO Financial Group

The opening example describes BMO Financial Group as a vanguard company noted for its values and performance success. In Chapter 4 you learned more about the complex nature of the external environments faced by organizations like BMO Financial Group. You also learned how organizations can benefit from strong and positive cultures and from internal environments committed to managing diversity and inclusivity for all employees. All of this, of course, doesn't just happen. Great managers make it happen. And that is what *Management* is all about.

THE NEXT STEP
INTEGRATED LEARNING ACTIVITIES

Cases/Projects	Self-Assessments	Exercises in Teamwork
• UPS Case	• Diversity Awareness (#7)	• Defining Quality (#3)
• Project 1—Diversity Lessons	• Organizational Design Preferences (#17)	• Which Organization Culture Fits You? (#8)
• Project 7—Gender and Leadership	• Are You Cosmopolitan? (#18)	• Case of the Contingency Workforce (#22)

STUDY QUESTION SUMMARY

1. What is the external environment of organizations?

• Competitive advantage and distinctive competency can only be achieved by organizations that deal successfully with dynamic and complex environments.

• The external environment of organizations consists of both general and specific parts.

• The general environment includes background economic, socio-cultural, legal-political, technological, and natural environment conditions.

- The specific or task environment consists of suppliers, customers, competitors, regulators, and pressure groups that an organization interacts with.

- Environmental uncertainty challenges organizations and managers to be flexible and responsive to new and changing conditions.

2. What is a customer-driven organization?

- A customer-driven organization recognizes customer service and product quality as foundations of competitive advantage.

- Total quality operations address needs of both internal customers and external customers.

- Customer relationship management builds and maintains strategic relationships with customers.

- Supply chain management builds and maintains strategic relationships with suppliers.

3. What is a quality-driven organization?

- To compete in the global economy, organizations are increasingly expected to meet ISO 9000 quality standards.

- Total quality management makes quality a strategic objective of the organization and supports it by continuous improvement efforts.

- Total quality operations try to meet customers' needs—on time, the first time, and all the time.

- Quality circles are groups of employees working together to solve quality problems.

4. What is organizational culture?

- The organizational culture is an internal environment that establishes a personality for the organization and has a strong influence on the behaviour of its members.

- The observable culture is found in the rites, rituals, stories, heroes, and symbols of the organization.

- The core culture consists of the core values and fundamental beliefs on which the organization is based.

- In organizations with strong cultures, members behave with shared understandings that support the organizational objectives.

- Symbolic managers build shared values, and use stories, ceremonies, heroes, and language to reinforce these values.

5. How is diversity managed in a multicultural organization?

- The organizational culture should create a positive ethical climate, or shared set of understandings about what is considered ethical.

- Multicultural organizations operate through a culture that values pluralism and respects diversity.

- Organizations have many subcultures, including those based on occupational, functional, ethnic, racial, age, and gender differences in a diverse workforce.

- Challenges faced by organizational minorities include sexual harassment, pay discrimination, job discrimination, and the glass ceiling effect.

- Managing diversity is the process of developing a work environment that is inclusive and allows everyone to reach their full potential.

KEY TERMS REVIEW

Biculturalism (p. 100)

Competitive advantage (p. 85)

Continuous improvement (p. 92)

Core values (p. 95)

Customer relationship management (p. 90)

Diversity (p. 96)

Environmental uncertainty (p. 88)

Ethnocentrism (p. 98)

General environment (p. 85)

Glass ceiling (p. 99)

ISO certification (p. 90)

Managing diversity (p. 100)

Multicultural organization (p. 97)

Multiculturalism (p. 97)

Organizational culture (p. 93)

Quality circle (p. 92)

Specific environment (p. 86)

Stakeholders (p. 87)

Subcultures (p. 97)

Supply chain management (p. 90)

Symbolic leader (p. 95)

Total quality management (p. 91)

Value-based management (p. 95)

Value creation (p. 87)

SELF-TEST 4

MULTIPLE-CHOICE QUESTIONS:

1. The general environment of an organization would include _____.
   (a) population demographics (b) activist groups (c) competitors (d) customers

2. In terms of value creation for stakeholders, _____ have a major interest in a business firm's profits and losses.
   (a) employees (b) communities (c) owners (d) suppliers

3. Two dimensions that determine the level of environmental uncertainty are the number of factors in the external environment and the _____ of these factors.
   (a) location (b) rate of change (c) importance (d) interdependence

4. Benchmarking, continuous improvement, and reduced cycle times are examples of organizational practices that show a commitment to _____.
   (a) affirmative action (b) total quality management (c) cost containment (d) supply chain management

5. A quality standard that has become essential for world-class companies competing in global markets is _____.
   (a) the Deming Prize (b) the Baldrige Award (c) CRM (d) ISO certification

6. New computer technologies have made possible _____ that quickly and efficiently produces individualized products for customers.
   (a) flexible manufacturing (b) mass production (c) mass customization (d) design for disassembly

7. Planned and spontaneous ceremonies and celebrations of work achievements illustrate how _____ help build strong corporate cultures.
   (a) rewards (b) heroes (c) rites and rituals (d) core values

8. When managers at Disney World use language metaphors, telling workers they are "on stage" as "members of the cast," they are engaging in _____ leadership.
   (a) symbolic (b) competitive (c) multicultural (d) stakeholder

9. Pluralism and the absence of discrimination and prejudice in policies and practices are two important hallmarks of _____.
   (a) the glass ceiling effect (b) a multicultural organization (c) quality circles (d) affirmative action

10. When members of minority cultures feel that they have to behave in ways similar to the majority, this is called _____.
    (a) biculturalism (b) symbolic leadership (c) the glass ceiling effect (d) inclusivity

11. Wal-Mart's suppliers electronically access inventory data and sales forecasts in the stores and automatically ship replacement products. This is an example of IT utilization in _____.
    (a) supply chain management (b) customer relationship management (c) total quality management (d) strategic constituencies analysis

12. Whether a structure is tight or loose and whether decisions are change oriented or driven by the status quo are indicators of an organization's _____.
    (a) inclusivity (b) culture (c) competitive advantage (d) multiculturalism

13. Performance with honesty, innovation, and social responsibility are among the _____ often espoused in corporate mission statements.
    (a) core values (b) stakeholder interests (c) TQM practices (d) ISO standards

14. _____ means that an organization fully integrates members of minority cultures and majority cultures.
     (a) Equal employment opportunity (b) Managing diversity (c) Symbolic leadership (d) Pluralism

15. The beliefs that older workers are not creative and are more interested in routine jobs are examples of stereotypes that can create bad feelings among members of different _____ subcultures in organizations.
     (a) occupational (b) generational (c) gender (d) functional

SHORT-RESPONSE QUESTIONS:

16. What operating objectives are appropriate for an organization seeking competitive advantage through improved customer service?

17. What is the difference between an organization's external customers and its internal customers?

18. What is value-based management?

19. Why is it important for managers to understand subcultures in organizations?

APPLICATION QUESTION:

20. Two businesswomen, former college roommates, are discussing their jobs and careers over lunch. You overhear one saying to the other, "I work for a large corporation, while you own a small retail business. In my company there is a strong corporate culture and everyone feels its influence. In fact, we are always expected to act in ways that support the culture and serve as role models for others to do so as well. This includes a commitment to diversity and multi-culturalism. Because of the small size of your firm, things like corporate culture, diversity, and multiculturalism are not so important to worry about." Do you agree or disagree with this statement? Why?

Global Dimensions
of Management

Planning Ahead

After reading Chapter 5, you should be able to answer these questions in your own words.

1. What are the international management challenges of globalization?

2. What are the forms and opportunities of international business?

3. What are multinational corporations and what do they do?

4. What is culture and how does it relate to global diversity?

5. How do management practices and learning transfer across cultures?

Gildan
Taking on the giants

A Montreal based clothing company deciding to take on the Chinese manufacturing might. Seems foolish, right? Well that's exactly what Gildan is doing. Most experts agreed that high Canadian labour costs, together with the removal of quotas under the World Trade Organization's agreement on textiles and clothing (in 1995), meant a surefire decline in the North American textile business. Not so for Gildan Activewear Inc., which has not only survived, but is set to expand further by venturing into the world of retail. Until now, Gildan has focused on selling only into the screen printing channel. How did they take on the giants?

Starting in 1999, the company undertook a global survey of clothing prices. "The first thing we did from Day 1 was to make sure that we benchmarked ourselves against the global market," says Glenn Chamandy, the CEO of Gildan. Gildan worked diligently to achieve their current level of pricing, which is approximately 35 percent lower than their Chinese competitors, in the US market.

To maintain its competitive advantage and remain a global player, Gildan recognized that it also had to establish operations offshore, first in Honduras in 1997, later expanding to Mexico, Haiti, the Dominican Republic, and Nicaragua. Locating offshore was not clear sailing. Initially, they were accused of poor working conditions and infringements on workers' rights, which may have negatively impacted the company's share price at the time. However, Gildan worked hard to develop a good working relationship and positive reputation for corporate social responsibility with non-governmental organizations, and joined the Fair Labor Association.

The strategic placement of these facilities has allowed Gildan to benefit from bilateral and multilateral trade agreements. It can ship duty-free anywhere in North America, the European Union, and Australia. This, together with fair labour practices and advanced technology, has kept the Chinese giants at bay. As Chamandy notes, 2005 was the year in which Gildan not only began to truly achieve its goals in economic terms but also reinforced its excellent financial performance by positioning itself "as a leader in corporate social responsibility and governance." [1]

IN THE WORKPLACE

You are waiting for a friend to tell you over lunch about her adventures teaching English in Korea. She's home for a few weeks before heading back to finish her contract in Korea.

As you wait, you remember the emails she sent you just after she arrived in Korea. These notes described how, after some initial reservations, she was having lots of fun and learning to survive and thrive in Korea.

You are then caught completely off-guard when she arrives and immediately complains about the way "they" do things "over there." Everything from how people bump into you, to having to drink tea and watch gloomy Korean movies. You tell your friend she is going through another adjustment stage. She asks, "Will the next stage be better than this?" How do you respond?

●●● Chapter 5   LEARNING PREVIEW   ●●●

There is more to Gildan than its manufacturing centres. Standing behind the T-shirts and clothing line is a large operation that depends on worldwide networks of suppliers and subcontractors to produce its products. But as Gildan strives for world markets it must continue to be well managed and to maintain high ethical standards. In Chapter 5 you will learn about international management with special attention to multinational corporations and the implications of global cultural diversity.

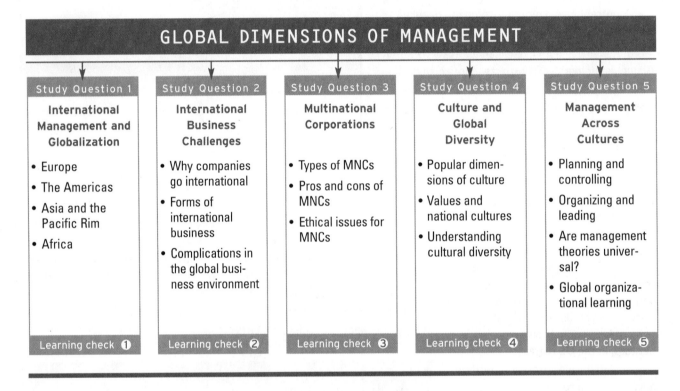

GLOBAL DIMENSIONS OF MANAGEMENT

Study Question 1	Study Question 2	Study Question 3	Study Question 4	Study Question 5
International Management and Globalization	**International Business Challenges**	**Multinational Corporations**	**Culture and Global Diversity**	**Management Across Cultures**
• Europe • The Americas • Asia and the Pacific Rim • Africa	• Why companies go international • Forms of international business • Complications in the global business environment	• Types of MNCs • Pros and cons of MNCs • Ethical issues for MNCs	• Popular dimensions of culture • Values and national cultures • Understanding cultural diversity	• Planning and controlling • Organizing and leading • Are management theories universal? • Global organizational learning
Learning check ❶	Learning check ❷	Learning check ❸	Learning check ❹	Learning check ❺

There is no doubt about it. We live and work in a global community, one that grows smaller and more immediately accessible by the day. The Internet and television bring on-the-spot news from around the world into our homes, 24 hours a day. The world's newspapers, from *The Globe and Mail*, to *El Financiero* (Mexico), to *Le Monde* (France), to the *Japan Times* can be read at the touch of a keyboard on your PC. It is possible to board a plane in Vancouver and fly non-stop to Beijing; it is sometimes less expensive to fly from Montreal to Paris than Montreal to Toronto. Colleges and universities offer a growing variety of study-abroad programs. For example, students at St. Francis Xavier University travel to places such as Grenada, Mexico, and Cuba to further understand global issues.

This world of international opportunities isn't just for tourists and travellers; it has major implications for businesses and those who work for them. Just take a look at the automobile industry. The Chrysler PT Cruiser is built in Mexico for Daimler-Chrysler of Germany; Ford owns Volvo; Toyota has produced more than 10 million cars at its North American plants; the "big three" Japanese automakers—Honda, Nissan, Toyota—get as much as 80 to 90 percent of their profits from sales in North America. And when the last of the original Volkswagen Beetles was made in mid-2003, it wasn't a German band that heralded its departure to the museum. *Mariachi* music greeted the car as it rolled off the line at Volkswagen's Puebla, Mexico, plant.[2]

The same trends and patterns are evident in other industries and countries. National boundaries are fast blurring as businesses of all sizes and types now travel the trade routes of the world.

Astute business investors know all this and more. They buy and sell only with awareness of the latest financial news from Hong Kong, London, Tokyo, New York, Sao Paulo, Johannesburg, and other financial centres of the world. There is no doubt that we live and work today in a truly global village. You, like the rest of us, must get connected with its implications for everyday living and careers.

And, what does the world think of Canada's place in the world economy? The Merrill Lynch Misery Index ranks nations based on unemployment, inflation, budgets, and trade balance; an economy with an increasing index is in poor economic shape. According to this index, Canada ranks second-best in the developed world with Japan at the top; this rating shows to the world that the Canadian economy is strong and vibrant. Merrill's chief North American economist, David Rosenberg, states that because of the volatility in Japan's economic fortunes, Canada is the most likely recipient of foreign-equity investment dollars in the next few years. It appears that the world is noticing what is happening in Canada, and likes it.[3]

INTERNATIONAL MANAGEMENT AND GLOBALIZATION

This is the age of the **global economy** in which resource supplies, product markets, and business competition are worldwide rather than purely local or national in scope.[4] It is also a time heavily influenced by the forces of **globalization**, the process of growing interdependence among these components in the global economy.[5] Harvard scholar and consultant Rosabeth Moss Kanter describes it as: "one of the most powerful and pervasive influences on nations, businesses, workplaces, communities, and lives…"[6]

■ In the **global economy**, resources, markets, and competition are worldwide in scope.

The global economy offers great opportunities for worldwide sourcing, production, and sales capabilities. But as businesses spread their reach around the world, the processes of globalization also bring many adjustments to traditional patterns.[7] Large multinational businesses are increasingly adopting transnational or "global" identities, rather than being identified with a national home. The growing strength and penetration of these businesses worldwide are viewed by some as a potential threat to national economies and their local business systems, labour markets, and cultures. All this adds up to great uncertainty as executives move into new and uncharted competitive territories. America Online's co-founder Stephen M. Case once described the scene: "I sometimes feel like I'm behind the wheel of a race car. One of the biggest challenges is there are no road signs to help navigate. And in fact… no one has yet determined which side of the road we're supposed to be on."[8]

■ **Globalization** is the process of growing interdependence among elements of the global economy.

The term used to describe management in organizations with business interests in more than one country is **international management**. There is no denying its importance. Procter & Gamble, for example, pursues a global strategy with a presence in more than 70 countries; the majority of McDonald's sales are now coming from outside North America, with some of its most profitable restaurants located in places like Moscow, Budapest, and Beijing. As the leaders of these and other companies press forward with global initiatives, the international management challenges and opportunities of working across borders—national and cultural—must be mastered. A new breed of manager, the **global manager**, is increasingly sought after. This is someone informed about international developments, transnational in outlook, competent in working with people from different cultures, and always aware of regional developments in a changing world.

■ **International management** involves managing operations in more than one country.

■ A **global manager** is culturally aware and informed about international affairs.

What about you? Are you prepared for the challenges of international management? Are you informed about the world and the forces of globalization?

●●● EUROPE

■ The **European Union** is a political and economic alliance of European countries.

The new Europe is a place of dramatic political and economic developments.[9] The **European Union** (EU) is expanding to 22 countries that agree to support mutual economic growth by removing barriers that previously limited cross-border trade and business development. As an economic union, the EU is putting the rest of the world on notice that European business is a global force to be reckoned with. Members are linked through favourable trade and customs laws intended to facilitate the free flow of workers, goods and services, and investments across national boundaries. Businesses in each member country have access to a market of over 375 million consumers.

■ The **Euro** is the common European currency.

Among the important business and economic developments in the EU are agreements to eliminate frontier controls and trade barriers, create uniform minimum technical product standards, open government procurement to businesses from all member countries, unify financial regulations, lift competitive barriers in banking and insurance, and offer a common currency—the **Euro**. The growing worldwide impact of the Euro is being watched carefully. Although there are still political and economic uncertainties, the expected regional benefits of an expanding EU include higher productivity, lower inflation, and steady growth.

take it to the case!

Bata Shoes
Growing one step at a time

Bata Shoes started in Czechoslovakia when three siblings decided to go into the shoemaking business. From these humble beginnings, Bata has grown to have a retail presence in over 50 countries and production factories in 26 countries, serving approximately 1 million customers each day and employing over 40,000 people. Since it began in 1894, Bata has sold over 14 billion pairs of shoes—enough for two pairs of shoes for everyone on the planet with a few billion left over for good measure. But it hasn't always been a rosy picture of prosperity and growth. Read the case in the *Management Learning Workbook* to learn about the real world of international business and development.

Source: With information from the corporate website: <www.bata.com>.

■ **NAFTA** is the North American Free Trade Agreement linking Canada, the United States, and Mexico in an economic alliance.

●●● THE AMERICAS

Canada, the United States, and Mexico are joined in the North American Free Trade Agreement (**NAFTA**). This agreement largely frees the flow of goods and services, workers, and investments within a region that has more potential consumers than its European rival, the EU. Getting approval of NAFTA from all three governments was not easy. Whereas Canadian firms worried about domination by US manufacturers, American politicians were concerned about the potential loss of jobs to Mexico. Some calls were made for more government legislation and support to protect domestic industries from foreign competition. While Mexicans feared that free trade would bring a further intrusion of US culture and values into their country, Americans complained that Mexican businesses did not operate by the same social standards—particularly with respect to environmental protection and the use of child labour.

At times an issue in NAFTA controversies, *maquiladoras* are foreign manufacturing plants allowed to operate in Mexico with special privileges in return for employing Mexican labour.[10] These firms import materials, components, and equipment duty free. They employ lower-cost Mexican labour to assemble these materials into finished products, which are then exported with duty paid only on the "value added" in Mexico. Critics of *maquiladoras* accuse them of exploiting Mexican workers and giving away jobs that would otherwise go to Canadians and Americans. They also point to high "social costs" as a continuing influx of workers overburdens services in Mexican border towns and the region becomes increasingly "Americanized." Advocates argue that *maquiladoras* increase employment and prosperity, and help develop skilled local workers.

> ■ *Maquiladoras* are foreign manufacturing plants that operate in Mexico with special privileges.

Optimism regarding business and economic growth extends throughout the Americas. Countries of the region are cutting tariffs, updating their economic policies, and welcoming foreign investors. An agreement has been reached by trade ministers to create a Free Trade Area of the Americas (FTAA), a proposed free-trade zone that would stretch from Point Barrow, Alaska, all the way to Tierra del Fuego, Chile. In addition, the MERCOSUR agreement links Bolivia, Brazil, Paraguay, Uruguay, and Argentina; the Andean Pact links Venezuela, Colombia, Equador, Peru, and Bolivia; and the Carribean Community, CARICOM, is growing as an economic linkage.

●●● ASIA AND THE PACIFIC RIM

When one looks toward Asia, China looms centre stage. The country of 1.3 billion people is the world's largest consumer marketplace. It is projected that China will top world performance charts for the next several years, growing by an average of 8.5–9 percent annually. However, another Asian giant, India, is not far behind as it cruises along at a 7–7.5 percent rate. While their economic structures differ noticeably, they do share a number of similarities. Both have economies that are growing at more than three times the average rate of other industrialized countries. Each nation has more people than the combined populations of Canada, the United States, the Eurozone (the collective group of countries that use the Euro as their common currency), and Japan. Combined, China and India add approximately 25 million people—a mini-Canada—to their economic base each year.[11] China's firms are major exporters of apparel and clothing and are direct competitors to firms like Gildan, featured in the chapter opener. It is also a top exporter of computers, electrical parts and components, telecommunications equipment, and sporting goods, among other products.[12] Over $120 billion worth of exports find their way annually from China to North America alone. But in Asia, one also has to recognize the historical strength of Japanese businesses—Honda, Toyota, Sony, to name just three—the growing prominence of firms like Samsung and Hyundai of South Korea, as well as other regional powers like Taiwan and Singapore. Together, they add another $200+ billion in exports to North America.

Elsewhere in Southeast Asia, countries like Malaysia and Thailand are prominent, Vietnam is fast advancing, and the Philippines is making a strategic move. With a high literacy rate, an educated workforce, and a population that speaks English, it intends to become a world centre for business process outsourcing. Goals include expanding its growing presence in global markets for medical transcription and accounting services, as well as customer call centres.[13] The 2003 agreement among 10 Southeast Asian nations to form an economic community along the lines of the EU model is designed to further growth in this region.

"Opportunity" is the watchword of the day wherever you travel or do business in Asia. Asian countries already represent a third of the global marketplace and rank as the world's top market for cars and telecommunications equipment. It is not just "low-cost" labour that attracts businesses to Asia; the growing availability of highly skilled "brainpower" is increasingly high on its list of advantages. India is a good example. The country is in the midst of economic expansion, with a high literacy rate and relatively inexpensive skilled labour. It is emerging as a world-class base for technology development and software engineering.

●●●● AFRICA

Africa (see *Figure 5.1*) is a continent in the news.[14] Although often the focus of reports on ethnic turmoil and civil strife in countries struggling along pathways to peace and development, the region beckons international investments. Whereas foreign businesses tend to avoid the risk of trouble spots, they are giving increased attention to stable countries with growing economics. One is Ghana, which has established a growing presence in the market for business process outsourcing.[15] On the discouraging side, the rates of economic growth in sub-Saharan Africa are among the lowest in the world; many parts of Africa suffer from terrible problems of poverty and the ravishment of a continuing AIDS epidemic. The region's need for sustained assistance from business investments and foreign aid is well established.

A report by two Harvard professors recently analyzed the foreign investment environment of Africa and concluded that the region's contextual problems are manageable.[16] "In fact they should be viewed as opportunities," says James A. Austin, one of the co-authors. He adds: "If a company has the managerial and organizational capabilities to deal with the region's unique business challenges, then it will be able to enter a promising market."[17]

The Southern African Development Community (SADC) links 14 countries of southern Africa in trade and economic development efforts. The objectives of SADC include harmonizing and rationalizing strategies for sustainable development among member

Figure 5.1 Africa, continent of opportunity.

AROUND THE WORLD

Botswana is in an enviable position compared with most other African countries. Since independence in 1966, it has been politically stable, boasts a multi-party democracy, and has enjoyed four decades of strong economic growth. In that time, it has been the fastest growing economy in the world. Botswana's economic success has come primarily from mining as it is the world's largest producer of gem-quality diamonds. Textiles, agriculture, and the financial services sector also offer new prospects for growth. As well, tourism is an increasingly important industry in Botswana, accounting for almost 12 percent of its gross domestic product. Botswana is keen to continue to sell itself internationally and show the benefits of investing there. With a Standard & Poor's "A" grade credit rating, Botswana is by far the best credit risk in Africa.

Botswana is just one of Africa's opportunities

Sources: Peter Biles, "Botswana: Africa's success story?," BBC news, March 7, 2005; U.S. State Department, "Background Note: Botswana," online at <www.state.gov/r/pa/ei/bgn/1830.htm#econ>.

countries.[18] Post-apartheid South Africa, in particular, has benefitted from political revival. A country of almost 50 million people and great natural resources, South Africa is experiencing economic recovery and attracting outside investors. It already accounts for half the continent's purchasing power.[19] Foreign investments in the country increased sharply after minority white rule ended and Nobel Prize winner Nelson Mandela became the nation's first black president.

BE SURE YOU CAN

• define the terms global economy and globalization • discuss the implications of globalization for international management • illustrate the significance of regional economic alliances by describing how NAFTA and the EU operate • discuss the pros and cons of *maquiladora* operations

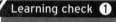 Learning check ❶

INTERNATIONAL BUSINESS CHALLENGES

John Chambers, CEO of Cisco Systems Inc., says: "I will put my jobs anywhere in the world where the right infrastructure is, with the right educated workforce, with the right supportive government."[20] Cisco and other firms like it are **international businesses**. They conduct for-profit transactions of goods and services across national boundaries.

▣ An **international business** conducts commercial transactions across national boundaries.

●●● WHY COMPANIES GO INTERNATIONAL

International businesses of all types and sizes are the foundations of world trade. They are the engines for moving raw materials, finished products, and specialized services from one country to another in the global economy. The reasons *why businesses go international* include these attractions of the marketplaces of the world:

• *Profits*—Global operations offer greater profit potential.

• *Customers*—Global operations offer new markets to sell products.

- *Suppliers*—Global operations offer access to needed raw materials.

- *Capital*—Global operations offer access to financial resources.

- *Labour*—Global operations offer access to lower labour costs.

CANADIAN COMPANY IN THE NEWS   **Toyota Canada Inc.**

MULTINATIONAL CORPORATION (MNC) COMMITS TO ONTARIO TOWNS

The towns of Simcoe and Woodstock, Ontario, are certainly benefitting from the expansion of one multinational corporation–Toyota Motor Corp. The Japanese carmaker's truck subsidiary Hino Motors Ltd. opened the first Japanese commercial truck assembly factory in Canada in Woodstock in 2006, hiring 45 people, with the possibility of another 15 to 20 jobs with the addition of a second shift. While it's not a major employer, analysts describe the move as an indication of the Japanese company's further commitment to Canada. Toyota also announced plans for a $50-million auto parts plant in Simcoe, with the creation of 250 jobs. Run by Toyotetsu Canada Inc., the auto parts plant will supply parts to the Toyota plant in Cambridge, Ontario, with another plant set to open in Woodstock in 2008.

Sources: Omar El Akkad, "Toyota to build auto parts factory in Ontario," *The Globe and Mail*, March 15, 2006, p. B4; Gary Norris, "Toyota opening truck plant in Woodstock, Ont.," Canadian Press, March 7, 2006.

●●● FORMS OF INTERNATIONAL BUSINESS

The common forms of international business are shown in *Figure 5.2*. When a business is just getting started internationally, global sourcing, exporting/importing, and licensing and franchising are the usual ways to begin. These are *market entry strategies* that involve the sale of goods or services to foreign markets but do not require expensive capital investments. Joint ventures and wholly owned subsidiaries are *direct investment strategies*. They require major capital commitments but create rights of ownership and control over operations in the foreign country.

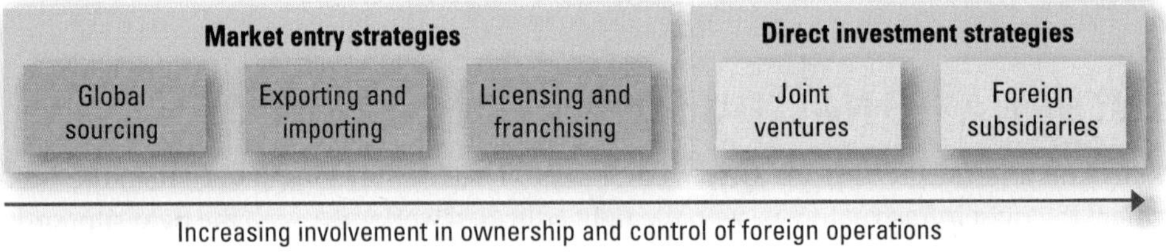

Figure 5.2 Common forms of international business–from market entry to direct investment strategies.

Market entry strategies			Direct investment strategies	
Global sourcing	Exporting and importing	Licensing and franchising	Joint ventures	Foreign subsidiaries

Increasing involvement in ownership and control of foreign operations

Market Entry Strategies

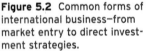 In **global sourcing**, materials or services are purchased around the world for local use.

A common first step into international business is **global sourcing**—the process of purchasing materials, manufacturing components, or business services from around the world. It is an international division of labour in which activities are performed in countries where they can be done well at the lowest cost. In manufacturing, global sourcing of components for cars may mean purchasing windshields and instrument panels from Mexico, and anti-lock braking systems from Germany. In services, it may mean setting up toll-free customer support call centres in the Philippines, or contracting for computer software programs in India. The goal of global sourcing is to take advantage of international wage gaps and the availability of skilled labour by contracting for goods and services in low-cost foreign locations.

A second form of international business involves **exporting**—selling locally made products in foreign markets, and/or **importing**—buying foreign-made products and selling them in domestic markets. Because the growth of export industries creates local jobs, governments often offer special advice and assistance to businesses that are trying to develop or expand their export markets. According to Statistics Canada, in 2006 Canada exported over $450 billion worth of goods, with the United States purchasing approximately 80 percent of that total. Our second trading partner, Japan, was a distant second place at 2 percent. Despite efforts to expand our trading partners, it is easy to see that the Canadian economy is extensively entwined with our neighbour to the south.[21]

Another form of international business is the **licensing agreement**, where foreign firms pay a fee for rights to make or sell another company's products in a specified region. The licence typically grants access to a unique manufacturing technology, special patent, or trademark. **Franchising** is a form of licensing in which the foreign firm buys the rights to use another's name and operating methods in its home country. As in domestic franchising agreements, firms like McDonald's, Wendy's, Subway, and others sell facility designs, equipment, product ingredients and recipes, and management systems to foreign investors, while retaining certain product and operating controls.

> ■ In **exporting**, local products are sold abroad.

> ■ **Importing** is the process of acquiring products abroad and selling them in domestic markets.

> ■ In a **licensing agreement** one firm pays a fee for rights to make or sell another company's products.
> ■ In **franchising** a fee is paid for rights to use another firm's name and operating methods.

Direct Investment Strategies

To establish a direct investment presence in a foreign country, many firms enter into **joint ventures**. These are co-ownership arrangements that pool resources and share risks and control for business operations. A joint venture may be established by equity purchases and/or direct investments by a foreign partner in an existing operation; it may also involve the creation of an entirely new business by a foreign and local partner. International joint ventures are *strategic alliances* that help partners gain things through co-operation that otherwise would be difficult to achieve independently. In return for its investment in a local operation, for example, the outside or foreign partner often gains both access to new markets and the assistance of a local partner who understands them. In return for its investment, the local partner often gains new technology as well as opportunities for its employees to learn new skills. *Manager's Notepad 5.1* offers a checklist for choosing joint venture partners.[22]

A **foreign subsidiary** is a local operation completely owned and controlled by a foreign firm. Like joint ventures, foreign subsidiaries may be formed through direct investment in start-up operations called *greenfield ventures*, or through equity purchases in existing ones. When making such investments, foreign firms are clearly taking a business risk. They must be confident that they possess the expertise needed to manage and conduct business affairs successfully in the new environment. This is where prior experience gained through joint ventures can prove very beneficial. Although establishing a foreign subsidiary represents the highest level of involvement in international operations, it can make very good business sense. Toyota recently agreed to open a second Canadian plant in Woodstock, Ontario. According to the president of Toyota Motor Corp., Katsuaki Watanabe, the expectation is to build 100,000 vehicles annually.[23] An auto analyst for a Japanese brokerage firm says: "It's a smart strategy to shift production to North America. They're reducing their exposure through building more in their regional markets, as well as being able to meet consumers' needs more quickly."[24]

> ■ A **joint venture** operates in a foreign country through co-ownership with local partners.

> ■ A **foreign subsidiary** is a local operation completely owned by a foreign firm.

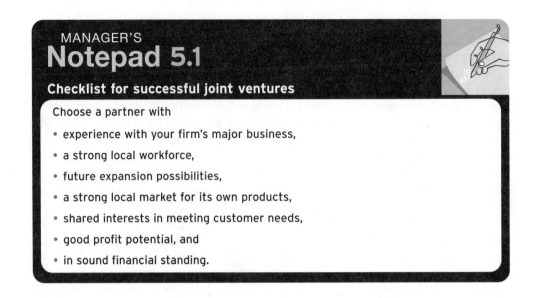

MANAGER'S
Notepad 5.1
Checklist for successful joint ventures

Choose a partner with

- experience with your firm's major business,
- a strong local workforce,
- future expansion possibilities,
- a strong local market for its own products,
- shared interests in meeting customer needs,
- good profit potential, and
- in sound financial standing.

●●● COMPLICATIONS IN THE GLOBAL BUSINESS ENVIRONMENT

The environment of international business in any form is complex and dynamic—and highly competitive. Global business executives must master task demands of operating with worldwide suppliers, distributors, customers, and competitors. They must understand and deal successfully with general environment differences in economic, legal-political, and educational systems, among other aspects of business infrastructure. Percy Barnevik, when chairman of the global corporation Asea Brown Boveri (ABB), once said: "Too many people think you can succeed in the long run just by exporting from America to Europe. But you need to establish yourself locally and become, for example, a Chinese, Indonesian, or Indian citizen."[25]

Differences in legal environments among nations create substantial international business challenges. Organizations are expected to abide by the laws of the host country in which they are operating. In the United States, for example, executives of foreign-owned companies must worry about antitrust issues that prevent competitors from regularly talking to one another. They also must deal with a variety of special laws regarding occupational health and safety, equal employment opportunity, sexual harassment, and other matters—all constraints potentially different from those they find at home.

The more home- and host-country laws differ, the more difficult and complex it is for international businesses to adapt to local ways. Common legal problems in international business involve incorporation practices and business ownership; negotiating and implementing contracts with foreign parties; protecting patents, trademarks, and copyrights; and handling foreign exchange restrictions. Intellectual property rights have long been a source of dispute between western businesses and China. Software piracy and copyright violations of CDs and books, for example, are well known. But General Motors recently had its own problems there. The firm's China executives noticed that a new model from a fast-growing local competitor—Chery Automobile, partially owned by GM's Chinese partner—looked very similar to one of their own cars due out in the near future. GM claims in local courts that their design was copied; the competitor denies the charges.[26]

When disputes between nations relate to international trade, they can end up before the **World Trade Organization**. This is a global institution established to promote free trade and

■ **World Trade Organization** member nations agree to negotiate and resolve disputes about tariffs and trade restrictions.

open markets around the world. In the WTO some 140+ members agree to give one another **most favoured nation status**—the most favourable treatment for imports and exports. Although members agree to ongoing negotiations and the reduction of tariffs and trade restrictions, trading relationships are often difficult. The WTO offers a mechanism for monitoring international trade and resolving disputes among countries. **Protectionism** in the form of political calls for tariffs and favourable treatments to help protect domestic businesses from foreign competition is a common and complicating theme. Government leaders, such as the prime minister of Canada, face internal political dilemmas involving the often-conflicting goals of seeking freer international trade while still protecting domestic industries. These dilemmas make it difficult to reach international agreement on trade matters, and create controversies for the WTO.

■ **Most favoured nation status** gives a trading partner most favourable treatment for imports and exports.

■ **Protectionism** is a call for tariffs and favourable treatments to protect domestic firms from foreign competition.

BE SURE YOU CAN
• list five reasons that companies pursue international business opportunities • describe and give examples of each of these international business strategies—global sourcing, exporting/importing, franchising/licensing, joint ventures, and foreign subsidiaries • explain the operations of the WTO • discuss how differences in legal environments can affect businesses operating internationally

✓ **Learning check ❷**

MULTINATIONAL CORPORATIONS

A true **multinational corporation** (MNC) is a business firm with extensive international operations in more than one foreign country. Premier MNCs found in annual listings such as *Fortune* magazine's Global 500 include such global giants as General Electric, Exxon, and Wal-Mart from the United States; Mitsubishi, Toyota, and NTT DoCoMo of Japan; DaimlerChrysler of Germany; Barrick Gold, En Cana Corp., and Enbridge International of Canada; and Royal Dutch/Shell Group of the Netherlands and Great Britain. Also important on the world scene are *multinational organizations* (MNOs)—like the International Federation of Red Cross and Red Crescent Societies, the United Nations, and the World Bank—whose non-profit missions and operations span the globe.

■ A **multinational corporation** is a business with extensive international operations in more than one foreign country.

●●● TYPES OF MULTINATIONAL CORPORATIONS

A typical MNC operates in many countries but has corporate headquarters in one home or host country. Microsoft, Apple Computer, and McDonald's are among the ready examples. Although deriving substantial sales and profits from international sources, these firms and others like them typically also have strong national identifications. But as the global economy grows more competitive, many multinationals are acting more like **transnational corporations**. They increasingly try to operate worldwide without being identified with one national home.[27] Executives of transnationals view the entire world as their domain for acquiring resources, locating production facilities, marketing goods and services, and promoting its brand image. They seek total integration of global operations, try to operate across borders without home-based prejudices, make major decisions from a global perspective, distribute work among worldwide points of excellence, and employ senior executives from many different countries. Nestlé is a good example in foods; Asea Brown Boveri (ABB) is another in diversified conglomerates. When one buys a Nestlé product in Brazil or has a neighbour working for ABB in Toronto, Ontario, who would know that both are actually registered Swiss companies?

■ A **transnational corporation** is an MNC that operates worldwide on a borderless basis.

●●● PROS AND CONS OF MULTINATIONAL CORPORATIONS

In this time when consumer demand, resource supplies, product flows, and labour markets increasingly span national boundaries, the actions of MNCs are increasingly influential in the global economy. The United Nations has reported that MNCs hold one-third of the world's productive assets and control 70 percent of world trade. Furthermore, more than 90 percent of these MNCs are based in the Northern Hemisphere. While this may bring a sense of both accomplishment and future opportunity to business leaders, it can also be very threatening to small and less-developed countries and their domestic industries.

Host-Country Issues

Ideally, global corporations and the countries that "host" their foreign operations should both benefit. *Figure 5.3* shows how things can and do go both right and wrong in MNC–host-country relationships. The *potential host-country benefits* include larger tax bases, increased employment opportunities, technology transfers, the introduction of new industries, and the development of local resources. The *potential host-country costs* include complaints that MNCs extract excessive profits, dominate the local economy, interfere with the local government, do not respect local customs and laws, fail to help domestic firms develop, hire the most talented of local personnel, and do not transfer their most advanced technologies.[28]

Of course executives of MNCs sometimes feel exploited as well in their relations with host countries. Consider China once again, a setting where major cultural, political, and economic differences confront the outsider.[29] Profits have proved elusive for some foreign investors; some have found it difficult to take profits out of the country; some have struggled to get the raw materials needed for operations.[30] The protection of intellectual property was mentioned earlier as an ongoing concern of foreign manufacturers, and managing relationships with Chinese government agencies can be very complicated.

Figure 5.3 What should go right and what can go wrong in MNC–host-country relationships.

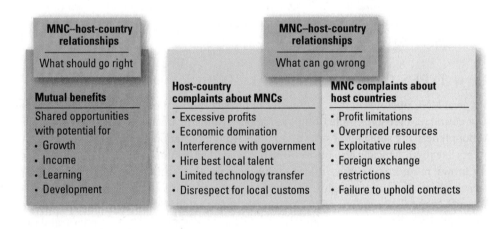

Home-Country Issues

MNCs may also encounter difficulties in the "home" country where their headquarters are located. Even as many MNCs try to operate more globally, home-country governments and citizens still tend to identify them with local and national interests. When an MNC outsources, cuts back, or closes a domestic operation to shift work to lower-cost international destinations, the loss of local jobs is controversial. Corporate decision makers are likely to be engaged by government and community leaders in critical debate about a firm's domestic social responsibilities. *Home-country criticisms of MNCs* include complaints about transferring jobs out of the country, shifting capital investments abroad, and engaging in corrupt practices in foreign settings.

●●● ETHICAL ISSUES FOR MULTINATIONAL CORPORATIONS

The ethical aspects of international business deserve special attention and were introduced in Chapter 3 on ethics and social responsibility. **Corruption**, engaging in illegal practice to further one's business interests, is a source of continuing controversy. The Canadian *Corruption of Foreign Public Officials Act* (1998) makes it illegal for firms and their managers to engage in corrupt practices overseas, including giving bribes and excessive commissions to foreign officials in return for business favours. This law specifically bans payoffs to foreign officials to obtain or keep business, provides punishments for executives who know about or are involved in such activities, and requires detailed accounting records for international business transactions. Critics, however, believe the law fails to recognize the "reality" of business as practised in many foreign nations. They complain that Canadian companies are at a competitive disadvantage because they can't offer the same "deals" as competitors from other nations—deals that locals may regard as standard business practices.

■ **Corruption** involves illegal practices to further one's business interests.

Sweatshops, business operations that employ workers at low wages for long hours and in poor working conditions, are another concern in the global business arena. Networks of outsourcing contracts are now common as manufacturers follow the world's low-cost labour supplies—countries like the Philippines, Sri Lanka, and Vietnam are popular destinations. Yet Nike, Inc., has learned that a global company will be held publicly accountable for the work standards and employment practices of its foreign subcontractors. Facing activist criticism, the company revised its labour practices after a review by the consulting firm GoodWorks International. Nike's website now offers reports and audit results on its international labour practices. Nike's international business web is extensive, including more than 750 manufacturing sites and contractors in some 50 countries.[31]

■ **Sweatshops** employ workers at very low wages, for long hours, and in poor working conditions.

Child labour, the full-time employment of children for work otherwise done by adults, is an international business ethics issue covered in Chapter 3. It has been made especially visible by activist concerns regarding the manufacture of handmade carpets in countries like Pakistan. Initiatives to eliminate child labour include an effort by the Rugmark Foundation to discourage purchases of carpets that do not carry its label. The "Rugmark" label is earned by a certification process to guarantee that a carpet manufacturer does not use illegal child labour.[32]

■ **Child labour** is the full-time employment of children for work otherwise done by adults.

Yet another ethical issue relates to global concerns for environmental protection. The world's citizenry expects global corporations to respect the natural environment. Industrial pollution of cities, hazardous waste, depletion of natural resources, and related concerns are now worldwide issues. The concept of **sustainable development** is a popular guideline advanced by activist groups. It is "development that meets the needs of the present without compromising the ability of future generations to meet their own needs."[33] As global corporate citizens, MNCs are increasingly expected to uphold high standards in dealing with sustainable development and protection of the natural environment—whenever and wherever they operate. The available guidelines for responsible environmental policies include **ISO 14000** certification standards of the International Organization for Standardization.

■ **Sustainable development** meets the needs of the present without hurting future generations.

■ **ISO 14000** offers a set of certification standards for responsible environmental policies.

BE SURE YOU CAN
• differentiate a multinational corporation from a transnational corporation • list at least three host-country complaints and three home-country complaints about MNC operations • define the terms corruption, sweatshop, and child labour • illustrate how each of these practices can create ethical problems for international businesses

✓ Learning check ❸

CULTURE AND GLOBAL DIVERSITY

■ **Culture** is a shared set of beliefs, values, and patterns of behaviour common to a group of people.

■ **Culture shock** is the confusion and discomfort a person experiences when in an unfamiliar culture.

■ **Ethnocentrism** is the tendency to consider one's culture as superior to others.

Culture is the shared set of beliefs, values, and patterns of behaviour common to a group of people. Anyone who has visited another country knows that cultural differences exist. **Culture shock**, the confusion and discomfort a person experiences when in an unfamiliar culture, is a reminder that many of these differences must be mastered just to travel comfortably around the world. But the business implications of cultural differences are also important to understand. An American exporter, for example, once went to see a Saudi Arabian official. He sat in the office with crossed legs and the sole of his shoe exposed—an unintentional sign of disrespect in the local culture. He passed documents to the host using his left hand, which Muslims consider unclean. And he refused to accept coffee when it was offered, suggesting criticism of the Saudi's hospitality. What was the price for these cultural miscues? He lost a $10 million contract to a Korean executive better versed in Arab ways.[34]

Ethnocentrism, the tendency to view one's culture as superior to others, is surprisingly common in international business. Local customs vary in too many ways for most of us to become true experts in the many cultures of our diverse world. Yet there are things we can do to respect differences, successfully conduct business abroad, and minimize culture shock. Self-awareness and reasonable sensitivity are the basic building blocks of cultural awareness, as suggested in *Manager's Notepad 5.2*.[35]

MANAGER'S
Notepad 5.2
Stages in adjusting to a new culture

- *Confusion:* First contacts with the new culture leave you anxious, uncomfortable, and in need of information and advice.
- *Small victories:* Continued interactions bring some "successes," and your confidence grows in handling daily affairs.
- *The honeymoon:* A time of wonderment, cultural immersion, and even infatuation, with local ways viewed positively.
- *Irritation and anger:* A time when the "negatives" overwhelm the "positives," and the new culture becomes a target of your criticism.
- *Reality:* A time of rebalancing; you are able to enjoy the new culture while accommodating its less desirable elements.

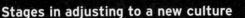

●●● POPULAR DIMENSIONS OF CULTURE

The first impressions of an international traveller often relate to language differences and difficulties. But other dimensions of popular culture quickly follow, including use of space, time orientation, religion, and contracts and agreements.[36] When executives at British Airways (BA) surveyed international customers, for example, a simple lesson emerged—don't assume people from different cultures will have the same dining habits and preferences. Japanese, for example, commented that BA's food was "not bad for Westerners." They also pointed out that the white china dishes were similar to those used in Japanese hospitals and prisons. "The further away from our Western culture we go, the less satisfied our customers are," said one BA marketing manager. "People from other cultures have felt looked down upon."[37]

Language

Language is a medium of culture. It provides access to the cultural understanding needed to conduct business and develop personal relationships. Not only do languages vary around the world; the same language (such as English) can vary in usage from one country to the next (as it does from North America to England to Australia). Although it isn't always possible to know a local language, such as Hungarian, it is increasingly usual in business dealings to find some common second language in which to communicate, such as English, French, German, or Spanish. The importance of good foreign language training is critical for the truly global manager. When Larry Johnston arrived in Paris to head up GE's medical equipment operations in Europe, the Middle East, and Africa, the first thing he did was study French intensively for a month. "I went from 7 a.m. to 8 p.m. and learned enough to converse," he says.[38]

According to anthropologist Edward T. Hall, there are systematic and important differences in the way cultures utilize language in communication.[39] He describes **low-context cultures** as those in which most communication takes place via the written or spoken word. In places like Canada, the United States, and Germany, the message is delivered in very precise wording. One has to listen and read carefully to best understand what the message sender intends. Things are quite different in **high-context cultures**, where much communication takes place through non-verbal and situational cues. In these cultures words communicate only a (sometimes small) part of the message. The rest must be interpreted from the situational "context"—body language, physical setting, and even the past relationships among those involved. This process is often time consuming and very deliberate. In high-context Japan, for example, much emphasis is given to social settings in which potential business partners develop a relationship and get to know one another; once this is accomplished, future deals can then be formed.

■ **Low-context cultures** emphasize communication via spoken or written words.

■ **High-context cultures** rely on non-verbal and situational cues as well as spoken or written words in communication.

Interpersonal Space

Hall considers the use of interpersonal space as one of the important "silent languages" of culture.[40] Arabs and many Latin Americans, for example, prefer to communicate at much closer distances than is standard in North American practice. Misunderstandings are possible if one person moves back as another moves forward to close the interpersonal distance between them. Some cultures of the world also value space more highly than others. Canadians tend to value large and private office space. The Japanese are highly efficient in using space; even executive offices are likely to be shared in major corporations.

Time Orientation

Time orientation is another of the silent languages of culture.[41] The way people approach and deal with time tends to vary widely. Mexicans, for example, may specify *hora Americana* on invitations if they want guests to appear at the appointed time; otherwise, it may be impolite to arrive punctually for a scheduled appointment. When working in Vietnam, punctuality is important and communicates respect for one's host.[42] Hall describes **monochronic cultures** in which people tend to do one thing at a time. The standard North American business practice is to schedule a meeting and give the visitor one's undivided attention for the allotted time.[43] In **polychronic cultures**, time is used to accomplish many different things at once. The North American visitor to an Egyptian client may be frustrated by continued interruptions as people flow in and out of the office and various transactions are made.

■ In **monochronic cultures** people tend to do one thing at a time.

■ In **polychronic cultures** time is used to accomplish many different things at once.

Religion

One should always be aware of religious traditions when visiting and working in other cultures. Religion is a major influence on many people's lives, and its impact may extend to practices regarding dress, food, and interpersonal behaviour. It is a source of ethical and moral teaching, with associated personal and institutional implications. "Islamic banks" in the Middle East, for example, service their customers without any interest charges to remain consistent with teachings of the *Koran*. The traveller and businessperson should always be sensitive to the rituals, holy days, and sabbath schedules of alternative religions. When working in Malaysia, for example, it is polite to schedule business dinners after 8 p.m. This allows Muslims to complete the evening prayer before dining. Similarly, it should be remembered that the Islamic holy month of Ramadan is a dawn-to-dusk time of fasting.

Contracts and Agreements

Cultures vary in their use of contracts and agreements. In Canada a contract is viewed as a final and binding statement of agreements. This tends to be consistent with practices of low-context cultures. But, in high-context cultures the written contract may be viewed as more of a starting point. Once in place it will continue to emerge and be modified as the parties work together over time. McDonald's once found this out when the Chinese government ignored the firm's lease on a restaurant site in downtown Beijing and tore down the building to make room for a development project. In Canada, furthermore, contracts are expected to be in writing. Requesting a written agreement from an Indonesian who has given his "word" may be considered disrespectful.

●●● VALUES AND NATIONAL CULTURES

As companies go global, their managers must become more global in viewpoints, experiences, and cultural appreciation. A German who travels frequently in the United States on business, for example, once told a *Wall Street Journal* reporter that he was surprised at how few of his American counterparts had travelled abroad and at how generally "non-global" they were. But he enjoyed the "friendliness and openness" of his American counterparts, as well as their tendency to "make quick decisions." Similarly, when Bob Hendry was sent to Germany to head General Motors' Opel Division he encountered work-style differences. The emphasis on short-term monthly and quarterly performance targets that he was familiar with, for example, clashed with the German focus on one-year and longer results.[44]

It is helpful to have a framework for understanding how cultural differences can influence management and organizational practices. Geert Hofstede, a Dutch scholar and international management consultant, studied personnel from a US-based MNC operating in 40 countries. First published in his book *Culture's Consequences: International Differences in Work-Related Values*, his research offers preliminary insights for understanding broad differences in national cultures.[45] *Figure 5.4* shows how selected countries rank on the five dimensions Hofstede now uses in his model.

1. *Power distance*—the degree to which a society accepts or rejects the unequal distribution of power among people in organizations and the institutions of society.

2. *Uncertainty avoidance*—the degree to which a society is uncomfortable with risk, change, and situational uncertainty, vs. having tolerance for them.

3. *Individualism-collectivism*—the degree to which a society emphasizes individual accomplishments and self-interests, vs. collective accomplishments and the interests of groups.

4. *Masculinity-femininity*—the degree to which a society values assertiveness and material success, vs. feelings and concern for relationships.[46]

5. *Time orientation*—the importance that a society attaches to the future vs the past and present.[47]

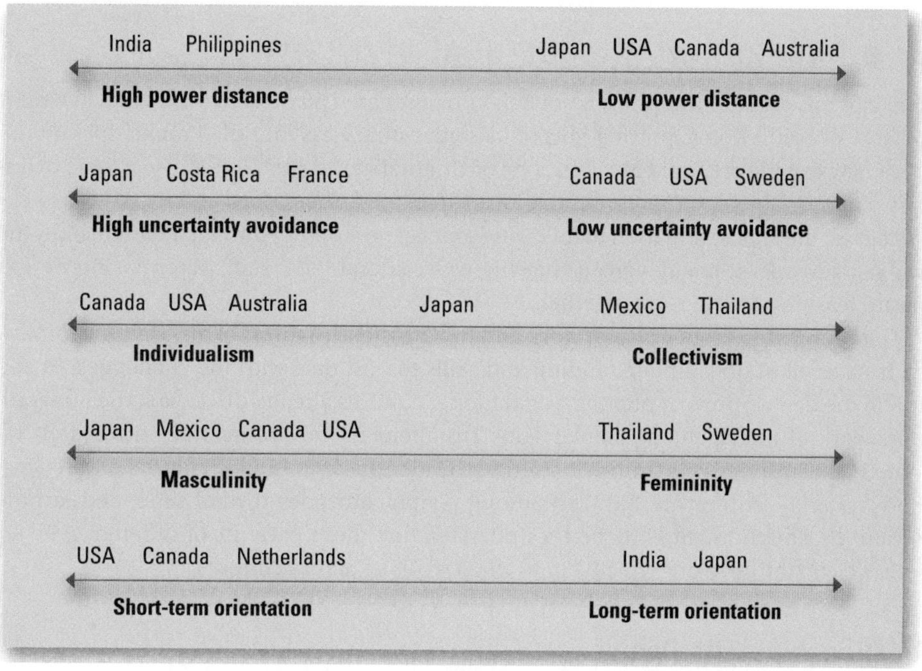

Figure 5.4 How countries compare on Hofstede's dimensions of national culture.

Looking at how Canadians scored on the Hofstede dimensions, Canada has Individualism (IDV) as our highest ranking score (80). This indicates Canadian society has a highly individualistic attitude and, in turn, comparatively weak bonds with others. Individualistic countries tend to be more self-reliant with people tending to look out primarily for themselves and close family members.

Canada's Power Distance (PDI) is relatively low with an index of 39 compared to a world average of 55. This indicates that Canadians see a greater equality between societal levels than many other countries. In Canada, people generally see that no one is any better than any other regardless of economic or cultural background. According to Hofstede this orientation results in more co-operative relations across all power levels and generally creates a stable cultural environment.

Canada scored 23 on Term Orientation. The average of this score is 45 among the other countries surveyed. This ranking indicates that Canadians focus on respecting tradition, fulfilling social obligations, and protecting their reputation as opposed to thrift and perseverence, which are valued more by long-term oriented societies.

Canadian Scores on the Five Dimensions were:

1. Power Distance: 39
2. Individualism: 80
3. Uncertainty Avoidance: 48
4. Masculinity: 52
5. Long term orientation: 23[48]

Hofstede's framework helps identify managerial implications of these potential cultural differences. For example, workers from high power-distance cultures such as Singapore can be expected to show great respect for elders and those senior in authority. In the more uncertainty-avoidance cultures like France, employment practices that increase job security are likely to be favoured. In highly individualistic societies like Canada and the United States, workers may be expected to emphasize self-interests more than group loyalty. Outsiders may also find that the workplace in masculine societies such as Japan displays more rigid gender stereotypes. Also, corporate strategies in more long-term cultures are likely to be just that—more long-term oriented.

●●● UNDERSTANDING CULTURAL DIVERSITY

Consider this scene.[49] Interbrew SA of Belgium purchased 50 percent ownership in Oriental Brewery of South Korea, putting four of its senior managers into the Korean operation. "It was a new experience," said Ms. Park, one of Oriental's local staff. It was also a clash of business cultures. The newcomers wanted locals to express their ideas and work toward clear objectives; the locals were used to following orders and working through relationships. After two years Ms. Park finally agreed that the western and local staff were making progress toward learning how to work together.

Stepping into cross-cultural work and managerial situations of any sort is complicated. It takes all of one's understanding and skills to best deal with the challenges. In addition to the descriptions of popular and national cultures already discussed, the integrative framework of management scholar Fons Trompenaars can be helpful. In research with some 15,000 respondents from 47 countries, he identifies systematic cultural differences in the ways relationships are handled among people, attitudes toward time, and attitudes toward the environment.[50] By better understanding these patterns of difference, he suggests we can improve our effectiveness when working across cultures.

Relationships with People

In his broad framework, Trompenaars identifies five major cultural differences in how people handle relationships with one another.

1. *Universalism vs. particularism*—the degree to which a culture emphasizes rules and consistency in relationships, or accepts flexibility and the bending of rules to fit circumstances.

2. *Individualism vs. collectivism*—the degree to which a culture emphasizes individual freedoms and responsibilities in relationships, or focuses more on group interests and consensus.

3. *Neutral vs. affective*—the degree to which a culture emphasizes objectivity and reserved detachment in relationships, or allows more emotionality and expressed feelings.

4. *Specific vs. diffuse*—the degree to which a culture emphasizes focused and in-depth relationships, or broader and more superficial ones.

5. *Achievement vs. prescription*—the degree to which a culture emphasizes an earned or performance-based status in relationships, or awards status based on social standing and non-performance factors.

Attitudes Toward Time

Attitudes toward time in the Trompenaars framework differ in the relative emphasis given to the present versus the past and future. In cultures that take a *sequential view*, time is considered a continuous and passing series of events. This view of time may be represented by a circle and the notion that time is recycling, a moment passed will return again. In cultures that take a *synchronic view*, by contrast, time takes on a greater sense of urgency. It is more linear, with a great interest in moving, from present to future. Pressures to resolve problems quickly so that time won't be "lost" are characteristic of synchronic cultures.

Attitudes Toward the Environment

Trompenaars also recognizes that cultures vary in their approach to the environment. In cultures that are *inner-directed*, people tend to view themselves as quite separate from nature. They are likely to consider the environment as something to be controlled or used for personal advantage. In cultures that are *outer-directed*, people tend to view themselves as part of nature. They are more likely to try to blend with or go along with the environment than to try to control it.

BE SURE YOU CAN   ✓ **Learning check** ❹

• define the term culture • explain how ethnocentrism can create difficulties for people working across cultures • differentiate between low-context and high-context cultures, and between monochronic and polychronic cultures • define Hofstede's five dimensions of value differences among national cultures • illustrate each dimension by contrasting North American culture with those of other countries • identify the major components in Trompenaars's model of cultural differences

---

MANAGEMENT ACROSS CULTURES

The management process—planning, organizing, leading, and controlling—is as relevant to international operations as to domestic ones. Yet as the preceding discussion of environment and culture should suggest, these functions must be applied appropriately from one country and culture to the next. **Comparative management** is the study of how management systematically differs among countries and/or cultures. Today we recognize the importance of learning about how management is practised around the world. Competition and the global economy have given rise to *global managers*, defined earlier as managers comfortable with cultural diversity, quick to find opportunities in unfamiliar settings, and

■ **Comparative management** studies how management practices differ among countries and cultures.

Canadian Managers
A Canadian Goes Global

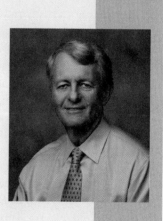

Henry "Hank" McKinnell, chairman and CEO of pharmaceutical company Pfizer Inc from 2001 to 2006, is the epitome of the global manager. Originally from Victoria, B.C., McKinnell worked at Pfizer's foreign offices for almost 14 years and speaks French, Japanese, and Arabic with some fluency. He joined Pfizer in 1971 in its Japan division, and then ran its business in Iran and Afghanistan, before becoming vice-president of the Asian division headquarters in Hong Kong. He then took a strategic planning position in New York, and eventually became CEO in 2001. His time abroad gave him a "great respect for diversity" and convinced him that a varied team could produce better results than either an individual or homogeneous group. To encourage employees to learn about other countries and to address the needs of patients and communities facing health challenges around the world, he started the Global Health Fellows program, which allows staff to use their skills in a six-month posting abroad.

Source: Zena Olijnyk, "Henry 'Hank' McKinnell," *Canadian Business*, March 2005.

able to marshal economic, social, technological, and other forces for the benefit of the organization.[51] As CEO of Willet International, a private UK-based company later bought over by Danaher Inc., Robert Willet maintained: "Our aim has always been to be a truly global company, not simply an exporter. We work very hard at developing and maintaining an international mindset that is shared by everyone—from senior management to staff."[52]

●●● PLANNING AND CONTROLLING

Planning and controlling are especially challenging in the complex environment of international businesses. Picture a home office in Vancouver. Foreign operations are scattered in Asia, Africa, South America, and Europe. Planning must somehow link the home office and foreign affiliates, while taking into account different countries, cultures, and needs. Increasingly, new technology facilitates the planning and control of global operations through vastly improved communications systems. Computer-based global networks and secure Web portals allow home and field offices to share databases, electronically transfer documents, hold virtual conferences, and make group decisions without face-to-face meetings.

■ **Currency risk** is possible loss because of fluctuating exchange rates.

Firms with investments in foreign countries must also factor into their planning the risks of doing business across political and economic borders. One risk is **currency risk**. As an export nation, Canada's economy is affected by the floating exchange rate between the Canadian dollar and foreign currencies, which impacts Canadian business greatly. In 2007, the Canadian dollar gained parity with the American dollar, making export products more expensive while making imports cheaper for the home market. This could potentially harm companies like Gildan, discussed in the opening vignette, who rely on the export market for their products.

■ **Political risk** is the possible loss of investment in or control over a foreign asset because of instability and political changes in the host country.

Another risk of international business is **political risk**, the potential loss of one's investment in or managerial control over a foreign asset because of instability and political changes in the host country. The major threats of political risk today come from terrorism, civil wars, armed conflicts and military disruptions, shifting government systems through elections or forced takeovers, and new laws and economic policies. **Political-risk analysis** is a planning process that forecasts the probability of disruptive events that can threaten the security of a foreign investment. The stakes in political risk analysis are quite high; even undertaking risk analysis is risky at best. For example, Danish companies suffered at the start of 2006 when they were boycotted by Muslim nations. This occurred after cartoons offensive to Muslims were published in Danish newspapers—something that even risk analysis could not have foreseen.

■ **Political-risk analysis** forecasts how political events may impact foreign investments.

●●● ORGANIZING AND LEADING

The same factors that challenge planning and controlling in the international arena also affect managerial efforts to organize and lead. The forces of globalization are complex indeed. For Caltex, it has meant closing a corporate headquarters in Dallas, Texas, and moving to Singapore. It has meant setting up a website development division in South Africa and an accounting division in the Philippines. Now part of Chevron-Texaco, the firm's goal is to leverage advancing technology and communications to build centres of excellence around the world.[53]

A common organizing approach for organizations just getting started in international business is to appoint a vice-president or other senior manager to oversee all foreign operations. This may be fine for limited international activity, but as global involvement expands, it usually requires a more complex arrangement. The *global area structure* shown in *Figure 5.5* arranges production and sales functions into separate geographical units. This allows activities in major areas of the world to be given special executive attention.

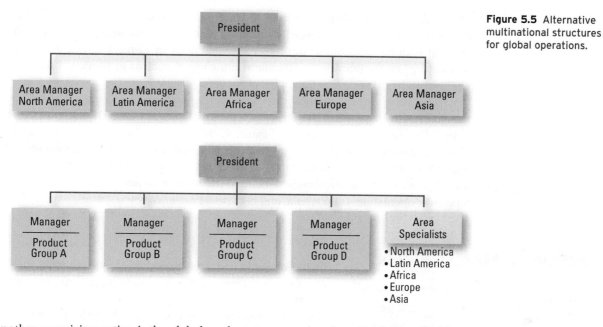

Figure 5.5 Alternative multinational structures for global operations.

Another organizing option is the *global product structure*, also shown in the figure. It gives worldwide responsibilities to product group managers, who are assisted by area specialists on the corporate staff. These specialists provide expert guidance on the unique needs of various countries or regions.

A guideline for staffing international operations can be stated this way: "Hire competent locals, use competent locals, and listen to competent locals." But in addition, global success also frequently depends on the work of **expatriates**—employees who live and work in foreign countries on short-term or long-term assignments. For progressive firms, assigning home office personnel to foreign operations is increasingly viewed as a strategic opportunity.[54] Not only does this offer the individuals challenging work experiences, it also helps bring into the executive suite culturally aware managers with truly global horizons and interpersonal networks of global contacts. Of course, not everyone performs well in an overseas assignment. Among the foundations for success are such personal attributes as a high degree of self-awareness and cultural sensitivity, a real desire to live and work abroad, family flexibility and support, as well as technical competence in one's job.

■ An **expatriate** lives and works in a foreign country.

●●● ARE MANAGEMENT THEORIES UNIVERSAL?

Management practices in North America and Western Europe frequently have been used as models around the world. Increasingly, however, a significant question is asked: "Are management theories universal?" Geert Hofstede, whose framework for understanding national cultures was introduced earlier, believes the answer is "No."[55] He worries that many theories are ethnocentric and fail to take into account cultural differences. For example, he argues that the North American emphasis on participation in leadership reflects the culture's moderate stance on power distance. National cultures with lower scores, such as Sweden and Israel, are characterized by even more "democratic" leadership initiatives. By contrast, the cultures of France and some Asian countries with higher power-distance scores are comfortable with hierarchy and less concerned with participative leadership.

Hofstede also points out that the motivation theories of American scholars tend to value individual performance. This is consistent with the high individualism found in some English-speaking countries such as Canada, the United States, and the United Kingdom.

Elsewhere, where values are more collectivist, the theories may be less applicable. Even a common value, such as the desire for increased humanization of work, may lead in different management directions. Until recently, practices in Canada largely emphasized redesigning jobs for individuals. Elsewhere in the world, such as in Sweden, the emphasis has been on redesigning jobs for groups of workers.

Consider as well the implications of transferring to Canada and other Western countries some of the Japanese management practices that have attracted great interest over the years.[56] Lifetime employment, gradual career advancement, and collective decision making have all been associated in one way or another with past successes in Japanese industry.[57] But as interesting as the practices may be, attempts to transfer them elsewhere must take into account the distinctive Japanese cultural traditions in which they emerged—such as long-term orientation, collectivism, and high power distance.[58]

PERSONAL MANAGEMENT

The complications of world events are ever-present reminders that **CULTURAL AWARENESS** is one of the great challenges of the 21st century. Consultant Richard Lewis warns of "cultural spectacles" that limit our vision, causing us to see and interpret things with the biases of our own culture.[63] You must learn to take off the spectacles and broaden your cultural horizons. The college and university campus is a great place to start. Its rich community of international students can take you around the world every day. Do you know, for example, that in Asian cultures Confucian values like the following are very influential?[64]

- *Harmony*—works well in a group, doesn't disrupt group order, puts group before self-interests.

- *Hierarchy*—accepts authority and hierarchical nature of society, doesn't challenge superiors.

- *Benevolence*—acts in a kind and understanding way toward others, paternalistic, willing to teach and help subordinates.

- *Loyalty*—loyal to organization and supervisor, dedicated to job, grateful for job and support of superior.

- *Learning*—eager for new knowledge, works hard to learn new job skills, strives for high performance.

Get to know yourself better

Complete Self-Assessments #8—**Global Readiness Index**, and #9—**Time Orientation** from the Workbook and Personal Management Activity #5 on the companion website.

●●● GLOBAL ORGANIZATIONAL LEARNING

In the dynamic and ever-expanding global economy, cultural awareness is helping to facilitate more informed transfers of management and organizational practices. We live at a fortunate time when managers around the world are realizing they have much to share with and learn from one another. Global organizational learning is a timely and relevant theme. This point is evident in the following words of Kenichi Ohmae, noted Japanese management consultant and author of *The Borderless World:*[59]

> *Companies can learn from one another, particularly from other excellent companies, both at home and abroad. The industrialized world is becoming increasingly homogeneous in terms of customer needs and social infrastructure, and only truly excellent companies can compete effectively in the global marketplace.*

Yes, we do have a lot to learn from one another.[60] Yet it must be learned with full appreciation of the constraints and opportunities of different cultures and country environments. Like the North American management practices before them, Japanese approaches and those from other cultures must be studied and adapted for local use very carefully. This applies to the way management is practised in Mexico, South Africa, Indonesia, Hungary, or any other part of the world. As Hofstede states: "Disregard of other cultures is a luxury only the strong can afford… increase in cultural awareness represents an intellectual and spiritual gain."[61]

When it comes to global organizational learning, however, not everyone and not every organization is ready. In some international businesses, **ethnocentric attitudes** still predominate.[62] Managers tend to view things from the perspective that the best approaches are always found at home. They fail to respect other practices and people, they tend to keep control of foreign operations at home, and they find little to learn from their international experiences. In other businesses, **polycentric attitudes** predominate. In these settings, managers respect the knowledge and practices of locals and allow them to largely run the operation in their countries. Learning, however, is still limited in that there is little transfer of experience from one location to the next. In the truly global business, **geocentric attitudes** create a rich global learning environment. Managers show a collaborative approach that links all international operations into a vast learning network, rich in information sharing. The emphasis is on deriving maximum advantage from best practices and the best people, wherever in the world they may be located.

Geocentric attitudes, displayed by managers and instilled in the corporate culture, offer the most opportunities for truly global organizational learning. Always, however, the approach to learning should be an alert, open, inquiring, and cautious one. It is important to both identify the potential merits of management practices found in other countries and understand how cultural differences may affect their success or failure when applied elsewhere. We should always be looking everywhere for new ideas. But we should hesitate to accept any practice, no matter how well it appears to work somewhere else, as a universal prescription to action. Indeed, the goal of comparative management studies is not to find universal principles. It is to help develop creative and critical thinking about the way managers around the world do things and about whether they can and should be doing them better.

■ **Ethnocentric attitudes** consider practices of the home country the best.

■ **Polycentric attitudes** assume locals know the best ways to manage in their countries.

■ **Geocentric attitudes** value talent and best practices from all over the world.

BE SURE YOU CAN

• discuss the international management implications of political risk • discuss the challenges of expatriate work • describe the differences between a global area structure and global product structure as ways of organizing for international operations • defend an answer to the question: "Do North American management theories apply universally around the world?"

✓ Learning check ❺

●●● Chapter 5   STUDY GUIDE

WHERE WE'VE BEEN

Back to Gildan Activewear Inc.

In the opening vignette, Gildan showed that Canadian companies can compete internationally by understanding the global economy and embracing new ways of managing. In Chapter 5 you learned about regional economic alliances and the complexities of international business, including the ethical issues faced by MNCs. You also learned about culture and how to examine differences among national cultures. Perhaps most importantly, you have been well introduced to a theme that must stay with you throughout your study of management—the importance of cross-cultural understanding and sensitivity.

THE NEXT STEP
INTEGRATED LEARNING ACTIVITIES

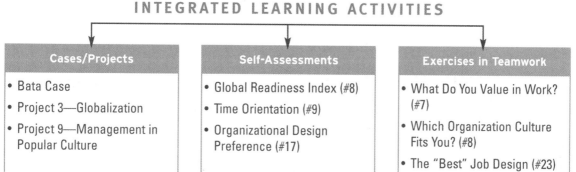

Cases/Projects	Self-Assessments	Exercises in Teamwork
• Bata Case	• Global Readiness Index (#8)	• What Do You Value in Work? (#7)
• Project 3—Globalization	• Time Orientation (#9)	• Which Organization Culture Fits You? (#8)
• Project 9—Management in Popular Culture	• Organizational Design Preference (#17)	• The "Best" Job Design (#23)

STUDY QUESTION SUMMARY

1. What are the international management challenges of globalization?

- International management is practised in organizations that conduct business in more than one country.

- Global managers are informed about international developments, transnational in outlook, competent in working with people from different cultures, and always aware of regional developments in a changing world.

- The global economy is making the diverse countries of the world increasingly interdependent regarding resource supplies, product markets, and business competition.

- The global economy is now strongly influenced by regional developments that involve growing economic integration in Europe, the Americas, and Asia, and the economic emergence of Africa.

2. What are the forms and opportunities of international business?

- Five forms of international business are global sourcing, exporting and importing, licensing and franchising, joint ventures, and wholly owned subsidiaries.

- The market entry strategies of global sourcing, exporting/importing, and licensing are common for firms wanting to get started internationally.

- Direct investment strategies to establish joint ventures or wholly owned subsidiaries in foreign countries represent substantial commitments to international operations.

- Global operations are influenced by important environmental differences among the economic, legal-political, and educational systems of countries.

3. What are multinational corporations and what do they do?

- A multinational corporation (MNC) is a business with extensive operations in more than one foreign country.

- True MNCs are global firms with worldwide missions and strategies that earn a substantial part of their revenues abroad.

- MNCs offer potential benefits to host countries in broader tax bases, new technologies, employment opportunities; MNCs can also disadvantage host countries if they interfere in local government, extract excessive profits, and dominate the local economy.

- *Corruption of Foreign Public Officials Act* prohibits Canadian MNCs from engaging in corrupt practices abroad.

4. What is culture and how does it relate to global diversity?

- The dimensions of popular culture include language, use of space, time orientation, religion, and the nature of contracts.

- Hofstede's dimensions of value differences in national cultures include power distance, uncertainty avoidance, individualism-collectivism, masculinity-femininity, and time orientation.

- Trompenaars's framework of cultural differences focuses on how people handle relationships with one another, their attitudes toward time, and their attitudes toward the environment.

5. How do management practices and learning transfer across cultures?

- The management process must be used appropriately and applied with sensitivity to local cultures and situations.

- The field of comparative management studies how management is practised around the world and how management ideas are transferred from one country or culture to the next.

- Management practices are influenced by cultural values; practices that are successful in one culture may work less well in others.

- The concept of global management learning has much to offer as the "borderless" world begins to emerge and as the management practices of diverse countries and cultures become more visible.

KEY TERMS REVIEW

Child labour (p. 119)

Comparative management (p. 125)

Corruption (p. 119)

Culture (p. 120)

Culture shock (p. 120)

Currency risk (p. 126)

Ethnocentric attitudes (p. 129)

Ethnocentrism (p. 120)

Euro (p. 110)

European Union (p. 110)

Expatriate (p. 127)

Exporting (p. 115)

Foreign subsidiary (p. 115)

Franchising (p. 115)

Geocentric attitudes (p. 129)

Global economy (p. 109)

Global manager (p. 109)

Global sourcing (p. 114)

Globalization (p. 109)

High-context culture (p. 121)

Importing (p. 115)

International business (p. 113)

International management (p. 109)

ISO 14000 (p. 119)

Joint ventures (p. 115)

Licensing agreement (p. 115)

Low-context culture (p. 121)

Maquiladora (p. 111)

Monochronic culture (p. 121)

Most favoured nation status (p. 117)

Multinational corporation (p. 117)

NAFTA (p. 110)

Political risk (p. 126)

Political-risk analysis (p. 126)

Polycentric attitude (p. 129)

Polychronic culture (p. 121)

Protectionism (p. 117)

Sustainable development (p. 119)

Sweatshop (p. 119)

Transnational corporation (p. 117)

World Trade Organization (p. 116)

SELF-TEST 5

MULTIPLE-CHOICE QUESTIONS:

1. In addition to gaining new markets, the reasons why businesses go international include the search for _____.
    (a) political risk (b) protectionism (c) lower labour costs (d) most favoured nation status

2. A _____ is a foreign firm that operates with special privileges in Mexico in return for agreeing to employ Mexican labour.
    (a) *keiretsu* (b) *maquiladora* (c) *jacaranda* (d) *zapatista*

3. A common form of international business that falls into the category of a direct investment strategy is _____.
    (a) exporting (b) joint venturing (c) licensing (d) global sourcing

4. The World Trade Organization, or WTO, would most likely become involved in disputes between countries over _____.
    (a) exchange rates (b) ethnocentrism (c) nationalization (d) tariffs and protectionism

5. If a new government seizes all foreign assets in the country and nationalizes them, the loss to foreign firms is a _____ risk of international business.
    (a) multinational (b) political (c) currency (d) social

6. In _____ cultures, members tend to do one thing at a time; in _____ cultures, members tend to do many things at once.
    (a) monochronic, polychronic (b) polycentric, geocentric (c) collectivist, individualist (d) neutral, affective

7. Business complaints about copyright protection and intellectual property rights in some countries illustrate how differences in _____ can impact international operations.
    (a) legal environments (b) political stability (c) sustainable development (d) economic systems

8. A firm operating with separate vice-presidents for Asian, African, and European divisions is using a global _____ structure.
    (a) product (b) functional (c) area (d) matrix

9. In Hofstede's study of national cultures, America was found to be highly _____ compared with other countries in his sample.
(a) individualistic (b) collectivist (c) feminine (d) long-term oriented

10. It is considered _____ when a foreign visitor takes offence at a local custom such as dining with one's fingers, considering it inferior to practices of his or her own culture.
(a) universalist (b) prescriptive (c) monochronic (d) enthnocentric

11. When a company buys cotton in Egypt and has pants sewn from it in Sri Lanka according to designs made in Italy for sale in the United State by catalogue orders, this form of international business is known as _____.
(a) licensing (b) importing (c) joint venturing (d) global sourcing

12. The difference between an international business and a transnational corporation is that the transnational _____.
(a) operates without a strong national identity (b) does business in only one or two foreign countries (c) is led by managers with ethnocentric attitudes (d) is ISO 14000 certified

13. The *Corruption of Foreign Public Officials Act* makes it illegal for _____.
(a) Canadians to contract with sweatshop operations abroad (b) foreign businesses to pay bribes to Canadian government officials (c) businesses to make "payoffs" abroad to gain international business contracts (d) foreign businesses to steal intellectual property from firms operating in their countries

14. In a high-context culture one would expect to find _____.
(a) low uncertainty avoidance (b) belief in achievement (c) an inner-directed orientation toward nature (d) emphasis on non-verbal as well as verbal communication

15. Hofstede would describe a culture in which members respect age and authority and in which workers defer to the preferences of their supervisors or team leaders as _____.
(a) low masculinity (b) high particularism (c) high power distance (d) monochronic

SHORT-RESPONSE QUESTIONS:

16. Why is NAFTA important for Canadian businesses?

17. Why do host countries sometimes complain about the operations of MNCs within their borders?

18. In what ways is the "power-distance" dimension of national culture important in management?

19. Choose a region of the world (Europe, the Americas, Africa, Asia) and describe its significance in the global economy.

APPLICATION QUESTION:

20. Kim has just returned from her first business trip to Japan. While there, she was impressed with the use of quality circles and work teams. Now back in British Columbia, she would like to start the same practices in her canoe-manufacturing company of 75 employees. Based on the discussion of culture and management in this chapter, what advice would you offer Kim?

Entrepreneurship and Small Business

Planning Ahead

After reading Chapter 6, you should be able to answer these questions in your own words.

1. What is entrepreneurship?

2. What is special about small businesses?

3. How does one start a new venture?

4. What resources support entrepreneurship and business development?

ACE

Support for the budding student entrepreneur

Do you see yourself as a Bill Gates, a James Pattison, a Richard Branson, or a Frank Stronach? Are you still at college or university? ACE (Advancing Canadian Entrepreneurship) may be the group for you to join.

Founded in 1987, this national not-for-profit organization has the stated goal of "teaching and igniting young Canadians to create brighter futures for themselves and their communities."

Located at 50 colleges and universities across Canada, there are over 80,000 students involved in ACE Projects with more than 2,000 student leaders on 49 ACE teams donating 55,000 volunteer hours. In 2000, ACE developed a strategic alliance with Students in Free Enterprise (SIFE), a non-profit group that has student teams involved in more than 500 SIFE projects located on university campuses in over 40 countries. Through the alliance, ACE can operate SIFE programs, in which student teams led by faculty advisors are challenged to develop community outreach projects based on five main educational topics:

- Market Economics
- Success Skills
- Entrepreneurship
- Financial Literacy
- Business Ethics

The projects are presented at both national and global competitions.

The 2005 SIFE Canada National Champions, from Wilfrid Laurier University, in Waterloo, Ontario developed numerous local initiatives and outreach programs in countries like Grenada and Egypt. So far, almost $700,000 has been reinvested into ACE communities.

For Joseph Fung, a winner of ACE's Student Entrepreneur of the Year Award, it has meant the opening of many doors. While a full-time student, he was the co-owner of Lewis Media, a web development company based in the Kitchener-Waterloo area. On winning the award he said, "It is a great opportunity for any student entrepreneur who wants to increase the profile of their business quickly and in a positive manner." This award, sponsored by CIBC, is one of two programs run by ACE.

As Brock University Student Alicia Konefal notes, "ACE has driven me to set my goals high and pursue them with the utmost passion." There is no doubt that ACE provides a great start to a promising business career. [1]

IN THE WORKPLACE

Your reputation is growing in your company after only a short time. Your ability to deal with a variety of challenges has caught the eye of senior members. Marc Ranger, the head of the "intrapreneur team," stops by to ask if you'd like to apply to run a start-up intrapreneur project. Flattered, you say you want some time to think about it. Marc says no problem, but please let him know by 5:00 p.m. You say that seems a rather short time to make a decision. Surprised, Marc says maybe he was wrong and that you might not have what it takes to be a successful entrepreneur. You say you'll let him know by 5:00 p.m. As Marc leaves, you wonder what the characteristics of a successful entrepreneur are. Do you have them?

We will discover that entrepreneurs like Frank Stronach at Magna International and Richard Branson at Virgin took risks. They invested their time and their own money to get their companies started. In Chapter 6 you will learn about entrepreneurship and the taking of business risks to pursue one's dreams. The chapter gives special attention to the small business context and the many opportunities it offers for people, including you, to one day start and own their own businesses.

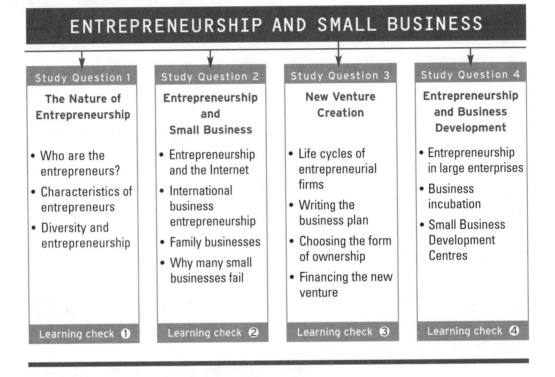

ENTREPRENEURSHIP AND SMALL BUSINESS

Study Question 1	Study Question 2	Study Question 3	Study Question 4
The Nature of Entrepreneurship	**Entrepreneurship and Small Business**	**New Venture Creation**	**Entrepreneurship and Business Development**
• Who are the entrepreneurs? • Characteristics of entrepreneurs • Diversity and entrepreneurship	• Entrepreneurship and the Internet • International business entrepreneurship • Family businesses • Why many small businesses fail	• Life cycles of entrepreneurial firms • Writing the business plan • Choosing the form of ownership • Financing the new venture	• Entrepreneurship in large enterprises • Business incubation • Small Business Development Centres
Learning check ❶	Learning check ❷	Learning check ❸	Learning check ❹

ACE highlights that getting involved with a local chapter "enables university and college students to reach their full potential by helping others reach theirs."[2] Through ACE, students are able to develop valuable hands-on leadership experience, gain business confidence, and network in a unique way. These networking opportunities include meeting CEOs from around the world at the SIFE conference, and attending national and international competitions in places like Paris and Barcelona. In turn, ACE team members' activities positively impact their local and international communities by helping to improve overall quality of life. This total experience equips ACE alumni to develop into successful entrepreneurs. ACEers, as they are also known, may also find themselves being recruited by leading companies, both large and small.

THE NATURE OF ENTREPRENEURSHIP

Today's dynamic environment demands that organizations and their managers adapt and renew themselves continually to succeed over time. People and organizations must change frequently and at a rapidly accelerating pace. Success in a highly competitive business environment, in particular, depends on **entrepreneurship**. This term is used to describe strategic thinking and risk-taking behaviour that result in the creation of new opportunities for individuals and/or organizations. H. Wayne Huizenga, a creator of three Fortune 500 companies, a five-time recipient of *Financial World* magazine's CEO of the Year, and the 2005 recipient of Ernst & Young's World Entrepreneur of the Year, describes it this way: "An important part of being an entrepreneur is a gut instinct that allows you to believe in your heart that something will work even though everyone else says it will not. You say, 'I am going to make sure it works. I am going to go out there and make it happen'."[3] These opportunities are illustrated in the success stories of business ventures that grew into large companies, such as the now-familiar Tim Hortons and Federal Express, or in successful products like 3M's popular Post-it® notes.

■ **Entrepreneurship** is dynamic, risk-taking, creative, growth-oriented behaviour.

●●● WHO ARE THE ENTREPRENEURS?

An **entrepreneur** is a risk-taking individual who takes action to pursue opportunities others fail to recognize, or even view as problems or threats. In the business context, an entrepreneur starts new ventures that bring to life new product or service ideas. Researchers are interested in the characteristics of entrepreneurs. They want to know what it takes to achieve entrepreneurial success.

■ An **entrepreneur** is willing to pursue opportunities in situations others view as problems or threats.

Before examining the findings, though, let's meet some real high-profile entrepreneurs. Their stories are rich with ideas for all of us to consider. Although the people and accomplishments are different, they have something in common. These entrepreneurs each built successful long-term businesses from good ideas and hard work.[4]

When Frank Stronach was 22 he left his native Austria to come to Montreal. With just a few hundred dollars, a suitcase, and an entrepreneurial willingness to work hard, he drew from his toolmaking know-how to build what is one of the world's largest automotive parts manufacturing companies. His company, Magna International Inc., has $6 billion in annual sales, 24,000 employees, and strategic alliances around the world. He did all of this by holding true to his vision of building a culture known as Fair Enterprise, which ensures the rights of employees, management, and investors to share in the profits they all help produce. Stronach wanted to give every employee a share of the company's profits, in a way making each of them a part-owner of the business with a stake in the company's success. It helped propel Magna to the world stage and enshrine Stronach as one of Canada's premier entrepreneurs.[5]

Want to start an airline? Richard Branson did, calling it Virgin Atlantic. But he started first in his native England with a student literary magazine and small mail-order record business. Since then, he's built "Virgin" into one of the world's most recognized brand names. Today, the Virgin Group is a business conglomerate employing some 25,000 people around the globe. It includes over 200 companies, including Virgin Mobile, Virgin Records, and even Virgin Cola. It's all very creative and ambitious, but that's Branson. "I love to learn things I know little about," he says.

Heather Reisman was born in Montreal and received her university education at McGill University. In 1979 she co-founded Paradigm Consulting, a strategy and change-management firm. Paradigm was the world's first strategic change consultancy and helped develop many organizational change strategies used today. In 1992, Reisman became president of Cott Corporation. During her time at the helm, Cott grew from a Canadian-based regional bottler to become the world's largest retailer-branded beverage supplier. In 1996, Reisman returned to her entrepreneurial roots and launched Indigo Books & Music Inc., combining two of her lifelong passions. Using a strong growth and change strategy, Indigo is now the largest book retailer in Canada, operating bookstores all across Canada.[6]

It's hard to do anything in Nova Scotia without stumbling over something Sobey. Nova Scotians buy their groceries at Sobeys stores; their conveniences at Needs, a Sobey-owned chain; their prescription drugs at Sobeys' Lawtons chain. If they go to a shopping mall, it is, likely as not, owned by a Sobey real estate company. The family even owns a chain of movie theatres. Frank Sobey changed the face of grocery and retailing in the Maritimes. Starting with only a small family butcher shop he worked hard at making it successful. Sobey believed in growing his company's business one customer at a time—he would pull over on the highway and help anyone in distress. His family carried on this neighbourly way of doing business and now Sobeys is the second-largest grocery chain in Canada.[7]

McMaster graduate Teresa Cascioli was the chair and chief executive officer of Lakeport Brewing Limited Partnership based in Hamilton, Ontario. This small brewery made big waves in the Ontario beer market before being purchased by Labatt in 2007. Cascioli took over a company that was in bankruptcy protection and made it profitable by cutting prices and expanding its market share through innovative ideas. Under Cascioli's guidance, Lakeport was once ranked one of Canada's fastest growing companies by *Profit* magazine. Cascioli herself has also been recognized as an "Entrepreneur of the Year" by Ernst & Young and inducted into the Canadian Sales Professional Association's Hall of Fame.[8]

Tim Horton opened his first doughnut and coffee store in 1964 in Hamilton, Ontario. Ron Joyce, a former police constable, saw through a newspaper advertisement that the NHL hockey player was looking for help in running his store. The two teamed up and Joyce proceeded to take out a $10,000 loan from the credit union to invest in the store. In 1965, Joyce took over the original Tim Hortons store with aspirations of expanding it to include 10 outlets. He acquired the whole operation in 1976 and drawing on unique products such as Timbits, creative marketing strategies like "Roll up the Rim," and a partnership with Dave Thomas of Wendy's, Joyce grew the company into Canada's largest national chain of coffee and doughnut shops, with over 2,000 stores across Canada and the United States.[9]

●●● CHARACTERISTICS OF ENTREPRENEURS

Do you find any common patterns in the prior examples? A common image of an entrepreneur is as the founder of a new business enterprise that achieves large-scale success, like the ones just mentioned. But, entrepreneurs also operate on a smaller and less public scale. Those who take the risk of buying a local McDonald's or Subway sandwich franchise, opening a small retail shop, or going into a self-employed service business are also entrepreneurs. Similarly, anyone who assumes responsibility for introducing a new product or change in operations within an organization is also demonstrating the qualities of entrepreneurship.

Obviously there's a lot to learn about entrepreneurs and entrepreneurship. Starting with the individual, however, indications are that entrepreneurs tend to share certain attitudes and personal characteristics. The general profile is of an individual who is very self-confident, determined, resilient, adaptable, and driven by excellence.[10] You should be able to identify these attributes in the prior examples. As shown in *Figure 6.1*, the typical personality traits and characteristics of entrepreneurs include the following:[11]

Figure 6.1 Personality traits and characteristics of entrepreneurs.

- *Internal locus of control:* Entrepreneurs believe that they are in control of their own destiny; they are self-directing and like autonomy.

- *High energy level:* Entrepreneurs are persistent, hard working, and willing to exert extraordinary efforts to succeed.

- *High need for achievement:* Entrepreneurs are motivated to accomplish challenging goals; they thrive on performance feedback.

- *Tolerance for ambiguity:* Entrepreneurs are risk takers; they tolerate situations with high degrees of uncertainty.

PERSONAL MANAGEMENT

Not everyone is comfortable with **RISK TAKING**. The uncertainty of risky situations is unsettling, and the anxieties are threatening for some of us. But risks, small and large, are a part of everyday living. In school and around campus there are many opportunities to explore your openness to risk and entrepreneurial tendencies. What will it take for you to start your own business or propose a new venture to your employer? Two former managers of Footlocker stores took the risk, and it paid off handsomely.[16] After noticing that customers kept asking for sports caps unavailable in stores, Glenn Campbell and Scott Molander decided to start a store of their own—Hat World. "People thought we were crazy," Campbell says. But Hat World took off, selling over 6,000 caps in two months. The entrepreneurs opened four more stores within a year. At last check, Campbell and Molander's risk turned into a firm with annual sales of $150+ million. Could this story be yours someday?

Get to know yourself better

Complete Self-Assessment #10—**Entrepreneurship Orientation**, and Exercise #8—**Which Organization Culture Fits You?**, from the Workbook and Personal Management Activity #6 on the companion website.

- *Self-confidence:* Entrepreneurs feel competent, believe in themselves, and are willing to make decisions.

- *Passion and action orientation:* Entrepreneurs try to act ahead of problems; they want to get things done and not waste valuable time.

- *Self-reliance and desire for independence:* Entrepreneurs want independence; they are self-reliant; they want to be their own boss, not work for others.

- *Flexibility:* Entrepreneurs are willing to admit problems and errors, and to change a course of action when plans aren't working.

In addition, research also suggests that entrepreneurs have unique backgrounds and personal experiences.[12] *Childhood experiences and family environment* seem to make a difference. Evidence links entrepreneurs with parents who were entrepreneurial and self-employed. Similarly, entrepreneurs are often raised in families that encourage responsibility, initiative, and independence. Another issue is *career or work history*. Entrepreneurs who try one venture often go on to others. Prior work experience in the business area or industry is helpful. Entrepreneurs also tend to emerge during certain *windows of career opportunity*. Most start their businesses between the ages of 22 and 45, an age span that seems to allow for risk taking. However, age is no barrier. When Tony DeSio was 50 he founded the Mail Boxes Etc. chain. He sold it for $300 million when he was 67 and suffering heart problems. Within a year he launched PixArts, another franchise chain, based on photography and art.[13]

Finally, a report in the *Harvard Business Review* suggests that entrepreneurs may have unique and *deeply embedded life interests*. The article describes entrepreneurs as having strong interests in creative production—enjoying project initiation, working with the unknown, and finding unconventional solutions. They also have strong interests in enterprise control—finding enjoyment from running things. The combination of creative production and enterprise control is characteristic of people who want to start things and move things toward a goal.[14]

Undoubtedly, entrepreneurs seek independence and the sense of mastery that comes with success. That seems to keep driving Tony DeSio in the example above. When asked by a reporter what he liked most about entrepreneurship, he replied: "Being able to make decisions without having to go through layers of corporate hierarchy—just being a master of your own destiny."[15]

●●● DIVERSITY AND ENTREPRENEURSHIP

Entrepreneurship is rich with diversity, and it grows richer by the day. In comparison with other countries, women in Canada make up a larger share of the self-employed population with over one-third of self-employed Canadians in 2002 being women. According to

MANAGER'S
Notepad 6.1

Challenging the myths about entrepreneurs

- *Entrepreneurs are born, not made.* Not true! Talent gained and enhanced by experience is a foundation for entrepreneurial success.

- *Entrepreneurs are gamblers.* Not true! Entrepreneurs are risk takers, but the risks are informed and calculated.

- *Money is the key to entrepreneurial success.* Not true! Money is no guarantee of success: There's a lot more to it than that; many entrepreneurs start with very little.

- *You have to be young to be an entrepreneur.* Not true! Age is no barrier to entrepreneurship; with age often comes experience, contacts, and other useful resources.

- *You have to have a degree in business to be an entrepreneur.* Not true! You may not need a degree at all; although a business degree is not necessary, it helps to study and understand business fundamentals.

Statistics Canada, there are more than 821,000 women entrepreneurs in Canada and growing; the number of women who are self-employed rose at a rate of over 8 percent annually. Women entrepreneurs are growing in number everywhere: they make up 38 percent of the self-employed Aboriginal population, 45 percent of ownership of Canadian small and medium enterprises (SMEs), and 31 percent ownership of both knowledge-based industry (KBI) firms and 31 percent of manufacturing firms.[17]

Clearly, entrepreneurship offers women opportunities of striking out on their own; it is also a pathway to opportunity that may be blocked otherwise. Among women leaving private-sector employment to strike out on their own, 33 percent said they were not being taken seriously by their prior employer and 29 percent said they had experienced "glass ceiling" issues.[18] In *Women Business Owners of Color: Challenges and Accomplishments*, the motivations of women of colour to pursue entrepreneurship because of glass ceiling problems are highlighted. These include not being recognized or valued by their prior employers, not being taken seriously, and seeing others promoted ahead of them.[19]

A report by Industry Canada, based on 2001 Census data, shows that entrepreneurship is opening business doors for visible minorities in Canada.[20] In that year, SMEs owned by visible minorities employed more than 500,000 people and generated revenues of more than $48.5 billion, an important contribution to Canada's economy. About 7 percent of Canada's 1.5 million SMEs were owned by visible minorities in 2001, and the percentage is growing as this group is now entering the SME marketplace at more than one and a half times the rate per year of other entrepreneurs. While most heavily concentrated in the service-based industries, the minority-owned SMEs are also twice as likely to be in a knowledge-based industry and are more likely to invest in research and development than are other SMEs. See *Manager's Notepad 6.1* for some challenges to common myths about entrepreneurship.[21]

BE SURE YOU CAN

• define the term entrepreneurship • list key personal characteristics of entrepreneurs • explain the influence of background and experience on entrepreneurs • discuss opportunities for entrepreneurship by women and minorities

✔ Learning check ❶

ENTREPRENEURSHIP AND SMALL BUSINESS

While there is no agreed upon definition of small business, it is generally accepted that organizations with under 10 employees are referred to as *microenterprises*, those with fewer than 100 employees are categorized as being small, while organizations with 100–500 employees are regarded as *medium-sized enterprises*.

The small business sector is very important in most nations of the world. Among other things, small businesses offer major economic advantages. According to Statistics Canada, in Canada just over 50 percent of the private labour force work in small businesses with an additional 16 percent working in medium-sized businesses.[22] Smaller businesses are especially prevalent in the service and retailing sectors of the economy. Higher costs of entry make them less common in other industries such as manufacturing and transportation.

There are many reasons why people pursue entrepreneurship and launch their own businesses. One study reports the following motivations: #1—wanting to be your own boss and controlling your future; #2—going to work for a family-owned business; and #3—seeking to fulfill a dream.[23] Only a very small percentage of respondents indicated that they had no other choice, such as having been laid off when their employer downsized.

▪ A **franchise** is when one business owner sells to another the right to operate the same business in another location.

Once a decision is made to go the small business route, the most common ways to get involved are: (1) start one, (2) buy an existing one, or (3) buy and run a **franchise**—where a business owner sells to another the right to operate the same business in another location. A franchise runs under the original owner's business name and guidance. In return, the franchise parent receives a share of income or a flat fee from the franchisee.

Canadian Managers

From Humble Beginnings to Toronto Landmark

No trip to Toronto is complete without a visit to Honest Ed's discount department store on Bloor Street, or for the more cultured, a show at the Royal Alexandra or Princess of Wales theatres. The entrepreneur behind these contrasting businesses was Ed Mirvish, the late Canadian icon and master of self-promotion. Despite his modest beginnings as a high school dropout working in his Russian immigrant parents' grocery store, Mirvish founded Canada's first discount retail establishment—Honest Ed's, "a one-of-a-kind bargain centre that has everything from wine to twine"—in the 1940s. He went on to save the Royal Alexandra Theatre from demolition in 1963, build the Princess of Wales Theatre with his son David in 1993, and then develop Mirvish Village around Honest Ed's.

Source: "The Life and Times of Ed Mirvish," CBC Website (www.cbc.ca); Mirvish Enterprises news release, "City commemorates Ed Mirvish's 90th birthday with a plaque at Honest Ed's," July 16, 2004

●●● ENTREPRENEURSHIP AND THE INTERNET

Have you started a "dot-com" today? The Internet has opened a whole new array of entrepreneurial possibilities. Just take a look at the action on eBay and imagine how many people are now running small trading businesses from their homes. It is estimated that a majority of small firms are conducting business over the Internet. Many of these firms are existing firms that modified traditional ways to pursue new Internet-driven opportunities. For some of these, the old ways of operating from a bricks-and-mortar retail establishment have given way to entirely online business activities.

Internet entrepreneurship isn't limited to trading through eBay or trying to create the next amazon.com. A growing area for Internet entrepreneurship is B2B, specialized business-to-business websites that link buyers and sellers. The opportunities for B2B entrepreneurship are many. If interested, you just need to let your creativity go to work.[24]

●●● INTERNATIONAL BUSINESS ENTREPRENEURSHIP

In the last chapter the reasons why businesses go international were discussed. The same global opportunities exist for smaller businesses. They also often find that international business brings opportunities for expanded markets, additional financing, access to quality and possibly lower-cost resources, access to labour and technical expertise, and locations for low-cost manufacturing or outsourcing. The Internet now makes selling abroad relatively easy; today's advanced distribution systems also make product delivery quick and efficient. Additionally, smaller businesses can find alliance opportunities in strategic ventures with foreign partners.

As the economies of the world's countries improve and the overall standards of living rise, consumer demand for goods and services grows as well. Governments, federal and provincial, encourage small businesses to explore and expand export activities. For example, in Ontario the Ministry of Economic Development offers business consulting services to small and mid-sized companies in the manufacturing and service industries. In eastern Canada, Team Canada Atlantic, a partnership of the four Atlantic provinces and the Atlantic Canada Opportunities Agency, optimizes export opportunities by coordinating trade missions and other trade-related activities to increase export opportunities for Atlantic Canadian companies.

Many smaller companies are seeking diversification opportunities abroad. With diversification comes some insurance against the risk of economic slowdown in any one area. If domestic business declines, the hope is that international business will take up the slack. Of course, it takes investment to move any business, small or large, toward international opportunities. One has to invest in travel, communication, and time to build relationships and gain expertise. But there is considerable support available. International Trade Canada, with regional offices in all provinces, provides trade development advice through one-on-one consultations, market and industry information, and advice on export financing. Many other resources are available to those trying to get started in international business. You just have to look.

●●● FAMILY BUSINESSES

Family businesses, ones owned and financially controlled by family members, represent the largest percentage of businesses operating worldwide. Family businesses must solve the same problems of other small or large businesses—meeting the challenges of strategy, competitive advantage, and operational excellence. When everything goes right, the family firm is almost an ideal situation—everyone working together, sharing values and a common goal, and knowing that what they do benefits the family. But it doesn't always work out this way or stay this way as a business changes hands over successive generations. Indeed, family businesses often face quite unique problems.

"Okay, Dad, so he's your brother. But does that mean we have to put up with inferior work and an erratic schedule that we would never tolerate from anyone else in the business?"[25] This conversation introduces a problem that can all too often set the stage for failure in a family

▪ A **family business** is owned and controlled by members of a family.

business—the *family business feud*. Simply put, members of the controlling family get into disagreements about work responsibilities, business strategy, operating approaches, finances, or other matters. The example is indicative of an intergenerational problem, but the feud can be between spouses, among siblings, between parents and children. It really doesn't matter. Unless disagreements are resolved satisfactorily among family members and to the benefit of the business itself, the firm will have difficulty surviving in a highly competitive environment.

■ **The succession problem** is the issue of who will run the business when the current head leaves.

Another significant problem faced by family businesses is the **succession problem**—transferring leadership from one generation to the next. A survey of small and mid-sized family businesses indicated that 66 percent planned on keeping the business within the family.[26] The management question is: How will the assets be distributed and who will run the business when the current head leaves? Although this problem is not specific to the small firm, it is especially significant in the family business context. The data on succession are eye-opening. About 30 percent of family firms survive to the second generation; only 12 percent survive to the third; only 3 percent are expected to survive beyond that.[27] In Canada, the Sobey family has been a real success story of how to plan a successful transfer of the leadership reins from one generation to the next; on the opposite end of the continuum might be the McCain family who, although keeping the business profitable, did not have such an amicable succession.

■ **A succession plan** describes how the leadership transition and related financial matters will be handled.

A family business that has been in operation for some time is a source of both business momentum and financial wealth. Both must be maintained in the succession process. Business advisors recommend a **succession plan**—a formal statement that describes how the leadership transition and related financial matters will be handled when the time for changeover arrives. *A succession plan should include* at least procedures for choosing or designating the firm's new leadership, legal aspects of any ownership transfer, and any financial and estate plans relating to the transfer. The foundations for effective implementation of a succession plan are set up well ahead of the need to use it. The plan should be shared and understood among all affected by it. The chosen successor should be prepared through experience and training to perform the new role when needed.

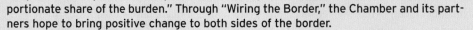

AROUND THE WORLD

Chamber of Commerce connects businesses across borders

Through a special program called "Wiring the Border," the United States-Mexico Chamber of Commerce is helping border companies tap the e-commerce marketplace. The Chamber's president, Albert C. Zapanta, says: "This initiative will help small businesses reach the international marketplace and compete effectively around the world." Major US and Mexican corporations, including IBM and TelMex, are helping to sponsor the program. The partners are contributing Web-enabling components. The member small businesses will be joined in a virtual network that will utilize e-commerce to increase sales, profits, and employment. Zapanta says: "Communities along the border have not shared in the economic growth enjoyed by most Americans the past several years, but they have borne a disproportionate share of the burden." Through "Wiring the Border," the Chamber and its partners hope to bring positive change to both sides of the border.

Source: Information from Scott Williams, "Program to Help Firms Enter the Internet Marketplace," *Hispanic Business* (August 2000); and information on the program website: <www.usmcoc.org/wiringdescription.html>

●●● WHY MANY SMALL BUSINESSES FAIL

Small businesses have a high failure rate—one high enough to be scary. A high proportion of new businesses fail in their first five years of operation. Part of this is a "counting" issue—the government counts as a "failure" any business that closes, whether it is due to the death or retirement of an owner, sale to someone else, or the inability to earn a profit.[28] Nevertheless, the fact remains: a lot of small business start-ups don't make it. And as shown in *Figure 6.2*, most of the failures are due to bad judgement and management mistakes made by entrepreneurs and owners. The following errors are common causes of small business failures.[29]

- *Lack of experience*—not having sufficient know-how to run a business in the chosen market or area.

- *Lack of expertise*—not having expertise in the essentials of business operations, including finance, purchasing, selling, and production.

- *Lack of strategy and strategic leadership*—not taking the time to craft a vision and mission, or formulate and properly implement strategy.

- *Poor financial control*—not keeping track of the numbers and failure to control business finances.

- *Growing too fast*—not taking the time to consolidate a position, fine-tune the organization, and systematically meet the challenges of growth.

- *Insufficient commitment*—not devoting enough time to the requirements of running a competitive business.

- *Ethical failure*—falling prey to the temptations of fraud, deception, and embezzlement.

Figure 6.2 Eight reasons why many small businesses fail.

BE SURE YOU CAN

• define a small business • illustrate opportunities for entrepreneurship on the Internet and in international business • discuss the succession problem in family-owned businesses and possible ways to deal with it • list several reasons why many small businesses fail

✔ Learning check ❷

NEW VENTURE CREATION

Now that the reasons for business failure have been described, let's talk about doing it right. Whether your interest is low-tech or high-tech, online or offline, opportunities for new ventures are always there for the true entrepreneur. To pursue entrepreneurship and start a new venture, you need good ideas and the courage to give them a chance. But you must also be prepared to meet and master the test of strategy and competitive advantage. Can you identify a *market niche* that is being missed by other established firms? Can you identify a *new market* that has not yet been discovered by existing firms? Can you generate **first-mover advantage** by exploiting a niche or entering a market before competitors? These are among the questions that entrepreneurs must ask and answer in the process of beginning a new venture. Of course, a focus on the customer is critical, too, as suggested in *Manager's Notepad 6.2*.[30]

■ **A first-mover advantage** comes from being first to exploit a niche or enter a market.

●●● LIFE CYCLES OF ENTREPRENEURIAL FIRMS

Figure 6.3 describes the stages common to the life cycles of entrepreneurial companies. It shows the relatively predictable progression of the small business.[31] The firm begins with the *birth stage*—where the entrepreneur struggles to get the new venture established and survive long enough to test the viability of the underlying business model in the marketplace. The firm then passes into the *breakthough stage*—where the business model begins to work well, growth is experienced, and the complexity of managing the business operation expands significantly. Next comes the *maturity stage*—where the entrepreneur experiences the advantages of market success and financial stability, while also facing continuing management challenges of remaining competitive in a changing environment.

MANAGER'S
Notepad 6.2

Questions that keep a new venture focused on its customers

- Who is your customer?
- How will you reach customers in key market segments?
- What determines customer choices to buy your product/service?
- Why is your product/service a compelling choice for the customer?
- How will you price your product/service for the customer?
- How much does it cost to make and deliver your product/service?
- How much does it cost to attract a customer?
- How much does it cost to support and retain a customer?

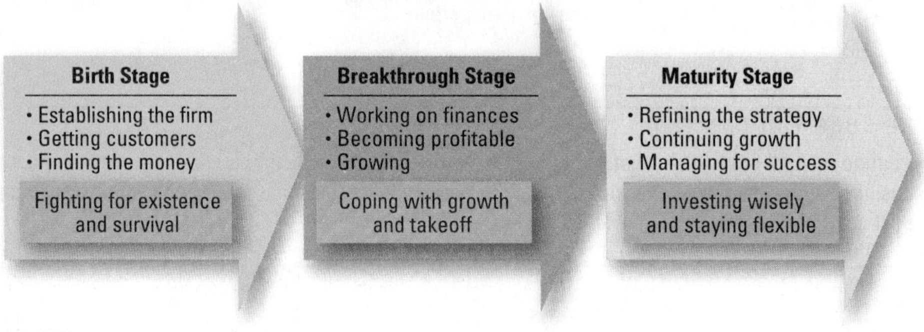

Figure 6.3 Stages in the life cycle of an entrepreneurial firm.

Birth Stage	**Breakthrough Stage**	**Maturity Stage**
• Establishing the firm • Getting customers • Finding the money	• Working on finances • Becoming profitable • Growing	• Refining the strategy • Continuing growth • Managing for success
Fighting for existence and survival	Coping with growth and takeoff	Investing wisely and staying flexible

Entrepreneurs often face control and management dilemmas when their firms experience growth, including possible diversification or global expansion. They encounter a variation of the succession problem described earlier for family businesses. This time the problem is succession from entrepreneurial leadership to professional strategic leadership. The former brings the venture into being and sees it through the early stages of life; the latter manages and leads the venture into maturity as an ever-evolving and perhaps still-growing corporate enterprise. If the entrepreneur is incapable of meeting or unwilling to meet the firm's leadership needs in later life-cycle stages, continued business survival and success may well depend on the business being sold or management control being passed to professionals.

●●● WRITING THE BUSINESS PLAN

When people start new businesses, or even start new units within existing ones, they can greatly benefit from a good **business plan**. This is a plan that describes the details needed to obtain start-up financing and operate a new business.[32] Banks and other financiers want to see a business plan before they loan money or invest in a new venture; senior managers want to see a business plan before they allocate scarce organizational resources to support a new entrepreneurial project. Importantly, the detailed thinking required to prepare a business plan can contribute to the success of the new initiative. As an old adage states, "If you fail to plan, you plan to fail."

■ A **business plan** describes the direction for a new business and the financing needed to operate it.

MANAGER'S
Notepad 6.3

What to include in a business plan

- *Executive summary*–overview of business purpose and highlight of key elements of the plan

- *Industry analysis*–nature of the industry, including economic trends, important legal or regulatory issues, and potential risks

- *Company description*–mission, owners, and legal form

- *Products and services description*–major goods or services, with special focus on uniqueness vis-à-vis competition

- *Market description*–size of market, competitor strengths and weaknesses, five-year sales goals

- *Marketing strategy*–product characteristics, distribution, promotion, pricing, and market research

- *Operations description*–manufacturing or service methods, supplies and suppliers, and control procedures

- *Staffing description*–management and staffing skills needed and available, compensation, human resource systems

- *Financial projection*–cash flow projections for one to five years, break-even points, and phased investment capital

- *Capital needs*–amount of funds needed to run the business, amount available, amount requested from new sources

- *Milestones*–a timetable of dates showing when key stages of new venture will be completed

Although there is no single template for a successful business plan, there is general agreement on the framework presented in *Manager's Notepad 6.3*.[33] Any business plan should have an executive summary, cover certain business fundamentals, be well-organized with headings, be easy to read, and be no more than about 20 pages in length. One of the great advantages of a business plan, of course, is forcing the entrepreneur to think through important issues and challenges before starting out. In addition to advice you find in books and magazines, there are many online resources available to assist in the development of a business plan. Among the alternatives are American Express Small Business Services, businesstown.com, and bizplanit.com.

●●● CHOOSING THE FORM OF OWNERSHIP

One of the important planning choices that must be made in starting a new venture is the legal form of ownership. There are a number of alternatives, and the choice among them involves careful consideration of their respective advantages and disadvantages. Briefly, the ownership forms include the following.

■ A **sole proprietorship** is an individual pursuing business for a profit.

A **sole proprietorship** is simply an individual or a married couple pursuing business for a profit. This does not involve incorporation. One does business, for example, under a personal name—such as "Tiana Lopez Designs." A sole proprietorship is simple to start, run, and terminate. However, the business owner is personally liable for business debts and claims. This is the most common form of small business ownership in Canada.

■ A **partnership** is when two or more people agree to contribute resources to start and operate a business together.

A **partnership** is formed when two or more people agree to contribute resources to start and operate a business together. Most typically it is backed by a legal and written partnership agreement. Business partners agree on the contribution of resources and skills to the new venture and on the sharing of profits and losses. In a *general partnership*, the simplest and most common form, they also share management responsibilities. A *limited partnership* consists of a general partner and one or more "limited" partners who do not participate in day-to-day business management. They share in profits, but their losses are limited to the amount of their investment. A *limited liability partnership*, common among professionals such as accountants and lawyers, limits the liability of one partner for the negligence of another.

■ A **corporation** is a legal entity that exists separately from its owners.

A **corporation**, commonly identified by the "Inc." designation in a name, is a legal entity that exists separately from its owners. The corporation can be for-profit, such as Microsoft Inc., or not-for-profit, such as the Canadian Red Cross Society. The corporate form offers two major advantages: (1) it grants the organization certain legal rights (e.g., to engage in contracts), and (2) the corporation becomes responsible for its own liabilities. This separates the owners from personal liability and gives the firm a life of its own that can extend beyond that of its owners. The disadvantage of incorporation rests largely with the cost of incorporating and the complexity of the documentation required to operate an incorporated business.

■ A **limited liability corporation** (LLC) is a hybrid business form combining advantages of the sole propietorship, partnership, and corporation.

Recently, the **limited liability corporation** (LLC) has gained popularity. A limited liability corporation combines the advantages of the other forms—sole proprietorship, partnership, and corporation. For liability purposes, it functions like a corporation, protecting the assets of owners against claims made against the company. For tax purposes, it functions as a partnership in the case of multiple owners and as a sole proprietorship in the case of a single owner.

●●● FINANCING THE NEW VENTURE

■ **Debt financing** involves borrowing money that must be repaid over time with interest.

Starting a new venture takes money, and that money often must be raised. The cost of start-up will most likely exceed the amount available from personal sources. There are two major ways the entrepreneur can obtain outside financing for a new venture. **Debt financing** involves going into debt by borrowing money from another person, a bank, or a financial institution. This loan must be paid back over time with interest. A loan also requires collateral that pledges business assets or personal assets, such as a home, to secure the loan in case of default. **Equity financing** involves giving ownership shares in the business to outsiders in return for outside investment monies. This money does not need to be paid back. It is an investment, and the investor assumes the risk for potential gains and losses. In return for taking that risk, the equity investor gains some proportionate ownership control.

> ■ **Equity financing** involves exchanging ownership shares for outside investment monies.

Equity financing is usually obtained from **venture capitalists**, companies that pool capital and make investments in new ventures in return for an equity stake in the business. Typically, venture capitalists finance only a very small proportion of new ventures. They tend to focus on relatively large investments, such as $1 million or more, and they usually take a management role in order to grow the business and add value as soon as possible. Sometimes that value is returned when a fast-growing firm gains a solid market base and becomes a candidate for an **initial public offering**, or IPO. This is when shares of stock in the business are first sold to the public and then begin trading on a major stock exchange. When an IPO is successful and the share prices are bid up by the market, the original investments of the venture capitalist and entrepreneur rise in value. The anticipation of such return on investment is a large part of the venture capitalist's motivation; indeed, it is the nature of the venture capital business.

> ■ **Venture capitalists** make large investments in new ventures in return for an equity stake in the business.

> ■ An **initial public offering** (IPO) is an initial selling of shares of stock to the public at large.

take it to the case!

Hannah's Ice Cream
Entrepreneurs face many challenges

Do you dream of owning your own business? As our fictional Ike Telloni found out when he bought Hannah's Ice Cream, there is more to being an entrepreneur than just wanting to run a business. As a kid, Ike dreamt of being his own boss and while in school he excelled at business courses and received numerous awards for entrepreneurship. After starting his career at Waterloo Ice Cream Company, Ike felt it was time to realize his dream and bought a successful business in his hometown of Elgin Beach, Ontario. Despite his business background, Ike found he was unprepared for the challenges of owning a small business. Read the case in the *Management Learning Workbook* to see how well-prepared you are to be your own boss!

Of the many venture capital firms, very few specifically seek investments in women-owned companies. Even though women are starting more new businesses than ever before, they don't get as much of the available venture capital as men. When venture capital isn't available to the entrepreneur, male or female, another important financing option is the **angel investor**. This is a wealthy individual who is willing to make an investment in return for equity in a new venture. Angel investors are especially common and helpful in the very early start-up stage. Their presence can help raise the confidence and interests of other venture capitalists and attract additional venture funding that would otherwise not be available. For

> ■ An **angel investor** is a wealthy individual willing to invest in return for equity in a new venture.

example, when Liz Cobb wanted to start her sales compensation firm, Incentive Systems, she contacted 15 to 20 venture capital firms. She was interviewed by 10 and turned down by all of them. After she located $250,000 from two angel investors, the venture capital firms got interested again. She was able to obtain her first $2 million in financing and has since built the firm into a 70-plus employee business.[34]

Learning check ③

BE SURE YOU CAN
• explain the concept of first-mover advantage in new venture creation • illustrate new venture life-cycle stages from birth to breakthrough to maturity • identify the major elements in a business plan • differentiate between common forms of small business ownership—sole proprietorship, partnership, and corporation • differentiate between debt financing and equity financing • explain the roles of venture capitalists and angel investors in new venture financing

ENTREPRENEURSHIP AND BUSINESS DEVELOPMENT

Entrepreneurship is indispensable to a healthy and growing economy, whether one is talking about a local community or an entire nation. It provides the creative spark to launch the small businesses and new ventures that are so important to job creation and economic development. It also provides the engine that drives innovation and business development within large enterprises.

CANADIAN COMPANY IN THE NEWS   Nk'Mip Cellars

ABORIGINAL WINERY PROVES FRUITFUL

Nk'Mip (pronounced in-ka-meep) Cellars, the first Aboriginal-owned and -operated vintner in North America, is a joint venture between the Osoyoos Indian Band and Vincor International, the maker of Jackson-Triggs and Inniskillin wines. Although the B.C. winery opened in August 2002, the band had been growing grapes for decades. It planted 93 hectares in 1968, growing grapes for other wineries. But in 2000, it started producing its own wine. By 2004, Nk'Mip Cellars was cultivating about 460 hectares annually. The Osoyoos Indian Band (Nk'Mip in the Okanagan language) has about 370 members living on its reserve. Economic activity has traditionally included ranching, trading, and farming; now the band is known for growing quality grapes and producing quality wines. In their first four years of production, Nk'Mip wines received several awards and accolades, and all have the Vintners Quality Alliance seal.

Source: D. Grant Black, "Native winery breaks new ground in the Okanagan," *The Globe and Mail*, June 5, 2004.

●●● ENTREPRENEURSHIP IN LARGE ENTERPRISES

Just like their smaller counterparts, large organizations depend on the entrepreneurial spirit to drive innovation for sustained competitive advantage. High performance in dynamic and competitive environments increasingly depends on the creative contributions of workers who are willing to assume risk and take initiative. Yet, paradoxically, the natural tendencies of very large and complex systems may be toward stability, rigidity, and avoidance of risk.

The concept of **intrapreneurship** describes entrepreneurial behaviour by people and subunits operating within large organizations.[35] Through the efforts of *intrapreneurs*, large organizations are able to turn new ideas into profitable new products, services, and business ventures. At Trilogy Software Inc., for example, talented engineers are hired directly from college. They attend Trilogy University for three months, learning about the company and its mission, executives, and expectations. They are told that they are responsible for creating the company's new revenues. The "university" experience is designed to start the creative process and build networks for entrepreneurship and internal business development. So far Trilogy has created from within itself six successful new ventures.[36]

Managers often find that gaining a competitive edge and success through intrapreneurship depends on the ability of large organizations to act like small ones. To do this, they create small subunits, often called **skunkworks**, in which teams are allowed to work together in a unique setting that is highly creative and free of the operating restrictions of the larger parent organization. A classic example occurred at Apple Computer Inc., where a small group of enthusiastic employees was once sent off to a separate facility in Cupertino, California. Their mandate was straightforward: to create a state-of-the-art, user-friendly personal computer. The group operated free of the firm's normal product development bureaucracy, set its own norms, and worked together without outside interference. The "Jolly Roger" was even raised over their building as a symbol of independence. It worked. This team brought the now-famous Macintosh computer into being.

> ■ **Intrapreneurship** is entrepreneurial behaviour displayed by people or subunits within large organizations.

> ■ **Skunkworks** are teams allowed to work creatively together, free of constraints from the larger organization.

●●● BUSINESS INCUBATION

One of the advantages of intrapreneurship is that it takes place in a larger organizational environment that can be highly supportive in terms of money and other startup resources. Individual entrepreneurs, who must start on their own, face quite a different set of challenges. Even though entrepreneurship and new venture creation are creative and exciting prospects, they are also potentially daunting in complexity and required resources.

One way that the motivation toward entrepreneurship can be maintained is through the support of a **business incubator**. This is a special facility that offers space, a variety of shared administrative services, and management advice to help small businesses get started. Some incubators are focused on specific businesses such as technology, manufacturing, or services; some are in more rural areas, others are city based. But regardless of focus and location, incubators share the common goal of helping to build successful new businesses that create jobs and improve economic development. They pursue this goal by nurturing start-up businesses in the incubators to help them to grow more quickly and become healthy enough to survive on their own. And, of course, the expected benefits include job and wealth creation in the economies of local communities.

> ■ **Business incubators** offer space, shared services, and advice to help small businesses get started.

●●● SMALL BUSINESS DEVELOPMENT CENTRES

With small business playing such an important economic role, a variety of resources are available to promote their development. **Small Business Development Centres** (SBDCs) offer guidance to entrepreneurs and small business owners—actual and prospective—in how to set up and successfully run a business operation. Often these centres are associated with universities or colleges. For example, in Antigonish, Nova Scotia, the Saint Francis Xavier Enterprise Development Centre (XEDC) is a valuable resource for individuals

> ■ **Small business development centres** offer guidance and support to small business owners in how to set up and run a business operation.

considering starting a business, for existing small and medium-sized business owners interested in growth or facing challenges in their business, as well as for not-for-profit community development organizations. They offer opportunities for students to become involved as consultants and learn first-hand the nature of small business and entrepreneurship.

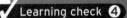

Learning check ④

BE SURE YOU CAN

• define the term intrapreneurship and differentiate it from entrepreneurship • explain the purpose of business incubators • explain how small business development centres try to help people start and operate small businesses

●●● Chapter 6 STUDY GUIDE

WHERE WE'VE BEEN

Back to ACE

The opening example of ACE showed how you can start your entrepreneurial journey while still at school. In Chapter 6, and through its many examples, you learned about entrepreneurship and the characteristics of entrepreneurs. You learned some of the basic elements of starting a new venture, and you learned about the nature of business ownership. Importantly, throughout the chapter you have been exposed to many issues and examples introducing the world of career opportunity that exists in entrepreneurship and small business ownership.

THE NEXT STEP
INTEGRATED LEARNING ACTIVITIES

Cases/Projects	Self-Assessments	Exercises in Teamwork
• Hannah's Ice Cream	• Entrepreneurship Orientation (#10) • Turbulence Tolerance Test (#16) • Internal/External Control (#26)	• Strategic Scenarios (#12) • Work vs. Family (#17) • Why Do We Work? (#21)

STUDY QUESTION SUMMARY

1. What is entrepreneurship?

• Entrepreneurship is risk-taking behaviour that results in the creation of new opportunities for individuals and/or organizations.

• An entrepreneur is someone who takes risks to pursue opportunities in situations others may view as problems or threats.

• The examples of entrepreneurs like Frank

Stronach, Richard Branson, Heather Reisman, and Teresa Cascioli can be a source of learning and inspiration for others.

- Entrepreneurs tend to be creative people who are self-confident, determined, resilient, adaptable, and driven to excel; they like to be masters of their own destinies.

- Entrepreneurship is rich with diversity, with women and minority-owned business start-ups increasing in numbers.

2. What is special about small businesses?

- Entrepreneurship results in the founding of many small business enterprises that offer job creation and other benefits to economies.

- The Internet has opened a whole new array of entrepreneurial possibilities, including online buying and selling and the more formal pursuit of dot-com businesses.

- Smaller businesses are pursuing more global opportunities in the quest for expanded markets, access to labour and technical expertise, and locations for low-cost manufacturing or outsourcing.

- Family businesses that are owned and financially controlled by family members represent the largest percentage of businesses operating worldwide.

- A significant problem faced by family businesses is the succession problem of transferring leadership from one generation to the next.

- Small businesses have a high failure rate; as many as 60 to 80 percent of new businesses fail in their first five years of operation.

- Small business failures are largely due to poor management, when owners make bad decisions on major business matters.

3. How does one start a new venture?

- Entrepreneurial firms tend to follow the life-cycle stages of birth, breakthrough, and maturity, with each stage offering different management challenges.

- New start-ups should be guided by a good business plan that describes the intended nature of the business, how it will operate, and how financing will be obtained.

- An important choice is the form of business ownership, with the proprietorship, corporate, and limited liability forms offering different advantages and disadvantages.

- Two basic ways of financing a new venture are through debt financing, by taking loans, and equity financing, which exchanges ownership shares in return for outside investment.

- Venture capitalists pool capital and make investments in new ventures in return for an equity stake in the business.

- The angel investor is a wealthy individual who is willing to invest money in return for equity in a new venture.

4. What resources support entrepreneurship and business development?

- Intrapreneurship, or entrepreneurial behaviour within larger organizations, is important in today's competitive environment.

- Business incubators offer space, shared services, and advice to small businesses in the start-up stages.

- Small businesses can get a variety of forms of support and assistance from small business development centres funded by federal and provincial government sources.

KEY TERMS REVIEW

Angel investor (p. 149)

Business incubator (p. 151)

Business plan (p. 147)

Corporation (p. 148)

Debt financing (p. 148)

Entrepreneur (p. 137)

Entrepreneurship (p. 137)

Equity financing (p. 149)

Family business (p. 143)

First-mover advantage (p. 146)

Franchise (p. 142)

Initial public offering (IPO) (p. 149)

Intrapreneurship (p. 151)

Limited liability corporation (p. 148)

Partnership (p. 148)

Skunkworks (p. 151)

Small Business Development Centre (p. 151)

Sole proprietorship (p. 148)

Succession plan (p. 144)

Succession problem (p. 144)

Venture capitalists (p. 149)

SELF-TEST 6

MULTIPLE-CHOICE QUESTIONS:

1. _____ is among the personality characteristics commonly found among entrepreneurs.
    (a) External locus of control (b) Inflexibility (c) Self-confidence (d) low tolerance for ambiguity

2. When an entrepreneur is comfortable with uncertainty and willing to take risks, these are indicators of someone with a(n) _____.
    (a) high tolerance for ambiguity (b) internal locus of control (c) need for achievement (d) action orientation

3. Organizations with fewer than 100 employees are referred to as _____.
    (a) medium-sized enterprises (b) small businesses (c) microenterprises (d) skunkworks

4. When a business owner sells to another person the right to operate that business in another location, this is a _____.
    (a) conglomerate (b) franchise (c) joint venture (d) limited partnership

5. A small business owner who is concerned about passing the business on to heirs after retirement or death should prepare a formal _____ plan.
    (a) retirement (b) succession (c) franchising (d) liquidation

6. Among the most common reasons that new small business start-ups often fail is _____.
    (a) lack of business expertise (b) strict financial controls (c) slow growth (d) high ethical standards

7. When a new business is quick to capture a market niche before competitors, this is called _____.
    (a) intrapreneurship (b) an initial public offering (c) succession planning (d) first-mover advantage

8. When a small business is just starting, the business owner is typically struggling to _____.
    (a) gain acceptance in the marketplace (b) find partners for expansion (c) prepare an initial public offering (d) bring professional skills into the management team

9. A venture capitalist who receives an ownership share in return for investing in a new business is providing _____ financing.
    (a) debt (b) equity (c) corporate (d) partnership

10. _____ is a term used to describe a small group of people operating with independence and in the expectation of being highly creative within a large organization.
    (a) Skunkworks (b) Product team (c) Focus group (d) Leadership council

11. _____ take ownership shares in a new venture in return for providing the entrepreneur with critical start-up funds.
    (a) Business incubators (b) Angel investors (c) SBDCs (d) Intrapreneurs

12. Among the forms of small business ownership, only a _____ protects the owners from any personal liabilities for business losses.
    (a) sole proprietorship (b) franchise (c) limited partnership (d) corporation

13. The first component of a good business plan is usually_____.
    (a) an industry analysis (b) a marketing strategy (c) an executive summary (d) a set of milestones

14. Data on current trends in small business ownership in Canada would most likely show that _____.
    (a) the numbers of women- and minority-owned businesses are declining (b) the majority of small businesses conduct some business by Internet (c) large businesses create more jobs than small businesses (d) very few small businesses engage in international import/export activities

15. In _____ financing, the entrepreneur borrows money as a loan that must eventually be paid back to the lender.

    (a) debt (b) equity (c) partnership (d) IPO

SHORT-RESPONSE QUESTIONS:

16. What is the relationship between diversity and entrepreneurship?

17. What are the major stages in the life cycle of an entrepreneurial firm, and what are the leadership challenges at each stage?

18. What are the advantages of choosing a limited partnership form of small business ownership?

19. How can a large corporation stimulate entrepreneurship within itself?

APPLICATION QUESTION:

20. Assume for the moment that you have a great idea for a potential Internet-based start-up business. In discussing the idea with a friend, she advises you to be very careful to tie your business idea to potential customers and then describe it well in a business plan. "After all," she says, "you won't succeed without customers and you'll never get a chance to succeed if you can't attract financial backers through a good business plan." With these words to the wise, you proceed. What questions will you ask and answer to ensure that you are customer-focused in this business? What are the major areas that you would address in writing your initial business plan?

Information and Decision Making

●●● CHAPTER 7 STUDY QUESTIONS

1. How is information technology changing the workplace?

2. What is the role of information in the management process?

3. How do managers use information to make decisions?

4. What are the steps in the decision-making process?

5. What are the current issues in managerial decision making?

Planning Ahead

After reading Chapter 7, you should be able to answer these questions in your own words.

Chapters-Indigo
A passion for books leads to success

Do you love books? Heather Reisman apparently does and she used this love to launch Indigo Books in 1996, the first bookstore in Canada to sell music and gifts, and have licensed cafés. The company's stated goal is "to create a true booklovers' haven—a place to discover books, music and more that might, in the rush of life, have gone undiscovered. A place that reflects the best of a small proprietor-run shop bundled with the selection of a true emporium." From this focused beginning, Reisman has gone on to establish the largest bookstore chain in Canada.

What were some of the decisions she made to reach this milestone? In 2001, Reisman purchased Chapters, a big-box book retailer (itself a merger between SmithBooks and Coles) and with it Chapters Online as well to create Indigo Books & Music, Inc. as a corporate entity. At the start, the new company's operations were run on the existing Chapters IT infrastructure. However, a new enterprise system was put in place by the end of 2003 and resulted in increased sales and improved inventory tracking. Using technology, Chapters-Indigo can also focus on delivering the right books to the right location, in the right quantities, at the right time. The online division, chapters.indigo.ca, is now one of Canada's top sites for books, music, videos, and DVDs and it has a strong affiliate program, allowing independent websites to link with this larger organization and secure a revenue stream. Other initiatives undertaken by Indigo are the marketing of Heather's picks and the iRewards program, one of Canada's largest paid loyalty programs at over one million members. The membership provides an ongoing discount to booklovers,

and other incentives, which can be used at all locations operated by Indigo as well as online. The company recently introduced a new online toy store, to complement its "edutainment" approach to its children's business. Launched in early October 2006, the online store features over 2,000 items for children up to 12 years of age.

The decisions made by Reisman have not gone unchallenged. Search the net and you will find commentary ranging from accusations of monopoly to customer backlash against the removal of sofas. Despite this feedback, Reisman has high hopes for the future, "I am cautiously bullish on our industry. I believe consumers value their opportunity to read books." With the company's continuing growth reports, perhaps Reisman's love of books and decision tactics will result in long-term financial success as well.[1]

IN THE WORKPLACE

Your co-worker Janet Hill in the sales department approaches you. She's noticed that on Mondays and Wednesdays this past month, the company's bookstore sold significantly more history books than the other days of the week. Janet asks you for some insight into why that would be. You pull up the work roster and notice that Deepak Patel was working on Mondays and Wednesdays this past month. You tell Janet that Deepak is a real "history buff" and that it may have been his enthusiasm for the subject that was creating interest in history books on those days. Janet thanks you for turning "data" into "information" and making it useful, and wonders if the company should hire Deepak full-time. You are not sure what she means by turning data into information.

Chapter 7   LEARNING PREVIEW

Heather Reisman made many decisions as she shaped Chapters-Indigo into the company it is today. At each step of the way, she combined talent and business insight with risk and environmental awareness. She has gathered information effectively to turn her plans into realities. In Chapter 7 you will learn about information and decision making, with special attention to developments in information technology.

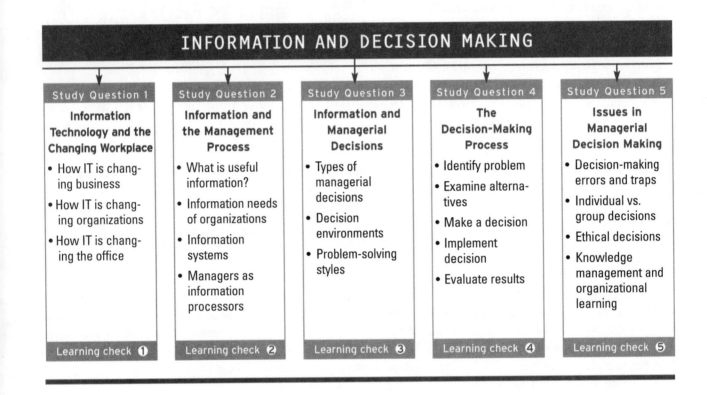

INFORMATION AND DECISION MAKING

Study Question 1	Study Question 2	Study Question 3	Study Question 4	Study Question 5
Information Technology and the Changing Workplace	**Information and the Management Process**	**Information and Managerial Decisions**	**The Decision-Making Process**	**Issues in Managerial Decision Making**
• How IT is changing business • How IT is changing organizations • How IT is changing the office	• What is useful information? • Information needs of organizations • Information systems • Managers as information processors	• Types of managerial decisions • Decision environments • Problem-solving styles	• Identify problem • Examine alternatives • Make a decision • Implement decision • Evaluate results	• Decision-making errors and traps • Individual vs. group decisions • Ethical decisions • Knowledge management and organizational learning
Learning check ❶	Learning check ❷	Learning check ❸	Learning check ❹	Learning check ❺

We live in an era of change. Society is in what futurist Alvin Toffler calls the *third wave* of development—information-driven, digital, networked, and continuously evolving.[2] An important key to performance in this new world is **information technology**, or "IT," and the way it is utilized. We live and work at a time when computers make more information about more things available to more people more quickly than ever before. The question is this: How well do we take advantage of it? Consider this description of how the world of business has been competitively changed by fast-paced developments.[3]

■ **Information technology** is the use of electronic devices that aid in the creation, management, and use of information.

> *Product life cycles are compressing and windows of market opportunity are slamming shut faster than ever before. Streamlined businesses are collapsing two and three jobs into one and asking managers to supervise more operations, across larger geographic expanses. Customers are demanding instant answers, personalized attention, and customized solutions. The only way for companies to maintain momentum, stay ahead of the market, and compete successfully in this unforgiving business environment is to find new and faster ways of sharing critical information and leveraging knowledge resources.*

INFORMATION TECHNOLOGY AND THE CHANGING WORKPLACE

Management scholar and consultant Peter Drucker said that in our IT-driven economy "the productivity of knowledge and knowledge workers" is the decisive competitive factor.[4] A **knowledge worker** is one whose value to organizations rests with intellect, not physical capabilities. Knowledge workers add to an organization's **intellectual capital**, first defined in Chapter 1 as the collective brainpower or shared knowledge of a workforce that can be used to create wealth.[5]

■ **Knowledge workers** add value to organizations through intellect.

Both knowledge and intellectual capital are irreplaceable organizational resources. They grow from information that, today, increasingly moves at high speed through electronic networks that link each of us to the world at large with an access and intensity never before possible. Thus, what Drucker called "the productivity of knowledge and knowledge workers" depends on two "must have" competencies: (1) *computer competency*—the ability to understand computers and to use them to their best advantage; and (2) *information competency*—the ability to utilize technology to locate, retrieve, evaluate, organize, and analyze information for decision making.

■ **Intellectual capital** is the collective brainpower or shared knowledge of a workforce.

●●● HOW IT IS CHANGING BUSINESS

One of the most significant business developments of all time is **electronic commerce**, or "e-commerce." This is the process of buying and selling goods and services electronically through use of the Internet. Business transactions between buyers and sellers are completed online rather than face-to-face. In *business-to-consumer, e-commerce,* or "B2C," businesses like Chapters-Indigo and Dell engage in e-retailing, selling directly to customers over the Internet. In *business-to-business e-commerce,* or "B2B," businesses use the Internet to collaborate and make transactions with one another. The following are the stages of development in e-commerce:[6]

■ **Electronic commerce** is buying and selling goods and services through use of the Internet.

1. *Secure an online identity:* Firms have a Web address and most likely a posted home page.

2. *Establish a Web presence:* Firms use their home page for advertising or promotional purposes but do not allow online queries or ordering.

3. *Enable e-commerce:* Firms engage in e-commerce with websites allowing visitors to order products online.

4. *Provide e-commerce and customer relationship management:* Firms use their websites to serve customers who, for example, check orders or inventory levels online.

5. *Utilize a service application model:* Firms use advanced websites to serve business functions such as financial and operations management.

●●● HOW IT IS CHANGING ORGANIZATIONS

Information technology is changing organizations by breaking down barriers.[7] As shown in *Figure 7.1,* within organizations this means that people working in different departments, levels, and physical locations can more easily communicate and share information. It also means that the organization can operate with fewer middle managers whose jobs otherwise would be to facilitate these information flows; computers now do the job. IT-intensive organizations

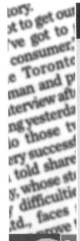

CANADIAN COMPANY   **Toromont Industries**
IN THE NEWS

IT IMPROVES TRADITIONAL OPERATIONS

Toromont Industries, a Toronto construction equipment rental company, has developed custom-built software, transforming the way it does business. The Web-based software is accessible from anywhere and easy to use. With the sales management system, the sales teams can track customer accounts, and management can manipulate daily data, resulting in new marketing approaches. In the distribution centre, orders for parts, based on delivery priority and where they're stocked, are transmitted wirelessly from a Web-based order system to computers on inventory-pickers' wrists. The warehouse has increased its volumes without physically expanding. It also identified almost $1 million in unaccounted-for inventory. With the financial planning application, managers from six operating companies can drag-and-drop their budget plans onto a Web page, where they are automatically consolidated and balanced for the finance department.

Source: Andrew Wahl, "The Best Managers in Canada: Top in Technology," *Canadian Business*, April 26–May 9, 2004, Vol. 77, Iss. 9.

are "flatter" and operate with fewer levels than their more traditional organizational counterparts. This creates opportunities for competitive advantage by faster decision making, better use of timely information, and better coordination of decisions and actions.

IT also breaks barriers between organizations and key elements in the external environment. It plays an important role in *customer relationship management* by quickly and accurately providing information for decision makers regarding customer needs, preferences, and satisfactions. It helps manage and control costs in all aspects of *supply chain management* from initiation of purchase, to logistics and transportation, to point of delivery and ultimate use. IT also allows outsourcing and other business contracts to be continuously and efficiently monitored.

Figure 7.1 Information technology is breaking barriers and changing organizations.

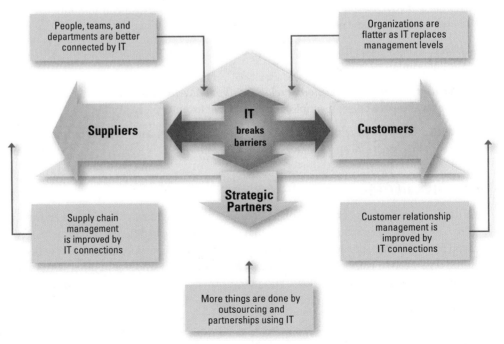

●●● HOW IT IS CHANGING THE OFFICE

Progressive organizations are doing all they can to design work settings for high performance in an environment where "speed to market," "quick response," "fast cycle time," and "time-based competition" are top priorities.[8] They drive investments in IT that have dramatically changed what most of us still call "the office."

Bell Canada's *flex*Space program redefines the word "office" for its employees. Bell equips each *flex*Space office so employees can find desk space, get access to the network, print presentations, or make phone calls, allowing workers the flexibility to work from head office, home, or at one of six satellite offices in Ontario and Quebec.

And that's not all. There are more developments coming to the networked office every day, and you most probably are already familiar with them. **Instant messaging**, instantaneous communication among persons online at the same time, isn't just for friends; it is a work facilitator as well. **Peer-to-peer file sharing** (P2P), PCs connected directly to one another over the Internet, gained fame as a way for friends to swap music and video files. It is now becoming indispensable as a way for workers to share information and otherwise collaborate "peer-to-peer."

At Nortel, the company's Multimedia Communications Server uses voice over Internet protocol (VoIP) to allow telecommuters to make calls from anywhere, and a "find me–follow me" feature lets colleagues and customers know where they are and what they are doing. Instant messenger and other IP features allow workers to easily set up video and teleconferences with colleagues, while white board and other application sharing programs encourage team communication and collaboration.[9]

> ■ **Instant messaging** is instantaneous communication between people online at the same time.
>
> ■ **Peer-to-peer file sharing** connects PCs directly to one another over the Internet.

BE SURE YOU CAN

• define the terms electronic commerce, B2B, and B2C • discuss how IT is breaking barriers within organizations and between organizations and their environments • describe the way IT is changing the office

✔ Learning check ❶

INFORMATION AND THE MANAGEMENT PROCESS

Organizations are changing as continuing developments in information technology exert their influence. Information departments, or centres, are now mainstream on organization charts. The number and variety of information career fields is rapidly expanding. Managers are increasingly expected to excel in their information processing roles. All of this, and more, is characteristic of the great opportunities of an information age.

●●● WHAT IS USEFUL INFORMATION?

Data are raw facts and observations. **Information** is data made useful and meaningful for decision making. In the music industry, for example, lots of data are available on the demographic profiles of customers—such as which age groups are buying which CDs and where they are buying them. Not everyone with access to this data, however, uses it well. But those who do may gain competitive advantage, perhaps by changing their advertising because younger customers do a lot of buying on the Internet while older customers shop mainly in retail stores.

> ■ **Data** are raw facts and observations.
>
> ■ **Information** is data made useful for decision making.

The management process of planning, organizing, leading, and controlling is ultimately driven by information, not data alone. Managers need good information, and they need it all the time. Information that is truly useful meets the test of these five criteria:

1. *Timely*—the information is available when needed; it meets deadlines for decision making and action.

2. *High quality*—the information is accurate, and it is reliable; it can be used with confidence.

3. *Complete*—the information is complete and sufficient for the task at hand; it is as up-to-date as possible.

4. *Relevant*—the information is appropriate for the task at hand; it is free from extraneous or irrelevant materials.

5. *Understandable*—the information is clear and easily understood by the user; it is free from unnecessary detail.

●●● INFORMATION NEEDS OF ORGANIZATIONS

Driven largely by IT, information serves the variety of needs described in *Figure 7.2*. At the organization's boundaries, information in the external environment is accessed. Managers use this *intelligence information* to deal effectively with competitors and key stakeholders such as government agencies, creditors, suppliers, and stockholders. Peter Drucker said that "a winning strategy will require information about events and conditions outside the institution," and that organizations must have "rigorous methods for gathering and analyzing outside information."[10] Organizations also send many types of *public information* to stakeholders and the external environment. This serves a variety of purposes ranging from image building to product advertising to financial reporting for taxes.

Within organizations, people need vast amounts of information to make decisions and solve problems in their daily work. The ability of IT to gather and move information quickly allows top levels to stay informed while freeing lower levels to make speedy decisions and take the actions they need to best perform their jobs. Silicon Valley giant and Cisco Systems' CEO John Chambers, for example, points out that he always has the information he needs in order to be in control—be it information on earnings, expenses, profitability, gross margins, and more. He also says, importantly: "Because I have my data in that format, every one of my employees can make decisions that might have had to come all the way to the president.

Figure 7.2 External and internal information needs of organizations.

| Intelligence information—gathered from stakeholders and external environment | Internal information—flows up, down, around, and across organizations | Public information—disseminated to stakeholders and external environment |

Internal and external information flows are essential to problem solving and decision making in organizations

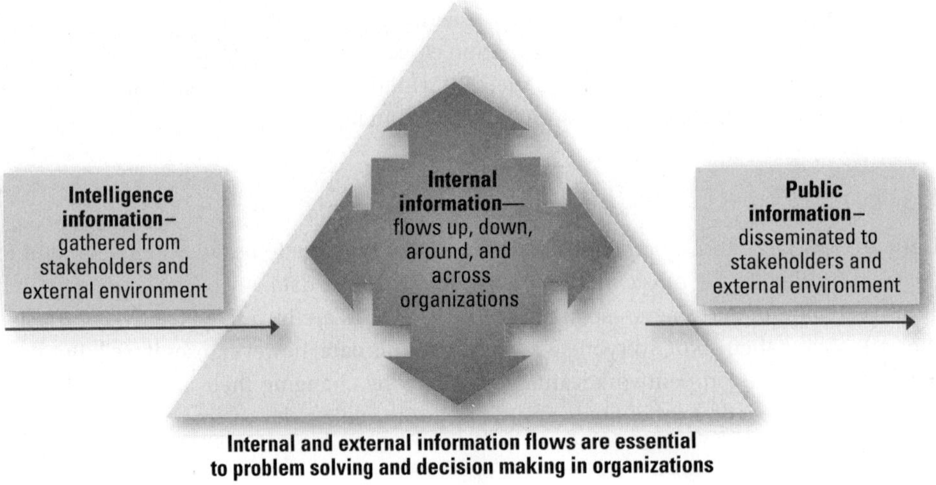

...Quicker decision making at lower levels will translate into higher profit margins. ...Companies that don't do that will be non-competitive."[11]

●●● INFORMATION SYSTEMS

In order to perform well, people in any work setting, large or small, must have available to them the right information at the right time and in the right place. **Information systems** use the latest in information technology to collect, organize, and distribute data in such a way that they become meaningful as information. **Management information systems**, or MIS, meet the specific information needs of managers as they make a variety of day-to-day decisions. Although it is important to avoid common mistakes (see *Manager's Notepad 7.1*), today's developments in MIS make possible performance levels that are truly extraordinary. C.R. England, Inc., a long-haul refrigerated trucking company, for example, uses a computerized MIS to monitor more than 500 aspects of organizational performance. The system tracks everything from billing accuracy to arrival times to driver satisfaction with company maintenance on their vehicles. Says CEO Dean England: "Our view was, if we could measure it, we could manage it."[12]

■ **Information systems** use IT to collect, organize, and distribute data for use in decision making.

■ **Management information systems** meet the information needs of managers in daily decisions.

MANAGER'S
Notepad 7.1

Avoiding common information systems mistakes

- Don't assume more information is always better.
- Don't assume that computers eliminate human judgement.
- Don't assume that the newest technology is always best.
- Don't assume that nothing will ever go wrong with your computer.
- Don't assume that everyone understands how the system works.

Decision Support and Expert Systems

A **decision support system** (DSS) is an interactive information system that allows users to organize and analyze data for solving complex and sometimes unstructured problems. Decision support systems are now available to assist in such business decisions as mergers and acquisitions, plant expansions, new product developments, and stock portfolio management, among many others. A fast-growing application involves *group decision support systems* (GDSS) that facilitate group efforts to solve complex and unstructured problems. GDSS software, called **groupware**, allows several people to simultaneously access a file or database and work together virtually. It facilitates information exchange, group decision making, work scheduling, and other forms of group activity without the requirement of face-to-face meetings.

An exciting area is *artificial intelligence* (AI), a field of science that is interested in building computer systems with the capacity to reason the way people do. **Expert systems** use AI to mimic the thinking of human experts, even to the point of dealing with ambiguities and difficult issues of judgement. In so doing, they offer consistent and "expert" decision-making advice to the user. Some use a complicated set of "if . . . then" rules developed by human experts to analyze problems. A good example is automatic approval for credit card purchases. Behind this system is an AI platform that analyzes the purchaser's credit worthiness using a set of predetermined rules, the same ones that a human expert would apply.

■ **Decision support systems** help users organize and analyze data for problem solving.

■ **Groupware** is software that facilitates group collaboration and problem solving.

■ **Expert systems** allow computers to mimic the thinking of human experts for applied problem solving.

Web Portals and Networks

The growth of the World Wide Web has created many advantages in the area of information systems. Rather than relying solely on their own networks for computer interfacing, organizations are actively utilizing Web portals to facilitate information processing. It is now very common for organizations to have **intranets** and **corporate portals** that allow employees, by password access, to share databases and communicate electronically. The goal is to efficiently improve integration and communication throughout the organization, while making it easy for employees to access key services. At Hewlett-Packard, for example, a corporate portal has saved over $50 million in reduced paperwork and administrative costs. Employees use the portal to stay up to date on company news, access benefit information, participate in focus groups and special surveys, and locate one another for business communications.[13]

Extranets and **enterprise portals** allow communication and data sharing between the organization and special elements in its external environment. They typically link organizations with strategic partners, vendors, outsourcers, suppliers, and consultants. An important and rapidly expanding development in this area is called **electronic data interchange,** or EDI. It uses controlled access to enterprise portals and supporting software to enable firms to electronically transact business with one another, for example by sharing purchase orders, bills, receipt confirmations, and payments. The goals of EDI include improved transaction speed and cost savings. In the retailing industry where profit margins are tiny, Wal-Mart aggressively pursues these goals as a state-of-the art user of EDI. Its suppliers are required to purchase the necessary software and then electronically work with the firm to handle all order, purchasing, and delivery details.[14]

■ **Intranets** and **corporate portals** use the Web for communication and data sharing within an organization.

■ **Extranets** and **enterprise portals** use the Web for communication and data sharing between the organization and its environment.

■ **Electronic data interchange** uses controlled access to enterprise portals to enable firms to electronically transact business with one another.

●●● MANAGERS AS INFORMATION PROCESSORS

The manager's job as shown in *Figure 7.3* is a nerve centre of information flows, with information being continually gathered, given, and received from many sources. All of the managerial roles identified by Henry Mintzberg and discussed in Chapter 1—interpersonal, decisional, and informational—involve communication and information processing.[15] So too, do all

Figure 7.3 The manager as an information-processing nerve centre.

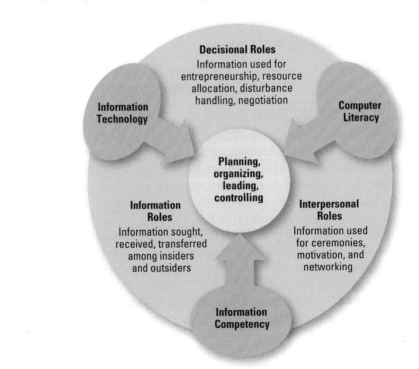

aspects of the management process—planning, organizing, leading, and controlling. Success in management is increasingly tied to the opportunities of IT.

- *Planning advantages*—better and more timely access to useful information, involving more people in the planning process.

- *Organizing advantages*—more ongoing and informed communication among all parts, improving coordination and integration.

- *Leading advantages*—more frequent and better communication with staff and stakeholders, keeping objectives clear.

- *Controlling advantages*—more immediate measures of performance results, allowing real-time solutions to problems.

BE SURE YOU CAN
- differentiate data and information • list the criteria of useful information • describe the information needs of organizations • explain the role of information systems in organizations • illustrate the use of corporate portals and enterprise portals • describe how IT influences the four functions of management

✓ Learning check ❷

INFORMATION AND MANAGERIAL DECISIONS

One way to describe what managers do is that they use information to solve a continuous stream of daily problems. The most obvious problem situation is a *performance deficiency*; that is, when actual performance is less than desired. For example, a manager faces a possible problem when turnover or absenteeism suddenly increases in the work unit, when a subordinate's daily output decreases, or when a higher executive complains about something that has been said or done. Another important problem situation emerges as a *performance opportunity* when an actual situation either turns out better than anticipated or offers the potential to be so.

The challenge in dealing with any performance deficiency or performance opportunity is to proceed with effective **problem solving**—the process of identifying a discrepancy between an actual and desired state of affairs and then taking action to resolve the deficiency or taking advantage of the opportunity. Success in problem solving is dependent on the right information being available to the right people at the right times so that they can make good problem-solving decisions. A **decision**, to be precise, is a choice among alternative possible courses of action. In today's IT-enriched organizations, information systems assist managers in gathering data, turning them into useful information, and utilizing that information individually and collaboratively to make problem-solving decisions.

▦ **Problem solving** involves identifying and taking action to resolve problems.

▦ A **decision** is a choice among possible alternative courses of action.

●●● TYPES OF MANAGERIAL DECISIONS

Managers make different types of decisions in their day-to-day work. **Programmed decisions** use solutions already available from past experience to solve **structured problems**—ones that are familiar, straightforward, and clear with respect to information needs. These problems are routine; although perhaps not predictable, they can at least be anticipated. This means that decisions can be planned or programmed in advance to be implemented as needed. In human resource management, for example, problems are common whenever decisions are made on pay raises and promotions, vacation requests, committee assignments, and the like. Knowing this, forward-looking managers plan ahead on how to handle complaints and conflicts when and if they should arise.

▦ A **programmed decision** applies a solution from past experience to a routine problem.

▦ **Structured problems** are straightforward and clear in information needs.

MANAGER'S
Notepad 7.2

Six rules for crisis management

1. *Figure out what is going on:* Take the time to understand the situation, what's happening, and the conditions under which the crisis must be resolved.

2. *Remember that speed matters:* Attack the crisis as quickly as possible, trying to catch it when it is as small as possible.

3. *Remember that slow counts, too:* Know when to back off and wait for a better opportunity to make progress with the crisis.

4. *Respect the danger of the unfamiliar:* Understand that the most dangerous crisis is the all-new territory where you and others have never been before.

5. *Value the skeptic:* Don't look for and get too comfortable with agreement; appreciate skeptics and let them help you to see things differently.

6. *Be ready to "fight fire with fire":* When things are going wrong but others don't seem to care, you may have to start a crisis of your own to get their attention.

▨ **Unstructured problems** have ambiguities and information deficiencies.

Managers must also deal with new or unusual situations that present **unstructured problems**, full of ambiguities and information deficiencies. These problems require **nonprogrammed decisions** that craft novel solutions to meet the demands of the unique situation at hand. Most problems faced by higher-level managers are of this type, often involving choice of strategies and objectives in situations of some uncertainty.

▨ A **nonprogrammed decision** applies a specific solution crafted for a unique problem.

An extreme type of nonprogrammed decision must be made in times of **crisis**—the occurrence of an unexpected problem that can lead to disaster if not resolved quickly and appropriately. Terrorism in a post–9/11 world, outbreaks of workplace violence, man-made environmental catastrophes, ethical scandals, and IT failures are examples. The ability to handle crises (see *Manager's Notepad 7.2*) may be the ultimate test of a manager's problem-solving capabilities. Unfortunately, research indicates that managers may react to crises by doing the wrong things. They isolate themselves and try to solve the problem alone or in a small "closed" group.[16] This denies them access to crucial information and assistance at the very time they are most needed. The crisis can even be accentuated when more problems are created because critical decisions are made with poor or inadequate information and from a limited perspective. The organizational consequences of alienated customers, lost profits, damaged reputations, and increased costs can be very severe.

▨ A **crisis** is an unexpected problem that can lead to disaster if not resolved quickly and appropriately.

When the power went out at the offices of Ottawa-based Magma Communications Ltd., the Internet service provider went on with business as usual. The emergency diesel generators were automatically started, staff members were immediately reallocated to reassure customers, and an order was placed to replenish the two-day supply of generator fuel. When the power came back on 12 hours later, Ron Ethier, Magma's vice-president of technology, stated, "The blackout wasn't a disaster for us; it was more of a hands-on test of our emergency plan."[17]

▨ **Crisis management** is preparation for the management of crises that threaten an organization's health and well-being.

For these and other reasons, many organizations are developing formal **crisis management** programs. They are designed to help managers and others prepare for unexpected high-impact events that threaten an organization's health and well-being. Anticipation is one aspect of crisis management; preparation is another. People can be assigned ahead of time to *crisis management teams*, and *crisis management plans* can be developed to deal with various contingencies. Just as police departments and community groups plan ahead and train to best handle civil and natural disasters, so too can managers and work teams plan ahead and train to best deal with organizational crises.[18]

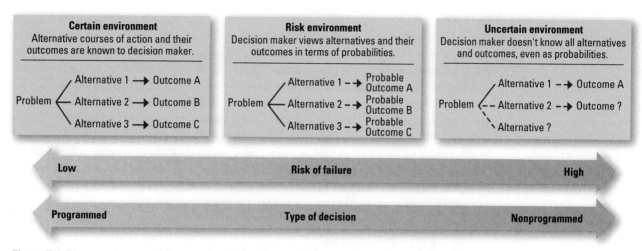

Figure 7.4 Three environments for managerial decision making and problem solving.

●●● DECISION ENVIRONMENTS

Figure 7.4 shows three different decision environments—certainty, risk, and uncertainty. Although managers make decisions in each, the conditions of risk and uncertainty are common at higher management levels where problems are more complex and unstructured. Former Coca-Cola CEO Roberto Goizueta, for example, was known as a risk taker. Among his risky moves were introducing Diet Coke to the market, changing the formula of Coca-Cola to create New Coke, and then reversing direction after New Coke flopped.[19]

The decision to market any new product is made in conditions quite different from the relative predictability of a **certain environment**. This is an ideal decision situation where factual information is available about the possible alternative courses of action and their outcomes. The decision maker's task is simply to study the alternatives and choose the best solution. But very few managerial problems are like this. It is more common to face a **risk environment** where facts and information on action alternatives and their consequences are incomplete, but

■ A **certain environment** offers complete information on possible action alternatives and their consequences.

■ A **risk environment** lacks complete information but offers "probabilities" of the likely outcomes for possible action alternatives.

Canadian Managers
Establishing an IT Tradition

The history of Mississauga, Ontario-based metals distributor Russel Metals Inc. dates back to 1866 and a one-man iron-trading operation. Today, the company has to manage inventories, meet just-in-time demands, and provide customized steel processing at 58 metals service centres in Canada and four in the United States. When Maureen Kelly joined Russel Metals in 1998 as vice president of information systems, her first task was to replace the 20-year-old Enterprise Resource Planning system with one that was Y2K-compliant, which she completed by July 1, 1999. She and her 29 staff members have digitized the company's paper systems with central document management, electronic fund transfers, and e-mail, and a purchasing portal now provides branches with immediate access to inventory data. And, while making these investments, Kelly has reduced IT costs each year.

Source: Andrew Wahl and John Gray, "Top in technology 2005: Maureen Kelly, Russel Metals Inc.," *Canadian Business*, April 25–May 8, 2005.

some estimates of "probabilities" can be made. A *probability* is the degree of likelihood (e.g., 4 chances out of 10) that an event will occur. Risk is typical for entrepreneurs and organizations that depend on ideas and continued innovation for their success. Steps can be taken to reduce risk in many situations. In the case of a new Coke product, for example, the firm can make the go-ahead decision only after receiving favourable reports from special focus groups testing it.

When facts are few and information is so poor that managers are unable even to assign probabilities to the likely outcomes of alternatives, an **uncertain environment** exists. This is the most difficult decision-making condition.[20] The high level of uncertainty forces managers to rely heavily on creativity in solving problems. Because uncertainty requires unique, novel, and often totally innovative alternatives, groups are frequently used for problem solving. In all cases, the responses to uncertainty depend greatly on intuition, judgement, informed guessing, and hunches—all of which leave considerable room for error.

◗ An **uncertain environment** lacks so much information that it is difficult to assign probabilities to the likely outcomes of alternatives.

●●● PROBLEM-SOLVING STYLES

In practice, managers display three quite different approaches or "styles" in the way they process information and deal with problems. Some are *problem avoiders* who ignore information that would otherwise signal the presence of an opportunity or performance deficiency. They are inactive in information gathering, not wanting to make decisions and deal with problems. *Problem solvers*, by contrast, are willing to make decisions and try to solve problems, but only when forced to by the situation. They are reactive in gathering information and responding to problems after they occur. They may deal reasonably well with performance deficiencies, but they miss many performance opportunities. *Problem seekers* actively process information and constantly look for problems to solve or opportunities to explore. True problem seekers are proactive and forward thinking. They anticipate problems and opportunities and take appropriate action to gain the advantage. Success at problem seeking is one of the ways exceptional managers distinguish themselves from the merely good ones.

Managers also differ in tendencies toward "systematic" and "intuitive" thinking. In **systematic thinking** a person approaches problems in a rational, step-by-step, and analytical fashion. This type of thinking involves breaking a complex problem into smaller components and then addressing them in a logical and integrated fashion. Managers who are systematic can be expected to make a plan before taking action and then to search for information to facilitate problem solving in a step-by-step fashion.

◗ **Systematic thinking** approaches problems in a rational and analytical fashion.

Someone using **intuitive thinking**, by contrast, is more flexible and spontaneous and also may be quite creative.[21] This type of thinking allows us to respond imaginatively to a problem based on a quick and broad evaluation of the situation and the possible alternative courses of action. Managers who are intuitive can be expected to deal with many aspects of a problem at once, jump quickly from one issue to another, and consider "hunches" based on experience or spontaneous ideas. This approach tends to work best in situations of high uncertainty where facts are limited and few decision precedents exist.

◗ **Intuitive thinking** approaches problems in a flexible and spontaneous fashion.

Senior managers, in particular, must deal with portfolios of problems and opportunities that consist of multiple and interrelated issues. This requires *multidimensional thinking*, or the ability to view many problems at once, in relationship to one another, and across long and short time horizons.[22] The best managers "map" multiple problems into a network that can be actively managed over time as priorities, events, and demands continuously change. And importantly, they are able to make decisions and take actions in the short run that benefit longer-run objectives. They avoid being sidetracked while sorting through a shifting mix of daily problems. This requires skill at **strategic opportunism**—the ability to remain focused on long-term objectives while being flexible enough to resolve short-term problems and opportunities in a timely manner.[23]

◗ **Strategic opportunism** focuses on long-term objectives while being flexible in dealing with short-term problems.

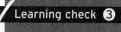

THE DECISION-MAKING PROCESS

The **decision-making process** involves a set of activities that begins with identification of a problem, includes making a decision, and ends with the evaluation of results.[24] As shown in *Figure 7.5*, the steps in managerial decision making are to (1) identify and define the problem, (2) generate and evaluate alternative solutions, (3) choose a preferred course of action and conduct the "ethics double-check," (4) implement the decision, and (5) evaluate results. Importantly, Step 3 in this model includes a built-in "checkpoint" as a way to verify the ethical aspects of a decision before any action is taken. Working with the following short-but-true case will help put all five steps into perspective.

> *The Ajax Case.* On December 31, the Ajax Company decided to close down its Murphysboro plant. Market conditions were forcing layoffs, and the company could not find a buyer for the plant. Of 172 employees, some had been with the company as long as 18 years, others as little as 6 months. All were to be terminated. Under company policy, they would be given severance pay equal to one week's pay per year of service. Top management faced a difficult problem: how to minimize the negative impact of the plant closing on employees, their families, and the small town of Murphysboro.

This case reflects how competition, changing times, and the forces of globalization can take their toll on organizations, the people that work for them, and the communities in which they operate. Think about how you would feel as the CEO of Ajax Company contemplating this decision, as one of the affected employees, and as the mayor of this small town.

■ The **decision-making process** begins with identification of a problem and ends with evaluation of implemented solutions.

Figure 7.5 Steps in managerial decision making and problem solving.

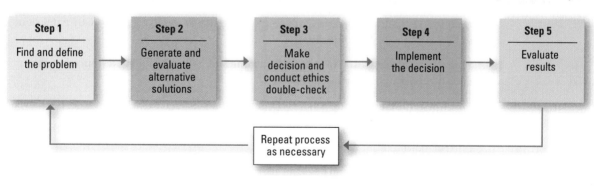

●●● IDENTIFY AND DEFINE THE PROBLEM

The first step in decision making is to find and define the problem. This is a stage of information gathering, information processing, and deliberation.[25] It is important at this step to clarify goals by identifying exactly what a decision should accomplish. The more specific the goals, the easier it is to evaluate results after the decision is actually implemented. Importantly, the way a problem is defined can have a major impact on how it is resolved.

Three common mistakes occur in this critical first step in decision making. *Mistake number one* is defining the problem too broadly or too narrowly. To take a classic example, the problem stated as "Build a better mousetrap" might be better defined as "Get rid of the mice." That is, managers should define problems in ways that give them the best possible range of problem-solving options. *Mistake number two* is focusing on symptoms instead of causes. Symptoms are indicators that problems may exist, but they shouldn't be mistaken for the problems themselves. Managers should be able to spot problem symptoms (e.g., a drop in performance). But instead of treating symptoms (such as simply encouraging higher performance), managers should address their root causes (such as discovering the worker's need for training in the use of a complex new computer system). *Mistake number three* is choosing the wrong problem to deal with. Managers should set priorities and deal with the most important problems first. They should also give priority to problems that are truly solvable.

> *Back to the Ajax Case.* Closing the Ajax plant will put a substantial number of people from this small community of Murphysboro out of work. The unemployment created will have a negative impact on individuals, their families, and the community as a whole. The loss of the Ajax tax base will further hurt the community. The local financial implications of the plant closure will be great. The problem for Ajax management is how to minimize the adverse impact of the plant closing on the employees, their families, and the community.

●●● GENERATE AND EVALUATE ALTERNATIVE COURSES OF ACTION

Once the problem is defined, it is time to assemble the facts and information that will be helpful for problem solving. It is important here to clarify exactly what is known and what needs to be known. Extensive information gathering should identify alternative courses of action, as well as their anticipated consequences. The process of evaluating alternatives often benefits from a *stakeholder analysis*. Key stakeholders in the problem should be identified and the effects of each possible course of action on them considered. Another useful approach for the evaluation of alternatives is **cost-benefit analysis**, the comparison of what an alternative will cost in relation to the expected benefits. At a minimum, the benefits of an alternative should be greater than its costs. Typical criteria for evaluating alternatives include the following:

■ **Cost-benefit analysis** involves comparing the costs and benefits of each potential course of action.

- *Benefits:* What are the "benefits" of using the alternative to solve a performance deficiency or take advantage of an opportunity?

- *Costs:* What are the "costs" of implementing the alternative, including resource investments as well as potential negative side effects?

- *Timeliness:* How fast will the benefits occur and how soon can a positive impact be achieved?

- *Acceptability:* To what extent will the alternative be accepted and supported by those who must work with it?

- *Ethical soundness:* How well does the alternative meet acceptable ethical criteria in the eyes of the various stakeholders?

The end result of this step can only be as good as the quality of the options considered; the better the pool of alternatives, the more likely that a good solution will be achieved. A common error is abandoning the search for alternatives too quickly. This often happens under pressures of time and other circumstances. But just because an alternative is convenient doesn't make it the best. It could have damaging side effects, or it might not be as good as others that might be discovered with extra effort. One way to minimize this error is through participation and involvement, bringing more people into the process, and bringing more information and perspectives to bear on the problem.

> *Back to the Ajax Case.* The Ajax plant is going to be closed. Among the possible alternatives that can be considered are (1) close the plant on schedule and be done with it; (2) delay the plant closing until all efforts have been made to sell it to another firm; (3) offer to sell the plant to the employees and/or local interests; (4) close the plant and offer transfers to other Ajax plant locations; or (5) close the plant, offer transfers, and help the employees find new jobs in and around Murphysboro.

●●● DECIDE ON A PREFERRED COURSE OF ACTION

This is the point of choice, where an actual decision is made to select a preferred course of action. Just how this is done, and by whom, must be successfully resolved in each problem situation. Management theory recognizes differences between the classical and behavioural models of decision making shown in *Figure 7.6*. The **classical decision model** views the manager as acting rationally in a certain world. Here, the manager faces a clearly defined problem and knows all possible action alternatives as well as their consequences. As a result, he or she makes an **optimizing decision** that gives the absolute best solution to the problem. The classical approach is a rational model that assumes perfect information is available for decision making.

Behavioural scientists question these assumptions. Perhaps best represented by the work of Herbert Simon, they recognize limits to our human information-processing capabilities.[26] These *cognitive limitations* make it hard for managers to become fully informed and make perfectly rational decisions. They create a *bounded rationality* such that managerial decisions are rational only within the boundaries defined by the available information. The **behavioural decision model**, accordingly, assumes that people act only in terms of what they perceive about a given situation. Because such perceptions are frequently imperfect, the decision maker has only partial knowledge about the available action alternatives and their consequences. Consequently, the first alternative that appears to give a satisfactory resolution of the problem is likely to be chosen. Simon, who won a Nobel Prize for his work, calls this the tendency toward **satisficing decisions**—choosing the first satisfactory alternative that comes to your attention. This model seems especially accurate in describing how people make decisions about ambiguous problems in risky and uncertain conditions.

> *Back to the Ajax Case.* Management at Ajax decided to follow alternative five as described in Step 2 of the decision-making process. They would close the plant, offer transfers to company plants in another state, and offer to help displaced employees find new jobs in and around Murphysboro.

■ The **classical decision model** describes decision making with complete information.

■ An **optimizing decision** chooses the alternative giving the absolute best solution to a problem.

■ The **behavioural decision model** describes decision making with limited information and bounded rationality.

■ A **satisficing decision** chooses the first satisfactory alternative that comes to one's attention.

Classical Model

- Structured problem
- Clearly defined
- Certain environment
- Complete information
- All alternatives and consequences known

Optimizing Decision
Choose absolute best among alternatives

Rationality
Acts in perfect world

Manager as decision maker

Bounded rationality
Acts with cognitive limitations

Behavioural Model

- Unstructured problem
- Not clearly defined
- Uncertain environment
- Incomplete information
- Not all alternatives and consequences known

Satisficing Decision
Choose first "satisfactory" alternative

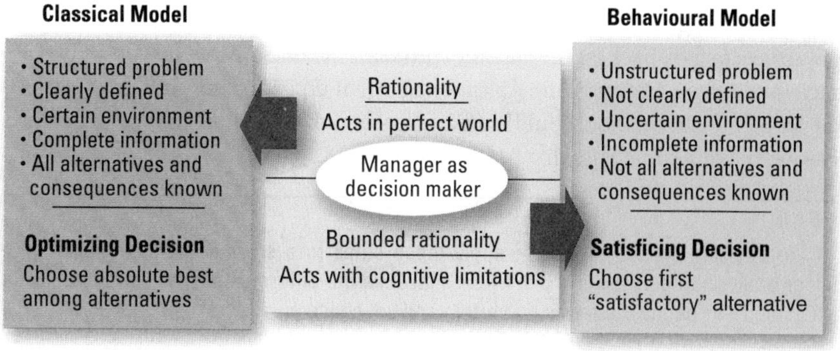

Figure 7.6 Differences in the classical and behavioural models of managerial decision making.

PERSONAL MANAGEMENT

Managers must have the **SELF-CONFIDENCE** to not only make decisions but also to implement them. Too many of us find all sorts of excuses for doing everything but that—we have difficulty deciding and we have difficulty acting. Opportunities to improve and develop your self-confidence abound, especially through involvement in the many student organizations on your campus. Carole Clay Winters was the first member of her family to go to college. On the encouragement of an economics professor, she joined Students in Free Enterprise (SIFE) and ended up on a team teaching business concepts to elementary school children in the local community.[27] Her team was chosen to participate in a national competition. They didn't win, but Carole did. "I felt my life had changed," she said. "I realized that if I could answer all the questions being posed by some of the country's most powerful executives, I had what I needed to become an executive myself." Carole went on to become a manager at KPMG. What about you? Do you have the self-confidence to make decisions relating to your career goals and future success? Are you taking full advantage of opportunities, on campus and off, to experience the responsibilities of leadership and gain confidence in your decision-making capabilities?

Get to know yourself better

Complete Self-Assessments #11—**Your Intuitive Ability,** and #12—**Assertiveness**, from the Workbook and Personal Management Activity #7 on the companion website.

●●● IMPLEMENT THE DECISION

Once a preferred solution is chosen, actions must be taken to fully implement it. Nothing new can or will happen unless action is taken to actually solve the problem. Managers not only need the determination and creativity to arrive at a decision, they also need the ability and willingness to implement it.

The "ways" in which previous steps have been accomplished can have a powerful impact on this stage of implementation. Difficulties encountered at this point can often be traced back to the *lack-of-participation error*. This is a failure to adequately involve in the process those persons whose support is necessary to implement the decision. Managers who use participation wisely get the right people involved in problem solving right from the beginning. When they do, implementation typically follows quickly, smoothly, and to everyone's satisfaction. Participation in decision making not only makes everyone better informed, it also builds the commitments needed for implementation.

> *Back to the Ajax Case.* Ajax ran an ad in the local and regional newspapers for several days. The ad called attention to an "Ajax skill bank" composed of "qualified, dedicated, and well-motivated employees with a variety of skills and experiences." Interested employers were urged to contact Ajax for further information.

●●● EVALUATE RESULTS

The decision-making process is not complete until results are evaluated. If the desired results are not achieved and/or if undesired side effects occur, corrective action should be taken. In this sense, evaluation is a form of managerial control. It involves gathering data to measure performance results against goals. Both the positive and negative outcomes should be examined. If the original choice appears inadequate, it is time to reassess and return to earlier steps. In this way, problem solving becomes a dynamic and ongoing activity within the management process. Evaluation is always easier, furthermore, when clear goals, measurable targets, and timetables were established to begin with.

Back to the Ajax Case. The advertisement ran for some 15 days. The plant's industrial relations manager commented, "I've been very pleased with the results." That's all we know. You can look back on the case and problem-solving process just described and judge for yourself. How well did Ajax management do in dealing with this very difficult problem? Perhaps you would have approached the situation and the five steps in decision making somewhat differently.

✓ Learning check ❹

BE SURE YOU CAN
• list the steps in the decision-making process • apply these steps to a sample decision-making situation • explain stakeholder analysis and cost-benefit analysis • discuss the differences between the classical and behavioural decision models • define the terms optimizing and satisfying

ISSUES IN MANAGERIAL DECISION MAKING

In settings rich in information technology but complicated by risk and uncertainty, managers with their limited human capacities, face many decision-making challenges. It helps to be aware of the common decision-making errors and traps, the advantages and disadvantages of individual and group decision making, the imperative of ethical decision making, and the growing importance of knowledge management and organizational learning.

●●● DECISION-MAKING ERRORS AND TRAPS

Faced with limited information, time, and even energy, people often use simplifying strategies for decision making. These strategies, known as **heuristics**, can cause decision-making errors.[28] The *availability heuristic* occurs when people use information "readily available" from memory as a basis for assessing a current event or situation. An example is deciding not to invest in a new product based on your recollection of how a similar new product performed in the recent past. The potential bias is that the readily available information may be fallible and irrelevant. The new product that recently failed may have been a good idea that was released to market at the wrong time of year.

■ **Heuristics** are strategies for simplifying decision making.

The *representativeness heuristic* occurs when people assess the likelihood of something occurring based on its similarity to a stereotyped set of occurrences. An example is deciding to hire someone for a job vacancy simply because he or she graduated from the same school attended by your last and most successful new hire. The potential bias is that the representative stereotype may mask the truly important factors relevant to the decision. For instance, the abilities and career expectations of the newly hired person may not fit the job requirements.

The *anchoring and adjustment heuristic* involves making decisions based on adjustments to a previously existing value or starting point. An example is setting a new salary level for an employee by simply raising the prior year's salary by a reasonable percentage. This may inappropriately bias a decision toward only incremental movement from the starting point. For instance, the individual's market value may be substantially higher than the existing salary. An incremental adjustment won't keep this person from looking for another job.

In addition to the biases of judgemental heuristics, managers can suffer from **framing error** when making decisions. Framing occurs when a problem is evaluated and resolved in the context in which it is perceived—either positive or negative. An example from the world of marketing is a product that data show has a 40-percent market share. A negative frame views the product as being deficient because it is missing 60 percent of the market. The likely discussion and problem solving in this frame would focus on the question: "What are we doing wrong?" Alternatively, the frame could be a positive one, looking at the 40-percent share as a good accomplishment. In this case the discussion is more likely to proceed with the question: "How do we do things better?" Sometimes people use framing as a tactic for presenting information in a way that gets other people to think inside the desired frame. In politics this is often referred to as "spinning" the data. In the marketing example, the data could be "spun" to the negative or positive by a presenter in an attempt to influence the decision-making process one way or the other.

■ **Framing error** is solving a problem in the context perceived.

Good managers are also aware of another decision-making trap known as **escalating commitment**. This is a decision to increase effort and perhaps apply more resources to pursue a course of action that is not working.[29] In such cases, managers let the momentum of the situation overwhelm them. They are unable to decide to "call it quits," even when experience otherwise indicates that this is the most appropriate thing to do. *Manager's Notepad 7.3* offers advice on avoiding tendencies toward escalating commitments to previously chosen courses of action.

■ **Escalating commitment** is the continuation of a course of action even though it is not working.

MANAGER'S
Notepad 7.3

How to avoid the escalation trap

- Set advance limits on your involvement and commitment to a particular course of action; stick with these limits.

- Make your own decisions; don't follow the lead of others, since they are also prone to escalation.

- Carefully determine just why you are continuing a course of action; if there are insufficient reasons to continue, don't.

- Remind yourself of what a course of action is costing; consider saving these costs as a reason to discontinue.

- Watch for escalation tendencies; be on guard against their influence on both you and others involved in the course of action.

●●● INDIVIDUAL VS. GROUP DECISION MAKING

One of the important issues in decision making is the choice of whether to make the decision individually or with the participation of a group. The best managers and team leaders don't limit themselves to just one way. Instead, they switch back and forth among individual and group decision making to best fit the problems at hand. A managerial skill is the ability to choose the "right" decision method—one that provides for a timely and quality decision, and one to which people involved in the implementation will be highly committed. To do this well, however, managers must understand both the potential assets and potential liabilities of moving from individual to more group-oriented decision making.[30]

The potential *advantages of group decision making* are highly significant, and they should be actively sought whenever time and other circumstances permit. Team decisions make greater amounts of knowledge and expertise available to solve problems. They expand the number of action alternatives that are examined; they help to avoid tunnel vision and con-

take it to the case!

Spin Master

Spin Master turns fun into opportunities

Spin Master, Canada's largest toymaker, is the result of a dream by three university friends to build a successful global corporation in the highly competitive toy market. In 1994, the three founders, Ronnen Harary, Anton Rabie, and Ben Varadi, combined a willingness to take risks with comprehensive hands-on market research to develop original products and capitalize on new opportunities. Spin Master has grown into an award-winning organization that strategically blends best-selling brands such as Air Hogs, Bella Dancerella, and Marshmallow, and partnerships with companies  such as McDonald's, Marvel, and Hershey to offer a range of toys that appeal to the kid in everyone. With its 300 employees, offices across the world, and over $300 million in sales, Spin Master is poised to play head to head with industry giants. Read the case in the *Workbook* and learn how to dream big dreams!

Source: With information from the corporate website: <www.spinmaster.com>.

sideration of only limited options. Team decisions increase the understanding and acceptance of outcomes by members. And importantly, team decisions increase the commitments of members to work hard to implement final plans.

The *potential disadvantages of group decision making* can be traced largely to the difficulties that can be experienced in a group process. In a team decision there may be social pressure to conform. Some individuals may feel intimidated or compelled to go along with the apparent wishes of others. There may be minority domination, where some members feel forced or "railroaded" to accept a decision advocated by one vocal individual or small coalition. Another problem that might occur is "groupthink," where cohesion among group members and a desire for unanimity overrides their motivation to realistically appraise a situation.[31] Also, there is no doubt that the time required to make team decisions can sometimes be a disadvantage. As more people are involved in the dialogue and discussion, decision making takes longer. This added time may be costly, even prohibitively so, in certain circumstances.[32]

●●● ETHICAL DECISION MAKING

Chapter 3 was devoted to ethics and social responsibility issues in management. As a reminder, however, it is important to restate the expectation that any decision should be ethical. It should at least meet the test described in Step 3 of decision making as the "ethics double-check." This involves asking and answering two straightforward but powerful *spotlight questions:* (1) "How would I feel if my family found out about this decision?", and (2) "How would I feel if this decision were published in the local newspaper?" The Josephson Institute model for ethical decision making suggests a third question to further strengthen the ethics double-check: "Think of the person you know or know of (in real life or fiction) who has the strongest character and best ethical judgement. Then ask yourself—what would that person do in your situation?"[33]

Although it adds time to decision making, the ethics double-check is necessary to ensure that the ethical aspects of a problem are properly considered in all situations. It is also consistent with the demanding moral standards of modern society. A willingness to pause to examine the ethics of a proposed decision may well result in both a better decision and the prevention of costly litigation. Ethicist Gerald Cavanaugh and his associates suggest that managers can proceed with the most confidence when the following criteria are met.[34]

1. *Utility*—Does the decision satisfy all constituents or stakeholders?

2. *Rights*—Does the decision respect the rights and duties of everyone?

3. *Justice*—Is the decision consistent with the canons of justice?

4. *Caring*—Is the decision consistent with my responsibilities to care?

●●● KNOWLEDGE MANAGEMENT AND ORGANIZATIONAL LEARNING

Now that the process of managerial decision making is clear, let's return to its context—a technology-driven world rich with information and demanding in the pace and uncertainty of change. This is the setting in which knowledge workers with intellectual capital become the most critical assets of organizations. Management theorist Peter Drucker, however, warned us that "knowledge constantly makes itself obsolete."[35] His message must be taken to heart. People and organizations cannot rest on past laurels; future success will be earned only by those who continually learn through experience.

The term **knowledge management** describes the processes through which organizations develop, organize, and share knowledge to achieve competitive advantage.[36] The significance of knowledge management as a strategic and integrating force in organizations is represented by the emergence of a new executive job title—*chief knowledge officer* (CKO). The CKO is

■ **Knowledge management** is the processes using intellectual capital for competitive advantage.

responsible for energizing learning processes and making sure that an organization's portfolio of intellectual assets are well managed and continually enhanced. These assets include such things as patents, intellectual property rights, trade secrets, and special processes and methods, as well as the accumulated knowledge and understanding of the entire workforce.

Knowledge management requires the creation of an organizational culture that truly values learning. Progressive organizations strive to build the foundations of what consultant Peter Senge calls a true **learning organization**. This is an organization, first described in Chapter 2, that "by virtue of people, values, and systems is able to continuously change and improve its performance based upon the lessons of experience."[37] Browne says that organizations can learn from many sources. They can learn from their own experience. They can learn from the experiences of their contractors, suppliers, partners, and customers. And they can learn from firms in unrelated businesses.[38] All of this, of course, depends on a willingness to seek out learning opportunities from these sources and to make information sharing an expected and valued work behaviour.

■ A **learning organization** continuously changes and improves using the lessons of experience.

✓ **Learning check ⑤**

BE SURE YOU CAN
• explain the availability, representativeness, anchoring, and adjustment heuristics • illustrate the concepts of framing error and escalating commitment in decision making • list questions that can be asked to double check the ethics of a decision • discuss why the best organizations today give high priority to knowledge management and organizational learning

---

●●● Chapter 7 STUDY GUIDE

WHERE WE'VE BEEN

Back to Chapters-Indigo

The opening example of how Heather Reisman turned her love of books into a national best-selling organization shows the importance of understanding the environment and being knowledgeable when taking risks and making decisions. In Chapter 7 you learned about the information needs of organizations and how new developments in information technology are changing organizations and the way people work. You have also learned how managers use information in the decision-making process, with special attention to decision errors and traps, ethical decision making, and decision making by individuals and groups.

THE NEXT STEP
INTEGRATED LEARNING ACTIVITIES

Cases/Projects	Self-Assessments	Exercises in Teamwork
• Spin Master Case	• Your Intuitive Ability (#11)	• Decision-Making Biases (#11)
• Project 10—Service Learning	• Assertiveness (#12)	• The Future Workplace (#14)
	• Facts and Inferences (#14)	• Dots and Squares Puzzle (#15)
	• Cognitive Style (#25)	• Lost at Sea (#26)

STUDY QUESTION SUMMARY

1. How is information technology changing the workplace?

- A major and rapidly growing force in the economy are e-businesses, which use the Internet to engage in business-to-consumer and business-to-business electronic commerce.

- Within organizations and between organizations IT is breaking barriers to speed workflows and cut costs.

- Today's "electronic" offices with e-mail, instant messaging, and networked computer systems are changing the way work is accomplished in and by organizations.

2. What is the role of information in the management process?

- Information is data made useful for decision making.

- Organizations need and use internal, public, and intelligence information.

- Management information systems (MIS) collect, organize, store, and distribute data to meet the information needs of managers.

- Intranets, extranets, and Web portals allow people to share databases and communicate electronically within an organization and between the organization and its environment.

3. How do managers use information to make decisions?

- A problem is a discrepancy between an actual and a desired state of affairs.

- The most threatening type of problem is the crisis, which occurs unexpectedly and can lead to disaster if it is not handled quickly and properly.

- Managers face structured and unstructured problems in environments of certainty, risk, and uncertainty.

- Managers vary in their willingness to deal with problems, and in their use of systematic and intuitive thinking.

4. What are the steps in the decision-making process?

- The steps in the decision-making process are: find and define the problem, generate and evaluate alternatives, decide on the preferred course of action, implement the decision, and evaluate the results.

- An optimizing decision, following the classical model, chooses the absolute best solution from a known set of alternatives.

- A satisfying decision, following the behavioural decision model, chooses the first satisfactory alternative that comes to attention.

5. What are the current issues in managerial decision making?

- Judgemental heuristics, framing errors, and escalating commitment can bias decision making.

- Group decisions offer the potential advantages of greater information and expanded commitment, but they are often slower than individual decisions.

- Decision makers should always take time to double-check the ethics of their decisions.

- Knowledge management captures, develops, and uses knowledge for competitive advantage; a learning organization is committed to continuous change and improvement based on the lessons of experience.

KEY TERMS REVIEW

Behavioural decision model (p. 171)

Certain environment (p. 167)

Classical decision model (p. 171)

Corporate portals (p. 164)

Cost-benefit analysis (p. 170)

Crisis (p. 166)

Crisis management (p. 166)

Data (p. 161)

Decision (p. 165)

Decision-making process (p. 169)

Decision support system (p. 163)

Electronic commerce (p. 159)

Electronic data interchange (p. 164)

Enterprise portals (p. 174)

Escalating commitment (p. 173)

Expert system (p. 163)

Extranet (p. 164)

Framing error (p. 173)

Groupware (p. 163)

Heuristics (p. 173)

Information (p. 161)

Information systems (p. 163)

Information technology (p. 158)

Instant messaging (p. 161)

Intellectual capital (p. 159)

Intranet (p. 164)

Intuitive thinking (p. 168)

Knowledge management (p. 175)

Knowledge worker (p. 159)

Learning organization (p. 176)

Management information systems (p. 163)

Nonprogrammed decision (p. 166)

Optimizing decision (p. 171)

Peer-to-peer file sharing (p. 161)

Problem solving (p. 165)

Programmed decision (p. 165)

Risk environment (p. 167)

Satisficing decision (p. 171)

Strategic opportunism (p. 168)

Structured problem (p. 165)

Systematic thinking (p. 168)

Uncertain environment (p. 168)

Unstructured problem (p. 166)

SELF-TEST 7

MULTIPLE-CHOICE QUESTIONS:

1. _____ is the collective brainpower or shared knowledge of an organization and its workforce.
   (a) Artificial intelligence (b) Groupware (c) Intellectual capital (d) Intelligence information

2. _____ are special computer programs that use "if . . . then" rules to help users analyze and solve problems.
   (a) Expert systems (b) Heuristics (c) Intranets (d) Web portals

3. A manager who is reactive and works hard to address problems after they occur is known as a _____.
   (a) problem seeker (b) problem avoider (c) problem solver (d) problem manager

4. When businesses like Chapters-Indigo and Dell use the Internet to sell products directly to customers, they are pursuing a form of e-commerce known as _____.
   (a) optimizing (b) B2B (c) B2C (d) networking

5. A problem is a discrepancy between a(n) _____ situation and a desired situation.
   (a) unexpected (b) past (c) actual (d) anticipated

6. A(n) _____ thinker approaches problems in a rational and analytic fashion.
   (a) systematic (b) intuitive (c) internal (d) external

7. The first step in the decision-making process is to _____.
   (a) identify alternatives (b) evaluate results (c) find and define the problem (d) choose a solution

8. Being asked to develop a plan to increase international sales of a product is an example of the types of _____ problems that managers must be prepared to deal with.
   (a) routine (b) unstructured (c) crisis (d) structured

9. Costs, timeliness, and _____ are among the recommended criteria for evaluating alternative courses of action.
   (a) ethical soundness (b) competitiveness (c) availability (d) simplicity

10. The _____ decision model views managers as making optimizing decisions, whereas the _____ decision model views them as making satisfying decisions.
    (a) behavioural, human relations (b) classical, behavioural (c) heuristic, humanistic (d) quantitative, behavioural

11. Top managers in organizations commonly use information to make decisions about _____.
    (a) strategy formulation (b) operational plans (c) day-to-day operations (d) short-term plans

12. Among the ways IT is changing organizations today, _____ is one of its most noteworthy characteristics.
    (a) eliminating the need for top managers (b) reducing the amount of information available for decision making
    (c) breaking down barriers internally and externally (d) decreasing the need for environmental awareness

13. When a problem is addressed according to the positive or negative context in which it is presented, this is an example of _____.
    (a) framing error (b) escalating commitment (c) availability and adjustment (d) strategic opportunism

14. A manager who asks whether or not the decision will satisfy all stakeholders is using the criterion of _____ to check the ethical soundness of the intended course of action.
    (a) justice (b) rights (c) cost vs. benefit (d) utility

15. Among the environments for managerial decision making, certainty is the most favourable and it can be addressed through _____ decisions.
    (a) programmed (b) risk (c) satisficing (d) intuitive

SHORT-RESPONSE QUESTIONS:

16. What is the difference between an optimizing decision and a satisficing decision?

17. How can a manager double-check the ethics of a decision?

18. How would a manager use systematic thinking and intuitive thinking in problem solving?

19. How can the members of an organization be trained in crisis management?

APPLICATION QUESTION:

20. As a participant in a new "mentoring" program between your university and a local high school, you have volunteered to give a presentation to a class on the challenges in the new "electronic office." The goal is to sensitize them to developments in IT and motivate them to take the best advantage of their high school program so as to prepare themselves for the workplace of the future. What will you say to them?

Planning and Controlling

Planning Ahead

After reading Chapter 8, you should be able to answer these questions in your own words.

1. How do managers plan?

2. What types of plans do managers use?

3. What are the useful planning tools and techniques?

4. What is the control process?

5. What are the common organizational controls?

Cognos Inc.
Crunching the numbers to succeed

The aim of Cognos Inc., a software company operating from Ottawa, Ontario, is to help businesses "crunch the numbers" in order to yield better organizational planning and control. Established in 1969, Cognos is now located in over 135 countries, with over 3,500 employees.

With businesses facing an ever-changing marketplace, Cognos has set out to help companies gain a flexible approach to their strategic plans by providing software to analyze business data. A world leader in business intelligence and performance planning software, the company provides businesses with a competitive advantage by integrating key areas of budgeting, performance, and sales so companies can analyze the numbers to monitor and re-engineer strategic direction. This ensures resources are directed toward areas that are financially and commercially viable. According to their website, "Cognos is the only company to support all these key management activities with a complete solution."

What is Cognos's own plan? They continue to research and develop new software. Recently, they launched Cognos 8 Business Intelligence, a product they state delivers "the complete range of BI capabilities: reporting, analyzing, scorecarding, dashboarding, business event management." The company has also created the Cognos Innovation Centre, a venue for executives and senior managers to dialogue and to create, implement, and sustain various innovative practices.

With customers in all sectors of industry, including Yamaha, Lufthansa, and Dow Chemical, the company looks set to take on the big enterprise resource planners (ERPs) and even Microsoft. As Philip Howard notes, "What Cognos has recognized is that planning is more than just a financial activity—that it is something that needs to spread across the enterprise and be coordinated across multiple departments. However, appreciating that fact and supporting it in principle in the planning software is one thing; supporting it in practice is another. This is where the Cognos blueprints come in, enabling users to adopt these practices relatively easily." It sounds as if Cognos has a plan.[1]

IN THE WORKPLACE

You are busy answering that stack of emails that appear daily when your colleague Chen from across the aisle starts saying rather loudly, "If you fail to plan, plan on failing—and right now I am failing!" Being the neighbourly type (and also not wanting to answer those emails), you ask what is going on with the planning and failing comment.

Chen confides in you that a project that he has been asked to do is in trouble because he did not think things through very well. He wonders what he could do to ensure this does not happen again. You suggest that he might make use of a number of planning tools and techniques. "Can you give me a few examples"? Chen asks. What tools and techniques do you suggest he try?

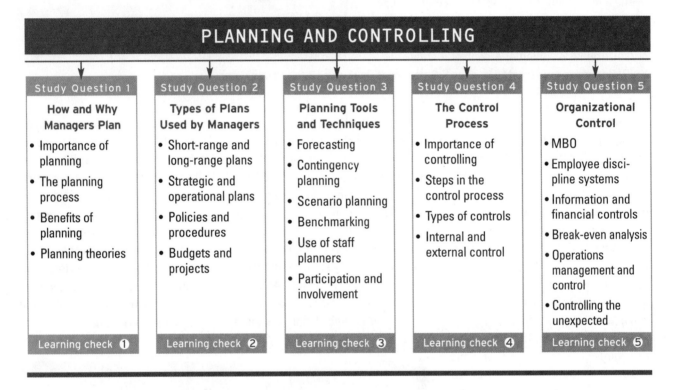

••• Chapter 8   LEARNING PREVIEW   •••

To survive and succeed, Cognos knows it has to plan for the future by constantly reinventing itself and its products. In Chapter 8 you will learn how managers use planning to help turn insight and opportunity into real performance accomplishments. You will find also that what you learn about planning has important personal applications. And you will learn why the management function of controlling is essential if we are to ensure that things do, in fact, happen according to plans.

PLANNING AND CONTROLLING

Study Question 1	Study Question 2	Study Question 3	Study Question 4	Study Question 5
How and Why Managers Plan	**Types of Plans Used by Managers**	**Planning Tools and Techniques**	**The Control Process**	**Organizational Control**
• Importance of planning	• Short-range and long-range plans	• Forecasting	• Importance of controlling	• MBO
• The planning process	• Strategic and operational plans	• Contingency planning	• Steps in the control process	• Employee discipline systems
• Benefits of planning	• Policies and procedures	• Scenario planning	• Types of controls	• Information and financial controls
• Planning theories	• Budgets and projects	• Benchmarking	• Internal and external control	• Break-even analysis
		• Use of staff planners		• Operations management and control
		• Participation and involvement		• Controlling the unexpected
Learning check ❶	Learning check ❷	Learning check ❸	Learning check ❹	Learning check ❺

In his book *Leading the Revolution*,[2] management consultant Gary Hamel argues that many of today's companies won't make it in the long run. "Organizations that succeed in this new century will be as different from industrial-era organizations as those companies themselves were different from craft-based industries," he says. "Companies are going to have to re-invent themselves much more frequently than before."[3] Cognos seems to be meeting this challenge. Although there are no guarantees about the future, it keeps changing to stay on top of its markets.

Managers need the ability to look ahead, make good plans, and then help others meet the challenges of the future. With the future uncertain, however, the likelihood is that even the best of plans will have to be changed at some point. Thus, managers also need the courage to be flexible in response to new circumstances and the discipline to maintain control even as situations become hectic and the performance pressures stay unrelenting. In the ever-changing technology industry, for example, CEO T. J. Rodgers of Cypress Semiconductor Corp., which has six offices in Canada, is known for valuing both performance goals and accountability. Cypress employees work with clear and quantified work goals, which they help set. Rodgers believes the system helps find problems before they interfere with performance. He says: "Managers monitor the goals, look for problems, and expect people who fall behind to ask for help before they lose control of, or damage, a major project."[4]

HOW AND WHY MANAGERS PLAN

In Chapter 1 the management process was described as planning, organizing, leading, and controlling the use of resources to achieve performance objectives. The first of these functions, **planning**, sets the stage for the others by providing a sense of direction. It is a process of setting objectives and determining how to best accomplish them. Said a bit differently, planning involves deciding exactly what you want to accomplish and how to best go about it.

> ■ **Planning** is the process of setting objectives and determining how to accomplish them.

●●● IMPORTANCE OF PLANNING

When planning is done well it creates a solid platform for the other management functions: *organizing*—allocating and arranging resources to accomplish tasks; *leading*—guiding the efforts of human resources to ensure high levels of task accomplishment; and *controlling*—monitoring task accomplishments and taking necessary corrective action.

The centrality of planning in management, as shown in *Figure 8.1*, is important to understand. In today's demanding organizational and career environments it is essential to stay one step ahead of the competition. This involves striving always to become better at what you are doing and to be action oriented. An Eaton Corporation annual report, for example, once stated: "Planning at Eaton means taking the hard decisions before events force them upon you, and anticipating the future needs of the market before the demand asserts itself."[5]

●●● THE PLANNING PROCESS

In the planning process, **objectives** identify the specific results, or desired outcomes, that one intends to achieve. The **plan** is a statement of action steps to be taken in order to accomplish the objectives. The steps in the systematic planning process include the following:

> ■ **Objectives** are specific results that one wishes to achieve.
>
> ■ A **plan** is a statement of intended means for accomplishing objectives.

1. *Define your objectives:* Identify desired outcomes or results in very specific ways. Know where you want to go; know how far off the mark you are at various points along the way and be specific enough to know exactly when you have arrived.

2. *Determine where you stand vis-à-vis objectives:* Evaluate current accomplishments relative to the desired results. Know where you stand in reaching the objectives; know what strengths work in your favour and what weaknesses may hold you back.

3. *Develop premises regarding future conditions:* Try to anticipate future events. Generate alternative "scenarios" for what may happen; identify, for each scenario, things that may help or hinder progress toward your objectives.

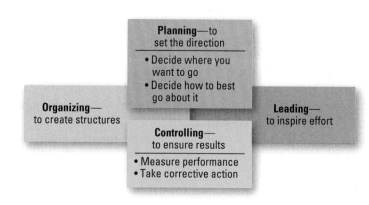

Figure 8.1 The roles of planning and controlling in the management process.

4. *Analyze and choose among action alternatives:* List and carefully evaluate the possible actions that may be taken. Choose the alternative(s) most likely to accomplish your objectives; describe step-by-step what must be done to follow the chosen course of action.

5. *Implement the plan and evaluate results:* Take action and carefully measure your progress toward your objectives. Do what the plan requires; evaluate results, take corrective action, and revise plans as needed.

The planning process just described is an application of the decision-making process discussed in Chapter 7. It is a systematic way to approach two important tasks: (1) setting performance objectives and (2) deciding how to best achieve them. This is not something managers do while working alone in quiet rooms, free from distractions, and at scheduled times. Planning should be ongoing, continuously done even while dealing with an otherwise hectic and demanding work setting.[6] Importantly, the best planning is always done with the active participation and involvement of those people whose work efforts will eventually determine whether or not the objectives are accomplished.

CANADIAN COMPANY IN THE NEWS   Air Canada

AIRLINE'S RESTRUCTURING PUTS IT BACK IN THE AIR

Air Canada successfully recovered from bankruptcy protection in 2004 largely because of a creative and effective change management plan, which included reduced operating costs, a stronger balance sheet, corporate reorganization, and a fleet renewal and marketing strategy. "We're emerging from CCAA [bankruptcy] focused and well on our way to becoming a profitable, growing and competitive company in a rapidly changing industry," Robert Milton, then chairman, president, and CEO of ACE Aviation Holdings Inc., said at the time. "We have not only reduced our cost structure and strengthened our balance sheet; we have fundamentally reinvented who we are." Air Canada's various business segments—Aeroplan, Air Canada Jazz, Touram, Air Canada Technical Services, Air Canada Cargo, and Air Canada Ground-handling Services—now operate as separate legal entities under parent holding company ACE Aviation Holdings Inc. Along with the creation of ACE came new by-laws and a new board of directors. Air Canada developed their plan and were successful at implementing it.

Source: Air Canada news release, Sept. 30, 2004; Schermerhorn et al., "Renewed Airline Takes Flight," *Organizational Behaviour* (Toronto: John Wiley & Sons Canada, 2005), p. 380.

●●● BENEFITS OF PLANNING

Organizations in today's dynamic times are facing pressures from many sources. Externally, these include ethical expectations, government regulations, ever-more-complex technologies, the uncertainties of a global economy, changing technologies, and the sheer cost of investments in labour, capital, and other supporting resources. Internally, they include the quest for operating efficiencies, new structures and technologies, alternative work arrangements, greater diversity in the workplace, and related managerial challenges. As you would expect, planning in such conditions offers a number of benefits.

Decima Research Inc. is a company focused on its core strengths: telephone survey and research. It has used its planning process to evolve and meet the market's changing needs: balancing customers' need for more precision with the fact that fewer people want to answer phone surveys. Decima, listed as one of Canada's best managed companies, is showing focus and innovation by building a large panel of Canadians willing to do telephone surveys, thereby providing researchers with a steady pool of respondents.[7]

Planning Improves Focus and Flexibility

Good planning improves focus and flexibility, both of which are important for performance success. An *organization with focus* knows what it does best, knows the needs of its customers, and knows how to serve them well. An *individual with focus* knows where he or she wants to go in a career or situation, and is able to retain that objective even when difficulties arise. An *organization with flexibility* is willing and able to change and adapt to shifting circumstances, and operates with an orientation toward the future rather than the past. An *individual with flexibility* adjusts career plans to fit new and developing opportunities.

Planning Improves Action Orientation

Planning is a way for people and organizations to stay ahead of the competition and always become better at what they are doing. It helps avoid the complacency trap of simply being carried along by the flow of events or of being distracted by successes or failures of the moment. It keeps the future visible as a performance target and reminds us that the best decisions are often made before events force them upon us. Management consultant Stephen R. Covey talks about the importance of priorities. He points out that the most successful executives "zero in on what they do that 'adds value' to an organization." Instead of working on too many things, they work on the things that really count. Covey says that good planning makes us more (1) *results oriented*—creating a performance-oriented sense of direction; (2) *priority oriented*—making sure the most important things get first attention; (3) *advantage oriented*—ensuring that all resources are used to best advantage; and (4) *change oriented*—anticipating problems and opportunities so they can be best dealt with.[8]

Planning Improves Coordination

Planning improves coordination. The many different individuals, groups, and subsystems in organizations are each doing many different things at the same time. But even as they pursue their specific tasks and objectives, their accomplishments must add up to meaningful contributions to the needs of the organization as a whole. Good planning throughout an organization creates a **means–ends chain** or *hierarchy of objectives* in which lower-level objectives lead to the accomplishment of higher-level ones. Higher-level objectives as *ends* are directly tied to lower-level objectives as the means for their accomplishment. *Figure 8.2* uses the example of quality management to show how a means–ends chain helps guide and integrate quality efforts within a large manufacturing firm.

■ In a **means–ends chain**, lower-level objectives help accomplish higher-level ones.

Figure 8.2 A sample means–ends chain for total quality management.

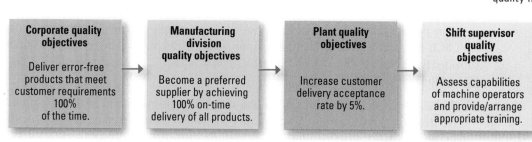

Corporate quality objectives	Manufacturing division quality objectives	Plant quality objectives	Shift supervisor quality objectives
Deliver error-free products that meet customer requirements 100% of the time.	Become a preferred supplier by achieving 100% on-time delivery of all products.	Increase customer delivery acceptance rate by 5%.	Assess capabilities of machine operators and provide/arrange appropriate training.

Planning Improves Time Management

One of the side benefits that planning offers is better time management. Lewis Platt, former chairman of Hewlett-Packard, says: "Basically, the whole day is a series of choices."[9] These choices have to be made in ways that allocate your time to the most important priorities. Platt says that he was "ruthless about priorities" and that you "have to continually work to optimize your time."

Most of us have experienced the difficulties of balancing available time with the many commitments and opportunities we would like to fulfill. It is easy to lose track of time and fall prey to what consultants identify as "time wasters." Too many of us allow our time to be dominated by other people and/or by non-essential activities.[10] "To-do" lists can help, but they have to contain the right things. In daily living and in management, it is important to distinguish between things that you *must do* (top priority), *should do* (high priority), would be *nice to do* (low priority), and really *don't need to do* (no priority).

Planning Improves Control

When planning is done well it facilitates control, making it easier to measure performance results and take action to improve things as necessary. Planning helps make this possible by defining the objectives along with the specific actions through which they are to be pursued. If results are less than expected, either the objectives or the action being taken, or both, can be evaluated and then adjusted through the control process. In this way planning and controlling work closely together in the management process. Without planning, control lacks a framework for measuring how well things are going and what could be done to make them go better. Without control, planning lacks the follow-through needed to ensure that things work out as planned.

●●● PLANNING THEORIES

■ **Rational comprehensive planning (RCP)** focuses on a logical decision-making approach and advocates a holistic approach to problem solving.

Two different theoretical approaches to planning are rational comprehensive planning and incrementalism. **Rational comprehensive planning** (RCP) focuses on a logical decision-making approach and advocates that problem solving should be looked at from a holistic or integrated systems viewpoint. RCP uses conceptual or mathematical models that relate ends (objectives) to means (resources and constraints) with a heavy reliance on statistical analysis. Planners using this approach gather information from the environment in order to run models that will allow them to determine what the future will be like so that the organization may be adapted accordingly.

RCP's major advantage is its simplicity. By following a logical, deliberate process, this type of planning is easily understood, the analytical techniques easy to use, and the corresponding plan of action easy to defend. RCP is, however, somewhat unrealistic. It can only be applied to relatively simple problems. In the real world, the limitations of resources, information, and time make it extremely difficult to use RCP in its purest form. Caveats and assumptions abound when using this approach, as the statistical modelling tools used cannot address the many subtle nuances of the complex world that businesses operate within. The costs of developing more comprehensive models often exceed the benefits derived from undertaking this analysis.

The perspective of *incrementalism* is to "muddle through." Recognizing the problems with RCP, planners examined alternative approaches. Eminent sociologist Amitai Etzioni provided the foundation for an incrementalist approach with his six key procedures for "disjointed incrementalism."

1. Rather than attempting a comprehensive survey and the evaluation of all alternatives, the decision maker focuses only on those policies that differ incrementally from existing policies.

2. Only a relatively small number of policy alternatives are considered.

3. For each policy alternative, only a restricted number of "important" consequences are evaluated.

4. The problem confronting the decision maker is continually redefined: incrementalism allows for countless ends–means and means–ends adjustments, which, in effect, make the problem more manageable.

5. Thus, there is no one decision or "right" solution but a "never-ending series of attacks" on the issues at hand through serial analyses and evaluation.

6. As such, incremental decision making is described as remedial, geared more to the alleviation of present, concrete social imperfections than to the promotion of future goals.[11]

Incremental planning's strength is that, rather than trying to be both rational and comprehensive, it looks at decision making as it generally occurs—quickly and with imperfect information. The model recognizes that planning is continually being undertaken and revised. Thus, changes are made in small doses rather than through a radical action, as is proposed with RCP. Incrementalism has fewer information demands and examines the consequences of smaller change, both of which allow decision makers to act more quickly in response to environmental changes. However, critics state that incremental planning is limited in scope as it generally addresses only a small range of alternatives. By focusing only on the very near future, incremental planning fails to take advantage of innovations and innovating thinking. Small steps are taken rather than big and bold ones that might be necessary.

In practice, planners initially examine a problem using an incremental planning approach and switch over to be more comprehensive depending upon the depth of the problem. Planners thus take advantage of the strengths of both approaches while attempting to avoid the weaknesses of each. This collectivist approach blends both types to yield successful planning. Some planners operate in an opposite direction—they use the RCP approach first to develop an "official plan" and then utilize an incremental approach in daily planning practice in order to successfully achieve their goal.[12]

BE SURE YOU CAN

• define planning as a management function • list the steps in the formal planning process • illustrate the benefits of planning for a business or organization that is familiar to you • illustrate the benefits of planning for personal career development

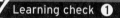 ✓ **Learning check ❶**

TYPES OF PLANS USED BY MANAGERS

Managers face different planning challenges in the flow and pace of activities in organizations. In some cases the planning environment is stable and quite predictable; in others it is more dynamic and uncertain. A variety of plans are available to meet these different needs.

●●● SHORT-RANGE AND LONG-RANGE PLANS

A rule of thumb is that *short-range plans* cover one year or less, *intermediate-range plans* cover one to two years, and *long-range plans* look three or more years into the future. Top management is most likely to be involved in setting long-range plans and directions for the organization as a whole, while lower management levels focus more on short-range plans

PERSONAL MANAGEMENT

Time is one of our most precious resources, and **TIME MANAGEMENT** is an essential skill in today's high-pressure and fast-paced world of work. Some 77 percent of managers in one survey said that the new digital age has increased the number of decisions they have to make; 43 percent complained there was less time available to make them. Others say that 20 percent of their telephone time is wasted.[13] Of course, you have to be careful in defining "waste." It isn't a waste of time to occasionally relax, take a breather from work, and find humour and pleasure in social interaction. Such breaks help us gather energies to do well in our work. But it is a waste to let friends dominate your time so that you don't work on a term paper until it is too late to write a really good one, or delay a decision to apply for an internship until the deadline is passed. Perhaps you are one of those who plans to do so many things in a day that you never get to the most important ones. Perhaps you don't plan, let events take you where they may, and on many days don't accomplish much at all. Learning to manage your time better will serve you very well in the future, both at work and in your personal life.

Get to know yourself better

Complete Self-Assessment #13—**Time Management Profile,** and Exercise #9—**Beating the Time Wasters**, from the Workbook and Personal Management Activity #8 on the companion website.

that help achieve long-term objectives. But everyone should understand an organization's long-term plans. In the absence of a hierarchy of objectives tied to a long-range plan, there is always a risk that the pressures of daily events may create confusion and divert attention from important tasks. In other words, without a sense of long-term direction, people can end up working hard but without achieving significant results.

EllisDon Corp. is a good example of a company that looks to the future. Five years ago, this Ontario construction company decided to change their business model and become a client-focused company, a new idea in this industry sector. They are now benefiting from increased profits and new markets, including setting up a permanent office in Dubai.

Management researcher Elliott Jaques suggests that people vary in their capability to think out, organize, and work through events of different time horizons.[14] In fact, he believes that most people work comfortably with only three-month time spans; a smaller group works well with a one-year span; and only about one person in several million can handle a 20-year time frame. These are provocative ideas. Although a team leader's planning challenges may rest mainly in the weekly or monthly range, a chief executive is expected to have a vision extending several years into the future. Career progress to higher management levels requires the conceptual skills to work well with longer-range time frames.[15]

Complexities and uncertainties in today's environments are putting pressure on these planning horizons. In an increasingly global economy, planning opportunities and challenges are often worldwide in scope, not just local. And, of course, the information age is ever present in its planning implications. We now talk about planning in *Internet time*, where businesses are continually changing and updating plans. Even top managers now face the reality that Internet time keeps making the "long" range of planning shorter and shorter.

●●● STRATEGIC AND OPERATIONAL PLANS

■ A **strategic plan** identifies long-term directions for the organization.

Plans differ not only in time horizons but also in scope. **Strategic plans** set broad, comprehensive, and longer-term action directions. Strategic planning by top management involves determining objectives for the entire organization and describing what and where the organization wants to be in the future. There was a time, for example, when many large businesses strategically sought to diversify into unrelated areas. A successful oil firm might have acquired an office products company or a successful cereal manufacturer might have acquired an apparel company. In the next chapter, "Strategic Management," we will examine the process through which such strategic choices are made and how they can be analyzed. For now, suffice it to say that diversification strategies haven't always proved successful. Many companies following them have since reversed course, choosing instead to strategically focus on core areas of expertise. Take for example A&W Food Services of Canada Inc., which wants to be the number-one burger choice of the baby boom generation and is doing so by creating a new/old relationship with the drive-in generation. Over the last 15 years, its strategic plan for attracting baby boomers has included expanding its free-standing street presence with retro designs and "cruising events." Initially focusing on British Columbia, the chain is now bringing these ideas to Ontario and Quebec.

Operational plans define what needs to be done in specific functions or work units to implement strategic plans. Typical operational plans in a business firm include: *production plans*—dealing with the methods and technology needed by people in their work; *financial plans*—dealing with money required to support various operations; *facilities plans*—dealing with facilities and work layouts; *marketing plans*—dealing with the requirements of selling and distributing goods or services; and *human resource plans*—dealing with the recruitment, selection, and placement of people into various jobs.

■ An **operational plan** identifies activities to implement strategic plans.

●●● POLICIES AND PROCEDURES

Among the many plans in organizations, *standing plans* in the form of organizational policies and procedures are designed for use over and over again. A **policy** communicates broad guidelines for making decisions and taking action in specific circumstances. For example, typical human resource policies address such matters as employee hiring, termination, performance appraisals, pay increases, promotions, and discipline. Another policy area of special organizational consequence is sexual harassment. Enlightened employers take great pains to clearly spell out their policies on sexual harassment and the methods for implementing them. When Judith Nitsch started her own engineering consulting business, for example, she defined a sexual harassment policy, took a hard line in its enforcement, and appointed both a male and a female employee for others to talk with about sexual harassment concerns.[16]

■ A **policy** is a standing plan that communicates broad guidelines for decisions and action.

Rules or **procedures** describe exactly what actions are to be taken in specific situations. They are often found stated in employee handbooks or manuals as "SOPs"—standard operating procedures. Whereas a policy sets a broad guideline for action, procedures define precise actions to be taken. In the prior example, Judith Nitsch will want to put in place procedures that ensure everyone receives fair, equal, and nondiscriminatory treatment under the sexual harassment policy. Everyone should know how to file a sexual harassment complaint and how that complaint will be handled.

■ A **procedure** or **rule** precisely describes actions that are to be taken in specific situations.

●●● BUDGETS AND PROJECTS

In contrast to standing plans, *single-use plans* are used once, serving the needs and objectives of well-defined situations in a timely manner. **Budgets** are single-use plans that commit resources to activities, projects, or programs. They are powerful tools that allocate scarce resources among multiple and often competing uses. Good managers are able to bargain for, and obtain, adequate budgets to support the needs of their work units or teams. They also achieve performance objectives while keeping within the allocated budget.

■ A **budget** is a plan that commits resources to projects or activities.

A *fixed budget* allocates a fixed amount of resources for a specific purpose. For example, a manager may have a $25,000 budget for equipment purchases in a given year. A *flexible budget* allows the allocation of resources to vary in proportion with various levels of activity. For example, a manager may have flexibility to hire extra temporary workers if production orders exceed a certain volume.

A common problem with budgets is that resource allocations get "rolled over" from one budgeting period to the next, often without a rigorous performance review. A **zero-based budget** deals with this problem by approaching each new budget period as if it were brand new. There is no guarantee that any past funding will be renewed; all proposals compete anew for available funds at the start of each new budget cycle. In a major division of the company Campbell Soup, for example, managers using zero-based budgeting once discovered that 10 percent of the marketing budget was going to sales promotions no longer relevant to current product lines.

■ A **zero-based budget** allocates resources as if each budget were brand new.

■ **Projects** are one-time activities that have clear beginning and end points.

■ **Project management** makes sure that activities required to complete a project are accomplished on time and correctly.

A lot of work in organizations takes the form of **projects**, one-time activities that have clear beginning and end points. Examples are the completion of a new student activities building on a campus, the development of a new computer software program, or the implementation of a new advertising campaign for a sports team. **Project management** involves making sure that the activities required to complete a project are completed on time, within budget, and in ways that otherwise meet objectives. Managers of projects make extensive use of *project schedules* that define specific task objectives, link activities to be accomplished with due dates, and identify the amounts and time of resource requirements.

Learning check ②

BE SURE YOU CAN

• differentiate short-range and long-range plans • differentiate strategic and operational plans and explain their relationships to one another • define the terms policy and procedure, and give an example of each in the university setting • explain the unique operation of a zero-based budget

PLANNING TOOLS AND TECHNIQUES

The benefits of planning are best realized when the foundations are strong. The useful tools and techniques of managerial planning include forecasting, contingency planning, scenarios, benchmarking, participative planning, and the use of staff planners.

●●● FORECASTING

■ **Forecasting** attempts to predict the future.

Forecasting is the process of predicting what will happen in the future.[17] All plans involve forecasts of some sort. Periodicals such as *Business Week*, *Fortune*, *Canadian Business*, and *The Economist* regularly report forecasts of economic conditions, interest rates, unemployment, and trade deficits, among other issues. Some are based on *qualitative forecasting*, which uses expert opinions to predict the future. Others involve *quantitative forecasting*, which uses mathematical models and statistical analysis of historical data and surveys to predict future events. Although useful, all forecasts should be treated cautiously. They are

AROUND THE WORLD

There may be more to competition than meets the eye

Coke and Pepsi spend hundreds of millions of dollars on advertising as they engage one another in the ongoing "Cola War." It may seem that they have nothing to worry about but each other and a few discounters. Not so. There is an ever-changing world out there, and more than 50 percent of their revenues come internationally. Now factor into the planning equation current events, and what do you get? Mecca Cola and Qibla Cola for one thing! Both new colas entered European markets riding a wave of resentment of US brands and multinationals. The founder of Qibla says: "By choosing to boycott major brands, consumers are sending an important signal: that the exploitation of Muslims cannot continue unchecked." Although Coke and Pepsi may have little to fear from these competitors, the emerging international consumer voice has to be heard inside the executive suites of all multinational companies.

Source: Information from Associated Press, "Cola Jihad Bubbling in Europe," *Columbus Dispatch* (February 11, 2003), pp. C1, C2.

planning aids, not substitutes. It is said that a music agent once told Elvis Presley: "You ought to go back to driving a truck because you ain't going nowhere." He was obviously mistaken. That's the problem with forecasts—they can be wrong. In the final analysis, forecasting always relies on human judgement. Planning involves deciding what to do about the implications of forecasts once they are made.

●●● CONTINGENCY PLANNING

Planning, by definition, involves thinking ahead. But the more uncertain the planning environment, the more likely that one's original assumptions, forecasts, and intentions may prove inadequate or wrong. **Contingency planning** identifies alternative courses of action that can be implemented to meet the needs of changing circumstances. Although one can't always predict when things will go wrong, it can be anticipated that they will. It is highly unlikely that any plan will ever be perfect; changes in the environment will sooner or later occur, as will crises and emergencies. And when they do, the best managers and organizations have contingency plans ready to be implemented. Contingency plans contain "trigger points" that indicate when pre-selected alternative plans should be activated.

■ **Contingency planning** identifies alternative courses of action to take when things go wrong.

●●● SCENARIO PLANNING

A long-term version of contingency planning, called **scenario planning**, involves identifying several alternative future scenarios or states of affairs that may occur. Plans are then made to deal with each should it actually occur.[18] When the Heart and Stroke Foundation of Ontario set out to design a new model for health care funding, they wanted to challenge the organization to think in different ways about the future. A scenario planning process helped the board and other invited experts to rehearse strategic development plans and tactics in five different but realistic scenarios from the world of cardiovascular research and health care in 2020. This scenario planning helped the foundation balance tools, evidence, and insight in order to develop a new way of doing business that would take them into the future.[19]

■ **Scenario planning** identifies alternative future scenarios and makes plans to deal with each.

●●● BENCHMARKING

All too often planners become too comfortable with the ways things are going and overconfident that the past is a good indicator of the future. Successful planning must challenge the status quo; it cannot simply accept things as they are. One way to do this is through **benchmarking**, a technique that makes use of external comparisons to better evaluate one's current performance and identify possible actions for the future.[20] The purpose of benchmarking is to find out what other people and organizations are doing very well, and plan how to incorporate these ideas into one's own operations. One benchmarking technique is to search for **best practices**, those things done by competitors and non-competitors alike that help them to achieve superior performance. This powerful planning technique is a way for progressive companies to learn from other "excellent" companies. The best-run organizations also emphasize internal benchmarking that encourages all members and work units to learn and improve by sharing one another's best practices.

■ **Benchmarking** uses external comparisons to gain insights for planning.

■ **Best practices** are things that lead to superior performance.

●●● USE OF STAFF PLANNERS

As organizations grow, there is a corresponding need to increase the sophistication of the planning system itself. In some cases, staff planners are employed to help coordinate planning for the organization as a whole or for one of its major components. These planning specialists are skilled in all steps of the planning process, as well as planning tools and techniques. They can help bring focus and energy to accomplish important, often strategic, planning tasks. But one risk is a tendency for a communication "gap" to develop between staff planners and line managers. Unless everyone works closely together, the resulting plans may be inadequate and people may lack commitment to implement the plans no matter how good they are.

●●● PARTICIPATION AND INVOLVEMENT

■ **Participatory planning** includes the persons who will be affected by plans and/or who will implement them.

"Participation" is a key word in the planning process. **Participatory planning** includes, in all planning steps, the people who will be affected by the plans and/or who will be asked to help implement them. This process, as shown in *Figure 8.3*, brings many benefits to the organization. Participation can increase the creativity and information available for planning. It can also increase the understanding and acceptance of plans, as well as commitment to their success. Even though participatory planning takes more time, it can improve results by improving implementation. When 7-Eleven executives planned for new "upscale" products and services such as selling fancy meals-to-go, they received a hard lesson. Although their ideas sounded good at the top, franchisees balked at the shop level. The executives learned the value of taking time to involve franchise owners in the process of planning new corporate strategies.[21] At Mackinnon Transport Inc. in Guelph, Ontario, participatory planning has resulted in an employee value-driven culture. All employees participate in the planning process and are regularly updated about the company's program toward its goals.

Figure 8.3 How participation and involvement help build commitments to plans.

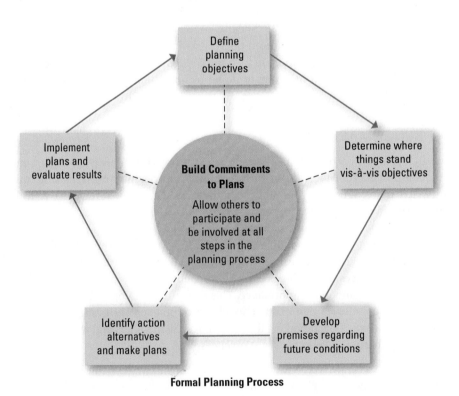

Formal Planning Process

BE SURE YOU CAN

• define the terms forecasting, contingency planning, scenario planning, and benchmarking • explain the value of contingency planning and scenario planning • explain the concept of participatory planning and defend its importance in organizations today

✓ Learning check ❸

THE CONTROL PROCESS

"Keeping in touch . . . Staying informed . . . Being in control." In addition to planning, these are important responsibilities for every manager. But "control" is a word like "power." If you aren't careful when it is used, it leaves a negative connotation. However, it is important to know that control plays a positive and necessary role in the management process. To have things "under control" is good; for things to be "out of control" is generally bad.

IMPORTANCE OF CONTROLLING

In the management process, **controlling** is a process of measuring performance and taking action to ensure desired results. Its purpose is straightforward—to make sure that plans are achieved, that actual performance meets or surpasses objectives. The foundation of control is information. Henry Schacht, former CEO of Cummins Engine Company, once discussed control in terms of what he called "friendly facts." He stated, "Facts that reinforce what you are doing . . . are nice, because they help in terms of psychic reward. Facts that raise alarms are equally friendly, because they give you clues about how to respond, how to change, and where to spend the resources."[22]

■ **Controlling** is the process of measuring performance and taking action to ensure desired results.

If you refer back to *Figure 8.1*, it shows how controlling fits in with the other management functions. Planning sets the directions and allocates resources. Organizing brings people and material resources together in working combinations. Leading inspires people to best utilize these resources. Controlling sees to it that the right things happen, in the right way, and at the right time. It helps ensure that performance by individuals and groups is consistent with plans. It helps ensure that accomplishments throughout an organization are coordinated in means–ends fashion. And, it helps ensure that people comply with organizational policies and procedures.

Effective control is also important to organizational learning. It offers the great opportunity of learning from experience. Consider, for example, the program of **after-action review** pioneered by the U.S. Army and now utilized by the Canadian military, firefighters, and in many corporate settings. This is a structured review of lessons learned and results accomplished on a completed project, task force, or special operation. Participants are asked to answer questions like: "What was the intent?" "What actually happened?" "What did we learn?"[23] The review helps make continuous improvement a part of the organizational culture. It encourages everyone involved to take responsibility for their performance efforts and accomplishments.

■ An **after-action review** identifies lessons learned in a completed project, task force, or special operation.

STEPS IN THE CONTROL PROCESS

The process of management control involves the four steps shown in *Figure 8.4*: (1) establish objectives and standards; (2) measure actual performance; (3) compare results with objectives and standards; and (4) take corrective action as needed. While essential to management, the process applies equally well to personal affairs and careers. Think about it. Without career objectives, how do you know where you really want to go? How can you allocate your time and other resources to take best advantage of available opportunities? Without measurement, how can you assess any progress being made? How can you adjust current behaviour to improve prospects for future results?

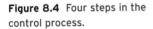

Figure 8.4 Four steps in the control process.

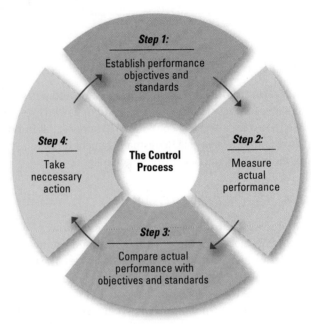

Step 1: Establish Objectives and Standards

The control process begins with planning, when performance objectives and standards for measuring them are set. It can't start without them. Performance objectives should represent key results that one wants to accomplish. The word "key" in the prior sentence is important. The focus in planning should be on describing "critical" or "essential" results that will make a substantial difference in the success of the organization. Standards are important too. As key results are identified, one also has to specify the standards and measures that will be used to evaluate their accomplishment. BMO Financial Group, for example, uses a diversity index to quantify performance on diversity issues. By setting strategic direction for quantitative and qualitative diversity goals, BMO measures executive performance against those goals on a quarterly and annual basis.[24]

> ■ An **output standard** measures performance results in terms of quantity, quality, cost, or time.

In the control process, **output standards** measure performance results in terms of outcomes like quantity, quality, cost, or time of accomplished work. BMO's use of the diversity index to rate executive performance is one example; others include percentage error rate, dollar deviation from budgeted expenditures, and the number of units produced or customers serviced in a time period. **Input standards**, by contrast, measure effort in terms of the amount of work expended in task performance. They are used in situations where outputs are difficult or expensive to measure. Examples of input standards include conformance to rules and procedures, efficiency in the use of resources, and work attendance or punctuality.

> ■ An **input standard** measures work efforts that go into a performance task.

Step 2: Measure Actual Performance

The second step in the control process is to measure actual performance. The goal is to accurately measure the performance results (output standards) and/or the performance efforts (input standards). Measurement must be accurate enough to spot significant differences between what is really taking place and what was originally planned. Without it, effective control is not possible. When Linda Sanford was appointed head of IBM's sales force, she came with an admirable performance record earned during a 22-year career with the company. Notably, Sanford grew up on a family farm, where she developed an appreciation for measuring results. "At the end of the day, you saw what you did, knew how many rows of strawberries you picked." At IBM she was known for walking around the factory just to see "at the end of the day how many machines were going out of the back dock."[25]

Step 3: Compare Results with Objectives and Standards

Step 3 in the control process is to compare objectives with results. This step can be expressed as the following *control equation*: Need for action = Desired performance − Actual performance. Sometimes managers make a *historical comparison*, using past performance as a basis for evaluating current performance. A *relative comparison* uses the performance achievements of other persons, work units, or organizations as the evaluation benchmarks. An *engineering comparison* uses standards set scientifically through such methods as time and motion studies. The delivery routines of Canada Post drivers, for example, are carefully measured in terms of expected minutes per delivery on various routes.

Step 4: Take Corrective Action

The final step in the control process is to take any action necessary to correct problems or make improvements. **Management by exception** is the practice of giving attention to situations that show the greatest need for action. It can save valuable time, energy, and other resources by focusing attention on high-priority areas. Managers should be alert to two types of exceptions. The first is a *problem situation* in which actual performance is below the standard. The reasons for this must be understood so corrective action can restore performance to the desired level. The second is an *opportunity situation* in which actual performance is above the standard. The reasons for this must also be understood, with the goal of continuing high levels of accomplishment in the future.

■ **Management by exception** focuses attention on substantial differences between actual and desired performance.

●●● TYPES OF CONTROLS

Figure 8.5 shows three major types of managerial controls—feedforward, concurrent, and feedback.[26] Each equates to a different phase of the organization's input-throughput-output cycle. And each offers significant opportunities for taking action to ensure high performance.

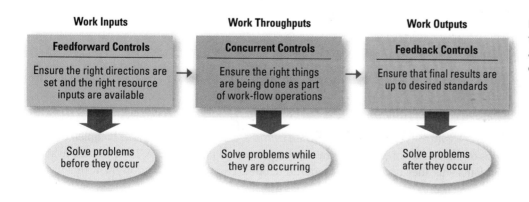

Figure 8.5 The role of feedforward, concurrent, and feedback controls in organizations.

Feedforward Controls

■ **Feedforward control** ensures that directions and resources are right before the work begins.

Feedforward controls, also called *preliminary controls*, take place before a work activity begins. They ensure that objectives are clear, that proper directions are established, and that the right resources are available to accomplish them. Feedforward controls are preventive in nature. The goal is to solve problems before they occur by asking an important but often-neglected question: "What needs to be done before we begin?" This is a forward-thinking and proactive approach to control. At McDonald's, for example, preliminary control of food ingredients plays an important role in the firm's quality program. The company requires that suppliers of its hamburger buns produce them to exact specifications, covering everything from texture to uniformity of color. Even in overseas markets, the firm works hard to develop local suppliers that can offer dependable quality.[27]

Concurrent Controls

■ **Concurrent control** focuses on what happens during the work process.

Concurrent controls focus on what happens during the work process. Sometimes called *steering controls*, they make sure things are being done according to plan. The goal is to solve problems as they are occurring. The key question is "What can we do to improve things right now? At McDonald's, ever-present shift leaders provide concurrent control through direct supervision. They constantly observe what is taking place even while helping out with the work. They are trained to intervene immediately when something is not done right and to correct things on the spot. Detailed instruction manuals also "steer" workers in the right directions as their jobs are performed.

take it to the case!

Wal-Mart Stores, Inc.

Self-management works at the number-one retailer

Numbers count at Wal-Mart, a firm that takes its financial performance very seriously. Top management at the firm founded by Sam Walton has to; that's part of the deal when you're number one in a global industry. And that company has no intention of resting on its past laurels. A recent observer says: "Wal-Mart is gaining momentum. This fast company is becoming a faster company. Wal-Mart grows a Fortune 100 corporation each year. The company is as strong as ever." Nancy Handley once supervised the men's department at a suburban St. Louis Wal-Mart store. She put in long hours but liked the responsibility and recognition that came with the job. "I'm proud of who I've made myself into and the department I've created," she said.

Source: Douglas McGregor, *The Human Side of Enterprise* (New York: McGraw-Hill, 2005).

Feedback Controls

■ **Feedback control** takes place after an action is completed.

Feedback controls, also called *post-action controls*, take place after work is completed. They focus on the quality of end results rather than on inputs and activities. The goals are to solve problems after they occur and prevent future ones. They ask the question "Now that we are finished, how well did we do?" Restaurants, for example, ask how you liked a meal...after it is eaten; final course evaluations tell instructors how well they performed...after the course is over; a budget summary identifies cost overruns...after a project is completed. In these and other circumstances the feedback provided by the control process is useful information for improving things in the future.

●●● INTERNAL AND EXTERNAL CONTROL

Managers have two broad options with respect to control. They can rely on people to control their own behaviour. This strategy of **internal control** allows motivated individuals and groups to exercise self-discipline in fulfilling job expectations. Alternatively, managers can take direct action to control the behaviour of others. This strategy of **external control** occurs through personal supervision and the use of formal administrative systems. Effective control typically involves a combination of both. However, the new workplace with its emphasis on participation, empowerment, and involvement places increased reliance on internal control.

■ **Internal control** occurs through self-discipline and self-control.

■ **External control** occurs through direct supervision or administrative systems.

Developing performance group norms can be a very effective internal control strategy. However, an internal control strategy requires a high degree of trust. When people are expected to work on their own and exercise self-control, managers must give them the freedom to do so. According to Douglas McGregor's Theory Y perspective, introduced in Chapter 2, people are ready and willing to exercise self-control in their work.[28] But he also points out that they are most likely to do this when they participate in setting performance objectives and standards. Furthermore, the potential for self-control is increased when capable people have a clear sense of organizational mission, know their goals, and have the resources necessary to do their jobs well. It is also enhanced by participative organizational cultures in which everyone treats each other with respect and consideration.

BE SURE YOU CAN
• define controlling as a management function • list the steps in the control process • explain where and why planning is important to controlling • explain the difference between output standards and input standards • illustrate how a fast-food restaurant utilizes three types of controls—feedforward, concurrent, and feedback • explain the difference between internal control and external control

✔ Learning check ❹

ORGANIZATIONAL CONTROL

Organizations benefit from the use of comprehensive and system-wide controls. Among the approaches are management by objectives, employee discipline systems, information and financial analysis, break-even analysis, and the techniques of operations management.

●●● MBO: INTEGRATED PLANNING AND CONTROLLING

A useful technique for integrating planning and controlling in day-to-day practice is **management by objectives** (MBO). This is a structured process of regular communication in which a supervisor/team leader and subordinates/team members jointly set performance objectives and review results accomplished.[29] As shown in *Figure 8.6*, MBO creates an agreement between the two parties regarding (1) performance objectives for a given time period, (2) plans through which they will be accomplished, (3) standards for measuring whether they have been accomplished, and (4) procedures for reviewing performance results. Both parties work closely together to fulfill the terms of the agreement.

■ **Management by objectives** is a process of joint objective setting between a superior and subordinate.

Figure 8.6
Management by objectives as an integrated planning and control framework.

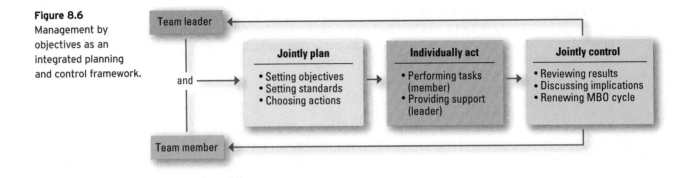

Performance Objectives in MBO

The way objectives are described and how they are established will both influence the success of MBO. Three types of objectives may be specified in an MBO contract. *Improvement objectives* document intentions for improving performance in a specific way. An example is "to reduce quality rejects by 10 percent." *Personal development objectives* pertain to personal growth activities, often those resulting in expanded job knowledge or skills. An example is "to learn the latest version of a computer spreadsheet package." Some MBO contracts also include *maintenance objectives* that formally express intentions to maintain performance at an existing level. In all cases, performance objectives in MBO are written and formally agreed upon. They also meet the following five criteria of a *SMART goal* or performance objective:

1. *Specific*—targets a key result to be accomplished

2. *Measurable*—there is a quantifiable aspect to the goal

3. *Attainable*—target is something that is realistic yet challenging

4. *Referred to regularly*—is continually discussed and progress noted

5. *Time defined*—identifies a date for achieving the desired result

One of the more difficult aspects of MBO relates to the need to state performance objectives as specifically and quantitatively as possible. Ideally this involves agreement on a *measurable end product*, for example: "to reduce housekeeping supply costs by 5 percent by the end of the fiscal year." But performance in some jobs, particularly managerial ones, is hard to quantify. Rather than abandon MBO in such cases, it is often possible to agree on performance objectives that are stated as *verifiable work activities*. The accomplishment of the activities serves as an indicator of progress under the performance objective. An example is "to improve communications with my subordinates in the next three months by holding weekly group meetings." Whereas it can be difficult to measure "improved communications," it is easy to document whether the "weekly group meetings" have been held.

MBO Pros and Cons

MBO is one of the most talked about and debated management concepts.[30] As a result, good advice is available. Things to avoid include tying MBO to pay, focusing too much attention on easy objectives, requiring excessive paperwork, and having supervisors simply tell subordinates their objectives. The advantages are also clear; MBO focuses workers on the most important tasks and objectives, and it focuses supervisors on areas of support that can truly help their subordinates meet the agreed-upon objectives. Because the process involves direct face-to-face communication, MBO contributes to relationship building. By giving people the opportunity to participate in decisions that affect their work, MBO encourages self-management.[31] One of the things that research is most clear about, in fact, is that participation in goal setting creates motivation to fulfill one's performance obligations.[32]

●●● EMPLOYEE DISCIPLINE SYSTEMS

Absenteeism…tardiness…sloppy work…the list of undesirable conduct can go on to even more extreme actions: falsifying records…sexual harassment…embezzlement. All are examples of behaviours that can and should be formally addressed through **discipline**, the act of influencing behaviour through reprimand. When discipline is handled in a fair, consistent, and systematic way, it is a useful form of managerial control. One way to be consistent in disciplinary situations is to remember the "hot stove rules" in *Manager's Notepad 8.1*. They rest on a simple understanding: "When a stove is hot, don't touch it." Everyone knows that when this rule is violated, you get burned—immediately, consistently, but usually not beyond the possibility of repair.[33]

■ **Discipline** is the act of influencing behaviour through reprimand.

Progressive discipline ties reprimands to the severity and frequency of the employee's infractions. Penalties for misbehaviour vary according to how significant it is and how often it occurs. The goal is to achieve compliance with organizational expectations through the least extreme reprimand possible. For example, the ultimate penalty of "discharge" would be reserved for the most severe behaviours (e.g., criminal code violations such as theft) or for repeated infractions of a less severe nature (e.g., being continually late for work and failing to respond to a series of written reprimands and/or suspensions).

■ **Progressive discipline** ties reprimands to the severity and frequency of misbehaviour.

MANAGER'S
Notepad 8.1

"Hot stove rules" of employee discipline

- A reprimand should be immediate; a hot stove burns the first time you touch it.

- A reprimand should be directed toward someone's actions, not the individual's personality; a hot stove doesn't hold grudges, doesn't try to humiliate people, and doesn't accept excuses.

- A reprimand should be consistently applied; a hot stove burns anyone who touches it, and it does so every time.

- A reprimand should be informative; a hot stove lets a person know what to do to avoid getting burned in the future—"don't touch."

- A reprimand should occur in a supportive setting; a hot stove conveys warmth but with an inflexible rule—"don't touch."

- A reprimand should support realistic rules; the don't-touch-a-hot-stove rule isn't a power play, a whim, or an emotion of the moment; it is a necessary rule of reason.

●●● INFORMATION AND FINANCIAL CONTROLS

The pressure is ever present for all organizations to use their resources well and to achieve high performance. In business, the analysis of a firm's financial performance is an important aspect of managerial control. At a minimum, managers should be able to understand the following financial performance measures: (1) *liquidity*—ability to generate cash to pay bills; (2) *leverage*—ability to earn more in returns than the cost of debt; (3) *asset management*—ability to use resources efficiently and operate at minimum cost; and (4) *profitability*—ability to earn revenues greater than costs.

These financial performance indicators can be assessed using a variety of financial ratios, including those shown in *Manager's Notepad 8.2*. Such ratios provide a framework for historical comparisons within the firm and for external benchmarking relative to industry performance. They can also be used to set financial targets or goals to be shared with employees and tracked to indicate success or failure in their endeavours. Rather than keep financial results hidden, the management team at telecommunications service provider Globalive Communications Corp. shares financial information with its employees and customers. The Toronto-based company is owned by its employees, customers, and suppliers and these important stakeholders always know how the company is doing. This shareholder mix encourages a greater focus on improving the business, and has resulted in Globalive's revenue having grown from $10 million to $45 million in just one year, earning them a spot as one of Canada's fastest growing companies.

MANAGER'S
Notepad 8.2
Popular financial ratios [with preferred directions ↑ or ↓]

Liquidity:

- Current ratio = Current assets/Current liabilities

↑ You want more assets and fewer liabilities.

Leverage:

- Debt ratio = Total debts/Total assets

↓ You want fewer debts and more assets.

Asset Management:

- Inventory turnover = Sales/Average inventory

↑ You want more sales and lower inventory.

Profitability:

- Net margin = Net profit after taxes/Sales
- Return on investment (ROI) = Net profit after taxes/Total assets

↑ You want as much profit as possible.

●●● BREAK-EVEN ANALYSIS

■ **Break-even analysis** calculates the point at which sales revenues cover costs.

A very common method for maintaining control over business operations is **break-even analysis**—the calculation of the point at which sales revenues are sufficient to cover costs. The graph in *Figure 8.7* shows the *break-even point* where losses end and one begins to make a profit. Obviously, the lower the break-even point, the better; the further one moves beyond the break-even point in actual performance, the better. A break-even point (BEP) is calculated by dividing total fixed costs (FC) by price (P) minus variable costs (VC). The formula is: BEP = FC/(P − VC).

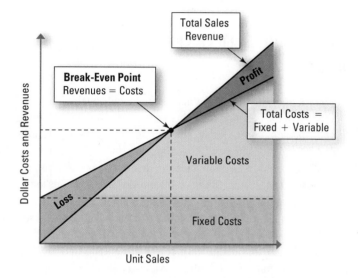

Figure 8.7 Graphical approach to break-even analysis.

Managers use break-even analysis in many ways. A very common situation is for someone in a firm to propose a new product or a new program initiative. Before giving approval, higher managers often ask: "What is your break-even point?" Familiarity with basic accounting principles is helpful in performing the analysis required to answer this question. For example, for a proposed new product you can calculate the sales volume required to break even at a targeted pricing point and also examine the impact of measures to control costs. Set up a spreadsheet with the target price of $8 per unit, fixed costs of $10,000, and variable costs of $4 per unit. According to the formula, the break-even point for these numbers is 2,500 units. But if you can reduce the variable costs to $3 per unit, the break-even point falls to 2,000 units, allowing you to earn profits much earlier in the cycle. Try experimenting with different "what-if" scenarios on your spreadsheet. This is exactly the type of analysis that will be expected of you as a matter of routine in business.

●●● OPERATIONS MANAGEMENT AND CONTROL

Control is integral to operations management, where the emphasis is on the efficient transformation of resource inputs into product or service outputs. The areas of purchasing control, inventory control, and statistical quality control are all operations management priorities.

Purchasing Control

Rising cost of materials is a fact of life in today's economy. Controlling these costs through efficient purchasing management is an important productivity tool. Like any individual, a thrifty organization must be concerned about how much it pays for what it buys. To leverage buying power, more organizations are centralizing purchasing to allow buying in volume. They are focusing on a small number of suppliers with whom they negotiate special contracts, gain quality assurances, and get preferred service. They are also finding ways to work together in supplier-purchaser partnerships. It is now more common, for example, that parts suppliers keep warehouses in their customer's facilities. The customer provides the space; the supplier does the rest. The benefits to the customer are lower purchasing costs and preferred service; the supplier gains an exclusive customer contract and more sales volume.

Canadian Managers

Adjusting for Differences

Twenty years ago, Réal Plourde was Alimentation Couche-Tard Inc.'s director of technical services, ensuring the lights stayed on and the roof didn't leak at the 10 Quebec convenience stores. Today, as chief operating officer, Plourde ensures the company's 4,796 locations across Canada and the United States run smoothly. Key to Couche-Tard's success has been tailoring each store—whether it's a Mac's in Toronto or a Circle K in Dayton, Ohio—to the individual needs of its local market. Each outlet has a unique design and can stock and promote items differently. This helps stores in one market learn from the success of others. For example, some US operations brought in their own automatic teller machines (ATMs), finding them to be a solid revenue source. Now, all Couche-Tard stores are getting their own ATMs. Plourde allows each store a measure of control—with excellent results!

Source: John Gray, Laura Bogomolny, and Andrew Wahl, "Top COO 2005: Réal Plourde, Alimentation Couche-Tard Inc.," *Canadian Business*, April 25–May 8, 2005.

Inventory Control

◾ Inventory control by **economic order quantity** orders replacements whenever inventory level falls to a predetermined point.

◾ **Just-in-time scheduling** minimizes inventory by routing materials to workstations "just in time" to be used.

Inventory is the amount of materials or products kept in storage. Organizations maintain inventories of raw materials, work in process, and finished goods. The goal of inventory control is to make sure that an inventory is just the right size to meet performance needs, thus minimizing the cost. The **economic order quantity** (EOQ) method of inventory control involves ordering a fixed number of items every time an inventory level falls to a predetermined point. When this point is reached, a decision is automatically made (typically by computer) to place a standard order to replenish the stock. The order sizes are mathematically calculated to minimize costs of inventory. The best example is the local supermarket, where hundreds of daily orders are routinely made on this basis. Another approach to inventory control is **just-in-time scheduling** (JIT), made popular by the Japanese. JIT systems reduce costs and improve workflow by scheduling materials to arrive at a workstation or facility "just in time" to be used. Because almost no inventories are maintained, the just-in-time approach is an important productivity tool.

Statistical Quality Control

◾ **Quality control** checks processes, materials, products, and services to ensure that they meet high standards.

Consistent with the total quality management theme in today's workplace, the practice of **quality control** involves checking processes, materials, products, and services to ensure that they meet high standards. This responsibility applies to all aspects of operations, from the selection of raw materials and supplies right down to the last task performed to deliver the finished good or service. In *statistical quality control*, the process is supported by rigorous statistical analysis. Typically this means taking samples of work, measuring quality in the samples, and then determining the acceptability of results. Unacceptable results in a sample would trigger the need for investigation and corrective action. The power of statistics allows the sampling to be efficiently used as the basis for decision making. At General Electric, for example, a Six Sigma program means that statistically the firm's quality performance will tolerate no more than 3.4 defects per million—a perfection rate of 99.9997 percent! As tough as it sounds, "Six Sigma" is a common quality standard for the new workplace.

●●● CONTROLLING THE UNEXPECTED

Controlling the unexpected seems to be a bit of an oxymoron. How can one control something that one cannot foresee happening? Karl Weick, a noted organizational psychologist, and colleagues have studied how organizations can help to manage or control the unexpected. In his studies of organizations where failure has high costs, such as aircraft carriers and nuclear power plants, Weick has found that confronting the unexpected is a key management control strategy. When something unusual happens, rather than dismiss it, Weick recommends that organizations become preoccupied with it. Organizations that effectively spot the unusual and then quickly adapt to meet the changed environment will become successful or develop into a **highly reliable organization** (HRO). In particular, HROs have five things that they are mindful or alert toward.

■ A **highly reliable organization** (HRO) is one that spots unexpected occurrences and reacts quickly to adapt to changing environments and avoid trouble.

- *Preoccupation with failure:* Rather than focus on organizational successes, HROs do exactly the opposite. HROs encourage members to be wary of success and to be preoccupied with failure. Fundamentally, HROs attend to negative deviations in any of their control systems, and when found, they are reported quickly. It is noticing small things that are going wrong that become the early warning signals for deepening trouble. These unexpected events are then studied, no matter how small they might seem, to see if they might build into something consequential. HROs then swiftly react to anything that does not fit with their expectations. By encouraging people to look at their own lapses and errors, HROs begin to understand where they are vulnerable and are able to take action to overcome weaknesses.

- *Commitment to resistance:* HROs have a commitment to bounce back from setbacks. They recognize that surprises are lurking and rather than be caught off guard when they arrive, HROs immediately focus on resistance or overcoming the surprise. There is no blame game. "Whose fault was that?" is not open for discussion. Rather, it is "What can we do to solve this problem?" Central to this commitment to resistance is improvization: HROs use what is available to combat the setback.

- *Sensitivity to operations:* HROs attend to the connection between actions and outcomes, both immediate and long-term. Rather than build elaborate contingency plans, HROs spend their time considering the outcome of present actions; they look at what might happen as a result of events being put into motion today. They focus on interconnectedness—what happens next after a chain of events has started. They concentrate on the immediate and the corresponding emerging events rather than planning for possible outcomes.

- *Deference to expertise:* HROs actively listen to their experts, who are often the people working on the front line. Front liners have first-hand knowledge of what the organization is facing, which provides them with a fuller picture of the problem. This perspective allows them to develop bold moves to solve developing problems. As people at the top rarely have this important ground-based view, HROs ensure that decisions migrate to the front-line experts. Decisions are shifted away from formal authority and are given to experts and to those with experience.

- *Reluctance to simplify:* Rather than look for simple solutions or redefine a problem in understandable ways, HROs are reluctant to accept simplification. Rather than define problems quickly and then get everyone to see the problem the same way, HROs recognize that it takes complexity to understand complexity. Key to building on complexity is to foster diverse perspectives on the problem. HROs bring in a variety of people who have different expertise to listen to each other, argue, reconcile differences, look at things again, and argue some more. They become adaptable by fostering complexity rather than simplicity.

To become an HRO, Weick says that all areas of an organization need to have "mindfulness," a struggle for a new alertness. To rate the mindfulness of an organization, either one you have worked for or one you are studying, take this quiz. Score 1 point for "Not at all"; 2 points for "To some extent"; and 3 points for "A great deal."

1. There is an organizational sense of susceptibility to the unexpected.

2. Everyone feels accountable for reliability.

3. Leaders pay as much attention to managing the unexpected events as they do to achieving formal organizational goals.

4. People at all levels of our organization value quality.

5. We have spent time identifying how our activities could harm our organization, employees, customers, other interested parties, and the environment at large.

6. We pay attention to when and why our employees, customers, or other interested parties might feel peeved at our disenfranchised organization.

7. There is widespread agreement among the firm's members on what shouldn't go wrong.

8. There is widespread agreement among the firm's members on what could go wrong.

A total score higher than 16 indicates an exemplary mindful company culture. A score lower than 10 suggests a need for immediate improvement.[34]

Learning check 5

BE SURE YOU CAN

• define the term management by objectives • illustrate how MBO operates in the relationship between a team leader and a team member • explain how a progressive discipline system operates • name the common financial ratios used in organizational control • complete a break-even analysis • define the terms economic order quantity and just-in-time delivery • explain the importance of purchasing control, inventory control, and statistical quality control in organizations • identify the key traits of an HRO

Back to Cognos Inc.

The opening vignette shows how Cognos successfully helps companies plan and control their businesses better. It also shows the importance of staying in touch with an ever-changing environment and updating plans to keep pace with new opportunities. In Chapter 8 you learned about planning and controlling as management functions. You learned about the different types of plans, as well as the important planning tools and techniques. You also learned how control systems facilitate organizational performance. Importantly, you have also gained awareness of how planning and controlling can help with your personal affairs and career development.

THE NEXT STEP
INTEGRATED LEARNING ACTIVITIES

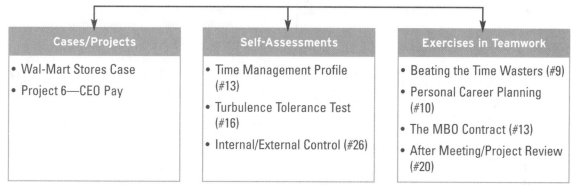

Cases/Projects	Self-Assessments	Exercises in Teamwork
• Wal-Mart Stores Case • Project 6—CEO Pay	• Time Management Profile (#13) • Turbulence Tolerance Test (#16) • Internal/External Control (#26)	• Beating the Time Wasters (#9) • Personal Career Planning (#10) • The MBO Contract (#13) • After Meeting/Project Review (#20)

STUDY QUESTION SUMMARY

1. How do managers plan?

• Planning is the process of setting performance objectives and determining what should be done to accomplish them.

• A plan is a set of intended actions for accomplishing important objectives.

• Planning sets the stage for the other management functions—organizing, leading, and controlling.

• The steps in the planning process are (1) define your objectives, (2) determine where you stand vis-à-vis objectives, (3) develop your premises regarding future conditions, (4) identify and choose among alternative ways of accomplishing objectives, and (5) implement action plans and evaluate results.

• The benefits of planning include better focus and flexibility, action orientation, coordination, control, and time management.

2. What types of plans do managers use?

• Short-range plans tend to cover a year or less, while long-range plans extend up to five years or more.

• Strategic plans set critical long-range directions; operational plans are designed to implement strategic plans.

• Organizational policies, such as a sexual harassment policy, are plans that set guidelines for the behaviour of organizational members.

• Organizational procedures and rules are plans that describe actions to be taken in specific situations, such as the steps to be taken when persons believe they have been sexually harassed.

- Organizational budgets are plans that allocate resources to activities or projects.

3. What are the useful planning tools and techniques?

- Forecasting, which attempts to predict what might happen in the future, is a planning aid but not a planning substitute.

- Contingency planning identifies alternative courses of action that can be implemented if and when circumstances change.

- Scenario planning analyzes the implications of alternative versions of the future.

- Planning through benchmarking utilizes external comparisons to identify desirable action directions.

- Participation and involvement open the planning process to valuable inputs from people whose efforts are essential to the effective implementation of plans.

4. What is the control process?

- Controlling is the process of measuring performance and taking corrective action as needed.

- The four steps in the control process are (1) establish performance objectives, (2) measure actual performance, (3) compare results with objectives, (4) take action to resolve problems or explore opportunities.

- Feedforward controls are accomplished before a work activity begins; they ensure that directions are clear and that the right resources are available to accomplish them.

- Concurrent controls make sure that things are being done correctly; they allow corrective actions to be taken while the work is being done.

- Feedback controls take place after an action is completed; they address the question "Now that we are finished, how well did we do and what did we learn for the future?"

- External control is accomplished through personal supervision and administrative systems.

- Internal control is self-control and occurs as people take personal responsibility for their work.

5. What are the common organizational controls?

- Management by objectives is a process through which supervisors work with their subordinates to "jointly" set performance objectives and review performance results.

- The MBO process is highly participatory and should clarify performance objectives for a subordinate while identifying support that should be provided by a supervisor.

- Discipline is the process of influencing behaviour through reprimand; it should be handled in a fair and progressive way.

- Financial control of business performance is facilitated by analysis of financial ratios, such as those dealing with liquidity, assets, and profitability.

- Operations control focuses on efficiencies in purchasing and inventory management, as well as on statistical approaches to quality control.

KEY TERMS REVIEW

After-action review (p. 193)

Benchmarking (p. 191)

Best practices (p. 191)

Break-even analysis (p. 200)

Budget (p. 189)

Concurrent control (p. 196)

Contingency planning (p. 191)

Controlling (p. 193)

Discipline (p. 199)

Economic order quantity (p. 202)

External control (p. 197)

Feedback control (p. 196)

Feedforward control (p. 196)

Forecasting (p. 190)

Highly reliable organization (HRO) (p. 203)

Input standards (p. 194)

Internal control (p. 197)

Just-in-time scheduling (p. 202)

Management by exception (p. 195)

Management by objectives (MBO) (p. 197)

Means-ends chain (p. 185)

Objectives (p. 183)

Operational plan (p. 189)

Output standards (p. 194)

Participatory planning (p. 192)

Plan (p. 183)

Planning (p. 183)

Policy (p. 189)

Procedure or rule (p. 204)

Progressive discipline (p. 199)

Project (p. 199)

Project management (p. 190)

Quality control (p. 202)

Rational comprehensive planning (RCP) (p. 186)

Rule (p. 189)

Scenario planning (p. 191)

Strategic plan (p. 188)

Zero-based budget (p. 189)

SELF-TEST 8

MULTIPLE-CHOICE QUESTIONS:

1. Planning is the process of _____ and _____.   *d*
   (a) developing premises about the future, evaluating them (b) measuring results, taking corrective action (c) measuring past performance, targeting future performance (d) setting objectives, deciding how to accomplish them

2. The benefits of planning include _____.   *a*
   (a) improved focus (b) lower labour costs (c) more accurate forecasts (d) guaranteed profits

3. In order to help implement its strategy, a business firm would likely develop a(n) _____ plan for the marketing function.   *b*
   (a) IT (b) operational (c) productivity (d) zero-based

4. _____ planning identifies alternative courses of action that can be taken if and when certain situations arise.   *d*
   (a) Benchmark (b) Participative (c) Strategic (d) Contingency

5. The first step in the control process is to _____.   *b*
   (a) measure actual performance (b) establish objectives and standards (c) compare results with objectives (d) take corrective action

6. The practice of giving attention to situations showing the greatest need for action is called management by _____.   *d*
   (a) objectives (b) results (c) efficiency (d) exception

7. A "No Smoking" rule and a sexual harassment policy are examples of _____ plans used by organizations.   *c*
   (a) long-range (b) single-use (c) standing plan (d) operational

8. A manager following the "hot stove rules" of progressive discipline would _____.   *c*
   (a) avoid giving the employee too much information about what was done wrong (b) stay flexible, reprimanding only at random (c) focus the reprimand on actions, not personality (d) delay reprimands until something positive can also be discussed.

9. Review of an employee's performance accomplishments in an MBO system is done by _____.   *c*
   (a) the employee (b) the employee's supervisor (c) the employee and the supervisor (d) the employee, the supervisor, and a lawyer

10. A good performance objective is written in such a way that it _____.   *d*
    (a) has no precise timetable (b) is general and not too specific (c) is almost impossible to accomplish (d) can be easily measured

11. When a manager is asked to justify a new budget proposal on the basis of projected activities rather than past practices, this is an example of _____ budgeting.   *a*
    (a) zero-based (b) variable (c) fixed (d) contingency

12. One of the benefits of participatory planning is _____.   *d*
    (a) reduced time for planning (b) less need for forecasting (c) greater attention to contingencies (d) more commitment to implementation

13. When an automobile manufacturer is careful to purchase only the highest-quality raw materials to be used in production, this is an example of _____ control.   *c*
    (a) concurrent (b) statistical (c) inventory (d) feedforward

14. In break-even analysis, the break-even point occurs where _____.   *b*
    (a) fixed costs = variable costs (b) profits = expenses (c) assets = liabilities (d) revenues = total costs

15. A manager is failing to live up to the concept of MBO when he or she _____.
   (a) sets performance objectives for subordinates (b) actively supports subordinates in their work (c) jointly reviews performance results with subordinates (d) keeps a written record of subordinates' performance objectives

SHORT-RESPONSE QUESTIONS:

16. List the five steps in the planning process, and give examples of each.

17. How might planning through benchmarking be used by the owner/manager of a local bookstore?

18. How does Douglas McGregor's Theory Y relate to the concept of internal control?

19. How does a progressive discipline system work?

APPLICATION QUESTION:

20. Put yourself in the position of a management trainer. You are asked to make a short presentation to the local Small Business Enterprise Association at its biweekly luncheon. The topic you are to speak on is "How Each of You Can Use Management by Objectives for Better Planning and Control." What will you tell them and why?

Strategic Management

Planning Ahead

After reading Chapter 9, you should be able to answer these questions in your own words.

1. What are the foundations of strategic competitiveness?

2. What is the strategic management process?

3. What types of strategies are used by organizations?

4. How are strategies formulated?

5. What are current issues in strategy implementation?

TAXI

Invites you to be a part of the future

Taxi is a hot fast-driving company. Founded in 1992 as an independent advertising company, it initially focused on the Montreal market. At the time, that market lent itself well to the company's strategic aim of being a "niche agency for niche challenger clients." However, Taxi, which is now based in Toronto, is no longer simply a niche agency; it is a powerful agency for a lot of very powerful brands. This fact lies behind the company's recent expansions into Calgary, Vancouver, and New York City, and the decision to re-establish in Montreal.

Strategically, why has the company decided to expand? The Calgary office was established to better serve its client WestJet; the Vancouver office to serve Telus; and the Montreal office was re-established because Pfizer is located there and because it wants to be a truly national agency. The New York office is Taxi's first move into the US market. The company sees New York as an "answer to a growing agency that simply needs more legroom."

Bringing an office to a client is not the only strategic concept that Taxi has adopted. Their name, Taxi, reflects their philosophy that small accountable teams are the best way to attract and service clients: the right number of Taxi employees to work with a client is the same as the number of employees who can fit, with the client, into the back of a cab. That, however, is not the end of Taxi's strategic thinking on company organization. As the number of employees in their Toronto office approaches 150, company chairman Paul Lavoie is quoted as saying, "I do not want to grow the agency

more than 150 per office." Lavoie strongly believes in the logic of "Dunbar's Number," the theory of British anthropologist Robin Dunbar that states that 150 represents the limit of how many people any one individual can maintain stable relationships with. Accordingly, Taxi has started up another branch office in Toronto called Taxi 2. While Toronto's Rob Guenette coordinates both offices, each is encouraged to

develop and think independently.

Taxi's ongoing creative strategy is to "doubt the conventional, create the exceptional." Clearly, winning *Strategy* magazine's "Agency of the Year" honours for the fourth year, and being ranked the #2 independent advertising agency overall in the world, it would seem that the company is on the right strategic track. Somebody hail me a Taxi![1]

IN THE WORKPLACE

As a reward for all of your hard work at your company over the last several months, your boss Darren Smith has asked you to head up a new project team. The team's task is to review and recommend action plans to present to senior management on how to improve the products that your company produces. Darren mentions that this review should start with Peter Drucker's five questions to ask when formulating a strategy. You agree, and recall reading about those questions in a management course. As Darren leaves your cubicle, you try to remember what those questions are. You reach for your management text and start to search for the answer.

●●● **Chapter 9** | LEARNING PREVIEW | ●●●

Start small, find the right clients, experiment, get bigger, get recognized, win awards, focus internationally, be different, turn category paradigms upside down; it sounds like a strategic plan for an independent advertising firm. This chapter introduces you to the issues of strategy and strategic management. It discusses strategy formulation and implementation, with special attention to alternative types of strategies and frameworks for strategy selection.

STRATEGIC MANAGEMENT

Study Question 1	Study Question 2	Study Question 3	Study Question 4	Study Question 5
Strategic Competitiveness	**The Strategic Management Process**	**Strategies Used by Organizations**	**Strategy Formulation**	**Strategy Implementation**
• What is strategy? • Strategic management • Strategic management goals	• Analysis of mission, values, and objectives • Analysis of resources and capabilities • Analysis of industry and environment	• Levels of strategy • Growth and diversification • Restructuring and divestiture • Global strategies • Co-operation • E-business	• Porter's generic strategies • Portfolio planning • Adaptive strategies • Incrementalism and emergent strategy	• Management practices and systems • Corporate governance • Strategic leadership
Learning check ❶	Learning check ❷	Learning check ❸	Learning check ❹	Learning check ❺

Let's change industries for a moment and move from Taxi advertising to the retailing world. Surely you are familiar with Wal-Mart, the world's largest retailer and the recommended case study for Chapter 8. Wal-Mart's master plan is elegant in its simplicity: to deliver consistently low prices and high customer service. An important foundation is use of the latest technology. Inventories are monitored around the clock, and a world-class distribution system ensures that stores are rarely out of the items customers are seeking. All systems are rallied around Wal-Mart's goals—low prices and high customer service. While the firm's competitors are asking, "How can we keep up?" the strategic visionaries at Wal-Mart are asking "How can we stay ahead?"

Even Wal-Mart can't rest on past laurels.[2] Success today is no guarantee of success tomorrow. We will surely see many changes in competitive retailing in the years ahead; we're already seeing many today. Similar forces and challenges confront managers in all settings, Taxi among them. Today's environment places a great premium on effective "strategy" and "strategic management" as prerequisites for organizational success. "If you want to make a difference as a leader," says *Fast Company* magazine, "you've got to make time for strategy."[3]

STRATEGIC COMPETITIVENESS

An organization with **competitive advantage** operates with an attribute or combination of attributes that allows it to outperform its rivals. At Wal-Mart, for example, one source of such an advantage is information technology that allows the retailer to quickly track sales and monitor inventories. In other industries, Dell Computer eliminates wholesale supplier markups by marketing directly to consumers; Toyota's shorter cycle times allow it to carry smaller amounts of work-in-process inventory. The goal for any organization, however, is not just to achieve competitive advantage. It is to make it sustainable, even as rivals attempt to duplicate and copy a success story. A *sustainable competitive advantage* is one that is difficult for competitors to imitate. At Wal-Mart again, the firm's use of IT is continuously improved. Competitors have trouble catching up, let alone getting ahead.

In Canada, Tim Hortons has a sustainable competitive advantage—it's called the "double double." With over 2,600 locations, the Tim Hortons' brand is a familiar feature in most Canadian cities. At "Tims" they work hard at making the company "Canada's coffee shop," with excellent results. In 2005, Tim Hortons held over 75 percent of the quick service coffee sector in Canada, making this brand hard to beat.[4] With this kind of penetration, it's no wonder that the company has won the top spot in both the 2004 and 2005 *Canadian Business* best-managed-brand surveys. [5]

> ■ A **competitive advantage** comes from operating in successful ways that are difficult to imitate.

●●● WHAT IS STRATEGY?

A **strategy** is a comprehensive action plan that identifies long-term direction for an organization and guides resource utilization to accomplish goals with sustainable competitive advantage. It focuses attention on the competitive environment and represents a "best guess" about what must be done to ensure future success in the face of rivalry, even as conditions change. Importantly, a strategy provides the plan for allocating and using resources with consistent **strategic intent**—that is, with all organizational energies directed toward a unifying and compelling target or goal.[6] At Coca-Cola, for example, strategic intent has been described as "To put a Coke within 'arm's reach' of every consumer in the world." Given the focus provided by this strategic intent, we would not expect Coca-Cola to be diversifying by investing in snack foods, as does its archrival PepsiCo.

In our fast-paced world of globalization and changing technologies, the "long-term" aspect of strategy is becoming ever shorter. As it does so, the challenges to the strategist become even greater. It used to be that companies could count on traditional "build-and-sell" business models that put them in control. In the early days of the automobile industry, for example, Henry Ford once said: "The customer can have any colour he wants as long as it's black." His firm, quite literally, was in the driver's seat. Today things have changed and strategy is increasingly driven by customers and flexibility. Stephen Haeckel, director of strategic studies at IBM's Advanced Business Institute, once described the shift this way: "It's a difference between a bus, which follows a set route, and a taxi, which goes where customers tell it to go."[7]

> ■ A **strategy** is a comprehensive plan guiding resource allocation to achieve long-term organization goals.
>
> ■ **Strategic intent** focuses and applies organizational energies on a unifying and compelling goal.

●●● STRATEGIC MANAGEMENT

In the case both of Taxi and Wal-Mart, crafting strategy may seem a deceptively simple task: find out what customers want, then provide it for them at the best prices and service. In practice, this task is made complex and risky by the forces and uncertainties of competitive environments.[8] Every strategist must remember that at the same time that one is trying to create competitive advantage for an organization, competitors are always trying to do the same. This gives rise to demands for strategies that are "bold," "aggressive," "fast-moving," and "innovative." But call them what you will, strategies don't just happen. They must be created. And strategies alone don't automatically bring success. They must be both well chosen and well implemented.

■ **Strategic management** is the process of formulating and implementing strategies.

Strategic management is the process of formulating and implementing strategies to accomplish long-term goals and sustain competitive advantage. The essence of strategic management is looking ahead, understanding the environment and the organization, effectively positioning the organization for competitive advantage in changing times, and then achieving it.

take it to the case!

Toyota Canada
Striving for continuous improvement
Toyota Canada's vision is to make things better: at work, at home, and in the community. It does so by incorporating *kaizen*, a passionate commitment to continuous improvement, into every decision. Toyota has been able to build strategies that focus on maintaining a balance between all stakeholders and a commitment to quality. From its start as a small Japanese company in 1938 to its introduction to Canada in 1965, Toyota has thrived in the highly competitive automotive industry by concentrating its resources on developing cost reduction strategies while at the same time pioneering innovative designs and new technologies. Committed to the vision of being the largest automotive manufacturer in the world by 2010, right now it is the second-largest automaker worldwide. Learn more about "The Toyota Way" of continuous improvement in the case in the *Management Learning Workbook*.

Source: With information from the corporate website: <www.toyota.ca/cgi>

●●● STRATEGIC MANAGEMENT GOALS

Michael Porter, Harvard scholar and strategy consultant, says that "sound strategy starts with having the right goal."[9] He argues that the ultimate goal for any business should be superior profitability. This creates value for investors in the form of **above-average returns**, returns that exceed what an investor could earn by investing in alternative opportunities of equivalent risk.[10]

■ **Above-average returns** exceed what could be earned from alternative investments of equivalent risk.

The ability to earn above-average returns is based in part on the competitive nature of organizational environments. Businesses compete in environments that vary in the following ways.[11] In a *monopoly environment*, there is only one player and no competition. This creates absolute competitive advantage that delivers sustainable and even excessive business profits. The U.S. Justice Department's antitrust lawsuit against Microsoft Corporation argued that the firm achieved actual or close to monopoly status in respect to the market for computer operating systems. An *oligopoly environment* contains a few players who compete against one another. Firms within an oligopoly sustain long-term competitive advantages within defined market segments. In the absence of competition within these segments, they can also reap excessive business profits. This describes conditions in the breakfast cereals market, for example. The industry is dominated by large players—Kellogg's, General Mills, and Quaker Oats—that control much of the market. It is difficult for new players to break in. From the customer's standpoint, both monopoly and oligopoly are disadvantageous. The lack of competition may keep prices high and product/service innovations low.

The global economy has helped to create for many businesses today an *environment of hypercompetition.*[12] This is an environment in which there are at least several players who directly compete with one another. An example is the fast-food industry, where McDonald's, Burger King, Wendy's, and many other restaurant chains all compete for largely the same customers. Because the competition is direct and intense, any competitive advantage that is realized is temporary. Successful strategies are often copied and firms must continue to find new strategies that deliver new sources of competitive advantage, even while trying to defend existing ones. McDonald's, for example, has had to mount an aggressive strategic campaign. The attack has come from healthy alternative fast-food companies like Subway Inc. To respond, McDonald's incorporated healthier foods into their line-up.[13] In hypercompetition, there are always some winners and some losers. Business profits can be attractive but intermittent. The customer generally gains in this environment, through lower prices and more product/service innovation.

BE SURE YOU CAN   ✔ Learning check ❶

• define the terms competitive advantage, strategy, and strategic management • explain the concept of sustained competitive advantage • explain the significance of above-average returns as strategic business goals
• differentiate monopoly, oligopoly, and hypercompetition as competitive environments

THE STRATEGIC MANAGEMENT PROCESS

Strategic management is successful when good strategies are crafted from insightful understandings of the competitive environment of the organization, and when these strategies are well implemented. *Figure 9.1* describes the steps involved in fulfilling the two major responsibilities of the strategic management process—strategy formulation and strategy implementation.

The first strategic management responsibility is **strategy formulation**, the process of creating strategy. This involves assessing existing strategies, organization, and environment to develop new strategies capable of delivering future competitive advantage. Peter Drucker

▪ **Strategy formulation** is the process of creating strategies.

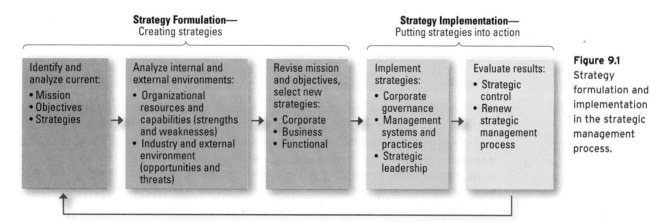

Strategy Formulation—
Creating strategies

Strategy Implementation—
Putting strategies into action

Identify and analyze current:
• Mission
• Objectives
• Strategies

Analyze internal and external environments:
• Organizational resources and capabilities (strengths and weaknesses)
• Industry and external environment (opportunities and threats)

Revise mission and objectives, select new strategies:
• Corporate
• Business
• Functional

Implement strategies:
• Corporate governance
• Management systems and practices
• Strategic leadership

Evaluate results:
• Strategic control
• Renew strategic management process

Figure 9.1
Strategy formulation and implementation in the strategic management process.

associated this process with a set of five strategic questions: (1) *What is our business mission?* (2) *Who are our customers?* (3) *What do our customers consider "value"?* (4) *What have been our results?* (5) *What is our plan?*[14]

■ **Strategy implementation** is the process of putting strategies into action.

The second strategic management responsibility is **strategy implementation**, the process of allocating resources and putting strategies into action. Once strategies are created, they must be successfully acted upon to achieve the desired results. As Drucker said, "The future will not just happen if one wishes hard enough. It requires decision—now. It imposes risk—now. It requires action—now. It demands allocation of resources, and above all, of human resources—now. It requires work—now."[15] Every organizational and management system must be mobilized to support and reinforce the accomplishment of strategies. All resources must be well utilized to achieve maximum impact on performance. All of this, in turn, requires a commitment to the full range of strategic management tasks listed in *Manager's Notepad 9.1.*[16]

MANAGER'S
Notepad 9.1
Five strategic management tasks

1. Identify organizational mission and objectives.
   Ask: "What business are we in? Where do we want to go?"

2. Assess current performance vis-à-vis mission and objectives.
   Ask: "How well are we currently doing?"

3. Create strategic plans to accomplish purpose and objectives.
   Ask: "How can we get where we really want to be?"

4. Implement the strategic plans.
   Ask: "Has everything been done that needs to be done?"

5. Evaluate results; change strategic plans and/or implementation processes as necessary.
   Ask: "Are things working out as planned? What can be improved?"

●●● ANALYSIS OF MISSION, VALUES, AND OBJECTIVES

The strategic management process begins with a careful review and clarification of organizational mission, values, and objectives.[17] This sets the stage for critically assessing the organization's resources and capabilities as well as competitive opportunities and threats in the external environment.

Mission

■ The **mission** is the organization's reason for existence in society.

As first discussed in Chapter 1, the **mission** or purpose of an organization may be described as its reason for existence in society. Strategy consultant Michael Hammer believes that a mission should represent what the strategy or underlying business model is trying to accomplish. He suggests asking: "What are we moving to?" "What is our dream?" "What kind of a difference do we want to make in the world?" "What do we want to be known for?"[18]

The best organizations have a clear sense of mission, and they utilize resources with clear strategic intent in respect to its fulfillment. Starbucks's mission is to be "the premier purveyor of the finest coffee in the world while maintaining our uncompromising principles as we grow." The mission of the Canadian Red Cross is "to improve the lives of vulnerable people by mobilizing the power of humanity in Canada and around the world."[19] NORPAC Controls, declared one of Canada's "best managed companies" in 2005, is an instrumentation and controls manufacturer based in Burnaby, British Columbia. Its mission is to "[be] results driven,…leading by example, …encourage empowerment and a positive attitude, and exceed customer expectations,…to deliver best-in-class products, services and value to our customers and stakeholders."[20]

A good *mission statement* identifies the *domain* in which the organization intends to operate—including the *customers* it intends to serve, the *products* and/or *services* it intends to provide, and the *location* in which it intends to operate. The mission statement should also communicate the underlying philosophy that will guide employees in these operations. An important test of a mission is how well it serves the organization's **stakeholders**. You should recall that these are individuals and groups—including customers, shareholders, suppliers, creditors, community groups, and others—who are directly affected by the organization and its strategic accomplishments. In the strategic management process, the stakeholder test can be done as a *strategic constituencies analysis*. Here, the specific interests of each stakeholder are assessed along with the organization's record in responding to them. *Figure 9.2* gives an example of how stakeholder interests can be reflected in the mission of a business firm.

■ **Stakeholders** are individuals and groups directly affected by an organization and its accomplishments.

Figure 9.2 How external stakeholders can be valued as strategic constituencies of organizations.

Employees
We respect the individuality of each employee … creativity and productivity are encouraged, valued, and rewarded.

Communities
We are committed to being caring and supportive corporate citizens within the worldwide communities in which we operate.

Mission

Shareholders
We are dedicated to … performing in a manner that will enhance returns on investments.

Customers
We are committed to providing superior value in our products and services.

Suppliers
We think of our suppliers as partners who share our goal of … highest quality.

Core Values

Behaviour in, and by, organizations will always be affected in part by *values*, which are broad beliefs about what is or is not appropriate. **Organizational culture** was first defined in Chapter 4 as the predominant value system of the organization as a whole.[21] Through organizational cultures, the values of managers and other members are shaped and pointed in common directions. In strategic management, the presence of strong core values for an organization helps build institutional identity. It gives character to an organization in the eyes of its employees and external stakeholders, and it backs up the mission statement. Shared values also help guide the behaviour of organization members in meaningful and consistent ways. For example, Canadian company Merck Frosst backs up its mission with a public commitment to core values that include preservation and improvement of human life, scientific excellence, ethics and integrity, and profits from work that benefits humanity.

■ **Organizational culture** is the system of shared beliefs and values that guides behaviour in organizations.

Objectives

■ **Operating objectives** are specific results that organizations try to accomplish.

Whereas a mission statement sets forth an official purpose for the organization and the core values describe appropriate standards of behaviour for its accomplishment, **operating objectives** direct activities toward key and specific performance results. These objectives are shorter-term targets against which actual performance results can be measured as indicators of progress and continuous improvement. According to Peter Drucker, the *operating objectives of a business* might include the following:[22]

- *Profitability*—producing at a net profit in business.
- *Market share*—gaining and holding a specific market share.
- *Human talent*—recruiting and maintaining a high-quality workforce.
- *Financial health*—acquiring capital; earning positive returns.
- *Cost efficiency*—using resources well to operate at low cost.
- *Product quality*—producing high-quality goods or services.
- *Innovation*—developing new products and/or processes.
- *Social responsibility*—making a positive contribution to society.

●●● ANALYSIS OF ORGANIZATIONAL RESOURCES AND CAPABILITIES

■ A **SWOT analysis** examines organizational strengths and weaknesses, and environmental opportunities and threats.

The strategic management process always involves careful analysis of organizational resources and capabilities. This can be approached by a technique known as **SWOT analysis**: the internal analysis of organizational Strengths and Weaknesses as well as the external analysis of environmental Opportunities and Threats.

■ A **core competency** is a special strength that gives an organization a competitive advantage.

As shown in *Figure 9.3*, a SWOT analysis begins with a systematic evaluation of the organization's resources and capabilities. A major goal is to identify **core competencies** in the form

Figure 9.3 SWOT analysis of strengths, weaknesses, opportunities, and threats.

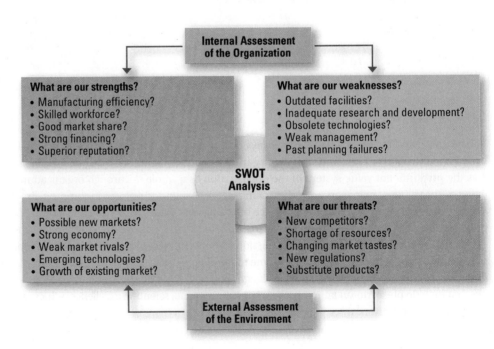

Internal Assessment of the Organization

What are our strengths?
- Manufacturing efficiency?
- Skilled workforce?
- Good market share?
- Strong financing?
- Superior reputation?

What are our weaknesses?
- Outdated facilities?
- Inadequate research and development?
- Obsolete technologies?
- Weak management?
- Past planning failures?

SWOT Analysis

What are our opportunities?
- Possible new markets?
- Strong economy?
- Weak market rivals?
- Emerging technologies?
- Growth of existing market?

What are our threats?
- New competitors?
- Shortage of resources?
- Changing market tastes?
- New regulations?
- Substitute products?

External Assessment of the Environment

of special strengths that the organization has or does exceptionally well, in comparison with competitors. They are capabilities that by virtue of being rare, costly to imitate, and non-substitutable, become viable sources of competitive advantage.[23] Core competencies may be found in special knowledge or expertise, superior technologies, efficient manufacturing technologies, or unique product distribution systems, among many other possibilities. But always, and as with the notion of strategy itself, they must be viewed relative to the competition. Organizations need core competencies that do important things better than the competition and that are very difficult for competitors to duplicate. Organizational weaknesses, of course, are the other side of the picture. They must also be identified to gain a realistic perspective on the formulation of strategies. The goal in strategy formulation is to create strategies that leverage core competencies for competitive advantage by building upon organizational strengths and minimizing the impact of weaknesses.

●●● ANALYSIS OF INDUSTRY AND ENVIRONMENT

A SWOT analysis is not complete until opportunities and threats in the external environment are also analyzed. They can be found among *macroenvironment* factors such as technology, government, social structures, population demographics, the global economy, and the natural environment. They can also include developments in the *industry environment* of resource suppliers, competitors, and customers. As shown in *Figure 9.3*, opportunities may exist as possible new markets, a strong economy, weaknesses in competitors, and emerging technologies. Weaknesses may be identified in such things as the emergence of new competitors, resource scarcities, changing customer tastes, and new government regulations, among other possibilities.

Scholar and consultant Michael Porter believes that the critical issue in respect to the external environment is how it impacts competition within the industry. He offers the five forces model shown in *Figure 9.4* as a way of adding sophistication to a strategic analysis of the environment.[24] His framework for competitive industry analysis directs attention toward understanding the following forces:

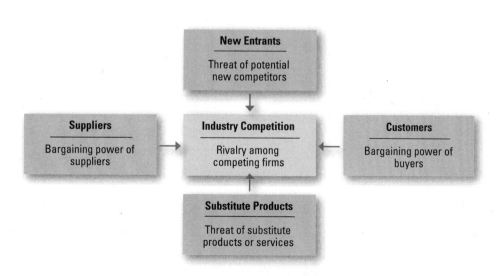

Figure 9.4 Porter's model of five strategic forces affecting industry competition.

Source: Adapted with permission of The Free Press, a Division of Simon & Schuster, Inc., from *Competitive Strategy* by Michael E. Porter. Copyright © 1980, 1998 by The Free Press.

1. *Industry competitors*—intensity of rivalry among firms in the industry.

2. *New entrants*—threats of new competitors entering the market.

3. *Suppliers*—bargaining power of suppliers.

4. *Customers*—bargaining power of buyers.

5. *Substitutes*—threats of substitute products or services.

From Porter's perspective, the foundations for any successful strategy rest with a clear understanding of these competitive environmental forces. He calls this the "industry structure." The strategic management challenge is to position an organization strategically within its industry, taking into account the implications of forces that make it more or less attractive. In general, an *unattractive industry* is one in which rivalry among competitors is intense, substantial threats exist in the form of possible new entrants and substitute products, and suppliers and buyers are very powerful in bargaining over such things as prices and quality. An *attractive industry*, by contrast, has less existing competition, few threats from new entrants or substitutes, and low bargaining power among suppliers and buyers. By systematically analyzing industry attractiveness in respect to the five forces, Porter believes that strategies can be chosen to give the organization a competitive advantage relative to its rivals.

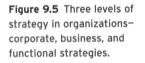

BE SURE YOU CAN

• differentiate strategy formulation from strategy implementation • list the major components in the strategic management process • explain what a mission statement is and illustrate how a good mission statement appeals to stakeholders • list several operating objectives of organizations • define the term core competencies • explain a SWOT analysis and use it to assess the strategic situation of an organization familiar to you • explain how Porter's five forces model can be used to assess the attractiveness of an industry

STRATEGIES USED BY ORGANIZATIONS

The strategic management process encompasses the three levels of strategy shown in *Figure 9.5*. Strategies are formulated and implemented at the organizational or corporate level, business level, and functional level. All should be integrated in means–end fashion to accomplish objectives and create sustainable competitive advantage.

Figure 9.5 Three levels of strategy in organizations—corporate, business, and functional strategies.

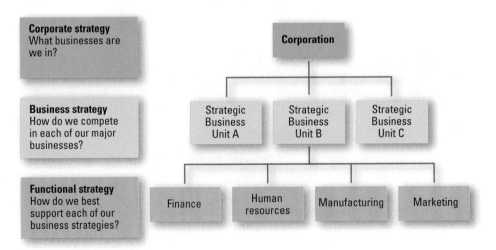

Canadian Managers

Successful Strategy Execution

Canadian Tire CEO Wayne Sales's growth plan for 2005–09 was met with confident enthusiasm by the investment community. After all, under Sales—who joined the company in 1991 and became CEO in 2000—Canadian Tire's stock value has quadrupled from a low of $15 to about $60 in 2005. The company's previous CEO, Stephen Bachand, had developed a capital-intensive strategy for reviving the retailer, the main feature of which was engineering a major retrofit of its outlets. Sales stuck to Bachand's basic strategy, focusing on improving stores through renovation and more assortment. Bachand now credits Sales for making the plan work.

Source: Zena Olijnyk, "Top CEO 2005: Wayne Sales, Canadian Tire Corp. Ltd.," *Canadian Business*, April 25–May 8, 2005.

●●● LEVELS OF STRATEGY

The level of **corporate strategy** directs the organization as a whole toward sustainable competitive advantage. For a business it describes the scope of operations by answering the following *strategic question*: "In what industries and markets should we compete?" The purpose of corporate strategy is to set direction and guide resource allocations for the entire enterprise. In large, complex organizations, corporate strategy identifies how the company intends to compete across multiple industries and markets. At General Electric (GE), for example, the firm pursues global business interests in aircraft engines, appliances, capital services, lighting, medical systems, broadcasting, plastics, and power systems, among others. Typical strategic decisions at the corporate level relate to the allocation of resources for acquisitions, new business development, divestitures, and the like across this business portfolio.

As one of Canada's 50 "best managed companies," CCI Thermal Technologies Inc. is an example of a company making strategic moves through acquisitions.[25] CCI's strong commitment to organic and global growth has seen them make four acquisitions in as many years, to become a major player in the North American industrial heating equipment market.[26]

Business strategy is the strategy for a single business unit or product line. It describes strategic intent to compete within a specific industry or market. Large *conglomerates* like GE are composed of many businesses, with many differences among them in product lines and even industries. The term **strategic business unit** (SBU) is often used to describe a single business firm or a component that operates with a major business line within a larger enterprise. The selection of strategy at the business level involves answering the *strategic question*: "How are we going to compete for customers in this industry and market?" Typical business strategy decisions include choices about product/service mix, facility locations, and new technologies. In single-business enterprises, business strategy is the corporate strategy.

Functional strategy guides the use of organizational resources to implement business strategy. This level of strategy focuses on activities within a specific functional area of operations. The standard business functions of marketing, manufacturing, finance, and human resources shown in *Figure 9.5* illustrate this level of strategy. The *strategic question* to be answered in selecting functional strategies is: "How can we best utilize resources to

■ A **corporate strategy** sets long-term direction for the total enterprise.

■ A **business strategy** identifies how a division or strategic business unit will compete in its product or service domain.

■ A **strategic business unit** (SBU) is a major business area that operates with some autonomy.

■ A **functional strategy** guides activities within one specific area of operations.

implement our business strategy?" Answers to this question typically involve the choice of management practices within each function that improves operating efficiency, product or service quality, customer service, or innovativeness.

●●● GROWTH AND DIVERSIFICATION STRATEGIES

■ **A growth strategy** involves expansion of the organization's current operations.

One of the most common and popular of the grand or master strategies followed by organizations at the corporate or business levels is growth.[27] **Growth strategies** pursue an increase in size and the expansion of current operations. They are popular in part because growth is viewed as necessary for long-run survival in some industries. While other companies were wondering about refocusing their western supply businesses, Lammle's Western Wear and Tack took a step forward and grew their business. Based in Calgary, Alberta, the company is now one of North America's top 10 western-wear retailers, growing from four stores to 23 stores across western Canada.

■ Growth through **concentration** is within the same business area.

One approach to growth is through **concentration**, where expansion is within the same business area. McDonald's, Wal-Mart, Starbucks, and others are pursuing aggressive growth strategies while still concentrating on their primary business areas. And importantly, they recognize the limits to growth in domestic markets and are expanding globally into markets and countries around the world.

■ Growth through **diversification** is by acquisition of or investment in new and different business areas.

Growth can also be pursued through **diversification**, where expansion takes place through the acquisition of, or investment in, new and different business areas. A strategy of *related diversification* involves growth by acquiring new businesses or entering business areas that are related to what one already does. This strategy seeks the advantages of growth in areas that utilize core competencies and existing skills. An example is the acquisition of Tropicana by PepsiCo. Although Tropicana specializes in fruit juices, the business is related to PepsiCo's expertise in the beverages industry. Another example is the Wendy's purchase of the Tim Hortons chain, and the subsequent building campaign that resulted in many instances where both franchises are located in a single building. A strategy of *unrelated diversification* involves growth by acquiring businesses or entering business areas that are different from what one already does.

■ Growth through **vertical integration** is by acquiring suppliers or distributors.

Diversification can also take the form of **vertical integration**, where a business acquires suppliers (*backward vertical integration*) or distributors (*forward vertical integration*). Backward vertical integration has been common in the automobile industry as firms purchased suppliers to ensure quality and control over the availability of key parts. In beverages, both Coca-Cola and PepsiCo have pursued forward vertical integration by purchasing some of their major bottlers.

There is a tendency to equate growth with effectiveness, but that is not necessarily true. Any growth strategy, whether by concentration or some form of diversification, must be well planned and well managed to achieve the desired results. Increased size of operation in any form adds challenge to the management process. Diversification, in particular, brings the difficulties of complexity and the need to manage and integrate very dissimilar operations. Research indicates that business performance may decline with too much unrelated diversification.[28]

●●● RESTRUCTURING AND DIVESTITURE STRATEGIES

■ **A retrenchment strategy** changes operations to correct weaknesses.

When organizations are in trouble, perhaps experiencing problems brought about by difficulties managing growth, some sort of readjustment must be made. Among the master strategies used by organizations, a **retrenchment strategy** seeks to correct weaknesses by making changes to current ways of operating. The goal is most often to reverse or change an approach that isn't working and to reorganize to compete better in the future. The most extreme form of retrenchment is *liquidation*, where business ceases and assets are sold to pay creditors. Less extreme and more common is **restructuring** of some sort. This involves making major changes to reduce the scale and/or mix of operations, with the twin goals of consolidating to gain short-term efficiencies and gaining time to prepare new strategies to improve future success.

Restructuring is sometimes accomplished by **downsizing**, which decreases the size of operations.[29] The expected benefits are reduced costs and improved operating efficiency. A common way to downsize is by cutting the size of the workforce. Research has shown that this is most successful when the workforce is reduced strategically or in a way that improves focus on key performance objectives.[30] Downsizing with a strategic focus is sometimes referred to as *rightsizing*. This contrasts with the less well-regarded approach of simply cutting staff "across the board."

Restructuring by **divestiture** involves selling off parts of the organization to refocus on core competencies, cut costs, and improve operating efficiency. This is a common strategy for organizations that find they have become over-diversified and are encountering problems managing the complexity of operations. It is also a way for organizations to take advantage of the value of internal assets by selling to a component that can stand on its own as an independent business.

■ **Restructuring** reduces the scale and/or mix of operations.

■ **Downsizing** decreases the size of operations.

■ **Divestiture** sells off parts of the organization to refocus attention on core business areas.

●●● GLOBAL STRATEGIES

Very few businesses operate today without some exposure to, and direct involvement in, international operations. A key aspect of strategy, therefore, becomes how the firm approaches the global economy and its mix of business risks and opportunities. Very often, a grand or master strategy of growth is pursued with the support of an accompanying global strategy.[31]

An easy way to spot differences in global strategies is to notice how products are developed and advertised around the world. A firm pursuing a **globalization strategy** tends to view the world as one large market, trying as much as possible to standardize products and their advertising for use everywhere. Authority for major management decisions will largely reside with corporate headquarters. The latest Gillette razors, for example, are typically sold and advertised similarly around the world. This reflects a somewhat *ethnocentric* view that assumes that everyone everywhere wants the same thing that one has developed and sold successfully at home.

■ A **globalization strategy** adopts standardized products and advertising for use worldwide.

Firms using a **multidomestic strategy** try to customize products and their advertising as much as possible to fit the local needs of different countries or regions. They distribute authority for major decisions to local and area managers to provide this differentiation. This is a popular strategy for many consumer goods companies—Procter & Gamble, Unilever—that vary their products according to consumer preferences in different countries and cultures. This reflects a more *polycentric view*, one showing respect for both market diversity and the capabilities of locals to best interpret their strategic implications.

■ A **multidomestic strategy** customizes products and advertising to best fit local needs.

A third approach to international business is the **transnational strategy** that seeks balance among efficiencies in global operations and responsiveness to local markets. The *transnational firm*, first described in Chapter 5, tries to operate without a strong national identity and to blend with the global economy to fully tap its business potential. Material resources and human capital are acquired worldwide; manufacturing and other business functions are performed wherever in the world they can be done best at lowest cost. Ford, for example, draws upon design, manufacturing, and distribution expertise all over the world to build car "platforms" that can then be efficiently modified to meet regional tastes. Such a transnational strategy reflects a *geocentric view* that respects diversity and values talents around the world. Transnational firms typically operate in a highly networked way, with information and learning continually flowing between headquarters and subsidiaries, and among the subsidiaries themselves.

■ A **transnational strategy** seeks efficiencies of global operations with attention to local markets.

●●● CO-OPERATIVE STRATEGIES

▦ In a **strategic alliance** organizations join together in partnership to pursue an area of mutual interest.

One of the trends today is toward more co-operation among organizations, and *international joint ventures* are a common form of international business. They are one among many forms of **strategic alliances** in which two or more organizations join together in partnership to pursue an area of mutual interest. One way to co-operate strategically is through *outsourcing alliances*, contracting to purchase important services from another organization. Many organizations today, for example, are outsourcing their IT function to firms like EDS and IBM in the belief that these services are better provided by a firm that specializes and maintains its expertise in this area. Co-operation in the supply chain also takes the form of *supplier alliances*, in which preferred supplier relationships guarantee a smooth and timely flow of quality supplies among alliance partners. Another common approach today is co-operation in *distribution alliances*, in which firms join together to provide products or services, or accomplish sales and distribution.

●●● E-BUSINESS STRATEGIES

▦ An **e-business strategy** strategically uses the Internet to gain competitive advantage.

Without a doubt, one of the most frequently asked questions these days for the business executive is: "What is your **e-business strategy**?" This is the strategic use of the Internet to gain competitive advantage.[32] As introduced in Chapter 7, popular e-business strategies involve B2B (business-to-business) and B2C (business-to-customer) applications. **B2B business strategies** use IT and Web portals to vertically link organizations with members of their supply chains. When Dell Computer sets up special website services that allow its major corporate customers to manage their accounts online, when Wal-Mart suppliers are linked to the firm's information systems and manage inventories for their own products electronically, and even when a business uses an online auction site to bid for supplies at the cheapest prices, they are utilizing B2B in various forms. B2B is the largest e-business component in the economy, and its benefits apply to large and small organizations alike.

▦ A **B2B business strategy** uses IT and Web portals to link organizations vertically in supply chains.

▦ A **B2C business strategy** uses IT and Web portals to link businesses with customers.

Most of us probably are more aware of **B2C business strategies** that use IT and Web portals to link organizations with their customers. A common B2C strategy has already been illustrated several times in this book—*e-tailing*, or the sale of goods directly to customers via

---

MANAGER'S
Notepad 9.2
Web-based business models

- *Brokerage*—bringing buyers and sellers together to make transactions (e.g., globeautos.com).

- *Advertising*—providing information or services while generating revenue from advertising (e.g., Yahoo!).

- *Merchant model*—selling products wholesale and retail through the Web, e-tailing (e.g., Chapters-Indigo and hbc.com).

- *Subscription model*—selling access to a website through subscription (e.g., *Canadian Business* online).

- *Infomediary model*—collecting information on users and selling it to other businesses (e.g., epinions.com).

the Internet. But, importantly, there is more to success with B2C than simply having a website that advertises products for customer purchase. The B2C strategy must be fully integrated with supporting functional strategies and operations. Among the e-tailers, for example, Dell has set a benchmarking standard that is very hard for competitors to duplicate. The easy-to-use Dell website allows customization of an individual's computer order, in effect offering a design-your-own-product capability. Then a highly efficient and streamlined manufacturing and distribution system takes over to build and ship the computer within three business days. And all this is backed by highly efficient customer service. Although many companies have tried copycat strategies, Dell sustains its competitive advantage with continual improvements to a state-of-the-art and fully integrated e-business strategy.

Manager's Notepad 9.2 lists some of the more common Web-based business models that are available, along with examples of each.[33] In considering the opportunities, however, it is important to keep the Dell story in mind. A lot more is required to achieve success with e-business than simply having IT support and a good website. Whether one is talking B2B or B2C, success with e-business requires both a good strategy and the capacity to implement the strategy extremely well.

BE SURE YOU CAN
• differentiate the three levels of strategy—corporate, business, and functional • list and explain the major types of growth and diversification strategies, and restructuring and divestiture strategies • list and give examples of major global strategies • define the term strategic alliance and explain how co-operation is used as a business strategy • explain B2B and B2C as forms of e-business strategy

✔ Learning check ❸

STRATEGY FORMULATION

Michael Porter says: "The company without a strategy is willing to try anything."[34] With a good strategy in place, by contrast, the resources of the entire organization can be focused on the overall goal: superior profitability or above-average returns. Whether one is talking about building e-business strategies for the new economy or crafting strategies for more traditional operations, it is always important to remember this goal and the need for sustainable competitive advantage. The major *opportunities for competitive advantage* are found in the following areas, which should always be considered in the strategy formulation process:[35]

• *Cost and quality*—where strategy drives an emphasis on operating efficiency and/or product or service quality.

• *Knowledge and speed*—where strategy drives an emphasis on innovation and speed of delivery to market for new ideas.

• *Barriers to entry*—where strategy drives an emphasis on creating a market stronghold that is protected from entry by others.

• *Financial resources*—where strategy drives an emphasis on investments and/or loss sustainment that competitors can't match.

It is important to remember that advantages gained in today's global and information-age economy of intense competition must be considered temporary, at best. Things change too fast. Any advantage of the moment will sooner or later be eroded as new market demands, copycat strategies, and innovations by rivals take their competitive tolls.[36] The challenge of achieving sustainable competitive advantage is thus a dynamic one. Strategies must be continually revisited, updated, and changed. This process of strategy formulation is facilitated by a number of strategic planning models or approaches.

●●● PORTER'S GENERIC STRATEGIES

Michael Porter's five forces model for industry analysis (refer back to *Figure 9.4*) helps answer the question: "Is this an attractive industry for us to compete in?" Within an industry, however, the strategic challenge becomes positioning one's firm and products relative to competitors. The question for strategy formulation becomes: "How can we best compete for customers in this industry?" Porter advises managers to answer this question by using his generic strategies framework, shown in *Figure 9.6*.[37]

According to Porter, business-level strategic decisions are driven by two basic factors: (1) *market scope—ask:* "How broad or narrow is your market or target market?" (2) *source of competitive advantage—ask:* "Will you compete for competitive advantage by lower price or product uniqueness?" As shown in the figure, these factors combine to create the following four generic strategies that organizations can pursue. The examples in the figure and shown here are of competitive positions within the soft-drink industry.

1. **Differentiation**—where the organization's resources and attention are directed toward making its products appear different from those of the competition (*example*: Coke, Pepsi).

2. **Cost leadership**—where the organization's resources and attention are directed toward minimizing costs to operate more efficiently than the competition (*example*: President's Choice Cola).

3. **Focused differentiation**—where the organization concentrates on one special market segment and tries to offer customers in that segment a unique product (*example*: A&W Root Beer, Canada Dry).

4. **Focused cost leadership**—where the organization concentrates on one special market segment and tries in that segment to be the provider with lowest costs (*example*: Red Cherry Pop).

■ A **differentiation strategy** offers products that are unique and different from the competition.

Organizations pursuing a **differentiation strategy** seek competitive advantage through uniqueness. They try to develop goods and services that are clearly different from the competition. The objective is to attract customers who become loyal to the organization's products and lose interest in those of competitors. This strategy requires organizational strengths in

Figure 9.6 Porter's generic strategies framework: soft-drink industry examples.

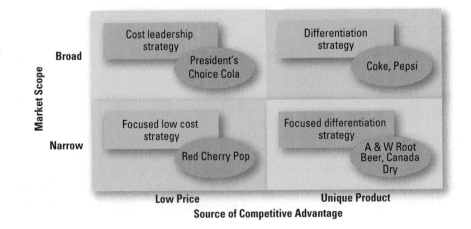

marketing, research and development, and creativity. Its success depends on continuing customer perceptions of product quality and uniqueness. An example in the apparel industry is Polo Ralph Lauren, retailer of upscale classic fashions and accessories. In Ralph Lauren's words, "Polo redefined how American style and quality is perceived. Polo has always been about selling quality products by creating worlds and inviting our customers to be part of our dream."[38]

Organizations pursuing a **cost leadership strategy** try to have lower costs than competitors and therefore achieve higher profits. The objective is to continuously improve the operating efficiencies of production, distribution, and other organizational systems. This requires tight cost and managerial controls as well as products that are easy to manufacture and distribute. In retailing, Wal-Mart aims to keep its costs so low that it can always offer customers the lowest prices and still make a reasonable profit. Most discounters operate with 18 to 20 percent gross margins. Wal-Mart can accept less and still make the same or higher returns.

■ A **cost leadership strategy** seeks to operate with lower costs than competitors.

Organizations pursuing **focus strategies** concentrate on a special market segment with the objective of serving its needs better than anyone else. The strategies focus organizational resources and expertise on a particular customer group, geographical region, or product or service line. They seek competitive advantage in that market segment through product differentiation or cost leadership. In 1996, WestJet borrowed the business model of the successful low-cost carrier Southwest Airlines and adapted it to fit Canadian expectations. By taking out business class and food services, offering low fares, and flying into smaller airports, WestJet focused on keeping customer service high and costs low. This no-frills approach has helped WestJet grow to become Canada's second largest airline, with revenues of $1.1 billion in 2005.[39]

■ A **focused differentiation strategy** offers a unique product to a special market segment.

■ A **focused cost leadership strategy** seeks the lowest costs of operations within a special market segment.

CANADIAN COMPANY IN THE NEWS Oxford Frozen Foods

FAMILY FRUIT COMPANY GOES GLOBAL

Strategy has played a large part in the growth of Oxford Frozen Foods. With intense marketing efforts and several trade trips to Asia, the Nova Scotia company has become a major supplier to Japan's largest jam manufacturer. It has had annual exports of more than $62 million to countries throughout Europe and Asia. "The seed of our family-run business was planted in a small Nova Scotia town blessed with ideal conditions for growing wild blueberries. The year was 1968 and Oxford Frozen Foods was a small company with plans to make this delicious fruit the natural pick of consumers around the world," says President John Bragg. "Today, we're the world's largest supplier of frozen wild blueberries." Oxford Frozen Foods is also one of North America's major producers of premium frozen carrots and onion rings, and has developed its own cranberry operation.

Source: Foreign Affairs and International Trade Canada website, "Why Trade Matters—Wild for Blueberries," *Stories of the Week*, Sept. 22, 2003; <www.dfait-maeci.gc.ca>

●●● PORTFOLIO PLANNING

In a single-product or single-business firm, the strategic context is one industry. Corporate strategy and business strategy are the same, and resources are allocated on that basis. When firms operate in multiple industries with many products or services, they become internally more complex and often larger in size. This makes resource allocation a more challenging strategic management task, since the mix of businesses must be well managed. The strategy

■ A **portfolio planning** approach seeks the best mix of investments among alternative business opportunities.

problem is similar to that faced by an individual with limited money who must choose among alternative stocks, bonds, and real estate in a personal investment portfolio. In multibusiness situations, strategy formulation also involves **portfolio planning** to allocate scarce resources among competing uses.[40]

BCG Matrix

■ The **BCG matrix** analyzes business opportunities according to market growth rate and market share.

Figure 9.7 summarizes an approach to business portfolio planning developed by the Boston Consulting Group and known as the **BCG matrix**. This framework analyzes business opportunities according to industry or market growth rate and market share.[41] As shown in the figure, this comparison results in four possible business conditions, with each being associated with a strategic implication: (1) *stars*—high-market-share/high-growth businesses; (2) *cash cows*—high-market-share/low-growth businesses; (3) *question marks*—low-market-share/high-growth businesses; and (4) *dogs*—low-market-share/low-growth businesses.

Figure 9.7 The BCG matrix approach to corporate strategy formulation.

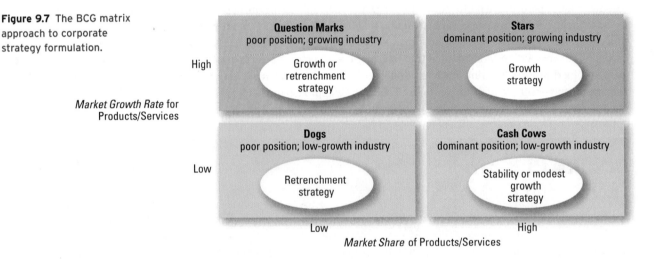

Market Growth Rate for Products/Services

Market Share of Products/Services

Stars are high-market-share businesses in high-growth markets. They produce large profits through substantial penetration of expanding markets. The preferred strategy for stars is growth, and further resource investments in them are recommended. *Question marks* are low-market-share businesses in high-growth markets. They do not produce much profit but compete in rapidly growing markets. They are the source of difficult strategic decisions. The preferred strategy is growth, but the risk exists that further investments will not result in improved market share. Only the most promising question marks should be targeted for growth; others are candidates for retrenchment by restructuring or divestiture.

Cash cows are high-market-share businesses in low-growth markets. They produce large profits and a strong cash flow. Because the markets offer little growth opportunity, the preferred strategy is stability or modest growth. "Cows" should be "milked" to generate cash that can be used to support investments in stars and question marks. *Dogs* are low-market-share businesses in low-growth markets. They do not produce much profit, and they show little potential for future improvement. The preferred strategy for dogs is retrenchment by divestiture.

●●● ADAPTIVE STRATEGIES

The Miles and Snow adaptive model of strategy formulation suggests that organizations pursue strategies that best fit with their external environments.[42] A well-chosen strategy allows an organization to successfully adapt to environmental challenges. The *prospector strategy* involves pursuing innovation and new opportunities in the face of risk and with prospects for growth. This is best suited to a dynamic and high-potential environment. A prospector "leads" an industry by using existing technology to new advantage and creating new products to which competitors must respond. This contrasts with a *defender strategy*, in which an organization tries to protect current market share by emphasizing existing products and without seeking growth. Defenders, like many small local retailers, try to maintain their operating domains with only slight changes over time. As a result, many suffer long-term decline in the face of competition. Defence is a protective strategy, suited only for a stable environment and perhaps declining industries.

The *analyzer strategy* seeks to maintain the stability of a core business while exploring selective opportunities for innovation and change. This strategy lies between the prospector and reactor strategies. It is a "follow-the-leader-when-things-look-good" approach. Many of the "clone" makers in the personal computer industry are analyzers; that is, they wait to see what the industry leaders do and how well it works out before modifying their own operations. Organizations pursuing a *reactor strategy* have no real strategy of their own. They simply respond to competitive pressures in order to survive. This is a "change-as-last-resort" approach. Reactors are slow to adapt to environmental changes and are the least desirable types in the Miles and Snow model.

●●● INCREMENTALISM AND EMERGENT STRATEGY

Not all strategies are created in systematic and deliberate fashion and then implemented step by step. Instead, strategies sometimes take shape, change, and develop over time as modest adjustments to past patterns. James Brian Quinn calls this a process of *incrementalism,*

AROUND THE WORLD

In the world of the Internet, eBay, Inc. lives up to its billing as "the world's online marketplace." On any given day over 12 million items are for sale on its website, the most visited on the Internet; online members transact over $15 billion in sales annually, worldwide. Not bad for a company that started in 1995 with a business model that almost seemed too simple to be right: Carry no inventory; just offer an electronic means for buyers and sellers to meet—for a fee. CEO Meg Whitman describes eBay's mission as: "to provide a global trading platform where practically anyone can trade practically anything." The company maintains dedicated local sites in many countries from Singapore to Spain. Although others may try to copy the eBay strategy, its first-mover advantage and global brand make it hard to beat.

A great business model travels the trade routes of the world

Source: Information and quotes from <www.ebay.com/community/aboutebay/ index.html>.

whereby modest and incremental changes in strategy occur as managers learn from experience and make adjustments.[43] This approach has much in common with Henry Mintzberg's and John Kotter's descriptions of managerial behaviour, as described in Chapter 1.[44] They view managers as planning and acting in complex interpersonal networks and in hectic, fast-paced work settings. Given these challenges, effective managers must have the capacity to stay focused on long-term objectives while still remaining flexible enough to master short-run problems and opportunities as they occur.

■ An **emergent strategy** develops over time as managers learn from and respond to experience.

Such reasoning has led Mintzberg to identify what he calls **emergent strategies**.[45] These are strategies that develop progressively over time as "streams" of decisions made by managers as they learn from and respond to work situations. There is an important element of "craftsmanship" here that Mintzberg worries may be overlooked by managers who choose and discard strategies in rapid succession while using the formal planning models. He also believes that incremental or emergent strategic planning allows managers and organizations to become really good at implementing strategies, not just formulating them.

✓ Learning check ④

BE SURE YOU CAN
• explain the four generic strategies in Porter's model • illustrate how these strategies use products in a market familiar to you • describe the BCG matrix for portfolio planning and use it to analyze strategic opportunities for a business • differentiate among the prospector, defender, analyzer, and reactor strategies • explain the concepts of incrementalism and emergent strategy

---

STRATEGY IMPLEMENTATION

No strategy, no matter how well formulated, can achieve long-term success if it is not properly implemented. This includes the willingness to exercise control and make modifications as required to meet the needs of changing conditions. Current issues in strategy implementation include excellence in all management systems and practices, the responsibilities of corporate governance, and the importance of strategic leadership.

●●● MANAGEMENT PRACTICES AND SYSTEMS

The rest of *Management* is about strategy implementation. In order to successfully put strategies into action, the entire organization and all of its resources must be mobilized in support of them. This, in effect, involves the complete management process from planning and controlling through organizing and leading. No matter how well or elegantly selected, a strategy requires supporting structures, the right technology, a good allocation of tasks and workflow designs, and the right people to staff all aspects of operations. The strategy needs to be enthusiastically supported by leaders who are capable of motivating everyone, building individual performance commitments, and utilizing teams and teamwork to their best advantage. And the strategy needs to be well- and continually communicated to all relevant persons and parties. Only with such total system support for implementation can strategies succeed in today's challenging and highly competitive environments.

Failures of substance and failures of process are common pitfalls that hinder strategy implementation. *Failures of substance* reflect inadequate attention to the major strategic planning elements—analysis of mission and purpose, core values and corporate culture, organizational strengths and weaknesses, and environmental opportunities and threats. *Failures of process* reflect poor handling of the ways in which the various aspects of strategic planning were accomplished. An important process failure is the *lack of participation error*. This is failure to include key persons in the strategic planning effort.[46] As a result, their lack of commitment to all-important action follow-through may severely hurt strategy implementation. Process failure also occurs with too much centralization of planning in top management or too much delegation of planning activities to staff planners or separate planning departments. Another process failure is the tendency to get so bogged down in details that the planning process becomes an end in itself instead of a means to an end. This is sometimes called "goal displacement."

●●●○ CORPORATE GOVERNANCE

In the wake of the ethics scandals in business, organizations today are experiencing new pressures at the level of **corporate governance**. As discussed in earlier chapters, this is the system of control and performance monitoring of top management that is maintained by boards of directors and other major stakeholder representatives. In businesses, for example, corporate governance is enacted by boards, institutional investors in a firm's assets, and other ownership interests. Each in its own way is a point of accountability for top management.[47]

Boards of directors play major roles in corporate governance. They are formally charged with ensuring that an organization operates in the best interests of its owners and/or the representative public in the case of non-profit organizations. Controversies sometimes arise over the role of *inside directors*, who are chosen from the senior management of the organization, and *outside directors*, who are chosen from other organizations and positions external to the organization. In some cases insiders may have too much control; in others the outsiders may be selected because they are friends of top management or at least sympathetic to them. The concern is that the boards may be too compliant in endorsing or confirming the strategic initiatives of top management. Today, board members are increasingly expected to exercise control and take active roles in ensuring that the strategic management of an enterprise is successful. They are also being selected because of special expertise that they can bring to the governance process.

If anything, the current trend is toward greater emphasis on the responsibilities of corporate governance. Top managers probably feel more performance accountability today than ever before to boards of directors and other stakeholder interest groups. Furthermore, this accountability relates not only to financial performance but also to broader ethical and social responsibility concerns. At GE, for example, CEO Jeffrey Immelt makes it a practice to absent himself at times from directors' meetings.[48] His predecessor, Jack Welch, always wanted to be present when directors met, but Immelt believes differently. His practice helps ensure that the governance responsibilities of the board, including oversight of the CEO's decisions and actions, are independently exercised.

> ▨ **Corporate governance** is the system of control and performance monitoring of top management.

●●●○ STRATEGIC LEADERSHIP

Effective strategy implementation depends on the full commitment of all managers to support and lead strategic initiatives within their areas of supervisory responsibility. In our dynamic and often-uncertain environment, the premium is on **strategic leadership**—the capability to inspire people to successfully engage in a process of continuous change, performance enhancement, and implementation of organizational strategies.[49] The broad issues associated with strategic leadership are so important that Part 5 of *Management* is devoted in its entirety to leadership and issues related to leadership development—including leadership models, motivation, communication, interpersonal dynamics, teamwork, and change leadership.

Porter argues that the CEO of a business has to be the chief strategist, someone who provides strategic leadership.[50] He describes the task in the following way. A strategic leader has to be the *guardian of trade-offs*. It is the leader's job to make sure that the organization's

> ▨ **Strategic leadership** inspires people to continuously change, refine, and improve strategies and their implementation.

resources are allocated in ways consistent with the strategy. This requires the discipline to sort through many competing ideas and alternatives to stay on course and not get side-tracked. A strategic leader also needs to *create a sense of urgency*, not allowing the organization and its members to grow slow and complacent. Even when doing well, the leader keeps the focus on getting better and being alert to conditions that require adjustments to the strategy. A strategic leader needs to *make sure that everyone understands the strategy*. Unless strategies are understood, the daily tasks and contributions of people lose context and purpose. Everyone might work very hard, but without alignment to strategy the impact is dispersed rather than advancing in a common direction to accomplish the goals. Importantly, a strategic leader must *be a teacher*. It is the leader's job to teach the strategy and make it a "cause," says Porter. In order for strategy to work, it must become an ever-present commitment throughout the organization. This means that a strategic leader must *be a great communicator*. Everyone must understand the strategy and how it makes their organization different from others.

Finally, it is important to note that the challenges faced by organizations today are so complex that it is difficult for any one individual to fulfill all strategic leadership needs. Strategic management is increasingly viewed as a team leadership responsibility. When Michael Dell founded Dell Computer, he did it in his dormitory room at university. Now the firm operates globally with $30 billion in sales. Dell is still Chairman and CEO, but he operates with a top management team. "I don't think you could do it with one person," he says, "there's way too much to be done."[51] As discussed in Chapter 16 on teams and teamwork, it takes hard work and special circumstances to create a real team, at the top or anywhere else in the organization.[52] Top management teams must work up to their full potential in order to bring the full advantages of teamwork to strategic leadership. Dell believes his top management team has mastered the challenge. "We bounce ideas off each other," he says, "and at the end of the day if we say who did this, the only right answer is that we all did. Three heads are better than one."

PERSONAL MANAGEMENT

CRITICAL THINKING is essential for executive leadership success. It is an analytical skill that involves the ability to gather and interpret information for decision making in a problem context. A good way to develop this skill is through case studies and problem-solving projects in your courses. But beware! One of the risks of our information-rich environment is overreliance on what we hear or read—especially when it comes from the Web. A lot of what circulates on the Web is anecdotal, superficial, irrelevant, and even just plain inaccurate. You must be disciplined, cautious, and discerning in interpreting the credibility and usefulness of any information that you retrieve. Once you understand this and are willing to invest the time for critical thinking, the Web offers a world of opportunities. Consider your personal career strategy: How well prepared are you to succeed in the *future* job market, not just the present one?

Get to know yourself better

Complete Self-Assessment #14—**Facts and Inferences**, and Exercise #10—**Personal Career Planning**, from the Workbook and Personal Management Activity #9 on the companion website.

✓ Learning check ⑤

BE SURE YOU CAN
• explain how the management process supports strategy implementation • define the term corporate governance • explain why boards of directors sometimes fail in their governance responsibilities • define the term strategic leadership • list the responsibilities of a strategic leader in today's organizations

WHERE WE'VE BEEN

Back to Taxi

The opening vignette, Taxi, introduced you to a firm that has successfully followed a growth strategy by differentiating themselves from others. In Chapter 9 you learned more about the concept of strategy and its relationship to the achievement of sustainable competitive advantage. You also learned how the strategic management process analyzes organization and environment, and utilizes various frameworks to select effective strategies. Finally, you learned that even the best strategies deliver high-performance results only when they are well implemented.

THE NEXT STEP

INTEGRATED LEARNING ACTIVITIES

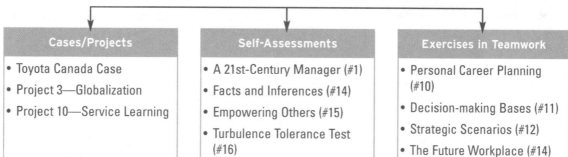

Cases/Projects	Self-Assessments	Exercises in Teamwork
• Toyota Canada Case	• A 21st-Century Manager (#1)	• Personal Career Planning (#10)
• Project 3—Globalization	• Facts and Inferences (#14)	• Decision-making Bases (#11)
• Project 10—Service Learning	• Empowering Others (#15)	• Strategic Scenarios (#12)
	• Turbulence Tolerance Test (#16)	• The Future Workplace (#14)

STUDY QUESTION SUMMARY

1. What are the foundations of strategic competitiveness?

• Competitive advantage is achieved by operating in ways difficult for competitors to imitate.

• A strategy is a comprehensive plan that sets long-term direction and guides resource allocation for sustainable competitive advantage.

• Strategic intent directs organizational resources and energies toward a compelling goal.

• The strategic goals of a business should include superior profitability and the generation of above-average returns for investors.

2. What is the strategic management process?

• Strategic management is the process of formulating and implementing strategies that achieve goals in a competitive environment.

• The strategic management process begins with analysis of mission, clarification of core values, and identification of objectives.

• A SWOT analysis systematically assesses organizational resources and capabilities and industry/environmental opportunities and threats.

• Porter's five forces model analyzes industry attractiveness in terms of competititors, new entrants, substitute products, and the bargaining powers of suppliers and buyers.

3. What types of strategies are used by organizations?

• Corporate strategy sets direction for an entire organization; business strategy sets direction for a business division or product/service line; functional strategy sets direction for the operational support of business and corporate strategies.

• The grand or master strategies used by organizations include growth—pursuing expansion through concentration and diversification; they also include retrenchment—pursuing ways to scale back operations through restructuring and divestiture.

• Global strategies take advantage of international business opportunities; co-operative strategies, such as international joint ventures, use strategic alliances for performance gains.

- E-business strategies use IT and the Internet to pursue competitive advantage.

4. How are strategies formulated?

- The three options in Porter's model of competitive strategy are: differentiation—distinguishing one's products from the competition; cost leadership—minimizing costs relative to the competition; and focus—concentrating on a special market segment.

- The BCG matrix is a portfolio planning approach that classifies businesses or product lines as "stars," "cash cows," "question marks," or "dogs."

- The adaptive model focuses on the congruence of prospector, defender, analyzer, or reactor strategies with demands of the external environment.

- The incremental or emergent model recognizes that many strategies are formulated and implemented incrementally over time.

5. What are current issues in strategy implementation?

- Management practices and systems—including the functions of planning, organizing, leading, and controlling—must be mobilized to support strategy implementation.

- Pitfalls that inhibit strategy implementation include failures of substance—such as poor analysis of the environment; and failures of process—such as lack of participation in the planning process.

- Boards of directors play important roles in corporate governance, monitoring top management, and organizational strategies and performance.

- Strategic leadership inspires the process of continuous evaluation and improvement of strategies and their implementation.

- Success in strategic leadership requires the ability to manage trade-offs in resource allocations, maintain a sense of urgency in strategy implementation, and effectively communicate the strategy to key constituencies.

KEY TERMS REVIEW

Above-average returns (p. 214)

B2B business strategy (p. 224)

B2C business strategy (p. 224)

BCG matrix (p. 228)

Business strategy (p. 221)

Competitive advantage (p. 213)

Concentration (p. 222)

Core competency (p. 218)

Corporate governance (p. 231)

Corporate strategy (p. 221)

Cost leadership strategy (p. 227)

Differentiation strategy (p. 226)

Diversification (p. 222)

Divestiture (p. 223)

Downsizing (p. 223)

E-business strategy (p. 224)

Emergent strategy (p. 230)

Focused cost leadership strategy (p. 227)

Focused differentiation strategy (p. 227)

Functional strategy (p. 221)

Globalization strategy (p. 223)

Growth strategy (p. 222)

Mission (p. 216)

Multidomestic strategy (p. 223)

Operating objectives (p. 218)

Organizational culture (p. 217)

Portfolio planning (p. 228)

Restructuring (p. 223)

Retrenchment strategy (p. 222)

Stakeholders (p. 217)

Strategic alliance (p. 224)

Strategic business unit (SBU) (p. 221)

Strategic intent (p. 213)

Strategic leadership (p. 231)

Strategic management (p. 214)

Strategy (p. 213)

Strategy formulation (p. 215)

Strategy implementation (p. 216)

SWOT analysis (p. 218)

Transnational strategy (p. 223)

Vertical integration (p. 222)

SELF-TEST 9

MULTIPLE-CHOICE QUESTIONS:

1. The most appropriate first question to ask in strategic planning is _____.
   (a) "Where do we want to be in the future?" (b) "How well are we currently doing?" (c) "How can we get where we want to be?" (d) "Why aren't we doing better?"

2. The ability of a firm to consistently outperform its rivals is called _____.
   (a) vertical integration (b) competitive advantage (c) incrementalism (d) strategic intent

c

3. In a complex conglomerate business such as General Electric, a(n) _____ -level strategy sets strategic direction for a strategic business unit or product division.
    (a) institutional (b) corporate (c) business (d) functional

c

4. An organization that is downsizing to reduce costs is implementing a grand strategy of _____.
    (a) growth (b) cost differentiation (c) retrenchment (d) stability

5. The _____ is a predominant value system for an organization as a whole.   *c*
    (a) strategy (b) core competency (c) mission (d) organizational culture

6. A _____ in the BCG matrix would have a high market share in a low-growth market.   *c*
    (a) dog (b) cash cow (c) question mark (d) star

7. In Porter's five forces framework, which of the following increases industry attractiveness?   *d*
    (a) many rivals (b) many substitute products (c) low bargaining power of suppliers (d) few barriers to entry

8. When PepsiCo acquired Tropicana, a maker of fruit juice, the firm's strategy was one of _____.   *a*
    (a) related diversification (b) concentration (c) vertical integration (d) co-operation

9. Cost efficiency and product quality are two examples of _____ objectives of organizations.   *b*
    (a) strategic (b) operating (c) performance (d) long-term

10. The customer generally gains through the lower prices and greater innovation characteristic of _____ environments.
    (a) monopoly (b) oligopoly (c) hypercompetition (d) downsizing   *c*

11. In the Miles and Snow model of adaptive strategy, the _____ strategy is largely a copycat approach that seeks to do whatever seems to be working well for someone else.   *d*
    (a) prospector (b) reactor (c) defender (d) analyzer

12. The role of the board of directors as an oversight body that holds top executives accountable for the success of business strategies is called _____.   *b*
    (a) strategic leadership (b) corporate governance (c) incrementalism (d) strategic management

13. Among the global strategies that might be pursued by international businesses, the _____ strategy is the most targeted on local needs, local management, and local products.   *d*
    (a) ethnocentric (b) transnational (c) geocentric (d) multidomestic

14. Restructuring by downsizing operations and reducing staff is a form of _____ strategy.   *a*
    (a) retrenchment (b) growth (c) concentration (d) incremental

15. According to Porter's model of generic strategies, a firm that wants to compete with its rivals by selling a very low priced product would need to succesfully implement a _____ strategy.
    (a) retrenchment (b) differentiation (c) cost leadership (d) diversification   *c*

SHORT-RESPONSE QUESTIONS:

16. What is the difference between corporate strategy and functional strategy?

17. How would a manager perform a SWOT analysis?

18. Explain the difference between B2B and B2C as e-business strategies.

19. What is strategic leadership?

APPLICATION QUESTION:

20. Kim Harris owns and operates a small retail store selling the outdoor clothing of a Canadian manufacturer to a predominately college and university student market. Lately, a large department store outside of town has started selling similar but lower-priced clothing manufactured in China, Thailand, and Bangladesh. Kim believes he is starting to lose business to this store. Assume you are part of a student team assigned to do a management class project for Kim. His question for the team is: "How can I best deal with my strategic management challenges in this situation?" How will you reply?

Organizing

Planning Ahead

After reading Chapter 10, you should be able to answer these questions in your own words.

1. What is organizing as a management function?

2. What are the major types of organization structures?

3. What are the new developments in organization structures?

4. What organizing trends are changing the workplace?

Edward Jones
Structures supporting strategies

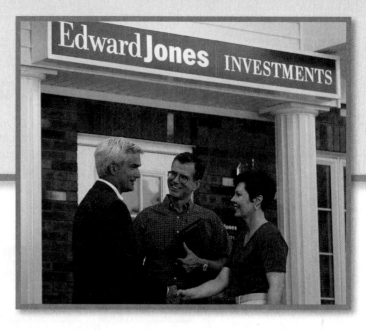

Edward Jones is an investment firm that does not operate like other investment firms. Its way of organizing its business sets them apart from the rest. Rather than develop large offices with many employees, Edward Jones has opened up many smaller offices, each staffed with one investment representative and one branch office administrator. Edward Jones's core strategic belief is that face-to-face interaction with clients is the best way to build their business; something best done at small, highly personal, focused centres. Offices are generally staffed by one investment representative who is a licensed broker and at least one office administrator. Some branches may have additional brokers and office staff depending on the level of business. Edward Jones believes that the one-broker-per-office model allows clients the opportunity to choose their broker and then to deal only with that broker.

With a strong core surrounded by largely independent satellite units, the Edward Jones structure is unique. Noted organizational theorist Peter Drucker described this company as "a confederation of highly autonomous entrepreneurial units bound together by a highly centralized core of values and services." And their approach is working. In the 1980s they were a small regional firm in the United States, with just over 300 offices. Today, Edward Jones has nearly 10,000 offices in three countries, including Canada. Edward Jones established its first office in Canada in 1994, and today it has more than 550 branches here.

Their satellite set-up appeals to employees of Edward Jones. *Report on Business* magazine recently named it one of the "50 Best Employers in Canada." Employees like working for the company because of the family atmosphere. Edward Jones also has a strong emphasis on work/life balance, which allows employees flexible work scheduling, training for staff, and realistic sales expectations.

Edward Jones's way of organizing also seems to be working for its clients. Edward Jones ranked "Highest in Investor Satisfaction with Full Service Brokerage Firms" by J.D. Power and Associates. The J.D. Power and Associates 2006 Canadian Full Service Investor Satisfaction Study is based on responses from 5,190 investors who used one of the 14 firms profiled in the study. It is easy to see that Edward Jones has found both an inventive and a successful way to organize.[1]

IN THE WORKPLACE

Your boss Darren Smith has just returned from a conference in California. For a moment you think about your future career and dream about the business trips you would like to take to distant destinations. Darren brings you quickly back to your work as he has another task for you to accomplish. "There was a lot of talk about 'matrix' structures at the conference. I want you to write a short report on its advantages and disadvantages. We might think about implementing it here." Some day it will be your turn to ask for reports to be written, but for now it is your time to write them. What do you say in your report about the pros and cons of matrix structures?

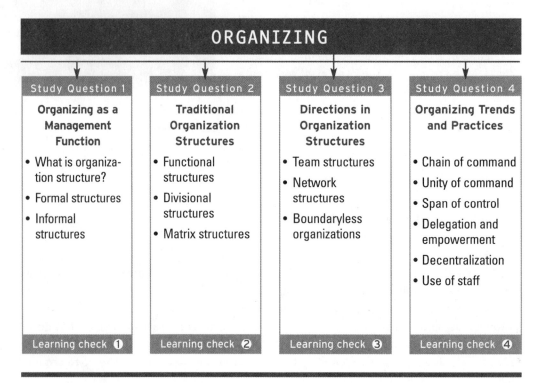

●●● Chapter 10 **LEARNING PREVIEW** ●●●

The opening example of Edward Jones shows how one firm has organized itself for high performance in the financial services industry. Part of the challenge faced by the company is to maintain success with its entrepreneurial strategy and small-firm ways even while experiencing the pressures of growth. This chapter introduces you to organizing as a management function. It reviews the traditional ways of structuring organizations as well as new directions such as those taken by Edward Jones. Current trends and organizing practices in the new workplace are also described.

ORGANIZING

Study Question 1	Study Question 2	Study Question 3	Study Question 4
Organizing as a Management Function	**Traditional Organization Structures**	**Directions in Organization Structures**	**Organizing Trends and Practices**
• What is organization structure? • Formal structures • Informal structures	• Functional structures • Divisional structures • Matrix structures	• Team structures • Network structures • Boundaryless organizations	• Chain of command • Unity of command • Span of control • Delegation and empowerment • Decentralization • Use of staff
Learning check ❶	Learning check ❷	Learning check ❸	Learning check ❹

Management scholar and consultant Henry Mintzberg points out that organizations are changing very quickly in today's world and people within them are struggling to find their place.[2] His point is that people need to understand how their organizations work if they are to work well within them. Mintzberg notes some common questions: "What parts connect to one another?" "How should processes and people come together?" "Whose ideas have to flow where?" These and related questions raise critical issues about organization structures and how well they meet an organization's performance needs.

The organizing approach of Edward Jones—management through a strong central core surrounded by small and autonomous units—is one entrepreneurial benchmark. By building a well-focused yet market-responsive structure, the firm has established and sustained a niche in the highly competitive financial services industry. But this is only one of the ways to structure for success. There are many options as organizations in all industries try new forms in the quest for sustained competitive advantage. Some are using designs that we will discuss as team, network, or even "boundaryless" and "virtual" organizations. Others involve downsizing, rightsizing, and delayering organizations in the search for productivity gains.

Among the best organizations, those that consistently deliver above-average returns and outperform their competitors, one does find consistent themes.[3] They emphasize empowerment, support for employees, responsiveness to client or customer needs, flexibility in dealing with a dynamic environment, and continual attention to quality improvements. They strive for positive cultures and high quality-of-work-life experiences for members and employees. And, importantly, they accept that nothing is constant, at least not for long. They are always seeking new ways of organizing the workplace to best support strategies and achieve high-performance goals.

ORGANIZING AS A MANAGEMENT FUNCTION

Organizing is the process of arranging people and other resources to work together to accomplish a goal. As one of the basic functions of management, it involves both creating a division of labour for tasks to be performed and then coordinating results to achieve a common purpose. *Figure 10.1* shows the central role that organizing plays in the management process. Once plans are created, the manager's task is to see to it that they are carried out. Given a clear mission, core values, objectives, and strategy, *organizing* begins the process of implementation by clarifying jobs and working relationships. It identifies who is to do what, who is in charge of whom, and how different people and parts of the organization relate to and work with one another. All of this, of course, can be done in different ways. The strategic leadership challenge is to choose the best organizational form to fit the strategy and other situational demands.

> ■ **Organizing** arranges people and resources to work toward a goal.

●●● WHAT IS ORGANIZATION STRUCTURE?

The way in which the various parts of an organization are formally arranged is usually referred to as the **organization structure**. It is the system of tasks, workflows, reporting relationships, and communication channels that link together the work of diverse individuals and groups. Any structure should both allocate tasks through a division of labour and provide for the coordination of performance results. A structure that does both of these things well is an important asset, helping to implement an organization's strategy.[4] Unfortunately, it is easier to talk about good structures than it is to actually create them. This is why you often read and hear about organizations changing their structures in an attempt to improve performance. There is no one best structure that meets the needs of all circumstances; structure must be addressed in a contingency fashion. As environments and situations change, structures must often be changed too. To make good choices, a manager must understand how structures work and know the available alternatives.

> ■ **Organization structure** is a system of tasks, reporting relationships, and communication linkages.

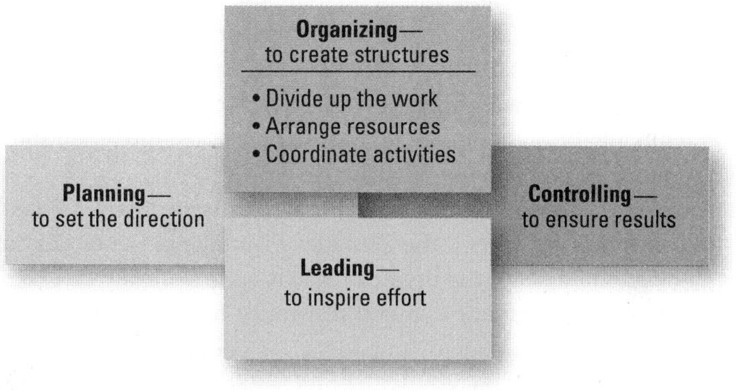

Figure 10.1 Organizing viewed in relationship with the other management functions.

Organizing—
to create structures

• Divide up the work
• Arrange resources
• Coordinate activities

Planning—
to set the direction

Controlling—
to ensure results

Leading—
to inspire effort

●●● FORMAL STRUCTURES

▥ An **organization chart** describes the arrangement of work positions within an organization.

You may know the concept of structure best in the form of an **organization chart.** This is a diagram that shows reporting relationships and the formal arrangement of work positions within an organization.[5] A typical organization chart identifies various positions and job titles as well as the lines of authority and communication between them. This is the **formal structure,** or the structure of the organization in its official state. It represents the way the organization is intended to function. By reading an organization chart, you can learn the basics of an organization's formal structure, including the following:

▥ **Formal structure** is the official structure of the organization.

- *Division of work:* Positions and titles show work responsibilities.

- *Supervisory relationships:* Lines show who reports to whom.

- *Communication channels:* Lines show formal communication flows.

- *Major subunits:* Positions reporting to a common manager are shown.

- *Levels of management:* Vertical layers of management are shown.

●●● INFORMAL STRUCTURES

▥ **Informal structure** is the set of unofficial relationships among an organization's members.

Behind every formal structure typically lies an **informal structure**. This is a "shadow" organization made up of the unofficial, but often critical, working relationships between organizational members. If the informal structure could be drawn, it would show who talks to and interacts regularly with whom regardless of their formal titles and relationships. The lines of the informal structure would cut across levels and move from side to side. They would show people meeting for coffee, in exercise groups, and in friendship groups, among other possibilities. Importantly, no organization can be fully understood without gaining insight into the informal structure as well as the formal one.[6]

Informal structures can be very helpful in getting work accomplished. Indeed, they may be essential in many ways to organizational success. This is especially true during times of change, when out-of-date formal structures may fail to provide the support people need to deal with new or unusual situations. Because it takes time to change or modify formal structures, this happens quite often. In many cases, the informal structure helps fill the void. Through the emergent and spontaneous relationships of informal structures, people benefit in task performance by being in personal contact with others who can help them get things done when necessary. They gain the advantages of *informal learning* that takes place while working and interacting together throughout the workday. Informal structures are also helpful in giving people access to interpersonal networks of emotional support and friendship that satisfy important social needs.

Nortel Networks, headquartered in Brampton, Ontario, recognizes the value of internal networking in increasing learning within their organization. Among the methods Nortel uses to promote the sharing of knowledge and experience among staff are social events, locating a project's staff in close proximity to each other, setting up informal coffee groups, and organizing formal meetings to discuss common concerns and important issues. Nortel also ensures networking throughout their global operations by implementing quarterly get-togethers and by using video conferencing extensively.[7]

Of course, informal structures also have potential disadvantages. Because they exist outside the formal authority system, the activities of informal structures can sometimes work against the best interests of the organization as a whole. They can be susceptible to rumour, carry inaccurate information, breed resistance to change, and even divert work efforts from important objectives. Also, "outsiders," or people who are left out of informal groupings, may feel less a part of daily activities and suffer a loss of satisfaction. Some North

American managers of Japanese firms, for example, have complained about being excluded from what they call the "shadow cabinet"—an informal group of Japanese executives who hold the real power to get things done and sometimes act to the exclusion of others.[8]

> **BE SURE YOU CAN**
>
> • define organizing as a management function • explain the difference between formal and informal structures • discuss the potential advantages and disadvantages of informal structures in organizations

✓ Learning check ❶

TRADITIONAL ORGANIZATION STRUCTURES

A traditional principle of organizing is that performance improves when people are allowed to specialize and become expert in specific jobs or tasks. Given this division of labour, however, decisions must then be made on **departmentalization**, how to group work positions into formal teams or departments that are linked together in a coordinated way. These decisions have traditionally resulted in three major types of organizational structures—the functional, divisional, and matrix structures.[9]

▣ **Departmentalization** is the process of grouping together people and jobs into work units.

●●● FUNCTIONAL STRUCTURES

In **functional structures**, people with similar skills and performing similar tasks are grouped together into formal work units. Members of functional departments share technical expertise, interests, and responsibilities. The first example in *Figure 10.2* shows a functional structure common in business firms: top management is arranged by the functions of marketing,

▣ A **functional structure** groups together people with similar skills who perform similar tasks.

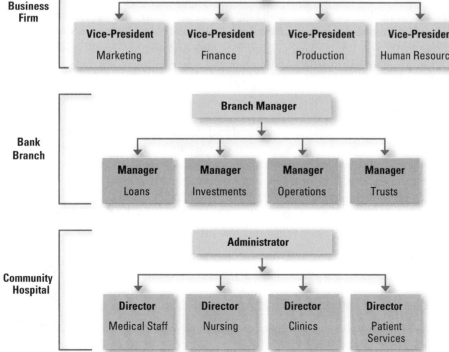

Figure 10.2 Functional structures in a business, bank branch, and community hospital.

finance, production, and human resources. In this functional structure, manufacturing problems are the responsibility of the production vice-president, marketing problems are the province of the marketing vice-president, and so on. The key point is that members of each function work within their areas of expertise. If each function does its work properly, the expectation is that the business will operate successfully.

Functional structures are not limited to businesses. The figure also shows how this form of departmentalization can be used in additional types of organizations, such as banks and hospitals. Functional structures typically work well for small organizations that produce only one or a few products or services. They also tend to work best in relatively stable environments where problems are predictable and the demands for change and innovation are limited. The major *advantages of a functional structure* include the following:

- Economies of scale with efficient use of resources.

- Task assignments consistent with expertise and training.

- High-quality technical problem solving.

- In-depth training and skill development within functions.

- Clear career paths within functions.

■ The **functional chimneys problem** is a lack of communication and coordination across functions.

There are also potential *disadvantages of functional structures*. Common problems include difficulties in pinpointing responsibilities for things like cost containment, product or service quality, timeliness, and innovation. A significant concern is with the **functional chimneys problem**—lack of communication, coordination, and problem solving across functions. Because the functions become formalized, not only on an organization chart but also in the mindsets of people, the sense of co-operation and common purpose breaks down. The total system perspective is lost to self-centred and narrow viewpoints. When problems occur between functions, they are too often referred up to higher levels for resolution rather than being addressed by people at the same level. This slows decision making and problem solving, and can result in a loss of advantage in competitive situations. For example, when Ford took over as the new owner of Jaguar it had to resolve many quality problems. The quality turnaround took longer than anticipated, in part because of what Jaguar's chairman called "excessive compartmentalization." In building cars, the different departments did very little talking and working with one another. Ford's response was to push for more interdepartmental coordination and consensus decision making.[10]

●●● DIVISIONAL STRUCTURES

■ A **divisional structure** groups together people working on the same product, in the same area, with similar customers, or on the same processes.

A second organizational alternative is the **divisional structure**. It groups together people who work on the same product or process, serve similar customers, and/or are located in the same area or geographical region. As illustrated in *Figure 10.3*, divisional structures are common in complex organizations with diverse operations that extend across many products, territories, customers, and work processes.[11]

Divisional structures attempt to avoid problems common to functional structures. The potential *advantages of divisional structures* include the following:

- More flexibility in responding to environmental changes.

- Improved coordination across functional departments.

- Clear points of responsibility for product or service delivery.

- Expertise focused on specific customers, products, and regions.

- Greater ease in changing size by adding or deleting divisions.

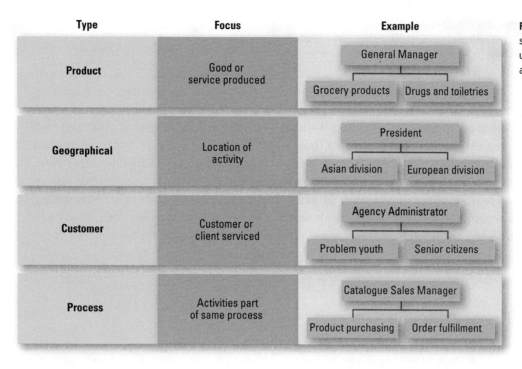

Type	Focus	Example
Product	Good or service produced	General Manager → Grocery products / Drugs and toiletries
Geographical	Location of activity	President → Asian division / European division
Customer	Customer or client serviced	Agency Administrator → Problem youth / Senior citizens
Process	Activities part of same process	Catalogue Sales Manager → Product purchasing / Order fulfillment

Figure 10.3 Divisional structures based on product, geography, customer, and process.

As with other alternatives, there are potential *disadvantages of divisional structures*. They can reduce economies of scale and increase costs through the duplication of resources and efforts across divisions. They can also create unhealthy rivalries as divisions compete for resources and top-management attention, and as they emphasize division needs to the detriment of the goals of the organization as a whole.

Product Structures

Product structures, sometimes called *market structures*, group together jobs and activities related to a single product or service. They clearly identify costs, profits, problems, and successes in a market area with a central point of accountability. Consequently, managers are encouraged to be responsive to changing market demands and customer tastes. Common in large organizations, product structures may even extend into global operations. When taking over as H.J. Heinz's new CEO, William R. Johnson became concerned about the company's international performance. He decided a change in structure could help improve performance. The existing structure that emphasized countries and regions was changed to global product divisions. The choice was based on his belief that a product structure would bring the best brand management to all countries and increase co-operation around the world within product businesses.

■ **A product structure** groups together people and jobs related to a single product or service.

Geographical Structures

Geographical structures, sometimes called *area structures*, group together jobs and activities being performed in the same location or geographical region. They are typically used when there is a need to differentiate products or services in various locations, such as in different regions of a country. They are also quite common in international operations, where they help to focus attention on the unique cultures and requirements of particular regions. As UPS operations expanded worldwide, for example, the company announced a change from a product to geographical organizational structure. Two geographical divisions were created—the Americas and Europe/Asia. Each area was given responsibility for its own logistics, sales, and other business functions.

■ **A geographical structure** groups together people and jobs performed in the same location.

Customer Structures

■ **A customer structure** groups together people and jobs that serve the same customers or clients.

Customer structures, sometimes also called *market structures* or *product structures*, group together jobs and activities that are serving the same customers or clients. The major appeal is the ability to best serve the special needs of the different customer groups. This is a common form of structure for complex businesses in the consumer products industries. 3M Corporation structures itself to focus attention around the world on its six business areas: consumer and office products, display and graphics products, electronic and communications solutions, health care products and services, industrial and transportation services, and security and safety services. Customer structures are also useful in the services sector. For example, banks use them to give separate attention to consumer and commercial loan customers. The example used in *Figure 10.3* also shows a government agency serving different client populations.

Process Structures

A *work process* is a group of tasks related to one another that collectively creates something of value to a customer.[12] An example is order fulfillment, for example, when you telephone a catalogue retailer and request a particular item. The process of order fulfillment takes the order from point of initiation by the customer to point of fulfillment by a delivered product. A **process structure** groups together jobs and activities that are part of the same processes. In the example of *Figure 10.3*, this might take the form of product-purchasing teams, order-fulfillment teams, and systems-support teams for the mail-order catalogue business. The importance of understanding work processes and designing process-driven organizations has been popularized by management consultant and author Michael Hammer.[13] The essentials of Hammer's ideas on work process design are discussed in the next chapter.

■ **A process structure** groups jobs and activities that are part of the same processes.

■ **A matrix structure** combines functional and divisional approaches to emphasize project or program teams.

●●● MATRIX STRUCTURES

The **matrix structure**, often called the *matrix organization*, combines the functional and divisional structures just described. In effect, it is an attempt to gain the advantages and minimize

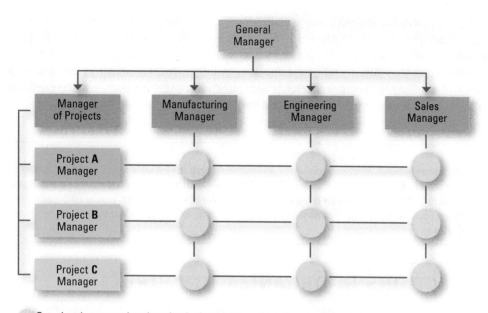

Figure 10.4 Matrix structure in a small multiproject business firm.

Functional personnel assigned to both projects and functional departments

the disadvantages of each. This is accomplished in the matrix by using permanent cross-functional teams to support specific products, projects, or programs.[14] As shown in *Figure 10.4*, workers in a matrix structure belong to at least two formal groups at the same time—a functional group and a product, program, or project team. They also report to two bosses—one within the function and the other within the team.

The matrix organization has gained a strong foothold in the workplace, with applications in such diverse settings as manufacturing (e.g., aerospace, electronics, pharmaceuticals), service industries (e.g., banking, brokerage, retailing), professional fields (e.g., accounting, advertising, law), and the non-profit sector (e.g., city, provincial, and federal agencies, hospitals, universities). Matrix structures are also found in multinational corporations, where they offer the flexibility to deal with regional differences as well as multiple product, program, or project needs.

The main contribution of matrix structures to organizational performance lies with the cross-functional teams whose members work closely together to share expertise and information in a timely manner to solve problems. The potential *advantages of matrix structures* include the following:

- Better co-operation across functions.

- Improved decision making as problem solving takes place at the team level, where the best information is available.

- Increased flexibility in adding, removing, and/or changing operations to meet changing demands.

- Better customer service, since there is always a program, product, or project manager informed and available to answer questions.

- Better performance accountability through the program, product, or project managers.

- Improved strategic management, since top managers are freed from unnecessary problem solving to focus time on strategic issues.

Predictably, there are also potential *disadvantages of matrix structures*. The two-boss system is susceptible to power struggles, as functional supervisors and team leaders vie with one another to exercise authority. The two-boss system can also be frustrating for matrix members if it creates task confusion and conflicting work priorities. Team meetings in the matrix are also time consuming. Teams may develop "groupitis," or strong team loyalties that cause a loss of focus on larger organizational goals. And the requirements of adding the team leaders to a matrix structure can result in increased costs.[15]

✓ **Learning check** ❷

BE SURE YOU CAN
• explain the differences between functional, divisional, and matrix structures • list advantages and disadvantages of a functional structure, and draw a chart to show its use in an organization familiar to you • list advantages and disadvantages of a divisional structure • draw a chart to show use of each divisional type in an organization familiar to you • list advantages and disadvantages of a matrix structure, and draw a chart to show its use in an organization familiar to you

DIRECTIONS IN ORGANIZATION STRUCTURES

The realities of a global economy and the demands of strategies driven by hypercompetition are putting increasing pressures on organization structures. The performance demands are for more speed to market, greater customer orientation, constant productivity improvements, better technology utilization, and more. The environment is unrelenting in such demands. As a result, managers are continually searching for new ways to better structure their organizations.

Structural innovation is always important in the search for productivity improvement and competitive advantage. The right structure is a performance asset; the wrong one is a liability. Today, the vertical and control-oriented structures of the past are proving less and less sufficient to master the tasks at hand. The matrix structure was a first step toward improving flexibility and problem solving through better cross-functional integration. It is now part of a broader movement toward more horizontal structures that decrease hierarchy, increase empowerment, and better mobilize technology and the talents of people to drive organizational performance. *Manager's Notepad 10.1* offers guidelines for tapping the opportunities of horizontal structures.[16]

MANAGER'S
Notepad 10.1

Guidelines for mobilizing horizontal structures

• Focus the organization around processes, not functions.

• Put people in charge of core processes.

• Decrease hierarchy and increase the use of teams.

• Empower people to make decisions critical to performance.

• Utilize information technology.

• Emphasize multi-skilling and multiple competencies.

• Teach people how to work in partnership with others.

• Build a culture of openness, collaboration, and performance commitment.

●●● TEAM STRUCTURES

As the traditional vertical structures give way to more horizontal ones, teams are serving as the basic building blocks.[17] Organizations with **team structures** extensively use both permanent and temporary teams to solve problems, complete special projects, and accomplish day-to-day tasks.[18] As illustrated in *Figure 10.5*, these are often **cross-functional teams** composed of members from different areas of work responsibility.[19] The intention is to break down the functional chimneys, or barriers, inside the organization and create more effective lateral relations for problem solving and work performance. There are also often **project teams** that are convened for a particular task or "project" and are disbanded once the task is completed. The intention here is to quickly convene people with the needed talents and focus their efforts intensely to solve a problem or take advantage of a special opportunity.

There are many potential *advantages of team structures*. They help eliminate difficulties with communication and decision making due to the functional chimneys problem described earlier. Team assignments help to break down barriers between operating departments as people from different parts of an organization get to know one another. They can also boost

■ A **team structure** uses permanent and temporary cross-functional teams to improve lateral relations.

■ A **cross-functional team** brings together members from different functional departments.

■ **Project teams** are convened for a particular task or project and disbanded once it is completed.

Figure 10.5 How a team structure uses cross-functional teams for improved lateral relations.

```
                        ┌──────────────┐
                        │    Plant     │
                        │   Manager    │
                        └──────────────┘
     ┌──────────────┬──────────┴──────────┬──────────────┐
┌──────────┐  ┌──────────┐          ┌──────────┐  ┌──────────────┐
│Manufac-  │  │  Sales   │          │Engineer- │  │Human Resource│
│turing    │  │ Manager  │          │ing       │  │  Manager     │
│Manager   │  │          │          │Manager   │  │              │
└──────────┘  └──────────┘          └──────────┘  └──────────────┘
```

New product development team

Valuing diversity task force

◄——————— Team assignments ———————►

AROUND THE WORLD

Intel is a well-known global competitor in the dynamic computer chip industry. But a visit to the firm's website is an eye opener. A quick look finds a listing of over 70 locations worldwide, from Belarus to the Philippines to Tajikistan. A fast-moving company in an industry that never sleeps, the firm taps the talents of the globe to keep its chips ahead of the pack. Intel relies heavily on a team organization; hierarchy takes a back seat to teamwork. Says one team member, "We report to each other." This commitment knows no boundaries. The County Kildare plant in Ireland was named recently by *Fortune* magazine as one of 10 "Great Companies to Work For" in Europe. Judges highlighted the importance of egalitarianism at the Irish facility, stating: "Intel has brought to Ireland the Silicon Valley culture of no reserved parking spaces, no executive dining rooms, and small cubicles for all employees. Everyone is on a first-name basis."

Team organization becomes part of borderless world

Source: Information and quotes from corporate website and <www.intel.com/ireland>

morale; people working in teams often experience a greater sense of involvement and identi-fication, increasing their enthusiasm for the job. Because teams focus shared knowledge and expertise on specific problems, they can also improve the speed and quality of decisions in many situations. After a research team at Polaroid Corporation developed a new medical imaging system in three years when most had predicted it would take six, a senior executive said, "Our researchers are not any smarter, but by working together they get the value of each other's intelligence almost instantaneously."[20]

The complexities of teams and teamwork contribute to the potential *disadvantages of team structures*. These include conflicting loyalties for persons with both team and function-al assignments. They also include issues of time management and group process. By their very nature, teams spend a lot of time in meetings. Not all of this time is productive. How well team members spend their time together often depends on the quality of interpersonal relations, group dynamics, and team management. All of these concerns are manageable, as will be described in Chapter 16 on teams and teamwork.

●●● NETWORK STRUCTURES

■ **A network structure** uses IT to link with networks of outside suppliers and service contractors.

Organizations using a **network structure** operate with a central core that is linked through "networks" of relationships with outside contractors and suppliers of essential services.[21] The old model was for organizations to own everything. The new model is to own only the most essential or "core" components of the business, and to engage in strategic alliances and "out-sourcing" to provide the rest. The *strategic alliance*, discussed in the last chapter, is a co-oper-ative strategy through which partners do things of mutual value for one another. For example, Bombardier's recreational products division began developing strategic supplier alliances in 1994, initially with just four subcontractors. Since then, Bombardier has increased the num-ber of supplier partnerships and has developed a true network of firms around itself. The syn-ergy generated by these relationships has promoted shared innovation, and, under the leadership of subcontractors, a number of products have been developed or improved to the benefit of all the partners.[22] **Outsourcing** is the contracting of business functions to outside

■ **Outsourcing** is when a business function is contract-ed to an outside supplier.

suppliers. For example, a bank may contract with local firms to provide mailroom, cafeteria, and legal services; an airline might contract out customer service jobs at various airports.

Figure 10.6 illustrates a network structure as it might work for a mail-order company sell-ing lawn and deck furniture through a catalogue. The firm itself is very small, consisting of a rel-atively few full-time core employees working from a central headquarters. Beyond that, it is structured as a network of outsourcing and partner relationships, maintained operationally using the latest in information technology. Merchandise is designed on contract with a furni-ture design firm—which responds quickly as designs are shared and customized via computer networking; it is manufactured and packaged by subcontractors located around the world—wherever materials, quality, and cost are found at best advantage; stock is maintained and shipped from a contract warehouse—ensuring quality storage and on-time expert shipping; all of the accounting and financial details are managed on contract with an outside firm—provid-ing better technical expertise than the firm could afford to employ on a full-time basis; and the quarterly catalogue is designed, printed, and mailed co-operatively as a strategic alliance with two other firms that sell different home furnishings with a related price appeal. All of this, of course, is supported by a company website also maintained by an outside contractor.

The creative use of information technology adds to the potential *advantages of network structures*. With the technological edge, the mail-order company in the prior example can operate with fewer full-time employees and less-complex internal systems. Network struc-tures are thus very lean and streamlined. They help organizations stay cost competitive through reduced overhead and increased operating efficiency. Network concepts allow organ-izations to employ outsourcing strategies and contract out specialized business functions

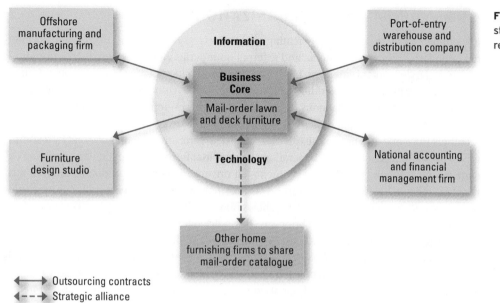

Figure 10.6 A network structure for a Web-based retail business.

rather than maintain full-time staff to do them. Information technology now makes it easy to manage these contracts and business alliances, even across great distances. Within the operating core of a network structure, furthermore, a variety of interesting jobs are created for those who must coordinate the entire system of relationships.

The potential *disadvantages of network structures* largely lie with the demands of new management responsibilities. The more complex the business or mission of the organization, the more complicated the network of contracts and alliances that must be maintained. It may be difficult to control and coordinate among them. If one part of the network breaks down or fails to deliver, the entire system suffers the consequences. Also, there is the potential for loss of control over activities contracted out and for a lack of loyalty to develop among contractors who are used infrequently rather than on a long-term basis. Some worry that outsourcing can become so aggressive as to be dangerous to the firm, especially when ever-more-critical activities such as finance, logistics, and human resource management are outsourced. *Manager's Notepad 10.2* lists the "seven deadly sins" of outsourcing that were developed by research on the practice.[23] Overall, the conclusion is that outsourcing works well, but, like anything else, it must be strategically directed and then controlled for results.

MANAGER'S
Notepad 10.2

Seven deadly sins of outsourcing

1. Outsourcing activities that are part of the core.

2. Outsourcing to untrustworthy vendors.

3. Not having good contracts with the vendor.

4. Overlooking impact on existing employees.

5. Not maintaining adequate supervision; losing control to vendors.

6. Overlooking hidden costs of managing contracts.

7. Failing to anticipate need to change vendors, cease outsourcing.

●●● BOUNDARYLESS ORGANIZATIONS

■ A **boundaryless organization** eliminates internal boundaries among subsystems and external boundaries with the external environment.

It is popular today to speak about creating a **boundaryless organization** that eliminates internal boundaries among subsystems and external boundaries with the external environment.[24] The boundaryless organization can be viewed as a combination of the team and network structures just described, with the addition of "temporariness." Within the organization, teamwork and communication—spontaneous, as needed, and intense—replace formal lines of authority. There is an absence of boundaries that traditionally and structurally separate organizational members from one another. In the external context, organizational needs are met by a shifting mix of outsourcing contracts and operating alliances that form and disband with changing circumstances. A "photograph" that documents an organization's configuration of external relationships today will look different from one taken tomorrow, as the form naturally adjusts to new pressures and circumstances. *Figure 10.7* shows how the absence of internal and external barriers helps people work in ways that bring speed and flexibility to the boundaryless firm.

Key requirements of boundaryless organizations are the absence of hierarchy, empowerment of team members, technology utilization, and acceptance of impermanence. Work is accomplished by empowered people who come together voluntarily and temporarily to apply their expertise to a task, gather additional expertise from whatever sources may be required to perform it successfully, and stay together only as long as the task is a work in process. The focus is on talent for the task. The assumption is that empowered people working together without bureaucratic restrictions can accomplish great things. Such a work setting is supposed to encourage creativity, quality, timeliness, and flexibility, while reducing inefficiencies and increasing speed. At General Electric, for example, the drive toward boundaryless operations is supported in part by aggressive "digitization." The firm is moving more and more administrative work onto the Web—where it can be done faster and by persons directly involved. Intermediaries in the form of support personnel are not needed.[25]

Knowledge sharing is both a goal and an essential component of the boundaryless organization. One way to think of this is in the context of a very small organization, perhaps a start-up. In the small firm, everyone pitches in to help out as needed and when appropriate to get things done. There are no formal assignments, and there are no job titles or job descriptions standing in the way. People with talent work together as needed to get the job done. The boundaryless organization, in its pure form, is just like that. Even in the larger organizational context, meetings and spontaneous sharing are happening continuously; perhaps thousands of people working together in hundreds of teams form and disband as needed. At consulting

Figure 10.7 The boundaryless organization eliminates internal and external barriers.

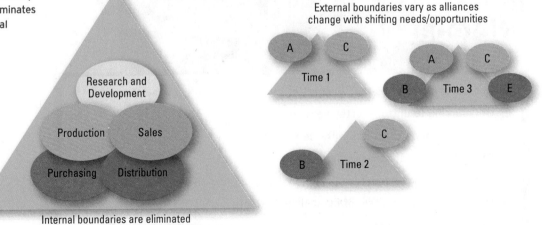

Internal boundaries are eliminated as people work together as needed

External boundaries vary as alliances change with shifting needs/opportunities

giant PricewaterhouseCoopers, for example, knowledge sharing brings together 160,000 partners spread across 150 countries in a vast virtual learning and problem-solving network. Partners collaborate electronically through online databases where information is stored, problems posted, and questions asked and answered in real time by those with experience and knowledge relevant to the problem at hand. Technology makes collaboration instantaneous and always possible, breaking down boundaries that might otherwise slow or impede the firm's performance.[26]

In the organization/environment interface, boundaryless operations emerge in a special form that is sometimes called the **virtual organization**.[27] This is an organization that operates in a shifting network of external alliances that are engaged as needed using IT and the Internet. The boundaries that traditionally separate a firm from its suppliers, customers, and even competitors are largely eliminated. Virtual organizations come into being "as needed" when alliances are called into action to meet specific operating needs and objectives. When the work is complete, the alliance rests until next called into action. The virtual organization operates in this manner with the mix of mobilized alliances continuously shifting, and with an expansive pool of potential alliances always ready to be called upon as needed. Operating as a virtual organization, Athena Sustainable Materials Institute has earned itself an international reputation for its work on the sustainability of building materials. This small Canadian organization has done that without a large staff, fancy offices, or even laboratories. Athena brings specialists, primarily from universities, together to work on a specific project or contract. Once the project is completed, the specialists return to their regular work until Athena needs their skills again.[28]

> ■ A **virtual organization** uses IT and the Internet to engage a shifting network of strategic alliances.

Canadian Managers

Decentralization from Head Office Leads to Quiet Success

Robert Ogilvie, chairman of Toromont Industries Ltd., has been quietly managing one of the country's best performing companies. The Concord, Ontario-based operator of Caterpillar heavy-equipment dealerships actually operates two business segments: the Equipment Group, which includes the equipment rentals and dealerships, and the Compression Group, specializing in compression, process, and industrial and recreational refrigeration systems. According to Ogilvie, credit for Toromont's success goes to the company's business operators, who are given a lot of autonomy by head office. Each business unit is run by its own president. "Our job," says Ogilvie, "is to choose which businesses to invest in and set the culture and framework to motivate those guys." Ogilvie's vision of employee empowerment goes further. Soon after joining Toromont, Ogilvie overhauled the bonus calculation system, removing criteria that employees could not control, like stock performance. The company now measures and rewards employees based on absolute performance only.

Source: Jeff Sanford and John Gray, "Top CFO 2005," *Canadian Business*, April 25 – May 8, 2005.

BE SURE YOU CAN

- describe how organizations can include cross-functional teams and project teams in their structures
- define the term network structure • illustrate how a new venture, such as a Web-based retailer, might use a network structure to organize its various operations • discuss the potential advantages and disadvantages of following a network approach • explain the concept of the boundaryless organization

✔ Learning check ❸

ORGANIZING TRENDS AND PRACTICES

■ The **upside-down pyramid** puts customers at the top, served by workers whose managers support them.

When structures are modified, refined, and abandoned in the search for new ones, the organizing practices that create and implement them must change too. In Chapter 1 the concept of the **upside-down pyramid** was introduced as an example of the new directions in management. By putting customers on top, served by workers in the middle, who are in turn supported by managers at the bottom, this notion tries to refocus attention on the marketplace and customer needs. Although more of a concept than a depiction of an actual structure, such thinking is representative of forces shaping new directions in how the modern workplace is organized. Among the organizing trends to be discussed next, a common theme runs throughout—making the adjustments needed to streamline operations for cost efficiency, higher performance, and increased participation by workers.

●●● SHORTER CHAINS OF COMMAND

■ The **chain of command** links all persons with successively higher levels of authority.

A typical organization chart shows the **chain of command**, or the line of authority that vertically links each position with successively higher levels of management. The classical school of management suggests that the chain of command should operate according to the *scalar principle*: there should be a clear and unbroken chain of command linking every person in the organization with successively higher levels of authority, up to and including the top manager.

When organizations grow in size they tend to get taller, as more and more levels of management are added to the chain of command. This increases overhead costs; it tends to decrease communication and access between top and bottom levels; it can greatly slow decision making; and it can lead to a loss of contact with the client or customer. These are all reasons why "tall" organizations with many levels of management are often criticized for inefficiencies and poor productivity. The current trend is toward shorter chains of command.

Trend. Organizations are being "streamlined" by cutting unnecessary levels of management; flatter, more horizontal structures are viewed as a competitive advantage.

take it to the case!

Nike
Spreading out to stay together

The next time you are looking for a company that uses outsourcing to capitalize on their core competencies, look no further than your feet. With one of the world's most recognized brands, their trademark "swoosh," Nike is among the most successful companies in North America. But how can a company that outsources most of their production remain connected to their products and their customers' needs? By focusing on what they do best! Nike adopted a decentralized structure in order to focus resources directly on their core competencies: comprehensive market research, advertising, and innovative research and design. As a result, Nike continues to dominate the highly competitive athletic market.

●●● LESS UNITY OF COMMAND

Another classical management principle describes how the chain of command should operate in daily practice. The *unity-of-command principle* states that each person in an organization should report to one, and only one, supervisor. This notion of "one person–one boss" is a foundation of the traditional pyramid form of organization. It is intended to avoid the confusion potentially created when a person gets work directions from more than one source. Unity of command is supposed to ensure that everyone clearly understands assignments and does not get conflicting instructions. It is violated, for example, when a senior manager bypasses someone's immediate supervisor to give him or her orders. This can create confusion for the subordinate and also undermine the supervisor's authority.

The "two-boss" system of matrix structure is a clear violation of unity of command. Whereas the classical advice is to avoid creating multiple reporting relationships, the matrix concept creates them by design. It does so in an attempt to improve lateral relations and teamwork in special programs or projects. Unity of command is also less predominant in the team structure and in other arrangements that emphasize the use of cross-functional teams and task forces. The current trend is for less, not more, unity of command in organizations.

Trend. Organizations are using more cross-functional teams, task forces, and horizontal structures, and they are becoming more customer conscious; as they do so, employees often find themselves working for more than one "boss."

●●● WIDER SPANS OF CONTROL

The **span of control** is the number of persons directly reporting to a manager. When span of control is "narrow," only a few people are under a manager's immediate supervision; a "wide" span of control indicates that the manager supervises many people. There was a time in the history of management thought when people searched for the ideal span of control. Although the magic number was never found, this *span-of-control principle* evolved: there is a limit to the number of people one manager can effectively supervise; care should be exercised to keep the span of control within manageable limits.

■ **Span of control** is the number of subordinates directly reporting to a manager.

Figure 10.8 shows the relationship between span of control and the number of levels in the chain of command. *Flat structures* have wider spans of control and fewer levels of management; *tall structures* have narrow spans of control and many levels of management. Because tall organizations have more managers, they are more costly. They are also generally

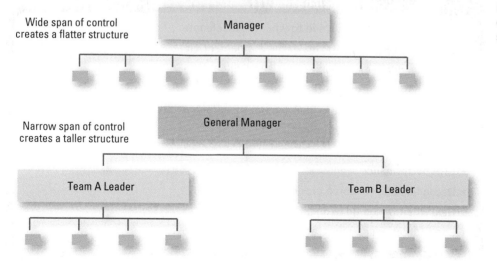

Figure 10.8 Spans of control in "flat" versus "tall" structures.

Wide span of control creates a flatter structure — Manager

Narrow span of control creates a taller structure — General Manager — Team A Leader — Team B Leader

viewed as less efficient, less flexible, and less customer sensitive than flat organizations. Before making spans of control smaller, therefore, serious thought should always be given to both the cost of the added management overhead and the potential disadvantages of a taller chain of command. When spans of control are increased, by contrast, overhead costs are reduced. Workers with less direct supervision in flatter structures also benefit from more empowerment and independence.[29]

   Trend. Many organizations are shifting to wider spans of control as levels of management are eliminated; managers are taking responsibility for larger numbers of subordinates who operate with less direct supervision.

●●● MORE DELEGATION AND EMPOWERMENT

■ **Delegation** is the process of distributing and entrusting work to other persons.

All managers must decide what work they should do themselves and what should be left for others. At issue here is **delegation**—the process of entrusting work to others by giving them the right to make decisions and take action. There are three steps to delegation. In *step 1, the manager assigns responsibility* by carefully explaining the work or duties someone else is expected to do. This *responsibility* is an expectation for the other person to perform assigned tasks. In *step 2, the manager grants authority to act.* Along with the assigned task, the right to take necessary actions (for example, to spend money, direct the work of others, use resources) is given to the other person. *Authority* is a right to act in ways needed to carry out the assigned tasks. In *step 3, the manager creates accountability.* By accepting an assignment, the person takes on a direct obligation to the manager to complete the job as agreed upon. *Accountability*, originally defined in Chapter 1, is the requirement to answer to a supervisor for performance results.

   A classical principle of organization warns managers not to delegate without giving the subordinate sufficient authority to perform. When insufficient authority is delegated, it will be very hard for someone to live up to performance expectations. They simply don't have the authority needed to get the job done. The *authority-and-responsibility principle* states that authority should equal responsibility when work is delegated from a supervisor to a subordinate. Useful guidelines for delegating are offered in *Manager's Notepad 10.3.*[30]

MANAGER'S
Notepad 10.3

Useful guidelines for delegating

- Carefully choose the person to whom you delegate.
- Define the responsibility; make the assignment clear.
- Agree on performance objectives and standards.
- Agree on a performance timetable.
- Give authority; allow the other person to act independently.
- Show trust in the other person.
- Provide performance support.
- Give performance feedback.
- Recognize and reinforce progress.
- Help when things go wrong.
- Don't forget *your* accountability for performance results.

A common management failure is unwillingness to delegate. Whether due to a lack of trust in others or to a manager's inflexibility in the way things get done, failure to delegate can be damaging. It overloads the manager with work that could be done by others; it also denies others many opportunities to fully utilize their talents on the job. When well done, by contrast, delegation leads to empowerment, in that people have the freedom to contribute ideas and do their jobs in the best possible ways. This involvement can increase job satisfaction for the individual and frequently results in better job performance.

Trend. Managers in progressive organizations are delegating more; they are finding more ways to empower people at all levels to make more decisions affecting themselves and their work.

■ **Centralization** is the concentration of authority for most decisions at the top level of an organization.

■ **Decentralization** is the dispersion of authority to make decisions throughout all organization levels.

●●● DECENTRALIZATION WITH CENTRALIZATION

A question frequently asked is: "Should most decisions be made at the top levels of an organization, or should they be dispersed by extensive delegation throughout all levels of management?" The former approach is referred to as **centralization**; the latter is called **decentralization**. There is no classical principle on centralization and decentralization. The traditional pyramid form of organization may give the impression of being a highly centralized structure, while decentralization is characteristic of newer structures and many recent organizing trends. But the issue doesn't have to be framed as an either/or choice. Today's organizations can operate with greater decentralization without giving up centralized control. This is facilitated by developments in information technology.

With computer networks and advanced information systems, managers at higher levels can more easily stay informed about a wide range of day-to-day performance matters. Because they have information on results readily available, they can allow more decentralization in decision making.[31] If something goes wrong, presumably the information systems will sound an alarm and allow corrective action to be taken quickly. Using such a decentralized approach, Golder Associates has become one of the world's most successful engineering consulting firms. With the company president based in Calgary and over 70 offices worldwide, Golder relies on individual office and manager autonomy in order to respond to the unique needs of their international clientele. By decentralizing while at the same time stressing high levels of internal communication, coordination, and decision making, Golder ensures that management teams keep connected concerning the wants and needs of both the organization and its customers.[32]

Trend. Whereas delegation, empowerment, and horizontal structures are contributing to more decentralization in organizations, advances in information technology simultaneously allow for the retention of centralized control.

PERSONAL MANAGEMENT

It takes a lot of trust to be comfortable with **EMPOWERMENT**. But if you aren't willing and able to empower others, you'll not only compromise your own performance but also add to the stress of daily work. Empowerment involves allowing and helping others to do things, even things that you might be very good at doing yourself. The beauty of organizations is synergy—bringing together the contributions of many people to achieve something that is much greater than what any individual can accomplish alone. Empowerment gives synergy a chance. But many people, perhaps even you, suffer from control anxiety. They don't empower others because they fear losing control over a task or situation. In groups, they want or try to do everything by themselves; they are afraid to trust other team members with important tasks. Being "unwilling to let go," they try to do too much, with the risk of missed deadlines and even poor performance; they deny others opportunities to contribute, losing the benefits of their talents and often alienating them in the process. Does this description apply to you? Now is a good time to think seriously about your personal style—are you someone who empowers others, or do you suffer from control anxiety and an unwillingness to delegate?

Get to know yourself better

Complete Assessment #15—**Empowering Others**, and Exercise #15—**Leading Through Participation** from the Workbook and Personal Management Activity #10 on the companion website.

●●● REDUCED USE OF STAFF

When it comes to coordination and control in organizations, the issue of line-staff relationships is important. Chapter 1 described the role of staff as providing expert advice and guidance to line personnel. This can help ensure that performance standards are maintained in areas of staff expertise. **Specialized staff** perform a technical service or provide special problem-solving expertise for other parts of the organization. This could be a single person, such as a corporate safety director, or a complete unit, such as a corporate safety department. Many organizations rely on staff specialists to maintain coordination and control over a variety of matters. In a large retail chain, line managers in each store typically make daily operating decisions regarding direct sales of merchandise. But staff specialists at the corporate or regional levels provide direction and support so that all the stores operate with the same credit, purchasing, employment, and advertising procedures.

■ **Specialized staff** provide technical expertise for other parts of the organization.

Organizations may also employ **personal staff**, individuals appointed in "assistant-to" positions with the purpose of providing special support to higher-level managers. Such assistants help by following up on administrative details and performing other duties as assigned. They can benefit also in terms of career development, through the mentoring relationships that such assignments offer. An organization, for example, might select promising junior managers as temporary administrative assistants to senior managers. This helps them gain valuable experience at the same time that they are facilitating the work of executives.

■ **Personal staff** are "assistant-to" positions that support senior managers.

Problems in line-staff distinctions can and do arise. In too many cases, organizations find that the staff grows to the point where it costs more in administrative overhead than it is worth. This is why staff cutbacks are common in downsizing and other turnaround efforts. There are also cases where conflicts in line-staff relationships cause difficulties. This often occurs when line and staff managers disagree over the extent of staff authority. At the one extreme, staff has purely *advisory authority* and can "suggest" but not "dictate." At the other extreme, it has *functional authority* to actually "require" that others do as requested within the boundaries of staff expertise. For example, a human resource department may advise line managers on the desired qualifications of new workers being hired (advisory authority); the department will likely require the managers to follow employment equity guidelines in the hiring process (functional authority).

There is no one best solution to the problem of how to divide work between line and staff responsibilities. What is best for any organization will be a cost-effective staff component that satisfies, but doesn't overreact to, needs for specialized technical assistance to line operations.

Trend. Organizations are reducing the size of staff; they are seeking lower costs and increased operating efficiency by employing fewer personnel and using smaller staff units.

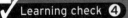

BE SURE YOU CAN

• define the terms chain of command, unity of command, span of control, delegation, empowerment, decentralization, centralization, and staff • describe the organizational trends that relate to each term • discuss the significance of these trends and practices for people and the new workplace

●●● Chapter 10 STUDY GUIDE

Back to Edward Jones

The opening example of Edward Jones described the challenges of organizing to achieve competitive advantage. It suggests that any structure must meet the needs of the organization with respect to situational demands and opportunities. In this chapter you learned the traditional types of organizational structures—functional, divisional, and matrix. You learned about the new team, network, and boundaryless structures that are appearing. And you learned the current trends and practices that are changing the way people work together in today's organizations.

THE NEXT STEP
INTEGRATED LEARNING ACTIVITIES

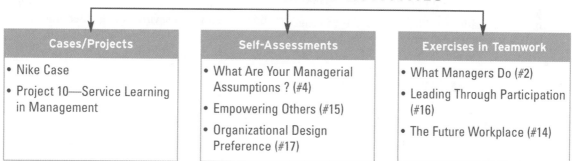

Cases/Projects	Self-Assessments	Exercises in Teamwork
• Nike Case • Project 10—Service Learning in Management	• What Are Your Managerial Assumptions ? (#4) • Empowering Others (#15) • Organizational Design Preference (#17)	• What Managers Do (#2) • Leading Through Participation (#16) • The Future Workplace (#14)

STUDY QUESTION SUMMARY

1. What is organizing as a management function?

• Organizing is the process of arranging people and resources to work toward a common goal.

• Organizing decisions divide up the work that needs to be done, allocate people and resources to do it, and coordinate results to achieve productivity.

• Structure is the system of tasks, reporting relationships, and communication that links people and positions within an organization.

• The formal structure, such as shown on an organization chart, describes how an organization is supposed to work.

• The informal structure of organization consists of the unofficial relationships that develop among members.

2. What are the major types of organization structures?

• Departmentalization is the process of grouping people together in formal work units or teams.

• In functional structures, people with similar skills who perform similar activities are grouped together under a common manager.

• In divisional structures, people who work on a similar product, work in the same geographical region, serve the same customers, or participate in the same work process are grouped together under common managers.

• A matrix structure combines the functional and divisional approaches to create permanent cross-functional project teams.

3. What are the new developments in organization structures?

- Increasing complexity and greater rates of change in the environment are challenging the performance capabilities of traditional organization structures.

- New developments emphasize more horizontal structures that utilize teams and technology to best advantage.

- Team structures use cross-functional teams and task forces to improve lateral relations and improve problem solving at all levels.

- Network structures use contracted services and strategic alliances to support a core business or organizational centre.

- Boundaryless organizations combine team and network structures with the advantages of technology to accomplish temporary tasks and projects.

- Virtual organizations utilize IT and the Internet to mobilize a shifting mix of strategic alliances to accomplish specific tasks and projects.

4. What organizing trends are changing the workplace?

- Traditional vertical command-and-control structures are giving way to more horizontal structures emphasizing employee involvement and flexibility.

- Many organizations are now operating with shorter chains of command and less unity of command.

- Many organizations are now operating with wider spans of control and fewer levels of management.

- The emphasis in more organizations today is on effective delegation and empowerment.

- Advances in information systems make it possible to operate with decentralization while still maintaining centralized control.

- Reducing the size of staff is a trend in organizations seeking cost savings and greater efficiency.

KEY TERMS REVIEW

Boundaryless organization (p. 250)

Centralization (p. 255)

Chain of command (p. 252)

Cross-functional teams (p. 247)

Customer structure (p. 244)

Decentralization (p. 255)

Delegation (p. 254)

Departmentalization (p. 241)

Divisional structure (p. 242)

Formal structure (p. 240)

Functional chimneys problem (p. 242)

Functional structure (p. 241)

Geographical structure (p. 243)

Informal structure (p. 240)

Matrix structure (p. 244)

Network structure (p. 248)

Organization chart (p. 240)

Organization structure (p. 239)

Organizing (p. 239)

Outsourcing (p. 248)

Personal staff (p. 256)

Process structure (p. 244)

Product structure (p. 243)

Project teams (p. 247)

Span of control (p. 253)

Specialized staff (p. 256)

Team structure (p. 247)

Upside-down pyramid (p. 252)

Virtual organization (p. 251)

SELF-TEST 10

MULTIPLE-CHOICE QUESTIONS:

1. The main purpose of organizing as a management function is to _____.
    (a) make sure that results match plans (b) arrange people and resources to accomplish work (c) create enthusiasm for the work to be done (d) match strategies with operational plans

2. _____ is the system of tasks, reporting relationships, and communication that links together the various parts of an organization.
    (a) Structure (b) Staff (c) Decentralization (d) Centralization

3. Transmission of rumours and resistance to change is a potential disadvantage often associated with _____.
    (a) virtual organizations (b) informal structures (c) delegation (d) specialized staff

4. An organization chart showing vice-presidents of marketing, finance, manufacturing, and purchasing all reporting to the president is depicting a _____ structure.
    (a) functional (b) matrix (c) network (d) product

5. The "two-boss" system of reporting relationships is found in the _____ structure.
    (a) functional (b) matrix (c) network (d) product

6. A manufacturing business with a functional structure has recently developed two new product lines. The president of the company might consider shifting to a(n) _____ structure to gain a stronger focus on each product.
    (a) virtual (b) informal (c) divisional (d) network

7. Better lower-level teamwork and more top-level strategic management are among the expected advantages of a _____ structure.
    (a) divisional (b) matrix (c) geographical (d) product

8. "Tall" organizations tend to have long chains of command and _____ spans of control.
    (a) wide (b) narrow (c) informal (d) centralized

9. The unity-of-command principle is intentionally violated in the _____ structure.
    (a) network (b) matrix (c) geographical (d) product

10. In delegation, _____ is the right of a subordinate to act in ways needed to carry out the assigned tasks.
    (a) authority (b) responsibility (c) accountability (d) centrality

11. The functional chimneys problem occurs when people in different functions _____.
    (a) fail to communicate with one another (b) try to help each other work with customers (c) spend too much time coordinating decisions (d) focus on products rather than functions

12. A _____ structure tries to combine the best elements of the functional and divisional forms.
    (a) matrix (b) boundaryless (c) team (d) virtual

13. Outsourcing plays a central role in the _____ organization.
    (a) functional (b) divisional (c) network (d) team

14. A student volunteers to gather information on a company for a group case analysis project. The other members of the group agree and tell her that she can choose the information sources. This group is giving the student _____ to fulfill the agreed-upon task.
    (a) responsibility (b) accountability (c) authority (d) decentralization

15. The current trend in the use of staff in organizations is to _____.
    (a) give personnel more functional authority over line operations (b) reduce the number of personnel overall (c) better utilize IT to give staff more centralized control (d) combine all staff functions in one department

SHORT-RESPONSE QUESTIONS:

16. What is the difference between a product divisional structure and a geographical or area divisional structure?
17. What are symptoms that might indicate a functional structure is causing problems for the organization?
18. Explain by example the concept of a network organization structure.
19. What positive results might be expected when levels of management are reduced and the chain of command shortened in an organization?

APPLICATION QUESTION:

20. Faisal Shams supervises a group of seven project engineers. His unit is experiencing a heavy workload as the demand for different versions of one of his firm's computer components is growing. Faisal finds that he doesn't have time to follow up on all design details for each version. Up until now he has tried to do this all by himself. Two of the engineers have shown interest in helping him coordinate work on the various designs. As a consultant, what would you advise Faisal in terms of delegating work to them?

Organizational Design and Work Processes

Planning Ahead

After reading Chapter 11, you should be able to answer these questions in your own words.

1. What are the essentials of organizational design?

2. How do contingency factors influence organizational design?

3. What are the major issues in subsystem design?

4. How can work processes be re-engineered?

KPMG International
Design for integration, empowerment, and flexibility

After the technology sector, the changes that have taken place in the accounting profession over the past 15 years are unparalleled in any other industry. Accountants are now key members of the strategic planning team, and no longer the backroom bean counters of yesterday.

In Canada, KPMG International, a global firm providing tax, audit, and advisory services, has worked hard to negotiate the changing accounting landscape. KPMG's roots date back to 1840; today, the company has offices in 35 communities across Canada, generating revenues of about $886 million. The professional staff number around 5,000; positions at the firm are highly sought after—not just in Canada, but in all the 148 countries it services.

To stay on top, KPMG organizes for high performance and staffs its business with talented professionals committed to excellence. KPMG's client services are organized into multidisciplinary teams; each team is focused on individual industry sectors designed to better serve every client's business. KPMG's organization is clearly a hybrid as it uses a client-centred industry sector while still providing key product services such as auditing, tax, and consulting. For example, KPMG's audit practice helps clients manage risk by first thoroughly understanding their business and then converting that information into insights to improve client competence and performance.

Leadership at KPMG also recognizes the design challenges of matching the career opportunities of the new workplace with the diversity of today's generation of university graduates. Look under the career section at the KPMG Canadian website, and find the section for university students, "campus recruiting." The recruitment section also has a strong emphasis on the values of the compa-

ny, stating, "What really sets KPMG apart is our shared set of values—our values define us as a firm and help to maintain our status as leaders in terms of the services we provide and the industries we serve." These values include working together, bringing out the best in each other, respect, challenging assumptions, open and honest communication, a commitment to community, being a

responsible corporate citizen, and acting with integrity.

KPMG knows that "one style doesn't fit all," and obviously values a good fit between its employees and the firm. By doing so, it keeps talent a main source of competitive advantage, and having good people allows KPMG to adapt to the changing times and to keep its clients satisfied.[1]

IN THE WORKPLACE

Your colleague Julie Steinberg stops by for a coffee and a chat. Julie shares that she is taking MBA classes at night and has prepared a "case analysis problem" for her classmates using a hypothetical company. She was wondering if you would read through it to see if it makes sense.

As you read the case it appears that the organization has a vertical structure, is focused on

efficiency and control, and is operating in an environment that has high uncertainty. You tell Julie that the case reads well and is clear. While she does not expect you to answer an MBA-level case, she wonders what you think would be a course of action for the firm. Always willing to take up a challenge, you offer some advice. What do you suggest this company might do?

●●● Chapter 11   LEARNING PREVIEW   ●●●

The example of KPMG shows how top organizations pay attention to the special interests of prospective employees. The message is that the firm will be adaptable and will do its best to fit work opportunities to the goals of talented persons. In this chapter you will learn about contingency factors in organizational design, including environment, strategy, technology, size and life cycle, and people. You will also learn the major design differences between bureaucratic and adaptive organizations, the dynamics of differentiation and integration in subsystems design, and the concept of process re-engineering as an approach to work process design.

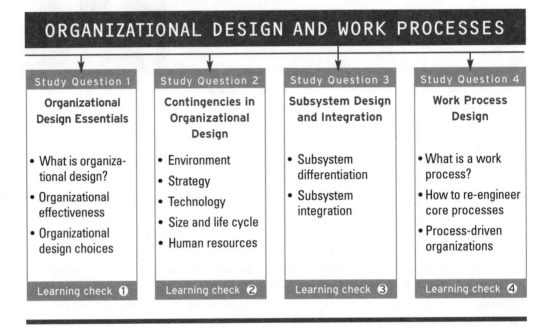

ORGANIZATIONAL DESIGN AND WORK PROCESSES

Study Question 1	Study Question 2	Study Question 3	Study Question 4
Organizational Design Essentials	**Contingencies in Organizational Design**	**Subsystem Design and Integration**	**Work Process Design**
• What is organizational design? • Organizational effectiveness • Organizational design choices	• Environment • Strategy • Technology • Size and life cycle • Human resources	• Subsystem differentiation • Subsystem integration	• What is a work process? • How to re-engineer core processes • Process-driven organizations
Learning check ❶	Learning check ❷	Learning check ❸	Learning check ❹

If you are in London, England, don't be surprised to find that St. Luke's isn't a church, it's an advertising agency. But it's also a unique one. Every employee is a part owner; a six-member board elected by staff members governs the company. Everyone's name is listed on the stationery—from the creative director to receptionist. The culture is informal, permeated by creativity. Workspaces are designed with common areas to maximize interaction and connectivity. Everyone focuses on great service to customers. One member of the firm describes working there as like "the difference between going to grade school and going to the university. At school the bell goes 'ding' and tells you what to do. We have no bell. Like the university, as long as you create great stuff, we don't care how you do it." You can expect this configuration—small in size and locally focused—to make St. Luke's quick, nimble, and creative.[2]

Now travel to Switzerland and visit the headquarters of Nestlé.[3] The global food giant has a product mix of beverages, ice cream, prepared foods, chocolates, pet care, and pharmaceuticals. It sells around the world—33 percent in the Americas, 32 percent in Europe, 17 percent in Asia and Africa, and 18 percent elsewhere. A stark contrast to St. Luke's in size and global reach, Nestlé might be described as one of the world's greatest organizational design challenges. CEO Peter Brabeck-Letmathe, a 35-year career veteran of the firm, recently reorganized in an attempt to boost profits and improve focus in its worldwide operations. In the past, the firm was decentralized into national companies. The new structure reconfigures them into three world regions, with the goal of gaining more co-operation and greater efficiencies. A corporate

IT initiative supports the new structure, linking employees worldwide in a knowledge management and information system. In Nestlé's competitive environment, just as with St. Luke's, success depends on the ability to continuously achieve integration, empowerment, and flexibility.

Organizations everywhere are adjusting to best meet new competitive demands. Changing times require flexible and well-integrated organizations that can deliver high-quality products and services while still innovating for sustained future performance. Traditional structures are being flattened, networks are being developed, IT is being utilized, and decision making is being moved to the points where knowledge exists. The goals are clear—improved teamwork, more creativity, shorter product development cycles, better customer service, and higher performance overall. Yet, organizations still face widely varying problems and opportunities. There is no one best way to structure and manage them. The key to success is finding the best design to master the unique situational needs and challenges for each organization.[4]

ORGANIZATIONAL DESIGN ESSENTIALS

Just as organizations vary in size and type, so too do the variety of problems and opportunities that they face. This is why they use the different types of structures described in Chapter 10—from the traditional functional, divisional, and matrix structures, to the team and network structures, and even beyond to the boundaryless organization. It is why they change structures to try to best fit the demands of new circumstances in a dynamic environment. And it is why we see more and more organizations trying to operate in ways that improve problem solving and flexibility—more sharing of tasks, reduced emphasis on hierarchy, greater emphasis on lateral communication, more teamwork, and more decentralization of decision making and empowerment. An example of this organizational flexibility is DBG Canada Limited. DBG is a major supplier of automotive, heavy truck, and value-added metal assembly industries operating out of Mississauga, Ontario. The company has associates, not employees, who are building dynamic relationships with customers. Flexibility, problem solving, and effective empowerment has resulted in the company gaining the reputation as a company able to "turn on a dime."[5]

●●● WHAT IS ORGANIZATIONAL DESIGN?

Organizational design is the process of choosing and implementing structures that best arrange resources to accomplish the organization's mission and objectives.[6] Because every organization faces its own set of unique problems and opportunities, the best design at any moment is the one that achieves a good match between structure and situation. As shown in *Figure 11.1*, this includes taking into consideration the implications of environment, strategies, people, technology, and size.[7] The process of organizational design is thus a problem-solving activity, one that should be approached in a contingency fashion that takes all of these factors into account. There is no universal design that applies in all circumstances. The goal is to achieve a best fit between structure and the unique situation faced by each organization.

■ **Organizational design** is the process of creating structures that accomplish the organization's mission and objectives.

●●● ORGANIZATIONAL EFFECTIVENESS

The ultimate goal of organizational design should be to achieve **organizational effectiveness**—sustainable high performance in using resources to accomplish the mission and objectives. Theorists view and analyze organizational effectiveness from different perspectives.[8] The *systems resource approach* looks at the input side and defines effectiveness in terms of success in acquiring needed resources from the organization's environment. The *internal process*

■ **Organizational effectiveness** is sustainable high performance in accomplishing the mission and objectives.

Figure 11.1 A framework for organizational design—aligning structures with situational contingencies.

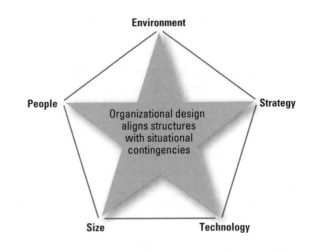

approach looks at the transformation process and examines how efficiently resources are utilized to produce goods and/or services. The *goal approach* looks at the output side to measure achievement of key operating objectives. And the *strategic constituencies approach* looks to the environment to analyze the impact of the organization on key stakeholders and their interests. Although they point in different directions, each of these approaches offers a framework for assessing how well an actual or proposed design is working.

Organizational effectiveness can also be evaluated according to specific criteria that set important performance benchmarks over time.[9] In the short run, the criteria focus on performance effectiveness in goal accomplishment and performance efficiency in resource utilization, as well as stakeholder satisfaction—including customers, employees, owners, and society at large. In the medium term, two more criteria become important: adaptability in the face of changing environments, and development of people and systems to meet new challenges. And in the long run, the effectiveness criterion is survival under conditions of uncertainty. For example, at the same time that Quebec-based Groupe Germain opened its first boutique hotel in Toronto, the tourist industry was hit by the unexpected SARS outbreak. Management recognized that their proposed strategy needed to change in order to adapt to the pressing environmental challenge. Rather than do things "in-house" with salaried employees, the company outsourced and made use of subcontractors for many necessary tasks. This internal process approach helped manage the company's cash flow with positive results; the family business survived and is now looking to expand its Ontario operations.[10]

Any organizational design should advance organizational effectiveness. Although there is no one universal design that applies in all circumstances, this does not mean that a given design—one in use or proposed—shouldn't be rigorously evaluated. In fact, quite the opposite applies. A design is a matter of choice, and that choice can be for the better or for the worse. Managers as decision makers need to make good organizational design choices; they need to make them with the goal of organizational effectiveness always in mind; and they need to make them with the assistance of an analytical framework that helps them sort through the many design alternatives that exist. In organization theory, these alternatives are broadly framed in the distinction between bureaucratic designs at one extreme and adaptive designs at the other.

●●● ORGANIZATIONAL DESIGN CHOICES

■ A **bureaucracy** emphasizes formal authority, order, fairness, and efficiency.

As first introduced in the discussion on historical foundations of management in Chapter 2, a **bureaucracy** is a form of organization based on logic, order, and the legitimate use of formal authority. Its distinguishing features include a clear-cut division of labour, strict hierarchy of authority, formal rules and procedures, and promotion based on competency. According to sociologist Max Weber, bureaucracies were supposed to be orderly, fair, and highly efficient.[11] In short, they were a model form of organization. Yet if you use the term "bureaucracy" today, it may well be interpreted with a negative connotation. If you call someone a "bureaucrat," it may well be considered an insult. Instead of operating efficiently, the bureaucracies that we know are often associated with "red tape"; instead of being orderly and fair, they are often seen as cumbersome and impersonal to the point of insensitivity to customer or client needs. And the bureaucrats? Don't we assume that they work only according to rules, diligently following procedures and avoiding any opportunities to take initiative or demonstrate creativity?

Research recognizes that there are limits to bureaucracy, particularly in their tendencies to become unwieldy and rigid.[12] Instead of viewing all bureaucratic structures as inevitably flawed, however, management theory asks the contingency questions: (1) When is a bureaucratic form a good choice for an organization? (2) What alternatives exist when it is not a good choice?

Pioneering research conducted in England during the early 1960s by Tom Burns and George Stalker helps answer these questions.[13] After investigating 20 manufacturing firms, they concluded that two quite different organizational forms could be successful, depending on the nature of a firm's external environment. A more bureaucratic form, which Burns and Stalker called *mechanistic*, thrived when the environment was stable. But it experienced difficulty when the environment was rapidly changing and uncertain. In these dynamic situations, a much less bureaucratic form, called *organic*, performed best. *Figure 11.2* portrays these two approaches as opposite extremes on a continuum of organizational design alternatives.

take it to the case!

World-class entrepreneur places his "BET" on the future

It takes an entrepreneur to start a business, but it takes quality people and the right design to keep it running … and growing. Robert Johnson, founder of BET Holdings II, Inc., knows that for sure and the company that he founded is the first African-American company to provide quality television programming, entertainment products, publishing, and Internet services specifically designed to appeal to African-American interests. The company owns and operates four television networks, including BET cable network, BET Films, a film production house, BET Event Productions, and BET.com, the top African-American Internet portal. The company sold Arabesque Books, its line of African-American romance novels, to Harlequin, Inc. in 2005. In November 2000, Johnson sold BET Holdings to Viacom for $3 billion. He stayed on as chairman and CEO of BET till early 2006 when he officially ended his employment with the company that he founded more than 25 years ago.

Source: Information from "BET.com Ranked #1 in Unique Visitors Among African American Sites," PR Newswire (June 6, 2000); <www.Bet.com>, and <www.viacom.com>

Figure 11.2 A continuum of organizational design alternatives—from bureaucratic to adaptive organizations.

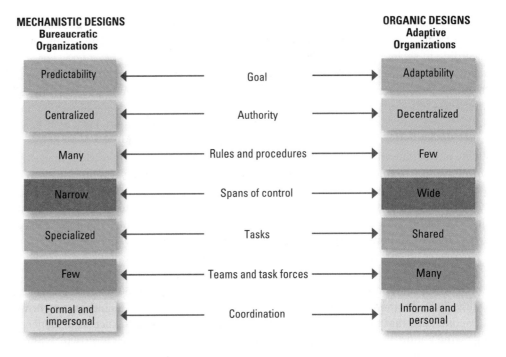

MECHANISTIC DESIGNS
Bureaucratic Organizations

ORGANIC DESIGNS
Adaptive Organizations

Mechanistic		Organic
Predictability	Goal	Adaptability
Centralized	Authority	Decentralized
Many	Rules and procedures	Few
Narrow	Spans of control	Wide
Specialized	Tasks	Shared
Few	Teams and task forces	Many
Formal and impersonal	Coordination	Informal and personal

Mechanistic Designs

■ **A mechanistic design** is centralized with many rules and procedures, a clear-cut division of labour, narrow spans of control, and formal coordination.

Organizations with more **mechanistic designs** are highly bureaucratic in nature. As shown in the figure, they typically operate with more centralized authority, many rules and procedures, a precise division of labour, narrow spans of control, and formal means of coordination. Mechanistic designs are described as "tight" structures of the traditional vertical or pyramid form.[14] For a good example, visit your local fast-food restaurant. A relatively small operation, each store operates quite like others in the franchise chain and according to rules established by the corporate management. You will notice that service personnel work in orderly and disciplined ways, guided by training, rules and procedures, and close supervision by crew leaders who work alongside them. Even their appearances are carefully regulated, with everyone working in a standardized uniform. These restaurants perform well as they repetitively deliver items that are part of their standard menus. You quickly encounter the limits, however, if you try to order something not on the menu. The chains also encounter difficulty when consumer tastes change or take on regional preferences that are different from what the corporate menu provides. Adjustments to the system take a long time.

The limits of mechanistic designs and their tight vertical structures are especially apparent in organizations that must operate in dynamic, often uncertain, environments. It's hard, for example, to find a technology company, consumer products firm, financial services business, or dot.com retailer that isn't making continual adjustments in operations and organizational design. Things keep changing on them, and organizational effectiveness depends on being able to change with the times. Mechanistic designs find this hard to do.

Organic Designs

Dee Hock, the founder of Visa International, says: "We can't run 21st-century society with 17th-century notions of organization."[15] Harvard scholar and consultant Rosabeth Moss Kanter notes

that the ability to respond quickly to shifting environmental challenges often distinguishes successful organizations from less successful ones:[16]

> *The organizations now emerging as successful will be, above all, flexible; they will need to be able to bring particular resources together quickly, on the basis of short-term recognition of new requirements and the necessary capacities to deal with them...The balance between static plans—which appears to reduce the need for effective reaction—and structural flexibility needs to shift toward the latter.*

The trend is toward **organic designs**, as portrayed in *Figure 11.2*, having more decentralized authority, fewer rules and procedures, less precise division of labour, wider spans of control, and more personal means of coordination. These create more **adaptive organizations** that operate with horizontal structures and with cultures that encourage worker empowerment and teamwork. They are described as relatively loose systems in which a lot of work gets done through informal structures and networks of interpersonal contacts.[17] Organic designs work well for organizations facing dynamic environments that demand flexibility in dealing with changing conditions. They are also increasingly popular in the new workplace, where the demands of total quality management and competitive advantage place more emphasis on internal teamwork and responsiveness to customers.

Above all, adaptive organizations are built upon a foundation of trust that people will do the right things on their own initiative. They move organizational design in the direction of what some might call *self-organization*, where the focus is on freeing otherwise capable people from unnecessarily centralized control and restrictions. Moving toward the adaptive form means letting workers take over production scheduling and problem solving; it means letting workers set up their own control systems; it means letting workers use their ideas to improve customer service. In the ultimately adaptive organizations, it means that members are given the freedom to do what they can do best—get the job done. This helps create what has been described in earlier chapters as a **learning organization**, one designed for continuous adaptation through problem solving, innovation, and learning.[18]

■ An **organic design** is decentralized with fewer rules and procedures, open divisions of labour, wide spans of control, and more personal coordination.

■ An **adaptive organization** operates with a minimum of bureaucratic features and encourages worker empowerment and teamwork.

■ A **learning organization** is designed for continuous adaptation through problem solving, innovation, and learning.

Canadian Managers
Unique Artistry Becomes Booming Industry

By taking chances and staying true to his artistic vision, Guy Laliberté has transformed Cirque du Soleil from the group of street performers he founded in 1984 to an international business and cultural phenomenon. Under Laliberté's guidance as CEO, Cirque du Soleil has reinvented and revolutionized the circus arts. By 2006, it had five permanent and seven touring shows, including a Las Vegas premiere of its 13th production, based on the music of the Beatles, and a show in Niagara Falls. The business employs more than 3,000 people worldwide, including 900 artists. Since 1984, the Cirque has performed for more than 50 million spectators. Its touring shows have made 250 stops in more than 100 cities. And, the business has branched out with Cirque du Soleil Images, a multimedia division, and Cirque du Soleil Musique, a recording company. It is also targetting another niche—merchandising and licensing.

Sources: Information from <www.cirquedusoleil.com>; Matthew Hays, "Goodbye big top, hello arena," *The Globe and Mail*, January 23, 2006; Brigitte Bélanger, Department of Foreign Affairs and International Trade, April 14, 1999.

Learning check ①

BE SURE YOU CAN
• define the terms organizational design and organizational effectiveness • explain alternative approaches and criteria for evaluating organizational effectiveness • differentiate the characteristics of bureaucratic designs and adaptive designs • discuss the implications of the Burns and Stalker study for organizational design • illustrate the types of situations in which the mechanistic design and the organic design work best

CONTINGENCIES IN ORGANIZATIONAL DESIGN

Good organizational design decisions should result in supportive structures that satisfy situational demands and advance organizational effectiveness. This is true contingency thinking. Among the contingency factors in the organizational design checklist featured in *Manager's Notepad 11.1* are the environment, strategy, technology, size and life cycle, and human resources.

MANAGER'S
Notepad 11.1
Organizational design checklist

Check 1: Does the design fit well with the major problems and opportunities of the external environment?

Check 2: Does the design support the implementation of strategies and the accomplishment of key operating objectives?

Check 3: Does the design support core technologies and allow them to be used to best advantage?

Check 4: Can the design handle changes in organizational size and different stages in the organizational life cycle?

Check 5: Does the design support and empower workers, and allow their talents to be used to best advantage?

●●● ENVIRONMENT

The organization's external environment and the degree of uncertainty it offers are of undeniable importance in organizational design.[19] A *certain environment* is composed of relatively stable and predictable elements. As a result, an organization can succeed with relatively few changes in the goods or services produced or in the manner of production over time. Bureaucratic organizations and mechanistic designs are quite adequate under such conditions. An *uncertain environment* will have more dynamic and less predictable elements. Changes occur frequently and may catch decision makers by surprise. As a result, organizations must be flexible and responsive over relatively short time horizons. This requires more adaptive organizations and organic designs. *Figure 11.3* summarizes these relationships, showing how increasing uncertainty in organizational environments calls for more horizontal and adaptive designs.

Due to uncertainty, especially around international tariffs, forestry is a tough industry to be in these days. Still, Hayes Forest Services Ltd., a full-service forest services company operating from Duncan, B.C., is doing well and outperforming its competitors by "embracing the

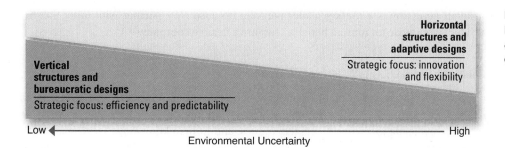

Figure 11.3
Environmental uncertainty and the performance of vertical and horizontal designs.

challenge of change." In an industry facing many transformations, Hayes has become innovative by making the company a "one-stop" supplier, and by focusing on new approaches to doing old things, such as helicopter logging. Working successfully in an uncertain environment has helped make them one of the 50 best-managed companies in Canada.[20]

●●● STRATEGY

The nature of organizational strategies and objectives is an important design contingency. Research on these contingency relationships is often traced to the pioneering work of Alfred Chandler Jr., who analyzed the histories of DuPont, General Motors, Sears, and Standard Oil.[21] Chandler's conclusion that "structure follows strategy" is a key element of organizational design. An organization's structure must support its strategy if the desired results are to be achieved.[22]

When strategy is stability oriented, the choice of organizational design is based on the premise that little significant change will be occurring in the external environment. This means that plans can be set and operations programmed to be routinely implemented. To best support this strategic approach, the organization should be structured to operate in well-defined and predictable ways. This is most characteristic of bureaucratic organizations that use more mechanistic design alternatives.

When strategy is growth oriented and when strategy is likely to change frequently, the situation as a whole becomes more complex, fluid, and uncertain. Operating objectives are likely to include the need for innovation and flexible responses to changing competition in the environment. Operations and plans are likely to have short life spans and require frequent and even continuous modification over time. The most appropriate structure is one that allows for internal flexibility and freedom to create new ways of doing things. This is most characteristic of the empowerment found in adaptive organizations using more organic design alternatives.

SkyWave Mobile Communication Inc. is an organic organization that has revolutionized the tracking of ships and trucks with their DMR-200 series, the world's first D+ satellite terminal with an integrated antenna and scripting capability for fixed and mobile asset tracking, monitoring, and control. This innovative

PERSONAL MANAGEMENT

It is easy to make decisions when you have perfect information. But in the new world of work, you will often face unstructured problems and have to make decisions with incomplete information under uncertain conditions. Depending on your **TOLERANCE FOR AMBIGUITY**, you may be comfortable or uncomfortable dealing with these new realities. It takes personal flexibility and lots of confidence to cope well with unpredictability. Some people have a hard time dealing with the unfamiliar. They prefer to work with directions that minimize ambiguity and provide clear decision-making rules; they like the structure of mechanistic organizations with bureaucratic features. Other people are willing and able to perform in less structured settings that give them lots of flexibility in responding to changing situations; they like the freedom of organic organizations designed for adaptation. You must find a good fit between your personal preferences and the nature of the organizations in which you choose to work. To achieve this fit, you have to both know yourself and be able to read organizational cultures and structures. And whatever your tolerance for ambiguity may be, the best time to explore these issues of person–organization fit is now, before you take your first or next job.

Get to know yourself better

Complete Self-Assessments #16—**Turbulence Tolerance Test**, and #17—**Organizational Design Preferences**, from the Workbook and Personal Management Activity #11 from the companion website.

Canadian company is a market leader partially because they partner with other solution providers worldwide for mutual benefit. They are a flexible company.[23]

●●● TECHNOLOGY

■ **Technology** includes equipment, knowledge, and work methods that transform inputs into outputs.

Technology is the combination of knowledge, skills, equipment, computers, and work methods used to transform resource inputs into organizational outputs. It is the way tasks are accomplished using tools, machines, techniques, and human know-how. The availability of appropriate technology is a cornerstone of productivity, and the nature of the core technologies in use must be considered in organizational design.

In the early 1960s, Joan Woodward conducted a study of technology and structure in over 100 English manufacturing firms. She classified core *manufacturing technology* into three categories.[24] In **small-batch production**, such as a racing bicycle shop, a variety of custom products are tailor-made to order. Each item, or batch of items, is made somewhat differently to fit customer specifications. The equipment used may not be elaborate, but a high level of worker skill is often needed. In **mass production**, the organization produces a large number of uniform products in an assembly-line system. Workers are highly dependent on one another, as the product passes from stage to stage until completion. Equipment may be sophisticated, and workers often follow detailed instructions while performing simplified jobs. Organizations using continuous-process production are highly automated. They produce a few products by continuously feeding raw materials—such as liquids, solids, and gases—through a highly automated production system with largely computerized controls. Such systems are equipment intensive, but can often be operated by a relatively small labour force. Classic examples are automated chemical plants, steel mills, oil refineries, and power plants.

■ **Small-batch production** manufactures a variety of products crafted to fit customer specifications.

■ **Mass production** manufactures a large number of uniform products with an assembly-line system.

■ In **continuous-process production** raw materials are continuously transformed by an automated system.

Woodward found that it was imperative to have the right combination of structure and technology to achieve organizational success. The best small-batch and **continuous-process production** plants in her study had more flexible organic structures; the best mass-production operations had more rigid mechanistic structures. The implications of this research have become known as the *technological imperative*: technology is a major influence on organizational structure.

The importance of technology for organizational design applies in services as well as manufacturing, although the core *service technologies* are slightly different.[25] In health care, education, and related services, an **intensive technology** focuses the efforts of many people with special expertise on the needs of patients or clients. In banks, real-estate firms, insurance companies, employment agencies, and others like them, a **mediating technology** links together parties seeking a mutually beneficial exchange of values—typically a buyer and seller. Finally, a **long-linked technology** can function like mass production, where a client is passed from point to point for various aspects of service delivery.

■ **Intensive technology** focuses the efforts and talents of many people to serve clients.

■ **Mediating technology** links together people in a beneficial exchange of values.

■ In **long-linked technology** a client moves from point to point during service delivery.

●●● SIZE AND LIFE CYCLE

Typically measured by number of employees, organizational size is another contingency factor in organizational design.[26] Although research indicates that larger organizations tend to have more mechanistic structures than smaller ones, it is also clear that this is not always best for them.[27] In fact, a perplexing managerial concern is that organizations tend to become more bureaucratic as they grow in size, and consequently have more difficulty adapting to changing environments. It is especially important to understand the design implications of the **organizational life cycle**, or the evolution of an organization over time through different stages of growth.

■ In the **organizational life cycle** an organization passes through different stages from birth to maturity.

ORGANIZED GROWTH LEADS TO OIL RICHES

In 1880, the merging of 16 southwestern Ontario oil refiners led to the creation of the Imperial Oil Company Limited. Since that time, Imperial Oil has been a major contributor to the petroleum industry's growth. Its landmark discovery of oil at Leduc, Alberta signalled the beginning of the modern Canadian petroleum industry. The company also pioneered development of the Alberta oil sands through its role in the creation of Syncrude and the development of large-scale, in-situ bitumen recovery at Cold Lake. With initiatives like these, Imperial has become one of the largest producers of crude oil in Canada, a major producer of natural gas, the largest refiner and marketer of petroleum products, and a significant presence in the petro-chemical industry. It distributes more than 700 products through a Canada-wide network of approximately 2,100 Esso service stations, 295 commercial bulk plants, and 30 distribution terminals. All of this could only be achieved through effective organizational design.

Source: Information from <www.imperialoil.ca>

The appeal of a biological life-cycle model is obvious. It explains that organizations are born, attempt to grow using many different forms, and eventually die. The theoretical under-pinning of this model is primarily deterministic in that it describes organizations as passing from one stage to the next over time.

Larry Greiner's work provides the basic foundations for the life cycle of any organization. He looked at both evolutionary and revolutionary factors that influence organizational development. He proposed that growing organizations move through five distinct stages of development. Each phase is characterized by a relatively calm period of growth followed by a management crisis that, in turn, ushers in the next phase. The cycle is as follows: [28]

1. Growth through creativity, followed by a crisis of leadership;

2. Growth through direction, followed by a crisis of autonomy;

3. Growth through delegation, followed by a crisis of control;

4. Growth through coordination, followed by a crisis of red tape;

5. Growth through collaboration; followed by a crisis of psychological saturation among employees.

The last crisis may be resolved by using new structures and programs that allow employees the opportunity to periodically rest, reflect, and revitalize themselves.

Another approach to life cycle follows a four-staged model. The stages in the organizational life cycle can be described as follows:

1. *Birth stage*—when the organization is founded by an entrepreneur.

2. *Youth stage*—when the organization starts to grow rapidly.

3. *Mid-life stage*—when the organization has grown large with success.

4. *Maturity stage*—when the organization stabilizes at a large size.[29]

In its *birth stage* the founder usually runs the organization. It stays relatively small, and the structure is quite simple. The organization starts to grow rapidly during the *youth stage*, and management responsibilities extend among more people. Here, the simple structure begins to exhibit the stresses of change. An organization in the *mid-life stage* is even larger, with a more complex and increasingly formal structure. More levels appear in the chain of command, and the founder may have difficulty remaining in control. In the *maturity stage*, the organization stabilizes in size, typically with a mechanistic structure. It runs the risk of becoming complacent and slow in competitive markets. Bureaucratic tendencies toward stability may lead an organization at this stage toward decline. Steps must be taken to counteract these tendencies and provide for needed creativity and innovation.

One way of coping with the disadvantages of a large organization is *downsizing*; that is, taking actions to reduce the scope of operations and number of employees. This response is often used when top management is challenged to reduce costs quickly and increase productivity.[30] But, perhaps more significantly, good managers in many organizations find unique ways to overcome the disadvantages of large size before the crisis of downsizing hits. They are creative in fostering **intrapreneurship**, described in Chapter 6 as the pursuit of entrepreneurial behaviour by individuals and subunits within large organizations.[31] They also find ways for smaller entrepreneurial units to operate with freedom and autonomy within the larger organizational framework. **Simultaneous systems**, for example, are organizations that utilize both mechanistic and organic designs to meet the need for production efficiency and continued innovation. This "loose–tight" concept in organizational design is depicted in *Figure 11.4*.

It is important to note that researchers have found that an opposite, or non-deterministic, life-cycle model of organizations also exists. With this model it is important to view the organization's development as a general growth and decline rather than a life cycle. Key to understanding organizational life cycles is an appreciation of how activities and structure will change over time as organizations try to match internal activities to changes in external conditions. A life cycles theory forms a road map, identifying critical transitional points for organizations and the pitfalls they should seek to avoid as they grow in size and complexity.

▓ **Intrapreneurship** is entrepreneurial behaviour by individuals and subunits within large organizations.

▓ In **simultaneous systems** mechanistic and organic designs operate together in an organization.

Figure 11.4
Simultaneous "loose–tight" properties of team structures support efficiency and innovation.

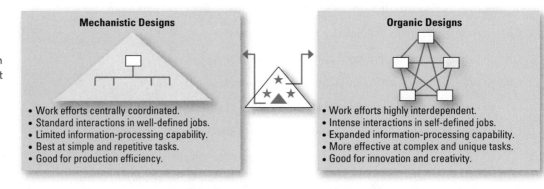

●●● HUMAN RESOURCES

Another contingency factor in organizational design is people—the human resources that staff the organization for action. A good organizational design provides people with the supporting structures they need to achieve both high performance and satisfaction in their work. Modern management theory views people-structure relationships in a contingency fashion. The prevailing argument is that there should be a good "fit" between organizational structures and the human resources.[32]

An important human resource issue in organizational design is skill. Any design should allow the expertise and talents of organizational members to be unlocked and utilized to the fullest. Especially in the age of information and knowledge workers, high-involvement organic designs with their emphasis on empowerment are crucial. When IBM purchased the software firm Lotus, for example, the intention was to turn it into a building block for the firm's networking business. But Lotus was small, and IBM was huge. The whole thing had to be carefully handled or IBM might lose many of the talented people who created the popular LotusNotes and related products. The solution was to adapt the design to fit the people. IBM gave Lotus the space it needed to retain the characteristics of a creative software house. Said the firm's head of software at the time: "You have to keep the people, so you have to ask yourself why it is they like working there."[33]

BE SURE YOU CAN
• explain the contingency relationships between strategy and organizational design • differentiate among small-batch production, mass production, and continuous-process production • differentiate among intensive, mediating, and long-linked technologies in service industries • explain the concept of simultaneous systems and the loose–tight concept in organizational design

✓ Learning check ❷

SUBSYSTEM DESIGN AND INTEGRATION

Organizations are composed of **subsystems**, such as a department or work unit headed by a manager, that operate as smaller parts of a larger and total organizational system. Ideally, the work of subsystems serves the needs of the larger organization. Ideally, too, the work of each subsystem supports the work of others. Things don't always work out this way, however. Another challenge of organizational design is to create subsystems and coordinate relationships so that the entire organization's interests are best met.

■ A **subsystem** is a work unit or smaller component within a larger organization.

AROUND THE WORLD

Most car rental companies have been designed to serve tourists, in locations such as airports and city centres. But in 1957, American entrepreneur Jack Taylor spotted a whole in the market while working at a St. Louis car dealership. He started renting cars to local customers whose vehicles were being serviced. Today, Enterprise Rent-a-Car has grown to be the biggest vehicle rental company in North America, and it's expanded into Europe, with some $9 billion in annual global revenues. One key to Enterprise's success in such a competitive industry is to run a decentralized operation with local offices (now numbering some 6,900) near where people live and work, as well as at airports. All share the core value of customer satisfaction. Employees are encouraged to act like entrepreneurs, and compensation and career advancement are tied to local customer service levels and financial results. "Few companies of our size encourage such autonomy so far out into the organization," the company says.

Source: With information from the company website: <http://aboutus.enterprise.com>.

Decentralization and entrepreneurial thinking add up to success

Important research in this area was reported in 1967 by Paul Lawrence and Jay Lorsch of Harvard University.[34] They studied 10 firms in three different industries—plastics, consumer goods, and containers. The firms were chosen because they differed in performance. The industries were chosen because they faced different levels of environmental uncertainty. The plastics industry was uncertain; the containers industry was more certain; the consumer goods industry was moderately uncertain. The results of the Lawrence and Lorsch study can be summarized as follows.

First, the total system structures of successful firms in each industry matched their respective environmental challenges. Successful plastics firms in uncertain environments had more organic designs; successful container firms in certain environments had more mechanistic designs. This result was consistent with the earlier research by Burns and Stalker already discussed in this chapter.[35] Second, Lawrence and Lorsch found that subsystem structures in the successful firms matched the challenges of their respective subenvironments. Subsystems within the successful firms assumed different structures to accommodate the special problems and opportunities of their operating situations. Third, the researchers found that subsystems in the successful firms worked well with one another, even though they were also very different from one another.

●●● SUBSYSTEM DIFFERENTIATION

Figure 11.5 depicts operating differences among three divisions in one of the firms studied by Lawrence and Lorsch. It shows how research and development, manufacturing, and sales subunits operate differently in response to unique needs. This illustrates **differentiation**, which is the degree of difference that exists between the internal components of the organization.

There are four common *sources of subsystem differentiation*. First, the subsystems may have *differences in time orientation*. In a business firm, for example, the manufacturing subsystem may have a shorter-term outlook than does the research and development group. These differences can make it difficult for personnel from the two units to work well together. Second, the different tasks assigned to work units may also result in *differences in objectives*. For example, cost-conscious production managers and volume-conscious marketing managers may have difficulty agreeing on solutions to common problems. Third, *differences in interpersonal orientation* can affect subsystem relations. To the extent that patterns of

■ **Differentiation** is the degree of difference between subsystems in an organization.

Figure 11.5 Subsystem differentiation among research and development (R&D), manufacturing, and sales divisions.

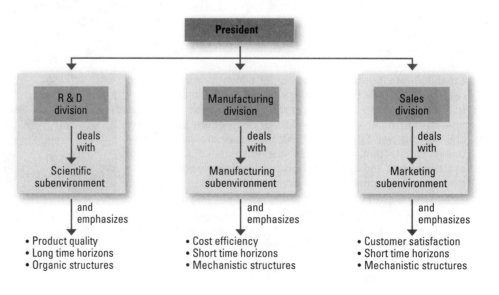

communication, decision making, and social interaction vary, it may be harder for personnel from different subsystems to work together. And fourth, *differences in formal structure* can also affect subsystem behaviours. Someone who is used to flexible problem solving in an organic setting may find it very frustrating to work with a manager from a mechanistic setting who is used to strict rules.

●●● SUBSYSTEM INTEGRATION

The term **integration** in organization theory refers to the level of coordination achieved among an organization's internal components. Organizational design involves the creation of both differentiated structures and appropriate integrating mechanisms. A basic *organizational design paradox*, however, makes this a particularly challenging managerial task. Increased differentiation among organizational subsystems creates the need for greater integration; however, integration becomes harder to achieve as differentiation increases.

Manager's Notepad 11.2 identifies several mechanisms for achieving subsystem integration.[36] Integrating mechanisms that rely on vertical coordination and the use of authority relationships work best when differentiation is low. They include use of rules and procedures, hierarchical referral, and planning. Integrating mechanisms that emphasize horizontal coordination and improved lateral relations work better when differentiation is high.[37] They include the use of direct contact between managers, liaison roles, task forces, teams, and matrix structures.

■ **Integration** is the level of coordination achieved between subsystems in an organization.

MANAGER'S
Notepad 11.2

How to improve subsystem integration

- *Rules and procedures:* Clearly specify required activities.

- *Hierarchical referral:* Refer problems upward to a common superior.

- *Planning:* Set targets that keep everyone headed in the same direction.

- *Direct contact:* Have subunit managers coordinate directly.

- *Liaison roles:* Assign formal coordinators to link subunits together.

- *Task forces:* Form temporary task forces to coordinate activities and solve problems on a timetable.

- *Teams:* Form permanent teams with the authority to coordinate and solve problems over time.

- *Matrix organizations:* Create a matrix structure to improve coordination on specific programs.

BE SURE YOU CAN
- explain the difference between a system and a subsystem • define the terms differentiation and integration
- discuss the implications of the Lawrence and Lorsch study for subsystem design • illustrate how subsystem differentiation might operate in a typical business • list several ways to improve subsystem integration in organizations

✔ Learning check **3**

WORK PROCESS DESIGN

■ **Process re-engineering** systematically analyzes work processes to design new and better ones.

From the emphasis on subsystems integration and more cross-functional collaboration in organizational design has come a popular development known as business **process re-engineering**.[38] This is defined by consultant Michael Hammer as the systematic and complete analysis of work processes and the design of new and better ones.[39] The goal of a re-engineering effort is to focus attention on the future, on customers, and on improved ways of doing things. It tries to break people and mindsets away from habits, preoccupation with past accomplishments, and tendencies to continue implementing old and outmoded ways of doing things. Simply put, re-engineering is a way of changing the way work is carried out in organizations.

●●● WHAT IS A WORK PROCESS?

■ A **work process** is a related group of tasks that together create a value for the customer.

In his book *Beyond Reengineering*, Michael Hammer defines a **work process** as "a related group of tasks that together create a result of value for the customer."[40] They are the things people do to turn resource inputs into goods or services for customers. Hammer highlights the following key words in the implications of his definition: (1) *group*—tasks are viewed as part of a group rather than in isolation; (2) *together*—everyone must share a common goal; (3) *result*—the focus is on what is accomplished, not on activities; (4) *customer*—processes serve customers, and their perspectives are the ones that really count.

■ **Workflow** is the movement of work from one point to another in a system.

The concept of **workflow**, or the way work moves from one point to another in manufacturing or service delivery, is central to the understanding of processes.[41] The various parts of a work process must all be completed to achieve the desired results, and they must typically be completed in a given order. An important starting point for a re-engineering effort is to diagram or map these workflows as they actually take place. Then each step can be systematically analyzed to determine whether it is adding value, to consider ways of eliminating or combining steps, and to find ways to use technology to improve efficiency. At PeopleSoft, for example, paper forms are definitely out; the goal is to eliminate them as much as possible. Employees are even able to order their own supplies through a direct Web link to Office Depot. The firm's chief information officer once said: "Nobody jumps out of bed in the morning and says, 'I want to go to work and fill out forms.' We create systems that let people be brilliant rather than push paper."[42]

●●● HOW TO RE-ENGINEER CORE PROCESSES

■ **Process value analysis** identifies and evaluates core processes for their performance contributions.

Given the mission, objectives, and strategies of an organization, business process re-engineering can be used to regularly assess and fine-tune work processes to ensure that they directly add value to operations. Through a technique called **process value analysis**, core processes are identified and carefully evaluated for their performance contributions. Each step in a workflow is examined. Unless a step is found to be important, useful, and contributing to the value added, it is eliminated. Process value analysis typically involves the following steps:[43]

1. Identify the core processes.
2. Map the core processes in respect to workflows.
3. Evaluate all tasks for the core processes.
4. Search for ways to eliminate unnecessary tasks or work.
5. Search for ways to eliminate delays, errors, and misunderstandings.
6. Search for efficiencies in how work is shared and transferred among people and departments.

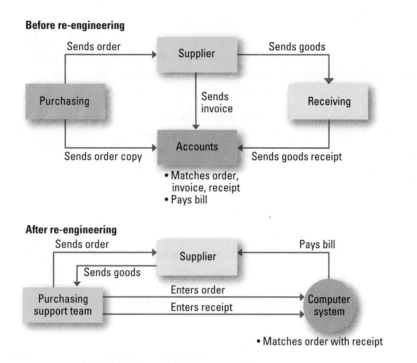

Figure 11.6 How re-engineering can streamline core business processes.

Figure 11.6 shows an example of how re-engineering and better use of computer technology can streamline a purchasing operation. A purchase order should result in at least three value-added outcomes: order fulfillment, a paid bill, and a satisfied supplier. Work to be successfully accomplished includes such things as ordering, shipping, receiving, billing, and payment. A traditional business system might have purchasing, receiving, and accounts payable as separate functions, with each communicating with each other and the supplier. Alternatively, process value analysis might result in re-engineering that designs a new purchasing support team whose members handle the same work more efficiently with the support of the latest computer technology.[44]

●●● PROCESS-DRIVEN ORGANIZATIONS

Customers, teamwork, and efficiency are central to Hammer's notion of process re-engineering. He describes the case of Aetna Life & Casualty Company, where a complex system of tasks and processes once took as much as 28 days to accomplish.[45] Customer service requests were handled in step-by-step fashion by many different persons. After an analysis of workflows, the process was redesigned into a "one and done" format where a single customer service provider handled each request from start to finish. One of Aetna's customer account managers said after the change was made: "Now we can see the customers as individual people. It's no longer 'us' and 'them.'"[46]

Hammer also describes re-engineering at a unit of Verizon Communications. Before re-engineering, customer inquiries for telephone service and repairs required extensive consultation between technicians and their supervisors. After process value analysis, technicians were formed into geographical teams that handled their own scheduling, service delivery, and reporting. They were given cellular telephones and laptop computers to assist in managing their work, resulting in the elimination of a number of costly supervisory jobs. The technicians enthusiastically responded to the changes and opportunities. "The fact that you've got four or five people zoned in a certain geographical area," said one, "means that we get personally familiar with our customers' equipment and problems."[47]

The essence of process re-engineering is to locate control for processes with an identifiable group of people, and to focus each person and the entire system on meeting customer needs and expectations. It tries to eliminate duplication of work and systems bottlenecks to reduce costs, increase efficiency, and build capacity for change. Hammer describes the *process-driven organization* in the following words:[48]

> *Its intrinsic customer focus and its commitment to outcome measurement make it vigilant and proactive in perceiving the need for change; the process owner, freed from other responsibilities and wielding the power of process design, is an institutionalized agent of change; and employees who have an appreciation for customers and who are measured on outcomes are flexible and adaptable.*

✓ **Learning check ④**

BE SURE YOU CAN

• define the terms process re-engineering and work process • draw a map of the workflow in an organization familiar to you • explain how process value analysis can be used to streamline workflows and improve work performance

●●● Chapter 11 STUDY GUIDE

WHERE WE'VE BEEN

Back to KPMG

The opening example of KPMG International highlighted the importance of fitting organizational design with the people who intimately deliver high-performance outcomes. In Chapter 11 you learned the differences between bureaucratic and adaptive organizations, including the notions of mechanistic and organic designs. You also learned more about the concept of contingency thinking in management, with a special focus on how designs must successfully fit environment, strategy, technology, size and life cycle, and people. You also leaned about subsystem design and process re-engineering in organizations.

THE NEXT STEP
INTEGRATED LEARNING ACTIVITIES

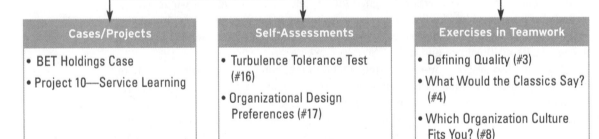

Cases/Projects	Self-Assessments	Exercises in Teamwork
• BET Holdings Case • Project 10—Service Learning	• Turbulence Tolerance Test (#16) • Organizational Design Preferences (#17)	• Defining Quality (#3) • What Would the Classics Say? (#4) • Which Organization Culture Fits You? (#8)

STUDY QUESTION SUMMARY

1. What are the essentials of organizational design?

- Organizational design is the process of choosing and implementing structures that best use resources to serve the mission and purpose.

- Bureaucratic organizational designs are vertical and mechanistic; they work best for routine and predictable tasks.

- Adaptive organizational designs are horizontal and organic; they perform best in conditions requiring change and flexibility.

2. How do contingency factors influence organizational design?

- Environment, strategy, technology, size, and people are all contingency factors influencing organizational design.

- Certain environments lend themselves to vertical and mechanistic organizational designs; uncertain environments require more horizontal and adaptive organizational designs.

- Technology—including the use of knowledge, equipment, and work methods in the transformation process—is an important consideration in organizational design.

- Although organizations tend to become more mechanistic as they grow in size, design efforts must be used to allow for innovation and creativity in changing environments.

3. What are the major issues in subsystem design?

- Organizations are composed of multiple subsystems that must work well together.

- Differentiation is the degree of difference that exists between various subsystems; integration is the level of coordination achieved among them.

- As organizations become more highly differentiated, they have a greater need for integration, but as differentiation increases, integration is harder to accomplish.

- Low levels of differentiation can be integrated through authority relationships and vertical organizational designs.

- Greater differentiation requires more intense integration through horizontal designs, with an emphasis on cross-functional teams and lateral relations.

4. How can work processes be re-engineered?

- A work process is a related group of tasks that together create value for a customer.

- Business process engineering is the systematic and complete analysis of work processes and the design of new and better ones.

- In process value analysis all elements of a process and its workflows are examined to identify their exact contributions to key performance results.

- Re-engineering eliminates unnecessary work steps, combines others, and uses technology to gain efficiency and reduce costs.

KEY TERMS REVIEW

Adaptive organization (p. 267)

Bureaucracy (p. 264)

Continuous-process production (p. 270)

Differentiation (p. 274)

Integration (p. 275)

Intensive technology (p. 270)

Intrapreneurship (p. 272)

Learning organization (p. 267)

Long-linked technology (p. 270)

Mass production (p. 270)

Mechanistic design (p. 266)

Mediating technology (p. 270)

Organic design (p. 267)

Organizational design (p. 263)

Organizational effectiveness (p. 263)

Organizational life cycle (p. 270)

Process re-engineering (p. 276)

Process value analysis (p. 276)

Simultaneous systems (p. 272)

Small-batch production (p. 270)

Subsystem (p. 273)

Technology (p. 270)

Work process (p. 276)

Workflow (p. 276)

SELF-TEST 11

MULTIPLE-CHOICE QUESTIONS:

1. The bureaucratic organization described by Max Weber is similar to the _____ organization described by Burns and Stalker.
    (a) adaptive (b) mechanistic (c) organic (d) learning

2. Teamwork, task forces, and empowerment are common in organizations operating with _____.
    (a) mechanistic designs (b) strict hierarchy (c) vertical structures (d) organic designs

3. The production method characteristic of an oil refinery is an example of what Woodward referred to as _____ technology.
    (a) intensive (b) continuous-process (c) mass-production (d) small-batch

4. As organizations grow in size, they tend to become more _____ in design, although this is not always best for them.
    (a) mechanistic (b) organic (c) adaptive (d) simultaneous

5. A basic paradox in subsystem design is that as differentiation increases, the need for _____ also increases but is harder to accomplish.
    (a) cost efficiency (b) innovation (c) integration (d) transformation

6. A(n) _____ organizational design works best in _____ environments.
    (a) flexible, stable (b) adaptive, uncertain (c) mechanistic, dynamic (d) organic, certain

7. A simple structure tends to work well when an organization is in the _____ stage of its life cycle.
    (a) birth (b) mid-life (c) maturity (d) youth

8. When the members of a marketing department pursue sales volume objectives and those in manufacturing pursue cost efficiency objectives, this is an example of _____.
    (a) simultaneous systems (b) subsystems differentiation (c) long-linked technology (d) small-batch production

9. A work process is defined as a related group of tasks that together create value for _____.
    (a) shareholders (b) customers (c) workers (d) society

10. The first step in process value analysis is to _____.
    (a) look for ways to eliminate unnecessary tasks (b) map or diagram the workflows (c) identify core processes (d) look for efficiencies in transferring work among people and departments

11. In the _____ approach to organizational effectiveness, the focus is on how well an organization satisfies customers and external stakeholders.
    (a) systems resource (b) strategic constituencies (c) process re-engineering (d) goal

12. After the short-term criteria of performance effectiveness and efficiency are met, an organizational design should next satisfy the organizational effectiveness criteria of _____ .
    (a) cost and quality control (b) stability and survival (c) adaptability and development (d) shareholder value and profit maximization

13. A traditional vertical structure is the most appropriate choice when an organization is pursuing a strategic focus on _____ .
    (a) intrapreneurship (b) innovation (c) stability (d) flexibility

14. A small Web-design firm that creates one-of-a-kind websites for customers is an example of a _____ technology in Woodward's classification scheme.
    (a) small-batch (b) continuous-process (c) long-linked (d) mediating

15. The major situational contingencies that affect the choice of organizational design include strategy, size, environment, technology, and _____.
    (a) performance (b) people (c) differentiation (d) workflow

SHORT-RESPONSE QUESTIONS:

16. Explain the practical significance of this statement: "Organizational design should always be addressed in contingency fashion."

17. What difference does environment make in organizational design?

18. Describe the relationship between differentiation and integration as issues in subsystem design.

19. If you were a re-engineering consultant, how would you describe the steps in a typical approach to process value analysis?

APPLICATION QUESTION:

20. Two business women, former university roommates, are discussing their jobs and careers over lunch. You overhear one saying to the other: "I work for a large corporation. It is bureaucratic and very authority driven. However, I have to say that it is also very successful. I like working there." Her friend responded: "My, I wouldn't like working there at all. In my organization things are very flexible and the structures are loose. We have a lot of freedom and the focus on operations is much more horizontal than vertical. And we, too, are very successful." After listening to the conversation and using insights from management theory, how can these two very different "success stories" be explained?

12

Human Resource Management

●●● CHAPTER 12 STUDY QUESTIONS

Planning Ahead

After reading Chapter 12, you should be able to answer these questions in your own words.

1. Why do people make the difference?

2. What is strategic human resource management?

3. How do organizations attract a quality workforce?

4. How do organizations develop a quality workforce?

5. How do organizations maintain a quality workforce?

Dofasco

"Take care of people, they'll take care of business"

This is an often used line, but in the case of Dofasco, a Canadian steel producer located in Hamilton, Ontario, it really is true. Featured yearly among the 50 "best companies to work for," Dofasco has developed a successful strategy of not only watching the financial measures, but of also monitoring its impact on the environment and ensuring employee productivity and job satisfaction.

Many initiatives help to ensure its employees remain satisfied. Decision making has been put in the hands of line workers with the removal of middle management and the development of cross-functional teams with responsibility for quality control. As John Mayberry, Dofasco's retired CEO, states, "People can make a phenomenal difference if you can tap into them, if you stop telling them to come to work, put their brains in a box, and do whatever the supervisor says."

Training and leadership are also important, and the company is preparing for the skills shortage expected as the baby boom generation begins to retire by, among other things, emphasizing its apprenticeship program. Dofasco spends about $13 million a year on training and development.

What about employee health and safety? Dofasco is number one according to Canada's National Quality Institute (NQI), which gives out Healthy Workplace awards. At Dofasco, volunteers run wellness initiatives including workshops in back care, nutrition, yoga, relaxation techniques, and tai chi. The company has also decreased its lost time due to injuries from 7 hours for every 200,000 hours worked in 1991, to 2.34 hours in 2001.

Employees are also proud of how Dofasco works to make the broader community better. "They see how we behave in the community, and they see that it's consistent with the way we behave with them," states Mayberry. He further notes that the company has earned its employees' trust, and that the deep values of the company are clearly being carried out, not just within the company, but also out into the community.

Though small by comparison, the company has continued to outperform its major competitors. It seems that Dofasco's motto, "Our product is steel, our strength is people," really does ring true.[1]

IN THE WORKPLACE

Naomi has stopped by your office for a chat. You have been very impressed by her knowledge of the company and her ability to always get things done on time. In your conversation, she says she is frustrated because she is being overlooked for senior management positions. Naomi laments: "It doesn't seem fair that I have done all of the things asked of me, and more, yet I am not getting promoted. What else can I do?" You wonder what might be happening in the company to cause such stress in an excellent employee. You ask yourself, "If I were in charge, what could I do to ensure that people know how they are doing and that the right people get promoted?"

●●● Chapter 12 LEARNING PREVIEW ●●●

Dofasco has made its mark in a highly competitive industry not only by focusing on financial and environmental measures, but through a concentrated and innovative approach to motivating their employees. By empowering their employees to make decisions and providing training and leadership opportunities, Dofasco's competitive strength is their people. In this chapter you will learn about the process of human resource management through which managers attract, develop, and maintain a talented workforce. You will also learn about the complex legal environment within which such human resource management decisions are made.

HUMAN RESOURCE MANAGEMENT

Study Question 1	Study Question 2	Study Question 3	Study Question 4	Study Question 5
Why People Make the Difference	**Human Resource Management**	**Attracting a Quality Workforce**	**Developing a Quality Workforce**	**Maintaining a Quality Workforce**
• Valuing human capital • The diversity advantage	• HRM process • Strategic HRM • Laws against employment discrimination • Current legal issues in HRM	• Human resource planning • The recruiting process • How to make selection decisions	• Employee orientation • Training and development • Performance management systems	• Career development • Work–life balance • Compensation and benefits • Retention and turnover • Labour–management relations
Learning check ❶	Learning check ❷	Learning check ❸	Learning check ❹	Learning check ❺

Today, perhaps more than ever before, the pressures of global competition and social change are influencing not just the organizations in which we work but the very nature of employment itself. In his book *The Future of Success*, Robert Reich calls this "the age of the terrific deal."[2] He also describes a shift away from a system in which people work loyally as traditional "employees" for "employers" who provide them career-long job and employment security.[3] In the emerging system we become sellers of our services (talents) to those buyers (employers) who are willing to pay for them. Those who do "buy" are looking for the very best people, whose capabilities and motivations match the demands of high-performance organizations. Reich is talking about changes to the **social contract**, or expectations of the employee-employer relationship. As today's organizations reconfigure around networks, teams, projects, flexibility, speed, and efficiency, the social contract is changing. For the individual, this means an emphasis on skills, responsibility, continuous learning, and mobility. For the organization, it means providing development opportunities, challenging work assignments, the best in resource support, and incentive compensation.[4]

All of this, of course, affects your future career. "Create a brand called 'You,'" "Build a portfolio of skills," "Protect your mobility," "Take charge of your destiny," "Add value to your

■ The **social contract** reflects expectations in the employee-employer relationship.

organization," advise the career gurus.[5] The advice is on target, but the really tough question is, "Are you ready?" Test yourself by asking and answering these *career readiness questions*: Who am I? What do I want? What have I done? What do I know? What can I do? Why should someone hire me?

WHY PEOPLE MAKE THE DIFFERENCE

People have to be a top priority in any organization with high-performance aspirations. Testimonials like these say it all: "*People* are our most important asset"; "It's *people* who make the difference"; "It's the *people* who determine whether our company thrives or languishes." Found on websites, in annual reports, and in executive speeches, they communicate respect for people and the talents they bring to organizations.

●●● VALUING HUMAN CAPITAL

A strong foundation of **human capital**—the economic value of people with job-relevant abilities, knowledge, experience, ideas, energies, and commitments—is essential to any organization's long-term performance success. Consider the strategic leadership implications of these comments made by Jeffrey Pfeffer in his book *The Human Equation: Building Profits by Putting People First*:[6]

> *The key to managing people in ways that lead to profit, productivity, innovation, and real organizational learning ultimately lies in how you think about your organization and its people. …When you look at your people, do you see costs to be reduced?…Or, when you look at your people do you see intelligent, motivated, trustworthy individuals—the most critical and valuable strategic assets your organization can have?*

In an *Academy of Management Executive* article entitled "Putting People First for Organizational Success," Jeffrey Pfeffer and John F. Veiga state: "There is a substantial and rapidly expanding body of evidence . . . that speaks to the strong connection between how firms manage their people and the economic results achieved."[7] They forcefully argue that organizations perform better when they treat their members better. The management practices associated with successful organizations are employment security, decentralization, use of teams, good compensation, extensive training, and information sharing.[8] James Baron and David Kreps also highlight the primacy of people in their book *Strategic Human Resources: Frameworks for General Managers*.[9] Stating that "human resources are key to organizational success or failure," they summarize empirical research showing a relationship between positive human resource policies and higher organizational performance.

●●● THE DIVERSITY ADVANTAGE

The best employers and the best managers know that to succeed in today's challenging times they must place a primacy on people.[10] This means valuing diversity and being fully inclusive of all people with the talent and desire to do good work. Job-relevant talent is not restricted because of anyone's race, gender, religion, marital or parental status, sexual orientation, ethnicity, or other diversity characteristics. And anytime these characteristics interfere with finding, hiring, and utilizing the best employees, the loss will be someone else's gain.

Respect for people in all of their diversity is a major theme in the book *Proversity: Getting Past Face Value and Finding the Soul of People–A Manager's Journey*, by author and consultant Lawrence Otis Graham.[11] He suggests that managers committed to building high-perform-

■ Human capital is the economic value of people with job-relevant abilities, knowledge, ideas, energies, and commitments.

ance work environments should take a simple test. The question is: which of the following qualities would you look for in anyone who works for you—work ethic, ambition and energy, knowledge, creativity, motivation, sincerity, outlook, collegiality and collaborativeness, curiosity, judgement and maturity, and integrity? In answering, you most likely selected all of these qualities, or at least you should have. The next test question is—where can you find people with these workplace qualities? The correct answer is, "everywhere."[12]

Canadian company Pelmorex Incorporated is known for being proactive in the field of equity and diversity. The company, which operates The Weather Network, won an Employment Equity Merit Award, presented by the Conference Board of Canada. The award recognizes "the importance of opening up the workplace to all our citizens, regardless of gender, race, culture or physical attributes."[13] Along with goals and policies, educational training, and outreach programs, many prominent on-air personalities form designated groups to deal with issues surrounding diversity in the workplace.

Diversity consultant and author R. Roosevelt Thomas puts the challenge this way: "Managers must find ways to get the highest level of contribution from their workers. And they will not be able to do that unless they are aware of the many ways that their understanding of diversity relates to how well, or how poorly, people contribute." Thomas goes further to identify what he calls the *diversity rationale* that must drive organizations today:[14]

> *To thrive in an increasingly unfriendly marketplace, companies must make it a priority to create the kind of environment that will attract the best new talent and will make it possible for employees to make their fullest contributions.*

Canadian Managers

Instilling Employee Pride

TD Bank Financial Group offers its employees an attractive compensation package, with competitive salaries and an employee stock purchase plan. But Teri Currie, executive vice-president of human resources, says that what makes TD's employees happiest is their pride in where they work, something she attributes to the bank's support of employee volunteerism. TD allows employees paid time off for volunteer activities. And, after volunteering with an organization for at least 40 hours in a year, employees can apply for a grant for the charity they support. "Our program allows them the flexibility in their schedule to be out in the community donating their time, and backing that activity up with corporate funding," says Currie. "Employees like to work for winning organizations, and winning organizations tend to create engaged employees, which produces results, which enhances shareholder value."

Source: Peter Evans, "Best workplaces 2006: Lessons from some of the best—TD Bank Financial Group," *Canadian Business*, April 10–23, 2006, p. 77.

✓ **Learning check ①**

BE SURE YOU CAN

• define the terms social contract and human capital • explain the logic behind this position: organizations perform better when they treat their people better • discuss how and why workforce diversity can be a source of performance advantage

HUMAN RESOURCE MANAGEMENT

A marketing manager at Ideo, an industrial design firm, once said: "If you hire the right people … if you've got the right fit…then everything will take care of itself."[15] It really isn't quite that simple, but one fact of management remains very clear—if an organization doesn't have the right people available to do the required work, it has very little chance of long-term success.

●●● HUMAN RESOURCE MANAGEMENT PROCESS

The process of **human resource management**, or HRM, involves attracting, developing, and maintaining a talented and energetic workforce. The basic goal of human resource management is to build organizational performance capacity by raising human capital, and to ensure that highly capable and enthusiastic people are always available. The three major responsibilities of human resource management are as follows:

1. *Attracting a quality workforce*—involves human resource planning as well as employee recruitment and selection.

2. *Developing a quality workforce*—involves employee orientation, training and development, and performance appraisal.

3. *Maintaining a quality workforce*—involves career development, work–life balance, compensation and benefits, retention and turnover, and labour–management relations.

The area of human resource management provides many career opportunities. HRM departments are common in most organizations. HRM specialists are increasingly important in an environment complicated by legal issues, labour shortages, economic turmoil, changing corporate strategies, changing personal values, new expectations, and more. As outsourcing of professional services becomes more popular, a growing number of firms provide specialized HRM services such as recruiting, compensation, outplacement, and the like. The Canadian Council of Human Resources Associations (CCHRA) is the result of the collaborative efforts of 10 provincial and specialist human resources associations that currently represent the interests of more than 30,000 professionals across Canada.[16] One of the more dynamic members is the Human Resources Professionals Association of Ontario (HRPAO). The mission of the organization is to set standards and enhance the profession while ensuring its membership is updated on the ever changing field of human resources.

■ **Human resource management** is the process of attracting, developing, and maintaining a high-quality workforce.

●●● STRATEGIC HUMAN RESOURCE MANAGEMENT

All organizations, at all times, need to have the right people available to do the work required to achieve and sustain competitive advantage. Today, this challenge is increasingly addressed by making the human resources function an integral component of strategic management. **Strategic human resource management** mobilizes human capital through the HRM process to best implement organizational strategies.[17] One indicator that the HRM process is truly strategic to the organization is when the HRM function is headed by a senior executive reporting directly to the chief executive officer. When Robert Nardelli took over as CEO of Home Depot, for example, the first person he hired into the senior executive suite was Denis Donovan, who became the firm's executive vice-president for human resources. Donovan says, "CEOs and boards of directors are learning that human resources can be one of your

■ **Strategic human resource management** mobilizes human capital to implement organizational strategies.

PERSONAL MANAGEMENT

PROFESSIONALISM! The code of ethics of the Human Resources Professionals Association of Ontario (www.hrpao.com) suggests the HR professional should meet the following requirements:

1. *Competence*   HR practitioners must maintain competence in carrying out professional responsibilities and ensure that services provided are within the limits of their knowledge, experience, and skill.

2. *Legal Requirements*   Adhere to any statutory acts, regulations, or by-laws that relate to the field of Human Resources Management as well as to all civil and criminal laws, regulations and statutes that apply in their jurisdiction.

3. *Dignity in the Workplace*   Support, promote, and apply the principles of human rights, equity, dignity, and respect in the workplace, within the profession, and in society as a whole.

4. *Balancing Interests*   Strive to balance organizational and employee needs and interests in the practice of their profession.

5. *Confidentiality*   Hold in strict confidence all confidential information acquired in the course of the performance of their duties and not divulge confidential information unless required by law.

6. *Conflict of Interest*   Avoid or disclose a potential conflict of interest that might influence or might be perceived to influence personal actions or judgements.

7. *Professional Growth and Support of Other Professionals*   Maintain personal and professional growth in Human Resources Management by engaging in activities that enhance the credibility and value of the profession.

8. *Enforcement*   The Canadian Council of Human Resources Associations works collaboratively with its Member Associations to develop and enforce high standards of ethical practice.

Get to know yourself better

Complete Self-Assessments #18—**Are You Cosmopolitan?**, and #19—**Performance Appraisal Assumptions** from the Workbook and Personal Management Activity #12 on the companion website.

biggest game-changers in terms of competitive advantage."[18] The strategic importance of HRM has been further accentuated by the spate of corporate ethics scandals. "It was a failure of people and that isn't lost on those in the executive suite," says Susan Meisinger, president of the Society for Human Resource Management.[19]

●●● LAWS AGAINST EMPLOYMENT DISCRIMINATION

Discrimination in employment occurs when someone is denied a job or a job assignment for reasons that are not job relevant. The *Canadian Human Rights Act* makes it illegal for employers to discriminate in hiring, promotion, and termination of employment based on prohibited grounds. A sample of major grounds on which discrimination is prohibited is provided in *Figure 12.1*. In Canada, federal legislation often provides the framework for provinces and municipalities when drafting their own legislation, which may vary slightly from province to province. These acts provide for the right to employment without regard to race, colour, national origin, religion, gender, age, or physical and mental ability. The intent is to ensure all citizens the right to gain and keep employment based only on their ability to do the job and their performance once on the job. Each provincial human rights commission has the power to impose remedies on organizations that do not provide a timely resolution to any discrimination charges brought against them. For example, the British Columbia Human Rights Tribunal has the power to order an organization to cease the discriminatory behaviour; make available the right, opportunity, or privilege that was denied; compensate for any wages lost or any expenses incurred; and provide damages for injury to feelings and self-respect.[20]

Organizations are expected to show **employment equity** by giving preference in employment to four designated groups—Aboriginals, women, visible minorities, and people with physical/mental disability. The purpose of the *Employment Equity Act* is to "achieve equality in the workplace so that no person shall be denied employment opportunities or benefits for reasons unrelated to ability and, in the fulfillment of that goal, to correct the conditions of disadvantage in employment experienced by women, aboriginal peoples, persons with disabilities, and members of visible minorities by giving effect to the principle that employment equity means more than treating persons in the same way but also requires special measures and the accommodation of differences."[21] The *Employment Equity Act* applies to federal government departments and agencies, and to private sector employers that are governed by federal legislation, such as banks, broadcasters, and transportation companies, as well as

Prohibited Grounds for Discrimination	Provinces
Race or colour	All provinces
Religion	All provinces
Physical or mental disability	All provinces
Age if 18–64/65	All provinces except Ont., Que., and Man.
Sex (includes pregnancy and childbirth)	All provinces
Marital status	All provinces
Dependence on drugs/alcohol	All except Y.T. and N.W.T.
Family status	All except N.B. and N.L.
Sexual orientation	All except N.W.T.
National or ethnic origin	All except B.C. and Alta.
Ancestry or place of origin	Y.T., B.C., Alta., Man., Sask., N.W.T., Ont., N.B.
Language	Y.T., Ont., Que.
Social condition or origin	Que., N.L.
Source of income	Alta., Sask., Man., Que., P.E.I., N.S.
Political belief	Y.T., B.C., Man., Que., N.S., P.E.I., N.L.
Criminal conviction	Y.T., B.C., Que., P.E.I.
Pardoned conviction	B.C., N.W.T., Ont.

Source: <www.chrc-ccdp.ca>

Figure 12.1 A sample of prohibited grounds of employment discrimination in Canadian provinces.

Aboriginal band councils. Criticisms tend to focus on the use of group membership (e.g., female or minority status) as a criterion in employment decisions.[22] The issues raised include claims of reverse discrimination by members of majority populations. White males, for example, may claim that preferential treatment given to minorities in a particular situation interferes with their individual rights.

As a general rule, the *Canadian Human Rights Act* does not restrict an employer's right to establish **bona fide occupational** requirements. These are criteria for employment that can be clearly justified as being related to a person's capacity to perform a job. The use of bona fide occupational requirements based on race and colour is not allowed under any circumstances; those based on gender, religion, and age are very difficult to support.[23]

●●● CURRENT LEGAL ISSUES IN HUMAN RESOURCE MANAGEMENT

All aspects of human resource management must be accomplished within the legal framework. Failure to do so is not only unjustified in a free society, it can also be a very expensive mistake resulting in fines and penalties. As a reminder, *Manager's Notepad 12.1* identifies questions that are considered illegal—or at least inappropriate—for an interviewer to ask during a job interview.[24] Of course, the Canadian legal and regulatory environment is constantly changing. A committed manager or human resource professional should always stay informed on the following and other issues of legal and ethical consequence.[25]

Sexual harassment occurs when people experience conduct or language of a sexual nature that affects their employment situation. Sexual harassment can be defined as behaviour that creates a hostile work environment, interferes with a person's ability to do a job, or

■ **Discrimination** occurs when someone is denied a job or job assignment for reasons not job relevant.

■ **Employment equity** is an effort to give preference in employment to Aboriginals, women, visible minorities, and people with physical/mental disability.

■ **Bona fide occupational requirements** are employment criteria justified by the capacity to perform a job.

■ **Sexual harassment** is behaviour of a sexual nature that affects a person's employment situation.

MANAGER'S
Notepad 12.1

Illegal or inappropriate (and acceptable) questions when interviewing a job candidate

- *Race:* No questions regarding race or colour are appropriate

- *Religion/creed:* No questions regarding religion or observance of religious holidays are appropriate. It is okay to ask if the shifts and days required will pose a problem.

- *National origin:* It is inappropriate to ask about ethnic origin or nationality. It is okay to ask if they are legally entitled to work in Canada.

- *Sex:* No questions regarding sexual orientation are appropriate.

- *Marital status:* May not ask about marital status or children. May ask if the travel and overtime expectations for the position will pose a problem.

- *Family planning:* No questions regarding present or future plans are allowed.

- *Age:* May not ask an applicant's age. May ask if they are between the ages of 18 and 65.

- *Arrest:* Inappropriate to ask if the applicant has ever been arrested. May ask if they have ever been convicted of a crime (relevant to job performance) for which they have not received a pardon.

- *Birthplace:* No questions regarding birthplace or the birthplace of parents or spouse.

- *Disability:* May not ask about specific disabilities. It is acceptable to ask if the applicant has any condition that could affect their ability to perform the major requirements of the job.

interferes with their promotion potential. Organizations should have clear sexual harassment policies in place along with fair and equitable procedures for implementing them. Both the *Canadian Human Rights Act* and the Canada Labour Code protect employees from sexual harassment in the workplace.[26]

Pay equity provides that men and women in the same organization should be paid equally for doing equal work in terms of required skills, responsibilities, and working conditions. But a lingering issue involving gender disparities in pay involves **comparable worth**, the notion that persons performing jobs of similar importance should be paid at comparable levels. Why should a long-distance truck driver, for example, be paid more than an elementary teacher in a public school? Does it make any difference that the former is a traditionally male occupation and the latter a traditionally female occupation? Advocates of comparable worth argue that such historical disparities are due to gender bias. They would like to have the issue legally resolved. Most provinces have three laws that address equal pay: a labour standards code, which applies to the private and public sectors; a human rights code addressing general discrimination; and a pay equity act, which applies to the broader civil service.[27]

The legal status and employee entitlements of *part-time* workers and **independent contractors** are also being debated. In today's era of downsizing, outsourcing, and projects, more and more persons are hired as temporary workers who work under contract to an organization and do not become part of its permanent workforce. They work only "as needed." But, a problem occurs when they are engaged regularly by the same organization and become what

■ **Comparable worth** holds that persons performing jobs of similar importance should be paid at comparable levels.

■ **Independent contractors** are hired on temporary contracts and are not part of the organization's permanent workforce, but they are also not covered under basic employment standards legislation.

many now call *permatemps*. Even though regularly employed, they work without benefits such as health coverage and pension eligibilities. A number of legal cases are now before the courts seeking to make such independent contractors eligible for benefits.

Workplace privacy is the right of individuals to privacy on the job.[28] It is quite acceptable for employers to monitor the work performance and behaviour of their employees. But employer practices can become invasive and cross legal and ethical lines, especially with the capabilities of information technology. Computers can easily monitor emails and Internet searches to track personal and unauthorized usage; they can identify who is called by telephone and how long conversations last; they can document work performance moment to moment; and they can easily do more. All of this information, furthermore, can be stored in vast databases that make it available to others, even without the individual's permission. The legal status of such IT surveillance is being debated. Until things are cleared up, one consultant recommends the best approach for everyone is, "Assume you have no privacy at work."[29]

> ■ **Workplace privacy** is the right to privacy while at work.

BE SURE YOU CAN
• explain the human resource management process • define the terms discrimination, employment equity, and bona fide occupational requirement • explain arguments for and against employment equity • identify major laws that protect against discrimination in employment • discuss current legal issues of sexual harassment, comparable worth, and independent contractors

✔ Learning check ❷

ATTRACTING A QUALITY WORKFORCE

The first responsibility of human resource management is to attract to the organization a high-quality workforce. Lee Valley Tools, with stores in 11 Canadian cities, scrutinizes potential employees' belief systems before they are hired. Interviews at the company often consist of questions regarding character, respect, and trust. As founder Leonard Lee comments, "You can do almost anything with a person who has the right basic instincts, and you can do practically nothing with someone who doesn't."[30] To attract the right people to its workforce, an organization must first know exactly what it is looking for—it must have a clear understanding of the jobs to be done and the talents required to do them well. Then it must have the systems in place to excel at employee recruitment and selection.

●●● HUMAN RESOURCE PLANNING

Human resource planning is the process of analyzing an organization's human resource needs and determining how to best fill them. Effective and strategic human resource planning ensures that the best people are always in place when needed by the organization. The major elements in this process are shown in *Figure 12.2*.

Strategic human resource planning begins with a review of organizational mission, objectives, and strategies. This establishes a frame of reference for forecasting human resource needs and labour supplies. Ultimately, the planning process should help managers identify staffing requirements, assess the existing workforce, and determine what additions and/or replacements are required to meet future needs. GE Medical Systems uses a multigenerational staffing plan. For every new product plan there is a human resource plan associated with it—one that covers all generations of the product's anticipated life.[31]

The foundations for human resource planning are set by **job analysis**—the orderly study of job facts to determine just what is done, when, where, how, why, and by whom in existing or potential new jobs.[32] The job analysis provides useful information that can then be used to write and/or update **job descriptions.** These are written statements of job duties

> ■ **Human resource planning** analyzes staffing needs and identifies actions to fill those needs.

> ■ **Job analysis** studies exactly what is done in a job, and why.

> ■ A **job description** details the duties and responsibilities of a job holder.

Figure 12.2 Steps in strategic human resource planning.

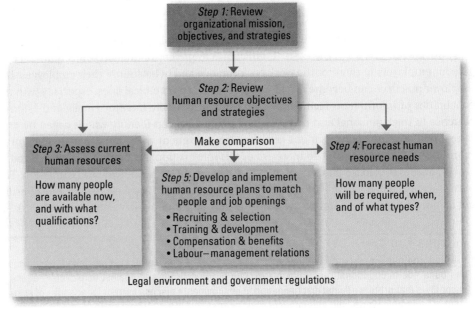

Step 1: Review organizational mission, objectives, and strategies

Step 2: Review human resource objectives and strategies

Make comparison

Step 3: Assess current human resources

How many people are available now, and with what qualifications?

Step 5: Develop and implement human resource plans to match people and job openings
• Recruiting & selection
• Training & development
• Compensation & benefits
• Labour–management relations

Step 4: Forecast human resource needs

How many people will be required, when, and of what types?

Legal environment and government regulations

■ A **job specification** lists the qualifications required of a job holder.

and responsibilities. The information in a job analysis can also be used to create **job specifications**. These are lists of the qualifications—such as education, prior experience, and skill requirements—needed by any person hired for, or placed in, a given job.

●●● THE RECRUITING PROCESS

■ **Recruitment** is a set of activities designed to attract a qualified pool of job applicants.

Recruitment is a set of activities designed to attract a *qualified* pool of job applicants to an organization. Emphasis on the word "qualified" is important. Effective recruiting should bring employment opportunities to the attention of people whose abilities and skills meet job specifications. The three steps in a typical recruitment process are (1) advertisement of a job vacancy, (2) preliminary contact with potential job candidates, and (3) initial screening to create a pool of qualified applicants. In college and university recruiting, for example, advertising is done by the firm posting short job descriptions in print or online through campus placement centres. Preliminary contact involves a short 20- to 30-minute interview, during which the candidate presents a resumé and briefly explains his or her job qualifications. Successful candidates at this stage are usually invited for further interviews during a formal visit to the organization.

External and Internal Recruitment

College and university recruiting is an example of *external recruitment* in which job candidates are sought from outside the hiring organization. Websites like workopolis.com and Monster.ca, newspapers, employment agencies, colleges, universities, technical training centres, personal contacts, walk-ins, employee referrals, and even persons in competing organizations are all sources of external recruits. Labour markets and recruiting are increasingly global in the new economy. When Nokia, the Finnish mobile-phone maker, needed high-tech talent, it posted all job openings on a website and received thousands of resumés from all over the world. The head of Nokia's recruiting strategy said, "There are no geographical boundaries anymore."[33]

Internal recruitment seeks applicants from inside the organization. For Pfizer Canada, the biggest recruiting challenge is finding individuals who fit in with the corporate culture. Pfizer emphasizes internal recruiting in order to identify candidates who not only have the technical skills required for the position, but who also have a demonstrated focus on performance and leadership flexibility that fits into their culture.[34] Most organizations have a procedure for announcing vacancies through newsletters, electronic bulletin boards, and the like. They also rely on managers to recommend subordinates as candidates for advancement. Internal recruitment creates opportunities for long-term career paths. Consider the story of Robert Goizueta, a former CEO of Coca-Cola. He made his way to the top over a 43-year career in the firm, an example of how loyalty and hard work can pay off.[35]

Both recruitment strategies offer potential advantages and disadvantages. External recruiting brings in outsiders with fresh perspectives. It also provides access to specialized expertise or work experience not otherwise available from insiders. Internal recruitment is usually less expensive. It also deals with persons whose performance records are well established. A history of serious internal recruitment also builds employees' loyalty and motivation, showing that one can advance by working hard and doing well when given responsibility.

Realistic Job Previews

In what may be called *traditional recruitment*, the emphasis is on selling the organization to job applicants. The emphasis is on the most positive features of the job and organization. Bias may even occur as the best features are exaggerated while negative features are avoided or even concealed. This form of recruitment may create unrealistic expectations that cause costly turnover when new hires become disillusioned and quit. The individual suffers a career disruption; the employer suffers lost productivity and the added costs of recruiting again.

The alternative is to provide **realistic job previews** that give candidates all the pertinent information about the job and organization without distortion and before the job is accepted.[36] Instead of "selling" only positive features, this approach tries to be open and balanced in describing the job and organization. Both favourable and unfavourable aspects are covered. The interviewer in a realistic job preview might use phrases such as: "Of course, there are some downsides…" "Things don't always go the way we hope…" "Something that you will want to be prepared for is…" "We have found that some new hires had difficulty with…." This type of conversation helps the candidate establish "realistic" job expectations and better prepare for the inevitable "ups and downs" of a new job. Higher levels of early job satisfaction and less inclination to leave prematurely are among the expected benefits. At Prudential Grand Valley Realty in Kitchener, Ontario, Keith Church uses a job simulation to both attract quality applicants and make better hiring decisions. The online video-based assessment simulates the entire sales cycle, from building a rapport with the client all the way to closing the sale. The job simulation helps to evaluate the applicant on their ability to understand client needs, handle objections, and negotiate. It also allows the applicant to make a more informed decision, improving the fit between the candidate and the job.[37]

> ■ **Realistic job previews** provide job candidates with all pertinent information about a job and organization.

●●● HOW TO MAKE SELECTION DECISIONS

The process of **selection** involves choosing, from a pool of applicants, the person or persons who offer the greatest performance potential. Steps in a typical selection process are shown in *Figure 12.3*. They are (1) completion of a formal application form, (2) interviewing, (3) testing, (4) reference checks, (5) physical examination, and (6) final analysis and decision to hire or reject. The best employers exercise extreme care in making selection decisions, seeking the best fit between individual and organization.

> ■ **Selection** is choosing whom to hire from a pool of qualified job applicants.

Figure 12.3 Steps in the selection process: the case of a rejected job applicant.

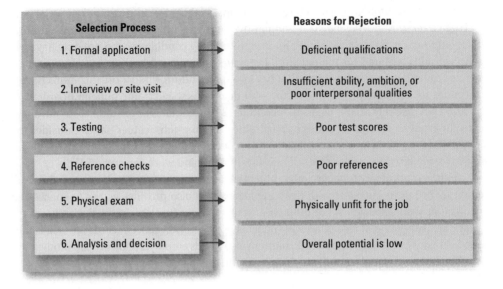

Application Forms

The application form declares the individual as a formal candidate for a job. It documents the applicant's personal history and qualifications. The personal resumé is often included with the job application. This important document should accurately summarize an applicant's special qualifications. As a job applicant, you should exercise great care in preparing your resumé for job searches. See the Student Portfolio section in the end-of-text *Management Learning Workbook* for advice. As a recruiter, you should also learn how to screen applications and resumés for insights that can help you make good selection decisions.

Interviews

Interviews are times in the selection process when both the job applicant and potential employer can learn a lot about one another. However, they can be difficult for both parties. Sometimes interviewers ask the wrong things, sometimes they talk too much, sometimes the wrong people do the interviewing, and sometimes their personal biases prevent an applicant's capabilities from being fully considered. Interviewees fail, too. They may be unprepared, they may be poor communicators, or they may lack interpersonal skills. An increasingly common and challenging interview setting for job applicants is highlighted in *Manager's Notepad 12.2—* the telephone interview.

■ **Reliability** means a selection device gives consistent results over repeated measures.

■ **Validity** means scores on a selection device have demonstrated links with future job performance.

■ An **assessment centre** examines how job candidates handle simulated work situations.

Employment Tests

Testing is often used in the screening of job applicants. Some of the common employment tests are designed to identify intelligence, aptitudes, personality, and interests. Whenever tests are used, the goal should be to gather information that will help predict the applicant's eventual performance success. Like any selection device, tests should meet the criteria of reliability and validity. **Reliability** means that the device is consistent in measurement; it returns the same results time after time. **Validity** means that there is a demonstrable relationship between a person's score or rating on a selection device and his or her eventual job performance. In simple terms, validity means that a good test score really does predict good performance.

New developments in testing extend the process into actual demonstrations of job-relevant skills and personal characteristics. An **assessment centre** evaluates a person's

MANAGER'S
Notepad 12.2

How to succeed in a telephone interview

- Be prepared ahead of time—study the organization, carefully list your strengths and capabilities.

- Take the call in private—make sure you are in a quiet room, with privacy and without the possibility of interruptions.

- Dress professionally—don't be casual; dressing right increases confidence and sets a tone for your side of the conversation.

- Practise your interview "voice"—your impression will be made quickly; how you sound counts; it even helps to stand up while you talk.

- Have reference materials handy—your resumé and other supporting documents should be within easy reach.

- Have a list of questions ready—don't be caught hesitating; intersperse your best questions during the interview.

- Ask what happens next—find out how to follow up by telephone, email, etc.; ask what other information you can provide.

potential by observing his or her performance in experiential activities designed to simulate daily work. A related approach is **work sampling**, which asks applicants to work on actual job tasks while being graded by observers on their performance. When Mercedes opened a new plant, it set up job-specific exercises to determine who had the best of the required skills and attitudes.[38] One was a tire-changing test, with colour-coded bolts and a set of instructions. As Charlene Paige took the test, she went slowly and carefully followed directions; two men with her changed the tires really fast. Charlene got the job and soon worked into a team leader position.[39]

■ In **work sampling** applicants are evaluated while performing actual work tasks.

Reference and Background Checks

Reference checks are inquiries to previous employers, academic advisors, co-workers, and/or acquaintances regarding the qualifications, experience, and past work records of a job applicant. Although they may be biased if friends are prearranged "to say the right things if called," reference checks are important. The Society for Human Resource Management estimates that 25 percent of job applications and resumés contain errors.[40] Infocheck Ltd., in their second annual resumé fraud study, found that 33 percent of final candidates had purposefully embellished their resumé.[41] Reference checks can better inform the potential employer. They can also help add credibility to the candidate if they back up what is said in an application.

Physical Examinations

Most organizations that do require medical/physical examinations are required to make it a post-offer condition of employment and justify this requirement. Under the Human Rights Code, employers cannot discriminate based on an assumption of physical disability. The same goes for drug testing, where the onus is on the employer to prove it is relevant to the position. This is often difficult to do, and also a significant privacy issue.

Final Decisions to Hire or Reject

The best selection decisions are most likely to be those involving extensive consultation among an applicant, future manager, or team leader and co-workers, as well as the human resource staff. Importantly, the emphasis in selection should be comprehensive and should focus on the person's capacity to perform well. Just as a "good fit" can produce long-term advantage, a "bad fit" can be the source of many long-term problems.

✓ Learning check ❸

BE SURE YOU CAN
• explain the difference between internal recruitment and external recruitment • discuss the value of realistic job previews to employers and job candidates • differentiate reliability and validity as two criteria of selection devices • illustrate the operation of an assessment centre • discuss the importance of conducting background and reference checks

DEVELOPING A QUALITY WORKFORCE

■ **Socialization** systematically influences the expectations, behaviour, and attitudes of new employees.

When people join an organization, they must "learn the ropes" and become familiar with "the way things are done." It is important to help newcomers fit into the work environment in a way that furthers their development and performance potential. **Socialization** is the process of influencing the expectations, behaviour, and attitudes of a new employee in a desirable way.[42]

●●● EMPLOYEE ORIENTATION

■ **Orientation** familiarizes new employees with jobs, co-workers, and organizational policies and services.

Socialization of newcomers begins with **orientation**—a set of activities designed to familiarize new employees with their jobs, co-workers, and key aspects of the organization as a whole. This includes clarifying mission and culture, explaining operating objectives and job expectations, and communicating policies and procedures. At the Disney World Resort in Buena Vista, Florida, each employee is carefully selected and trained to provide high-quality customer service as a "cast member." During orientation, newly hired employees are taught the corporate culture. They learn that everyone employed by the company, regardless of her or his specific job—be it entertainer, ticket seller, or groundskeeper—is there "to make the customer happy." The company's interviewers say that they place a premium on personality. "We can train for skills," says an HRM specialist. "We want people who are enthusiastic, who have pride in their work, who can take charge of a situation without supervision."[43]

The first six months of employment are often crucial in determining how well someone is going to fit in and perform over the long run. It is a time when the original expectations are tested and patterns are set for future relationships between an individual and employer. Unfortunately, orientation is sometimes neglected and newcomers are often left to fend for themselves. They may learn job and organizational routines on their own or through casual interactions with co-workers, and they may acquire job attitudes the same way.[44] The result is that otherwise well-intentioned and capable persons may learn the wrong things and pick up bad attitudes and habits. A good orientation, like Disney's, can set the stage for high performance, job satisfaction, and work enthusiasm.

●●● TRAINING AND DEVELOPMENT

■ **Training** provides learning opportunities to acquire and improve job-related skills.

Training is a set of activities that helps people acquire and improve job-related skills. This applies both to initial training of an employee and to upgrading or improving skills to meet changing job requirements. Progressive organizations invest in extensive training and development programs to ensure that their workers always have the capabilities needed to perform well.

On-the-Job Training

On-the-job training takes place in the work setting while someone is doing a job. A common approach is job rotation that allows people to spend time working in different jobs and thus expanding the range of their job capabilities. Another is **coaching**, in which an experienced person provides performance advice to someone else. In 2003, the Campbell Soup Company of Canada brought in a formal coaching strategy that started at the executive level and filtered down through the organization. A five-month Inspired Growth leadership program, just one of the four pillars of the initiative, has helped employees create a higher sense of awareness of their own values and strengths, and has re-engaged them in the organization. As a result Campbell's can better nurture and retain top talent, improve business, and encourage innovation.[45] One form of coaching is **mentoring**, in which early-career employees are formally assigned as proteges to senior persons. The mentoring relationship gives them regular access to advice on developing skills and becoming better informed about the organization. **Modelling** is an informal type of coaching. It occurs when someone demonstrates, through day-to-day personal behaviour, that which is expected of others. One way to learn managerial skills, for example, is to observe and practise the techniques displayed by good managers. Modelling is a very important influence on behaviour in organizations. A good example is how the behaviours of senior managers help set the ethical culture and standards for other employees.

> ■ **Coaching** occurs as an experienced person offers performance advice to a less-experienced person.

> ■ **Mentoring** assigns early career employees as proteges to more senior ones.

> ■ **Modelling** uses personal behaviour to demonstrate performance expected of others.

Off-the-Job Training

Off-the-job training is accomplished outside the work setting. An important form is **management development**, designed to improve a person's knowledge and skill in the fundamentals of management. For example, *beginning managers* often benefit from training that emphasizes team leadership and communication; *middle managers* may benefit from training to better understand multi-functional viewpoints; *top managers* may benefit from

> ■ **Management development** is training to improve knowledge and skills in the management process.

advanced management training to sharpen their decision-making and negotiating skills, and to expand their awareness of corporate strategy and direction. At the Center for Creative Leadership, managers learn by participating in the "looking glass" simulation that models the pressures of daily work. The simulation is followed by extensive debriefings and discussions in which participants give feedback to one another. One participant commented, "You can look in the mirror but you don't see yourself. People have to say how you look."[46]

●●● PERFORMANCE MANAGEMENT SYSTEMS

An important part of human resource management is design and implementation of a successful **performance management system**. This is a system that ensures that performance standards and objectives are set, that performance is regularly assessed for accomplishments, and that actions are taken to improve future performance.

Purpose of Performance Appraisal

The process of formally assessing someone's work accomplishments and providing feedback is **performance appraisal**. It serves both evaluation and development purposes. The *evaluation purpose* is intended to let people know where they stand relative to performance objectives and standards. The *development purpose* is intended to assist in their training and continued personal development.[47]

The evaluation purpose of performance appraisal focuses on past performance and measures results against standards. Performance is documented for the record and to establish a basis for allocating rewards. The manager acts in a *judgemental role* in which he or she gives a direct evaluation of another person's accomplishments. The development purpose of performance appraisal, by contrast, focuses on future performance and the clarification of success standards. It is a way of discovering performance obstacles and identifying training and development opportunities. Here the manager acts in a counselling role, focusing on the other person's developmental needs.

Like employment tests, any performance appraisal method can fulfill these purposes only when the criteria of *reliability* and *validity* are met. To be reliable, the method should consistently yield the same result, over time and/or for different raters; to be valid, it should be unbiased and measure only factors directly relevant to job performance. Both these criteria are especially important in today's complex legal environment. A manager who hires, fires, or promotes someone is increasingly called upon to defend such actions—sometimes in response to lawsuits alleging that the actions were discriminatory. At a minimum, written documentation of performance appraisals and a record of consistent past actions will be required to back up any contested evaluations.

Performance Appraisal Methods

Organizations use a variety of performance appraisal methods.[48] One of the simplest is a **graphic rating scale** in which appraisers complete checklists of traits or performance characteristics. A manager rates the individual on each item using a numerical score. Although this approach is quick and easy to complete, its reliability and validity are questionable.

A more advanced approach is the **behaviourally anchored rating scale** (BARS), which describes actual behaviours that exemplify various levels of performance achievement in a job. Look at the case of a customer service representative illustrated in *Figure 12.4*. "Extremely poor" performance is clearly defined as rude or disrespectful treatment of a customer. Because performance assessments are anchored to specific descriptions of work behaviour, a

> ■ A **performance management system** sets standards, assesses results, and plans for performance improvements.

> ■ **Performance appraisal** is the process of formally evaluating performance and providing feedback to a job holder.

> ■ A **graphic rating scale** uses a checklist of traits or characteristics to evaluate performance.

> ■ A **behaviourally anchored rating scale** (BARS) uses specific descriptions of actual behaviours to rate various levels of performance.

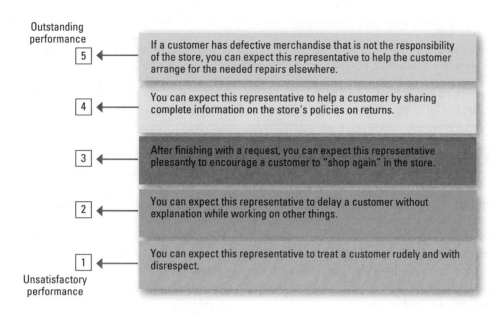

Outstanding
performance

5 — If a customer has defective merchandise that is not the responsibility of the store, you can expect this representative to help the customer arrange for the needed repairs elsewhere.

4 — You can expect this representative to help a customer by sharing complete information on the store's policies on returns.

3 — After finishing with a request, you can expect this representative pleasantly to encourage a customer to "shop again" in the store.

2 — You can expect this representative to delay a customer without explanation while working on other things.

1 — You can expect this representative to treat a customer rudely and with disrespect.

Unsatisfactory
performance

Figure 12.4 Sample behaviourally anchored rating scale for performance appraisal.

BARS is more reliable and valid than the graphic rating scale. The behavioural anchors can also be helpful in training people to master job skills of demonstrated performance importance.

The **critical-incident technique** involves keeping a running log or inventory of effective and ineffective job behaviours. By creating a written record of positive and negative performance examples, this method documents success or failure patterns that can be specifically discussed with the individual. Using the case of the customer service representative again, a critical-incidents log might contain the following types of entries: *Positive example*—"Took extraordinary care of a customer who had purchased a defective item from a company store in another city"; *negative example*—"Acted rudely in dismissing the complaint of a customer who felt that a sale item was erroneously advertised."

■ The **critical-incident technique** keeps a log of someone's effective and ineffective job behaviours.

Some performance management systems use **multiperson comparisons**, which formally compare one person's performance with that of one or more others. Such comparisons can be used on their own or in combination with some other method. They can also be done in different ways. In *rank ordering*, all persons being rated are arranged in order of performance achievement. The best performer goes at the top of the list, the worst performer at the bottom; no ties are allowed. In *paired comparisons*, each person is formally compared with every other person and rated as either the superior or the weaker member of the pair. After all paired comparisons are made, each person is assigned a summary ranking based on the number of superior scores achieved. In *forced distribution*, each person is placed into a frequency distribution that requires that a certain percentage fall into specific performance classifications, such as top 10 percent, next 40 percent, next 40 percent, and bottom 10 percent.

■ A **multiperson comparison** compares one person's performance with that of others.

Not all performance appraisals are completed only by one's immediate boss. It is increasingly popular today to expand the role of a job's stakeholders in the appraisal process. The new workplace often involves use of *peer appraisal*, including in the process others who work regularly and directly with a job holder, and *upward appraisal*, including in the process subordinates reporting to the job holder. An even broader stakeholder approach is known as **360° feedback**, where superiors, subordinates, peers, and even internal and external customers are involved in the appraisal of a job holder's performance.[49]

■ **360° feedback** includes in the appraisal process superiors, subordinates, peers, and even customers.

MAINTAINING A QUALITY WORKFORCE

It is not enough to attract and develop workers with the talents to achieve high-performance results for the short term only. They must be successfully retained, nurtured, and managed for long-term effectiveness. When adverse turnover occurs and talented workers leave to pursue other opportunities, the resulting costs for the employer can be staggering. When the Society for Human Resource Management surveyed employers to identify the most effective tools for maintaining a quality workforce, they found the following: good benefits—especially health care, competitive salaries, flexible work schedules and personal time off, and opportunities for training and development.[50]

●●● CAREER DEVELOPMENT

■ A **career** is a sequence of jobs that constitutes what a person does for a living.

In his book *The Age of Unreason*, British scholar and consultant Charles Handy discusses dramatic new developments in the world of work and careers. Specifically, Handy says, "The times are changing and we must change with them."[51] A **career** is a sequence of jobs and work pursuits that constitutes what a person does for a living. For many of us, a career begins on an anticipatory basis with our formal education. From there it progresses into an initial job choice and any number of subsequent choices that may involve changes in task assignments, employing organizations, and even occupations. A *career path* is a sequence of jobs held over time during a career. Career paths vary between those that are pursued internally with the same employers and those pursued externally among various employers. Sobeys Inc., a national grocery retailer based in Stellarton, N.S., has developed career ladders to support its people, performance, and development strategy. With over 35,000 employees in more than 1,300 company stores and franchises across Canada, Sobeys's objective is to better define career paths for both store and office employees. Stephanie Curtis Sood, a HR advisor for the company, says, "We want to better position Sobeys as an organization where you can build a rewarding career."[52] Although many organizations place great emphasis on making long-term career opportunities available to their employees, Handy believes that external career paths will be increasingly important in the future.

■ **Career planning** is the process of matching career goals and individual capabilities with opportunities for their fulfillment.

Career planning is the process of systematically matching career goals and individual capabilities with opportunities for their fulfillment. It involves answering questions such as "Who am I?," "Where do I want to go?," and "How do I get there?" While some suggest that a career should be allowed to progress in a somewhat random but always opportunistic way, others view a career as something to be rationally planned and pursued in a logical step-by-step fashion. In fact, a well-managed career will probably include elements of each. The carefully thought-out plan can point you in a general career direction; an eye for opportunity can fill in the details along the way.

■ A **career plateau** is a position from which someone is unlikely to move to a higher level of work responsibility.

When you think about adult life stages or transitions, you should recognize that sooner or later most people's careers level off. A **career plateau** is a position from which someone is unlikely to move to a higher level of work responsibility.[53] Three common reasons for career plateaus are personal choice, limited abilities, and lack of opportunity. For some, the plateau may occur at a point in life when it suits their individual needs. For others, such as employees

take it to the case!

RBC Financial Group
Taking care of people makes good business sense
Started in 1864, Royal Bank of Canada (part of the RBC Financial Group) has grown to become one of Canada's largest banks, holding over $450 billion in assets and employing over 60,000 people worldwide. To ensure continued growth, RBC implements strategic human resources policies and practices with ambitious goals to increase the diversity and flexibility of its workforce. At present, half of all managers at RBC are women, and women hold over one third of senior management positions, with an additional nine percent being held by visible minorities. RBC is also committed to employee development through a comprehensive recognition program and a total rewards philosophy, with HR policies that encourage flexibility in compensation, benefits, professional development, and work-life balance. Does focusing on employee development help RBC succeed? Read the case in the *Management Learning Workbook* to find out!

Source: With information from the corporate website: <www.rbc.com>.

within 10 to 15 years of retirement age, plateaus can be very frustrating. Progressive employers seek ways to engage them with new opportunities in lateral moves, mentoring assignments, and even overseas jobs. Susan Peters, vice-president for executive development at GE, says: "Suddenly they come to a stage when they may have more flexibility to take a foreign assignment or do something they couldn't at a younger age."[54] She strongly believes in the value of broad experience and the willingness to pursue opportunities through lateral career moves.

●●● WORK–LIFE BALANCE

"Hiring good people is tough," starts an article in the *Harvard Business Review*. The sentence finishes with, "keeping them can be even tougher."[55] A very important retention issue given today's fast-paced and complicated lifestyles is **work–life balance**—how people balance the demands of careers with their personal and family needs. "Family" in this context includes not just children but also elderly parents and other relatives in need of care. Human resource practices that support a healthy work–life balance are increasingly valued, with the chapter case on the SAS Institute a good example.

■ **Work–life balance** involves balancing career demands with personal and family needs.

    Included among work–life balance concerns are the unique needs of *single parents*, who must balance parenting responsibilities with a job, and *dual-career couples*, who must balance the career needs and opportunities of each partner. The special situations of both working mothers and working fathers are also being recognized.[56] Not surprisingly, the "family-friendliness" of an employer is now frequently and justifiably used as a screening criterion by job candidates. *Business Week*, *Maclean's*, and *Fortune* are among the magazines annually ranking employers on this criterion.

●●● COMPENSATION AND BENEFITS

Good compensation and benefit systems attract qualified people to the organization and help retain them. **Base compensation**, in the form of salary or hourly wages, can help get

■ **Base compensation** is a salary or hourly wage paid to an individual.

■ **Fringe benefits** are non-monetary forms of compensation such as life insurance and retirement plans.

■ **Flexible benefits** programs allow employees to choose from a range of benefit options.

■ **Family-friendly benefits** help employees achieve better work–life balance.

■ **Employee assistance programs** help employees cope with personal stresses and problems.

the right people into jobs to begin with and keep them there by making outside opportunities less attractive. Unless an organization's prevailing wage and salary structure is competitive in the relevant labour markets, it will be difficult to attract and retain a staff of highly competent workers. Also important are **fringe benefits**, the additional nonwage or nonsalary forms of compensation. Benefit packages can constitute some 30 percent or more of a typical worker's earnings. They usually include various options on disability protection, life insurance, and retirement plans.

The ever-rising cost of fringe benefits, particularly employee medical benefits, is a major worry for employers. Some are attempting to gain control over health care costs by encouraging healthy lifestyles. An increasingly common approach, overall, is **flexible benefits**, sometimes known as *cafeteria benefits*, which lets the employee choose a set of benefits within a certain dollar amount. The growing significance of work–life balance in the new social contract is also reflected in a trend toward more **family-friendly benefits** that help employees better balance work and nonwork responsibilities. These include child care, eldercare, flexible schedules, parental leave, and part-time employment options, among others. The best employers also offer **employee assistance programs** that help employees deal with troublesome personal problems. EAPs may include assistance in dealing with stress, counselling on alcohol and substance abuse problems, referrals for domestic violence and sexual abuse, family and marital counselling, and advice on community resources.

CANADIAN COMPANY IN THE NEWS   Pratt & Whitney Canada

PUTTING EMPLOYEES FIRST

In addition to having access to fitness centres, daycare, and recreation clubs, employees at Pratt & Whitney Canada can sign up for a variety of courses and academic programs, including flying lessons! P&WC was the first company in Canada to offer employees free first-aid training during work hours. The company has about 10 reward programs designed to recognize staff for personal and collective achievements. For example, the "Pioneers of Our Future" program rewards successful teams that have helped the company achieve its business objectives. P&WC also provides funding for staff members who want to become adoptive parents. And it encourages employees to commit to their communities through programs like matching gift, mini-grants, and volunteer team efforts.

Source: "An Employer of Choice," *Canadian Business*, Advertising Supplement, Nov. 21–Dec. 4, 2005.

●●● **RETENTION AND TURNOVER**

The several steps in the human resource management process both conclude and recycle with *replacement* decisions. These involve the management of promotions, transfers, terminations, layoffs, and retirements. Any replacement situation is an opportunity to review human resource plans, update job analyses, rewrite job descriptions and job specifications, and ensure that the best people are selected to perform the required tasks.

Some replacement decisions shift people between positions within the organization. *Promotion* is movement to a higher-level position; *transfer* is movement to a different job at a similar level of responsibility. Another set of replacement decisions relates to *retirement*, something most people look forward to…until it is close at hand. Then the prospect of being retired often raises fears and apprehensions. Many organizations offer special counselling and other forms of support for retiring employees, including advice on company benefits, money management, estate planning, and use of leisure time.

The most extreme replacement decisions involve *termination*, the involuntary and permanent dismissal of an employee. In some cases the termination is based on performance problems. The person involved is not meeting the requirements of the job or has violated key organizational policy. In other cases the termination may be due to financial conditions of the employer, such as those requiring downsizing or restructuring. The persons involved may be performing well but are being terminated as part of a workforce reduction. Where possible, organizations may provide outplacement services to help terminated employees find other jobs. In any and all cases, terminations should be handled fairly according to organizational policies and in full legal compliance. They should show respect for the person being dismissed, who may well find it hard to accept the decision.

●●● LABOUR–MANAGEMENT RELATIONS

A final aspect of human resource management involves the role of organized labour. **Labour unions** are organizations, to which workers belong, that deal with employers on the workers' behalf.[57] Although they used to be associated primarily with industrial and business occupations, labour unions now represent such public-sector employees as teachers, university professors, police officers, and government workers. They are important forces in the modern workplace both in Canada and around the world. About 30 percent of Canadian workers belong to a union; the figures are around 13 percent for the United States and closer to 25 percent in Great Britain.[58]

> ■ A **labour union** is an organization that deals with employers on the workers' collective behalf.

Labour unions act as a collective "voice" for members in dealing with employers. They serve as bargaining agents that negotiate legal contracts affecting many aspects of the employment relationship. These **labour contracts**, for example, typically specify the rights and obligations of employees and management with respect to wages, work hours, work rules, seniority, hiring, grievances, and other conditions of employment. All of this has implications for management. In a unionized work setting, the labour contract and its legal implications must be considered when making human resource management decisions.

> ■ A **labour contract** is a formal agreement between a union and employer about the terms of work for union members.

The foundation of any labour and management relationship is **collective bargaining**, which is the process of negotiating, administering, and interpreting labour contracts. Labour contracts and the collective bargaining process—from negotiating a new contract to resolving disputes under an existing one—are major influences on human resource management in unionized work settings. In Canada, national and international unions are closely governed by the Canadian Labour Congress, which promotes unionism and protection of member rights. In addition, the Canada Labour Code, provincial labour relations acts, and provincial acts like the *Trade Unions Act* in Saskatchewan or the *Labour Relations Act* in Ontario provides guidelines for employer and unions regarding certification, negotiation and management of collective agreements, and arbitration.[59]

> ■ **Collective bargaining** is the process of negotiating, administering, and interpreting a labour contract.

The collective bargaining process typically occurs in face-to-face meetings between labour and management representatives. During this time, a variety of demands, proposals, and counterproposals are exchanged. Several rounds of bargaining may be required before a contract is reached or a dispute over a contract issue is resolved. And, as you might expect, the process can lead to problems. In *Figure 12.5*, labour and management are viewed as "win-lose" adversaries destined to be in opposition and possessed of certain weapons with which to fight one another. If labour–management relations take this form, a lot of energy on both sides can be expended in prolonged conflict. This adversarial approach is, to some extent, giving way to a new and more progressive era of greater co-operation. Each side seems more willing to understand the need for co-operation and mutual adjustment to new and challenging times.

Figure 12.5 The traditional adversarial view of labour–management relations.

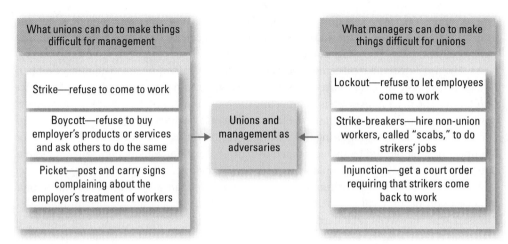

What unions can do to make things difficult for management

- Strike—refuse to come to work
- Boycott—refuse to buy employer's products or services and ask others to do the same
- Picket—post and carry signs complaining about the employer's treatment of workers

Unions and management as adversaries

What managers can do to make things difficult for unions

- Lockout—refuse to let employees come to work
- Strike-breakers—hire non-union workers, called "scabs," to do strikers' jobs
- Injunction—get a court order requiring that strikers come back to work

✓ Learning check ⑤

BE SURE YOU CAN

• define the terms career plateau and work–life balance • discuss the significance of each term for the human resource management process • explain why compensation and benefits are important elements in human resource management • define the terms labour union, labour contract, and collective bargaining • compare the adversarial and co-operative approaches to labour–management relations

●●● Chapter 12 STUDY GUIDE

WHERE WE'VE BEEN

Back to Dofasco

The opening example of Dofasco introduced how organizations can outperform the competition by highlighting the importance of human resource activities within their strategic organizational goals. In this chapter you learned about the human resource management process, the legal environment that governs this process, and the managerial responsibilities through which decisions are made and actions taken to ensure that organizations always attract, develop, and maintain a talented workforce capable of creating high-performance results.

THE NEXT STEP
INTEGRATED LEARNING ACTIVITIES

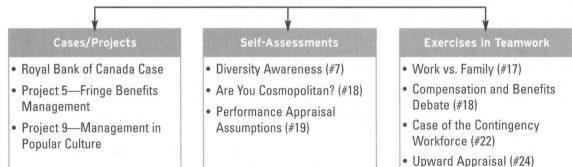

Cases/Projects

- Royal Bank of Canada Case
- Project 5—Fringe Benefits Management
- Project 9—Management in Popular Culture

Self-Assessments

- Diversity Awareness (#7)
- Are You Cosmopolitan? (#18)
- Performance Appraisal Assumptions (#19)

Exercises in Teamwork

- Work vs. Family (#17)
- Compensation and Benefits Debate (#18)
- Case of the Contingency Workforce (#22)
- Upward Appraisal (#24)

STUDY QUESTION SUMMARY

1. Why do people make the difference?

- Even in this age of information, high technology, and globalization, people are irreplaceable assets that make organizations work.

- Organizations with positive human resource policies and practices are gaining significant performance advantages.

- The challenges of complexity and uncertainty in highly competitive environments are best met by a diverse and talented workforce.

- The diversity advantage is gained only when the talents of all persons, regardless of personal characteristics, are respected and given the opportunity to be displayed.

2. What is strategic human resource management?

- The human resource management process involves attracting, developing, and maintaining a quality workforce.

- Human resource management becomes strategic when it is integrated into the organization's strategic leadership.

- Human resource management is influenced by a complex and changing legal environment.

- Employment equity guarantees people the right to employment and advancement without discrimination.

- Current legal issues in HRM include sexual harassment, comparable worth, rights of independent contractors, and employee privacy.

3. How do organizations attract a quality workforce?

- Human resource planning is the process of analyzing staffing needs and identifying actions to satisfy these needs over time.

- The purpose of human resource planning is to make sure the organization always has people with the right abilities available to do the required work.

- Recruitment is the process of attracting qualified job candidates to fill vacant positions.

- Realistic job previews provide candidates with accurate information on the job and organization.

- Managers use interviews, employment tests, and references to help make selection decisions; the use of assessment centres and work sampling is becoming more common.

4. How do organizations develop a quality workforce?

- Orientation is the process of formally introducing new employees to their jobs, performance expectations, and the organization.

- On-the-job training includes coaching, apprenticeship, modelling, and mentoring; off-the-job training includes formal programs, such as management development courses.

- Performance management systems establish work standards and the means for assessing performance results.

- Common performance appraisal methods are graphic rating scales, narratives, behaviourally anchored rating scales, and multiperson comparisons.

5. How do organizations maintain a quality workforce?

- Career planning systematically matches individual career goals and capabilities with opportunities for their fulfillment.

- Programs that address work–life balance and the complex demands of job and family responsibilities are increasingly important in human resource management.

- Compensation and benefits packages must be continually updated so that the organization stays competitive in labour markets.

- Whenever workers must be replaced through promotions, transfers, retirements, and/or terminations, the goal should be to treat everyone fairly while ensuring that remaining jobs are filled with the best personnel available.

- In collective bargaining situations, labour–management relations should be positively approached and handled with all due consideration of applicable laws.

KEY TERMS REVIEW

Assessment centre (p. 294)

Base compensation (p. 301)

Behaviourally anchored rating scale (BARS) (p. 298)

Bona fide occupational requirements (p. 289)

Career (p. 300)

Career planning (p. 300)

Career plateau (p. 300)

Coaching (p. 297)

Collective bargaining (p. 303)

Comparable worth (p. 290)

Critical-incident technique (p. 299)

Discrimination (p. 289)

Employee assistance program (p. 302)

Employment equity (p. 289)

Family-friendly benefits (p. 302)

Flexible benefits (p. 302)

Fringe benefits (p. 302)

Graphic rating scale (p. 298)

Human capital (p. 285)

Human resource management (p. 287)

Human resource planning (p. 291)

Independent contractor (p. 290)

Job analysis (p. 291)

Job description (p. 291)

Job specification (p. 292)

Labour contract (p. 303)

Labour union (p. 303)

Management development (p. 297)

Mentoring (p. 297)

Modelling (p. 297)

Multiperson comparison (p. 299)

Orientation (p. 296)

Performance appraisal (p. 298)

Performance management system (p. 298)

Realistic job preview (p. 293)

Recruitment (p. 292)

Reliability (p. 294)

Selection (p. 293)

Sexual harassment (p. 289)

Social contract (p. 284)

Socialization (p. 296)

Strategic human resource management (p. 287)

360° feedback (p. 299)

Training (p. 296)

Validity (p. 294)

Work sampling (p. 295)

Work–life balance (p. 301)

Workplace privacy (p. 291)

SELF-TEST 12

MULTIPLE-CHOICE QUESTIONS:

1. Human resource management is the process of _____, developing, and maintaining a high-quality workforce.
    (a) attracting (b) compensating (c) appraising (d) selecting

2. A _____ is a criterion that can be legally justified for use in screening candidates for employment.
    (a) job description (b) bona fide occupational requirement (c) job specification (d) BARS

3. _____ programs are designed to ensure employment equity for persons historically unrepresented in the workforce.
    (a) Realistic recruiting (b) External recruiting (c) Employment equity (d) Employee assistance

4. An employment test that yields different results over time when taken by the same person should be replaced because it lacks _____.
    (a) validity (b) specificity (c) realism (d) reliability

5. The assessment centre approach to employee selection relies heavily on _____.
    (a) pencil-and-paper tests (b) simulations and experiential exercises (c) 360° feedback (d) formal one-on-one interviews

6. _____ is a form of on-the-job training wherein an individual learns by observing others who demonstrate desirable job behaviours.
    (a) Mentoring (b) Work sampling (c) Modelling (d) Simulation

7. The first step in human resource planning is to _____.
    (a) forecast human resource needs (b) forecast labour supplies (c) assess the existing workforce (d) review organizational mission, objectives, and strategies

8. Socialization of newcomers occurs during the _____ step of the staffing process.
    (a) recruiting (b) orientation (c) selecting (d) training

9. In human resource planning, a(n) _____ is used to determine exactly what is done in an existing job.
    (a) critical-incident technique (b) assessment centre (c) job analysis (d) multiperson comparison

10. In what is called the new "social contract" between employers and employees, the implications for the individual include accepting more personal responsibility for _____.
    (a) learning and mobility (b) salary negotiation (c) labour–management relations (d) socialization

11. The _____ purpose of performance appraisal is being addressed when a manager describes training options that might help an employee improve future performance.
    (a) development (b) evaluation (c) judgemental (d) legal

12. When a team leader is required to rate 10 percent of team members as "superior," 80 percent as "good," and 10 percent as "unacceptable" for their performance on a project, this is an example of the _____ approach to performance appraisal.
    (a) graphic (b) forced distribution (c) behaviourally anchored rating scale (d) realistic

13. An employee with family problems that are starting to interfere with work would be pleased to learn that his employer had a(n) _____ plan to help on such matters.
    (a) employee assistance (b) cafeteria benefits (c) comparable worth (d) collective bargaining

14. A manager who _____ is displaying a commitment to valuing human capital.
    (a) believes payroll costs should be reduced wherever possible (b) is always looking for new ways to replace people with machines (c) protects workers from stress by withholding from them information about the organization's performance (d) views people as assets to be nurtured and developed over time

SHORT-RESPONSE QUESTIONS:

15. How do internal recruitment and external recruitment compare in terms of advantages and disadvantages for the employer?

16. Why is orientation an important part of the staffing process?

17. What is the difference between the graphic rating scale and the BARS as performance appraisal methods?

18. How does mentoring work as a form of on-the-job training?

APPLICATION QUESTION:

19. Sy Smith is not doing well in his job. The problems began to appear shortly after Sy's job was changed from a manual to a computer-based operation. He has tried hard, but is just not doing well in learning to use the computer and meet performance expectations. As a 55-year-old employee with over 30 years with the company, Sy is both popular and influential among his work peers. Along with his performance problems, you have also noticed the appearance of some negative attitudes, including a tendency for Sy to sometimes "badmouth" the firm. As Sy's manager, what options would you consider in terms of dealing with the issue of his retention in the job and in the company? What would you do and why?

13

Leading

●●● CHAPTER 13 STUDY QUESTIONS

1. What is the nature of leadership?

2. What are the important leadership traits and behaviours?

3. What are the contingency theories of leadership?

4. What is transformational leadership?

5. What are current issues in leadership development?

Planning Ahead

After reading Chapter 13, you should be able to answer these questions in your own words.

Leading with vision,

Cordon bleu, and spirituality

J.-Robert Ouimet of Ouimet-Cordon Bleu Foods is a leader with the unique vision of "reconciling human happiness with business profitability." As a strategic leader, Ouimet's accomplishments have earned him the Order of Quebec, the Order of Canada, and directorships on the boards of a number of organizations. He has expanded his small family business to become one of the top 50 food companies in Canada. Ouimet is quoted as saying, "I have only four competitors: Campbell's, Heinz, Maple Leaf, and Chef Boyardee.... They are Goliaths, we are David."

Ouimet isn't known only for his strategic leadership, but more for the personal vision that has always been a part of his business career. Personal faith is important to Ouimet, and he has sought the advice of spiritual leaders such as the Dalai Lama and Mother Teresa, who made a private visit to one of his plants in 1988. Spiritual principles have led Ouimet in developing a number of the management tools he advocates, including silence or meditation rooms, gestures of reconciliation, time set aside for reflection and/or prayer, and authentic communication. Ouimet believes these tools are an important way to "increase not only human happiness and well-being, but company profitability." To prove his theories, Ouimet tested them while writing his Ph.D. thesis. He has taken his ideas on the road, speaking to other companies and leaders and also to more than 167 public conferences and presentations in North America, Europe, the Middle East, the Far East, and Asia.

It is not just his 400 employees who benefit from Ouimet's strong belief and vision, his customers do

as well. He notes, "[our] experience reconciling human happiness with business profitability has influenced the content of our product, the packaging, the pricing, and the promotion." The logo on the beef gravy states, "Cordon Bleu has you at heart." This packaging reflects that the product is low in fat and salt content, but also that the company combines the goal of profitability with efforts to provide information that satisfies the needs of the consumer. "That's the process that will

lead to further transformation," notes Ouimet.

While not everyone is accepting of Ouimet's philosophy, there can be no doubt about his success. By seeing "consumers as individual human beings—very precious, one by one" and not only as potential profits, and perhaps by advising business leaders to "seek guidance from on high, not just from the bottom line," Ouimet has created a leadership profile that is all his own.[1]

IN THE WORKPLACE

Sheri Coombs is sitting in your cubicle and lamenting that she doesn't have the power to get things done. She has lots of great ideas that seem to go nowhere and finds it frustrating. She is not the type of person who likes to just respond to questions asked; she wants to make things happen but has no title to allow her to command people to do things. In one of your reflective moods, you offer that position power is only one way to get things done. Since she does not have "reward, coercive, or legitimate" power, she will have to work on influencing people in other ways. "Such as?" Sheri asks. You loan Sheri your copy of the Management text and ask her to review the two bases of personal power.

●●● **Chapter 13** ●●●

J.-Robert Ouimet exemplifies the importance of leadership through unique personal vision and values, and commitment to his employees and customers. Ouimet is an example of a leader who invests himself fully in the responsibilities of leadership. In this chapter you will learn about leadership concepts and the various approaches taken by scholars to understand leadership effectiveness. You will learn about the current issues in leadership development, and you will also be asked to reflect on your personal capacities to lead with excellence.

LEADING				
Study Question 1	Study Question 2	Study Question 3	Study Question 4	Study Question 5
The Nature of Leadership	**Leadership Traits and Behaviours**	**Contingency Approaches to Leadership**	**Transformational Leadership**	**Current Issues in Leadership Development**
• Leadership and vision • Power and influence • Ethics and the limits to power • Leadership and empowerment	• Search for leadership traits • Focus on leader behaviours • Classic leadership styles	• Fiedler's contingency model • Hersey-Blanchard situational leadership model • House's path-goal leadership theory • Vroom-Jago leader-participation model	• Transformational and transactional leadership • Qualities of a transformational leader	• Emotional intelligence • Gender and leadership • Drucker's "old-fashioned" leadership • Moral leadership
Learning check ❶	Learning check ❷	Learning check ❸	Learning check ❹	Learning check ❺

Rob McEwen, a former CEO and Chairman of Goldcorp Inc., described his leadership style by saying, "Challenge the NORM! I have pushed all of Goldcorp's employees to test the validity of entrenched assumptions within our mining industry. My goal is to engage the collective wisdom of Goldcorp's workforce to identify and implement alternative methods that are faster, more productive and more profitable. When achieved, this hard-earned success perpetuates growth. When we recognize the unique qualities of others, we become less inclined to believe that we alone know what is best."[2] Under his leadership, Goldcorp Inc., headquartered in Vancouver, has become a gold producer with one of the lowest production costs in the world. By valuing and respecting people, we learn how to provide them with meaningful work and opportunities. This leadership lesson extends to all types and sizes of organizations. Great leaders bring out the best in people. Consultant and author Tom Peters says that the leader is "rarely—possibly never?—the best performer."[3] They don't have to be; they thrive through, and by, the successes of others.

THE NATURE OF LEADERSHIP

Warren Bennis, a respected scholar and consultant, claims that too many North American corporations are "over-managed and under-led." The late Grace Hopper, a computer scientist and the first female admiral in the U.S. Navy, said, "You manage things; you lead people."[4] A glance at the shelves in your local bookstore will quickly confirm that **leadership**, the process of inspiring others to work hard to accomplish important tasks, is one of the most popular management topics. As shown in *Figure 13.1*, it is also one of the four functions that constitutes the management process. Planning sets the direction and objectives; organizing brings the resources together to turn plans into action; *leading* builds the commitments and enthusiasm for people to apply their talents to help accomplish plans; controlling makes sure things turn out right.

■ **Leadership** is the process of inspiring others to work hard to accomplish important tasks.

Managers today must lead under new and difficult conditions. The time frames for getting things accomplished are becoming shorter; leaders are expected to get things right the first time, with second chances few and far between; the problems to be resolved through leadership are complex, ambiguous, and multi-dimensional; leaders are expected to be long-term oriented even while meeting demands for short-term performance results.[5] Anyone aspiring to career success in leadership must rise to these challenges, and more, becoming good at communication, interpersonal relations, motivation, teamwork, and change—all topics in this final part of *Management*.

●●● LEADERSHIP AND VISION

"Great leaders," it is said, "get extraordinary things done in organizations by inspiring and motivating others toward a common purpose."[6] Frequently today, leadership is associated with **vision**—a future that one hopes to create or achieve in order to improve upon the present state of affairs. The term **visionary leadership** describes a leader who brings to the situation a clear and compelling sense of the future as well as an understanding of the actions needed to get there successfully.[7] But simply having the vision of a desirable future is not enough. Truly great leaders are extraordinarily good at turning their visions into accomplishments. This involves the ability to communicate the vision in such a way that others are willing to work hard to achieve it. Visionary leaders, simply put, inspire others to take the actions necessary to turn vision into reality. At General Electric, for example, an "A" leader is considered to be someone "…with vision and the ability to articulate that vision to the team, so vividly and powerfully that it also becomes their vision."[8]

■ A **vision** is a clear sense of the future.

■ **Visionary leadership** brings to the situation a clear sense of the future and an understanding of how to get there.

The five principles[9] for meeting the challenges of visionary leadership are:

- *Challenge the process:* Be a pioneer; encourage innovation and support people who have ideas.

- *Show enthusiasm:* Inspire others through personal enthusiasm to share in a common vision.

- *Help others to act:* Be a team player and support the efforts and talents of others.

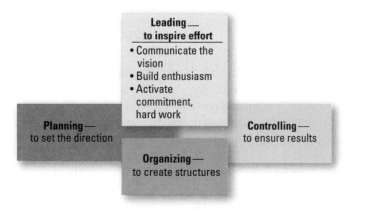

Figure 13.1 Leading viewed in relationship to the other management functions.

- *Set the example:* Provide a consistent model of how others can and should act.

- *Celebrate achievements:* Bring emotion into the workplace and rally "hearts" as well as "minds."

The suggestions go beyond a manager's responsibilities for making long-term plans and drafting budgets, putting structures in place, assigning people to jobs, and making sure that results are consistent with plans. Leading with vision means doing all these things and more. It means having a clear vision, communicating that vision to all concerned, and getting people motivated and inspired to pursue the vision in their daily work. Visionary leadership means bringing meaning to people's work, making what they do worthy and valuable. Bonnie DuPont, a vice-president and high-ranking member of Enbridge's corporate leadership team, is a leader by example and one of the most senior women in the energy sector. Dupont believes that leadership involves setting a course, providing a vision, and motivating people by giving them objectives to achieve, the tools to do the job, and the incentives to succeed.[10]

●●● POWER AND INFLUENCE

■ **Power** is the ability to get someone else to do something you want done or to make things happen the way you want.

The foundations of effective leadership lie in the way a manager uses power to influence the behaviour of other people. **Power** is the ability to get someone else to do something you want done. It is the ability to make things happen the way you want them to.[11] Research recognizes that a need for power is essential to executive success.[12] But this need for power is not a desire to control for the sake of personal satisfaction; it is a desire to influence and control others for the good of the group or organization as a whole. This "positive" face of power is the foundation of effective leadership. *Figure 13.2* shows that leaders gain power from both the positions they hold and from their personal qualities.[13]

Figure 13.2 Sources of position power and personal power used by managers.

Power of the POSITION: Based on things managers can offer to others.	Power of the PERSON: Based on how managers are viewed by others.
Rewards: "If you do what I ask, I'll give you a reward."	**Expertise** — as a source of special knowledge and information.
Coercion: "If you don't do what I ask, I'll punish you."	**Reference** — as a person with whom others like to identify.
Legitimacy: "Because I am the boss, you *must* do as I ask."	

Sources of Position Power

A manager's official status, or position, in the organization's hierarchy of authority is an important source of power. Although anyone holding a managerial position theoretically has this power, how well it is used will vary from one person to the next. Consequently, leadership success will vary as well. The three bases of *position power* are reward power, coercive power, and legitimate power.

■ **Reward power** is the capacity to offer something of value as a means of influencing other people.

Reward power is the ability to influence through rewards. It is the capability to offer something of value—a positive outcome—as a means of influencing the behaviour of other people. This involves the control of rewards or resources such as pay raises, bonuses, promotions, special assignments, and verbal or written compliments. To mobilize reward power, a manager says, in effect, "If you do what I ask, I'll give you a reward."

■ **Coercive power** is the capacity to punish or withhold positive outcomes as a means of influencing other people.

Coercive power is the ability to influence through punishment. It is the capacity to punish or withhold positive outcomes as a way to influence the behaviour of other people. A manager may attempt to coerce someone by threatening him or her with verbal reprimands, pay penalties, and even termination. To mobilize coercive power, a manager says, in effect, "If you don't do what I want, I'll punish you."

Legitimate power is the ability to influence through authority—the right, by virtue of one's organizational position or status, to exercise control over persons in subordinate positions. It is the capacity to influence the behaviour of other people by virtue of the rights of office. To mobilize legitimate power, a manager says, in effect, "I am the boss, therefore you are supposed to do as I ask."

Sources of Personal Power

The unique personal qualities of a manager are further sources of power. In fact, a truly successful leader is very good at building and using the two bases of *personal power*—expert power and referent power.

Expert power is the ability to influence through special expertise. It is the capacity to influence the behaviour of other people because of one's knowledge and skills. Expertise derives from the possession of technical understanding or information pertinent to the issue at hand. It is developed by acquiring relevant skills or competencies and by gaining a central position in relevant information networks. It is maintained by protecting one's credibility and not overstepping the boundaries of true expertise. When a manager uses expert power, the implied message is, "You should do what I want because of my special expertise or information." Rose M. Patten, senior executive vice-president of Human Resources and head of Strategic Management for BMO Financial Group, is an example of an individual developing expert leadership power early in their career. She credits her significant volunteer activity at an early age as key in developing her leadership ability. These volunteer activities resulted in a number of leadership assignments and learning opportunities. While starting early provided the basis for leadership, Patten also believes that being in the right place at the right time is important. But, this holds true only if you are willing to tackle the challenge of change with courage and plunge yourself into uncharted waters. In 2005, she was named to the list of Canada's most powerful women, while the *Human Resource Executive's* "Honour Roll" recognized her leadership in establishing workforce diversity as an integral and strategic part of BMO.[14]

Referent power is the ability to influence through identification. It is the capacity to influence the behaviour of other people because they admire you and want to identify positively with you. Reference is a power derived from charisma or interpersonal attractiveness. It is developed and maintained through good interpersonal relations that encourage the admiration and respect of others. When a manager uses referent power, the implied message is, "You should do what I want in order to maintain a positive self-defined relationship with me."

◾ **Legitimate power** is the capacity to influence other people by virtue of formal authority, or the rights of office.

◾ **Expert power** is the capacity to influence other people because of specialized knowledge.

◾ **Referent power** is the capacity to influence other people because of their desire to identify personally with you.

PERSONAL MANAGEMENT

Leadership is an interpersonal process. You either lead well or poorly in large part due to your ability to relate well to other people. Furthermore, in today's high-performance work settings, with their emphasis on horizontal structures, cross-functional teams, and projects, leading requires skillful **NETWORKING**. Within teams, across functions, and in day-to-day work encounters the best leaders get things done because they build and maintain positive working relationships with others. In the social context of organizations, there is very little you can do by yourself; the vast majority of work gets done because people in your networks help you out. For some of us, networking is as natural as walking down the street. For others, it is a big challenge in the intimidating realm of interpersonal relationships. But even if you fall into this last category, the fact remains: to be a successful leader you need networking skills. Don't underestimate the challenge; be prepared for leadership. Do you have confidence in these networking skills?

- *Network identification*—knowing and finding the right people to work with.
- *Network building*—engaging others and relating to them in positive ways.
- *Network maintenance*—actively nurturing and supporting others in their work.

Get to know yourself better

Complete Self-Assessment #20—**T-P Leadership Questionnaire**, and #22—**Least Preferred Co-Worker Scale**, from the Workbook and Personal Management Activity #13 on the companion website.

Turning Power into Influence

To succeed at leadership, managers must both acquire all types of power and use them appropriately.[15] The best leaders understand that use of the various power bases results in quite different outcomes. When one relies on rewards and legitimacy to influence others, the likely outcome is temporary compliance. The follower will do what the leader requests, but only so long as the reward continues and/or the legitimacy persists. When one relies on coercion, compliance is also temporary and dependent on the continued threat of punishment. In this case, however, the compliance is often accompanied by resentment. The use of expert and referent power has the most enduring results, creating commitment rather than compliance. Followers respond positively because of internalized understanding or beliefs that create a long-lasting impact on behaviour.

Position power and the compliance it generates are often insufficient for managers to achieve and sustain needed influence. Personal power and the resulting commitment are what often make the difference between leadership success and mediocrity. This is particularly true in today's horizontal organizations with their emphasis on teamwork and co-operation. Four points to keep in mind when building your managerial power are as follows: (1) there is no substitute for expertise, (2) likable personal qualities are very important, (3) effort and hard work breed respect, and (4) personal behaviour must match expressed values.[16]

In organizations, power and influence are also linked to where one fits and how one acts in the structures and networks of the workplace.[17] *Centrality* is important. Managers gain power by establishing networks of interpersonal contacts and getting involved in the information flows within them. They avoid becoming isolated. *Criticality* is important. To gain power, managers must take good care of others who are dependent on them. They support them exceptionally well by doing things that add value to the work setting. *Visibility* is also important. It helps to become known as an influential person in the organization. Managers gain power by performing well in formal presentations, on key task forces or committees, and in special assignments that display their talents and capabilities.

●●● ETHICS AND THE LIMITS TO POWER

On the issue of ethics and the limits to power, it is always helpful to remember Chester Barnard's *acceptance theory of authority*. He identifies four conditions that determine whether a leader's directives will be followed and true influence achieved:[18] the other person must (1) truly understand the directive, (2) feel capable of carrying out the directive, (3) believe that the directive is in the organization's best interests, and (4) believe that the directive is consistent with personal values.

In Chapter 3 it was noted that many ethical dilemmas begin when leaders and managers pressure followers to do questionable things. Using the acceptance theory of authority as a starting point, the ethical question a follower must always be prepared to ask is, "Where do I (or will I) draw the line; at what point do I (or will I) refuse to comply with requests?" Someday you may face a situation in which you are asked by someone in authority to do something that violates personal ethics and/or even the law. Can you…will you…when will you, say "no"? After all, as Barnard said, it is "acceptance" that establishes the limits of managerial power.

●●● LEADERSHIP AND EMPOWERMENT

■ **Empowerment** enables others to gain and use decision-making power.

At many points in this book we have talked about **empowerment**, the process through which managers enable and help others to gain power and achieve influence within the

MANAGER'S
Notepad 13.1

How to empower others

- Get others involved in selecting their work assignments and the methods for accomplishing tasks.

- Create an environment of co-operation, information sharing, discussion, and shared ownership of goals.

- Encourage others to take initiative, make decisions, and use their knowledge.

- When problems arise, find out what others think and let them help design the solutions.

- Stay out of the way; give others the freedom to put their ideas and solutions into practice.

- Maintain high morale and confidence by recognizing successes and encouraging high performance.

organization. Effective leaders empower others by providing them with the information, responsibility, authority, and trust to make decisions and act independently. They know that when people feel empowered to act, they tend to follow through with commitment and high-quality work. They also realize that power in organizations is not a "zero-sum" quantity; in order for someone to gain power, it isn't necessary for someone else to give it up. Indeed, today's high-performance organizations thrive by mobilizing power throughout all ranks of employees.

Derek Oland, CEO and chairman of Moosehead Breweries, has a management style that is collegial. He doesn't believe in the "one genius that leads the company" model. Rather, he strives to get the very best people around him, provides them with direction, and then lets them do their thing.[19] When asked how Suncor Energy came to be named as a "best in class" company, Darcie Park, the co-manager of the company's corporate sustainability report, said, "It starts at the top with leadership and commitment, and then every Suncor employee is expected to do his or her part."[20] Both are talking about leadership through empowerment—allowing and helping people to use their experience, knowledge, and judgement to make a real difference in daily workplace affairs. *Manager's Notepad 13.1* offers tips on how leaders can empower others.[21] Doing so requires respect for the talents and creativity of others. And it requires the confidence to let people work with initiative in responsible jobs, participate in decisions affecting their work, and make reasonable choices regarding their work-life balance.

BE SURE YOU CAN
- define the term vision • explain the concept of visionary leadership • define the term power • illustrate three types of position power and discuss how managers use each • illustrate two types of personal power and discuss how managers use each • explain the implications of Barnard's acceptance theory of authority for ethical behaviour in organizations • define the term empowerment • explain why managers benefit by empowering others

Learning check ❶

LEADERSHIP TRAITS AND BEHAVIOURS

For centuries, people have recognized that some persons perform very well as leaders, whereas others do not. The question still debated is, "Why?" Historically, the issue of leadership success has been studied from the perspective of the trait, behavioural, and contingency approaches. Each takes a slightly different tack in attempting to explain leadership effectiveness and identify the pathways to leadership development.

●●● SEARCH FOR LEADERSHIP TRAITS

An early direction in leadership research involved the search for universal traits or distinguishing personal characteristics that would separate effective and ineffective leaders.[22] Sometimes called the *great person theory*, the notion was to identify successful leaders and then determine what made them great.

Briefly, the results of many years of research in this direction can be summarized as follows. Physical characteristics such as a person's height, weight, and physique make no difference in determining leadership success. On the other hand, certain personal traits do seem to differentiate leaders, although they must always be considered along with situational factors. A study, by Jim Kouzes and Barry Posner, of over 3,400 managers, for example, found that followers rather consistently admired leaders who were honest, competent, forward-looking, inspiring, and credible.[23] In a comprehensive review of research to date, Shelley Kirkpatrick and Edwin Locke further identify these personal traits as being common among successful leaders.[24]

- *Drive:* Successful leaders have high energy, display initiative, and are tenacious.

- *Self-confidence:* Successful leaders trust themselves and have confidence in their abilities.

- *Creativity:* Successful leaders are creative and original in their thinking.

- *Cognitive ability:* Successful leaders have the intelligence to integrate and interpret information.

- *Business knowledge:* Successful leaders know their industry and its technical foundations.

- *Motivation:* Successful leaders enjoy influencing others to achieve shared goals.

- *Flexibility:* Successful leaders adapt to fit the needs of followers and demands of situations.

- *Honesty and integrity:* Successful leaders are trustworthy; they are honest, predictable, and dependable.

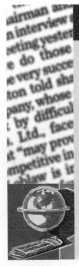

CANADIAN COMPANY
IN THE NEWS   Inco Ltd.

GROOMING TOMORROW'S LEADERS

With today's aging workforce, companies need to consider who among their employees will lead the company in the future. Canada's largest nickel company, Inco Ltd., launched a Trailblazers program in 2001, to groom high-potential employees for leadership roles. Participants are given an individual development plan, as well as mentoring and coaching over 18 months as they work in a more demanding role. The goal is to prepare them for advanced positions in two to five years, rather than the usual eight to ten years. The program's success is evident in its expansion from an Ontario initiative to Inco's worldwide operations.

Source: "Developing Tomorrow's Leaders," *Canadian Business*, Advertising Supplement, Jan. 17–30, 2005, Vol. 78, Iss. 2.

●●● FOCUS ON LEADERSHIP BEHAVIOURS

Researchers next turned their attention toward how leaders behave when working with followers. Work in this tradition investigated **leadership styles**—the recurring patterns of behaviours exhibited by leaders.[25] If the best style could be identified, the implications were straightforward and practical—train leaders to become skilled at using it.

Most leader-behaviour research focused on two dimensions of leadership style: (1) concern for the task to be accomplished and (2) concern for the people doing the work. The terminology used to describe these dimensions varies among many studies. Concern for task is sometimes called "initiating structure," "job-centredness," and "task orientation"; concern for people is sometimes called "consideration," "employee centredness," and "relationship orientation." But, regardless of the terminology, the behaviours characteristic of each dimension are quite clear. A *leader high in concern for task* plans and defines work to be done, assigns task responsibilities, sets clear work standards, urges task completion, and monitors performance results. By contrast, a *leader high in concern for people* is warm and supportive toward followers, maintains good social relations with them, respects their feelings, is sensitive to their needs, and shows trust in them.

The results of leader behaviour research at first suggested that followers of people-oriented leaders would be more productive and satisfied than those working for more task-oriented leaders.[26] Later results, however, suggested that truly effective leaders were high in both concern for people and concern for task. *Figure 13.3* describes one of the popular versions of this conclusion—the Leadership Grid of Robert Blake and Jane Mouton.[27] This grid describes alternative leadership styles that managers display. It is designed to assist in the process of leadership development. The approach uses assessments (such as #20 in the *Management Learning Workbook*) to first determine where someone falls with respect to people and task concerns. Then a training program is designed to help shift the person's style in the preferred direction of becoming strong on both dimensions. Blake and Mouton called this preferred style *team management*. This leader shares decisions with subordinates, encourages participation, and supports the teamwork needed for high levels of task accomplishment. Today, this would be a manager who "empowers" others.

■ **Leadership style** is the recurring pattern of behaviours exhibited by a leader.

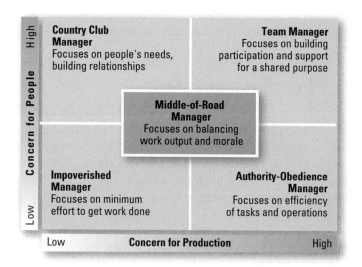

Figure 13.3 Managerial styles in Blake and Mouton's Leadership Grid.

CLASSIC LEADERSHIP STYLES

■ A leader with an **autocratic style** acts in unilateral command-and-control fashion.

■ A leader with a **laissez-faire style** displays a "do the best you can and don't bother me" attitude.

■ A leader with a **democratic style** encourages participation with an emphasis on both task accomplishment and development of people.

Even today, when people describe the leaders with whom they work, their vocabulary includes three classic styles of leadership from the behavioural leadership theories.[28] A leader with an **autocratic style** emphasizes task over people, keeps authority and information to himself or herself, and acts in unilateral command-and-control fashion. A leader with a **laissez-faire style** does just the opposite, showing little concern for task, letting the group make decisions, and acting with a "do the best you can and don't bother me" attitude. In contrast to both, a leader with a **democratic style** is committed to task and people, getting things done while sharing information, encouraging participation in decision making, and otherwise helping others develop their skills and capabilities. You might wonder which style works best. The answer is debatable. Under the leadership styles of former CEOs Cedric Ritchie and Peter Godsoe, Scotiabank didn't just climb from being the smallest of Canada's "big five," it grew to be the second largest of the banks. But throughout the process, these two CEOs left managers in the dark about what was going on. Scotiabank's current CEO, Richard Waugh, has a leadership style that is much more democratic. "My style is, and will be, different than theirs," he says. "I'm broadening it out. We're more diverse, with a great team of people." Waugh's style has already brought a relaxed atmosphere and greater dialogue to board meetings. But others, watching Waugh, say his style may jar with Scotia's culture. "Somebody has to be the boss," says one fund manager with a stake in the bank. "Waugh is a very solid guy, but I don't believe he has the kind of force of presence that Ritchie and Godsoe had."[29] An important personal question, of course, is, "What type of leader are you?" And perhaps even more importantly, "How would the people with whom you work and study describe your style—autocratic, laissez-faire, or democratic?"

✓ Learning check ❷

BE SURE YOU CAN
• contrast the trait and leader behaviour approaches to leadership research • identify five personal traits common among successful leaders • illustrate leader behaviours consistent with a high concern for task • illustrate leader behaviours consistent with a high concern for people • explain the leadership development implications of Blake and Mouton's Leadership Grid • describe three classic leadership styles

CONTINGENCY APPROACHES TO LEADERSHIP

As leadership research continued, scholars recognized the need to probe beyond leader behaviours and examine yet another question: "When and under what circumstances is a particular leadership style preferable to others?" They developed the following *contingency approaches*, which share the goal of understanding the conditions for leadership success in different situations.

FIEDLER'S CONTINGENCY MODEL

An early contingency leadership model developed by Fred Fiedler proposed that good leadership depends on a match between leadership style and situational demands.[30] Leadership style in Fiedler's model is measured on the *least-preferred co-worker scale*, known as the LPC scale. It describes tendencies to behave either as a task-motivated (low LPC score) or relationship-motivated (high LPC score) leader. This "either/or" concept is important. Fiedler believes that leadership style is part of one's personality; therefore, it is relatively enduring and difficult to change. He doesn't place much hope in trying to train a task-motivated leader to behave in a relationship-motivated manner, or vice versa. Rather, Fiedler believes that the key to leadership success is putting our existing styles to work in

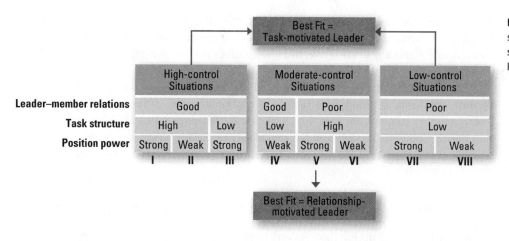

Figure 13.4 Matching leadership style and situation—summary predictions from Fiedler's contingency theory.

situations for which they are the best "fit." This is true contingency leadership thinking with the goal of successfully matching one's style with situational demands.

Understanding Leadership Situations

In Fiedler's model, the amount of control a situation allows the leader is a critical issue in determining the correct style-situation fit. Three contingency variables are used to diagnose situational control. The *quality of leader–member relations* (good or poor) measures the degree to which the group supports the leader. The *degree of task structure* (high or low) measures the extent to which task goals, procedures, and guidelines are clearly spelled out. The *amount of position power* (strong or weak) measures the degree to which the position gives the leader power to reward and punish subordinates. *Figure 13.4* shows eight leadership situations that result from different combinations of these variables. They range from the most favourable situation of high control (good leader–member relations, high task structure, strong position power) to the least favourable situation of low control (poor leader–member relations, low task structure, weak position power).

Matching Leadership Style and Situation

Figure 13.4 also summarizes Fiedler's extensive research on the contingency relationships between situation control, leadership style, and leader effectiveness. Note that neither the task-oriented nor the relationship-oriented leadership style is effective all the time. Instead, each style appears to work best when used in the right situation. The results can be stated as two propositions. *Proposition 1* is that a task-oriented leader will be most successful in either very favourable (high-control) or very unfavourable (low-control) situations. *Proposition 2* is that a relationship-oriented leader will be most successful in situations of moderate control.

Assume, for example, that you are the leader of a team of bank tellers. The tellers seem highly supportive of you, and their job is clearly defined regarding what needs to be done. You have the authority to evaluate their performance and to make pay and promotion recommendations. This is a high-control situation consisting of good leader–member relations, high task structure, and strong position power. *Figure 13.4* shows that a task-motivated leader would be most effective in this situation.

Now take another example. Suppose that you are chairperson of a committee asked to improve labour–management relations in a manufacturing plant. Although the goal is clear, no one can say for sure how to accomplish it. Task structure is low. Because committee members are free to quit any time they want, the chairperson has little position power. Because not all members believe the committee is necessary, poor leader–member relations are apparent. According to the figure, this low-control situation also calls for a task-motivated leader.

Finally, assume that you are the new head of a retail section in a large department store. Because you were selected over one of the popular sales clerks you now supervise, leader–member relations are poor. Task structure is high since the clerk's job is well defined. Your position power is low because the clerks work under a seniority system and fixed wage schedule. The figure shows that this moderate-control situation requires a relationship-motivated leader.

●●● HERSEY-BLANCHARD SITUATIONAL LEADERSHIP MODEL

In contrast to Fiedler's notion that leadership style is hard to change, the Hersey-Blanchard situational leadership model suggests that successful leaders do adjust their styles. And they do so based on the *maturity* of followers, indicated by their readiness to perform in a given situation.[31] "Readiness," in this sense, is based on how able and willing or confident followers are to perform required tasks. As shown in *Figure 13.5*, the possible leadership styles that result from different combinations of task-oriented and relationship-oriented behaviours are as follows:

* *Delegating*—allowing the group to take responsibility for task decisions; a low-task, low-relationship style.

* *Participating*—emphasizing shared ideas and participative decisions on task directions; a low-task, high-relationship style.

* *Selling*—explaining task directions in a supportive and persuasive way; a high-task, high-relationship style.

* *Telling*—giving specific task directions and closely supervising work; a high-task, low-relationship style.

Managers using this model must be able to implement the alternative leadership styles as needed. The *delegating style* works best in high-readiness situations of able and willing or confident followers; the *telling style* works best at the other extreme of low readiness, where followers are unable and unwilling or insecure. The *participating style* is recommended for low-to-moderate readiness (followers able but unwilling or insecure) and the *selling style* for moderate-to-high readiness (followers unable but willing or confident). Hersey and Blanchard further believe that leadership styles should be adjusted as followers change over

Figure 13.5 Leadership implications of the Hersey-Blanchard situational leadership model.

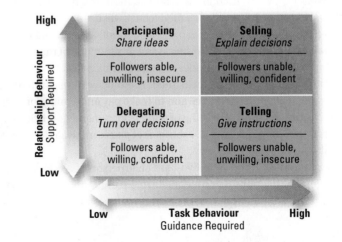

time. The model also implies that if the correct styles are used in lower-readiness situations, followers will "mature" and grow in ability, willingness, and confidence. This allows the leader to become less directive as followers mature. Although the Hersey-Blanchard model is intuitively appealing, limited research has been accomplished on it to date.[32]

●●● HOUSE'S PATH-GOAL LEADERSHIP THEORY

A third contingency leadership approach is the path-goal theory advanced by Robert House.[33] This theory suggests that an effective leader is one who clarifies paths through which followers can achieve both task-related and personal goals. The best leaders raise motivation and help followers move along these paths. They remove any barriers that stand in the way and provide appropriate rewards for task accomplishment. Path-goal theorists believe leaders should be flexible and move back and forth among four leadership styles to create positive "path-goal" linkages.

- *Directive leadership*—letting subordinates know what is expected; giving directions on what to do and how; scheduling work to be done; maintaining definite standards of performance; clarifying the leader's role in the group.

- *Supportive leadership*—doing things to make work more pleasant; treating group members as equals; being friendly and approachable; showing concern for the well-being of subordinates.

- *Achievement-oriented leadership*—setting challenging goals; expecting the highest levels of performance; emphasizing continuous improvement in performance; displaying confidence in meeting high standards.

- *Participative leadership*—involving subordinates in decision making; consulting with subordinates; asking for suggestions from subordinates; using these suggestions when making a decision.

Path-Goal Predictions and Managerial Implications

The path-goal theory, summarized in *Figure 13.6*, advises managers to use leadership styles that fit situational needs. This means that the leader adds value by contributing things that are missing from the situation or that need strengthening; she or he specifically avoids redundant behaviours. For example, when team members are expert and competent at their tasks, it is unnecessary and even dysfunctional for the leader to tell them how to do things.

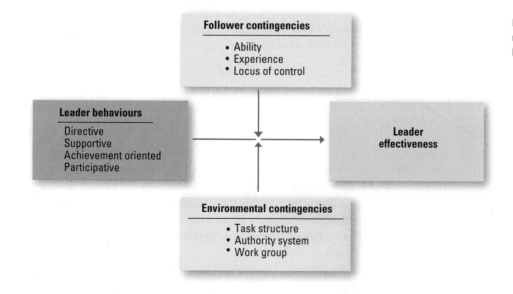

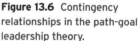
Figure 13.6 Contingency relationships in the path-goal leadership theory.

The important contingencies for making good path-goal leadership choices include follower characteristics (ability, experience, and locus of control) and work environment characteristics (task structure, authority system, and work group). For example, the match of leader behaviours and situation might take the following forms.[34] When *job assignments* are unclear, directive leadership is appropriate to clarify task objectives and expected rewards. When *worker self-confidence* is low, supportive leadership is appropriate to increase confidence by emphasizing individual abilities and offering needed assistance. When *performance incentives* are poor, participative leadership is appropriate to clarify individual needs and identify appropriate rewards. When *task challenge* is insufficient in a job, achievement-oriented leadership is appropriate to set goals and raise performance aspirations.

Substitutes for Leadership

■ **Substitutes for leadership** are factors in the work setting that direct work efforts without the involvement of a leader.

Path-goal theory has also contributed to the recognition of what are called **substitutes for leadership**.[35] These are aspects of the work setting and the people involved that can reduce the need for a leader's personal involvement. In effect, they make leadership from the "outside" unnecessary because leadership is already provided from within the situation. Possible substitutes for leadership include *subordinate characteristics* such as ability, experience, and independence; *task characteristics* such as routineness and availability of feedback; and *organizational characteristics* such as clarity of plans and formalization of rules and procedures. When these substitutes are present, managers should avoid duplicating them. Instead, they should concentrate on other and more important things.

●●● VROOM-JAGO LEADER-PARTICIPATION MODEL

The Vroom-Jago leader-participation model is designed to help a leader choose the decision-making method that best fits the problem being faced.[36] The key issue is on the amount of decision-making participation allowed followers. The broad choices are for the leader to make an **authority**, **consultative**, or **group decision**.[37] In its current version, the model views a manager as leading effectively when making the right selection from among the following decision-making options:

■ An **authority decision** is made by the leader and then communicated to the group.

- *Decide alone*—this is an authority decision; the manager decides how to solve the problem and communicates the decision to the group.

■ A **consultative decision** is made by a leader after receiving information, advice, or opinions from group members.

- *Consult individually*—the manager makes the decision after sharing the problem and consulting individually with group members to get their suggestions.

- *Consult with group*—the manager makes the decision after convening the group, sharing the problem, and consulting with everyone to get their suggestions.

■ A **group decision** is made by group members themselves.

- *Facilitate*—the manager convenes the group, shares the problem, and then facilitates group discussion to make a decision.

- *Delegate*—the manager convenes the group and delegates to group members the authority to define the problem and make a decision.

In true contingency fashion, no one decision method is considered by the Vroom-Jago model as universally superior to any others. Each of the five decision methods is appropriate in certain situations, and each has its advantages and disadvantages.[38] Leadership success results when the decision type correctly matches the characteristics of the problem to be solved. The key rules guiding the choice relate to (1) *decision quality*—based on who has the information needed for problem solving; (2) *decision acceptance*—based on the importance of subordinate acceptance of the decision to its eventual implementation; and (3) *decision time*—based on the time available to make and implement the decision.

As shown in *Figure 13.7*, the more authority-oriented decisions work best when leaders personally have the expertise needed to solve the problem, they are confident and capable of acting alone, others are likely to accept and implement the decision they make, and little or no time is available for discussion. By contrast, in the following situations the more group-oriented and participative decision methods are recommended:

• The leader lacks sufficient expertise and information to solve this problem alone.

• The problem is unclear and help is needed to clarify the situation.

• Acceptance of the decision and commitment by others are necessary for implementation.

• Adequate time is available to allow for true participation.

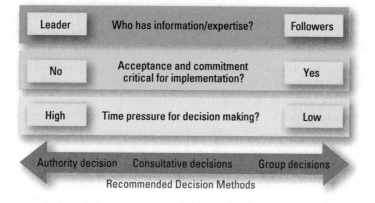

Figure 13.7 Leadership implications of Vroom-Jago leader-participation model.

The more participative decision methods offer important benefits.[39] They help improve decision quality by bringing more information to bear on the problem. They help improve decision acceptance as participants gain understanding and become committed to the process. They also contribute to the development of leadership potential in others through the experience gained by active participation in the problem-solving process. However, there is a potential cost of lost efficiency. The greater the participation, the more time required for the decision process. Leaders do not always have sufficient time available; some problems must be resolved immediately. In such cases the authority decision may be the only option.[40]

BE SURE YOU CAN

• contrast the leader behaviour and contingency approaches to leadership research • explain the relationship between leadership style and a person's score on Fiedler's least-preferred co-worker scale • explain Fiedler's contingency thinking on matching leadership style and situation • identify the four leadership styles in the Hersey-Blanchard situational model • explain House's path-goal theory • illustrate the behaviours of directive, supportive, achievement-oriented, and participative leadership styles • define the term substitutes for leadership • contrast the authority, consultative, and group decisions in the Vroom-Jago model • explain when more participative decisions work best

TRANSFORMATIONAL LEADERSHIP

There is a great deal of interest today in "superleaders," persons whose visions and strong personalities have an extraordinary impact on others. They are often called **charismatic leaders** because of their special powers to inspire others in exceptional ways. Charisma was

■ A **charismatic leader** develops special leader–follower relationships and inspires followers in extraordinary ways.

traditionally thought of as being limited to a few lucky persons who were born with it. Today, it is considered part of a broader set of special personal leadership that can be developed with foresight and practice.

●●● TRANSFORMATIONAL AND TRANSACTIONAL LEADERSHIP

■ **Transactional leadership** directs the efforts of others through tasks, rewards, and structures.

Leadership scholars James MacGregor Burns and Bernard Bass suggest that the research and models we have discussed so far tend toward **transactional leadership**.[41] The impression is that if you learn the frameworks you can then apply them systematically to keep others moving forward to implement plans and achieve performance goals. Managers with this approach to leadership change styles, adjust tasks, and allocate rewards to achieve positive influence. Notably absent from this description is any evidence of "enthusiasm" and "inspiration," more emotional qualities that are characteristic of superleaders having charismatic appeal. Importantly, these are the very qualities that Burns and Bass associate with **transformational leadership**. This describes someone who is truly inspirational as a leader, who is personally excited about what they are doing, and who arouses others to seek extraordinary performance accomplishments. A transformational leader uses charisma and related qualities to raise aspirations and shift people and organizational systems into new high-performance patterns. The presence of transformational leadership is reflected in followers who are enthusiastic about the leader and his or her ideas, who work very hard to support them, who remain loyal and devoted, and who strive for superior performance accomplishments.

■ **Transformational leadership** is inspirational and arouses extraordinary effort and performance.

The transactional and transformational leadership approaches are not mutually exclusive. On its own, transactional leadership is probably insufficient to meet fully the leadership challenges and demands of today's dynamic work environments. Rather, it is a foundation or building block for solid day-to-day leadership. But in a context of continuous and often large-scale change, the additional and inspirational impact of transformational leadership becomes essential. One way to describe this in a classroom situation is the following. Skill at transactional leadership will earn you a B, allowing you to routinely lead people quite well. Moving from B to A leadership, however, requires additional excellence in transformational leadership.

take it to the case!

Lakeport Brewing Income Fund
Great leadership equals great results

What do you get when you mix a great leader and a great product together? You get Lakeport Brewing Income Fund. New to the brewing business, Teresa Cascioli took the helm of Hamilton-based Lakeport Brewing in 1999 and in six short years turned it into a presence in a market dominated by giants such as Labatt and Molson. By focusing on the value-priced market and using her now famous "24 for $24" pricing strategy, Lakeport shot from  bankruptcy protection to become the third-largest brewery in Ontario in 2006. Cascioli took the company public as an income fund in 2004, expanding Lakeport's opportunities for flexibility and growth. Cascioli has received top entrepreneur awards from organizations such as *Profit* and *Chatelaine* magazines, Ernst & Young, and Canada's Venture Capital and Private Equity Association, and in 2006 was recognized as one of Canada's Most Powerful Women. Find out how she did it in the case in the *Management Learning Workbook*.

Source: Natalia Williams, "Teresa Cascioli," *Strategy* (May 2006), p. 56. "Business is Brewing," *ImPRESSions* (Lakeport Brewing; August 2006 to December 2006). "Labatt Brewing Company Limited acquires Lakeport Brewing Income Fund for cash offer of $28.00 per unit," news release, Canada Newswire (February 1, 2007).

●●● QUALITIES OF A TRANSFORMATIONAL LEADER

The goal of excellence in transformational leadership offers a distinct management challenge, with important personal development implications. It is not enough to possess leadership traits, know the leadership behaviours, and understand leadership contingencies. Any manager must also be prepared to lead in an inspirational way and with a compelling personality. The transformational leader provides a strong sense of vision and a contagious enthusiasm that substantially raises the confidence, aspirations, and performance commitments of followers. The special qualities characteristic of transformational leaders include the following:[42]

- *Vision*—having ideas and a clear sense of direction; communicating them to others; developing excitement about accomplishing shared "dreams."

- *Charisma*—using the power of personal reference and emotion to arouse others' enthusiasm, faith, loyalty, pride, and trust in themselves.

- *Symbolism*—identifying "heroes" and holding spontaneous and planned ceremonies to celebrate excellence and high achievement.

- *Empowerment*—helping others develop by removing performance obstacles, sharing responsibilities, and delegating truly challenging work.

- *Intellectual stimulation*—gaining the involvement of others by creating awareness of problems and stirring their imaginations.

- *Integrity*—being honest and credible, acting consistently out of personal conviction, and following through on commitments.

BE SURE YOU CAN

- define the terms transformational leadership and transactional leadership • explain when transformational leadership becomes essential • identify the special personal qualities of transformational leaders

✓ Learning check ❹

CURRENT ISSUES IN LEADERSHIP DEVELOPMENT

A number of issues and themes related to leadership development add further context to the many insights of this chapter. Of particular interest are research on both emotional intelligence and the relationship between gender and leadership, as well as practical discussions of the everyday work of a leader and the importance of ethical leadership in our society.

●●● EMOTIONAL INTELLIGENCE

An area of leadership development that is currently very popular is **emotional intelligence**, first discussed in Chapter 1 as part of the essential human skills of managers. Popularized by the work of Daniel Goleman, "EI" is defined as "the ability to manage ourselves and our relationships effectively."[43] According to his research, emotional intelligence is an important influence on leadership effectiveness, especially in more senior management positions. In Goleman's words, "the higher the rank of the person considered to be a star performer, the more emotional intelligence capabilities showed up as the reason for his or her effectiveness."[44] This is a strong endorsement for considering whether or not EI is one of your leadership assets. Important too is Goleman's belief that emotional intelligence skills can be learned.

■ **Emotional intelligence** is the ability to manage our emotions in social relationships.

For purposes of research and training, Goleman breaks emotional intelligence down into five critical components.[45] He argues that each of us should strive for competency in each component and thereby maximize our ability to work well in relationships with others. The critical components of EI are the following:

- *Self-awareness*—understanding our own moods and emotions, and understanding their impact on our work and on others.

- *Self-regulation*—thinking before we act and controlling otherwise disruptive impulses.

- *Motivation*—working hard with persistence and for reasons other than money and status.

- *Empathy*—understanding the emotions of others and using this understanding to better relate to them.

- *Social skill*—establishing rapport with others and building good relationships and networks.

●●● GENDER AND LEADERSHIP

One of the leadership themes of continuing interest deals with the question of whether gender influences leadership styles and/or effectiveness. Sara Levinson, president of NFL Properties Inc., for example, once asked the all-male members of her management team, "Is my leadership style different from a man's?" "Yes," they replied, suggesting that the very fact that she was asking the question was evidence of the difference. They also indicated that her leadership style emphasized communication, and gathering ideas and opinions from others. When Levinson probed further by asking, "Is this a distinctly 'female' trait?", they said that they thought it was.[46]

The evidence clearly supports the fact that both women and men can be effective leaders.[47] As suggested in the prior example, however, they may tend toward somewhat different styles.[48] Victor Vroom and his colleagues have investigated gender differences in respect to the leader-participation model discussed earlier.[49] They find women managers to be significantly more participative than their male counterparts. Other studies report that peers, subordinates, and supervisors of female leaders rate them higher than men on motivating others, fostering communication, listening to others, and producing high-quality work.[50] This style has been called *interactive leadership*.[51] Leaders with this style display behaviours typically considered democratic and participative—showing respect for others, caring for others, and sharing power and information with others. They focus on building consensus and good interpersonal relations through communication and involvement. The interactive style has qualities in common with the transformational leadership just discussed.[52] An interactive leader tends to use personal power, gaining influence over others through support, and interpersonal relationships. Men, by contrast, may tend toward more transactional approaches, relying more on directive and assertive behaviours, and using position power in a traditional "command and control" way.

Given the emphasis on shared power, communication, co-operation, and participation in the new-form organizations of today, these results are provocative. The interactive leadership style seems to be an excellent fit with the demands of a diverse workforce and the new workplace. As Harvard professor and consultant Rosabeth Moss Kanter says, "Women get high ratings on exactly those skills required to succeed in the Global Information Age, where teamwork and partnering are so important."[53] Gender issues aside, it seems clear that future leadership success for anyone will rest on one's capacity to lead through openness, positive relationships, support, and empowerment.

Canadian Managers

Leading through Innovation

David Patchell-Evans, founder and CEO of London, Ontario-based GoodLife Fitness Clubs, has built Canada's largest fitness chain by doing things differently. "In my business, people don't want a typical CEO," says Patchell-Evans, who prefers to be called "Patch." Innovation is the hallmark of his leadership style. He has acquired exclusive Canadian rights to Visual Fitness Planner, a software tool that allows clients to picture themselves before and after they've met their fitness goals. Other new ways to attract and retain customers Patchell-Evans has implemented include free DVD rentals, babysitting and tanning services, women-only fitness facilities, and a Web-based nutrition program. He's also planning to recycle energy from hot water, which he estimates will save $6,000 to $20,000 per year at seven locations retrofitted with the technology.

Source: Erin Pooley, "Most innovative CEO 2005: David Patchell-Evans, GoodLife Fitness Clubs," *Canadian Business*, April 25–May 8, 2005.

●●●● DRUCKER'S "OLD-FASHIONED" LEADERSHIP

Peter Drucker offered a time-tested and very pragmatic view of leadership. It is based on what he referred to as a "good old-fashioned" look at the plain hard work it takes to be a successful leader. Consider, for example, his description of a telephone conversation with a potential consulting client. "We'd want you to run a seminar for us on how one acquires charisma," she said. Drucker's response was not what she expected. He advised her that there was more to leadership than the popular emphasis on personal "dash" or charisma. In fact, he said that "leadership…is work."[54]

Drucker's observations remind us that leadership effectiveness must have strong foundations. First, he believed that the basic building block of effective leadership is *defining and establishing a sense of mission*. A good leader sets the goals, priorities, and standards. A good leader keeps them all clear and visible, and maintains them. In Drucker's words, "The leader's first task is to be the trumpet that sounds a clear sound." Second, he believed in *accepting leadership as a responsibility rather than a rank*. Good leaders surround themselves with talented people. They are not afraid to develop strong and capable subordinates. And, they do not blame others when things go wrong. As Drucker said, "The buck stops here" is still a good adage to remember. Third, he stressed the importance of *earning and keeping the trust of others*. The key here is the leader's personal integrity. The followers of good leaders trust them. This means that they believe the leader means what he or she says and that his or her actions will be consistent with what is said. In Drucker's words again, "Effective leadership… is not based on being clever; it is based primarily on being consistent."

●●●● MORAL LEADERSHIP

As discussed in Chapter 3, society today is unforgiving in its demands that organizations be run with **ethical leadership**—that is, leadership by moral standards that meet the ethical test of being "good" and not "bad," of being "right" and not "wrong."[55] The expectation is that anyone in a leadership position will practise high ethical standards of behaviour, help to build and

■ **Ethical leadership** is always "good" and "right" by moral standards.

AROUND THE WORLD

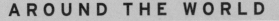

Developing great leadership from within

Some say that great leaders are born, not made, but don't tell that to Natura, the Brazil-based cosmetics company that's achieving runaway success in its home country and across Latin America. Recently named by *Fortune* magazine as the best company in Latin America for developing strong leaders, Natura says its "management style is characterized by a dauntless, visionary disposition to mobilize large social networks," including its more than 500,000 consultants who sell the products to some 50 million consumers. With a strong commitment to sustainable development and "social transformation," Natura says it "should develop, with even more commitment, our capacity to find, train and retain leaders who are aware of their role in the global community." Another challenge the leaders face is accelerated growth: Natura's gross revenues expanded by more than 129 percent in a recent three-year period and it has expanded into France, the birthplace of modern cosmetics.

Source: "The Top Companies for Leaders 2007," *Fortune* magazine, online at <http://money.cnn.com/magazines/fortune/leadership/2007/index.html>; Natura Annual Report 2005, online at the company website: <www.natura.net>.

maintain an ethical organizational culture, and both help and require others to behave ethically in their work. *Management* has communicated throughout an essential belief about success in work and in life—long-term, sustainable success can only be built upon a foundation of solid ethical behaviour. As a leader, you should not try to be ethical out of fear of being caught doing something wrong; you should want to be ethical because of the freedom and success that it brings. Ethical leaders have little to fear when the inevitable problems and traumas of daily work appear. They can act with confidence, always knowing that their actions are beyond reproach.

> ■ **Integrity** in leadership is honesty, credibility, and consistency in putting values into action.

Ethical leadership begins with personal integrity, a concept fundamental to the notions of both transformational and good old-fashioned leadership. A leader with **integrity** is honest, credible, and consistent in putting values into action. When a leader has integrity, he or she earns the trust of followers. And when followers believe leaders are trustworthy, they are willing to commit themselves to behave in ways that live up to the leader's expectations. For managers in our high-pressure and competitive work environments, nothing can substitute for leadership strongly anchored in personal integrity. When viewed through the lens of what is truly the right thing to do, even the most difficult decisions become easier.

John W. Gardner talks with great insight about further "moral aspects" of leadership.[56] He does so with great respect for people and the talents that they bring with them to the workplace. "Most people in most organizations most of the time," Gardner writes, "are more stale than they know, more bored than they care to admit." Leaders, according to Gardner, have a moral obligation to build performance capacities by awakening the potential of each individual—to urge each person "to take the initiative in performing leader-like acts." He points out that high expectations tend to generate high performance. It is the leader's job to remove "obstacles to our effective functioning—to help individuals see and pursue shared purposes."

> ■ **Authentic leadership** activates positive psychological states to achieve self-awareness and positive self-regulation.

The concept of **authentic leadership** advanced by Fred Luthans and Bruce Avolio is relevant in this same context.[57] Authentic leadership activates performance through the positive psychological states of confidence, hope, optimism, and resilience. It enhances self-awareness and self-development by the leader and by her or his associates. The resulting positive self-regulation helps authentic leaders to clearly frame moral dilemmas, transparently respond to them, and serve as ethical role models.[58] There is no doubt that ethical leadership has such authenticity and is also strongly anchored in a true commitment to people. Pat Daniel, President and Chief Executive Officer of Enbridge Inc., is considered an authentic leader. He is known to have high integrity, a deep sense of service to his employees, the community, the environment, and a view that each of Enbridge's 4,000 employees has the potential to be a leader.[59]

BE SURE YOU CAN

• explain how emotional intelligence contributes to leadership success • discuss alternative views of the relationship between gender and leadership • list Drucker's three essentials of good old-fashioned leadership • define the term integrity and discuss it as a foundation for moral leadership

✓ Learning check ❺

●●● Chapter 13 STUDY GUIDE

WHERE WE'VE BEEN

Back to J.-Robert Ouimet

The opening example of J.-Robert Ouimet illustrates that leadership is a competitive tool that provides support for meaningful personal and organizational performance. In this chapter you learned about the trait and leader behaviour approaches to leadership, as well as important contingency models as developed by Fiedler, Hersey-Blanchard, House, and Vroom-Jago. You also learned the difference between transformational and transactional leadership, and were introduced to current issues in leadership development, including emotional intelligence, gender differences, and moral foundations.

THE NEXT STEP
INTEGRATED LEARNING ACTIVITIES

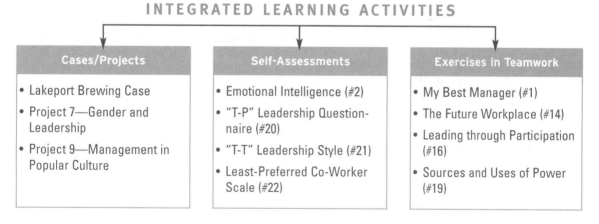

Cases/Projects	Self-Assessments	Exercises in Teamwork
• Lakeport Brewing Case	• Emotional Intelligence (#2)	• My Best Manager (#1)
• Project 7—Gender and Leadership	• "T-P" Leadership Questionnaire (#20)	• The Future Workplace (#14)
• Project 9—Management in Popular Culture	• "T-T" Leadership Style (#21)	• Leading through Participation (#16)
	• Least-Preferred Co-Worker Scale (#22)	• Sources and Uses of Power (#19)

STUDY QUESTION SUMMARY

1. What is the nature of leadership?

- Leadership is the process of inspiring others to work hard to accomplish important tasks.

- The ability to communicate a vision, a clear sense of the future, is increasingly considered to be an essential ingredient of effective leadership.

- Power is the ability to get others to do what you want them to do through leadership.

- Managerial power equals position power plus personal power.

- Sources of position power include rewards, coercion, and legitimacy or formal authority; sources of personal power include expertise and reference.

- Effective leaders empower others; that is, they help and allow others to make job-related decisions on their own.

2. What are the important leadership traits and behaviours?

- Early leadership research searched unsuccessfully for a set of personal traits that would always differentiate successful and unsuccessful leaders.

- Traits that do seem to have a positive impact on leadership include drive, integrity, and self-confidence.

- Research on leader behaviours focused on alternative leadership styles based on concerns for task and concerns for people.

- One suggestion of leader-behaviour researchers is that effective leaders will be good at team-based or participative leadership that is high in both task and people concerns.

3. What are the contingency theories of leadership?

- Contingency leadership approaches point out that no one leadership style always works best; the best style is one that properly matches the demands of each unique situation.

- Fiedler's contingency model describes how situa-

tional differences in task structure, position power, and leader–member relations may influence which leadership style works best.

- House's path-goal theory points out that leaders should add value to situations by responding with supportive, directive, achievement-oriented, and/or participative styles as needed.

- The Hersey-Blanchard situational model recommends using task-oriented and people-oriented behaviours, depending on the "maturity" levels of followers.

- The Vroom-Jago leader-participation theory advises leaders to choose decision-making methods—individual, consultative, group—that best fit the problems they are trying to solve.

4. What is transformational leadership?

- Charismatic leadership creates a truly inspirational relationship between leader and followers.

- Transactional leadership focuses on tasks, rewards, and structures to influence follower behaviour.

- Transformational leaders use charisma and emotion to inspire others toward extraordinary efforts in support of change and performance excellence.

5. What are current issues in leadership development?

- Emotional intelligence, the ability to manage our relationships and ourselves effectively, is an important leadership capability.

- The interactive leadership style often associated with women emphasizes communication, involvement, and interpersonal respect, all things consistent with the demands of the new workplace.

- Drucker and others remind us that leadership is "hard work" that always requires a personal commitment to consistently meeting high ethical and moral standards.

KEY TERMS REVIEW

Authentic leadership (p. 328)

Authority decision (p. 322)

Autocratic style (p. 318)

Charismatic leader (p. 323)

Coercive power (p. 312)

Consultative decision (p. 322)

Democratic style (p. 318)

Emotional intelligence (p. 325)

Empowerment (p. 314)

Ethical leadership (p. 327)

Expert power (p. 313)

Group decision (p. 322)

Integrity (p. 328)

Laissez-faire style (p. 318)

Leadership (p. 311)

Leadership style (p. 317)

Legitimate power (p. 313)

Power (p. 312)

Referent power (p. 313)

Reward power (p. 312)

Substitutes for leadership (p. 322)

Transactional leadership (p. 324)

Transformational leadership (p. 324)

Vision (p. 311)

Visionary leadership (p. 311)

SELF-TEST 13

MULTIPLE-CHOICE QUESTIONS:

1. Someone with a clear sense of the future and the actions needed to get there is considered a _____ leader.
   (a) task-oriented (b) people-oriented (c) transactional (d) visionary

2. Managerial power = _____ power × _____ power.
   (a) reward, punishment (b) reward, expert (c) legitimate, position (d) position, personal

3. A manager who says "Because I am the boss, you must do what I ask" is relying on _____ power.
   (a) reward (b) legitimate (c) expert (d) referent

4. The personal traits now considered important for managerial success include _____.
   (a) self-confidence (b) gender (c) age (d) personality

5. According to the Blake and Mouton model of leader behaviours, the most successful leader is one who acts with _____.
   (a) high initiating structure (b) high consideration (c) high concern for task and high concern for people
   (d) low job stress and high task goals

6. In Fiedler's contingency model, both highly favourable and highly unfavourable leadership situations are best dealt with by a _____ leader.
   (a) task-oriented (b) laissez-faire (c) participative (d) relationship-oriented

7. Directive leadership and achievement-oriented leadership are among the options in House's _____ theory of leadership.
   (a) trait (b) path-goal (c) transformational (d) leader-participation

8. Vision, charisma, integrity, and symbolism are all on the list of attributes typically associated with _____ leaders.
   (a) contingency (b) old-fashioned (c) transformational (d) transactional

9. _____ leadership theory suggests that leadership success is achieved by correctly matching leadership style with situations.
   (a) Trait (b) Fiedler's (c) Transformational (d) Blake and Mouton's

10. In the leader-behaviour approaches to leadership, someone who does a very good job of planning work, setting standards, and monitoring results would be considered a(n) _____ leader.
    (a) task-oriented (b) control-oriented (c) achievement-oriented (d) employee-centred

11. When a leader assumes that others will do as she asks because they want to positively identify with her, she is relying on _____ power to influence their behaviour.
    (a) expert (b) referent (c) legitimate (d) reward

12. The interactive leadership style often associated with women is characterized by _____.
    (a) inclusion and information sharing (b) use of rewards and punishments (c) command and control
    (d) emphasis on position power

13. A leader whose actions indicate an attitude of "do as you want and don't bother me" would be described as having a(n) _____ leadership style.
    (a) autocratic (b) country club (c) democratic (d) laissez-faire

14. The critical contingency variable in the Hersey-Blanchard situational model of leadership is _____.
    (a) followers' maturity (b) LPC (c) task structure (d) emotional intelligence

15. A leader who _____ would be described as achievement oriented in the path-goal theory.
    (a) works hard to achieve high performance (b) sets challenging goals for others (c) gives directions and monitors results (d) builds commitment through participation

SHORT-RESPONSE QUESTIONS:

16. Why does a person need both position power and personal power to achieve long-term managerial effectiveness?
17. What is the major insight offered by the Vroom-Jago leader-participation model?
18. What are the three variables that Fiedler's contingency model uses to diagnose the favourability of leadership situations, and what does each mean?
19. How does Peter Drucker's view of "good old-fashioned leadership" differ from the popular concept of transformational leadership?

APPLICATION QUESTION:

20. When Marcel Henry took over as leader of a new product development team, he was both excited and apprehensive. "I wonder," he said to himself on the first day in his new assignment, "if I can meet the challenges of leadership." Later that day, Marcel shares this concern with you during a coffee break. Based on the insights of this chapter, how would you describe to him the implications for his personal leadership development of current thinking on transformational leadership and moral leadership?

Motivation—
Theory and Practice

●●● CHAPTER 14 STUDY QUESTIONS

Planning Ahead

After reading Chapter 14, you should be able to answer these questions in your own words.

1. What is motivation?

2. What are the different types of individual needs?

3. What are the process theories of motivation?

4. What role does reinforcement play in motivation?

5. What are the challenges of motivation in the new workplace?

Genentech

Passion for science and people

What does it take to make it to the top of the "best companies to work for" lists produced by publications such as *Fortune*, *Science*, *Scientist*, and *Essence*, and the *San Francisco Business Times*? Genentech did it by attracting and keeping an energized and motivated staff.

Founded in 1976, Genentech's motivational culture has been its competitive advantage. Founders Bob Swanson and Herb Boyer knew the success of their venture depended on luring and keeping big-brain bioscience talent. Art Levinson continued this tradition when he became CEO in 1995. Levinson maintained the focus on championing the science, creating a stream of new drugs, and winning over employees. This focus has paid off. Genentech is not just the very first biotechnology company, it is the brightest star in the industry, with year-end revenues approaching $6.6 billion in 2006—three times higher than four years ago.

Genentech pours a tremendous amount of energy into creating a culture that motivates and supports people with passion. The atmosphere is casual and collegial, and employees don't get assignments—they receive "appointments." They traverse the grounds by shuttle bus and bicycles provided by the company. Employees can visit the on-site libraries and a bank, use company subsidized daycare and cafeterias, or draw on the concierge service to help with personal errands. At Genentech, every milestone calls for celebration—and on very big occasions, very big celebrity bands. After an unusual run of drug approvals, the parking lot in front of Building 9 became the site of a rock concert featuring Elton John, Mary J. Blige, and Matchbox 20.

Genentech looks for people like Ellen Filvaroff, a senior scientist in molecular oncology. Her walls are decorated with pictures of her patients and her toddler. The perks she likes most are little things—like being able to purchase and mail birthday cards from the company store. But the biggest perk by far, she says, is having colleagues who can help crack the science. Collaboration at Genentech is easy and encouraged; sabbaticals keep creativity alive and stave off burnout; and scientists and engineers are encouraged to pursue pet projects.

While Genentech offers flexible medical benefits, long-term disability, and life insurance, they recognize that different things motivate different people. They provide employee recognition through a corporate bonus program, as well as cash bonuses when extraordinary milestones are reached. They offer stock purchase plans, flexible-spending accounts, discounts for cellular phones, vacations to Disneyland, legal services, and even pet insurance.

With all that Genentech has to offer it is no wonder it has been on many "100 Best Companies to Work For" lists for the past seven consecutive years.[1]

IN THE WORKPLACE

You remember your management instructor saying that "giving goals is the best way to motivate your workforce," but somehow, that comment seems hollow at the moment. You look down at the 17 goals that your boss Darren Smith has dropped on your desk. Some look challenging, some are too easy, and "the Big Four," as Darren called them, are so difficult that you doubt you could ever complete them. Instead of motivating you, these goals have deflated you. How could your instructor have been so wrong? However, you remember that your instructor also said "there is nothing more valuable than good theory." Reflecting on this point, you look at the motivational theories talked about in class to see what might be causing your lack of motivation.

●●● **Chapter 14**   LEARNING PREVIEW   ●●●

The chapter opening example of Genentech demonstrates how management commitment to employees shown through the development of a supportive culture, the celebration of successes, an appreciation of individuality, and recognition that different things motivate different people pays off. In this chapter you will learn about the concept of motivation. You will examine the main content, process, and reinforcement theories that help to explain motivation to work. You will also gain an understanding of their practical implications.

MOTIVATION—THEORY AND PRACTICE

Study Question 1	Study Question 2	Study Question 3	Study Question 4	Study Question 5
What Is Motivation?	**Content Theories of Motivation**	**Process Theories of Motivation**	**Reinforcement Theory of Motivation**	**Motivation in the New Workplace**
• Motivation and rewards • Rewards and performance	• Hierarchy of needs theory • ERG theory • Two-factor theory • Acquired needs theory • Q & A on content theories	• Equity theory • Expectancy theory • Goal-setting theory	• Reinforcement strategies • Positive reinforcement • Punishment • Ethical issues in reinforcement	• Integrated motivation model • Pay for performance • Incentive compensation systems
Learning check ❶	Learning check ❷	Learning check ❸	Learning check ❹	Learning check ❺

Why do some people work enthusiastically, often doing more than required to turn out an extraordinary performance? Why do others hold back and do the minimum needed to avoid reprimand or termination? How can a team leader or manager build a high-performance work setting? What can be done to ensure that the highest possible performance is achieved by every person in every job on every workday? These questions are, or should be, asked by managers in all work settings. Good answers begin with a true respect for people, with all of their talents and diversity, as the human capital of organizations. The best managers already know this. Like the opening example of Genentech, the work cultures they create invariably reflect an awareness that "productivity through people" is an irreplaceable foundation for long-term success. Consider these comments by those who know what it means to lead a high-performance organization.[2]

> *When people feel connected to something with a purpose greater than themselves, it inspires them to reach for levels they might not otherwise obtain…Our business is based on human potential.*

George Zimmer, founder and CEO of Men's Warehouse

No business goal is worth sacrificing your values. If you have to treat people poorly, or cut corners in your dealings with customers, forget it…You can build an organization based on mutual loyalty…but you can't do it if you treat people as disposable.

Patrick Kelly, CEO of PSS/World Medical, Inc.

In an increasingly competitive environment, it is vitally important that organizations take full advantage of the considerable potential inherent in their people.

Graham Dodd, Canadian practice leader at Watson Wyatt Canada

It is easy to say as a leader, or write in a mission statement, that "people are our most important asset." But the proof comes when actions back up the words. This means consistently demonstrating that one's organization is committed to people, that it offers a truly "motivational" work environment. Realistically, however, this task isn't always easy. The workplace often becomes complicated as the intricacies of human psychology come to play in daily events and situations. Sometimes a great employee who was motivated and energized turns into a dead-weight, pulling the company down. His ideas have dried up, he mopes around, and his only contribution to organizational functioning is relaying last night's hockey scores. Chances are he's checked out mentally from the company—something human-resource practitioners call "disengagement." Many would fire this slacker—or maybe not, says Jocelyn Bérard, managing director of DDI Canada, a human-resource consulting firm in Toronto. "Letting somebody go is not pleasant, and it can be very costly as well," says Bérard. "If you lose the person, you lose the expertise and sometimes even a client, and that's worse." Bérard suggests a better strategy would be to figure why the employee has changed and start working on getting the employee back psychologically.[3]

WHAT IS MOTIVATION?

The term **motivation** is used in management theory to describe forces within the individual that account for the level, direction, and persistence of effort expended at work. Simply put, a highly motivated person works hard at a job; an unmotivated person does not. A manager who leads through motivation does so by creating conditions under which other people feel consistently inspired to work hard. Obviously, a highly motivated workforce is indispensable to the achievement of sustained high-performance results.

■ **Motivation** accounts for the level, direction, and persistence of effort expended at work.

●●● MOTIVATION AND REWARDS

A *reward* is a work outcome of positive value to the individual. A motivational work setting is rich in rewards for people whose performance accomplishments help meet organizational objectives. In management, it is useful to distinguish between two types of rewards, extrinsic and intrinsic. **Extrinsic rewards** are externally administered. They are valued outcomes given to someone by another person, typically, a supervisor or higher-level manager. Common workplace examples are pay bonuses, promotions, time off, special assignments, office fixtures, awards, verbal praise, and recognition. The motivational stimulus of these extrinsic rewards originates outside of the individual; the rewards are made available by another person or by the organizational system.[4]

■ An **extrinsic reward** is provided by someone else.

Located in Midland, Ontario, Baytech Plastics engineers, manufactures, finishes, and assembles high-quality, custom-molded plastic components for both domestic and international markets. The company has remained successful through periods of rapid change by

take it to the case!

SC Johnson Canada
Motivating employees through work-life balance
With its Canadian head office located in Brantford, Ontario, SC Johnson Canada represents over 100 years of family history. Started in 1886 as a flooring company, SC Johnson has become the market leader in home care products including famous brands such as Pledge, Glade, and Raid. SC Johnson attributes its success to motivating and developing its employees by treating them like family. The company goes beyond standard benefits like salary and health care, and takes a more holistic approach to motivating and retaining employees by balancing their personal and professional needs. SC Johnson Canada was recognized as a best company to work for by *Canadian Business* magazine in 2007, and has been listed as one of *Report on Business*'s 50 best employers in Canada for six consecutive years. How does this focus on employees contribute to the success of SC Johnson? Find out by reading the case in the *Management Learning Workbook*.

Source: With information from the corporate website: <www.scjohnson.com>. Andrew Wahl, Joe Castaldo, Zena Olijnyk, Erin Pooley, et al., "The Best Workplaces in Canada 2007," *Canadian Business* (April 23, 2007), p. 39.

retaining and motivating its high-quality workforce. How does this company minimize employee turnover while maximizing productivity? It places a priority on a number of extrinsic initiatives, including competitive wages, pension plan, and health and dental benefits; as well as an innovative pay-for-performance system developed in co-operation with the union. The result is happy employees and a turnover rate of about 1.2 percent.[5]

■ An **intrinsic reward** occurs naturally during job performance.

Intrinsic rewards, by contrast, are self-administered. They occur "naturally" as a person performs a task, and are, in this sense, built directly into the job itself. The major sources of intrinsic rewards are the feelings of competency, personal development, and self-control people experience in their work.[6] In contrast to extrinsic rewards, the motivational stimulus of intrinsic rewards is internal and does not depend on the actions of some other person. Being self-administered, they offer the great advantage and power of "motivating from within." An air traffic controller, for example, says: "I don't know of anything I'd rather be doing. I love working the airplanes."[7]

●●● REWARDS AND PERFORMANCE

Starbucks seems to have the recipe right—not just for coffee, but also for rewards and performance. The company offers a stock option plan to all its employees. Called "bean stock," the incentive plan offers employees stock options linked to their base pay. This means they can buy the company's stock at a fixed price in the future; if the market value is higher than the price of their option, they gain. Thus, they should be motivated to do things that help the firm perform best. CEO Howard Schultz says the plan has had a positive impact on attitudes and performance. The phrase "bean-stocking it" is even used by employees when they find ways to reduce costs or increase sales. Schultz is committed to the motivational value of this innovative reward plan.[8]

There are many possible ways to creatively and directly link rewards and performance in the new workplace; that is, to establish *performance-contingent rewards*. To take full advantage of the possibilities, however, managers must (1) respect diversity and individual differences in order to best understand what people want from work, and (2) allocate rewards in ways that satisfy the interests of both individuals and the organization. A variety of motivation theories provide insights into this complex process. The *content theories of motivation* help us to understand human needs and how people with different needs may respond to different work situations. The *process theories of motivation* describe how people give meaning to rewards and then make decisions on various work-related behaviours. The *reinforcement theory of motivation* focuses on the environment as a major source of rewards that influence human behaviour.

> **BE SURE YOU CAN**
> • define the term motivation • differentiate extrinsic and intrinsic rewards • explain the concept of perform-   ✓ Learning check ❶
> ance-contingent rewards • differentiate the basic approaches of the content, process, and reinforcement
> theories

CONTENT THEORIES OF MOTIVATION

Most discussions of motivation begin with the concept of individual **needs**—the unfulfilled physiological or psychological desires of an individual. Content theories of motivation use individual needs to explain the behaviours and attitudes of people at work. Although each of the following theories discusses a slightly different set of needs, all agree that needs cause tensions that influence attitudes and behaviour. Good managers and leaders establish conditions in which people are able to satisfy important needs through their work. They also eliminate work obstacles that interfere with the satisfaction of important needs.

■ A **need** is an unfulfilled physiological or psychological desire.

●●● HIERARCHY OF NEEDS THEORY

The theory of human needs developed by Abraham Maslow was introduced in Chapter 2 as an important foundation of the history of management thought. According to his hierarchy of human needs, **lower-order needs** include physiological, safety, and social concerns, and **higher-order needs** include esteem and self-actualization concerns.[9] Whereas lower-order needs are desires for social and physical well-being, the higher-order needs are desires for psychological development and growth.

Maslow uses two principles to describe how these needs affect human behaviour. The *deficit principle* states that a satisfied need is not a motivator of behaviour. People are expected to act in ways that satisfy deprived needs; that is, needs for which a "deficit" exists. The *progression principle* states that a need at one level does not become activated until the next lower-level need is already satisfied. People are expected to advance step-by-step up the hierarchy in their search for need satisfactions. At the level of self-actualization, the more these needs are satisfied, the stronger they are supposed to grow. According to Maslow, a person should continue to be motivated by opportunities for self-fulfillment as long as the other needs remain satisfied. Although research has not verified the strict deficit and progression principles, Maslow's ideas are very helpful for understanding the needs of people at work and considering what can be done to satisfy them. His theory advises managers to recognize that deprived needs may result in negative attitudes and behaviours. By the same token, opportunities for need satisfaction may have positive motivational consequences. *Figure 14.1* illustrates how managers can use Maslow's ideas to better meet the needs of the people with whom they work. Notice that the higher-order self-actualization needs are served entirely by intrinsic rewards. The esteem needs are served by both intrinsic and extrinsic rewards. Lower-order needs are served solely by extrinsic rewards.

■ **Lower-order needs** are physiological, safety, and social needs in Maslow's hierarchy.

■ **Higher-order needs** are esteem and self-actualization needs in Maslow's hierarchy.

Figure 14.1 Opportunities for satisfaction in Maslow's hierarchy of human needs.

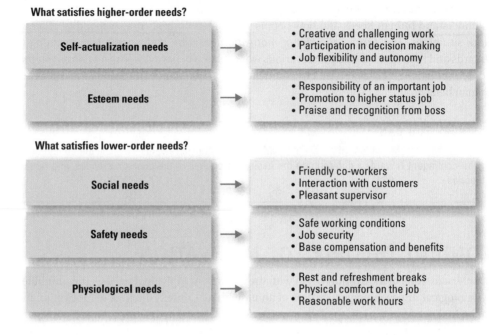

What satisfies higher-order needs?

Self-actualization needs →
- Creative and challenging work
- Participation in decision making
- Job flexibility and autonomy

Esteem needs →
- Responsibility of an important job
- Promotion to higher status job
- Praise and recognition from boss

What satisfies lower-order needs?

Social needs →
- Friendly co-workers
- Interaction with customers
- Pleasant supervisor

Safety needs →
- Safe working conditions
- Job security
- Base compensation and benefits

Physiological needs →
- Rest and refreshment breaks
- Physical comfort on the job
- Reasonable work hours

●●● ERG THEORY

One of the most promising efforts to build on Maslow's work is the ERG theory proposed by Clayton Alderfer.[10] This theory collapses Maslow's five needs categories into three. *Existence needs* are desires for physiological and material well-being. *Relatedness needs* are desires for satisfying interpersonal relationships. *Growth needs* are desires for continued psychological growth and development. Alderfer's ERG theory also differs from Maslow's theory in other respects. ERG does not assume that lower-level needs must be satisfied before higher-level needs become activated; any or all types of needs can influence individual behaviour at a given time. Alderfer also does not assume that satisfied needs lose their motivational impact. ERG theory contains a *frustration-regression principle*, according to which an already-satisfied lower-level need can become reactivated and influence behaviour when a higher-level need cannot be satisfied. Alderfer's approach offers an additional means for understanding human needs and their influence on people at work.

▪ A **satisfier factor** is found in job content, such as a sense of achievement, recognition, responsibility, advancement, or personal growth.

▪ A **hygiene factor** is found in the job context, such as working conditions, interpersonal relations, organizational policies, and salary.

●●● TWO-FACTOR THEORY

The two-factor theory of Frederick Herzberg was developed from a pattern identified in the responses of almost 4,000 people to questions about their work.[11] When questioned about what "turned them on," they tended to identify things relating to the nature of the job itself. Herzberg calls these **satisfier factors**. When questioned about what "turned them off," they tended to identify things relating more to the work setting. Herzberg calls these **hygiene factors**.

As shown in *Figure 14.2*, the two-factor theory associates hygiene factors, or sources of *job dissatisfaction*, with aspects of *job context*. The *hygiene factors* include such things as working conditions, interpersonal relations, organizational policies and administration, technical quality of supervision, and base wage or salary. These factors contribute to more or less job dissatisfaction. Herzberg argues that improving them, such as by adding piped in music or

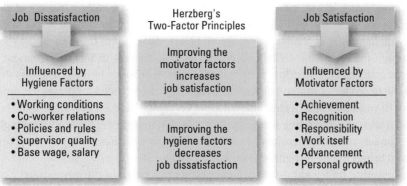

Figure 14.2 Herzberg's two-factor theory.

implementing a no-smoking policy, can make people less dissatisfied with these aspects of their work. But this will not increase job satisfaction. That requires attention to an entirely different set of factors and managerial initiatives.

To improve motivation, Herzberg advises managers to focus on the satisfier factors. By making improvements in *job content* he believes that job satisfaction and performance can be raised. The important *satisfier factors* include such things as a sense of achievement, feelings of recognition, a sense of responsibility, the opportunity for advancement, and feelings of personal growth.

Scholars have criticized Herzberg's theory as being method-bound and difficult to replicate.[12] For his part, Herzberg reports confirming studies in countries located in Europe, Africa, the Middle East, and Asia.[13] At the very least, the two-factor theory remains a useful reminder that there are two important aspects of all jobs: *job content*, what people do in terms of job tasks; and *job context*, the work setting in which they do it. Herzberg's advice to managers is still timely: (1) always correct poor context to eliminate actual or potential sources of job dissatisfaction; and (2) be sure to build satisfier factors into job content to maximize opportunities for job satisfaction. The two-factor theory also cautions managers not to expect too much by way of motivational improvements from investments in things like special office fixtures, attractive lounges for breaks, and even high base salaries. Instead, it focuses attention on the nature of the job itself and on such things as responsibility and personal growth as opportunities for higher-order need satisfaction.

●●● ACQUIRED NEEDS THEORY

In the late 1940s, David McClelland and his colleagues began experimenting with the Thematic Apperception Test (TAT) as a way of examining human needs. The TAT asks people to view pictures and write stories about what they see. The stories are then content analyzed for themes that display individual needs.[14] From this research, McClelland identified three needs that are central to his approach to motivation. **Need for Achievement** is the desire to do something better or more efficiently, to solve problems, or to master complex tasks. **Need for Power** is the desire to control other people, to influence their behaviour, or to be responsible for them. **Need for Affiliation** is the desire to establish and maintain friendly and warm relations with other people.

According to McClelland, people acquire or develop these needs over time as a result of individual life experiences. He also associates each need with a distinct set of work preferences. Managers are encouraged to recognize the strength of each need in themselves and in other people. Attempts can then be made to create work environments responsive to them. People high in the need for achievement, for example, like to put their competencies to work,

■ **Need for Achievement** is the desire to do something better, to solve problems, or to master complex tasks.

■ **Need for Power** is the desire to control, influence, or be responsible for other people.

■ **Need for Affiliation** is the desire to establish and maintain good relations with people.

they take moderate risks in competitive situations, and they are willing to work alone. As a result, the work preferences of high-need achievers include (1) individual responsibility for results, (2) achievable but challenging goals, and (3) feedback on performance.

Through his research, McClelland concludes that success in top management is not based on a concern for individual achievement alone. It requires broader interests that also relate to the needs for power and affiliation. People high in the need for power are motivated to behave in ways that have a clear impact on other people and events. They enjoy being in control of a situation and being recognized for this responsibility. A person with a high need for power prefers work that involves control over other persons, has an impact on people and events, and brings public recognition and attention.

Importantly, McClelland distinguishes between two forms of the power need. The *need for "personal" power* is exploitative and involves manipulation for the pure sake of personal gratification. This type of power need is not successful in management. By contrast, the *need for "social" power* is the positive face of power. It involves the use of power in a socially responsible way, one that is directed toward group or organizational objectives rather than personal ones. This need for social power is essential to managerial leadership.

People high in the need for affiliation seek companionship, social approval, and satisfying interpersonal relationships. They take a special interest in work that involves interpersonal relationships, work that provides for companionship, and work that brings social approval.

McClelland believes that people very high in the need for affiliation alone may not make the best managers; their desires for social approval and friendship may complicate decision making. There are times when managers and leaders must decide and act in ways that other persons may disagree with. To the extent that the need for affiliation interferes with someone's ability to make these decisions, managerial effectiveness will be sacrificed. Thus, the successful executive, in McClelland's view, is likely to possess a high need for social power that is greater than an otherwise strong need for affiliation.

●●● QUESTIONS AND ANSWERS ON CONTENT THEORIES

Figure 14.3 shows how the human needs identified by Maslow, Alderfer, Herzberg, and McClelland compare with one another. Although the terminology varies, there is a lot of common ground. The insights of the theories can and should be used together to add to our understanding of human needs in the workplace. By way of summary, the following questions and answers further clarify the content theories and their managerial implications.[15]

"How many different individual needs are there?" Research has not yet identified a perfect list of individual needs at work. But, as a manager, you can use the ideas of Maslow,

Figure 14.3 Comparison of Maslow's, Alderfer's, Herzberg's, and McClelland's motivation theories.

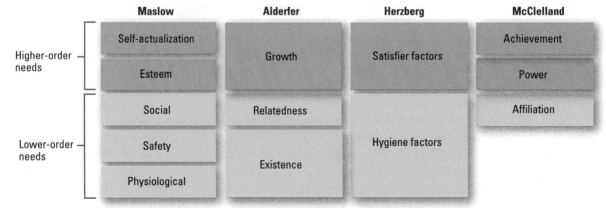

Alderfer, Herzberg, and McClelland to better understand the various needs that people may bring with them to the work setting. *"Can a work outcome or reward satisfy more than one need?"* Yes, work outcomes or rewards can satisfy more than one need. Pay is a good example. It is a source of performance feedback for the high need achiever. It can be a source of personal security for someone with strong existence needs. It can also be used indirectly to obtain things that satisfy social and ego needs. *"Is there a hierarchy of needs?"* Research does not support the precise five-step hierarchy of needs postulated by Maslow. It seems more legitimate to view human needs as operating in a flexible hierarchy, such as the one in Alderfer's ERG theory. However, it is useful to distinguish between the motivational properties of lower-order and higher-order needs. *"How important are the various needs?"* Research is inconclusive as to the importance of different needs. Individuals vary widely in this regard. They may also value needs differently at different times and at different ages or career stages. This is another reason why managers should use the insights of all the content theories to understand the differing needs of people at work.

> **BE SURE YOU CAN**
> • define the term need • describe work practices that satisfy higher-order and lower-order needs in Maslow's ✔ **Learning check ❷**
> hierarchy • contrast Maslow's hierarchy with ERG theory • describe work practices that influence hygiene factors and satisfier factors in Herzberg's two-factor theory • define needs for achievement, affiliation, and power in McClelland's theory • differentiate the needs for personal and social power • describe work practices that satisfy a person with a high need for achievement • compare the common ground among the content theories of Maslow, Alderfer, Herzberg, and McClelland

PROCESS THEORIES OF MOTIVATION

Although the details vary, each of the content theories can help managers better understand individual differences and deal positively with them. The process theories add to this understanding. The equity, expectancy, and goal-setting theories offer advice and insight on how people actually make choices to work hard or not, based on their individual preferences, the available rewards, and possible work outcomes.

●●● EQUITY THEORY

The equity theory of motivation is best known in management through the work of J. Stacy Adams.[16] It is based on the logic of social comparisons and the notion that perceived inequity is a motivating state. That is, when people believe that they have been unfairly treated in comparison to others, they will be motivated to eliminate the discomfort and restore a sense of perceived equity to the situation. The classic example is pay. The equity question is, "In comparison with others, how fairly am I being compensated for the work that I do?" According to the equity theory, an individual who perceives that she or he is being treated unfairly in comparison to others will be motivated to act in ways that reduce the perceived inequity.

Figure 14.4 shows how the equity dynamic works in the form of input-to-outcome comparisons. These equity comparisons are especially common whenever managers allocate extrinsic rewards, things like compensation, benefits, preferred job assignments, and work privileges. The comparison points may be co-workers in the group, workers elsewhere in the organization, and even persons employed by other organizations. Perceived inequities occur whenever people feel that the rewards received for their work efforts are unfair given the rewards others appear to be getting. Adams predicts that people will try to deal with perceived negative inequity by any one or more of the following:

Figure 14.4 Equity theory and the role of social comparison.

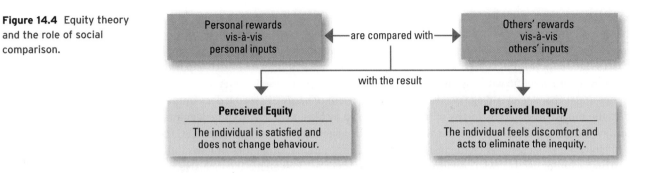

PERSONAL MANAGEMENT

It is very difficult to say that someone completely lacks **INITIATIVE.** Each of us has to display a certain amount of initiative just to survive each day. But the initiative of people at work varies greatly, just as it does among students. For you the issue is: do you have the self-initiative to work hard and apply your talents to achieve high performance in school, in a job, on an assigned task? Don't hide from the answer. The way you work now in school or in a job is a good predictor of the future.

Part of the key to initiative lies in a good person–job fit; that is, finding the right job in the right career field. The rest, however, is all up to you. Only you can decide that you want to work really hard. Look at the following criteria for someone high in self-initiative. Consider how you behave as a student or in a job. Can you honestly say that each statement accurately describes you?

- Looks for problems, and fixes them.
- Does more than required; works beyond expectations.
- Helps others when they are stuck or overwhelmed.
- Tries to do things better; is not comfortable with the status quo.
- Thinks ahead; crafts ideas and makes plans for the future.

Get to know yourself better

Complete Self-Assessments #23—**Student Engagement Survey,** and #24—**Job Design Choices,** and #23—**Best Job Design,** from the Workbook and Personal Management Activity #14 on the companion website.

- Changing their work inputs by putting less effort into their jobs.
- Changing the rewards received by asking for better treatment.
- Changing the comparison points to make things seem better.
- Changing the situation by leaving the job.

Research on equity theory has largely been accomplished in the laboratory. It is most conclusive with respect to perceived negative inequity. People who feel underpaid, for example, experience a sense of anger. This causes them to try to restore perceived equity to the situation by pursuing one or more of the actions described in the above list, such as reducing current work efforts to compensate for the missing rewards or even quitting the job.[17] There is also evidence that the equity dynamic occurs among people who feel overpaid. This time the perceived inequity is associated with a sense of guilt. The attempt to restore perceived equity may involve, for example, increasing the quantity or quality of work, taking on more difficult assignments, or working overtime.

A key point in the equity theory is that people behave according to their perceptions. What influences individual behaviour is not the reward's absolute value or the manager's intentions; the recipient's perceptions determine the motivational outcomes. Rewards perceived as equitable should have a positive result on satisfaction and performance; those perceived as inequitable may create dissatisfaction and cause performance problems.

Informed managers anticipate perceived negative inequities whenever especially visible rewards such as pay or promotions are allocated. Instead of letting equity dynamics get out of hand, they try to manage the perceptions. They carefully communicate the intended value of rewards being given, clarify the performance appraisals upon which they are based, and suggest appropriate comparison points.

In respect to pay, two equity situations mentioned earlier in the book are worth remembering. First is *gender equity*. It is well established that women, on the average, earn less than men. This difference is most evident in occupations traditionally dominated by men, such as the legal professions, but it also includes ones where females have traditionally held most jobs, such as teaching. Second is *comparable worth*. This is the concept that people doing jobs of similar value based on required education, training, and skills (such as nursing and accounting) should receive similar pay. Advocates of comparable worth claim that it corrects historical pay inequities and is a natural extension of the "equal-pay-for-equal-work" concept. Critics claim that "similar value" is too difficult to define and that the dramatic restructuring of wage scales would have a negative economic impact on society.

●●● EXPECTANCY THEORY

Victor Vroom's expectancy theory of motivation asks a central question: what determines the willingness of an individual to work hard at tasks important to the organization?[18] In response, the theory indicates that "people will do what they can do when they want to do it." More specifically, Vroom suggests that the motivation to work depends on the relationships among the *three expectancy factors*, depicted in *Figure 14.5* and described here:

- Expectancy—a person's belief that working hard will result in a desired level of task performance being achieved (this is sometimes called effort-performance expectancy).

- Instrumentality—a person's belief that successful performance will be followed by rewards and other potential outcomes (this is sometimes called performance-outcome expectancy).

- Valence—the value a person assigns to the possible rewards and other work-related outcomes.

> ■ **Expectancy** is a person's belief that working hard will result in high task performance.
>
> ■ **Instrumentality** is a person's belief that various outcomes will occur as a result of task performance.
>
> ■ **Valence** is the value a person assigns to work-related outcomes.

In the expectancy theory, motivation *(M)*, expectancy *(E)*, instrumentality *(I)*, and valence *(V)* are related to one another in a multiplicative fashion: $M = E \times I \times V$. In other words, motivation is determined by expectancy times instrumentality times valence. This multiplier effect has important managerial implications. Mathematically speaking, a zero at any location on the right side of the equation (that is, for *E*, *I*, or *V*) will result in zero motivation. Managers are thus advised to act in ways that (1) maximize expectancy—people must believe that if they try, they can perform; (2) maximize instrumentality—people must perceive that high performance will be followed by certain outcomes; and (3) maximize valence—people must value the outcomes. Not one of these factors can be left unattended.

Suppose, for example, that a manager is wondering whether or not the prospect of earning a promotion will be motivational to a subordinate. A typical assumption is that people will work hard to earn a promotion. But is this necessarily true? Expectancy theory predicts that a person's motivation to work hard for a promotion will be low if any one or more of the following three conditions apply. First, *if expectancy is low, motivation will suffer*. The person may feel that he or she cannot achieve the performance level necessary to get promoted. So why try? Second, *if instrumentality is low, motivation will suffer*. The person may lack confidence

Figure 14.5 Elements in the expectancy theory of motivation.

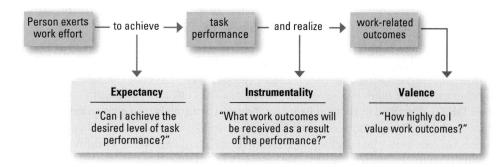

Person exerts work effort — to achieve → task performance — and realize → work-related outcomes

Expectancy
"Can I achieve the desired level of task performance?"

Instrumentality
"What work outcomes will be received as a result of the performance?"

Valence
"How highly do I value work outcomes?"

that a high level of task performance will result in being promoted. So why try? Third, *if valence is low, motivation will suffer.* The person may place little value on receiving a promotion. It simply isn't much of a reward. So, once again, why try?

As shown in *Figure 14.6*, the management implications of expectancy theory include being willing to work with each individual to maximize his or her expectancies, instrumentalities, and valences in ways that support organizational objectives. The theory reminds managers that different people answer the question "Why should I work hard today?" in different ways. The implication is that every person must be respected as an individual with unique needs, preferences, and concerns regarding work. Knowing this, a manager can try to customize work environments to best fit individual needs and preferences.

Figure 14.6 Managerial implications of expectancy theory.

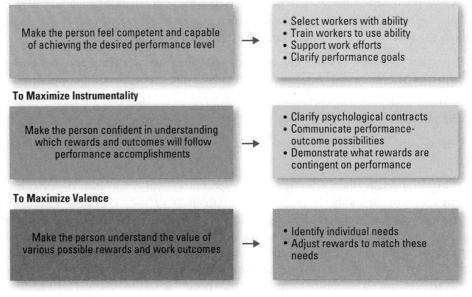

To Maximize Expectancy

Make the person feel competent and capable of achieving the desired performance level

→

- Select workers with ability
- Train workers to use ability
- Support work efforts
- Clarify performance goals

To Maximize Instrumentality

Make the person confident in understanding which rewards and outcomes will follow performance accomplishments

→

- Clarify psychological contracts
- Communicate performance-outcome possibilities
- Demonstrate what rewards are contingent on performance

To Maximize Valence

Make the person understand the value of various possible rewards and work outcomes

→

- Identify individual needs
- Adjust rewards to match these needs

●●● GOAL-SETTING THEORY

The goal-setting theory described by Edwin Locke focuses on the motivational properties of task goals.[19] The basic premise is that task goals can be highly motivating *if* they are properly set and *if* they are well managed. Goals give direction to people in their work. Goals clarify the performance expectations between a supervisor and subordinate, between co-workers, and across subunits in an organization. Goals establish a frame of reference for task feedback. Goals also provide a foundation for behavioural self-management.[20] In these and related ways, Locke believes goal setting can enhance individual work performance and job satisfaction.

To achieve the motivational benefits of goal setting, research by Locke and his associates indicates that managers and team leaders must work with others to set the right goals in the right ways. The keys in this respect largely relate to *goal specificity, goal difficulty, goal acceptance*, and *goal commitment*. These are among the goal-setting recommendations provided in *Manager's Notepad 14.1*. Participation is a major element in applying these concepts to unlock the motivational value of task goals. The concept of management by objectives (MBO), described in Chapter 8 on planning and controlling, is a good example. When done well, MBO brings supervisors and subordinates together in a joint and participative process of goal setting and performance review. Research indicates that a positive impact is most likely to occur when the participation in MBO (1) allows for increased understanding of specific and difficult goals and (2) provides for greater acceptance of the goals and a sense of commitment to them. Along with participation, the opportunity to receive feedback on goal accomplishment is also essential to motivation.

Managers should be aware of the participation options in goal setting. It may not always be possible to allow participation when selecting exactly which goals need to be pursued, but it may be possible to allow participation in the decisions about how to best pursue them. Furthermore, the constraints of time and other factors operating in some situations may not allow for participation. In these settings, Locke's research suggests that workers will respond positively to externally imposed goals if supervisors assigning them are trusted and if workers believe they will be adequately supported in their attempts to achieve them.

MANAGER'S
Notepad 14.1
How to make goal setting work for you

- *Set specific goals:* They lead to higher performance than more generally stated ones, such as "Do your best."

- *Set challenging goals:* When viewed as realistic and attainable, more difficult goals lead to higher performance than do easy goals.

- *Build goal acceptance and commitment:* People work harder for goals they accept and believe in; they resist goals forced upon them.

- *Clarify goal priorities:* Make sure that expectations are clear as to which goals should be accomplished first, and why.

- *Provide feedback on goal accomplishment:* Make sure that people know how well they are doing in respect to goal accomplishment.

- *Reward goal accomplishment:* Don't let positive accomplishments pass unnoticed; reward people for doing what they set out to do.

BE SURE YOU CAN
• explain the role of social comparison in Adams's equity theory • apply the equity theory to explain how people with felt negative inequity behave • define the terms expectancy, instrumentality, valence • explain the implications of Vroom's expectancy theory: $M = E \times I \times V$ • explain Locke's goal-setting theory • describe the fit between goal-setting theory and MBO

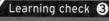 Learning check ❸

REINFORCEMENT THEORY OF MOTIVATION

The content and process theories are concerned with explaining "why" people do things in terms of satisfying needs, resolving felt inequities, and/or pursuing positive expectancies and task goals. Reinforcement theory, by contrast, views human behaviour as determined by its environmental consequences. Instead of looking within the individual to explain motivation, it focuses on the external environment and the consequences it holds for the individual. The basic premises of reinforcement theory are based on what E. L. Thorndike called the **law of effect**: behaviour that results in a pleasant outcome is likely to be repeated; behaviour that results in an unpleasant outcome is not likely to be repeated.[21]

■ The **law of effect** states that behaviour followed by pleasant consequences is likely to be repeated; behaviour followed by unpleasant consequences is not.

●●● REINFORCEMENT STRATEGIES

▪ **Operant conditioning** is the control of behaviour by manipulating its consequences.

▪ **Positive reinforcement** strengthens a behaviour by making a desirable consequence contingent on its occurrence.

▪ **Negative reinforcement** strengthens a behaviour by making the avoidance of an undesirable consequence contingent on its occurrence.

▪ **Punishment** discourages a behaviour by making an unpleasant consequence contingent on its occurrence.

▪ **Extinction** discourages a behaviour by making the removal of a desirable consequence contingent on its occurrence.

Psychologist B. F. Skinner popularized the concept of **operant conditioning** as the process of applying the law of effect to control behaviour by manipulating its consequences.[22] You may think of operant conditioning as learning by reinforcement. In management, the goal is to use reinforcement principles to systematically reinforce desirable work behaviour and discourage undesirable work behaviour.[23]

Four strategies of reinforcement are used in operant conditioning. **Positive reinforcement** strengthens or increases the frequency of desirable behaviour by making a pleasant consequence contingent on its occurrence. *Example:* A manager nods to express approval to someone who makes a useful comment during a staff meeting. **Negative reinforcement** increases the frequency of or strengthens desirable behaviour by making the avoidance of an unpleasant consequence contingent on its occurrence. *Example:* A manager who has been nagging a worker every day about tardiness does not nag when the worker comes to work on time. **Punishment** decreases the frequency of or eliminates an undesirable behaviour by making an unpleasant consequence contingent on its occurrence. *Example:* A manager issues a written reprimand to an employee whose careless work creates quality problems. **Extinction** decreases the frequency of, or eliminates, an undesirable behaviour by making the removal of a pleasant consequence contingent on its occurrence. *Example:* A manager observes that a disruptive employee is receiving social approval from co-workers; the manager counsels co-workers to stop giving this approval.

Figure 14.7 shows how these four reinforcement strategies can be applied in management. The supervisor's goal in the example is to improve work quality as part of a TQM program. Notice how the supervisor can use each of the strategies to influence continuous improvement practices among employees. Note, too, that both positive and negative reinforcement strategies strengthen desirable behaviour when it occurs. The punishment and extinction strategies weaken or eliminate undesirable behaviours.

Figure 14.7 Applying reinforcement strategies: case of total quality management.

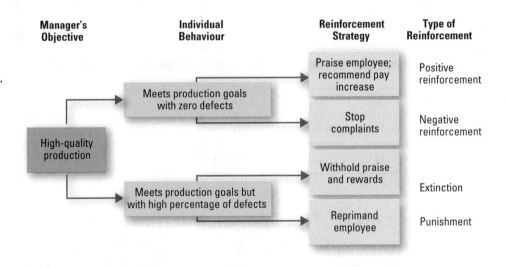

●●● POSITIVE REINFORCEMENT

Among the reinforcement strategies, positive reinforcement deserves special attention. It should be a central part of any manager's motivational strategy. For example, Pfizer Canada, a pharmaceutical company with its head office in Kirkland, Quebec, regularly organizes an overseas trip for representatives (and their spouses) who successfully achieve their annual goals.

There are two important laws of positive reinforcement. First, the *law of contingent reinforcement* states that for a reward to have maximum reinforcing value, it must be delivered only if the desired behaviour is exhibited. Second, the *law of immediate reinforcement* states that the more immediate the delivery of a reward after the occurrence of a desirable behaviour, the greater the reinforcing value of the reward. A study from Wichita State University discovered that the most powerful motivator is a personalized, instant recognition from either one's co-workers or manager.[24] Managers should use these laws to full advantage in the everyday pursuit of the benefits of positive reinforcement. Several useful guidelines are presented in *Manager's Notepad 14.2*.

The power of positive reinforcement can be mobilized through a process known as **shaping**. This is the creation of a new behaviour by the positive reinforcement of successive approximations to it. The timing of positive reinforcement can also make a difference in its impact. A *continuous reinforcement schedule* administers a reward each time a desired behaviour occurs. An *intermittent reinforcement schedule* rewards behaviour only periodically. In general, a manager can expect that continuous reinforcement will elicit a desired behaviour more quickly than will intermittent reinforcement. Also, behaviour acquired under an intermittent schedule will be more permanent than will behaviour acquired under a continuous schedule. One way to succeed with a shaping strategy, for example, is to give reinforcement on a continuous basis until the desired behaviour is achieved. Then an intermittent schedule can be used to maintain the behaviour at the new level.

■ **Shaping** is positive reinforcement of successive approximations to the desired behaviour.

MANAGER'S Notepad 14.2

Guidelines for positive reinforcement...and punishment

Positive Reinforcement:

- Clearly identify desired work behaviours.
- Maintain a diverse inventory of rewards.
- Inform everyone of what must be done to get rewards.
- Recognize individual differences when allocating rewards.
- Follow the laws of immediate and contingent reinforcement.

Punishment:

- Tell the person what is being done wrong.
- Tell the person what is being done right.
- Make sure the punishment matches the behaviour.
- Administer the punishment in private.
- Follow the laws of immediate and contingent reinforcement.

●●●● PUNISHMENT

As a reinforcement strategy, punishment attempts to eliminate undesirable behaviour by making an unpleasant consequence contingent with its occurrence. To punish an employee, for example, a manager may deny a valued reward, such as verbal praise or merit pay, or administer an unpleasant outcome, such as a verbal reprimand or pay reduction. Like positive reinforcement, punishment can be done poorly or it can be done well. All too often, it is probably done poorly. If you look back to *Manager's Notepad 14.2*, it offers guidance on how to best handle punishment as a reinforcement strategy.

●●● ETHICAL ISSUES IN REINFORCEMENT

The use of reinforcement techniques in work settings has produced many success stories of improved safety, decreased absenteeism and tardiness, and increased productivity.[25] But there are still debates over both the results and the ethics of controlling human behaviour. Opponents are concerned that the use of operant conditioning principles ignores the individuality of people, restricts their freedom of choice, and fails to recognize that people can be motivated by things other than extrinsic rewards. Advocates attack the criticisms straight on. They agree that reinforcement involves the control of behaviour, but they argue that control is part of every manager's job. The real question, they say, is whether it is ethical to not control behaviour well enough so that the goals of both the organization and the individual are well served. Even as research continues, the value of reinforcement techniques is undeniable. This is especially true when they are combined with the insights of the other motivation theories discussed in this chapter.[26]

✔ **Learning check ④**

BE SURE YOU CAN
• define the terms law of effect and operant conditioning • illustrate how positive reinforcement, negative reinforcement, punishment, and extinction are used to influence work behaviour • explain the reinforcement technique of shaping • describe how managers should use the laws of immediate and contingent reinforcement when allocating rewards

MOTIVATION IN THE NEW WORKPLACE

The changes taking place in organizations have been mentioned many times so far in *Management*—horizontal structures, primacy of people, importance of teamwork, high-performance goals, adaptability and speed, worker empowerment, and high technology. All these

Canadian Managers
Motivator Extraordinaire!

Toronto Argonauts coach and former CFL most outstanding player, Michael "Pinball" Clemons, is a leader both on and off the football field. A man of unquestionable character, he is an excellent motivator for his players, for community groups, and for corporate clients.

Clemons's aptitude for motivational speaking is indisputable. Sports commentator Mark Lee observes that "a head coach's job, in most respects, is to be a guy who can rally everybody around one cause. The Argos's turnaround shows [Michael Clemons is] a guy with great spirit and a great leader."

Clemons's presentations are captivating and empowering. How does he do it? Clemons communicates through heartfelt stories offered in a passionate voice and with a contagious smile. He focuses on the importance of teamwork. At barely 168 cm and 78 kg, he inspires his listeners by showing that it is possible to beat the odds and that, with effort, all things are possible.

Source: With information from www.speakers.ca and "Pinball Clemons keeps inspiring Argos" <www.cbc.ca/sports>. Retrieved February 9, 2007.

developments and more are creating new work environments in which people search for meaning, rewards, and valuable contributions. The workforce is changing as well. More work is being done by part-timers; there is an increasing divide between low-skill, low-pay workers and high-skill, high-pay workers; the number of older workers is growing; and volunteers are playing increasingly important roles in the non-profit service organizations of communities. Managers must rise to the challenge of creating motivational environments in these new realities. The following integrated motivational model is a helpful point of reference. It pulls together the best insights from all motivation theories, allowing them to be applied to good advantage in a manager's unique circumstances.

●●● INTEGRATED MODEL OF MOTIVATION

Figure 14.8 shows how each of the theoretical perspectives discussed so far can be combined into one model of motivational dynamics. In this figure, motivation leads to effort that, when combined with appropriate individual abilities and organizational support, leads to performance. The motivational impact of any rewards received for this performance depends on equity and reinforcement considerations. Ultimately, satisfaction with rewards should lead to increased motivation to work hard in the future. Among the motivation issues that can be addressed within this integrating framework, perhaps none receives as much attention as compensation.[27] There are many advantages, both individual and organizational, to be gained from a truly motivational compensation scheme. But in practice, the link between motivation and compensation can be quite complicated.

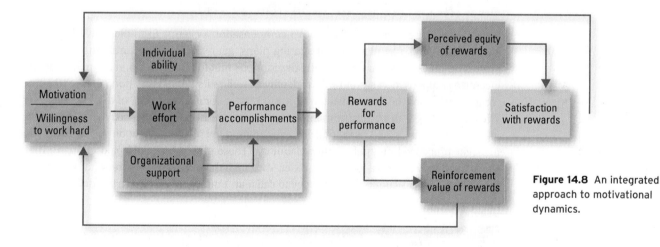

Figure 14.8 An integrated approach to motivational dynamics.

●●● PAY FOR PERFORMANCE

The notion of paying people for their performance is consistent with the equity, expectancy, and reinforcement theories.[28] Formally defined, **merit pay** is a compensation system that awards pay increases in proportion to individual performance contributions. By allocating pay increases in this way, managers are attempting to recognize and positively reinforce high performers. They are also attempting to remind low performers of their lack of achievement, and send a signal that they must do better in the future. In principle, it makes sense to reward people in proportion to their work contributions. But, because of the difficulty of actually linking pay with performance in a contingent and equitable manner, merit pay does not always achieve the desired results.

■ **Merit pay** awards pay increases in proportion to performance contributions.

A successful merit pay system must have a solid foundation in agreed-upon and well-defined "performance measures." Any weakness in the performance appraisal methods can undermine a merit pay system. There must also be consistency in applying merit pay at all levels of the organization. Failure to do so undermines the system's credibility. There is a lot of concern today, for example, that CEO pay isn't adequately linked to performance. Magazines like *Business Week* and *Fortune* regularly report on the issues. The impression of some is that CEOs are well rewarded no matter how well the company performs. A critical report by *Responsible Wealth* once cited a dramatic example. Honeywell CEO Michael Bonsignore made some $54 million in total compensation the same year that his firm laid off 11,600 workers worldwide.[29] Fortunately, there have been some improvements. A Watson Wyatt study on the latest trends in executive compensation found that, "Canadian organizations are answering the call of increasingly vocal stakeholder groups to improve management and disclosure of executive compensation practices…our study clearly demonstrates that the pay-for-performance philosophy is taking hold and companies are making strides in aligning CEO compensation to corporate performance."[30]

For these and related reasons, not everyone believes in merit pay. John Whitney, author of *The Trust Factor*, suggests that pay-for-performance may not work very well. While pointing out that market forces should determine base pay, Whitney believes that annual increases should be an equal percentage of base. This communicates a universal sense of importance to all employees. And it helps to avoid frustrations and complaints when merit increases are tied to performance differences. Says Whitney, "Quibbling over whether someone should get a 4.7 percent raise or 5.1 percent is a colossal waste of time."[31]

●●● INCENTIVE COMPENSATION SYSTEMS

Organizations use a variety of incentive compensation systems. Examples include pay for knowledge, bonus pay plans, profit-sharing plans, gain-sharing plans, and employee stock ownership plans.[32] As you consider the descriptions that follow, however, remember that any incentive compensation system will work only as well as its implementation. The well-known compensation scholar and consultant Edward Lawler, for example, tells of this experience.[33] While consulting with a furniture manufacturing plant, he became convinced that a "gain sharing" incentive plan would be helpful and thus advised the plant manager on starting one. The manager proceeded only reluctantly, claiming, "These guys are already paid enough…they should be happy to have a job." Says Lawler, "Although the program was somewhat successful, the plant manager's continuing tendency to call it an 'employee bribe program' definitely limited its success."

CANADIAN COMPANY IN THE NEWS   Flight Centre

RECOGNIZING GOOD WORK

Motivating employees sometimes requires more creativity than simply handing out cash bonuses for a job well done. The travel retailer Flight Centre has some innovative ideas, combining both monetary compensation and other incentives, to motivate its young workforce. A monthly "Buzz Night" recognizes high achievers with feedback and gift certificates. And, at the end of the year, a black-tie ball provides top performers with cash bonuses, free airline tickets, and a grand prize of a car. The "ultra-high" achievers go to a global ball. Sometimes an entire unit is given this honour in order to illustrate the importance of teamwork.

Source: "Developing Tomorrow's Leaders," *Canadian Business*, Advertising Supplement, January 17-30, 2005.

Pay for Knowledge

Consistent with the emphasis on human capital, some organizations now emphasize paying for knowledge. A concept called **skills-based pay** pays workers according to the number of job-relevant skills they master. For example, Westbridge PET Containers, a privately owned Calgary company specializing in food, beverage, and personal care markets, introduced a pay-for-knowledge system. When employees become qualified in another job at Westbridge they are given a financial reward. Cross-trained employees go back to their regular job, but receive extra pay. Interested workers are able to train for all of the positions in the plant. The system has been well received by the employees, with a 100 percent satisfaction rate noted in a recent survey. The company is also happy with the arrangement because the system provides them with a flexible workforce, high employee retention and competitiveness, and increased morale.[34]

■ **Skills-based pay** is a system of paying workers according to the number of job-relevant skills they master.

Bonus Pay

Bonus pay plans provide one-time or lump-sum payments to employees based on the accomplishment of specific performance targets or some other extraordinary contribution, such as an idea for a work improvement. They typically do not increase base salary or wages. Bonuses have been most common at the executive level, but they are now being used more extensively. Corning, for example, has tried rewarding individual achievements with on-the-spot bonuses of 3 to 6 percent of someone's pay. As director of risk management and prevention for the firm, Peter Maier gave about 40 percent of his subordinates individual bonuses in a year. He says, "If someone has done a spiffy job, you need to recognize them."[35]

Profit Sharing

Profit-sharing plans distribute to some or all employees a proportion of net profits earned by the organization during a stated performance period. The exact amount typically varies according to

AROUND THE WORLD

The Cleveland, Ohio-based Lincoln Electric Company, which manufactures arc welding equipment, among other things, has the oldest pay-for-performance system in the United States. And it's still admired and studied. Employees are compensated with a base pay plus bonuses and stock options tied to individual, team, and company performance. Production workers are paid on a piecework basis, but with daily incentives, they can earn more than $100,000 a year. Faulty items returned by customers are tracked to an individual, who is then docked pay. In 1959, the company introduced guaranteed lifelong employment for workers with three years' service and has not had a layoff since. Lincoln Electric, which now operates in 19 countries, including Canada, is felt by some to have one of the most highly productive, compensated, and skilled workforces in the world. And the company is profiting, too, with nearly $2 billion in worldwide sales in 2006.

Incentive pay rewards employees and employer

Source: Deborah Sherman, "Pioneering Synergy: The Lincoln Electric Company," February 22, 2002, online at <http://futurepositive.synearth.net/2002/02/27>; company website at: <www.lincolnelectric.com>.

the level of profits and each person's base compensation. At the marketing services firm Valassis Communications Inc., a member of *Fortune's* "100 Best Companies to Work For," every employee, from the press operator right up to the CEO, is eligible for profit sharing that runs from 10 to 25 percent of pay. In Langley, B.C., Freybe Gourmet Foods has used employee profit sharing to motivate employees for over 25 years.[36]

Gain Sharing

Gain-sharing plans extend the profit-sharing concept by allowing groups of employees to share in any savings or "gains" realized through their efforts to reduce costs and increase productivity. Specific formulas are used to calculate both the performance contributions and gain-sharing awards. The classic example is the Scanlon plan, which usually results in 75 percent of gains being distributed to workers and 25 percent being kept by the company.

Employee Stock Ownership

Employee stock ownership plans involve employees in ownership through the purchase of stock in the companies that employ them. Whereas formal "ESOP" plans are often used as financing schemes to save jobs and prevent business closings, stock ownership by employees is an important performance incentive. It can be motivating to have an ownership share in one's place of employment. An approach to employee ownership through **stock options** gives the option holder the right to buy shares of stock at a future date at a fixed price. This links ownership directly with a performance incentive, since employees holding stock options presumably are motivated to work hard to raise the price of the firm's stock. When the price has risen they can exercise their options and buy the stock at a discount, thus realizing a financial gain. Stock options are most common in senior executive compensation, but their use is spreading to include lower-level employees.

■ **Stock options** give the right to purchase shares at a fixed price in the future.

The Hay Group reports that the most admired companies in North America are also ones that offer stock options to a greater proportion of their work forces. Intel, Merck, and Kimberly-Clark are examples of global firms that allow all of their employees to have access to options.[37] One of the issues with stock options, however, is risk. If and when a company's shares perform poorly, the options are worth less; their motivational value is largely eliminated. In 1993, when Canadian Airlines was on the verge of bankruptcy, its employees agreed to pay concessions in exchange for equity in the company. This worked to resolve the company's financial troubles for a time, but before long the airline was in financial difficulty once again and it was eventually taken over by Air Canada. In the end, the stock options granted to employees were essentially worthless.[38]

When the technology companies experienced a downturn in the stock market, for example, many employees were disappointed with incentive pay that was tied to stock options. One result is a resurgence of interest in cash bonuses. How would you like to someday receive a letter like this one, once sent to two top executives by Amazon.com's chairman Jeff Bezos? "In recognition and appreciation of your contributions," his letter read, "Amazon.com will pay you a special bonus in the amount of $1,000,000."[39] Not bad for a performance incentive!

✓ **Learning check 5**

BE SURE YOU CAN
• construct an integrative model of motivation that includes ideas of the content, process, and reinforcement theories • apply this model to describe how pay-for-performance systems should work • differentiate among skill-based pay, bonus pay, profit sharing, gain sharing, and stock options as incentive compensation systems

●●● Chapter 14 STUDY GUIDE

WHERE WE'VE BEEN

Back to Genentech

The opening example of Genentech offers a benchmark example of leadership commitment to motivation and support of a firm's employees. The commitment extended by Genentech's founders has been returned multiple times in the form of sustained performance by the company. In this chapter you learned how content theories explain motivation in respect to human needs, and how equity and expectancy theories focus on the decisions people make to work or not to work hard. You learned the important principles underlying reinforcement theory and the special importance of positive reinforcement in the workplace. You also learned about the motivational issues in pay-for-performance and incentive compensation systems.

THE NEXT STEP
INTEGRATED LEARNING ACTIVITIES

Cases/Projects	Self-Assessments	Exercises in Teamwork
• SC Johnson Canada Case	• Organizational Design Preference (#17)	• What Do You Value in Work? (#7)
• Project 6—Controversies in CEO Pay	• Student Engagement Survey (#23)	• Work vs. Family (#17)
• Project 9—Management in Popular Culture	• Job Design Choices (#24)	• Compensation and Benefits Debate (#18)
• Project 10—Service Learning		• Why Do We Work? (#21)

STUDY QUESTION SUMMARY

1. What is motivation?

- Motivation involves the level, direction, and persistence of effort expended at work; simply put, a highly motivated person works hard.

- Extrinsic rewards are given by another person; intrinsic rewards derive naturally from the work itself.

- To maximize the motivational impact of rewards, they should be allocated in ways that respond to individual needs.

- The three major types of motivation theories are the content, process, and reinforcement theories.

2. What are the different types of individual needs?

- Maslow's hierarchy of human needs suggests a progression from lower-order physiological, safety, and social needs to higher-order ego and self-actualization needs.

- Alderfer's ERG theory identifies existence, relatedness, and growth needs.

- Herzberg's two-factor theory points out the importance of both job content and job context to motivation and performance.

- McClelland's acquired needs theory identifies the needs for achievement, affiliation, and power, all of which may influence what a person desires from work.

3. What are the process theories of motivation?

- Adams's equity theory recognizes that social comparisons take place when rewards are distributed in the workplace.

- People who feel inequitably treated are motivated to act in ways that reduce the sense of inequity; perceived negative inequity may result in someone working less hard in the future.

- Vroom's expectancy theory states that Motivation = Expectancy × Instrumentality × Valence.

- Expectancy theory encourages managers to make sure that any rewards offered for motivational purposes are achievable, predictable, and individually valued.

- Locke's goal-setting theory emphasizes the motivational power of goals; task goals should be specific rather than ambiguous, difficult but achievable, and set through participatory means.

4. What role does reinforcement play in motivation?

- Reinforcement theory recognizes that human behaviour is influenced by its environmental consequences.

- The law of effect states that behaviour followed by a pleasant consequence is likely to be repeated; behaviour followed by an unpleasant consequence is unlikely to be repeated.

- Reinforcement strategies used by managers include positive reinforcement, negative reinforcement, punishment, and extinction.

- Positive reinforcement works best when applied according to the laws of contingent and immediate reinforcement.

5. What are the challenges of motivation in the new workplace?

- The insights of content, process, and reinforcement theories can be integrated in a model of motivational dynamics.

- Merit pay plans tie pay increases to performance accomplishments.

- Incentive compensation programs, such as bonuses, gain sharing, and profit sharing, allow workers to benefit materially from improved organizational profits and productivity.

- Pay-for-knowledge systems link pay to the mastery of job-relevant skills.

KEY TERMS REVIEW

Expectancy (p. 345)	Lower-order needs (p. 339)	Operant conditioning (p. 348)
Extinction (p. 348)	Merit pay (p. 351)	Positive reinforcement (p. 348)
Extrinsic reward (p. 337)	Motivation (p. 337)	Punishment (p. 348)
Higher-order needs (p. 339)	Need (p. 339)	Satisfier factor (p. 340)
Hygiene factor (p. 340)	Need for Achievement (p. 341)	Shaping (p. 349)
Instrumentality (p. 345)	Need for Affiliation (p. 341)	Skills-based pay (p. 353)
Intrinsic reward (p. 338)	Need for Power (p. 341)	Stock options (p. 354)
Law of effect (p. 347)	Negative reinforcement (p. 348)	Valence (p. 345)

SELF-TEST 14

MULTIPLE-CHOICE QUESTIONS:

1. Lower-order needs in Maslow's hierarchy correspond to _____ needs in ERG theory.
    (a) growth (b) affiliation (c) existence (d) achievement

2. A worker high in need for _____ power in McClelland's theory tries to use power for the good of the organization.
    (a) position (b) expert (c) personal (d) social

3. In the _____ theory of motivation, an individual who feels under-rewarded relative to a co-worker might be expected to reduce his or her performance in the future.
    (a) ERG (b) acquired needs (c) two-factor (d) equity

4.   Which of the following is a correct match?
     (a) McClelland—ERG theory (b) Skinner—reinforcement theory (c) Vroom—equity theory
     (d) Locke—expectancy theory
5.   The expectancy theory of motivation says that motivation = expectancy × _____ × _____.
     (a) rewards, valence (b) instrumentality, valence (c) equity, instrumentality (d) rrewards, instrumentality
6.   The law of _____ states that behaviour followed by a positive consequence is likely to be repeated, whereas
     behaviour followed by an undesirable consequence is not likely to be repeated.
     (a) reinforcement (b) contingency (c) goal setting (d) effect
7.   _____is a positive reinforcement strategy that rewards successive approximations to a desirable behaviour.
     (a) Extinction (b) Negative reinforcement (c) Shaping (d) Merit pay
8.   A _____ pay plan gives bonuses based on cost savings or productivity increases that workers help to generate.
     (a) merit (b) gain-sharing (c) base (d) skills-based
9.   In Herzberg's two-factor theory, base pay is considered a(n) _____ factor.
     (a) valence (b) satisfier (c) equity (d) hygiene
10. Jobs high in _____ rewards naturally provide workers with higher-order need satisfactions.
     (a) intrinsic (b) extrinsic (c) monetary (d) existence
11. When a team member shows what would be called strong ego needs in Maslow's hierarchy, the team leader should
     find ways to link work on the team task with _____.
     (a) compensation tied to group performance (b) individual praise and recognition for work well done
     (c) lots of social interaction with other team members (d) challenging individual performance goals
12. When someone has a high and positive "expectancy" in the expectancy theory of motivation, this means that the per-
     son _____.
     (a) believes he or she can meet performance expectations (b) highly values the rewards being offered
     (c) sees a relationship between high performance and the available rewards (d) believes that rewards are equitable
13. In goal-setting theory, the goal of "becoming more productive in my work" would not be considered a source of moti-
     vation since it fails the criterion of goal _____.
     (a) acceptance (b) specificity (c) challenge (d) commitment
14. B. F. Skinner would argue that "getting a paycheque on Friday" reinforces a person for coming to work on Friday, but
     would not reinforce the person for doing an extraordinary job on Tuesday. This is because the Friday paycheque fails
     the law of _____ reinforcement.
     (a) negative (b) continuous (c) immediate (d) intermittent
15. In the integrated model of motivation, a person will be satisfied with rewards only if they are _____.
     (a) perceived as equitable (b) high in instrumentality (c) meeting growth needs (d) improving on hygiene factors

SHORT-RESPONSE QUESTIONS:

16. What preferences does a person high in the need for achievement bring to the workplace?
17. Why is participation important to goal-setting theory?
18. What is motivation to work?
19. What is the managerial significance of Herzberg's distinction between job content and job context factors?

APPLICATION QUESTION:

20. How can a manager combine the powers of goal setting and positive reinforcement to create a highly motivational
     work environment for a group of workers with high needs for achievement?

Individual Behaviour and Performance

●●● CHAPTER 15 STUDY QUESTIONS

Planning Ahead

After reading Chapter 15, you should be able to answer these questions in your own words.

1. How do we understand people at work?

2. What should we know about work attitudes and behaviour?

3. What are the alternative approaches to job design?

4. How can jobs be enriched?

5. How can work be scheduled to improve work–life balance?

Monitor Company

Unlocking everyone's performance potential

Monitor Company isn't just another of the world's top strategic management consulting firms. It's a firm with a difference, and a major part of that difference is a genuine respect for knowledge. Where is the knowledge located? In the minds of each and every one of the firm's 1,000-plus employees, as well as with their clients.

Essential to Monitor's talent development strategy is to provide people with a work environment that meets their needs, doesn't inhibit them with performance obstacles, and is full of learning opportunities. Says Alan Kantrow, chief knowledge officer for Monitor: "The employees we are trying to attract expect to have a series of careers. If Monitor can't provide outlets for their ambitions, they'll go elsewhere. So by design, all the roles, titles, and clusters of activities are transitory."

Consulting jobs at Monitor are complex, and the deadlines are often tight. No one ever knows for sure who is the team expert. Everyone has to work together, while depending on each other to do their best. The team that successfully helped Bermuda turn around its flagging tourism industry was headed by project coordinator Joseph Babiec. About the experience he says: "We were a team of equals. It didn't matter who was in Bermuda the longest. I worked for you. Then you worked for me."

It had to be that way. The team was dealing with different and some-times warring government units, labour unions, outside investors, and industry representatives. Whereas strictly defined roles and a rigid hierarchy of authority would have made the task almost impossible, the knowledge-based approach of Monitor's consulting team worked wonders for the client, and did so quickly.

Monitor employees work for a firm dedicated to talent, a firm that states that part of its mission is "creating personal competitive advantage—in the form of unique skills and insights—for each of our employees." Monitor has offices in 27 major cities around the world, including one in Toronto.[1]

IN THE WORKPLACE

Your roommate is not feeling the same about her co-op work experience as you. Leslie complains that her job involves doing the same thing (analyzing marketing reports) over and over again. Every Monday, a new set of numbers comes in from each retail outlet. Leslie compiles them, compares them with the numbers from the past six weeks, and highlights significant differences. Every Friday afternoon, she then walks her report to her boss, who says thank you, and then she returns to her desk until 5:00 p.m., when she goes home for the weekend. It's too bad that her boss doesn't understand the "core characteristics model" by Hackman and Oldham that you offer. How might Leslie's boss enrich her job?

●●● Chapter 15   LEARNING PREVIEW   ●●●

The chapter opening example of Monitor Company introduced life inside a professional consulting firm. Monitor consultants solve complex and ambiguous problems for client organizations. Although their work is intense and demanding, respect for talent and the freedom to make decisions add a high performance edge. In this chapter you will learn more about the meaning of work, quality of work life, job satisfaction, and individual performance. You will also learn about job designs and work arrangements that can improve the fit between work demands and individual capabilities.

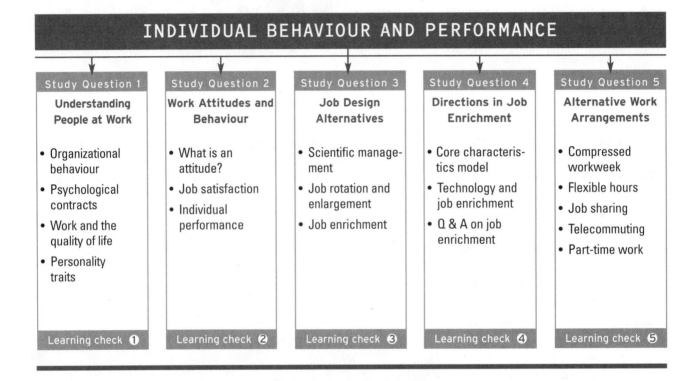

INDIVIDUAL BEHAVIOUR AND PERFORMANCE

Study Question 1	Study Question 2	Study Question 3	Study Question 4	Study Question 5
Understanding People at Work	**Work Attitudes and Behaviour**	**Job Design Alternatives**	**Directions in Job Enrichment**	**Alternative Work Arrangements**
• Organizational behaviour • Psychological contracts • Work and the quality of life • Personality traits	• What is an attitude? • Job satisfaction • Individual performance	• Scientific management • Job rotation and enlargement • Job enrichment	• Core characteristics model • Technology and job enrichment • Q & A on job enrichment	• Compressed workweek • Flexible hours • Job sharing • Telecommuting • Part-time work
Learning check ❶	Learning check ❷	Learning check ❸	Learning check ❹	Learning check ❺

For managers in organizations of all types and sizes, a critical pathway toward performance improvement is better mobilizing and unlocking the great potential of human talent.[2] The ideal situation is a loyal and talented workforce that is committed to organizational goals and highly motivated to work hard on their behalf. But saying this is one thing; achieving it is quite another. Even in the best of circumstances the management of human resources is a challenging task. In order for human capital to have an impact on organizational performance, it must be supported, nurtured, and allowed to work to its best advantage. All too often it is not, observe scholars Jeffrey Pfeffer and Charles O'Reilly. They believe that too many organizations underperform because they operate with great untapped "hidden value" in human resources; they fail to take full advantage of the talent they already have available.[3] They criticize organizations "with smart, motivated, hard-working, decent people who nevertheless don't perform very well because the company doesn't let them shine and doesn't really capitalize on their talent and motivation." O'Reilly and Pfeffer also praise true high-performance organizations as ones able to "produce extraordinary results from almost everybody."

UNDERSTANDING PEOPLE AT WORK

What do you think about when you see or hear the word "work"? Is it a "turn-on" or a "turn-off"? Some people might regard work as an exciting place to be; others might see it only as a necessary evil. It is noteworthy that there are no health care organizations on the lists of best places to work in Canada. A recent report notes that the quality of work life for health care workers has deteriorated to the point where it makes it difficult to recruit and retain staff. A discussion paper, "Creating High Quality Health Care Workplaces," prepared by the Canadian Policy Research Networks (CPRN), highlights that health care professionals are the least likely to describe their work environment as healthy. The reasons, say the authors, are because of poor labour relations, low levels of trust, high workload, lack of control over work, psychological distress, and burnout. The negative work experience of health care workers threatens the viability of the health care system.[4]

The CPRN directs our attention toward an unfortunate fact of life in the modern workplace—some people, too many people, work under conditions that fail to provide them with respect and satisfaction. A central premise of *Management* is that it doesn't have to be this way. People at work can achieve both high performance and job satisfaction. When managers value people and create high-quality work environments that respect people's needs and potential, everyone gains.

●●● ORGANIZATIONAL BEHAVIOUR

The present and following chapters on individuals, groups, and interpersonal dynamics will draw upon concepts and insights from **organizational behaviour**, the study of individuals and groups in organizations. Called "OB" for short, it is an applied scientific discipline that seeks both to explain human behaviour in organizations and to make practical suggestions for influencing it. Research in OB addresses such outcomes or dependent variables as individual and team performance, job satisfaction, group morale, absenteeism, turnover, organizational citizenship, organizational commitment, and other matters of individual, organizational, and social consequence. The foundations of OB as a scientific discipline are as follows:[5]

■ **Organizational behaviour** is the study of individuals and groups in organizations.

1. *An interdisciplinary body of knowledge*—OB draws insights from the social sciences and related areas.

2. *Use of scientific methods*—The knowledge base of OB is created by scientific methods using rigorous concepts and disciplined analysis.

3. *Focus on practical applications*—OB strives to make a positive difference by improving the performance of organizations and their members.

4. *Contingency thinking*—OB respects individual differences, seeking the best fits between management practices and situational complexities.

One of the important contingency issues in OB is the notion of *person–job fit*, finding a good match of individual interests and capabilities with job characteristics. For example, Rich DeVault, a manager at Stryker Instruments, a worldwide company manufacturing medical devices, noticed that an employee's interpersonal talents weren't being well utilized. After DeVault moved him to another job that required good human relations skills, the employee saved Stryker $1 million in outsourcing fees. Says DeVault: "The look on his face when he's working is different—he's much more absorbed in what he's doing. His new position allows him to use his talents by coordinating a number of in-house and subcontractor resources. His enthusiasm stepped up as well as his impact."[6] Stryker Canada has its headquarters in Hamilton, Ontario.

◎●● PSYCHOLOGICAL CONTRACTS

The effective management of person–job fit begins with the nature of the employment relationship itself. Work should provide a mutual and positive exchange of value between people and organizations. This sense of mutual benefit is reflected in the **psychological contract,** or set of expectations held by the individual about what will be given and received in the employment relationship.[7] The ideal work situation is one in which the exchange of values in the psychological contract is considered fair. When the psychological contract is unbalanced or broken, however, morale problems easily develop. This problem surfaced in Japan, where workers historically enjoyed high job security and, in return, put in long work hours at great personal sacrifice. But when the Japanese economy experienced difficulty and companies cut back on job protections, worker morale declined. The psychological contract shared between workers and employers had been damaged.[8]

Figure 15.1 shows that a healthy psychological contract offers a balance between individual contributions made to the organization and inducements received in return. *Contributions* are work activities, such as effort, time, creativity, and loyalty, that make the individual a valuable human resource. *Inducements* are things the organization gives to the individual in exchange for these contributions. Typical inducements include pay, fringe benefits, training, opportunities for personal growth and advancement, and job security. Such inducements should be valued by employees and should make it worthwhile for them to work hard for the organization.

■ A **psychological contract** is the set of individual expectations about the employment relationship.

Figure 15.1 Components in the psychological contract.

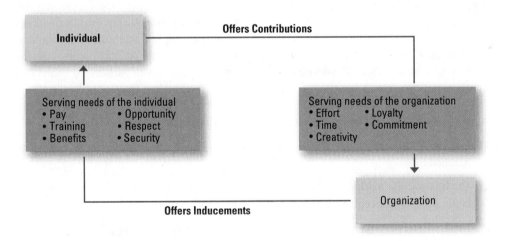

◎●● WORK AND THE QUALITY OF LIFE

The term "quality of work life" (QWL) was first used in Chapter 1 to describe the overall quality of human experiences in the workplace. Most people spend many hours a week, and many years of their lives, at work. What happens to them at work, how they are treated, and what their work is like are influences on their overall quality of life.[9] Our experiences at work can, and often do, spill over to affect our non-work activities and lives, just as our non-work experiences sometimes affect our attitudes and performance at work.

Anyone who serves as a manager must accept that the job carries a high level of social responsibility. Poor management practices can diminish a person's overall quality of life, not just the quality of work life; good management, by contrast, has the potential to enhance both.

If you think this is an overstatement, consider a steelworker's compelling words once shared with the noted author Studs Terkel:[10]

> *When I come home, know what I do for the first twenty minutes? Fake it. I put on a smile. I got a kid three years old. If I feel bad, I can't take it out on the kid. Kids are born innocent of everything but birth. You can't take it out on your wife either. That is why you go to a tavern. You want to release it there rather than do it at home. What does an actor do when he's got a bad movie? I got a bad movie every day.*

In contrast to the steelworker, here are Ed Cox's comments made on the anniversary of his 30 years of working for Roots Canada, a Toronto-based clothing company founded by Don Green and Michael Budman: "I love working at Roots because of the close-knit family and team atmosphere," says Cox. "Don and Michael really make me feel like part of the group. I appreciate their open-door policy. I can walk into their offices and get greeted like a friend rather than an employee. The Roots environment is so unique. That's why I enjoy working for Roots and look forward to each new workday."[11] Today's managers are expected to help create work environments within which people have positive experiences while performing to high levels of expectation. The themes of this chapter all relate in one way or another to this goal.

●●● PERSONALITY TRAITS

"Of course he's a bad fit for the job; with a personality like that, he doesn't work well with others." "Put Shoshanna on the project; her personality is perfect for the intensity that we expect from the team." These are examples of everyday conversations about people at work, with the key word being **personality**—the combination or overall profile of characteristics that makes one person unique from every other. Individual personalities and variations among them are important managerial considerations in any work setting. It is common and helpful in this regard to understand what psychologists call the *Big Five personality traits*.[12]

> ■ **Personality** is the profile of characteristics making a person unique from others.

- *Extroversion*—The degree to which someone is outgoing, sociable, and assertive. An extrovert is comfortable and confident in interpersonal relationships; an introvert is more withdrawn and reserved.

> ■ **Extroversion** is being outgoing, sociable, and assertive.

- *Agreeableness*—The degree to which someone is good-natured, co-operative, and trusting. An agreeable person gets along well with others; a disagreeable person is a source of conflict and discomfort for others.

> ■ **Agreeableness** is being good-natured, co-operative, and trusting.

- *Conscientiousness*—The degree to which someone is responsible, dependable, and careful. A conscientious person focuses on what can be accomplished and meets commitments; a person who lacks conscientiousness is careless, often trying to do too much and failing, or doing little.

> ■ **Conscientiousness** is being responsible, dependable, and careful.

- *Emotional stability*—The degree to which someone is relaxed, secure, and unworried. A person who is emotionally stable is calm and confident; a person lacking in emotional stability is anxious, nervous, and tense.

> ■ **Emotional stability** is being relaxed, secure, and unworried.

- *Openness*—The degree to which someone is curious, open to new ideas, and imaginative. An open person is broad-minded, receptive to new things, open to change; a person who lacks openness is narrow-minded, has few interests, and is resistant to change.

> ■ **Openness** is being curious, receptive to new ideas, and imaginative.

You can easily spot these personality traits in people with whom you work, study, and socialize. But don't forget that they also apply to you; others have impressions of your personality on these very same dimensions. In the social context of the workplace, managers must

Figure 15.2 The "Big Five" and five more personality dimensions that influence human behaviour at work.

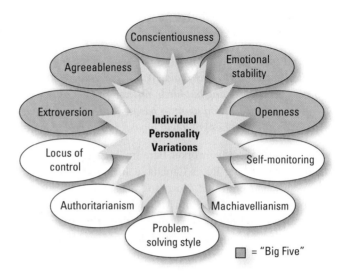

PERSONAL MANAGEMENT

Your **PROBLEM-SOLVING STYLE** is likely to differ from those of people you study and work with. It is important to understand your style and learn about problems that can occur as styles clash when you work with others. Which of the four master problem-solving styles shown here best describes you?[18]

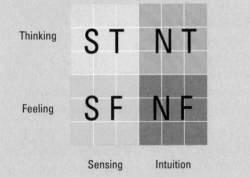

- *Sensation-Thinker:* STs take a realistic approach to problem solving, preferring "facts," clear goals, and certainty.
- *Intuitive-Thinker:* NTs are comfortable with abstraction and unstructured situations, tending to be idealistic and to avoid details.
- *Intuitive-Feeler:* NFs are insightful, like to deal with broad issues, and value flexibility and human relationships.
- *Sensation-Feeler:* SFs emphasize analysis using facts, while being open communicators and respectful of feelings and values.

Get to know yourself better

Complete Self-Assessments #25—**Cognitive Style,** and #26—**Internal–External Control,** from the Workbook and Personal Management Activity #15 on the companion website.

be able to understand and respond to these personality differences when making job assignments, building teams, and otherwise engaging in the daily give-and-take of work. Psychologists also use the Big Five to steer people in the direction of career choices that provide the best personality–job fits.

Figure 15.2 displays the Big Five along with five other personality dimensions that can make a further difference in how people work and how well they work together in organizations.[13] Scholars have a strong interest in **locus of control**, recognizing that some people believe they are in control of their destinies while others believe that what happens to them is beyond their control.[14] "Internals" are more self-confident and accept responsibility for their own actions, while "externals" are more prone to blame others and outside forces for what happens to them. Interestingly, research suggests that internals tend to be more satisfied and less alienated from their work.

Authoritarianism is the degree to which a person defers to authority and accepts status differences.[15] Someone with an authoritarian personality would tend to act rigidly and be control oriented when in a leadership capacity; this same person would be subservient and follow the rules when in a follower capacity. The tendency of people with an authoritarian personality to obey orders can be problematic if they follow a supervisor's directives to the point of acting unethically—or even illegally.

In his 16th-century book *The Prince*, Niccolo Machiavelli gained lasting fame for giving advice on how to use power to achieve personal goals.[16] **Machiavellianism** describes the extent to which someone is emotionally detached and manipulative in using power.[17] A person with a "high-Mach" personality is usually viewed as exploitative and unconcerned about others, with the guiding rule being that the end justifies the means. A person with a "low-Mach" personality, by contrast, would be deferential in allowing others to exert power over them.

The psychologist Carl Jung pointed out that people display significant differences in **problem-solving styles**, or the way they gather and evaluate information for decision making.[19] Information is gathered by *sensation* (emphasizing details, facts, and routine) or by *intuition* (looking for the "big picture" and being willing to deal with various possibilities). Information is evaluated by *thinking* (using reason and analysis) or by *feeling* (responding to the feelings and desires of others). Because these differences are so extreme, it is not surprising that people approach their jobs in different ways and have difficulty, at times, working with one another. Many organizations use the Myers-Briggs Type Indicator, a 100-question survey instrument, to measure variations in problem-solving styles. This test helps employees to both understand their own problem-solving styles and learn how to work more productively with people with different styles.

Finally, **self-monitoring** reflects the degree to which someone is able to adjust and modify behaviour in response to the situation and external factors.[20] A person high in self-monitoring tends to be a learner, comfortable with feedback, and both willing and able to change. Because high self-monitors are flexible in changing behaviour from one situation to the next, it may be hard to get a clear reading of where they stand. A person low in self-monitoring, by contrast, is predictable, tending to act consistently regardless of circumstances.

■ **Locus of control** is the extent to which one believes that what happens is within one's control.

■ **Authoritarianism** is the degree to which a person tends to defer to authority.

■ **Machiavellianism** is the extent to which someone is emotionally detached and manipulative in using power.

■ A **problem-solving style** is the way in which a person gathers and evaluates information when making decisions.

BE SURE YOU CAN
• define the terms organizational behaviour, psychological contract, and personality • explain the benefits of a healthy psychological contract • discuss the managerial implications of the quality of work life concept • list the Big Five personality traits and give work-related examples of each • list an additional five personality traits and give work-related examples for each

✔ Learning check ❶

WORK ATTITUDES AND BEHAVIOUR

When Deborah Alexander joined Scotiabank as an executive vice-president in June 2002, she was immediately required to deal with a tense stand-off with an offshore government partner. She saw this not as a problem but more as an opportunity. Using her ability to understand situations and to get in and get the job done, she was instrumental in providing a successful resolution for Scotiabank. She reflected that, despite this being a difficult problem for the bank, it was a timely opening for her as a new executive. "It helped me get to know Scotiabank's senior people very quickly...and show them how I could contribute." Having a positive attitude helped Alexander overcome a tough situation.[21]

■ **Self-monitoring** is the degree to which someone is able to adjust behaviour in response to external factors.

●●● WHAT IS AN ATTITUDE?

An **attitude** is a predisposition to act in a certain way toward people and things in one's environment.[22] In the case of Deborah Alexander, for example, she was predisposed to take risk and embrace challenges. This "positive" attitude influenced her behaviour when dealing with the inevitable problems, choices, and opportunities of work and career. To fully understand attitudes, positive or negative, you must recognize their three components. First, the *cognitive component* reflects a belief or opinion. You might believe, for example, that your management course is very interesting. Second, the *affective* or *emotional component* of an attitude reflects a specific feeling. For example, you might feel very good about being a management major. Third, the *behavioural component* of an attitude reflects an intention to behave consistently with the belief and feeling. Using the same example again, you might say to yourself: "I am going to work hard and try to get an A in all my management courses."

■ An **attitude** is a predisposition to act in a certain way.

CANADIAN COMPANY IN THE NEWS   The Forzani Group Ltd.

CORE VALUES DRIVE PERFORMANCE

In 1974, John Forzani and three Calgary Stampeder teammates opened "Forzani's Locker Room," a 1,200-square-foot store in Calgary. The business grew steadily, expanding from strictly selling athletic footwear to include clothing, licensed apparel, and sports equipment. Today, The Forzani Group Ltd. is Canada's largest retailer of sporting goods, operating stores under four corporate banners—Sport Chek, Sports Experts, Coast Mountain Sports, and Sport Mart. It is also a franchisor under the banners Sports Experts, Intersport, RnR, Econosports, and Tech Shop. The company's core values drive the performance of its employees. It aims for bold performance targets. It ensures that all business areas are constantly re-evaluated. It encourages individual initiatives and risk taking in an environment that is forgiving of mistakes. And it invests in its people, placing them outside of their "comfort zone" so that they and the company may progress faster.

Source: Information from <www.forzanigroup.com>

Importantly, the intentions reflected in an attitude may or may not be confirmed in one's actual behaviour. Despite having a positive attitude and all good intentions, the demands of family, friends, or leisure activities might use up the time you would otherwise need to devote to studying hard enough to get an A in your management courses. Thus, you might fail to live up to your own expectations. In fact, the psychological concept of **cognitive dissonance** describes the discomfort felt when one's attitude and behaviour are inconsistent.[23] For most people, dissonance is very uncomfortable and results in changing the attitude to fit the behaviour ("Oh, I really don't like management that much anyway"), changing future behaviour to fit the attitude (dropping out of intramural sports to get extra study time), or rationalizing to force the two to be compatible ("Management is an okay major, but being a manager also requires the experience I'm gaining in my extracurricular activities").

> ▨ **Cognitive dissonance** is discomfort felt when attitude and behaviour are inconsistent.

●●● JOB SATISFACTION

People hold attitudes about many things in the workplace—bosses, each other, tasks, policies, goals, and more. A comprehensive work attitude is **job satisfaction**, the degree to which an individual feels positive or negative about various aspects of work.[24] The evaluative points of reference in job satisfaction are such things as pay, co-workers, supervisor, work setting, advancement opportunities, and workload. A poll run by workopolis.com, and developed by Environics Research, found some unsettling statistics: 17 percent of respondents indicated that they disliked their job so much, they dreaded the thought of going to work. A further 32 percent thought of their job as only a means to earn a living and not a career with long-term potential. An overwhelming 64 percent said they see little or no opportunity for advancement, and 35 percent rated their job so routine that they get no exposure to new experiences.[25]

> ▨ **Job satisfaction** is the degree to which an individual feels positive or negative about a job.

In terms of consequences, researchers know that there is a strong relationship between job satisfaction and *absenteeism*. Workers who are more satisfied with their jobs are absent less often than those who are dissatisfied. There is also a relationship between job satisfaction and *turnover*. Satisfied workers are more likely to stay, and dissatisfied workers are more likely to quit their jobs. Both of these findings are important since absenteeism and turnover are costly in terms of the recruitment and training needed to replace workers, as well as in the productivity lost while new workers are learning how to perform up to expectations. One study reports that changing retention rates up or down results in magnified changes to corporate earnings. The author warns about the adverse impact on corporate performance of declining employee loyalty and "revolving door" defections.[26]

Closely related to job satisfaction are two other concepts with quality of work life implications. **Job involvement** is defined as the extent to which an individual is dedicated to a job. Someone with high job involvement, for example, would be expected to work beyond expectations to complete a special project. **Organizational commitment** is defined as the loyalty of an individual to the organization itself. Individuals with a high organizational commitment would identify strongly with the organization and take pride in considering themselves a member. In respect to the consequences again, a survey of 55,000 workers by the Gallup Organization found evidence that attitudes reflecting job involvement and commitment correlated with higher profits for their employers. The four attitudes that counted most were believing one has the opportunity to do one's best every day, believing one's opinions count, believing fellow workers are committed to quality, and believing there is a direct connection between one's work and the company's mission.[27]

> ■ **Job involvement** is the extent to which an individual is dedicated to a job.

> ■ **Organizational commitment** is the loyalty of an individual to the organization.

take it to the case!

Steinway & Sons
Craftwork, tradition, and time build grand pianos

Stop in at Steinway & Sons online and take their factory tour. You'll see how the finest in individual craftwork, the ingenuity of patented designs and methods, and the very best of teamwork still combine to build what may be the world's most famous pianos. The firm remains true to its history, dating to its founding in 1853 by Henry Engelhard Steinway. Over half the firm's 114 patents were in place before 1900. The traditions of skilled craftspeople building handmade pianos continue today. Highly skilled workers bend and shape the very best wood using time-tested techniques, taking eight months to finish a concert grand. Skill, patience, the best materials, and modern organization allow the firm to produce some 5,000 pianos a year worldwide.

Source: Information from James Barron, "Mystery at Steinway," *International Herald Tribune* (May 12, 2003), p. 2; see also <www.steinway.com>.

●●● INDIVIDUAL PERFORMANCE

The following sign once hung in a tavern near a Ford Motor Company plant: "I spend 40 hours a week here—am I supposed to work too?" The message behind these words is an important one in management: it is one thing for people to come to work and even to be satisfied with their jobs; it is quite another for them to work hard and achieve high performance. **Job performance** is measured as the quantity and quality of tasks accomplished by an individual or group. It is, so to speak, the "bottom line" for people at work. And the important managerial question becomes: What factors determine individual performance?

> ■ **Job performance** is the quantity and quality of tasks accomplished.

In answering this question, the following *Individual Performance Equation* is a good starting point: *Performance = Ability × Support × Effort*.[28] The logic of this equation is straightforward and very practical. If high performance is to be achieved in any work setting, the individual must possess the right abilities—creating the *capacity* to perform; work hard at the task—showing the *willingness* to perform; and have the necessary support—creating the *opportunity* to perform.[29] All three factors are important and necessary; failure to provide for any one or more is likely to cause performance losses.

Performance Begins with Ability

Ability establishes an individual's capacity to perform at a high level of accomplishment. As discussed in Chapter 12 on human resource management, proper employee selection brings people with the right abilities to a job; poor selection does not. Good training and development keep people's skills up to date and job relevant; poor or insufficient training does not. The best managers never let a job vacancy or training opportunity pass without giving it serious attention. The best managers make sure, every day, that all jobs under their supervision are staffed up to the moment with talented people.

Performance Requires Support

Even the most capable and hard-working individual will not achieve the highest performance levels unless proper support is available. Support creates a work environment rich in opportunities to apply one's talents to maximum advantage. To fully utilize their abilities workers need sufficient resources, clear goals and directions, freedom from unnecessary rules and job constraints, appropriate technologies, and performance feedback. Providing these and other forms of direct work support is a basic managerial responsibility. The best information on the need for support, of course, comes from the workers themselves. Wouldn't it be nice to hear more managers speak the following words in everyday conversations with their subordinates: "How can I help you today?" Bill Falconer, Organizational Development vice-president at Nova Scotia's Valley Credit Union, asks that question daily. For example, the organization had a teller who was having trouble balancing funds adequately. Recognizing that as a teller's accuracy improves, overall performance improves as well, Falconer sat down with the employee in a supportive environment and also matched her with a branch manager to act as her coach. Working closely with the manager, the employee's performance improved. Falconer believes that his job was to encourage the employee and foster positive performance by showing an interest in the individual, not just in her performance.[30]

Performance Involves Effort

The willingness to work hard at a task is an essential component of the high-performance workplace. But the decision to exert work effort rests squarely with the individual alone; it is the ultimate test of the motivation theories discussed in Chapter 14. All any manager (or teacher or parent) can do is attempt to create the conditions under which the answer to the all-important question—"Should I work hard today?"—is more often "Yes" than "No." And quite frankly, the most powerful and enduring "Yes" is the one driven by forces within the individual—intrinsic motivation—rather than by outside initiatives such as supervisory appeals, offers of monetary reward, or threats of punishment. Good managers understand this reality as they build jobs for people in organizations.

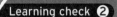

Learning check ❷

BE SURE YOU CAN

• define the terms attitude, job satisfaction, and job performance • list the three components of an attitude • explain cognitive dissonance • explain the potential consequences of high and low job satisfaction • explain the multiplication signs in the individual performance equation: $P = A \times S \times E$ • illustrate how managers can positively influence performance through each factor in this equation

JOB DESIGN ALTERNATIVES

A **job** is a collection of tasks performed in support of organizational objectives. The process of **job design** is one of creating or defining jobs by assigning specific work tasks to individuals and groups. Job design uses the insights of motivation theories discussed in the last chapter to help accomplish two major goals—high levels of both job satisfaction and job performance. Jobs can and should be designed so that satisfaction and performance go hand in hand. This is in many ways an exercise in "fit." A good job design provides a good fit between the individual worker and the task requirements. *Figure 15.3* shows a continuum of job design alternatives—job simplification, job enlargement and rotation, and job enrichment.

■ A **job** is the collection of tasks a person performs in support of organizational objectives.

■ **Job design** is the allocation of specific work tasks to individuals and groups.

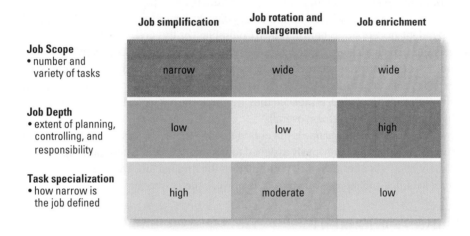

Figure 15.3 A continuum of job design alternatives.

	Job simplification	Job rotation and enlargement	Job enrichment
Job Scope • number and variety of tasks	narrow	wide	wide
Job Depth • extent of planning, controlling, and responsibility	low	low	high
Task specialization • how narrow is the job defined	high	moderate	low

●●● SCIENTIFIC MANAGEMENT

Job simplification involves standardizing work procedures and employing people in well-defined and highly specialized tasks. This is an extension of the scientific management approach discussed in Chapter 2. Simplified jobs are narrow in *job scope*—that is, the number and variety of different tasks a person performs. Many employees around the world earn their livings working at highly simplified tasks, often on assembly lines. The most extreme form of job simplification is **automation**, or the total mechanization of a job.

■ **Job simplification** employs people in clearly defined and very specialized tasks.

■ **Automation** is the total mechanization of a job.

The logic of job simplification is straightforward. Because the jobs don't require complex skills, workers should be easier and quicker to train, less difficult to supervise, and easy to replace if they leave. Furthermore, because tasks are well defined, workers should become good at them while performing the same work over and over again. Consider the case of Cindy Vang, who works on an assembly line for Medtronics, Inc. She works in a dust-free room making a specialized medical component. She is certified on five of 14 job skills in her department. At any given time, however, she performs one of them, for example, feeding small devices by tweezers into special containers. It is tedious work without much challenge. But Vang says: "I like it." Importantly, she notes that the job doesn't interfere with her home life with a husband and three sons. Her economic needs are met in a low-stress job and comfortable work environment.[31]

Situations don't always work out this well in highly simplified jobs. Productivity can suffer as unhappy workers drive up costs through absenteeism and turnover, and through poor performance caused by boredom and alienation. Although simplified jobs appeal to some people, disadvantages can develop with structured and repetitive tasks.

●●● JOB ROTATION AND JOB ENLARGEMENT

■ **Job rotation** increases task variety by periodically shifting workers between different jobs.

One way to move beyond simplification in job design is to broaden the scope through **job rotation**, increasing task variety by periodically shifting workers between jobs involving different task assignments. Job rotation can be done on a regular schedule; it can also be done periodically or occasionally. The latter approach is often used in training to inform people about jobs performed by others. Relatively few employed Canadians engage in job rotation or cross-training. While 15 percent say they "occasionally" participate in such workplace practices, only 6 percent report doing so on a "frequent" basis. This form of flexible work organization is slightly more common among workers in large firms. For instance, those employed in firms with fewer than 20 employees are least likely to be engaged in job rotation or cross-training, with 84 percent of them indicating that they never do so, compared with 80 percent of workers in firms with 500 or more employees.[32] However, one Canadian company that does is Thrifty Foods Ltd. An independent grocery store chain in British Columbia, Thrifty Foods believes in training their managers through application as well as more formal training. In the company's job rotation program, assistant store management trainees spend time in each of eight departments, rotating from the meat department to the deli, seafood, produce, and other departments until everyone, the trainee included, is satisfied that the employee has a good grounding in the practical challenges facing the business overall.[33]

■ **Job enlargement** increases task variety by combining into one job two or more tasks previously assigned to separate workers.

Another way to broaden scope is **job enlargement**—increasing task variety by combining two or more tasks that were previously assigned to separate workers. Often these are tasks done immediately before or after the work performed in the original job. This is sometimes called *horizontal loading*—pulling prework and/or later work stages into the job.

●●● JOB ENRICHMENT

Frederick Herzberg, whose two-factor theory of motivation was discussed in Chapter 14, questions the motivational value of horizontally loading jobs through enlargement and rotation. "Why," he asks, "should a worker become motivated when one or more meaningless tasks are added to previously existing ones or when work assignments are rotated among equally meaningless tasks?" By contrast, he says, "If you want people to do a good job, give them a good job to do."[34] He argues that this is best done through **job enrichment**, the practice of expanding job content to create more opportunities for satisfaction. TD Bank recognized that their employees wanted more control over their careers. They designed a self-service website that included interactive diagnostic tools, advice, and information to

■ **Job enrichment** increases job depth by adding work planning and evaluating duties normally performed by the supervisor.

MANAGER'S
Notepad 15.1

Job enrichment checklist

- *Check 1:* Remove controls that limit people's discretion in their work.
- *Check 2:* Grant people authority to make decisions about their work.
- *Check 3:* Make people understand their performance accountability.
- *Check 4:* Allow people to do "whole" tasks or complete units of work.
- *Check 5:* Make performance feedback available.

enable employees to figure out how to overcome career challenges. This tool allows employees and managers to identify options such as skills development, career shifts, or job enrichment to help employees understand both themselves better, and what will increase their satisfaction with their job.[35]

In contrast to job enlargement and rotation, job enrichment focuses not just on job scope but also on *job depth*, that is, the extent to which task planning and evaluating duties are performed by the individual worker rather than the supervisor. Changes designed to increase job depth are sometimes referred to as *vertical loading*. Herzberg's recommendations for enriching jobs are found in *Manager's Notepad 15.1*.

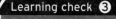

BE SURE YOU CAN

• illustrate a job designed by scientific management • illustrate jobs designed by job rotation and job enlargement • illustrate a job designed by Herzberg's concept of job enrichment • explain the job satisfaction implications of job design by simplification, enlargement, rotation, and enrichment

✔ Learning check ❸

DIRECTIONS IN JOB ENRICHMENT

Modern management theory takes job enrichment a step beyond the suggestions of Frederick Herzberg. Most importantly, it adopts a contingency perspective and recognizes that job enrichment may not be best for everyone. Among the directions in job design, the core characteristics model developed by J. Richard Hackman and his associates offers a way for managers to create jobs, enriched or otherwise, that best fit the needs of people and organizations.[36]

●●● CORE CHARACTERISTICS MODEL

The model described in *Figure 15.4* offers a diagnostic approach to job enrichment. A job that is high in the five core characteristics is considered enriched; the lower a job scores on these characteristics, the less enriched it is. The *five core job characteristics* are as follows:

1. *Skill variety*—the degree to which a job requires a variety of different activities to carry out the work, and involves the use of a number of different skills and talents of the individual.

2. *Task identity*—the degree to which the job requires completion of a "whole" and identifiable piece of work, one that involves doing a job from beginning to end with a visible outcome.

3. *Task significance*—the degree to which the job has a substantial impact on the lives or work of other people elsewhere in the organization or in the external environment.

4. *Autonomy*—the degree to which the job gives the individual freedom, independence, and discretion in scheduling work and in choosing procedures for carrying it out.

5. *Feedback from the job itself*—the degree to which work activities required by the job result in the individual obtaining direct and clear information on his or her performance.

According to this model, job satisfaction and performance are influenced by three critical psychological states: (1) experienced meaningfulness of the work; (2) experienced responsibility for the outcomes of the work; and (3) knowledge of actual results of work activities. These, in turn, are influenced by the presence or absence of the five core job characteristics. In true contingency fashion, however, the core characteristics will not affect all people in the

Figure 15.4 Job design and individual work outcomes using the core characteristics model.

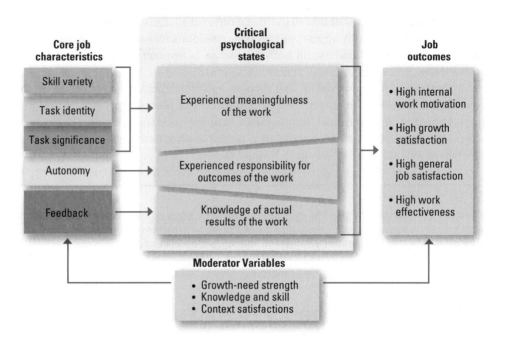

Source: Hackman, J.R./Oldham, G.R., WORK REDESIGN © 1980, p. 90. Reprinted by permission of Pearson Education, Inc., Upper Saddle River, New Jersey.

same way. Generally speaking, people who respond most favourably to enriched jobs will have strong higher-order needs, appropriate job knowledge and skills, and be otherwise satisfied with job context. One of the key contingency or moderator variables in the model is **growth-need strength**, described in Alderfer's ERG theory (see Chapter 14) as the degree to which an individual seeks psychological growth in his or her work. The expectation is that people with strong growth needs will respond most positively to enriched jobs.

When job enrichment is a good job design choice, Hackman and his colleagues recommend five ways to improve the core characteristics. First, you can *form natural units of work.* Make sure that the tasks people perform are logically related to one another and provide a

■ **Growth-need strength** is the desire to achieve psychological growth in one's work.

Canadian Managers
From E-Commerce Billionaire to Film Producer

Jeff Skoll's Participant Productions was well represented at the 2006 Academy Awards, with the films *North Country* and *Syriana* each receiving two nominations, and *Good Night, and Good Luck* receiving six. Not bad for a Canadian who ventured into film production just a few years ago; this is Skoll's "second act." Born in Montreal and raised in Toronto, Skoll had ambitions of becoming a writer but decided he needed to make money first. He studied electrical engineering, and then pursued an MBA. In 1995, at the age of 31, he joined a new company, called AuctionWeb, as its president. Skoll wrote the business plan for what would become eBay Inc. Less than two months after eBay went public in 1998, the company was worth $5.2 billion, making Skoll's 22-percent slice worth $1.14 billion. He left eBay in 2001, free to focus on writing. But, between the Skoll Foundation—a venture capital fund for businesses with a social-justice agenda—and managing his fortune, he couldn't find the time. He ventured into making politically engaged and socially conscious movies instead.

Source: Chris Shulgan, "Mr. Skoll goes to Hollywood," *The Globe and Mail*, Feb. 21, 2006.

clear and meaningful task identity. Second, try to *combine tasks*. Expand job responsibilities by pulling together, into one larger job, a number of smaller tasks previously done by others. Third, *establish client relationships*. Put people in contact with others who, as clients inside and/or outside the organization, use the results of their work. Fourth, *open feedback channels*. Provide opportunities for people to receive performance feedback as they work and to learn how performance changes over time. Fifth, *practise vertical loading*. Give people more control over their work by increasing their authority to perform the planning and controlling previously done by supervisors.

AROUND THE WORLD

Teaching high sales performance

There are few jobs in any workplace more focused on individual performance than the salesperson. For Canon, the global electronics firm, its targets for salespeople were for years based on volume. But as its product differentiation with competitors started to blur, the company realized it needed to excel at customer service. Canon's European operations hired a consultant to create a customized Sales Academy. The curriculum developed key competencies for each sales role; account managers hone their skills in relationship management and negotiation, for example. Sales staff learn to think as partners and consultants to Canon's retailers, working together to develop marketing plans and in-store displays, which boosts sales and customer satisfaction. The Sales Academy is also linked with employee development plans and performance appraisals. Says Joris de Haas, the European HR Director for Canon's Consumer Business, "The academy is at the heart of the business, creating effective development opportunities for our employees, together with the right motivation and spirit for world class customer partnership."

Source: "Achieving High Performance by Transforming the Sales Organization," Accenture, 2007, available online at <www.accenture.com>.

●●● TECHNOLOGY AND JOB ENRICHMENT

On the important issue of technology, the managerial challenge is quite clear: job design should proceed with the goal of increasing productivity through integrated **sociotechnical systems**.[37] These are job designs that use technology to best advantage while still treating people with respect and allowing their human talents to be applied to their fullest potential. The continuing inroads made by computers into the workplace are changing structures, workflows, and the mix of skills needed in many settings. Consider the special case of *robotics*—the use of computer-controlled machines to completely automate work tasks previously performed by hand. Such automation of work is the most extreme form of job simplification and has both its limits and critics. On the positive side, such technology offers an opportunity to take over many routine tasks previously assigned to individuals and thereby frees human talents for more enriched job assignments. In this and other ways, technology utilization and job enrichment can be complementary strategies.

■ A **sociotechnical system** integrates technology and human resources in high-performance systems.

●●● QUESTIONS AND ANSWERS ON JOB ENRICHMENT

"Is it expensive to implement job enrichment?" Job enrichment can be costly. The cost grows as the required changes in technology, workflow, and other facilities become more complex.

"Will people demand more pay for doing enriched jobs?" Herzberg believes that if people are being paid truly competitive wages (i.e., if pay dissatisfaction does not already exist), the satisfactions of performing enriched tasks will be adequate compensation for the increased work involved. But any job-enrichment program should be approached with recognition that pay may be an issue for the people involved.[38]

"Should everyone's job be enriched?" No, contingency counts. The people most likely to respond favourably to job enrichment are those seeking higher-order or growth-need satisfactions at work and who have the levels of training, education, and ability required to perform the enriched job.

"What do the unions say about job enrichment?" Suffice it to say that the following comments made some years ago by one union official are still worth consideration. "Better wages, shorter hours, vested pensions, a right to have a say in their working conditions, the right to be promoted on the basis of seniority, and all the rest. That's the kind of job enrichment that unions believe in."[39] However, the level of union–employee involvement at the planning stages can facilitate union acceptance of change and innovation at the workplace level.

✓ **Learning check ➍**

BE SURE YOU CAN

• list and describe the five core job characteristics • explain the relationship between these characteristics and job enrichment • explain how a person's growth needs, skills, and context satisfaction can affect their responses to these characteristics • apply the core characteristics model to a job situation and recommend ways to improve job satisfaction and performance • answer the question: should everyone's job be enriched?

ALTERNATIVE WORK ARRANGEMENTS

Not only is the content of jobs changing for people in today's workplace, the context is changing too. Among the more significant developments is the emergence of a number of alternative ways for people to schedule their work time.[40] And "flexibility" is the key word. This is especially important as employers deal with work–life balance issues affecting today's highly diverse workforce. Many are finding that alternative work schedules can help attract and retain the best workers.

●●● THE COMPRESSED WORKWEEK

■ A **compressed workweek** allows a full-time job to be completed in less than five days.

A **compressed workweek** is any work schedule that allows a full-time job to be completed in less than the standard five days of 8-hour shifts.[41] Its most common form is the "4–40;" that is, accomplishing 40 hours of work in four 10-hour days. One advantage of the 4–40 schedule is that the employee receives three consecutive days off from work each week. This benefits the individual through more leisure time and lower commuting costs. The organization should also benefit through lower absenteeism and any improved performance that may result. Potential disadvantages include increased fatigue and family adjustment problems for the individual, as well as increased scheduling problems, possible customer complaints, and union objections against the organization.

Twice a month, Susan Shaughnessy, a mother of five, wakes up without the alarm telling her it's time to go to work. On these days, Shaughnessy, who is a lawyer in the tax litigation directorate of Justice Canada, finds the time to do any number of personal projects like shopping or studying for her master's degree in taxation at HEC in Montreal. She has these days to herself because she has chosen to work a flexible work arrangement offered by her employer. She now earns 90 percent of her salary and works 90 percent of the time. "A flexible work arrangement allows employees to do personal business that they might have to do during work time," said Gary Johns, Concordia University research chair in management. "This helps them out, vis à vis their family and their employer."[42]

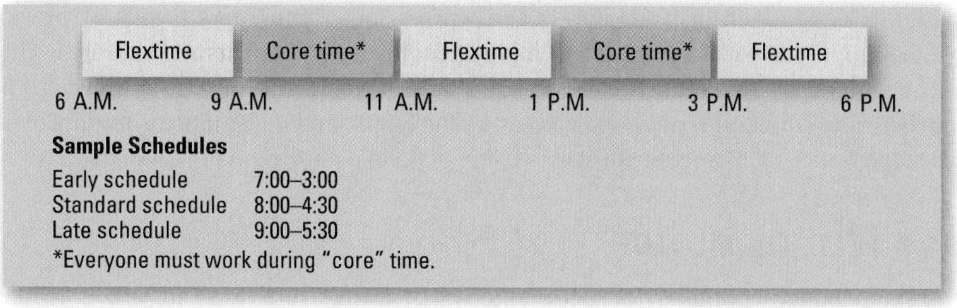

Flextime	Core time*	Flextime	Core time*	Flextime

6 A.M.   9 A.M.   11 A.M.   1 P.M.   3 P.M.   6 P.M.

Sample Schedules
Early schedule   7:00–3:00
Standard schedule   8:00–4:30
Late schedule   9:00–5:30
*Everyone must work during "core" time.

Figure 15.5 A sample flexible working hours schedule.

●●● FLEXIBLE WORKING HOURS

The term **flexible working hours**, also called *flexitime* or *flextime*, describes any work schedule that gives employees some choice in the pattern of their daily work hours. A sample flexible working schedule offers choices of starting and ending times, such as the program depicted in *Figure 15.5*. Employees in this example work four hours of "core" time, or the time they must be present at work. In this case, core time falls between 9 and 11 a.m. and 1 and 3 p.m. They are then free to choose another four work hours from "flextime" blocks. Such flexible schedules give employees greater autonomy while ensuring that they maintain work responsibility. Some may choose to come in earlier and leave earlier, while still completing an 8-hour day; others may choose to start later in the morning and leave later. In between these extremes are opportunities to attend to personal affairs, such as dental appointments, home emergencies, visits to children's schools, and so on.

■ **Flexible working hours** give employees some choice in daily work hours.

Flexible hours help organizations attract and retain talented employees whose lives are complicated by personal responsibilities. These include dual-career couples, single parents with child-care complications, and employees who are care providers for elderly parents. All top 100 companies in *Working Mother* magazine's list of best employers for working moms offer flexible scheduling. Reports indicate that flexibility in dealing with non-work obligations reduces stress and unwanted job turnover. At the women's sports apparel company Athleta, for example, a low turnover rate compared with the industry average is attributed to flexible scheduling.[43]

●●● JOB SHARING

Another work scheduling alternative is **job sharing**, where one full-time job is split between two or more persons. This often involves each person working one-half day, but it can also be done on weekly or monthly sharing arrangements. Organizations benefit by employing talented people who would otherwise be unable to work. The qualified specialist who is also a parent may be unable to stay away from home for a full workday but may be able to work a half day. Job sharing allows two such persons to be employed as one, often to great benefit. The Conference Board of Canada estimates that 20 percent of Canadian organizations allow job sharing and that the majority of arrangements involve women.[44]

■ **Job sharing** splits one job between two people.

Job sharing should not be confused with a more controversial concept called *work sharing*. This involves an agreement between employees who face layoffs or terminations to cut back their work hours so they can all keep their jobs. Instead of losing 20 percent of a firm's workforce to temporary layoffs in an unexpected business downturn, for example, a work-sharing program would cut everyone's hours by 20 percent to keep them all employed. This allows employers to retain trained and loyal workers even when forced to temporarily economize by reducing labour costs. For employees whose seniority could protect them from layoff, the disadvantage is lost earnings. For those who would otherwise be terminated, however, it provides continued work—albeit with reduced earnings—and with a preferred employer. In Canada, work-sharing programs are provided for under the *Employment Insurance Act*. Work sharing is designed to help employers and workers avert temporary layoffs by providing income support to workers eligible for Employment Insurance benefits and who are willing to work a temporarily reduced workweek. Work-sharing agreements must be approved by both employee and employer representatives and by the Employment Insurance Commission, and can range from 6 to 26 weeks with an extension of up to a maximum of 38 weeks.[45]

●●● TELECOMMUTING

■ **Telecommuting** involves using IT to work at home or outside the office.

It is increasingly popular for people to work away from a fixed office location. **Telecommuting,** sometimes called *flexiplace*, is a work arrangement that allows at least a portion of scheduled work hours to be completed outside the office. Often this is facilitated by information technology that allows one to work from home while linked with customers and a central office. Telecommuting frees the job holder from the normal constraints of commuting, fixed hours, special work attire, and even direct contact with supervisors. It is popular, for example, among computer programmers and is found increasingly in such diverse areas as marketing, financial analysis, and administrative services. London, Ontario-based Info-Tech Research Group classifies nearly 40 percent of all workers in Canada and the US as "mobile," meaning they routinely do at least 20 percent of their "core business functions" remotely.[46] New terms are even becoming associated with telecommuting practices. We speak of *hotelling* when telecommuters come to the central office and use temporary office facilities; we also refer to *virtual offices* that include everything from an office at home to a mobile workspace in an automobile.

Overall, there is no doubt that telecommuting is here to stay as an important aspect of the continually developing new workplace. When asked what they like, telecommuters tend to report increased productivity, fewer distractions, the freedom to be your own boss, and the benefit of having more time for themselves. A study by Cisco Systems Inc. and economist OMNI Consulting Group reported that using mobile data services increased global workforce productivity by an average of 13.4 percent.[47] On the negative side, telecommuters cite working too much, having less time to themselves, difficulty separating work and personal life, and having less time for family.[48] Other considerations for the individual include feelings of isolation and loss of visibility for promotion. Managers, in turn, may be required

---

MANAGER'S
Notepad 15.2

How to make telecommuting work for you

- Treat telecommuting like any work day; keep regular hours.
- Limit non-work distractions; set up private space dedicated to work.
- Establish positive routines and work habits; be disciplined.
- Report regularly to your boss and main office; don't lose touch.
- Seek out human contact; don't become isolated.
- Use technology: instant messaging, intranet links, Net meetings.
- Keep your freedoms and responsibilities in balance.
- Reward yourself with time off; let flexibility be an advantage.

to change their routines and procedures to accommodate the challenges of supervising people from a distance. One telecommuter's advice to others is: "You have to have self-discipline and pride in what you do, but you also have to have a boss that trusts you enough to get out of the way."[49] IBM Canada has leveraged its telecommuting program to annually save $20 million in actual operating costs and over 500,000 square feet of real estate. "In a company like IBM, it's particularly important that we have telecommuting options," says Susan Turner, IBM Canada's diversity and workplace programs executive. "Future employees are looking for this flexibility."[50] *Manager's Notepad 15.2* offers several guidelines for how to make telecommuting work for you.[51]

●●● PART-TIME WORK

The growing use of temporary workers is another striking employment trend, and it has a controversial side. **Part-time work** is done on any schedule less than the standard 40-hour workweek, and that does not qualify the individual as a full-time employee. Many employers rely on **contingency workers**—part-timers or *permatemps* who supplement the full-time workforce, often on a long-term basis. According to Statistics Canada, approximately 30 percent of the population is employed on a part-time basis and, over the last 20 years, part-time employment has grown by a ratio of three to one over full-time employment. In Canada, part-time is defined as employees who normally work under 30 hours per week.[52] No longer limited to the traditional areas of clerical services, sales personnel, and unskilled labour, these workers serve an increasingly broad range of employer needs. It is now possible to hire, on a part-time basis, everything from executive support, such as a chief financial officer, to such special expertise as engineering, computer programming, and market research.

Because part-time or contingency workers can be easily hired, contracted with, and/or terminated in response to changing needs, many employers like the flexibility they offer in controlling labour costs and dealing with cyclical demand. On the other hand, some worry that temporaries lack the commitment of permanent workers and often reduce company productivity. Perhaps the most controversial issue of the part-time work trend relates to the different treatment part-timers often receive from employers. They may be paid less than their full-time counterparts, and many do not receive important benefits, such as health care, life insurance, pension plans, and paid vacations.

■ **Part-time work** is temporary employment for less than the standard 40-hour workweek.

■ **Contingency workers** are employed on a part-time and temporary basis to supplement a permanent workforce.

BE SURE YOU CAN

• describe the compressed workweek, flexible work hours, job sharing, and telecommuting as alternative work schedules • discuss the potential advantages and disadvantages of each to both employers and employees • discuss the significance of part-time contingency workers in the economy

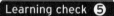 ✔ Learning check ❺

●●● Chapter 15

WHERE WE'VE BEEN

Back to Monitor Company

The opening example of the Monitor Company showed how jobs and work environments can be designed to meet the needs of highly talented people. Monitor illustrates that designing jobs to fit people pays off in both job satisfaction and high levels of performance accomplishment. In this chapter you learned about psychological contracts, attitudes, personality, the nature of job satisfaction, and factors influencing individual performance. You learned alternative job design approaches, with specific attention to job enrichment. You also learned about alternative work arrangements available in the new workplace.

THE NEXT STEP
INTEGRATED LEARNING ACTIVITIES

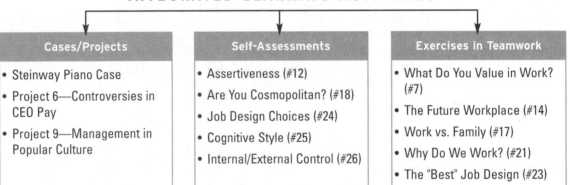

Cases/Projects	Self-Assessments	Exercises in Teamwork
• Steinway Piano Case	• Assertiveness (#12)	• What Do You Value in Work? (#7)
• Project 6—Controversies in CEO Pay	• Are You Cosmopolitan? (#18)	• The Future Workplace (#14)
• Project 9—Management in Popular Culture	• Job Design Choices (#24)	• Work vs. Family (#17)
	• Cognitive Style (#25)	• Why Do We Work? (#21)
	• Internal/External Control (#26)	• The "Best" Job Design (#23)

STUDY QUESTION SUMMARY

1. How do we understand people at work?

• Organizational behaviour is the study of individuals and groups in organizations.

• Work is an exchange of values between individuals and organizations.

• A healthy psychological contract occurs when a person's contributions—such as time and effort, and inducements—such as pay and respect, are in balance.

• What happens to people at work, their quality of work life, is an important influence on their quality of life overall.

• The Big Five personality factors are extroversion, agreeableness, conscientiousness, emotional stability, and openness.

• Additional personality dimensions of work significance are locus of control, authoritarianism, Machiavellianism, problem-solving style, and self-monitoring.

2. What should we know about work attitudes and behaviour?

• An attitude is a predisposition to respond in a certain way to people and things.

• Cognitive dissonance occurs when a person's attitude and behaviour are inconsistent.

• Job satisfaction is an important work attitude, reflecting a person's evaluation of the job, co-workers, and other aspects of the work setting.

• Job satisfaction influences such behaviours as work attendance and turnover, and is related to other attitudes such as job involvement and organizational commitment.

- The individual performance equation states: *Performance = Ability × Support × Effort.*

3. What are the alternative approaches to job design?

- Job design is the process of creating or defining jobs by assigning specific work tasks to individuals and groups.

- Jobs should be designed so workers enjoy high levels of both job performance and job satisfaction.

- Job simplification creates narrow and repetitive jobs consisting of well-defined tasks with many routine operations, such as the typical assembly-line job.

- Job enlargement allows individuals to perform a broader range of simplified tasks; job rotation allows individuals to shift among different jobs of similar skill levels.

- Job enrichment results in more meaningful jobs that give people more autonomy in decision making and broader task responsibilities.

4. How can jobs be enriched?

- The diagnostic approach to job enrichment involves analyzing jobs according to five core characteristics: skill variety, task identity, task significance, autonomy, and feedback.

- Jobs deficient in one or more of these core characteristics can be redesigned to improve their level of enrichment.

- Jobs can be enriched by forming natural work units, combining tasks, establishing client relationships, opening feedback channels, and vertically loading to give workers more planning and controlling responsibilities.

- Job enrichment does not work for everyone; it works best for people with strong growth needs—the desire to achieve psychological growth in their work.

5. How can work be scheduled to improve work-life balance?

- Alternative work schedules can make work hours less inconvenient and enable organizations to respond better to individual needs and personal responsibilities.

- The compressed workweek allows 40 hours of work to be completed in only four days' time.

- Flexible working hours allow people to adjust the starting and ending times of their daily schedules.

- Job sharing allows two people to share one job.

- Telecommuting allows people to work at home or in mobile offices through computer links with their employers and/or customers.

- An increasing number of people work on part-time schedules as part of a contingency workforce.

KEY TERMS REVIEW

Agreeableness (p. 363)

Attitude (p. 365)

Authoritarianism (p. 365)

Automation (p. 369)

Cognitive dissonance (p. 366)

Compressed workweek (p. 374)

Conscientiousness (p. 363)

Contingency worker (p. 377)

Emotional stability (p. 363)

Extroversion (p. 363)

Flexible working hours (p. 375)

Growth-need strength (p. 372)

Job (p. 369)

Job design (p. 369)

Job enlargement (p. 370)

Job enrichment (p. 370)

Job involvement (p. 367)

Job performance (p. 367)

Job rotation (p. 370)

Job satisfaction (p. 366)

Job sharing (p. 375)

Job simplification (p. 369)

Locus of control (p. 365)

Machiavellianism (p. 365)

Openness (p. 363)

Organizational behaviour (p. 361)

Organizational commitment (p. 367)

Part-time work (p. 377)

Personality (p. 363)

Problem-solving style (p. 365)

Psychological contract (p. 362)

Self-monitoring (p. 365)

Sociotechnical system (p. 373)

Telecommuting (p. 376)

SELF-TEST 15

MULTIPLE-CHOICE QUESTIONS:

1. Interest in organizational behaviour on individual differences and good person–job fits reflects a commitment to _____.

   (a) sociotechnical systems (b) an interdisciplinary knowledge base (c) use of scientific methods (d) high quality of work life

2. A manager's job design goals should include establishing conditions for workers to achieve high levels of both task performance and _____.

   (a) financial gain (b) social interaction (c) job satisfaction (d) job security

3. Vertical loading of a job is most associated with _____.

   (a) bringing prework into the job (b) bringing later work stages into the job (c) bringing higher-level or managerial work into the job (d) raising standards for high performance

4. The _____ strategy of job design allows workers to shift among a variety of jobs requiring essentially the same skills.

   (a) job simplification (b) job enlargement (c) job rotation (d) job sharing

5. The addition of more planning and evaluating responsibilities to a job is an example of the _____ job design strategy.

   (a) job enrichment (b) job enlargement (c) job rotation (d) job sharing

6. _____ is one of the core characteristics that should be improved upon in order to enrich a job.

   (a) Work–life balance (b) Task significance (c) Growth-need strength (d) Automation

7. Workers in a compressed workweek typically work 40 hours in _____ days.

   (a) 3 (b) 4 (c) 5 (d) a flexible number of

8. Another term used to describe part-time workers is _____.

   (a) contingency workers (b) virtual workers (c) flexible workers (d) secondary workers

9. _____ is where two workers split one job on an arranged work schedule; _____ is where a group of workers accept reduced individual work hours in order to avoid layoffs.

   (a) Job rotation, job sharing (b) Job sharing, work sharing (c) Job enrichment, job sharing (d) Job splitting, job simplification

10. Hotelling is a development associated with the growing importance of _____ in the new workplace.

   (a) part-time work (b) telecommuting (c) compressed workweeks (d) flexible working hours

11. A person with a high _____ personality would be unemotional and willing to manipulate others to achieve personal goals.

   (a) extrovert (b) sensation-thinking (c) self-monitoring (d) Machiavellian

12. Among the Big Five personality traits, _____ indicates someone who is responsible, dependable, and careful in respect to tasks.

   (a) authoritarianism (b) agreeableness (c) conscientiousness (d) emotional stability

13.   The _____ component of an attitude indicates a person's belief about someone or something.
      (a) cognitive (b) emotional (c) affective (d) behavioural

14.   The term used to describe the discomfort someone feels when his or her behaviour is inconsistent with an expressed attitude is _____.
      (a) alienation (b) cognitive dissonance (c) job dissatisfaction (d) person–job imbalance

15.   A manager who asks subordinates the question "How can I help you today?" will get answers useful in addressing the _____ factor in the Individual Performance Equation.
      (a) motivation (b) effort (c) support (d) ability

SHORT-RESPONSE QUESTIONS:

16.   What is a "healthy" psychological contract?

17.   What difference does growth-need strength make in the job enrichment process?

18.   Which three of the Big Five personality traits do you believe most affect how well people work together in organizations, and why?

19.   Why might an employer not want to offer employees the option of working on a compressed workweek schedule?

APPLICATION QUESTION:

20.   Kurt Swenson has just attended a management development program in which the following equation was discussed: *Performance = Ability × Support × Effort*. As a plant manager, he is interested in implementing the concept. He plans to hold a meeting for all of his team leaders to explain the implications of this equation. If you were Kurt, how would you explain the importance of each performance factor—ability, support, effort—and how would you explain the significance of the multiplication signs in the equation?

Teams and Teamwork

●●● CHAPTER 16 STUDY QUESTIONS

1. How do teams contribute to organizations?

2. What are current trends in the use of teams?

3. How do teams work?

4. How do teams make decisions?

5. What are the challenges of leading high-performance teams?

Planning Ahead

After reading Chapter 16, you should be able to answer these questions in your own words.

C.O.R.E. Digital Pictures

Teamwork in a pod

A sign with the Walt Disney logo proudly announcing, "All reels locked!" hangs on the wall at C.O.R.E. Digital Pictures's King Street West headquarters in Toronto. That poster indicates that a feature animated film has been completed. The film, Walt Disney Pictures's *The Wild*, opened in April 2006 on 3,500 movie screens across North America. It was made at C.O.R.E.'s Toronto studio with computer-generated imagery (CGI), the kind of 3-D animation used in movies like *Shrek* and *Finding Nemo*.

C.O.R.E., now a leading creator of digital visual effects and animation for feature film and television, was founded in 1994 by four partners armed with passion and ambition: Bob Munroe, John Mariella, Kyle Menzies, and actor, director, and writer William Shatner. Since then, C.O.R.E. has produced award-winning work for more than 55 feature films, including Columbia Pictures's *Fly Away Home*, Twentieth Century Fox's *Dr. Dolittle* and *X-Men*, Universal Pictures's *Nutty Professor II: The Klumps*, and Sony Pictures's *Resident Evil: Apocalypse*.

The Wild is one of the most complex CGI movies ever made, and with a budget of US $80 million, it is the largest feature animated movie produced in Canada. It took two and a half years between the time the project was given the green light by Disney to the time the poster with "all reels locked" could be put on display. Four hundred employees, including digital artists, renderers, digital lighting technicians, and software developers, worked at C.O.R.E. at the peak of production.

How did the company manage so many people, within such tight deadlines, to create such outstanding results? Ron Estey, C.O.R.E.'s manag-

ing director, attributes it to structure and strategy, stating, "Our structure is beyond flat. The president, a shareholder and partner, works for the production manager. The VP works for the production manager, side by side with the animators and artists. It's a true matrix organization, and as democratic as we can make it."

To facilitate this structure, the workspaces at C.O.R.E. are organized as pods, with three or four employees in each pod, but not necessarily working on the same proj-

ect. Estey explains, "We certainly try to put a junior with a senior so there is always a mix, and that provides the opportunity to roll back and say 'what does this button do?' or 'you know, this animation's not working right, what do you think?' We want that type of collaboration, the ability to self-criticize and group criticize in small teams—the way critical review would be done in an art school or an environment where you're collectively responsible for the outcome."[1]

IN THE WORKPLACE

A vice president in your company, Katherine Dombaj, has just asked you to be the team leader of the Spring Celebration event. This annual event is the company's way of celebrating the start of a new fiscal year and looking back on the successes of the past year. New products and projects, company goals and objectives, and superior performers are all high-

lighted in a company-wide luncheon held off-site.

You attended last year's event and it was fun—there was good food, lively presentations, and lots of heartfelt backslapping. As you think about putting your team together, you reflect on the things you know about developing a high-performing team. What are the key points you need to consider?

●●● **Chapter 16** LEARNING PREVIEW ●●●

In the chapter opening example of C.O.R.E. Digital Pictures, you were able to peek into a leading company in the film industry to see how they use teams to achieve success. You saw how C.O.R.E aligns organizational structure, strategy, and decision making to energize talent and encourage a high degree of fluidity and creativity as an essential part of a high-performance system. In this chapter you will learn more about the nature of teams, the types of teams found in organizations, and new directions in the use of teams. You will learn about team effectiveness, and how norms, cohesion, decision making, communication, and group processes influence team accomplishments and, in turn, the satisfactions of members.

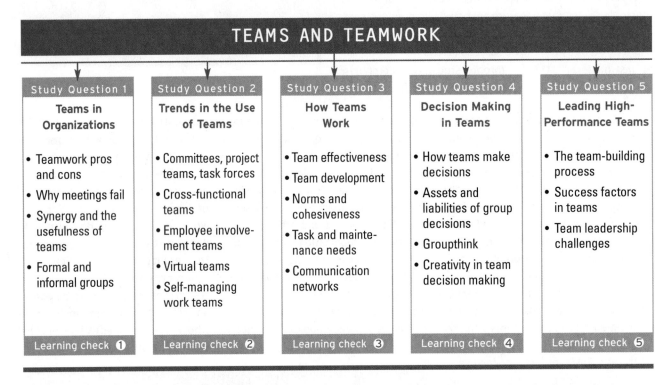

TEAMS AND TEAMWORK

Study Question 1	Study Question 2	Study Question 3	Study Question 4	Study Question 5
Teams in Organizations	**Trends in the Use of Teams**	**How Teams Work**	**Decision Making in Teams**	**Leading High-Performance Teams**
• Teamwork pros and cons • Why meetings fail • Synergy and the usefulness of teams • Formal and informal groups	• Committees, project teams, task forces • Cross-functional teams • Employee involvement teams • Virtual teams • Self-managing work teams	• Team effectiveness • Team development • Norms and cohesiveness • Task and maintenance needs • Communication networks	• How teams make decisions • Assets and liabilities of group decisions • Groupthink • Creativity in team decision making	• The team-building process • Success factors in teams • Team leadership challenges
Learning check ❶	Learning check ❷	Learning check ❸	Learning check ❹	Learning check ❺

People have the need to work in teams. There is a desire to work with others and enjoy the benefits of your work and your successes together, these . . . satisfactions are as important today as they have ever been.

Andy Grove, former Chairman of Intel, Inc.

I learned a long time ago that in team sports or in business, a group working together can always defeat a team of individuals even if the individuals, by themselves, are better than your team . . . If you're going to empower people and you don't have teamwork, you're dead.

John Chambers, CEO of Cisco Systems

As these opening quotes suggest, the new workplace is rich in teams and teamwork.[2] To build high-performance organizations driven by speed, innovation, efficiency, spontaneity, and continuous change, the great potential of teams and teamwork must be harnessed. But even as we recognize that finding the best ways to utilize teams as performance resources is an important managerial task, we must also admit that it is not always easy to successfully lead through teamwork.

Just the words "*group*" and "*team*" elicit both positive and negative reactions in the minds of many people. Although it is said that "two heads are better than one," we are also warned that "too many cooks spoil the broth." The true skeptic can be heard to say: "A camel is a horse put together by a committee." Against this somewhat humorous background lies a most important point: teams are both rich in performance potential and very complex in the way they work.[3] Consider, too, these realities. Many people prefer to work in teams rather than independently; over 60 percent of the average worker's time is spent in a team environment; even though most workers spend at least some time in teams, less than half receive training in group dynamics.[4]

TEAMS IN ORGANIZATIONS

Most tasks in organizations are well beyond the capabilities of individuals alone. Managerial success is always earned, in substantial part, through success at mobilizing, leading, and supporting people as they work together in groups. The new organizational designs and cultures require it, as does any true commitment to empowerment and employee involvement.[5] There is no doubt that teams are indispensable to the new workplace. The question for managers, and the guiding theme of this chapter, thus becomes: How do we make sure that teams and teamwork are utilized to everyone's best advantage? Managing large projects using teams is part of what Pomerleau Inc., a Quebec construction company, does best. In particular, Pomerleau utilizes client-responsive project teams to ensure that there are many people listening to the needs of their customers. Established in 1964, Pomerleau has successfully delivered over 1,500 construction projects, with current projects including the enlargement of Montreal's Pierre Elliott Trudeau International Airport.[6]

Before proceeding, let's be specific about the terminology. A **team** is a small group of people with complementary skills, who work together to accomplish shared goals while holding themselves mutually accountable for performance results.[7] **Teamwork** is the process of people working together to accomplish these goals.

■ A **team** is a collection of people who regularly interact to pursue common goals.

■ **Teamwork** is the process of people actively working together to accomplish common goals.

●●● TEAMWORK PROS AND CONS

Figure 16.1 shows four important roles that managers must perform in order to fully master the challenges of teams and teamwork. These roles, along with examples, are (1) *supervisor*—serving as the appointed head of a formal work unit; (2) *facilitator*—serving as the peer leader and networking hub for a special task force; (3) *participant*—serving as a helpful, contributing member of a project team; and (4) *coach*—serving as the external convenor or sponsor of a problem-solving team staffed by others.

Experience has taught all of us that serving in these roles isn't always easy and that things don't always work out as intended. Teams and teamwork are not problem free. For example, who hasn't encountered **social loafing**—the presence of "free-riders" who slack off because

■ **Social loafing** is the tendency of some people to avoid responsibility by "free-riding" in groups.

Figure 16.1 Team and teamwork roles for managers.

Supervisor

Network facilitator

Helpful participant

External coach

How managers get involved with teams and teamwork

responsibility is diffused in teams and others are present to do the work?[8] To overcome social loafing, it is key that group members recognize the importance of the project, and that they establish a connection with the team. To do that, J.D. Rothwell recommends getting everyone involved by having each member select a specific, meaningful task. Rothwell suggests that allowing choice affords personal control, that focusing on a specific task fosters obligation, and the fact that it is a meaningful task signifies importance—all of which serve to connect the individual to the task and, in turn, to the group.[9] The time we spend in groups can be productive and satisfying, but to make it so we must understand the complex nature of groups and their internal dynamics.[10]

An important management skill is knowing *when* a team is the best choice for a task. Another is knowing *how* to work with and manage the team to best accomplish that task. Take social loafing as an example. What can a leader or other concerned team member do when someone is free-riding? It's not easy, but the problem can be addressed. Actions can be taken to make individual contributions more visible, reward individuals for their contributions, make task assignments more interesting, and keep group size small so that free-riders are more visible to peer pressure and leader evaluation.[11]

Other problems are also common when we work in groups and teams. Personality conflicts and individual differences in work styles can disrupt the team. Tasks are not always clear. Ambiguous agendas and/or ill-defined problems can cause teams to work too long on the wrong things. Not everyone is always ready to work. Sometimes the issue is lack of motivation, but it may also be conflicts with other work deadlines and priorities. Low enthusiasm for group work may also be caused by a lack of team organization or progress, as well as by meetings that lack purpose and members who come unprepared. These and other difficulties can easily turn the great potential of teams into frustration and failure.

●●● WHY MEETINGS FAIL

One of the best examples of group work in organizations is the ever-present meeting.[12] But what do you think when someone says, "Let's have a meeting"? Are you ready, apprehensive, or even perturbed? Meetings are a hard fact of the workplace, especially in today's horizontal, flexible, and team-oriented structures. But all too often, those who must attend do not view the call to yet another meeting enthusiastically. A survey by Office Team, for example, found that 27 percent of respondents viewed meetings as their biggest time wasters, ranking ahead of unnecessary interruptions.[13] "We have the most ineffective meetings of any company," says a technology executive. "We just seem to meet and meet and meet and we never seem to do anything," says another in the package delivery industry. "We realize our meetings are unproductive. A consulting firm is trying to help us. But we've got a long way to go," says yet another corporate manager.[14]

PERSONAL MANAGEMENT

No one can deny that teams are indispensable in today's organizations. And importantly, you cannot deny that a large part of your career success will depend on your skills at working in and leading teams. The question of the day is: Are you ready for truly valuable **TEAM CONTRIBUTIONS**? Consider this list of critical skills that you must have in order to contribute significantly to the success of work teams:

- Good at encouraging and motivating others.
- Good at accepting suggestions.
- Good at listening to different points of view.
- Good at communicating information and ideas.
- Good at persuasion.
- Good at conflict resolution and negotiating.
- Good at building consensus.
- Good at fulfilling commitments.

Ask yourself the tough questions. In your classes and/or at work, are you making these contributions to the teams in which you are asked to participate? Push the question even further. Ask others who know and work with you to assess your performance and contributions as a group member. What suggestions do they have for how you could improve your team contributions?

Get to know yourself better

Complete Self-Assessment #27—**Team Leader Skills**, and Exercises #26—**Lost at Sea**, and #27—**Work Team Dynamics**, from the Workbook and Personal Management Activity #16 on the companion website.

MANAGER'S
Notepad 16.1
Seven sins of deadly meetings

1. People arrive late, leave early, and don't take things seriously.
2. The meeting is too long, sometimes twice as long as necessary.
3. People don't stay on topic; they digress and are easily distracted.
4. The discussion lacks candour; people are unwilling to tell the truth.
5. The right information isn't available, so decisions are postponed.
6. Nothing happens when the meeting is over; no one puts decisions into action.
7. Things never get better; the same mistakes are made meeting after meeting.

Consider the list of typical meeting problems described in *Manager's Notepad 16.1*.[15] You might even be able to add to the list from personal experience in student groups and work teams. But remember, in your career it will be important for you to make the most of meetings as a leader and as a member. Meetings can and should be places where information is shared, decisions get made, and people gain understanding of one another. And this can be accomplished without "wasting" time. The material in this chapter offers a useful knowledge base about group dynamics that can be helpful in making your meetings effective. But as with all group activities in organizations, good things don't happen by chance. People have to work hard and work together to make their meetings productive and rewarding.

●●●● SYNERGY AND THE USEFULNESS OF TEAMS

Synergy is the creation of a whole that is greater than the sum of its parts. Teamwork in our society makes available everything from aircraft to the Internet to music videos. It all happens because of synergy, the pooling of individual talents and efforts to create extraordinary results. Synergy occurs when a team uses its membership resources to the fullest and thereby achieves through collective action far more than could otherwise be achieved. This is very good for organizations and it can also be very good for their members. Being part of a team can have a strong influence on individual attitudes and behaviours. When the experience is positive, working in and being part of a team helps satisfy important individual needs. Sometimes these are needs that may be difficult to meet in the regular work setting. Thus, in terms of both performance and satisfaction, the usefulness of teams is extensive. They offer:[16]

- more resources for problem solving,
- improved creativity and innovation,
- improved quality of decision making,
- greater commitments to tasks,
- higher motivation through collective action,
- better control and work discipline, and
- more individual need satisfaction.

▥ **Synergy** is the creation of a whole greater than the sum of its individual parts.

■ A **quality circle** is a team of employees who meet periodically to discuss ways of improving work quality.

A popular form of employee involvement team is the **quality circle**, a group of workers who meet regularly to discuss and plan specific ways to improve work quality.[26] After receiving special training in problem solving, team processes, and quality issues, members of the quality circle try to come up with suggestions that can be implemented to raise productivity through quality improvements. Quality circles became popular in North America, in part, because of their success in Japanese management.

●●● VIRTUAL TEAMS

■ Members of a **virtual team** work together and solve problems through computer-based interactions.

A newer form of group that is increasingly common in today's organizations is the **virtual team**—sometimes called a *computer-mediated group* or *electronic group network*.[27] This is a team of people who work together and solve problems largely through computer-mediated, rather than face-to-face, interactions. The use of virtual teams is changing the way many committees, task forces, and other problem-solving teams function. Working in virtual environments, team members in dispersed locations can easily address problems and seek consensus on how to best deal with them. Virtual teams operate just like other teams in respect to what gets done; how things get done, however, is different and this can be a source of both potential advantages and disadvantages.[28]

In terms of potential advantages, virtual teams can save time and travel expenses. They can allow members to work collectively in a time-efficient fashion, and without interpersonal difficulties that might otherwise occur—especially when the issues are controversial. Nortel Networks has been at the forefront of using virtual teams. One of the main reasons, according to HR director Dale Pratt, is that "there's a phenomenal cost saving for people not having to meet face-to-face." Other benefits she noted include a speedy dissemination of information, enhanced knowledge sharing within the organization, closer customer relationships due to the transcendence of time barriers, potential for full-time and part-time employees to work together, recruitment of talent regardless of location, and the possibility of working from home more frequently.[29] Virtual teams can also be easily expanded to include additional experts as needed, and the discussions and information shared among team members can be stored online for continuous updating and access. When problems do occur in virtual teams, they often arise because members have difficulty establishing good working relationships. Relations among team members can become depersonalized as the lack of face-to-face interaction limits the role of emotions and non-verbal cues in the communication process.[30]

Following some basic guidelines can help ensure that the advantages of virtual teams outweigh their disadvantages. The critical ingredients relate to the creation of positive impressions and the development of trust among team members with limited face-to-face meeting opportunities.[31]

- Virtual teams should begin with social messaging that allows members to exchange information about themselves to personalize the process.

- Virtual team members should be assigned clear roles so that they can focus while working alone and also know what others are doing.

- Virtual team members must join and engage the team with positive attitudes that support a willingness to work hard to meet team goals.

■ Members of a **self-managing work team** have the authority to make decisions about how they share and complete their work.

●●● SELF-MANAGING WORK TEAMS

In a growing number of organizations, traditional work units consisting of first-level supervisors and their immediate subordinates are disappearing. They are being replaced with **self-managing work teams**. Sometimes called *autonomous work groups*, these are teams of

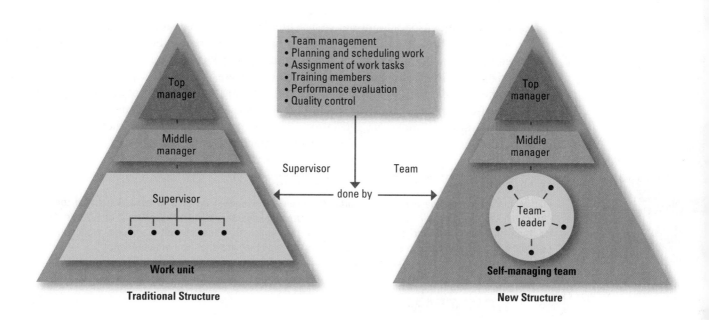

workers whose jobs have been redesigned to create a high degree of task interdependence and who have been given authority to make many decisions about how they go about doing the required work.[32]

Self-managing teams operate with participative decision making, shared tasks, and the responsibility for many of the managerial tasks performed by supervisors in more traditional settings. The "self-management" responsibilities include planning and scheduling work, training members in various tasks, sharing tasks, meeting performance goals, ensuring high quality, and solving day-to-day operating problems. In some settings, the team's authority may even extend to "hiring" and "firing" its members when necessary. A key feature is *multi-tasking*, in which team members each have the skills to perform several different jobs. As shown in *Figure 16.2*, typical characteristics of self-managing teams are as follows:

- Members are held collectively accountable for performance results.

- Members have discretion in distributing tasks within the team.

- Members have discretion in scheduling work within the team.

- Members are able to perform more than one job on the team.

- Members train one another to develop multiple job skills.

- Members evaluate one another's performance contributions.

- Members are responsible for the total quality of team products.

Within a self-managing team the emphasis is always on participation. The leader and members are expected to work together not only to do the required work but also to make the decisions that determine how it gets done. A true self-managing team emphasizes team decision making, shared tasks, high involvement, and collective responsibility for accomplished results. The expected advantages include better performance, decreased costs, and higher morale. Of course, these results are not guaranteed. Managing the transition to self-managing teams from more traditional work settings isn't always easy. The process requires leadership committed to both empowerment and a lot of support for those learning to work in new ways. For example, at the City of Grande Prairie, Alberta, self-managing teams are

Figure 16.2 Organizational and management implications of self-managing work teams.

part of the municipal administrative structure. The Taxation, By-law, Engineering, and most recently the Leisure Services departments have all converted to being self-managing. To educate the public about this change, the municipality has a large amount of information on the benefits of self-managing teams on their website.[33] As the concept of self-managing teams spreads globally, researchers are also examining the receptivity of different cultures to self-management concepts.[34] Such cultural dimensions as high-power distance and individualism, for example, may generate resistance that must be considered when implementing this and other team-based organizational practices.

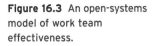

BE SURE YOU CAN
• differentiate a committee from a task force • explain the expected benefits of cross-functional teams • explain how a quality circle operates • explain the potential advantages and disadvantages of virtual teams for their members and for organizations • list the characteristics of self-managing work teams • explain why organizations use self-managing teams and how they are changing organizations

HOW TEAMS WORK

Regardless of its form and purpose, any team must achieve three key results—perform tasks, satisfy members, and remain viable for the future.[35] On the *performance* side, a work group or team is expected to transform resource inputs (such as ideas, materials, and objects) into product outputs (such as a report, decision, service, or commodity) that have some value to the organization. The members of a team should also be able to experience *satisfaction* from both these performance results and their participation in the process. And, in respect to *future viability*, the team should have a social fabric and work climate that makes members willing and able to work well together in the future, again and again as needed.

●●● WHAT IS AN EFFECTIVE TEAM?

■ An **effective team** achieves high levels of task performance, membership satisfaction, and future viability.

An **effective team** is one that achieves and maintains high levels of task performance, member satisfaction, and viability for future action.[36] *Figure 16.3* shows how any team can be viewed as an open system that transforms various resource inputs into these outcomes. Among the

Figure 16.3 An open-systems model of work team effectiveness.

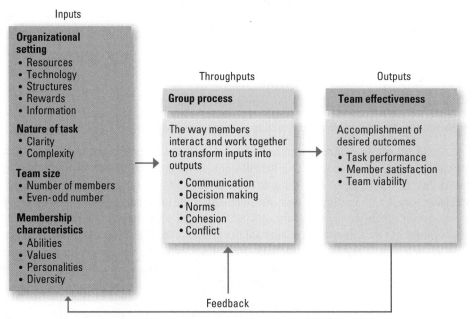

important inputs are such things as the organizational setting, the nature of the task, the team size, and the membership characteristics.[37] Each of these factors influences the group process and helps set the stage for the accomplishment of group outcomes.

Group Inputs

The *nature of the task* is always important. It affects how well a team can focus its efforts and how intense the group process needs to be to get the job done. Clearly defined tasks make it easier for team members to combine their work efforts. Complex tasks require more information exchange and intense interaction than do simpler tasks. The *organizational setting* can also affect how team members relate to one another and apply their skills toward task accomplishment. A key issue is the amount of support provided in terms of information, material resources, technology, organization structures, available rewards, and spatial arrangements. Increasingly, for example, organizations are being architecturally designed to directly facilitate teamwork. At SEI Investments, employees work in a large, open space without cubicles or dividers; each has a private set of office furniture and fixtures—but all on wheels; all technology easily plugs and unplugs from suspended power beams that run overhead. Project teams convene and disband as needed, and people easily meet and converse intensely, with the ebb and flow of work, all day.[38]

Team size affects how members work together, handle disagreements, and reach agreements. The number of potential interactions increases geometrically as teams increase in size, and communications become more congested. Teams larger than about six or seven members can be difficult to manage for the purpose of creative problem solving. When voting is required, teams with odd numbers of members help prevent "ties." In all teams, the *membership characteristics* are also important. Teams must have members with the right abilities, or skill mix, to master and perform tasks well. They must also have values and personalities that are sufficiently compatible for everyone to work well together.

Group Process

Although having the right inputs available to a team is important, it is not a guarantee of effectiveness. **Group process** counts too. This is the way the members of any team actually work together as they transform inputs into outputs. Also called *group dynamics*, the process aspects of any group or team include how members communicate with one another, make decisions, and handle conflicts, among other things. When the process breaks down and the internal dynamics fail in any way, team effectiveness can suffer. This *Team Effectiveness Equation* is a helpful reminder: Team effectiveness = quality of inputs + (process gains − process losses).

> ■ **Group process** is the way team members work together to accomplish tasks.

Team Diversity

Team diversity, in the form of different values, personalities, experiences, demographics, and cultures among the membership, can present significant group process challenges. The more homogeneous the team—the more similar the members are to one another—the easier it is to manage relationships. As team diversity increases, so too does the complexity of interpersonal relationships among members. But with the complications also come special opportunities. The more heterogeneous the team—the more diversity among members—the greater the variety of available ideas, perspectives, and experiences that can add value to problem solving and task performance.

In teamwork, as with organizations at large, the diversity lesson is very clear. There is a lot to gain when membership diversity is valued and well managed. The process challenge is to maximize the advantages of team diversity while minimizing its potential disadvantages. In the international arena, for example, research indicates that culturally diverse work teams have more difficulty learning how to work well together than do culturally homogeneous teams.[39] They tend to struggle more in the early stages of working together. But once the process challenges are successfully mastered, the diverse teams eventually prove to be more creative than the homogeneous ones.

●●● STAGES OF TEAM DEVELOPMENT

A synthesis of research on small groups suggests that there are five distinct phases in the life cycle of any team:[40]

1. *Forming*—a stage of initial orientation and interpersonal testing.

2. *Storming*—a stage of conflict over tasks and working as a team.

3. *Norming*—a stage of consolidation around task and operating agendas.

4. *Performing*—a stage of teamwork and focused task performance.

5. *Adjourning*—a stage of task completion and disengagement.

Forming Stage

The forming stage involves the first entry of individual members into a team. This is a stage of initial task orientation and interpersonal testing. As individuals come together for the first time or two, they ask a number of questions: "What can or does the team offer me?" "What will I be asked to contribute?" "Can my needs be met while my efforts serve the task needs of the team?"

In the forming stage, people begin to identify with other members and with the team itself. They are concerned about getting acquainted, establishing interpersonal relationships, discovering what is considered acceptable behaviour, and learning how others perceive the team's task. This may also be a time when some members rely on, or become temporarily dependent on, another member who appears "powerful" or especially "knowledgeable." Such things as prior experience with team members in other contexts and individual impressions of organization philosophies, goals, and policies may also affect member relationships in new work teams. Difficulties in the forming stage tend to be greater in more culturally and demographically diverse teams.

Storming Stage

The storming stage of team development is a period of high emotionality. Tension often emerges between members over tasks and interpersonal concerns. There may be periods of outright hostility and infighting. Coalitions or cliques may form around personalities or interests. Subteams form around areas of agreement and disagreement involving group tasks and/or the manner of operations. Conflict may develop as individuals compete to impose their preferences on others and to become influential in the group's status structure.

Important changes occur in the storming stage as task agendas become clarified and members begin to understand one another's interpersonal styles. Here attention begins to shift toward obstacles that may stand in the way of task accomplishment. Efforts are made to find ways to meet team goals while also satisfying individual needs. Failure in the storming stage can be a lasting liability, whereas success in the storming stage can set a strong foundation for later team effectiveness.

Canadian Managers
Supporting a Volunteer Team for Better Health Services

Running a charitable foundation takes lots of organization and teamwork. Just ask Bill Hallett. As President and CEO of the Niagara Health Systems Foundation, Hallett is responsible for designing and managing the major fundraising campaign "It's our Time" in support of a number of health care initiatives in the Niagara region of Ontario.

With any aggressive campaign seeking to raise large amounts of money, Hallett believes that the key to success is commitment to relationship building. In order to establish relationships that are critical to the success of the Foundation's initiatives, he has worked with the Niagara Health System Board of Trustees, volunteers, and staff at local hospital boards to recruit a team of community leaders to serve as the Foundation's board of directors. In addition, Hallett focuses on supporting strong partnerships with individual donors, local hospital foundations, auxiliaries, and municipal governments. Bill Hallett recognizes that fundraising involves both "friend raising" and getting the right team together.

Source: With information from the corporate website www.niagarahealth.on.ca and from "Great Expectations," *Philanthropic Trends*, Spring 2005.

Norming Stage

Co-operation is an important issue for teams in the norming stage. At this point, members of the team begin to become coordinated as a working unit and tend to operate with shared rules of conduct. The team feels a sense of leadership, with each member starting to play useful roles. Most interpersonal hostilities give way to a precarious balancing of forces as norming builds initial integration. Harmony is emphasized, but minority viewpoints may be discouraged.

In the norming stage, members are likely to develop initial feelings of closeness, a plan for the division of labour, and a sense of shared expectations. This helps protect the team from disintegration. Holding the team together may become even more important than successful task accomplishment.

Performing Stage

Teams in the performing stage are more mature, organized, and well functioning. This is a stage of total integration in which team members are able to deal in creative ways with both complex tasks and any interpersonal conflicts. The team operates with a clear and stable structure, and members are motivated by team goals.

The primary challenges of teams in the performing stage are to continue refining the operations and relationships essential to working as an integrated unit. Such teams need to remain coordinated with the larger organization and adapt successfully to changing conditions over time. A team that has achieved total integration will score high on the criteria of team maturity shown in *Figure 16.4*.[41]

Adjourning Stage

The final stage of team development is adjourning, when team members prepare to achieve closure and disband. Ideally, temporary committees, task forces, and project teams disband with a sense that important goals have been accomplished. This may be an emotional time,

Figure 16.4 Criteria for assessing the maturity of a team.

		Very poor			Very good	
1.	Trust among members	1	2	3	4	5
2.	Feedback mechanisms	1	2	3	4	5
3.	Open communications	1	2	3	4	5
4.	Approach to decisions	1	2	3	4	5
5.	Leadership sharing	1	2	3	4	5
6.	Acceptance of goals	1	2	3	4	5
7.	Valuing diversity	1	2	3	4	5
8.	Member cohesiveness	1	2	3	4	5
9.	Support for each other	1	2	3	4	5
10.	Performance norms	1	2	3	4	5
		Where you don't want to be			Where you do want to be	

and disbandment should be managed with this possibility in mind. For members who have worked together intensely for a period of time, breaking up the close relationships may be painful. In all cases, the team would like to disband with members feeling they would work with one another again sometime in the future. Members should be acknowledged for their contributions and praised for the group's overall success.

●●● NORMS AND COHESIVENESS

■ A **norm** is a behaviour, rule, or standard expected to be followed by team members.

A **norm** is a behaviour expected of team members.[42] It is a "rule" or "standard" that guides their behaviour. When violated, a norm may be enforced with reprimands and other sanctions. In the extreme, violation of a norm can result in a member being expelled from a team or socially ostracized by other members. The *performance norm*, which defines the level of work effort and performance that team members are expected to contribute, is extremely important. In general, work groups and teams with positive performance norms are more successful in accomplishing task objectives than are teams with negative performance norms. Other important team norms relate to such things as helpfulness, participation, timeliness, quality, and innovation.

Team leaders should help and encourage members to develop norms that support organizational objectives. During the forming and storming steps of development, for example, norms relating to membership issues such as expected attendance and levels of commitment are important. By the time the stage of performing is reached, norms relating to adaptability and change become most relevant. The following are guidelines for *how to build positive group norms*:[43]

• Act as a positive role model.

• Reinforce the desired behaviours with rewards.

• Control results by performance reviews and regular feedback.

• Train and orient new members to adopt desired behaviours.

- Recruit and select new members who exhibit the desired behaviours.

- Hold regular meetings to discuss progress and ways of improvement.

- Use team decision-making methods to reach agreement.

Team members vary in the degree to which they accept and adhere to group norms. Conformity to norms is largely determined by the strength of group **cohesiveness**, the degree to which members are attracted to be, and motivated to remain, part of a team.[44] Persons in a highly cohesive team value their membership and strive to maintain positive relationships with other team members. They experience satisfaction from team identification and interpersonal relationships. Because of this they tend to conform to the norms. Importantly, this can be good or bad for organizations; it depends on whether or not the performance norm is positive.

Look at *Figure 16.5*. When the performance norm of a team is positive, high cohesion and the resulting conformity to norms has a beneficial effect on overall team performance. This is a "best-case" scenario for both the manager and the organization. Competent team members work hard and reinforce one another's task accomplishments while experiencing satisfaction with the team. But when the performance norm is negative in a cohesive team, high conformity to the norm can have undesirable results. The figure shows this as a "worst-case" scenario where team performance suffers from restricted work efforts by members. Between these two extremes are mixed situations of moderate to low performance. To ensure employee buy-in and participation into their team philosophy and development, TELUS implemented their Team Machine. This web-based program allows employees to "recognize the outstanding performance, extraordinary efforts, and exceptional results that support our TELUS Values." Put forth by fellow employees, each individual or team member receives Team Machine Points that can either be redeemed or accumulated from the Team Machine Reward Selection.[45] The program has been successful in improving employee buy-in, motivation, and satisfaction.

To achieve and maintain the best-case scenario shown in *Figure 16.5*, managers should be skilled at influencing both the norms and cohesiveness of any team. They will want to build and maintain high cohesiveness in teams whose performance norms are positive. Guidelines on *how to increase cohesion* include the following:

- Induce agreement on team goals.

- Increase membership homogeneity.

- Increase interactions among members.

> ▦ **Cohesiveness** is the degree to which members are attracted to and motivated to remain part of a team.

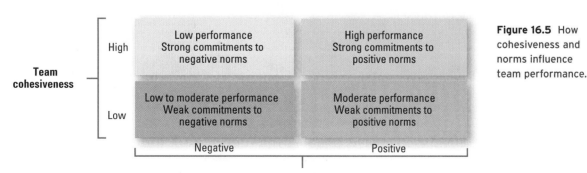

Figure 16.5 How cohesiveness and norms influence team performance.

- Decrease team size.

- Introduce competition with other teams.

- Reward team rather than individual results.

- Provide physical isolation from other teams.

●●● TASK AND MAINTENANCE NEEDS

■ A **task activity** is an action taken by a team member that directly contributes to the group's performance purpose.

Research on the social psychology of groups identifies two types of activities that are essential if team members are to work well together over time.[46] **Task activities** contribute directly to the team's performance purpose, and **maintenance activities** support the emotional life of the team as an ongoing social system. Although the team leader or supervisor will often handle them, the responsibility for both types of activities should be shared and distributed among all team members. Anyone can help lead a team by acting in ways that satisfy its task and maintenance needs. This concept of *distributed leadership in teams* makes every member continually responsible for both recognizing when task or maintenance activities are needed and taking actions to provide them.

■ A **maintenance activity** is an action taken by a team member that supports the emotional life of the group.

Figure 16.6 offers useful insights on distributed leadership in teams. Leading through task activities involves making an effort to define and solve problems and advance work toward performance results. Without the relevant task activities, such as initiating agendas, sharing information, and others listed in the figure, teams will have difficulty accomplishing their objectives. Leading through maintenance activities, by contrast, helps strengthen and perpetuate the team as a social system. When maintenance activities such as encouraging others and reducing tensions are performed well, good interpersonal relationships are achieved and the ability of the team to stay together over the longer term is ensured.

Both team task and maintenance activities stand in distinct contrast to the *dysfunctional activities* also described in *Figure 16.6*. Activities such as withdrawing and horsing around are usually self-serving to the individual member. They detract from, rather than enhance, team effectiveness. Unfortunately, very few teams are immune to dysfunctional behaviour by members. Everyone shares in the responsibility for minimizing its occurrence and meeting the distributed leadership needs of a team by contributing functional task and maintenance behaviours.

Figure 16.6 Distributed leadership helps teams meet task and maintenance needs.

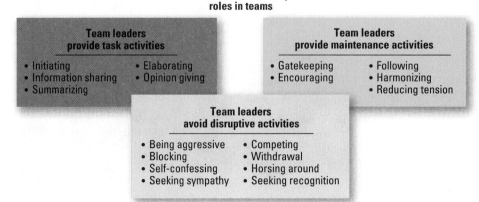

Distributed leadership roles in teams

Team leaders provide task activities
- Initiating
- Information sharing
- Summarizing
- Elaborating
- Opinion giving

Team leaders provide maintenance activities
- Gatekeeping
- Encouraging
- Following
- Harmonizing
- Reducing tension

Team leaders avoid disruptive activities
- Being aggressive
- Blocking
- Self-confessing
- Seeking sympathy
- Competing
- Withdrawal
- Horsing around
- Seeking recognition

●●● COMMUNICATION NETWORKS

Figure 16.7 depicts three interaction patterns and communication networks that are common in teams.[47] When teams are interacting intensively and their members are working closely together on tasks, close coordination of activities is needed. This need is best met by a **decentralized communication network** in which all members communicate directly with one another. Sometimes this is called the *all-channel* or *star communication network*. At other times and in other situations team members work on tasks independently, with the required work being divided up among them. Activities are coordinated and results pooled by a central point of control. Most communication flows back and forth between individual members and this hub or centre point. This creates a **centralized communication network** as shown in the figure. Sometimes this is called a *wheel* or *chain communication structure*. When teams are composed of subgroups experiencing issue-specific disagreements, such as a temporary debate over the best means to achieve a goal, the resulting interaction pattern often involves a *restricted communication network*. Here, polarized subgroups contest one another and may even engage in antagonistic relations. Communication between the subgroups is limited and biased, with negative consequences for group process and effectiveness.

The best teams use communication networks in the right ways, at the right times, and for the right tasks. Centralized communication networks seem to work better on simple tasks.[48] These tasks require little creativity, information processing, and problem solving and lend themselves to more centralized control. The reverse is true for more complex tasks, where interacting groups do better. Here, the decentralized networks work well since they are able to support the more intense interactions and information sharing required to perform

> ▦ A **decentralized communication network** allows all members to communicate directly with one another.

> ▦ In a **centralized communication network**, communication flows only between individual members and a hub or centre point.

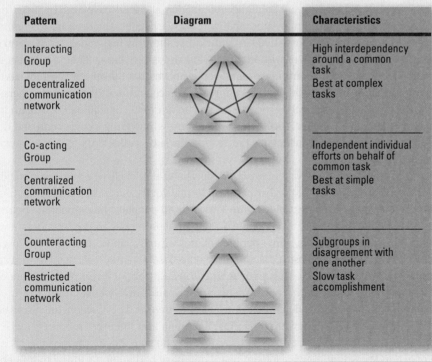

Pattern	Diagram	Characteristics
Interacting Group ──── Decentralized communication network		High interdependency around a common task ──── Best at complex tasks
Co-acting Group ──── Centralized communication network		Independent individual efforts on behalf of common task ──── Best at simple tasks
Counteracting Group ──── Restricted communication network		Subgroups in disagreement with one another ──── Slow task accomplishment

Figure 16.7 Interaction patterns and communication networks in teams.

Source: John R. Schermerhorn, Jr., James G. Hunt, and Richard N. Osborn, *Organizational Behavior*, 8th ed. (New York: Wiley, 2003), p. 347. Used by permission.

complicated tasks. When teams get complacent, the conflict among co-acting groups can be a source of creativity and critical evaluation. But when subgroups have difficulty communicating with one another, task accomplishment typically suffers for the short run at least.

✓ **Learning check ❸**

BE SURE YOU CAN

• define the term group effectiveness • identify inputs that influence group effectiveness • define the term group process, and explain its influence on team effectiveness • discuss how membership diversity influences team effectiveness • list five stages of group development • illustrate how group members act in each stage • define the term group norm and list ways to build positive group norms • define the term cohesiveness and list ways to increase and decrease group cohesion • explain how norms and cohesiveness interact to influence group performance • differentiate task, maintenance, and disruptive activities by group members • describe how and when groups should use decentralized and centralized communication networks

---

DECISION MAKING IN TEAMS

■ **Decision making** is the process of making choices among alternative courses of action.

Decision making, discussed extensively in Chapter 7, is the process of making choices among alternative possible courses of action. It is one of the most important group processes. It is also complicated by the fact that decisions in teams can be made in several different ways.

●●● HOW TEAMS MAKE DECISIONS

Edgar Schein, a respected scholar and consultant, notes that teams make decisions by at least six methods: lack of response, authority rule, minority rule, majority rule, consensus, and unanimity.[49] In *decision by lack of response*, one idea after another is suggested without any discussion taking place. When the team finally accepts an idea, all others have been bypassed and discarded by simple lack of response rather than by critical evaluation. In *decision by authority rule*, the leader, manager, committee head, or some other authority figure makes a decision for the team. This can be done with or without discussion and is very time efficient. Whether the decision is a good one or a bad one, however, depends on whether the authority figure has the necessary information and on how well this approach is accepted by other team members. In *decision by minority rule*, two or three people are able to dominate or "railroad" the team into making a mutually agreeable decision. This is often done by providing a suggestion and then forcing quick agreement by challenging the team with such statements as "Does anyone object?…Let's go ahead, then."

One of the most common ways teams make decisions, especially when early signs of disagreement arise, is *decision by majority rule*. Here, formal voting may take place, or members may be polled to find the majority viewpoint. This method parallels the democratic political system and is often used without awareness of its potential problems. The very process of voting can create coalitions; that is, some people will be "winners" and others will be "losers" when the final vote is tallied. Those in the minority—the "losers"—may feel left out or discarded without having had a fair say. They may be unenthusiastic about implementing the decision of the "majority," and lingering resentments may impair team effectiveness in the future.

Teams are often encouraged to follow *decision by consensus*. This is where full discussion leads to one alternative being favoured by most members and the other members agree to support it. When a consensus is reached, even those who may have opposed the chosen course of action know that they have been heard and have had an opportunity to influence the decision outcome. Such consensus does not require unanimity. But it does require that team members be able to argue, engage in reasonable conflict, and still get along with and respect one another.[50] And it requires that there be the opportunity for any dissenting members to know that they have been able to speak and that they have been listened to. At the student-run and -funded Alberta Public Interest Research Group (APIRG), decisions are made by consensus. APIRG believes that consensus does not mean everyone thinks that the decision made is necessarily the best one possible or even that everyone is sure it will work. What it does believe is that, in making decisions, no one should feel that their position on the matter was misunderstood or that it wasn't given a proper hearing.[51]

A *decision by unanimity* may be the ideal state of affairs. Here, all team members agree on the course of action to be taken. This is a logically perfect method for decision making in teams, but it is also extremely difficult to attain in actual practice. One of the reasons that teams sometimes turn to authority decisions, majority voting, or even minority decisions, in fact, is the difficulty of managing the team process to achieve consensus or unanimity.

●●● ASSETS AND LIABILITIES OF GROUP DECISIONS

The best teams don't limit themselves to just one decision-making method. Instead, they vary methods to best fit the problems at hand, in true contingency management fashion. A very important team leadership skill is the ability to help a team choose the "best" decision method—one that provides for a timely and quality decision and one to which the members are highly committed. This reasoning is consistent with the Vroom-Jago leader-participation model discussed in Chapter 13.[52] You should recall that this model describes how leaders should utilize the full range of individual, consultative, and group decision methods as they resolve daily problems. To do this well, however, team leaders must understand the potential assets and potential liabilities of group decisions.[53]

The potential *advantages of group decision making* are significant. Because of this, the general argument is that team decisions should be sought whenever time and other circumstances permit. Team decisions make greater amounts of information, knowledge, and expertise available to solve problems. They expand the number of action alternatives that are examined; they help groups to avoid tunnel vision and tendencies to consider only a limited

AROUND THE WORLD

Teaming up for worldwide soccer success

The enormous success of the Real Madrid soccer team on the field is rivalled only by its success off the field. The Spanish club is not only the winningest team in European soccer history, but it's the richest soccer team in the world, pulling in 292 million Euros in 2005–06. The 100-year-old club has developed into one of the world's most recognizable brands in any type of business, spawning a video game, TV channel, and even a movie. Real Madrid players, employees, shareholders (who are members of the public), advertisers, and its loyal fans stick to traditional values of honesty, discipline, fighting spirit, leadership, camaraderie, chivalry, nobility, fair play, continual self-improvement, and respect for adversaries. The century-old team spirit inspires Real Madrid's backroom employees. In fact, it's said that if a management directive is ever unclear, employees instinctively know what to do because the values are so enshrined.

Source: "Real Madrid stays at the top," Deloitte and Touche press release, Feb. 8, 2007; Kimio Kase, Ignacio Urrutia de Hoyos, Carlos Martí Sanchís, and Magdalena Opazo Bretón, "The proto-image of Real Madrid: Implications for marketing and management," *International Journal of Sports Marketing and Sponsorship*, April 2007, pp. 212–233; corporate website: <www.realmadrid.com>.

range of options. Team decisions increase the understanding and acceptance of outcomes by members. And importantly, team decisions increase the commitments of members to follow through to implement the decision once made. Simply put, team decisions can result in quality decisions that all members work hard to make successful.

The potential *disadvantages of group decision making* largely trace to the difficulties that can be experienced in group process. In a team decision there may be social pressure to conform. Individual members may feel intimidated or compelled to go along with the apparent wishes of others. There may be minority domination, where some members feel forced or "railroaded" to accept a decision advocated by one vocal individual or small coalition. Also, the time required to make team decisions can sometimes be a disadvantage. As more people are involved in the dialogue and discussion, decision making takes longer. This added time may be costly, even prohibitively so, in certain circumstances.[54]

●●● GROUPTHINK

A high level of cohesiveness can sometimes be a disadvantage during decision making. Members of very cohesive teams feel so strongly about the group that they may not want to do anything that might detract from feelings of goodwill. This may cause them to publicly agree with actual or suggested courses of action, while privately having serious doubts about them. Strong feelings of team loyalty can make it hard for members to criticize and evaluate one another's ideas and suggestions. Unfortunately, there are times when desires to hold the team together at all costs and avoid disagreements may result in poor decisions.

■ **Groupthink** is a tendency for highly cohesive teams to lose their evaluative capabilities.

Psychologist Irving Janis calls this phenomenon **groupthink**, the tendency for highly cohesive groups to lose their critical evaluative capabilities.[55] You should be alert to spot the following *symptoms of groupthink* when they occur in your decision-making teams:

- *Illusions of invulnerability:* Members assume that the team is too good for criticism or beyond attack.

- *Rationalizing unpleasant and disconfirming data:* Members refuse to accept contradictory data or to thoroughly consider alternatives.

- *Belief in inherent group morality:* Members act as though the group is inherently right and above reproach.

- *Stereotyping competitors as weak, evil, and stupid:* Members refuse to look realistically at other groups.

- *Applying direct pressure to deviants to conform to group wishes:* Members refuse to tolerate anyone who suggests the team may be wrong.

- *Self-censorship by members:* Members refuse to communicate personal concerns to the whole team.

- *Illusions of unanimity:* Members accept consensus prematurely, without testing its completeness.

- *Mind guarding:* Members protect the team from hearing disturbing ideas or outside viewpoints.

Groupthink can occur anywhere. On January 28, 1986, the space shuttle Challenger exploded in mid-air, killing all seven astronauts on board. The disaster resulted in one of the most in-depth aviation accident investigations in history. One of the most damning indictments to emerge was the extent to which a groupthink mentality by senior project leaders contributed to the disaster.[56] When and if you encounter groupthink, Janis suggests taking action along the lines shown in *Manager's Notepad 16.3*.

MANAGER'S
Notepad 16.3

How to avoid groupthink

- Assign the role of critical evaluator to each team member; encourage a sharing of viewpoints.

- Don't, as a leader, seem partial to one course of action; do absent yourself from meetings at times to allow free discussion.

- Create subteams to work on the same problems and then share their proposed solutions.

- Have team members discuss issues with outsiders and report back on their reactions.

- Invite outside experts to observe team activities and react to team processes and decisions.

- Assign one member to play a "devil's advocate" role at each team meeting.

- Hold a "second-chance" meeting after consensus is apparently achieved to review the decision.

●●● CREATIVITY IN TEAM DECISION MAKING

Among the potential benefits that teams can bring to organizations is increased creativity. Two techniques that are particularly helpful for creativity in decision making are brainstorming and the nominal group technique.[57] Both can now be pursued in computer-mediated or virtual team discussions, as well as in face-to-face formats.

In **brainstorming,** teams of 5 to 10 members meet to generate ideas. Brainstorming teams typically operate within these guidelines. *All criticism is ruled out*—judgement or evaluation of ideas must be withheld until the idea-generation process has been completed. "*Freewheeling" is welcomed*—the wilder or more radical the idea, the better. *Quantity is important*—the greater the number of ideas, the greater the likelihood of obtaining a superior idea. *Building on one another's ideas is encouraged*—participants should suggest how ideas of others can be turned into better ideas, or how two or more ideas can be joined into still another hybrid idea.

■ **Brainstorming** engages group members in an open, spontaneous discussion of problems and ideas.

By prohibiting criticism, the brainstorming method reduces fears of ridicule or failure on the part of individuals. Ideally, this results in more enthusiasm, involvement, and a freer flow of ideas among members. But there are times when team members have very different opinions and goals. The differences may be so extreme that a brainstorming meeting might deteriorate into antagonistic arguments and harmful conflicts. In such cases, a **nominal group technique** could help. This approach uses a highly structured meeting agenda to allow everyone to contribute ideas without the interference of evaluative comments by others. Participants are first asked to work alone and respond in writing with possible solutions to a stated problem. Ideas are then shared in round-robin fashion without any criticism or discussion; all ideas are recorded as they are presented. Ideas are next discussed and clarified in round-robin sequence, with no evaluative comments allowed. Next, members individually and silently follow a written voting procedure that allows for all alternatives to be rated or ranked in priority order. Finally, the last two steps are repeated as needed to further clarify the process.

■ The **nominal group technique** structures interaction among team members discussing problems and ideas.

LEADING HIGH-PERFORMANCE TEAMS

When we think of the word "team," sporting teams often come to mind. And we know these teams certainly have their share of problems. Members slack off or become disgruntled; even world-champion teams have losing streaks; and, the most highly talented players sometimes lose motivation, quibble with other team members, and lapse into performance slumps. When these things happen, the owners, managers, and players are apt to take corrective action to "rebuild the team" and restore what we have called team effectiveness. Work teams are teams in a similar sense. Even the most mature work team is likely to experience problems over time. When such difficulties arise, structured efforts at team building can help.

●●● THE TEAM-BUILDING PROCESS

▦ **Team building** is a sequence of collaborative activities to gather and analyze data on a team and make changes to increase its effectiveness.

Team building is a sequence of planned activities used to gather and analyze data on the functioning of a team, and to implement constructive changes to increase its operating effectiveness.[58] Most systematic approaches to team building follow the steps described in *Figure 16.8*. The cycle begins with awareness that a problem may exist or may develop within the team. Members then work together to gather and analyze data so that the problem is fully understood. Action plans are made by members and collectively implemented. Results are evaluated by team members working together. Any difficulties or new problems that are discovered serve to recycle the team-building process. Consider this added detail to the case featured in *Figure 16.8*.

> The consultant received a call from the hospital's director of personnel. He indicated that a new hospital president felt the top management team lacked cohesiveness and was not working well together as a team. The consultant agreed to facilitate a team-building activity that would include a day-long retreat at a nearby resort hotel. The process began when the consultant conducted interviews with the president and other members of the executive team. During the retreat, the consultant reported these results to the team as a whole. He indicated that the hospital's goals were generally understood by all but that they weren't clear enough to allow agreement on action priorities. Furthermore, he reported that interpersonal problems between the director of nursing services and the director of administration were making it difficult for the team to work together comfortably. These and other issues were addressed by the team at the retreat. Working sometimes in small subteams, and at other times together as a whole, they agreed first of all that action should be taken to clarify the hospital's overall mission and create a priority list of objectives for the current year. Led by the president, activity on this task would involve all team members and was targeted for completion within a month. The president asked that progress on the action plans be reviewed at each of the next three monthly executive staff meetings. Everyone agreed.

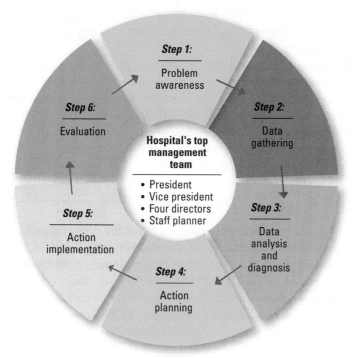

Figure 16.8 Steps in the team-building process: case of the hospital top management team.

This example introduces team building as a way to assess a work team's functioning and take corrective action to improve its effectiveness. It can and should become a regular work routine. There are many ways to gather data on team functioning, including structured and unstructured interviews, questionnaires, and team meetings. Regardless of the method used, the basic principle of team building remains the same. The process requires

take it to the case!

Big Bertha's team hits a long ball

He has been described as "a man of vision, yet very focused with the willingness to undertake challenges others couldn't—or wouldn't—with a work-hard ethic that inspired us all." Ely Callaway, founder of Callaway Golf, maker of the famous "Big Bertha" driver, certainly was special. The goal he infused in his firm is continuous improvement, doing better than competitors and the firm's own past work. Callaway remains self-described as committed to producing golf products that are "Demonstrably Superior and Pleasingly Different," and to providing golfers with "A better game by design." Even as the firm has grown from a group of 5 in 1982 to over 3,000 employees today, it strives for a family atmosphere and a comfortable, enjoyable culture. New members of the Callaway Golf team are expected to have integrity, be honest and daring, and to work hard, with enthusiasm and a sense of personal accountability.

Source: Information from <www.callawaygolf.com>

that a careful and collaborative assessment of the team's inputs, processes, and results be made. All members should participate in data gathering, assist in data analysis, and collectively decide on actions to be taken.

Sometimes teamwork can be improved when people share the challenges of unusual and even physically demanding experiences. Outward Bound is famous for hands-on action learning, in a wilderness setting. More than a million people from companies that include Gulf Canada, Wood Gundy, and Maple Leaf Foods have taken part in its intensive outdoor education programs. Year-round, Outward Bound offers courses across Canada and tailors each course to meet individual company goals—perhaps to energize a stale team or help build trust between budding business partners.[59]

●●● SUCCESS FACTORS IN TEAMS

Among the many developments in the workplace today, the continuing effort to refine and apply creative team concepts is high on most executives' action agendas. But whether the group or team is working at the top, bottom, cross-functionally, or in direct customer service, high-performance results can't be left to chance. There are too many forces in the environment and group dynamics that can lead teams astray. Team success is only achieved through the special efforts of leaders and members alike. We know, for example, that high-performance teams generally share these characteristics:[60]

- a clear and elevating goal,

- a task-driven and results-oriented structure,

- competent and committed members who work hard,

- a collaborative climate,

- high standards of excellence,

- external support and recognition, and

- strong, principled leadership.

WHAT IT TAKES TO BE THE BEST

Blast Radius, a global technology firm with Canadian headquarters in Vancouver, realized that service excellence and teamwork were critical to achieving corporate goals. To reinforce this message the CEO and the HR department defined these behaviours and included them in the performance management process. In addition, project managers provided feedback on these behaviours at the end of each project and provided cash rewards to teams of employees who demonstrated high levels of performance. To further support integrated recognition messages, employees nominated their peers and teams for awards in these areas.

Source: Natalie Michael, "Ring a bell and employees will deliver," *Canadian HR Reporter*, Aug. 14, 2006, Vol. 19, Iss. 14, pp. 17–18.

●●●● TEAM LEADERSHIP CHALLENGES

The last point on this list—the need for strong and principled leadership—may be the key to them all. In their book, *Teamwork: What Can Go Right/What Can Go Wrong*, Carl Larson and Frank LaFasto state: "The right person in a leadership role can add tremendous value to any collective effort, even to the point of sparking the outcome with an intangible kind of magic."[61] They further point out that leaders of high-performing teams share many characteristics with the "transformational leader" examined in Chapter 13.

Successful team leaders *establish a clear vision of the future*. This vision serves as a goal that inspires hard work and the quest for performance excellence; it creates a sense of shared purpose. Successful team leaders help to *create change*. They are dissatisfied with the status quo, influence team members toward similar dissatisfaction, and infuse the team with the motivation to change in order to become better. Finally, successful team leaders *unleash talent*. They make sure the team is staffed with members who have the right skills and abilities. And they make sure these people are highly motivated to use their talents to achieve the group's performance objectives.

The best leaders know that teams are hard work, but that they are also worth it. You don't get a high-performing team by just bringing a group of people together and giving them a shared name or title. Leaders of high-performance teams create supportive climates in which team members know what to expect from the leader and each other, and know what the leader expects from them. They empower team members. By personal example they demonstrate the importance of setting aside self-interests to support the team's goals. And, they view team building as an ongoing leadership responsibility. An important aspect of this responsibility is developing future leaders for the team. Joe Liemandt, founder and CEO of the software firm Trilogy, Inc., says: "As Trilogy grew, one of the most important lessons we learned is that hiring for raw talent isn't enough. We had to build leaders. I believe you should always work to replace yourself."[62]

BE SURE YOU CAN

• define the term team building • illustrate how managers can use team building to improve group effectiveness • list three things that successful leaders do to create and maintain high-performance teams

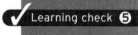 Learning check **5**

●●● **Chapter 16** STUDY GUIDE

WHERE WE'VE BEEN

Back to C.O.R.E

The opening example of C.O.R.E. Digital Pictures showed talented individuals working together in a highly creative setting. It is also indicated that high performance by an organization depends on more than the involvement of talented individuals; it requires that they be blended together into effective teams. In this chapter you learned about the nature of teams and different types of teams found in organizations. You learned about group effectiveness, the stages of team development, and the input factors that influence team performance. You also learned about group processes and how leaders build high-performing teams that sustain themselves with satisfied members.

THE NEXT STEP
INTEGRATED LEARNING ACTIVITIES

Cases/Projects	**Self-Assessments**	**Exercises in Teamwork**
• Callaway Golf Case • Project 8—Superstars on the Team • Project 9—Management in Popular Culture	• Emotional Intelligence (#2) • T-T Leadership Style (#21) • Team Leader Skills (#27)	• Leading through Participation (#16) • Lost at Sea (#26) • Work Team Dynamics (#27)

STUDY QUESTION SUMMARY

1. How do teams contribute to organizations?

• A team is a collection of people working together to accomplish a common goal.

• Organizations operate as interlocking networks of formal work groups, which offer many benefits to the organizations and to their members.

• Teams help organizations through synergy in task performance, the creation of a whole that is greater than the sum of its parts.

• Teams help satisfy important needs for their members, providing various types of job support and social satisfactions.

• Social loafing and other problems can limit the performance of teams.

2. What are current trends in the use of teams?

• Teams are important mechanisms of empowerment and participation in the workplace.

• Committees and task forces are used to facilitate operations and allow special projects to be completed with creativity.

• Cross-functional teams bring members together from different departments and help improve lateral relations and integration in organizations.

• Employee involvement teams, such as the quality circle, allow employees to provide important insights into daily problem solving.

• New developments in information technology are making virtual teams, or computer-mediated teams, more commonplace.

- Self-managing teams are changing organizations by allowing team members to perform many tasks previously reserved for their supervisors.

3. How do teams work?

- An effective team achieves high levels of task performance, member satisfaction, and team viability.
- Important team input factors include the organizational setting, nature of the task, size, and membership characteristics.
- A team matures through various stages of development, including forming, storming, norming, performing, and adjourning.
- Norms are the standards or rules of conduct that influence the behaviour of team members; cohesion is the attractiveness of the team to its members.
- In highly cohesive teams, members tend to conform to norms; the best situation for a manager or leader is a team with positive performance norms and high cohesiveness.
- Distributed leadership in serving a team's task and maintenance needs helps in achieving long-term effectiveness.
- Effective teams make use of alternative communication networks to best complete tasks.

4. How do teams make decisions?

- Teams can make decisions by lack of response, authority rule, minority rule, majority rule, consensus, and unanimity.
- The potential advantages of group decision making include having more information available and generating more understanding and commitment.
- The potential liabilities to group decision making include social pressures to conform and greater time requirements.
- Groupthink is a tendency of members of highly cohesive teams to lose their critical evaluative capabilities and make poor decisions.
- Techniques for improving creativity in teams include brainstorming and the nominal group technique.

5. What are the challenges of leading high-performance teams?

- Team building helps team members develop action plans for improving the way they work together and the results they accomplish.
- The team-building process should be data based and collaborative, involving a high level of participation by all team members.
- High-performance work teams have a clear and shared sense of purpose as well as a strong internal commitment to its accomplishment.

KEY TERMS REVIEW

Brainstorming (p. 403)

Centralized communication network (p. 399)

Cohesiveness (p. 397)

Committee (p. 388)

Cross-functional team (p. 389)

Decentralized communication network (p. 399)

Decision making (p. 400)

Effective team (p. 392)

Employee involvement team (p. 389)

Formal group (p. 388)

Group process (p. 393)

Groupthink (p. 402)

Informal group (p. 388)

Maintenance activity (p. 398)

Nominal group technique (p. 403)

Norm (p. 396)

Project team (p. 389)

Quality circle (p. 390)

Self-managing work team (p. 390)

Social loafing (p. 385)

Synergy (p. 387)

Task activity (p. 398)

Task force (p. 389)

Team (p. 385)

Team building (p. 404)

Teamwork (p. 385)

Virtual team (p. 390)

SELF-TEST 16

MULTIPLE-CHOICE QUESTIONS:

1. When a group of people is able to achieve more than what its members could by working individually, this is called _____.
   (a) social loafing (b) consensus (c) viability (d) synergy

2. In an organization operating with self-managing teams, the traditional role of _____ is replaced by the role of team leader.
   (a) chief executive officer (b) first-line supervisor (c) middle manager (d) general manager

3. An effective team is defined as one that achieves high levels of task performance, member satisfaction, and _____.
   (a) resource efficiency (b) team viability (c) consensus (d) creativity

4. In the open-systems model of teams, the _____ is an important input factor.
   (a) communication network (b) decision-making method (c) performance norm (d) set of membership characteristics

5. A basic rule of team dynamics states that the greater the _____ in a team, the greater the conformity to norms.
   (a) membership diversity (b) cohesiveness (c) task structure (d) competition among members

6. Groupthink is most likely to occur in teams that are _____.
   (a) large in size (b) diverse in membership (c) high performing (d) highly cohesive

7. Gatekeeping is an example of a _____ activity that can help teams work effectively over time.
   (a) task (b) maintenance (c) team-building (d) decision-making

8. Members of a team tend to become more motivated and able to deal with conflict during the _____ stage of team development.
   (a) forming (b) norming (c) performing (d) adjourning

9. One way for a manager to build positive norms within a team is to _____.
   (a) act as a positive role model (b) increase group size (c) introduce groupthink (d) isolate the team from others

10. When teams are highly cohesive, _____.
    (a) members are high performers (b) members tend to be satisfied with their team membership (c) members have positive norms (d) the group achieves its goals

11. A "quality circle" is an example of how organizations try to use _____ teams for performance advantage.
    (a) virtual (b) informal (c) employee involvement (d) self-managing

12. It would be common to find members of self-managing work teams engaged in _____.
    (a) social loafing (b) multi-tasking (c) centralized communication (d) decision by authority rule

13. The "team effectiveness equation" states: Team effectiveness = quality of inputs + (_____ − process losses).
    (a) process gains (b) leadership impact (c) membership ability (d) problem complexity

14. A _____ decision is one in which all members agree on the course of action to be taken.
    (a) consensus (b) unanimity (c) majority (d) synergy

15. To increase the cohesiveness of a group, a manager would be best off _____.
    (a) starting competition with other groups (b) increasing the group size (c) acting as a positive role model (d) introducing a new member

SHORT-RESPONSE QUESTIONS:

16.   How can a manager improve team effectiveness by modifying inputs?

17.   What is the relationship among a team's cohesiveness, performance norms, and performance results?

18.   How would a manager know that a team is suffering from groupthink (give two symptoms) and what could the manager do about it (give two responses)?

19.   What makes a self-managing team different from a traditional work team?

APPLICATION QUESTION:

20.   Marcos Martinez has just been appointed manager of a production team operating the 11 p.m. to 7 a.m. shift in a large manufacturing firm. An experienced manager, Marcos is concerned that the team members really like and get along well with one another, but they also appear to be restricting their task outputs to the minimum acceptable levels. What could Marcos do to improve things in this situation and why should he do them?

Communication and Interpersonal Skills

●●● CHAPTER 17 STUDY QUESTIONS

1. What is the communication process?

2. How can communication be improved?

3. How does perception influence communication?

4. How can we deal positively with conflict?

5. How can we negotiate successful agreements?

Planning Ahead

After reading Chapter 17, you should be able to answer these questions in your own words.

Center for Creative Leadership

Lead the way with communication

The importance of communication and interpersonal skills in leadership development is mainstream at the internationally regarded Center for Creative Leadership. The Center's mission is to "advance the understanding, practice and development of leadership for the benefit of society worldwide." Branches in North America, Asia, Europe, as well as network associates—such as the Niagara Institute in Ontario—expand the Center's reach to managers worldwide and contribute to its global reputation for excellence. Leaders need to be able to communicate effectively and use interpersonal skills to engage others in their work. The Center for Creative Leadership helps managers gain better insights into their interpersonal styles and build leadership skills for personal and organizational success.

After 23 years with his organization, Dean Marion, a plant manager with BGF Industries, realized that his entire career had been driven by the goal of becoming plant manager. He recognizes that "because I was always focused on that, I had high expectations of myself and I put pressure on everybody around me to live up to those same expectations." Through personal coaching, Marion's focus turned to improving relationships with his peers and supervisors, and helping others to succeed. "I'm still a performance-driven person who looks at the bottom line," he emphasizes, "but the difference is that I'm not out there hammering at people." Similarly, The Women's Leadership Program offered Ellen Magnis an experience that gained her some much needed balance between her job and her personal life, and that at the same time gave her staff new opportunities to stand up and take charge and shine. She explains, "I come to work now and know I'm making a difference to them."

The Center for Creative Leadership was founded on the initiative of H. Smith Richardson, Jr., a successful executive. He believed, "what organizations needed was not just leadership for the present and the near future, but a kind of innovative leadership with a broader focus and a longer view. Such leadership would be concerned not with profits, markets, and business strategies alone, but with the place of business in society."[1]

IN THE WORKPLACE

As you sit around the table with your team, discussing preparations for the Spring Celebration, you notice that there are a lot of unhappy faces. Disagreement is high. No one appears to be willing to change their point of view on which strategy is the best one to make the event a success. Some want to make it a "green" or eco-friendly event while others are hoping for a more traditional gathering.

While it has been a good exercise, you are finding that the discussion is now falling into a dysfunctional level of conflict. You know you have to get the team to move forward on this issue; the Spring Celebration is coming quickly and a decision has to be made soon. What should you do next?

●●● **Chapter 17** LEARNING PREVIEW ●●●

The chapter opening example of the Center for Creative Leadership introduced an organization devoted to leadership training that makes a difference—a real difference in the behaviour of leaders. The Center uses a variety of learning approaches to help participants better understand themselves and their behaviour when working with other persons. In this chapter you will learn about the communication process, communication barriers, and ways to become effective in interpersonal communication. You will learn about perception and how it influences communication through stereotypes and other perceptual distortions. You will also learn about the processes of conflict and negotiation, and how they can be engaged in positive and successful ways.

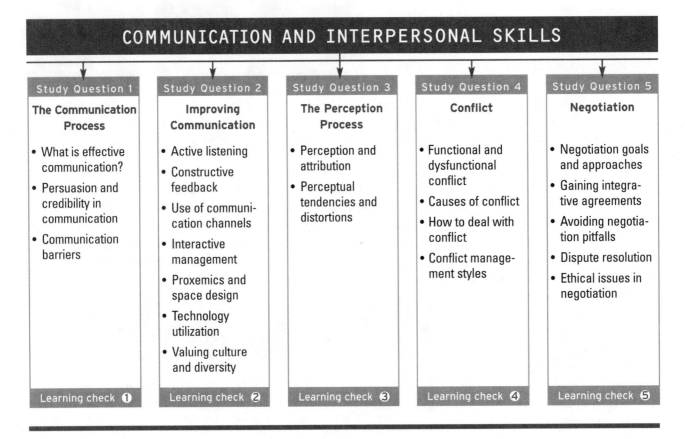

COMMUNICATION AND INTERPERSONAL SKILLS

Study Question 1	Study Question 2	Study Question 3	Study Question 4	Study Question 5
The Communication Process	**Improving Communication**	**The Perception Process**	**Conflict**	**Negotiation**
• What is effective communication? • Persuasion and credibility in communication • Communication barriers	• Active listening • Constructive feedback • Use of communication channels • Interactive management • Proxemics and space design • Technology utilization • Valuing culture and diversity	• Perception and attribution • Perceptual tendencies and distortions	• Functional and dysfunctional conflict • Causes of conflict • How to deal with conflict • Conflict management styles	• Negotiation goals and approaches • Gaining integrative agreements • Avoiding negotiation pitfalls • Dispute resolution • Ethical issues in negotiation
Learning check ❶	Learning check ❷	Learning check ❸	Learning check ❹	Learning check ❺

Anyone heading into the new workplace must understand that the work of managers and team leaders is highly interpersonal and communication intensive. Whether you work at the top, building support for strategies and organizational goals, or at lower levels, interacting with others to support their work efforts and your own, communication and interpersonal skills are essential to your personal toolkit. Think back to the descriptions of managerial work by Henry Mintzberg, John Kotter, and others as discussed in Chapter 1. For Mintzberg, managerial success involves performing well as an information "nerve centre," gathering information from and disseminating information to internal and external sources.[2] For Kotter, it depends largely on one's ability to build and maintain a complex web of interpersonal networks with insiders and outsiders so as to implement work priorities and agendas.[3] Says Pam Alexander, CEO of Alexander Ogilvy Public Relations Worldwide:

"Relationships are the most powerful form of media. Ideas will only get you so far these days. Count on personal relationships to carry you further."[4]

The ability to communicate well both orally and in writing is a critical managerial skill and the foundation of effective leadership.[5] Through communication, people exchange and share information with one another and influence one another's attitudes, behaviours, and understandings. Communication allows managers to establish and maintain interpersonal relationships, listen to others, and otherwise gain the information needed to create an inspirational workplace. No manager can handle conflict, negotiate successfully, and succeed at leadership without being a good communicator. Any student portfolio should include adequate testimony to one's abilities to communicate well in interpersonal relationships, in various forms of writing and public speaking, and increasingly through the electronic medium of the computer.

THE COMMUNICATION PROCESS

Communication is an interpersonal process of sending and receiving symbols with messages attached to them. In more practical terms, the key elements in the communication process are shown in *Figure 17.1*. They include a *sender*, who is responsible for encoding an intended *message* into meaningful symbols, both verbal and non-verbal. The message is sent through a *communication channel* to a *receiver*, who then decodes or interprets its *meaning*. This interpretation, importantly, may or may not match the sender's original intentions. *Feedback*, when present, reverses the process and conveys the receiver's response back to the sender. Another way to view the communication process is as a series of questions. "Who?" (sender) "says what?" (message) "in what way?" (channel) "to whom?" (receiver) "with what result?" (interpreted meaning).

▪ **Communication** is the process of sending and receiving symbols with meanings attached.

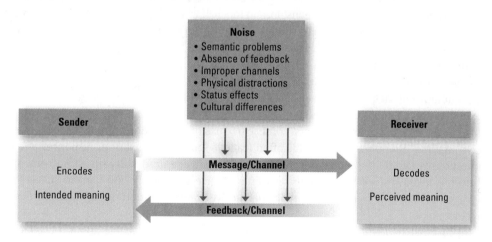

Figure 17.1 The interactive two-way process of interpersonal communication.

●●● WHAT IS EFFECTIVE COMMUNICATION?

Effective communication occurs when the message is fully understood. The intended meaning of the sender and the interpreted meaning of the receiver are one and the same. However, the goal in communication—effectiveness—is not always achieved. **Efficient communication** occurs at minimum cost in terms of resources expended. Time, in particular, is an important resource in the communication process. Picture your instructor taking the time to communi-

▪ In **effective communication** the intended meaning is fully understood by the receiver.

▪ **Efficient communication** occurs at minimum cost.

cate individually with each student about this chapter. It would be virtually impossible. Even if it were possible, it would be costly. This is why managers often leave voicemail messages and interact by email rather than visit their subordinates personally. Simply put, these alternatives are more efficient ways to communicate than through one-on-one and face-to-face communications. With the goal of transforming TELUS from a regional, western Canada-based company into a national telecommunications products and services provider, CEO Daren Entwistle focused on establishing an effective communication system. The process began with a weekly e-letter to employees, and, over the course of a two-year period, a CEO mailbox was established so that all company employees now have the opportunity to communicate directly with the CEO's office.[6]

One problem is that efficient communications are not always effective. A low-cost approach such as an email note to a distribution list may save time, but it does not always result in everyone getting the same meaning from the message. Without opportunities to ask questions and clarify the message, erroneous interpretations are possible. By the same token, an effective communication may not always be efficient. If a work team leader visits each team member individually to explain a new change in procedures, this may guarantee that everyone truly understands the change. But it may also be very costly in the demands it makes on the leader's time. A team meeting would be more efficient. In these and other ways, potential trade-offs between effectiveness and efficiency must be recognized in communication.

●●● PERSUASION AND CREDIBILITY IN COMMUNICATION

■ **Persuasion** is presenting a message in a manner that causes the other person to support it.

Communication is not always just about sharing information or being "heard"; it often includes the desire of one party to influence or motivate the other in a desired way. Especially in management, one of the most important purposes of communication is **persuasion**, getting someone else to support the message being presented.[7]

Much of what happens in today's horizontal structures and organic designs is outside of the formal supervisor–subordinate relationship, and much of what happens within it is in the context of empowerment. Managers get things done by working with and persuading others who are their peers, teammates, co-workers. They get things done more by convincing than by order-giving. Furthermore, they must be able to persuade others over and over again in the dynamic and complex workplace; once is not enough.

In terms of the power bases discussed in Chapter 13 on leadership, personal powers of expertise and reference are essential to the art of effective persuasion. Scholar and consultant Jay Conger says that many managers "confuse persuasion with taking bold stands and aggressive arguing." He points out that this often leads to "counter persuasion" responses and to questions regarding the manager's credibility.[8] And without **credibility**—trust, respect, and integrity in the eyes of others—he sees little chance that persuasion can be successful. Conger's advice is to build credibility for persuasive communication through expertise and relationships.

■ **Credibility** is trust, respect, and integrity in the eyes of others.

To build *credibility through expertise*, you must be knowledgeable about the issue in question and/or have a successful track record in dealing with similar issues in the past. In a hiring situation where you are trying to persuade team members to select candidate A rather than B, for example, you had better be able to defend your reasons. And it will always be better if your past recommendations turned out to be good ones. To build *credibility through relationships*, you must have a good working relationship with the person to be persuaded. The iron rule of reference power should be remembered: it is always easier to get someone to do what you want if they like you. To return to the prior example, if you have to persuade your boss to support a special bonus package to attract candidates, a good relationship will add credibility to your request.

■ **Noise** is anything that interferes with the communication process.

■ A **communication channel** is a medium through which the sender conveys a message to the receiver.

●●● COMMUNICATION BARRIERS

Communication is a shared and two-way process that requires effort and skill on the part of both the sender and the receiver. **Noise**, as previously shown in *Figure 17.1*, is anything that interferes with the effectiveness of the communication process. For example, when Yoshihiro Wada was president of Mazda Corporation, he once met with representatives of the firm's American joint-venture partner, Ford. But he had to use an interpreter. He estimated that 20 percent of his intended meaning was lost in the exchange between himself and the interpreter, and another 20 percent was lost between the interpreter and the Americans, with whom he was ultimately trying to communicate.[9] In addition to the obvious problems when different languages are involved, common sources of noise in communication include poor choice of channels, poor written or oral expression, failure to recognize non-verbal signals, physical distractions, and status effects.

Poor Choice of Channels

A **communication channel** is the medium through which a message is conveyed from sender to receiver. Good managers choose the right communication channel, or combination of channels, to accomplish their intended purpose in a given situation.[10] In general, *written channels* are acceptable for simple messages that are easy to convey and for those that require extensive dissemination quickly. They are also important as documentation when formal policies or directives are being conveyed. *Spoken channels* work best for messages that are complex and difficult to convey, and where immediate feedback to the sender is valuable. They are also more personal and can create a supportive, even inspirational, emotional climate.

Poor Written or Oral Expression

Communication will be effective only to the extent that the sender expresses a message in a way that can be clearly understood by the receiver. This means that words must be well chosen and properly used to express the sender's intentions. Consider the following "bafflegab" found among some executive communications.

> *A business report said:* "Consumer elements are continuing to stress the fundamental necessity of a stabilization of the price structure at a lower level than exists at the present time." (*Translation:* Consumers keep saying that prices must go down and stay down.)

> *A manager said:* "Substantial economies were effected in this division by increasing the time interval between

PERSONAL MANAGEMENT

COMMUNICATION and **INTERPERSONAL SKILLS** top the lists of characteristics looked for in employment candidates by corporate recruiters today. Yet there are some worrisome statistics out there. An amazing 81 percent of university professors in one survey rated high school graduates as "fair" or "poor" in writing clearly; 78 percent rated students the same in spelling and use of grammar. In an American Management Association survey, managers rated their bosses only slightly above average (3.51 on a 5-point scale) on these important dimensions of communication—transforming ideas into words, credibility, listening and asking questions, and written and oral presentations.[11] There is no doubt that we are in very challenging times when it comes to finding internships and full-time jobs in a streamlined economy. Strong communication and interpersonal skills could differentiate you from others wanting the same job. What about it? Can you convince a recruiter that you have the skills you need to run effective meetings, write informative reports, use email correctly, deliver persuasive presentations, conduct job interviews, work well with others on a team, keep conflicts constructive and negotiations positive, network with peers and mentors, and otherwise communicate enthusiasm to the people with whom you work?

Get to know yourself better

Complete Self-Assessments #12—**Assertiveness** and #28—**Conflict Management Styles** from the Workbook and Personal Management Activity #17 on the companion website.

MANAGER'S
Notepad 17.1

How to make a successful presentation

- *Be prepared:* Know what you want to say; know how you want to say it; rehearse saying it.
- *Set the right tone:* Act audience centred; make eye contact; be pleasant and confident.
- *Sequence points:* State your purpose; make important points; follow with details; then summarize.
- *Support your points:* Give specific reasons for your points; state them in understandable terms.
- *Accent the presentation:* Use good visual aids; provide supporting "handouts" when possible.
- *Add the right amount of polish:* Attend to details; have room, materials, and arrangements ready to go.
- *Check your technology:* Check everything ahead of time; make sure it works and know how to use it.
- *Don't bet on the Internet:* Beware of plans to make real-time Internet visits; save sites on a disk and use a browser to open the file.
- *Be professional:* Be on time; wear appropriate attire; act organized, confident, and enthusiastic.

distribution of data-eliciting forms to business entities." (*Translation:* The division saved money by sending out fewer questionnaires.)

Both written and oral communication require skill. It isn't easy, for example, to write a concise letter or to express one's thoughts in an email report. Any such message can easily be misunderstood. It takes practice and hard work to express yourself well. The same holds true for oral communication that takes place in telephone calls, face-to-face meetings, formal briefings, video conferences, and the like. *Manager's Notepad 17.1* identifies guidelines for an important communication situation—the executive briefing or formal presentation.[12]

Failure to Recognize Non-verbal Signals

■ **Non-verbal communication** takes place through gestures and body language.

Non-verbal communication takes place through such things as hand movements, facial expressions, body posture, eye contact, and the use of interpersonal space. It can be a powerful means of transmitting messages. Eye contact or voice intonation can be used intentionally to accent special parts of an oral communication. The astute observer notes the "body language" expressed by other persons. At times our body may be "talking" for us even as we otherwise maintain silence. And when we do speak, our body may sometimes "say" different things than our words convey. A **mixed message** occurs when a person's words communicate

■ A **mixed message** results when words communicate one message, while actions, body language, or appearance communicate something else.

one message while his or her actions, body language, appearance, or use of interpersonal space communicate something else. Watch how people behave in a meeting. A person who feels under attack may move back in a chair or lean away from the presumed antagonist, even while expressing verbal agreement. All of this is done quite unconsciously, but it sends a message to those alert enough to pick it up.

Canadian Managers

Canadian's Communication Skills Put Her on Top Internationally

Ann Godbehere has the communications skills critical for today's style of CFO, says Simone Lauper, media relations officer at Swiss Reinsurance Co., the 140-year-old Zurich-based reinsurance giant. Godbehere is a core member of the Swiss Reinsurance management team that, in mid-2006, expected to finalize a $6.8-billion takeover of General Electric Co.'s Insurance Solutions unit. Her communications skills will be crucial in navigating the regulatory and integration hurdles involved with this takeover.

Godbehere was rated by *Institutional Investor* magazine as the leading CFO in the European insurance sector in 2004, an award she says reflects the team she has assembled. "I encourage people to say openly if they don't understand something," she says. "I'm not afraid to say 'I don't get it.'" This self-effacing but direct, inclusive, and tough-minded style represents traits of effective communications skills found in a good manager.

Sources: Gordon Pitts, "Canadians find influence, top careers in foreign lands," *The Globe and Mail*, January 16, 2006.

Non-verbal channels probably play a more important part in communication than most people recognize. One researcher indicates that gestures alone may make up as much as 70 percent of communication.[13] In fact, a potential side effect of the growing use of electronic mail, computer networking, and other communication technologies is that gestures and other non-verbal signals that may add important meaning to the communication event are lost.

Physical Distractions

Any number of physical distractions can interfere with the effectiveness of a communication attempt. Some of these distractions, such as telephone interruptions, drop-in visitors, and lack of privacy, are evident in the following conversation between an employee, George, and his manager:[14]

> *Okay, George,* let's hear your problem [phone rings, boss picks it up, promises to deliver a report "just as soon as I can get it done"]. Uh, now, where were we—oh, you're having a problem with your technician. She's [manager's secretary brings in some papers that need his immediate signature; secretary leaves] . . . you say she's overstressed lately, wants to leave...I tell you what, George, why don't you [phone rings again, lunch partner drops by]...uh, take a stab at handling it yourself...I've got to go now.

Besides what may have been poor intentions in the first place, the manager in this example did not do a good job of communicating with George. This problem could be easily corrected. If George has something important to say, the manager should set aside adequate time for the meeting. Additional interruptions such as telephone calls and drop-in visitors could be eliminated by issuing appropriate instructions to the secretary. Many communication distractions can be avoided or at least minimized through proper planning.

Status Effects

"Criticize my boss? I don't have the right to." "I'd get fired." "It's her company, not mine." As suggested in these comments, the hierarchy of authority in organizations creates another potential barrier to effective communications. Consider the "corporate cover-up" once discovered at an electronics company. Product shipments were being predated and papers falsified to meet unrealistic sales targets set by the president. His managers knew the targets were impossible to attain, but at least 20 persons in the organization co-operated in the deception. It was months before the top found out. What happened in this case is **filtering**—the intentional distortion of information to make it appear favourable to the recipient.

▨ **Filtering** is the intentional distortion of information to make it appear most favourable to the recipient.

The presence of such information filtering is often found in communications between lower and higher levels in organizations. Tom Peters, the popular management author and consultant, has called such information distortion "Management Enemy Number 1."[15] Simply put, it most often involves someone "telling the boss what he or she wants to hear." Whether the reason behind this is a fear of retribution for bringing bad news, an unwillingness to identify personal mistakes, or just a general desire to please, the end result is the same. The person receiving filtered communications can end up making poor decisions because of a biased and inaccurate information base.

✓ Learning check ❶

BE SURE YOU CAN
• describe the communication process and identify its key components • differentiate effective and efficient communication • explain the role of credibility in persuasive communication • list the common sources of noise that create barriers to effective communication • illustrate how the barriers might affect communication between a team leader and team members • explain how mixed messages and filtering can interfere with communication in organizations

IMPROVING COMMUNICATION

A number of things can be done to overcome barriers and improve the process of communication. They include active listening, making constructive use of feedback, opening upward communication channels, understanding proxemics and the use of space, utilizing technology, and valuing diversity.

●●● ACTIVE LISTENING

Managers must be very good at listening. When people "talk," they are trying to communicate something. That "something" may or may not be what they are saying. **Active listening** is the process of taking action to help someone say exactly what he or she really means. It involves being sincere in listening to find the full meaning of what is being said. It also involves being disciplined in controlling emotions and withholding premature evaluations or interpretations. There are five rules for becoming an active listener:[16]

▨ **Active listening** helps the source of a message say what he or she really means.

1. *Listen for message content:* Try to hear exactly what content is being conveyed in the message.

2. *Listen for feelings:* Try to identify how the source feels about the content in the message.

3. *Respond to feelings:* Let the source know that her or his feelings are being recognized.

4. *Note all cues:* Be sensitive to non-verbal and verbal messages; be alert for mixed messages.

5. *Paraphrase and restate:* State back to the source what you think you are hearing.

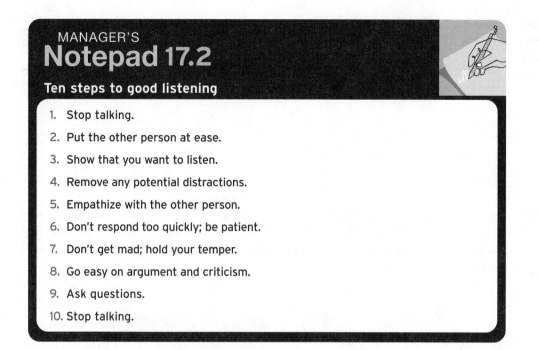

MANAGER'S
Notepad 17.2

Ten steps to good listening

1. Stop talking.

2. Put the other person at ease.

3. Show that you want to listen.

4. Remove any potential distractions.

5. Empathize with the other person.

6. Don't respond too quickly; be patient.

7. Don't get mad; hold your temper.

8. Go easy on argument and criticism.

9. Ask questions.

10. Stop talking.

Different responses to the following two questions contrast how a "passive" listener and an "active" listener might act in real workplace conversations. Question 1: "Don't you think employees should be promoted on the basis of seniority?" *Passive listener's response:* "No, I don't!" *Active listener's response:* "It seems to you that they should, I take it?" Question 2: "What does the supervisor expect us to do about these out-of-date computers?" *Passive listener's response:* "Do the best you can, I guess." *Active listener's response:* "You're pretty disgusted with those machines, aren't you?" These examples show how active listening can facilitate communication in difficult circumstances, rather than discourage it. *Manager's Notepad 17.2* offers more guidelines for good listening.

●●● CONSTRUCTIVE FEEDBACK

The process of telling other people how you feel about something they did or said, or about the situation in general, is called **feedback.** The art of giving feedback is an indispensable skill, particularly for managers who must regularly give feedback to other people. Often this takes the form of performance feedback given as evaluations and appraisals. When poorly done, such feedback can be threatening to the recipient and cause resentment. When properly done, feedback—even performance criticism—can be listened to, accepted, and used to good advantage by the receiver.[17]

■ **Feedback** is the process of telling someone else how you feel about something that person did or said.

There are ways to help ensure that feedback is useful and constructive rather than harmful. To begin with, the sender must learn to recognize when the feedback he or she is about to offer will really benefit the receiver and when it will mainly satisfy some personal need. A supervisor who berates a computer programmer for errors, for example, actually may be angry about personally failing to give clear instruction in the first place. Also, a manager should make sure that any feedback is considered by the recipient as understandable, acceptable, and plausible. *Guidelines for giving "constructive" feedback* include the following:[18]

• Give feedback directly, and with real feeling, based on trust between you and the receiver.

• Make sure that feedback is specific rather than general; use good, clear, and preferably recent examples to make your points.

- Give feedback at a time when the receiver seems most willing or able to accept it.

- Make sure the feedback is valid; limit it to things the receiver can be expected to do something about.

- Give feedback in small doses; never give more than the receiver can handle at any particular time.

●●● USE OF COMMUNICATION CHANNELS

■ **Channel richness** is the capacity of a communication channel to effectively carry information.

Channel richness is the capacity of a communication channel to carry information in an effective manner.[19] *Figure 17.2* shows that face-to-face communication is very high in richness, enabling two-way interaction and real-time feedback. Formal reports and memos are very low in richness, due to impersonal one-way interaction with limited opportunity for feedback. Managers need to understand the limits of the possible channels and choose wisely when using them for communication.

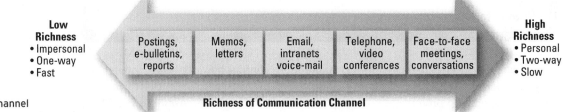

Figure 17.2 Channel richness and the use of communication media.

●●● INTERACTIVE MANAGEMENT

Interactive management approaches use a variety of means to keep communication channels open between organizational levels. A popular choice is **management by wandering around** (MBWA)—dealing directly with subordinates by regularly spending time walking around and talking with them about work-related matters. MBWA involves finding out for yourself what is going on in face-to-face communications. The basic objectives are to break down status barriers, increase the frequency of interpersonal contact, and get more and better information from lower-level sources. Of course, this requires a trusting relationship. Terry Curtis, president of EION Inc., believes in MBWA. In one of his previous positions as head of the IT department, he would take one day a month and shadow one of his employees. He would go where his employee went and do what they did. He said that "I would find out more stuff that day than all the other days of the month."[20]

■ In **management by wandering around** (MBWA) managers spend time outside of their offices to meet and talk with workers at all levels.

Management practices designed to open channels and improve upward communications have traditionally involved *open office hours*, whereby busy senior executives like Patricia Gallup, CEO of PC Connection Inc., set aside time in their calendars to welcome walk-in visits during certain hours each week.[21] Today this approach can be expanded to include *online discussion forums* and "chat rooms" that are open at certain hours. Programs of regular *employee group meetings* are also helpful. Here, a rotating schedule of "shirtsleeve" meetings brings top managers into face-to-face contact with mixed employee groups throughout an organization. The face-to-face groups can be supplemented by *computer-mediated meetings* and *video conferences*, which serve similar purposes, overcoming time and distance limitations to communication. In some cases, a comprehensive communications program includes an *employee advisory council* composed of members elected by their fellow employees. Such councils meet with management on a regular schedule to discuss and react to new policies and programs that will affect employees.

At Vancity, Canada's largest credit union, the opportunity to take part in the television program, *Back to the Floor*, was looked upon as a chance to accomplish two goals—first, to connect the CEO with employees through a non-corporate program, and second, to gain a higher external profile by showing why the company was a great place to work. Paula Martin, vice-president of Public Affairs and Corporate Communications notes, "It was a perfect opportunity to help employees understand the business through the program's storyline. It wasn't part of the business plan for the employee communication program, but we saw an opportunity to do something spontaneous to support the company culture." Valuing communication as a key part of the company's culture has helped Vancity be named "Best employer in Canada for 2005" by *Maclean's* magazine.[22]

When executives suspect that they are having communication problems, *communication consultants* can be hired to conduct interviews and surveys of employees on their behalf. Productivity was chronically low at Rodebec, a copper rod manufacturing plant based in Saint-Romuald, Quebec, despite significant investment in capital improvements and training. Outside consultants were brought in to assess the problem and found there was a direct correlation between the low productivity and poor communication among management, supervisors, and employees.[23]

Another interactive approach that seeks to broaden the awareness of "bosses" regarding the feelings and perceptions of other people that they work closely with is **360-degree feedback**, discussed in Chapter 12.[24] This typically involves upward appraisals done by a manager's subordinates as well as additional feedback from peers, internal and external customers, and higher-ups. A self-assessment is also part of the process. The goal of 360-degree feedback is to provide the manager with information that can be used for constructive improvement. Managers who have participated in the process often express surprise at what they learn. Some have found themselves perceived as lacking vision, having bad tempers, being bad listeners, and lacking flexibility.[25] Eric Djukastein, co-founder and president of Victoria, B.C.-based Contech Electronics, found 360-degree feedback helpful. "It was illuminating and scary looking at the results—when your staff say you don't follow through on your commitments, that hurts," he says. "I was terrible at delivering so many things that a conscientious worker needs, such as regular performance reviews and wage reviews. I had a bad habit of doing things impulsively." Djukastein does see a bright side: "The good news is that it enabled me to open my eyes to things that were instrumental in changing my mental attitude."[26]

■ **360° feedback** includes views of bosses, peers, and subordinates in performance appraisals.

●●● PROXEMICS AND SPACE DESIGN

An important but sometimes neglected part of communication involves proxemics, or the use of space.[27] The distance between people conveys varying intentions in terms of intimacy, openness, and status. And the physical layout of an office is an often-overlooked form of nonverbal communication. Check it out. Offices with chairs available for side-by-side seating convey different messages from those where the manager's chair sits behind the desk and those for visitors sit facing it in front.

Office or workspace architecture is an important influence on communication and behaviour. Architects and consultants specializing in *organizational ecology* are helping executives build offices conducive to the intense communication needed today. When Sun Microsystems built its San Jose, California facility, public spaces were designed to encourage communication among persons from different departments. Many meeting areas have no walls, and most of the walls that exist are glass. As manager of planning and research, Ann Bamesberger said: "We were creating a way to get these people to communicate with each other more." Importantly, the Sun project involved not only the assistance of expert architectural consultants, but also extensive inputs and suggestions from the employees themselves. The results seem to justify the effort. A senior technical writer, Terry Davidson, commented: "This is the most productive workspace I have ever been in."[28]

●●● TECHNOLOGY UTILIZATION

When IBM surveyed employees to find out how they learned what was going on at the company, executives were not surprised that co-workers were perceived as credible and useful sources. But they were surprised that the firm's intranet ranked equally high. IBM's internal websites were ranked higher than news briefs, company memos, and information from managers.[29] The new age of communication is one of email, voice mail, instant messaging, teleconferencing, online discussions, video conferencing, virtual or computer-mediated meetings, intranets, and Web portals. And the many implications of technology utilization must be understood.

Technology offers the power of the *electronic grapevine*, speeding messages and information from person to person. When the members of a Grade 6 class in Taylorsville, North Carolina (population 1,566), sent out the email message, "Hi!…We are curious to see where in the world our email will travel," they were surprised. Over a half-million replies flooded in, overwhelming not only the students but the school's computer system also.[30] Messages fly with equal speed and intensity around organizations. The results can be both functional—when the information is accurate and useful; and dysfunctional—when the information is false, distorted, or simply based on rumour. Managers should be quick to correct misimpressions and inaccuracies; they should also positively utilize the electronic grapevines as ways to quickly transfer factual and relevant information among organizational members.

Knowing how and when to use email may well be the biggest communication issue for people in organizations today. Purpose and privacy are two concerns. Employers are concerned that too much work time gets spent handling personal email; employees are concerned that employers are eavesdropping on their email messages. The best advice comes down to this: (1) find out the employer's policy on personal email and follow it; (2) don't assume that you ever have email privacy at work. Another major concern is email workload, which can be overwhelming. At Intel, for example, managers discovered that some employees faced up to 300 email messages a day and spent some two and one-half hours per day dealing with them. The firm initiated a training program to improve email utilization and efficiency.[31] Tips on managing your email include the following:[32]

- Read items only once.

- Take action immediately to answer, move to folders, or delete.

- Purge folders regularly of useless messages.

- Send group mail and use "reply to all" only when really necessary.

- Get off distribution lists without value to your work.

- Send short messages in the subject line, avoiding a full-text message.

- Put large files on websites, instead of sending as attachments.

- Use IM, instant messaging, as an email alternative.

- Don't forget the basic rule of email privacy: there isn't any.

●●● VALUING CULTURE AND DIVERSITY

Workforce diversity and globalization are two of the most talked-about trends in modern society. Communicating under conditions of diversity, where the sender and receiver are part of different cultures, is certainly a significant challenge. Cross-cultural communication was first discussed in Chapter 5 on the global dimensions of management. It is useful to recall that a major source of difficulty is **ethnocentrism**, the tendency to consider one's culture superior to any and all others. Ethnocentrism can adversely affect communication in at least three major ways: (1) it may cause someone to not listen well to what others have to say; (2) it may cause someone to address or speak with others in ways that alienate them; and (3) it may lead to the use of inappropriate stereotypes when dealing with persons from another culture.[33]

■ **Ethnocentrism** is the tendency to consider one's culture superior to any and all others.

For years, cultural challenges have been recognized by international travellers and executives. But as we know, you don't have to travel abroad to come face to face with communication and cultural diversity. The importance of cross-cultural communication skills applies at home just as much as it does in a foreign country. Just going to work is a cross-cultural journey for most of us today. The workplace abounds with subcultures based on gender, age, ethnicity, race, and other factors. All are a source of different perspectives, experiences, values, and expectations that can complicate the communication process. When the sender and receiver are unable to empathize with one another's cultures they will have difficulties understanding when and why certain words, gestures, and messages are misinterpreted.

Adept managers recognize the challenges surrounding communications. When Janet Plante, CEO of Davco Machine Ltd., was faced with a shortage of skilled journeymen labourers she knew she had to expand her recruiting strategy. As part of that new strategy, Davco took part in the Government of Alberta's Foreign Worker Readiness Program, travelling to Germany to hire skilled workers willing to work in Canada. Plante recognized that successfully incorporating global workers into the existing workforce would require some understanding of cultural differences. To ease the transition, Davco managers went through a significant amount of cultural sensitivity training: "We're trying to train our leaders to make the environment comfortable for everybody."[34]

> **BE SURE YOU CAN**
> • define the term active listening • list the rules for active listening • illustrate how the guidelines for constructive feedback can be used when dealing with a subordinate having performance problems • explain how MBWA can improve upward communication • explain how proxemics and space design influence communication • discuss the influence of technology utilization on communication • explain the impact of ethnocentrism on communication

✔ **Learning check ❷**

THE PERCEPTION PROCESS

Perception is the process through which people receive and interpret information from the environment. It is the way we form impressions about ourselves, other people, and daily life experiences. And it is the way we process information to make the decisions that ultimately guide our actions.[35] As shown in *Figure 17.3*, perception acts as a screen or filter through which information passes before it has an impact on communication, decision making, and action. Because perceptions are influenced by such things as cultural background, values, and other personal and situational circumstances, people can and do perceive the same things or situations differently. And importantly, people behave according to their perceptions.

■ **Perception** is the process through which people receive, organize, and interpret information from the environment.

Figure 17.3 Perception and communication.

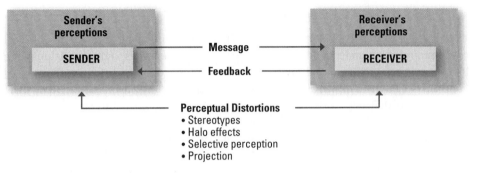

Perceptual Distortions
• Stereotypes
• Halo effects
• Selective perception
• Projection

●●● PERCEPTION AND ATTRIBUTION

One of the ways in which perception exerts its influence is through *attribution,* the process of developing explanations for events. It is natural for people to try to explain what they observe and the things that happen to them. The fact that people can perceive the same things quite differently has an important influence on attributions and their ultimate influence on behaviour.

In social psychology, attribution theory describes how people try to explain their own behaviour and that of others.[36] One of its significant applications is in the context of people's performance at work. Fundamental **attribution error** occurs when observers blame another person's performance failures more on internal factors relating to the individual than on external factors relating to the environment. In the case of someone who is producing poor-quality work, for example, a supervisor might blame a lack of job skills or laziness—an unwillingness to work hard enough. In response, the supervisor is likely to try to resolve the problem through training, motivation, or even replacement. The attribution error leads to the neglect of possible external explanations, for example, that the poor-quality work was caused by unrealistic time pressures or substandard technology. Opportunities to improve upon these factors through managerial action will thus be missed.

Another confounding aspect of perception and attribution occurs as a **self-serving bias**. This happens when individuals blame their personal failures or problems on external causes and attribute their successes to internal causes. You might think of this tendency the next time you "blame" your instructor for a poor course grade. The self-serving bias is harmful when it causes us to give insufficient attention to the need for personal change and development. While readily taking credit for successes, we are often too quick to focus on the environment to explain away our failures.

■ Fundamental **attribution error** overestimates internal factors and underestimates external factors as influences on someone's behaviour.

■ **Self-serving bias** explains personal success by internal causes and personal failures by external causes.

●●● PERCEPTUAL TENDENCIES AND DISTORTIONS

In addition to the attribution errors just discussed, a variety of perceptual tendencies and distortions can also influence communication and workplace behaviour. Of particular interest are the use of stereotypes, halo effects, selective perception, and projection.

Stereotypes

A **stereotype** occurs when someone is identified with a group or category, and then oversimplified attributes associated with the group or category are used to describe the individual. We all use stereotypes and they are not always negative or ill-intended. But those based on such factors as gender, age, and race can, and unfortunately still do, bias the perceptions of people in some work settings.

■ A **stereotype** is when attributes commonly associated with a group are assigned to an individual.

The *glass ceiling*, mentioned in Chapter 1 as an invisible barrier to career advancement, still exists. Legitimate questions can be asked about *racial and ethnic stereotypes* and about the slow progress of minority managers within corporate North America. According to a survey conducted by Catalyst Canada Inc., a research group that focuses on women's issues, there has been little change in the number of women in positions of leadership in the corporate world. "Change has been slow, but it is getting to the point where it is going to change. I think it's a tipping-point question," notes Lorna Marsden, president of York University and board member of Manulife Financial Corp. "The number of women on FP500 boards clearly does not reflect their true impact on the Canadian economy as wage earners, managers, professionals, consumers, investors and business owners," said Sonya Kunkel, senior director of Catalyst Canada.[37] Why is this happening? Another Catalyst study of opportunities for women in global business points to gender stereotypes that place women at a disadvantage to men for these types of opportunities. There is a misplaced assumption that women lack the ability and/or willingness for working in international positions.[38] Although employment barriers caused by gender stereotypes are falling, women may still suffer from false impressions and biases imposed on them. Even everyday behaviour may be misconstrued. Consider this example: "*He's* talking with co-workers." (*Interpretation:* He's discussing a new deal.) "*She's* talking with co-workers." (*Interpretation:* She's gossiping.)[39]

Ability stereotypes and *age stereotypes* also exist in the workplace. A candidate with a disability may be overlooked by a recruiter even though her skills are perfect for the job. A talented older worker may not be promoted because a manager assumes older workers are cautious and tend to avoid risk. For those employers who break through stereotypes to find the true value in people, the rewards are there. A Conference Board survey of workers 50 and older, for example, found that 72 percent felt they could take on additional responsibilities, and two-thirds were interested in further training and development.[40]

Halo Effects

A **halo effect** occurs when one attribute is used to develop an overall impression of a person or situation. When meeting someone new, for example, the halo effect may cause one trait, such as a pleasant smile, to result in a positive first impression. By contrast, a particular hairstyle or manner of dressing may create a negative reaction. Halo effects cause the same problem for managers as do stereotypes; that is, individual differences become obscured. This is especially significant in performance evaluations. One factor, such as a person's punctuality, may become the "halo" for a positive overall performance assessment. Even though the general conclusion seems to make sense, it may or may not be true in a given circumstance.

■ A **halo effect** occurs when one attribute is used to develop an overall impression of a person or situation.

Selective Perception

Selective perception is the tendency to single out for attention those aspects of a situation or person that reinforce or appear consistent with one's existing beliefs, values, or needs.[41] Information that makes us uncomfortable is screened out. What this often means in an organization is that people from different departments or functions—such as marketing and manufacturing—tend to see things from their own points of view and fail to recognize other points of view. Like the other perceptual distortions, selective perception can bias a manager's view of situations and individuals. One way to reduce its impact is to be sure to gather additional opinions from other people.

■ **Selective perception** is the tendency to define problems from one's own point of view.

■ **Projection i:**
ment of persor
other individua

✓ Learning chec

■ **Conflict** is a
over issues of
and/or an emc
antagonism.

■ **Substantive**
involves disag
goals, resourc
policies, proce
assignments.

■ **Emotional c**
from feelings
distrust, dislik
resentment as
personality cla

■ **Functional c**
constructive a
task performa

■ **Dysfunction**
destructive an
performance.

●●● **Chapter 17** STUDY GUIDE

WHERE WE'VE BEEN

Back to Center for Creative Leadership

The opening example of the Center for Creative Leadership confirmed once again that leadership begins with one's ability to work well with other people. In this chapter you learned about interpersonal communication, with an emphasis on dealing with barriers and achieving communication effectiveness. You learned about perception and how perceptual distortions can influence communication and behaviour. You also learned about the processes of conflict and negotiation, including how each can be engaged positively in the work setting.

THE NEXT STEP
INTEGRATED LEARNING ACTIVITIES

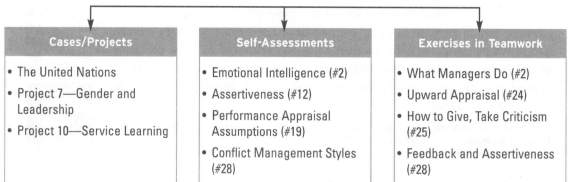

Cases/Projects	Self-Assessments	Exercises in Teamwork
• The United Nations • Project 7—Gender and Leadership • Project 10—Service Learning	• Emotional Intelligence (#2) • Assertiveness (#12) • Performance Appraisal Assumptions (#19) • Conflict Management Styles (#28)	• What Managers Do (#2) • Upward Appraisal (#24) • How to Give, Take Criticism (#25) • Feedback and Assertiveness (#28)

STUDY QUESTION SUMMARY

1. What is the communication process?

• Communication is the interpersonal process of sending and receiving symbols with messages attached to them.

• Effective communication occurs when the sender and the receiver of a message both interpret it in the same way; efficient communication occurs when the message is sent at low cost for the sender.

• Persuasive communication results in the recipient acting as intended by the sender.

• Credibility earned by expertise and good relationships is essential to persuasive communication.

• Noise is anything that interferes with the effectiveness of communication; it is caused by poor utilization of channels, poor written or oral expression, physical distractions, and status effects.

2. How can communication be improved?

• Active listening, through reflecting back and paraphrasing, can help overcome barriers and improve communication.

• Interactive management through MBWA and use of structured meetings, suggestion systems, and advisory councils can improve upward communication.

• Office architecture and physical space can be used and designed to improve communication in organizations.

• Information technology, such as email and intranets, can improve communication in organizations, but it must be well used.

• The negative influences of ethnocentrism on communication can be offset by greater cross-cultural awareness and sensitivity.

3. How does perception influence communication?

• Perception acts as a filter through which all communication passes as it travels from one person to the next.

• Because people tend to perceive things differently, the same message may be interpreted quite differently by different people.

• Fundamental attribution error occurs when we blame others for performance problems while excluding possible external causes; self-serving bias occurs when, in judging our own performance, we take personal credit for successes and blame failures on external factors.

• Stereotypes, projections, halo effects, and selective perception can distort perceptions and reduce communication effectiveness.

4. How can we deal positively with conflict?

• Conflict occurs as disagreements over substantive or emotional issues.

• Moderate levels of conflict are functional for performance and creativity; too little or too much conflict becomes dysfunctional.

• Conflict may be managed through structural approaches that involve changing people, goals, resources, or work arrangements.

• Personal conflict management styles include avoidance, accommodation, compromise, competition, and collaboration.

• True conflict resolution involves problem solving through a win-win collaborative approach.

5. How can we negotiate successful agreements?

• Negotiation is the process of making decisions in situations in which the participants have different preferences.

• Both substance goals, those concerned with outcomes, and relationship goals, those concerned with processes, are important in successful negotiation.

• Effective negotiation occurs when issues of substance are resolved and the process results in good working relationships.

• Distributive approaches to negotiation emphasize win-lose outcomes; integrative approaches to negotiation emphasize win-win outcomes.

• Mediation and arbitration offer structured approaches to dispute resolution.

KEY TERMS REVIEW

Accommodation (p. 430)

Active listening (p. 420)

Arbitration (p. 434)

Attribution error (p. 426)

Avoidance (p. 430)

Bargaining zone (p. 433)

BATNA (p. 433)

Channel richness (p. 422)

Collaboration (p. 430)

Communication (p. 415)

Communication channel (p. 416)

Competition (p. 430)

Compromise (p. 430)

Conflict (p. 428)

Conflict resolution (p. 430)

Credibility (p. 416)

Distributive negotiation (p. 432)

Dysfunctional conflict (p. 428)

Effective communication (p. 415)

Efficient communication (p. 415)

Emotional conflict (p. 428)

Ethnocentrism (p. 425)

Feedback (p. 421)

Filtering (p. 420)

Functional conflict (p. 428)

Halo effect (p. 427)

Integrative negotiation (p. 432)

Lose-lose conflict (p. 431)

Management by wandering around (p. 422)

Mediation (p. 434)

Mixed message (p. 418)

Negotiation (p. 432)

Noise (p. 416)

Non-verbal communication (p. 418)

Perception (p. 425)

Persuasion (p. 416)

Principled negotiation (p. 432)

Projection (p. 428)

Selective perception (p. 427)

Self-serving bias (p. 426)

Stereotype (p. 426)

Substantive conflict (p. 428)

360˚ feedback (p. 423)

Win-lose conflict (p. 431)

Win-win conflict (p. 431)

SELF-TEST 17

MULTIPLE-CHOICE QUESTIONS:

1. The use of paraphrasing and reflecting back what someone else says in communication is characteristic of _____.
    (a) mixed messages (b) active listening (c) projection (d) lose-lose conflict

2. When the intended meaning of the sender and the interpreted meaning of the receiver are the same, communication is _____.
    (a) effective (b) persuasive (c) selective (d) efficient

3. Constructive feedback is _____.
    (a) general rather than specific (b) indirect rather than direct (c) given in small doses (d) given any time the sender is ready

4. When a manager uses email to send a message that is better delivered in person, the communication process suffers from _____.
    (a) semantic problems (b) a poor choice of communication channels (c) physical distractions (d) information overload

5. _____ is a form of interactive management that helps improve upward communication.
    (a) Attribution (b) Mediation (c) MBWA (d) BATNA

6. Cross-cultural communication may run into difficulties because of _____, or the tendency to consider one's culture superior to others.
    (a) selective perception (b) ethnocentrism (c) mixed messages (d) projection

7. An appeal to superordinate goals is an example of a(n) _____ approach to conflict management.
    (a) avoidance (b) structural (c) dysfunctional (d) self-serving

8. The conflict management style with the greatest potential for true conflict resolution involves _____.
    (a) compromise (b) competition (c) smoothing (d) collaboration

9. When a person is highly co-operative but not very assertive in approaching conflict, the conflict management style is referred to as _____.
    (a) avoidance (b) authoritative (c) smoothing (d) collaboration

10. The three criteria of an effective negotiation are quality, cost, and _____.
    (a) harmony (b) timeliness (c) efficiency (d) effectiveness

11. In order to be truly and consistently persuasive when communicating with others in the workplace, a manager should build credibility by _____.
    (a) making sure the rewards for compliance are clear (b) making sure the penalties for non-compliance are clear (c) making sure that they know who is the boss (d) making sure that good relationships have been established with them

12. Among the 10 rules for good listening described in the chapter, _____ is both #1 and #10.
    (a) "Stop talking" (b) "Be patient" (c) "Ask questions" (d) "Empathize"

13. A manager who understands the importance of proxemics in communication would be likely to _____.
    (a) avoid sending mixed messages (b) arrange work spaces so as to encourage interaction (c) be very careful in the choice of written and spoken words (d) make frequent use of email messages to keep people well informed

14. Self-serving bias is a form of attribution error that involves _____.
    (a) blaming yourself for problems caused by others (b) blaming the environment for problems you caused (c) choosing to communicate one-way instead of two-way (d) projecting one's values onto others

15. A conflict is most likely to be functional and have a positive impact on group performance when it is _____.
    (a) based on emotions (b) resolved by arbitration (c) caused by resource scarcities (d) of moderate intensity

SHORT-RESPONSE QUESTIONS:

16. Briefly describe what a manager would do to be an "active listener" when communicating with subordinates.

17. What is the difference between the halo effect and selective perception?

18. How do tendencies toward assertiveness and co-operativeness in conflict management result in win-lose, lose-lose, and win-win outcomes?

19. What is the difference between substance and relationship goals in negotiation?

APPLICATION QUESTION:

20. After being promoted to store manager for a new branch of a large department store chain, Harold Welsch was concerned about communication in the store. Six department heads reported directly to him, and 50 full-time and part-time sales associates reported to them. Given this structure, Harold worried about staying informed about all store operations, not just those coming to his attention as senior manager. What steps might Harold take to establish and maintain an effective system of upward communication in his store?

Change Leadership

Planning Ahead

After reading Chapter 18, you should be able to answer these questions in your own words.

1. What are the challenges of strategic leadership and innovation?

2. What is the nature of organizational change?

3. How can planned organizational change be managed?

4. What is organization development?

5. How can stress be managed in a change environment?

Meridian Credit Union

The call that changed the face of the neighbourhood credit union

where real people build lives™

It started in 2004, when Niagara Credit Union received a call that would change the way many Ontarians looked at their neighbourhood credit union. HEPCOE, Ontario's third largest credit union, approached Niagara Credit Union, Ontario's second largest, to discuss a merger. With the financial services marketplace expanding both nationally and internationally, financial institutions were under pressure to remain competitive. Both credit unions saw an opportunity to strategically position the new organization as a significant competitor in Ontario's financial services industry.

As a result, Meridian Credit Union was launched in April 2005—the largest credit union in Ontario and the third largest in Canada, with 180,000 members, over 1,000 employees, and $3.5 billion in assets. From the beginning, it seemed like a perfect fit of vision, culture, and leadership. Don Ariss, chairman of HEPCOE, remarks, "We share the same values, including a strong commitment to providing the highest level of personalized services to our members and to being an employer of choice." Sean Jackson, president and CEO of Niagara Credit Union, saw the merger as a watershed moment in the history of credit unions in the province: "This merger will give us the resources to reinvent neighbourhood banking in Ontario."

Any merger, however, is not without challenges. It was obvious to both organizations that a comprehensive approach to change was needed, as well as significant support from all members, shareholders, and employees. The innovation and creativity with which these challenges were addressed illustrate why Meridian Credit Union is so successful. Under the leadership of Jackson, Meridian sent out a series of mailings addressing members' concerns. Humour and light-hearted reassurances were used

to position the new organization as one with a friendly personality, right down to the smile within the new Meridian logo.

Addressing employees' specific concerns, Jackson stated, "No employee will be laid off as a result of this merger. Every branch employee will keep his or her job. Every corporate office employee will be offered a job in the new credit union." Both corporate offices were kept open to minimize disruption for employees.

The response from members to these strategies was overwhelmingly positive. More than two-thirds of

the members and shareholders at both credit unions voted in favour of the proposed amalgamation. Gord Hunchak, vice-president of Production Development and Delivery for Meridian says, "There is always that great fear that once you change the situation or merge, you'll lose that momentum. But we haven't. Growth amongst our membership base in terms of assets has grown faster than the typical membership growth. We've actually deepened our relationship with our memberships since this merger, which is exciting."[1]

IN THE WORKPLACE

As you join the "water cooler gang" for the morning discussion, it is apparent that a hot topic is being debated: how to change the provincial and national election process. A colleague of yours, Hameeda Mahmood, says she feels that we need to change how we elect our representatives to government in Canada.

Not wishing to create an argument, you agree with her but

say that it will be very difficult to enact this change. She asks you why. You offer that the thought of change usually brings out strong resistance in people. Probing further, Hameeda asks why people resist change. You offer that there are any number of reasons why this is so. What are some reasons why people may be hesitant to change?

●●● Chapter 18   LEARNING PREVIEW   ●●●

In the chapter opening example of Meridian Credit Union, you were introduced to the challenges of strategic change and the importance of leadership and compromise in making change work. The successful merger that led to the formation of Meridian shows that leadership capabilities must extend beyond having a good sense of strategy and vision. They need to include a full understanding of what is needed to transform an organization, as well as a sensitivity to the broader impact of strategic change. In Chapter 18 you will learn about how strategic leadership supports change, creativity, and innovation in organizations. You will learn about change leaders, change strategies, and resistance to change. You will learn about the process of organization development. You will also learn about the stress that comes with change in the workplace and how stress can be managed constructively.

CHANGE LEADERSHIP

Study Question 1	Study Question 2	Study Question 3	Study Question 4	Study Question 5
Strategic Leadership and Innovation	**Organizational Change**	**Leading Planned Change**	**Organization Development**	**Stress and Stress Management**
• What is strategic leadership? • Creativity and innovation • Characteristics of innovative organizations	• Change leaders • Models of change leadership • Transformational and incremental change • Forces and targets for change	• Phases of planned change • Change strategies • Resistance to change • Challenges of technological change	• Organization development goals • How organization development works • Organization development interventions	• Sources of stress • Consequences of stress • Stress management strategies
Learning check ❶	Learning check ❷	Learning check ❸	Learning check ❹	Learning check ❺

When a group of Japanese students drove out of Tokyo one day, the event wouldn't have seemed remarkable to bystanders. But when they arrived, some 900 kilometres later, on the northern island of Hokkaido, Mitsubishi's president was extremely pleased. The students' car, powered by a new engine technology, had made the trip without refuelling! In fact, there was fuel to spare in the gas tank. It was an important breakthrough for the company. For a long time engineers had known the feat was technically possible, but they didn't know how to do it. Finally, through hard work, through a lot of information sharing and problem solving, and through learning, they found the answer.[2]

Novel answers to perplexing problems move people, organizations, and societies continuously ahead in our dynamic and very challenging world. We are living and working at a time when intellectual capital, knowledge management, and learning organizations are taking centre stage. And rightfully so. Harvard scholars Michael Beer and Nitin Nohria observe, "The new economy has ushered in great business opportunities and great turmoil. Not since the Industrial Revolution have the stakes of dealing with change been so high. Most traditional organizations have accepted, in theory at least, that they must either change or die."[3] Speaking from the vantage point of a corporate leader always looking toward the future, John Chambers, CEO of Cisco Systems, would no doubt agree. "Companies that are successful will have cultures that thrive on change," he says, "even though change makes most people uncomfortable."[4]

Unfortunately, and even though the watchwords of today continue to be *change, change,* and *change,* many organizations and too many leaders are slow in responding to the challenge. Creating positive change in organizations is not easy. Change involves risk, complexity, uncertainty, anxiety, and stress. Leading organizations on the pathways of change takes great understanding, discipline, and commitment to creativity and human ingenuity. In his book *The Circle of Innovation,* consultant Tom Peters warns that we must refocus the attention of managers and leaders away from past accomplishments and toward the role of innovation as the primary source of competitive advantage. Doing well in the past, simply put, is no guarantee of future success.[5] The future is the issue in this final chapter of *Management*—organizational futures, managerial futures, and your future. It is time to inquire into your readiness to master the challenges of change in the evolving new workplace.

STRATEGIC LEADERSHIP AND INNOVATION

At the World Economic Forum, a famous and futuristic think tank for global business, government, and civic leaders held in Davos, Switzerland, the popular buzzwords were "business webs," "value networks," "molecular organizations," and more. The following trends and possibilities were prominent among observations about the changing nature of business in the new economy.[6]

Companies that design and brand their own products, build and package them, and then deliver them to customers will soon no longer exist.

Companies (now) have the ability to strip down their business to its essence, to focus on where the greatest value creation (and profits) lies.

Extraneous functions can be eliminated through partnerships and newly supercharged forms of outsourcing.

Instead of one big monolithic entity, companies start to look like clusters of distributed capabilities.

There are those who might go so far as to say that the corporation as we have traditionally known it is dead, or at least dying. For sure the traditional forms, practices, and systems of the past are being replaced by dramatic new developments driven by the forces of information technology and the relentless pressures of global competitiveness. And this is all happening very, very fast. No leader in any organization, no matter how big or small and whether operating for-profit or not-for-profit, can fail to take notice.

●●● WHAT IS STRATEGIC LEADERSHIP?

Although the points and details may differ, the conclusion reached by futurists is the same. The years ahead will be radically different from those past. We and our organizations must be prepared not only to change, but to change continuously and successfully in the face of ever-present uncertainties. In earlier chapters we discussed the benefits of what Peter Senge calls **learning organizations**—ones that mobilize people, values, and systems to achieve continuous change and performance improvements driven by the lessons of experience.[7] Albert Einstein

■ A **learning organization** utilizes people, values, and systems to continuously change and improve its performance.

was once quoted as saying, "The significant problems we have cannot be solved at the same level of thinking with which we created them." Even though he was speaking about the state of the world, his statement is equally important for businesses striving to succeed in this ever-changing and extremely competitive economic environment. Whether you are a manufacturer or provide a service, your industry requires a dynamic learning strategy that harnesses the knowledge of its people and is an integral component of the firm's strategic plan. Now more than ever before, businesses must learn from their experiences and adapt to change in order to survive and prosper.[8] This is the ideal; it is the target; it is what organizations should be like. It is what leaders everywhere should strive for as they help and move and push organizations forward into the complicated world of tomorrow. CIBC has always been "the bank that service built," but the vision it first articulated in the early 1990s—becoming a customer-obsessed company, driven by the customer, close to the customer, and with ever-strengthening relationships with the customers—went far beyond tradition. Hubert Saint-Onge, the vice-president responsible for CIBC's leadership development during this period, said of CIBC's early learning organization efforts, "We never discussed learning organizations at the bank, but talked about enhancing organizational capability."[9]

■ **Strategic leadership** creates the capacity for ongoing strategic change.

Scholars R. Duane Ireland and Michael Hitt describe **strategic leadership** as the "ability to anticipate, envision, maintain flexibility, think strategically, and work with others to initiate changes that will create a viable future for the organization."[10] Strategic leaders are change leaders who build learning organizations and keep them competitive even in difficult and uncertain times. The goal is to make a core competency out of the ability to successfully and continuously change. But this isn't just pushing change for the sake of change; the change must have a strategic and customer-driven purpose. Spencer Stuart, a company that is a global specialist in board counsel and recruitment, says, "The harsh reality is that during tough economic times there is no room for organizations that aren't continuously reinventing themselves...It is no longer merely desirable to develop an organizational culture that embraces new ideas and establishes the structures necessary to implement innovation. It is imperative for the survival of a company."[11] *Manager's Notepad 18.1* highlights strategic leadership components that best prepare managers to meet this challenge.[12]

MANAGER'S
Notepad 18.1

Six components of strategic leadership

- Determining the organization's purpose or vision.
- Exploiting and maintaining the organization's core competencies.
- Developing the organization's human capital.
- Sustaining an effective organizational culture.
- Emphasizing and displaying ethical practices.
- Establishing balanced organizational controls.

●●● CREATIVITY AND INNOVATION

Sustainable competitive advantage in a change environment is earned in part through organizational cultures and human capital that unlock the full powers of creativity and innovation.

Creativity is the generation of a novel idea or unique approach to solving problems or crafting opportunities.[13] It is one of the great assets of human capital. People have ideas; people possess ingenuity; people have the capacity to invent. Creativity is what allows us to turn technologies and other resources into unique processes and products that differentiate the accomplishments of any one organization from those of the next.

Creativity exerts its influence in organizations through **innovation**, the process of creating new ideas and putting them into practice.[14] Management consultant Peter Drucker called innovation "an effort to create purposeful, focused change in an enterprise's economic or social potential."[15] Said a bit differently, it is the act of converting new ideas into usable applications with positive economic or social consequences. Consider two very different examples.

> *Groove Networks, Inc. has been described as "Napster for business", and founder Ray Ozzie is sometimes called the "wizard of peer-to-peer computing." After watching his son play multiplayer games on the Web and his daughter send instant messages, Ozzie realized the potential and created new software devoted to "P2P" collaboration in business. Before this he had created Lotus Notes, now owned by IBM.[16]*

> *What happens when the digital age meets the developing world? Progress, at least if you are part of the Grameen Bank network in Bangladesh. Most of the country's 68,000 villages have no phone service; the average annual income is about $200. That is changing through an innovative program. The Grameen Bank makes loans to women entrepreneurs to allow them to buy and operate a cellular telephone, each typically serving an entire village. The bank's goal is twofold: to receive an economic return on its investment and to contribute to economic development. The model is now spreading to serve the rural poor in other nations.[17]*

Innovation, in and by organizations, occurs in two broad forms: (1) **process innovations**, which result in better ways of doing things; and (2) **product innovations**, which result in the creation of new or improved goods and services. The management of both requires active encouragement and support for *invention*—the act of discovery; and for *application*—the act of use. Managers need to be concerned about investing and building new work environments that stimulate creativity and an ongoing stream of new ideas. They must also make sure that good ideas for new or modified processes and products are actually implemented. One way to describe the full set of responsibilities for the innovation process is in these five steps, constituting what consultant Gary Hamel calls the *wheel of innovation*.[18]

1. *Imagining*—thinking about new possibilities; making discoveries by ingenuity or communication with others; extending existing ways.

2. *Designing*—testing ideas in concept; discussing them with peers, customers, clients, or technical experts; building initial models, prototypes, or samples.

3. *Experimenting*—examining practicality and financial value through experiments and feasibility studies.

4. *Assessing*—identifying strengths and weaknesses, potential costs and benefits, and potential markets or applications, and making constructive changes.

5. *Scaling*—gearing up and implementing new processes; putting to work what has been learned; commercializing new products or services.

One of the major requirements of successful innovation is that the entire process meets real needs of the organization and its marketplace. New ideas alone are not sufficient to guarantee success in this setting; they must be relevant and they must be well implemented in

■ **Creativity** is the generation of a novel idea or unique approach that solves a problem or crafts an opportunity.

■ **Innovation** is the process of taking a new idea and putting it into practice.

■ **Process innovation** results in better ways of doing things.

■ **Product innovation** results in new or improved goods or services.

■ **Commercializing innovation** turns ideas into economic value added.

order to improve organizational performance. In business, **commercializing innovation** is the process of turning new ideas into products or processes that can increase profits through greater sales or reduced costs.[19] For example, 3M Corporation generates over one-third of its revenues from products that didn't exist four years ago. The firm, for whom product innovation is a way of life, owes its success to the imagination of employees like Art Fry. He's the person whose creativity turned an adhesive that "wasn't sticky enough" into the blockbuster product known worldwide today as Post-It Notes.® *Figure 18.1* uses the example of new product development to highlight the various steps of commercializing innovation.

World-class technology and innovations produced by Canadian companies are helping NASA scientists ensure both the productivity and safety of future space missions, and are maintaining Canada's international reputation for technological know-how. The Canadarm, with its extension-boom tipped with two laser camera systems (one of which is Canadian), is designed to inspect the shuttles for possible damage while in flight as well as assist with construction and maintenance of the International Space Station. The laser camera system, designed by Ottawa-based Neptec, uses a state-of-the-art scanning technique. The extended boom was built in Brampton, Ontario, by MDA, a company with experience in developing space-borne robotic manipulators. Space activities like these contribute to Canada's present and future success in the global knowledge economy by inspiring students to pursue studies and careers in science and technology.

Figure 18.1 Process of commercializing innovation in organizations: the case of new product development.

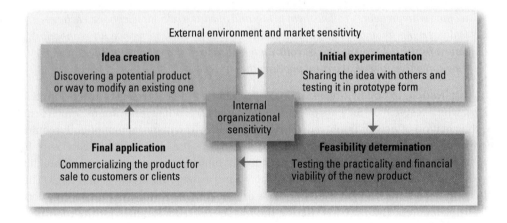

●●● CHARACTERISTICS OF INNOVATIVE ORGANIZATIONS

Innovative organizations like 3M, Johnson & Johnson, Apple Computer, and others are great at mobilizing talent and intellectual capital to support creativity and entrepreneurship. Their managers at all levels are masters at actively leading the innovation process.[20] In highly innovative organizations, the *corporate strategy and culture support innovation*. The strategies of the organization, the visions and values of senior management, and the framework of policies and expectations emphasize an entrepreneurial spirit. Innovation is expected, failure is accepted, and the organization is willing to take risks. Johnson & Johnson's former CEO James Burke once said, "I try to give people the feeling that it's okay to fail, that it's important to fail." His key point is that managers should eliminate risk-averse climates and replace them with organizational cultures in which innovation is a norm.

In highly innovative organizations, *organization structures support innovation.* More and more large organizations are trying to capture the structural flexibility of smaller ones. They are striving for more organic operations that emphasize lateral communications and extensively use cross-functional teams and task forces. In particular, research and development, historically a separate and isolated function, is being integrated into a team setting. As Peter Drucker pointed out, "Successful innovations…are now being turned out by cross-functional teams with people from marketing, manufacturing, and finance participating in research work from the very beginning."[21]

In highly innovative organizations, *top management supports innovation.* In the case of 3M, for example, many top managers have been the innovators and product champions in the company's past. They understand the innovation process, are tolerant of criticisms and differences of opinion, and take all possible steps to keep the goals clear and the pressure on. The key, once again, is to allow the creative potential of people to operate fully.

In highly innovative organizations, the *organization's staffing supports innovation.* Organizations need different kinds of people to support the innovation process. The critical innovation roles to be filled include the following:[22]

- *Idea generators*—people who create new insights from internal discovery or external awareness, or both.

- *Information gatekeepers*—people who serve as links between people and groups within the organization, and with external sources.

- *Product champions*—people who advocate and push for change and innovation, and for the adoption of specific product or process ideas.

- *Project managers*—people who perform technical functions needed to keep an innovative project on track with necessary resource support.

- *Innovation leaders*—people who encourage, sponsor, and coach others to keep the innovation values, goals, and energies in place.

AROUND THE WORLD

Japan's Mitsubishi Corporation has for years been a leader in alternative fuel technologies for its automobiles, as described at the start of this chapter. But now the company is driving into new territories by investing in what it sees as other high-growth industries around the world. In 2007, Mitsubishi established a Business Innovation Group to become a "new industry innovator," conducting research and development in fields such as nanotechnology, information and communication technology, environment and water, medical and health care, and even food services. Among its business lines are new services for mobile phones, and services for "active senior citizens." Mitsubishi is confronting change not only in the global economy but in broader society, "aggressively tackling innovation and advancement in global industrial technology, as well as the changing social environment that surrounds us such as an aging society with fewer children and environmental problems on a global scale," the company says.

Source: With information from the corporate website, <www.mitsubishicorp.com>.

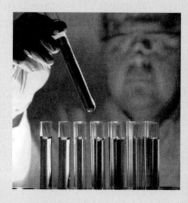

Driving growth into new industries

ORGANIZATIONAL CHANGE

According to Peter Drucker, purposeful innovation should add value to organizations and soci-ety.[23] This positive message makes change sound almost a matter of routine, something read-ily accepted by everyone involved. But what are the realities of trying to systematically change organizations and the behaviours of people within them? When Angel Martinez became CEO of Rockport Company, for example, he sought to change traditional ways that were not aligned with future competition. Rather than embrace the changes he sponsored, employees resisted. Martinez said they "gave lip service to my ideas and hoped I'd go away."[24] Consider also what once happened at Bank of America after the company announced a large quarterly operating loss. Its new CEO at the time, Samuel Armacost, complained about the lack of "agents of change" among his top managers. Claiming that managers seemed more interested in taking orders than initiating change, he said: "I came away quite distressed from my first couple of management meetings. Not only couldn't I get conflict, I couldn't even get comment. They were all waiting to see which way the wind blew."[25]

●●● CHANGE LEADERS

■ A **change leader** is a **change agent** who tries to change the behaviour of another person or social system.

A **change leader** is a **change agent** who takes leadership responsibility for changing the existing pattern of behaviour of another person or social system. Change agents make things happen, and part of every manager's job is to act as a change leader in the work set-ting. This requires being alert to situations or to people needing change, being open to good ideas and opportunities, and being ready and able to support the implementation of new ideas in actual practice. *Figure 18.2* contrasts a true "change leader" with a "status quo manager." The former is forward-looking, proactive, and embraces new ideas; the latter is backward-looking, reactive, and comfortable with habit. Obviously, the new workplace demands change leadership at all levels of management.

Figure 18.2 Change leaders versus status quo managers.

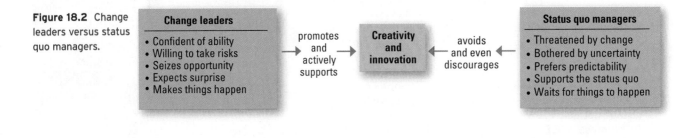

●●● MODELS OF CHANGE LEADERSHIP

In Chapter 16 on teams and teamwork, we discussed the concept of distributed leadership in teams. The point was that every team member has the potential to lead by serving group needs for task and maintenance activities. The same notion applies when it comes to change leadership. The responsibilities for change leadership are ideally distributed and shared by all managers, top to bottom, in any organization.

Top-Down Change

In **top-down change**, senior managers initiate changes with the goal of comprehensive impact on the organization and its performance capabilities. This is the domain of strategic leadership as discussed earlier in the chapter. Importantly, however, reports indicate that some 70 percent or more of large-scale change efforts actually fail.[26] The most common reason is poor implementation. The success of top-down change is usually determined by the willingness of middle-level and lower-level workers to actively support top-management initiatives. Change programs have little chance of success without the support of those who must implement them. Any change that is driven from the top runs the risk of being perceived as insensitive to the needs of lower-level personnel. It can easily fail if implementation suffers from excessive resistance and insufficient commitments to change. Thus, it is not enough to simply mandate change from the top; action must be taken to earn the support of others throughout the organization.

■ In **top-down change**, the change initiatives come from senior management.

Bottom-Up Change

In **bottom-up change** the initiatives for change come from any and all parts of the organization, not just top management. This type of change is essential to organizational innovation and is very useful in terms of adapting operations and technologies to the changing requirements of work. It is made possible by management commitments to empowerment, involvement, and participation, as discussed in earlier chapters. For example, at Johnson Controls Inc., Jason Moncer was given the nickname "Mr. Kaizen" by his co-workers.[27] The nickname refers to a Japanese practice of continuous improvement. Moncer earned it by offering many ideas for changes in his work area. At his plant, workers contributed over 200 suggestions that were

■ In **bottom-up change**, change initiatives come from all levels in the organization.

Canadian Managers
Leadership Team Brings Organization Together

Royal Bank of Canada's CEO Gord Nixon and COO Barbara Stymiest are the team behind one of the biggest corporate shakeups in the bank's history. Nixon, who became CEO in 2001, found that various business heads were making decisions and acquisitions in isolation. Not surprisingly, the bank's performance suffered. By 2004, RBC lagged behind the other Canadian banks in performance (registering a 6% decline in profit) and suffered a credit downgrade from Standard & Poor's. Nixon went through head office from top to bottom, eventually letting 1,600 people go. He personally recruited Stymiest from the Toronto Stock Exchange. Under Nixon and Stymiest's leadership, RBC has become more centralized; no acquisitions are made unless they work for the bank as a whole. "Business does not happen through silos," says Stymiest. "When you think of broader enterprise strategy, you have to think across the entire organization. It's a return to that old term, general management."

Source: Jeff Sanford, "A Royal Return," *Canadian Business*, Summer 2006, p. 42.

implemented in just one year alone. The company is committed to the belief that workers should be encouraged to use their job knowledge and common sense to improve things. In other words, when the workers talk at Johnson Controls, managers listen.

Integrated Change Leadership

The most successful and enduring change leadership is that which can harness the advantages of both top-down and bottom-up change. Top-down initiatives may be needed to break traditional patterns and implement difficult economic adjustments; bottom-up initiatives are necessary to build institutional capability for sustainable change and organizational learning. When first taking over as CEO of General Electric in 1981, Jack Welch began an aggressive top-down restructuring that led to major workforce cuts and a trimmer organization structure. Once underway, however, this evolved into bottom-up change focusing on employee involvement. He started a widely benchmarked program called Work-Out to invigorate a process of continuous reassessment and planned change.[28] In Work-Out sessions employees confront their managers in a "town meeting" format, with the manager in front listening to suggestions for removing performance obstacles and improving operations. The managers are expected to respond immediately to the suggestions and support positive change initiatives raised during the session.

CANADIAN COMPANY
IN THE NEWS   Inmet Mining Corp.

MINING TURNAROUND

In early 2007 Inmet Mining Corp. was largely debt-free, had millions of dollars in cash reserves, and its stock was worth more than $62 per share. It wasn't always this way. During the late 1990s, the company endured poor metals prices, write-downs, and an unsuccessful attempt to rid itself of the Troilus gold mine in Quebec. Inmet itself had to back away from Antamina, a copper-zinc project in Peru in which the company had staked its future. Change was needed.

In 2000, Richard Ross took over as CEO and helped stabilize the company. But there was little cash, its stock was at $1.75, and its mines weren't operating well. Under Ross's steady change focus Inmet began a dramatic turnaround. It has increased revenue through acquisitions, undertaken greater explorations, increased production capacity, and also improved safety at its mines by decreasing lost time due to injuries. Ross's patient management style is credited for this spectacular change of direction.

Source: Matther McClearn, "The Best Managers in Canada: Top Execs, Inmet Mining," *Canadian Business*, April 26–May 9, 2004, Vol. 77, Iss. 9 and with information from the corporate website <www.inmetmining.com>.

●●● TRANSFORMATIONAL AND INCREMENTAL CHANGE

Some changes occur spontaneously in organizations, largely in response to unanticipated events. These *unplanned changes* can be disruptive, such as a wildcat strike that results in a plant closure. But they can also be beneficial, such as an interpersonal conflict that results in a decision to try a new procedure or work process. Good managers do their best to take advantage of opportunities for such **reactive change**, doing a good job of responding to events as, or after, they occur. But the really great managers are not satisfied with being reac-

■ **Reactive change** responds to events as or after they occur.

tive. They are forward thinking and always alert to potential future problems and opportunities. They offer organizations proactive leadership that activates **planned change**—taking steps to best align the organization with anticipated future challenges.[29] They are always on the alert for **performance gaps,** or discrepancies between desired and actual states of affairs. Performance gaps may represent problems to be resolved or opportunities to be explored. In both cases, proactive change leaders take action in the present to deal with performance gaps in ways that improve future organizational performance.

> ■ **Planned change** aligns the organization with anticipated future challenges.

There are two major types of planned organizational change. The first is radical or frame-breaking **transformational change**—that which results in a major and comprehensive redirection of the organization.[30] Transformational change is led from the top and designed to change the basic character of the organization. It results in fundamental shifts in strategies, culture, structures, and even the underlying sense of purpose or mission. A good example is the case of Meridian Credit Union described in the chapter opener. As you would expect, transformational change is intense, highly stressful, and very complex to achieve. *Manager's Notepad 18.2* offers several lessons learned from studies of large-scale transformational change in business.[31]

> ■ A **performance gap** is a discrepancy between a desired and actual state of affairs.

> ■ **Transformational change** results in a major and comprehensive redirection of the organization.

MANAGER'S
Notepad 18.2

How to lead transformational change

- Establish a sense of urgency for change.
- Form a powerful coalition to lead the change.
- Create and communicate a change vision.
- Empower others to move change forward.
- Celebrate short-term "wins" and recognize those who help.
- Build on success; align people and systems with new ways.
- Stay with it; keep the message consistent; champion the vision.

The second type of planned change in organizations is **incremental change**. Rather than radical transformation of an organization, this type of change bends and nudges existing systems and practices to better align them with emerging problems and opportunities. Leadership of incremental change focuses on building upon existing ways of doing things with the goal of improvement, doing them better in the future. Common incremental changes in organizations involve new products, new processes, new technologies, and new work systems. The quality concept of continuous improvement is closely linked with this notion of incremental change.

> ■ **Incremental change** bends and adjusts existing ways to improve performance.

●●● FORCES AND TARGETS FOR CHANGE

The impetus for organizational change, transformational or incremental, can arise from a variety of external forces.[32] These include globalization, market competition, local economic conditions, government laws and regulations, technological developments, market trends, and social forces and values, among others. As an organization's general and specific environments develop and change over time, the organization must adapt as well. Internal forces for change are important too. Indeed, any change in one part of the organization as a complex system—perhaps a change initiated in response to one or more of the external forces just identified—can often create the need for change in another part of the system. The common *organizational targets for change*—tasks, people, culture, technology, and structure—are highly interrelated:[33]

- *Tasks*—the nature of work as represented by organizational mission, objectives, and strategy, and the job designs for individuals and groups.
- *People*—the attitudes and competencies of the employees and the human resource systems that support them.
- *Culture*—the value system for the organization as a whole, and the norms guiding individual and group behaviour.
- *Technology*—the operations and information technology used to support job designs, arrange workflows, and integrate people and machines in systems.
- *Structure*—the configuration of the organization as a complex system, including its design features and lines of authority and communications.

Ralph Fehr, CEO of Elias Woodwork in Manitoba, credits the company's culture of embracing change with their success. For this custom woodworking company, change came about by necessity rather than by design. In keeping up with new technology, ongoing developments in the product line, and rapidly changing customer demands, the organization needed to be able to adapt continuously in order to remain competitive. Fehr says, "Now everyone seems to thrive on change. That translates into new products being manufactured by people who get excited about them."[34]

✓ **Learning check ❷**

BE SURE YOU CAN

- define the term change agent • discuss the pros and cons of top-down change and of bottom-up change
- differentiate planned and unplanned change • differentiate transformational and incremental change
- list common organizational targets for change

LEADING PLANNED CHANGE

The many complications of change in organizations begin with human nature. People tend to act habitually and in stable ways over time. They may not want to change even when circumstances require it. As a manager and change agent, you will need to recognize and deal with such tendencies in order to successfully lead planned change.

●●● PHASES OF PLANNED CHANGE

Kurt Lewin, a noted psychologist, recommends that any planned change effort be viewed as a process with the three phases shown in *Figure 18.3*.[35] Lewin's three phases of planned change are (1) *unfreezing*—preparing a system for change; (2) *changing*—making actual changes in the system; and (3) *refreezing*—stabilizing the system after change.

Unfreezing

■ **Unfreezing** is the phase during which a situation is prepared for change.

In order for change to be successful, people must be ready for it. Planned change has little chance for long-term success unless people are open to doing things differently. **Unfreezing** is the stage in which a situation is prepared for change and the needs for change are developed.

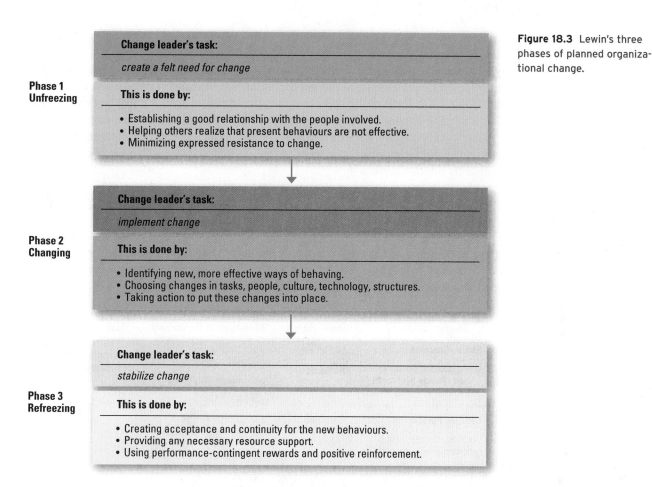

Figure 18.3 Lewin's three phases of planned organizational change.

It can be facilitated in several ways: through environmental pressures for change, declining performance, the recognition that problems or opportunities exist, and the observation of behavioural models that display alternative approaches. When handled well, conflict can be an important unfreezing force in organizations. It often helps people break old habits and recognize alternative ways of thinking about or doing things.

Changing

In the **changing** phase, something new takes place in a system and change is actually implemented. This is the point at which managers initiate changes in such organizational targets as tasks, people, culture, technology, and structure. This phase is ideally reached after unfreezing, with a good diagnosis of a problem and a careful examination of alternatives. However, Lewin believes that many change agents enter the changing phase prematurely, are too quick to change things, and therefore end up creating resistance to change. When managers implement change before people feel a need for it, there is an increased likelihood of failure.

■ **Changing** is the phase where a planned change actually takes place.

Refreezing

The final stage in the planned change process is **refreezing**. Here, the manager is concerned about stabilizing the change and creating the conditions for its long-term continuity. Refreezing is accomplished by linking change with appropriate rewards for performance, positive reinforcement, and necessary resource support. It is also important in this phase to

■ **Refreezing** is the phase at which change is stabilized.

evaluate results carefully, provide feedback to the people involved, and make any required modifications in the original change. When refreezing is done poorly, changes are too easily forgotten or abandoned with the passage of time. When it is done well, change should be more long lasting. However, in this era of continuous pressure for rapid market responses, refreezing the planned change process may prove difficult. Author Ron Knowles proposes that refreezing implies a return to a previously frozen state, but this is clearly unrealistic and not what Lewin intended. He envisioned a continuous process of unfreezing, changing, and refreezing, during which one set of changes is followed by another set of changes in a constantly evolving pattern.[36]

●●● CHANGE STRATEGIES

The act of actually changing, or moving people to do things differently, can be pursued in different ways. *Figure 18.4* summarizes three common change strategies known as force-coercion, rational persuasion, and shared power.[37] Managers, as change agents, should understand that each can have very different consequences.

Figure 18.4 Alternative change strategies and their leadership implications.

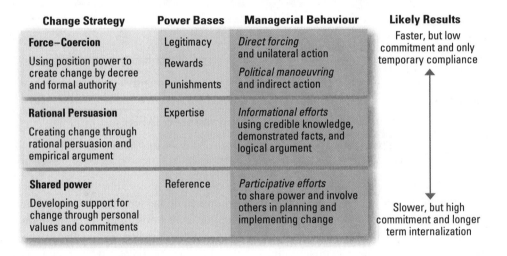

Change Strategy	Power Bases	Managerial Behaviour	Likely Results
Force–Coercion Using position power to create change by decree and formal authority	Legitimacy Rewards Punishments	*Direct forcing* and unilateral action *Political manoeuvring* and indirect action	Faster, but low commitment and only temporary compliance
Rational Persuasion Creating change through rational persuasion and empirical argument	Expertise	*Informational efforts* using credible knowledge, demonstrated facts, and logical argument	
Shared power Developing support for change through personal values and commitments	Reference	*Participative efforts* to share power and involve others in planning and implementing change	Slower, but high commitment and longer term internalization

Force-Coercion Strategies

A **force-coercion strategy** pursues change through formal authority and/or the use of rewards or punishments.

A **force-coercion strategy** uses the power bases of legitimacy, rewards, and punishments as the primary inducements to change. A change agent that seeks to create change through force-coercion believes that people are basically motivated by self-interest and by what the situation offers in terms of potential personal gains or losses.[38] This change agent believes that people change only in response to such motives, tries to find out where their vested interests lie, and then puts the pressure on. Once a weakness is found, it is exploited.

In a *direct forcing strategy*, the change agent takes direct and unilateral action to "command" that change take place. This involves the exercise of formal authority or legitimate power, offering special rewards and/or threatening punishment. In *political manoeuvring*, the change agent works indirectly to gain special advantage over other persons and thereby make them change. This involves bargaining, obtaining control of important resources, forming alliances, or granting small favours.

Any force-coercion strategy, on its own, produces limited results. Although it can be implemented rather quickly, most people respond to force-coercion out of fear of punishment or hope for a reward. This usually results in only temporary compliance with the change agent's desires. The new behaviour continues only so long as the opportunity for rewards and punishments is present. For this reason, force-coercion is most useful as an unfreezing device that helps people break old patterns of behaviour and gain initial impetus to try new ones. The example of General Electric's Work-Out program, noted earlier, applies here.[39] Jack Welch started Work-Out to create a forum for active employee empowerment of continuous change. But he didn't make the program optional; participation in Work-Out was mandatory from the start. Welch used his authority as leader to initiate the program because he was confident it would survive and prosper on its own—once it was experienced. Part of his commitment to change leadership was a willingness to use authority to unfreeze situations and get new things started.

take it to the case!

BC Ferries
Weathering ongoing change

For British Columbia Ferry Services, becoming the world's largest ferry service has been a very rough ride. Started in 1960, BC Ferries has weathered major growth, continuous financial difficulties, hasty leadership changes, and a movement from government to independent ownership. When David Hahn took the helm of BC Ferries in 2003, the company was struggling to survive. Hahn met that challenge head on and instituted changes in everything from improving customer service to establishing real independence from the government. These changes were often met with resistance, whether from employees or government, but they doubled the company's revenues. But the tragic sinking of one of its ships in 2006, resulting in the death of two passengers, turned Hahn's focus from growth to deeper concerns about safety, training, risk management, and employee relations issues. Read the case in the *Management Learning Workbook* to find out how BC Ferries has weathered the storm of ongoing change.

Source: "About BC Ferries," on the BC Ferries website, <www.bcferries.com/about/>.

Rational Persuasion Strategies

Change agents using a **rational persuasion strategy** attempt to bring about change through persuasion backed by special knowledge, empirical data, and rational argument. A change agent following this strategy believes that people are inherently rational and are guided by reason in their actions and decision making. Once a specific course of action is demonstrated to be in a person's self-interest, the change agent assumes that reason and rationality will cause the person to adopt it. Thus, he or she uses information and facts to communicate the essential desirability of change.

> ■ A **rational persuasion strategy** pursues change through empirical data and rational argument.

The likely outcome of rational persuasion is eventual compliance with reasonable commitment. When successful, a rational persuasion strategy helps both unfreeze and refreeze a change situation. Although slower than force-coercion, it tends to result in longer-lasting and more internalized change. To be successful, a manager using rational persuasion must convince others that the cost-benefit value of a planned change is high and that it will leave them better off than before. This power can come directly from the change agent if she or he has personal credibility as an "expert." If not, it can be obtained in the form of consultants and other outside experts, or from credible demonstration projects and benchmarks. The magic of

Walt Disney World, for example, extends to more than family fun and holidays. Many firms use Disney as a benchmark to demonstrate to their own employees how changes can improve operations. A Ford vice-president says, "Disney's track record is one of the best in the country as far as dealing with customers." The firm sends managers to Disney to learn about customer loyalty, hoping to drive customer service initiatives of their own.[40] In this sense, the power of rational persuasion is straightforward: if it works for Disney, why can't it work for us?

Shared Power Strategies

■ **A shared power strategy** pursues change by participation in assessing change needs, values, and goals.

A **shared power strategy** engages people in a collaborative process of identifying values, assumptions, and goals from which support for change will naturally emerge. The process is slow, but it is likely to yield high commitment. Sometimes called a *normative re-educative strategy*, this approach is based on empowerment and is highly participative in nature. It relies on involving others in examining personal needs and values, group norms, and operating goals as they relate to the issues at hand. Power is shared by the change agent and other persons as they work together to develop a new consensus to support needed change.

Managers using shared power as an approach to planned change need referent power and the skills to work effectively in groups. They must be comfortable allowing others to participate in making decisions that affect the planned change and the way it is implemented. Because it entails a high level of involvement, this strategy is often quite time consuming. But importantly, power sharing is likely to result in a longer-lasting and internalized change.

A change agent who shares power begins by recognizing that people have varied needs and complex motivations. He or she believes people behave as they do because of socio-cultural norms and commitments to the expectations of others. Changes in organizations are understood to inevitably involve changes in attitudes, values, skills, and significant relationships, not just changes in knowledge, information, or intellectual rationales for action and practice. Thus, when seeking to change others, this change agent is sensitive to the way group pressures can support or inhibit change. In working with people, every attempt is made to gather their opinions, identify their feelings and expectations, and incorporate them fully into the change process.

The great "power" of sharing power in the change process lies with unlocking the creativity and experience of people within the system. Unfortunately, many managers are hesitant to engage this process for fear of losing control or of having to compromise on important organizational goals. Harvard scholar Teresa M. Amabile, however, points out that managers and change leaders should have the confidence to share power regarding means and processes, but not overall goals. "People will be more creative," she says, "if you give them freedom to decide how to climb particular mountains. You needn't let them choose which mountains to climb."[41]

●●● RESISTANCE TO CHANGE

Change typically brings with it resistance. When people resist change, furthermore, they are most often defending something that is important and that appears threatened. A change of work schedules for workers in ON Semiconductor's plant, for example, may not have seemed like much to top management. But to the workers it was significant enough to bring about an organizing attempt by the Teamsters Union. When management delved into the issues, they found that workers viewed changes in weekend work schedules as threatening to their personal lives. With inputs from the workers, the problem was resolved satisfactorily.[42]

There are any number of reasons why people in organizations may resist planned change. Some of the more common ones are shown in *Manager's Notepad 18.3*. Change

MANAGER'S
Notepad 18.3

Why people may resist change

- *Fear of the unknown*—not understanding what is happening or what comes next.

- *Disrupted habits*—feeling upset when old ways of doing things can't be followed.

- *Loss of confidence*—feeling incapable of performing well under the new ways of doing things.

- *Loss of control*—feeling that things are being done "to" you rather than "by" or "with" you.

- *Poor timing*—feeling overwhelmed by the situation or that things are moving too fast.

- *Work overload*—not having the physical or psychic energy to commit to the change.

- *Loss of face*—feeling inadequate or humiliated because it appears that the "old" ways weren't "good" ways.

- *Lack of purpose*—not seeing a reason for the change and/or not understanding its benefits.

agents and managers often view such resistance as something that must be "overcome" in order for change to be successful. But, resistance is better viewed as feedback that the informed change agent can use to plan or modify change to best fit situational needs and goals. When resistance appears, it usually means that something can be done to achieve a better "fit" among the planned change, the situation, and the people involved. Consider the implications of this conversation reported by Jim Stam, a shift-work consultant with Circadian Technologies: *Manager*—"Come on, Jim, there must be one schedule that's the right schedule for this industry." *Jim*—"Yes, it's the one the people in the plant pick."[43]

Once resistance to change is recognized and understood, it can be dealt with in various ways.[44] Among the alternatives for effectively managing resistance, the *education and communication* approach uses discussions, presentations, and demonstrations to educate people beforehand about a change. *Participation and involvement* allow others to contribute ideas and help design and implement the change. The *facilitation and support* approach involves providing encouragement and training, actively listening to problems and complaints, and helping to overcome performance pressures. *Facilitation and agreement* provides incentives that appeal to those who are actively resisting or ready to resist. It also makes trade-offs in exchange for assurances that change will not be blocked. *Manipulation and co-optation* try to covertly influence others by providing information selectively and structuring events in favour of the desired change. *Explicit and implicit coercion* forces people to accept change by threatening resistors with a variety of undesirable consequences if they do not go along as asked. Obviously, the last two approaches carry great risk and potential for negative side effects.

●●● CHALLENGES OF TECHNOLOGICAL CHANGE

Ongoing technological change is a way of life in today's organizations, but it also brings special challenges to change leaders. For the full advantages of new technologies to be realized, a good fit must be achieved with work needs, practices, and people. This, in turn, requires sensitivity to resistance and continual gathering of information so that appropriate adjustments can be made during the time a new technology is being implemented. The demands of managing technological change have been described using the analogy of contrasting styles between navigators from the Micronesian island of Truk and their European counterparts.[45]

> *The European navigator works from a plan, relates all moves during a voyage to the plan, and tries to always stay "on course." When something unexpected happens, the plan is revised systematically, and the new plan followed again until the navigator finds the ship to be off course. The Trukese navigator, by contrast, starts with an objective and moves off in its general direction. Always alert to information from waves, clouds, winds, etc., the navigator senses subtle changes in conditions and steers and alters the ship's course continually to reach the ultimate objective.*

Like the navigators of Truk, technological change may best be approached as an ongoing process that will inevitably require improvisation as things are being implemented. New technologies are often designed external to the organization in which they are to be used. The implications of such a technology for a local application may be difficult to anticipate and plan for ahead of time. A technology that is attractive in concept may appear complicated to the new users; the full extent of its benefits and/or inadequacies may not become known until it is tried. This, in turn, means that the change leader and manager should be alert to resistance, should continually gather and process information relating to the change, and should be willing to customize the new technology to best meet the needs of the local situation.[46]

✓ Learning check ❸

BE SURE YOU CAN
• identify Lewin's phases of planned change • discuss a change leader's action responsibilities for each phase • explain the force-coercion, rational persuasion, and shared power change strategies • discuss the pros and cons of each change strategy • list several reasons why people resist change • identify strategies for dealing with resistance to change • discuss the challenges of technological change

ORGANIZATION DEVELOPMENT

■ **Organization development** is a comprehensive effort to improve an organization's ability to solve problems and improve performance.

There will always be times when the members of organizations should sit together and systematically reflect on strengths and weaknesses, performance accomplishments and failures, and the future. One way to ensure that this happens in a participative and action-oriented environment is through **organization development**. This is a comprehensive approach to planned organizational change that involves the application of behavioural science in a systematic and long-range effort to improve organizational effectiveness.[47] "OD" is an important way for leaders to share power to advance planned change agendas, foster creativity and innovation, and continuously improve organizational performance. Although it often involves the assistance of a consultant with special training, all managers can and should include OD in their change leadership agendas.

●●● ORGANIZATION DEVELOPMENT GOALS

Two goals are pursued simultaneously in organization development. The *outcome goals of OD* focus on task accomplishments, while the *process goals of OD* focus on the way people work together. The second goal strongly differentiates OD from more general attempts at planned change in organizations. You may think of OD as a form of "planned change plus," with the "plus" meaning that change is accomplished in such a way that organization members develop a capacity for continued self-renewal. That is, OD tries to achieve change in ways that help organization members become more active and self-reliant in their ability to continue changing in the future. What also makes OD unique is its commitment to strong humanistic values and established principles of behavioural science. OD is committed to improving organizations through freedom of choice, shared power, and self-reliance, and by taking the best advantage of what we know about human behaviour in organizations.

●●● HOW ORGANIZATION DEVELOPMENT WORKS

Figure 18.5 presents a general model of OD and shows its relationship to Lewin's three phases of planned change. To begin the OD process successfully, any consultant or facilitator must first *establish a working relationship* with members of the client system. The next step is *diagnosis*—gathering and analyzing data to assess the situation and set appropriate change objectives. This helps with unfreezing as well as pinpointing appropriate directions for action. Diagnosis leads to active *intervention*, wherein change objectives are pursued through a variety of specific interventions, a number of which will be discussed shortly. Also essential to any OD effort is *evaluation*. This is the examination of the process to determine whether things are proceeding as desired and whether further action is needed. Eventually, the OD consultant or facilitator should *achieve a terminal relationship* that leaves the client able to function on its own. If OD has been well done, the system and its members should be better prepared to manage their ongoing need for self-renewal and development.

Figure 18.5 Organization development and the planned change process.

The success or failure of any OD program lies in part with the strength of its methodological foundations. As shown in *Figure 18.6*, these foundations rest on **action research**—the process of systematically collecting data on an organization, feeding it back to the members for action planning, and evaluating results by collecting more data and repeating the process as necessary. Action research is initiated when someone senses a performance gap and decides to analyze the situation to understand its problems and opportunities. Data gathering can be done in several ways. Interviews are a common means of gathering data in action research. Formal written surveys of employee attitudes and needs are also growing in popularity. Many such "climate," "attitude," or "morale" questionnaires have been tested for reliability and validity. Some have even been used so extensively that norms are available so that one organization can compare its results with those from a broad sample of counterparts.

■ **Action research** is a collaborative process of collecting data, using it for action planning, and evaluating the results.

Figure 18.6 Action research as a foundation of organization development.

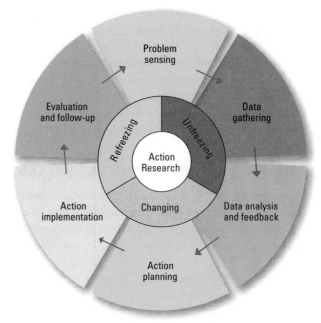

●●● ORGANIZATION DEVELOPMENT INTERVENTIONS

In many ways, organization development is employee involvement in action. The process involves respect for people and commitments to their full participation in self-directed change efforts. The process is activated by a variety of **OD interventions** that directly facilitate participatory change. Importantly, these interventions are linked to concepts and ideas discussed elsewhere in this book and that are well represented in the practices and approaches of the new workplace.[48]

■ An **OD intervention** is a structured activity that helps create change for organization development.

Individual Interventions

Organization development practitioners recognize that needs for personal growth and development are most likely to be satisfied in a supportive and challenging work environment. They also accept the premise that most people are capable of assuming responsibility for their own actions and of making positive contributions to organizational performance. Based on these principles, some of the more popular OD interventions designed to help improve individual effectiveness include the following:

• *Sensitivity training*—unstructured sessions (T-groups) where participants learn interpersonal skills and increased sensitivity to other people.

• *Management training*—structured educational opportunities for developing important managerial skills and competencies.

• *Role negotiation*—structured interactions to clarify and negotiate role expectations among people who work together.

• *Job redesign*—realigning task components to better fit the needs and capabilities of individuals.

• *Career planning*—structured advice and discussion sessions to help individuals plan career paths and personal development programs.

Team Interventions

The team plays a very important role in organization development. OD practitioners recognize two principles in this respect. First, teams are viewed as important vehicles for helping people satisfy important needs. Second, it is believed that improved collaboration within and among teams can improve organizational performance. Selected OD interventions designed to improve team effectiveness include the following:

- *Team building*—structured experiences to help team members set goals, improve interpersonal relations, and become a better-functioning team.

- *Process consultation*—third-party observation and advice on critical team processes (e.g., communication, conflict, and decision making).

- *Intergroup team building*—structured experiences to help two or more teams set shared goals, reduce conflict, improve intergroup relations, and become better coordinated.

Organization-Wide Interventions

At the level of the total organization, OD practitioners operate on the premise that any changes in one part of the system will also affect other parts. The organization's culture is considered to have an important impact on member attitudes and morale. And it is believed that structures and jobs can be designed to bring together people, technology, and systems in highly productive and satisfying working combinations. Some of the OD interventions with an emphasis on overall organizational effectiveness include the following:

- *Survey feedback*—comprehensive and systematic data collection to identify attitudes and needs, analyze results, and plan for constructive action.

- *Confrontation meeting*—one-day intensive, structured meetings to gather data on workplace problems and plan for constructive actions.

- *Structural redesign*—realigning the organization structure to meet the needs of environmental and contextual forces.

- *Management by objectives*—Formalizing MBO throughout the organization to link individual, group, and organizational objectives.

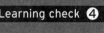

BE SURE YOU CAN

• define the term organization development • differentiate outcome and process goals of OD • explain the steps in the OD process • explain the role of action research in OD • list OD interventions focusing on individuals and on teams • list organization-wide OD interventions

STRESS AND STRESS MANAGEMENT

With the ever-present and ever-changing demands of working in the new economy, it is not surprising that people are experiencing more stress in their daily lives. Formally defined, **stress** is a state of tension experienced by individuals facing extraordinary demands, constraints, or opportunities.[49] Any look toward your future work career would be incomplete without considering stress as a challenge that you are sure to encounter along the way—and a challenge you

■ **Stress** is a state of tension experienced by individuals facing extraordinary demands, constraints, or opportunities.

must be prepared to help others learn to deal with. In his book *The Future of Success*, for example, Robert Reich says that even though the new economy gives us much to celebrate, its "rewards are coming at the price of lives that are more frenzied, less secure, more economically divergent, more socially stratified."[50] At centre stage in this milieu stand job stress and its implications for the managerial role. Consider this statement by a psychologist who worked with top-level managers having alcohol abuse problems: "All executives deal with stress. They wouldn't be executives if they didn't. Some handle it well, others handle it poorly."[51]

Is workplace stress a problem in Canada? The quick answer is yes. Over 30 percent of working Canadians cited too many demands placed on them and long work hours as their main sources of stress, while a further 10 percent cited a fear of being laid off from their job as their central source of stress. A further 15 percent cited poor interpersonal relations and 13 percent cited risk of accident or injury as their key sources of stress. Canadian managers and professionals were significantly more likely to report stress from too many demands or hours than were workers in health occupations, who were seven times more likely to cite fear of accident or injury. [52]

●●● SOURCES OF STRESS

■ A **stressor** is anything that causes stress.

Stressors are things that cause stress. Whether they originate directly from a change environment, other aspects of the work setting, or in personal and non-work situations, stressors have the potential to influence our work attitudes, behaviour, job performance, and even health.

Work factors have an obvious potential to create job stress. Some 34 percent of workers in one survey said that their jobs were so stressful that they were thinking of quitting.[53] We often experience such stress in long hours of work, excessive emails, unrealistic work deadlines, difficult bosses or co-workers, unwelcome or unfamiliar work, and unrelenting change.[54] It is also associated with excessively high or low task demands, role conflicts or ambiguities, poor interpersonal relations, or career progress that is too slow or too fast. Stress tends to be high during periods of work overload, when office politics are common, and among persons working for organizations undergoing staff cutbacks and downsizing. Two of the common work-related stress syndromes are (1) *set up to fail*—where the performance expectations are impossible or the support is totally inadequate to the task; and (2) *mistaken identity*—where the individual ends up in a job that doesn't at all match talents or that he or she simply doesn't like.[55]

■ A **Type A personality** is a person oriented toward extreme achievement, impatience, and perfectionism.

A variety of *personal factors* are also sources of potential stress for people at work. Such individual characteristics as needs, capabilities, and personality can influence how one perceives and responds to work and change. Researchers, for example, identify a **Type A personality** that is high in achievement orientation, impatience, and perfectionism. Type A persons are likely to create stress in circumstances that others find relatively stress-free. Type A's, in this sense, bring stress on themselves. The stressful behaviour patterns of *Type A personalities* include the following:[56]

- Always moving, walking, and eating rapidly.

- Acting impatient, hurrying others, disliking waiting.

- Doing, or trying to do, several things at once.

- Feeling guilty when relaxing.

- Trying to schedule more in less time.

- Using nervous gestures such as a clenched fist.

- Hurrying or interrupting the speech of others.

Finally, stress from *non-work factors* can have spillover effects that affect people at work. Stressful life situations including such things as family events (e.g., the birth of a new child), economics (e.g., a sudden loss of extra income), and personal affairs (e.g., a preoccupation with a bad relationship) are often sources of emotional strain. Depending on the individual and his or her ability to deal with them, preoccupation with such situations can affect one's work and add to the stress of work–life conflicts.

●●● CONSEQUENCES OF STRESS

The discussion of stress so far may give the impression that it always acts as a negative influence on our lives. But like conflict, stress actually has two faces—one constructive and one destructive.[57] Consider the analogy of a violin.[58] When a violin string is too loose, the sound produced by even the most skilled player is weak and raspy. When the string is too tight, however, the sound gets shrill and the string might even snap. But when the tension on the string is just right, neither too loose nor too tight, a most beautiful sound is created. With just enough stress, in other words, performance is optimized.

The same argument tends to hold in the workplace. **Constructive stress**, sometimes called *eustress*, acts in a positive way for the individual and/or the organization. It occurs in moderation and proves energizing and performance enhancing.[59] The stress is sufficient to encourage increased effort, stimulate creativity, and enhance diligence in one's work, while not overwhelming the individual and causing negative outcomes. Individuals with a Type A personality, for example, are likely to work long hours and to be less satisfied with poor performance. For them, challenging task demands imposed by a supervisor may elicit higher levels of task accomplishment. Even non-work stressors, such as new family responsibilities, may cause them to work harder in anticipation of greater financial rewards.

Just like tuning the violin string, however, achieving the right balance of stress for each person and situation is difficult. The question is, "When is a little stress too much stress?" **Destructive stress**, or *distress*, is dysfunctional. It occurs as intense or long-term stress that, as shown in *Figure 18.7*, overloads and breaks down a person's physical and mental systems. Destructive stress can lead to **job burnout**—a form of physical and mental exhaustion that can be incapacitating both personally and in respect to one's work. Productivity can suffer as people react to very intense stress through turnover, absenteeism, errors, accidents, dissatisfaction, and reduced performance. Today as well, there is increased concern for another consequence of excessive stress, **workplace rage**—overtly aggressive behaviour toward co-workers and the work setting in general. Lost tempers are a common example; the unfortunate extremes are tragedies involving physical harm to others.[60]

Medical research is also concerned that too much stress can reduce resistance to disease and increase the likelihood of physical and/or mental illness. It may contribute to health problems such as hypertension, ulcers, substance abuse, overeating, depression, and muscle aches, among others.[61] Also important to understand is that excessive work stress can have *spillover*

PERSONAL MANAGEMENT

It may strike you as odd to talk here about personal **STRENGTH AND ENERGY**. But the fact is that it isn't easy to work today. One national survey of American workers, for example, found 54 percent feeling overworked, 55 percent overwhelmed by their workloads, 56 percent not having enough time to complete their work, 59 percent not having enough time for reflection, and 45 percent having to do too many things at once. At a minimum this reminds us that work in the 21st century can be very stressful. And just as to play tennis or some other sport, we have to get and stay in shape for work. This means building strength and energy to best handle the inevitable strains and anxieties of organizational changes, job pressures, and the potential conflicts between work demands and personal affairs.

- Is it hard to relax after a day in class?

- Does it take effort to concentrate in your spare time?

- Do you lay awake thinking and worrying about events of the day?

- Are you so tired that you are unable to join friends or family in leisure activities?

Any "yes" answer indicates the need to do a better job of building and sustaining your capacities to handle heavy workloads. And if you think things are tough as a student, get ready. The real challenges lie ahead!

Get to know yourself better

Complete Self-Assessments #29—**Stress Self-Test**, and #30—**Work–Life Balance**, from the Workbook and Personal Management Activity #18 on the companion website.

■ **Constructive stress** acts in a positive way to increase effort, stimulate creativity, and encourage diligence in one's work.

■ **Destructive stress** impairs the performance of an individual.

■ **Job burnout** is physical and mental exhaustion from work stress.

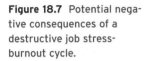
Workplace rage is aggressive behaviour toward co-workers or the work setting.

effects on one's personal life. A study of dual-career couples found that one partner's work experiences can have psychological consequences for the other; as one's work stress increases, the partner is likely to experience stress too.[62] The bottom line is that any stress we experience at work is contagious; it can affect one's spouse, family, and friends. The wife of a company controller, for example, went through a time when her husband was stressed by a boss who was overly critical. "He was angry, really angry when he came home," she says. His mood affected her and their young child and created what she called "one of the worst times in our seven-year marriage."[63]

Figure 18.7 Potential negative consequences of a destructive job stress-burnout cycle.

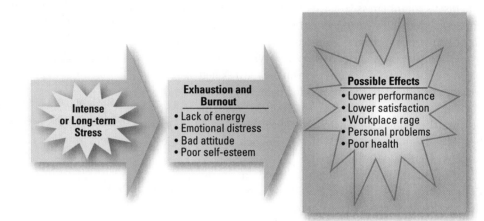

STRESS MANAGEMENT STRATEGIES

The best stress management is to prevent it from reaching excessive levels in the first place. Stressors emerging from personal and non-work factors must be identified so that action can be taken to prevent them or minimize their negative consequences. Family difficulties, for example, may be relieved by a change of work schedule, or the anxiety they cause may be reduced by an understanding supervisor. Also, people sometimes need help in combating the tendency toward "working too much." They need to be reminded not to forgo vacations or not to work excessive overtime.

Among the work factors with the greatest potential to cause excessive stress are role ambiguities, conflicts, and overloads. *Role clarification* through a management-by-objectives approach can work to good advantage here. By bringing the supervisor and subordinate together in face-to-face, task-oriented communications, MBO offers an opportunity both to spot stressors and to take action to reduce or eliminate them. Another common stressor is a poor fit between individual abilities and job demands. In this case, job redesign may be helpful to better configure task requirements. Alternatively, changing jobs altogether can help achieve a better person–job fit.

Personal wellness is the pursuit of one's full potential through a personal-health promotion program.

Personal wellness is a term used to describe the pursuit of one's physical and mental potential through a personal health-promotion program. This form of *preventative stress management* recognizes the individual's responsibility to enhance his or her personal health through a disciplined approach to such things as smoking, alcohol use, diet, exercise, and physical fitness. The essence of personal wellness is a lifestyle that reflects a true commitment to health. And it makes a great deal of sense. Those who aggressively maintain their personal wellness are better prepared to deal with the inevitable stresses of work, work–life conflicts, and organizational changes. In a national wellness survey of Canadian companies, 83 percent of respondents said their company offered at least one "wellness initiative," such as stress-management techniques, weight-control programs, fitness incentives, or nutrition awareness. That's a huge increase from 64 percent back in 2000.[64] Expectations are that investments in wellness programs benefit both the organization and its employees. B.C. Hydro, for instance, reports that the return on investment for its employee wellness program is $3 to $4 for every dollar invested. That's a common result for many wellness programs, which have been expanding significantly in recent years. But some, such as Canada Life's, get up to $6 back. The savings come from reduced absenteeism along with fewer extended health benefit and disability payouts.[65]

BE SURE YOU CAN

• define the term stress • identify the common stressors found in work and in personal life • describe a person with a Type A personality • differentiate constructive and destructive stress • explain the destructive nature of job burnout and workplace rage • discuss personal wellness as a stress management strategy

✔ Learning check ➎

●●● Chapter 18 STUDY GUIDE

WHERE WE'VE BEEN

Back to Meridian Credit Union

The opening example of Meridian Credit Union brought the issues of change leadership centre stage in your study of management. In this chapter you learned about the challenges of strategic leadership and innovation. You learned the responsibilities of leading change, including understanding the phases of planned change, the nature of resistance to change, and the alternative change strategies. You also learned about organization development and how important it is to manage stress in work settings undergoing the pressures of change.

THE NEXT STEP
INTEGRATED LEARNING ACTIVITIES

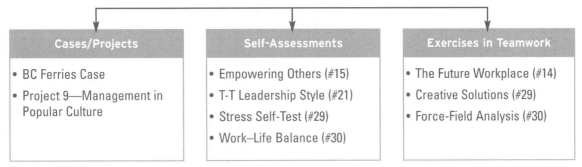

Cases/Projects	Self-Assessments	Exercises in Teamwork
• BC Ferries Case	• Empowering Others (#15)	• The Future Workplace (#14)
• Project 9—Management in Popular Culture	• T-T Leadership Style (#21)	• Creative Solutions (#29)
	• Stress Self-Test (#29)	• Force-Field Analysis (#30)
	• Work–Life Balance (#30)	

STUDY QUESTION SUMMARY

1. What are the challenges of strategic leadership and innovation?

- The future will be like our past—always unpredictable, very challenging, and full of continuous change.

- A learning organization is one in which people, values, and systems support innovation and continuous change based upon the lessons of experience.

- Organizations need strategic leaders who work with a strategic direction to initiate and successfully implement changes that help organizations perform well in changing environments.

- Innovation allows creative ideas to be turned into products and/or processes that benefit organizations and their customers.

- Highly innovative organizations tend to have supportive cultures, strategies, structures, staffing, and top management.

- The possible barriers to innovation in organizations include a lack of top-management support, excessive bureaucracy, short time horizons, and vested interests.

2. What is the nature of organizational change?

- Change leaders are change agents who take responsibility for helping to change the behaviour of people and organizational systems.

- Managers should be able to spot change opportunities and lead the process of planned change in their areas of work responsibilities.

- Although organizational change can proceed with a top-down emphasis, inputs from all levels of responsibility are essential to achieve successful implementation.

- Transformational change is led from the top and makes radical changes in organizational directions; incremental change is led from all levels and makes continuing adjustments to existing ways and practices.

- The many possible targets for change include organizational tasks, people, cultures, technologies, and structures.

3. How can planned organizational change be managed?

- Lewin's three phases of planned change are unfreezing—preparing a system for change; changing—making a change; and refreezing—stabilizing the system with a new change in place.

- Good change agents understand the nature of force-coercion, rational persuasion, and shared power change strategies.

- People resist change for a variety of reasons, including fear of the unknown and force of habit.

- Good change agents deal with resistance positively and in a variety of ways, including education, participation, facilitation, manipulation, and coercion.

- Success with technological change requires an openness to resistance and willingness to improvise as implementation proceeds.

4. What is organization development?

- Organization development (OD) is a comprehensive approach to planned organization change that uses principles of behavioural science to improve organizational effectiveness over the long term.

- Outcome goals of OD focus on improved task accomplishment; process goals of OD focus on improvements in the way people work together to accomplish important tasks.

- The OD process involves action research wherein people work together to collect and analyze data on system performance and decide what actions to take to improve things.

- OD interventions are structured activities that help people work together to accomplish change; they may be implemented at the individual, group, and/or organizational levels.

5. How can stress be managed in a change environment?

- Stress occurs as the tension accompanying extraordinary demands, constraints, or opportunities builds.

- Stress can be destructive or constructive; a moderate level of stress typically has a positive impact on performance.

- Stressors are found in a variety of work, personal, and non-work situations.

- For some people, having a Type A personality creates stress as a result of continual feelings of impatience and pressure.

- Stress can be effectively managed through both prevention and coping strategies, including a commitment to personal wellness.

KEY TERMS REVIEW

Action research (p. 459)

Bottom-up change (p. 449)

Change agent (p. 448)

Change leader (p. 448)

Changing (p. 453)

Commercializing innovation (p. 446)

Constructive stress (p. 463)

Creativity (p. 445)

Destructive stress (p. 463)

Force-coercion strategy (p. 454)

Incremental change (p. 451)

Innovation (p. 445)

Job burnout (p. 463)

Learning organization (p. 443)

OD interventions (p. 460)

Organization development (p. 458)

Performance gap (p. 451)

Personal wellness (p. 464)

Planned change (p. 451)

Process innovations (p. 445)

Product innovations (p. 445)

Rational persuasion strategy (p. 455)

Reactive change (p. 451)

Refreezing (p. 453)

Shared power strategy (p. 456)

Strategic leadership (p. 444)

Stress (p. 461)

Stressor (p. 462)

Top-down change (p. 449)

Transformational change (p. 451)

Type A personality (p. 463)

Unfreezing (p. 452)

Workplace rage (p. 464)

SELF-TEST 18

MULTIPLE-CHOICE QUESTIONS:

1. In organizations, product innovation (creating new goods or services) and _____ innovation (creating new ways of doing things) are important.
   (a) commercializing (b) process (c) quality (d) task

2. The first step in Hamel's "wheel of innovation" is _____.
   (a) imagining (b) assessing (c) experimenting (d) scaling

3. An executive pursuing transformational change would give highest priority to which one of these change targets?
   (a) an out-of-date policy (b) the organizational culture (c) technology support for a new MIS (d) job designs for individuals in a customer service department

4. A manager using a force-coercion strategy will rely on the power of _____ to bring about change.
   (a) expertise (b) reference (c) rewards, punishments, or authority (d) information

5. The most participative of the planned change strategies is _____.
   (a) force-coercion (b) rational persuasion (c) shared power (d) command and control

6. Trying to covertly influence others, offering only selective information, and/or structuring events in favour of the desired change are ways of dealing with resistance by _____.
   (a) participation (b) manipulation and co-optation (c) force-coercion (d) facilitation

7. In organization development both _____ and _____ goals are important.
   (a) task, maintenance (b) management, labour (c) outcome, process (d) profit, market share

8. Sensitivity training and role negotiation are examples of organization development interventions at the _____ level.
   (a) individual (b) group (c) system-wide (d) organization

9. The concept of empowerment is most often associated with the _____ strategy of planned change.
   (a) political manoeuvring (b) rational persuasion (c) direct forcing (d) normative–re-educative

10. Unfreezing occurs during the _____ step of organizational development.
     (a) diagnosis (b) intervention (c) evaluation (d) termination

11. The quality concept of continuous improvement is most consistent with the notion of _____.
     (a) incremental change (b) transformational change (c) radical change (d) reactive change

12. True internalization and commitment to a planned change is most likely to occur when a manager uses a(n) _____ change strategy.
     (a) education and communication (b) rational persuasion (c) manipulation and co-optation (d) shared power

13. Through _____, the stress people experience in their personal lives can create problems for them at work and the stress experienced at work can create problems for their personal lives.
     (a) eustress (b) refreezing (c) spillover effects (d) action research

14. As a stress management strategy, MBO would be especially useful in helping people deal with _____.
     (a) role ambiguities (b) workplace rage (c) personal wellness (d) resistance to change

15. Learning organizations that sustain themselves through positive change are made possible by strong and continuing _____.
     (a) force-coercion (b) stress (c) strategic leadership (d) project management

SHORT-RESPONSE QUESTIONS:

16. What are the three phases of change described by Lewin, and what are their implications for change leadership?

17. What are the major differences in the potential outcomes of force-coercion, rational persuasion, and shared power strategies of planned change?

18. What does the statement "OD equals planned change plus" mean?

19. Why is it important for a manager to understand the Type A personality?

APPLICATION QUESTION:

20. As a newly appointed manager in any work setting, you are likely to spot many things that "could be done better" and to have many "new ideas" that you would like to implement. Based on the ideas presented in this chapter, how should you go about effecting successful planned change in such situations?

INSIDE:

Integrated Case

Cases for Critical Thinking

Active Learning Projects

Exercises in Teamwork

Self-Assessments

Student Portfolio Builder

MANAGEMENT LEARNING
WORKBOOK

Management Learning Workbook

Integrated Case

RIM Fights to Manage Intellectual Property W-4

Cases for Critical Thinking

1. Apple Inc.—Where people and design create the future W-13

2. The Coca-Cola Company—Coke gets back to business W-16

3. Barenaked Ladies—Changing the world one song at a time W-18

4. United Parcel Service—Where technology rules a total quality road W-21

5. Bata—One step at a time W-24

6. Hannah's Ice Cream—A hypothetical study of entrepreneurship W-26

7. Spin Master—Turning fun into opportunities W-28

8. Wal-Mart—Self-management works at the number-one retailer W-31

9. Toyota Canada Inc.—Making things better W-33

10. Nike—Spreading out to stay together W-36

11. BET Holdings—World-class entrepreneur places "BET" on the future W-39

12. Royal Bank of Canada—Progressive HR makes good business sense W-41

13. Lakeport Brewing Income Fund—A case of great leadership W-43

14. SC Johnson Canada—Where employees are family W-47

15. Steinway & Sons—Craftwork, tradition, and time build grand pianos W-50

16. Callaway Golf—Big Bertha's team hits a long ball W-52

17. The United Nations—Conflict and negotiation in the global community W-54

18. British Columbia Ferry Services—Navigating the changing times W-58

Active Learning Projects

1. Diversity Lessons W-62

2. Corporate Social Responsibility W-63

3. Globalization Pros and Cons W-63

4. Diversity Management W-64

5. Fringe Benefits W-64

6. Controversies in CEO Pay W-65

7. Gender and Leadership W-65

8. Superstars on the Team W-66

9. Management in Popular Culture W-66

10. Service Learning in Management W-67

Exercises in Teamwork

1. My Best Manager W-68

2. What Managers Do W-69

3. Defining Quality W-69

4. What Would the Classics Say? W-70

5. The Great Management History Debate W-70

6. Confronting Ethical Dilemmas W-71

7. What Do You Value in Work? W-71

8. Which Organizational Culture Fits You? W-72

9. Beating the Time Wasters W-73

10. Personal Career Planning W-73

11. Decision-Making Biases W-74

12. Strategic Scenarios W-75

13. The MBO Contract W-75

14. The Future Workplace W-76

15. Dots and Squares Puzzle W-76

16. Leading Through Participation W-77

17. Work vs. Family—You Be the Judge W-78

18. Compensation and Benefits Debate W-79

19. Sources and Uses of Power W-79

20. After Meeting/Project Review W-80

21. Why Do We Work? W-81

22. The Case of the Contingency Workforce W-81

23. The "Best" Job Design W-82

24. Upward Appraisal W-82

25. How to Give, and Take, Criticism W-83

26. Lost at Sea W-83

27. Work Team Dynamics W-84

28. Feedback and Assertiveness W-84

29. Creative Solutions W-85

30. Force-Field Analysis W-86

13. Time Management Profile W-103

14. Facts and Inferences W-104

15. Empowering Others W-105

16. Turbulence Tolerance Test W-106

17. Organizational Design Preference W-107

18. Are You Cosmopolitan? W-108

19. Performance Appraisal Assumptions W-109

20. "T-P" Leadership Questionnaire W-110

21. "T-T" Leadership Style W-112

22. Least-Preferred Co-worker Scale W-113

23. Student Engagement Survey W-114

24. Job Design Choices W-115

25. Cognitive Style W-117

26. Internal/External Control W-118

27. Team Leader Skills W-119

28. Conflict Management Styles W-120

29. Stress Self-Test W-121

30. Work-Life Balance W-122

Self-Assessments

1. A 21st-Century Manager? W-88

2. Emotional Intelligence W-89

3. Learning Tendencies W-91

4. What Are Your Managerial Assumptions? W-92

5. Terminal Values W-93

6. Instrumental Values W-95

7. Diversity Awareness W-97

8. Global Readiness Index W-98

9. Time Orientation W-99

10. Entrepreneurship Orientation W-100

11. Your Intuitive Ability W-101

12. Assertiveness W-102

Student Portfolio Builder

What Is a Student Portfolio?

Planning Your Student Portfolio W-125

Resumé Writing Guide W-125

Interview Preparation Guide W-126

Skill and Outcome Assessment Framework W-126

Getting Started With Your Student Portfolio

Portfolio Format W-128

Career Development Plan—A Portfolio Project W-129

Sample Portfolio Components W-130

RIM Fights to Manage Intellectual Property

Mike Lazaridis, founder of Research in Motion (RIM), sits in his office in Waterloo, Ontario. He is staring at a letter he has just received from a company called Visto claiming a patent infringement.[1] It was just a short time ago that RIM and another company named NTP settled their high profile patent dispute, allowing RIM to continue selling its wildly popular BlackBerry wireless email devices in the United States. But the lawsuit cost RIM $612.5 million in a one-time lump sum to NTP for the use of its technology.[2] Now Lazaridis thinks to himself, "Here we go again."

THE PLAYERS

The story of Mike Lazaridis, inventor, entrepreneur, and multimillionaire, began when he arrived in Canada at age 5 with his Greek parents and three suitcases.[3] He became both an inventor and an entrepreneur at a very young age;[4] he constructed a working pendulum clock out of Lego at age 8[5] and around the age of 10, he and a friend set out to build force fields like the ones they had seen on Star Trek. Lazaridis's passion for wireless technology began in his high-school electronics class. His teacher ran the local amateur radio and television club, and Lazaridis would work in his labs sending signals between Windsor and Detroit.[6]

His first taste of entrepreneurial success came in high school. As a participant of Reach for the Top, an inter-school TV quiz show, Lazaridis was frustrated that the buzzer was too slow and unresponsive, so he decided to design a better one. The show adopted his design, which was a vastly superior switching device that locked out other respondents and flashed a light after the first person buzzed. This invention paid for his first year tuition at the University of Waterloo.[7]

When he arrived at university, Lazaridis was already thinking far beyond the heavy course material and partying that occupied most of his fellow electrical engineering and computer science students.[8] "RIM was part of a long-term plan for Mike Lazaridis," said Larry Smith, an associate economics professor at Waterloo and an early mentor of Lazaridis. "He always intended to start and operate his own company."[9]

In the midst of a recession, Lazaridis, like many of his fellow students, feared becoming a jobless graduate. He was always after his friends to go out and start their own companies. A friend finally asked him, "Mike, if you feel so strongly about it, why don't you start a company?"[10]

In his final year of university, that's exactly what he did. Lazaridis dropped out in 1984 to start his own company with his partner and high school friend, Douglas Fregin, after accepting a $600,000 contract with General Motors to design industrial displays for use in its automotive assembly line.[11] Lazaridis wanted his company to be called "something Research." But all the good names seemed to have been taken so he flipped it around and came up with Research In Motion, a name that seems to have predicted his breakthrough product and his rush to success.[12] Lazaridis is the science mastermind, the production guru, the dreamer, and the one who will find solutions to the customers' problems.[13]

The other main RIM personality is Jim Balsillie. A graduate of the University of Toronto and the Harvard School of Business, Balsillie met and got to know Lazaridis in 1989 as a RIM customer.[14] The two worked well together and in 1992, Lazaridis succeeded in bringing the skilled negotiator Balsillie to the fledgling company as co-CEO. While Lazaridis had the technical knowledge, Balsillie brought his unique brand of salesmanship to the company.[15] Those who know RIM attribute much of its success to the complementary relationship of its two CEOs.[16]

Balsillie brings the business smarts. He is the business maven who as a young man mortgaged his house and invested much of his net worth into Lazaridis's fledgling operation. Balsillie is the corporate strategist, the financial wizard, the negotiator, and the face of the company on Wall Street.[17] Like Lazaridis, Balsillie sees himself an entrepreneur, bringing with him a focus on sales, products, channels, and the markets they are designed to address.[18]

THE COMPANY

Located on the outskirts of Waterloo, RIM's now sprawling complex more closely resembles a suburban outlet mall than the headquarters of one of the most innovative corporations. But within the understated facility is where RIM churns out BlackBerry wireless email devices for the world.[19]

In 1984, the Internet as we know it didn't exist; businesspeople on the road relied on pay phones and hotel phones to stay connected to the office or their customers. Even Lazaridis didn't envisage a world

where you would use a little black device to communicate by email or phone or log onto the Internet.[20] But every entrepreneur looks for opportunities and knows there is real value in solving those problems.[21]

One night shortly after the birth of his first child in 1997, Lazaridis had an epiphany about a wireless email device small enough to fit in a pocket. He spent the night in his basement working on the concept and emailed the plan to his office.[22] Over the next several years, Lazaridis and Balsillie worked tirelessly to turn a bulky prototype into the BlackBerry's sleek and user-friendly current incarnation.[23]

RIM began working with branding strategists in preparation for the official launch of BlackBerry.[24] The first BlackBerry was released in early 1999, running on the Mobitex network, and was immediately successful because it did something no other wireless email device had done. It had just one mailbox, eliminating the need for separate wireless and corporate mailboxes.[25]

While it took five years for RIM to sign up one million subscribers, by 2004 it took less than 10 months to sign up its next million.[26] Today over 50,000 organizations and 3 million subscribers count on a BlackBerry to receive and deliver email messages on the spot.[27]

INDUSTRY AND PATENTS

With increasing competition and market volatility, the drive for organizations to promote and protect innovation has found the patent process becoming a strategic tool in gaining and maintaining market share. A patent has become an increasingly potent weapon for economic warfare, allowing organizations to turn profits through licensing technology or software to competitors but also to control competition by launching infringement suits.[28] Legal experts say that over the past decade, a great number of doubtful patents have been issued in the US. Now, numerous holding companies that own these questionable patents make it their business to try to force companies to pay damages or licence fees by launching infringement suits.[29]

For years, RIM had managed its hold on the market by successfully forcing would-be competitors into court, alleging infringement of its proprietary intellectual property (IP). While RIM is aggressive in enforcing what it sees as patent infringement, its executives insist they aren't trying to wall the technology in, just stake a firm claim so that everyone else has to pay to use it.[30]

RIM is something of a legend for its vigorous use of the courts as a weapon against competitors, so much so that in certain circles it is known as "Lawsuit in Motion."[31] In 2002 alone, RIM filed a total of four separate suits against competitor Good Technologies over allegations of unfair competition and patent infringement. RIM has also filed suit against rival Handspring over alleged patent infringement, although the suit was subsequently dropped after Handspring agreed to use RIM's keyboard.[32] RIM also drove rival Glenayre Electronics right out of the wireless email space altogether after winning a patent dispute.[33]

RIM is fighting for the right to own a piece of the booming wireless email market. Intellectual property is quickly taking its place as a strategic rather than defensive device. Staking a claim to IP has become a profit driver not only for RIM but also for giants such as IBM, Microsoft, Lucent, and the Dow Chemical Company.[34]

ENTER NTP: FIRST CONTACT

RIM first became aware of NTP after receiving a letter from it dated January 27, 2000 inviting RIM to license some of NTP's patents. The only documentation accompanying NTP's letter was a collection of seemingly random marketing materials printed from RIM's website. According to RIM, it promptly responded to NTP with a request for documentation that would explain how NTP's patents would apply to RIM's products. When NTP failed to respond, RIM had no further communication with the company.[35]

WHO IS NTP?

Tom Campana, NTP's founder, loved fixing things as a boy. While others played baseball or joined Boy Scouts, Campana spent his time tinkering with appliances around the family home in Chicago or heading over to a neighbour's house to work on an old car.[36] His father fondly recalls the time his son and a friend built a crude computer in the basement of the family home with machine parts assembled in an old cabinet.[37]

Like Lazaridis, Campana went on to be an inventor and entrepreneur. By the early 1980s, Campana's company, ESA, had developed a paging system that could be used nationally. At the time, pager companies operated on different frequencies, making it impossible to use the same pager in a different city. Campana invented a receiving system that worked on radio waves and allowed pagers to be used across the US. The device was among the first of 50 patents ESA took out.[38]

In 1985, Campana also helped start another company called Telefind Corp. and the two companies developed more innovations to ESA's paging system, including one that could receive up to 14 text messages with a maximum of 500 characters each.[39] However, Campana was a better inventor than businessman and Telefind folded at the end of 1991. Owed nearly half a million dollars, Campana walked away from the bankruptcy with only Telefind's paging technology.[40]

That's when Campana met Washington lawyer Donald Stout. Stout had spent four years as an examiner in the United States Patent and Trademark Office before opening his own successful practice. In 1992, Campana and Stout formed New Technology Products, or NTP. Its only notable asset was a bunch of dusty patents. From the beginning, NTP was never about making things or selling things. It was about protecting potentially valuable ideas, some of which dealt with sending messages to wireless devices.[41]

It's clear that while Campana and Lazaridis share many similarities, their common bond—a drive to make a mark as innovators—is the key factor in turning what should have been a routine legal dispute into an ill-fated battle of wills.[42]

BACK TO THE CHALLENGE

In now-active discussions, NTP said RIM ignored its letter while the Canadian company countered that an internal review concluded it wasn't infringing on NTP's patents. RIM officials insisted they told NTP that but RIM couldn't produce any evidence that it had ever acknowledged NTP's inquiries.[43] However, RIM wasn't the only one that received the unusual letter: apparently NTP approached as many as 40 companies in the wireless space with offers to license and warnings about patent infringement. There was some speculation that RIM was simply a juicy target for NTP, sufficiently prosperous to make going after it worthwhile, but small enough that it couldn't steamroll NTP in the way that larger companies like Motorola or Ericsson might.[44]

THE LEGAL BATTLE TIMELINE

Like many other large conflicts, a variety of smaller campaigns were fought along the way to the decisive ending.

2001

In November 2001, NTP sent RIM a formal notice that it had filed an infringement case in U.S. District Court.[45] RIM's entrepreneurial bosses stood their ground. They regarded NTP as a vile patent "troll"—a company with dormant patents that preys on successful technology companies to extort fees from a hot-selling product.[46] In a press release, RIM stated that it believed that NTP's complaint was unsubstantiated and it would file a legal response to the case.[47] RIM and NTP hurtled toward a court date in Richmond, Virginia. RIM hired a large, venerable Cleveland-based law firm that had a proven track record for wearing down less well-financed opponents with paper filings and delays.[48]

2002

From the outset, RIM and its lawyers didn't seem to take NTP seriously. The company was convinced NTP's patents were junk because they codified technology that was already widely in use by RIM and countless others. In legal jargon, it felt that NTP's patents were "prior art," and therefore invalid.[49] RIM's case hinged on proving that Campana's patents were not valid because other people had already invented wireless email by the time he applied for his patents in 1991. One of RIM's key witnesses was David Keeney, whose company TeckNow had mastered an email process called System for Automated Messages, or SAM, in 1987.[50]

During the trial, RIM's lawyers brought Keeney in to perform a dramatic demonstration for the jury. Using two old laptop computers and a pager, he explained how he could send a text message using SAM. Then he typed "Tommy, the deal is closed," which quickly appeared on the pager.[51] The demonstration was crucial to RIM's case, which was that Keeney's work had predated Campana's by at least four years, making his 1991 patents invalid.

However, to get the demonstration to work, TeckNow and RIM had to secretly swap in newer software. NTP's lawyer spotted the discrepancy and cornered Keeney and RIM officials during cross-examination. After Keeney spent a few more minutes struggling to explain how the newer version was installed, Judge James Spencer cut Keeney off and told the jury to leave the room. "I'll count to 10. I don't want to yell at you," the judge said, admonishing RIM's legal team for the deception.[52] Then he called the jury

members back in and told them to disregard the RIM demonstration.

The demo that was supposed to seal RIM's case became the turning point of the trial. The judge told jurors that the defendant's key piece of evidence was fabricated.[53] In the end, the US jury took only five hours to find in favour of NTP and awarded it a one-time payment of US $23 million, plus unspecified damages totalling another US $30.7 million.[54] NTP applied to Judge Spencer to have the damages "enhanced," in part because of RIM's actions during the trial. The judge agreed, saying the botched demonstration was "fraudulent" and that RIM had "consistently engaged in a variety of questionable litigation tactics throughout the course of this action."[55]

Yet Lazaridis and RIM still didn't settle. Friends and colleagues say Lazaridis is uncompromising by nature. "Mike is the kind of guy who doesn't make business compromises. You know how people plead guilty, even when they know they're innocent, just to get a reduced sentence—Mike wouldn't do that," says Bill Frezza, who worked with RIM on prototype wireless devices in the early 1990s while with Ericsson Canada Ltd.[56] RIM staunchly maintained that it had not infringed any patents. Balsillie called NTP's patents invalid and said there were enough legal errors in the case to give RIM grounds for an appeal.[57]

An NTP lawyer at the time said that based on the court's ruling, he would be seeking an injunction, which would keep RIM from selling its BlackBerry in the US. The judge was also scheduled to review the jury's award, which, depending on the outcome, could triple the award for NTP or dismiss the case.[58] In response to the threat of an injunction, Balsillie said that he thought the chances it could actually happen in the hearings slated for 2003 was extremely improbable. Balsillie further commented that "we intend to seek a review of the verdict and are confident that we will prevail. We believe that in further review the verdict will be overturned."[59]

2003

With the battle between NTP and RIM heating up, U.S. House of Representatives Chief Administrative Officer James Eagan III sent a letter to lawyers on both sides imploring them to settle their differences amicably and pleading with NTP that any injunction that interfered with U.S. Congress's BlackBerrys could jeopardize public interest.[60] The U.S. patent office, under pressure to defend its process, announced that it would review some of NTP's patents, a rare move that some observers ascribed to some BlackBerry fans in very high places.[61] For NTP, this meant that out of the five patents that made it to trial, four were to be re-examined by the patent office.[62]

This news was positive for RIM and added further momentum to its claims that NTP's patents were invalid. In response, NTP said the patent re-examination was routine, the key patents in dispute weren't among those being reviewed, and that its patent was "broad in scope, in that it covers everything that RIM is doing."[63] To help resolve this long-standing battle, Judge Spencer ordered RIM and NTP into mediation.[64]

The courts responded later in the year, denying RIM's motion to overturn the jury verdict and awarding NTP enhanced damages on top of the original $23.1 million. It also ordered RIM to pay 80 percent of NTP's legal fees, or about $5 million.[65] However, the award was stayed pending an appeal, as was an injunction that would have prevented RIM from making, using, or selling handheld devices, services, or software in the US.[66]

As the legal battle between RIM and NTP heated up, a judge for the U.S. District Court for Eastern District of Virginia found that NTP would face irreparable harm if an injunction was not issued. The court added that an injunction was in the public interest because it promotes the protection of rights gained through the patent process.[67] Alternatively, the courts also found that RIM would be irreparably injured without a stay of the injunction pending an appeal.[68] This ruling favoured RIM and allowed RIM to continue selling its products and services in the US without interruption until the issue was resolved.[69]

After the judge's ruling, RIM's pleased lawyers stated, "RIM has always disputed the validity and infringement of the NTP patents and we continue to believe the jury verdict was wrong as both a matter of law and fact."[70]

2004

The U.S. Court of Appeals for the Federal Circuit found that RIM indeed infringed upon NTP's patents, and it lifted the District Court's injunction and referred the case back to the lower court.[71] This was not good for RIM because the case was being sent back to the court that had already ruled in favour of NTP in the first place.[72]

2005

Finally, in March 2005, both sides reached a $450 million patent suit settlement and it seemed like the battle was finally over.[73] The deal seemed designed to make the best of what had become an extremely volatile situation. For a price, RIM and its partners could continue to sell its products, services, and infrastructure free from any claim by NTP or any claims that NTP may have against wireless carriers, partners, or third-party devices that use RIM's BlackBerry Connect or BlackBerry Built-In technology. This meant that RIM could continue to move forward with major partners like Nokia, which started licensing BlackBerry software.[74]

Not surprisingly, given the antagonism that existed between RIM and NTP, the settlement quickly became another dispute and the companies reached an impasse in efforts to finalize the details of the agreement.[75] RIM said it would take legal action to enforce the agreement, accusing NTP of refusing to live up to it. RIM insisted that as it wasn't seeking to reduce the amount of damages or make changes to the pact, the original agreement should remain binding and unambiguous, allowing RIM to carry on with its business free from further litigation or payments to NTP.[76] NTP responded that the deal was being interpreted differently by the two sides regarding virtually every significant provision.[77]

With the threat of an injunction still hanging over it, RIM was left in a precarious position. If the courts ruled against it, RIM could be forced to stop selling the BlackBerry in the US, a market that accounted for about two-thirds of its revenue. To counter any customer concerns about the loss of service, RIM announced that backup technology was in place to keep US BlackBerrys running should the NTP settlement fall apart. Balsillie reassured customers that the alternative technology was designed not to infringe on patents held by NTP.[78]

To further complicate matters, in the same year, RIM scored a small victory when the U.S. Patent and Trademark Office said that it had rejected another patent claim from NTP.[79] At this point, RIM's fight began to attract some very high-powered supporters. Intel Corp. asked the court to reconsider the decision that found RIM guilty of patent infringement. Because RIM operates in Canada, yet offers service to the US market, Intel recommended that the U.S. Court of Appeals in Washington re-examine RIM's case because US courts hadn't properly enforced or defined cross-border patent law. Intel also said the U.S. Congress, not the courts, should set extraterritorial law.[80] NTP countered this support by saying that Intel's filing was late, misleading, and should not be considered. NTP alleged that Intel misrepresented itself by saying it had no direct interest in the outcome of this dispute.[81]

More attention brought even more high-powered support. The Canadian government, Microsoft Corp., Seven Networks, and the Information Technology Association of Canada also submitted court documents to support RIM's case.[82] The US government even said that a US ban on the popular BlackBerry could put essential government services in jeopardy at the local,

state, and federal levels. The federal government asked for 90 days' notice before a US trial court enforced the injunction in the US to ensure public workers could keep using the devices.[83]

The Canadian government weighed in as well and took the extraordinary measure of filing a brief in support of RIM. Like Intel, it was concerned that the case raised the question of whether US patent law could reach over the border. Since BlackBerry emails are routed through RIM's servers in Waterloo, the technology may fall outside of American patent jurisdiction. Because NTP and RIM eventually settled their dispute, that question was never answered by the courts.[84]

When the U.S. patent office finished its review of the five NTP patents, it had rejected all the claims in all of the patents. It looked like RIM had finally won. Still, a victory was premature as NTP had the right to challenge the patent office's decision.[85]

The situation was becoming intense for RIM. With increased competition from Microsoft, Motorola, and a slew of companies that were readying competitive wireless email devices, RIM had to settle soon.[86] RIM's attempt to enforce a $450 million settlement with NTP was denied by an American judge who had to return to the issues of whether to block sales of the email device in the US. Judge Spencer said the court found that the parties did not have a valid and enforceable settlement of agreement and that he would schedule further hearings to consider the remaining issues between the parties.[87]

2006

The Supreme Court declined to hear RIM's contention that the lower court erred in its judgement that US patent law applied to companies whose operations are based in Canada.[88] Judge Spencer made it quite clear that he wanted the parties to settle the matter. Despite industry and government support, he dismissed RIM's claims that the world would end if he granted an injunction, halting RIM's operations in the US. Judge Spencer basically told them to use telephones—still a useful invention after 130 years![89]

With the injunction a reality, RIM and NTP announced late one Friday night that they had settled their high-profile patent dispute by RIM agreeing to pay $612.5 million in a one-time lump sum for the use of the technology, effectively averting a shutdown of the BlackBerry system in the US.[90]

NTP stated, "We are pleased to have reached an amicable settlement with RIM…We believe that the settlement is in the best interest of all parties, including the US government and all other BlackBerry users in the US."[91] RIM executives were also relieved.

THE AFTERMATH?

With the lawsuit finally settled and RIM safe to continue service to the US, the question of what exactly happened and why still remains.

What prompted RIM to settle and why it didn't do so earlier will no doubt be debated by litigation pundits for years to come. RIM's final willingness to pay, although perhaps a good move in putting the matter behind it, contradicts what it maintained all along—that it would not pay.[92] RIM had painted NTP as opportunistic. RIM's stand appeared to be bolstered by the decisions of the U.S. patent office that struck down most of NTP's claims of infringement, but perhaps it recognized that while these decisions could be appealed, reversals of rulings are virtually unknown.[93] But the fact remains that two levels of judiciary found RIM liable for patent infringement. The fact that the patent office felt differently was irrelevant—the issue became how much RIM should pay for the licence to use NTP IP and what amount of damages appropriately reflected its transgressions.[94]

In the end RIM had no cards left to play. With Judge Spencer's patience fading and the threat of an injunction and a court-imposed settlement hanging over its head, RIM knew it had to act. With more than 70 percent of its customer base in the US, it could not allow its US operations to be terminated for any amount of time.[95]

So why did RIM make the decision to fight rather than settle when it first had the chance?

There are many speculative reasons why. One is the lack of independence of the board of directors. RIM is a corporate ecosystem of more than 4,500 employees and 4.9 million subscribers that needs to be properly managed and held accountable by its board.[96] RIM's board of directors is made up of 10 directors, six of whom are insiders (employees of RIM, including both founders Michael Lazaridis and James Balsillie). Balsillie's refusal to bend, together with his and the company's insider clout and majority on the board, no doubt coloured the decision-making process and set up the chain of events that led to the prolonged legal battle.[97]

THE SECOND ROUND

As Mike Lazaridis reaches for the phone to call Jim Balsillie, he looks once again at the letter. They are being sued for patent infringements, this time from a company called Visto. In short order, he finds out that NTP has a stake in Visto. After the outcome of their last "dance" with NTP, Mike Lazaridis ponders what to do now.

1 Tony Smith, "Visto sues Seven, targets RIM," *Register Hardware* (May 2, 2006), on the Web, <www.reghardware.co.uk/2006/05/02/visto_sues_seven_rim/>.

2 "RIM settles with NTP Inc.," *Telegram* (May 4, 2006), retrieved from ABI Inform on August 6, 2006.

3 Barry McKenna, Paul Waldie, and Simon Avery, "Patently absurd," *Globe and Mail* (January 28, 2006), on the Web, <www.blackberryforums.com/blackberry-news/25186-2006-01-28-patently-absurd.html>.

4 Dominic White, "Keeping a finger on the pulse means less wear on the thumbs: The brains and heart behind the BlackBerry pocket computer is evangelical about creative uses of new technology," *The Telegraph* (January 23, 2004), on the Web, <www.telegraph.co.uk/money/main.jhtml?xml=/money/2004/01/23/prof24.xml>.

5 McKenna, Waldie, and Avery, op. cit.

6 Ibid.

7 Chris Hornsey, *Ottawa Citizen* (January 2, 2004).

8 McKenna, Waldie, and Avery, op. cit.

9 Ibid.

10 Ibid.

11 Hornsey, op. cit.

12 McKenna, Waldie, and Avery, op. cit.

13 Anne Marie Squeo and Elena Cherney, "Blackberry Gambles Patent Office Will Be On Its Side in Court," *Wall Street Journal* (January 17, 2006), retrieved from ABI Inform on August 20, 2006.

14 John Greenwood, "James Balsillie & Michael Lazaridis [CEO scorecard, #1]," *Financial Post Business* (November 2005), retrieved from ABI Inform on August 6, 2006.

15 Cindy Waxer, "BlackBerry against the World," *Chief Executive* (October 2005), retrieved from ABI Inform on August 6, 2006.

16 Squeo and Cherney, op. cit.

17 Ibid.

18 "Visionary," *Marketing* magazine (January 16, 2006).

19 Waxer, op. cit.

20 Sarah Scott, "Shock of the new: Offend hierarchies. Make mistakes. Break rules. Let freedom ring. The secrets of successful innovators," *National Post Business* (August 2002), retrieved from ABI Inform on August 6, 2006.

[21] Scott, op. cit.

[22] White, op. cit.

[23] Waxer, op. cit.

[24] Ibid.

[25] "Research In Motion," on the Wikipedia website, <http://en.wikipedia.ord/wiki/Research_In_Motion>.

[26] Andy Holloway, "Top in sales 2005: Don Morrison, Research in Motion," *Canadian Business* (April 25–May 8, 2005), retrieved from ABI Inform on August 6, 2006.

[27] Waxer, op. cit.

[28] Kevin Libin, "RIM's patent wars," *Canadian Business* (September 2, 2003), retrieved from ABI Inform on August 6, 2006.

[29] Robert Thompson, "RIM share down after patent verdict: Debate rages over possible fallout from court findings," (November 23, 2003), retrieved from ABI Inform on August 6, 2006.

[30] Libin, op. cit.

[31] Ibid.

[32] Albert Leonardo, "RIM heading back to court," *Network World Canada* (February 7, 2003), retrieved from ABI Inform on August 6, 2006.

[33] Libin, op. cit.

[34] Libin, op. cit.

[35] "RIM Comments on Patent Complaint," Canada Newswire (November 21, 2001).

[36] McKenna, Waldie, and Avery, op. cit.

[37] Ibid.

[38] Ibid.

[39] Ibid.

[40] Ibid.

[41] Ibid.

[42] Ibid.

[43] Ibid.

[44] Libin, op. cit.

[45] Canada Newswire, op. cit.

[46] McKenna, Waldie, and Avery, op. cit.

[47] Canada Newswire, op. cit.

[48] McKenna, Waldie, and Avery, op. cit.

[49] Ibid.

[50] Ibid.

[51] Ibid.

[52] Ibid.

[53] Ibid.

[54] Andy Holloway, "Is this the end? RIM's future has never looked bleaker," *Canadian Business* (January 30–February 12, 2006), on the Web, <www.canadianbusiness.com/technology/companies/article.jsp?content=20060130_74246_74246>.

[55] McKenna, Waldie, and Avery, op. cit.

[56] Ibid.

[57] Robert Thompson, "RIM loses US patent lawsuit: $US 23.1M damages: BlackBerry maker may face sales ban, denies infringement," *National Post* (November 22, 2002), retrieved from ABI Inform on August 6, 2006.

[58] Thompson, November 22, 2002, op. cit.

[59] Thompson, November 22, 2002, op. cit.

[60] Libin, op. cit.

[61] Libin, op. cit.

[62] David Paddon, "US patent office to review four patents at centre of jury award against RIM," (January 14, 2003), retrieved from ABI Inform on August 6, 2006.

[63] Paddon, op. cit.

[64] "RIM told to mediate patent-infringement suit," *Calgary Herald* (March 3, 2003), retrieved from ABI Inform on August 6, 2006.

[65] "Research In Motion Ltd.: Damages Boosted $8.9 Million in Patent Dispute with NTP," *Wall Street Journal* (May 27, 2003), retrieved from ABI Inform on August 6, 2006.

[66] "Injunction stayed, RIM claims victory in suit," *St. Catharines Standard* (August 6, 2003), retrieved from ABI Inform on August 6, 2006.

[67] Robert Thompson, "Court orders BlackBerry sales injunction: Ruling stayed until appeal," *National Post* (August 6, 2003), retrieved from ABI Inform on August 6, 2006.

68 Thompson, August 6, 2003, op. cit.

69 *St. Catharines Standard*, August 6, 2003, op. cit.

70 Thompson, August 6, 2003, op. cit.

71 Andy Holloway, January 30–February 12, 2006, op. cit.

72 Kevin Restivo, "Canadian BlackBerry maker strikes out in US court," (October 27, 2005), retrieved from ABI Inform on August 6, 2006.

73 Mark Heinzl, "BlackBerry Maker Seeks Enforcement of Patent Accord," *Wall Street Journal* (June 10, 2005), retrieved from ABI Inform on August 6, 2006.

74 Sarah Lysecki, "RIM deals lifts cloud over BlackBerry," *Computer Dealer News* (April 1, 2005), retrieved from ABI Inform on August 6, 2006.

75 Heinzl, op. cit.

76 Ibid.

77 Steve Erwin, "Research in Motion asks court to complete US$450M settlement with NTP," Canadian Press (June 9, 2005), retrieved from ABI Inform on August 6, 2006.

78 "BlackBerry back-up plan in motion," *Ottawa Citizen* (June 18, 2005), retrieved from ABI Inform on August 6, 2006.

79 Kevin Restivo, "RIM hurt by bad numbers: Share sink over forecasts, subscriber growth," *National Post* (September 30, 2005), retrieved from ABI Inform on August 6, 2006.

80 Kevin Restivo, "Intel back RIM in NTP court case," *National Post* (September 2, 2005), retrieved from ABI Inform on August 6, 2006.

81 Restivo, September 2, 2005, op. cit.

82 Ibid.

83 "US Government opposes BlackBerry Ban," *Calgary Herald* (November 12, 2005), retrieved from ABI Inform on August 6, 2006.

84 Katherine Macklem, "Patent Predators," *Maclean's* (March 28, 2005), retrieved from ABI Inform on August 6, 2006.

85 Restivo, September 30, 2005, op. cit.

86 Restivo, October 27, 2005, op. cit.

87 David Paddon, "BlackBerry uncertainty continues as judge says RIM's deal with NTP is invalid," (November 30, 2005), retrieved from ABI Inform on August 6, 2006.

88 Andy Holloway, January 30–February 12, 2006, op. cit.

89 Richard Powers, "Recklessness in motion," *National Post* (March 7, 2006), retrieved from ABI Inform on August 2, 2006.

90 *Telegram*, op. cit.

91 Ibid.

92 Powers, op. cit.

93 Ibid.

94 Ibid.

95 Ibid.

96 Andy Holloway, "Time to Grow up," *Canadian Business* (March 13–March 26, 2006), retrieved from ABI Inform on August 6, 2006.

97 Ibid.

CASES FOR CRITICAL THINKING

CASE 1

Apple Inc.: Where People and Design Create the Future

Apple Inc. exists, paradoxically, as both one of America's greatest business successes and one of its greatest failures to achieve potential. This company ignited the personal computer industry in the 1970s,[1] almost bringing corporate giants such as IBM and Digital Equipment to their knees. At the same time, the history of Apple also demonstrates opportunities that were lost. In this way, Apple Inc. represents a fascinating microcosm of a business as it works to capitalize on its strengths while, at the same time, continuously reinventing itself.

CORPORATE HISTORY

The history of Apple Inc. is one of passion; passion among its founders, its employees, and its loyal users.[2] A pair of Stevens, both of whom showed an interest in electronics from an early age, started the company. Steven Wozniak and Steven Jobs initially utilized their skills at Hewlett Packard and Atari, respectively. Naming their company after the Apple I, the first personal computer built by Wozniak, the two men formed Apple Computer on April 1, 1976.

From its earliest days, the Apple Computer company placed an extreme emphasis on new and innovative styling in its computer offerings. Jobs took a personal interest in the development of new products, including the Lisa and the legendary Macintosh (Mac) with its graphical user interface and 3.5-inch floppy disk. The passion that Apple is so famous for was clearly evident in the design of the Mac. Project teams worked around the clock to develop this machine. The use of graphical icons to create simplified user commands for the Mac was an immensely popular alternative to the command-line structure of DOS. The launch of the Mac, with its increased speed through the use of a Motorola chip and expandable hardware, invigorated Apple's sales. In tandem with the LaserWriter, the first affordable PostScript laser printer for the Mac, and Aldus's Pagemaker, one of the first desktop publishing programs, the Mac presented an ideal method of publishing at a reasonable cost.

When IBM entered the personal computer (PC) market, Jobs recognized the threat it posed to Apple and realized that it was time for Apple to "grow up" and operate in a more business-like fashion. In early 1983, he persuaded John Sculley, then president of Pepsi-Cola, to join Apple as president. The two men clashed almost from the start, and in 1985 Jobs left the company.

In the meantime, IBM continued to develop its products, and by the 1990s IBM PCs and clones were saturating the market. In addition to this competition, Microsoft launched Windows 3.0, a greatly improved version of the Wintel operating system, for use on IBM PCs and clones. Apple had contemplated licensing its Mac operating system to other computer manufacturers and making it run on Intel-based machines, but the idea was rejected—a decision that would ultimately result in Microsoft Windows's domination of the market.

INNOVATIVE DESIGN TO THE RESCUE

Apple continued to rely on its innovative design ideas in order to remain competitive throughout this period. In the 1990s, Apple introduced both the very popular PowerBook notebook computer line and the unsuccessful Newton personal digital assistant. Sculley, having lost interest in the day-to-day operations of Apple, was replaced with Michael Spindler, who had been at Apple since 1980. As chief operating officer, Spindler oversaw a number of innovations, including the PowerMac family—the first Macs to be based on the PowerPC chip, an extremely fast processor that was co-developed with IBM and Motorola. The PowerPC processor allowed Macs to compete with, and in many cases surpass, the speed of Intel's processors. Apple eventually did license its operating system to a number of Mac cloners, but never in significant numbers. After a difficult time in the mid-1990s, Spindler was replaced by Gil Amelio, the former president of National Semiconductor. This set the stage for one of the most famous turnarounds in corporate history.

JOBS'S RETURN

After leaving Apple, Steven Jobs had started NeXT Computer and produced an advanced personal computer with a sleek, innovative design. However, entering the market late in the game and requiring proprietary software, the device never gained a large following and went through many changes in direction. During this time, Jobs also co-founded Pixar Animation Studios. Along with Walt Disney Studios, Pixar produced a number of successful movies, including the popular Toy Story.[3]

In late 1996, Apple announced the purchase of NeXT and Jobs returned to Apple in an unofficial capacity as advisor to the president. However, when Gil Amelio resigned a year later, Jobs accepted the role of "interim CEO" of Apple Computer and wasted no time in making his return felt.

Among a number of changes he made at Apple, Jobs announced an alliance with Apple's former rival, Microsoft. In exchange for US$150 million in Apple stock, Microsoft and Apple worked out a five-year patent cross-licence for their graphical interface operating systems. He also revoked all licences allowing the production of Mac clones, and started offering Macs for sale over the Web. In addition to many new product offerings, Jobs introduced the iMac, with a revolutionary see-through design that has proved popular among consumers through all of its various incarnations. This was soon followed by the iBook, a similarly styled portable computer. By introducing an attractive—and powerful—line of computers at entry-level price points, Apple was once again viewed as an industry innovator.[4]

Unfortunately, however, Apple remains a relatively small player in the personal computer industry. While its computers are very popular among a dedicated set of users, it still commands only a little over 5 percent of the total computer market.[5] It remains locked in a pattern of continual boom and bust cycles, always dependent on its ability to turn out a stream of new product hits.

WHAT DOES THE FUTURE HOLD?

Apple is faced with a stark reality—can it continue to offer both hardware and software solutions in a rapidly changing technology environment? Its early decision to keep its technology proprietary, as opposed to IBM's decision to support an open architecture system, has proved to be a costly strategy to support in the long run.

Some critics argued that Apple should reinvent itself once again, this time concentrating on software. It did that once before, and its OS X operating system and iLife software have proved immensely popular among loyal enthusiasts and first-time users alike. And instead of trying to fight the Wintel system, Apple simply joined it; its new line of Intel-based Macs are faster and more efficient than equivalently powered PCs, and the recent models are able to run Windows XP with the help of software patches. By doing this, Apple cleverly turned a widely held principle of the computer industry on its ear. Years earlier, when Windows licensed its operating system to multiple hardware vendors, Microsoft founder Bill Gates stated that hardware was irrelevant, so long as you had the right operating system. But now, by introducing computers that run OS X and Windows operating systems with equal precision, Steve Jobs is countering that the right hardware will run any operating system.

Part of Apple's new corporate strategy, developed in the face of a massive slowdown in the technology industry, involves taking advantage of the explosion of personal electronic devices (CD players, MP3 players, cell phones, digital cameras, DVD players, and so on) through building Mac applications that add value to those devices. Just as iMovie adds tremendous value to digital cameras, iDVD adds value to DVD players and iTunes adds value to CD and MP3 players. However, Apple recognized the size of the PC market that is not being reached with its Mac applications, and has made iPod and iTunes into Windows-compatible products. In its first week, iTunes sold 1.5 million songs and captured 80 percent of the market share of legal music download.

It is Apple's hope that making its products, including the popular iPhone, the "digital hub" of the new "digital lifestyle" will revitalize Apple's sales and guarantee the company's long-term security. But can the company retain its lead in the valuable music-player niche, especially with Microsoft's commitment to innovation? And though Apple's designs are widely lauded by both critics and customers, will it ever earn a double-digit share of the desktop computer market? Hop online or stroll down to an Apple Store to get a taste of Apple's future.

REVIEW QUESTIONS

1. Why is Apple not a dominant provider of personal computers?

2. Was Apple's decision to use Intel processors, which allow the computers to run either Apple or Windows operating systems, a wise choice? Why or why not?

3. Do you believe that Apple Inc. functions as an open system? Support your answer with specific evidence.

YOU DO THE RESEARCH

1. Locate five sources on the Web that discuss Apple and the history of the personal computer market.

2. Who are the new competitors for Apple as it expands its "digital" presence?

---

[1] Apple Inc., on the Web, <www.apple.com>.
[2] Ibid.
[3] Pixar Animation Studio on the Web, <www.pixar.com>.
[4] Apple Inc., op. cit.
[5] "Apple Computer," *Business Week*, on the Web, April 2006, <www.businessweek.com>.

CASE 2

The Coca-Cola Company: Coke Gets Back to Business

With production facilities in over 200 countries in the world, there are few symbols as internationally recognized as the ubiquitous Coke bottle.[1] To put this into perspective, another American icon, McDonald's, has locations in only 119 countries.[2] As one of the world's best-known brands, Coca-Cola has capitalized on opportunities and thrived. However, the process has not been without upheavals. When Roberto Goizueta, CEO of Coca-Cola for 17 years, passed away on October 18, 1997 after a short battle with lung cancer, the future of the company looked uncertain. During Goizueta's tenure at Coca-Cola, the market value of the company had dramatically increased from US$4 billion to over US$164 billion.[3] This made him one of the greatest value creators in history. While the appointment of CFO Douglas Ivester as his replacement did not immediately allay the concerns of the financial market, the value of Coke stock continued to increase until mid-1998. Since then, the value of the stock has declined. The question, then and now, on many investors' minds remains: "Can Coke recapture its previous growth pace and stock value without Goizueta's legendary leadership?"

COCA-COLA'S GLOBAL DOMINANCE

The larger a company is the harder it is to continue to grow at a steady pace. This continues to be the major challenge facing the Coca-Cola Company. In 2005, both profits and volume reached a record high for the company.[4] In that year, annual per capita consumption of Coca-Cola products increased slightly in the North American, African, and Latin American markets. In East Asia, South Asia, and the Pacific Rim, both volume and annual per capita consumption decreased in the same period, while in the European Union, volumes and consumption remained steady. The greatest gains in 2005 were seen in the North Asia, Eurasia, and Middle East markets. The highest levels of per capita consumption are still found in North America, Europe, and Latin America.

However, in spite of the fact that there is a much lower consumption rate internationally than there is in the United States, more than 70 percent of Coca-Cola's income is generated outside of the United States.[5] This is primarily due to population differentials among the world's regions. Coca-Cola, recognizing the importance of international sales, has been very sensitive to local market conditions in developing products that will meet the varied taste preferences of consumers in different countries. In fact, Coca-Cola produces more than 400 brands worldwide in addition to its flagship brands, Coke and Diet Coke.[6] The bottling and distribution system is also adapted to local needs. For instance, all bottlers are local companies either independently owned or only partially owned by the Coca-Cola Company. In this way, Coca-Cola gains the benefits of intrinsic local knowledge. The distribution systems range from boats in Indonesia, four-legged power in the Andes, to fleets of trucks in the United States. In each case, local conditions are considered. Coca-Cola prides itself on acting as a local citizen in a global marketplace.

COKE'S BUSINESS

Coca-Cola has achieved its dominance in the global marketplace through its consistent loyalty to the Coke heritage and the image and standards that it conveys.

Coca-Cola, historically, has not been a company noted for innovation; it was almost 100 years after the creation of Coke that it introduced Diet Coke. After the disastrous introduction of New Coke, there was reluctance to tamper with the original Coke formula. As Douglas Daft, former chairman and CEO, explained in his 2002 letter to share owners, "Responsibility for the world's most beloved and valuable brand requires extreme care in how, when, and why we extend it. We don't risk consumer loyalty to the brand or seek an artificial bump in volume by spinning out product after product to chase the latest fad."[7] These sentiments are no different today under Neville Isdell's leadership.

Historically, carbonated beverages have been the backbone of the Coca-Cola Company; in 2005 they accounted for 80 percent of sales.[8] Coca-Cola's acknowledgment of changing consumer tastes, however, has fostered a continued expansion of its line of noncarbonated beverages. Growth in sales of noncarbonated beverages varied across their portfolio in 2005. The largest increase was seen in energy drinks, with growth of 200 percent, making Coke number three in the United States energy drinks market in less than a year. This growth has been fuelled both internally and through acquisitions and licensing agreements.[9] Coca-Cola is hoping to achieve profitability through economies of scale and by capitalizing on its existing distribution system.

The Coca-Cola Company has positioned itself for growth by moving key decision making closer to local markets and by fostering deeper connections to consumers. It has also restructured, with a management team coordinating a new, nimble, and entrepreneurial network. As one of his first acts during his time as CEO, Daft axed 6,000 employees, many of them middle and senior managers at its headquarters in Atlanta. There is now, under Isdell's leadership, a 15-person executive management team in place, including six executive vice-presidents who are chief operating officers for the Eurasian, African, North American, Pacific, European Union, and the Latin American groups. Twenty-five division and operations presidents report to the chief operating officers in each of the international regions.[10]

This group of individuals, along with Coca-Cola employees and partners worldwide, are responsible for implementing what Isdell calls the "Manifesto for Growth" that was developed in 2004.[11] The manifesto includes statements concerning the mission, vision, values, capabilities, incentives, goals, metrics, and growth paths of the company. Sustainable growth for Coca-Cola is defined in terms of the five P's: Profit—maximum return for the shareholder; People—be a great place to work; Partners—nurture mutual loyalty; Portfolio—brands that anticipate and satisfy people's

needs; and Planet—responsible global citizens who make a difference. The manifesto also provides a 10-year objective for each. According to Isdell, all five elements must be equal, obvious, and interconnected with each component of Coke's business model. *Products* are what Coke wants in the marketplace, and they also make possible what the company aspires to become over the long term. The *portfolio* of brands that are made available to consumers through Coke's *partners* will allow the company to generate the profits it needs to reach its goals for *people* and the *planet*. As part of the Manifesto for Growth, Isdell and his team have identified strategic growth paths: accelerate the growth rate of core brands, especially Coke's historical product, carbonated beverages; expand the portfolio of products; develop products, such as tea and soy beverages, in the health awareness area; nurture production system health in all the markets; create customer value; and develop adjacent businesses, such as iCoke and ingredient licensing.[12]

Will the restructuring and the new strategic initiatives identified by Neville Isdell help Coca-Cola achieve its mission of "benefiting and refreshing everyone it touches," as well as regain the growth and value experienced under Roberto Goizueta?

REVIEW QUESTIONS

1. Apply Henri Fayol's five rules of management to the Coca-Cola case.

2. Consider the following quote from Coca-Cola's statement on diversity: "The Coca-Cola Company commits to excel among *Fortune* 500 companies in promoting and fostering

equal opportunity in compensation, promotion, and career advancement for all employees in all levels and areas of the business, regardless of race, color, gender, religion, age, national origin, or disability, and to promote and foster an environment of inclusion, respect, and freedom from retaliation."[13] Relate this quote to the case and to the behavioural approaches to management.

3. How does Coca-Cola score on the eight attributes of performance excellence?

4. Do you think Neville Isdell will be successful in regaining the growth and value experienced under Roberto Goizueta?

YOU DO THE RESEARCH

1. While stock prices have declined since 1998, what has happened to revenues and income over the same period?

2. What are Coca-Cola's underlying beliefs? See the message at <www.thecocacolacompany.com/ourcompany/ourbeliefs.html>.

3. Read Coca-Cola's statement on diversity at <www.thecoca-colacompany.com/ourcompany/ourDiversity.html>.
   What insights does it provide?

[1] Annual Report 2005, on the Web, <www.thecoca-colacompany.com/investors/annual_other_reports.html>.

[2] McDonald's website, <www.mcdonalds.com>.

[3] "Coke CEO Roberto Goizueta Dies at 65," on the Web, October 18, 1997, <www.cnn.com>.

[4] Annual Report 2005, op. cit.

[5] Ibid.

[6] "Brands," on the Web, <www.thecoca-colacompany.com>.

[7] Annual Report 2002, on the Web, op. cit.

[8] Andrew Ward, "Coke hopes for next real thing," *National Post* (March 31, 2006), p. FP.7.

[9] "2005 Annual Review," on the Web, <www.thecoca-colacompany.com/citizenship/company_reports.html>.

[10] "Leadership," on the Web, <www.thecoca-colacompany.com/ourcompany>.

[11] "Manifesto for Growth," on the Web, <www.thecoca-colacompany.com/ourcompany.>.

[12] Speech by Neville Isdell, on the Web, <www.thecoca-colacompany.com/presscenter/viewpoints_isdell_cies2006.html.>.

[13] "Diversity," Task Force Report, on the Web, <www.thecoca-colacompany.com/ourcompany>.

CASE 3

Barenaked Ladies: Changing the World One Song at a Time

With sales of over 12 million records, the Barenaked Ladies are one of Canada's most successful bands. Not your typical rock stars, these five males are self-effacing celebrities and nice lads who devote their spare time to their families and supporting local causes such as wind power and the New Democratic Party. They're so Canadian it hurts.[1] With continued popularity worldwide, can this quintessentially Canadian band continue their success while promoting a more ethical focus?

A CHEEKY BEGINNING

An oddball success story, the Ladies (actually five males: Steven Page, Ed Robertson, Tyler Stewart, and brothers Jim and Andy Creeggan) defied music and industry norms from the start. Working from the basement rec rooms of their parents' homes, in 1991 the group released an independent cassette, which sold an unprecedented 80,000 copies domestically. Almost unheard of for a new act, their debut album, Gordon, sold 500,000 copies in Canada.[2]

Formed in 1988 and then largely written off by the mid-1990s as a novelty act, the group lost founding member Andy Creeggan, who left the band in 1995 to further study music. With new keyboard player Kevin Hearn in tow, the group headed south of the border only to find greater fame. American audiences welcomed the band's melodic songs and tongue-in-cheek lyrics. Although the Ladies' US breakthrough came with its 1996 live recording, Rock Spectacle, it was the next album that catapulted them well into music's upper echelons. Featuring the hyperactive rap of One Week, a No. 1 hit on the US Billboard charts, the four-million-selling Stunt established the Ladies as superstars capable of filling arenas and stadiums from Portland, Oregon, to Poughkeepsie, New York.[3]

Their sense of humour has, on occasion, plunged the Barenaked Ladies into the hot waters of political correctness: their ironic name got the group banned from Toronto's city hall early in their career when one official decreed that it objectified women. More recently, Métis leaders objected to a line from "If I Had $1,000,000," a satirical song that calls the wearing of fur "cruel," because they said that it threatened their livelihood.[4]

"That got us into a lot of trouble in Canada," said guitarist Page. "We ended up having First Nations people—the Dene, the Métis, and also the Inuit up in the Northwest Territories—threaten to picket outside of our show because fur is a traditional way of life that fuels their economy. They were really upset about that line. You do start learning to be careful or choose your words wisely, and really have a reason for them, even the ones that seem non-sensical."[5]

MEANING FOR THE MASSES

Over the last decade, the Ladies have taken a more personal, serious approach to their music. Now, the band's songs tend to be more thoughtful. "Some of it is born out of frustration with the glibness of modern culture and knowing how much we participated in that," concedes Page. "As a songwriter, I asked myself whether I've put enough of my heart in the music in the past, or whether I've spent too much time trying to shield the emotional side of things." One of the themes of their album Maroon was about taking action—going out and doing something, instead of sitting and talking about it.[6]

Page and Robertson have lent their faces to an information campaign sponsored by the non-profit organization Artists Against Racism. And recently, along with Stewart, they made a series of public service announcements on behalf of World Vision, the Third World relief agency.[7] "For us," says Page, "with the events going on in the world and our country's unfortunate slide to the right of the spectrum, it was inevitable that we carried on with some of the political themes we explore. But for me, it was truly about making those situations personal."[8]

According to Robertson, Page, the band's most engaged activist, is its "social and political watchdog." While a music superstar may seem an unlikely participant in serious dialogue over the need to balance corporate, social, and environmental agendas, Page's role and approach

shows a trend toward broadening the array of stakeholders working together to better society. "We couldn't succeed without the protest singer, without the grass-roots, without the anger and fear that sometimes generates change," Page says. "But I also have an opportunity as a mainstream pop singer to bridge a gap between the place where public opinion starts and corporate, provincial, and national policy gets made."[9]

Page says he knows fans come for a laugh, but he hopes they're also willing to at least listen to the band's message. The singer has long been vocal about his progressive views, campaigning with the NDP, wearing a "Vote Solar" shirt on stage, serving on the board of directors for World Wildlife Fund Canada, and participating in WindShare, a renewable-energy co-op in his hometown of Toronto.[10]

"We need to reduce our overall demand on the planet's resources and we have realized that only with more people making better consumer choices will such environmental initiatives become economic successes," Page explains. "We are proud to work with companies who show dedication to our planet and who understand that sustainability is the only way forward."[11]

A GREENER FUTURE

Barenaked Planet is the Barenaked Ladies' campaign to communicate to fans about environmental and social issues that have become increasingly important to them. On their Barenaked Planet tour, the Ladies collaborated with Reverb, a non-profit organization, to coordinate several different "greening" mechanisms, such as helping fuel the tour buses and trucks with

biodiesel, offsetting the energy used at each show with wind power, recycling, and using compostable materials backstage.[12]

At first, the band just set up an eco-village at concerts, offering fans an opportunity to meet not-for-profits and companies with new products with a green focus. "But then we're standing there on stage saying, 'Go check out the eco-village,' and backstage, there's all this waste. Our industry had never really paid any attention to the amount of waste that goes on—whether it's food waste or the fact that you have buses and trucks and, of course, air travel," Page says. "So we decided to work with Reverb a little closer this time and have them help us design a smaller footprint for our tour."[13]

So why are the Ladies doing all of this? It's their way of addressing the serious threats of global warming, industrial pollution, forest destruction, our overdependence on oil, and a host of other challenges.[14] "We're looking forward to reducing the amount of waste and CO_2 emissions we create on tour," says bassist/vocalist Jim Creeggan. "Now that technologies like biodiesel, renewable energy, and compostable products are available, it has made it possible for us to take action against environmental threats like global warming and deforestation. Ultimately, at the end of a tour, all we would like to leave behind is our music."[15]

To help offset carbon emissions, fans can buy a Barenaked Planet offset bumper sticker at the eco-village, which will allow them to neutralize the carbon emissions from the drive to and from the show. Since its inception, Barenaked Ladies fans have bought enough stickers to neutralize more than 1.6 million kilometres of driving![16]

But Barenaked Planet is not just for the fans. The band has committed to a number of environmental initiatives such as the use of biodiesel in all of the band's trucks and buses, recycling and the use of compostables backstage, organic merchandise, printed materials on recycled papers with soy inks, and wind energy offset for every show through their partners at Native-Energy, a Native American energy company. Through these partnerships, the band has neutralized 300 tonnes of CO_2 by offsetting the power consumed at the concerts and 27,000 kilograms of CO_2 were kept from going into the atmosphere by fuelling the touring fleet with biodiesel. The band also sells organic cotton merchandise and biodegradable food service items, recycles computer paper and donations of partially used batteries, and even collects used guitar strings and has them re-crafted into unique, artisan bracelets.[17] Barenaked Ladies leaves no stone unturned in their quest for a greener planet.

REVIEW QUESTIONS

1. Could the Barenaked Ladies' environmental values be considered ethical behaviour?

2. Using the four alternative views of ethical behaviour, describe which view would be closest to the Barenaked Ladies' philosophy.

3. What factors influence the Barenaked Ladies' ethical behaviour?

YOU DO THE RESEARCH

1. Can the Barenaked Ladies' approach to ethical management work in the business world?

2. Find five Internet sites that discuss ethics and social responsibility, and identify an important ethical lesson or insight that is provided on each site.

[1] Brian D. Johnson, "Barenaked brains," *Maclean's* (October 20, 2003), p. 58.

[2] Nicholas Jennings, "Naked ambition," *Maclean's* (March 8, 1993), p. 54.

[3] Nicholas Jennings, "Ladies on top: Canada's Barenaked Ladies are riding high with a new album, a documentary, and a new maturity," *Maclean's* (September 25, 2000), p. 66.

[4] Jennings, 1993, op. cit.

[5] Sarah van Schagen, "The Barenaked Truth: Barenaked Ladies vocalist Steven Page lays bare his hopes for a green future," *Grist* (December 18, 2006), on the Web, <http://grist.org/news/maindish/2006/12/18/BNL/index.html>.

[6] Jennings, 2000, op. cit.

[7] Ibid.

[8] Barenaked Ladies website, <www.bnlmusic.com/news/>.

[9] Randall Anthony Mang, "Common Ground," *The Globe and Mail* (June 27, 2005), on the Web, <http://www.cbsr.bc.ca/files/CSR-CanadaPartnerships-toGMFINAL.pdf>.

[10] van Schagen, op. cit.

[11] "'Barenaked Ladies Are Me' CD covers printed on Domtar EarthChoice® environmentally responsible paper," Domtar news release (September 12, 2006), on the Domtar website, <http://www.domtar.com/en/paper/products/earthchoice/3122.asp>.

[12] Barenaked Planet website, <www.reverbrock.org/barenakedplanet/>.

[13] van Schagen, op. cit.

[14] "Bare Naked [sic] Ladies Charge The Planet: Full-blown environmentally friendly tour unveiled," *IGN Music* (October 5, 2006), on the Web, <http://music.ign.com/articles/737/737423p1.html>.

[15] Ibid.

[16] Barenaked Ladies website, op. cit.

[17] Ibid.

CASE 4

United Parcel Service: Where Technology Rules a Total Quality Road

United Parcel Service (UPS), the world's largest package distribution company, transports more than 3.75 billion parcels and documents annually. With more than 427,000 employees worldwide, 1,788 operating facilities, 1,838 daily flights, 91,700 vehicles, and the world's largest private communications system, UPS provides service in more than 200 countries.[1] How does UPS control such a vast and extended enterprise and still fulfill its commitment to serving the needs of the global marketplace?

CORPORATE HISTORY

In 1907, there was a great need for private messenger and delivery services. Only a few homes had private telephones, and luggage, packages, and personal messages had to be carried by hand. The U.S. Postal Service did not yet have the parcel post system. To help meet this need, an enterprising 19-year-old, James E. "Jim" Casey, borrowed $100 from a friend and established the American Messenger Company in Seattle, Washington. Despite stiff competition, the company did well, largely because of Jim Casey's strict policies on customer courtesy, reliability, round-the-clock service, and low rates. These principles, which guide UPS even today, are summarized by Jim's slogan: "Best Service and Lowest Rates."[2]

Obsessed with efficiency from the beginning, the company pioneered the concept of consolidated delivery—combining packages addressed to certain neighbourhoods onto one delivery vehicle. In this way, manpower and motorized equipment could be used more efficiently. The 1930s brought more growth. By this time, UPS provided delivery services in all major American West Coast cities, and a foothold had been established on the other coast with a consolidated delivery service in the New York City area. Many innovations were

adopted, including the first mechanical system for package sorting. During this time, accountant George D. Smith joined the firm and helped make financial cost control the cornerstone of all planning decisions. The name United Parcel Service was adopted—"United" to emphasize the unity of the company's operations in each city, "Parcel" to identify the nature of the business, and "Service" to indicate what was provided to customers.[3] In 1975, Toronto was Canada's first city to enjoy UPS services and UPS's first international location.

In 1953, UPS resumed air service, which it had discontinued during the Depression, offering two-day service to major cities on the east and west coasts. Packages flew in the cargo holds of regularly scheduled airlines. Called UPS Blue Label Air, the service grew and by 1978 it was available in every state of the US, including Alaska and Hawaii. The demand for air parcel delivery increased in the 1980s at the same time that federal deregulation of the airline industry created new opportunities for UPS. Deregulation resulted in the established airlines reducing the number of flights being offered or abandoning routes altogether. To ensure dependability, UPS began to assemble its own jet cargo fleet, the largest in the industry. With growing demand

for faster service, UPS entered the overnight air delivery business, and by 1985 UPS Next Day Air service was available in continental US and Puerto Rico; Alaska and Hawaii were added later. That same year, UPS entered a new era, adding international air package and document service, linking the United States and six European nations.

UPS TODAY

In 1988, UPS received authorization from the U.S. Federal Aviation Administration (FAA) to operate its own aircraft, thus officially becoming an airline. Recruiting the best people available, UPS merged a number of different organizational cultures and procedures into a seamless operation called UPS Airline. UPS Airline was the fastest-growing airline in FAA history, formed in little more than one year with all the necessary technology and support systems. UPS Airline features some of the most advanced information systems in the world to support flight planning, scheduling, and load handling.[4]

Today, the UPS system moves more than 14 million packages and documents daily around the globe. Packages are processed using advanced information technology and are transported by the company's own aircraft, chartered aircraft, and a fleet of delivery vehicles. While international package delivery operations constitute a substantial part of UPS's business, an important segment of the business is providing supply chain solutions for UPS customers.[5] In 2003, the company introduced a new brand logo representing a new, evolved UPS and adopted the acronym UPS as its formal name, indicating its broad range of capabilities and services beyond package delivery.[6] Today, UPS emphasizes its customer service orientation with the advertising slogan: "What can brown do for you?"

INNOVATIONS AT UPS

Known for its technological innovations, UPS keeps its package delivery and non-package operations on the cutting edge. Technology at UPS spans an incredible range, from specially designed package delivery vehicles to global computer and communications systems. UPS Worldport is the latest example of technology being used to increase efficiency and quality in the company's package operations. Located in Louisville, Kentucky, Worldport is a 360,000 square metre facility outfitted with overhead cameras to read smart labels and process documents, small packages, and irregular-shaped objects at a rate of over 300,000 packages per hour as they move along conveyors with astounding speed. Worldport also allows UPS to consolidate volume at a single location, thereby enabling the company to use larger and more efficient aircraft and streamlining the sorting at regional hubs throughout the world. UPS has planned a one billion dollar expansion of World-

port to be completed by 2010, building an additional 90,000 million square metres of space and increasing the number of conveyers to more than 32,000.[7]

UPS Supply Chain Solutions, the company's non-package operation, targets a variety of supply chain challenges faced by its customers, including helping them manage overseas suppliers, the logistics of post-sales parts and servicing, and order processing. This operation also coordinates transportation, vendors, contracts, and shipments, and simplifies international trade and regulatory compliance. UPS Supply Chain Solutions relies on a physical and virtual infrastructure for managing the flow of goods, information, and funds for different customers.[8] For example, through UPS Trade Direct Cross Border, Canadian company G3 was able to boost efficiency and reduce costs in the shipment of high-end backcountry ski equipment from Canada to hundreds of specialty shops and resorts throughout the United States. UPS consolidated shipments in Canada before moving them through customs, then repacked individual orders in the US and shipped them at domestic rates. This streamlined G3's supply chain, enhanced customer service, and greatly reduced the company's costs.[9] Another supply chain solution was provided to TeddyCrafters, enabling that company to better manage the transportation and distribution of supplies from Asian and North American vendors. UPS designed a comprehensive inbound distribution system for Teddy-Crafters that improved inventory management and provided for weekly restocking of the chain's

retail stores. In each of these cases, and many others, UPS uses its own technological expertise in the transportation and distribution of documents and packages to help other companies achieve efficient, rapid, and low-cost solutions for all stages of their supply chains.[10]

THREE TRENDS DRIVING THE INDUSTRY

Frederick Smith of FedEx, a UPS competitor, identifies three trends driving the package delivery business: globalization, cost cutting, and Internet commerce.[11] *Globalization* will cause the world express-transportation market to explode to more than US$150 billion in value. While DHL Worldwide Express is a major player in the international market, UPS and FedEx are expanding at a rapid pace. Lee Hibbets of Air Cargo Management Group in Seattle states, "FedEx is seen as more aggressive, whereas UPS is a little bit more methodical and long term."[12] *Cost cutting* among customer firms, primarily by cutting inventory, fits into the package-firms' delivery systems. Technology plays a significant part in a delivery company's ability to assist customers in cutting their inventories. UPS and FedEx are competing fiercely in using technology to facilitate cost-cutting efforts. *Internet commerce*, the third trend, generates a huge need for shipping. Package delivery companies hope to capture the lion's share of the Internet commerce shipping business.

It remains to be seen who will win out in the package delivery wars, but UPS is a leader in the market. Its ability to track packages around the world is a testament to the value of technology in the workplace. With technological innovations generating higher productivity, the future for package delivery remains bright. Moreover, with attention being given to the challenges of supply chain management, package delivery companies like UPS can apply their technological expertise in developing additional business opportunities.

REVIEW QUESTIONS

1. Describe UPS's competitive advantage.

2. How does UPS approach customer relationship management?

3. How does technology enable UPS to be a quality-driven organization?

YOU DO THE RESEARCH

1. Describe the general environmental factors that affect UPS and its competitors in the package delivery industry.

2. Identify the stakeholders for UPS, and explain how those stakeholders potentially influence the company.

3. Describe the organizational culture at UPS and the role that it plays in the company's success.

[1] "UPS Fact Sheet," Media Kits on the Web, <www.pressroom.ups.com>.

[2] United Parcel Service homepage, <www.ups.com>.

[3] Rachael Kamuf, "UPS Upping Employment as well as Technology," *Business First*, March 9, 1998.

[4] Information on the history of UPS services taken from the company website, <www.ups.com>.

[5] "Company History," About UPS on the Web, op. cit.

[6] "The UPS Logo: A Brief History," Fact Sheet on the Web, op. cit.

[7] "UPS Worldport Expansion Project," Fact Sheet on the Web, op. cit.

[8] UPS Supply Chain Solutions on the Web, op. cit.

[9] Consumer Goods and Retail Case Studies, on the Web, <www.ups-scs.com/solutions/case_consumer.html>.

[10] Ibid.

[11] Karen Walker, "Brown is Beautiful," *Airline Business* (November 1997), p. 46.

[12] Ibid.

CASE 5

Bata: One Step at a Time

With head offices in Toronto, Bata Ltd. has a worldwide reach. Its operations span five continents managed by four regional business units, with more than 40 production facilities across 26 countries. Bata serves more than 1 million customers per day. While impressive, Bata is not the company it once was. Can Bata, with annual sales of roughly $3 billion, successfully maintain operations in 4,600 stores spread across 68 countries?[1]

T.&A. BATA SHOE COMPANY

In 1894, siblings Tomáš, Anna, and Antonín Bata registered the T.&A. Bata Shoe Company in Zlin, Czechoslovakia. From the beginning, Bata Shoe Company brought innovation and creativity to century-old traditions of the one-man cobbler's workshop. The next year, Tomáš took over sole leadership when brother Antonín joined the army, followed shortly by Anna, who left the company after she got married. The year 1909 brought expansion for Bata, with the first export sales through agencies in Germany, the Balkans, and in the Middle East.[2]

By 1917, sales had reached 2 million pairs of shoes per year produced by some 5,000 employees. Over the next two decades, the company continued to grow by importing advanced production equipment, and creating prosperity in the communities in which it operated by building stores, housing, schools, and hospitals. The company expanded its international operations again in 1929 by building factories in Switzerland, Germany, England, France, Yugoslavia, Poland, the Netherlands, the United States, and India. By 1939, Bata operated 63 companies in various industries, but footwear remained the core business, with 60 million pairs sold per year in more than 30 countries.[3]

COMING TO CANADA

With Tomáš's death in 1932, his son, Thomas Bata, took over the company leadership and further diversified into the production of tires, aircraft, bicycles, and machineries. Fleeing wartorn Europe in the late 1930s with about 100 Czech workers and their families, Thomas Bata landed in Canada, where he set up a flagship shoe-making plant in Batawa, a town he christened in eastern Ontario. Batawa slowly became the quintessential company town, and in its heyday in the 1960s, the population reached 1,200. The company made four million pairs of shoes and boots a year, which were sold across Canada and around the world. Bata owned all the land within the town, 480 hectares, and built cookie-cutter bungalows for the workers to rent, adding schools and churches for the families. Workers played on Bata baseball and hockey teams and shopped at the company-owned grocery store.[4]

THE UPS AND DOWNS OF BATA

By 1960, Bata's headquarters were officially relocated in Toronto under the leadership of Thomas Bata and the company focused on expanding its international reach through new factories serving new local markets.[6] During its heyday, Bata was the world's largest shoemaker, with the Canadian operation hitting its peak in the late 1970s when it produced about 4.6 million pairs of dress shoes and boots. In the early 1980s, Bata operated 250 stores across Canada and was considered a Canadian icon and a family-destination store.

But the company, with estimated annual sales of $3 billion in 68 countries, couldn't compete with a flood of Chinese imports being offered at lower-priced retailers.[7] Due to this increased competition, product trend missteps, and succession issues, operations waned over the years, leading to losses in the millions in the 1990s. This all lead to a painful restructuring, and the company closed the Batawa facility in 1999.[8]

However, Bata was not willing to be complacent and slowly disappear. By 2000, Bata had expanded into Russia, Poland, Croatia, and Slovenia, as well into new markets in China, with the opening of the Bata procurement centre in Guanzhou and a distribution partnership for the opening of Bata retail stores.[9] Recognizing the increased competition from discount retailers such as Wal-Mart Canada and Payless Shoes, the once-giant Bata chain began phasing out the last 30 shoe stores it operated in Canada. Instead, Bata focused on its 160 Athletes World stores across the country. While the firm said it may also eventually return to Canada with the superstore concept it now operates in Europe, for the moment it will introduce Web shopping from Bata Europe.

The closing of Bata's remaining stores in Canada came as no surprise to consultant Anthony Stokan of the Toronto-based Anthony Russell Inc.[11] Stokan said the lack of consistency in being either a family-shoe destination or a casual-shoe store also contributed to the company's retail demise.[12] "They couldn't quite figure out who they were," Stokan said. "Historically, they were a great family shoe store in the Sixties, Seventies and even in the early Eighties. But they haven't had any direction in terms of their footwear collection in the last 15 years, and they had so many different store formats."[13] In addition, the company went through a number of management changes in the 1990s, bringing in people from outside its ranks until Thomas Bata Jr., grandson of the founder, returned to take over in 2001, having left the company when his efforts to take it public and raise its marketing profile were opposed by several board members.[14]

Despite succession changes and competitive challenges, Bata still remains one of Canada's great family business success stories, with a formidable footprint. Across the globe, Bata employs more than 50,000 people and makes 140 million pairs of shoes a year in 46 facilities. This now also includes the Czech Republic, where Bata received a hero's welcome after returning to restart operations.[15]

REVIEW QUESTIONS

1. Describe Bata's international business strategy. Would you consider Bata a multinational corporation?

2. If you were Bata's top management, how would you deal with successfully managing business units in four very different geographic regions?

3. What benefits and challenges do you foresee if Bata continues its global expansion strategy?

YOU DO THE RESEARCH

1. How successful is Bata against competitors in North America?

2. How should Bata reinvent its image if it decides to re-enter the Canadian market?

3. Should businesses like Bata receive protection from the Canadian government against overseas competition?

[1] Brian Dunn, "Bata to close units; Aldo to merge nameplates," *Footwear News* (March 28, 2005), p. 50.

[2] "Bata Heritage – 1894 to Now," on the Bata website, <www.bata.com/about_us/heritage/heritage_1894_now.php>.

[3] Ibid.

[4] Thomas Watson, "Bata shoes," *Canadian Business* (September 2, 2003), p. 69.

[5] Tanya Davies, "When the jobs go," *Maclean's* (August 14, 2000), p. 23.

[6] "Bata Heritage – 1894 to Now," op. cit.

[7] "Bata to close remaining stores in Canada," CBC News (March 15, 2005), on the CBC website, <www.cbc.ca/money/story/2005/03/15/bata-050315.html>.

[8] Watson, op. cit.

[9] "Bata Heritage – 1894 to Now," op. cit.

[10] CBC News, op. cit.

[11] Ibid.

[12] Ibid.

[13] Ibid.

[14] Ibid.

[15] Watson, op. cit.

CASE 6

Hannah's Ice Cream: A Hypothetical Study of Entrepreneurship

Forty years after inheriting the small restaurant called Hannah's from her parents, Hannah Bryant had grown the business from a small lunch counter to a thriving enterprise in Elgin Beach, on the shores of Lake Huron in Ontario. An icon on the main street, Hannah's is a small café-style restaurant that sells ice cream cones, sundaes, milkshakes, and other ice cream products. Hannah's had thrived in part due to its location, but primarily it had been successful because the owner was well liked by the community, customers, and her staff.

One of the reasons for Bryant's success was her treatment of her employees. She compensated the workers above minimum wage, provided incentives, held employee improvement meetings, and listened to the staff's ideas. This was really important because Bryant hired mostly teenagers. Since most of the customers were teenagers and families with small children, Bryant knew the kids would listen to teenagers because they would not be intimidated. Other customers responded well to her staff because they were enthusiastic, motivated, and friendly, and provided great customer service.

Bryant's business was a great success. In her last year, she had after-tax profits of $150,000.

ENTER IKE TELLONI

Ever since he was a kid growing up in Elgin Beach, Ike Telloni had dreamed of following in his parents' footsteps and running his own business. In elementary school, he got a taste of the entrepreneurial life by washing cars and shovelling walkways in his neighbourhood. By high school, he was managing a team of local kids and had a roster of steady clients across the community. He had excelled at his business courses in high school and continued his business studies at the University of

Ottawa, receiving numerous awards for student entrepreneurship, involvement, and leadership.

After graduation, Telloni began his career at the Waterloo Ice Cream Company, moving quickly from a sales representative to regional sales director for southern Ontario. While Telloni enjoyed his job, he felt there was little opportunity for growth with the company. In addition, 10 years of constant travelling had started to take a toll on him and his young family. Realizing he needed a change, Telloni began to look for other opportunities closer to home when he found that Hannah's Ice Cream was for sale. Since his parents and family still lived in Elgin Beach, Telloni thought it would be an ideal place to raise his three small children.

Telloni knew that owning any small business is a risk but he felt that Hannah's would allow him to combine his entrepreneurial dream with the experience he gained while working at the Waterloo Ice Cream Company. Being self-employed and moving to Elgin Beach would mean a big change for Telloni and his family, but he felt the chance to be his own boss was well worth the risk. Telloni had some money saved, and after discussing the purchase with his friends and family, he took out a bank loan and put in an offer on Hannah's. By the end of the week,

Telloni was once again a small business owner.

ADJUSTMENTS

Telloni was glad to leave the corporate world behind. He had become tired of the constant travel and lack of control. A small business appealed to him because he could be self-directed and would not have to report to a boss. Telloni felt his strengths were in sales (from his old company), accounting, and long-term planning. While he knew a lot about the financial aspects, Telloni was having difficulty understanding the day-to-day running of the business. He had heard that he should develop a business plan, but he felt confident that with his skills and experience, he would learn about local markets, suppliers, and customer trends as he went along.

As months passed, Telloni was going into the shop less and less. He found the café hectic, crowded, and was frustrated that his employees constantly asked him to explain what he wanted them to do. To compensate for his not being there, he promoted one of his best sales staff, Nafeeza Shafie, to assistant manager. Shafie had worked in the shop for five years while studying management part-time at a local college. She was highly committed to Hannah's success and was extremely well respected by employees and customers alike.

While this arrangement worked for a while, over the next year business began to noticeably decline. The first problem was Telloni's relationship with his staff and customers. Despite his background in sales, he came across as cold, uncommunicative, and short-tempered with both customers and staff. In one instance, Telloni screamed at an employee for making a simple mistake and called him "stupid" in front of number of customers in the busy store. The employee immediately quit and when a customer tried to intervene, Telloni yelled at her to butt out. Word of the incident spread quickly and Telloni was repeatedly asked about it when he attended the Chamber of Commerce meeting later that month. Even with decreased customer volume and increased turnover, Telloni continued to feel that his management style was effective. His employees needed to learn how the business world functioned and that they would be expected to work hard if they wanted to stay at Hannah's.

The next problem arose when Telloni reviewed the financial records. Revenues were down 22 percent and profits, 35 percent. Telloni's reaction was to substitute cheaper alternatives for some of Hannah's best-selling products. He also cancelled the employee bonus program and the weekly improvement meetings to save money. He felt that these were just "extras" he could no longer afford. He also called off the monthly picnic for the employees and their families.

Finally, Telloni overheard a rumour about another ice cream shop opening up in the town and that

Shafie had been approached about becoming a part owner. With the decline in business and subsequent financial difficulties, Telloni was increasingly becoming aware that he didn't have the skills to run Hannah's successfully. Given that their relationship had become strained over the past few months, Telloni became very concerned about losing Shafie.

THE BEGINNING OF THE END

The situation came to a head a few weeks later. Telloni had asked Shafie for her help in creating a marketing campaign for Hannah's famous Canada Day celebration. Shafie took the project and developed an innovative campaign that included flyers, newspaper advertising, coupons, and contests that would attract customers into the store. There was a lot of excitement surrounding the upcoming Canada Day celebration and she was very proud of what she had accomplished. However, at a Chamber of Commerce meeting shortly before the event, Telloni took credit for Shafie's ideas. Shafie confronted him immediately after the meeting and he openly dismissed her contribution, saying that she was merely an employee of Hannah's, not the owner. Shafie was furious with Telloni and quit. Word soon spread around the small community about what Telloni had done and the Canada Day celebration was first time in the history of Hannah's that it operated at a loss.

A few days later, Telloni opened his mail to find an advertisement for a new ice cream store opening down the street from Hannah's. At the bottom of the flyer it announced

that the new store was co-owned by Nafeeza Shafie and Hannah Bryant. He knew that with Shafie's skills and Bryant's reputation, this new store could put him out of business.

REVIEW QUESTIONS

1. Would you classify Telloni as a classic entrepreneur? What characteristics of an entrepreneur does Telloni exhibit?

2. What are some of the reasons that Telloni's business failed? What could he have done to prevent it?

3. What alternative ownership strategies should Telloni have entertained? Be sure to support your answer.

YOU DO THE RESEARCH

1. Drawing from the information in the hypothetical case and your own knowledge of your local community, prepare a business plan for "Your Town's Ice Cream."

The authors express their deep appreciation to Lynda Anstett for developing this case.

CASE 7

Spin Master: Turning Fun into Opportunities

Spin Master, Canada's most celebrated and largest toymaker, is the result of the desire of three young entrepreneurs to prove not only that they can grow a global corporation in a very competitive industry, but that they can stay human while doing so.[1] Over the past 10 years, Spin Master has become an internationally recognized company, selecting, developing, and marketing toys globally. Spin Master's success has stemmed largely from its willingness to take risks and market innovative, original products that are above all fun.[2]

Winner of numerous Toy of the Year honours, as well as a two-time ranking as one of Canada's 50 Best Managed Private Companies, Spin Master is poised to develop the long-term brands and discipline that will assure it a permanent place in the global toy market alongside giants such as Hasbro and Mattel.[3] Even with sales of over $300 million and 300 employees spread throughout offices in Toronto, New York, Paris, London, Hong Kong, and China,[4] that's no easy task. How did Spin Master capitalize on these opportunities to achieve success in this highly competitive market?

THE SEEDS OF GROWTH

The roots of Spin Master date back to 1994, when three university friends, Ronnen Harary, Anton Rabie, and Ben Varadi set out to build a business. Their first product was The Earth Buddy. This product was "a small, pantyhose-covered head filled with grass seeds that sprouted hair when watered."[5] With Earth Buddy's vaguely environmental cachet, Rabie figured it would be a perfect fit for the urban-adventurer image espoused by Roots Canada Ltd., a company founded by Michael Budman and Don Green. Budman allowed Rabie and Harary to test-market Earth Buddies in Roots stores. They were a hit! Next

came a 500,000 order from K-Mart in the United States, so soon operations moved from Harary's kitchen to a factory staffed by 200 employees working around the clock.[6] With $1.8 million in sales within the first six months, the Earth Buddy was an unqualified hit.[7]

So how do you follow up a pantyhosed sprouting head? With Devil Sticks of course! Using a grassroots marketing campaign, students were enlisted to travel across North America and demonstrate the baton-like toy at public events. Spin Master once again had huge success, selling more than 250,000 Devil Sticks in just six months.[8]

In 1996, two British inventors introduced an air-pressured airplane to Spin Master. The prototype the inventors sent to Toronto was, Harary says, "a Canada Dry ginger ale bottle with foam wings—it still had the label on it." But the partners at Spin Master saw opportunity. "The one thing that did appeal to me wasn't so much the item itself as the state of the category," Varadi says. On the top end were gasoline-powered planes; on the low end were $3 rubber-band-and-balsawood "aircraft." Varadi figured there had to be something in the middle. "If we could pull this off, we'd be like pioneers in this category," he said. "We also realized that this would elevate the level of the company in

terms of how people saw us."[9] With time, effort, and faith, the Air Hogs brand was born in 1998, with the release of the Sky Shark. The toy was both a popular and critical success, earning a prestigious spot on *Popular Science's* annual list of the Top 100 Innovations in Science in Technology.[10]

Drawing from the success of Air Hogs, Spin Master continued to blend in-house creativity with innovative marketing partnerships and became adept at modernizing former toy classics such as the legendary Shrinky Dinks and refuelling toy-buyers' imaginations. Demonstrating that Spin Master had not forgotten its grassroots past, the collectible wiggly characters Mighty Beanz were introduced in 2003. Using the same philosophy and marketing techniques as Devil Sticks, Spin Master began distributing the Beanz across North America, and they have literally been flying off the shelves, with more than 10 million sold. Spin Master also created a new Marshmallow children's furniture division, producing the successful Flip-Open Sofa and innovative new items such as the High-Back Chair and Cube Couch.[11]

Capitalizing on its considerable strengths, Spin Master also licenses some of the world's leading brands, which continues to be an integral part of their strategy to drive growth. Spin Master has teamed up with Disney, HIT Entertainment (The Wiggles), McDonald's, Marvel, Hershey, and others in delivering products ranging from Sponge Bob Square Pants-inspired Bounce 'Rounds to the McDonald's McFlurry Maker. Further growth has been driven by other Spin Master best-selling brands, such as Aquadoodle™, Bella Dancerella, Black Belts, 7-11™ Slurpee Maker, and Moon Sand.[12]

PICKING WINNERS

So how do you pick a winning toy? "It's the hardest thing in the world," says Varadi. "You have to look at the product line's history, trends, competition. Is it a basic improvement on something else or does it take it in a new direction? In the end, it's a gut feel."[13]

The US$20 billion North American toy market is highly competitive and contracting by 3 percent a year. Customers are fickle and easily bored, making the lifespan of a typical toy today just 18 months. As a result, Spin Master has to reinvent 70 percent of its product line every year.[14]

While global sales have grown rapidly, an increasing international presence is driven through innovative deployment of strategic alliances. Spin Master is a great example of growth through creative alliances rather than bricks and mortar. "A lot of our global alliances are predicated on the reputation of the company," says Harary. "We're known for our strength in sales, product performance, and quality marketing. We'll get the awareness of a product out."[15]

To fuel growth, Spin Master has sought strategic relationships with a broad spectrum of industry players, from inventors to toy brokers, international distributors to manufacturers, all the way to retailers and brand licensors. As a result, Spin Master has been rewarded with growth and accolades in an industry that often leaves new participants reeling.[16]

There's a culture of "How do we do this?" not "Why we can't do this" at Spin Master. "It's really refreshing," says Professor Ken Wong of Queen's University's School of Business. He credits the Spin Master leaders trusting their instincts and listening to all available external inputs, rather than just to formal, conventional market research, in forging their consistent success.[17]

Strategic intelligence-gathering also gives Spin Master an innovation edge. Rabie spends a few days every two months prowling retail stores, eyeing merchandise trends and chatting up retailers. One frequent source is Jon Levy, co-founder of Mastermind Toys, a specialty retailer in Toronto. "They are fantastically connected to all areas of their business," says Levy. "They care about my market and really want to know what makes my market tick. That's very unusual." He says every conversation with Rabie starts with genuine personal warmth before moving quickly to rapidfire questions such as "What's your best-selling item? What do you think is going to be hot this fall?"[18]

Rabie's insatiable curiosity created one of Spin Master's biggest breakthroughs. An Australian distributor revealed he was seeing a lot of action in kids' flip-out foam sofas. Any toymaker that could slap popular character logos on these items, he said, would have a runaway hit. Capitalizing on that idea, in 1996, Spin Master created a new division, Marshmallow, to produce kids' furniture and décor accessories, from pop-up Winnie the Pooh storage hampers to Disney Princess canopy beds.[19] Marshmallow racked up $20 million in sales.

Not one to rest on their past successes, Spin Master is seeking out kids online and counting on them to be the chief marketers of future products. "This is where the market is going," says a Spin Master executive.[20] Spin Master Ltd. considered more than a dozen iPod-friendly toys but decided to market just two for 2006: IDrum and IMix. They serve as protective plastic cases for the iPod and also function as tools to enhance the tunes. The IDrum, which features a drum pad on the back of the case, allows a child to create beats and rhythms, while IMix lets the children create scratching DJ sounds over the music.[21]

WHAT'S NEXT?

"We have such a large desire for growth," says Rabie, "we feel that if we can harness the world's ideas, we can grow faster than we would by growing on ideas developed internally."[22]

In 2004, only a decade after its inception, Spin Master entered the ranks of the world's top 10 toy manufacturers, relying on a global team of skilled, passionate employees to drive and support growth with confidence, enthusiasm, and energy. Despite its runaway success, the spirit in which the company was founded has not changed. Spin Master remains a youthful, hip, energetic organization, willing to take risks, eager to innovate, and always looking to pursue new and exciting ideas.[23]

Adding to Spin Master's commercial success is an impressive collection of awards and accolades, including citations as one of the Top 40 leaders under 40 (1999), Ernst & Young Entrepreneurs of the Year (1999), #10 on *Profit* magazine's 100 Fastest Growing Private Companies, one of Canada's 50 Best Managed Private Companies (2001–2003), and several major toy awards, including the 2002 TOTY (Toy of the Year) for Catch-A-Bubble (Outdoor Toy of the Year), and 2003 TOTYs for Bounce 'Round (Outdoor Toy of the Year) and Regenerator (Vehicle of the Year).[24]

REVIEW QUESTIONS

1. Describe the key decisions that Harary, Rabie, and Varadi faced in the start-up of their company. Looking at the decision environment, were these more programmed or non-programmed decisions types?

2. As a result of Spin Master's success, what decision errors and traps might be a problem for them in the future?

3. The three founders have found a way to agree so far. What decision-making challenges might they face in the future?

YOU DO THE RESEARCH

1. How does Spin Master develop new product ideas?

2. How might Spin Master further use information technology to help fuel continuing global expansion?

3. Examine the top toys for the past 10 years. Can you see a trend in the industry? What might be the next big hit?

[1] Rick Spence, "Inside the Tornado," *Profit* (December 2005), p. 40.

[2] "About Spin Master," on the Spin Master website, <www.spinmastertoys.co.uk/sections.jsp?about>.

[3] Spence, op. cit.

[4] "News and Promotions," on the Spin Master website, <www.spinmaster.com/spinHq/news.htm>.

[5] "A Brief History of Spin Master," on the Spin Master website, <http://www.spinmaster.com/spinHq/hr/aboutspinmaster.htm>.

[6] Shawna Steinberg and Joe Chidley, "Fun for the money," *Canadian Business* (December 11, 1998), p. 44.

[7] "A Brief History of Spin Master," op. cit.

[8] Ibid.

[9] Steinberg and Chidley, op. cit.

[10] "A Brief History of Spin Master," op. cit.

[11] Ibid.

[12] "News and Promotions," op. cit.

[13] Spence, op. cit.

[14] Ibid.

[15] Anthony Grnak, John Hughes, and Douglas Hunter, "Lessons from the sandbox," *National Post* (January 28, 2006), p. FW2.

[16] Ibid.

[17] Maneesh Mehta, "Growth by design: How good design drives company growth," *Ivey Business Journal* (January/February 2006), on the Web, <www.iveybusinessjournal.com/article.asp?intArticle_ID=602>.

[18] Spence, op. cit.

[19] Ibid.

[20] Jennifer Alsever, "Flying off the Shelves," *Business 2.0* (December 2006), p. 47.

[21] "Toy makers hitch to iPod," *Victoria Times-Colonist* (February 19, 2006), p. A11.

[22] Grnak, Hughes, and Hunter, op. cit.

[23] "A Brief History of Spin Master," op. cit.

[24] Ibid.

CASE 8

Wal-Mart: Self-Management Works at the Number-One Retailer

Wal-Mart, first opened in 1962 by Sam Walton in Rogers, Arkansas, has become the largest retailer in the world, with more than 6,500 store locations and approximately 1.8 million associates worldwide.[1] After the death of Sam Walton in 1992, Wal-Mart continues to be successful, reaching record annual sales of US$312.4 billion and earnings of US$11.2 billion.[2] Maintaining this phenomenal growth presents a significant challenge to Wal-Mart's current leadership.

CARRYING ON SAM WALTON'S LEGACY

In his 1990 letter to Wal-Mart stockholders, then-CEO David Glass laid out the company's philosophy: "We approach this new, exciting decade of the '90s much as we did in the '80s—focused on only two main objectives: (a) providing the customers what they want, when they want it, all at a value; and (b) treating each other as we would hope to be treated, acknowledging our total dependency on our associate partners to sustain our success."[3] Following in Sam Walton's footsteps, Glass believed that the traditional format of organization—employee commitment, cost control, carefully planned locations for new stores, and attention to customer needs and desires—would enable Wal-Mart to enjoy continued success.

Wal-Mart's success came through paying careful attention to its market niche: customers looking for quality at a bargain price. Customers did not have to wait for a sale to realize savings at Wal-Mart. As Glass looked ahead to the 1990s, he recognized the opportunities and threats that confronted Wal-Mart. Many of its stores were located in smaller towns, primarily throughout the American south and midwestern states. While the traditional geographical markets served by

Wal-Mart were not saturated, growth in these areas was limited. Any strategy to achieve continuing growth would have to include expansion into additional geographical regions. In 1993, the company added the 91-store Pace Membership Warehouse chain, which it purchased from Kmart.[4] Competition was increasing as smaller regional chains such as Costco and Price Club merged and opened stores in many of the same markets as Wal-Mart.[5] Glass recognized that existing stores might have to introduce new product lines and higher-priced products in order to achieve year-to-year sales growth.

Wal-Mart has experimented with numerous retail formats over the years. Today, the company is made up of five retail divisions and five specialty divisions. The retail divisions include Wal-Mart Stores; SAM's Clubs, a membership warehouse; Neighborhood Markets, selling groceries, pharmaceuticals, and general merchandise; International Division; and Walmart.com, an on-line version of the neighbourhood Wal-Mart store. There are also three specialty divisions, Tire & Lube Express, Wal-Mart Optical, and Wal-Mart Pharmacy, that typically operated within the Wal-Mart stores, supercentres, and SAM's Club outlets.

Wal-Mart has also worked to develop internationally. In March

1994, the company bought 122 Canadian Woolco stores, formerly owned by Woolworth Corp., the largest single purchase Wal-Mart had made.[6] This international expansion continued, and in 2003, Wal-Mart's international division was the second largest of the five with respect to sales and earnings. Today, the almost 2,600 international locations have reported US$62.7 billion in sales and an operating profit of US$3.3 billion.[7]

Wal-Mart subscribes to the corporate policy "buy American whenever possible." Nonetheless, it has a global purchasing system that allows it to effectively coordinate its entire worldwide supply chain and to share its buying power and merchandise network with all its operations throughout the world.[8] The company has set up an inventory control procedure based on a satellite communication system that links all stores with the Bentonville, Arkansas, headquarters. The satellite system is also used to transmit messages and training materials from headquarters, facilitate communications among stores, and can even be used to track the company's delivery trucks. In addition, Wal-Mart has an online system that links the company's computer systems with its suppliers. Because of its use of innovative technology, Wal-Mart has gained a competitive advantage in the speed with which it delivers goods to its customers.

While each new Wal-Mart brings jobs into communities, there are also other, negative, effects. A 1991 *Wall Street Journal* article noted that many small retailers are forced to close after a Wal-Mart opens nearby.[9] In one Wisconsin town, the large department store J. C. Penney lost 50 percent of its Christmas sales and closed down when Wal-Mart opened. In an Iowa town, four clothing and shoe stores, a hardware store, a drug store, and a dime store all went out of business as a result of Wal-Mart's arrival. Citizens of many communities across North America have successfully worked together to delay or change Wal-Mart's plans, or even prevented the retail giant from locating in the area altogether.

Wal-Mart has faced considerable cultural resistance for its low-paying, part-time jobs and the disproportionately small number of its employees who qualify for full-time benefits, such as insurance. In response, Wal-Mart has made an inexpensive, "value plan" health insurance available to its employees. For about $25 a month, the plan covers a limited number of prescriptions before a deductible applies, but it also includes some negative cost-sharing features.[10]

Even Wal-Mart's "Bring it home to the USA" buying program produced controversy when an NBC news program found clothing that had been made overseas hanging under a "Made in the USA" sign in 11 Wal-Mart stores. In addition, a buying program video showed children sewing at a Wal-Mart supplier's factory in Bangladesh. Wal-Mart insisted that its supplier was obeying local labour laws, which allowed 14-year-olds to work. A company official had also paid a surprise visit to the factory and not found any problems. Then-CEO David Glass stated, "I can't tell you today that illegal child labour hasn't happened someplace, somewhere. All we can do is try our best to prevent it."[11]

SAM'S CULTURAL LEGACY

Wal-Mart's success is built upon its culture. Rob Walton, the company's current chairman of the board, says, "Although Wal-Mart has grown large, we still focus daily on the culture and values established by my father, Sam Walton."[12] Sam Walton founded and built Wal-Mart around three basic beliefs: *respect for the individual, service to our customers, and striving for excellence.* Wal-Mart's slogan that "our people make the difference" reflects the company's respect for, and commitment to, its employees. Diversity is also highly valued. Wal-Mart's philosophy of customer service emphasizes the lowest possible prices along with the best possible service to each and every customer. Lee Scott, Wal-Mart's current president and CEO, observes, "Sam was never satisfied that prices were as low as they needed to be or that our product's quality was as high as they deserved—he believed in the concept of striving for excellence before it became a fashionable concept."[13]

Three critical elements in Wal-Mart's approach to customer service are the *sundown rule*, the *ten-foot rule*, and *every day low prices*. The *sundown rule* means Wal-Mart sets a standard of accomplishing tasks on the same day that the need arises—in short, responding to requests by sundown on the day it receives them. The *ten-foot rule* promises that if an employee comes within 10 feet, or three metres, of a customer, the employee must look the customer in the eye and ask if the person would like to be helped. *Every day low prices* is another important operating philosophy. Wal-Mart believes that by lowering markup, it will earn more because of increased volume, thereby bringing consumers added value for the dollar every day.[14]

Although Wal-Mart has enjoyed phenomenal success, there is no guarantee that it will continue to do so in the future. As the company's annual report points out, preserving and advancing the *every day low prices* concept and helping thousands of new associates to embrace the customer-centred Wal-Mart culture are essential for the company's continued growth.[15] But given the ever-increasing pressures of business, as well as a growing tide of resistance to Wal-Mart's competitive practices, how long can the company stay on top? Chances are there's a Wal-Mart nearby, so stop in and see what you think.

REVIEW QUESTIONS

1. What are Wal-Mart's key objectives? How have Wal-Mart's managerial philosophies and principles enabled it to pursue these key objectives?

2. How do planning and controlling seem to be linked at Wal-Mart?

3. In what ways does Wal-Mart save money through purchasing control?

YOU DO THE RESEARCH

1. Wal-Mart's expansion into the grocery business has caused some problems for Canadian grocers. What has Loblaws or Sobeys done from a planning or control perspective to better compete with Wal-Mart?

2. How might Wal-Mart use scenario planning to assist them as they look to expand into other countries?

[1] "The Wal-Mart Story," on the Web, September 28, 2006, <www.walmartfacts.com>.

[2] "Financial Results," on the Web, <www.walmartfacts.com>.

[3] "Wal-Mart Picks Up the PACE," *Business Week* (November 15, 1993), p. 45.

[4] Ibid.

[5] Wendy Zellner, "Warehouse Clubs Butt Heads—and Reach for the Ice Pack," *Business Week* (April 19, 1993), p. 68.

[6] William C. Symonds, "Invasion of the Retail Snatchers," *Business Week* (May 9, 1994), pp. 72–73.

[7] "International Operations," on the Web, <www.walmartstores.com>.

[8] 2003 Annual Report, <www.walmartstores.com>, p. 3.

[9] Barbara Marsh, "Merchants Mobilize to Battle Wal-Mart in a Small Community," *Wall Street Journal* (June 5, 1991), p. A1.

[10] Victoria Colliver, "Health insurance for $25: Wal-Mart offers various lower-cost coverage plans for workers," *San Francisco Chronicle* (October 25, 2005).

[11] Bill Saporito, "David Glass Won't Crack Under Fire," *Fortune* (February 8, 1993), pp. 75, 78.

[12] 2003 Annual Report, op. cit.

[13] Wal-Mart website, op. cit.

[14] Ibid.

[15] 2003 Annual Report, op. cit.

CASE 9

Toyota Canada Inc.: Making Things Better

Toyota Canada's vision is to make things better: at work, at home, in the community, and even in the world at large.[1] This philosophy draws on Toyota's global corporate philosophy of *kaizen*–the Japanese word for continuous improvement–which it applies to all aspects of its business.[2] In addition to its respect for people, continuous improvement is built into "The Toyota Way," the company's mission and the values it delivers to customers, shareholders, fellow team members, business partners, and the global community.[3]

Toyota's goal is to capture 15 percent of the global car market by 2010.[4] While this might seem high in a market with ever-increasing competition and limited growth, Toyota is confident it will be successful. To achieve this goal, Toyota continues to develop competitive strategies that balance its vision and goals.

Can Toyota successfully develop initiatives to become the acknowledged leader in the highly competitive automotive market?

AUTOMOTIVE PIONEERS

Back in 1938 when Kiichiro Toyoda, the founder of Toyota Motor Corp., instructed his understudy, Eiji Toyoda, to build a factory on land cleared from a red-pine forest in central Japan, neither realized they were about to make history. That plant, located in what is now called Toyota City, pioneered concepts such as just-in-time inventory control, *kaizen* continuous improvement, and *kanban* (or signboards) labelling of parts to make the assembly line more efficient—all disciplines common today in factories from Detroit to Stuttgart, and essential to the Toyota Way.[5]

Moving to Canada in 1965 with just two models and an inventory of 755 cars,[6] Toyota Canada Inc. (TCI) has expanded significantly over the past 40 years. Today, Toyota offers 16 models and in 2006 it sold more than 195,000 vehicles in Canada. Nine of these models are built in North America; two, Corolla and Matrix, are built in Canada by Toyota Motor Manufacturing Canada Inc. (TMMC) in Cambridge, Ontario.[7]

Toyota, now the world's second-largest automaker and eighth-largest company, directly employs more than 5,000 Canadians, with an additional 8,000 people across Canada working at independent dealerships. With a head office in Scarborough, Ontario and five zone offices across Canada, TCI oversees all divisions of Toyota's sales, marketing, parts, and service, as well as its Lexus luxury car division, and industrial equipment operations.[8]

A COMPETITIVE MARKET

The automobile industry in North America is undergoing rapid technological transformation and is currently faced with the challenges of increased deregulation, accelerating globalization, and ever-changing consumer tastes.[9]

After decades of dominance, the "Big Three" automakers—General Motors, Ford, and Daimler-Chrysler—are now struggling with diminishing market share, listing the huge burden of legacy costs and the inability to adjust their structural costs as the main culprits for massive financial losses.[10] In 2005, GM, the world's largest automaker, incurred the highest loss ever of US$8.6 billion. This resulted in the elimination of 30,000 jobs and the scaling back of operations in 12 fa-

cilities. Ford also reported a record loss of US$1.5 billion in 2005, while DaimlerChrysler fell short of expectations.[11]

In contrast, Toyota does not have the "legacy" costs that GM has to bear and is instead able to focus on future growth. In 2006, Toyota posted record earnings for its fiscal year, as its sales grew across all key regions.[12] Toyota commands the largest market capitalization (almost US$173.6 billion as of December 31, 2005), which is more than 14.3 times that of GM.[13]

STRATEGY: THE TOYOTA WAY

TCI's vision is to be North America's most admired company, distinguished by its culture and the satisfaction of all of its stakeholders. To do this, Toyota ensures that all major decisions are focused on maintaining a balance among stakeholders: customers, suppliers, team members, shareholders, and the community. TCI has undertaken strategic approaches toward productivity and profitability while maintaining its deep commitment to the environment and the community.[14]

TCI focuses on achieving cost reductions through economies of scale and flexible production using the Toyota Production System (TPS). TPS, well known and copied in the automotive industry, is an integrated approach to production that manages equipment, materials, and people in the most efficient manner.[15] TPS is a continuous process built on two main principles: just-in-time production and jidoka, the concept of building quality directly into the process itself.[16] It also incorporates *kaizen*, or continuous improvement, to identify and eliminate waste in all

areas. The company does this by making a task simpler and easier to perform. Toyota currently uses a very high-tech production engineering system called Vcomm, allowing possible problems to be predicted and corrected before actual production begins, which significantly enhances product quality and efficiency. Toyota's technological prowess is likely to continue relative to its rivals into the foreseeable future.[17]

Toyota also believes that the principal form of motivation for improvement is derived from learning to appreciate how much waste exists around you in all the work you and your organization do every day.[18] Expanding on this philosophy, Toyota has committed to protecting the environment and ensuring that its automobile manufacturing operations are safe for its team members, the community, and the environment.[19] By pioneering the most advanced environmental technologies, Toyota is committed to creating a society where people can live safely, securely, and comfortably. Toyota is a driving force in the market for hybrid cars that use electricity and gasoline, promoting the appeal of environmentally friendly cars throughout the world and gaining a larger number of Toyota fans.[20]

Toyota is also adept at developing new brands appealing to different segments of customers within a given target market. When Toyota entered the North American market in large volumes, it offered limited choices and was not distinct. But Toyota soon established itself by targeting more sophisticated customers by introducing the Lexus line of products in 1989, which became the best-selling luxury car in just five years, surpassing American and European brands.[21]

Toyota has also learned some lessons from its own global penetration and from the achievements and failures of the Big Three in expanding into foreign markets. The first lesson is to have a flexible line of products that address the special needs of the target market. In one of its five value concepts, Toyota emphasizes that customers always come first and tries to forge close partnerships with them and strive to exceed their expectations. Toyota always attempts to venture into new products to gain the favour of its target customers long before they actually become household names.[22]

MEASURING SUCCESS

Will Toyota's current strategies successfully establish a dominant market position in the global automotive industry? Given the current growth rate, Toyota is expected to soon overtake GM in market share for the first time.[23] In 2004, Toyota moved into second position just behind GM, with passenger car sales of 1.018 million units.[24]

Toyota also generates the highest revenue and income per employee of $674,000 and $540,000, respectively, which is far ahead of the industry average as well as all of its competitors. While GM ranks second in terms of revenue generated per employee, its income per employee is, however, at negative $10,000.[25] As well, of the six largest car manufacturers, Toyota has the highest capacity utilization of 107 percent. Daimler-Chrysler follows with a distant second at 90 percent, while GM, the lowest, is at 85 percent.[26]

To achieve its future goals, Toyota must not only focus on introducing a new generation of brands that appeal to differentiated market segments, but it also must establish and increase its market shares in emerging markets. In established markets such as North America and Japan, Toyota focuses on products that are environmental friendly and are more appealing to the younger generation. In other markets offering significant growth potential, such as China and India, Toyota has successfully combined its brand with the image of durability

and reliability and offers its products at an affordable cost. These qualities, coupled with its flexible manufacturing, allow Toyota to penetrate into and match the needs of targeted local and regional markets through its network of manufacturing centres around the globe.[27] It is a company on the move.

REVIEW QUESTIONS

1. Prepare a SWOT analysis of TCI.

2. What are TCI's core competencies? Who are its stakeholders?

3. Prepare a Porter's Model of Five Strategic Forces for the automotive industry in Canada.

YOU DO THE RESEARCH

1. Using the Internet, research and briefly describe TCI's Global Vision for 2010. What important strategies from the chapter are included in TCI's vision?

2. Find TCI's mission statement. In your opinion, is this a good mission statement? Why?

[1] "Make things better," on the Toyota Canada website, <www.toyota.ca/cgi-bin/WebObjects/WWW.woa/6/wo/Home.AboutToyota-fy6NmBbjaSWqye6BTWoMKM/0.9?fmg%2fabout%2findex%2ehtml>.

[2] "Toyota Canada Inc.: 'make things better,'" news release from Canada Newswire, February 14, 2007.

[3] "Join our team," on the Toyota Canada website, <www.toyota.ca/cgi-bin/WebObjects/WWW.woa/18/wo/Home.TMMC-s0PuCFCmIQuDOetfURpmv0/11.13.7.11.2.7.5>.

[4] Hailu Regassa and Ahmad Amhadian, "Comparative Study of American and Japanese Auto Industry: General Motors Versus Toyota Motors Corporations," *The Business Review* (summer 2007), p. 1.

[5] Chester Dawson, "Blazing the Toyota Way: The world's carmakers follow the pattern set by Kiichiro and Eiji Toyoda, *Business Week* (May 24, 2004), p. 22.

[6] "Our commitment to Canada," on the Toyota Canada website, <www.toyota.ca/cgi-bin/WebObjects/WWW.woa/7/wo/Home.About-Toyota-t4Y8QMn1NS4Jtzotp5qVrw/3.9?a130000e%2ehtml>.

[7] Ibid.

[8] Ibid.

[9] Regassa and Ahmadian, op. cit.

[10] Ibid.

[11] Ibid.

[12] Ibid.

[13] Ibid.

[14] "Who we are," on the Toyota Canada website, <www.toyota.ca/cgi-bin/WebObjects/WWW.woa/7/wo/Home.TMMC-vzk5b9bmL848cnZZ52ttHw/7.13?t124000e%2ehtml>.

[15] Regassa and Ahmadian, op. cit.

[16] "How we build," on the Toyota Canada website, <www.toyota.ca/cgi-bin/WebObjects/WWW.woa/14/wo/Home.TMMC-SahVwzEg5q33tjZ9EbrRDM/9.13?t141000e%2ehtml>.

[17] Regassa and Ahmadian, op. cit.

[18] George Koenigsaecker, "Sustaining Lean," *Manufacturing Engineering* (May 2007), p. 117.

[19] "Commitment to the environment," on the Toyota Canada website, <www.toyota.ca/cgi-bin/WebObjects/WWW.woa/14/wo/Home.TMMC-Dme2MraOrbYlw5AcKbYs20/0.13?t151000e%2ehtml>.

[20] Regassa and Ahmadian, op. cit.

[21] Ibid.

[22] Ibid.

[23] Ibid.

[24] Ibid.

[25] Ibid.

[26] Ibid.

[27] Ibid.

CASE 10

Nike: Spreading Out to Stay Together

Nike is, indisputably, a giant in the athletics industry. Yet the Portland, Oregon, company has grown so large precisely because it knows how to stay small. By focusing on its core competencies, and outsourcing the rest, Nike has managed to become a sharply focused industry leader. But can it keep the lead?

WHAT DO YOU CALL A COMPANY OF THINKERS?

It's not a joke or a riddle. Rather, it's a conundrum that applies to one of the most successful companies in the United States. Nike is known worldwide for its products, none of which it actually makes. This begs two questions: if you don't make anything, what do you actually do, and if you outsource everything, what's left?

For starters, what's left is a whole lot of brand recognition. Nike, know by its trademark "swoosh," is still among the most recognized brands in the world and an industry leader in the US$57 billion sports footwear and apparel market. And with a 33 percent market share it dominates the global athletic shoe market.[1]

Since captivating the shoe-buying public in the early 1980s with indomitable spokesperson Michael Jordan, Nike continues to outpace the athletic shoe competition while branding an ever-widening universe of sports equipment, apparel, and paraphernalia. The omnipresent swoosh graces everything from bumper stickers, to sunglasses, to high school sports uniforms.

Not long after the introduction of its hit shoe, Air Jordans, the first strains of the "Just Do It" ad campaign sealed Nike's reputation as a megabrand. Nike made the strategic image shift from simply selling products to embodying love of sport, self-discipline, ambition, and other desirable traits of athleticism. It was also among the first in a long line of brands to latch on to the strategy of representing, in its advertising, the freedom of self-expression that can be had through the use of its products.

Advertising has played no small part in Nike's continued success. In the United States alone, Nike recently spent US$85 million annually on advertising,[2] with a recent combined total of US$213 million in measured media, according to TNS Media Intelligence.[3]

By comparison, Adidas spent US$47 million and Reebok spent US$26 million.[4]

Portland ad agency Wieden + Kennedy has been instrumental in creating and perpetuating Nike's image, so much so that the agency has a large division, in-house, at Nike headquarters. This intimate relationship allows the ad designers to focus solely on Nike work, and it gives them unparalleled access to executives, researchers, and anyone else who might provide the inspiration for the next successful advertisement.

WHAT'S LEFT, THEN?

Although Nike has cleverly kept its ad agency close to home, it has relied on outsourcing for many of the non-executive responsibilities in order to reduce overhead. Actually, Nike took outsourcing to a new level, now barely producing any of its products in its own factories. All of its shoes, for instance, are made by subcontractors. Although this allocation of production hasn't had a negative impact on the quality of the shoes, it has harmed Nike's reputation among fair-trade critics.

After initial allegations of sweatshop labour conditions surfaced at Nike-sponsored factories, the company tried to reach out and reason with its more moderate critics. But this approach failed, and Nike found itself in the unenviable position of trying to defend its outsourcing practices while at the same time keeping details of the locations of its favoured production shops from the competition. In a bold move designed to convert the critics, Nike announced that it would post information on its website about all of the approximately 750 factories it uses to make the shoes, apparel, and other sporting goods that it sells. It released this data alongside a comprehensive new corporate responsibility report summarizing the environmental and labour situations of its contract factories.[5]

"This is a significant step that will blow away the myth that companies can't release their factory names because it's proprietary information," said Charles Kernaghan, executive director of the National Labor Committee, a New York-based anti-sweatshop group that has been no friend to Nike over the years. "If Nike can do it, so can Wal-Mart and all the rest."[6]

JORDAN ISN'T FOREVER

Knowing that shoe sales alone wouldn't be enough to sustain continued growth, Nike made the lateral move to learn more about its customers' involvement in sports and what needs it might be able to fill. Banking on the star power of the swoosh, Nike has successfully branded apparel, sporting goods, sunglasses, and even an MP3 player made by Philips. Like many large companies that have found themselves dealing with the limitations of their brands, Nike realized that it would have to successfully identify new needs in the market and also be able to supply creative and desirable solutions.

To achieve this, Nike has branched into merchandising arenas previously unexplored by the company. Taking up the company's original name once again, it quietly launched the Blue Ribbon Sports line of urban-themed apparel. Sold only at high-end shops, the line seeks to fill a niche only recently discovered by the Adidas–Stella McCartney collaboration.[7]

In keeping with the times, John R. Hoke III, head of Nike's design team, is encouraging his designers to develop environmentally sustainable designs. This may come as a surprise to anyone who has ever thought about how much foam and plastic goes into the average Nike sneaker, but a corporate-wide mission called "Considered" has designers rethinking the toxic materials used to put the spring in millions of steps. "I'm very passionate about this idea," Hoke said. "We are going to challenge ourselves to think a little bit differently about the way we create products."[8]

NIPPING AT NIKE'S HEELS

But despite its success, it hasn't been all roses for Nike recently. Feeling the need to step down, Phil Knight handed the reins to Bill Perez, former CEO of SC Johnson, who became the first outsider recruited for the executive tier since Nike's founding in 1968. But after barely a year on the job, Knight, who stayed close as chairman of the board, decided Perez couldn't "get his arms around the company." Citing numerous other conflicts, Knight accepted Perez's resignation and promoted Mark Parker, a 27-year veteran who was co-president of the Nike brand, as a replacement.[9]

Pressures are mounting from outside its Beaverton, Oregon, headquarters as well. German rival Adidas drew a few strides closer to Nike with the purchase of Reebok for approximately US$3.8 billion.[10] Joining forces will collectively now help the two brands negotiate shelf space and other sales issues in North American stores, as well as give them a size advantage in price discussion with Asian manufacturers.

With recent combined global sales of US$12 billion, the new, combined company isn't far behind Nike's US$14 billion in sales.[11] According to Jon Hickey, senior vice-president of sports and entertainment marketing for the ad agency Mullen, Nike now has its "first real, legitimate threat since the '80s. There's no way either one would even approach Nike, much less overtake them, on their own," he said. "But now, Nike has to respond. This new, combined entity has a chance to make a run. Now, it's game on."[12]

But when faced with a challenge, Nike simply knocks its bat against its cleats and steps up to the plate. "Our focus is on growing our own business," said Nike spokesperson Alan Marks. "Of course we're in a competitive business, but we win by staying focused on our strategies and our consumers. And from that perspective nothing has changed."[13]

PUTTING IT ALL TOGETHER

Nike has balanced its immense size and the tremendous pressures for success by attaining a decentralized corporate structure. Individual business centres—such as research, production, and marketing—are free to focus on their core competencies, free the effects of being such a large company. Similarly, Nike has found continued success in the marketplace by moving away from being viewed simply as a huge sneaker company, instead positioning itself as a brand meeting the evolving needs of athletes. Will Nike continue to profit from an increasingly decentralized business model, or will it spread itself so thin that the competition will overtake it?

REVIEW QUESTIONS

1. If a sporting good can be used in a sporting event, and especially if that event can be televised, Nike has likely made such a product and added a swoosh to it. But in this day and age, are there any sporting products that Nike would do better not to produce? Explain your reasoning.

2. Nike's long-running "Just Do It" tagline establishes the brand—and therefore its products—as a means of self-expression, implying that "Our products help you be you." This has worked thus far for Nike, but this strategy is ubiquitous in the marketplace and is used to sell everything from yogurt to plastic surgery. Select and defend one of the following positions:

   a) This is an advantageous strategy for Nike because it adequately represents customers' perceptions of the Nike brand and its products.

   b) This strategy works against Nike's best interests and prevents customers from forming their own associations with Nike products. Whichever you choose, you may not cite the length of the "Just Do It" campaign as evidence for your point.

3. If you were charged today with the task of creating an athletics company comparable to Nike and were given the budget to do so, would you adopt the same decentralized structure as Nike? Why or why not?

YOU DO THE RESEARCH

1. Nike's reputation was marred by allegations that they were running "sweatshops." What did they do to overcome this problem?

2. Do other shoe manufacturing companies organize themselves similar to Nike?

[1] "Adidas-Reebok Merger Lets Rivals Nip at Nike's Heels," *USA Today* (August 4, 2005).

[2] Ibid.

[3] Rich Thomaselli, "Deal Sets Stage for Full-Scale War with Nike," *Advertising Age*, vol. 76 (August 8, 2005).

[4] "Adidas-Reebok Merger," op. cit.

[5] Aaron Bernstein, "Nike Names Names," *Business Week Online* (April 13, 2005).

[6] Ibid.

[7] Rich Thomaselli, "Nike Launches Upscale Urban Street Wear Line," *Advertising Age*, vol. 76 (August 1, 2005).

[8] Stanley Holmes, "Green Foot Forward," *Business Week* (November 28, 2005).

[9] "Nike Replaces CEO After 13 Months," *USA Today* (January 24, 2006).

[10] "Just Doing It," *Economist*, vol. 376 (August 6, 2005).

[11] "Adidas-Reebok Merger," op. cit.

[12] "Deal Sets Stage," op. cit.

[13] "Adidas-Reebok Merger," op. cit.

CASE 11

BET Holdings: World-Class Entrepreneur Places "BET" on the Future

Robert Johnson, born the ninth in a family of 10 children in Hickory, Mississippi, is a true rags-to-riches success story. His father, Archie, chopped wood while his mother taught school. Ultimately, their search for a better life led them to Freeport, Illinois, a predominantly white working-class neighbourhood. Archie supplemented his factory jobs by operating his own junkyard on the predominantly black east side of town. Edna Johnson got a job at Burgess Battery, and although she eventually secured a job for Robert at the battery firm, he knew it wasn't for him.[1]

ROBERT JOHNSON'S JOURNEY TO BECOMING AN ENTREPRENEUR

Bob Johnson showed an enterprising nature at an early age, delivering papers, mowing lawns, and cleaning out tents at local fairs. At Freeport High School, he was an honours student and entered the University of Illinois upon graduation. Virgil Hemphill, his freshman roommate, commented: "He was not overly slick, overly smooth. He was kind of innocent and naïve. His strength was being able to talk to different types of people. I went to Freeport with him, and he could communicate with the regular people and with the suit-and-tie people."[2]

Johnson did well at university, studying history, holding several work-study jobs, and participating in Kappa Alpha Psi, a black fraternity. After graduation in 1968, he was admitted to a two-year program at Princeton University's Woodrow Wilson School of Public and International Affairs. He had a full scholarship plus expenses but dropped out after the first semester to marry his college sweetheart, Sheila Crump, a former cheerleader and a gifted violinist. He eventually returned to Princeton to earn his Master's degree in public administration in 1972.[3]

He moved on to Washington, D.C., to first work at the Corporation for Public Broadcasting and then at the Washington Urban League, where the director, Sterling Tucker, appreciated Johnson's ability to think both "micro-ly and macro-ly" while still "thinking like a visionary" in pursuing larger goals.[4] Moving on to work for the Congressional Black Caucus, Johnson became impressed with the possibilities for black power that lay in television—cable in particular. In 1976, he began working as a lobbyist for the National Cable Television Association (NCTA), where he gained valuable insight into the cable industry.

At the NCTA's 1979 convention, Johnson met Bob Rosencrans, president of UA-Columbia Cablevision. While Bob Johnson had a strong idea for providing cable programming to minority audiences, he had no satellite time. Rosencrans, on the other hand, was looking for programs to support his local franchises and to fill some unused slots on one of the cable TV satellites. According to Rosencrans, "I just said, 'Bob, you're on. Let's go.' I don't think we even charged him. We knew he couldn't afford much, and for us, it was a plus because it gave us more ammunition to sell cable. The industry was not attracting minority customers."[5]

With US$15,000 from a consulting contract that he received upon his departure from NCTA, Robert Johnson launched Black Entertainment Television (BET) at 11:00 p.m. on January 8, 1980. The first BET show was a 1974 African safari movie, *Visit to a Chief's Son.* Initially, BET aired for only two hours on Friday nights. The shows bounced off an RCA satellite and into 3.8 million homes served by Rosencrans's franchises. Johnson received his first crucial financing from John Malone of TCI in the form of a US$380,000 loan plus US$120,000 for a 20 percent ownership in BET.[6]

To raise capital in the 1980s, Johnson sold off pieces of BET to Time Inc. and Taft Broadcasting for more than US$10 million. However, from the start, controversy over programming followed Johnson with his heavy reliance on music videos (60 percent of total programming), gospel and religious programs, infomercials, and reruns of older shows such as *Sanford and Son* and *227.*[7]

THE GROWTH OF BET HOLDINGS

Robert Johnson had grand plans for BET, seeking to turn the enterprise into what marketers call an umbrella brand.[8] The firm published two national magazines that reached 250,000 readers: *Young Sisters and Brothers* for teens and *Emerge* for affluent adults. BET also had interests in film production, electronic retailing, and radio. The first BET Sound Stage restaurant opened in suburban Washington and another in Disney World in Orlando. With the Hilton hotel chain as a partner, Johnson explored opening a casino in Las Vegas, Nevada. Johnson wanted to capture a share of black consumers' disposable income, valued at US$425 billion annually. To do this, he partnered primarily with big names as such Disney, Hilton, Blockbuster, Microsoft, and others. "You simply cannot get big anymore by being 100 percent black-owned anything," Johnson claimed.[9] His Black Entertainment Television cable station provided the perfect medium to target this increasingly affluent black audience.

BET Inc. aims to become the leading African-American multimedia entertainment company and is committed to establishing the most valued consumer brand within the African-American marketplace."[10]

Black Entertainment Television, aimed toward serving the African-American community, remains at the core of the BET business empire. As of late 2005, Black Entertainment Television has reached more than 80 million cable subscribers in the United States.[11]

Included among this subscriber base are more than 90 percent of all black households that have cable hookups. BET's related digital cable businesses include BET on Jazz, BET Gospel, BET Classic Soul, BET International, and BET Hip Hop. BET Books publishes literature with African-American themes written by African-American authors. BET Pictures produces documentaries on African-American themes and made-for-TV movies. BET Interactive, a partnership between BET, Microsoft, Liberty Digital Media, News Corporation, and USA Networks created the Internet portal BET.com, the leading online site for African-Americans.[12]

The company grew into such a success story that Viacom Inc. purchased it for US$3 billion in November 2001. Until his retirement in 2005, Robert Johnson remained chairman and CEO of the Viacom subsidiary, reporting to Viacom's then president and chief operating officer, Mel Karmazin.[13] Debra Lee, former president and COO, took control of BET in 2006. Johnson stated, "I could not have chosen a better chief executive and outstanding leader to succeed me at BET than Debra Lee. I am convinced that BET's legacy is in great hands."[14] Karmazin described the acquisition of BET Holdings as "a

strategically perfect fit. . . . . Viacom is home to the industry's most creative and distinctive branded programming, the perfect environment for BET's television and online business to grow and prosper."[15]

REVIEW QUESTIONS

1. Is a mechanistic organizational design or an organic organizational design more appropriate for BET? Explain your answer.

2. How might environment and strategy influence BET's organizational design?

3. As a multi-faceted, multimedia entertainment company, what challenges regarding differentiation and integration does BET likely face?

YOU DO THE RESEARCH

1. Was Robert Johnson correct in selling his BET Holdings to Viacom?

2. Will BET Interactive become a major force on the Web?

3. What's next for Robert Johnson?

[1] Peter Perl, "His Way," *Washington Post* (December 14, 1997), Magazine Section, W08.
[2] Ibid.
[3] Ibid.
[4] Ibid.
[5] Ibid.
[6] Ibid.
[7] Ibid.
[8] Adam Zagorin, "BET's Too Hot a Property," *Time* (October 20, 1997), p. 80.
[9] Perl, op. cit.
[10] "The Facts," Viacom Website, <www.viacom.com/thefacts>.
[11] Ibid.
[12] Robert L. Johnson, Founder, on the Web, <www.bet.com/articles>.
[13] Joe Flint, "Viacom Changes Leadership at BET and Spike TV," *Wall Street Journal* (January 31, 2005), p. B4.
[14] "Debra Lee Assumes Helm of Black America's Network," on the Web, <www.bet.com/News/debra_lee.htm>.
[15] Carol King, "Viacom Acquires BET Holdings," on the Web, <www.internetnews.com/bus-news>.

CASE 12

Royal Bank of Canada: Progressive HR Makes Good Business Sense

Starting in 1864 as a small group of enterprising Halifax merchants, Royal Bank of Canada (RBC) continues to be one of Canada's largest banks, holding over $448 billion in assets. Specializing in personal and business banking, full-service brokerage services, insurance, and corporate and investment banking, RBC serves over 12 million customers per day. RBC has a strong commitment to its 60,000 employees worldwide through progressive human resources strategies, policies, and practices.[1] With over 13,000 resumés pouring in a month, RBC is committed to remaining an employer of choice in Canada. It does this through a strong commitment to diversity, total rewards philosophy, and recognition.

DIVERSITY

For RBC, diversity in its workforce is one of its greatest competitive advantages for developing intellectual capital and ensuring continued growth, not only within Canada but around the world.[2] RBC creates workplaces where employees can realize their full potential, achieve their aspirations, and make significant contributions while developing their own unique personal abilities.[3]

RBC's focus on diversity dates back to the early 1970s when it developed an internal task force on the status of women, followed by a focus on employment equity groups in the 1980s and comprehensive work–life initiatives in the 1990s.[4] The appointment of a woman as manager of a Montreal branch in 1968 opened the doors for other women to be promoted into management positions. The creation of the Advisory Task Force on the Status of Women in Royal Bank of Canada in 1977 examined the bank's systems and practices toward women, the first of its kind for a Canadian bank.[5] Today, RBC continues to strive to build and sustain an inclusive work environment in many ways. For example, it was a founding sponsor of Career Bridge, which provides a four-month Canadian internship to foreign-trained professionals to help them integrate into the Canadian workforce. RBC also established a Diversity Leadership Council in 2001 to help identify and develop strategic diversity initiatives.[6]

Having a workforce that fully reflects the clients and communities a business serves is a basic premise of diversity. At RBC, nearly one-third of senior management (vice-presidents and above) are women, and 9 percent are visible minorities. Approximately half of all managers are women, and RBC has set ambitious goals to continue to increase the representation of both women and visible minorities in senior management and to develop upcoming talent.[7]

TOTAL REWARDS

When developing a total rewards philosophy in 2002, Royal Bank wanted to be sure it was meeting the needs of all employees when it comes to pay, benefits, and work–life balance. RBC surveyed 16,000 of its employees to get solid data. The results showed a dominant theme: flexibility. Employees wanted choice and flexibility, and for management to recognize that needs change over the course of a career.[8]

"It is not enough anymore to focus on traditional notions of remuneration like pay and benefits," says Zabeen Hirji,[9] Chief Human Resources Officer for RBC.[10] "We need to be competitive, but things like pay can easily be duplicated by other companies if they want to attract a person. When we look at things from the perspective of employee relationship management, we would look at career-life cycle," she says.[11]

Today, RBC's total rewards package includes compensation, benefits, professional development, and a variety of work–life initiatives, and is all about creating the combination that is right for each individual employee.[12] When employees sign in to the company's HR Web portal, they're presented with the total rewards quadrant and can then enter into one of the four sections. Hirji says about 9 out of 10 employees visit the site at least once a month.[13]

RBC benefits are competitive, with the flexibility to add additional coverage to suit employees' personal needs, enabling them to customize their benefits package to suit their own situation. Basic life and disability benefits, a pension plan, and health and dental plans are all available with several options. If additional life or accident insurance is needed, all employees have the option to purchase more.[14]

RBC also provides its staff with employee assistance and work–life support services,[15] enabling workers to manage multiple responsibilities of work, home, and the community. RBC believes that investing in work–life policies, programs, and resources allows it to respond to the changing workforce and workplace. Strategic HR policies enable RBC to attract, retain, and engage employees, and reduce stress and short-term absenteeism—all of which increase individual and organizational effectiveness.[16]

RECOGNITION FOR EMPLOYEES

There is also a very different rewards and recognition philosophy at RBC. Since the late 1980s, the bank has tried to make recognition and rewards an integral part of its corporate culture. As a former president made it clear years ago, recognition would not be something that comes and goes with the economic tides, arguing that it's more important to thank employees when times are tough. Since then, the company has stayed true to that commitment, keeping the recognition budget almost unchanged for more than 15 years.[17]

The important element of RBC's program is that the recognition is done by the manager. The managers and leaders know best what behaviours deserve special attention so decisions about recognition are made in the field, not at head office. Managers know there is a mixture of team and individual reward options available, but it's up to them to decide on what behaviours to reward and in what measure. One of the strongest elements of the recognition program is the nomination system: employees are nominated for recognition by a co-worker or manager. Using a points system, employees have maximum choice in what rewards they receive.[18] "It's not about the item that the person is getting," Hirji says, "it's about how the manager uses that opportunity to say, 'Great, you've been with us for two years. We're really pleased about that.'"[19] RBC believes that recognition has a role in creating positive morale and minimizing turnover.

RECOGNITION FOR RBC

Does RBC's focus on employees contribute to its success? The answer is yes! In 2006 RBC was named one of Canada's most admired corporate cultures for the second year in a row.[20] That same year, RBC was also recognized as one of the top employers for workplace diversity by *The Canadian Immigrant Magazine*,[21] and in an annual survey conducted by Ipsos Reid for KPMG, RBC was named one of Canada's most respected corporations for a fourth year in a row.[22]

REVIEW QUESTIONS

1. Using the three major responsibilities of human resources management, describe how RBC can be considered an employer of choice.

2. Assume you are hired as a consultant to create a plan to improve the development of RBC's workforce. What recommendations would you make for RBC to further develop its workforce? Explain your reasoning.

3. How does RBC work to maintain its workforce? Do you think the strategy is effective? Why or why not?

YOU DO THE RESEARCH

1. Compare RBC with Bank of Montreal (BMO), a competitor in the banking industry, in terms of approaches to attracting, developing, and maintaining a diverse workforce.

2. Why does BMO take the approach that it does? Why does RBC take the approach that it does?

3. Would the RBC approach to attracting, developing, and maintaining a diverse workforce be adaptable to any company in any industry? Why or why not?

[1] RBC Financial Group, Corporate Profile, on the Web, <www.rbc.com/aboutus/index.html>.
[2] Zabeen Hirji, "Growth and innovation rests on diversity: A look at how RBC has leveraged its diverse workforce," *Canadian HR Reporter* (December 18, 2006), pp. 18–9.
[3] RBC Financial Group, Careers: Diversity: Diversity in Action, on the Web, <www.rbc.com/uniquecareers/diversity/action.html>.
[4] Hirji, op. cit.
[5] RBC Financial Group, History: Quick to the Frontier: 1960 to 1979, on the Web, <www.rbc.com/history/quicktofrontier/glbl_stage.html>.
[6] Hirji, op. cit.
[7] Ibid.

[8] Todd Humber, "Banking on a benefits redesign: RBC organizes pay, benefits, training, work environment into a single package," *Canadian HR Reporter* (February 23, 2004), p. G1.

[9] "HR leaders talk," *Canadian HR Reporter* (February 10, 2003), pp. 15–8.

[10] RBC Financial Group, Executive Profiles: Zabeen Hirji: Chief Human Resources Officer, on the Web, <www.rbc.com/newsroom/down2-zabeen_hirji.html>.

[11] "HR leaders talk," op. cit.

[12] RBC Financial Group, Careers: Welcome to Total Rewards, on the Web, <www.rbc.com/uniquecareers/meetrbc/totrewards.html>.

[13] Humber, op. cit.

[14] RBC Financial Group, Careers: Total Rewards: My Pay, on the Web, <www.rbc.com/uniquecareers/meetrbc/pay.html>.

[15] RBC Financial Group, Careers: Total Rewards: My Workplace, on the Web, <www.rbc.com/uniquecareers/meetrbc/workplace.html>.

[16] RBC Financial Group, Careers: Diversity: Work/Life Solutions, on the Web, <www.rbc.com/uniquecareers/diversity/solutions-overview.html>.

[17] David Brown, "RBC's recognition department oversees rewarding culture," *Canadian HR Reporter* (March 14, 2005), pp. 7–8.

[18] Ibid.

[19] Humber, op. cit.

[20] RBC Financial Group, "RBC named one of Canada's most admired corporate cultures," news release, October 10, 2006, on the Web, <www.rbc.com/aboutus/20061010CorpCulture.html>.

[21] RBC Financial Group, "TCIM's 2006 Top Employers for Workplace Diversity," on the Web, <www.rbc.com/uniquecareers/meetrbc/rbc_awardse.pdf>.

[22] RBC Financial Group, "RBC named Canada's Most Respected Corporation fourth year in a row," news release, February 1, 2006, on the Web, <www.rbc.com/newsroom/20060201respected.html>.

CASE 13

Lakeport Brewing Income Fund: A Case of Great Leadership

Canada's $8-billion beer industry is in the throes of a massive change. While frontrunners Molson and Labatt each hold about 42 percent market share, a small, but growing, group of local craft breweries are creating serious competition for the big players.[1] In response, major brewers are rushing to add more discount and imported brands just to retain their market share. Now with as many as 300 brands in most beer stores, there has never been more choice for consumers, or competition for their loyalty.[2]

Located in Hamilton, Ontario, Lakeport Brewing Income Fund is an independent brewer and producer of alcoholic and non-alcoholic products.[3] In addition to its own namesake line, which includes Lakeport Pilsner, Honey Lager, Light, Strong, and Red, Lakeport also produces and markets Steeler Lager, Brava Mexican Style, and Wee Willy.[4]

ENTER TERESA CASCIOLI

When Teresa Cascioli took the helm of Lakeport Brewery in 1999, the company was $18 million in debt, under bankruptcy protection, and held virtually no clout in the Ontario beer market.[5] Under her leadership, Lakeport emerged from its financial woes to become the third-largest brewer in Ontario in 2006, with gross revenues that rose to $32.6 million from $21.6 million a year earlier. The company's success, due in part to its aggressive dollar-a-bottle pricing strategy, has vaulted Cascioli into one of the top businesswomen in the country.[6] So what does it take to succeed as a leader?

After graduating with a commerce degree in 1983 from nearby McMaster University, Cascioli worked in finance and administration with the City of Hamilton for a number of years,[7] before moving into finance at Philip Services, a Hamilton-based recycling and environmental-services firm.[8]

In the summer of 1999, Cascioli had just quit her job at Philips to attend law school. Before she could get started, however, acquaintances working on restructuring the troubled Lakeport asked her to investigate the viability of the business. She did and the lenders were so impressed that they asked her to stay and run the company.[9] "I knew the investors at Lakeport and they felt that it was important, given the history of the company, to have someone with a financial background in the role," says Cascioli.[10]

Her first task as leader was to learn what it took to succeed in a completely new industry. "My father used to tell me, 'Teresa, don't teach Michelangelo how to paint; you need to take advice from people who know.'" So true to form, she asked the guys on the plant floor.[11]

Faced with the daunting challenge of turning Lakeport around, her financial background, while impressive, wouldn't be enough to get the company back on its feet. There were also marketing issues, low employee morale, and competitors to deal with. "You either are an entrepreneur, or you're not," says Cascioli. "You have to have the leadership skills and that's what it takes."[12]

In an industry that Cascioli calls "way too competitive" for mentoring, she had to work hard, learn quickly, and lead aggressively in order to succeed.[13] Under her guidance, Lakeport manufactured other beverages. It also redesigned the label and reduced the price of its beer about $12 from that of leading Canadians brands: to $24 for 24 beers, the cheapest legally allowed in the province.[14] How did she come up with the idea? "I was sitting with a stack of newspapers and every one of them was saturated with beer ads saying, '$5 Off.' And I kept thinking, 'Off what?'," recalls Cascioli. "There was no clear message as to what the price of beer was."[15]

In 2002, Lakeport started selling its most popular Honey Lager beer with the new pricing slogan "24 for $24," and since has made huge inroads in Ontario by selling into the value-priced market. "The market at the time was overlooked by big brewers, who priced their beer as much as $10 higher, then offered frequent specials of $5 or $7 off a case," she said.[16]

When asked why she decided to focus solely on discount brands, Cascioli admits, "I'd love to tell you it was a grand strategy, but it was desperation. In 2002, we thought this was a way to keep people employed by getting more volume in the plant. Our 24 for $24 campaign was a good way to get attention without spending a lot on marketing. Then we realized it could be profitable."[17]

BREWING SUCCESS

With Lakeport leading the way, it is estimated that the value beer market now makes up more than 20 percent of all the brew sold in Canada (about 30 percent in Ontario, and more than 40 percent in Alberta). While value-priced brands have smaller margins than premium brands, they make up for it with higher volumes, making the discount market very lucrative.[18]

It has been very profitable indeed. On the strength of its flagship brands (Honey Lager, Pilsener, and Lakeport Light), its market share has increased from just over 1 percent in 2000 to approximately 11 percent in March 2006, with two of the brewery's brands on The Beer Store's Top 10 bestseller list.[19] "We've seen a dramatic shift in the market over to quality ales that feature a lower price point," says Cascioli.[20]

For cynics who think Lakeport's success can only be attributed to price, consider this: today 26 competing brands advertise the same price, compared with 11 when Lakeport first started this strategy. The difference is Lakeport has cleverly tied price with quality. That combination is represented in Lakeport's "Great Beer. Fair Prices" tag line.[21]

By 2004, Cascioli was looking for a business partner to support her ambitious plans for expanding the brewery. She found it in Ven-Growth, a Toronto-based venture capital firm, which helped her buy up the equity stake belonging to the original silent partners,[22] assuming sole ownership.[23]

In addition to buying out the 82 percent of the company held by private investors, Cascioli said the deal gave Lakeport access to the money and support that it needed for growth—support that former lenders just weren't willing to give to a business that once almost collapsed under nearly $18 million in debt.[24] "We're not the same company we were five years ago, but every time I wanted to do something with the former lenders I had to spend more and more time explaining it," she said.[25]

Lakeport Brewing Income Fund, which spun off from private predecessor, Lakeport Brewing Co., has done remarkably well in the highly competitive Ontario beer market, with consumers moving away from mainstream beers such as Molson Canadian and Labatt Blue and toward cheaper alternatives.[26] While some people have questioned whether Lakeport has what it takes to keep going after the major breweries, so far the numbers speak for themselves: 20 percent growth in sales every year since 2001 and 16 percent growth in cash flow.[27]

ARE LEADERS BORN OR MADE?

While many people marvel at the immense success of Lakeport and the unique tactics that have become Cascioli's legacy, particularly as a woman in the male-dominated corporate world, Cascioli is a little less surprised. "So what that I'm a woman? Irrespective of gender, it's still about hard work," she says. And hard work, along with her marketing savvy, aptitude for numbers, and ability to make quick decisions, is what has come to define her.[28]

"I don't see it as a man's business, let's start with that," says Cascioli, who is one of only two female members of the Brewers Association of Canada. "I'm a woman in business ... I'm going to tell you straight out, you're not going to win any points by thinking there's a man's world and a women's world. The world we live in today is about competency, having the right skills, no whining, hard work, and sacrifice. That's it.," Cascioli says.[29] "Quite frankly I'm just a woman who ... works very hard. I'm just a regular human being dealing with the challenges of running a business."[30]

She takes this business very personally and feels that the company's success and failures are a direct reflection on her. "I have difficulty separating my successes and achievements from those of the business," says Cascioli. In an industry with a lot of big players, Cascioli is always under stress. Like everyone else, she has her good days and her bad days. She tries to minimize stress by being proactive about the things she can control. "You do the best you can and [don't] worry about the stuff you can't control," says Cascioli.[31]

So what does it take to lead a rapidly growing company? "I start between 8 a.m. and 8:30 a.m. and finish between 7 p.m. and 7:30 p.m." she says. "I don't work on weekends but I'm always on call." She also recognizes where her time is best spent. "I don't have to socialize for work because we specialize in the take-home market. I didn't get here by sitting and chatting with people. I can count the number of times on one hand that I've done that in the past eight years."[32]

Cascioli admits that she loves being a leader. In fact, she can recall several instances from her formative years when she was asked about her future aspirations. "Whenever people would ask me what I wanted to be, I would always say I want to be the boss." And she certainly is.[33]

She revels in the power she wields and in the myriad challenges she encounters at any given time. Making decisions is her forte and developing clever marketing strategies is something she's built her reputation on.[34]

Asked what she enjoys most about her job, she's candid.[35] "The best part is winning and beating the competition. The big breweries would love nothing more than to see me fail. My management team is committed to winning and we love the challenge of the game."[36]

EARNING ACCOLADES

For Cascioli, the winnings can be measured in more ways that one. "It's about market shares and gains, yet it's also about the response we receive from our customers."[37]

With winning often comes recognition. Teresa Cascioli's awards include being named top

female entrepreneur by *Profit* and *Chatelaine* magazines. In 2004, Cascioli was named Entrepreneur of the Year by Ernst & Young in the Turnaround Category and in 2005 the Canadian Professional Sales Association inducted her into the Sales Hall of Fame. The Ontario Chamber of Commerce recognized Lakeport in the category of Outstanding Business Achievement in 2004. In 2006, Cascioli was named Entrepreneur of the Year by Canada's Venture Capital and Private Equity Association. As well, *Profit* ranked Lakeport among Canada's Fastest Growing Companies.

Her advice to future leaders: if you don't have the expertise, get it. Recognize your strengths and don't be afraid to go elsewhere to get the resources that you don't have. Even with smaller companies, people can't be expected to know everything. "When in doubt, contract out," says Cascioli.[38]

UPDATE

In February 2007, Labatt Brewing Company Limited bid to acquire all of outstanding units of Lakeport Brewing Income Fund at a purchase price of $28.00 per unit in cash for an aggregate price of just over $201.4 million.[39] By late March, the takeover was complete and Teresa Cascioli resigned after seven years as Lakeport's CEO.[40]

REVIEW QUESTIONS

1. What role has leadership played in the success of Lakeport Brewing?

2. Define and describe the sources of power you think Teresa Cascioli uses.

3. What leadership traits do you think best describe Cascioli as a leader and why?

4. Choose a leadership style that best describes Cascioli. Does she fit more than one leadership style? If so, what styles?

5. Would you consider Cascioli a transformational or transactional leader? Why?

6. Do you think that gender has played a role in Cascioli's success as a leader? If so, why?

YOU DO THE RESEARCH

1. What is Teresa Cascioli doing now?

2. How is Lakeport doing under Labatt Brewery's leadership?

1 Dana Flavelle, "Beer and loathing," *Toronto Star* (May 19, 2006), p. A01.

2 Ibid.

3 "Lakeport Brewing Corporation," *The Globe and Mail* (June 23, 1998), p. B10.

4 "Our Products," on the Lakeport website, <www.lakeportbrewing.ca>.

5 Scott Deveau, "A top brewer," *National Post* (February 2, 2007), p. FP3.

6 Natalia Williams, "Teresa Cascioli," *Strategy* (May 2006), p. 56.

7 Deveau, op. cit.

8 Christine Baker, "Pouring on success at Lakeport Beverages," *BusinessWoman Canada* (Fall 2003), pp. 20–21, on the Web, <www.connectuscanada.com/articles/BWC-33E.pdf>.

9 Amanda Lang, "Trailblazer: When she wants to think big thoughts—like how to turn the stodgy old beer industry on its head—Lakeport CEO Teresa Cascioli heads to the hills," *Report on Business* magazine (March 2006), p. 12.

10 Baker, op. cit.

11 Lang, op. cit.

12 Baker, op. cit.

13 Ibid.

14 Deveau, op. cit.

15 Chris Daniels, "Small-town Beer, Big Impact," *Marketing* (December 12–19, 2005), p. 22.

16 Kristin Goff, "Pouring cold water on idea that business is a 'man's world'," *Ottawa Citizen* (March 16, 2006), p. D3.

17 Libby Znaimer, "Shaking up the old-boy's beer club," *National Post* (August 26, 2006), p FW5.

18 John Intini, "Cheap is beautiful," *Maclean's* (November 14, 2005), p. 102.

19 "Teresa Cascioli of Lakeport Brewing Income Fund Awarded CVCA 'Entrepreneur of the Year' Award," news release from Canada's Venture Capital & Private Equity Association (June 2, 2006), on the CVCA website, <www.cvca.ca/files/News/EOYA_2006_Release_FINAL.pdf>.

20 Jack Kohane, "Tale of the ale," *Food in Canada* (September 2005), p. 48.

21 Daniels, op. cit.

22 Lang, op. cit.

23 Deveau, op. cit.

24 "Saviour takes helm at Lakeport Brewing," *St. Catharines Standard* (January 7, 2005), p. D6.

25 Ibid.

26 Romina Maurino, "Lakeport Brewing's growth plans in Ontario; focus on pricing and distribution," Canadian Press (April 21, 2006).

27 Lang, op. cit.

28 "Business is Brewing," *ImPRESSions* (Lakeport Brewing; August 2006 to December 2006).

29 Goff, op. cit.

30 Steve Arnold, "Hamilton still proud of brewery's saviour," *Toronto Star* (February 2, 2007), p. F1.

31 Baker, op. cit.

32 Znaimer, op. cit.

33 "Business is Brewing," op. cit.

34 Ibid.

35 Ibid.

36 Znaimer, op. cit.

37 "Business is Brewing," op. cit.

38 Baker, op. cit.

39 "Labatt Brewing Company Limited acquires Lakeport Brewing Income Fund for cash offer of $28.00 per unit," news release, Canada Newswire (February 1, 2007).

40 "'Buck a beer' will continue," *Toronto Star* (March 31, 2007), p. D20.

CASE 14

SC Johnson Canada: Where Employees Are Family

For more than 100 years, SC Johnson and Son Ltd. has been a privately held family business; five generations later it is still run by the Johnson family, with Dr. H. Fisk Johnson recently installed as the current Chairman and CEO of the company.[1] SC Johnson is a market leader in the sale of home care products. With its stable of dozens of household products, including famous brands such as Pledge, Glade, Edge, Raid, OFF!, Windex, and Ziploc, the company enjoys a dominant share of the market in more than 10 key categories in which it competes.[2]

In Canada, SC Johnson's head office is housed in Brantford, Ontario and its manufacturing facility produces the Glade line of candles, as well as other product lines under the Raid and OFF! brand names. The company also has regional sales offices in Montreal and Calgary and a smaller manufacturing facility in Varennes, Que., which produces the Ziploc brand of food storage products.[3]

BUILDING FROM THE FLOOR UP

In 1886, Samuel Curtis Johnson purchased a parquet flooring business in Racine, Wisconsin, starting SC Johnson on the road to its present success.[4] In response to customers' questions about the care of their floors, he developed his own Johnson's Prepared Paste Wax, taking the first step toward product diversification. Sales of his waxes soon outpaced those of the company's parquet flooring.[5] Later, Johnson's son, Herbert Fisk Johnson, Sr., joined the family firm, creating SC Johnson and Son. He helped his father realize the opportunities that lay in markets outside the United States, establishing the first international subsidiary in England in 1914, followed by Australia in 1917.[6]

In 1920, H.F. Johnson, Sr. rode a train headed to Toronto to search for a suitable location for his Canadian operations. During the trip, he happened to strike up a conversation with M.M. McBride, the mayor of Brantford. The mayor urged H.F. Johnson, Sr. to get off the train at Brantford instead of completing the trip to Toronto. He did, and was so impressed by the town—and the mayor—that he decided to establish SC Johnson's Canadian operations there.[7] Since that chance encounter, "Canadian Johnson," as it is often referred to by SC Johnson employees, has continued to be an integral part of the company's growth.

To the senior leaders of SC Johnson, the key to its long-term health has always been its commitment to taking care of people, whether employees or customers. In 1927, H.F. Johnson, Sr. summarized the company's guiding principles: "The goodwill of the people is the only enduring thing in any business. It is the sole substance. The rest is shadow." These beliefs continue to be consistently practised by the Johnson family and employees, who still proudly refer to H.F. Johnson, Sr.'s famous speech, saying that its meaning rings as true today as it did 80 years ago.[8]

EMPLOYEES ARE ITS GREATEST STRENGTH

SC Johnson knows that successfully motivating employees does not end with just offering competitive compensation and benefits. As a recognized leader in providing for the welfare of its employees, the company has a long track record of treating employees like family.[9] Beginning with the introduction of paid vacations in 1900 and profit sharing and group life insurance benefits in 1917,[10] the company has continued to adopt cutting-edge programs and policies designed to motivate, develop, and retain employees. Shirley Harries Langley, vice-president of human resources, believes that SC Johnson works hard to go beyond the "standard stuff like flex and summer hours and casual Fridays," offering a more holistic approach to satisfy employees' personal and professional needs.[11]

Harries Langley considers it her duty to safeguard the beliefs of the Johnson family. As a privately held company, she says, "They're able to support the ideas of how we treat people, and it allows us to be different from many public companies, because we don't have to answer to shareholders. We have a family, and the family is going to be able to be much more sensitive to people's needs."[12]

For example, to contribute to employees' sense of well-being, SC Johnson offers on-site dry cleaning and massage therapy to all employees at the Brantford facility.[13] Another Canadian-only program is called Kids' Camps, which operate on holidays such as Easter Monday and school breaks, when daycare is closed. Instead of forcing workers to choose between finding alternative childcare or taking vacation time, for a nominal fee employees can bring their children to work where they are taken care of by qualified YMCA staff. "We allow our employees to have a relationship with us that provides them with a situation where there are fewer work/life trade-offs," Harries Langley says.[14]

To create a greater sense of community at work, the F.F. (Bud) Wiley Recreation Centre encourages employees to get together to play ball hockey and volleyball in the gym during a lunch break, or try ping pong and air hockey in the common area during breaks. Employees can also play squash, join a fitness class, or just work out in the weight room.[15]

To balance employee needs in a challenging work environment, two Fridays per month, SC Johnson has a "no meeting-day" policy. This allows employees to be more productive leading into the weekends, decreasing the need to take work home.[16] It also gives employees the opportunity to regularly revisit their job goals to ensure they are on the right track. "I had the opportunity to step back and see whether I was doing the right things," recalls Cynthia Georgeson, an SC Johnson official.[17]

SC Johnson has long recognized training and development as key to encouraging employees to continue to challenge themselves. The company offers a number of programs through the Johnson Learning Institute Canada that foster its commitment to lifelong employee development. SC Johnson Canada's current core curriculum of training programs includes sessions such as Stephen Covey's 7 Habits of Highly Effective People, and function-specific training focuses on formal, on-the-job training. For employees interested in expanding their opportunities with the company, personal development courses help improve their skills in strategic thinking, leadership, communication, presentation, and computer operation, just to name a few.[18]

SC Johnson Canada also believes in building opportunities for their employees through cross-functional assignments that broaden their skills as well as their overall knowledge of company processes. Employees on the manufacturing end, for example, have moved into human resources, while those working in sales have made the jump to marketing.[19]

"We're trying to prepare our own people and grow our own talent wherever possible," says Harries Langley. "One of our goals is to have our non-entry positions filled internally. That speaks to a very high focus on our succession development planning of our people."[20] Due to the organization's carefully honed talent development strategies, 9 out of 10 positions are filled internally.[21]

Although fairness at work is most often equated with tangibles such as salary, benefits, and perks, SC Johnson focuses on developing

an open and transparent approach toward the way decisions are made and relationships are handled.[22] In a workplace where job titles and seniority levels vary so widely—approximately half of SC Johnson's employees work in manufacturing—the perception of fairness is not always an easy task. To address this, managers are provided with diversity tool kits to stimulate discussion among all employees about fairness in all areas of interaction, including training, communication, retention, and advancement. But regardless of whether they are on the assembly line or in a corner office, all staff members are given the same opportunities for training, mentorship, and profit-sharing. "The whole idea is to create an environment that is attracting, retaining, and developing the best people, and that's by respecting and valuing everyone's individual differences and similarities," says Harries Langley. "It's just about making everything that we do—whether it be internally or externally—as inclusive as possible," she says. "One of the things we teach our employees is that no matter who's walking in the door, you must treat them respectfully."[23]

AN EMPLOYER OF CHOICE

Does the focus on treating employees as family pay off? Definitely! SC Johnson's ability to motivate employees toward exceptional performance has established the company as a major player in the home care market. In addition, the loyalty and dedication shown by its employees means that SC Johnson does not have to spend money hiring. One quarter of its employees have worked there for more than 15 years. As well, in its entire history, the company has never had to lay off any workers.[24]

In addition to remaining a top player, SC Johnson has also become an employer of choice. In Canada, in addition to being named a best company to work for by *Canadian Business* magazine in 2007,[25] SC Johnson Canada has also been named as one of *Report on Business's* 50 Best Employers in Canada for six consecutive years.[26] This winning philosophy extends to other countries as well, with SC Johnson listed among top employers in the United States, Argentina, Chile, Europe, Latin America, and Mexico.[27]

REVIEW QUESTIONS

1. Using any one of the content theories of motivation, describe how SC Johnson meets both the lower order and higher order needs of its employees.

2. Pretend you are a consultant and SC Johnson has asked you to recommend new programs to improve its ability to motivate employees. Outline its current practices and provide recommendations to add to or improve its programs.

YOU DO THE RESEARCH

1. What companies are on the current *Canadian Business* magazine's list of best workplaces? What things are these companies doing to motivate their employees?

2. Research other major competitors of SC Johnson and compare their strategies for motivating employees.

[1] "About SC Johnson," on the SC Johnson and Son website, <www.scjohnson.com/family/>.

[2] "SC Johnson Canada's 80th anniversary," *Canadian Grocer* (May 2000), p. S1.

[3] Ibid.

[4] "Milestones," on the SC Johnson and Son website, <www.scjohnson.com/milestones/>.

[5] "SC Johnson Canada's 80th anniversary," op. cit.

[6] Ibid.

[7] Ibid.

[8] Ibid.

[9] Ibid.

[10] "Milestones," op. cit.

[11] "SC Johnson Canada's 80th anniversary," op. cit.

[12] Ibid.

[13] Ibid.

[14] Andy Holloway, "S.C. Johnson and Son Ltd.," *Canadian Business* (April 10–23, 2006), p. 81.

[15] "SC Johnson Canada's 80th anniversary," op. cit.

[16] "We offer an innovative environment," on the SC Johnson and Son website, <www.scjohnsonwax.com/careers/car_aie.asp>.

[17] Joann S. Lublin and Rachel Emma Silverman, "Your Career Matters: The Jungle," *Wall Street Journal* (December 28, 1999), p. B6.

[18] "SC Johnson Canada's 80th anniversary," op. cit.

[19] Ibid.

[20] Ibid.

[21] Nancy R. Lockwood, "Talent Management: Driver for Organizational Success," *HR Magazine* (June 2006), p. S1.

[22] Andrew Wahl, Joe Castaldo, Zena Olijnyk, Erin Pooley, et al., "The Best Workplaces in Canada 2007," *Canadian Business* (April 23, 2007), p. 39.

[23] Ibid.

[24] "SC Johnson Canada's 80th anniversary," op. cit.

[25] Wahl, Castaldo, Olijnyk, Pooley, et al., op. cit.

[26] "50 Best employers in Canada," on the Hewitt Associates website, <http://was7.hewitt.com/bestemployers/canada/the_list_2006.htm>.

[27] "Winning recognition as a great place to work," on the SC Johnson and Son website, <www.scjohnson.com/pr06/GPTW_winning.asp>.

CASE 15

Steinway & Sons: Craftwork, Tradition, and Time Build Grand Pianos

Steinway & Sons remains one of the best-known producers of concert pianos in the world. Throughout its great history, the company has shown a distinctive talent for innovation, as evidenced by its more than 100 patents, and is known for quality workmanship. In an age of mass production, Steinway continues to manufacture a limited number of handmade pianos in a unique testament to individual craftsmanship. However, some rival piano makers have tried to challenge Steinway's dominance of the concert piano market.[1] Can Steinway continue its cherished ways, or will it need to adjust to new circumstances?

A LONG AND GOLDEN HISTORY

German immigrant Heinrich "Henry" Steinway founded Steinway & Sons in 1853. Henry was a master cabinetmaker who built his first piano in the kitchen of his home in Seesen, Germany. He had built 482 pianos by the time he established Steinway & Sons. The first piano produced by the company, number 483, was sold to a New York family for $500. It is now displayed at New York City's Metropolitan Museum of Art.

Steinway & Son's unique quality became obvious early in the history of the firm, as the company won a number of gold medals in several American and European exhibitions in 1855. The company gained further international recognition in 1867 at the Paris Exhibition when it was awarded the prestigious "Grand Gold Medal of Honor" for excellence in manufacturing and engineering. Henry Steinway developed his pianos using emerging technical and scientific research, including the acoustical theories of the renowned physicist Hermann von Helmhotz. The Steinway factory today still uses many of the craftsmanship techniques handed down from previous generations.[2]

As a result of two world wars, the Depression, and the emergence of radio and television, there was a decline in demand for pianos from the 1920s onward.[3] Steinway & Sons was sold to CBS in 1968. Many concert artists complained that the quality of the pianos had suffered as a result of that ownership. Pianists talked of the "Teflon controversy" when Steinway replaced some fabric innards with Teflon (it now coats the Teflon with fabric). Steinway was sold by CBS to a group of private investors in 1985, and many experts voiced the opinion that Steinway's legendary quality was returning. By this time Yamaha Corporation was also selling concert pianos in direct competition to Steinway. Larry Fine, a piano expert, argued that "a Steinway has a kind of sustained, singing tone that a Yamaha doesn't have. Yamaha has a more brittle tone in the treble that some jazz pianists prefer."[4]

THE STEINWAY FACTORY

Today, even with increased competition, the making of a Steinway piano follows the Steinway tradition. Every grand piano takes more than a year to complete and incorporates more than 1,000 details that set a Steinway apart from its competitors. A tour of the Steinway factory is a trip back through time, as the key steps in the process of crafting a piano and many of the manufacturing techniques have not been changed since 1853.[5]

Using a method that was patented in 1878, the piano manufacturing process begins with the creation of the inner and outer piano rims that give a grand piano its distinctive shape; this is known as the piano case. Eighteen layers of rock maple, each 6.7 metres in length, are laminated together and then formed into the piano shape on a giant vise. The rim-bending team centres the wood on the vise and forces it into place with the aid of wood clamps.

Meanwhile, the soundboard is carefully hand formed by an expert craftsman. It must be slightly thinner at the edges so that it can vibrate properly once it is glued to the piano's inner rim. The bridge of the soundboard is notched for the piano strings before the soundboard can be placed into the piano case. A highly skilled craftsman, with years of training, performs this operation because precision is so essential to the quality of the piano's sound.

A wooden brace assembly is crafted to fit inside the piano case to help support the 155 kilogram cast-iron plate that provides the rigid and stable foundation for approximately 18,000 kilograms of tension from the piano strings. This brace is secured to the rim of the piano with fine carpentry joinery and maple dowels, and any necessary adjustments are made before final installation of the plate.

After the soundboard and cast-iron plate are properly fitted in the piano case, the piano wires are installed, using both a machine-guided stringer and appropriate hand tools. Next, the felt hammers are formed using glue and a copper forming tool. The felt hammers are then put on the hammer shanks and dampers are installed to prevent unintentional vibration of the piano strings. A master technician, using mirrors to see while reaching underneath the piano, painstakingly matches the damper felts to the strings and then adjusts the levers that control each of the dampers.

Next, the keyboard is calibrated by inserting lead weights into the body of each key so that the pressure required to push a key down is the same for every key. Subsequently, a master "voicer" will adjust the tone quality of each key. This is done by sticking the hammer's felt with a small row of needles to reduce the stiffness of the felt to achieve a more mellow tone, or by applying a small amount of lacquer to the felt for the opposite effect. Finally, a technician regulates the tone by turning the tuning pins to adjust string tension.

Steinway's process of making a grand piano is complex, requiring numerous steps and procedures that must be performed by highly skilled craftsmen. True craftsmen produce the world's finest quality concert pianos. However, not everyone wants or can afford a Steinway piano. What has Steinway & Sons done to reach other markets while maintaining the Steinway reputation for product quality?

EXPANSION BEYOND THE CLASSIC STEINWAY PIANOS

In recent years, Steinway developed the Boston Piano in an attempt to broaden its market. Steinway & Sons designed Boston Pianos using the latest computer technology and then outsourced the manufacturing to Kawai, the second-largest Japanese piano maker. By transferring its quality and knowledge of building pianos to the Boston Piano operation, Steinway was able to open up a whole new market. The Boston Piano venture demonstrated that Steinway's core competence of hand craftsmanship could be applied in a newer, high-technology manner to a lower-priced market niche.[6] In early 2001, Steinway & Sons introduced a third line of pianos, called the Essex, to complement its Steinway and Boston lines. The Essex line now offers eight grand and 18 upright models ranging in price from US$5,200 to $17,800. With the Essex, Steinway now provides pianos for every level of musical ability and budget.[7]

Having been sold again in 1995, Steinway & Sons was then merged with the Selmer Company, a manufacturer of woodwind, stringed, and percussion instruments.[8] With this merger, Steinway & Sons is now a stronger and more diversified firm. The question remains, however, can the company continue to operate in the way that has proved successful over the past 150 years?

REVIEW QUESTIONS

1. The equation specifying that Performance = Ability × Support × Effort is known as the individual performance equation. Using this equation, explain the exceptional performance that is required of, and exhibited by, the craftsmen at Steinway.

2. Use the core job characteristics model to explain the implications of Steinway's piano manufacturing process for work motivation and behaviour.

3. How does Steinway's piano manufacturing process exhibit the need for teamwork? How does this relate to job enrichment?

YOU DO THE RESEARCH

1. How does Steinway continue its emphasis on craftsmanship in this age of mass production?

2. Can any of Steinway's processes be transferred to other companies?

3. What other consumer products appear to be using a Steinway approach to producing its products?

---

[1] M. Cox, "Steinway Faces Yamaha Push in Piano Market," *Wall Street Journal* (January 19, 1988).

[2] Steinway & Sons on the Web, <www.steinway.com>.

[3] Steinway Musical Properties Inc. company history on the Web, <www.fundinguniverse.com>.

[4] M. Cox, op. cit.

[5] "Factory Tour," on the web, <www.steinway.com>.

[6] "Boston Piano," on the web, op. cit.

[7] "Steinway Unveils Essex Piano," Business Wire (January 23, 2001) and Steinway & Sons website, op. cit.

[8] Steinway Musical Properties Inc. company history, op. cit.

CASE 16

Callaway Golf: Big Bertha's Team Hits a Long Ball

Callaway Golf Company designs, creates, builds, and sells what founder Ely Callaway would have called "Demonstrably Superior and Pleasingly Different" golf products. Today, for Callaway Golf this means "any club, ball, or putter in the Callaway Golf family must be a significant improvement not only upon the products of our competitors, but also our own."[1] How does the company achieve its goals of manufacturing and distributing demonstrably superior and pleasingly different golf products?

CALLAWAY'S DSPD PHILOSOPHY

In 1982, after a long business career in textiles and wine making, Ely Callaway bought a 50 percent interest in Hickory Stick USA, a small pitching wedge and putter manufacturing operation. Callaway's goal was to bring his philosophy of making demonstrably superior and pleasingly different (DSPD) products to golfing.

The DSPD philosophy was based on his previous business experiences and served as the primary guiding principle for Callaway Golf, the company that grew out of Hickory Stick USA.[2] This philosophy provides an important foundation for Callaway Golf's corporate mission: "Callaway Golf Company is driven to be a world class organization that designs, develops, makes, and delivers demonstrably superior and pleasingly different golf products that incorporate breakthrough technologies and backs those products with noticeably superior customer service. We share every golfer's passion for the game, and commit our talents and technology to increasing the satisfaction and enjoyment all golfers derive from pursuing that passion."[3]

IMPLEMENTING THE DSPD PHILOSOPHY

Callaway Golf's numerous innovations "revolutionized the industry with friendly clubs that helped golfers of all abilities find more enjoyment and a few more great shots in their game."[4] These innovations included the 2-Ball putter and the HX aerodynamic cover pattern on golf balls. Perhaps the company's most publicized innovation was the Big Bertha driver with its large, forgiving stainless steel head.

Capitalizing on the design and manufacturing of "demonstrably superior and pleasingly different golf products," Callaway Golf continued to grow. It went public with its stock in 1992, also the year it acquired Odyssey Putters. Callaway entered the golf ball market in 2000.[5] In 2003, Calloway further expanded with the purchase of the Top-Flite Golf Company.[6] According to George Fellows, company president and CEO, in 2006 the company experienced "gains in woods, balls, and accessories and we were able to maintain our number one market position in irons and putters."[7]

Callaway Golf operates in 107 countries, building on Ely Callaway's vision of helping the average golfer find more enjoyment in the game. Ely Callaway, now deceased, retired from the company in 2001. His vision continues at Callaway Golf, first through the leadership of his hand-picked successor Ron Drapeu, and then with George Fellows, who took over as CEO in 2005.

TEAMWORK AT CALLAWAY GOLF

Teamwork at Callaway Golf is built around five different areas: research and development, information systems, manufacturing, sales, and general/administrative services. The *research and development team*—responsible for designing, building prototypes, and testing the company's innovative, premium golf equipment—draws on the engineering, analytical, and computer skills of people trained in a wide range of industries. The *information systems team* supplies the company's information needs around the clock using various computer applications. The *manufacturing team* achieves levels of efficiency, innovation, and safety that are at the top of the golf industry, using the latest manufacturing and assembly techniques. The manufacturing team members have backgrounds in industrial, mechanical, electrical, and process engineering, as well as in chemistry and aerodynamics, among other fields. The *sales team* spans the world, providing golf retailers with the latest innovations in golf equipment and the highest quality service. The *general/administrative team*—helping to build and grow the company by supporting the activities of the other teams—consists of accountants, legal experts, artists, human resource generalists, receptionists, writers, and others.[8]

While the backgrounds of the members of these teams reflect considerable diversity, all of the team members share some common characteristics. Callaway Golf looks for "integrity, honesty, daring, enthusiasm, accountability and hard work" in its employees. In addition, the company seeks to keep a "healthy balance between career and play," recognizing that this results in "happier people who are more productive in every aspect of their lives."[9] Thus far, Callaway Golf has used both similarities and differences among it employees to forge five very effective teams. Will Callaway be able to maintain this balance in the future, or will diversity be sacrificed for commonality, or commonality for diversity?

REVIEW QUESTIONS

1. What is the DSPD philosophy? Explain how the operations of the different teams reflect the DSPD philosophy.

2. What team member characteristics does Callaway Golf consider to be important? Why do these characteristics seem to be important?

3. Consider the question at the very end of the case: "Will Callaway be able to maintain this balance in the future, or will diversity be sacrificed for commonality, or commonality for diversity?" What is the most reasonable answer to this question? Why?

YOU DO THE RESEARCH

1. Identify a competitor of Callaway Golf. How does Callaway Golf's DSPD philosophy compare with the fundamental management philosophy of the competitor? What managerial insights do you gain from making this comparison?

2. Use the Callaway Golf competitor that you identified for the previous question. How does Callaway Golf's emphasis on teamwork compare with the competitor's approach to organizing and utilizing the talents of its employees? What insights about teamwork does this comparison provide?

[1] "Our Founder," on the Web, <www.callawaygolf.com>.

[2] "History," on the Web, <www.callawaygolf.com>.

[3] "Investor Relations," on the Web, <www.callawaygolf.com>.

[4] "History," op. cit.

[5] Ibid.

[6] "Business Brief—Callaway Golf: Bankruptcy Court Approval Is Given to Acquire Top-Flite," *Wall Street Journal* (September 5, 2003), p. 1.

[7] "Callaway Golf Releases Preliminary," on the Web, <www.callawaygolf.com>.

[8] "Callaway Golf Teams," on the Web, <www.callawaygolf.com>.

[9] "Careers," on the Web, <www.callawaygolf.com>.

The United Nations: Conflict and Negotiation in the Global Community

The United Nations (UN),[1] like its precursor the League of Nations, was established after a devastating world war in order to promote co-operation, peace, and security among its member countries. With 51 countries participating, the UN officially came into existence on October 24, 1945. Now, with over 192 members, it includes most countries in the world. Member countries accept the obligations of the UN Charter, an international treaty that sets out basic principles of international relations. It is an organization that truly embraces the concepts of diversity, co-operation, and conflict resolution and prevention. However, the UN does much more than resolve conflict. Looking at the major headings on its home page you find, in addition to peace and security, emphases on economic and social development, human rights, humanitarian affairs, and international law.[2]

A WORLD ORDER—HOW DOES IT WORK?

The United Nations is made up of six main branches:

- General Assembly—This body considers critical international problems.

  Each member country has one vote and key decisions require a two-thirds majority, while for lesser matters a simple majority is sufficient. In recent years there has been a striving for consensus decision making, in an effort to promote harmony.

- Security Council—The 15-member council has primary responsibility for maintaining international peace and security. Five of the member countries— China, France, the Russian Federation, the United Kingdom, and the United States—are permanent members; the other 10 are elected for two-year terms. Under the UN Charter, members are obligated to follow the Security Council's directives. Decisions require nine "yes" votes, and any permanent member can veto a decision. The Security Council tries to exhaust all possibilities for resolution prior to authorizing the use of force. The possibilities short of force include negotiation, mediation, reference to the International Court of Justice, and economic pressure.

- Economic and Social Council— The 54-member council coordinates the economic and social work of the UN system. Members are elected for three-year terms.

- Trusteeship Council—This council was formed to administer 11 trust territories. When the final territory became self-governing in 1994, the rules of procedure were changed. The current council is composed of the five permanent members of the Security Council and meets only if needed.

- International Court of Justice— Often called the World Court, this body is responsible for deciding disputes between countries, when the countries involved agree to participate. The 15 judges, elected jointly by the General Assembly and Security Council, make decisions that those appearing before them are obligated to accept.

- Secretariat—Headed by the elected Secretary-General, the staff of the Secretariat handles the administrative work of the United Nations.

In addition to these branches, there are a number of other agencies and programs, such as the International Monetary Fund and the World Health Organization, that are linked to the UN through co-operative agreements. These organizations, along with the UN's six branches, subunits, programs, and funds, form the UN system. The UN system promotes human rights, protects the environment, fights disease, fosters economic development, and reduces poverty, in addition to preserving world peace and security.[3]

The UN's greatest opportunity for impact lies in its ability to influence international public opinion. Through the UN, world conflicts are discussed on a world stage with a world audience. However, that does not guarantee that conflict can be prevented or that peacekeeping is a simple exercise. In fact, one of the organization's most inclusive experiences to date involved engaging in conflict. The UN served as a focal point in arranging a coalition of nations to counter Iraq's invasion and occupation of Kuwait in the early 1990s. Under the auspices of the Security Council, 34 nations provided the military forces necessary for Operation Desert Storm and drove

Saddam Hussein's forces out of Kuwait. Former U.S. President George H. W. Bush's claim of a "New World Order" as a result of the outcome did not come to pass.

Peacekeeping, sometimes a very dangerous enterprise, can be of short duration or last for decades. As many as 2,312 peacekeepers have died since the inception of the UN, with more UN peacekeepers dying in 2005 than in any other year of the past decade.[4] In that year there were 17 peacekeeping missions in operation, including two in Asia, three in the Middle East, three in Europe, and six in Africa.[5] Two of those have been in operation for decades; the mission at the India–Pakistan border began in 1949, and UN peacekeepers have been in Cyprus since 1964. It seems that the goal of durable peace may be difficult to achieve.

OTHER CONFLICTS

While the Security Council has the primary responsibility for maintaining international peace and security, the Security Council itself is not always at peace. After the September 11, 2001, terrorist attacks on the World Trade Center and the Pentagon, the Security Council speedily adopted a resolution that obligated member countries to ensure that terrorists would be brought to justice. However, the dissension among Security Council members regarding the appropriate action to take against Iraq subsequent to September 11 was newsworthy and unresolved. Some members wished to continue trying to settle the matter peacefully through diplomatic means but, in the end, the United States and its allies took non-sanctioned action

against Saddam Hussein. In December 2006, in his final speech as outgoing Secretary-General for the United Nations, Kofi Annan remained critical of the US involvement in the Iraq war.[6] It remains to be seen, under the leadership of the new Secretary-General Ban Ki-Moon, whether there will be any lasting breach in relations among members or damage to the power and prestige of the UN. The UN Security Council has implicitly accepted the situation by adopting resolutions indicating its willingness to continue to be involved in the process of stabilizing a postwar Iraq.

The structure of the Security Council, its funding, and its priorities are also a source of conflict within the UN. While the UN provides an infrastructure that transcends national borders, thereby encouraging international solutions to world problems, many smaller countries argue against domination by the larger nations, particularly by the Security Council's permanent membership.

In reaction to pressure from a number of nations, including the United States, the UN launched a reform movement in the late 1990s. Discussions on financing, operations, and Security Council makeup continue, but often to the frustration of the smaller countries. These frustrations are best expressed by quotations taken from the speeches made during the General Assembly's September 22 to October 7, 1997 debate on UN reform.[7] The following quotes illustrate the frustration felt over the power of the Security Council and the lack of transparency in its actions:

If reform of the [Security] Council is to be truly comprehensive and consistent with the spirit and realities of our time, then we must seek to remove—or at least, as a first step, restrict—the use of the veto power. Democracy in the United Nations is a mockery if the voice of the majority is rendered meaningless by the narrow interests of the dominant few. (Minister for Foreign Affairs of Malaysia, HE Dato' Seri Abdullah bin Haji Ahmad Badawi)

We also believe that real reform of the Security Council should aim above all at ensuring that the decision-making machinery and processes have the transparency, effectiveness and pluralism that must characterize every democratic institution. This includes, among other specific measures, the limitation of the veto power of the Council's permanent members, and for timelier and more effective action to prevent international conflicts at the request of any State Member of the Organization. (President of the Republic of Ecuador, HE Mr. Fabian Alarcon Rivera)

We would similarly like to see certain restrictions placed on the use of the veto. We understand that all efforts at restructuring and reform in the United Nations, however, should be focused on economic growth and development. In addition, my country is calling for a reversal in the diminishing role of the General Assembly. The accountability of the Security Council to the General Assembly must be re-emphasized, and the General Assembly should more actively assert its role in the maintenance of international peace and security. (Chair of the delegation of Antigua and Barbuda, HE Mr. Patrick Albert Lewis)

Another source of dissension among UN members is the direction of the UN toward goals that are not immediately related to maintaining peace and security. The United States withheld its dues, for a number of years, in protest against certain UN policies and the level of administrative waste within its programs. The disagreement concerning the funding and priorities of the UN is illustrated in the following quotes drawn from the same debate, in which implicit reference also is made to the withholding of funds by United States and other member countries:[8]

The situation of the United Nations social sphere is the most worrisome. The greatest burden of the Organization's budgetary crisis has fallen upon the bodies involved whose financing has dropped by many millions of dollars during the present decade.... In a world where 1.3 billion people still survive on less than a dollar a day, in a world where, for the price of one combat plane, 57,000 children in Africa can be fed for a year, it is impossible to conceive of a reform of the United Nations whose priority is not to strengthen the work of its institutions and programmes dedicated to social issues. (President of the Republic of Colombia, HE Mr. Ernesto Samper Pisano, also Chair of the Non-Aligned Movement)

While we are deeply engaged in this process of reform we must not lose sight of the fundamental goals that impelled us to undertake it in the first place: to enhance the organization's ability to foster development and to address the root causes of poverty and conflict. Reform should not become a euphemism for budget slashing or an excuse for certain Member States to renege on their financial obligations to the Organization. (Minister for Foreign Affairs of Indonesia, HE Mr. Ali Alatas)

Jamaica also endorses the need for measures to improve efficiency, and we have no quarrel with reform to streamline and rationalize the system. In welcoming these steps, we must however emphasize that reform is not synonymous with cost cutting. Reform is not about doing less; it is about doing better. (Prime Minister of Jamaica, The Right Honourable Percival James Patterson)

If the United Nations is to be reformed and made effective, then adequate financing is a matter of top priority. We therefore appeal to all Member States to pay their dues in full, on time, and without conditions. (First Deputy Prime Minister and Minister for Foreign Affairs of Uganda, HE The Honourable Iriya Kategaya)

It is apparent that considerable concern exists over the funding, the organization, and the role of the UN. But does that mean that the UN has failed?

THE FUTURE

Even in the face of frustration, it appears that most members continue to believe that the UN still represents the world's best opportunity to create a climate of communication and dispute resolution across national borders and to promote worldwide well-being. They recognize that the UN has had notable success in a variety of areas, including both the Nuclear Non-Proliferation Treaty (1968) and the Comprehensive Nuclear-Test-Ban Treaty (1996), the promotion of democracy, the improvement of world health, and the resolution of conflicts within and between member nations.

In response to the Programme for Reform launched in 1997, there have been three phases of reform spearheaded by the Secretary-General. The first, *Strengthening of the United Nations: an agenda for further change* focuses on the aim of adapting the internal structures and culture of the United Nations to new expectations and new challenges. Since then, there have been some important achievements—not least of these being the Millennium Declaration itself. This document contains a clear set of priorities, including precise, time-bound development goals in key areas—such as peace, security and disarmament, economic development and poverty eradication, environmental protection, and human rights, among others—that serve as a common policy framework for the entire United Nations system.[9]

The second phase of reform began in 2005 with the document *In Larger Freedom: Towards Development, Security, and Human Rights for all,* which reviewed the progress to date toward the goals of the Millennium Declaration and attempted to revitalize consensus on key challenges and priorities in converting ideas into collective action. Target areas for reform are found under four headings: *Freedom from want, Freedom from fear, Freedom to live in dignity,* and *Strengthening the United Nations.*[10]

The final phase, *Investing in the United Nations,* responded to requests for change made at the 2005 World Summit. While generating some improvements, previous reforms have primarily addressed the symptoms rather than the causes of the United Nations weaknesses, leading this report to recommend a massive restructuring of the United Nations Secretariat.[11]

Despite the focus on reform, crisis and scandal continue to plague the United Nations. In 2003, the UN was badly divided because of the US-led action in Iraq. Mr. Annan came under savage criticism both from the US, for his opposition to the war, and from the rest of the world, for failing to oppose it enough. In August 2003, the UN office in Baghdad was bombed, killing many of its brightest stars.[12] In 2004, evidence came to light of UN mismanagement over Iraq's oil-for-food program, resulting in investigations of bribery and other charges against eight senior UN procurement officials. In the same year, the head of the UN budget oversight committee was indicted on money-laundering charges, and another official pleaded guilty to skimming nearly US$1 million off UN contracts. The UN's own office of Internal Oversight found that UN peacekeeping operations had mismanaged some US$300 million in expenditures.[13] Critics continue to claim that the reforms and recommendations made by the Secretary-General in response to its internal difficulties will make no difference as they would not resolve the fundamental problems of the United Nations.[14]

Will the member countries, under the new leadership of Ban Ki-Moon, continue to support the UN, to join forces, and to seize the opportunities to revitalize the organization? Will Ban Ki-Moon be able to achieve a United Nations that is, in Kofi Annan's words, a "unique and universal instrument for concerted action in pursuit of the betterment of humankind"?[15] Or has the United Nations been irreparably damaged—and destined to go the way of the League of Nations?

REVIEW QUESTIONS

1. What is the difference between mediation and negotiation? Can you find an effective use of each by the UN?

2. Based on the quotes given, how would you classify the general debate on reform in terms of conflict management styles?

3. If reform does occur, how do you think the reform will be perceived: lose–lose, win–lose, or win–win?

4. What suggestions might you make to the UN to improve communication and conflict resolution?

YOU DO THE RESEARCH

1. What does the most recent Security Council resolution about Iraq indicate regarding the UN's involvement in that area?

2. In how many peacekeeping operations is the UN currently involved?

3. How many member countries are currently in arrears in their payments to the UN?

4. What are the current issues on the UN agenda?

[1] "About the United Nations," on the Web, <www.un.org>.

[2] Ibid.

[3] Ibid.

[4] "Message by the Secretary-General: 2006 International Day of United Nations Peacekeepers," on the Web, <www.un.org/Depts/dpko/peacekeepers06/SG_message06.pdf>.

[5] "Peacekeeping," on the Web, <www.un.org/peace/>.

[6] Steven Edwards, "Annan uses swan song to dump on Bush," CanWest News Service on the Web, December 12, 2006.

[7] "Selected Quotations on the Subject of UN Reform," <www.globalpolicy.org/reform/quotes.htm>.

[8] Ibid.

[9] "Millennium Declaration," on the Web, <www.un.org/millenniumgoals/background.html>.

[10] "In Larger Freedom," on the Web, <www.un.org/largerfreedom/summary.html>.

[11] "Investing in the United Nations," on the Web, <www.un.org/reform/investinginun/summary.shtml>.

[12] Mark Turner, "In the Spotlight Kofi Annan: Gamble of a peacemaker," *Financial Times* (August 28, 2006), p. 32.

[13] "Kofi and UN 'Ideals'," *Wall Street Journal* (December 14, 2006), p. A.20.

[14] Ryan Gawn, "A Year of Bold Decision? What UN Reform Would Have Looked Like," *Peace Magazine,* vol. 21 (Oct-Dec 2005), p. 16.

[15] "Selected Quotations on the Subject of UN Reform," op. cit.

CASE 18

British Columbia Ferry Services: Navigating the Changing Times

What began in 1960 as a two-vessel, 200-employee, and two-terminal operation has grown into one of the largest, most sophisticated ferry transportation systems in the world.[1] Today, British Columbia Ferry Services has 36 vessels and provides service to more than 47 destinations that are some of the most fun, fascinating, and often remote corners of the British Columbia coast. The staff complement now exceeds 4,700 in the summer and their commitment to customer safety and service has never been stronger.[2] President and CEO David Hahn has been instrumental in turning BC Ferries from a troubled Crown corporation to a successful independent business. Can Hahn sustain the company's forward momentum in the face of significant organizational and environmental changes?

BC FERRIES THROUGH THE YEARS

Recognizing the need for continued reliable ferry service on the west coast of British Columbia, Premier W.A.C. Bennett announced on July 18, 1958, that the British Columbia Ferry Authority would take over service under mandate from the provincial government.[3]

Starting out with just two ships, the new ferry system began operating under the name "British Columbia Toll Authority Ferry System." The service linked Victoria, the provincial capital on Vancouver Island, with the City of Vancouver and the rest of the mainland,[4] operating essentially a marine extension to the province's public highways system.[5]

Official service began during one of the windiest, rainiest days in June 1960, but the vessels kept to their schedules and carried their passengers safely to their destinations. With local airports fogged in much of the time, the ferry system quickly attracted customers who found it more convenient and less expensive than taking a plane. By the end of first year, the fledgling organization managed to turn a profit and growth followed quickly.[6]

Despite its early success, the ferry system was plagued by poor service and inefficient operations, issues compounded by the fact that almost every employee function, from deck swabbers to ship captains, was separated into a different union. Yet by 1985, the rechristened BC Ferry Corp. became was one of the world's largest ferry operations. Despite extensive growth, BC Ferry Corp.'s financial difficulties continued. Tolls covered only a fraction of the corporation's operating costs, with the balance covered by grants from the provincial and federal governments.[7]

Year after year, the BC Ferry Corp.'s financial situation grew worse. In 2000, the corporation lost a staggering $300 million. Meanwhile, its debt had reached $1.1 billion. While the government wrote off the debt and increased the corporation's annual subsidy from $50 million to $72 million, it still wasn't enough. BC Ferries lost another $22.6 million in 2001. The entire organizational system was floundering and it only took one glance at the balance sheets to show why.[8]

By 2002, BC Ferries was technically insolvent. Bob Lingwood, the corporation's third president and CEO in three years, was dismissed by the new Liberal government. A year later, the corporation was dismantled and replaced with the new British Columbia Ferry Services Inc. David Emerson, a successful executive and Canada's current Minister of International Trade, was appointed chairman.[9] It was apparent to Emerson that in order to survive, BC Ferries desperately needed a new direction. It also needed the right leadership to steer the company through a sea of significant change.

PUBLIC TO PRIVATE OWNERSHIP

In April 2, 2003, after intense examination by the provincial government and the BC Ferries' board of directors, the new British Columbia Ferry Services Inc. was officially relaunched as a new independent commercial company.[10]

In addition to helping redesign the company's management structure, Emerson was also tasked to find a new leader. While more than 150 resumés crossed his desk, Emerson and the BC Ferries board hired David Hahn, a former New York vice-president for Ogden Aviation Services. Although Hahn knew next to nothing about the company's operations, Emerson felt that he seemed like someone who was "willing to go down into the engine rooms." He also believed that

Hahn's no-nonsense style of leadership fit the skills needed to lead BC Ferries through the tough times ahead.[11]

Hahn not only went down to the engine room, he went everywhere. "When I was interviewing, I came out here and I rode the ferries," he recalls. "I found their condition not what one would have expected. Particularly the washrooms. They just weren't maintained." Hahn felt the whole operation looked battered. "It wasn't just one ship, or two ships. It was everything." Hahn saw that was just the tip of the iceberg. "I spent a lot of time watching the employees," says Hahn. "There was a morale problem. On-time performance was horrible."[12]

Once in charge, Hahn wasted no time making changes, even if they seemed trivial. He had the washrooms cleaned up. Efforts to market the service were improved. Extra night sailings were added to coincide with major events and customer surveys were introduced, providing the company with valuable feedback.[13] He also incorporated live, onboard announcements to let passengers know when a ferry departed late and why. At first, he says, the ferry workers were resistant. They "didn't see the value in it. Why would that be useful? They never had to do it before, blah, blah, blah," Hahn says. "People want to know what the status is. That's a pretty basic service principle."[14]

While focusing on improving customer services, Hahn still had to tackle the three major challenges. The first was establishing real independence from government. Attempts to interfere with his mandate came from everywhere. "Everyone from an MLA to local politicians, they all wanted to add

their two cents. You still had some people who felt they could tell BC Ferries how to behave and act and try to tell us what we'd have to do around purchasing something or [making] a policy change." In his typical style, Hahn states, "I don't have the time to waste with that nonsense. We don't cater to government. We cater to the public."[15]

The next priority was taking on his employees' largest and most militant labour union. Despite a long history of poor labour relations, Hahn demanded changes to a new collective agreement under negotiation with the Marine Workers' Union, which represented about 4,300 ferry workers. In addition to a long-term contract, Hahn wanted concessions that would save the company money. He also wanted the ability to contract out certain positions to non-union workers. Talks stalled between BC Ferries management and the union, resulting in a wildcat strike in December 2003, right before the busy holiday season. The whole ferry system shut down but Hahn stood his ground, supported by public sentiment. For the public, illegal pickets meant more than just inconvenience, it meant that businesses would suffer and some people would lose access to medical care. The ferry workers went back to work, and the union agreed to binding arbitration. In October 2004, a mediator instituted a seven-year contract, giving total wage increases of just 6 percent over the period. Layoffs and wage and benefit rollbacks were not included in the deal.[16]

The final priority Hahn wanted to tackle was to implement a fleet and terminal improvement plan. With the current fleet of ships averaging over 32 years of age, the company needed new ships; the last

large vessels it had commissioned had entered service in the early 1990s. Since then, passenger trips had peaked at about 22 million a year. To boost revenue, the company had to increase capacity significantly if it was to increase loads. In 2004, Hahn decided to commission 22 new vessels, costing $1.8 billion, with another $400 million marked for ferry terminal improvements. Some of the system's terminals had already been dramatically revamped but Hahn says the biggest improvements are still to come. "The best thing that will happen for the company is when the new ships arrive."[17]

THE PAYOFF

All of Hahn's efforts had started to pay off. In 2003, 76 percent of customers reported they were satisfied with BC Ferries. In 2005, satisfaction levels reached 86 percent. He attributes the success in part to some changes he thought were obvious. "We make announcements on board the ships, saying when we're leaving and what the arrival time is," Hahn says. "Before it was like some kind of big mystery, which I couldn't understand. ...We've also equipped 17 of our vessels with defibrillators. That says we care about our customers."

There has also been a steady increase in BC Ferries' net earnings, from $28 million in 2004 to $49.9 million in 2006.[18]

Hahn knows his straight-to-the-point manner can be offensive, but he says he doesn't care. In fact, he believes his direct approach has helped contribute to the turnaround at BC Ferries. "I was probably rude to some people," Hahn says. "Especially to those in government, who still felt we could do things the old way."[19]

TRAGIC CRISIS

However, balance sheets are only one measure of health, and gains like these looked trivial when compared with the catastrophe that lay ahead.

For three years, David Hahn's efforts to turn the newly privatized BC Ferry Services into an efficient, customer-friendly operation had been mostly on track. Then the worst happened. In March 2006, one of its ships, Queen of the North, hit a rock and sank in the deep, cold waters off tiny Gil Island, 135 kilometres south of Prince Rupert.[20]

According to the ship's manifest, there were 102 passengers and crew members on board. As one of the worst accidents in BC Ferries' history was unfolding, Hahn was front and centre trying to hold the company together. Two passengers were missing. Hours passed. Then a day. The missing couple had not been found and it appeared certain they had gone down with the ship.[21]

Since the tragic sinking, Hahn has focused on finding out what the three bridge crew members were doing in the crucial final 14 minutes when Queen of the North should have changed course at Sainty Point, but instead rammed into Gil Island. He has even threatened to discipline the crew members for refusing to take part in the corporation's internal investigation.[22]

He refuses to accept union claims that management failed to properly train the crew on newly installed equipment. And he has maintained that view, despite a Transportation Safety Board advisory that said bridge crew members were confused on how to use a new steering mode selector switch and turned off an electronic chart display monitor because they didn't know how to use the screen's dimmer switch.[23]

The most recent accident isn't the first time ferry safety has been called into question under Hahn's watch. In July 2005, the Queen of Oak Bay lost power and ran into a West Vancouver marina, damaging two dozen pleasure craft. The accident was recorded and broadcast around the world on CNN.[24]

THE FUTURE

While the accident and its aftermath will not ruin BC Ferries, they have shifted attention away from the company's forward momentum to deeper concerns about safety. The incident has also reignited battles between management and the unions.[25]

The federal Transportation Safety Board investigated the sinking but its report was not released at the time of writing. However, the safety review ordered by BC Ferries recommended the company put safety at the top of its list in every facet of the company.[26]

The 70-page report, written by former B.C. auditor general George Morfitt, said the company's safety management system needs a top-to-bottom review. It also cites problems with risk management, inadequate shift handovers, a lack of training for the company's accident investigators, and internal audits that deal with paper trails rather than observing "live" drills and inspections.[27]

The report noted that while the company's system of practices, protocols, and procedures required under the International Safety Code was adopted a decade ago, BC Ferries management neglected to ensure sufficient buy-in from employees to transform it from a series of manuals and checklists into a fleet-wide approach embraced by workers.[28]

To address this, Hahn says BC Ferries will implement the 41 recommendations in the Morfitt report, including addressing the relationship between the corporation and its employees. While many of the union–management issues pre-date Hahn's arrival, the company and union are committed to resolving their differences.[29] Recognizing that dysfunction between the union and management "poses a significant impediment to resolving operational safety issues and continuously improving the safety management system,"[30] Hahn and union president Jackie Miller have endorsed the report and promised to work together to implement the recommendations.[31]

On the complimentary side, the report says the company sets safe practices as a goal, operates its fleet safely overall, buys the best emergency equipment, and has laudable plans for its own training centre.[32] It remains to be seen how those goals will be set into practice.

BC Ferries remains deeply committed to safety, but is prepared to do more to address Morfitt's report, Hahn says. "How you make (safety) culturally a stronger part of an organization is you start every meeting by talking about safety," he says. "Every element of work, whether you're in the finance department or the marketing department—not just on the ships—has to think safety first."[33]

While the report concludes overall that BC Ferries operates a safe transportation system, Hahn agrees "there are a number of areas identified in this report where safety and related administrative processes and procedures should be strengthened."[34]

Despite total revenue climbing to $579.2 million in 2006, up from $564.5 million the previous year,[35] Hahn wears the success as much as he bears the weight of what happened with the Queen of the North. "I think about the Queen of the North and the two people who died every day," Hahn says. "Not just once, about 10 times a day."[36]

It's hard to predict what the accident will mean for Hahn's turnaround efforts and his tenure at BC Ferries. Watching how he's handled this crisis, however, it's clear he'll continue using the combative approach that has worked well for him so far.[37]

REVIEW QUESTIONS

1. Describe the internal and external forces for change faced by BC Ferries.

2. Did Hahn follow Kurt Lewin's approach to planned change? Support your answer.

3. What change strategy approach did Hahn make primary use of at BC Ferries?

YOU DO THE RESEARCH

1. Despite numerous challenges, BC Ferries has apparently turned its fortunes around. Do you think the changes instituted by David Hahn have helped or harmed BC Ferries' long-term success?

---

[1] "About BC Ferries," on the BC Ferries website, <www.bcferries.com/about/>.

[2] "Our history," on the BC Ferries website, <www.bcferries.bc.ca/corporate/history/history.html>.

[3] Ibid.

[4] Ibid.

[5] Brian Hutchinson, "Uncharted Waters," *Financial Post Business* (September 2006), p. 40.

[6] "Our history," op. cit.

[7] Hutchinson, op. cit.

[8] Ibid.

[9] Ibid.

[10] "Our history," op. cit.

[11] Hutchinson, op. cit.

[12] Ibid.

[13] Ibid.

[14] Ibid.

[15] Ibid.

[16] Ibid.

[17] Ibid.

[18] Ibid.

[19] Ibid.

[20] Ibid.

[21] Ibid.

[22] Cindy E. Harnett, "Ferry boss steers through rough waters," *Victoria Times-Colonist* (December 24, 2006), p. D7.

[23] Ibid.

[24] Hutchinson, op. cit.

[25] Ibid.

[26] Dirk Meissner, "B.C. Ferries president says company will implement 41 safety recommendations," Canadian Press (January 22, 2007).

[27] Christina Montgomery, "B.C. Ferries, union agree to act on safety report," CanWest News (January 23, 2007).

[28] Ibid.

[29] Meissner, op. cit.

[30] Ibid.

[31] Montgomery, op. cit.

[32] Ibid.

[33] Meissner, op. cit.

[34] Ibid.

[35] "Big things are happening in B.C.," *Marine Log* (October 2006), p. 19.

[36] Harnett, op. cit.

[37] Hutchinson, op. cit.

ACTIVE LEARNING PROJECTS

Diversity Lessons—"What Have We Learned?"

QUESTION

What are the current "facts" in terms of progress for visible minorities, the disabled, Aboriginals, and women in the workplace? What lessions of diversity have been learned? What are the "best" employers doing?

Possible Research Directions

- Examine case studies of employers reported as having strong diversity programs. What do they have in common? What do they do differently?

- Find out what we know about how well people of different racial, ethnic, gender, lifestyle, physical abilities, and generational groups work together. What are the common problems, if any? What concerns do managers and workers have?

- Get specific data on how the "glass ceiling" affects the careers of women and members of diverse groups in various occupational settings. Analyze the data and develop the implications.

- Take a critical look at the substance of diversity training programs. What do these programs try to accomplish, and how? Are they working or not, and how do we know?

PROJECT 2

Corporate Social Responsibility—"What's the Status?"

QUESTION

Where do businesses stand today with respect to the criteria for evaluating social responsibility discussed in the textbook?

Possible Research Directions

- Create a scale that could be used to measure the social responsibility performance of an organization. Review the scholarly research in this area, but also include your own ideas and expectations.

- Use your scale to research and evaluate the "status" of major organizations and local ones on social responsibility performance. How well are they doing? Would you use them as models of social responsibility for others to follow, or not?

- Conduct research to identify current examples of the "best" and the "worst" organizations in terms of performance or social responsibility criteria. Pursue this investigation on a(n) (a) international, (b) national, and/or (c) local scale.

PROJECT 3

Globalization—"What Are the Pros and Cons?"

QUESTION

"Globalization" is frequently in the news. You can easily read or listen to both advocates and opponents. What is the bottom line? Is globalization good or bad, and for whom?

Possible Research Directions

- What does the term "globalization" mean? Review various definitions and find the common ground.

- Read and study the scholarly arguments about globalization. Summarize what the scholars say about the forces and consequences of globalization in the past, present, and future.

- Examine current events relating to globalization. Summarize the issues and arguments. What is the positive side of globalization? What are the negatives that some might call its "dark" side?

- Consider globalization from the perspective of your local community or one of its major employers. Is globalization a threat or an opportunity, and why?

- Take a position on globalization. State what you believe to be the best course for government and business leaders to take. Justify your position.

PROJECT 4

Diversity Management—"Where Do We Go from Here?"

QUESTION

Organizational researchers argue that it is time to move beyond employment equity and learn how to "manage diversity." There are a lot of issues that may be raised in this context—issues of equal employment opportunity, hiring quotas, reverse discrimination, and others. What is the status of managing diversity today?

Possible Research Directions

- Read articles on the subject of managing diversity. Make sure you are clear on the term "employment equity" and its legal underpinnings. Research the topic, identify the relevant laws, and make a history line to chart its development over time.

- Examine current debates on employment equity. What are the issues? How are the "for" and "against" positions being argued?

- Identify legal cases where reverse discrimination has been charged. How have they been resolved and with what apparent human resource management implications?

- Look at actual organizational policies on diversity. Analyze them and identify the common ground. Prepare a policy development guideline for use by human resource managers.

- As you ponder these issues and controversies be sure to engage different perspectives. Talk to and read about people of different "majority" and "minority" groups. Find out how they view these things—and why.

PROJECT 5

Fringe Benefits—"How Can They Be Managed?"

QUESTION

Employers complain that the rising cost of "fringe benefits" is a major concern. Is this concern legitimate? If so, how can fringe benefits be best managed?

Possible Research Directions

- Find out exactly what constitutes "fringe benefits" as part of the typical compensation package. Look in the literature and also talk to local employers. Find out what percentage of a typical salary is represented in fringe benefits.

- Find and interview two or three human resource managers in your community. Ask them to describe their fringe benefits programs and how they manage fringe benefits costs. What do they see happening in the future? What do they recommend? Talk to two or three workers from different employers in your community. Find out how things look to them and what they recommend.

- Pick a specific benefit such as dental benefits. What are the facts? How are employers trying to manage the rising cost? What are the implications for workers?

- Examine the union positions on fringe benefits. How is this issue reflected in major labour negotiations? What are the results of major recent negotiations?

- Look at fringe benefits from the perspective of temporary, part-time, or contingent workers. What do they get? What do they want? How are they affected by rising costs?

PROJECT 6

CEO Pay—"Is It Too High?"

QUESTION

What is happening in the area of executive compensation? Are CEOs paid too much? Are they paid for "performance," or are they paid for something else?

Possible Research Directions

- Check the latest reports on CEO pay. Get the facts and prepare a briefing report as if you were writing a short informative article for *Canadian Business* magazine. The title of your article should be "Status Report: Where We Stand Today on CEO Pay."

- Address the pay-for-performance issue. Do corporate CEOs get paid for performance or for something else? What do the researchers say? What do the business periodicals say? Find some examples to explain and defend your answers to these questions.

- Take a position: Should a limit be set on CEO pay? If no, why not? If yes, what type of limit do we set? Who, if anyone, should set these limits—company boards of directors, or someone else?

- Examine the same issues in the government setting. Are premiers and prime ministers paid too much?

PROJECT 7

Gender and Leadership—"Is There a Difference?"

QUESTION

Do men and women lead differently?

Possible Research Directions

- Review the discussion on gender and leadership in the textbook, Chapter 13. Find and read the articles cited in the endnotes. Then, update this literature by finding and reading the most recent scholarly findings and reports.

- Interview managers from organizations in your local community. Ask them whether men and women lead differently. Ask them to give you specific examples to justify their answers. Look for patterns and differences. Do male managers and female managers answer the question similarly?

- Interview workers from organizations in your local community. Ask them the question. Ask them to give you specific examples to justify their answers. Look for patterns and differences. Do male workers and female workers answer the question similarly? Do the same for students—pressing them to share insights and examples from their experiences in course study groups and student organizations.

- Summarize your findings. Describe the implications of your findings in terms of leadership development for both men and women.

PROJECT 8

Superstars on the Team—"What Do They Mean?"

QUESTION

Do we want a "superstar" on our team?

Possible Research Directions

- Everywhere you look—in entertainment, in sports, and in business—a lot of attention these days goes to the superstars. What is the record of teams and groups with superstars? Do they really outperform the rest?

- What is the real impact of a superstar's presence on a team or in the workplace? What do they add? What do they cost? Consider the potential costs of having a superstar on a team in the equation: Benefits − Costs = Value. What is the bottom line of having a superstar on the team?

- Interview the athletic coaches on your campus. Ask them whether having a superstar means outperforming others. Compare and contrast their answers. Interview players from various teams. Do the same for them.

- Develop a set of guidelines for creating team effectiveness for a situation where a superstar is present. Be thorough and practical. Can you give advice good enough to ensure that a superstar always creates super performance for the team or work group or organization?

PROJECT 9

Management in Popular Culture—"Seeing Ourselves Through Our Pastimes"

QUESTION

What management insights are found in popular culture and reflected in our everyday living?

Possible Research Directions

- Listen to music. Pick out themes that reflect important management concepts and theories. Put them together in a multimedia report that presents your music choices and describes their messages about management and working today.

- Watch television. Look again for the management themes. In a report, describe what popular television programs have to say about management and working. Also consider TV advertisements. How do they use and present workplace themes to help communicate their messages?

- Read the comics, also looking for management themes. Compare and contrast management and working in two or three popular comic strips.

- Read a best-selling novel. Find examples of management and work themes in the novel. Report on what the author's characters and their experiences say about people at work.

- Watch a film or video. Again, find examples of management and work themes. In a report describe the message of the movie in respect to management and work today.

Note: These ideas are borrowed from the extensive work in this area by Dr. Robert (Lenie) Holbrook of Ohio University.

PROJECT 10

Service Learning in Management—"Learning from Volunteering"

QUESTION

What can you learn about management and leadership by working as a volunteer for a local community organization?

Possible Research Directions

- Explore service learning opportunities on your campus. Talk to your instructor about how to add a service learning component to your management course.

- List the nonprofit organizations in your community that might benefit from volunteers. Contact one or more of them and make inquiries as to how you might help them. Do it, and then report back on what you learned as a result of the experience that is relevant to management and leadership.

- Locate the primary schools in your community or region. Contact the school principals and ask how you might be able to help teachers working with students in Grades 1–6. Do it, and then report back on what you learned with respect to personal management and leadership development.

- For either the nonprofit organization or the primary school, form a group of students who share similar interests in service learning. Volunteer as a group to help the organization and prepare a team report on what you learned.

- Take the initiative. Create service learning ideas of your own—to be pursued individually or as part of a team. While working as a volunteer always keep your eyes and ears open for learning opportunities. Continually ask—"What is happening here in respect to: leadership, morale, motivation, teamwork, conflict, interpersonal dynamics, organization culture and structures, and more?"

EXERCISES IN TEAMWORK

EXERCISE 1

My Best Manager

PREPARATION

Working alone, make a list of the *behavioural attributes* that describe the best manager you have ever worked for. This could be someone you worked for in a full-time or part-time job, summer job, volunteer job, student organization, or whatever. If you have trouble identifying an actual manager, make a list of behavioural attributes of the type of manager you would most like to work for in your next job.

INSTRUCTIONS

Form into groups as assigned by your instructor, or work with a nearby classmate. Share your list of attributes and listen to the lists of others. Be sure to ask questions and make comments on items of special interest. Work together to create a master list that combines the unique attributes of the "best" managers experienced by members of your group. Have a spokesperson share that list with the rest of the class.

Source: Adapted from John R. Schermerhorn, Jr., James G. Hunt, and Richard N. Osborn, *Managing Organizational Behavior*, 3rd ed. (New York: Wiley, 1988), pp. 32–33. Used by permission.

EXERCISE 2

What Managers Do

PREPARATION

Think about the questions that follow. Record your answers in the spaces provided.

1. How much of a typical manager's time would you expect to be allocated to these relationships? (total should = 100%)

___% of time working with subordinates

___% of time working with boss

___% of time working with peers and outsiders

2. How many hours per week does the average manager work? ___ hours

3. What amount of a manager's time is typically spent in the following activities? (total should = 100%)

___% in scheduled meetings

___% in unscheduled meetings

___% doing desk work

___% talking on the telephone

___% walking around the organization/ work site

INSTRUCTIONS

Talk over your responses with a nearby classmate. Explore the similarities and differences in your answers. Be prepared to participate in a class discussion led by your instructor.

EXERCISE 3

Defining Quality

PREPARATION

Write your definition of the word quality here.
QUALITY =

INSTRUCTIONS

Form groups as assigned by your instructor. (1) Have each group member present a definition of the word "quality." After everyone has presented, come up with a consensus definition of *quality*. That is, determine and write down one definition of the word with which every member can agree. (2) Next, have the group assume the position of top manager in each of the following organizations. Use the group's *quality* definition to state for each a *quality objective* that can guide the behaviour of members in producing high-"quality" goods and/or services for customers or clients. Elect a spokesperson to share group results with the class as a whole.

Organizations:

a. A college of business administration

b. A community hospital

c. A retail sporting goods store

d. A fast-food franchise restaurant

e. A Canada Post branch

f. A full-service bank branch

g. A student-apartment rental company

h. A used textbook store

i. A computer software firm

EXERCISE 4

What Would the Classics Say?

PREPARATION

Consider this situation:

Six months into his new job, Bob, a laboratory worker, is performing just well enough to avoid being fired. When hired he was carefully selected and had the abilities required to do the job really well. At first Bob was enthusiastic about his new job, but now he isn't performing up to this high potential. Fran, his supervisor, is concerned and wonders what can be done to improve this situation.

INSTRUCTIONS

Assume the identify of one of the following persons: Frederick Taylor, Henri Fayol, Max Weber, Abraham Maslow, Chris Argyris. Assume that *as this person* you have been asked by Fran for advice on the management situation just described.

Answer these questions as you think your assumed identity would respond. Be prepared to share your answers in class and to defend them based on the text's discussion of this person's views.

1. As (*your assumed identity*), what are your basic beliefs about good management and organizational practices?

2. As (*your assumed identity*), what do you perceive may be wrong in this situation that would account for Bob's low performance?

3. As (*your assumed identity*), what could be done to improve Bob's future job performance?

EXERCISE 5

The Great Management History Debate

PREPARATION

Consider the question "What is the best thing a manager can do to improve productivity in her or his work unit?"

INSTRUCTIONS

The instructor will assign you, individually or in a group, to one of the following positions. Complete the missing information as if you were the management theorist referred to. Be prepared to argue and defend your position before the class.

- Position A: "Mary Parker Follett offers the best insight into the question. Her advice would be to … " (advice to be filled in by you or the group).

- Position B: "Max Weber's ideal bureaucracy offers the best insight into the question. His advice would be to …" (advice to be filled in by you or the group).

- Position C: "Henri Fayol offers the best insight into the question. His advice would be to . . . " (advice to be filled in by you or the group).

- Position D: "The Hawthorne studies offer the best insight into the question. Elton Mayo's advice would be to …" (advice to be filled in by you or the group).

EXERCISE 6

Confronting Ethical Dilemmas

PREPARATION

Read and indicate your response to each of the situations below.

a. Pierre Tremblay, vice president of a large construction firm, receives in the mail a large envelope marked "personal." It contains a competitor's cost data for a project that both firms will be bidding on shortly. The data are accompanied by a note from one of Pierre's subordinates saying: "This is the real thing!" Pierre knows that the data could be a major advantage to his firm in preparing a bid that can win the contract. *What should he do?*

b. Kay Smith is one of your top-performing subordinates. She has shared with you her desire to apply for promotion to a new position just announced in a different division of the company. This will be tough on you since recent budget cuts mean you will be unable to replace anyone who leaves, at least for quite some time. Kay knows this and in all fairness has asked your permission before she submits an application. It is rumoured that the son of a good friend of your boss is going to apply for the job. Although his credentials are less impressive than Kay's, the likelihood is that he will get the job if she doesn't apply. *What will you do?*

c. Marty Jose got caught in a bind. She was pleased to represent her firm as head of the local community development committee. In fact, her supervisor's boss once held this position and told her in a hallway conversation, "Do your best and give them every support possible." Going along with this, Marty agreed to pick up the bill (several hundred dollars) for a dinner meeting with local civic and business leaders. Shortly therafter, her supervisor informed everyone that the entertainment budget was being eliminated in a cost-saving effort. Marty, not wanting to renege on supporting the community development committee, was able to charge the dinner bill to an advertising budget. Eventually, an internal auditor discovered the mistake and reported it to you, the personnel director. Marty is scheduled to meet with you in a few minutes. *What will you do?*

INSTRUCTIONS

Working alone, make the requested decisions in each of these incidents. Think carefully about your justification for the decision. Meet in a group assigned by your instructor. Share your decisions and justifications in each case with other group members. Listen to theirs. Try to reach a group consensus on what to do in each situation and why. Be prepared to share the group decisions, and any dissenting views, in general class discussion.

EXERCISE 7

What Do You Value in Work?

PREPARATION

Rank order the nine items in terms of how important (9 = most important) they would be to you in a job. How important is it to you to have a job that:

___ Is respected by other people?

___ Encourages continued development of knowledge and skills?

___ Provides job security?

___ Provides a feeling of accomplishment?

___ Provides the opportunity to earn a high income?

(a) The president drafted the 8 objectives and submitted them to Chang for review.

(b) The president and Chang thoroughly discussed the 8 objectives in proposal form before they were finalized.

(c) The president and Chang scheduled a meeting in 6 months to review Chang's progress on the objectives.

(d) The president didn't discuss the objectives with Chang again until the scheduled meeting was held.

(e) The president told Chang his annual raise would depend entirely on the extent to which these objectives were achieved.

3. Share and discuss your responses to parts 1 and 2 of the exercise with a nearby classmate. Reconcile any differences of opinion by referring back to the chapter discussion of MBO. Await further class discussion.

EXERCISE 14

The Future Workplace

INSTRUCTIONS

Form groups as assigned by the instructor. Brainstorm to develop a master list of the major characteristics you expect to find in the future workplace in the year 2020. Use this list as background for completing the following tasks:

1. Write a one-paragraph description of what the typical "Workplace 2020 manager's" workday will be like.

2. Draw a "picture" representing what the "Workplace 2020 organization" will look like.

Choose a spokesperson to share your results with the class as a whole and explain their implications for the class members.

EXERCISE 15

Dots and Squares Puzzle

INSTRUCTIONS

1. Shown here is a collection of 16 dots. Study the figure to determine how many "squares" can be created by connecting the dots.

2. Draw as many squares as you can find in the figure while making sure a dot is at every corner of every square. Count the squares and write this number in the margin to the right of the figure.

3. Share your results with those of a classmate sitting nearby. Indicate the location of squares missed by either one of you.

4. Based on this discussion, redraw your figure to show the maximum number of possible squares. Count them and write this number to the left of the figure.

5. Await further class discussion led by your instructor.

EXERCISE 16

Leading Through Participation

PREPARATION

Read each of the following vignettes. Write in the margin whether you think the leader should handle the situation with an individual decision (I), consultative decision (C), or group decision (G).

VIGNETTE I

You are a general supervisor in charge of a large team laying an oil pipeline. It is now necessary to estimate your expected rate of progress in order to schedule material deliveries to the next field site. You know the nature of the terrain you will be travelling and have the historical data needed to calculate the mean and variance in the rate of speed over the type of terrain. Given these two variables, it is a simple matter to calculate the earliest and latest times at which materials and support facilities will be needed at the next site. It is important that your estimate be reasonably accurate; underestimates result in idle supervisors and workers, and overestimates result in materials being tied up for a period of time before they are to be used. Progress has been good, and your 5 supervisors along with the other members of the gang stand to receive substantial bonuses if the project is completed ahead of schedule.

VIGNETTE II

You are supervising the work of 12 engineers. Their formal training and work experience are very similar, permitting you to use them interchangeably on projects. Yesterday, your manager informed you that a request had been received from an overseas affiliate for 4 engineers to go abroad on extended loan for a period of 6 to 8 months. He argued and you agreed that for a number of reasons this request should be filled from your group. All your engineers are capable of handling this assignment, and from the standpoint of present and future projects there is no particular reason that any one should be retained over any other. The problem is complicated by the fact that the overseas assignment is in what is generally regarded in the company as an undesirable location.

VIGNETTE III

You are the head of a staff unit reporting to the vice president of finance. He has asked you to provide a report on the firm's current portfolio including recommendations for changes in the selection criteria currently employed. Doubts have been raised about the efficiency of the existing system in the current market conditions, and there is considerable dissatisfaction with prevailing rates of return. You plan to write the report, but at the moment you are quite perplexed about the approach to take. Your own specialty is the bond market, and it is clear to you that a detailed knowledge of the equity market, which you lack, would greatly enhance the value of the report. Fortunately, 4 members of your staff are specialists in different segments of the equity market. Together, they possess a vast amount of knowledge about the intricacies of investment. However, they seldom agree on the best way to achieve anything when it comes to the stock market. Whereas they are obviously conscientious as well as knowledgeable, they have major differences when it comes to investment philosophy and strategy. The report is due in 6 weeks. You have already begun to familiarize yourself with the firm's current portfolio and have been provided by management with a specific set of constraints that any portfolio must satisfy. Your immediate problem is to come up with some alternatives to the firm's present practices and select the most promising ones for detailed analysis in your report.

VIGNETTE IV

You are on the division manager's staff and work on a wide variety of problems of both an administrative and technical nature. You have been given the assignment of developing a universal method to be used in each of the 5 plants in the division for manually reading equipment registers, recording the readings, and transmitting the scoring to a centralized information system. All plants are located in a relatively small geographical region. Until now there has been a high error rate in the reading and/or transmittal of the data. Some locations have considerably higher error rates than others, and the methods used to record and transmit the data vary between plants. It is probable, therefore, that part of the error variance is a function of specific local conditions rather than anything else, and this will complicate the establishment of any system common to all plants. You have the information on error rates but no information on the local practices that generate these errors or on the local conditions that necessitate the different practices. Everyone would benefit from an improvement in the quality of the data because they are used in a number of important decisions. Your contacts with the plants are through the quality control supervisors responsible for collecting the data. They are a conscientious group committed to doing their jobs well but are highly sensitive to interference on the part of higher management in their own operations. Any solution that does not receive the active support of the various plant supervisors is unlikely to reduce the error rate significantly.

INSTRUCTIONS

Form groups as assigned by the instructor. Share your choices with other group members and try to achieve a consensus on how the leader should best handle each situation. Refer back to the discussion of the Vroom-Jago "leader-participation" theory presented in Chapter 13. Analyze each vignette according to their ideas. Do you come to any different conclusions? If so, why? Nominate a spokesperson to share your results in general class discussion.

Source: Victor H. Vroom and Arthur G. Jago, *The New Leadership* (Englewood Cliffs, NJ: Prentice Hall, 1988).

EXERCISE 17

Work vs. Family—You Be the Judge

1. Read the following situation.

   Joanna, a single parent, was hired to work 8:15 a.m. to 5:30 p.m. weekdays selling computers for a firm. Her employer extended her workday until 6:30 p.m. on weekdays and added 8:15 a.m. to 2:30 p.m. on Saturday. Joanna refused to work the extra hours, saying that she had a six-year-old son and that so many work hours would lead to neglect. The employer said this was a special request during a difficult period and that all employees needed to share in helping out during the "crunch." Still refusing to work the extra hours, Joanna was fired.

2. You be the judge in this case. Take an individual position on the following questions:

   Should Joanna be allowed to work only the hours agreed to when she was hired? Or is the employer correct in asking all employees, regardless of family status, to work the extra hours? Why?

3. Form into groups as assigned by the instructor. Share your responses to the questions and try to develop a group consensus. Be sure to have a rationale for the position the group adopts. Appoint a spokesperson who can share results with the class. Be prepared to participate in open class discussion.

Source: This case scenario is from Sue Shellenbarger, "Employees Challenge Policies on Family and Get Hard Lessons," *Wall Street Journal* (December 17, 1997), p. B1.

EXERCISE 18

Compensation and Benefits Debate

PREPARATION

Consider the following quotations.

On compensation: "A basic rule of thumb should be—pay at least as much, and perhaps a bit more, in base wage or salary than what competitors are offering."

On benefits: "When benefits are attractive or at least adequate, the organization is in a better position to employ highly qualified people."

INSTRUCTIONS

Form groups as assigned by the instructor. Each will be given either one of the preceding position statements or one of the following alternatives.

On compensation: "Given the importance of controlling costs, organizations can benefit by paying as little as possible for labour."

On benefits: "Given the rising cost of health-care and other benefit programs and the increasing difficulty many organizations have staying in business, it is best to minimize paid benefits and let employees handle more of the cost on their own."

Each group should prepare to debate a counterpoint group on its assigned position. After time is allocated to prepare for the debate, each group will present its opening positions. Each will then be allowed one rebuttal period to respond to the other group. General class discussion on the role of compensation and benefits in the modern organization will follow.

EXERCISE 19

Sources and Uses of Power

PREPARATION

Consider *the way you have behaved* in each of the situations described below. They may be from a full-time or part-time job, student organization or class group, sports team, or whatever. If you do not have an experience of the type described, try to imagine yourself in one; think about how you would expect yourself to behave.

1. You needed to get a peer to do something you wanted that person to do but were worried he or she didn't want to do it.

2. You needed to get a subordinate to do something you wanted her or him to do but were worried the subordinate didn't want to do it.

3. You needed to get your boss to do something you wanted him or her to do but were worried the boss didn't want to do it.

INSTRUCTIONS

Form into groups as assigned by the instructor. Start with situation 1 and have all members of the group share their approaches. Determine what specific sources of power (see Chapter 13) were used. Note any patterns in group members' responses. Discuss what is required to be successful in this situation. Do the same for situations 2 and 3. Note any special differences in how situations 1, 2, and 3 should be or could be handled. Choose a spokesperson to share results in general class discussion.

After Meeting/Project Review

PREPARATION

After participating in a meeting or a group project, complete the following assessment.

1. How satisfied are *you* with the outcome of the meeting project?

Not at all satisfied						Totally satisfied
1	2	3	4	5	6	7

2. How do you think *other members of the meeting/project group would rate you* in terms of your influence on what took place?

No influence						Very high influence
1	2	3	4	5	6	7

3. In your opinion, how *ethical* is any decision that was reached?

Highly *unethical*						Highly ethical
1	2	3	4	5	6	7

4. To what extent did you feel "*pushed into*" going along with the decision?

Not pushed into it at all						Very pushed into it
1	2	3	4	5	6	7

5. How *committed* are *you* to the agreements reached?

Not at all committed						Highly committed
1	2	3	4	5	6	7

6. Did you understand what was expected of you as a member of the meeting or project group?

Not at all clear						Perfectly clear
1	2	3	4	5	6	7

7. Were participants in the meeting/project group discussions listening to each other?

Never						Always
1	2	3	4	5	6	7

8. Were participants in the meeting/project group discussions honest and open in communicating with one another?

Never						Always
1	2	3	4	5	6	7

9. Was the meeting/project completed efficiently?

Not at all						Very much
1	2	3	4	5	6	7

10. Was the outcome of the meeting/project something that you felt proud to be a part of?

Not at all						Very much
1	2	3	4	5	6	7

INSTRUCTIONS

In groups (actual meeting/project group or as assigned by the instructor) share results and discuss their implications (a) for you, and (b) for the effectiveness of meetings and group project work in general.

Source: Developed from Roy J. Lewicki, Donald D. Bowen, Douglas T. Hall, and Francine S. Hall, *Experiences in Management and Organizational Behavior*, 4th ed. (New York: Wiley, 1997), pp. 195–197.

EXERCISE 21

Why Do We Work?

PREPARATION

Read the following "ancient story."

In days of old a wandering youth happened upon a group of men working in a quarry. Stopping by the first man, he said, "What are you doing?" The worker grimaced and groaned as he replied, "I am trying to shape this stone, and it is backbreaking work." Moving to the next man, he repeated the question. This man showed little emotion as he answered, "I am shaping a stone for a building." Moving to the third man, our traveller heard him singing as he worked. "What are you doing?" asked the youth. "I am helping to build a cathedral," the man proudly replied.

INSTRUCTIONS

In groups assigned by your instructor, discuss this short story. Ask and answer the question: "What are the lessons of this ancient story for (a) workers and (b) managers of today?" Ask members of the group to role-play each of the stonecutters, respectively, while they answer a second question asked by the youth: "Why are you working?" Have someone in the group be prepared to report and share the group's responses with the class as a whole.

Source: Developed from Brian Dumaine, "Why Do We Work," *Fortune* (December 26, 1994), pp. 196–204.

EXERCISE 22

The Case of the Contingency Workforce

PREPARATION

Part-time and contingency work is a rising percentage of the total employment in Canada. Go to the library and read about the current use of part-time and contingency workers in business and industry. Ideally, go to the Internet, enter a government website, like Statistics Canada, and locate some current statistics on the size of the contingent labour force, the proportion that is self-employed and part-time, and the proportion of part-timers who are voluntary and involuntary.

INSTRUCTIONS

In your assigned work group, pool the available information on the contingency workforce. Discuss the information. Discuss one another's viewpoints on the subject as well as its personal and social implications. Be prepared to participate in a classroom "dialogue session" in which your group will be asked to role-play one of the following positions:

a. Vice president for human resources of a large discount retailer hiring contingency workers.

b. Owner of a local specialty music shop hiring contingency workers.

c. Recent graduate of your college or university working as a contingency employee at the discount retailer in (a).

d. Single parent with two children in elementary school, working as a contingency employee of the music shop in (b).

The question to be answered by the (a) and (b) groups is "What does the contingency workforce mean to me?" The question to be answered by the (c) and (d) groups is "What does being a contingency worker mean to me?"

EXERCISE 23

The "Best" Job Design

PREPARATION

Use the left-hand column to rank the following job characteristics in the order most important *to you* (1 = highest to 10 = lowest). Then use the right-hand column to rank them in the order in which you think they are most important *to others*.

___ Variety of tasks   ___

___ Performance feedback   ___

___ Autonomy/freedom in work   ___

___ Working on a team   ___

___ Having responsibility   ___

___ Making friends on the job   ___

___ Doing all of a job, not part   ___

___ Importance of job to others   ___

___ Having resources to do well   ___

___ Flexible work schedule   ___

INSTRUCTIONS

Form work groups as assigned by your instructor. Share your rankings with other group members. Discuss where you have different individual preferences and where your impressions differ from the preferences of others. Are there any major patterns in your group—for either the "personal" or the "other" rankings? Develop group consensus rankings for each column. Designate a spokesperson to share the group rankings and results of any discussion with the rest of the class.

Source: Developed from John M. Ivancevich and Michael T. Matteson, *Organizational Behavior and Management*, 2nd ed. (Homewood, IL: BPI/Irwin, 1990), p. 500.

EXERCISE 24

Upward Appraisal

INSTRUCTIONS

Form into work groups as assigned by the instructor. The instructor will then leave the room. As a group, complete the following tasks:

1. Within each group create a master list of comments, problems, issues, and concerns about the course experience to date that members would like to communicate with the instructor.

2. Select one person from the group to act as spokesperson and give your feedback to the instructor when he or she returns to the classroom.

3. The spokespersons from all the groups should meet to decide how the room should be physically arranged (placement of tables, chairs, etc.) for the feedback session. This should allow the spokespersons and instructor to communicate while they are being observed by other class members.

4. While the spokespersons are meeting, members remaining in the groups should discuss what they expect to observe during the feedback session.

5. The classroom should be rearranged. The instructor should be invited in.

6. Spokespersons should deliver feedback to the instructor while observers make notes.

7. After the feedback session is complete, the instructor will call on observers for comments, ask the spokespersons for their reactions, and engage the class in general discussion about the exercise and its implications.

Source: Developed from Eugene Owens, "Upward Appraisal: An Exercise in Subordinate's Critique of Superior's Performance," *Exchange: The Organizational Behavior Teaching Journal*, vol. 3 (1978), pp. 41–42.

EXERCISE 25

How to Give, and Take, Criticism

PREPARATION

The "criticism session" may well be the toughest test of a manager's communication skills. Picture Setting 1—you and a subordinate meeting to review a problem with the subordinate's performance. Now picture Setting 2—you and your boss meeting to review a problem with *your* performance. Both situations require communication skills in giving and receiving feedback. Even the most experienced person can have difficulty, and the situations can end as futile gripe sessions that cause hard feelings. The question is "How can such 'criticism sessions' be handled in a positive manner that encourages improved performance ... and good feelings?"

INSTRUCTIONS

Form into groups as assigned by the instructor. Focus on either Setting 1 or Setting 2, or both, as also assigned by the instructor. First, answer the question from the perspective assigned. Second, develop a series of action guidelines that could best be used to handle situations of this type. Third, prepare and present a mini-management training session to demonstrate the (a) unsuccessful and (b) successful use of these guidelines.

If time permits, outside of class prepare a more extensive management training session that includes a videotape demonstration of your assigned criticism setting being handled first poorly and then very well. Support the videotape with additional written handouts and an oral presentation to help your classmates better understand the communication skills needed to successfully give and take criticism in work settings.

EXERCISE 26

Lost at Sea

CONSIDER THIS SITUATION

You are adrift on a private yacht in the South Pacific when a fire of unknown origin destroys the yacht and most of its contents. You and a small group of survivors are now in a large raft with oars. Your location is unclear, but you estimate that you are about 1,500 km south-southwest of the nearest land. One person has just found in her pockets 5 $1 coins and a packet of matches. Everyone else's pockets are empty. The items at the right are available to you on the raft.

INSTRUCTIONS

1. *Working alone*, rank in Column **A** the 15 items in order of their importance to your survival ("1" is most important and "15" is least important).

2. *Working in an assigned group*, arrive at a "team" ranking of the 15 items and record this ranking in Column **B**. Appoint one person as group spokesperson to report your group rankings to the class.

3. *Do not write in Column **C*** until further instructions are provided by your instructor.

Source: Adapted from "Lost at Sea: A Consensus-Seeking Task," in *The 1975 Handbook for Group Facilitators*, University Associates, Inc.

	A	B	C
Sextant	____	____	____
Shaving mirror	____	____	____
25 litres water	____	____	____
Mosquito netting	____	____	____
1 survival meal	____	____	____
Maps of Pacific Ocean	____	____	____
Flotable seat cushion	____	____	____
10 litres oil-gas mix	____	____	____
Small transistor radio	____	____	____
Shark repellent	____	____	____
2 square metres black plastic	____	____	____
1 litre 20-proof rum	____	____	____
5 metres nylon rope	____	____	____
24 chocolate bars	____	____	____
Fishing kit	____	____	____

EXERCISE 27

Work Team Dynamics

PREPARATION

Think about your course work group, a work group you are involved in for another course, or any other group suggested by the instructor. Indicate how often each of the following statements accurately reflects your experience in the group. Use this scale:

1 = Always   2 = Frequently   3 = Sometimes
4 = Never

____ **1.** My ideas get a fair hearing.

____ **2.** I am encouraged to give innovative ideas and take risks.

____ **3.** Diverse opinions within the group are encouraged.

____ **4.** I have all the responsibility I want.

____ **5.** There is a lot of favouritism shown in the group.

____ **6.** Members trust one another to do their assigned work.

____ **7.** The group sets high standards of performance excellence.

____ **8.** People share and change jobs a lot in the group.

____ **9.** You can make mistakes and learn from them in this group.

____ **10.** This group has good operating rules.

INSTRUCTIONS

Form groups as assigned by your instructor. Ideally, this will be the group you have just rated. Have all group members share their ratings, and make one master rating for the group as a whole. Circle the items over which there are the biggest differences of opinion. Discuss those items and try to find out why they exist. In general, the better a group scores on this instrument, the higher its creative potential. If everyone has rated the same group, make a list of the five most important things members can do to improve its operations in the future. Nominate a spokesperson to summarize the group discussion for the class as a whole.

_____

Source: Adapted from William Dyer, *Team Building*, 2nd ed. (Reading, MA: Addison-Wesley, 1987), pp. 123–125.

EXERCISE 28

Feedback and Assertiveness

PREPARATION

Indicate the degree of discomfort you would feel in each situation below by circling the appropriate number:

1. high discomfort

2. some discomfort

3. undecided

4. very little discomfort

5. no discomfort

1 2 3 4 5   **1.** Telling an employee who is also a friend that she or he must stop coming to work late.

1 2 3 4 5   **2.** Talking to an employee about his or her performance on the job.

1 2 3 4 5   **3.** Asking an employee if she or he has any comments about your rating of her or his performance.

1 2 3 4 5   **4.** Telling an employee who has problems in dealing with other employees that he or she should do something about it.

1 2 3 4 5   **5.** Responding to an employee who is upset over your rating of his or her performance.

1 2 3 4 5   **6.** An employee's becoming emotional and defensive when you tell her or him about mistakes on the job.

1 2 3 4 5   **7.** Giving a rating that indicates improvement is needed to an employee who has failed to meet minimum requirements of the job.

1 2 3 4 5   **8.** Letting a subordinate talk during an appraisal interview.

1 2 3 4 5   **9.** An employee's challenging you to justify your evaluation in the middle of an appraisal interview.

1 2 3 4 5   **10.** Recommending that an employee be discharged.

1 2 3 4 5   **11.** Telling an employee that you are uncomfortable with the role of having to judge his or her performance.

1 2 3 4 5   **12.** Telling an employee that her or his performance can be improved.

1 2 3 4 5   **13.** Telling an employee that you will not tolerate his or her taking extended coffee breaks.

1 2 3 4 5   **14.** Telling an employee that you will not tolerate her or his making personal telephone calls on company time.

INSTRUCTIONS

Form three-person teams as assigned by the instructor. Identify the 3 behaviours with which they indicate the most discomfort. Then each team member should practise performing these behaviours with another member, while the third member acts as an observer. Be direct, but try to perform the behaviour in an appropriate way. Listen to feedback from the observer and try the behaviours again, perhaps with different members of the group. When finished, discuss the exercise overall. Be prepared to participate in further class discussion.

Source: Adapted from Judith R. Gordan, *A Diagnostic Approach to Organizational Behavior,* 3rd edition (Boston: Allyn & Bacon, 1991).

EXERCISE 29

Creative Solutions

INSTRUCTIONS

Complete these 5 tasks while working alone. Be prepared to present and explain your responses in class.

1. Divide the following shape into four pieces of exactly the same size.

2. Without lifting your pencil from the paper, draw no more than 4 lines that cross through all of the following dots.

3. Draw the design for a machine that will turn the pages of your textbook so you can eat a snack while studying.

4. Why would a wheelbarrow ever be designed this way?

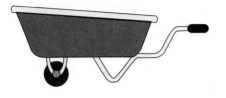

5. Turn the following into words.

(a) ___ program

(b) r\e\a\d\i\n\g

(c) ECNALG

(d)   j
        u
    yousme
        t

(e) stand
        i

OPTIONAL INSTRUCTIONS

After working alone, share your responses with a nearby classmate or with a group. See if you can develop different and/or better solutions based on this exchange of ideas.

_____

Source: Ideas 2 and 5 found in Russell L. Ackoff, *The Art of Problem Solving* (New York: Wiley, 1978); ideas 1 and 4 found in Edward De Bono, *Lateral Thinking: Creativity Step by Step* (New York: Harper & Row, 1970); source for 5 is unknown.

EXERCISE 30

Force-Field Analysis

INSTRUCTIONS

1. Form into your class discussion groups.

2. Review the concept of force-field analysis—the consideration of forces driving in support of a planned change and forces resisting the change.

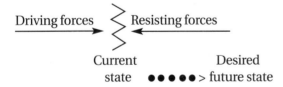

3. Use this force-field analysis worksheet in the assignment:

List of Driving Forces (those supporting the change)

_____

_____ … list as many as you can think of

List of Resisting Forces (those working against the change)

_____

_____ … list as many as you can think of

4. Apply force-field analysis and make your lists of driving and resisting forces for one of the following situations:

(a) Due to rapid advances in Web-based computer technologies, the possibility exists that the course you are presently taking could be in part offered online. This would mean a reduction in the number of required class sessions but an increase in students' responsibility for completing learning activities and assignments through computer mediation.

(b) A new owner has just taken over a small walk-in-and-buy-by-the-slice pizza shop in a college town. There are eight employees, three of whom are full-time and five of whom are part-timers. The shop is open seven days a week from 10:30 a.m. to 10:30 p.m. each day. The new owner believes there is a market niche available for late-night pizza and would like to stay open each night until 2 a.m.

(c) A situation assigned by the instructor.

5. Choose the three driving forces that are most significant to the proposed change. For each force develop ideas on how it could be further increased or mobilized in support of the change.

6. Choose the three resisting forces that are most significant to the proposed change. For each force develop ideas on how it could be reduced or turned into a driving force.

7. Be prepared to participate in a class discussion led by the instructor.

ASSESSMENT 1

A 21st-Century Manager?

INSTRUCTIONS

Rate yourself on the following personal characteristics. Use this scale.

S = Strong, I am very confident with this one.

G = Good, but I still have room to grow.

W = Weak, I really need work on this one.

U = Unsure, I just don't know.

1. *Resistance to stress:* The ability to get work done even under stressful conditions.

2. *Tolerance for uncertainty:* The ability to get work done even under ambiguous and uncertain conditions.

3. *Social objectivity:* The ability to act free of racial, ethnic, gender, and other prejudices or biases.

4. *Inner work standards:* The ability to personally set and work to high performance standards.

5. *Stamina:* The ability to sustain long work hours.

6. *Adaptability:* The ability to be flexible and adapt to changes.

7. *Self-confidence:* The ability to be consistently decisive and display one's personal presence.

8. *Self-objectivity:* The ability to evaluate personal strengths and weaknesses and to understand one's motives and skills relative to a job.

9. *Introspection:* The ability to learn from experience, awareness, and self-study.

10. *Entrepreneurism:* The ability to address problems and take advantage of opportunities for constructive change.

SCORING

Give yourself 1 point for each S, and 1/2 point for each G. Do not give yourself points for W and U responses. Total your points and enter the result here [PMF = ___].

INTERPRETATION

This assessment offers a self-described *profile of your management foundations* (PMF). Are you a perfect 10, or is your PMF score something less than that? There shouldn't be too many 10s around. Ask someone who knows you to assess you on this instrument. You may be surprised at the differences between your PMF score as you described it and your PMF score as described by someone else. Most of us, realistically speaking, must work hard to grow and develop continually in these and related management foundations. This list is a good starting point as you consider where and how to further pursue the development of your managerial skills and competencies. The items on the list are recommended by the American Assembly of Collegiate Schools of Business (AACSB) as the skills and personal characteristics that should be nurtured in college and university students of business administration. Their success—and yours—as 21st-century managers may well rest on (1) an initial awareness of the importance of these basic management foundations and (2) a willingness to strive continually to strengthen them throughout the work career.

Source: See *Outcome Measurement Project*, Phase I and Phase II Reports (St. Louis: American Assembly of Collegiate Schools of Business, 1986 and 1987).

ASSESSMENT 2

Emotional Intelligence

INSTRUCTIONS

Rate yourself on how well you are able to display the abilities for each item listed below. As you score each item, try to think of actual situations in which you have been called upon to use the ability. Use the following scale.

1	2	3	4	5	6	7
Low Ability		Neutral		High Ability		

1 2 3 4 5 6 7   **1.** Identify changes in physiological arousal.

1 2 3 4 5 6 7   **2.** Relax when under pressure in situations.

1 2 3 4 5 6 7   **3.** Act productively when angry.

1 2 3 4 5 6 7   **4.** Act productively in situations that arouse anxiety.

1 2 3 4 5 6 7   **5.** Calm yourself quickly when angry.

1 2 3 4 5 6 7   **6.** Associate different physical cues with different emotions.

1 2 3 4 5 6 7   **7.** Use internal "talk" to affect your emotional states.

1 2 3 4 5 6 7   **8.** Communicate your feelings effectively.

1 2 3 4 5 6 7   **9.** Reflect on negative feelings without being distressed.

1 2 3 4 5 6 7   **10.** Stay calm when you are the target of anger from others.

1 2 3 4 5 6 7   **11.** Know when you are thinking negatively.

1 2 3 4 5 6 7   **12.** Know when your "self-talk" is instructional.

1 2 3 4 5 6 7   **13.** Know when you are becoming angry.

1 2 3 4 5 6 7   **14.** Know how you interpret events you encounter.

1 2 3 4 5 6 7   **15.** Know what senses you are currently using.

1 2 3 4 5 6 7   **16.** Accurately communicate what you experience.

1 2 3 4 5 6 7   **17.** Identify what information influences your interpretations.

1 2 3 4 5 6 7   **18.** Identify when you experience mood shifts.

1 2 3 4 5 6 7   **19.** Know when you become defensive.

1 2 3 4 5 6 7   **20.** Know the impact your behaviour has on others.

1 2 3 4 5 6 7   **21.** Know when you communicate incongruently.

1 2 3 4 5 6 7   **22.** "Gear up" at will.

1 2 3 4 5 6 7   **23.** Regroup quickly after a setback.

1 2 3 4 5 6 7   **24.** Complete long-term tasks in designated time frames.

1 2 3 4 5 6 7   **25.** Produce high energy when doing uninteresting work.

1 2 3 4 5 6 7   **26.** Stop or change ineffective habits.

1 2 3 4 5 6 7   **27.** Develop new and more productive patterns of behaviour.

1 2 3 4 5 6 7   **28.** Follow words with actions.

1 2 3 4 5 6 7   **29.** Work out conflicts.

1 2 3 4 5 6 7   **30.** Develop consensus with others.

1 2 3 4 5 6 7   **31.** Mediate conflict between others.

1 2 3 4 5 6 7   **32.** Exhibit effective interpersonal communication skills.

1 2 3 4 5 6 7   **33.** Articulate the thoughts of a group.

1 2 3 4 5 6 7   **34.** Influence others, directly or indirectly.

1 2 3 4 5 6 7   **35.** Build trust with others.

1 2 3 4 5 6 7   **36.** Build support teams.

1 2 3 4 5 6 7   **37.** Make others feel good.

1 2 3 4 5 6 7   **38.** Provide advice and support to others, as needed.

1 2 3 4 5 6 7   **39.** Accurately reflect people's feelings back to them.

1 2 3 4 5 6 7   **40.** Recognize when others are distressed.

1 2 3 4 5 6 7   **41.** Help others manage their emotions.

1 2 3 4 5 6 7   **42.** Show empathy to others.

1 2 3 4 5 6 7   **43.** Engage in intimate conversations with others.

1 2 3 4 5 6 7   **44.** Help a group to manage emotions.

1 2 3 4 5 6 7   **45.** Detect incongruence between others' emotions or feelings and their behaviours.

SCORING

This instrument measures six dimensions of your emotional intelligence. Find your scores as follows.

Self-awareness—Add scores for items 1, 6, 11, 12, 13, 14, 15, 16, 17, 18, 19, 20, 21

Managing emotions—Add scores for items 1, 2, 3, 4, 5, 7, 9, 10, 13, 27

Self-motivation—Add scores for items 7, 22, 23, 25, 26, 27, 28

Relating well—Add scores for items 8, 10, 16, 19, 20, 29, 30, 31, 32, 33, 34, 35, 36, 37, 38, 39, 42, 43, 44, 45

Emotional mentoring—Add scores for items 8, 10, 16, 18, 34, 35, 37, 38, 39, 40, 41, 44, 45

INTERPRETATION

The prior scoring indicates your self-perceived abilities in these dimensions of emotional intelligence. To further examine your tendencies, go back for each dimension and sum the number of responses you had that were 4 and lower (suggesting lower ability), and sum the number of responses you had that were 5 or better (suggesting higher ability). This gives you an indication by dimension of where you may have room to grow and develop your emotional intelligence abilities.

Source: Scale from Hendrie Weisinger, *Emotional Intelligence at Work* (San Francisco: Jossey-Bass, 1998), pp. 214–15. Used by permission.

ASSESSMENT 3

Learning Tendencies

INSTRUCTIONS

In each of the following pairs, distribute 10 points between the two statements to best describe how you like to learn. For example:

_3_ (a) I like to read.

_7_ (b) I like to listen to lectures.

1. _____ (a) I like to learn through working with other people and being engaged in concrete experiences.

   _____ (b) I like to learn through logical analysis and systematic attempts to understand a situation.

2. _____ (a) I like to learn by observing things, viewing them from different perspectives, and finding meaning in situations.

   _____ (b) I like to learn by taking risks, getting things done, and influencing events through actions taken.

SCORING

Place "dots" on the following graph to record the above scores: "Doing" = 2b.   "Watching" = 1b.   "Feeling" = 1a.   "Thinking" = 2a. Connect the dots to plot your learning tendencies.

INTERPRETATION

This activity provides a first impression of your learning tendencies or style. Four possible learning styles are identified on the graph—convergers, accommodators, divergers, and assimilators. Consider the following descriptions for their accuracy in describing you. For a truly good reading on your learning tendencies, ask several others to complete the Step 1 questions for you, and then assess how their results compare with your own perceptions.

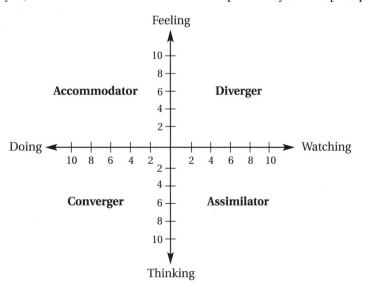

Convergers—combined tendencies toward abstract conceptualization (thinking) and active experimentation (doing). They like to learn in practical situations. They prefer to deal with technical issues and solve problems through systematic investigation of alternatives. Good at experimentation, finding new ways of doing things, making decisions.

Accommodators—combine concrete experience (feeling) with active experimentation (doing). They like to learn from hands-on experience. They prefer "gut" responses to problems rather than systematic analysis of alternatives. Good at influencing others, committing to goals, seeking opportunities.

Divergers—combine concrete experience (feeling) with reflective observation (watching). They like to learn from observation. They prefer to participate in brainstorming and imaginative information gathering. Good at listening, imagining, and being sensitive to feelings.

Assimilators—combine abstract conceptualization (thinking) with reflective observation (watching). They like to learn through information. They prefer ideas and concepts to people and value logical reasoning. Good at organizing information, building models, and analyzing data.

Source: Developed from David A. Kolb, "Learning Style Inventory" (Boston, MA: McBer & Company, 1985); see also his article "On Management and the Learning Process," in David A. Kolb, Irwin M. Rubin, and James M. McIntyre, eds., *Organizational Psychology: A Book of Readings*, 2nd ed. (Englewood Cliffs, NJ: Prentice-Hall, 1974), pp. 27–42.

ASSESSMENT 4

What Are Your Managerial Assumptions?

INSTRUCTIONS

Read the following statements. Use the space in the margins to write "Yes" if you agree with the statement, or "No" if you disagree with it. Force yourself to take a "yes" or "no" position. Do this for every statement.

1. Are good pay and a secure job enough to satisfy most workers?

2. Should a manager help and coach subordinates in their work?

3. Do most people like real responsibility in their jobs?

4. Are most people afraid to learn new things in their jobs?

5. Should managers let subordinates control the quality of their work?

6. Do most people dislike work?

7. Are most people creative?

8. Should a manager closely supervise and direct the work of subordinates?

9. Do most people tend to resist change?

10. Do most people work only as hard as they have to?

11. Should workers be allowed to set their own job goals?

12. Are most people happiest off the job?

13. Do most workers really care about the organization they work for?

14. Should a manager help subordinates advance and grow in their jobs?

SCORING

Count the number of "yes" responses to items 1, 4, 6, 8, 9, 10, 12; write that number here as [X = ___]. Count the number of "yes" responses to items 2, 3, 5, 7, 11, 13, 14; write that score here [Y = ___].

INTERPRETATION

This assessment sheds insight into your orientation toward Douglas McGregor's Theory X (your "X" score) and Theory Y (your "Y" score) assumptions. You should review the discussion of McGregor's thinking in Chapter 2 and consider further the ways in which you are likely to behave toward other people at work. Think, in particular, about the types of "self-fulfilling prophecies" you are likely to create.

ASSESSMENT 5

Terminal Values Survey

INSTRUCTIONS

Rate each of the following values in terms of its importance to you. Think about each value *in terms of its importance as a guiding principle in your life.* As you work, consider each value in relation to all the other values listed in the survey.

TERMINAL VALUES

		1	2	3	4	5	6	7
1.	A comfortable life	Of lesser importance					Of greater importance	
2.	An exciting life	Of lesser importance					Of greater importance	
3.	A sense of accomplishment	Of lesser importance					Of greater importance	
4.	A world at peace	Of lesser importance					Of greater importance	
5.	A world of beauty	Of lesser importance					Of greater importance	
6.	Equality	Of lesser importance					Of greater importance	
7.	Family security	Of lesser importance					Of greater importance	
8.	Freedom	Of lesser importance					Of greater importance	

9. Happiness

1	2	3	4	5	6	7
Of lesser importance					Of greater importance	

10. Inner harmony

1	2	3	4	5	6	7
Of lesser importance					Of greater importance	

11. Mature love

1	2	3	4	5	6	7
Of lesser importance					Of greater importance	

12. National security

1	2	3	4	5	6	7
Of lesser importance					Of greater importance	

13. Pleasure

1	2	3	4	5	6	7
Of lesser importance					Of greater importance	

14. Salvation

1	2	3	4	5	6	7
Of lesser importance					Of greater importance	

15. Self-respect

1	2	3	4	5	6	7
Of lesser importance					Of greater importance	

16. Social recognition

1	2	3	4	5	6	7
Of lesser importance					Of greater importance	

17. True friendship

1	2	3	4	5	6	7
Of lesser importance					Of greater importance	

18. Wisdom

1	2	3	4	5	6	7
Of lesser importance					Of greater importance	

SCORING

To score this instrument, you must multiply your score for each item times a "weight"—e.g. (#3 × 5) = your new question 3 score.

1. Calculate your Personal Values Score as: (#1 × 5) + (#2 × 4) + (#3 × 4) + (#7) + (#8) + (#9 × 4) + (#10 × 5) + (#11 × 4) + (#13 × 5) + (#14 × 3) + (#15 × 5) + (#16 × 3) + (#17 × 4) + (#18 × 5)

2. Calculate your Social Values Score as: (#4 × 5) + (#5 × 3) + (#6 × 5) + (#12 × 5)

3. Calculate your Terminal Values Score as: Personal Values − Social Values

INTERPRETATION

Terminal values reflect a person's preferences concerning the "ends" to be achieved. They are the goals individuals would like to achieve in their lifetimes.

Different value items receive different weights in this scale. (Example: "A comfortable life" receives a weight of "5" while "Freedom" receives a weight of "1.") Your score on Personal Values has your Social Values score subtracted from it to determine your Terminal Values score.

_____

Source: Adapted from James Weber, "Management Value Orientations: A Typology and Assessment," *International Journal of Value Based Management*, vol. 3, no. 2 (1990), pp. 37–54.

ASSESSMENT 6

Instrumental Values Survey

INSTRUCTIONS

Rate each of the following values in terms of its importance to you. Think about each value in terms of its importance as a guiding principle in your life. As you work, consider each value in relation to all the other values listed in the survey.

INSTRUMENTAL VALUES

1. Ambitious

1	2	3	4	5	6	7
Of lesser importance					Of greater importance	

2. Broadminded

1	2	3	4	5	6	7
Of lesser importance					Of greater importance	

3. Capable

1	2	3	4	5	6	7
Of lesser importance					Of greater importance	

4. Cheerful

1	2	3	4	5	6	7
Of lesser importance					Of greater importance	

5. Clean

1	2	3	4	5	6	7
Of lesser importance					Of greater importance	

6. Courageous

1	2	3	4	5	6	7
Of lesser importance					Of greater importance	

7. Forgiving

1	2	3	4	5	6	7
Of lesser importance					Of greater importance	

8. Helpful

1	2	3	4	5	6	7
Of lesser importance					Of greater importance	

9. Honest

1	2	3	4	5	6	7
Of lesser importance					Of greater importance	

10. Imaginative

1	2	3	4	5	6	7
Of lesser importance					Of greater importance	

11. Independent

1	2	3	4	5	6	7
Of lesser importance					Of greater importance	

12. Intellectual

1	2	3	4	5	6	7
Of lesser importance					Of greater importance	

13. Logical

1	2	3	4	5	6	7
Of lesser importance					Of greater importance	

14. Loving

1	2	3	4	5	6	7
Of lesser importance					Of greater importance	

15. Obedient

1	2	3	4	5	6	7
Of lesser importance					Of greater importance	

16. Polite

1	2	3	4	5	6	7
Of lesser importance					Of greater importance	

17. Responsible

1	2	3	4	5	6	7
Of lesser importance					Of greater importance	

18. Self-controlled

1	2	3	4	5	6	7
Of lesser importance					Of greater importance	

SCORING

To score this instrument, you must multiply your score for each item times a "weight"—e.g. (#3 × 5) = your new question 3 score.

1. Calculate your Competence Values Score as: (#1 × 5) + (#2 × 2) + (#3 × 5) + (#10 × 5) + (#11 × 5) + (#12 × 5) + (#13 × 5) + (#17 × 4)

2. Calculate your Moral Values Score as: (#4 × 4) + (#5 × 3) + (#6 × 2) + (#7 × 5) + (#8 × 5) + (#9 × 2) + (#14 × 5) + (#15) + (#16 × 3)

3. Calculate your Instrumental Values Score as: Competence Values − Moral Values

INTERPRETATION

Instrumental Values are defined as the "means" for achieving desired ends. They represent how you might go about achieving your important end states, depending on the relative importance you attach to the instrumental values.

Different value items receive different weights in this scale. (Example: "Ambitious" receives a weight of "5" while "Obedient" receives a weight of "1.") Your score on Competence Values has your Moral Values score subtracted from it to determine your Instrumental Values score.

Source: Adapted from James Weber, "Management Value Orientations: A Typology and Assessment," *International Journal of Value Based Management*, vol. 3, no. 2 (1990), pp. 37–54.

ASSESSMENT 7

Diversity Awareness

INSTRUCTIONS

Complete the following questionnaire.

DIVERSITY AWARENESS CHECKLIST

Consider where you work or go to school as the setting for the following questions. Indicate "O" for often, "S" for sometimes, and "N" for never in response to each of the following questions as they pertain to the setting.

____ 1. How often have you heard jokes or remarks about other people that you consider offensive?

____ 2. How often do you hear men "talk down" to women in an attempt to keep them in an inferior status?

____ 3. How often have you felt personal discomfort as the object of sexual harassment?

____ 4. How often do you work or study with Asians or Black Canadians?

____ 5. How often have you felt disadvantaged because members of ethnic groups other than yours were given special treatment?

____ 6. How often have you seen a woman put in an uncomfortable situation because of unwelcome advances by a man?

____ 7. How often does it seem that Asians, francophones, Caucasians, women, men, and members of minority demographic groups seem to "stick together" during work breaks or other leisure situations?

____ 8. How often do you feel uncomfortable about something you did and/or said to someone of the opposite sex or a member of an ethnic or racial group other than yours?

____ 9. How often do you feel efforts are made in this setting to raise the level of cross-cultural understanding among people who work and/or study together?

____ 10. How often do you step in to communicate concerns to others when you feel actions and/or words are used to the disadvantage of minorities?

SCORING

There are no correct answers for the Diversity Awareness Checklist.

INTERPRETATION

In the diversity checklist, the key issue is the extent to which you are "sensitive" to diversity issues in the workplace or university. Are you comfortable with your responses? How do you think others in your class responded? Why not share your responses with others and examine different viewpoints on this important issue?

Source: Items for the WV Cultural Awareness Quiz selected from a longer version by James P. Morgan, Jr., and published by University Associates, 1987.

ASSESSMENT 8

Global Readiness Index

INSTRUCTIONS

Rate yourself on each of the following items to establish a baseline measurement of your readiness to participate in the global work environment.

RATING SCALE

1 = Very Poor

2 = Poor

3 = Acceptable

4 = Good

5 = Very Good

____ **1.** I understand my own culture in terms of its expectations, values, and influence on communication and relationships.

____ **2.** When someone presents me with a different point of view, I try to understand it rather than attack it.

____ **3.** I am comfortable dealing with situations where the available information is incomplete and the outcomes unpredictable.

____ **4.** I am open to new situations and am always looking for new information and learning opportunities.

____ **5.** I have a good understanding of the attitudes and perceptions toward my culture as they are held by people from other cultures.

____ **6.** I am always gathering information about other countries and cultures and trying to learn from them.

____ **7.** I am well informed regarding the major differences in government, political, and economic systems around the world.

____ **8.** I work hard to increase my understanding of people from other cultures.

____ **9.** I am able to adjust my communication style to work effectively with people from different cultures.

____ **10.** I can recognize when cultural differences are influencing working relationships and adjust my attitudes and behaviour accordingly.

SCORING

The goal is to score as close to a perfect "5" as possible on each of the three dimensions of global readiness. Develop your scores as follows.

Items $(1 + 2 + 3 + 4)/4$
= ___ Global Mindset Score

Items $(5 + 6 + 7)/3$
= ___ Global Knowledge Score

Items $(8 + 9 + 10)/3$
= ___ Global Work Skills Score

INTERPRETATION

To be successful in the 21st-century work environment, you must be comfortable with the global economy and the cultural diversity that it holds. This requires a *global mindset* that is receptive to and respectful of cultural differences, *global knowledge* that includes the continuing quest to know and learn more about other nations and cultures, and *global work skills* that allow you to work effectively across cultures.

_____

Source: Developed from "Is Your Company Really Global?", *Business Week* (December 1, 1997).

ASSESSMENT 9

Time Orientation

INSTRUCTIONS

This instrument examines your tendencies to favour "monochronic" or "polychronic" time orientations. Rate your tendencies for each item below using the following scale.

RATING SCALE

1 = Almost never

2 = Seldom

3 = Sometimes

4 = Usually

5 = Almost always

____ 1. I like to do one thing at a time.

____ 2. I have a strong tendency to build lifetime relationships.

____ 3. I concentrate on the job at hand.

____ 4. I base the level of promptness on the particular relationship.

____ 5. I take time commitments (deadlines, schedules) seriously.

____ 6. I borrow and lend things often and easily.

____ 7. I am committed to the job.

____ 8. Intimacy with family and friends is more important than respecting their privacy.

____ 9. I adhere closely to plans.

____ 10. I put obligations to family and friends before work concerns.

____ 11. I am concerned about not disturbing others (follow rules of privacy).

____ 12. I change plans often and easily.

____ 13. I emphasize promptness in meetings.

____ 14. I am committed to people and human relationships.

____ 15. I show great respect for private property (seldom borrow or lend).

____ 16. I am highly distractible and frequently interrupt what I am doing.

____ 17. I am comfortable with short-term relationships.

____ 18. I like to do many things at once.

SCORING

To obtain your monochronic time orientation score, sum results for items 1, 3, 5, 7, 9, 11, 13, 15, 17. To obtain your polychronic time orientation score, sum results for items 2, 4, 6, 8, 10, 12, 14, 16, 18.

INTERPRETATION

A person high in monochronic time orientation approaches time in a linear fashion with things dealt with one at a time in an orderly fashion. Time is viewed as a precious commodity, not to be wasted; this person values punctuality and promptness.

A person high in polychronic time orientation tends to do a number of things at once, intertwining them together in a dynamic process that considers changing circumstances. Commitments are viewed as objectives, but capable of adjustment when necessary.

Cultural differences in orientations toward time can be observed. Tendencies toward monochronic time orientation are common to North America and northern European cultures. Tendencies toward polychronic time orientation are common in cultures of the Middle East, Asia, and Latin America.

Source: Adapted from J. Ned Seelye and Alan Seelye-James. *Culture Clash* (Lincolnwood, IL: NTC Business Books, 1996).

ASSESSMENT 10

Entrepreneurship Orientation

INSTRUCTIONS

Answer the following questions.

1. What portion of your university expenses did you earn (or are you earning)?

   (a) 50% or more

   (b) less than 50%

   (c) none

2. In university, your academic performance was/is

   (a) above average.

   (b) average.

   (c) below average.

3. What is your basic reason for considering opening a business?

   (a) I want to make money.

   (b) I want to control my own destiny.

   (c) I hate the frustration of working for someone else.

4. Which phrase best describes your attitude toward work?

   (a) I can keep going as long as I need to; I don't mind working for something I want.

   (b) I can work hard for a while, but when I've had enough, I quit.

   (c) Hard work really doesn't get you anywhere.

5. How would you rate your organizing skills?

   (a) superorganized

   (b) above average

   (c) average

   (d) I do well if I can find half the things I look for

6. You are primarily a(n)

   (a) optimist.

   (b) pessimist.

   (c) neither.

7. You are faced with a challenging problem. As you work, you realize you are stuck. You will most likely

   (a) give up.

   (b) ask for help.

   (c) keep plugging; you'll figure it out.

8. You are playing a game with a group of friends. You are most interested in

   (a) winning.

   (b) playing well.

   (c) making sure that everyone has a good time.

   (d) cheating as much as possible.

9. How would you describe your feelings toward failure?

   (a) Fear of failure paralyzes me.

   (b) Failure can be a good learning experience.

   (c) Knowing that I might fail motivates me to work even harder.

   (d) "Damn the torpedoes! Full speed ahead."

10. Which phrase best describes you?

    (a) I need constant encouragement to get anything done.

    (b) If someone gets me started, I can keep going.

    (c) I am energetic and hard-working—a self-starter.

11. Which bet would you most likely accept?

    (a) a wager on a dog race

    (b) a wager on a racquetball game in which you play an opponent

    (c) Neither. I never make wagers.

12. At the Kentucky Derby, you would bet on

    (a) the 100-to-1 long shot.

    (b) the odds-on favourite.

    (c) the 3-to-1 shot.

    (d) none of the above.

SCORING

Give yourself 10 points for each of the following answers: 1a, 2a, 3c, 4a, 5a, 6a, 7c, 8a, 9c, 10c, 11b, 12c; total the scores and enter the results here [I = ___]. Give yourself 8 points for each of the following answers: 3b, 8b, 9b; total the scores and enter the results here [II = ___]. Give yourself 6 points for each of the following answers; 2b, 5b; total the scores and enter the results here [III = ___]. Give yourself 5 points for this answer: 1b; enter the result here [IV = ___]. Give yourself 4 points for this answer: 5c; enter the result here [V = ___]. Give yourself 2 points for each of the following answers: 2c, 3a, 4b, 6c, 9d, 10b, 11a, 12b; total the scores and enter the results here [VI = ___]. Any other scores are worth 0 points. Total your summary scores for I + II + III + IV + V + VI and enter the result here [EP = ___].

INTERPRETATION

This assessment offers an impression of your *entrepreneurial profile*, or EP. It compares your characteristics with those of typical entrepreneurs. Your instructor can provide further information on each question as well as some additional insights into the backgrounds of entrepreneurs. You may locate your EP score on the following grid.

100 +	= Entrepreneur extraordinaire
80–99	= Entrepreneur
60–79	= Potential entrepreneur
0–59	= Entrepreneur in the rough

Source: Instrument adapted from Norman M. Scarborough and Thomas W. Zimmerer, *Effective Small Business Management*, 3rd ed. (Columbus: Merrill, 1991), pp. 26–27.

ASSESSMENT 11

Your Intuitive Ability

INSTRUCTIONS

Complete this survey as quickly as you can. Be honest with yourself. For each question, select the response that most appeals to you.

1. When working on a project, do you prefer to

   (a) be told what the problem is but be left free to decide how to solve it?

   (b) get very clear instructions about how to go about solving the problem before you start?

2. When working on a project, do you prefer to work with colleagues who are

   (a) realistic?

   (b) imaginative?

3. Do you most admire people who are

   (a) creative?

   (b) careful?

4. Do the friends you choose tend to be

   (a) serious and hard working?

   (b) exciting and often emotional?

5. When you ask a colleague for advice on a problem you have, do you

   (a) seldom or never get upset if he or she questions your basic assumptions?

   (b) often get upset if he or she questions your basic assumptions?

6. When you start your day, do you

   (a) seldom make or follow a specific plan?

   (b) usually first make a plan to follow?

7. When working with numbers do you find that you

   (a) seldom or never make factual errors?

   (b) often make factual errors?

8. Do you find that you

   (a) seldom daydream during the day and really don't enjoy doing so when you do it?

   (b) frequently daydream during the day and enjoy doing so?

9. When working on a problem, do you

   (a) prefer to follow the instructions or rules when they are given to you?

(b) often enjoy circumventing the instructions or rules when they are given to you?

10. When you are trying to put something together, do you prefer to have

(a) step-by-step written instructions on how to assemble the item?

(b) a picture of how the item is supposed to look once assembled?

11. Do you find that the person who irritates you the most is the one who appears to be

(a) disorganized?

(b) organized?

12. When an unexpected crisis comes up that you have to deal with, do you

(a) feel anxious about the situation?

(b) feel excited by the challenge of the situation?

SCORING

Total the number of "a" responses circled for questions 1, 3, 5, 6, 11; enter the score here [A = ___]. Total the number of "b" responses for questions 2, 4, 7, 8, 9, 10,

12; enter the score here [B = ___]. Add your "a" and "b" scores and enter the sum here [A + B = ___]. This is your intuitive score. The highest possible intuitive score is 12; the lowest is 0.

INTERPRETATION

In his book *Intuition in Organizations* (Newbury Park, CA: Sage, 1989, pp. 10–11), Weston H. Agor states, "Traditional analytical techniques…are not as useful as they once were for guiding major decisions. … If you hope to be better prepared for tomorrow, then it only seems logical to pay some attention to the use and development of intuitive skills for decision making." Agor developed the preceding survey to help people assess their tendencies to use intuition in decision making. Your score offers a general impression of your strength in this area. It may also suggest a need to further develop your skill and comfort with more intuitive decision approaches.

_____

Source: AIM Survey (El Paso, TX: ENFP Enterprises, 1989). Copyright ©1989 by Weston H. Agor.

ASSESSMENT 12

Assertiveness

INSTRUCTIONS

This instrument measures tendencies toward aggressive, passive, and assertive behaviours in work situations. For each statement below, decide which of the following answers best fits you.

1 = Never true

2 = Sometimes true

3 = Often true

4 = Always true

____ 1. I respond with more modesty than I really feel when my work is complimented.

____ 2. If people are rude, I will be rude right back.

____ 3. Other people find me interesting.

____ 4. I find it difficult to speak up in a group of strangers.

____ 5. I don't mind using sarcasm if it helps me make a point.

____ 6. I ask for a raise when I feel I really deserve it.

____ 7. If others interrupt me when I am talking, I suffer in silence.

____ 8. If people criticize my work, I find a way to make them back down.

____ 9. I can express pride in my accomplishments without being boastful.

____ 10. People take advantage of me.

____ 11. I tell people what they want to hear if it helps me get what I want.

____ 12. I find it easy to ask for help.

____ 13. I lend things to others even when I don't really want to.

___ **14.** I win arguments by dominating the discussion.

___ **15.** I can express my true feelings to someone I really care for.

___ **16.** When I feel angry with other people, I bottle it up rather than express it.

___ **17.** When I criticize someone else's work, they get mad.

___ **18.** I feel confident in my ability to stand up for my rights.

SCORING

Obtain your scores as follows:

Aggressiveness tendency score—Add items 2, 5, 8, 11, 14, and 17

Passive tendency score—Add items 1, 4, 7, 10, 13, and 16

Assertiveness tendency score—Add items 3, 6, 9, 12, 15, and 18

INTERPRETATION

The maximum score in any single area is 24. The minimum score is 6. Try to find someone who knows you well. Have this person complete the instrument also as it relates to you. Compare his or her impression of you with your own score. What is this telling you about your behaviour tendencies in social situations?

Source: From Douglas T. Hall, Donald D. Bowen, Roy J. Lewicki, and Francine S. Hall, *Experiences in Management and Organizational Behaviour*, 2nd ed. (New York: Wiley, 1985). Used by permission.

ASSESSMENT 13

Time Management Profile

INSTRUCTIONS

Complete the following questionnaire by indicating "Y" (yes) or "N" (no) for each item. Force yourself to respond yes or no. Be frank and allow your responses to create an accurate picture of how you tend to respond to these kinds of situations.

___ **1.** When confronted with several items of similar urgency and importance, I tend to do the easiest one first.

___ **2.** I do the most important things during that part of the day when I know I perform best.

___ **3.** Most of the time I don't do things someone else can do; I delegate this type of work to others.

___ **4.** Even though meetings without a clear and useful purpose upset me, I put up with them.

___ **5.** I skim documents before reading them and don't complete any that offer a low return on my time investment.

___ **6.** I don't worry much if I don't accomplish at least one significant task each day.

___ **7.** I save the most trivial tasks for that time of day when my creative energy is lowest.

___ **8.** My workspace is neat and organized.

___ **9.** My office door is always "open"; I never work in complete privacy.

___ **10.** I schedule my time completely from start to finish every workday.

___ **11.** I don't like "to do" lists, preferring to respond to daily events as they occur.

___ **12.** I "block" a certain amount of time each day or week that is dedicated to high-priority activities.

SCORING

Count the number of "Y" responses to items 2, 3, 5, 7, 8, 12. [Enter that score here ___.] Count the number of

"N" responses to items 1, 4, 6, 9, 10, 11. [Enter that score here ___.] Add together the two scores.

INTERPRETATION

The higher the total score, the closer your behaviour matches recommended time management guidelines. Reread those items where your response did not match the desired one. Why don't they match? Do you have reasons why your behaviour in this instance should be different from the recommended time management guideline? Think about what you can do (and how easily it can be done) to adjust your behaviour to be more consistent with these guidelines. For further reading, see Alan Lakein, *How to Control Your Time and Your Life* (New York: David McKay, no date), and William Oncken, *Managing Management Time* (Englewood Cliffs, NJ: Prentice Hall, 1984).

_____

Source: Suggested by a discussion in Robert E. Quinn, Sue R. Faerman, Michael P. Thompson, and Michael R. McGrath, *Becoming a Master Manager: A Contemporary Framework* (New York: Wiley, 1990), pp. 75–76.

ASSESSMENT 14

Facts and Inferences

PREPARATION

Often, when we listen or speak, we don't distinguish between statements of fact and those of inference. Yet, there are great differences between the two. We create barriers to clear thinking when we treat inferences (guesses, opinions) as if they are facts. You may wish at this point to test your ability to distinguish facts from inferences by taking the accompanying fact-inference test based on those by Haney (1973).

INSTRUCTIONS

Carefully read the following report and the observations based on it. Indicate whether you think the observations are true, false, or doubtful on the basis of the information presented in the report. Write T if the observation is definitely true, F if the observation is definitely false, and ? if the observation may be either true or false. Judge each observation in order. Do not reread the observations after you have indicated your judgement, and do not change any of your answers.

A well-liked university instructor had just completed making up the final examinations and had turned off the lights in the office. Just then a tall, broad figure with dark glasses appeared and demanded the examination. The professor opened the drawer. Everything in the drawer was picked up, and the individual ran down the corridor. The president was notified immediately.

___ 1. The thief was tall, broad, and wore dark glasses.

___ 2. The professor turned off the lights.

___ 3. A tall figure demanded the examination.

___ 4. The examination was picked up by someone.

___ 5. The examination was picked up by the professor.

___ 6. A tall, broad figure appeared after the professor turned off the lights in the office.

___ 7. The man who opened the drawer was the professor.

___ 8. The professor ran down the corridor.

___ 9. The drawer was never actually opened.

___ 10. Three persons are referred to in this report.

When told to do so by your instructor, join a small work group. Now, help the group complete the same task by making a consensus decision on each item. Be sure to keep a separate record of the group's responses and your original individual responses.

SCORING

Your instructor will read the correct answers. Score both your individual and group responses.

INTERPRETATION

To begin, ask yourself if there was a difference between your answers and those of the group for each item. If so, why? Why do you think people, individually or in groups, may answer these questions incorrectly? Good planning depends on good decision making by the people doing the planning. Being able to distinguish "facts" and understand one's "inferences" are important steps toward improving the planning process. Involving others to help do the same can frequently assist in this process.

Source: From De Vito, Joseph A. *Messages: Building Interpersonal Communication Skills*, 6/e Published by Allyn and Bacon, Boston, MA. Copyright © 2005 by Pearson Education. Reprinted by permission of the publisher.

ASSESSMENT 15

Empowering Others

INSTRUCTIONS

Think of times when you have been in charge of a group—this could be a full-time or part-time work situation, a student work group, or whatever. Complete the following questionnaire by recording how you feel about each statement according to this scale:

1 = Strongly disagree 2 = Disagree 3 = Neutral 4 = Agree 5 = Strongly agree

When in charge of a group, I find that:

____ 1. Most of the time other people are too inexperienced to do things, so I prefer to do them myself.

____ 2. It often takes more time to explain things to others than to just do them myself.

____ 3. Mistakes made by others are costly, so I don't assign much work to them.

____ 4. Some things simply should not be delegated to others.

____ 5. I often get quicker action by doing a job myself.

____ 6. Many people are good only at very specific tasks and so can't be assigned additional responsibilities.

____ 7. Many people are too busy to take on additional work.

____ 8. Most people just aren't ready to handle additional responsibilities.

____ 9. In my position, I should be entitled to make my own decisions.

SCORING

Total your responses: enter the score here [____].

INTERPRETATION

This instrument gives an impression of your *willingness to delegate*. Possible scores range from 9 to 45. The higher your score, the more willing you appear to be to delegate to others. Willingness to delegate is an important managerial characteristic: It is essential if you—as a manager—are to "empower" others and give them opportunities to assume responsibility and exercise self-control in their work. With the growing importance of empowerment in the new workplace, your willingness to delegate is worth thinking about seriously. Be prepared to share your results and participate in general class discussion.

Source: Questionnaire adapted from L. Steinmetz and R. Todd, *First Line Management*, 4th ed. (Homewood, IL: BPI/Irwin, 1986), pp. 64–67.

ASSESSMENT 16

Turbulence Tolerance Test

INSTRUCTIONS

The following statements were made by a 37-year-old manager in a large, successful corporation. How would you like to have a job with these characteristics? Using the following scale, choose your response to the left of each statement.

0 = This feature would be very unpleasant for me.

1 = This feature would be somewhat unpleasant for me.

2 = I'd have no reaction to this feature one way or another.

3 = This would be enjoyable and acceptable most of the time.

4 = I would enjoy this very much; it's completely acceptable.

_____ 1. I regularly spend 30 to 40% of my time in meetings.

_____ 2. Eighteen months ago my job did not exist, and I have been essentially inventing it as I go along.

_____ 3. The responsibilities I either assume or am assigned consistently exceed the authority I have for discharging them.

_____ 4. At any given moment in my job, I have on the average about a dozen phone calls to be returned.

_____ 5. There seems to be very little relation in my job between the quality of my performance and my actual pay and fringe benefits.

_____ 6. About 2 weeks a year of formal management training is needed in my job just to stay current.

_____ 7. Because we have very effective employment equity policies in my company and because it is thoroughly multinational, my job consistently brings me into close working contact at a professional level with people of many races, ethnic groups and nationalities, and of both sexes.

_____ 8. There is no objective way to measure my effectiveness.

_____ 9. I report to three different bosses for different aspects of my job, and each has an equal say in my performance appraisal.

_____ 10. On average about a third of my time is spent dealing with unexpected emergencies that force all scheduled work to be postponed.

_____ 11. When I have to have a meeting of the people who report to me, it takes my secretary most of a day to find a time when we are all available, and even then, I have yet to have a meeting where everyone is present for the entire meeting.

_____ 12. The university degree I earned in preparation for this type of work is now obsolete, and I probably should go back for another degree.

_____ 13. My job requires that I absorb 100–200 pages of technical materials per week.

_____ 14. I am out of town overnight at least 1 night per week.

_____ 15. My department is so interdependent with several other departments in the company that all distinctions about which departments are responsible for which tasks are quite arbitrary.

_____ 16. In about a year I will probably get a promotion to a job in another division that has most of these same characteristics.

_____ 17. During the period of my employment here, either the entire company or the division I worked in has been reorganized every year or so.

_____ 18. While there are several possible promotions I can see ahead of me, I have no real career path in an objective sense.

_____ 19. While there are several possible promotions I can see ahead of me, I think I have no realistic chance of getting to the top levels of the company.

_____ 20. While I have many ideas about how to make things work better, I have no direct influence on either the business policies or the personnel policies that govern my division.

_____ **21.** My company has recently put in an "assessment centre" where I and all other managers will be required to go through an extensive battery of psychological tests to assess our potential.

_____ **22.** My company is a defendant in an anti-trust suit, and if the case comes to trial, I will probably have to testify about some decisions that were made a few years ago.

_____ **23.** Advanced computer and other electronic office technology is continually being introduced into my division, necessitating constant learning on my part.

_____ **24.** The computer terminal and screen I have in my office can be monitored in my bosses' offices without my knowledge.

SCORING

Add up all of your scores and then divide the total by 24. This is your "Turbulence Tolerance Test" (TTT) score.

INTERPRETATION

This instrument gives an impression of your tolerance for managing in turbulent times—something likely to characterize the world of work well into the new century. In general, the higher your TTT score, the more comfortable you seem to be with turbulence and change—a positive sign.

For comparison purposes, the average TTT scores for some 500 MBA students and young managers was 1.5-1.6. The test's author suggests TTT scores may be interpreted much like a grade point average in which 4.0 is a perfect "A". On this basis, a 1.5 is below a "C"! How did you do?

_____

Source: Peter B. Vail, *Managing as a Performance Art: New Ideas for a World of Chaotic Change* (San Francisco: Jossey-Bass, 1989), pp. 8–9. Used by permission.

ASSESSMENT 17

Organizational Design Preference

INSTRUCTIONS

In the margin near each item, write the number from the following scale that shows the extent to which the statement accurately describes your views.

5 = strongly agree

4 = agree somewhat

3 = undecided

2 = disagree somewhat

1 = strongly disagree

I prefer to work in an organization where

1. goals are defined by those in higher levels.

2. work methods and procedures are specified.

3. top management makes important decisions.

4. my loyalty counts as much as my ability to do the job.

5. clear lines of authority and responsibility are established.

6. top management is decisive and firm.

7. my career is pretty well planned out for me.

8. I can specialize.

9. my length of service is almost as important as my level of performance.

10. management is able to provide the information I need to do my job well.

11. a chain of command is well established.

12. rules and procedures are adhered to equally by everyone.

13. people accept the authority of a leader's position.

14. people are loyal to their boss.

15. people do as they have been instructed.

16. people clear things with their boss before going over his or her head.

SCORING

Total your scores for all questions. Enter the score here [___].

INTERPRETATION

This assessment measures your preference for working in an organization designed along "organic" or "mechanistic" lines (see Chapter 11). The higher your score (above 64), the more comfortable you are with a mechanistic design; the lower your score (below 48), the more comfortable you are with an organic design. Scores between 48 and 64 can go either way. This organizational design preference represents an important issue in the new workplace. Indications are that today's organizations are taking on more and more organic characteristics. Presumably, those of us who work in them will need to be comfortable with such designs.

Source: From *The Dynamics of Organizational Theory: Gaining a Macro*, 2nd edition by Veiga/Yanouzas, 1984, South-Western, a division of Thomson Learning.

ASSESSMENT 18

Are You Cosmopolitan?

INSTRUCTIONS

Answer the following questions.

1. You believe it is the right of the professional to make his or her own decisions about what is to be done on the job.

Strongly disagree 1 2 3 4 5 Strongly agree

2. You believe a professional should stay in an individual staff role regardless of the income sacrifice.

Strongly disagree 1 2 3 4 5 Strongly agree

3. You have no interest in moving up to a top administrative post.

Strongly disagree 1 2 3 4 5 Strongly agree

4. You believe that professionals are better evaluated by professional colleagues than by management.

Strongly disagree 1 2 3 4 5 Strongly agree

5. Your friends tend to be members of your profession.

Strongly disagree 1 2 3 4 5 Strongly agree

6. You would rather be known or get credit for your work outside rather than inside the company.

Strongly disagree 1 2 3 4 5 Strongly agree

7. You would feel better making a contribution to society than to your organization.

Strongly disagree 1 2 3 4 5 Strongly agree

8. Managers have no right to place time and cost schedules on professional contributors.

Strongly disagree 1 2 3 4 5 Strongly agree

SCORING

Add your score for each item to get a total score between 8 and 40.

INTERPRETATION

A "cosmopolitan" identifies with the career profession, and a "local" identifies with the employing organization. A score of 30–40 suggests a "cosmopolitan" work orientation, 10–20 a "local" orientation, and 20–30 a "mixed" orientation.

Source: Developed from Joseph A. Raelin, *The Clash of Cultures, Managers and Professionals*, (Boston: Harvard Business School Press, 1986).

ASSESSMENT 19

Performance Appraisal Assumptions

INSTRUCTIONS

In each of the following pairs of statements, check off the statement that best reflects your assumptions about performance evaluation.

Performance evaluation is

1. (a) a formal process that is done annually.
   (b) an informal process done continuously.

2. (a) a process that is planned for subordinates.
   (b) a process that is planned with subordinates.

3. (a) a required organizational procedure.
   (b) a process done regardless of requirements.

4. (a) a time to evaluate subordinates' performance.
   (b) a time for subordinates to evaluate their manager.

5. (a) a time to clarify standards.
   (b) a time to clarify the subordinate's career needs.

6. (a) a time to confront poor performance.
   (b) a time to express appreciation.

7. (a) an opportunity to clarify issues and provide direction and control.
   (b) an opportunity to increase enthusiasm and commitment.

8. (a) only as good as the organization's forms.
   (b) only as good as the manager's coaching skills.

SCORING

There is no formal scoring for this assessment, but there may be a pattern to your responses. Check them again.

INTERPRETATION

In general, the "a" responses represent a more traditional approach to performance appraisal that emphasizes its *evaluation* function. This role largely puts the supervisor in the role of documenting a subordinate's performance for control and administrative purposes. The "b" responses represent a more progressive approach that includes a strong emphasis on the *counselling* or *development* role. Here, the supervisor is concerned with helping the subordinate do better and with learning from the subordinate what he or she needs to be able to do better. There is more of an element of reciprocity in this role. It is quite consistent with new directions and values emerging in today's organizations.

Source: Developed in part from Robert E. Quinn, Sue R. Faerman, Michael P. Thompson, and Michael R. McGrath, *Becoming a Master Manager: A Contemporary Framework* (New York: Wiley, 1990), p. 187. Used by permission.

ASSESSMENT 20

"T-P" Leadership Questionnaire

INSTRUCTIONS

The following items describe aspects of leadership behaviour. Respond to each item according to the way you would most likely act if you were the leader of a work group. Circle whether you would most likely behave in the described way: always (A), frequently (F), occasionally (O), seldom (S), or never (N).

A F O S N   **1.** I would most likely act as the spokesperson of the group.

A F O S N   **2.** I would encourage overtime work.

A F O S N   **3.** I would allow members complete freedom in their work.

A F O S N   **4.** I would encourage the use of uniform procedures.

A F O S N   **5.** I would permit the members to use their own judgement in solving problems.

A F O S N   **6.** I would stress being ahead of competing groups.

A F O S N   **7.** I would speak as a representative of the group.

A F O S N   **8.** I would push members for greater effort.

A F O S N   **9.** I would try out my ideas in the group.

A F O S N   **10.** I would let the members do their work the way they think best.

A F O S N   **11.** I would be working hard for a promotion.

A F O S N   **12.** I would tolerate postponement and uncertainty.

A F O S N   **13.** I would speak for the group if there were visitors present.

A F O S N   **14.** I would keep the work moving at a rapid pace.

A F O S N   **15.** I would turn the members loose on a job and let them go to it.

A F O S N   **16.** I would settle conflicts when they occur in the group.

A F O S N   **17.** I would get swamped by details.

A F O S N   **18.** I would represent the group at outside meetings.

A F O S N   **19.** I would be reluctant to allow the members any freedom of action.

A F O S N   **20.** I would decide what should be done and how it should be done.

A F O S N   **21.** I would push for increased performance.

A F O S N   **22.** I would let some members have authority, which I could otherwise keep.

A F O S N   **23.** Things would usually turn out as I had predicted.

A F O S N   **24.** I would allow the group a high degree of initiative.

A F O S N   **25.** I would assign group members to particular tasks.

A F O S N   **26.** I would be willing to make changes.

A F O S N   **27.** I would ask the members to work harder.

A F O S N   **28.** I would trust the group members to exercise good judgement.

A F O S N   **29.** I would schedule the work to be done.

A F O S N   **30.** I would refuse to explain my actions.

A F O S N   **31.** I would persuade others that my ideas are to their advantage.

A F O S N   **32.** I would permit the group to set its own pace.

A F O S N   **33.** I would urge the group to beat its previous record.

A F O S N   **34.** I would act without consulting the group.

A F O S N   **35.** I would ask that group members
follow standard rules and regula-
tions.

SCORING/INTERPRETATION

Score the instrument as follows.

a. Write a "1" next to each of the following items if you
scored them as S (seldom) or N (never).
8, 12, 17, 18, 19, 30, 34, 35

b. Write a "1" next to each of the following items if you
scored them as A (always) or F (frequently).
1, 2, 3, 4, 5, 6, 7, 9, 10, 11, 13, 14, 15, 16, 20, 21, 22, 23,
24, 25, 26, 27, 28, 29, 31, 32, 33

c. Circle the "1" scores for the following items, and then
add them up to get your TOTAL "P" SCORE = ___.
3, 5, 8, 10, 15, 18, 19, 22, 23, 26, 28, 30, 32, 34, 35

d. Circle the "1" scores for the following items, and then
add them up to get your TOTAL "T" SCORE = ___.
1, 2, 4, 6, 7, 9, 11, 12, 13, 14, 16, 17, 20, 21, 23, 25, 27,
29, 31, 33

e. Record your scores on the following graph to develop
an indication of your tendencies toward task-oriented leadership, people-oriented leadership, and
shared leadership. Mark your T and P scores on the
appropriate lines, then draw a line between these two
points to determine your shared leadership score.

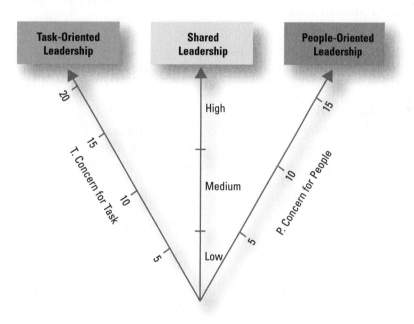

Source: Modified slightly from "T-P Leadership Questionnaire," University Associates, Inc., 1987.

ASSESSMENT 21

"T-T" Leadership Style

INSTRUCTIONS

For each of the following 10 pairs of statements, divide 5 points between the two according to your beliefs or perceptions of yourself or according to which of the two statements characterizes you better. The 5 points may be divided between the a and b statements in any one of the following ways: 5 for a, 0 for b; 4 for a, 1 for b; 3 for a, 2 for b; 1 for a, 4 for b; 0 for a, 5 for b, but not equally (2-1/2) between the two. Weigh your choices between the two according to which one characterizes you or your beliefs better.

1. (a) As leader I have a primary mission of maintaining stability.

   (b) As leader I have a primary mission of change.

2. (a) As leader I must cause events.

   (b) As leader I must facilitate events.

3. (a) I am concerned that my followers are rewarded equitably for their work.

   (b) I am concerned about what my followers want in life.

4. (a) My preference is to think long range: What might be.

   (b) My preference is to think short range: What is realistic.

5. (a) As a leader I spend considerable energy in managing separate but related goals.

   (b) As a leader I spend considerable energy in arousing hopes, expectations, and aspirations among my followers.

6. (a) Although not in a formal classroom sense, I believe that a significant part of my leadership is that of teacher.

   (b) I believe that a significant part of my leadership is that of facilitator.

7. (a) As leader I must engage with followers on an equal level of morality.

   (b) As leader I must represent a higher morality.

8. (a) I enjoy stimulating followers to want to do more.

   (b) I enjoy rewarding followers for a job well done.

9. (a) Leadership should be practical.

   (b) Leadership should be inspirational.

10. (a) What power I have to influence others comes primarily from my ability to get people to identify with me and my ideas.

    (b) What power I have to influence others comes primarily from my status and position.

SCORING

Circle your points for items 1b, 2a, 3b, 4a, 5b, 6a, 7b, 8a, 9b, 10a and add up the total points you allocated to these items; enter the score here [T = ___]. Next, add up the total points given to the uncircled items 1a, 2b, 3a, 4b, 5a, 6b, 7a, 8b, 9a, 10b; enter the score here [T = ___].

INTERPRETATION

This instrument gives an impression of your tendencies toward "transformational" leadership (your T score) and "transactional" leadership (your T score). You may want to refer to the discussion of these concepts in Chapter 13. Today, a lot of attention is being given to the transformational aspects of leadership—those personal qualities that inspire a sense of vision and the desire for extraordinary accomplishment in followers. The most successful leaders of the future will most likely be strong in both "T"s.

Source: Questionnaire by W. Warner Burke, Ph.D. Used by permission.

ASSESSMENT 22

Least-Preferred Co-worker Scale

INSTRUCTIONS

Think of all the different people with whom you have ever worked—in jobs, in social clubs, in student projects, or whatever. Next think of the one person with whom you could work least well—that is, the person with whom you had the most difficulty getting a job done. This is the one person—a peer, boss, or subordinate—with whom you would least want to work. Describe this person by circling numbers at the appropriate points on each of the following pairs of bipolar adjectives. Work rapidly. There are no right or wrong answers.

Pleasant	8 7 6 5 4 3 2 1	Unpleasant
Friendly	8 7 6 5 4 3 2 1	Unfriendly
Rejecting	1 2 3 4 5 6 7 8	Accepting
Tense	1 2 3 4 5 6 7 8	Relaxed
Distant	1 2 3 4 5 6 7 8	Close
Cold	1 2 3 4 5 6 7 8	Warm
Supportive	8 7 6 5 4 3 2 1	Hostile
Boring	1 2 3 4 5 6 7 8	Interesting
Quarrelsome	1 2 3 4 5 6 7 8	Harmonious
Gloomy	1 2 3 4 5 6 7 8	Cheerful
Open	8 7 6 5 4 3 2 1	Guarded
Backbiting	1 2 3 4 5 6 7 8	Loyal
Untrustworthy	1 2 3 4 5 6 7 8	Trustworthy
Considerate	8 7 6 5 4 3 2 1	Inconsiderate
Nasty	1 2 3 4 5 6 7 8	Nice
Agreeable	8 7 6 5 4 3 2 1	Disagreeable
Insincere	1 2 3 4 5 6 7 8	Sincere
Kind	8 7 6 5 4 3 2 1	Unkind

SCORING

This is called the "least-preferred co-worker scale" (LPC). Compute your LPC score by totalling all the numbers you circled; enter that score here [LPC = ___].

INTERPRETATION

The LPC scale is used by Fred Fiedler to identify a person's dominant leadership style (see Chapter 13). Fiedler believes that this style is a relatively fixed part of one's personality and is therefore difficult to change. This leads Fiedler to his contingency views, which suggest that the key to leadership success is finding (or creating) good "matches" between style and situation. If your score is 73 or above, Fiedler considers you a "relationship-motivated" leader; if your score is 64 or below, he considers you a "task-motivated" leader. If your score is between 65 and 72, Fiedler leaves it up to you to determine which leadership style is most like yours.

Source: Fred E. Fiedler and Martin M. Chemers, *Improving Leadership Effectiveness: The Leader Match Concept,* 2nd ed. (New York: Wiley, 1984).

ASSESSMENT 23

Student Engagement Survey

INSTRUCTIONS

Use the following scale to indicate the degree to which you agree with the following statements:

1—No agreement

2—Weak agreement

3—Some agreement

4—Considerable agreement

5—Very strong agreement

1. Do you know what is expected of you in this course?

2. Do you have the resources and support you need to do your coursework correctly?

3. In this course, do you have the opportunity to do what you do best all the time?

4. In the last week, have you received recognition or praise for doing good work in this course?

5. Does your instructor seem to care about you as a person?

6. Is there someone in the course who encourages your development?

7. In this course, do your opinions seem to count?

8. Does the mission/purpose of the course make you feel your study is important?

9. Are other students in the course committed to doing quality work?

10. Do you have a best friend in the course?

11. In the last six sessions, has someone talked to you about your progress in the course?

12. In this course, have you had opportunities to learn and grow?

SCORING

Score the instrument by adding up all your responses. A score of 0–24 suggests you are "actively disengaged" from the learning experience; a score of 25–47 suggests you are "moderately engaged"; a score of 48–60 indicates you are "actively engaged."

INTERPRETATION

This instrument suggests the degree to which you are actively "engaged" or "disengaged" from the learning opportunities of your course. It is a counterpart to a survey used by the Gallup Organization to measure the "engagement" of American workers. The Gallup results are surprising—indicating that up to 19% of US workers are actively disengaged, with the annual lost productivity estimated at some US $300 billion per year. One has to wonder: What are the costs of academic disengagement by students?

Source: This survey was developed from a set of "Gallup Engagement Questions" presented in John Thackray, "Feedback for Real," *Gallup Management Journal* (March 15, 2001), available online at http://gmj.gallup.com/content/811/Feedback-Real.aspx; data reported from James K. Harter, "The Cost of Disengaged Workers," Gallup Poll (March 13, 2001).

ASSESSMENT 24

Job Design Choices

INSTRUCTIONS

People differ in what they like and dislike about their jobs. Listed below are 12 pairs of jobs. For each pair, indicate which job you would prefer. Assume that everything else about the jobs is the same—pay attention only to the characteristics actually listed for each pair of jobs. If you would prefer the job in Column A, indicate how much you prefer it by putting a check mark in a blank to the left of the Neutral point. If you prefer the job in Column B, check one of the blanks to the right of Neutral. Check the Neutral blank only if you find the two jobs equally attractive or unattractive. Try to use the Neutral blank sparingly.

COLUMN A

1. A job that offers little or no challenge.

Strongly prefer A   Neutral   Strongly prefer B

2. A job that pays well.

Strongly prefer A   Neutral   Strongly prefer B

3. A job that often requires you to make important decisions.

Strongly prefer A   Neutral   Strongly prefer B

4. A job with little security in a somewhat unstable organization.

Strongly prefer A   Neutral   Strongly prefer B

5. A job in which greater responsibility is given to those who do the best work.

Strongly prefer A   Neutral   Strongly prefer B

6. A job with a supervisor who sometimes is highly critical.

Strongly prefer A   Neutral   Strongly prefer B

7. A very routine job.

Strongly prefer A   Neutral   Strongly prefer B

COLUMN B

A job that requires you to be completely isolated from coworkers.

A job that allows considerable opportunity to be creative and innovative.

A job in which there are many pleasant people to work with.

A job in which you have little or no opportunity to participate in decisions that affect your work.

A job in which greater responsibility is given to loyal employees who have the most seniority.

A job that does not require you to use much of your talent.

A job in which your co-workers are not very friendly.

8. A job with a supervisor who respects you and treats you fairly.

Strongly prefer A — Neutral — Strongly prefer B

A job that provides constant opportunities for you to learn new and interesting things.

9. A job that gives you a real chance to develop yourself personally.

Strongly prefer A — Neutral — Strongly prefer B

A job with excellent vacation and fringe benefits.

10. A job in which there is a real chance you could be laid off.

Strongly prefer A — Neutral — Strongly prefer B

A job that offers very little chance to do challenging work.

11. A job that gives you little freedom and independence to do your work in the way you think best.

Strongly prefer A — Neutral — Strongly prefer B

A job with poor working conditions.

12. A job with very satisfying teamwork.

Strongly prefer A — Neutral — Strongly prefer B

A job that allows you to use your skills and abilities to the fullest extent.

SCORING/INTERPRETATION

People differ in their need for psychological growth at work. This instrument measures the degree to which you seek growth-need satisfaction. Score your responses as follows:

For items 1, 2, 7, 8, 11, and 12 give yourself the following points for each item:

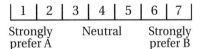

1	2	3	4	5	6	7

Strongly prefer A — Neutral — Strongly prefer B

For items 3, 4, 5, 6, 9, and 10 give yourself the following points for each item:

7	6	5	4	3	2	1

Strongly prefer A — Neutral — Strongly prefer B

Add up all of your scores and divide by 12 to find the average. If you score above 4.0, your desire for growth-need satisfaction through work tends to be high and you are likely to prefer an enriched job. If you score below 4.0, your desire for growth-need satisfaction through work tends to be low and you are likely to not be satisfied or motivated with an enriched job.

Source: Hackman, J.R./Oldham, G.R., WORK REDESIGN © 1980, pp. 275–294. Reprinted by permission of Pearson Education, Inc. Upper Saddle River, New Jersey.

Cognitive Style

INSTRUCTIONS

This assessment is designed to get an impression of your cognitive style, based on the work of psychologist Carl Jung. For each of the following 12 pairs, place a "1" next to the statement that best describes you. Do this for each pair even though the description you chose may not be perfect.

1. ___ (a) I prefer to learn from experience.

   ___ (b) I prefer to find meanings in facts and how they fit together.

2. ___ (a) I prefer to use my eyes, ears, and other senses to find out what is going on.

   ___ (b) I prefer to use imagination to come up with new ways to do things.

3. ___ (a) I prefer to use standard ways to deal with routine problems.

   ___ (b) I prefer to use novel ways to deal with new problems.

4. ___ (a) I prefer to learn from experience.

   ___ (b) I prefer to find meanings in facts and how they fit together.

5. ___ (a) I am patient with details but get impatient when they get complicated.

   ___ (b) I am impatient and jump to conclusions but am also creative, imaginative, and inventive.

6. ___ (a) I enjoy using skills already mastered more than learning new ones.

   ___ (b) I like learning new skills more than practising old ones.

7. ___ (a) I prefer to decide things logically.

   ___ (b) I prefer to decide things based on feelings and values.

8. ___ (a) I like to be treated with justice and fairness.

   ___ (b) I like to be praised and to please other people.

9. ___ (a) I sometimes neglect or hurt other people's feelings without realizing it.

   ___ (b) I am aware of other people's feelings.

10. ___ (a) I give more attention to ideas and things than to human relationships.

    ___ (b) I can predict how others will feel.

11. ___ (a) I do not need harmony; arguments and conflicts don't bother me.

    ___ (b) I value harmony and get upset by arguments and conflicts.

12. ___ (a) I am often described as analytical, impersonal, unemotional, objective, critical, hard-nosed, rational.

    ___ (b) I am often described as sympathetic, people-oriented, unorganized, uncritical, understanding, ethical.

SCORING

Sum your scores as follows, and record them in the space provided. (Note that the Sensing and Feeling scores will be recorded as negatives.)

(−   ) *Sensing* (*S Type*)   = 1a + 2a + 3a + 4a + 5a + 6a

(   ) *Intuitive* (*N Type*) = 1b + 2b + 3b + 4b + 5b + 6b

(   ) *Thinking* (*T Type*) = 7a + 8a + 9a + 10a + 11a + 12a

(−   ) *Feeling* (*F Type*)   = 7b + 8b + 9b + 10b + 11b + 12b

Plot your scores on the graph on the next page. Place an "X" at the point that indicates your suggested problem-solving style.

INTERPRETATION

This assessment examines cognitive style through the contrast of personal tendencies toward information gathering (sensation vs. intuition) and information evaluation (feeling vs. thinking) in one's approach to problem solving. The result is a classification of four master cognitive styles, with the following characteristics. Read the descriptions and consider the implications of your suggested style, including how well you might work with persons whose styles are very different.

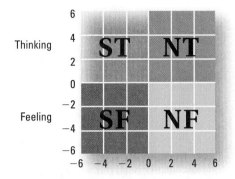

Sensation Thinkers: STs tend to emphasize the impersonal rather than the personal and take a realistic approach to problem solving. They like hard "facts," clear goals, certainty, and situations of high control.

Intuitive Thinkers: NTs are comfortable with abstraction and unstructured situations. They tend to be idealistic, prone toward intellectual and theoretical positions; they are logical and impersonal but also avoid details.

Intuitive Feelers: NFs prefer broad and global issues. They are insightful and tend to avoid details, being comfortable with intangibles; they value flexibility and human relationships.

Sensation Feelers: SFs tend to emphasize both analysis and human relations. They tend to be realistic and prefer facts; they are open communicators and sensitive to feelings and values.

_____

Source: Developed from Donald Bowen, "Learning and Problem-Solving: You're Never Too Jung," in Donald D. Bowen, Roy J. Lewicki, Donald T. Hall, and Francine S. Hall, eds., *Experiences in Management and Organizational Behaviour,* 4th ed. (New York: Wiley, 1997), pp. 7–13; and John W. Slocum, Jr., "Cognitive Style in Learning and Problem Solving," ibid., pp. 349–353.

ASSESSMENT 26

Internal/External Control

INSTRUCTIONS

Circle either "a" or "b" to indicate the item you most agree with in each pair of the following statements.

1. (a) Promotions are earned through hard work and persistence.

   (b) Making a lot of money is largely a matter of breaks.

2. (a) Many times the reactions of teachers seem haphazard to me.

   (b) In my experience I have noticed that there is usually a direct connection between how hard I study and the grades I get.

3. (a) The number of divorces indicates that more and more people are not trying to make their marriages work.

   (b) Marriage is largely a gamble.

4. (a) It is silly to think that one can really change another person's basic attitudes.

   (b) When I am right I can convince others.

5. (a) Getting promoted is really a matter of being a little luckier than the next guy.

   (b) In our society an individual's future earning power is dependent upon his or her ability.

6. (a) If one knows how to deal with people, they are really quite easily led.

   (b) I have little influence over the way other people behave.

7. (a) In my case the grades I make are the results of my own efforts; luck has little or nothing to do with it.

   (b) Sometimes I feel that I have little to do with the grades I get.

8. (a) People like me can change the course of world affairs if we make ourselves heard.

(b) It is only wishful thinking to believe that one can really influence what happens in society at large.

9. (a) Much of what happens to me is probably a matter of chance.

(b) I am the master of my fate.

10. (a) Getting along with people is a skill that must be practised.

(b) It is almost impossible to figure out how to please some people.

SCORING

Give 1 point for 1b, 2a, 3a, 4b, 5b, 6a, 7a, 8a, 9b, 10a.

8–10 = high *internal* locus of control

6–7 = moderate *internal* locus of control

5 = mixed locus of control

3–4 = moderte *external* locus of control

INTERPRETATION

This instrument offers an impression of your tendency toward an *internal locus of control* or *external locus of control*. Persons with a high internal locus of control tend to believe they have control over their own destinies. They may be most responsive to opportunities for greater self-control in the workplace. Persons with a high external locus of control tend to believe that what happens to them is largely in the hands of external people or forces. They may be less comfortable with self-control and more responsive to external controls in the workplace.

Source: Instrument from Julian P. Rotter, "External Control and Internal Control," *Psychology Today* (June 1971), p. 42.

ASSESSMENT 27

Team Leader Skills

INSTRUCTIONS

Consider your experience in groups and work teams. Ask: "What skills do I bring to team leadership situations?" Then, complete the following inventory by rating yourself on each item using this scale.

1 = Almost Never

2 = Seldom

3 = Sometimes

4 = Usually

5 = Almost Always

1 2 3 4 5   **1.** I facilitate communications with and among team members between team meetings.

1 2 3 4 5   **2.** I provide feedback/coaching to individual team members on their performance.

1 2 3 4 5   **3.** I encourage creative and "out-of-the-box" thinking.

1 2 3 4 5   **4.** I continue to clarify stakeholder needs/expectations.

1 2 3 4 5   **5.** I keep team members' responsibilities and activities focused within the team's objectives and goals.

1 2 3 4 5   **6.** I organize and run effective and productive team meetings.

1 2 3 4 5   **7.** I demonstrate integrity and personal commitment.

1 2 3 4 5   **8.** I have excellent persuasive and influence skills.

1 2 3 4 5   **9.** I respect and leverage the team's cross-functional diversity.

1 2 3 4 5   **10.** I recognize and reward individual contributions to team performance.

1 2 3 4 5   **11.** I use the appropriate decision-making style for specific issues.

1 2 3 4 5   **12.** I facilitate and encourage broader management with the team's key stakeholders.

1 2 3 4 5   **13.** I ensure that the team meets its team commitments.

1 2 3 4 5   **14.** I bring team issues and problems to the team's attention and focus on constructive problem solving.

1 2 3 4 5   **15.** I provide a clear vision and direction for the team.

SCORING

The inventory measures seven dimensions of team leadership. Add your scores for the items listed next to each dimension below to get an indication of your potential strengths and weaknesses.

1,9   Building the Team

2,10   Developing People

3,11   Team Problem Solving/Decision Making

4,12   Stakeholder Relations

5,13   Team Performance

6,14   Team Process

7,8,15   Providing Personal Leadership

INTERPRETATION

The higher the score, the more confident you are on the particular skill and leadership capability. When considering the score, ask yourself if others would rate you the same way. Consider giving this inventory to people who have worked with you in teams and have them rate you. Compare the results to your self-assessment. Also, remember that it is doubtful that any one team leader is capable of exhibiting all the skills listed above. More and more, organizations are emphasizing "top-management teams" that blend a variety of skills, rather than depending on the vision of the single, heroic leader figure. As long as the necessary leadership skills are represented within the membership, it is more likely that the team will be healthy and achieve high performance. Of course, the more skills you bring with you to team leadership situations, the better.

Source: Developed from Lynda McDermott, Nolan Brawley, and William Waite, *World-Class Teams: Working across Borders* (New York: Wiley, 1998).

ASSESSMENT 28

Conflict Management Styles

INSTRUCTIONS

Think of how you behave in conflict situations in which your wishes differ from those of one or more other persons. In the space to the left of each of the following statements, write the number from the following scale that indicates how likely you are to respond that way in a conflict situation.

1 = very unlikely   2 = unlikely

3 = likely   4 = very likely

_____   **1.** I am usually firm in pursuing my goals.

_____   **2.** I try to win my position.

_____   **3.** I give up some points in exchange for others.

_____   **4.** I feel that differences are not always worth worrying about.

_____   **5.** I try to find a position that is intermediate between the other person's and mine.

_____   **6.** In approaching negotiations, I try to be considerate of the other person's wishes.

_____   **7.** I try to show the logic and benefits of my positions.

___ **8.** I always lean toward a direct discussion of the problem.

___ **9.** I try to find a fair combination of gains and losses for both of us.

___ **10.** I attempt to work through our differences immediately.

___ **11.** I try to avoid creating unpleasantness for myself.

___ **12.** I try to soothe the other person's feelings and preserve our relationship.

___ **13.** I attempt to get all concerns and issues immediately out in the open.

___ **14.** I sometimes avoid taking positions that would create controversy.

___ **15.** I try not to hurt others' feelings.

SCORING

Total your scores for items 1, 2, 7; enter that score here [*Competing* = ___]. Total your scores for items 8, 10, 13; enter that score here [*Collaborating* = ___]. Total your scores for items 3, 5, 9; enter that score here [*Com-*

promising = ___]. Total your scores for items 4, 11, 14; enter that score here [*Avoiding* = ___]. Total your scores for items 6, 12, 15; enter that score here [*Accommodating* = ___].

INTERPRETATION

Each of the scores above corresponds to one of the conflict management styles discussed in Chapter 17. Research indicates that each style has a role to play in management but that the best overall conflict management approach is collaboration; only it can lead to problem solving and true conflict resolution. You should consider any patterns that may be evident in your scores and think about how to best handle the conflict situations in which you become involved.

Source: Adapted from Thomas-Kilmann, *Conflict Mode Instrument.* Copyright © 1974, Xicom, Inc., Tuxedo, NY 10987.

ASSESSMENT 29

Stress Self-Test

INSTRUCTIONS

Complete the following questionnaire. Circle the number that best represents your tendency to behave on each bipolar dimension.

Am casual about appointments	1 2 3 4 5 6 7 8	Am never late
Am not competitive	1 2 3 4 5 6 7 8	Am very competitive
Never feel rushed	1 2 3 4 5 6 7 8	Always feel rushed
Take things one at a time	1 2 3 4 5 6 7 8	Try to do many things at once
Do things slowly	1 2 3 4 5 6 7 8	Do things fast
Express feelings	1 2 3 4 5 6 7 8	"Sit on" feelings
Have many interests	1 2 3 4 5 6 7 8	Have few interests but work

SCORING

Total the numbers circled for all items, and multiply this by 3; enter the result here [___].

INTERPRETATION

This scale is designed to measure your personality tendency toward Type A or Type B behaviours. As described in Chapter 16, a Type A personality is associated with high stress. Persons who are Type A tend to bring stress on themselves even in situations where others are relatively stress-free. This is an important characteristic to be able to identify in yourself and in others.

Points	Personality
120+	A+
106 − 119	A
100 − 105	A−
90 − 99	B+
below 90	B

Source: Adapted from R. W. Bortner, "A Short Rating Scale as a Potential Measure of Type A Behaviour," *Journal of Chronic Diseases*, vol. 22 (1966), pp. 87–91.

ASSESSMENT 30

Work-Life Balance

INSTRUCTIONS

Complete this inventory by circling the number that indicates the extent to which you agree or disagree with each of the following statements.

1. How much time do you spend on nonwork-related activities such as taking care of family, spending time with friends, participating in sports, enjoying leisure time?

   Almost none/never   1   2   3   4   5   Very much/always

2. How often do family duties and nonwork responsibilities make you feel tired out?

   Almost none/never   1   2   3   4   5   Very much/always

3. How often do you feel short of time for family-related and nonwork activities?

   Almost none/never   1   2   3   4   5   Very much/always

4. How difficult is it for you to do everything you should as a family member and friend to others?

   Almost none/never   1   2   3   4   5   Very much/always

5. I often feel that I am being run ragged, with not enough time in a day to do everything and do it well.

   Almost none/never   1   2   3   4   5   Very much/always

6. I am given entirely too much work to do.

Almost none/never   1   2   3   4   5   Very much/always

7. How much conflict do you feel there is between the demands of your job and your family, and nonwork activities life?

Almost none/never   1   2   3   4   5   Very much/always

8. How much does your job situation interfere with your family life?

Almost none/never   1   2   3   4   5   Very much/always

9. How much does your family life and nonwork activities interfere with your job?

Almost none/never   1   2   3   4   5   Very much/always

SCORING

1. Family Demand Score: Total items #1, #2, #3, #4 and divide by 4.

2. Work Demand Score: Total items #5, #6 and divide by 2.

3. Work-Family Conflict Score: Total items #7, #8, #9 and divide by 3.

Your responses to items 1–4 are totalled and divided by 4, giving you the Life Demand score. Your responses to items 5–6 are totalled and divided by 2, resulting in your Work Demand score. Responses to items 7–9 are summed and divided by 3, giving your Work–Life conflict score.

INTERPRETATION

Compare yourself with these scores from a sample of Chinese and American workers.

	US	Chinese	Your Scores
Life Demand	3.53	2.58	4
Work Demand	2.83	2.98	4
Work–Life Conflict	2.53	2.30	4.67

Are there any suprises in this comparison?

Work–life conflict is defined as "a form of interrole conflict in which the role pressures from the work and family nonwork domains are mutually noncompatible in some respect." Demands of one role make it difficult to satisfy demands of the others.

Source: Based on Nini Yang, Chao D. Chen, Jaepil Choi, and Yimin Zou, "Sources of Work-Family Conflict: A Sino–U.S. Comparison of the Effects of Work and Family Demands," *Academy of Management Journal*, vol. 43, no. 1, pp. 113–123.

STUDENT PORTFOLIO BUILDER

What Is a Student Portfolio?

A *Student Portfolio* is a paper or electronic collection of documents that summarizes your academic and personal accomplishments in a way that effectively communicates with academic advisors and potential employers.[1] At a minimum, your portfolio should include the following:

• an up-to-date professional resumé

• a listing of courses in your major and related fields of study

• a listing of your extracurricular activities and any leadership positions

• documentation of your career readiness in terms of skills and learning outcomes

The purpose of a Student Portfolio is twofold—academic assessment and career readiness.

---

[1] The value and use of Student Portfolios are described by David S. Chappell and John R. Schermerhorn, Jr., in "Using Electronic Student Portfolios in Management Education: A Stakeholder Perspective," *Journal of Management Education*, vol. 23 (1999), pp. 651–62; and "Electronic Student Portfolios in Management Education" in Robert deFelippi and Charles Wrankel (eds.), *Educating Managers with Tomorrow's Technology* (Information Age Press, 2003), pp. 101–129.

1. *Academic Assessment Goal*   The Student Portfolio serves as an ongoing academic assessment tool that documents your learning and academic accomplishments. As you progress through a curriculum, the portfolio depicts the progress you are making in acquiring the skills and competencies necessary to be successful in life-long career pursuits. Over time, your portfolio will become increasingly sophisticated in the range and depth of learning and accomplishments that are documented. A well-prepared Student Portfolio is a very effective way of summarizing your academic achievements in consultation with both faculty advisors and professors.

2. *Career Readiness Goal*   The Student Portfolio serves as an important means of communicating your resumé and credentials to potential employers, as you search for both internship and full-time job opportunities. The portfolio is an effective career tool that offers value far beyond the standard resumé. Potential employers can readily examine multiple aspects of your accomplishments and skill sets in order to make a desired match. A professional and complete portfolio allows potential employers to easily review your background and range of skills and capabilities. It may convey your potential to a much greater depth and with a more positive impression than a traditional resumé. There is no doubt that a professional and substantive portfolio can help set you apart from the competition and attract the interest of employers.

PLANNING YOUR STUDENT PORTFOLIO

Your Student Portfolio should document, in a progressive and clear manner, your credentials and academic work. As you progress through the curriculum in your major and supplementary fields of study, the portfolio should be refined and materials added to display your most up-to-date skills, competencies, and accomplishments. Use of the *Management Skill and Outcome Assessment Framework*, described shortly, will help you to do this. Students should use the portfolio to store their coursework.

The closer you get to graduation, the entries in your portfolio should become more specific to your job and career goals. In this way, your portfolio becomes a dynamic and evolving career tool with value far beyond that of the standard resumé. We recommend that our students plan their portfolios to serve two immediate career purposes: (1) obtain a professional internship for the junior/senior year period while still a student, and (2) obtain their initial full-time job after graduation. A typical student of ours begins his or her portfolio as a sophomore in second year and then refines and adds to it throughout the program of study.

RESUMÉ WRITING GUIDE

The first thing that should go into your Student Portfolio is a professional resumé. Don't worry about how sophisticated or complete it is at first. The important things are to (1) get it started and (2) continue to build it as your experience grows. You will be surprised at how complete it will become with systematic attention and a personal commitment to take full advantage of the professional development opportunities available to you.

The following example should help get you started. It shows both a professional format and the types of things that can and should be included. We have also annotated the sample to show how an internship recruiter or potential employer might respond when reading the resumé for the first time. Wouldn't you like to have such positive reactions to the accomplishments and experiences documented in your resumé?

INTERVIEW PREPARATION GUIDE

You will know that your Student Portfolio was worthwhile and successful when it helps you land a preferred internship or your first-choice job. But the portfolio only helps get you to the point of a formal interview. The next step is doing well in it. In order to prepare for this step in the recruiting process, consider the following tips on job interviewing.[2]

- *Research the organization*—Make sure you read their recent literature, including annual reports; scan current news reports; and examine the industry and their major competitors.

- *Prepare to answer common interview questions*—Sample questions include: What do you really want to do in life? What do you consider your greatest strengths and weaknesses? How can you immediately contribute to our organization? Why did you choose your college or university? What are your interests outside of work? What was your most rewarding university experience? How would one of your professors describe you? What do you see yourself doing five years from now?

- *Dress for success*—Remember that impressions count, and first impressions often count the most. If you aren't sure what to wear or how to look, get advice from your professors and from career counsellors at your college or university.

- *Follow-up*—After the interview, send a "thank you" letter, ideally no longer than a week later. In the letter be sure to mention specific things about the organization that are important/insightful to you, and take the opportunity to clarify again where and how you believe you would fit as a valuable employee. Be prompt in providing any additional information requested during the interview.

SKILL AND OUTCOME ASSESSMENT FRAMEWORK

Skill and outcome assessment is an increasingly important part of management education. It allows you to document key academic accomplishments and career readiness for faculty review and for review by potential employers. Following guidelines of the AACSB, the International Association for Management Education, we suggest integrating into your portfolio specific documentation of your accomplishments in the following six areas of professional development.

---

[2] This section and the tips were recommended by Dr. Robert Lenie Holbrook of Ohio University.

RESUMÉ SAMPLE

■ Note: The annotations indicate positive reactions by a prospective employer to the information being provided.

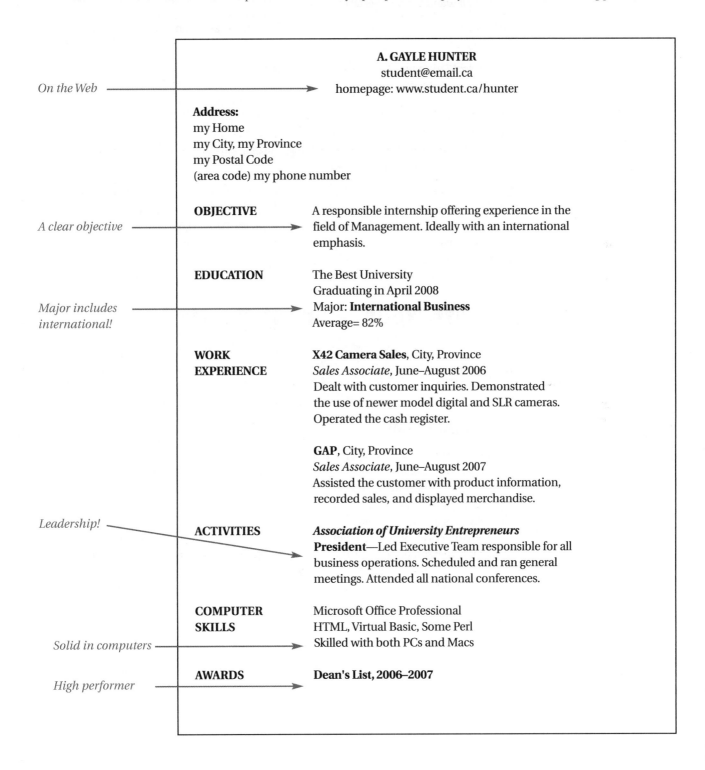

On the Web

A. GAYLE HUNTER
student@email.ca
homepage: www.student.ca/hunter

Address:
my Home
my City, my Province
my Postal Code
(area code) my phone number

A clear objective

OBJECTIVE — A responsible internship offering experience in the field of Management. Ideally with an international emphasis.

EDUCATION — The Best University
Graduating in April 2008

Major includes international!

Major: **International Business**
Average= 82%

WORK EXPERIENCE — **X42 Camera Sales**, City, Province
Sales Associate, June–August 2006
Dealt with customer inquiries. Demonstrated the use of newer model digital and SLR cameras. Operated the cash register.

GAP, City, Province
Sales Associate, June–August 2007
Assisted the customer with product information, recorded sales, and displayed merchandise.

Leadership!

ACTIVITIES — ***Association of University Entrepreneurs***
President—Led Executive Team responsible for all business operations. Scheduled and ran general meetings. Attended all national conferences.

COMPUTER SKILLS — Microsoft Office Professional
HTML, Virtual Basic, Some Perl

Solid in computers

Skilled with both PCs and Macs

High performer

AWARDS — **Dean's List, 2006–2007**

1. *Communication*—Demonstrates ability to share ideas and findings clearly in written and oral expression, and with technology utilization.

2. *Leadership*—Demonstrates ability to influence and support others to perform complex and ambiguous tasks.

3. *Teamwork*—Demonstrates ability to work effectively as a team member and as a team leader.

4. *Critical Thinking*—Demonstrates ability to gather and analyze information for creative problem solving.

5. *Self-Management*—Demonstrates ability to evaluate oneself, modify behaviour, and meet obligations.

6. *Professionalism*—Demonstrates ability to sustain a positive impression, instill confidence, and advance in a career.

The many learning resources and activities in this *Management Learning Workbook*—cases, projects, exercises, and self-assessments—relate to these skills and outcome assessment areas. There is no better time than the present to start participating in the learning experiences and documenting your results and accomplishments in your student portfolio.

Getting Started with Your Student Portfolio

The basic Student Portfolio consists of (1) a professional resumé and (2) a compendium of coursework samples that displays your career readiness skills and capabilities.

PORTFOLIO FORMAT

The easiest way to organize a paper portfolio is with a three-ring binder. This binder should be professional in appearance and have an attractive cover page that clearly identifies it as your student portfolio. The binder should be indexed with dividers that allow a reader to easily browse the resumé and other materials to gain a complete view of your special credentials.

In today's age of information technology and electronic communication, it is also highly recommended that you develop an online or *electronic portfolio*. This format allows you to communicate easily and effectively through the Internet with employers offering potential internship and job placements. An online version of your student portfolio can be displayed either on your personal website or on one provided by your university. Once you have created an electronic portfolio, it is easy to maintain. It is also something that will impress reviewers and help set you apart from the competition. At the very least, the use of an electronic portfolio communicates to potential employers that you are a full participant in this age of information technology.

MANAGEMENT SKILL AND OUTCOME ASSESSMENT FRAMEWORK

Communication – Demonstrates ability to share ideas and findings clearly in written and oral expression.

- Writing
- Oral presentation
- Giving and receiving feedback
- Technology utilization

Leading – Demonstrates ability to influence and support others to perform complex and ambiguous tasks.

- Diversity awareness
- Global awareness
- Project management
- Strategic leadership

Teamwork – Demonstrates ability to work effectively as a team member and a team leader.

- Team contribution
- Team leadership
- Conflict management
- Negotiation and consensus building

Critical Thinking – Demonstrates ability to gather and analyze information for creative problem solving.

- Problem solving
- Judgement and decision making
- Information gathering/interpretation
- Creativity and innovation

Self-Management – Demonstrates ability to evaluate oneself, modify behaviour, and meet obligations.

- Ethical understanding/behaviour
- Personal flexibility
- Tolerance for ambiguity
- Performance responsibility

Professionalism – Demonstrates ability to sustain a positive impression, instill confidence, and advance in a career.

- Personal presence
- Personal initiative
- Career management
- Unique "value added"

CAREER DEVELOPMENT PLAN—A PORTFOLIO PROJECT

A very good way to enhance your Student Portfolio is by completing the following project as part of your introductory management course, or on your own initiative. Called the "Career Development Plan," the objective of this project is to identify professional development opportunities that you can take advantage of to advance your personal career readiness.

Deliverable: Write and file in your Student Portfolio a two-part career development memorandum that is written in professional format and addressed to your instructor or to "prospective employer." The memorandum should do the following:

- *Part A*. Answer the question: "What are my personal strengths and weaknesses as a potential manager?"

  It is recommended that you use the *Management* Skill and Outcome Assessment Framework in structuring your analysis. It is recommended that you support your answer in part by analysis of results from your work with a selection of experiential exercises and self-assessments from this workbook. You can also supplement the analysis with other relevant personal insights.

- *Part B*. Answer the question: "How can I best take advantage of available opportunities to improve my managerial potential?"

  Make this answer as specific as possible. Describe a clear plan of action that encompasses the time available to you between now and graduation. This plan should include summer activities, as well as academic and extracurricular experiences. Your goal should be to build a resumé and complete portfolio that will best present you as a skilled and valuable candidate for the entry-level job that you would like in your chosen career field.

Evaluation: Your career development memorandum should be professional and error-free, and meet the highest standards of effective written communication. It should be sufficiently analytical in Part A to show serious consideration of your personal strengths and weaknesses in managerial potential at this point in time. It should be sufficiently detailed and in-depth in Part B so that you can objectively evaluate your progress step-by-step between now and graduation. Overall, it should be a career development plan you can be proud to formally include in your Student Portfolio. It should serve as a positive indicator of your professionalism.

SAMPLE PORTFOLIO COMPONENTS

The following samples document a range of accomplishments and capabilities. As with the sample resumé presented earlier, they are shown here with illustrative comments (written in red) that indicate how a prospective employer might react when reading them in print or viewing them online. As you look at these samples, ask: "How can I best display my course and academic accomplishments to document my learning and career readiness?"

WRITTEN ASSIGNMENT IN FRENCH

La Conception de L'Amour Pendant toute L'Histoire

La conception de l'amour pendant toute l'histoire est très intérresante, à voir. Pendant l'histoire, les formes de l'amour ont changé un peu, mais l'idée de base reste la même. Dans les ouvrages au XVIème siècle, on peut trouver des idées de l'amour qui sont semblables à la conception de l'amour dans notre société moderne. Avec une comparaison entre la poésie de Louise Labé et Ronsard au XVIème siècle, et le film Indochine, que Regis Wargnier a réalisé en 1992, on peut voir la conception de l'amour pendant l'histoire.

Second language skill!

INTERNATIONAL VIRTUAL TEAMWORK PROJECT

In my university management course I volunteered for a special assignment called the "International Virtual Teamwork Project." Through this experience I learned about cross-cultural issues in management and had the opportunity to experience the challenges of working as a member of a virtual team. The instructor's description of the project completed by my international virtual team follows.

Project Overview and Deliverables

This project requires extra effort to participate in an *international virtual team*. Students from each participating university will form into 4–5 person teams. Each team will complete a "domestic" project (Part A) and then participate in an "international" comparison project working with a team from the other university (Part B). A final report will be created by each pair of teams working together. The same final report will be submitted for grading. The final report will also be posted on the course website.

Shows high initiative!

Experienced with virtual groups

Cross-cultural awareness!

End Notes

CHAPTER 1 NOTES

1. Sources for the opening vignette:

   Patrick Sullivan, "Speech to CIPS," Toronto, November 13, 2003, on the Web, <www.cipstoronto.ca>.

   (November 2006). Information from the Workopolis website, <www.workopolis.com>.

TEXT NOTES

2. Information from the *Fast Company* website, <www.fastcompany.com>.

3. Charles O'Reilly III and Jeffrey Pfeffer, *Hidden Value: How Great Companies Achieve Extraordinary Results with Ordinary People* (Boston: Harvard Business School Press, 2000), p. 2.

4. For a research perspective see Denise M. Rousseau, "Organizational Behavior in the New Organizational Era," *Annual Review of Psychology*, vol. 48 (1997), pp. 515–46; for a consultant's perspective see Tom Peters, *The Circle of Innovation* (New York: Knopf, 1997); and Joan Magretta, *Managing in the New Economy* (Boston: Harvard Business School Press, 1999).

5. See Kevin Kelly, *New Rules for a New Economy: 10 Radical Strategies for a Connected World* (New York: Penguin, 1999).

6. Max DePree's books include *Leadership Is an Art* (New York: Dell, 1990) and *Leadership Jazz* (New York: Dell, 1993). See also Herman Miller's home page, <www.hermanmiller.com>.

7. Thomas A. Stewart, *Intellectual Capital: The Wealth of Organizations* (New York: Bantam, 1998).

8. See Peter F. Drucker, *The Changing World of the Executive* (New York: T.T. Times Books, 1982), and *The Profession of Management* (Cambridge, MA: Harvard Business School Press, 1997); and Francis Horibe, *Managing Knowledge Workers: New Skills and Attitudes to Unlock the Intellectual Capital in Your Organization* (New York: Wiley, 1999).

9. Kenichi Ohmae's books include *The Borderless World: Power and Strategy in the Interlinked Economy* (New York: Harper, 1989); *The End of the Nation State* (New York: Free Press, 1996); and *The Invisible Continent: Four Strategic Imperatives of the New Economy* (New York: Harper, 1999).

10. For information on Ballard Power Systems, see <www.ballard.com>.

11. For a discussion of globalization see Thomas L. Friedman, *The Lexus and the Olive Tree: Understanding Globalization* (New York: Bantam Doubleday Dell, 2000); and John Micklethwait and Adrian Woolridge, *A Future Perfect: The Challenges and Hidden Promise of Globalization* (New York: Crown, 2000).

12. Alfred E. Eckes, Jr., and Thomas W. Zeiler, *Globalization and the American Century* (Cambridge, UK: Cambridge University Press, 2003), pp. 1–2.

13. Michael E. Porter, *The Competitive Advantage of Nations: With a New Introduction* (New York: Free Press, 1998).

14. See, for example, Carl Shapiro and Hal R. Varian, *Information Rules: A Strategic Guide to the Network Economy* (Cambridge, MA: Harvard Business School Press, 1998).

15. *Workforce 2000: Work and Workers for the 21st Century* (Indianapolis: Towers Perrin/Hudson Institute, 1987).

16. Richard W. Judy and Carol D'Amico, eds., *Workforce 2020: Work and Workers for the 21st Century* (Indianapolis: Hudson Institute, 1997).

17. See Richard D. Bucher, *Diversity Consciousness: Opening Our Minds to People, Cultures, and Opportunities* (Upper Saddle River, NJ: Prentice-Hall, 2000).

18. View RS 1985, c H-6 of the Canadian Human Rights Act on the Web, <www.lois.justice.gc.ca>. (December 2006).

19. For a discussion of diversity issues, see R. Roosevelt Thomas, "From Affirmative Action to Affirming Diversity," *Harvard Business Review* (March–April 1990), pp. 107–17; and *Beyond Race and Gender: Unleashing the Power of Your Total Workforce by Managing Diversity* (New York: AMA-COM, 1992).

20. Quotations from Thomas, op. cit. (1990); and *Business Week* (August 8, 1990), p. 50, emphasis added.

21. Survey results reported in Rebecca Gomez, "Women Execs Increasing in Number, Survey Finds," *Columbus Dispatch* (November 19, 2002), p. D12.

22. Sue Shellenbarger, "Number of Women Managers Rises," *Wall Street Journal* (September 30, 2003), p. D2; "Best Companies for Women of Color," Working Mother Media on the Web, <www.workingmother.com>. (December 2006).

23. Stephanie N. Mehta, "What Minority Employees Really Want," *Fortune* (July 10, 2000), pp. 181–86.

24. Information from "Racism in Hiring Remains, Study Says," *Columbus Dispatch* (January 17, 2003), p. B2.

25. For background see Taylor Cox, Jr., "The Multicultural Organization," *Academy of Management Executive*, vol. 5 (1991), pp. 34–47; and *Cultural Diversity in Organizations: Theory, Research and Practice* (San Francisco: Berrett-Koehler, 1993).

26. For discussions of the glass ceiling effect see Ann M. Morrison, Randall P. White, and Ellen Van Velso, *Breaking the Glass Ceiling* (Reading, MA: Addison-Wesley, 1987); Anne E. Weiss, *The Glass Ceiling: A Look at Women in the Workforce* (New York: Twenty First Century, 1999); and Debra E. Meyerson and Joyce K. Fletcher, "A Modest Manifesto for Shattering the Glass Ceiling," *Harvard Business Review* (January–February 2000).

27. Judith B. Rosener, "Women Make Good Managers, So What?" *Business Week* (December 11, 2000), p. 24.

28. Portions adapted from John W. Dienhart and Terry Thomas, "Ethical Leadership: A Primer on Ethical Responsibility in Management," in John R. Schermerhorn, Jr., ed., *Management, 7th ed.* (New York: Wiley, 2002).

29. Judy and D'Amico, op. cit.

30. Credo selection from <www.jnj.com>.

31. Charles Handy, *The Age of Unreason* (Cambridge, MA: Harvard Business School Press, 1990).

32. "Is Your Job Your Calling?" *Fast Company* (February–March 1998), p. 108.

33. Tom Peters, "The New Wired World of Work," *Business Week* (August 28, 2000), pp. 172–73.

34. Robert Reich, "The Company of the Future," *Fast Company* (November 1998), p. 124ff.

35. Developed from Peters, op. cit. (2000).

36. For an overview of organizations and organization theory see W. Richard Scott, *Organizations; Rational, Natural and Open Systems, 4th ed.* (Englewood Cliffs, NJ: Prentice-Hall, 1998).

37. Ronald B. Lieber, "Why Employees Love These Companies," *Fortune* (January 12, 1998), pp. 72–74; and David Whitford, "A Human Place to Work," *Fortune* (January 8, 2001), pp. 108–20. See also <www.medtronic.com>.

38. For a discussion of organizations as systems, see Scott, op. cit. and Lane Tracy, *The Living Organization* (New York: Quorum Books, 1994).

39. Developed in part from Jay A. Conger, *Winning 'em Over: A New Model for Managing in the Age of Persuasion* (New York: Simon & Schuster, 1998), pp. 180–81; Stewart D. Friedman, Perry Christensen, and Jessica De Groot, "Work and Life: The End of the Zero-Sum Game," *Harvard Business Review* (November–December 1998), pp. 119–29; Chris Argyris, "Empowerment: The Emperor's New Clothers," *Harvard Business Review* (May–June 1998), pp. 98–105, and John A. Byrne, "Management by Web," *Business Week* (August 28, 2000), pp. 84–98.

40. Philip B. Crosby, *Quality Is Still Free: Making Quality Certain in Uncertain Times* (New York: McGraw-Hill, 1995). For a comprehensive review see Robert E. Cole and W. Richard Scott, eds., *The Quality Movement & Organization Theory* (Thousand Oaks, CA: Sage, 2000).

41. Jeffrey Pfeffer and John F. Veiga, "Putting People First for Organizational Success," *Academy of Management Executive*, vol. 13 (May 1999), pp. 37–48; and Jeffrey Pfeffer, *The Human Equation: Building Profits by Putting People First* (Boston: Harvard Business School Press, 1998).

42. "Workweek," *Wall Street Journal* (January 9, 2001), p. 1.

43. Henry Mintzberg, "The Manager's Job: Folklore and Fact," *Harvard Business Review*, vol. 53 (July–August 1975), p. 61. See also his book *The Nature of Managerial Work* (New York: Harper & Row, 1973, and Harper-Collins, 1997).

44. Hal Lancaster, "Middle Managers Are Back—But Now They're 'High-Impact' Players," *Wall Street Journal* (April 14, 1998), p. B1.

45. Information from David Whitford, "A Human Place to Work," *Fortune* (January 8, 2001), pp. 108–20.

46. Lancaster, op. cit.

47. For a perspective on the first-level manager's job, see Leonard A. Schlesinger and Janice A. Klein, "The First-Line Supervisor: Past, Present and Future," pp. 370–82, in Jay W. Lorsch, ed., *Handbook of Organizational Behavior* (Englewood Cliffs, NJ: Prentice-Hall, 1987). Research reported in "Remember Us?," *Economist* (February 1, 1992), p. 71.

48. Whitford, op. cit.

49. Stewart D. Friedman, Perry Christensen, and Jessica De Groot, "Work and Life: The End of the Zero-Sum Game," *Harvard Business Review* (November–December 1998), pp. 119–29.

50. For a classic study see Thomas A. Mahoney, Thomas H. Jerdee, and Stephen J. Carroll, "The Job(s) of Management," *Industrial Relations,* vol. 4 (February 1965), pp. 97–110.

51. This running example is developed from information from "Accountants Have Lives, Too, You Know," *Business Week* (February 23, 1998), pp. 88–90, and the Ernst & Young website <www.ey.com>.

52. Mintzberg, op. cit. (1973/1997), p. 30.

53. See, for example, John R. Veiga and Kathleen Dechant, "Wired World Woes: www.help," *Academy of Management Executive,* vol. 11 (August 1997), pp. 73–79.

54. See Mintzberg, op. cit (1973/1997); and Henry Mintzberg, "Covert Leadership: The Art of Managing Professionals," *Harvard Business Review* (November–December 1998), pp. 140–47; and, Jonathan Gosling and Henry Mintzberg,

"The Five Minds of a Manager," *Harvard Business Review* (November, 2003), pp. 1–9.

55. Mintzberg, op. cit. (1973/1997), p. 60.

56. For research on managerial work see Morgan W. McCall, Jr., Ann M. Morrison, and Robert L. Hannan, *Studies of Managerial Work: Results and Methods. Technical Report #9* (Greensboro, NC: Center for Creative Leadership, 1978), pp. 7–9. See also John P. Kotter, "What Effective General Managers Really Do," *Harvard Business Review* (November– December 1982), pp. 156–57.

57. Kotter, op. cit. p. 164. See also his book *The General Managers* (New York: Free Press, 1986); and David Barry, Catherine Durnell Crampton, and Stephen J. Carroll, "Navigating the Garbage Can: How Agendas Help Managers Cope with Job Realities," *Academy of Management Executive*, vol. 11 (May 1997), pp. 43–56.

58. To read more on the Johari Window, see R. P. Esposito, H. McAdoo, and L. Scher, "The Johari Window Test: A Research Note," *Journal of Humanistic Psychology*, vol. 18, no. 1 (1978), pp. 79–81.

59. Robert L. Katz, "Skills of an Effective Administrator," *Harvard Business Review* (September–October 1974), p. 94.

60. Hendrie Weisinger, *Emotional Intelligence at Work* (San Francisco: Jossey-Bass, 2000).

61. See Daniel Goleman's books *Emotional Intelligence* (New York: Bantam, 1995) and *Working with Emotional Intelligence* (New York: Bantam, 1998); and his articles "What Makes a Leader," *Harvard Business Review* (November–December 1998), pp. 93–102, and "Leadership That Makes a Difference," *Harvard Business Review* (March–April 2000), pp. 79–90, quote from p. 80.

62. Richard E. Boyatzis, *The Competent Manager: A Model for Effective Performance* (New York: Wiley, 1982). See also Jon P. Briscoe and Douglas T. Hall, "Grooming and Picking Leaders Using Competency Frameworks: Do They Work?", *Organizational Dynamics* (Autumn 1999), pp. 37–52.

CHAPTER 2 NOTES

1. Sources for the opening vignette:

   R. Alsop, "Ranking Corporate Reputations; Tech Companies Score High in Yearly Survey As Google Makes Its Debut in Third Place," *Wall Street Journal* (December 6, 2005).

   K.J. Delaney, "Google as—Get This—Value Play," *Wall Street Journal* (August 18, 2005).

   G. Robertson, "Yahoo's search for Net supremacy," *Globe and Mail* (December 10, 2005).

   "How Google's unsung hero won AOL deal," *Globe and Mail* (December 20, 2005).

TEXT NOTES

2. Pauline Graham, *Mary Parker Follett— Prophet of Management: A Celebration of Writings from the 1920s* (Boston: Harvard Business School Press, 1995).

3. For a timeline of twentieth-century management ideas see "75 Years of Management Ideas and Practices: 1922–1997," *Harvard Business Review,* supplement (September–October 1997).

4. A thorough review and critique of the history of management thought, including management in ancient civilizations, is provided by Daniel A. Wren, *The Evolution of Management Thought, 4th ed.* (New York: Wiley, 1993).

5. For a timeline of major people and themes see "75 Years of Management," op. cit.

6. For a sample of this work see Henry L. Gantt, *Industrial Leadership* (Easton, MD: Hive, 1921; Hive edition published in 1974); Henry C. Metcalfe and Lyndall Urwick, eds., *Dynamic Administration: The Collected Papers of Mary Parker Follett* (New York: Harper & Brothers, 1940); James D. Mooney, *The Principles of Administration, rev. ed.* (New York: Harper & Brothers, 1947); Lyndall Urwick, *The Elements of Administration* (New York: Harper & Brothers, 1943); and *The Golden Book of Management* (London: N. Neame, 1956).

7. References on Taylor's work are from Frederick W. Taylor, *The Principles of Scientific Management* (New York: W. W. Norton, 1967), originally published by Harper & Brothers in 1911. See Charles W. Wrege and Amedeo G. Perroni, "Taylor's Pig-Tale: A Historical Analysis of Frederick W. Taylor's Pig Iron Experiments," *Academy of Management Journal*, vol. 17 (March 1974), pp. 6–27 for a criticism. See Edwin A. Lock, "The Ideas of Frederick W. Taylor: An Evaluation," *Academy of Management Review*, vol. 7 (1982), p. 14 for an examination of the contemporary significance of Taylor's work. See also the biography, Robert Kanigel, *The One Best Way* (New York: Viking, 1997).

8. Kanigel, op. cit.

9. See Frank B. Gilbreth, *Motion Study* (New York: Van Nostrand, 1911).

10. Available in the English language as Henri Fayol, *General and Industrial Administration* (London: Pitman, 1949); subsequent discussion is based on M. B. Brodie, *Fayol on Administration* (London: Pitman, 1949).

11. M. P. Follett, *Freedom and Coordination* (London: Management Publications Trust, 1949).

12. Judith Garwood, "A Review of *Dynamic Administration: The Collected Papers of Mary Parker Follett,*" *New Management*, vol. 2 (1984), pp. 61–62; eulogy from Richard C. Cabot, "Follett, Mary Parker," *Encyclopaedia of Social Work, vol. 15*, p. 351.

13. Henderson and Talcott Parsons, eds. and trans., *Max Weber: The Theory of Social Economic Organization* (New York: Free Press, 1947).

14. Ibid., p. 337.

15. The Hawthorne studies are described in detail in F. J. Roethlisberger and William J. Dickson, *Management and the Worker* (Cambridge, MA: Harvard University Press, 1966); and G. Homans, *Fatigue of Workers* (New York: Reinhold, 1941). For an interview with three of the participants in the relay assembly test-room studies, see R. G. Greenwood, A. A. Bolton, and R. A. Greenwood, "Hawthorne a Half Century Later: 'Relay Assembly Participants Remember'," *Journal of Management*, vol. 9 (1983), pp. 217–31.

16. The criticisms of the Hawthorne studies are detailed in Alex Carey, "The Hawthorne Studies: A Radical Criticism," *American Sociological Review*, vol. 32 (1967), pp. 403–16; H. M. Parsons, "What Happened at Hawthorne?" *Science*, vol. 183 (1974), pp. 922–32; and B. Rice, "The Hawthorne Defect: Persistence of a Flawed Theory," *Psychology Today*, vol. 16 (1982), pp. 70–74. See also Wren, op. cit.

17. This discussion of Maslow's theory is based on Abraham H. Maslow, *Eupsychian Management* (Homewood, IL: Richard D. Irwin, 1965); and Abraham H. Maslow, *Motivation and Personality, 2nd ed.* (New York: Harper & Row, 1970).

18. Douglas McGregor, *The Human Side of Enterprise* (New York: McGraw-Hill, 1960).

19. See Gary Heil, Deborah F. Stevens, and Warren G. Bennis, *Douglas McGregor on Management: Revisiting the Human Side of Enterprise* (New York: Wiley, 2000).

20. Chris Argyris, *Personality and Organization* (New York: Harper & Row, 1957).

21. The ideas of Ludwig von Bertalanffy contributed to the emergence of this systems perspective on organizations. See his article, "The History and Status of General Systems Theory," *Academy of Management Journal*, vol. 15 (1972), pp. 407–26. This viewpoint is further developed by Daniel Katz and Robert L. Kahn in their classic book, *The Social Psychology of Organizations* (New York: Wiley, 1978). For an integrated systems view see Lane Tracy, *The Living Organization* (New York: Quorum Books, 1994). For an overview, see W. Richard Scott, *Organizations: Rational, Natural, and Open Systems, 4th ed.* (Upper Saddle River, NJ: Prentice-Hall, 1998).

22. Chester I. Barnard, *Functions of the Executive* (Cambridge, MA: Harvard University Press, 1938).

23. See discussion by Scott, op. cit., pp. 66–68.

24. Peter F. Drucker, "The Future That Has Already Happened," *Harvard Business Review*, vol. 75 (September–October

1997), pp. 20–24. See also Shaker A. Zahra, "An Interview with Peter Drucker," *Academy of Management Executive*, vol. 17 (2003), pp. 9–12.

25. For an overview, see Scott, op. cit., pp. 95–97.

26. For the classics see W. Edwards Deming, *Quality, Productivity, and Competitive Position* (Cambridge, MA: MIT Press, 1982); and Joseph M. Juran, *Quality Control Handbook, 3rd ed.* (New York: McGraw-Hill, 1979).

27. D. Wren, *The History of Management Thought* (Hoboken, NJ: Wiley, 2005).

28. Jay R. Gailbraith, "Designing the Networked Organization: Leveraging Size and Competencies" in Susan Albers Mohrman, Jay R. Galbraith, Edward E. Lawler III and Associates, *Tomorrow's Organization: Crafting Winning Capabilities in a Dynamic World* (San Francisco: Jossey-Bass, 1998), pp. 92–94.

29. Thomas J. Peters and Robert H. Waterman, Jr., *In Search of Excellence: Lessons from America's Best-Run Companies* (New York: Harper & Row, 1982). For a retrospective see William C. Bogner, "Tom Peters on the Real World of Business" and "Robert Waterman on Being Smart and Lucky," *Academy of Management Executive*, vol. 16 (2002), pp. 40–50.

30. William Ouchi, *Theory Z: How American Businesses Can Meet the Japanese Challenge* (Reading, MA: Addison-Wesley, 1981); and Richard Tanner Pascale and Anthony G. Athos, *The Art of Japanese Management: Applications for American Executives* (New York: Simon & Schuster, 1981).

31. Ouchi, op. cit.; see also the review by J. Bernard Keys, Luther Tray Denton, and Thomas R. Miller, "The Japanese Management Theory Jungle—Revisited," *Journal of Management*, vol. 20 (1994), pp. 373–402.

32. Peter Senge, *The Fifth Discipline* (New York: Harper, 1990).

33. John Gardner, *No Easy Victories* (New York: Harper & Row, 1968).

34. Quote from Allan H. Church, Executive Commentary, *Academy of Management Executive* (February 2002), p. 74.

35. Peter F. Drucker, "Looking Ahead: Implications of the Present," *Harvard Business Review* (September–October, 1997), pp. 18–32.

36. Quote from Ralph Z. Sorenson, "A Lifetime of Learning to Manage Effectively," *Wall Street Journal* (February 28, 1983), p. 18.

CHAPTER 3 NOTES

1. Sources for the opening vignette:

J. Bagnall, "Well Healed," *Canadian Business Magazine* (December 5, 2005).

Information from the Aldo website <www.aldoshoes.com>.

TEXT NOTES

2. Adapted from Terry Thomas, John W. Dienhart, and John R. Schermerhorn, Jr., "Leading Toward Ethical Behavior in Business," working paper (2003).

3. For more on the WorldCom debacle see Susan Pulliam, "A Staffer Ordered to Commit Fraud Balked, Then Caved," *Wall Street Journal* (June 23, 2003), pp. A1, A6; for more on the Andersen saga see Barbara Ley Toffler, *Final Accounting: Ambition, Greed and the Fall of Arthur Andersen* (New York: Broadway Books, 2003).

4. Mark Heinz, *Wall Street Journal*, (February 19, 1998), p. 1.

5. See the discussion by Lynn Sharpe Paine, "Managing for Organizational Integrity," *Harvard Business Review* (March–April 1994), pp. 106–117.

6. This quote is from an interview with Jana Matthews for the magazine of her alma mater, Earlham College. See "Business as an Ethical Activity," *Earlhamite* (Winter 2003), pp. 14–15.

7. Desmond Tutu, "Do More Than Win," *Fortune* (December 30, 1991), p. 59.

8. For an overview, see Linda K. Trevino and Katherine A. Nelson, *Managing Business Ethics, 3rd ed.* (New York: Wiley, 2003).

9. Ibid.

10. Milton Rokeach, *The Nature of Human Values* (New York: Free Press, 1973). See also W. C. Frederick and J. Weber, "The Values of Corporate Executives and Their Critics: An Empirical Description and Normative Implications," in W. C. Frederick and L. E. Preston, eds., *Business Ethics: Research Issues and Empirical Studies* (Greenwich, CT: JAI Press, 1990).

11. See Gerald F. Cavanagh, Dennis J. Moberg, and Manuel Velasquez, "The Ethics of Organizational Politics," *Academy of Management Review*, vol. 6 (1981), pp. 363–74; Justin G. Locknecker, Joseph A. McKinney, and Carlos W. Moore, "Egoism and Independence: Entrepreneurial Ethics," *Organizational Dynamics* (winter 1988), pp. 64–72; and Justin G. Locknecker, Joseph A. McKinney, and Carlos W. Moore, "The Generation Gap in Business Ethics," *Business Horizons* (September–October 1989), pp. 9–14.

12. Raymond L. Hilgert, "What Ever Happened to Ethics in Business and in Business Schools," *Diary of Alpha Kappa Psi* (April 1989), pp. 4–8.

13. Jerald Greenburg, "Organizational Justice: Yesterday, Today, and Tomorrow," *Journal of Management*, vol. 16, (1990) pp. 399–432; and Mary A. Konovsky, "Understanding Procedural Justice and Its Impact on Business Organizations," *Journal of Management*, vol. 26 (2000), pp. 489–511.

14. Interactional justice is described by Robert J. Bies, "The Predicament of Injustice: The Management of Moral Outrage," in L. L. Cummings & B. M. Staw, eds., *Research in Organizational Behavior*, vol. 9 (Greenwich, CT: JAI Press, 1987), pp. 289–319. The example is from Carol T. Kulik & Robert L. Holbrook, "Demographics in Service Encounters: Effects of Racial and Gender Congruence on Perceived Fairness," *Social Justice Research*, vol. 13 (2000), pp. 375–402.

15. Robert D. Haas, "Ethics—A Global Business Challenge," *Vital Speeches of the Day* (June 1, 1996), pp. 506–9.

16. Thomas Donaldson, "Values in Tension: Ethics Away from Home," *Harvard Business Review*, vol. 74 (September–October 1996), pp. 48–62.

17. Thomas Donaldson and Thomas W. Dunfee, "Towards a Unified Conception of Business Ethics:

Integrative Social Contracts Theory," *Academy of Management Review*, vol. 19 (1994), pp. 252–85.

18. Developed from Donaldson, op. cit.

19. Reported in Barbara Ley Toffler, "Tough Choices: Managers Talk Ethics," *New Management*, vol. 4 (1987), pp. 34–39. See also Barbara Ley Toffler, *Tough Choices: Managers Talk Ethics* (New York: Wiley, 1986).

20. See discussion by Trevino and Nelson, op. cit., pp. 47–62.

21. Information from Steven N. Brenner and Earl A. Mollander, "Is the Ethics of Business Changing?" *Harvard Business Review*, vol. 55 (January–February 1977).

22. Saul W. Gellerman, "Why 'Good' Managers Make Bad Ethical Choices," *Harvard Business Review*, vol. 64 (July–August, 1986), pp. 85–90.

23. Reported in Adam Smith, "Wall Street's Outrageous Fortunes," *Esquire* (April 1987), p. 73.

24. The Body Shop came under scrutiny over the degree to which its business practices actually live up to this charter and the company's self-promoted green image. See, for example, John Entine, "Shattered Image," *Business Ethics* (September–October 1994), pp. 23–28.

25. Steve Maich, "Selling Ethics at Nortel," *Maclean's* (January 24, 2005).

26. Information on this case from William M. Carley, "Antitrust Chief Says CEOs Should Tape All Phone Calls to Each Other," *Wall Street Journal* (February 15, 1983), p. 23; "American Air, Chief End Antitrust Suit, Agree Not to Discuss Fares with Rivals," *Wall Street Journal* (July 15, 1985), p. 4; "American Airlines Loses Its Pilot," *Economist* (April 18, 1998), p. 58.

27. Alan L. Otten, "Ethics on the Job: Companies Alert Employees to Potential Dilemmas," *Wall Street Journal* (July 14, 1986), p. 17; and "The Business Ethics Debate," *Newsweek* (May 25, 1987), p. 36.

28. See "Whistle-Blowers on Trial," *Business Week* (March 24, 1997), pp. 172–78; and "NLRB Judge Rules for Massachusetts Nurses in Whistle-Blowing Case," *American Nurse* (January–February 1998), p. 7.

29. Greg Watson, "Auditor, ad man heroes of Adscam," *Ottawa Sun* (November 1, 2005).

30. For a review of whistle-blowing, see Marcia P. Micelli and Janet P. Near, *Blowing the Whistle* (Lexington, MA: Lexington Books, 1992); see also Micelli and Near, "Whistleblowing: Reaping the Benefits," *Academy of Management Executive*, vol. 8 (August 1994), pp. 65–72.

31. Information from James A. Waters, "Catch 20.5: Mortality as an Organizational Phenomenon," *Organizational Dynamics*, vol. 6 (spring 1978), pp. 3–15.

32. Information from Ethics Resource Center, "Major Survey of America's Workers Finds Substantial Improvements in Ethics," *Wall Street Journal* (May 21, 2003).

33. Robert D. Gilbreath, "The Hollow Executive," *New Management*, vol. 4 (1987), pp. 24–28.

34. Information from <www.josephsoninstitute.org/MED/MED-2sixpillars.htm>.

35. Developed from recommendations of the Government Accountability Project reported in "Blowing the Whistle without Paying the Piper."

36. Quote taken from BCE's code of business conduct found on the company website, <www.bce.ca>. (December 2006).

37. Information taken from the Social Responsibility page of the corporate website, <www.gapinc.com>. (December 2006).

38. For a good review see Robert H. Miles, *Managing the Corporate Social Environment* (Englewood Cliffs, NJ: Prentice-Hall, 1987).

39. See Thomas Donaldson and Lee Preston, "The Stakeholder Theory of the Corporation," *Academy of Management Review*, vol. 20 (January 1995), pp. 65–91.

40. Information from Sustainable Development page of Natural Resources Canada on the Web, <www.nrcan.gc.ca>. (December 2006).

41. See Joel Makower, *Putting Social Responsibility to Work for Your Business and the World* (New

York: Simon & Schuster, 1994), pp. 17–18.

42. The historical framework of this discussion is developed from Keith Davis, "The Case for and against Business Assumption of Social Responsibility," *Academy of Management Journal* (June 1973), pp. 312–22; Keith Davis and William Frederick, *Business and Society: Management: Public Policy, Ethics, 5th ed.* (New York: McGraw-Hill, 1984). The debate is also discussed by Makower, op. cit., pp. 28–33. See also, "Civics 101," *Economist* (May 11, 1996), p. 61.

43. The Friedman quotation is from Milton Friedman, *Capitalism and Freedom* (Chicago: University of Chicago Press, 1962); the Samuelson quotation is from Paul A. Samuelson, "Love That Corporation," *Mountain Bell Magazine* (spring 1971). Both are cited in Davis, op. cit.

44. Davis and Frederick, quoted in op. cit.

45. See James K. Glassman, "When Ethics Meet Earnings," *International Herald Tribune* (May 24–25, 2003), p. 15.

46. See Makower, op. cit. (1994), pp. 71–75; and Sandra A. Waddock and Samuel B. Graves, "The Corporate Social Performance-Financial Performance Link," *Strategic Management Journal* (1997), pp. 303–19.

47. Davis, op. cit.

48. The "compliance–conviction" distinction is attributed to Mark Goyder in Martin Waller, "Much Corporate Responsibility Is Box-Ticking," *Times Business* (July 8, 2003), p. 21.

49. Archie B. Carroll, "A Three-Dimensional Model of Corporate Performance," *Academy of Management Review*, vol. 4 (1979), pp. 497–505. Carroll's continuing work in this area is most recently reported in Mark S. Schwartz and Archie B. Carroll, "Corporate Social Responsibility: A Three Domain Approach," *Business Ethics Quarterly*, vol. 13 (2003), pp. 503–530.

50. Elizabeth Gatewood and Archie B. Carroll, "The Anatomy of Corporate Social Response," *Business Horizons*, vol. 24 (September–October 1981), pp. 9–16.

51. David Bornstein, *How to Change the World: Social Entrepreneurs and the Power of New Ideas* (New York: Oxford University Press, 2004).

52. Information taken from <www.ashoka.org>.

53. C. Leadbeater, *The Rise of the Social Entrepreneur* (London: Demos 1997).

54. Judith Burns, "Everything You Wanted to Know About Corporate Governance... But Didn't Know to Ask," *Wall Street Journal* (October 27, 2003), p. R6.

55. See for example "Pay for Performance Report," *Institute of Management and Administration* (December, 2003).

CHAPTER 4 NOTES

1. Sources for the opening vignette:

   With information from the corporate websites <www2.bmo.com> and <www4.bmo.com> (November 22, 2006).

TEXT NOTES

2. Robert Reich, *The Future of Success* (New York: Knopf, 2001), p. 7.

3. Quote from *The New Blue* (IBM Annual Report, 1997), p. 8.

4. Reich, op. cit.

5. See Michael E. Porter, *Competitive Strategy: Techniques for Analyzing Industries and Competitors* (New York: Free Press, 1980); and *Competitive Advantage: Creating and Sustaining Superior Performance* (New York: Free Press, 1986); also, Richard A. D'Aveni, *Hyper-Competition: Managing the Dynamics of Strategic Maneuvering* (New York: Free Press, 1994).

6. Joseph M. Juran, "Made in U.S.A.: A Renaissance in Quality," *Harvard Business Review* (July–August 1993), pp. 42–50.

7. Michael Porter, *The Competitive Advantage of Nations* (New York: Free Press, 1989).

8. See Richard D. Bucher, *Diversity Consciousness: Opening Our Minds to People, Cultures, and Opportunities* (Upper Saddle River, NJ: Prentice-Hall, 2000), p. 201.

9. James D. Thompson, *Organizations in Action* (New York: McGraw-Hill, 1967); and Robert B. Duncan, "Characteristics of Organizational Environments and Perceived Environmental Uncertainty," *Administrative Science Quarterly*, vol. 17 (1972), pp. 313–27. For discussion of the implications of uncertainty see Hugh Courtney, Jane Kirkland, and Patrick Viguerie, "Strategy Under Uncertainty," *Harvard Business Review* (November–December 1997), pp. 67–79.

10. Quotation from a discussion by Richard J. Shonberger and Edward M. Knod, Jr., *Operations Management: Serving the Customer, 3rd ed.* (Plano, TX: Business Publications, 1988), p. 4.

11. Rosabeth Moss Kanter, "Transcending Business Boundaries: 12,000 World Managers View Change," *Harvard Business Review* (May–June 1991), pp. 151–64.

12. Reported in Jennifer Steinhauer, "The Undercover Shoppers," *New York Times* (February 4, 1998), pp. C1, C2.

13. Information from "How Marriott Never Forgets a Guest," *Business Week* (February 21, 2000), p. 74.

14. Roger D. Blackwell and Kristina Blackwell, "The Century of the Consumer: Converting Supply Chains into Demand Chains," *Supply Chain Management Review* (fall 1999).

15. See Joseph M. Juran, *Quality Control Handbook, 3rd ed.* (New York: McGraw-Hill, 1979) and "The Quality Trilogy: A Universal Approach to Managing for Quality," in H. Costin, ed., *Total Quality Management* (New York: Dryden, 1994); W. Edwards Derning, *Out of Crisis* (Cambridge, MA: MIT Press, 1986); and "Deming's Quality Manifesto," *Best of Business Quarterly*, vol. 12 (winter 1990–1991), pp. 6–10. See also Howard S. Gitlow and Shelly J. Gitlow, *The Deming Guide to Quality and Competitive Position* (Englewood Cliffs, NJ: Prentice-Hall, 1987); and Juran, op. cit. (1993).

16. See information on the Malcolm Baldrige National Quality Award, on the Web, <www.quality.nist.gov>; see also, "Does the Baldrige Award Really Work?" *Harvard Business Review* (January–February 1992), pp. 126–47.

17. Philip B. Crosby, *Quality Is Free* (New York: McGraw-Hill, 1979); *The Eternally Successful Organization* (New York: McGraw-Hill, 1988); and *Quality Is Still Free: Making Quality Certain in Uncertain Times* (New York: McGraw-Hill, 1995).

18. Rafael Aguay, *Dr. Deming: The American Who Taught the Japanese About Quality* (New York: Free Press, 1997); and W. Edwards Deming, op. cit. (1986).

19. See Edward E. Lawler III, Susan Albers Mohrman, and Gerald E. Ledford, Jr., *Employee Involvement and Total Quality Management: Practices and Results in Fortune 1000 Companies* (San Francisco: Jossey-Bass, 1992).

20. Edward E. Lawler III and Susan Albers Mohrman, "Quality Circles After the Fad," *Harvard Business Review* (January–February 1985), pp. 65–71.

21. Quotes from Arnold Kanarick, "The Far Side of Quality Circles." *Management Review*, vol. 70 (October 1981), pp. 16–17.

22. See B. Joseph Pine II, Bart Victor, and Andrew C. Boynton, "Making Mass Customization Work," *Harvard Business Review* (September–October 1993), pp. 108–19; and "The Agile Factory: Custom-made, Direct from the Plant," *Business Week,* special report on "21st Century Capitalism" (January 23, 1995), pp. 158–59; and Justin Martin, "Give 'Em *Exactly* What They Want," *Fortune* (November 10, 1997), p. 283.

23. Edgar H. Schein, "Organizational Culture," *American Psychologist*, vol. 45 (1990), pp. 109–19. See also Schein's *Organizational Culture and Leadership, 2nd ed.* (San Francisco: Jossey-Bass, 1997); and *The Corporate Culture Survival Guide* (San Francisco: Jossey-Bass, 1999).

24. James Collins and Jerry Porras, *Built to Last* (New York: Harper Business, 1994).

25. Schein, op. cit. (1997); Terrence E. Deal and Alan A. Kennedy, *Corporate Cultures: The Rites and Rituals of Corporate Life* (Reading, MA: Addison-Wesley, 1982); and Ralph Kilmann, *Beyond the Quick Fix* (San Francisco: Jossey-Bass, 1984).

26. In their book *Corporate Culture and Performance* (New York: Macmillan, 1992), John P. Kotter and James L. Heskett make the point that strong cultures have the desired effects over the long term only if they encourage adaptation to a changing environment. See also Collins and Porras, op. cit. (1994).

27. Andrew Wahl, "Stop the Rot: Advice for Turning Culture Around," *Canadian Business Magazine* (October 10–23, 2005).

28. Andrew Wahl, "Culture Shock: A Survey of Canadian Executives Reveals that Corporate Culture is in Need of Improvement," *Canadian Business Magazine* (October 10–23, 2005).

29. This is a simplified model developed from Schein, op. cit. (1997).

30. Wahl, op. cit.

31. James C. Collins and Jerry I. Porras, "Building Your Company's Vision," *Harvard Business Review* (September–October 1996), pp. 65–77.

32. Ralph H. Kilmann, Mary J. Saxton, and Roy Serpa, "Issues in Understanding and Changing Corporate Culture," *California Management Review*, vol. 28 (1986), pp. 87–94.

33. See Mary Kay Ash, *Mary Kay: You Can Have It All* (New York: Roseville, CA: Prima Publishing, 1995).

34. Lee Gardenswartz and Anita Rowe, *Managing Diversity: A Complete Desk Reference and Planning Guide* (Chicago: Irwin, 1993).

35. R. Roosevelt Thomas, Jr., *Beyond Race and Gender* (New York: AMACOM, 1992), p. 10; see also R. Roosevelt Thomas, Jr., "From 'Affirmative Action' to 'Affirming Diversity,'" *Harvard Business Review* (November–December 1990), pp. 107–17; R. Roosevelt Thomas, Jr., with Marjorie I. Woodruff, *Building a House for Diversity* (New York: AMACOM, 1999).

36. Thomas Kochan, Katerina Bezrukova, Robin Ely, Susan Jackson, Aparna Joshi, Karen Jehn, Jonathan Leonard, David Levine, and David Thomas, "The Effects of Diversity on Business Performance: Report of the Diversity Research Network," reported in SHRM Foundation Research Findings, on the Web, <www.shrm.org/foundation>. (December 2006).

37. Gardenswartz and Rowe, op. cit., p. 220.

38. Taylor Cox, Jr., *Cultural Diversity in Organizations* (San Francisco: Berrett Koehler, 1994).

39. Joseph A. Raelin, *Clash of Cultures* (Cambridge, MA: Harvard Business School Press, 1986).

40. Geert Hofstede, *Culture's Consequences* (Beverly Hills: Sage, 1982).

41. See Anthony Robbins and Joseph McClendon III, *Unlimited Power: A Black Choice* (New York: Free Press, 1997); and Augusto Failde and William Doyle, *Latino Success: Insights from America's Most Powerful Latino Executives* (New York: Free Press, 1996).

42. See, for example, the discussion in Ron Zembke, Claire Raines, and Bob Filipczak, *Generations at Work: Managing the Clash of Veterans, Boomers, Xers, and Nexters in Your Workplace* (New York: AMACOM, 1999); and Brian O'Reilly, "Meet the Future: It's Your Kids," *Fortune* (July 24, 2000), pp. 144–64.

43. Barbara Benedict Bunker, "Appreciating Diversity and Modifying Organizational Cultures: Men and Women at Work," Chapter 5 in Suresh Srivastva and David L. Cooperrider, eds., *Appreciative Management and Leadership* (San Francisco: Jossey-Bass, 1990).

44. See Gary N. Powell, *Women & Men in Management* (Thousand Oaks, CA: Sage, 1993) and Cliff Cheng, ed., *Masculinities in Organizations* (Thousand Oaks, CA: Sage, 1996). For added background, see also Sally Helgesen, *Everyday Revolutionaries: Working Women and the Transformation of American Life* (New York: Doubleday, 1998).

45. Stephanie N. Mehta, "What Minority Employees Really Want," *Fortune* (July 10, 2000), pp. 181–86.

46. Information from "The Bugs in Microsoft Culture," *Fortune* (January 8, 2001), p. 128.

47. Data reported in "How to Enable the Disabled," *Business Week* (November 6, 2000), p. 36.

48. This section is based on ideas set forth by Thomas, op. cit. (1992); and Thomas and Woodruff, op. cit. (1999).

49. Thomas, op. cit. (1992), p. 17.

50. Thomas and Woodruff, op. cit. (1999), pp. 211–26.

51. Based on ibid., pp. 11–12.

52. Survey reported in "The Most Inclusive Workplaces Generate the Most Loyal Employees," *Gallup Management Journal*, December 2001, on the Web, <gmj.gallup.com>. (December 2006).

53. "Diversity Today: Corporate Recruiting Practices in Inclusive Workplaces," *Fortune* (June 12, 2000), p. S4.

CHAPTER 5 NOTES

1. Sources for the opening vignette:

   J. Sanford, "Beat China on Cost: Gildan taps other labour pool and trade pacts," *Canadian Business Magazine* (November 7, 2005).

   J. Sanford and J. Gray, "Top CFO 2005: Lawrence Sellyn, Gildan Activewear Inc.," *Canadian Business Magazine* (April 25, 2005).

   Additional information from the Gildan website, <www.gildan.com>.

TEXT NOTES

2. Information from Lindsay Whipp and Kae Inoue, "Japan Carmakers to Expand U.S. Output," *International Herald Tribune* (May 23, 2003), p. B3.

3. Robin Blumenthal and Vito J. Racanelli, "O, Canada, Expect Funds to Flow to You," *Barron's*, vol. 86 (January 2, 2006), p. 11.

4. See Kenichi Ohmae, *The Evolving Global Economy* (Cambridge, MA: Harvard Business School Press, 1995).

5. For a discussion of globalization see Thomas L. Friedman, *The Lexus and the Olive Tree: Understanding Globalization* (New York: Bantam Doubleday Dell, 2000); and John Micklethwait and Adrian Woodridge, *A Future Perfect: The Challenges and*

Hidden Promise of Globalization (New York: Crown, 2000).

6. Rosabeth Moss Kanter, *World Class: Thinking Locally in the Global Economy* (New York: Simon & Schuster, 1995), preface.

7. See the discussion by Alfred E. Eckes, Jr., and Thomas W. Zeiler, *Globalization and the American Century* (Cambridge, UK: Cambridge University Press, 2003).

8. Quote from Jeffrey E. Garten, "The Mind of the CEO," *Business Week* (February 5, 2001), p. 106.

9. The *Economist* on the Web, <www.economist.com>, is a good weekly source of information on Europe.

10. A monthly publication that covers the *maquiladora* industries is the *Twin Plant News* (El Paso, Texas) on the Web, <www.twin-plant-news.com>.

11. Warren Jestin, Mary Webb, Aron Gampel, Pablo Bréard, "Keeping Canada Competitive—The Importance of Being Earnest," *Global Outlook* (December 2005), pp. 1, 15.

12. For an overview of business in China see John Studdard and James G. Shiro, *The New Silk Road: Secrets of Business Success in China Today* (New York: Wiley, 2000). Export data from "Surviving the Onslaught," *Wall Street Journal* (October 6, 2003), p. B1.

13. Information from Hiawatha Bray, "Philippines Vies for 'Back-Office' Operations," *International Herald Tribune* (May 23, 2003), p. 14.

14. The *Economist* on the Web, <www.economist.com>, is a good weekly source of information on Africa.

15. Bray, op. cit.

16. James A. Austin and John G. McLean, "Pathways to Business Success in Sub-Saharan Africa," *Journal of African Finance and Economic Development*, vol. 2 (1996), pp. 57–76.

17. Information from "International Business: Consider Africa," *Harvard Business Review*, vol. 76 (January–February 1998), pp. 16–18.

18. Information taken from MBendi, Information for Africa on the Web, <www.mbendi.co.za/orsadc.htm>. (December 2006).

19. See "Inside View: South Africa," *New York Times* (September 18, 2000), pp. A15–A17.

20. Quote from John A. Byrne, "Visionary vs. Visionary," *Business Week* (August 28, 2000), p. 210.

21. With information from <www.statcan.ca>. (July 2006).

22. Developed from Anthony J. F. O'Reilly, "Establishing Successful Joint Ventures in Developing Nations: A CEO's Perspective," *Columbia Journal of World Business* (spring 1988), pp. 65–71; and "Best Practices for Global Competitiveness," *Fortune* (March 30, 1998), pp. S1–S3, special advertising section.

23. CBC News on the Web, <www.cbc.ca>.

24. Whipp and Inoue, op. cit.

25. Quoted from "Own Words: Percy Barnevik, ABB and Investor," *Financial Times Limited* (1998).

26. Information from Karby Leggett, "U.S. Auto Makers Find Promise—and Peril—in China," *Wall Street Journal* (June 19, 2003), p. B1.

27. See Peter F. Drucker, "The Global Economy and the Nation-State," *Foreign Affairs,* vol. 76 (September–October 1997), pp. 159–71.

28. Adapted from R. Hall Mason. "Conflicts between Host Countries and Multinational Enterprise," *California Management Review*, vol. 17 (1974), pp. 6–7.

29. For a good overview, see Randall E. Stros, *Bulls in the China Shop and Other Sino-American Business Encounters* (New York: Pantheon, 1991); as well as Studdard and Shir, op. cit.

30. For an interesting discussion of one company's experience in China see Jim Mann, *Beijing Jeep: A Case Study of Western Business in China* (Boulder, CO: Westview Press, 1997).

31. Information from the corporate web-site, <www.nikeBiz.com/labor>. (December 2006).

32. "An Industry Monitors Child Labor," *New York Times* (October 16, 1997), pp. B1, B9; on the Web, <www.rug-mark.de>. (December 2006).

33. Definition from World Commission on Environment and Development, *Our Common Future* (Oxford: Oxford University Press, 1987).

34. Examples reported in Neil Chesanow, *The World-Class Executive* (New York: Rawson Associates, 1985).

35. Based on Barbara Benedict Bunker, "Appreciating Diversity and Modifying Organizational Cultures: Men and Women at Work," in Suresh Srivastiva and David L. Cooperrider, eds., *Appreciative Management and Leadership: The Power of Positive Thought and Action in Organizations* (San Francisco: Jossey-Bass, 1990), pp. 127–49.

36. For a good overview of the practical issues, see Richard D. Lewis, *The Cultural Imperative: Global Trends in the 21st Century* (Yarmouth, ME: Intercultural Press, 2002); and Martin J. Gannon, *Understanding Global Cultures* (Thousand Oaks, CA: Sage, 1994).

37. Information from Ronald B. Lieber, "Flying High, Going Global," *Fortune* (July 7, 1997), pp. 195–197.

38. See Gary P. Ferraro, "The Need for Linguistic Proficiency in Global Business," *Business Horizons* (May–June 1996), pp. 39–46; quote from Carol Hymowitz, "Companies Go Global, but Many Managers Just Don't Travel Well," *Wall Street Journal* (August 15, 2000), p. B1.

39. Edward T. Hall, *Beyond Culture* (New York: Doubleday, 1976).

40. Edward T. Hall, *The Silent Language* (New York: Anchor Books, 1959); *The Hidden Dimension* (New York: Anchor Books, 1969).

41. Hall, op. cit., (1959).

42. Lady Borton, "Learning to Work with Viet Nam," *The Academy of Management Executive*, vol. 14 (December 2000), pp. 20–31.

43. Edward T. Hall, *Hidden Differences* (New York: Doubleday, 1990).

44. Both examples from Hymowitz, op. cit.

45. Geert Hofstede, *Culture's Consequences* (Beverly Hills: Sage, 1984).

46. This dimension is explained more thoroughly by Geert Hofstede et al.,

Masculinity and Femininity: The Taboo Dimension of National Cultures (Thousand Oaks, CA.: Sage, 1998).

47. For an introduction to the fifth dimension, see Geert Hofstede and Michael H. Bond, "The Confucius Connection: From Cultural Roots to Economic Growth," *Organizational Dynamics*, vol. 16 (1988), pp. 4–21, which presents comparative data from Bond's "Chinese Values Survey."

48. With information from <www.geerthofstede.com/hofstede_canada.shtml>. (November 2006).

49. Michael Schuman, "How Interbrew Blended Disparate Ingredients in Korean Beer Venture," *Wall Street Journal* (July 24, 2000), pp. A1, A6.

50. Fons Trompenaars, *Riding the Waves of Culture: Understanding Cultural Diversity in Business* (London: Nicholas Brealey Publishing, 1993).

51. See Robert B. Reich, "Who Is Them?" *Harvard Business Review* (March–April 1991), pp. 77–88.

52. "Going International: Willett Systems Limited," *Fortune* (February 16, 1998), p. S6, special advertising section.

53. Mark Clifford and Majeet Kripalani, "Different Countries, Adjoining Cubicles," *Business Week* (August 28, 2000), pp. 182–184.

54. For a perspective on the role of women in expatriate managerial assignments, see Marianne Jelinek and Nancy J. Adler, "Women: World-Class Managers for Global Competition" *Academy of Management Executive* (February 1988), pp. 11–19.

55. Geert Hofstede, "Motivation, Leadership, and Organization," p. 43. See also Hofstede's "Cultural Constraints in Management Theories," *Academy of Management Review*, vol. 7 (1993), pp. 81–94.

56. The classics are William Ouchi, *Theory Z: How American Businesses Can Meet the Japanese Challenge* (Reading, MA: Addison-Wesley, 1981), and Richard Tanner Pascale and Anthony G. Athos, *The Art of Japanese Management: Applications for American Executives* (New York: Simon & Schuster, 1981). See also J. Bernard Keys, Luther Tray Denton, and Thomas R. Miller, "The Japanese Management Theory Jungle—Revisited," *Journal of Management*, vol. 20 (1994), pp. 373–402.

57. For a good discussion, see Chapters 4 and 5 in Miriam Erez and P. Christopher Earley, *Culture, Self-Identity, and Work* (New York: Oxford University Press, 1993).

58. For a good discussion of the historical context of Japanese management practices see Makoto Ohtsu, *Inside Japanese Business: A Narrative History 1960–2000* (Armonk, NY: M.E. Sharpe, 2002), pp. 39–41.

59. Quote from Kenichi Ohmae, "Japan's Admiration for U.S. Methods Is an Open Book," *Wall Street Journal* (October 10, 1983), p. 21. See also his book, *The Borderless World: Power and Strategy in the Interlinked Economy* (New York: Harper, 1989).

60. See, for example, Mzamo P. Mangaliso, "Building Competitive Advantage from ubuntu: Management lessons from South Africa," *Academy of Management Executive*, vol. 15 (2001), pp. 23–33.

61. Geert Hofstede, "A Reply to Goodstein and Hunt," *Organizational Dynamics*, vol. 10 (summer 1981), p. 68.

62. This discussion is based on Howard V. Perlmutter, "The Tortuous Evolution of the Multinational Corporation," *Columbia Journal of World Business*, vol. 4 (January–February, 1969).

63. Lewis, op. cit.

64. Information from Ohtsu, op. cit.

CHAPTER 6 NOTES

1. Sources for the opening vignette:

   SIFE website, <www.sife.org/canada>.

   ACE website, <www.acecanada.ca>.

TEXT NOTES

2. Information from <www.acecanada.ca>. (November 2006)

3. Speech at the Lloyd Greif Center for Entrepreneurial Studies, Marshall School of Business, University of Southern California, 1996.

4. Information from the corporate websites.

5. Information on Frank Stronach found on the Web, <www.empireclubfoundation.com>. (December 2006).

6. Information from <www.chapters.indigo.ca>. (November 2006).

7. Information from Stephen Kimber, "Bag-boy calls," *Globe and Mail* (September 26, 2003), pp. 66 and <www.sobeys.com>.

8. Information from <www.lakeportbrewing.ca> and Sasha Nagy, "Teresa Cascioli: Creativity was spawned from pure desperation," *Globe and Mail* on the Web, September 21, 2005, <www.theglobeandmail.com>. (November 2006).

9. Information from <www.timhortons.com>.

10. For a review and discussion of the entrepreneurial mind see Jeffry A. Timmons, *New Venture Creation: Entrepreneurship for the 21st Century* (New York: Irwin/McGraw-Hill, 1999), pp. 219–25.

11. See the review by Robert D. Hisrich and Michael P. Peters, *Entrepreneurship, 4th ed.* (New York: Irwin/McGraw-Hill, 1998), pp. 67–70; and Paulette Thomas, "Entrepreneurs' Biggest Problems and How They Solve Them," *Wall Street Journal Reports* (March 17, 2003), pp. R1, R2.

12. Based on research summarized by Hisrich and Peters, op. cit., pp. 70–74.

13. Information from Jim Hopkins, "Serial Entrepreneur Strikes Again at Age 70," *USA Today* (August 15, 2000).

14. Timothy Butler and James Waldroop, "Job Sculpting: The Art of Retaining Your Best People," *Harvard Business Review* (September–October 1999), pp. 144–52.

15. Hopkins, op. cit.

16. Information from Janet Whitman, "How Do You Handle Extraordinary Growth?" *Wall Street Journal Reports* (March 17, 2003), p. R3.

17. Information from the Standing Committee on the Status of Women, "Parental Benefits for Self-employed Women," on the Web, June 13, 2005, <www.wec.ca/taskforce.html>. (December 2006).

18. Hopkins, op. cit.

19. National Foundation for Women Business Owners, *Women Business Owners of Color: Challenges and Accomplishments* (1998).

20. Information from Industry Canada, Small Business Policy Branch, "Visible Minority Entrepreneurs," SME Financing Data Initiative, Small Business Financing Profiles, on the Web, March 2005, <www.strategis.ic.gc.ca>. (October 2006).

21. This list is developed from Timmons, op. cit, pp. 47–48; and Hisrich and Peters, op. cit., pp. 67–70.

22. Information from Industry Canada, "Key Small Business Statistics," Small Business Research and Policy, on the Web, January 2006, <www.strategis.ic.gs.ca>. (November 2006).

23. John Case, "The Rewards: Is it worth it to run your own business?" *Inc.*, State of Small Business Issue 2001 (May 15, 2001), pp. 50–51.

24. Julia Angwin, "Used-Car Auctioneers, Dealers Meet Online," *Wall Street Journal* (November 20, 2003), pp. B1, B13; and "Renaissance in Cyberspace," *Wall Street Journal* (November 20, 2003), p. B1.

25. Conversation from the case "Am I My Uncle's Keeper?" by Paul I. Karofsky (Northeastern University Center for Family Business); on the Web, <www.fambiz.com>. (December 2006).

26. Arthur Andersen, *Survey of Small and Mid-Sized Businesses: Trends for 2000* (2000).

27. Ibid.

28. George Gendron, "The Failure Myth," *Inc.* (January 2001), p. 13.

29. Based on Norman M. Scarborough and Thomas W. Zimmerer, *Effective Small Business Management* (Englewood Cliffs, NJ: Prentice-Hall, 2000), pp. 25–30; and Scott Clark, "Most Small-Business Failures Tied to Poor Management," *Business Journal* (April 10, 2000).

30. See, for example, John L. Nesheim, *High Tech Start Up* (New York: Free Press, 2000).

31. Discussion based on "The Life Cycle of Entrepreneurial Firms," in Ricky Griffin, ed., *Management, 6th ed.* (New York: Houghton Mifflin, 1999), pp. 309–10; and Neil C. Churchill and Virginia L. Lewis, "The Five Stages of Small Business Growth," *Harvard Business Review* (May–June 1993), pp. 30–50.

32. Developed from William S. Sahlman, "How to Write a Great Business Plan," *Harvard Business Review* (July–August 1997), pp. 98–108.

33. Standard components of business plans are described in many text sources such as Linda Pinson and Jerry Jinnett, *Anatomy of a Business Plan: A Step-by-Step Guide to Starting Smart, Building the Business, and Securing Your Company's Future, 4th ed.* (Dearbern Trade, 1999); Scarborough and Zimmerer, op. cit.; and on websites such as <www.americanexpress.com>, <www.businesstown.com>, and <www.bizplanit.com>.

34. "You've Come a Long Way Baby," *Business Week Frontier* (July 10, 2000).

35. Gifford Pinchot III, *Intrapreneuring, or Why You Don't Have to Leave the Corporation to Become an Entrepreneur* (New York: Harper & Row, 1985).

36. Information from John A. Byrne, "Management by Web," *Business Week* (August 28, 2000), pp. 84–97.

CHAPTER 7 NOTES

1. Sources for the opening vignette:

   Information from company website, <www.chaptersindigo.ca>.

   Ken Mark, "Indigo Books Starts a New Chapter," *Chain Store Age (*October 2005), p. 22A–23A.

   Rebecca Harris, "Indigo gets its wish...list," *Marketing*, vol. 110 (November 28, 2005), p. 4.

   Patricia MacInnis and Jennifer Brown, "Outsourcing: The Dating Game," *Computing Canada*, vol. 30 (April 9, 2004), pp. 12–18.

   Leah Eichler, "Cautiously, Respectfully Bullish," *Publishers Weekly* (April 29,

   2002).

   With information from <www.sap.com/industries/retail/pdf/ CS_IBM-Indigo.pdf>. (January 2007)

TEXT NOTES

2. See Alvin Toffler, *Powershift: Knowledge, Wealth, and Violence at the Edge of the 21st Century* (New York: Bantam Books, 1990).

3. "E-Meetings Redefine Productivity," *Fortune,* Special Advertising Section (February 5, 2001), p. S2.

4. Peter F. Drucker, "Looking Ahead: Implications of the Present," *Harvard Business Review* (September–October 1997), pp. 18–32. See also Shaker A. Zahra, "An Interview with Peter Drucker," *Academy of Management Executive*, vol. 17 (August 2003), pp. 9–12.

5. Thomas A. Stewart, *Intellectual Capital: The Wealth of Organizations* (New York: Doubleday, 1997).

6. Information from Robert W. Bly, "Does Your 'Second Generation' Site Get a Passing Grade?" (September 8, 2000).

7. See Susan G. Cohen and Don Mankin, "The Changing Nature of Work: Managing the Impact of Information Technology," Chapter 6 in Susan Albers Mohrman, Jay R. Galbraith, Edward E. Lawler III and Associates, *Tomorrow's Organization: Crafting Winning Capabilities in a Dynamic World* (San Francisco: Jossey-Bass, 1988), pp. 154–78.

8. See "Technology: The Best Way to Go," *Wall Street Journal Reports* (September 15, 2003).

9. Gerry Blackwell, "Telework," *IT Business Edge* on the Web, May 25, 2006, <www.itbusiness.ca>. (June 24, 2006).

10. Drucker, op. cit., "Looking Ahead" (1997), p. 22.

11. Information from John A. Byrne, "Visionary vs. Visionary," *Business Week* (August 28, 2000), pp. 210–14.

12. Jaclyn Fierman, "Winning Ideas from Maverick Managers," *Fortune* (February 6, 1995), pp. 66–80.

13. Information from Pui-Wing Tam, "Communication with Employees,"

Wall Street Journal (September 15, 2003), pp. R4, R10.

14. Ann Zimmerman, "To Sell Goods to Wal-Mart, Get on the Net," *Wall Street Journal* (November 21, 2003), pp. B1, B6.

15. Henry Mintzberg, *The Nature of Managerial Work* (New York: HarperCollins, 1997).

16. For scholarly reviews, see Dean Tjosvold, "Effects of Crisis Orientation on Managers' Approach to Controversy in Decision Making," *Academy of Management Journal*, vol. 27 (1984), pp. 130–38; and Ian I. Mitroff, Paul Shrivastava, and Firdaus E. Udwadia, "Effective Crisis Management," *Academy of Management Executive*, vol. 1 (1987), pp. 283–92.

17. Allan Britnell, "Crisis? What crisis?" *Profit*, vol. 22 (November 2003), pg. 77.

18. Developed from Anna Muoio, "Where There's Smoke It Helps to Have a Smoke Jumper," *Fast Company*, vol. 33, p. 290.

19. See David Greisling, *I'd Like to Buy the World a Coke: The Life and Leadership of Roberto Goizueta* (New York: Wiley, 1998).

20. See Hugh Courtney, Jane Kirkland, and Patrick Viguerie, "Strategy Under Uncertainty," *Harvard Business Review* (November–December 1997), pp. 67–79.

21. For a good discussion, see Watson H. Agor, *Intuition in Organizations: Leading and Managing Productively* (Newbury Park, CA: Sage, 1989); Herbert A. Simon, "Making Management Decisions: The Role of Intuition and Emotion," *Academy of Management Executive*, vol. 1 (1987), pp. 57–64; Orlando Behling and Norman L. Eckel, "Making Sense Out of Intuition," *Academy of Management Executive*, vol. 5 (1991), pp. 46–54.

22. Daniel J. Isenberg, "How Senior Managers Think," *Harvard Business Review*, vol. 62 (November–December 1984), pp. 81–90.

23. Daniel J. Isenberg, "The Tactics of Strategic Opportunism," *Harvard Business Review*, vol. 65 (March–April 1987), pp. 92–97.

24. See George P. Huber, *Managerial Decision Making* (Glenview, IL: Scott, Foresman 1975). For a comparison, see the steps in Xerox's problem-solving process as described in David A. Garvin, "Building a Learning Organization," *Harvard Business Review* (July–August 1993), pp. 78–91; and the Josephson model for ethical decision making, on the Web, <www.josephsoninstitute.org>.

25. Peter F. Drucker, *Innovation and Entrepreneurship: Practice and Principles* (New York: Harper & Row, 1985).

26. For a sample of Simon's work see Herbert A. Simon, *Administrative Behavior* (New York: Free Press, 1947); James G. March and Herbert A. Simon, *Organizations* (New York: Wiley, 1958); Herbert A. Simon, *The New Science of Management Decision* (New York: Harper, 1960).

27. Information from Carol Hymowitz, "Independent Program Puts College Students on Leadership Paths," *Wall Street Journal* (January 14, 2003), p. B1.

28. This presentation is based on the work of R. H. Hogarth, D. Kahneman, A. Tversky, and others, as discussed in Max H. Bazerman, *Judgment in Managerial Decision Making, 3rd ed.* (New York: Wiley, 1994).

29. Barry M. Staw, "The Escalation of Commitment to a Course of Action," *Academy of Management Review*, vol. 6 (1981), pp. 577–87; and Barry M. Staw and Jerry Ross, "Knowing When to Pull the Plug," *Harvard Business Review*, vol. 65 (March–April 1987), pp. 68–74.

30. The classic work is Norman R. Maier, "Assets and Liabilities in Group Problem Solving," *Psychological Review*, vol. 74 (1967), pp. 239–49.

31. I. Janis, *Groupthink: Psychological Studies of Policy Decisions and Fiascoes, 2nd ed.* (Boston: Houghton Mifflin, 1982).

32. Maier, op. cit.

33. Josephson, op. cit.

34. Based on Gerald F. Cavanagh, *American Business Values, 4th ed.* (Upper Saddle River, NJ: Prentice-Hall, 1998).

35. Peter F. Drucker, "The Future That Has Already Happened," *Harvard Business Review*, vol. 75 (September–October 1997), pp. 20–24; and Peter F. Drucker, Esther Dyson, Charles Handy, Paul Daffo, and Peter M. Senge, "Looking Ahead: Implications of the Present," *Harvard Business Review*, vol. 75 (September–October, 1997).

36. See, for example, Thomas H. Davenport and Laurence Prusak, *Working Knowledge: How Organizations Manage What They Know* (Cambridge, MA: Harvard Business School Press, 1997).

37. Peter Senge, *The Fifth Discipline* (New York: Harper, 1990).

38. Steven E. Prokesch, "Unleashing the Power of Learning," *Harvard Business Review* (September–October 1997), pp. 147–68.

CHAPTER 8 NOTES

1. Sources for the opening vignette:

Andrew Wahl, "A few modest proposals," *Canadian Business*, vol. 79 (December 26, 2005–January 15, 2006), p. 19.

"BSG aligns with Cognos to help drive Middle East channel," *Al Bawaba* (November 20, 2005), p. 1.

"Cognos ranked as a leader in performance management solutions," *Al Bawaba* (December 22, 2005), p. 1.

"Cognos unveils new blueprints for initiative and strategic long range planning," *Al Bawaba* (October 19, 2005), p. 1.

"Lufthansa Selects Cognos 8 Business Intelligence," news release on the Web, January 24, 2006 <www.cognos.com>. (December 2006).

TEXT NOTES

2. Gary Hamel, *Leading the Revolution* (Boston: Harvard Business School Press, 2000).

3. Quote from "Today's Companies Won't Make It, and Gary Hamel Knows Why," *Fortune* (September 4, 2000), pp. 386–87.

4. T. J. Rodgers, William Taylor, and Rick Foreman, "No Excuses Management," *World Executive's Digest* (May 1994) pp. 26–30.

5. Eaton Corporation Annual Report (1985).

6. Henry Mintzberg, "The Manager's Job: Folklore and Fact," *Harvard Business Review*, vol. 53 (July–August 1975), pp. 54–67; and Henry Mintzberg, "Planning on the Left Side and Managing on the Right," *Harvard Business Review*, vol. 54 (July–August 1976), pp. 46–55.

7. Carolyn Ryan, "The hunt for the no-telephone poll," Canada Votes, CBC on the Web, January 23, 2006, <www.cbc.ca>. (December 2006). With information from the corporate website <www.decima.com>.

8. Quote from Stephen Covey and Roger Merrill, "New Ways to Get Organized at Work," *USA Weekend* (February 6–8, 1998), p. 18. Books by Stephen R. Covey include *The 7 Habits of Highly Effective People: Powerful Lessons in Personal Change* (New York: Fireside, 1990); and Stephen R. Covey and Sandra Merril Covey, *The 7 Habits of Highly Effective Families: Building a Beautiful Family Culture in a Turbulent World* (New York: Golden Books, 1996).

9. Quotes from *Business Week* (August 8, 1994), pp. 78–86.

10. See William Oncken, Jr., and Donald L. Wass, "Management Time: Who's Got the Monkey?" *Harvard Business Review*, vol. 52 (September–October 1974), pp. 75–80; and featured as an HBR classic, *Harvard Business Review* (November–December 1999).

11. Amitai Etzioni, "Mixed Scanning: A 'Third' Approach to Decision-making," (1967) in Andreas Faludi, *A Reader in Planning Theory* (Pergamon Press, 1973), pp. 219–20.

12. Based on information from David Macleod, "Planning and Environmental Information," on the Web, <www3.sympatico.ca/david.macleod/PTHRY.HTM>. (December 2006).

13. Survey results from "Hurry Up and Decide," *Business Week* (May 14, 2001), p. 16.

14. See Elliot Jaques, *The Form of Time* (New York: Russak & Co., 1982). For an executive commentary on his research, see Walter Kiechel III, "How

Executives Think," *Fortune* (December 21, 1987), pp. 139–44.

15. See Henry Mintzberg, "Rounding Out the Manager's Job," *Sloan Management Review* (fall 1994), pp. 1–25.

16. Information from "Avoiding a Time Bomb: Sexual Harassment," *Business Week*, Enterprise issue (October 13, 1997), pp. ENT20–21.

17. For a thorough review of forecasting, see J. Scott Armstrong, *Long-Range Forecasting, 2nd ed.* (New York: Wiley, 1985).

18. The scenario-planning approach is described in Peter Schwartz, *The Art of the Long View* (New York: Doubleday/Currency, 1991); and Arie de Geus, *The Living Company: Habits for Survival in a Turbulent Business Environment* (Boston, MA: Harvard Business School Press, 1997).

19. Greg Williams, Joy Mabon, and Bev Heim-Myers, "Best Practice: Strategic planning in a complex environment: The health-care example," *Ivey Business Journal* on the Web, January–February 2006, < www.ivey-businessjournal.com>. (December 2006).

20. See, for example, Robert C. Camp, *Business Process Benchmarking* (Milwaukee: ASQ Quality Press 1994); Michael J. Spendolini, *The Benchmarking Book* (New York: AMA-COM, 1992); and Christopher E. Bogan and Michael J. English, *Benchmarking for Best Practices: Winning Through Innovative Adaptation* (New York: McGraw-Hill, 1994).

21. "How Classy Can 7-Eleven Get?" *Business Week* (September 1, 1997), pp. 74–75; and Kellie B. Gormly, "7-Eleven Moving Up a Grade," *Columbus Dispatch* (August 3, 2000), pp. C1–C2.

22. "The Renewal Factor: Friendly Fact, Congenial Controls," *Business Week* (September 14, 1987), p. 105.

23. Rob Cross and Lloyd Baird, "Technology Is Not Enough: Improving Performance by Building Institutional Memory," *Sloan Management Review* (spring 2000), p. 73.

24. "Forging the link between diversity and business strategy," BMO Financial Group website <www2.bmo.com>. (August 2006).

25. Information from Raju Narisetti, "For IBM, a Groundbreaking Sales Chief," *Wall Street Journal* (January 19, 1998), pp. B1, B5.

26. Based on discussion by Harold Koontz and Cyril O'Donnell in *Essentials of Management* (New York: McGraw-Hill, 1974), pp. 362–65; see also Cross and Baird, op. cit.

27. Information from Louis Lee, "I'm Proud of What I've Made Myself Into—What I've Created," *Wall Street Journal* (August 27, 1997), pp. B1, B5; and Jim Collins, "Bigger, Better, Faster," *Fast Company*, vol. 71 (June 2003), p. 74; on the Web, June 2003, <www.fastcompany.com>. (December 2006).

28. See John F. Love, *McDonald's: Behind the Arches* (New York: Bantam Books, 1986); and Ray Kroc and Robert Anderson, *Grinding It Out: The Making of McDonald's* (New York: St. Martin's Press, 1990).

29. See Dale D. McConkey, *How to Manage by Results, 3rd ed.* (New York: AMACOM, 1976); Stephen J. Carroll, Jr., and Henry J. Tosi, Jr., *Management by Objectives: Applications and Research* (New York: Macmillan, 1973); and Anthony P. Raia, *Managing by Objectives* (Glenview, IL: Scott, Foresman, 1974).

30. For a discussion of research, see Carroll and Tosi, op. cit.; Raia, op. cit., and Steven Kerr, "Overcoming the Dysfunctions of MBO," *Management by Objectives*, vol. 5 (1976). Information in part from Dylan Loeb McClain, "Job Forecast: Internet's Still Hot," *New York Times* (January 30, 2001), p. 9.

31. McGregor, op. cit.

32. The work on goal setting and motivation is summarized in Edwin A. Locke and Gary P. Latham, *Goal Setting: A Motivational Technique That Works!* (Englewood Cliffs, NJ: Prentice-Hall, 1984).

33. The "hot stove rules" are developed from R. Bruce McAfee and William Poffenberger, *Productivity Strategies:*

Enhancing Employee Job Performance (Englewood Cliffs, NJ: Prentice-Hall, 1982), pp. 54–55. They are originally attributed to Douglas McGregor, "Hot Stove Rules of Discipline," in G. Strauss and L. Sayles, eds., *Personnel: The Human Problems of Management* (Englewood Cliffs, NJ: Prentice-Hall, 1967).

34. Karl E. Weick and Kathleen M. Sutcliffe, *Managing the Unexpected: Assuring High Performance in an Age of Complexity* (San Francisco, CA: Jossey-Bass, 2001).

CHAPTER 9 NOTES

1. Sources for the opening vignette:

   Corporate website <www.taxi.ca>.

   Laura Bogomolny, "The Contenders," *Canadian Business*, vol. 77 (August 16–29, 2004), p. 55.

   Rae Ann Fera, "Splitting a Cab: Taxi Continues Canadian Dominance, Makes Splash in New York," *Boards* (January 2006), p. 32.

   Danny Kucharsky, "The long drive home," *Marketing* (November 22, 2004), p. 28.

   Paul-Mark Rendon, "New York story," *Marketing* (September 27, 2004), p. 7.

   Marcus Robinson, "Creative control: Zak Mroueh puts Taxi in the driver's seat," *Boards* (September 2005), p. 30.

   Natalia Williams, "Gold-Taxi Shocking Upset!" *Strategy* (December 2005), p. 39.

TEXT NOTES

2. Jim Collins, "Bigger, Better, Faster," *Fast Company*, vol. 71 (June 2003), p. 74; on the Web, <www.fastcompany.com>. (December 2006).

3. Keith H. Hammond, "Michael Porter's Big Ideas," *Fast Company* (March 2001), pp. 150–56; on the Web, <www.fastcompany.com>. (December 2006).

4. Jeff Sanford, "Want a piece of this?" *Canadian Business*, vol. 79 (February 13–26, 2006), p. 83.

5. Tara Perkins, "Investors to bet on Tim Hortons' growth prospects," Canadian Press (March 20, 2006); on the Web, <www.canada.com/topics/finance/story.html>. (December 2006).

6. Gary Hamel and C. K. Prahalad, "Strategic Intent," *Harvard Business Review* (May–June 1989), pp. 63–76.

7. Information and quotes from Marcia Stepanek, "How Fast Is Net Fast?" *Business Week E-Biz* (November 1, 1999), pp. EB52–EB54.

8. For research support, see Daniel H. Gray, "Uses and Misuses of Strategic Planning," *Harvard Business Review*, vol. 64 (January–February 1986), pp. 89–97.

9. Hammond, op. cit., p. 153.

10. Michael A. Hitt, R. Duane Ireland, and Robert E. Hoskisson, *Strategic Management: Competitiveness and Globalization* (Minneapolis: West, 1997), p. 5.

11. See Michael E. Porter, *Competitive Strategy: Techniques for Analyzing Industries and Competitors* (New York: Free Press, 1980), and *Competitive Advantage: Creating and Sustaining Superior Performance* (New York: Free Press, 1986); and Richard A. D'Aveni, *Hyper-Competition: Managing the Dynamics of Strategic Maneuvering* (New York: Free Press, 1994).

12. D'Aveni, op. cit.

13. Example from "Memorable Memo: McDonald's Sends Operators to War on Fries," *Wall Street Journal* (December 18, 1997), p. B1.

14. Peter F. Drucker, "Five Questions," *Executive Excellence* (November 6, 1994), pp. 6–7.

15. Peter F. Drucker, *Management: Tasks, Responsibilities, Practices* (New York: Harper & Row, 1973), p. 122.

16. Ibid.

17. See Laura Nash, "Mission Statements—Mirrors and Windows," *Harvard Business Review* (March–April 1988), pp. 155–6; James C. Collins and Jerry I. Porras, "Building Your Company's Vision," *Harvard Business Review* (September–October 1996), pp. 65–77; and James C. Collins and Jerry I. Porras, *Built to Last: Successful Habits of Visionary Companies* (New York: Harper Business, 1997).

18. Gary Hamel, *Leading the Revolution* (Boston, MA: Harvard Business School Press, 2000), pp. 72–73.

19. For a discussion of non-profit organization mission statements, see Peter F. Drucker, "Self-Assessment: The First Action Requirement of Leadership," Drucker Foundation Self-Assessment Tool, on the Web, <www.leader-toleader.org>. (December 2006).

20. Retrieved from <www.norpaccontrols.com/tcc>. (August 2006).

21. Terrence E. Deal and Allen A. Kennedy, *Corporate Cultures: The Rites and Rituals of Corporate Life* (Reading, MA: Addison-Wesley, 1982), p. 22. For more on organizational culture see Edgar H. Schein, *Organizational Culture and Leadership*, 2nd ed. (San Francisco: Jossey-Bass, 1997).

22. Peter F. Drucker's views on organizational objectives are expressed in his classic books *The Practice of Management* (New York: Harper & Row, 1954), and *Management: Tasks, Responsibilities, Practices* (New York: Harper & Row, 1973). For a more recent commentary, see his article, "Management: The Problems of Success," *Academy of Management Executive*, vol. 1 (1987), pp. 13–19.

23. C. K. Prahalad and Gary Hamel, "The Core Competencies of the Corporation," *Harvard Business Review* (May–June 1990), pp. 79–91; see also Hitt, et al., op. cit., pp. 99–103.

24. For a discussion of Michael Porter's approach to strategic planning, see his books *Competitive Strategy* and *Competitive Advantage*; his article, "What Is Strategy? *Harvard Business Review* (November–December, 1996), pp. 61–78; and Richard M. Hodgetts' interview, "A Conversation with Michael E. Porter: A Significant Extension Toward Operational Improvement and Positioning," *Organizational Dynamics* (summer 1999), pp. 24–33.

25. Based on information from a press release of February 3, 2006, on the Web, <www.ccithermal.com>. (December 2006).

26. David Finlayson, "Management kudos for CCI," *Edmonton Journal* (March 21, 2006); and on the Web, <www.ccithermal.com>. (December 2006).

27. The four grand strategies were original-

ly described by William F. Glueck, *Business Policy: Strategy Formulation and Management Action, 2nd ed.* (New York: McGraw-Hill, 1976).

28. Hitt et al., op. cit., p. 197.

29. See William McKinley, Carol M. Sanchez, and A. G. Schick, "Organizational Downsizing: Constraining, Cloning, Learning," *Academy of Management Executive,* vol. 9 (August 1995), pp. 32–44.

30. Kim S. Cameron, Sara J. Freeman, and A. K. Mishra, "Best Practices in White-Collar Downsizing: Managing Contradictions," *Academy of Management Executive,* vol. 4 (August 1991), pp. 57–73.

31. This strategy classification is found in Hitt, et al., op. cit.; the attitudes are from a discussion by Howard V. Perlmutter, "The Tortuous Evolution of the Multinational Corporation," *Columbia Journal of World Business,* vol. 4 (January–February 1969).

32. See Michael E. Porter, "Strategy and the Internet," *Harvard Business Review* (March 2001), pp. 63–78.

33. Information from Michael Rappa, Business Models on the Web, <www.digitalenterprise.org>. (December 2006).

34. Hammond, op. cit.

35. D'Aveni, op. cit.

36. D'Aveni, op. cit.

37. Porter, op cit. (1980), (1986), (1996).

38. Information from <www.polo.com>.

39. David Knibb, "Service Formula," *Airline Business,* vol. 21 (December 2005), p. 68.

40. Richard G. Hammermesh, "Making Planning Strategic," *Harvard Business Review,* vol. 64 (July–August 1986), pp. 115–120; and Richard G. Hammermesh, *Making Strategy Work* (New York: Wiley, 1986).

41. See Gerald B. Allan, "A Note on the Boston Consulting Group Concept of Competitive Analysis and Corporate Strategy," Harvard Business School, Intercollegiate Case Clearing House, ICCH9-175-175 (Boston: Harvard Business School, June 1976).

42. The adaptive model is described in Raymond E. Miles and Charles C. Snow's book, *Organizational Strategy, Structure, and Process* (New York: McGraw-Hill, 1978); and their articles, "Designing Strategic Human Resources Systems," *Organizational Dynamics,* vol. 13 (summer 1984), pp. 36–52; and "Fit, Failure, and the Hall of Fame," *California Management Review,* vol. 26 (spring 1984), pp. 10–28.

43. James Brian Quinn, "Strategic Change: Logical Incrementalism," *Sloan Management Review,* vol. 20 (fall 1978), pp. 7–21.

44. Henry Mintzberg, *The Nature of Managerial Work* (New York: Harper & Row, 1973); and John R. P. Kotter, *The General Managers* (New York: Free Press, 1982).

45. Henry Mintzberg, "Planning on the Left Side and Managing on the Right," *Business Review,* vol. 54 (July–August 1976), pp. 46–55; Henry Mintzberg and James A. Waters, "Of Strategies, Deliberate and Emergent," *Strategic Management Journal,* vol. 6 (1985), pp. 257–72; Henry Mintzberg, "Crafting Strategy," *Harvard Business Review,* vol. 65 (July–August 1987), pp. 66–75.

46. For research support, see Daniel H. Gray, "Uses and Misuses of Strategic Planning," *Harvard Business Review,* vol. 64 (January–February 1986), pp. 89–97.

47. For a discussion of corporate governance issues, see Hugh Sherman and Rajeswararao Chaganti, *Corporate Governance and the Timeliness of Change* (Westport, CT: Quorum Books, 1998).

48. See Carol Hyowitz, "GE Chief Is Charting His Own Strategy, Focusing on Technology," *Wall Street Journal* (September 23, 2003), p. B1.

49. See R. Duane Ireland and Michael A. Hitt, "Achieving and Maintaining Strategic Competitiveness in the 21st Century," *Academy of Management Executive,* vol. 13 (1999), pp. 43–57.

50. Hammond, op. cit.

51. Michael Dell quotes from Matt Murray, "As Huge Companies Keep Growing, CEOs Struggle to Keep Pace," *Wall Street Journal* (February 8, 2001), pp. A1, A6.

52. Jon R. Katzenbach, "The Myth of the Top Management Team," *Harvard Business Review* (November–December 1997), pp. 82–91.

CHAPTER 10 NOTES

1. Sources for the opening vignette:

From "Information and Statistics Fact Sheet" and "Edward Jones Again Named One of the '50 Best Employers in Canada'," on the Web, <www.edwardjones.com>. (November 2006).

TEXT NOTES

2. Henry Mintzberg and Ludo Van der Heyden, "Organigraphs: Drawing How Companies Really Work," *Harvard Business Review* (September–October 1999), pp. 87–94.

3. See, for example, Charles O'Reilly III and Jeffrey Pfeffer, *Hidden Value: How Great Companies Achieve Extraordinary Results with Ordinary People* (Boston: Harvard Business School Press, 2000); Jeffrey Pfeffer and John F. Veiga, "Putting People First for Organizational Success," *Academy of Management Executive,* vol. 13 (May 1999), pp. 37–48; Jeffrey Pfeffer, *The Human Equation: Building Profits by Putting People First* (Boston: Harvard Business School Press, 1998); Jeffrey Pfeffer, "When It Comes to 'Best Practices'— Why Do Smart Organizations Occasionally Do Dumb Things?" *Organizational Dynamics,* vol. 25 (summer 1996), pp. 33–44; and Michael Beer, "How to Develop an Organization Capable of Sustained High Performance: Embrace the Drive for Results—Capability Development Paradox," *Organizational Dynamics,* vol. 29 (spring 2001), pp. 233–247.

4. The classic work is Alfred D. Chandler's *Strategy and Structure* (Cambridge, MA: MIT Press, 1962).

5. See Alfred D. Chandler, Jr., "Origins of the Organization Chart," *Harvard Business Review* (March–April 1988), pp. 156–57.

6. See David Krackhardt and Jeffrey R. Hanson, "Informal Networks: The

Company Behind the Chart," *Harvard Business Review* (July–August 1993), pp. 104–11.

7. With information from George A. Neufeld, Peter A. Simeoni, and Marilyn A. Taylor, "High-performance research organization," *Research Technology Management*, vol. 44 (November–December 2001), pp. 42–53.

8. See Kenneth Noble, "A Clash of Styles: Japanese Companies in the U.S." *New York Times* (January 25, 1988), p. 7.

9. For a discussion of departmentalization, see H. I. Ansoff and R. G. Bradenburg, "A Language for Organization Design," *Management Science*, vol. 17 (August 1971), pp. B705–B731; Mariann Jelinek, "Organization Structure: The Basic Conformations," in Mariann Jelinek, Joseph A. Litterer, and Raymond E. Miles, eds., *Organizations by Design: Theory and Practice* (Plano, TX: Business Publications, 1981), pp. 293–302; Henry Mintzberg, "The Structuring of Organizations," in James Brian Quinn, Henry Mintzberg, and Robert M. James, eds., *The Strategy Process: Concepts, Contexts, and Cases* (Englewood Cliffs, NJ: Prentice-Hall, 1988), pp. 276–304.

10. Robert L. Simison, "Jaguar Slowly Sheds Outmoded Habits," *Wall Street Journal* (July 26, 1991), p. A6; and Richard Stevenson, "Ford Helps Jaguar Get Back Old Sheen," *International Herald Tribune* (December 14, 1994), p. 11.

11. These alternatives are well described by Mintzberg, op. cit.

12. The focus on process is described in Michael Hammer, *Beyond Reengineering* (New York: Harper Business, 1996).

13. Ibid.

14. Excellent reviews of matrix concepts are found in Stanley M. Davis and Paul R. Lawrence, *Matrix* (Reading, MA: Addison-Wesley, 1977); Paul R. Lawrence, Harvey F. Kolodny, and Stanley M. Davis, "The Human Side of the Matrix," *Organizational Dynamics*, vol. 6 (1977), pp. 43–61; and Harvey F. Kolodny, "Evolution to a Matrix Organization," *Academy of Management Review*, vol. 4 (1979), pp. 543–53.

15. Davis and Lawrence, op. cit.

16. Developed from Frank Ostroff, *The Horizontal Organization: What the Organization of the Future Looks Like and How It Delivers Value to Customers* (New York: Oxford University Press, 1999).

17. The nature of teams and teamwork is described in Jon R. Katzenbach and Douglas K. Smith, "The Discipline of Teams," *Harvard Business Review* (March–April 1993), pp. 111–20.

18. Susan Albers Mohrman, Susan G. Cohen, and Allan M. Mohrman, Jr., *Designing Team-Based Organizations* (San Francisco: Jossey-Bass, 1996).

19. See Glenn M. Parker, *Cross-Functional Teams* (San Francisco: Jossey-Bass, 1995).

20. Information from William Bridges, "The End of the Job," *Fortune* (September 19, 1994), pp. 62–74; Alan Deutschman, "The Managing Wisdom of High-Tech Superstars," *Fortune* (October 17, 1994), pp. 197–206.

21. See the discussion by Jay R. Galbraith, "Designing the Networked Organization: Leveraging Size and Competencies," in Susan Albers Mohrman, Jay R. Galbraith, Edward E. Lawler III and Associates, *Tomorrow's Organizations: Crafting Winning Strategies in a Dynamic World* (San Francisco: Jossey-Bass, 1998), pp. 76–102. See also Rupert F. Chisholm, *Developing Network Organizations: Learning from Practice and Theory* (Reading, MA: Addison-Wesley, 1998).

22. With information from Yvon Bigras, "Transforming SMEs," *CMA Management*, vol. 76 (September 2002), pp. 31–33.

23. See Jerome Barthelemy, "The Seven Deadly Sins of Outsourcing," *Academy of Management Executive*, vol. 17 (2003), pp. 87–98.

24. See Ron Ashkenas, Dave Ulrich, Todd Jick, and Steve Kerr, *The Boundaryless Organization: Breaking the Chains of Organizational Structure* (San Francisco: Jossey-Bass, 1996).

25. Robert Slater, *Jack Welch and the GE Way: Management Insights and Leadership Secrets from the Legendary CEO* (New York: 1998); and "Jack the Job-Killer Strikes Again," *Business Week* (February 12, 2001), p. 12.

26. Information from John A. Byrne, "Management by Web," *Business Week* (August 28, 2000), pp. 84–97.

27. See the collection of articles by Cary L. Cooper and Denise M. Rousseau, eds., *The Virtual Organization: Vol. 6, Trends in Organizational Behavior* (New York: Wiley, 2000).

28. See Korky Koroluk, "Canadian institute gains attention on world stage," *Daily Commercial News and Construction Record*, vol. 77 (September 17, 2004), p. GB1.

29. David Van Fleet, "Span of Management Research and Issues," *Academy of Management Journal*, vol. 26 (1983), pp. 546–52.

30. Developed from Roger Fritz, *Rate Your Executive Potential* (New York: Wiley, 1988), pp. 185–86; Roy J. Lewicki, Donald D. Bowen, Douglas T. Hall, and Francine S. Hall, *Experiences in Management and Organizational Behavior, 3rd ed.* (New York: Wiley, 1988), p. 144.

31. David North, "Is your head office a useless frill?", *Canadian Business*, vol. 70 (November 14, 1997), pp. 78–80.

32. See George P. Huber, "A Theory of Effects of Advanced Information Technologies on Organizational Design, Intelligence, and Decision Making," *Academy of Management Review*, vol. 15 (1990), pp. 67–71.

CHAPTER 11 NOTES

1. Sources for the opening vignette:

   Information from the company website, <www.kpmg.com> and <www.kpmg.ca >. (November 2006).

TEXT NOTES

2. Described by Andrew Ross Sorkin, "Gospel According to St. Luke's," *New York Times* (February 12, 1998), pp. C1, C7; see also the corporate website, <www.stlukes.co.uk>.

3. Information and quotes from corporate website and Judith Rehak, "A Swiss Giant Awakens with a Start," *International Herald Tribune* (May 3–4, 2003), pp. 13–14.

4. For a discussion of organization theory, see W. Richard Scott, *Organizations: Rational, Natural, and Open Systems, 4th ed.* (Upper Saddle River, NJ: Prentice-Hall, 1998).

5. Information taken from the corporate website, <www.dbgcanada.com>. (November 2006).

6. For a classic work see Jay R. Galbraith, *Organizational Design* (Reading, MA: Addison-Wesley, 1977).

7. This framework is based on Harold J. Leavitt, "Applied Organizational Change in Industry," in James G. March, *Handbook of Organizations* (New York: Rand-McNally, 1965), pp. 144–70; and Edward E. Lawler III, *From the Ground Up: Six Principles for the New Logic Corporation* (San Francisco: Jossey-Bass Publishers, 1996), pp. 44–50.

8. See the discussion in Gaerth Jones, *Organizaional Theory and Design, 3rd ed.* (Upper Saddle River, NJ: Prentice-Hall, 2001).

9. See the discussion in James L. Gibson, John M. Ivancevich, and James H. Donnelly, Jr., *Organizations: Behavior, Structure, Processes, 5th ed.* (Homewood, IL: Richard D. Irwin, 1991).

10. Peter Diekmeyer, "Hotelier Taps Demand for Quantity, Service," *National Post* (February 3, 2006).

11. Max Weber, *The Theory of Social and Economic Organization,* A. M. Henderson, trans., and H. T. Parsons (New York: Free Press, 1947).

12. For classic treatments of bureaucracy, see Alvin Gouldner, *Patterns of Industrial Bureaucracy* (New York: Free Press, 1954); and Robert K. Merton, *Social Theory and Social Structure* (New York: Free Press, 1957).

13. Tom Burns and George M. Stalker, *The Management of Innovation* (London: Tavistock, 1961; republished by Oxford University Press, London, 1994).

14. See Henry Mintzberg, *Structure in Fives: Designing Effective Organizations* (Englewood Cliffs, NJ: Prentice-Hall, 1983).

15. Information from Thomas Petzinger, Jr., "Self-Organization Will Free Employees to Act Like Bosses," *Wall Street Journal* (January 3, 1997), p. B1.

16. See Rosabeth Moss Kanter, *The Changing Masters* (New York: Simon & Schuster, 1983). Quotation from Rosabeth Moss Kanter and John D. Buck, "Reorganizing Part of Honeywell: From Strategy to Structure," *Organizational Dynamics*, vol. 13 (winter 1985), p. 6.

17. See for example, Jay R. Galbraith, Edward E. Lawler III and Associates, *Organizing for the Future* (San Francisco: Jossey-Bass Publishers, 1993); and Susan Albers Mohrman, Jay R. Galbraith, Edward E. Lawler III and Associates, *Tomorrow's Organizations: Crafting Winning Strategies in a Dynamic World* (San Francisco: Jossey-Bass, 1998).

18. Peter Senge, *The Fifth Discipline: The Art and Practice of the Learning Organization* (New York: Doubleday, 1994).

19. A classic treatment of environment and organizational design is found in James D. Thompson, *Organizations in Action* (New York: McGraw-Hill, 1967). See also Scott, op. cit., pp. 264–69.

20. Information and media release found on the corporate website, <www.hayes.bc.ca>.

21. Alfred D. Chandler, Jr., *Strategy and Structure: Chapter in the History of American Industrial Enterprise* (Cambridge, MA: MIT Press, 1962).

22. See, for example, Danny Miller, "Configurations of Strategy and Structure: Towards a Synthesis," *Strategic Management Journal*, vol. 7 (1986), pp. 233–49.

23. Information taken from the corporate website, <www.skywavemobile.com>. (November 2006).

24. Joan Woodward, *Industrial Organization: Theory and Practice* (London: Oxford University Press, 1965; republished by Oxford University Press, 1994).

25. This classification is from Thompson, op. cit.

26. See Peter M. Blau and Richard A. Schoennerr, *The Structure of Organizations* (New York: Basic Books, 1971); and Scott, op. cit., pp. 259–63.

27. D. E. Gumpert, "The Joys of Keeping the Company Small," *Harvard Business Review* (July–August 1986), pp. 6–8, 12–14.

28. L. Greiner, "Evolution and Revolution as Organizations Grow," *Harvard Business Review*, vol. 50 (1972), pp. 37–46.

29. John R. Kimberly and Robert H. Miles, *The Organizational Life Cycle* (San Francisco: Jossey-Bass, 1980).

30. Kim Cameron, Sarah J. Freeman, and Naneil K. Mishra, "Best Practices in White-Collar Downsizing: Managing Contradictions," *Academy of Management Executive*, vol. 5 (August 1991), pp. 57–73.

31. See Gifford Pinchot III, *Intrapreneuring: Or Why You Don't Have to Leave the Corporation to Become an Entrepreneur* (New York: Harper & Row, 1985).

32. See Jay Lorsch and John Morse, *Organizations and Their Members: A Contingency Approach* (New York: Harper & Row, 1974); and Scott, op. cit., pp. 263–64.

33. "The Rebirth of IBM," *Economist* (June 6, 1998), pp. 65–68.

34. Paul R. Lawrence and Jay W. Lorsch, *Organizations and Environment* (Boston: Division of Research, Graduate School of Business Administration, Harvard University, 1967).

35. Burns and Stalker, op. cit.

36. See Jay R. Galbraith, op. cit., and Susan Albers Mohrman, "Integrating Roles and Structure in the Lateral Organization," Chapter 5 in Jay R. Galbraith, Edward E. Lawler III and Associates, *Organizing for the Future* (San Francisco: Jossey-Bass Publishers, 1993).

37. For a good discussion of coordination and integration approaches, see Scott, op. cit., pp. 231–39.

38. Michael Hammer and James Champy, *Reengineering the Corporation: A Manifesto for Business Revolution, rev. ed.* (New York: Harper Business, 1999).

39. Michael Hammer, *Beyond Reengineering* (New York: Harper Business, 1997).

40. Ibid., p. 5; see also the discussion of processes in Gary Hamel, *Leading the Revolution* (Boston, MA: Harvard Business School Press, 2000).

41. Thomas M. Koulopoulos, *The Workflow Imperative* (New York: Van Nostrand Reinhold, 1995); Hammer, *Beyond Reengineering,* op. cit. (1997).

42. Paul Roberts, "Humane Technology—PeopleSoft," *Fast Company*, vol. 14 (1998), p. 122.

43. Ronni T. Marshak, "Workflow Business Process Reengineering," special advertising section, *Fortune* (1997).

44. A similar example is found in Hammer, op. cit. (1997), pp. 9–10.

45. Ibid., pp. 28–30.

46. Ibid., p. 29.

47. Ibid., p. 27.

48. Quote from Hammer and Company website, <www.hammerandco.com>.

CHAPTER 12 NOTES

1. Sources for the opening vignette:

   Anonymous, "Employee Wellness," *Canadian HR Reporter*, vol. 17 (February 23, 2004), pp. 9ff.

   David Brown, "Success Starts at the Middle," *Canadian HR Reporter*, vol. 16 (June 2, 2003), pp.1ff.

   Cheryl Dahle, "A Steelmaker's Heart of Gold," *Fast Company* (June 2003), pp. 46ff.

   S. Mingail, "Tackling Workplace Literacy a No-Brainer," *Canadian HR Reporter*, vol. 17 (November 22, 2004), pp. G3, G11.

   Raizel Robin, "Taking Care of Business: Dofasco is now a national leader in workplace health," *Canadian Business*, vol. 76 (November 24–December 7, 2003).

   Marilyn Scales, "Canada's Top 40," *Canadian Mining Journal*, vol. 124 (September 2003).

   Cindy Waxer, "Steelmaker Revives Apprentice Program to Address Graying Workforce, Forge Next Leaders," *Workforce Management*, vol. 85, pp. 40ff.

TEXT NOTES

2. Robert B. Reich, *The Future of Success* (New York: Knopf, 2000).

3. Robert B. Reich, "The Company of the Future," *Fast Company* (November 1998), pp. 124ff.

4. See Jeffrey Pfeffer, *The Human Equation: Building Profits by Putting People First* (Boston: Harvard University Press, 1998).

5. See, for example, Charles Handy, *The Age of Unreason* (Cambridge, MA: Harvard Business School Press, 1990); and Tom Peters, "The Brand Called You," *Fast Company* (August 1997), pp. 83ff.

6. Pfeffer, op. cit., p. 292.

7. Jeffrey Pfeffer and John F. Veiga, "Putting People First for Organizational Success," *Academy of Management Executive*, vol. 13 (May 1999), pp. 37–48.

8. Ibid; and Pfeffer, op. cit.

9. James N. Baron and David M. Kreps, *Strategic Human Resources: Frameworks for General Managers* (New York: Wiley, 1999).

10. R. Roosevelt Thomas, Jr., *Beyond Race and Gender* (New York: AMACOM, 1992).

11. Lawrence Otis Graham, *Proversity: Getting Past Face Value and Finding the Soul of People* (New York: Wiley, 1997).

12. See also R. Roosevelt Thomas Jr.'s books, op. cit.; and (with Marjorie I. Woodruff) *Building a House for Diversity* (New York: AMACOM, 1999); and Richard D. Bucher, *Diversity Consciousness* (Englewood Cliffs, NJ: Prentice-Hall, 2000).

13. "IBM Canada and Pelmorex Incorporated honoured at the Employment Equity Merit Awards," on the Web, October 9, 2003, <www.hrsdc.gc.ca>. (December 2006).

14. Thomas, op. cit., p. 4.

15. Quote from William Bridges, "The End of the Job," *Fortune* (September 19, 1994), p. 68.

16. Message from the president, found on the Canadian Council of Human Resources Associations website, <www.cchra-ccarh.ca>. (December 2006).

17. See Baron and Kreps, op. cit.

18. Quotes from Kris Maher, "Human-Resources Directors Are Assuming Strategic Roles," *Wall Street Journal* (June 17, 2003), p. B8.

19. Ibid.

20. Human Rights Program Part IV: Measures Adopted by the Governments of the Provinces: British Columbia, on the Web, <www.pch.gc.ca/progs>. (November 2006).

21. Taken from the Employment Equity Act, on the Web, <http://laws.justice.gc.ca>. (November 2006).

22. See the discussion by David A. DeCenzo and Stephen P. Robbins, *Human Resource Management, 6th ed.* (New York: Wiley, 1999), pp. 66–68, 81–83.

23. Ibid., pp. 77–79.

24. Information from "There Are Questions You Shouldn't Answer," *New York Times* (January 30, 2001), p. 2.

25. See discussion by DeCenzo and Robbins, op. cit., pp. 79–90.

26. Canadian Human Rights Commission, "Anti-Harassment Policies for the Workplace: An Employer's Guide," on the Web, March 2006, <www.chrc-ccdp.ca>. (November 2006).

27. Information on pay equity found on the Web, <www.workrights.ca>. (November 2006).

28. See Frederick S. Lane, *The Naked Employee: How Technology is Compromising Workplace Privacy* (New York: AMACOM, 2003).

29. Quote from George Myers, "Bookshelf," *Columbus Dispatch* (June 9, 2003), p. E6.

30. Kristen Goff, "'Strong Belief System' Key Factor in Quality Workforce, Lee Says," *Ottawa Citizen* (October 24, 2006), p. B3.

31. Information from Thomas A. Stewart, "In Search of Elusive Tech Workers," *Fortune* (February 16, 1998), pp. 171–72.

32. See Ernest McCormick, "Job and Task Analysis," in Marvin Dunnette, ed., *Handbook of Industrial and Organizational Psychology* (Chicago: Rand McNally, 1976), pp. 651–96.

33. Information from Gautam Naik, "India's Technology Whizzes Find Passage to Nokia," *Wall Street Journal* (August 1, 2000), p. B1.

34. Uyen Vu, "The drug sector's staffing remedies," *Canadian HR Reporter*, vol. 16 (February 10, 2003), pp. 1ff.

35. See David Greising, *I'd Like to Buy the World a Coke: The Life and Leadership of Roberto Goizueta* (New York: Wiley, 1998).

36. See John P. Wanous, *Organizational Entry: Recruitment, Selection, and Socialization of Newcomers* (Reading, MA: Addison-Wesley, 1980), pp. 34–44.

37. Ravit Abelman and Igor Kotlyar, "Simulation Turns Recruitment into a Two-Way Street: Applicants can get a better sense of the job while the company gets a sampling of how the candidate will perform," *Canadian HR Reporter*, vol. 16 (December 1, 2003), p. G6.

38. Information from Justin Martin, "Mercedes: Made in Alabama," *Fortune* (July 7, 1997), pp. 150–58.

39. Information from Kemba J. Dunham, "The Jungle: Focus on Recruitment, Pay and Getting Ahead," *Wall Street Journal* (September 23, 2003), p. B8.

40. Reported in "Would You Hire This Person Again?" *Business Week*, Enterprise issue (June 9, 1997), pp. ENT32.

41. Dwight Hamilton, "Have Résumés: Fact or fiction?" *CAmagazine*, vol. 133 (April 2000), p. 16; on the Web, <www.camagazine.com>. (December 2006).

42. For a scholarly review, see John Van Maanen and Edgar H. Schein, "Toward a Theory of Socialization," in Barry M.

Staw, ed., *Research in Organizational Behavior, vol. 1* (Greenwich, CT: JAI Press, 1979), pp. 209–64. For a practitioner's view, see Richard Pascale, "Fitting New Employees into the Company Culture," *Fortune* (May 28, 1984), pp. 28–42.

43. Quote from Ronald Henkoff, "Finding, Training, and Keeping the Best Service Workers," *Fortune* (October 3, 1994), pp. 110–22.

44. This involves the social information processing concept as discussed in Gerald R. Salancik and Jeffrey Pfeffer, "A Social Information Processing Approach to Job Attitudes and Task Design," *Administrative Science Quarterly*, vol. 23 (June 1978), pp. 224–53.

45. Andy Holloway, "Mirror, Mirror," *Canadian Business*, vol. 79 (Summer 2006), p. 175ff.

46. Quote from Peter Petre, "Games That Teach You to Manage," *Fortune* (October 29, 1984), pp. 65–72; see also, the "Looking Glass" description on the Center for Creative Leadership website, <www.ccl.org>.

47. See Larry L. Cummings and Donald P. Schwab, *Performance in Organizations: Determinants and Appraisal* (Glenview, IL: Scott, Foresman, 1973).

48. Dick Grote, "Performance Appraisal Reappraised," *Harvard Business Review Best Practice* (1999), Reprint F00105.

49. See Mark R. Edwards and Ann J. Ewen, *360-Degree Feedback: The Powerful New Tool for Employee Feedback and Performance Improvement* (New York: AMACOM, 1996).

50. Information from "What Are the Most Effective Retention Tools?" *Fortune* (October 9, 2000), p. S7.

51. Charles Handy, *The Age of Unreason* (Cambridge, MA: Harvard Business School Press, 1990), p. 55.

52. Claudine Kapel and Catherine Shepherd, "Career Ladders Create Common Language for Defining Jobs," *Canadian HR Reporter*, vol. 17 (June 14, 2004), p. 15.

53. See Thomas P. Ference, James A. F. Stoner, and E. Kirby Warren,

"Managing the Career Plateau," *Academy of Management Review*, vol. 2 (October 1977), pp. 602–12.

54. Information and quote from Carol Hymowitz, "Baby Boomers Seek New Ways to Escape Career Claustrophobia," *Wall Street Journal* (June 24, 2003), p. B1.

55. Timothy Butler and James Waldroop, "Job Sculpting: The Art of Retaining Your Best People," *Harvard Business Review* (September–October 1999), pp. 144–52.

56. See Betty Friedan, *Beyond Gender: The New Politics of Work and the Family* (Washington, DC: Woodrow Wilson Center Press, 1997); and James A. Levine, *Working Fathers: New Strategies for Balancing Work and Family* (Reading, MA: Addison-Wesley, 1997).

57. For reviews, see Richard B. Freeman and James L. Medoff, *What Do Unions Do?* (New York: Basic Books, 1984); Charles C. Heckscher, *The New Unionism* (New York: Basic Books, 1988); and Barry T. Hirsch, *Labor Unions and the Economic Performance of Firms* (Kalamazoo, MI: W.E. Upjohn Institute for Employment Research, 1991).

58. Yochi J. Dreazen, "Percentage of U.S. Workers in a Union Sank to Record Low of 13.5% Last Year," *Wall Street Journal* (January 19, 2001), p. A2.

59. D. Carter, G. England, B. Etherington, and G. Trudeau, *Labour Law in Canada* (The Hague, Netherlands: Kluwer Law International, Distributed by Butterworths Canada Ltd., 2002).

CHAPTER 13 NOTES

1. Source for the opening vignette:

Information and quotes from Philip Preville, "For God's sake," *Canadian Business*, vol. 72 (June 25–July 9, 1999), p. 58–61.

TEXT NOTES

2. Information from the corporate website, <www.goldcorp.com>; and "The Fast 50 Leaders," *Fast Company* on the Web, <www.fastcompany.com>. (December 2006).

3. Tom Peters, "Rule #3: Leadership Is Confusing as Hell," *Fast Company* (March 2001), pp. 124–40.

4. Quotations from Marshall Loeb, "Where Leaders Come From," *Fortune* (September 19, 1994), pp. 241–42; Genevieve Capowski, "Anatomy of a Leader: Where Are the Leaders of Tomorrow?" *Management Review* (March 1994), pp. 10–17. For additional thoughts, see Warren Bennis, *Why Leaders Can't Lead* (San Francisco: Jossey-Bass, 1996).

5. See Jean Lipman-Blumen, *Connective Leadership: Managing in a Changing World* (New York: Oxford University Press, 1996), pp. 3–11.

6. James M. Kouzes and Barry Z. Posner, "The Leadership Challenge," *Success* (April 1988), p. 68. See also their books *The Leadership Challenge: How to Get Extraordinary Things Done in Organizations* (San Francisco: Jossey-Bass, 1987); *Credibility: How Leaders Gain and Lose It; Why People Demand It* (San Francisco: Jossey-Bass, 1996); *Encouraging the Heart: A Leader's Guide to Rewarding and Recognizing Others* (San Francisco: Jossey-Bass, 1999).

7. Burt Nanus, *Visionary Leadership: Creating a Compelling Sense of Vision for Your Organization* (San Francisco: Jossey-Bass, 1992).

8. Quotation from the General Electric Company Annual Report (1997), p. 5. For more on Jack Welch's leadership approach at GE see *Jack Welch & the GE Way* (New York: McGraw-Hill, 1998).

9. See Kouzes and Posner, op. cit. and James C. Collins and Jerry I. Porras, "Building Your Company's Vision," *Harvard Business Review* (September–October 1996), pp. 65–77.

10. Bonnie Dupont, "Leadership—An Organization's Biggest Competitive Advantage," address given at the Faculty of Management Awards and Scholarship ceremony, University of Calgary, March 13, 2002, Calgary, Alberta.

11. Rosabeth Moss Kanter, "Power Failure in Management Circuits," *Harvard Business Review* (July–August 1979), pp. 65–75.

12. For a good managerial discussion of power, see David C. McClelland and David H. Burnham, "Power Is the Great Motivator," *Harvard Business Review* (March–April 1976), pp. 100–10.

13. The classic treatment of these power bases is John R. P. French, Jr. and Bertram Raven, "The Bases of Social Power," in Darwin Cartwright, ed., *Group Dynamics: Research and Theory* (Evanstion, IL: Row, Peterson, 1962), pp. 607–13. For managerial applications of this basic framework, see Gary Yukl and Tom Taber, "The Effective Use of Managerial Power," *Personnel*, vol. 60 (1983), pp. 37–49; and Robert C. Benfari, Harry E. Wilkinson, and Charles D. Orth, "The Effective Use of Power," *Business Horizons*, vol. 29 (1986), pp. 12–16; Gary A. Yukl, *Leadership in Organizations, 4th ed.* (Englewood Cliffs, NJ: Prentice-Hall, 1998), includes "information" as a separate, but related, power source.

14. Information from <www.wxnetwork.com>; and remarks by Rose Patten, Senior Executive Vice-President at BMO Financial Group to the Financial Women's Association of Chicago, February 24, 2005; available on the Web, <www2.bmo.com>. (December 2006).

15. Based on David A. Whetten and Kim S. Cameron, *Developing Management Skills, 2nd ed.* (New York: Harper-Collins, 1991), pp. 281–97.

16. Ibid., p. 282.

17. Ibid.

18. Chester A. Barnard, *Functions of the Executive* (Cambridge, MA: Harvard University Press, 1938).

19. Andy Holloway, "Live and Learn: Derek Oland," *Canadian Business* (October 24–November 6, 2005); available on the Web, <www.canadianbusiness.com>. (December 2006).

20. Jeff Sanford, "Clean and green: Suncor uses sustainability performance to track business," *Canadian Business* Online, February 22, 2006, <www.canadianbusiness.com>. (December 2006).

21. Jay A. Conger, "Leadership: The Art of Empowering Others," *Academy of Management Executive*, vol. 3 (1989), pp. 17–24.

22. The early work on leader traits is well represented in Ralph M. Stogdill, "Personal Factors Associated with Leadership: A Survey of the Literature," *Journal of Psychology*, vol. 25 (1948), pp. 35–71. See also Edwin E. Ghiselli, *Explorations in Management Talent* (Santa Monica, CA: Goodyear, 1971); and Shirley A. Kirkpatrick and Edwin A. Locke, "Leadership: Do Traits Really Matter?" *Academy of Management Executive* (1991), pp. 48–60.

23. See also John W. Gardner's article, "The Context and Attributes of Leadership," *New Management*, vol. 5 (1988), pp. 18–22; John P. Kotter, *The Leadership Factor* (New York: Free Press, 1988); and Bernard M. Bass, *Stogdill's Handbook of Leadership* (New York: Free Press, 1990).

24. Kirkpatrick and Locke, op. cit. (1991).

25. See, for example, Jan P. Muczyk and Bernie C. Reimann, "The Case for Directive Leadership," *Academy of Management Review*, vol. 12 (1987), pp. 637–47.

26. See Bass, op. cit.

27. Robert R. Blake and Jane Srygley Mouton, *The New Managerial Grid III* (Houston: Gulf Publishing, 1985).

28. This terminology comes from the classic studies by Kurt Lewin and his associates at the University of Iowa. See, for example, K. Lewin and R. Lippitt, "An Experimental Approach to the Study of Autocracy and Democracy: A Preliminary Note," *Sociometry*, vol. 1 (1938), pp. 292–300; K. Lewin, "Field Theory and Experiment in Social Psychology: Concepts and Methods," *American Journal of Sociology*, vol. 44 (1939), pp. 86–896; and K. Lewin, R. Lippitt, and R. K. White, "Patterns of Aggressive Behavior in Experimentally Created Social Climates," *Journal of Social Psychology*, vol. 10 (1939), pp. 271–301.

29. See Jason Kirby, "In the Vault," *Canadian Business*, vol. 77 (March 1–4, 2004), p. 68–72.

30. For a good discussion of this theory see Fred E. Fiedler, Martin M. Chemers, and Linda Mahar, *The Leadership Match Concept* (New York: Wiley, 1978); Fiedler's current contingency research

with the cognitive resource theory is summarized in Fred E. Fiedler and Joseph E. Garcia, *New Approaches to Effective Leadership* (New York: Wiley, 1987).

31. Paul Hersey and Kenneth H. Blanchard, *Management and Organizational Behavior* (Englewood Cliffs, NJ: Prentice-Hall, 1988). For an interview with Paul Hersey on the origins of the model, see John R. Schermerhorn, Jr., "Situational Leadership: Conversations with Paul Heresy," *Mid-American Journal of Business* (fall 1997), pp. 5–12.

32. See Claude L. Graeff, "The Situational Leadership Theory: A Critical View," *Academy of Management Review*, vol. 8 (1983), pp. 285–91.

33. See, for example, Robert J. House, "A Path-Goal Theory of Leader Effectiveness," *Administrative Sciences Quarterly*, vol. 16 (1971), pp. 321–38; Robert J. House and Terrence R. Mitchell, "Path-Goal Theory of Leadership," *Journal of Contemporary Business* (autumn 1974), pp. 81–97. The path-goal theory is reviewed by Bass, op. cit.; and Yukl, op. cit. A supportive review of research is offered in Julie Indvik, "Path-Goal Theory of Leadership; A Meta-Analysis," in John A. Pearce II and Richard B. Robinson, Jr., eds., *Academy of Management Best Paper Proceedings* (1986), pp. 189–92.

34. See the discussions of path-goal theory in Yukl, op. cit.; and Bernard M. Bass, "Leadership: Good, Better, Best," *Organizational Dynamics* (winter 1985), pp. 26–40.

35. See Steven Kerr and John Jermier, "Substitutes for Leadership: Their Meaning and Measurement," *Organizational Behavior and Human Performance*, vol. 22 (1978), pp. 375–403; Jon P. Howell and Peter W. Dorfman, "Leadership and Substitutes for Leadership among Professional and Nonprofessional Workers," *Journal of Applied Behavioral Science*, vol. 22 (1986), pp. 29–46.

36. Victor H. Vroom and Arthur G. Jago, *The New Leadership: Managing Participation in Organizations* (Englewood Cliffs, NJ: Prentice-Hall, 1988). This is based on earlier work by Victor H. Vroom, "A New Look in Managerial Decision-Making," *Organizational Dynamics* (spring 1973), pp. 66–80; and Victor H. Vroom and Phillip Yetton, *Leadership and Decision-Making* (Pittsburgh: University of Pittsburgh Press, 1973).

37. For a related discussion see Edgar H. Schein, *Process Consultation Revisited: Building the Helping Relationship* (Reading, MA: Addison-Wesley, 1999).

38. Vroom and Jago, op. cit.

39. For a review see Yukl, op. cit.

40. See the discussion by Victor H. Vroom, "Leadership and the Decision-Making Process," *Organizational Dynamics*, vol. 28 (2000), pp. 82–94.

41. The distinction was originally made by James McGregor Burns, *Leadership* (New York: Harper & Row, 1978) and was further developed by Bernard Bass, *Leadership and Performance Beyond Expectations* (New York: Free Press, 1985) and Bernard M. Bass, "Leadership: Good, Better, Best," *Organizational Dynamics* (winter 1985), pp. 26–40.

42. This list is based on Kouzes and Posner, op. cit.; Gardner, op. cit.

43. Daniel Goleman, "Leadership That Gets Results," *Harvard Business Review* (March–April 2000), pp. 78–90. See also his books *Emotional Intelligence* (New York: Bantam Books, 1995) and *Working with Emotional Intelligence* (New York: Bantam Books, 1998).

44. Daniel Goleman, "What Makes a Leader?" *Harvard Business Review* (November–December 1998), pp. 93–102.

45. Goleman, op. cit., (1998).

46. Information from "Women and Men, Work and Power," *Fast Company*, Issue 13 (1998), p. 71.

47. A. H. Eagley, S. J. Daran, and M. G. Makhijani, "Gender and the Effectiveness of Leaders: A Meta-Analysis," *Psychological Bulletin*, vol. 117 (1995), pp. 125–45.

48. Research on gender issues in leadership is reported in Sally Helgesen, *The Female Advantage: Women's Ways of Leadership* (New York: Doubleday, 1990); Judith B. Rosener, "Ways Women Lead," *Harvard Business Review* (November–December 1990), pp. 119–25; and Alice H. Eagly, Steven J. Karau, and Blair T. Johnson, "Gender and Leadership Style Among School Principals: A Meta Analysis," *Administrative Science Quarterly*, vol. 27 (1992), pp. 76–102; Jean Lipman-Blumen, *Connective Leadership: Managing in a Changing World* (New York: Oxford University Press, 1996); and Alice H. Eagley, Mary C. Johannesen-Smith, and Marloes L. van Engen, "Transformational, Transactional and Laissez-Faire Leadership: A Meta-Analysis of Women and Men," *Psychological Bulletin*, vol. 124 (2003), pp. 569–591.

49. Vroom, op. cit., (2000).

50. Data reported by Rochelle Sharpe, "As Women Rule," *Business Week* (November 20, 2000), p. 75.

51. Rosener, op. cit., (1990).

52. For debate on whether some transformational leadership qualities tend to be associated more with female than male leaders, see "Debate: Ways Women and Men Lead," *Harvard Business Review* (January–February 1991), pp. 150–60.

53. Quote from "As Leaders, Women Rule," *Business Week* (November 20, 2000), pp. 75–84. Rosabeth Moss Kanter is the author of *Men and Women of the Corporation, 2nd ed.* (New York: Basic Books, 1993).

54. Peter F. Drucker, "Leadership: More Doing than Dash," *Wall Street Journal* (January 6, 1988), p. 16. For a compendium of writings on leadership sponsored by the Drucker Foundation, see Frances Hesselbein, Marshall Goldsmith, and Richard Beckhard, *Leader of the Future* (San Francisco: Jossey-Bass, 1997).

55. Based on the discussion by John W. Dienhart and Terry Thomas, "Ethical Leadership: A Primer on Ethical Responsibility," in John R. Schermerhorn, Jr., *Management, 7th ed.* (New York: Wiley, 2003).

56. Gardner, op. cit.

57. Fred Luthans and Bruce Avolio, "Authentic Leadership: A Positive Development Approach," in K. S. Cameron, J. E. Dutton, and R. E. Quinn, eds., *Positive Organizational*

Scholarship (San Francisco, Berrett-Koehler, 2003), pp. 241–258.

58. Doug May, Adrian Chan, Timothy Hodges, and Bruce Avolio, "Developing the Moral Component of Authentic Leadership," *Organizational Dynamics*, vol. 32 (2003), pp. 247–60.

59. Conference Board of Canada, "Pat Daniel: An Authentic Voice," Leaders on Leadership series, July 2003, on the Web, <www.conferenceboard.ca>. (December 2006).

CHAPTER 14 NOTES

1. Sources for the opening vignette:

   B. Morris, "Genentec: The best place to work now," *Fortune* (January 20, 2006), p. 79; on the Web, <www.money.cnn.com>. (December 2006).

   Information from the corporate website, <www.gene.com>. (April, 2006).

TEXT NOTES

2. Quotes from Charles O'Reilly III and Jeffrey Pfeffer, *Hidden Value: How Great Companies Achieve Extraordinary Results Through Ordinary People* (Boston, MA: Harvard Business School Press, 2000), pp. 5–6.

3. A. Holloway, "Find out why your employee is disgruntled and fix it," *Canadian Business* (November 7–20, 2005).

4. For a comprehensive treatment of extrinsic rewards, see Bob Nelson, *1001 Ways to Reward Employees* (New York: Workman Publishing, 1994).

5. The Baytech case study is taken from "Employee Retention/Turnover and Knowledge Transfer Report," commissioned by the Canadian Plastics Sector Council, on the Web, <www.cpsc-ccsp.ca>. (November 2006).

6. For a research perspective, see Edward Deci, *Intrinsic Motivation* (New York: Plenum, 1975); Edward E. Lawler III, "The Design of Effective Reward Systems," in Jay W. Lorsch, ed., *Handbook of Organizational Behavior* (Englewood Cliffs, NJ: Prentice-Hall, 1987), pp. 255–71.

7. Michael Maccoby's book, *Why Work: Leading the New Generation* (New York: Simon & Schuster, 1988), deals extensively with this point of view.

8. Information from Ellen Graham, "Work May Be a Rat Race, But It's Not a Daily Grind," *Wall Street Journal* (September 19, 1997), pp. R1, R4. The story of Starbucks is told in Howard Schulz and Dori Jones Yang, *Pour Your Heart Into It: How Starbucks Built a Company One Cup at a Time* (New York: Hyperion, 1999).

9. See Abraham H. Maslow, *Eupsychian Management* (Homewood, IL: Richard D. Irwin, 1965); Abraham H. Maslow, *Motivation and Personality, 2nd ed.* (New York: Harper & Row, 1970). For a research perspective, see Mahmoud A. Wahba and Lawrence G. Bridwell, "Maslow Reconsidered: A Review of Research on the Need Hierarchy," *Organizational Behavior and Human Performance*, vol. 16 (1976), pp. 212–40.

10. See Clayton P. Alderfer, *Existence, Relatedness, and Growth* (New York: Free Press, 1972).

11. The complete two-factor theory is in Frederick Herzberg, Bernard Mausner, and Barbara Block Synderman, *The Motivation to Work, 2nd ed.* (New York: Wiley, 1967); Frederick Herzberg, "One More Time: How Do You Motivate Employees?" *Harvard Business Review* (January–February 1968), pp. 53–62; and reprinted as an HBR Classic (September–October 1987), pp. 109–20.

12. Critical reviews are provided by Robert J. House and Lawrence A. Wigdor, "Herzberg's Dual-Factor Theory of Job Satisfaction and Motivation: A Review of the Evidence and a Criticism," *Personnel Psychology*, vol. 20 (winter 1967), pp. 369–89; Steven Kerr, Anne Harlan, and Ralph Stogdill, "Preference for Motivator and Hygiene Factors in a Hypothetical Interview Situation," *Personnel Psychology*, vol. 27 (winter 1974), pp. 109–24.

13. Frederick Herzberg, "Workers' Needs: The Same around the World," *Industry Week* (September 21, 1987), pp. 29–32.

14. For a collection of McClelland's work, see David C. McClelland, *The Achieving Society* (New York: Van Nostrand, 1961); "Business Drive and National Achievement," *Harvard Business Review*, vol. 40 (July–August 1962), pp. 99–112; David C. McClelland and David H. Burnham, "Power is the Great Motivator," *Harvard Business Review* (March–April 1976), pp. 100–10; David C. McClelland, *Human Motivation* (Glenview, IL: Scott, Foresman, 1985); David C. McClelland and Richard E. Boyatsis, "The Leadership Motive Pattern and Long-Term Success in Management," *Journal of Applied Psychology*, vol. 67 (1982), pp. 737–43.

15. Developed originally from a discussion in Edward E. Lawler III, *Motivation in Work Organizations* (Monterey, CA: Brooks/Cole Publishing, 1973), pp. 30–36.

16. See, for example, J. Stacy Adams, "Toward an Understanding of Inequity," *Journal of Abnormal and Social Psychology*, vol. 67 (1963), pp. 422–36; J. Stacy Adams, "Inequity in Social Exchange," in L. Berkowitz, ed., *Advances in Experimental Social Psychology, vol. 2* (New York: Academic Press, 1965), pp. 267–300.

17. See, for example, J. W. Harder, "Play for Pay: Effects of Inequity in a Pay-for-Performance Context," *Administrative Science Quarterly*, vol. 37 (1992), pp. 321–35.

18. Victor H. Vroom, "Work and Motivation (New York: Wiley, 1964; republished by Jossey-Bass, 1994).

19. The work on goal-setting theory is well summarized in Edwin A. Locke and Gary P. Latham, *Goal Setting: A Motivational Technique That Works!* (Englewood Cliffs, NJ: Prentice Hall, 1984). See also Edwin A. Locke, Kenneth N. Shaw, Lisa A. Saari, and Gary P. Latham, "Goal Setting and Task Performance 1969–1980," *Psychological Bulletin*, vol. 90 (1981), pp. 125–52; Mark E. Tubbs, "Goal Setting: A Meta-Analytic Examination of the Empirical Evidence," *Journal of Applied Psychology*, vol. 71 (1986), pp. 474–83; and Terence R. Mitchell, Kenneth R. Thompson, and Jane George-Falvy, "Goal Setting: Theory and Practice," Chapter 9 in Cary L. Cooper and Edwin A. Locke, eds., *Industrial and Organizational Psychology: Linking Theory with Practice* (Malden, MA: Blackwell Business, 2000), pp. 211–249.

20. Gary P. Latham and Edwin A. Locke, "Self-Regulation Through Goal Setting," *Organizational Behavior and Human Decision Processes*, vol. 50 (1991), pp. 212–47.

21. E. L. Thorndike, *Animal Intelligence* (New York: Macmillan, 1911), p. 244.

22. See B. F. Skinner, *Walden Two* (New York: Macmillan, 1948); *Science and Human Behavior* (New York: Macmillan, 1953); *Contingencies of Reinforcement* (New York: Appleton-Century-Crofts, 1969).

23. OB mod is clearly explained in Fred Luthans and Robert Kreitner, *Organizational Behavior Modification* (Glenview, IL: Scott, Foresman, 1975); and Fred Luthans and Robert Kreitner, *Organizational Behavior Modification and Beyond* (Glenview, IL: Scott, Foresman, 1985); see also Fred Luthans and Alexander D. Stajkovic, "Reinforce for Performance: The Need to Go Beyond Pay and Even Rewards," *Academy of Management Executive*, vol. 13 (1999), pp. 49–57.

24. Andrea Nierenberg, "How to Motivate a Staff," on the Web, <www.selfmarketing.com>. (November 2006).

25. For a good review, see Lee W. Frederickson, ed., *Handbook of Organizational Behavior Management* (New York: Wiley-Innerscience, 1982); Luthans and Kreitner, op. cit. (1985); and Andrew D. Stajkovic and Fred Luthans, "A Meta-Analysis of the Effects of Organizational Behavior Modification on Task Performance 1975–95," *Academy of Management Journal*, vol. 40 (1997), pp. 122–49.

26. Edwin A. Locke, "The Myths of Behavior Mod in Organizations," *Academy of Management Review*, vol. 2 (October 1977), pp. 543–53.

27. For a discussion of compensation and performance, see Rosabeth Moss Kanter, "The Attack on Pay," *Harvard Business Review*, vol. 65 (March–April 1987), pp. 60–67; Edward E. Lawler III, *Strategic Pay* (San Francisco: Jossey-Bass, 1990).

28. Karthryn M. Bartol and Cathy C. Durham, "Incentives: Theory and Practice," Chapter 1 in Cooper and Locke, op. cit. (2000).

29. "As CEO Pay Rockets Higher, Shareholders Urge Companies to Share the Rewards More Widely," report by *Responsible Wealth* (April 5, 2000).

30. "Pay-For-Performance, Shareholder Scrutiny and Disclosure Requirements Impacting CEO Compensation," based on the annual Watson Wyatt study, "CEO Compensation Practices in the S&P/TSX Composite Index," on the Web, November 28, 2005, <www.watsonwyatt.com/news>. (November 2006).

31. Information from Jaclyn Fierman, "The Perilous New World of Fair Pay," *Fortune* (June 13, 1994), pp. 57–61.

32. Tove Helland Hammer, "New Developments in Profit Sharing, Gain Sharing, and Employee Ownership," Chapter 12 in John P. Campbell and Richard J. Campbell, eds., *Productivity in Organizations: New Perspective from Industrial and Organizational Psychology* (San Francisco: Jossey-Bass, 1988).

33. Edward E. Lawler III, *From the Ground Up: Six Principles for Building the New Logic Corporation* (San Francisco: Jossey-Bass, 1996), pp. 217–18. See also Lawler's *Rewarding Excellence* (San Francisco: Jossey-Bass, 2000).

34. Information from the "Employee Retention/Turnover and Knowledge Transfer Report," commissioned by the Canadian Plastics Sector Council, on the Web, <www.cpsc-ccsp.ca>. (November 2006).

35. Jaclyn Fierman, "The Perilous New World of Fair Pay," *Fortune* (June 13, 1994), pp. 57–61.

36. "Freybe Gourmet Foods Ltd.," *National Post* Entrepreneur Profile, on the Web, <www.canada.com/nationalpost/entrepreneur/freybe.html>. (November 2006).

37. Employee stock option information on the Web, <www.intel.com>. (November 2006).

38. Anonymous, "Planes, pains & automobiles," *Canadian Business*, vol. 76 (September 15, 2003), p. 104.

39. Information from Susan Pulliam, "New Dot-Com Mantra: 'Just Pay Me in Cash, Please,'" *Wall Street Journal* (November 28, 2000), p. C1.

CHAPTER 15 NOTES

1. Sources for the opening vignette:

   Neil Gross, "Mining a Company's Mother Lode of Talent," *Business Week* (August 8, 2000), pp. 135–37.

   Information from the corporate website, <www. monitor.com>.

TEXT NOTES

2. Jeffrey Pfeffer and John F. Veiga, "Putting People First for Organizational Success," *Academy of Management Executive,* vol. 13 (1999), pp. 37–48; see also Jeffrey Pfeffer, *The Human Equation: Building Profits by Putting People First* (Boston: Harvard University Press, 1998).

3. Charles O'Reilly III and Jeffrey Pfeffer, *Hidden Value: How Great Companies Achieve Extraordinary Results Through Ordinary People* (Boston: MA: Harvard Business School Publishing, 2000), p. 2.

4. Mieke Koehoorn, Graham Lowe, Kent V. Rondeau, and Grant Schellenberg, *Creating High-Quality Health Care Workplaces*, prepared for the Canadian Policy Research Networks on the Web, January 23, 2002, <www.cprn.com>. (December 2006).

5. See John R. Schermerhorn, Jr., James G. Hunt, and Richard N. Osborn, *Organizational Behavior, 8th ed.* (New York: Wiley 2003).

6. Steve Crabtree, "Stryker's Investment in Talent Pays Off," Gallup Management Journal on the Web, June 12, 2003, <www.gmj.gallup.com>. (December 2006).

7. John P. Kotter, "The Psychological Contract: Managing the Joining Up Process," *California Management Review*, vol. 15 (spring 1973), pp. 91–99; Denise Rousseau, ed., *Psychological Contracts in Organizations* (San Francisco: Jossey-Bass, 1995); Denise Rousseau, "Changing the Deal While Keeping the People," *Academy of Management Executive*, vol. 10 (1996), pp. 50–59; and Denise Rousseau and Rene Schalk, eds., *Psychological Contracts in Employment: Cross-Cultural Perspectives* (San Francisco: Jossey-Bass, 2000).

8. Linda Grant, "Unhappy in Japan," *Fortune* (January 13, 1997), p. 142.

9. For a thought provoking discussion of this issue, see Ben Hamper, *Rivethead: Tales from the Assembly Line* (New York: Warner, 1991).

10. Studs Terkel, *Working* (New York: Avon Books, 1975).

11. Information from the corporate website, <www.roots.com>.

12. See M. R. Barrick and M. K. Mount, "The Big Five Personality Dimensions and Job Performance: A Meta-Analysis," *Personnel Psychology*, vol. 44 (1991), pp. 1–26.

13. This discussion based in part on Schermerhorn, et al., op. cit., pp. 54–60.

14. J. B. Rotter, "Generalized Expectancies for Internal Versus External Control of Reinforcement," *Psychological Monographs*, vol. 80 (1966), pp. 1–28.

15. T. W. Adorno, E. Frenkel-Brunswick, D. J. Levinson, and R. N. Sanford, *The Authoritarian Personality* (New York: Harper & Row, 1950).

16. Niccolo Machiavelli, *The Prince,* trans. George Bull (Middlesex, UK: Penguin, 1961).

17. Richard Christie and Florence L. Geis, *Studies in Machiavellianism* (New York: Academic Press, 1970).

18. Developed from Donald Bowen, "Learning and Problem-Solving: You're Never Too Jung," in Donald D. Bowen, Roy J. Lewicki, Donald T. Hall, and Francine S. Hall, *Experiences in Management and Organizational Behavior, 4th ed.* (New York: Wiley 1997), pp. 7–13.

19. I. Briggs-Myers, *Introduction to Type* (Palo Alto, CA: Consulting Psychologists Press, 1980). For management applications and research, see William L. Gardner and Mark J. Martinko, "Using the Myers-Briggs Type Indicator to Study Managers: A Literature Review and Research Agenda," *Journal of Management,* vol. 22 (1996), pp. 45–83.

20. See M. Snyder, *Public Appearances/Private Realities: The Psychology of Self-Monitoring* (New York: Freeman, 1987).

21. "Deborah Alexander Gets the Job Done," *Osler Link* (Spring-Summer 2003); on the Web, <www.osler.com>. (April 2006).

22. Martin Fishbein and Icek Ajzen, *Belief, Attitude, Intention and Behavior: An Introduction to Theory and Research* (Reading, MA: Addison-Wesley, 1973).

23. See Leon Festinger, *A Theory of Cognitive Dissonance* (Palo Alto, CA: Stanford University Press, 1957).

24. For an overview, see Charles N. Greene, "The Satisfaction-Performance Controversy," *Business Horizons,* vol. 15 (1982), p. 31; Michelle T. Iaffaldano and Paul M. Muchinsky, "Job Satisfaction and Job Performance: A Meta Analysis," *Psychological Bulletin*, vol. 97 (1985), pp. 251–273; Paul E. Spector, *Job Satisfaction* (Thousand Oaks, CA: Sage, 1997); and Timothy A. Judge and Allan H. Church, "Job Satisfaction: Research and Practice," Chapter 7 in Cary L. Cooper and Edwin A. Locke, eds., *Industrial and Organizational Psychology: Linking Theory with Practice* (Malden, MA: Blackwell Business, 2000).

25. Information from Wallace Immen, "It's Time to Leave a Loveless Career," *Globe and Mail* (September 7, 2005), p. C1.

26. Data reported in "When Loyalty Erodes, So Do Profits," *Business Week* (August 13, 2001), p. 8.

27. Information from Sue Shellenbarger, "Employers Are Finding It Doesn't Cost Much to Make a Staff Happy," *Wall Street Journal* (November 19, 1997), p. B1. See also, "Special Consumer Survey Report: Job Satisfaction on the Decline," The Conference Board (July 2002). A summary is available on the Web, <www.readyminds.com>. (December 2006).

28. The Individual Performance Equation and its management and research implications are discussed in William L. Gardner and John R. Schermerhorn, Jr., "Strategic Operational Leadership and the Management of Supportive Work Environments," in Robert L. Phillips and James G. Hunt, eds., *Leadership: A Multi-Organizational–Level Perspective* (Beverly Hills, CA: Sage, 1992); Thomas N. Martin, John R. Schermerhorn, Jr., and Lars L. Larson, "Motivational Consequences of a Supportive Work Environment," in M. L. Maehr and C. Ames, eds., *Advances in Motivation and Achievement: Motivation Enhancing Environments, vol. 6* (Greenwich, CT: JAI Press, 1989); John R. Schermerhorn, Jr., "Team Development of High Performance Management," *Training & Development Journal,* vol. 40 (1986), pp. 38–41; and John R. Schermerhorn, Jr., William L. Gardner, and Thomas N. Martin, "Management Dialogues: Turning on the Marginal Performer, *Organizational Dynamics* (Summer 1990), pp. 47–59.

29. See Melvin Blumberg and Charles D. Pringle, "The Missing Opportunity in Organizational Research: Some Implications for a Theory of Work Motivation," *Academy of Management Review*, vol. 7 (1982), pp. 560–69.

30. Information from "Reasonable Work Demands Equals Happy Employees," *Canadian HR Reporter*, vol. 19 (May 22, 2006), p. 7.

31. Information from David Whitford, "A Human Place to Work," *Fortune* (January 8, 2001), pp. 108–20.

32. Job rotation information on the Web, <www.jobquality.ca>. (November 2006).

33. Information from David Kosub, "Putting Theory into Practice," *Canadian HR Reporter*, vol. 16 (January 13, 2003), p. 9.

34. See Frederick Herzberg, Bernard Mausner, and Barbara Block Synderman, *The Motivation to Work, 2nd ed.* (New York: Wiley, 1967). The quotation is from Frederick Herzberg, "One More Time: Employees?" *Harvard Business Review* (January–February 1968), pp. 53–62, and reprinted as an HBR Classic in (September–October 1987), pp. 109–20.

35. Information from David Brown, "TD gives employees tool to chart career paths," *Canadian HR Reporter*, vol. 18 (June 20, 2005), p. 11.

36. For a complete description of the core characteristics model, see J. Richard

Hackman and Greg R. Oldham, *Work Redesign* (Reading, MA: Addison-Wesley, 1980).

37. See Richard E. Walton, *Up and Running: Integrating Information Technology and the Organization* (Boston, MA: Harvard Business School Press, 1989); Richard Walton, "From Control to Commitment in the Workplace," *Harvard Business Review* (March–April 1985), pp. 77–94; and William A. Pasmore, *Designing Effective Organizations: A Sociotechnical Systems Perspective* (New York: Wiley, 1988).

38. Paul J. Champagne and Curt Tausky, "When Job Enrichment Doesn't Pay," *Personnel*, vol. 3 (January–February 1978), pp. 30–40.

39. Quote from William W. Winipsigner, "Job Enrichment: A Union View," in Karl O. Magnusen, ed., *Organizational Design, Development, and Behavior: A Situational View* (Glenview, IL: Scott, Foresman, 1977), p. 22.

40. Barney Olmsted and Suzanne Smith, *Creating a Flexible Workplace: How to Select and Manage Alternative Work Options* (New York: American Management Association, 1989).

41. See Allen R. Cohen and Herman Gadon, *Alternative Work Schedules: Integrating Individual and Organizational Needs* (Reading, MA: Addison-Wesley, 1978), p. 125; Simcha Ronen and Sophia B. Primps, "The Compressed Work Week as Organizational Change: Behavioral and Attitudinal Outcomes," *Academy of Management Review*, vol. 6 (1981), pp. 61–74.

42. Information from Donna Nebenzahl, "Workers, Companies Find Flex-time Offers Benefits," *Vancouver Sun* (December 27, 2003), p. H9.

43. Anusha Shrivastava, "Flextime is now Key Benefit for Mom-Friendly Employers," *The Columbus Dispatch* (September 23, 2003), p. C2; Sue Shellenbarger, "Number of Women Managers Rises," *Wall Street Journal* (September 30, 2003), p. D2.

44. Information from <www.conference-board.ca>.

45. Information from <www.hrsdc.gc.ca>. (December 2006).

46. Information from Ian Harvey and Ian Johnson, "Will the Workplace Ever Be the Same?" *Globe and Mail* (April 25, 2006).

47. Ibid.

48. For a review see Wayne F. Cascio, "Managing a Virtual Workplace," *Academy of Management Executive*, vol. 14 (2000), pp. 81–90.

49. Quote from Phil Porter, "Telecommuting Mom Is Part of a National Trend," *Columbus Dispatch* (November 29, 2000), pp. H1, H2.

50. Information from Robert Coleman, "Telecommuting Transitions," *CMA Management* (August–September 2004); on the Web, <www.management-mag.com>. (November 2006).

51. These guidelines are collected from a variety of sources for telecommuters such as InnoVisions Canada, on the Web, <www.ivc.ca>.

52. Information from <www.statcan.ca>.

CHAPTER 16 NOTES

1. Sources for the opening vignette:

   Based on an interview of Ron Estey conducted by the author.

   Information from Jared Mitchell, "Pixar, eh?" *Financial Post Business* (April 2006), pp. 34–39.

TEXT NOTES

2. Grove quote from John A. Bryne, "Visionary vs. Visionary," *Business Week* (August 28, 2000), pp. 210–14; Chambers quote from Charles O'Reilly III and Jeffrey Pfeffer, *Hidden Value: How Great Companies Achieve Extraordinary Results Through Ordinary People* (Boston, MA: Harvard Business School Publishing, 2000), p. 4.

3. See Edward E. Lawler III, *From the Ground Up: Six Principles for Building the New Logic Corporation* (San Francisco: Jossey-Bass, 1996), pp. 131ff.

4. Cited in Lynda C. McDermott, Nolan Brawley, and William A. Waite, *World-Class Teams: Working Across Borders* (New York: Wiley, 1998), p. 5.

5. See, for example, Edward E. Lawler III, Susan Albers Mohrman, and Gerald E. Ledford, Jr., *Employee Involvement and Total Quality Management: Practices and Results in Fortune 1000 Companies* (San Francisco: Jossey-Bass, 1992); Susan A. Mohrman, Susan A. Cohen, and Monty A. Mohrman, *Designing Team-based Organizations: New Forms for Knowledge Work* (San Francisco: Jossey-Bass, 1995).

6. Information from the corporate website, <www.pomerleau.ca>. (November 2006).

7. Jon R. Katzenbach and Douglas K. Smith, *The Wisdom of Teams: Creating the High Performance Organization* (Boston: Harvard Business School Press, 1993).

8. A classic work is Bib Latane, Kipling Williams, and Stephen Harkins, "Many Hands Make Light the Work: The Causes and Consequences of Social Loafing," *Journal of Personality and Social Psychology*, vol. 37 (1978), pp. 822–32.

9. J. D. Rothwell, *In the Company of Others: An Introduction to Communication*, 2nd ed. (New York: McGraw-Hill, 2004).

10. See Marvin E. Shaw, *Group Dynamics: The Psychology of Small Group Behavior*, 2nd ed. (New York: McGraw-Hill, 1976); Harold J. Leavitt, "Suppose We Took Groups More Seriously," in Eugene L. Cass and Frederick G. Zimmer, eds., *Man and Work in Society* (New York: Van Nostrand Reinhold, 1975), pp. 67–77.

11. John M. George, "Extrinsic and Intrinsic Origins of Perceived Social Loafing in Organizations," *Academy of Management Journal* (March, 1992), pp. 191–202; and W. Jack Duncan, "Why Some People Loaf in Groups While Others Loaf Alone," *Academy of Management Executive*, vol. 8 (1994), pp. 79–80.

12. For insights on how to conduct effective meetings see Mary A. De Vries, *How to Run a Meeting* (New York: Penguin, 1994).

13. Survey reported in "Meetings Among Top Ten Time Wasters," *San Francisco Business Times* (April 7, 2003).

14. Quotes from Eric Matson, "The Seven Sins of Deadly Meetings," *Fast Company* (April/May, 1996), p. 122.

15. Developed from ibid.

16. See Leavitt, op. cit.

17. The "linking pin" concept is introduced in Rensis Likert, *New Patterns of Management* (New York: McGraw-Hill, 1962).

18. See discussion by Susan G. Cohen and Don Mankin, "The Changing Nature of Work," in Susan Albers Mohrman, Jay R. Galbraith, Edward E. Lawler III and Associates, *Tomorrow's Organization: Crafting Winning Capabilities in a Dynamic World* (San Francisco: Jossey-Bass, 1998), pp. 154–78.

19. Information from "Diversity: America's Strength," special advertising section, *Fortune* (June 23, 1997); American Express corporate communication (1998).

20. Information from Matthew de Paula, "Diversity is About Equality, and That's Good for Bank Business," *USBanker* (June 2004), p. 32.

21. See Susan D. Van Raalte, "Preparing the Task Force to Get Good Results," *S.A.M. Advanced Management Journal*, vol. 47 (winter, 1982), pp. 11–16; Walter Kiechel III, "The Art of the Corporate Task Force," *Fortune* (January 28, 1991), pp. 104–6.

22. Developed from ibid.

23. Mohrman et al., op. cit.

24. Information from Jenny C. McCune, "Making Lemonade," *Management Review* (June 1997), pp. 49–53.

25. Information from TECSYS customer case studies on the Web, <www.tecsys.com>. (December 2006).

26. For a good discussion of quality circles, see Edward E. Lawler III and Susan A. Mohrman, "Quality Circles After the Fad," *Harvard Business Review*, vol. 63 (January–February, 1985), pp. 65–71; Edward E. Lawler III and Susan Albers Mohrman, "Employee Involvement, Reengineering, and TQM: Focusing on Capability Development," in Mohrman, et al. (1998), pp. 179–208.

27. See Wayne F. Cascio, "Managing a Virtual Workplace," *Academy of Management Executive*, vol. 14 (2000), pp. 81–90.

28. See Sheila Simsarian Webber, "Virtual Teams: A Meta-Analysis," SHRMOnline, October 24, 2005, <www.shrm.org>. (December 2006).

29. "Nortel and BP succeed through virtual teamwork," *Training Strategies for Tomorrow*, vol. 16 (May/June 2002), pp. 3–5.

30. R. Brent Gallupe and William H. Cooper, "Brainstorming Electronically," *Sloan Management Review* (winter, 1997), pp. 11–21; Cascio, op. cit.

31. Cascio, op. cit.

32. See, for example, Paul S. Goodman, Rukmini Devadas, and Terri L. Griffith Hughson, "Groups and Productivity: Analyzing the Effectiveness of Self-Managing Teams," Chapter 11 in John R. Campbell and Richard J. Campbell, *Productivity in Organizations* (San Francisco: Jossey-Bass, 1988); Jack Orsbrun, Linda Moran, Ed Musslewhite, and John H. Zenger, with Craig Perrin, *Self-Directed Work Teams: The New American Challenge* (Homewood, IL: Business One Irwin, 1990); Dale E. Yeatts and Cloyd Hyten, *High Performing Self-Managed Work Teams* (Thousand Oaks, CA: Sage, 1997).

33. Information from Grande Prairie website, <www.cityofgp.com>. (December 2006).

34. Bradley L. Kirkman and Debra L. Shapiro, "The Impact of Cultural Values on Employee Resistance to Teams: Toward a Model of Globalized Self-Managing Work Team Effectiveness," *Academy of Management Review*, vol. 22 (1997), pp. 730–57.

35. For a discussion of effectiveness in the context of top management teams, see Edward E. Lawler III, David Finegold, and Jay A. Conger, "Corporate Boards: Developing Effectiveness at the Top," in Mohrman, op. cit. (1998), pp. 23–50.

36. For a review of research on group effectiveness, see J. Richard Hackman, "The Design of Work Teams," in Jay W. Lorsch, ed., *Handbook of Organizational Behavior* (Englewood Cliffs, NJ: Prentice-Hall, 1987), pp. 315–42; and J. Richard Hackman, Ruth Wageman, Thomas M. Ruddy, and Charles L. Ray, "Team Effectiveness in Theory and Practice," Chapter 5 in Cary L. Cooper

and Edwin A. Locke, *Industrial and Organizational Psychology: Linking Theory with Practice* (Malden, MA: Blackwell, 2000).

37. Ibid; Lawler, et al., op. cit., 1998.

38. Example from "Designed for Interaction," *Fortune* (January 8, 2001), p. 150.

39. See Warren Watson, "Cultural Diversity's Impact on Interaction Process and Performance," *Academy of Management Journal*, vol. 16 (1993); and Christopher Earley and Elaine Mosakowski, "Creating Hybrid Team Structures: An Empirical Test of Transnational Team Functioning," *Academy of Management Journal*, vol. 5 (February 2000), pp. 26–49.

40. J. Steven Heinen and Eugene Jacobson, "A Model of Task Group Development in Complex Organizations and a Strategy of Implementation," *Academy of Management Review*, vol. 1 (1976), pp. 98–111; Bruce W. Tuckman, "Developmental Sequence in Small Groups," Psychological Bulletin, vol. 63 (1965), pp. 384–99; Bruce W. Tuckman and Mary Ann C. Jensen, "Stages of Small-Group Development Revisited," *Group & Organization Studies*, vol. 2 (1977), pp. 419–27.

41. See for example, Edgar Schein, *Process Consultation* (Reading, MA: Addison-Wesley, 1988); and Linda C. McDermott, Nolan Brawley, and William A. Waite, *World-Class Teams: Working Across Borders* (New York: Wiley, 1998).

42. For a good discussion, see Robert F. Allen and Saul Pilnick, "Confronting the Shadow Organization: How to Detect and Defeat Negative Norms," *Organizational Dynamics* (spring 1973), pp. 13–16.

43. See Schein, op. cit., pp. 76–79.

44. Marvin E. Shaw, *Group Dynamics: The Psychology of Small Group Behavior* (New York: McGraw-Hill, 1976).

45. Information from the coporate website, <www.telus.com>. (December 2006).

46. A classic work in this area is K. Benne and P. Sheets, *Journal of Social Issues, vol. 2* (1948), pp. 42–47; see also, Likert, op. cit., pp. 166–69; Schein, op. cit., pp. 49–56.

47. Based on John R. Schermerhorn, Jr., James G. Hunt, and Richard N. Osborn, *Organizational Behavior, 7th ed.* (New York: Wiley, 2000), pp. 345–46.

48. Research on communication networks is found in Alex Bavelas, "Communication Patterns in Task-Oriented Groups," *Journal of the Acoustical Society of America*, vol. 22 (1950), pp. 725–30; Shaw, op. cit.

49. Schein, op. cit., pp. 69–75.

50. See Kathleen M. Eisenhardt, Jean L. Kahwajy, and L. J. Bourgeois III, "How Management Teams Can Have a Good Fight," *Harvard Business Review* (July–August 1997), pp. 77–85.

51. The APIRIG consensus policy can be viewed on the Web, <www.apirg.org>. (December 2006.)

52. Victor H. Vroom and Arthur G. Jago, *The New Leadership: Managing Participation in Organizations* (Englewood Cliffs, NJ: Prentice Hall, 1988); Victor H. Vroom, "A New Look in Managerial Decision-Making," *Organizational Dynamics* (spring 1973), pp. 66–80; Victor H. Vroom and Phillip Yetton, *Leadership and Decision-Making* (Pittsburgh: University of Pittsburgh Press, 1973).

53. Norman F. Maier, "Assets and Liabilities in Group Problem Solving," *Psychological Review,* vol. 74 (1967), pp. 239–49.

54. Ibid.

55. See Irving L. Janis, "Groupthink," *Psychology Today* (November 1971), pp. 43–46; *Victims of Groupthink, 2nd ed.* (Boston: Houghton Mifflin, 1982).

56. Rosie Steeves, "Group Think Kills Healthy Corporate Decision-making and Weakens Companies," <www.exceptionalleadership.com/pdfs/groupthink_apr05.pdf>. (January 2007).

57. These techniques are well described in Andre L. Delbecq, Andrew H. Van de Ven, and David H. Gustafson, *Group Techniques for Program Planning* (Glenview, IL: Scott, Foresman, 1975).

58. A very good overview is provided by William D. Dyer, *Team-Building* (Reading, MA: Addison-Wesley, 1977).

59. Information on the Web, <www.out­wardbound.ca>. (November 2006).

60. Katzenbach and Smith, op. cit; see also Jon R. Katzenbach, "The Myth of the Top Management Team," *Harvard Business Review*, vol. 75 (November–December 1997), pp. 83–91.

61. Carl E. Larson and Frank M. J. LaFasto, *Team Work: What Must Go Right/What Can Go Wrong* (Newbury Park, CA: Sage, 1990).

62. Quote from "Teach Your Leaders that Their Main Priority Is to Energize and Grow Their Team Around Themselves," *Fast Company* (March, 2001), p. 95.

CHAPTER 17 NOTES

1. Sources for the opening vignette:

Quotes from *Business Week* (July 8, 1991), pp. 60–61.

Additional information from the Center's website, <www.ccl.org>.

TEXT NOTES

2. Henry Mintzberg, *The Nature of Managerial Work* (New York: Harper & Row, 1973).

3. John P. Kotter, "What Effective General Managers Really Do," *Harvard Business Review*, vol. 60 (November–December 1982), pp. 156–57; and *The General Managers* (New York: Macmillan, 1986).

4. "Relationships Are the Most Powerful Form of Media," *Fast Company* (March 2001), p. 100.

5. See Mintzberg, op. cit., Kotter, op. cit.

6. Mary Pat Barry, "Canadian Telephone Company Enhances Corporate Dialogue With CEO Mailbox," *Communication World*, vol. 21 (July–August 2004), p. 50–51.

7. Jay A. Conger, *Winning 'Em Over: A New Model for Managing in the Age of Persuasion* (New York: Simon & Schuster, 1998), pp. 24–79.

8. This discussion developed from ibid.

9. *Business Week* (February 10, 1992), pp. 102–8.

10. See Robert H. Lengel and Richard L. Daft, "The Selection of Communication

Media as an Executive Skill," *Academy of Management Executive,* vol. 2 (August 1988), pp. 225–32.

11. Survey information from "What Do Recruiters Want?" *BizEd* (November–December 2002), p. 9; "Much to Learn, Professors Say," *USA Today* (July 5, 2001), p. 8D; and AMA-Fast Response Survey, "The Passionate Organization," (September 26–29, 2000).

12. See Eric Matson, "Now That We Have Your Complete Attention," *Fast Company* (February–March 1997), pp. 124–32.

13. David McNeill, *Hand and Mind: What Gestures Reveal about Thought* (Chicago: University of Chicago Press, 1992).

14. Adapted from Richard V. Farace, Peter R. Monge, and Hamish M. Russell, *Communicating and Organizing* (Reading, MA: Addison-Wesley, 1977), pp. 97–98.

15. Tom Peters and Nancy Austin, *A Passion for Excellence* (New York: Random House, 1985).

16. This discussion is based on Carl R. Rogers and Richard E. Farson, "Active Listening" (Chicago: Industrial Relations Center of the University of Chicago, n.d.).

17. A useful source of guidelines is John J. Gabarro and Linda A. Hill, "Managing Performance," Note 9-96-022 (Boston, MA: Harvard Business School Publishing, n.d.).

18. Developed from John Anderson, "Giving and Receiving Feedback," in Paul R. Lawrence, Louis B. Barnes, and Jay W. Lorsch, eds., *Organizational Behavior and Administration, 3rd ed.* (Homewood, IL: Richard D. Irwin, 1976), p. 109.

19. See Lengel and Daft, op. cit. (1988).

20. Information from Terry Curtis, "Business Best Practices Applied to Sport," paper presented at Sport Leadership Sportif Quebec, 2005.

21. Information from Esther Wachs Book, "Leadership for the Millennium," *Working Woman* (March 1998), pp. 29–34.

22. Anonymous, "Going back to the floor to shape culture at Vancity," *Business*

Communicator, vol. 6 (October 2005), pp. 8–9.

23. Adam Appelbaum, Lessard Javeri, et al., "A Case Study Analysis of the Impact of Satisfaction and Organizational Citizenship on Productivity Management," *Research News*, vol. 28 (May 2005), pp. 1–26.

24. See Richard Lepsinger and Anntoinette D. Lucia, *The Art and Science of 360° Feedback* (San Francisco: Jossey-Bass, 1997).

25. Brian O'Reilly, "360° Feedback Can Change Your Life," *Fortune* (October 17, 1994), pp. 93–100.

26. Sue Bowness, "Full-circle feedback: 360-degree performance reviews," *Profit* (May 2006); on the Web, <www.canadianbusiness.com>. (December 2006).

27. A classic work on proxemics is Edward T. Hall's book, *The Hidden Dimension* (Garden City, NY: Doubleday, 1986).

28. Mirand Wewll, "Alternative Spaces Spawning Desk-Free Zones," *Columbus Dispatch* (May 18, 1998), pp. 10–11.

29. Information from Susan Stellin, "Intranets Nurture Companies from the Inside," *New York Times* (January 21, 2001), p. C4.

30. Example from Heidi A. Schuessler, "Social Studies Class Finds How Far EMail Travels," *New York Times* (February 22, 2001), p. D8.

31. Alison Overholt, "Intel's got (Too Much) Mail," *Fortune* (March 2001), pp. 56–58.

32. Developed from *Working Woman* (November 1995), p. 14; and Elizabeth Weinstein, "Help! I'm Drowing in E-Mail!" *Wall Street Journal* (January 10, 2002), pp. B1, B4.

33. See Edward T. Hall, *The Silent Language* (New York: Doubleday, 1973).

34. Anonymous, "*Workforce Development*," *Canadian HR Reporter*, vol. 18 (December 5, 2005), p. 7.

35. See H. R. Schiffman, *Sensation and Perception: An Integrated Approach, 3rd ed.* (New York: Wiley, 1990).

36. A good review is E. L. Jones, ed., *Attribution: Perceiving the Causes of Behavior* (Morristown, NJ: General Learning Press, 1972). See also John H. Harvey and Gifford Weary, "Current Issues in Attribution Theory and Research," *Annual Review of Psychology*, vol. 35 (1984), pp. 427–59.

37. With information from "Few Cracks in Glass Ceiling," CBC News, on the Web, March 1, 2006, <www.cbc.ca>. Based on the "2005 Catalyst Census of Women Board Directors of the FP500," and Virginia Gault, "Lots of Qualified Women, but Few Sit on Boards," *Globe and Mail* (March 2, 2006), B1.

38. Information from "Misconceptions About Women in the Global Arena Keep Their Numbers Low," Catalyst study on the Web, <www.catalyst-women.org/home.html>. (December 2006).

39. These examples are from Natasha Josefowitz, *Paths to Power* (Reading, MA: Addison-Wesley, 1980), p. 60. For more on gender issues see Gary N. Powell, ed., *Handbook of Gender and Work* (Thousand Oaks, CA: Sage, 1999).

40. Survey reported in Kelly Greene, "Age Is Still More Than a Number," *Wall Street Journal* (April 10, 2003), p. D2.

41. The classic work is Dewitt C. Dearborn and Herbert A. Simon, "Selective Perception: A Note on the Departmental Identification of Executives," *Sociometry*, vol. 21 (1958), pp. 140–44. See also J. P. Walsh, "Selectivity and Selective Perception: Belief Structures and Information Processing," *Academy of Management Journal*, vol. 24 (1988), pp. 453–70.

42. Richard E. Walton, *Interpersonal Peacemaking: Confrontations and Third-Party Consultation* (Reading, MA: Addison-Wesley, 1969), p. 2.

43. Information from Michael A. Roberto, "Making difficult decisions in turbulent times," *Ivey Business Journal*, vol. 66 (January–February 2002), pp. 15–20.

44. See Kenneth W. Thomas, "Conflict and Conflict Management," in M. D. Dunnett, ed., *Handbook of Industrial and Organizational Behavior* (Chicago; Rand McNally, 1976), pp. 889–935.

45. See Robert R. Blake and Jane Strygley Mouton, "The Fifth Achievement," *Journal of Applied Behavioral Science*, vol. 6 (1970), pp. 413–27; Alan C. Filley, *Interpersonal Conflict Resolution* (Glenview, IL: Scott, Foresman, 1975).

46. This discussion is based on Filley, op. cit.

47. Information from "A Tale of Two Hotels: Hilton and Delta," *UNITE HERE Reporter* (December 2004), p. 1; on the Web, <www.unitehere.ca>. (December 2006).

48. Portions of this treatment of negotiation originally adapted with permission from John R. Schermerhorn, Jr., James G. Hunt, and Richard N. Osborn, *Managing Organizational Behavior*, 4th ed. (New York: Wiley, 1991), pp. 382–87.

49. See Roger Fisher and William Ury; *Getting to Yes: Negotiating Agreement Without Giving In* (New York: Penguin, 1983); James A. Wall, Jr., *Negotiation: Theory and Practice* (Glenview, IL: Scott, Foresman, 1985); and William L. Ury, Jeanne M. Brett, and Stephen B. Goldberg, *Getting Disputes Resolved* (San Francisco: Jossey-Bass, 1997).

50. Fisher and Ury, op. cit.

51. Information from Julie Stauffer, "Making It Work" *National*, vol. 14 (September 2005), p. 32; on the Web, <www.cba.org/CBA/National/Main/>. (December 2006).

52. Fisher and Ury, op. cit.

53. Developed from Max H. Bazerman, *Judgment in Managerial Decision Making, 4th ed.* (New York: Wiley, 1998), Chapter 7.

54. Fisher and Ury, op. cit.

55. Roy J. Lewicki and Joseph A. Litterer, *Negotiation* (Homewood, IL: Irwin, 1985).

CHAPTER 18 NOTES

1. Sources for the opening vignette:

   With information from archived news releases dated February 16, 2005 and

April 4, 2005. Retrieved from <www.meridiancu.ca> (January 2007).

Susan Maclean, "In the Mail: Mailings Help Credit Union Members Smile on Mergers, Meridian Launch," *Direct Marketing News* (August 2005).

TEXT NOTES

2. Information from "On the Road to Innovation," in special advertising section, "Charting the Course: Global Business Sets Its Goals," *Fortune* (August 4, 1997).

3. Michael Beer and Nitin Nohria, "Cracking the Code of Change," *Harvard Business Review* (May–June 2000), pp. 133–41.

4. Quote from John A. Byrne, "Visionary vs. Visionary," *Business Week* (August 28, 2000), p. 210.

5. Tom Peters, *The Circle of Innovation* (New York: Knopf, 1997).

6. Quotes from David Kirkpatrick, "From Davos, Talk of Death," *Fortune* (March 5, 2001), pp. 180–82.

7. Peter Senge, *The Fifth Discipline* (New York: Harper, 1990).

8. Teresa Kirkwood and Ajay Pangarkar, "Workplace Learning: beyond the classroom," *CMA Management*, vol.77 (May 2003), p. 10.

9. Peter A.C. Smith, "The Learning Organization Ten Years On: A case study," *Learning Organization*, vol. 6 (1999), p. 217.

10. R. Duane Ireland and Michael A. Hitt, "Achieving and Maintaining Strategic Competitiveness in the 21st Century: The Role of Strategic Leadership," *Academy of Management Executive* (February 1999), pp. 43–57.

11. *Director's Breakfast Series: Testing the Limits of Innovation* (Toronto: Spencer Stuart, 2002).

12. Developed from Ireland & Hitt, op. cit.

13. See, for example, Roger von Oech, *A Whack on the Side of the Head* (New York: Warner Books, 1983) and *A Kick in the Seat of the Pants* (New York: Harper & Row, 1986).

14. See Peter F. Drucker, "The Discipline of Innovation," *Harvard Business* Review (November–December 1998), pp. 3–8.

15. Peter F. Drucker, *Management: Tasks, Responsibilities, and Practices* (New York: Harper & Row, 1973), p. 797.

16. Information from David Kirkpatrick, "Software's Humble Wizard Does It Again," *Fortune* (February 19, 2001), pp. 137–42.

17. Information from "Providing Rural Phone Service Profitably in Poor Countries," *Business Week* (December 18, 2000), special advertising section.

18. Based on Gary Hamel, *Leading the Revolution* (Boston, MA: Harvard Business School Press, 2000), pp. 293–95.

19. Based on Edward B. Roberts, "Managing Invention and Innovation," *Research Technology Management* (January– February 1988), pp. 1–19, and Hamel, op. cit.

20. This discussion is stimulated by James Brian Quinn, "Managing Innovation Controlled Chaos," *Harvard Business Review*, vol. 63 (May–June 1985). Selected quotations and examples from Kenneth Labich, "The Innovators," *Fortune* (June 6, 1988), pp. 49–64.

21. Peter F. Drucker, "Best R&D Is Business Driven," *Wall Street Journal*, (February 10, 1988), p. 11.

22. See Roberts, op. cit.

23. Drucker, op. cit., 1998.

24. Reported in Carol Hymowitz, "Task of Managing Changes in Workplace Takes a Careful Hand," *Wall Street Journal* (July 1, 1997), p. B1.

25. Reported in G. Christian Hill and Mike Tharp, "Stumbling Giant—Big Quarterly Deficit Stuns BankAmerica, Adds Pressure on Chief," *Wall Street Journal* (July 18, 1985), pp. 1–16.

26. Beer and Nohria, op. cit.; and "Change Management, An Inside Job," *Economist* (July 15, 2000), p. 61.

27. Reported in Robert Rose, "Kentucky Plant Workers Are Cranking Out Good Ideas," *Wall Street Journal* (August 13, 1996), p. B1.

28. Beer & Nohria, op. cit.

29. For a review of scholarly work on organizational change, see Arthur G. Bedian, "Organizational Change: A Review of Theory and Research," *Journal of Management*, vol. 25 (1999), pp. 293–315.

30. For a discussion of alternative types of change, see David A. Nadler and Michael L. Tushman, *Strategic Organizational Design* (Glenview, II: Scott, Foresman, 1988); John P. Kotter, "Leading Change: Why Transformations Efforts Fail," *Harvard Business Review* (March–April 1995), pp. 59–67; and W. Warner Burke, *Organization Change* (Thousand Oaks, CA: Sage, 2002).

31. Based on Kotter, op. cit.

32. See Edward E. Lawler III, "Strategic Choices for Changing Organizations," Chapter 12 in Allan M. Mohrman, Jr., Susan Albers Mohrman, Gerald E. Ledford, Jr., Thomas G. Cummings, Edward E. Lawler III and Associates, *Large Scale Organizational Change* (San Francisco: Jossey-Bass, 1989).

33. The classic description of organizations on these terms is by Harold J. Leavitt, "Applied Organizational Change in Industry: Structural, Technological and Humanistic Approaches," in James G. March, ed., *Handbook of Organizations* (Chicago: Rand McNally, 1965), pp. 1144–70.

34. Angela Lovell, "Winkler's Super Carpenter," *Manitoba Business*, vol. 28 (May 2006), p. 15.

35. Kurt Lewin, "Group Decision and Social Change," in G. E. Swanson, T. M. Newcomb and E. L. Hartley, eds., *Readings in Social Psychology* (New York: Holt, Rinehart, 1952), pp. 459–73.

36. Ron Knowles, "Continuous change," *CA Magazine*, vol.132 (May 1999), p. 43.

37. This discussion is based on Robert Chin and Kenneth D. Benne, "General Strategies for Effecting Changes in Human Systems," in Warren G. Bennis, Kenneth D. Benne, Robert Chin, and Kenneth E. Corey, eds., *The Planning*

of Change, 3rd ed. (New York: Holt, Rinehart; 1969), pp. 22–45.

38. The change agent descriptions here and following are developed from an exercise reported in J. William Pfeiffer and John E. Jones, *A Handbook of Structured Experiences for Human Relations Training*, vol. 2 (La Jolla, CA: University Associates, 1973).

39. Ram N. Aditya, Robert J. House, and Steven Kerr, "Theory and Practice of Leadership: Into the New Millennium," Chapter 6 in Cary L. Cooper and Edwin A. Locke, *Industrial and Organizational Psychology: Linking Theory with Practice* (Malden, MA: Blackwell, 2000).

40. Information from Mike Schneider, "Disney Teaching Excess Magic of Customer Service," *Columbus Dispatch* (December 17, 2000), p. G9.

41. Teresa M. Amabile, "How to Kill Creativity," *Harvard Business Review*, (September–October, 1998), pp. 77–87.

42. Sue Shellenbarger, "Some Employers Find Way to Ease Burden of Changing Shifts," *Wall Street Journal* (March 25, 1998), p. B1.

43. Ibid.

44. John P. Kotter and Leonard A. Schlesinger, "Choosing Strategies for Change," *Harvard Business Review*, vol. 57 (March–April 1979), pp. 109–12.

45. Wanda J. Orlikowski and J. Debra Hofman, "An Improvisational Model for Change Management: The Case of Groupware Technologies," *Sloan Management Review* (winter 1997), pp. 11–21.

46. Ibid.

47. Overviews of organization development are provided by W. Warner Burke, *Organization Development: A Normative View* (Reading, MA: Addison-Wesley, 1987); William Rothwell, Roland Sullivan, and Gary N. McLean, *Practicing Organization Development* (San Francisco: Jossey-Bass, 1995); and Wendell L. French and Cecil H. Bell, Jr., *Organization Development*, 6th ed. (Englewood Cliffs, NJ: Prentice-Hall, 1998).

48. See French and Bell, op. cit.

49. See Arthur P. Brief, Randall S. Schuler, and Mary Van Sell, *Managing Job Stress* (Boston: Little, Brown, 1981), pp. 7, 8.

50. Robert B. Reich, *The Future of Success* (New York: Knopf, 2000), p. 8.

51. Michael Weldholz, "Stress Increasingly Seen as Problem with Executives More Vulnerable," *Wall Street Journal* (September 28, 1982), p. 31.

52. "Sources of Workplace Stress," Statistics Canada on the Web, June 25, 2003, <www.statcan.ca>. (February 2006).

53. Sue Shellenbarger, "Do We Work More or Not? Either Way, We Feel Frazzled," *Wall Street Journal* (July 30, 1997), p. B1.

54. See, for example, "Desk Rage," *Business Week* (November 27, 2000), p. 12.

55. Carol Hymowitz, "Impossible Expectations and Unfulfilling Work Stress Managers, Too," *Wall Street Journal* (January 16, 2001), p. B1.

56. The classic work is Meyer Friedman and Ray Roseman, *Type A Behavior and Your Heart* (New York: Knopf, 1974).

57. See Hans Selye, *Stress in Health and Disease* (Boston: Butterworth, 1976).

58. Carol Hymowitz, "Can Workplace Stress Get Worse?" *Wall Street Journal* (January 16, 2001), pp. B1, B3.

59. See Steve M. Jex, *Stress and Job Performance* (San Francisco: Jossey-Bass, 1998).

60. The extreme case of "workplace violence" is discussed by Richard V. Denenberg and Mark Braverman, *The Violence-Prone Workplace* (Ithaca, NY: Cornell University Press, 1999).

61. See Daniel C. Ganster and Larry Murphy, "Workplace Interventions to Prevent Stress-Related Illness: Lessons from Research and Practice," Chapter 2 in Cooper and Locke, eds., op. cit. (2000).

62. Reported in Sue Shellenbarger, "Finding Ways to Keep a Partner's Job Stress from Hitting Home," *Wall Street Journal* (November 29, 2000), p. B1.

63. Quote from Shellenbarger, op. cit.

64. Raizel Robin, "Healthy, Wealthy and Wise," *Canadian Business* (December 2003), p. 129; on the Web, <www.candianbusiness.com>. (December 2006).

65. Ibid.

Photo Credits

Name Index

A

Adams, Barry, 66
Adams, J. Stacy, 343
Adlerfer, Clayton, 340
Alexander, Pam, 414
Allen, Michael, 96
Amabile, Teresa M., 456
Argyris, Chris, 38, 42–43
Ariss, Don, 441
Armacost, Samuel, 448
Athos, Anthony G., 48
Austin, James A., 112
Avolio, Bruce, 328

B

Babiec, Joseph, 359
Bachand, Stephen, 221
Balsillie, Jim, 5
Bamesberger, Ann, 424
Banks, Jordan, 94
Barnard, Chester, 44–45, 314
Barnevik, Percy, 116
Baron, James, 285
Barron, James, 367
Barry, Megan, 64
Bass, Bernard, 324
Beer, Michael, 442
Bélanger, Brigitte, 267
Bensadoun, Aldo, 55
Bérard, Jocelyn, 337
Bezos, Jeff, 354
Biles, Peter, 113
Black, D. Grant, 150
Blake, Robert, 317
Bogomolny, Laura, 202
Boyer, Herb, 335
Brabeck-Letmathe, Peter, 262
Bragg, John, 221
Branson, Richard, 137
Bretón, Magdalena Opazo, 401
Brin, Sergey, 31
Budman, Michael, 363
Burke, James, 446
Burns, James MacGregor, 324
Burns, Tom, 265

C

Callaway, Ely, 405
Campbell, Glenn, 140
Carroll, Archie, 71
Cascioli, Teresa, 138
Case, Stephen M., 109
Castaldo, Joe, 338
Chamandy, Glenn, 107
Chambers, John, 113, 162, 384, 443
Chandler, Alfred, Jr., 269
Clemons, Mike "Pinball," 350
Clifford, Paul, 431
Cobb, Liz, 150
Cohen, Herman, 66
Conger, Jay, 416
Connolly, Agnes, 66
Cornell, Camilla, 244
Covey, Stephen R., 185
Cox, Ed, 363

Crandall, Robert, 64
Crosby, Philip, 91
Currie, Teri, 286
Curtis, Terry, 422
Cutler, Allan, 66

D

Daniel, Pat, 325
Davidson, Terry, 424
Davis, Keith, 70
De Haas, Joris, 373
de Hoyos, Ignacio Urrutia, 401
DeVault, Rich, 361
Dell, Michael, 89, 232
Deming, W. Edward, 91
Demming, Edward, 46
DePree, Max, 6
Disney, Walt, 456
Djukastein, Eric, 423
Dodd, Graham, 337
Donaldson, Thomas, 60
Donovan, Denis, 287
Drucker, Peter, 50, 162, 175, 211, 215, 218, 237, 327, 445, 447
Duane, R., 444
Dunbar, Robin, 211
DuPont, Bonnie, 312

E

Einstein, Albert, 443
El Akkad, Omar, 114
England, Dean, 163
Entwistle, Daren, 416
Estey, Ron, 383
Etzioni, Amitai, 186
Evans, Peter, 286

F

Falconer, Bill, 368
Fayol, Henri, 35–36
Fehr, Ralph, 452
Fiedler, Fred, 318–320
Filvaroff, Ellen, 335
Fisher, Roger, 433
Follett, Mary Parker, 35
Ford, Henry, 33, 213
Forzani, John, 366
Friedman, Milton, 69
Fritz, Justine, 16
Fry, Art, 446
Fung, Joseph, 135

G

Gallup, Patricia, 422
Gardner, John, 49, 328
George, Bill, 15
Gerstner, Louis V., Jr., 85
Gilbreth, Frank and Lillian, 34
Godbehere, Ann, 419
Godsoe, Peter, 318
Goizueta, Roberto, 167, 293
Goleman, Daniel, 23, 325
Graham, Lawrence Otis, 285
Gray, John, 167, 202
Green, Don, 363

Greiner, Larry, 271
Grove, Andy, 384
Guenette, Rob, 211

H

Hackman, J. Richard, 371
Haeckel, Stephen, 213
Hahn, David, 455
Hall, Edward T., 121
Hallett, Bill, 395
Hamel, Gary, 182, 445
Hammer, Michael, 216, 276
Handley, Nancy, 196
Handy, Charles, 9, 300
Harary, Ronnen, 174
Hays, Matthew, 267
Hendry, Bob, 122
Harrington, Ann, 47
Herzberg, Frederick, 342, 371
Hitt, Michael, 444
Hock, Dee, 266
Hofstede, Geert, 122, 127–128
Holmes, Deborah K., 19, 20
Hopper, Grace, 310
Horton, Tim, 138
House, Robert, 321
Howard, Philip, 181
Huizenga, H. Wayne, 137
Hunchak, Gord, 441
Hunt, James G., 399

J

Jackson, Sean, 441
Janis, Irving, 402
Jaques, Elliott, 188
Jobs, Steven, 13
Johnson, Robert, 265
Johnson, William R., 243
Johnston, Larry, 121
Jones, Dave, 66
Joyce, Ron, 138
Jung, Carl, 365
Juran, Joseph, 46, 85

K

Kamenetz, Anya, 429
Kanter, Rosabeth Moss, 109, 266, 326
Kantrow, Alan, 359
Kase, Kimio, 401
Katz, Robert L., 22
Kellner, Peter, 96
Kelly, Maureen, 167
Kelly, Patrick, 337
Khosa, Veronica, 72
Kielburger, Marc, 74
Kirkpatrick, Shelley, 316
Knight, Charles, 428
Knowles, Ron, 454
Kochan, Thomas, 97
Konefal, Alicia, 135
Kotter, John, 21, 230, 414–415
Kouzes, Jim, 316
Krasner, James D., 149
Kreps, David, 285
Kunkel, Sonya, 427

L

LaFasto, Frank, 407
Laliberté, Guy, 267
Larson, Carl, 407
Laskawy, Philip A., 19
Lauper, Simone, 419
Lavoie, Paul, 211
Lawler, Edward, 352
Lawrence, Paul, 274
Lee, Leonard, 291
Lee, Mark, 350
Levinson, Art, 335
Levinson, Sara, 326
Lewin, Kurt, 454
Lewis, Richard, 128
Likert, Rensis, 388
Locke, Edwin, 316
Locke, John, 59
Lorsch, Jay, 274
Losey, Michael R., 101–102
Luthans, Fred, 328

M

Machiavelli, Niccolo, 364
Magnis, Ellen, 413
Mandela, Nelson, 113
Marion, Dean, 413
Marsden, Lorna, 427
Martin, Justin, 36
Martin, Paula, 423
Martinez, Angel, 448
Maslow, Abraham, 40–41, 339
Matthews, Jana, 57
Mayberry, John, 283
Mayo, Elton, 39
McClearn, Matther, 450
McClelland, David, 341
McEwen, Rob, 310
McGregor, Douglas, 38, 196
McGuire, Elizabeth, 432
McKinnell, Henry "Hank," 125
Meisinger, Susan, 288
Michael, Natalie, 406
Mill, John Stuart, 58
Milton, Robert, 184
Mintzberg, Henry, 15, 20, 21, 230, 238, 414
Mirvish, Ed, 142
Molander, Scott, 140
Molinaro, Kerri, 6
Moncer, Jason, 449
Mouton, Jane, 317

N

Nardelli, Robert, 287
Newsham, Margaret, 66
Nitsch, Judith, 187
Nixon, Gord, 449
Nohria, Nitin, 442
Norris, Gary, 114

O

Ogilvie, Robert, 251
Ohmae, Kenichi, 7, 128

Oland, Derek, 315
Oldham, Greg R., 372
Olijnyk, Zena, 125, 221, 338
O'Reilly, Charles, 360
Osborn, Richard N., 399
Ouchi, William, 48
Ouimet, J. Robert, 309
Ozzie, Ray, 445

P

Page, Larry, 31
Park, Darcie, 315
Pascale, Richard Tanner, 48
Patchell-Evans, David, 327
Patten, Rose M., 313
Peters, Susan, 301
Peters, Tom, 10, 47, 420, 443
Pfeffer, Jeffrey, 14, 285, 360
Pitts, Gordon, 419
Plante, Janet, 425
Platt, Lewis, 186
Plourde, Réal, 202
Pooley, Erin, 327, 338
Porter, Michael, 214, 219, 220, 226
Posner, Barry, 316
Pratt, Dale, 390
Putnam, Howard, 64

Q

Quinn, James Brian, 229

R

Rabie, Anton, 174
Reich, Robert, 11, 84, 284, 462
Reisman, Heather, 138, 157
Richardson, H. Smith, Jr., 413
Ritchie, Cedric, 318
Roddick, Anita, 63
Rodgers, T. J., 182
Rokeach, Milton, 58
Rosenberg, David, 109
Rosener, Judith, 8
Ross, Richard, 450
Rothwell, J. D., 386
Rottenberg, Linda, 96

S

Sabia, Michael, 67
Saint-Onge, Hubert, 444
Sales, Wayne, 221
Samuelson, Paul, 70
Sanchís, Carlos Martí, 401
Sanford, Jeff, 449
Sanford, Linda, 195
Schein, Edgar, 93, 400
Schermerhorn, John R., Jr., 399
Schultz, Howard, 338
Senge, Peter, 49, 176, 443
Shaughnessy, Susan, 374
Sheppard, Susan, 64
Shulgan, Chris, 372
Simon, Rafael, 42
Sherman, Deborah, 353
Skinner, B. F., 348

Skoll, Jeff, 372
Smith, Adam, 33
Sobey, Frank, 138
Soignet, Michel, 149
Sood, Stephanie Curtis, 300
Sorenson, Ralph, 50
Stalker, George, 274
Stam, Jim, 457
Steinway, Henry Engelhard, 367
Strauss, Marina, 6
Stronach, Frank, 137
Stymiest, Barbara, 449
Swanson, Bob, 335

T

Taylor, Andy, 273
Taylor, Frederick W., 33–35
Taylor, Jack, 273
Terkel, Studs, 363
Thomas, Dave, 138
Thomas, R. Roosevelt, Jr., 96, 100, 101, 286
Thomson, Sarah, 99
Thorndike, E. L., 347
Toffler, Alvin, 158
Trompenaars, Fons, 124–125
Turner, Susan, 377
Tutu, Desmond, 57

U

Ury, William, 433

V

Vang, Cindy, 369
Varadi, Ben, 174
Veiga, John F., 14, 285
Verschuren, Annette, 99
Vroom, Victor, 322, 345

W

Wada, Yoshihiro, 417
Wahl, Andrew, 42, 160, 167, 202, 338
Watanabe, Katsuaki, 115
Waterman, Robert, 47
Waugh, Richard, 318
Weber, Max, 37, 265
Weick, Karl, 203
Welch, Jack, 450, 455
Whitman, Meg, 229
Whitney, John, 352
Willet, Robert, 126
Williams, Natalia, 324
Williams, Scott, 144
Winters, Carole Clay, 172
Woodward, Joan, 270
Wren, Daniel, 33

Z

Zapanta, Albert C., 144
Zolli, Andrew, 429
Zimmer, George, 336

Subject Index

A

Ability stereotypes, 427
Above-average returns, 214
Absenteeism, 366
Acceptance theory of authority, 314
Accommodation, 430
Accommodative strategy, 72
Accountability, 16
ACE, 135
Achievement-oriented leadership, 321
Achievement vs. prescription, 124
Acquired needs theory, 341–342
Action research, 459
Active listening, 420–421
Adaptive organizations, 267
Adaptive strategies, 229
Adjourning stage, 395–396
Administration Industrielle et Générale (Fayol), 35–36
Administrative principles, 35–36
Administrator, 16
Advancing action, 101
Advancing Canadian Entrepreneurship (ACE), 135
Advisory authority, 256
Aetna Life & Casualty Company, 277
Africa, 112–113
After-action review, 193
Age of Unreason, The (Handy), 300
Age stereotypes, 427
Agile manufacturing, 92
Agreeableness, 363
AI, 163
Air Canada, 184
Alberta Public Interest Research Group (APIRG), 401
ALDO shoes, 55
Alimentation Couche-Tard, 202
All-channel communication network, 399
Alternative dispute resolution, 435
Alternative work arrangements, 374–377
Americas, 110–111
Analyzer strategy, 299
Anchoring and adjustment heuristic, 173
Andean Pact, 111
Angel investor, 149
Apple Computer, 13, 117, 151, 446
Application form, 294
Arbitration, 434–435
Area structure, 243
Argyris's theory of adult personality, 42–43
Art of Japanese Management, The (Pascale/Athos), 48
Arthur Andersen, 9, 57, 64
Artificial intelligence (AI), 163
Asea Brown Boveri (ABB), 117
Asia/Pacific Rim, 111–112
Assertiveness, 430
Assessing, 445
Assessment centre, 294–295

Athena Sustainable Materials Institute, 251
Attitude, 365
Attractive industry, 220
Attribution error, 426
Attribution theory, 426
Authentic leadership, 328
Authoritarianism, 364
Authority-and-responsibility principle, 254
Authority decision, 322
Autocratic style, 318
Autodesk, 297
Automation, 369
Autonomous work groups, 390
Autonomy, 371
Availability heuristics, 173
Avoidance, 430
A&W Food Services, 188

B

Background checks, 295
Backward vertical integration, 222
Bafflegab, 417
Ballard Power Systems, 7
Bank of Nova Scotia, 9
Barenaked Ladies, 58
Bargaining zone, 433
Barrick Gold, 117
BARS, 298–299
Base compensation, 301–302
Bata Shoes 110
BATNA, 433
Baytech Plastics, 337–338
B2B business strategy, 224–225
B2B e-commerce, 143, 159
B.C. Ferries, 455
B.C. Hydro, 465
B2C business strategy, 224–225
B2C e-commerce, 159
BCG matrix, 228
Behavioural decision model, 171,
Behavioural management approaches, 38–43
Behaviourally anchored rating scale (BARS), 298–299
Bell Canada, 161
Bell Canada Enterprises (BCE), 67
Benchmarking, 191
Best alternative to a negotiated agreement (BATNA), 433
Best practices, 191
BET Holdings II, Inc., 265
Beyond Race and Gender (Thomas), 96
Beyond Reengineering (Hammer), 276
Biculturalism, 100
Big Five personality traits, 363–364
Birth stage, 146, 271
Blast Radius, 406
BMO Financial Group, 83, 194
Board of directors, 231
Body Shop, 63
Bombardier, 248

Bona fide occupational requirements, 289
Bonus pay, 353
Borderless World, The (Ohmae), 128
Botswana, 113
Bottom-up change, 449
Boundaryless organization, 250–251
Brainstorming, 403
Bre-X, 9, 56
Break-even analysis, 200–201
Break-even point, 200, 201
Breakfast cereals market, 215
Breakthrough stage, 146
British Airways (BA), 120
British Columbia Ferry Services, 455
Budgets, 189
Bureaucracy, 37, 264–265
Bureaucratic organization, 37–38
Business incubation, 151
Business incubator, 151
Business plan, 147–148
Business strategy, 220, 221
Business-to-business e-commerce, 159
Business-to-consumer e-commerce, 159

C

Cafeteria benefits, 302
Callaway Golf, 405
Caltex, 126
Campbell Soup, 189, 297
Canadarm, 446
Canadian Airlines, 354
Canadian Council of Human Resources Associates (CCHRA), 287
Canadian Human Rights Act, 8, 290
Canadian Red Cross Society, 148, 217
Canadian Securities Administrators (CSA), 64
Canadian Tire, 221, 435
Canon, 373
Career, 300
Career development, 300–301
Career path, 300
Career planning, 300, 460
Career plateau, 300–301
Careers, 9–10
CARICOM, 111
Cash cows, 228
CCI Thermal Technologies, 221
Celebrity entrepreneurs, 137–138
Center for Creative Leadership, 298, 413
Centralization, 255
Centralized communication network, 399
Certain environment, 167, 268
Chain communication network, 399
Chain of command, 252
Challenger shuttle disaster, 403
Change. *See* organizational change
Change agent, 448
Change leaders, 448
Change strategies, 454–456
Changing, 453

Changing nature of managerial work, 17–18
Channel richness, 422,
Chapters-Indigo, 157
Charismatic leader, 323–324
Chat rooms, 422
Chemical Bank, 65
Chevron-Texaco, 126
Chief knowledge officer (CKO), 175
Child labour, 119
China, 111, 116
CIBC, 73, 444
Circle of Innovation, The (Peters), 443
Cirque du Soleil, 267
City of Grande Prairie, 391–392
Classical decision model, 171
Classical management approaches, 33–38
Classical view of social responsibility, 69
Co-operative strategies, 224
Co-operativeness, 430
Coaching, 297
Coca-Cola, 37,47, 167, 190, 213, 222,
Code of ethics, 67
Coercion, 457
Coercive power, 312–313
Cognitive dissonance, 366
Cognos, 181
Cohesiveness, 397
Collaboration, 430, 431
Collective bargaining, 303
Commercializing innovation, 445
Committee, 388–389
Communication, 415–425
    barriers, 417–420
    channel, 416, 417
    consultants, 423
    credibility, 416
    cultural challenges, 425
    defined, 415
    diversity, 425
    effective/efficient, 415–416
    feedback, 421
    interactive management, 422–423
    listening, 420–421
    networks, 399–400
    persuasion, 416
    process, 415
    proxemics, 423–424
    space design, 423–424
    technology utilization, 424
"Company of the Future, The" (Reich), 11
Comparable worth, 290, 345
Comparative management, 125
Compensation and benefits, 301–302
Competing objectives, 429
Competition, 430, 431
Competitive advantage, 84–85, 213
Compressed workweek, 374–375
Compromise, 430, 431
Computer-mediated group, 390

Computer-mediated meetings, 422
Concentration, 222
Conceptual skill, 23
Concurrent controls, 196
Conflict, 428–432
Conflict management styles, 430–432
Conflict of interest, 61
Conflict resolution, 430
Confrontation meeting, 461
Confucian values, 128
Conscientiousness, 363
Constructive conflict, 427
Constructive stress, 463
Consultative decision, 321
Consumer protection, 71
Content theories of motivation, 339–343
Contingency approaches to leadership,
    318–323
Contingency planning, 191
Contingency thinking, 45–46
Contingency workers, 377
Continuous improvement, 92
Continuous-process production, 270
Continuous reinforcement schedule, 349
Control equation, 195
Control process, 193–194
Controlling, 20, 193–204
    break-even analysis, 200–201
    defined, 193
    employee discipline, 199
    importance, 193
    information and financial controls,
        199–200
    internal vs. external control, 197
    MBO, 197–199
    operations management and control,
        201–203
    organizational control, 197–204
    planning, and, 185
    steps in process, 193–194
    types of controls, 195–197
    unexpected events, 203–204
C.O.R.E. Digital Pictures, 383
Core characteristics model, 371–373
Core competency, 218–219
Core culture, 95
Core values, 95, 217
Corning, 353
Corporate culture, 93–96
Corporate governance, 9, 76–77, 231
Corporate portals, 164
Corporate social responsibility, 67–74
    classical view, 69
    corporate governance, 76–77
    defined, 67
    evaluating performance, 71–72
    social entrepreneurship, 72–74
    social responsibility strategies, 71–72
    socio-economic view, 70
    stakeholder issues and analysis, 68–69

Corporate strategy, 221, 227, 228
Corporation, 148
Corruption, 119
Corruption of Foreign Public Officials Act,
    119
Cost-benefit analysis, 170
Cost leadership strategy, 227
Cott Corporation, 138
C.R. England, 163
"Creating High Quality Health Care
    Workplace," 361
Creativity, 444–445
Credibility, 416
Crisis, 166
Crisis management, 166
Crisis management plans, 166
Crisis management teams, 166
Critical-incident techniques, 24, 299
Critical thinking, 232
Cross-functional teams, 247, 389
Cultural awareness, 128
Cultural diversity, 124–126
Cultural relativism, 59
Culture, 120
Culture shock, 120
Culture's Consequences: International
    Differences in Work-Related Values
    (Hofstede), 122
Currency risk, 126
Current ration, 200
Customer confidence, 61
Customer-driven organizations, 88–90
Customer relations management (CRM),
    90, 160
Customer structure, 244
Customer wants, 89–90
Customers, 89
Cycle time, 92

D
DaimlerChrysler, 117
Data, 161
Davco Machine Ltd., 425
DBG Canada Limited, 263
Debate, 428
Debt financing, 148
Debt ratio, 200
Decentralization, 255
Decentralization with centralization, 255
Decentralized communication network, 399
Decima Research, 184
Decision, 165
Decision by authority rule, 400
Decision by consensus, 400
Decision by lack of response, 400
Decision by majority rule, 400
Decision by minority rule, 400
Decision by unanimity, 401

Decision environments, 167–168
Decision making, 165–167, 400
    decision environments, 167–168
    errors/traps, 173
    ethics, 175
    heuristics, 173
    individual vs. group, 174–175,
        400–404
    knowledge management, 175
    organizational learning, 175
    problem-solving styles, 168
    steps in process, 169–172
    teams, 400–404
    types of decisions, 165–166
Decision-making process, 169–172
Decision support system (DSS), 163
Decisional roles, 20
Defender strategy, 229
Defensive strategy, 72
Deficit principle, 40, 339
Delegating style, 320
Delegation, 254
Dell Computer, 89, 224–225, 232
Delta Hotel, 431
Deming Prize, 91–92
Deming's "14 points of equality," 92
Democratic style, 318
Departmentalization, 241
Design. *See* Organizational design
Design for disassembly, 92
Design for manufacturing, 92
Designing, 445
Destructive conflict, 428
Destructive stress, 463
Differentiation, 274
Differentiation strategy, 226
Direct investment strategies, 115
Directive leadership, 321
Discipline, 189
Discrimination, 8, 61, 288–289
Disney, 95
Disney World Resort, 296
Dispute resolution, 434–435
Distress, 463
Distribution alliances, 224
Distributive justice, 59
Distributive negotiation, 432
Diversification, 222
Diversity, 96. *See also* Workplace diversity
Diversity maturity, 101
Diversity rationale, 286
Diversity trends in socio-cultural
    environment, 86
Divestiture, 223
Divisional structure, 242–244
Dofasco, 283
Dogs, 228
Downsizing, 223, 272
Drucker's "old-fashioned" leadership, 327

DSS, 163
Dunbar's Number, 211
DuPont Canada, 69
*Dynamic Administration: The Collected
    Papers of Mary Parker Follett*, 37
Dysfunctional conflict, 427

E
E-business strategies, 224
E-commerce, 159
E-tailing, 224–225
EAP, 302
eBay, 229
eBay Canada, 94
Economic order quantity (EOQ), 202
EDI, 164
Edward Jones, 238–239
Effective communication, 415
Effective team, 392
Efficient communication, 415
EI, 325–326
80/20 rule, 46
Electronic commerce, 159
Electronic data interchange (EDI), 164
Electronic grapevine, 424
Electronic group network, 390
EllisDon Corp., 188
Email workload, 424
Emergent strategy, 230
Emotional conflict, 428
Emotional intelligence, 23
Emotional intelligence (EI), 325
Emotional stability, 363
Employee. *See* Human resource manage-
    ment (HRM)
Employee advisory council, 423
Employee assistance program (EAP), 302
Employee benefits, 301–302
Employee discipline, 199
Employee group, 422
Employee involvement teams, 389
Employee orientation, 296
Employee stock ownership, 354
Employment discrimination, 288–289
Employment equity, 288–289
Employment Equity Act, 75, 287–288
Employment interview, 290, 294
Employment tests, 294–295
Empowerment, 255, 314–315
En Cana, 117
Enbridge International, 117, 329
Endeavor Global, 96
Engineering comparison, 195
Enron, 9, 56, 64
Enterprise portals, 164
Enterprise Rent-a-Car, 273
Entrepreneur, 137
Entrepreneurship, 137
Entrepreneurship and small business,

142–152
    business incubation, 151
    business plan, 147–148
    celebrity entrepreneurs, 136–137
    characteristics of entrepreneurs,
        139–140
    diversity and entrepreneurship, 140–141
    failure—small business, 145
    family business, 143–144
    financing new ventures, 148–150
    form of ownership, 148
    international business entrepreneurship,
        143
    Internet and entrepreneurship, 142–143
    large enterprises and entrepreneurship,
        150–151
    myths, 141
    new venture creation, 146–150
    SBDCs, 151–152
Environment and competitive advantage,
    84–88
Environment of hypercompetition, 215
Environmental concern, 88
Environmental protection, 75, 111,119
Environmental Protection Act, 75
Environmental uncertainty, 88
EOQ, 202
Equity financing, 149
Equity theory, 343–345
ERG theory, 340, 372
Ernst & Young, 19
Escalating commitment, 173
Escalation trap, 174
ESOP, 354
Essential managerial skills, 22–23
Esteem needs, 41, 340
Ethical dilemma, 61
Ethical imperialism, 59
Ethical leadership, 327–328
Ethics, 8–9, 56–67. *See also* Corporate
   social responsibility
    alternative views of, 58–59
    checklist (ethical dilemmas), 65
    cultural issues, 59–60
    decision making, 175
    defined, 8–9, 57
    ethical behaviour, 57–58
    ethical codes, 67
    ethical role models, 66
    factors to consider, 62–64
    leadership, 327–328
    multinational corporations, 117–119
    negotiation, 435
    power, 314
    rationalization for unethical behaviour,
        61–62
    reinforcement, 350
    training, 65
    whistle-blower protection, 66

workplace ethical dilemmas, 61
Ethics advocate, 66
Ethics training, 65
Ethnic cultures, 98
Ethnocentric attitudes, 128
Ethnocentric view, 223
Ethnocentrism, 98, 120, 425
EU, 110
Euro, 110
Europe, 110
European Union (EU), 110
Eustress, 463
Evolution of Management Thought, The (Wren), 33
Executive briefing, 418
Existence needs, 340
Expatriate, 127
Expectancy, 345
Expectancy theory, 345–346
Experimenting, 445
Expert power, 313
Expert systems, 163
Exporting, 115
External control, 197
External customers, 89
External recruitment, 292–293
Extinction, 348
Extranet, 164
Extrinsic reward, 337
Extroversion, 363
Exxon, 117

F
Facilities plans, 189
Failures of process, 230
Failures of substance, 230
Fair labour practices, 75
Family business, 143–144
Family business feud, 144
Family-friendly benefits, 302
Fast-food industry, 215
Fayol's 14 principles of management, 36–37
Feedback, 421
Feedback controls, 196
Feedback from the job itself, 371
Feedforward controls, 196
Fielder's contingency model, 318–320
Fifth Discipline, The (Senge), 48–49
Filtering, 420
Financial plans, 189
Financial ratios, 200
Financing new venture, 148–149
First-line managers, 15–16
First-mover advantage, 146
Fixed budget, 189
Flat structure, 253–254
Flexible benefits, 302
Flexible budget, 189
Flexible manufacturing, 92

Flexible working hours, 375
Flexiplace, 376
Flexitime, 375
*flex*Space, 161
Flextime, 375
Flight Centre, 352
Focused cost leadership strategy, 227
Focused differentiation strategy, 227
Force-coercion strategy, 454–455
Forced distribution, 299
Forcing strategy, 454
Ford, 7, 242
Forecasting, 190
Foreign subsidiary, 115
Formal group, 388
Formal presentation, 418
Formal structure, 240
Forming stage, 394
Forward vertical integration, 222
Forzani Group, 366
Founding story, 96
4–40 schedule, 374
Four Seasons Hotel, 39
Framing error, 173
Franchise, 142
Franchising, 115
Free Trade Area of the Americas (FTAA), 111
Freybe Gourmet Foods, 354
Friendship groups, 388
Fiedler's contingency model, 318–319
Fringe benefits, 302
Frustration-regression principle, 340
FTAA, 111
Functional authority, 256
Functional chimneys problem, 242
Functional conflict, 428
Functional managers, 16
Functional strategy, 216
Functional structure, 241–242
Functional subcultures, 98
Functions of management, 18–21
Functions of the Executive (Barnard), 44
Future of Success, The (Reich), 84, 284, 462

G
Gain sharing, 354
Gap Inc., 67
GDSS, 163
GE Medical Systems, 291
Gender equity, 344–345
Gender subcultures, 98
General Electric, 15, 117, 221, 250, 311, 450, 455
General environment, 85–86
General managers, 16
General Motors, 122
General partnership, 148
Generational gaps, 98

Generational subcultures, 98
Genentech, 335
Geocentric attitudes, 128
Geocentric view, 223
Geographical structure, 243
Getting to Yes (Fisher/Ury), 433
Ghana, 112
Gildan Activewear Inc., 107
Glass ceiling, 99, 141, 427
Glass ceiling effect, 8
Global area structure, 126
Global awareness, 48
Global dimensions of management, 108–129
    Africa, 112–113
    Americas, 110–111
    Asia/Pacific Rim, 111–112
    complications, 116–117
    contracts and agreements, 122
    controlling, 126
    cultural diversity, 120–125
    direct investment strategies, 115
    entrepreneurship, 143
    ethical issues, 119
    Europe, 110
    global organizational learning, 128–129
    home-country issues, 118–119
    host-country issues, 118
    international management, 109–110
    interpersonal space, 121
    language, 121
    management theories, 127–128
    market entry strategies, 114–115
    multinational corporation (MNC), 117–119
    organizing, 126–127
    planning, 126
    religion, 122
    staffing, 127
    time orientation, 121
    universal values, 60
    values and national cultures, 122
    why companies go international, 113–114
Global economy, 109
Global manager, 109, 125–126
Global organizational learning, 128–129
Global product structure, 121
Global sourcing, 114
Global strategies, 223
Globalive Communications, 200
Globalization, 7, 109
Globalization strategy, 223
Goal displacement, 231
Goal-setting theory, 346–347
Goldcorp Inc., 310
Golder Associates, 225
GoodLife Fitness Clubs, 327
Google, 31
Government influence, 74–76

Grameen Bank, 445
Graphic rating scale, 298
Great person theory, 316
Greenfield ventures, 115
Groove Networks, 445
Group decision, 321
Group decision making, 174–175
Group decision support systems (GDSS), 163
Group process, 393
Groupe Germain, 264
Groupthink, 402–403
Groupware, 163
Growth and diversification strategies, 222
Growth needs, 340
Growth-need strength, 372
Growth strategy, 222
Gulf Canada, 406

H
Halo effect, 427
Hannah's Ice Cream, 149
Hat World, 140
Hawthorne effect, 40
Hawthorne studies, 39–40
Hayes Forest Services, 268–269
Hazardous Product Act, 75
Heart and Stroke Foundation of Ontario, 191
Heroes, 94
Hersey-Blanchard situational leadership model, 320–321
Herzberg's two-factor theory, 340–341
Heuristics, 173
Hierarchy of needs theory, 40–41, 339–340
Hierarchy of objectives, 185
High-context cultures, 121
Higher-order needs, 339
Highly reliable organization (HRO), 203
Hilton Hotel, 431
Hino Motors Ltd., 114
Historical comparison, 195
Home-country issues, 118–119
Home Depot, 69, 73, 287
Home Depot Canada, 99
Honda, 86, 94, 108
Honest Ed's, 142
Horizontal loading, 370
Horizontal structure, 246
Host-country issues, 118
Hotelling, 376
House's path-goal leadership theory, 321–323
HRM. See Human resource management (HRM)
HRO, 203
HRPAO, 287, 288
Hubbell Canada, 389
Human capital, 285
Human Equation: Building Profits by Putting People First, The (Pfeffer), 285

Human relations movement, 40
Human resource management (HRM), 284–304
    career development, 300–301
    compensation and benefits, 301–302
    defined, 287
    discrimination, 288–289
    diversity advantage, 285
    labour-management relations, 303–304
    legal issues, 289–291
    organizational design, 273–274
    orientation, 296
    performance appraisal, 298–300
    planning, 291–292
    recruiting process, 292–293
    retention and turnover, 302–303
    selection process, 293–296
    strategic, 287–288
    training and development, 296–297
    work-life balance, 301
Human resource management process, 287
Human resource plans, 189
Human resources management, 287–288
Human Resources Professional Association of Ontario (HRPAO), 287, 288
Human Side of Enterprise, The (McGregor), 41
Human skill, 23
Husky Injection Molding, 69
Hygiene factor, 340
Hyundai, 111

I
IBM, 7, 195, 273, 424
IBM Canada, 377
Idea generators, 447
IKEA, 6
Imagining, 445
Imperial Oil, 271
Importing, 115
Improvement objectives, 198
In Search of Excellence: Lessons from America's Best-Run Companies (Peters/Waterman), 47
Inco, 316
Incremental change, 451
Incremental planning, 186–187
Incrementalism, 186, 229
Independent contractors, 290–291
India, 111
Indigo Books & Music, 138
Individual behaviour and performance, 360–378
    alternative work arrangements, 374–377
    core characteristics model, 371–373
    individual performance, 367–368
    job design, 369
    job enlargement, 370

    job enrichment, 370–371
    job rotation, 370
    job satisfaction, 366
    OB, 361
    personality traits, 363–365
    psychological contract, 362
    quality of work life (QWL), 362
    scientific management, 369
    work attitude, 365–367
Individual performance, 367–368
Individual performance equation, 367–368
Individual vs. group decision making, 174–175
Individual with flexibility, 185
Individual with focus, 185
Individualism-collectivism, 122
Individualism view, 58
Individualism vs. collectivism, 124
Industry/environment analysis, 219–220
Influence, 314
Info-Tech Research Group, 376
Infocheck Ltd., 295
Infomediary model, 224
Informal group, 388
Informal network integration, 97
Informal structure, 240–241
Information, 161
Information and financial controls, 199–210
Information filtering, 420
Information gatekeepers, 447
Information systems, 163
Information technology (IT), 158–161
Informational roles, 20, 21
Initial public offering (IPO), 149
Initiative, 344
Inmet Mining, 450
Inner-directed culture, 125
Innovation, 445
Innovation leaders, 447
Input standard, 194
Instant messaging, 161
Instrumental values, 58
Instrumentality, 345
Integrated change leadership, 450
Integrated model of motivation, 351
Integration, 275
Integrative agreements, 433
Integrative negotiation, 432
Integrity, 328
Intel, 247, 424
Intellectual capital, 6, 159
Intelligence information, 162
Intensive technology, 270
Interactional justice, 59
Interactive management, 422–423
Interbrew SA, 124
Interest groups, 388
Intergroup team building, 461
Intermediate-range plans, 187

Intermittent reinforcement schedule, 349
Internal control, 197
Internal customers, 89
Internal recruitment, 292–293
International business, 113. *See* Global
    dimensions of management
International business entrepreneurship, 143
International joint ventures, 115, 224
International management, 109–110
Internet and entrepreneurship, 142–143
Internet time, 188
Interpersonal roles, 20
Interpersonal skills, 414–435
    communication, 415–425. *See also*
    Communication
    conflict, 428–432
    negotiation, 432–435
    perception process, 425–428
    personal management, 417
Interpersonal space, 121
Interview, 294
Intranet, 164
Intrapreneurship, 151, 272
Intrinsic reward, 338
Intuitive-feeler, 364
Intuitive-thinker, 364
Intuitive thinking, 168
Inventory, 202
Inventory control, 202
Inventory turnover, 200
IPO, 149
ISO certification, 90
ISO 14000, 119
IT, 159–161

J
Jaguar, 242
Japan, 115
JIT systems, 202
Job, 369
Job analysis, 291
Job burnout, 463
Job description, 291–292
Job design, 369
Job discrimination, 100
Job enlargement, 370
Job enrichment, 370–371
Job enrichment checklist, 370
Job interview, 290
Job involvement, 367
Job performance, 367
Job redesign, 460
Job rotation, 370
Job satisfaction, 366
Job sharing, 375
Job simplification, 369
Job specification, 292
Johari Window, 21
Johnson & Johnson, 9, 31, 446

Johnson Controls, 449
Joint venture, 115
Just-in-time scheduling (JIT), 202
Justice view, 59

K
Kickbacks, 61
Kimberly-Clark, 354
Knowledge management, 175
Knowledge sharing, 250–251
Knowledge worker, 6, 159
KPMG, 261

L
Labour contract, 303
Labour-management relations, 303–304
Labour union, 303
Lack of participation error, 172, 230
Laissez-faire style, 318
Lakeport Brewing Income Fund, 324
Lakeport Brewing Limited Partnership, 138
Language, 121
Language metaphors, 95
Law of contingent reinforcement, 349
Law of effect, 347
Law of immediate reinforcement, 349
Leadership, 311, 316–329
    behaviours, 316–317
    Grid, 317
    style, 317–318
    traits, 316–317
Leading, 19–20, 310–329
    contingency approaches to leadership,
        318–323
    Drucker's "old-fashioned" leadership,
        327
    EI, 325–326
    empowerment, 314–315
    ethics, 314, 325
    Fiedler's contingency model, 318–320
    gender, 326
    Hersey-Blanchard situational leadership
        model, 320–321
    House's path-goal leadership theory,
        321–322
    influence, 314
    leadership behaviours, 316–317
    leadership style, 317
    leadership traits, 316–317
    moral leadership, 327–328
    power, 312–314
    strategic leadership, 443–444
    substitutes for leadership, 322
    teams, 407
    transactional leadership, 324
    transformational leadership, 323–325
    vision, 311–312
    Vroom-Jago leader-participation
        model, 322–323

Leading the Revolution (Hamel), 182
Lean production, 92
Learning organization, 48–49, 176, 267, 443
Learning style, 49
Least-preferred co-worker scale (LPC
    scale), 318
Lee Valley Tools, 291
Legitimate power, 313
Lewis Media, 135
Licensing agreement, 115
Lifelong learning, 22
Limited liability corporation (LLC), 148
Limited liability partnership, 148
Limited partnership, 148
Lincoln Electric, 353
Line managers, 16
Linear programming, 43
Liquidation, 222
Listening, 420–421
LLC, 148
Lobbying, 76
Locus of control, 364
Long-linked technology, 270
Long-range plans, 187–188
Lose-lose conflict, 431
Lotus, 273
Low-context cultures, 121
Lower-order needs, 339
LPC scale, 318
Lucent Technologies, 39

M
Machiavellianism, 364
Mackinnon Transport, 192
Magma Communications, 166
Magna International, 137
Maintenance activity, 398
Maintenance objectives, 198
Malaysia, 111
Management, 18–20
Management by exception, 195
Management approaches. *See* Management
    theory
Management by objectives (MBO),
    197–199, 346–47, 461
Management by wandering around
    (MBWA), 422–423
Management development, 297
Management information systems, 161
Management learning framework, 24–25
Management Learning Workbook, 25
Management practices and systems,
    230–231
Management process, 18–22
Management science, 43–44
Management theory, 32–50
    administrative principles, 35–36
    Argyris's theory of adult personality,
        42–43

behavioural management approaches, 38–43
bureaucratic organization, 37–38
classical management approaches, 33–38
contingency thinking, 45–46
continuing management themes, 46–50
Fayol, 35–36
Follett, 37
global awareness, 48–50
Hawthorne studies, 39–40
human relations movement, 40
learning organization, 48–49
management science, 43–44
Maslow's hierarchy of needs, 40–42
modern management approaches, 44–46
organizations as systems, 44–45
quality and performance excellence, 46–47
quantitative management approaches, 43–44
scientific management, 33–35
Theory X/Theory Y, 41–42
21st century leadership, 49–50
Management training, 460
Manager
    competencies, 23–24
    decision making. See Decision making
    defined, 15–16
    essential skills, 22–23
    global, 109
    information processors, as, 164–165
    levels of, 15–16
    required attributes, 49–50
    roles, 20–21
    teams, 404, 407
    types of, 16
Managerial activities and roles, 20–21
Managerial agendas and networking, 20–22
Managerial competency, 23–24
Managerial performance, 16–17
Managing diversity, 100–102
Manipulation and co-optation, 457
Maple Leaf Foods, 406
Maquiladoras, 111
Market entry strategies, 114–115
Market structure, 244
Marketing plans, 189
Mary Kay Cosmetics, 96
Mary Parker Follett–Prophet of Management: A Celebration of Writings from the 1920s, 32
Masculinity-femininity, 123
Maslow's hierarchy of needs, 40–41
Mass customization, 92
Mass production, 270
Mathematical forecasting, 43
Matrix organization, 244–245

Matrix structure, 244–245
Maturity stage, 146, 271
MBO, 197–198, 346–347, 461
MBWA, 422–423
McDonald's, 109, 115, 122, 196, 215
MDA, 446
Means-ends chain, 185
Mecca Cola, 190
Mechanistic design, 265–266
Mediating technology, 270
Mediation, 434
Medical/physical examination, 295
Medium-sized enterprises, 142
Medtronics, 11, 369
Meetings, 386–387
Mentoring, 297
Mercedes Benz, 36
Merchant model, 224
Merck, 86, 95, 217, 354
MERCOSUR, 111
Meridian Credit Union, 441
Merit pay, 351–352
Merrill Lynch Misery Index, 109
Mexico, 110
Microenterprises, 142
Microsoft, 100, 117, 148, 214
Mid-life stage, 271
Middle managers, 15
Miles and Snow adaptive model of strategy formulation, 229
Mindfulness, 204
Minorities, 98–99, 141
Mission, 216
Mission statement, 216
Mitsubishi, 117, 447
Mixed message, 418
MNOs, 117
Modelling, 297
Modern management approaches, 44–46
Monitor Company, 359
Monochronic cultures, 121
Monopoly environment, 214
Moose Deer Point First Nations Sustainable Community Project, 69
Moral leadership, 327–328
Moral quality circles, 66
Moral-rights view, 59
Most favoured nation status, 117
Motion studies, 34
Motivation, 335–354
    acquired needs theory, 341–342
    content theories, 339–343
    defined, 337
    equity theory, 343–345
    ERG theory, 340
    expectancy theory, 345–346
    goal-setting theory, 346–347
    hierarchy of needs theory, 339–340
    incentive compensation systems, 352–354

    integrated model of, 351
    pay for performance, 351–352
    process theories, 343–347
    reinforcement theory, 347–350
    rewards, 337–339
    two-factor theory, 340–341
Mountain Equipment Co-op (MEC), 70
Multi-tasking, 391
Multicultural organization, 97
Multiculturalism, 97
Multidimensional thinking, 168
Multidomestic strategy, 223
Multinational corporation (MNC), 117–119
Multinational organizations (MNOs), 117
Multiperson comparisons, 299
Myers-Briggs Type Indicator, 365

N
NAFTA, 110–111
National cultures, 98
Natura, 328
Nature of Managerial Work, The (Mintzberg), 20
Need, 40–41, 339
Need for achievement, 341
Need for affiliation, 341
Need for personal power, 342
Need for power, 341
Need for social power, 342
Negative reinforcement, 348
Negotiation, 432–435
Neptec, 446
Nestlé, 117, 262
Net margin, 200–201
Network models, 43
Network structure, 248–249
Networking, 313
Neutral vs. affective, 124
New venture creation, 146–150
Niagara Health Systems Foundation, 395
Nike, 119, 252
Nk'Mip Cellars, 150
No Easy Victories (Gardner), 49
Noise, 416, 417
Nokia, 292
Nominal group technique, 403
Nonprogrammed decisions, 166
Non-verbal communication, 418
Nordstrom, 95
Norm, 396
Normative re-educative strategy, 456
Norming stage, 395
NORPAC Controls, 217
Nortel Networks, 64, 161, 240, 370
North American Free Trade Agreement (NAFTA), 110–111
NTT DoCoMo, 117

O

OB, 361
Objectives, 183, 218
Observable culture, 94–95
Obstructionist strategy, 72
Occupational health and safety, 75
Occupational Health and Safety Act, 75
Occupational subcultures, 98
OD, 458–461
OD intervention, 460
Off-the-job training, 297
Oligopoly environment, 214
Ombudsperson, 435
On-the-job training, 297
Online discussion forums, 422
Open office hours, 422
Open system, 11, 45
Openness, 363
Operant conditioning, 348
Operating objectives, 218
Operational plan, 189
Operations management and control, 201–204
Operations research, 43
Opportunity situation, 195
Optimizing decision, 171
Oral presentation, 417
Organic design, 265, 266–267
Organization, *See also* Organizing
    bureaucratic, 40
    changing nature of, 13
    defined, 11
    government, and, 74–76
    open system, as, 11, 44–45
    performance measures, 12–14
    upside-down pyramid, as, 18
Organization chart, 240
Organization development (OD), 458–461
Organization structure, 239. *See also* Organizing
Organization with flexibility, 185
Organization with focus, 185
Organizational behaviour (OB), 40, 361
Organizational change, 448–458
    bottom-up change, 449
    change leaders, 448–449
    change strategies, 454–456
    forces/targets for change, 451–452
    incremental change, 451
    integrated change leadership, 450
    OD, 458–461
    phases of planned change, 452–453
    resistance to change, 456–457
    technological change, 457–458
    top-down change, 449
    transformational change, 450–451
Organizational commitment, 367
Organizational control, 197–204
Organizational culture, 93–96, 217

Organizational design, 262–278
    checklist, 268
    defined, 263
    environment, 268–269
    framework, 264
    human resources, 272–273
    life cycle, 270–272
    mechanistic design, 265–266
    organic design, 265, 266–267
    organizational effectiveness, 263–264
    size, 270
    strategy, 269–270
    subsystem differentiation, 274–275
    subsystem integration, 275
    technology, 270
    work process design, 276–278
Organizational design checklist, 268
Organizational design paradox, 275
Organizational ecology, 423
Organizational effectiveness, 263–264
Organizational flexibility, 263
Organizational learning, 175
Organizational life cycle, 270–272
Organizational performance, 12
Organizational resources/capabilities, 218–219
Organizational ritual, 94
Organizational size, 270
Organizational stakeholders, 68
Organizational subcultures, 97–98
Organizing, 19, 238–256
    boundaryless organization, 250–251
    chain of command, 252
    customer structure, 244
    decentralization with centralization, 255
    delegation, 254
    divisional structure, 242–244
    formal structure, 240
    functional structure, 241–242
    geographical structure, 243–244
    horizontal structure, 246
    informal structure, 240–242
    matrix structure, 244–245
    network structure, 248–249
    process structure, 244
    product structure, 243
    span of control, 253–254
    staffing, 256
    team structure, 247–248
    unity of command, 253
    virtual organization, 251
Oriental Brewery, 124
Orientation, 296
Ouimet-Cordon Bleu Foods, 309
Outer-directed culture, 125
Outplacement services, 303
Output standard, 194
Outsourcing, 248, 249

Outsourcing alliances, 224
Outward Bound, 406
Oxford Frozen Foods, 227

P

PAC, 76
Paired comparisons, 299
PAR, 100
Pareto Principle, 46
Part-time work, 377
Participant Productions, 372
Participating style, 320
Participative leadership, 321
Participatory planning, 192
Partnership, 148
Pay discrimination, 99
Pay for knowledge, 353
Peer appraisal, 299
Peer-to-peer file sharing, 161
Pelmorex Incorporated, 286
People, 6
PeopleSoft, 276
PepsiCo, 190, 222
Perception, 425
Perception process, 425–428
Performance appraisal, 298–300
Performance-contingent rewards, 338
Performance deficiency, 165
Performance effectiveness, 12
Performance efficiency, 12
Performance excellence, 46
Performance gap, 451
Performance management systems, 298
Performance measures, 12
Performance norm, 396
Performance opportunity, 165
Performing stage, 395
Permatemps, 291, 377
Person-job fit, 361
Personal character, 66
Personal development objectives, 198
Personal power, 313–314
Personal staff, 256
Personal wellness, 464
Personality, 363
Personality and Organization (Argyris), 42
Personality traits, 363–365
Persuasion, 416
Pfizer Canada, 293, 348
Philippines, 111
Physical examination, 295
Physiological needs, 41, 340
Plan, 183
Planned change, 451
Planning, 19, 183–193
    benchmarking, 191
    benefits of, 184–185
    budgets, 189–190
    contingency planning, 191

defined, 183
forecasting, 190
importance, 183
participation and involvement, 192
policies and procedures, 189
projects, 190
scenario planning, 191
short-range *vs.* long-range plans, 187–188
staff planners, 191–192
steps in process, 183–184
strategic and operational plans, 188–189
theories, 186–187
Planning process, 183–184
Planning theories, 186–187
Pluralism, 97
Polaroid Corporation, 248
Policy, 189
Political action committees (PAC), 76
Political risk, 126
Political-risk analysis, 126
Polycentric attitudes, 128
Polycentric view, 223
Polychronic cultures, 121
Pomerleau, 385
Pop!Tech, 429
Porter's five forces model, 219
Porter's generic strategies, 226–227
Portfolio planning, 227–228
Position power, 312–313
Positive reinforcement, 348, 348–349
Post-action controls, 196
Power, 312–314
Power distance, 122
P2P file sharing, 161
Pratt & Whitney Canada, 302
Prejudice, 8
Preliminary controls, 196
PricewaterhouseCoopers, 73, 251
Principles of Scientific Management, The (Taylor), 33
Principled negotiation, 432
Proactive strategy, 72
Probability, 168
Problem avoiders, 168
Problem seekers, 168
Problem situation, 195
Problem solvers, 168
Problem solving, 165
Problem-solving styles, 168, 364–365
Procedural justice, 59
Procedure, 189
Process consultation, 461
Process failure, 230
Process innovation, 445
Process re-engineering, 276
Process structure, 244
Process theories of motivation, 343–347

Process value analysis, 276–277
Procter & Gamble, 109, 223
Product champions, 447
Product design, 97
Product innovation, 445
Product structure, 243, 244
Production plans, 189
Productivity, 12
Professionalism, 288
Profit sharing, 353
Programmed decision, 165
Progression principle, 41, 339
Progressive Aboriginal Relations (PAR), 100
Progressive discipline, 199
Project management, 190
Project managers, 15, 447
Project schedules, 190
Project team, 247, 389
Projection, 428
Projects, 190
Promotion, 302
Prospector strategy, 229
Protectionism, 117
Proversity: Getting Past Face Value and Finding the Soul of People - A Manager's Journey (Graham), 285
Proxemics, 423–424
Prudential Grand Valley Realty, 293
Psychological contract, 362
Public information, 162
Public relations campaigns, 76
Punishment, 348, 349–350
Purchasing control, 201–202
"Putting People First for Organizational Success" (Pfeffer/Veiga), 14, 285

Q
Qualitative forecasting, 190
Quality and performance excellence, 46–47
Quality circle, 92, 390
Quality control, 202
Quality cycle, 92
Quality-driven organizations, 90–92
Quality management, 92
Quality of work life (QWL), 17, 362–363
Quantitative forecasting, 190
Quantitative management approaches, 43–44
Questions marks, 228
Queuing theory, 43
Quibla Cola, 190
QWL, 17, 362

R
Race and ethnicity. *See* Workplace diversity
Racial and ethnic stereotypes, 427
Racial subcultures, 98
Rank ordering, 299
Rational comprehensive planning (RCP), 186

Rational persuasion strategy, 445–456
RBC, 449
RBC Financial Group, 301
Reactor strategy, 229
Real Madrid soccer team, 401
Realistic job previews, 293
Recruiting process, 292–293
Recruitment, 292
Reference checks, 295
Referent power, 313
Refreezing, 453–454
Reinforcement theory of motivation, 347–350
Related diversification, 222
Relatedness needs, 340
Relationship goals, 432
Relative comparison, 195
Reliability, 294
Religion, 122
Representativeness heuristics, 173
Research in Motion (RIM), 5
Resistance to change, 456–457
Resource scarcities, 429
Restricted communication network, 399
Restructuring, 223
Restructuring and divestiture strategies, 222–223
Retention and turnover, 302–303
Retirement, 302–303
Retrenchment strategy, 222
Reward power, 312
Rewards, 337–339
Rightsizing, 223
Risk environment, 167
Risk taking, 140
Rites and rituals, 94
Rodebec, 423
Role ambiguity, 428
Role clarification, 464
Role negotiation, 460
Roots Canada, 363
Royal Bank of Canada (RBC), 449
Royal Dutch/Shell Group, 117
Rugmark Foundation, 119
Rule, 189
"Run for the Cure" event, 73
Russel Metals, 167

S
Safety needs, 42, 340
Saint Francis Xavier Enterprise Development Centre (XEDC), 151
Sarbanes-Oxley Act, 64
Satisfier factor, 340
Satisficing decision, 171
SADC, 112
SBDC, 151
SBU, 221
SC Johnson Canada, 338
Scalar chain principle, 36

Scalar principle, 252
Scaling, 445
Scenario planning, 191
Scientific management, 33–35, 369
Scotiabank, 318, 365
SEI Investments, 393
Selection, 293
Selection process, 293–296
Selective perception, 427
Self-actualization needs, 42, 340
Self-awareness, 21
Self-confidence, 172
Self-fulfilling prophecies, 42
Self-managing work teams, 390–391
Self-monitoring, 365
Self-organization, 267
Self-serving bias, 426
Selling style, 320
Sensation-feeler, 364
Sensation-thinker, 364
Sensitivity training, 460
Sequential view of time, 124
Service technologies, 270
7-Eleven, 192
Sexual harassment, 61, 99, 189, 289–290
Shamrock organization, 9–10
Shaping, 349
Shared power strategy, 456
Short-range plans, 187–188
SIFE, 135
Simulations, 43
Simultaneous systems, 272
Singapore, 111
Six pillars of character, 66
Six Sigma, 203
Skill
    conceptual, 23
    defined, 23
    human, 23
    survival, 11
    technical, 23
Skill and outcome assessment, 23–24
Skill variety, 371
Skills-based pay, 353
Skunkworks, 151
SkyWave Mobile Communication, 269
Small-batch production, 270
Small business. *See* Entrepreneurship and
    small business
Small business development centre (SBDC),
    151–152
SMART goal, 198
Sobeys, 138, 144, 300
Social Accountability International, 75
Social entrepreneurship, 72–74
Social loafing, 385
Social needs, 41, 340
Social responsibility. *See* Corporate social
    responsibility
Social responsibility audit, 71

Social responsibility strategies, 71–72
Socialization, 296
Socio-economic view of social responsibility,
    70
Sociotechnical system, 373
Sole proprietorship, 148
Sony, 7, 95, 111
SOPs, 189
South Africa, 113
South Korea, 111
Southern African Development Community
    (SADC), 112
Southwest Airlines, 227
Space design, 423–424
Span of control, 253–254
Specialized staff, 256
Specific environment, 86–87
Specific *vs.* diffuse, 124
Spillover effects, 462
Spin Master, 174
Spotlight questions, 175
St. Luke's, 262
Staff managers, 16
Staff planners, 191–192
Staffing, 256
Stakeholder analysis, 170
Stakeholder issues and analysis, 68–69
Stakeholders, 87, 217
Standard operating procedures (SOPs), 189
Star communication network, 399
Starbucks, 216, 338
Stars, 228
Statistical quality control, 202–203
Status effects, 420
Steering controls, 196
Steinway & Sons, 367
Stereotype(s), 426–427
Stock options, 354
Stories, 94
Storming stage, 394
Strategic alliance, 115, 224, 248
Strategic business unit (SBU), 221
Strategic competitiveness, 213–215
Strategic constituencies analysis, 217
Strategic human resource management,
    287–288
*Strategic Human Resources: Frameworks for
    General Managers* (Baron/Kreps), 285
Strategic intent, 213
Strategic leadership, 231–232, 443–444
Strategic management, 212–232
    adaptive strategies, 229
    BCG matrix, 228
    co-operative strategies, 224
    core values, 217
    corporate governance, 231
    defined, 214
    e-business strategies, 224–225
    emergent strategy, 229–230
    global strategies, 223

    goals, 214–215
    growth and diversification strategies,
        222
    incrementalism, 229–230
    industry/environment analysis,
        219–220
    levels of strategy, 220–222
    management practices and systems,
        230–231
    mission, 216
    objectives, 218
    organizational resources/capabilities,
        218–219
    Porter's generic strategies, 226–227
    portfolio planning, 227–228
    restructuring and divestiture strategies,
        222–223
    strategic leadership, 231–232
    strategy formulation, 225–230
    strategy implementation, 230–232
Strategic management goals, 214–215
Strategic management process, 215–220
Strategic opportunism, 168
Strategic plan, 188
Strategy, 213
Strategy formulation, 219, 225–230
Strategy implementation, 216, 230–232
Stress/stress management, 461–465
Stressor, 462
Strong cultures, 93–94
Structural differentiation, 429
Structural integration, 97
Structural redesign, 461
Structured problems, 165
Stryker Instruments, 361–362
Students in Free Enterprise (SIFE), 135
Sub-Saharan Africa, 112
Subscription model, 224
Substance goals, 432
Substantive conflict, 428
Substitutes for leadership, 322
Subsystem, 44, 273
Subsystem differentiation, 274–275
Subsystem integration, 275
Subway, 115
Succession plan, 144
Succession problem, 144
Sun Microsystems, 423
Supervisor, 15–16
Supplier alliances, 224
Supply chain management, 90, 160
Support groups, 388
Supportive leadership, 321
Survey feedback, 461
Survival skills, 10
Sustainable competitive advantage, 213
Sustainable development, 119
Sweatshops, 119
Swiss Reinsurance Company, 419
SWOT analysis, 218

Symbolic leader, 95
Symbols, 94
Synchronic view of time, 125
Synergy, 387
System, 44
Systematic thinking, 168

T
Taiwan, 111
Tall structures, 253–254
Task activity, 398
Task environment, 87
Task force, 389
Task identity, 371
Task interdependencies, 429
Task significance, 371
Tateni Home Care Nursing Services, 72
Taxi, 211, 213
TD Bank Financial Group, 286, 370
Team, 385
Team-building process, 404–406
Team contributions, 386
Team decision making, 400–404
Team diversity, 393–394
Team leader, 15–16
Team management, 317
Team structure, 247–248
Teams/teamwork, 385–408
    cohesiveness, 397
    committee, 388–389
    communication networks, 399–400
    cross-functional teams, 389
    decision making, 400–404
    definitions, 385
    diversity, 393–394
    effectiveness, 392–394
    employee involvement teams, 389
    formal/informal groups, 388
    leadership challenges, 407
    meetings, 386–387
    norms, 396–397
    project team, 389
    pros/cons, 385–386
    self-managing work teams, 390–391
    size, 386
    stages of team development, 394–396
    success factors, 406–407
    synergy, 387
    task and maintenance needs, 398
    task force, 389
    team-building process, 404–406
    usefulness of teams, 387
    virtual teams, 390
Teamwork, 23, 385
*Teamwork: What Can Go Right/What Can
    Go Wrong* (Larson/LaFasto), 407
Technical skill, 23
Technological change, 457–458
Technological imperative, 270
Technology, 7, 270, 373

Technology utilization, 424
Telecommuting, 376–377
Telephone interview, 295
Telling style, 320
Telus, 46, 397, 416
Terminal values, 58
Termination, 303
Thailand, 111
Theory. *See* Management theory
Theory X, 41–42
Theory Y, 41–42, 197
Theory Z, 48
Theory Z (Ouchi), 48
3M, 244, 446, 447
3M Canada, 46
360° feedback, 299, 423
Thrifty Foods, 370
Tim Hortons, 138, 213,
Time management, 186, 188
Time orientation, 121, 123
Tolerance for ambiguity, 269
Top-down change, 449
Toromont Industries, 160, 251
Total quality management (TQM), 14, 46, 91
Toxic workplaces, 15
Toyota, 86, 114, 115, 214
Toyotetsu Canada, 114
TQM, 14, 46, 91
Traditional recruitment, 293
Training, 296
Training and development, 296–297
Transactional leadership, 324
Transfer, 302
Transformational change, 451
Transformational leadership, 324–325
Transnational corporation, 117
Transnational strategy, 223
Trilogy, 151, 407
Tropicana, 222
Trust Factor, The (Whitney), 352
Turnover, 366
21st century leadership, 49–50
Two-factor theory, 340–341
Type A personality, 462

U
Unattractive industry, 220
Uncertain environment, 168, 263
Uncertainty avoidance, 122
Unfreezing, 452–453
Unilever, 223
Union, 303
United Nations, 434
United Parcel Service (UPS), 35, 91, 243
Unity of command, 253
Unity of command principle, 36
Unity of direction principle, 36
Universalism, 59
Universalism vs. particularism, 124

Unrelated diversification, 222
Unresolved prior conflicts, 429
Unstructured problems, 166
Upside-down pyramid, 18, 252
Upward appraisal, 299
Utilitarian view, 58

V
Valassis Communications, 354
Valence, 345
Validity, 294
Value-based management, 95
Value chain, 46
Value creation, 12, 87
Values, 57–58
Valuing diversity, 101
Vancity, 423
Venture capitalists, 149
Verizon Communications, 277
Vertical integration, 222
Video conferences, 418
Vietnam, 111
Virgin Group, 137
Virtual offices, 376
Virtual organization, 251
Virtual teams, 390
Vision, 311–312
Visionary leadership, 311–312
Voice over internet protocol (VoIP), 161
VoIP, 161
Volunteer Now!, 74
Vroom-Jago leader-participation model,
    322–325

W
Wal-Mart, 87, 164, 196, 212, 224
Walt Disney World, 456
Weather Network, 286
Web-based business models, 224
Web portals, 164
Wendy's, 115, 222
Westbridge PET Containers, 353
Western Electric Company, 39
Western Wear and Tack, 222
WestJet, 94, 227
Wheel communication structure, 399
Wheel of innovation, 445
Whistle-blower, 66
Willet International, 126
Win-lose conflict, 431
Win-win conflict, 431
"Wiring the Border," 144
Women, 98–99. *See also* Workplace diversity
*Women Business Owners of Color:
    Challenges and Accomplishments*, 141
Wood Gundy, 406
Work attitude, 365–367
Work-life balance, 301
Work-Out, 450
Work process, 276

Work process design, 276–278
Work sampling, 295
Work sharing, 375
Workbrain, 244
Workflow, 276
Workforce 2000: Work and Workers for the 21st Century, 8
Workforce 2020, 8
Workopolis, 3
Workforce diversity, 8
Workplace diversity, 8

communication, 425
diversity maturity, 101
diversity trends in socio-cultural environment, 86
Workplace privacy, 291
Workplace rage, 463
World Trade Organization (WTO), 116–117
WorldCom, 9, 56
WTO, 116–117

X

XEDC, 151
Xerox Canada, 100
Xerox North American TeleWeb, 46

Y
Youth stage, 271

Z
Zenon Environment, 42
Zero-based budget, 189